*For Nael and Carole Piety
Thanks for your service to our
country and your care of its
warriors. Semper Fi
Ed Krekorian M.D.*

VIETNAM, A SURGEON'S ODYSSEY

Colonel Ed Krekorian, MC, USA (Retired)

D1737239

ATHENA PRESS
LONDON

VIETNAM, A SURGEON'S ODYSSEY
Copyright © Colonel Ed Krekorian, MC, USA (Retired) 2002

ISBN 1 932077 50 2

First Published 2002 by
ATHENA PRESS
Queen's House, 2 Holly Road
Twickenham TW1 4EG

Printed for Athena Press

VIETNAM, A SURGEON'S ODYSSEY

This book is gratefully dedicated to the following:

The United States Army medics and United States Navy corpsmen:
they never failed their wounded comrades, often at great risk to themselves.

The Air Ambulance flight crews of the United States Army,
Navy and Marine Corps who often braved hostile terrain,
deteriorating weather, and intense enemy fire to evacuate wounded comrades.

My son-in-law, New York/New Jersey Port Authority Police Officer
Alfonse Joseph Niedermeyer III, his brother officers and firemen,
killed in the line of duty at the World Trade Center, September 11, 2001.

"No greater love…"

Prologue

Saturday, October 16, 1996, 1156 hours
Auditorium, United States Army Medical Museum, Fort Sam Houston, Texas

Loud gasps shattered the academic quiet of the semi-dark auditorium when the slide flashed on the screen. Military and civilian surgeons strained to see better the image of a gaping wound in an adult neck. Torn muscles, transected arteries, veins, and nerves were viewed against a background of fresh and clotted blood. Fragments of gray-white cartilage and bits of muscle, once an intact larynx and vocal cords, lay partially obscured in the massively distorted anatomy.

Today was the final day of an army-sponsored symposium on head and neck war trauma. At the front of the auditorium, standing beside the lectern, James Paul (JP) Franklin, M.D., colonel, retired, Medical Corps, US Army, and Professor Emeritus, University of Colorado School of Medicine, was about to end the morning session with a challenge. He speared the slide with a red arrow projected from a laser pointer. "This injury is not as it might appear, a botched judicial beheading attempted from in front by a myopic executioner with a dull sword. The injury was produced by a metal shard from a Made-In-USA truck blown up by a Made-In-USA 155-millimeter artillery shell converted to a land mine by the Viet Cong."

Dr. Franklin paused to allow the impact of the slide to be dissipated before continuing. "The casualty, an eighteen-year-old private first class, was driving a jeep behind a truck in a convoy. The artillery shell, buried in the road, detonated just as the truck passed over it. Four soldiers in the truck were killed instantly; truck parts were blasted in all directions. A large piece came through the jeep's windshield and struck the driver in the anterior neck."

The red laser arrow indicated severed ends of narrow muscles at the front of the neck, then went to the thick oblique muscles at the sides. "The strap and sternomastoid muscles were cut bilaterally." The arrow moved to the clotted ends of a pale red tubular structure partially obscured by a torn dark blue sausage-like vessel. "The common carotid artery and internal jugular vein were transected on the right." The arrow then moved to the ends of a severed white elongated structure half the width of a pencil. "The right vagus nerve was transected, denervating the right side of the larynx, esophagus, stomach, and heart. Behind the carotid artery the right cervical sympathetic nerve was also cut." The arrow circled gray-white fragments of cartilage imbedded in torn bloody tissue. "The larynx was shattered; behind it the hypopharynx was cut through to the cervical spine."

"Jesus Christ," a voice whispered in the semi-darkness.

'You're right whoever you are. If ever help was needed from the Big Consultant in

7

the sky it was on this case," Dr. Franklin said, chuckling. 'Let me summarize the casualty's dilemma as this point. Blood that should have been going to the right brain geysered from the severed carotid artery with each heartbeat. Blood reaching the brain through the intact left carotid and vertebral arteries poured out through the torn internal jugular vein. Not only was the casualty rapidly losing his life's blood, he was at great risk of a massive stroke or fatal air embolus via the torn veins. His airway was obstructed because of the smashed larynx. What airway remained was flooded by blood, so he was also drowning as well. Other than those problems he was in good shape."

Dr. Franklin glanced at the illuminated clock on the far wall: 1157. Almost time for the lunch break. He continued, "A medic with the convoy forced a plastic breathing tube through the open neck and shattered larynx into the trachea, securing an airway He controlled bleeding with pressure over gauze pads on the neck. A Dust-off picked up the casualty and medic within fifteen minutes. En route to the 96th Evacuation Hospital in Phong Sahn the medic somehow maintained control of the hemorrhage and the airway. I'm not quite sure how he managed to do either, much less both. I doubt if any of us could have done as well."

The screen went dark; the dimmed auditorium lights brightened. "Time for lunch," Dr. Franklin announced. "I would urge all residents to make this case a matter of conversation during lunch. When we resume at 1330 hours I will call on chief residents to discuss the acute and long-term management of this type injury." Wearing a malicious grin Dr. Franklin surveyed the auditorium. "You navy types can expect a disproportionate number of questions. I would be surprised if the chief resident from Bethesda Naval Hospital wasn't given first opportunity to demonstrate what he knows… or doesn't know."

Near the front row, a lieutenant commander dressed in a white uniform, gold naval-aviator's wings on his short-sleeved shirt, slumped in his seat and groaned. In the back row, Dr. Franklin's wife, Kathy, smiled tolerantly. She knew her husband, an enlisted marine in World War II, could not resist an opportunity to tweak naval personnel, especially officers.

★

Saturday, October 16, 1996, 1930 hours
Officers' Club Parking Lot, Randolph Air Force Base, San Antonio, Texas

Colonel JP Franklin, M.D., Medical Corps, US Army, retired, swung the rented Ford Taurus sedan a third time through the officers' club parking lot without finding a vacant space. He turned to his wife beside him. "This reminds me of our first date at Bliss."

"That was almost fifty years ago," Kathy Franklin said, recalling the evening. "You were so shy for a second lieutenant."

"That was my 'aw shucks' act. It worked wonders on first dates."

"Really. Tell me more."

"Just kidding, honey. Find us a parking place now like you did then."

They continued to cruise slowly past rows of parked cars. A dozen cars ahead a set of tail lights glowed red, then white backup lights came on.

"There you go," Kathy said, pointing.

The Taurus leaped forward, arriving at the space as its former occupant pulled away. Braking aggressively, JP slewed the Taurus between a Cadillac and a Lincoln. "How's that for a coordinated maneuver?" he said smugly, glancing at his wife. Just at that moment the front bumper of the Taurus smacked the front bumper of the car in the opposite space, jarring both cars without damaging either.

An embarrassing interlude of silence was broken by Kathy. "JP, you really should wear those new glasses… especially when you park."

"Glasses are for old folks. I'm only seventy," he said, reaching to the back seat for his suit jacket. Opening his door he stepped out, slipped on the jacket and headed for the passenger-side door.

James Paul (JP) Franklin, five foot ten, weighed a wiry 154 pounds. His eleven-year-old gray suit fit much like the tailored army uniform he wore for so many years. Before that he had worn the uniform of a United States Marine. Dark brown thinning hair showed gray at the temples. Brown eyes reflected gentleness, compassion, humor, and sometimes sorrow. They gave no clue as to what those eyes had seen or what the man who possessed them had done. After twenty-eight years of active military duty and three wars, Colonel Franklin had retired to join the faculty of the University of Colorado School of Medicine as a professor. Twelve years later he retired again. Renowned over the world for his expertise in the management of trauma and tumors of the head and neck, he was frequently invited to medical schools as a visiting professor and to conferences to lecture.

In retirement, Dr. Franklin was regarded by his neighbors in Colorado as a kindly, dedicated, benign physician who had excelled at head and neck surgery. Only his family, military colleagues, and a few close civilian friends were aware of his activities as a teenaged marine in World War II, a combat officer during the Korean War, and a senior medical officer at Walter Reed and in South-east Asia during the Vietnam War.

Reaching the passenger side of the Taurus, Dr. Franklin opened the door for his wife. The mother of three grown boys and a girl, Kathy Franklin, retained her slender youthful figure, southern beauty, and gentle southern ways. A gifted artist and teacher, her paintings hung in galleries throughout the south-west. Three years younger than her husband, she was not only the daughter of a retired army lieutenant general but the sister of Dr. Franklin's best friend, now a retired artillery colonel. As she stepped from the Taurus Dr. Franklin surveyed her slender figure. "Miss Kathy," he said in his best John Wayne drawl, "you sure are a handsome woman."

Kathy responded in an exaggerated southern accent. "Why, Colonel Franklin, you do say the sweetest things. But suh, they would mean so much more if you were wearing your glasses."

Hand in hand Colonel (retired) and Mrs. JP Franklin walked through the parking lot and entered the Randolph Air Force Base Officers' Club.

Saturday, October 16, 1996, 2115 hours
Main Dining Room, Officers' Club, Randolph Air Force Base, Texas

JP leaned back in his chair, sighed and studied the remnants on his plate. "The broiled swordfish was outstanding… now if only I had a cigar"

"Didn't you see the sign in the lobby as we came in?" Kathy asked.

"Sign? What sign?"

"The one in the lobby that said there was absolutely no smoking permitted in the club."

JP shrugged. "I must have missed it."

"You really should wear the glasses Jim Beard prescribed," Kathy Franklin said, reaching across the table for her husband's hands. "This is the most relaxed I've seen you in the past three days."

"The symposium was hard work. I'm glad it's over."

"You really gave that navy commander a rough time this afternoon."

JP laughed. "I did, didn't I, but he gave back as good as he got, maybe better although I would never admit it."

'I saw the wings on his shirt," Kathy said. "Is he a flight surgeon?"

JP shook his head. "No. He was a Top Gun fighter pilot before going to medical school. He was elected AOA in his third year."

"The navy is lucky to have people of that caliber as doctors."

"The navy is going to lose him. After the symposium ended we had a serious conversation. He's getting out as soon as he pays back the navy for his training."

"I would have thought he was gung-ho navy."

"He's a very sincere young man who loves the navy, but he's seen integrity, honor, and commitment give way to expediency, social engineering, compromise, and poor leadership. He told me he did not want to be part of a second-rate navy."

Kathy Franklin remained quiet, but her face reflected understanding. She was acutely aware of the degradation of the armed forces, the reduction of its medical capabilities, and the erosion of lifetime medical care promised to active duty people, dependants, and retirees. She told her husband, "I know you feel the same way about the army. Unfortunately there's nothing you or I can do about it."

The waiter appeared with the check on a small tray. JP placed his credit card over the check. After the waiter left to process the credit card charge, JP suggested they reconnoiter the rest of the club before leaving. "It's supposed to be one of the nicest in the air force. Who knows when we'll be back."

When the waiter returned with the credit card and charge slip, JP added a hefty tip and signed the charge slip. Kathy reached over, picked up the charge slip and studied it, then laughed. "Your signature looks like the EKG tracing of someone about to have a cardiac arrest."

"No one can possibly forge my signature." Returning the charge card to his wallet,

JP stood up and went to Kathy's chair. "Come on, kid," he said, mimicking Humphrey Bogart, "let's case the joint."

"I recognized that one… Jimmy Cagney."

"Don't get smart with me, kid," he drawled, taking her arm.

Moments later they walked through a wide carpeted hall, its walls hung with paintings of military aircraft from World War I to Desert Storm. They stopped briefly to study each painting, then peeked into unoccupied small dining rooms. Oak paneling and furniture, dark red rugs and matching curtains gave the rooms an ambience of rustic elegance. Finally, they checked out a noisy bar packed with young officers. Most were dressed in slacks, sports shirts or sweat-stained flight suits. A few turned to stare at Kathy; she smiled and waved.

JP guided his wife towards a flight of stairs leading down. "Let's see what or who the air force is hiding in its basement." Descending the stairs, they were assaulted by waves of loud raucous laughter and the pungent odor of cigar smoke. At the bottom of the stairs JP turned to Kathy. "I thought there was no smoking in the club."

"That's what the sign said. Maybe these officers can't read."

"Air force pilots do have those kinds of reputations."

As they walked towards open double doors at the end of the hall, the sounds of fists and bottles banging on tables were added to laughter and shouts. The smell or cigar smoke became almost overwhelming. JP took Kathy's arm. "Let's take a peek at the rascals who would violate the sacred rules of this austere establishment."

Glancing through the open doorway, they saw clouds of cigar and cigarette smoke nestled over five long tables of diners at the far end of the room. The remainder of the room was empty save for folded tables and chairs leaning against a wall. They stepped inside for a better look. A few diners wore air force formal dress uniforms with mess jackets. Most were dressed in grotesque flight suits or uniforms ranging in color from midnight black to seasick green. Myriads of oversized campaign ribbons and squadron patches covered chests and sleeves. The officers appeared middle-aged or older, some old enough to be JP's contemporaries. No women were present.

Kathy turned to her husband. "Have you ever seen such a weird collection?"

"Not on this planet."

As they gaped at the bizarre group an officer wearing a robin-blue flight suit, oversized silver captain's bars on his shoulders, and pilot's wings so large that they covered his left chest, broke from the group and hurried towards them. "Sir, can I help you?" he asked as he approached.

JP introduced himself and Kathy, then apologized for intruding. "We were curious to see the gutsy individuals who dared ignore the sign in the lobby prohibiting smoking in the club."

"Sign? What sign, sir?" the captain asked innocently.

"Precisely. I didn't see any sign either when I walked in," JP said. "My wife told me about it when I expressed a longing for a cigar."

The captain reached into his blouse pocket, removed a long black cigar and passed it to JP. "My compliments, sir."

"Thank you, captain," JP said, accepting the cigar with alacrity. He swept the room with a glance. "What have we stumbled into?"

"Sir, you and Mrs. Franklin have stumbled into the annual banquet of the Goshawks. Are you familiar with the Goshawks, sir?"

JP studied the man and his absurd uniform. "I know a little about the Goshawks," he said quietly.

The captain beamed. "In that case you and Mrs. Franklin must join us for drinks.'

JP knew enough about the Goshawks – civilian pilots who flew in South-east Asia – to stay away from them. "That's very kind, captain, but we have a long drive back to Fort Sam tonight and an early flight to Denver in the morning."

As he and Kathy started to leave a loud gravely voice boomed from the head table. "Captain, secure those two and bring them here."

A vice clamped on JP's arm. He and Kathy were firmly escorted towards the head table. The man who ordered them brought forward stood up.

Kathy took one look at the man and groaned. "Oh no!"

It had been twenty-six years since she last saw Charles Sanderson. He was heavier now, his face wrinkled and his hair snow white, but she recognized him at once. Her husband's grin was wider than the open cargo door of a C–5 Galaxy.

The two men rushed to each other, hugged and pounded each other. Then Sanderson embraced Kathy. She kissed his cheek. "Charles, your breath stinks," she whispered. "What are you doing in that hideous flight suit?"

"Be quiet, woman and sit down," Sanderson ordered. The officers on each side of Sanderson's chair stood and held their chairs out for Kathy and JP. The sixty or so seated diners, in their absurd uniforms, became quiet, regarding the two intruders with amused curiosity. A glass of white wine was passed to Kathy and a cold bottle of beer to her husband.

JP felt an anxiety comparable to that of a trapped animal. His eyes searched for an escape route.

"Relax, Colonel," Sanderson said firmly. "Tonight you will be an honored guest of the Goshawks."

JP started to rise. "Time for us to go, Kathy."

Sanderson grabbed him by the shoulder. "Sit down, Colonel. That's an order."

"I outrank you, Sanderson. You can't order me to do anything."

"Wrong; I retired a brigadier general."

JP took a long swallow of beer, set the bottle down, burped, and regarded Sanderson critically. "The air force must have been hard up for general officers when they selected you. You can't land an airplane without trashing it."

Kathy interrupted. "JP, why do you want to leave?"

"Why? Because we have stumbled into the den of the most pathological pilots in the world, and that includes the air forces of our allies and adversaries, real and imagined." Glancing around the room at the collections of empty beer bottles covering the tables and the spectrum of weird uniforms, he groaned, "The lunatics have taken over the asylum."

Sanderson, still on his feet, rapped on a glass with his knife. "Gentlemen, gentlemen, your attention, please." Pausing for the noise to subside, he smiled

12

wickedly at JP. After briefly introducing JP and Kathy he continued, "Fate has delivered to us a man most deserving of recognition as an honored guest of this austere and dignified organization. Let me take a few minutes to tell you about the man who now sits before you sipping beer from a bottle instead of a glass." Sanderson chuckled. "That in itself should tell you something about him."

After puffing on his cigar, Sanderson set it down and went on, "Back in World War II, before most of you were born, another P–38 pilot, Dick Grundig, now a retired two-star general, and I ditched our planes near a small island in the Northern Solomons. We managed to swim to the island, but it just wasn't our day. The island was occupied by several hundred Imperial Japanese marines, most of whom started looking for Grundig and me. We would have been captured and probably executed if it hadn't been for a native named John Boreas." Sanderson paused.

The Goshawks were now all ears. Kathy Franklin's blue eyes were fixed on Sanderson.

"John Boreas hid us from the Japanese in a cave part way up a mountain. After nearly three months of hiding Grundig and I were almost dead from malnutrition, dysentery, and malaria. A Jap patrol at the base of the mountain spotted us and ordered us to surrender. When we didn't answer they fired mortars at the cave where we were hiding. We heard a bunch of grenades go off, bursts of automatic weapon fire and then quiet. Dick and I went further back in our cave, too weak to do anything more than wait to be killed."

Sanderson took a slug of beer and smiled at Kathy. He continued, "About an hour later someone at the cave's entrance shouted, 'Hey in there, the marines have landed.' Grundig and I were sure it was an English-speaking Jap with a Boston accent. We suspected a trap. Then the same person ordered, mind you, *ordered* officers of the United States Army Air Corps, 'Get your asses out here on the double or we'll leave you for the Japs.'"

General Sanderson's narrative was interrupted by three waiters who entered the room with pots of fresh coffee. After the pots were distributed the waiters left. Sanderson continued, "When Grundig and I came out of the cave who should be waiting for us but a teenage marine Pfc cradling a Thompson sub-machine gun and John Boreas, the native who had guided us to the cave. They moved Grundig and me down a steep cliff. I slipped and was headed for a fifty-foot drop when the marine grabbed me and stopped my fall. After we reached bottom we were led to a waiting patrol of marines. That evening Grundig and I were put in a rubber raft to be taken to a waiting PT boat. Before we got moving we came under fire from the shore. The sergeant in charge of the patrol and John Boreas were severely wounded. The marine and his two buddies got them into the raft with Grundig and me, then stayed behind to fight off the Japs so we could get away. I never had a chance to thank the marine or his buddies until later, much later."

The dining room had become quiet except for the clinking of cups placed on saucers and an occasional cough.

"Now fast forward to the Korean War," Sanderson said, "to April of 1951 and the Chinese spring offensive. I'm flying a T–6 as a FAC (forward air controller) in the 3rd

Infantry Division AO when this cool voice with a Boston accent came up on the emergency net with a Mayday. The voice belonged to a lieutenant in charge of a platoon of self-propelled automatic weapons – Dusters and Quad Fifties to those who served in South-east Asia. In a moment of great courage or utter stupidity, I have yet to decide which, the lieutenant took on two regiments of CCF to keep a battalion of Brits from being overrun. When the lieutenant realized his guns would run out of ammunition before the CCF ran out of troops, he had the good judgment to ask the United States Air Force for help. After I called in a flight of Bravo two sixes, and the air force saved him, his platoon, and the Brits, he went on to evacuate over a dozen severely wounded Brits to a MASH."

Kathy reached across Sanderson and squeezed her husband's hand. JP unwrapped his cigar. The officer next to him lit a match and held it to the cigar's end while JP puffed, emitting clouds of gray smoke. Kathy made a face to show her displeasure. JP blew a stream of smoke towards the ceiling, looked at his wife and grinned.

"Fast forward again," Sanderson said, "this time to the Vietnam War. Most of you know that I flew 0-One Bird Dogs as a FAC on my first tour. I pushed my luck one day and got shot down. That stuff happens as many of you can recall. When I crashed my shoulder harness failed and I hit my neck on the instrument panel. My larynx, voice box to those of you who never finished high school, was fractured. It was fixed at an army hospital in Vietnam. A couple of days after I was evacuated to Japan I started running a high fever. My neck swelled up and I couldn't breathe. To make matters worse, I became paralyzed, or thought I was. No one in Japan could figure out what was wrong or what to do. I was evacuated to Walter Reed Army Hospital to die. A hotshot army surgeon rushed me to the operating room and saved my life. During my convalescence he kept me from going berserk by taking me flying in an air force flying club T–34 – the military version of Beechcraft Bonanza with tandem seating, formerly used as a primary trainer. Would you believe he even allowed me to fly from the back seat?"

"That's the only place I'd let you fly from," a voice interrupted.

When the laughter subsided Sanderson went on. "Gentlemen, the story does not end at Walter Reed. During my second tour in Nam I heard about a division surgeon whose CG made the mistake of giving him a UH1H Huey and carte blanche to go wherever he wanted. This surgeon hadn't been in Vietnam four weeks when he crossed the sovereign border of Laos in violation of State Department agreements with the government of Laos and in violation of DOD regulations. He committed this nefarious offense in response to a Mayday from a SOG team which had rescued a severely injured Goshawk POW. An NVA guard tried to kill the Goshawk by cutting his throat because the Goshawk was too sick and weak to keep up with other POWs moving to a new camp. When the division surgeon's chopper couldn't land because of the terrain he rappelled a hundred feet through double canopy jungle to give emergency care to the Goshawk. Then he rigged some sort of sling on a rope lowered from his helicopter. He and the Goshawk were then extracted, flown to an aid station where the Goshawk was given emergency care, then flown to a hospital."

General Sanderson looked with disgust at his empty beer bottle, then at his cigar,

14

which had gone out. A just opened bottle of beer, foam spilling down its neck, was handed him. He took a long swig, then set the bottle down. It was obvious he was enjoying himself immensely. He continued, "Other SOG teams prowling the same area searching for POWs tangled with some NVA, then stumbled on to an NVA regimental headquarters. As soon as the SOG teams were extracted the B–52s did their wonderful thing. The bombardiers claimed they were aiming for targets in Vietnam and their bombs accidentally landed in Laos." Sanderson sucked on the unlit cigar stub and grinned knowingly. "So much for the proficiency of air force bombardiers."

He looked at JP for a long moment, then addressed the group again. "And now, gentlemen, the rest of the story, which you have probably guessed by now. The marine who rescued me and Dick Grundig on that Pacific island, the lieutenant whose butt I saved in Korea, the surgeon who saved my life at Walter Reed, the division surgeon who risked his career and put his life on the line to rescue an injured Goshawk in Laos, and God only knows what else he's done that we don't know about, sits before you now, quietly drinking your beer and smoking a cigar. I believe his record, excluding his flying proficiency which is marginal at best, is worthy of recognition as our honored guest this evening." He paused. "Do I hear a motion?"

A tall middle-aged officer with absurdly large major's leaves on his shoulders jumped up and walked briskly towards the head table. When JP saw him he paled. Slowly getting to his feet, he went to meet him, extending his hand. The major ignored the hand, embraced him in a fierce hug, then turned to address the tables. "I'm the guy the doctor broke all rules to save in Laos. Not only that, but when he got me to the hospital, damned if he didn't take me to the operating room and operate on me." He fingered a horizontal scar low on his neck. "I am honored to nominate him."

From somewhere in the room a voice called out, "Seconded."

"All in favor so respond."

The "yeas" were thunderous.

"The motion is carried." General Sanderson turned to JP "There is one final requirement which must be met before you can be recognized by this austere collection of aviators."

JP whispered to Kathy, "I was afraid of this."

Sanderson continued as though he hadn't heard. "You must prove you are aeronautically competent."

JP braced himself.

"You will be required to demonstrate two daylight and one night carrier landings."

"But I'm not a naval aviator," JP protested, "and I hate ships. They make me seasick."

Sanderson ignored the protest.

Six Goshawks stood up and went to the stack of long collapsed tables leaning against the wall. Dragging a table from the stack to the center of the room, they pulled out its legs and set the table upright. From willing contributors they collected beer, ice, and water, all of which were dumped along the length of the table.

JP stood up and removed his coat, tie, shirt, undershirt, shoes and socks. If Kathy hadn't been present he would have removed his trousers.

"The objective, sir," General Sanderson explained, "is to make a power-on approach to landing on the carrier deck with enough momentum to carry you the length of the deck. By flexing your legs at a propitious moment you will be trapped by a cane held horizontally by two of our most junior and less experienced Goshawks. Questions?"

"Yes, sir. Can I drag the carrier deck before attempting a landing… sir?'

"Of course," Sanderson said, stifling a smile. "A careful pilot will do that routinely before landing on a strange carrier or airfield. I'm gratified your flying judgment has improved since I last flew with you."

As JP walked behind Kathy's chair she grabbed his arm and pulled him down close. "You're as bad as the rest of these lunatics," she whispered.

Chapter One

Monday, April 14, 1969, 0535 hours
16th Avenue, Washington, District of Columbia

Lieutenant Colonel James Paul (JP) Franklin, M.D., Medical Corps, United States Army, pushed the Chevrolet Corvair van beyond the speed limit as he drove south on 16th Street towards Walter Reed Army Medical Center. With the roads clear of traffic at such an early hour he could break his record of eighteen minutes driving time from his quarters in Forest Glen to the west gate of the medical center. But the roads were not quite clear of traffic. Ahead he caught sight of a parked D.C. police car almost hidden against the background of trees and vegetation on a road from Rock Creek Park. "Sneaky rascal," he muttered, hitting the brakes. The speedometer needle dropped. By the time he passed the police car he was the image of a law-abiding citizen. A look in his rearview mirror showed no flashing red light behind him. A glance at the dashboard clock told him he would set no new record this morning, but at least he would have time for a quick cup of coffee before ward rounds.

When the Medical Center came into view, Lieutenant Colonel JP Franklin eased the van into the left lane, braked to let an oncoming car pass, then turned into the open gate. An armed MP stepped from a small brick guard house. Recognizing the box-shaped white van with its single broad red stripe, he came to attention, waved it through and saluted. Lieutenant Colonel Franklin snapped a return salute as he drove past. In his rearview mirror he caught a smile spreading across the MP's face. Almost every morning for the past two weeks he and the same MP saluted each other with progressive effort, each trying to outdo the other with the precision of his salute.

Every time Lieutenant Colonel Franklin entered the 114-acre campus of Walter Reed Army Medical Center he felt an immense flush of pride, for he had entered the most prestigious military medical center in the world. As the chief of the head and neck surgery service he was an integral part of that center. His service, with twelve residents and two staff, managed the care of an average of sixty inpatients. Close to a thousand patients were treated every month in the head and neck outpatient clinic. But supervision of patient care was only part of his duties. He was also the consultant to the Army Surgeon General, responsible for every aspect of his specialty worldwide, from procurement of equipment to assignment of 120 head and neck specialists. In moments of self-indulgence he sometimes remarked to himself, "Not bad for an ex-jarhead."

Staying scrupulously within the 20 mph speed limit, he partially circled a rotary dominated by the imposing statue of Major Walter Reed, conqueror of typhoid and yellow fever. Major Reed's dedication and accomplishments had inspired generations of army medical scientists. The statue itself was a constant reminder to Lieutenant

Colonel Franklin of the frailties of medicine. Walter Reed had died of peritonitis following surgery for a ruptured appendix.

Leaving the rotary he passed a block-long red brick building, the Army School of Nursing. Next came a motel-like structure, the guest house. Relatives of patients in the hospital had priority for accommodations there. Across the street a long driveway climbed past well-kept lawns, oak and pine trees to a sprawling officers' club. Hidden from the street by the main building were two tennis courts and a swimming pool. Beyond the club a cluster of evergreen trees partially obscured two large red brick buildings, the Walter Reed Army Institute of Research. Dozens of top scientists labored at the institute to follow in the traditions of Walter Reed. On the far side of the institute a white concrete windowless building squatted like an huge blockhouse, the AFIP – Armed Forces Institute of Pathology. Military and civilian doctors on its staff were world-renowned authorities on the pathology of virtually every disease known to mankind.

A second rotary, its interior blazing with thousands of red and yellow tulips around a working fountain, fed traffic past the hospital's main entrance. Greek columns reached up four floors to a red tile roof. The hospital, constructed of red brick, was laid out in the form of a giant four-story "E". The arms of the "E" housed most wards, clinics, and doctors' offices. Administrative offices, labs, and operating rooms were in the body.

Driving on, he turned left in front of a wooden cottage-like structure, the Walter Reed branch of the Riggs National Bank where he and Kathy shared a checking and a modest savings account. Beyond the bank he turned left again, passing the commissary, an aging red brick building. It was so small the number of shoppers allowed in at any one time had to be limited. After passing a large, partially filled parking lot, another left turn took the Corvair under an arch into a small quadrangle formed by the hospital's walls. The quadrangle had sufficient area for fourteen parking spaces. To have one of those spaces was the most coveted perk on the entire post. Only the commanding general, deputy commander, executive officer, and chiefs of major services were privileged to park in the quadrangle. JP eased the Corvair van into a space. bringing the front bumper almost in contact with the brick wall. A metal sign fixed to the wall at eye level read: CHIEF HEAD AND NECK SURGERY.

★

Monday, April 14, 1969, 0558 hours
Wards 20/21, Walter Reed Army Hospital, Washington D.C.

Leaving the elevator on the fourth floor, Lieutenant Colonel JP Franklin headed for Ward 21, the forty-bed enlisted ward of the Head and Neck Surgery Service. Ward 21 occupied the north wing with Ward 20, the forty-bed urology ward. Although each ward was separate, both shared the same nursing station and latrine. Pausing at the nursing station, JP wished the chief ward nurse, Major Mary Fenster, a cheerful good morning. As he started to leave, Major Fenster's drill sergeant's voice stopped him.

"Not so fast, Colonel."

Five feet tall, weighing about 100 pounds. Mary Fenster ran Wards 20 and 21 much as a battalion commander ran his battalion. It was easy to understand how she came to be a major at thirty and why at thirty-four she was on the list for lieutenant colonel from below the zone. A widow, her husband had been a navy seal killed in Vietnam. Childless and still very pretty, JP wondered why she didn't remarry. For the present she seemed totally committed to being a nurse. She had served two tours in Vietnam and recently volunteered for a third.

JP stepped into the glassed nursing station. "All I said was 'Good morning'."

"It may be a good morning unless you happen to be a patient on my wards and need to use the latrine."

JP groaned. "Not again."

"Yes, sir. All six commodes are obstructed. The urinals, shower, and sinks drains are backed up."

"Call the urologists; they're the obstruction specialists."

"This isn't funny, Colonel. It's the third time in as many weeks the latrine has been unusable."

"Have the post engineers been called?"

"They promised to be here at 0800."

"How are the patients managing?"

"Well, sir, since your clinic is just down the hall with two latrines, I had the AOD unlock the door and turn on the lights. Ambulatory patients have been using those latrines, the nurses' latrine. and latrines and showers on other wards. Non-ambulatory patients still use bedpans." She fixed JP with hazel eyes. "Colonel, when is something more than band-aid repairs going to be done?"

JP sighed, "I wish I knew Mary. Colonel Mangonis and I have been pressuring General Worden for the past year to get new plumbing and air conditioning for our wards."

"So what's the hang-up?"

"What it always has been – money. The general agreed our latrine facilities are inadequate and may even be a health hazard. He's been pleading with the SGO for additional funds to renovate parts of the hospital, but with new hospital construction about to begin, sinking money into this old barn is not a popular concept."

That clearly was not the answer Major Fenster was seeking. "Colonel, may I speak frankly?"

"You never asked my permission before," JP said, suppressing a grin,

Fenster ignored the remark. "Most of the patients on my wards are casualties from Vietnam. They have serious injuries. Forcing them to put up with inadequate toilets and shower facilities is immoral. And don't forget the summer months... the temperature and humidity on the wards is almost unbearable. You know what that does to our infection rate.

"Mary, believe me, Joe Mangonis and I have pushed the system to the edge of insubordination and have yet to reach first base."

Fenster would not give up. "The men on my wards served their country and paid a heavy price. Damn it, sir, they deserve better."

JP lowered his voice. "I'll tell you this much. Consider it classified."

"Oh?"

"Joe Mangonis and I have resorted to an alternative plan to circumvent certain obstacles."

"What does that mean?"

"In military vernacular it means we have gone to a flanking maneuver."

Fenster stared at him, then burst out laughing. "Why do I suspect some sort of Marine Corps deviancy?"

JP's face was the picture of innocence. "Mary, how could you think such a thing?" As he started to leave he told her, "Send me word if the engineers don't come through… so to speak."

Fenster returned to her charts, slowly shaking her head.

Back in the hall JP headed towards a dozen white-coated doctors gathering loosely around a wheeled chart rack outside Ward 21. A glance at his watch told him there would be no coffee before rounds. As he approached he was greeted with a subdued chorus of "Good morning, Colonel," followed by a plethora of exaggerated yawns.

"War is hell, gentlemen," JP responded. Suppressing a yawn of his own he nodded a greeting to his assistant, Major Dave Strickland. "Anything exciting happen over the weekend?"

"Yes, sir. Two medevacs from Vietnam on Saturday and two surgical emergencies yesterday."

"What were the emergencies?"

"A six-year-old boy with a severe dog bite of the upper neck was choppered in from Fort Belvoir. The dog crushed the larynx and tore the jugular. Just as we finished with him, a GI on the eye service began hemorrhaging from the nose and mouth. Both patients should be back on the wards by now. We'll see them on rounds."

"As old Dr. Mosher at Mass General used to say, 'The best cases come in at night and on weekends.' Anything else?"

"The AOD called at four this morning to alert us that an air evac 141 from Vietnam is due at Andrews Air Force Base at about 1900 hours. The breakdown for our service is eight EM and one officer. I passed that on to Roy."

Major Roy French, the chief resident for Ward 21, was thirty-four years old, married and the father of three children. A fighter pilot before going to medical school he had flown F–86s. Of average height and slight build, he was quiet in demeanor, cool under pressure, and lightning quick in response. He seemed the very antithesis of the traditional flamboyant fighter pilot. Deeply religious, he was a great role model for the younger doctors.

JP turned to him. "Roy, what's the bed availability on Ward 21?"

French glanced at a 2 x 4 card in his hand. "Before rounds I discharged two patients to duty, transferred three to Forest Glen, sent three more home on convalescent leave, and transferred two back to the orthopedic service. There are some other moves pending but I expect we should have enough beds by tonight for the air evacs: maybe even one or two extra."

20

JP nodded approval. "Be sure the air evacs are evaluated as soon as they're admitted. I'll be on staff call tonight. Call me to discuss evacs you believe should be added to tomorrow's OR schedule."

"Problem, sir."

"You know how I hate that word, Major French."

"Yes, sir, but there are times when no other word will suffice."

"Okay, let's have it."

"We have three long operations including a commando on the schedule for tomorrow. They will carry us to almost midnight. I don't believe any more cases can be added unless—"

JP interrupted. "Maybe the chief resident for the officers, women, and pediatric wards has an answer to that dilemma.

Major Terry O'Connel, USMA '59, responded without hesitating. "Commit the reserves, sir."

"Spoken like a true armor officer, but what does it mean?"

O'Connel smiled blandly. "Cancel outpatient clinic and use the doctors from it to make up a second operating team."

Captain Greg Brazelton, a hyperactive first year resident from Georgia, pleased at the idea of escaping from the drudge of a busy outpatient clinic to the excitement of an operating room, burst out, "All right."

JP fixed Brazelton with a disapproving look. "You just volunteered for the history question of the day."

Brazelton's subdued "Yes, sir" reflected past unhappy experiences with such questions.

"What was implied by Major French's use of the term 'commando' in describing one of the operations on tomorrow's schedule?"

Brazelton brightened. He had been studying the technique and anatomy of the operation for the past week. "Sir, commando is an idiom for a cancer operation that resects half the tongue, floor of mouth, adjacent mandible, and is combined with a radical neck dissection."

"So far so good," JP said, "but that was just a preliminary question. Now for the real one."

"I was afraid of that."

"Why is the operation called a commando?"

Brazelton stammered, "I suppose because it's so destructive in terms of anatomy, similar, in a sense, to the destruction achieved by British commando raids in World War II."

"Good try but a miss." JP scanned the doctors. "Anyone?"

Captain Craig Entarde cleared his throat. An intense, studious, third year resident, Entarde graduated from the Citadel as commandant of cadets before going to medical school.

"Go ahead, Craig."

"On August 14, 1942, Hayes Martin, then chief of head and neck surgery at Memorial Hospital in New York, did the first combined tongue, jaw, floor of mouth, and neck dissection ever done for cancer. He named the operation 'commando' in honor of the joint British–Canadian commando raid on Dieppe, France that took place the same day."

A mild applause followed.

Once started Entarde was hard to stop. Next to medicine, history was his passion. He continued, "Dr. Martin's operation was a success. The commando raid on Dieppe was not. In fact it was a dismal failure. Most of the commandos were killed or captured. Many of the captured were executed by the SS on Hitler's orders. However the raid did have a positive spin-off. It focused on major shortcomings of Allied intelligence and planning which were rectified for the Normandy invasion."

Again applause, but louder and more sustained.

"Don't encourage him," Roy French admonished. "We've got to get started on rounds today."

The cluster or white coats shuffled into the ward. Dave Strickland moved closer to his boss. "We almost lost the bleeder last night."

"Your use of the adverb 'almost' is reassuring."

"A nineteen-year-old air evac with a transverse wound of the face was admitted to the eye service on Saturday. Late yesterday he cut loose from the nose and mouth."

"Why was he on the eye service?"

"He's blind. Both eyes were removed in Vietnam."

JP remained quiet.

As the two walked into the ward behind the residents Dave Strickland told his boss, "The latrine is stopped up again."

"Mary Fenster dropped that on me this morning. All I can say right now is that Joe Mangonis and I are on it."

Strickland chuckled. "With the chief of urology and the chief of head and neck surgery working on the problem it's reassuring that the subject is covered from one end to the other."

JP threw his assistant a look of feigned reprimand. "That's disgusting."

Dave Strickland smiled. He liked his boss. In fact he liked the army and the Army Medical Corps. Four years ago he had entered active duty with the intent to serve his obligatory two years and leave for academic medicine. Challenged by the demands of military medicine and inspired by the dedication, judgment and skill of his army medical associates, he extended an additional two years. Then, much to the delight of his boss, he applied for a regular army commission.

JP selected Dave Strickland to be his assistant from a list of over sixty head and neck surgeons entering active duty from civilian life. Strickland, a tall, taciturn Vermonter, his triangular thin intellectual face made more intellectual by rimless glasses, had graduated from MIT with a degree in aeronautical engineering at age nineteen. He worked at McDonnell-Douglas for two years designing fighter aircraft for the navy before deciding to study medicine. After graduating from medical school with honors he completed a five-year head and neck surgery residency and then a two-year fellowship. Married to a nurse he met during his internship, he was the father of two girls. That he possessed a commercial-instrument pilot's license had nothing to do with his selection as assistant chief, it was merely coincidental. It was less of a coincidence that he joined the flying club at Andrews Air Force Base at the urging of his boss, a long time member.

Ward 21, by any criteria, could never be described as cheerful. Its high ceiling, cold fluorescent lights, and dull-green painted walls gave it a mournful depressing ambience. The new hospital would be a marked improvement, but it was two to three years away and of little comfort to the recovering wounded on Ward 21.

As JP passed near an open window he glimpsed an indistinct object just visible on the ledge outside. "Wait a second, Dave," he told Strickland. Going closer to the window he saw the outline of a six pack in a brown paper bag. A breeze fluttered open the bag and the word BEER became visible.

Alcohol was prohibited in the hospital except for medicinal purposes. A patient caught with alcohol in his possession would be subject to disciplinary action and the alcohol confiscated. JP hesitated, then turned away. The beer on the ledge clearly qualified for the medicinal category. He rejoined Strickland, much to the relief of several patients who were watching with more than a passing interest.

"See anything?" Strickland asked.

"Pigeons, Dave, just pigeons."

Chapter Two

Monday, 14 April, 1969, 0605 hours
Ward 21, Walter Reed Army Hospital, Washington D.C.

Major Roy French led to the first bed. The patient, a young soldier, sat leaning back against several pillows, his left eye hidden behind a black patch, his right eye watching the doctors. The left side of his face sagged noticeably and showed no movement while the right side moved normally. Saliva drooled intermittently from the left corner of his mouth. A plastic feeding tube exited the right nostril. The bed sheet, pulled up to his chest, was conspicuously flat below his mid-thighs.

While waiting for the doctors to assemble Roy French examined a 4" healing incision that extended from behind the left ear down into the upper neck. Satisfied there was no evidence of infection he leaned over to inspect a longer incision low in the neck which crossed from one side to the other. At its center the round open end of the trachea was attached to the skin by a circle of interrupted sutures. It resembled the open end of a garden hose. Straightening up, Roy French faced the doctors. "This is Pfc Dana Fabrezius, an eighteen-year-old infantryman," he began.

The patient turned his head so his right ear was towards French.

"A week ago he was point man on patrol in the Central Highlands when he triggered a mine. He sustained immediate traumatic above the knee amputations of both legs and was blown eight to ten feet into the air. On impacting the ground the front of his neck and left skull struck an unknown object. By the time he reached the 71st Evac at Pleiku he was in shock and acute respiratory distress. In addition to the obvious leg amputations he had fractures of the left skull base and mastoid, bleeding from the left ear canal, left facial paralysis, and an extensive bruise over the anterior neck."

Major French opened the chart, studied a page, then closed it and continued, "At the 71st all attempts to intubate him to relieve the airway obstruction failed. The head and neck surgeon began what he thought would be a quick tracheotomy. To his surprise he found a three-centimeter gap where the trachea should have been. The trachea had separated at the third tracheal ring with the lower segment retracted into the chest. It was grasped with an Allis clamp and brought up into the neck where it was intubated. During anesthesia induction an arrhythmia developed which rapidly progressed to cardiac arrest. After resuscitation he continued to demonstrate multiple arrhythmias, then arrested a second time. He was again resuscitated. Despite twelve units of blood and vasopressors, he remained unstable.

"The anesthesiologist and surgeons were concerned he would go into another cardiac arrest from which he could not be resuscitated. They decided to get him off the table as quickly as possible. While the orthopods debrided the legs to mid-thigh amputations, the head and neck surgeon sutured the distal end of the trachea to the skin above the sternal notch. The upper end of the trachea was anastamosed into the pharynx for drainage of secretions. The mastoid fractures and ear were debrided, irrigated and drained. Over the next forty-eight hours he stabilized. Three days later he was medevac'd directly here."

"Have the orthopods seen him?" JP asked.

"Yes, sir, Saturday night when he was admitted and twice yesterday. They plan revision of the stumps in two weeks."

"Why the patch over the left eye?" Captain Brazelton asked.

"Aesthetic reasons, mostly. He developed a corneal ulcer because of the inability to close the eye. The ophthalmologists put some ointment in the eye and taped it closed. They'll check the eye daily. The patch was an afterthought. They told Dana it would make him look distinguished, like the man in the shirt ads."

The right side of Fabrezio's face showed a smile, the left remained immobile.

"What's his status as of this morning?" JP asked.

"Unsettled, Colonel. Since he arrived he's had intermittent abdominal cramps, diarrhea, and temperature elevations as high as 103. A white count on blood drawn three hours ago was 22,000 with a shift to the left, a clear evidence of infection. A spinal tap was negative. An admission chest X-ray showed only a mild cloudiness of both lungs but nothing diagnostic of pneumonia. We bronchoscoped him anyway. The lungs were clear."

"What's your game plan?"

"Well, it's apparent he has an infection somewhere. We'll continue to work that up. Malaria, dysentery, septicemia, wound infection, and GU infection are being considered plus a few of the more exotic diseases endemic to South-east Asia. At least a dozen cultures from operative sites, blood and spinal fluid are cooking for aerobes and anaerobes. A contrast study of the upper GI tract is scheduled for this afternoon to rule out injury of the cervical esophagus. This morning he complained of abdominal pain. He had tenderness over the umbilicus, left upper quadrant, and referred to his shoulder on deep pressure. The general surgeons will be over in a few minutes to take a look at him."

"You think he might have an acute belly?"

"I know it's a long shot, but there is always the possibility of splenic injury or even a hot appendix. Flying F–86s taught me to be thorough, Colonel," French said.

"And I thought it was your training at Walter Reed. What will happen after the peripheral problems have been managed?"

"Schedule him for reconstruction of the airway. Sometime after that explore the left ear and mastoid, middle ear and facial nerve. Hopefully hearing in the left ear can be restored and the facial nerve repaired."

"Sounds good to me," JP said. He leaned towards the patient's right ear. "How does it sound to you, Dana?"

Fabrezio gave a thumbs up.

"If you have any questions write them down and give them to Major French. He has all the answers."

Again Fabrezio's right face smiled.

JP turned to the doctors. "Has anyone talked to his parents?"

"Yes, sir, yesterday," Roy French said. "His parents live in western Pennsylvania. They're leaving today to come down here. Greg got them a room at the guest house."

JP nodded and indicated they should move on.

Rolf Hanley, the most junior resident, pushed the wheeled chart rack to the next bed. The cluster of doctors shuffled behind him like a elk herd moving to the next forage The patient, a mildly obese man in his mid-thirties, was sitting up and leaning forward. A bulky dressing covered his neck except the lower part, where adhesive tape pulled it away from a tracheotomy tube. Every minute or two the patient lifted a large metal suction tube to his lips, flipped the switch on a suction machine next to his bed. and cleaned quantities of saliva from his mouth. A plastic nasogastric feeding tube exited the left nostril.

Roy French accepted a chart from Hanley, then motioned the group away from the man's hearing and that of the other patients. Holding the closed chart, he waited until the doctors formed around him, then began. "Melvin Lindquist is a thirty-four-year-old staff sergeant assigned to MACV in Saigon. Six days ago, after receiving a 'Dear John' letter from his wife, he got drunk and attempted suicide by cutting his throat with a razor blade. The cut was just under the mandible and extended from one side to the other, going through both sub-maxillary glands. It was fortuitous he chose to make the attempt outside the emergency room of the 3rd Field Hospital.

"He was found unconscious, bleeding profusely, with severe upper airway obstruction. During intubation for anesthesia it was noted that the tongue did not move and had retracted to the back of the pharynx, blocking the airway. Based on the location of the cut in the neck and the immobile tongue, it was presumed that both hypoglossal nerves were severed. Most of the bleeding was traced to a severed right lingual artery which was ligated. Definitive repair of the hypoglossal nerves was not done. The wound was irrigated, drains placed and the wound closed. A nasogastric tube was put down for feeding. He was medevac'd here for repair of the hypoglossal nerves and psychiatric follow-up.

"Findings on admission were the trach, closed incision in the upper neck with two Penrose drains, a non-moving tongue fixed at the back of the throat, complete inability to swallow, and unintelligible speech. Psychiatry saw him on Saturday. They interpreted his suicide attempt as a one-time event. A second attempt would be unlikely even though he was severely depressed. They started him on a short course of anti-depressants and will see him daily on the ward. When he's ambulatory he'll be followed in the psych clinic."

Major Dave Strickland scanned the herd for a victim, settling on a dark-complexioned resident wearing air force blues under his white coat. "Dr. Kaydenov, what does the literature tell us about managing bilateral severed hypoglossal nerves?"

"Not much. I did a search in the library yesterday and found only four articles published within the last fifteen years. Each reported one or two cases with equivocal results."

"What would be your recommendation to Sergeant Lindquist?"

"I would first tell him the facts of life."

"And those facts are?"

"He has a very uncommon injury. Effective treatment has yet to be determined, and a long period of rehabilitation can be anticipated. Then, using the rationale that there is nothing to lose and possibly much to gain, I would recommend the severed nerve ends be identified on both sides and anastamosed."

"Assuming the nerves are successfully repaired," Dave Strickland continued, "what problems can be anticipated?"

"The major problems will be maintaining nutrition, the airway, and unintelligible speech. At the rate at which nerves regenerate, it would be at least nine months to a year, probably longer, before any return of tongue function can be expected. Even then there would be a need for him to relearn how to swallow and learn how to articulate with an abnormally moving tongue. As for nutrition, the nasogastric tube could be left down but would cause ulceration, infection, and scar formation over such a long period. Acceptable alternatives are cervical esophagostomy and gastrostomy. I would recommend the latter."

JP turned to Dave Strickland. "What was your experience at Michigan with these types of injuries?"

"Only one case during my residency, Colonel. A drunk fell through a plate glass window and cut both hypoglossals. We did exactly what Lew recommended. The patient was discharged a month after admission with a gastrostomy and trach. He never returned."

"Our series of five here at Reed is slightly larger but not much more enlightening. In two patients the nerves were repaired with end-to-end anastamosis. A third patient required bilateral grafts. Those three were eventually decanulated, the earliest at eight months, the latest at sixteen. All three had moderate tongue atrophy and limited tongue motion, but were able to swallow soft foods and liquids. Speech was abnormal but understandable. A speech therapist continues to work with them to improve speech and swallowing. The fourth patient, wounded by an RPG frag, had such tissue destruction that nothing remotely resembling a nerve could be identified on either side. He still has his trach and gastrostomy, and is a full-time student at Duke. The fifth patient, a suicide attempt, was repaired with end-to-end anastamosis. An alcoholic and a drug user, he disappeared from the ward three weeks after surgery and never returned. Two years after he took off I received a short note from the VA hospital in Ashville notifying me that the patient died of a gunshot wound to the head. He still had a trach."

Dave Strickland turned to Roy French. "Well, Doctor, you heard the spectrum of your staff's modest experience and the recommendations of the junior air force resident. What are your intentions?"

French smiled smugly. "He's on Wednesday's operating schedule for exploration and bilateral repair of the hypoglossal nerves. The general surgeons will put in a gastrostomy."

The herd moved on. The next patient lay quietly in a semi-reclining position, a black eye patch over each eye. A bulky bloodstained dressing covered most of his neck. Rolf Hanley removed a chart from the rack and passed it to Roy French.

After glancing at some lab slips, French looked up. "Pfc Harold Bailey is a nineteen-year-old infantryman. Two weeks ago he was on patrol near the Laotian border when he was hit in the face by a high velocity bullet, presumably AK–47. The bullet entered below the right cheekbone, passed just under both eyes and exited the left cheekbone. He sustained extensive fractures of the mid-face, nose, sinuses, and orbits. He was medevac'd to the 94th Evac Hospital at Phu Thien. The fractures were reduced and stabilized. Both eyes were so severely damaged they were enucleated. He arrived this weekend and was admitted to the eye service.

"About 2300 hours last night he bled massively from his nose and mouth. We were called a few minutes later. Luckily we were in the doctors' lounge drinking coffee after finishing up the kid with the dog bite. We crashed into his right neck and ligated the external carotid artery. That stopped the bleeding as if turning off a faucet."

Rolf Hanley raised his hand. "If he was pouring blood out of his mouth and nose, how did you know to ligate the right external carotid and not the left?"

"The situation was desperate. Blood was coming out faster than we could pump it in. We had to do something fast. The bullet's path, based on entrance and exit wounds, was through the region of the internal maxillary artery on both sides. Ligating those vessels was not an option because of the technical difficulties operating in an area of fractures, bleeding, and tissue destruction. Since the internal max is a branch of the external carotid, which is easily accessible in the neck, we targeted the external carotid. We picked the right side because pressure over the right carotid diminished bleeding while pressure the left had no effect."

Hanley persisted. "But why did he bleed massively three weeks after being wounded and not at the time he was wounded?"

"You field that one, Greg," Roy French told the first year resident from Georgia.

"Thanks a lot," Brazelton said, clearing his throat. "After an artery is severed it goes into spasm, narrowing its diameter. A period of shock level blood pressure or no blood pressure will further reduce the flow of blood to the injured artery. Both facilitate clot formation. After two or three weeks the clot begins to dissolve. Arterial pressure will ultimately blow it out. A second explanation may be weakening of the arterial wall by shock waves from the bullet passing nearby. With time, the weakened wall bulges out as a false aneurysm and finally ruptures, like a balloon bursting."

JP asked Roy French, "Are you concerned the internal max on the left side may blow?"

"Yes, sir. We plan an angiogram this week. If it's suspicious we'll consider ligating the internal max on the left."

The patient suddenly sat straight up. "I hear you bastards talking about me. You had to muck around in my neck last night and stop the bleeding. You should have let me die. If I bleed again keep your fucking hands off me. No more surgery and no more tests. You tell that son of a bitch in charge I said so" He began to sob. "Just let me die. I want to die."

The vehemence of the outburst shocked patients and doctors. They looked to JP for his response. He merely shrugged. What could the army do to a war-blinded teenager? Send him back to Vietnam? He motioned Roy French away from the others.

"That's not the first time I've been called a son of a bitch, occasionally with some justification," JP told French, "but the talk of wanting to die is worrisome."

"I discussed that with the ophthalmology resident this morning, Colonel. While on their service, Bailey never mentioned wanting to die until yesterday. His fiancée came up from Virginia to spend a few days with him. The prospect of having to care for a blind husband with facial deformities for the rest of her life was more than she could handle. She stayed about a half hour, broke their engagement and left. It was after she left that he started talking about wanting to die. The psych resident saw him as an emergency last evening and was about to transfer him to their closed ward when he began to hemorrhage. He'll be transferred this morning after we change his dressing."

"Impress the psych people to call us at the first sign of bleeding," JP said. "We are not going to let him bleed to death, no matter what he says he wants."

"Yes, sir."

"And Roy, search out the idiot who assigned a blind kid who wants to die because his fiancée broke their engagement to a bed next to a depressed patient who attempted suicide because his wife sent him a 'Dear John'. When you identify him or her, be sufficiently explicit so there is never a repetition."

French reddened, accepting the reprimand even though not directed at him. As they walked to the next patient, a sixty-two-year-old master sergeant with a sixty pack year smoking history and advanced throat cancer, JP's pager beeped. His secretary's voice blasted out in a heavy Brooklyn accent. "Colonel, there's a Dr. Minter here who insists on seeing you right away. He says it's urgent; and Ricardo Diego just walked in."

Quieting the beeper's static, JP told Dave Strickland, "You have the rounds." As he walked past Harold Bailey's bed on the way out of the ward, he couldn't help but think back twenty-six years to World War II, when he was a seventeen-year-old marine stationed at Camp Pendleton in California. On his first liberty in San Diego he met a pre-law student named Ann Gallagher. By the time he sailed for the war in the Pacific a month later they were deeply in love. They almost married before he left: such wartime marriages were common.

But marines were taking heavy casualties in the Pacific. Chances were good he too would become a casualty. His love for Ann would not allow him to saddle her with a husband who might return from war with an injury so crippling he would be a burden for the rest of his life. Or a dead husband who left only packets of letters and a month of memories for his teenaged widow to treasure.

When he returned from the Pacific eighteen months later the love between the two had not only survived but had grown stronger. Then the war suddenly ended with an atomic bomb exploding over Hiroshima and Nagasaki. JP found himself a civilian in a university thousands of miles from Ann. While she excelled in law school, graduating first in her class, he became bored with academia. Instead of attending classes he hung out with other veteran students at a local tavern drinking beer and telling war stories. His grades deteriorated until he was threatened with expulsion. A cynical indifference impacted his relationship with Ann. After missing her graduation he quit writing to her. Three months later he received his own 'Dear John'.

JP stopped and looked back over his shoulder at Harold Bailey. He still sat in his bed, eye sockets hidden by black patches, staring into what would be a lifetime of darkness. A tidal wave of sorrow swept over JP. Fighting tears he turned and walked out of the ward.

Chapter Three

The inpatient Head and Neck Clinic was a hundred feet more or less down the hall from Ward 21. The clinic's proximity to the ward was a great convenience. Patients from Ward 21 were easily brought to the clinic for examinations, minor surgery and follow-up. Staff offices were located in the clinic, making the staff available for consultations and emergencies. At the far end of the clinic double doors opened. to a wide corridor that led to the operating suite. Serendipity or not, no other surgical service enjoyed such a strategic location.

Walking to the clinic, JP puzzled over why his secretary was at work so early. But then she had been around Walter Reed long enough to be privileged to set her own hours. Thelma Hoffberg, a childless overweight widow in her early sixties, was two years from retiring. An excellent secretary, she could take shorthand faster than JP could think, much less talk, and her typing was impeccable. Her last eighteen years as a civil servant was as secretary to a succession of chiefs of head and neck surgery She had but one shortcoming: she had never given up the concept of motherhood. As a result she adopted the twelve head and neck residents as her own grandchildren, freely dispensing advice or admonishments as she saw fit. The chief of head and neck surgery became the surrogate for the son she never had, and she treated him accordingly. Like most mothers and grandmothers she was very protective of her brood.

When JP entered the waiting room a young man wearing slacks, a sport shirt, and ball cap abruptly dropped a magazine on the chair beside him and stood up. Even a casual observer would have noticed that the right side of his face was collapsed inward. A black patch covered the eye socket. Five months earlier Pfc Ricardo Diego, age twenty, was diagnosed as having an aggressive malignancy of the right cheek with invasion of the eye and brain. After radical surgery removed the right upper jaw, cheekbone, eye socket, eye, base of skull, a small portion of the dura and frontal lobe, he was treated with radiation followed by repeated courses of chemotherapy. It had been a maximum effort to destroy a tumor that was a vicious killer. One month ago he was medically retired without evidence of tumor and returned to his home in Florida to be followed locally. That he returned so soon after discharge was ominous.

JP greeted Ricardo warmly. "Didn't you get enough of Walter Reed the last time you were here?"

"Yes, sir, but the doctor in Florida said I should come back and let you take a look at this." He lifted the eye patch revealing a deep cavity where the eye had been.

Taking a penlight from his white coat pocket, JP directed its beam into a deep cavity. Its roof showed pulsating brain covered by a well-healed skin graft. So far so good. The light shifted to the back wall. A multi-nodular purplish mass was clearly visible. Slipping the penlight back into his pocket, he ran fingers over both sides of Ricardo's neck. A walnut-sized, hard, fixed lump was just under the skin on the right. Ricardo's tumor was not only present at the operative site, it had spread to the neck. JP felt as though he had been kicked in the gut. He tried to keep his face from betraying his thoughts.

A grating nasal voice interrupted. "Dr. Franklin, I'm Dr. Minter. I must talk with you."

JP turned to see a somber man in his early thirties wearing a wrinkled dark suit. He was already showing pudginess of the face and gut. JP extended his hand. Minter's grip was limp and damp. Believing Minter a civilian head and neck surgeon scheduled to come on active duty in July, JP presumed he had come to discuss possible assignments. As a professional courtesy he introduced Ricardo. "He had surgery for embryonal rhabdomyosarcoma of the cheek followed by—"

Minter showed no interest in Ricardo and interrupted. "Dr. Franklin, I've been waiting over twenty minutes to see you. My time is valuable. Would you mind finishing your examination of this patient later?"

Momentarily taken aback by Minter's lack of courtesy, JP told Ricardo, "One of the other doctors will see you as soon as rounds are finished. How about a cup of coffee?"

"No thanks, sir. I remember your coffee from the last time, I'll just check out the magazines."

"They're probably the same ones that were here a month ago. If you change your mind about the coffee, see Thelma."

JP fixed Minter with a cold stare. "This way, Doctor." By the time they entered his office his ire had cooled: he vowed to kill Minter with hospitality. Indicating an army-issue "antique" chair for Minter he went behind his desk and sat down.

Mrs. Hoffberg came to the door and asked Minter if he would like some coffee.

"I don't drink caffeinated beverages," Minter snapped.

Well, bully for you. "Black for me, please," JP said. He leaned forward. "What can I do for you, Dr. Minter?"

"You are the head and neck surgery consultant to the Army Surgeon General, are you not?"

JP nodded.

"And as consultant you are responsible for the assignments of head and neck surgeons, are you not?"

"I may make recommendations for assignments based on background, training, experience, and unusual circumstances such as hardships, but it is the Surgeon General who makes the final decision. How does this affect you?"

Mrs. Hoffberg reappeared with a mug of steaming coffee and set it on the desk. JP waited for Minter to continue.

"I enrolled in the Berry plan at the beginning of my residency four years ago and will graduate this June. Technically I am obligated to serve two years of active duty after graduating. Last December I wrote the Surgeon General a letter requesting I be absolved of my military obligation unless I could be assigned to Walter Reed as assistant chief, and provided certain other conditions were met."

Minter's statement got JP's attention. "Really," he said icily, "and what might those conditions be?"

"I must be excused from all night call and have weekends off."

This guy can't be serious, JP thought. *No, he is serious.* "Was there some basis for this request, Dr. Minter?"

"In my December letter to the Surgeon General I stated that my wife Ellen is very fragile emotionally. According to her doctor, any stress will precipitate a psychiatric crisis. Just the contemplation of my active duty in July requires the use of sedatives and anti-depressants."

JP regretted having thought ill of Minter. The poor guy's wife was a definite problem. But why only Washington D.C. and Walter Reed?

Minter continued. "My wife has lived in the Chicago area with her parents all her life. She has never been away from home. With their encouragement she has become active in the ballet and theater arts. After she and I married her parents insisted we move in with them."

JP's sympathy for the man increased markedly.

"My wife and her parents agree that the only city comparable to Chicago in the arts is Washington D.C. The only assignment I feel would be commensurate with my high level of training and skills would be Walter Reed."

JP reached for his coffee mug and thoughtfully sipped. Out of curiosity more than anything else he asked, "Why would it be necessary for you to be excused from night call and weekend duty?"

"My wife is terrified of the dark. It's important I be with her to give her a feeling of security at night. And as I mentioned earlier, she is very dependent on her parents. She will agree to come to Washington only if she can be assured I can take her back to Chicago each weekend. All this was in my December letter to the Surgeon General."

"Did you receive a response?" JP asked.

"I did. A Lieutenant Colonel Joseph Macklin requested corroborative medical records and statements from psychiatrists involved in my wife's care. I wrote back that the material requested was privileged and I had no intention of sending it. Furthermore, I reminded him I was a medical doctor and my word should be good enough."

Joe Macklin was JP's MSC counterpart in the Surgeon General's office. They worked together on assignments for head and neck surgeons and related matters. A former enlisted marine, Macklin became an army infantry officer through ROTC and eventually commanded an infantry battalion in Vietnam. Severely wounded two years ago he lost a leg. JP learned of him through the ill-defined Marine Corps grapevine and visited him on the orthopedic ward. With JP's guidance Macklin successfully fought a medical discharge, transferred to the Medical Service Corps and now commanded a desk.

Macklin's response had been routine. JP reiterated the need for supportive medical

32

documents. "When we have that information and it confirms what you have told me," he said, "I'm sure something can be worked out. It may not be Walter Reed but…"

Minter's voice began rising with his temper. "I expected to be given more sympathetic consideration than that from a fellow physician. Assistant Chief at Walter Reed is the only assignment I will consider. By denying me that assignment you leave me no choice but to demand relief from my military obligation." He took an envelope from his coat pocket and threw it on JP's desk. "That contains a letter outlining the reasons I cannot honor my military commitment. With it is a statement from my wife's physician describing her psychiatric status. You wanted corroborative data. Now you have it." Minter settled back in his chair.

JP opened the envelope, unfolded Minter's letter, glanced at it and set it aside. It was the second letter that interested him. He read:

To Whom It May Concern

Ellen Minter has been my patient for twenty-nine years. It is my opinion she is emotionally and psychiatrically unstable. Any prolonged absence from her parents or move to a strange environment will precipitate a psychiatric crisis. She must remain in Chicago or a comparable environment, such as Washington D.C. For these reasons it is strongly recommended that her husband, Ray Minter, M.D., be assigned to Walter Reed Army Medical Center, Washington D.C. or released from his military obligation. Should the former be selected it is imperative Dr. Minter be free at night to provide emotional support for his wife, and free on weekends to bring his wife to visit her parents.

I.V. Turner, M.D.

JP stared at the letter, then reread it. He presumed Dr. Turner was a psychiatrist although there was no letterhead to indicate his specialty. Confused, he looked at Dr. Minter. "Your wife has been under the care of a psychiatrist a long time. How old is she?"

"She's twenty-nine."

"Your wife has been under the care of a psychiatrist since birth?"

Minter looked sheepish. "Dr. Turner is not a psychiatrist. He's a family practitioner."

"Did he deliver her?"

"No, but he was present at the birth."

This was becoming more and more bizarre. JP could not understand why Dr. Turner, a family practitioner, did not refer a patient as emotionally unstable as Minter's wife to a psychiatrist. "I don't understand," he told Minter, "is there a reason why Dr. Turner didn't refer your wife to a psychiatrist, or why you and her parents didn't take it upon yourselves to do so?"

Minter's demeanor began to shift perceptibly from offensive to defensive. He shifted in his chair, refused to make eye contact, and dropped his voice. "Dr. Turner," he began, "even though a family practitioner, is also very competent as a psychiatrist."

JP sipped his coffee. Something was not right here. Deciding to play a hunch, he fixed Minter with an accusing glare. "Dr. Minter, are you aware that making false or deceptive statements to military authorities may subject you to criminal prosecution, heavy fines, and imprisonment?"

Minter looked as if he would pass out.

JP bore in. "Who is Dr. Turner and what is this twenty-nine-year relationship with your wife?"

Guilt flashed across Minter's face. "Dr. Turner is my wife's father," he stammered. "He knows my wife's condition and how to manage it better than any psychiatrist could possibly know." Minter's voice rose in pitch and volume. "His paternal relation to my wife has nothing to do with the issues I'm bringing up."

"The hell it doesn't," JP said with the righteous anger of someone who realizes he has been deceived. His voice became low and threatening. "Are there any medical records to corroborate what you have told me about your wife's condition..." he waved Minter's letter, "or as stated in this?"

"There are no written medical records. Dr. Turner kept that information in his head," Minter reluctantly admitted.

"You said earlier you are technically obliged to serve two years' military service. You have that wrong, Dr. Minter. You are legally obliged to serve two years' military service. That obligation can only be absolved by the Department of Defense for proven compassionate reasons, with the burden of proof on you. Unless the assignment orders you receive from the Department of Army read otherwise, you will report to Fort Sam Houston for the medical officers' orientation course by 2400 hours on the date specified in those orders. For your information, Dr. Minter, 2400 hours is midnight. The big hand and little hand both will be on the number twelve and it will be dark outside. Should you fail to report on that date the Federal Bureau of Investigation will be notified that you are a deserter and a warrant will be issued for your arrest. The environment of a federal prison will be much more traumatic than anything you might encounter on a military post in this country or Vietnam."

Minter stood up, pale and shaking. "Vietnam? You can't send me to Vietnam. I'm too well trained. My parents have too much money invested in me. My attorneys will not permit it. You and the government will be held responsible for any aggravation of my wife's emotional condition."

"Shut up and sit down, Minter," JP ordered.

Minter slid into his chair and stared at JP.

"You have an alternative to active duty as a medical officer."

Hope flooded Minter's face.

"You can sign a document stating that you refuse to accept a commission as a captain, Medical Corps. That document will be sent to your draft board. Within forty-eight hours you will receive a notice of induction ordering you to report to Fort Jackson, South Carolina, for basic training." The image of Minter marching with an M–16 or cleaning latrines brought a grim smile to JP. His face quickly hardened; he stood up. "Now, Dr. Minter, get your sorry ass out of here before I decide to talk to the JAG and US Attorney about attempted fraud."

Minter jumped up and reached for the letters on the desk. JP's hand shot out and grabbed his wrist in such an iron grasp that Minter yelped. Opening a drawer with his other hand, JP took the letters, dropped them in the drawer, and closed it. "Those letters are now part of your official record. They may be used later as evidence of attempted fraud."

"You will hear from my attorney and my senator about this," Minter howled. He slammed his fist down on JP's desk with force, knocking the "In" basket off the desk. When it hit the floor its load of papers scattered. Turning, he strode angrily from the office, colliding with Dave Strickland in the doorway.

"Oops. Sorry," Strickland apologized.

Minter grunted and shoved Strickland aside. "Get the hell out of my way." Then he was gone.

JP chuckled. Dave Strickland held a black belt in karate. If he had wanted he could have decked Minter in the blink of an eye. Kneeling, he began picking up papers.

Strickland glanced at the vacant doorway, then at JP. "What's his problem?"

"He wants to replace you."

"What did you tell him?"

"I told him I'd think about it," JP said with a straight face. "Rounds over?"

"No, sir. I just got off the phone with Bill Dreicher at West Point."

JP replaced the In box on the desk, stuffed the papers into it, then sat down. "What did the master of subtle remarks call about?"

"A twenty-one-year-old senior cadet named Tom Carter has bled intermittently from his nose and mouth over the past forty-eight hours despite packing. He's had four units of blood and is now on his fifth. An angiogram done at the hospital in Newburg last night demonstrated an extensive vascular tumor of the nasopharynx, most likely juvenile angiofibroma The tumor extends into the cheek, base of skull, sphenoid sinus, and middle fossa. Seventy percent of its blood supply is from the right external carotid, ten percent from the left, and twenty percent from the intracranial segment of the right internal carotid artery. The tumor that extends into the cranial cavity is either indenting the temporal lobe or penetrating it."

"Sounds like a big one," JP said. "Is the surgery going to be done at one of the hospitals in New York City? They have some outstanding people."

"The cadet's mother pushed for that. She offered to pay for the surgery and hospitalization. Apparently she doesn't have a high opinion of military surgeons. Two very prominent specialists convinced her that the surgery should done here. They told her you and George Barfield pioneered the operation for those kinds of tumors and have the most experience removing them of anyone in the world."

"True," JP said, grinning modestly, "so when is the Mr. Carter due?"

"Sometime this evening; Bill wants to get him stabilized first. An army chopper will pick him up at the West Point hospital and take him to Stuart Air Force Base."

"I used to fly Navions out of Stuart when I was stationed at the Military Academy," JP reminisced. "Those were idyllic times. Some days I wish I were back there."

"Maybe it's good we can't go back, boss," Strickland said, then returned to cadet Carter. "An air force T–39 will take him from Stuart to Andrews and a chopper will bring him here from Andrews."

"Have the parents been notified?"

"The father is deceased. Bill talked with the mother this morning. She lives in California and is some sort of federal judge in the middle of a big-time trial. She was reluctant to leave the trial until Bill convinced her that her son was facing possible stroke, blindness, pituitary failure, or even death."

"That Dreicher can be so subtle," JP said, chuckling.

"She plans to leave tomorrow morning, arriving tomorrow night at Dulles."

"The surgery will be long over by then," JP said. "Want to give me a hand?"

Strickland's wide smile was taken as affirmative.

"Tell Terry O'Connel and Craig Entarde they will make up the rest of extracranial team. I'll alert George Barfield about doing the intracranial part. Cancel the commando for tomorrow and try to work it in towards the end of the week. If not, schedule him for the weekend and I'll staff it. You need a weekend off to spend with your family, go flying or whatever you do in your spare time."

"Right, boss," Strickland said, throwing a half-salute and leaving.

"And, Dave, make sure Dreicher sends the angiograms with the cadet."

JP settled back in his chair, slurped coffee, and reviewed his experience with juvenile angiofibroma. A rare vascular tumor, it developed at the upper part of the throat in male adolescents and young men. Although theoretically benign, it had the capacity to erode bone, invade the eye socket, push out the eyeball, invade the face, sinuses, nose, base of skull, and, in rare cases, the brain. The tumor was so infiltrated with blood-filled spaces that even a small biopsy could result in life-threatening hemorrhage. Tumors without brain invasion had been successfully removed at many centers for years. However, tumors with brain invasion had invariably resulted in fatal uncontrollable hemorrhage from incomplete removal or death from meningitis.

Six years ago JP and George Barfield, the assistant chief of neurosurgery, worked out a technique to jointly remove the tumors with brain invasion. Barfield removed the small intracranial extension and JP the massive extracranial portion. So far they had operated successfully on seven patients with no fatalities. It was the largest series in the world. After publishing the technique and results, the international reputations of both surgeons became firmly established.

Lieutenant Colonel George Barfield was one of JP's closest friends and surgical colleagues, Their families had lived in quarters next to each other at Forest Glen for five years. Each family had four children roughly the same ages. Louise Barfield, George's wife, and Kathy Franklin had become as close as sisters. The two families shared Thanksgiving and Christmas dinners, Easter egg hunts, Fourth of July celebrations, and backyard barbecues.

Now the Vietnam War was about to break up the dynamic duo of Franklin and Barfield. In two weeks George Barfield would leave for Vietnam to fill a vacancy as the division surgeon for an infantry division. Months ago JP had learned of the vacancy and requested to fill it. The Surgeon General refused to approve the request. "You're too valuable as chief at Walter Reed and my consultant," he told JP. However, assistant chiefs did not enjoy such immunity. When JP lamented to

George Barfield that his request had been turned down, George applied for the position and was accepted. JP had encouraged him, arguing the experience would enhance his career as a military officer and physician.

Taking a sip of coffee, he reached for the intercom. "Thelma, get me George Barfield in neurosurgery."

"Yes, sir. General Briggs's aide called a few minutes ago to say the general would be about forty-five minutes late."

Several minutes later Thelma's voice cracked from the intercom. "Colonel Barfield is on line one."

JP picked up the phone. "George, you had breakfast?"

"Just getting ready to leave for the mess hall."

"See you there in five minutes."

★

Monday, 14 April, 1969, 0805 hours
Mess Hall, Walter Reed Army Hospital, Washington D.C.

JP Franklin slid his tray on to the table opposite George Barfield, then sat down. Barfield, a six-foot bear of a man with black hair cut close, bushy black eyebrows, and a Wyatt Earp moustache, scrutinized the four slices of bacon, two fried eggs, grits, and three slices of toast piled on JP's tray. "You on a diet?" he asked.

JP grinned. "I have to store up food like a camel does water. I never know when I'm going to eat again." He became serious. "There's a West Point cadet with intracranial angiofibroma due to arrive some time this evening. He is in need of the army's most gifted neurosurgeon to snatch him from the jaws of death."

"I had an idea this breakfast meeting was not going to be a social occasion."

JP briefly reviewed the information he had received from Dave Strickland. "This may be a good case to be less radical in our surgery with the idea of keeping the cadet eligible to meet minimal physical standards for commissioning."

"I'll go along with that. I was never convinced some of the things we did were really necessary."

JP took out his pen and began outlining the main arterial supply or the neck and head on the tablecloth. "Here are some modifications to consider. Tell me what you think we can get away with." Moments later they were in deep conversation, pen sketches covering a fourth of the tablecloth. A heavy-set fortyish female in a white uniform and lieutenant colonel's silver leaves on her collar points appeared at their table, hands on hips.

"Colonel Franklin," she started off in a loud voice, "I warned you before not to draw on the tablecloth."

People at neighboring tables stopped eating and stared. George Barfield stood and picked up his tray. "Time for me to go."

"Coward," JP told him, then turned to the angry dietician. "Sorry, Colonel Duggan. You'll have to report me to the general. While you're doing it suggest he have me sent to Vietnam as fitting punishment."

Two doctors and a nurse at the next table applauded. Colonel Duggan glared at them. "You don't need to encourage him." Turning, she stalked off towards her office.

JP stood, bowed to the adjacent table, picked up his tray and left.

Chapter Four

Monday, 14 April, 1969, 0930 hours
Walter Reed Army Hospital, Washington D.C.

Leaving the mess hall, Lieutenant Colonel JP Franklin climbed the stairs to the third floor and entered the library. After a search of head and neck literature he found three articles on angiofibroma with intracranial extension. Two described a single case and both referred to the third, an article published by JP and George Barfield describing their technique. So much for the world literature. Returning the bound journals to the stacks, he headed to the anesthesia department by way of the head and neck clinic.

Climbing stairs to the fourth floor, he heard a strange intermittent grinding noise. When he reached the hall between the wards and clinic the noise was much louder. Curious, he traced the noise to the latrine. Two civilian workmen in overalls, one young and thin, the other much older and grossly obese, were on their knees manipulating an electric snake down the protruding pipe of a dismantled commode. "How is it going?" he shouted above the noise.

The grinding stopped. The two workmen turned to stare at him. "Not so good, Doc," the older workman answered. "These pipes must have been put in during the Civil War. They may shatter if we get too heavy with the snake."

"We have the same problems with humans," JP said. Wishing them good luck, he left. Entering the head and neck clinic, he glanced at the plethora of patients in the waiting room and kept moving before someone stopped him. He didn't make it past Thelma's office.

"Just a minute, Colonel," she called. JP stuck his head in the door.

"Don't forget General Briggs at eleven," Thelma reminded him.

"Have I ever forgotten an appointment?"

"I can list them if you like, starting with the chief justice…"

"Forget I asked. Have the general's medical records shown up?"

"Yes, sir. They're on your desk. Where are you going now?"

"Anesthesia. I need to discuss a case with Major Resniek."

He walked through the remainder of the clinic, opened one of the double doors and entered the corridor leading to the operating room suite. Reaching it, he turned left and headed for the anesthesia induction room where he hoped to find the assistant chief of anesthesia, Harry Resniek.

★

An emergency operation on a critical patient, especially one with a rare condition requiring complex surgery still considered in its infant stages, demanded an anesthesiologist in whom the surgeons had great confidence. Harry Resniek was that kind of anesthesiologist. Exceedingly competent, he not only stayed cool when situations became desperate, he was eccentric enough to make even the dullest operation interesting.

A Brooklyn native like Thelma Hoffberg, Resniek graduated from Columbia University at eighteen with a degree in mathematics and a Phi Beta Kappa key. For some unknown reason he became enamored of human physiology. Three years later, with major research and a slew of publications behind him, he received a PhD degree. Still in need of intellectual challenge, he left his beloved Brooklyn for the Johns Hopkins School of Medicine. Graduating with honors, he interned at Hopkins, completed a three-year anesthesia residency and a year of fellowship, during which he was protected from the draft by the Berry Plan. When payback time came, the army, to its credit, committed a most appropriate and logical act. It assigned him to Walter Reed as assistant chief of anesthesia. In addition to giving anesthesia on complicated cases, he supervised a dozen residents and an equal number of nurse anesthetists.

The anesthesia induction room was long and narrow. Four operating tables lined each side, each with its own anesthesia machine and cabinet filled with equipment and medications. Patients were put to sleep or given spinal anesthesia, then transported to an operating room ready to be positioned on the table and prepped. This permitted close supervision by a senior staff during induction, a critical phase of anesthesia. It also facilitated efficient use of operating room time. A resident scheduled to do the surgery had better be in the operating room waiting when the anesthetized patient arrived. If by some unfortunate event the resident was absent or late, his chief of service would receive a caustic telephone call from the assistant chief of anesthesia. Although a very junior major, Harry Resniek was not at all intimidated by lieutenant colonels, colonels, and even generals.

Inside the induction room JP saw only two patients being put to sleep. A third, lying on his side in the fetal position, was about to receive a spinal anesthetic. Major Resniek stood nearby watching, a 5'8" mother hen with coke bottle glasses and a walrus moustache. JP walked over and tossed him a cheery "Good morning, Harry".

Resniek turned. "Ah, the warrior surgeon." He looked at his wristwatch. "You have no other motive for showing up here other than to wish me a good morning?"

"How did anyone so young and brilliant become so cynical?"

"Working around surgeons like you. What's up, Colonel?"

"Just a short case that won't be much of a challenge. I hope you don't have plans for tonight."

"Come on, Colonel. Rhoda and I have tickets to the Ford Theatre."

JP acted as though he hadn't heard. "Let me tell you about the fascinating case coming from West Point…"

★

Monday, April 14, 1969, 1045 hours
Walter Reed Army Hospital, Washington D.C.

Back in his office JP checked his watch, then reviewed what he knew of four-star General Peter Briggs. The referring physician who phoned had provided background information. Briggs had graduated from the US Military Academy in 1943 in the upper tenth of his class. He then went through airborne training, joined the 82nd Airborne Division in time to make the jump into St. Mere Eglise. By the time the war ended he had been wounded three times, been awarded two Silver Stars, four Bronze Stars, and was a captain. After the war he commanded training companies, then attended Command and Staff College at Fort Leavenworth, Kansas. When the Korean War began he was promoted to major and shipped to Korea where he commanded a battalion in the 24th Infantry Division. On his second tour in Korea he served as a regimental S–3 (operations) then executive officer. Promoted to lieutenant colonel, he commanded a battalion until wounded and evacuated to Walter Reed. Then came a series of schools, command, Pentagon duty and Vietnam tours. Promotions followed. Two years ago he received his fourth star and was currently under consideration as NATO commander. JP considered General Briggs one hell of a soldier and paid him the ultimate compliment: he would have made a good marine.

He reached for the sealed manila envelope with the general's medical records. Opening the envelope, he removed the contents and began reading. Briggs was forty-nine years old with a history of smoking two to three packs of cigarettes a day since age twenty-two. Ten months earlier at another hospital he was diagnosed with cancer of the right vocal cord. The doctors recommended laryngectomy but General Briggs, desperate to save his voice and career, rejected the surgery in favor of radiation therapy. The cancer initially appeared to respond, but the vocal cord remained swollen and its movement limited. Then redness and ulceration developed. The vocal cord became paralyzed and airway obstruction followed.

Just as JP finished reading the general's records, Thelma's sharp voice jumped from the intercom. "Colonel, General Briggs is here."

JP crossed the hall to Thelma's office. A robust, mildly obese man in a civilian suit sat by Thelma's desk drinking coffee. He stood when JP walked in.

"General Briggs," JP said, extending his hand.

"Colonel Franklin. I've heard a lot of good things about you." The general's grip was firm.

"Sir, you're embarrassing me in front of Mrs. Hoffberg. She knows the truth." JP immediately noted that General Briggs's voice was hoarse and raspy. Even more alarming was wheezing on inspiration and expiration. Suppressing overt appearance of concern he told the general, "Let's go across the hall to my examining room. Bring your coffee if you like."

"I'd prefer a cigarette instead."

"Sir, from the sound of your voice your smoking days are over."

General Briggs gave JP a hard stare, then smiled. "Colonel, I like your style. Okay. You give the orders."

When they entered the examining room JP closed the door. He asked the general to remove his coat, tie and shirt, then sit in a chair somewhat resembling a dentist's chair. After the general was settled JP took a medical history. "Any shortness of breath?"

"Affirmative. I had to give up handball last month. I blamed it on old age catching up to me. Now climbing a flight of stairs is an effort."

"What about pain?"

"There's a steady dull pain in my throat. When I swallow it becomes sharp and my right ear aches. I keep clearing my throat as if a burr is stuck in it. Sometimes I cough to clear my throat and get up streaks of blood in my sputum."

After washing his hands JP examined the general's head, neck and chest. He was not surprised to see a fixed right vocal cord infiltrated by a beefy red ulcerated growth occluding half the airway. The growth extended to adjacent structures including the left vocal cord. Palpation of the neck disclosed two grape-sized lumps deep on the right. A third mass was felt in the right lobe of the thyroid gland. Efforts to move the Adam's apple from side to side were unsuccessful. Tumor and radiation scarring had fixed it to adjacent tissues. It was clear the general had a serious condition, a condition that would end his military career and possibly his life. "Let's go into to my office, sir," he told the general. "We need to talk."

The general seated himself in one of the two fake antique chairs in front of JP's desk. "What do you think, Colonel?" he asked in a raspy voice. The inflections suggested he already knew the answer.

JP dreaded answering. There were times when he wished he stayed an artillery officer or a marine, and this was one of those times.

"General," he began, "it's my impression that radiation therapy failed to control the vocal cord cancer. It has spread to the left side of the voice box, spilled over into the gullet, spread to the lymph nodes in the neck and to the thyroid gland. On the scale of life threat I would consider your condition a DEFCON TWO and close to DEFCON ONE."

"I was afraid of that. What about more radiation?"

JP shook his head. "You have had the maximum dosage. The only remaining option is radical surgery."

General Briggs grimaced at the words. "What does that mean?"

"Removal of the entire voice box, part of the pharynx and perhaps even part of the upper esophagus. It would be done in continuity with what is referred to as a radical neck dissection. That is, removal of the large thick muscle in the right neck, its underlying internal jugular vein, certain nerves, about forty lymph nodes, and the right lobe of the thyroid gland. I would not rule out a similar dissection on the left or chemotherapy after surgery."

General Briggs sat back in deep thought. "It sounds like you want to nuke my neck, Colonel."

JP smiled at the comparison. "You will lose your normal voice, but there are alternate means of communicating. The most practical is esophageal speech. It involves belching air to make sound, then forming words using the tongue and lips. There's a retired colonel, an active attorney, who had a laryngectomy four years ago. He developed excellent esophageal speech which allowed him to continue his law practice. Considering how sharp he is, it's fortunate he doesn't specialize in suing doctors. He will be contacting you for a lunch date if you have no objections. You will see how well he is able to communicate."

"What are the alternatives to esophageal speech?"

"One is a device that emits a low-pitched buzzing sound when a button is pressed. With the device held against the neck the sound produced can be molded into words. Voice is adequate for conversing but is a monotone much like a robot voice. The future is bright for innovative surgical techniques and devices that will serve as more effective sound producers."

"What about my remaining on active duty?"

This was the hardest part for JP to relay. Men like General Briggs had devoted their entire lives to serving their country. Now when he had the most to offer he could no longer serve.

"Army regulations do not permit it except under very unusual circumstances. There is an air force dental surgeon at Eglin who was allowed to continue on active duty even though he had a laryngectomy."

"So you think I may have a chance?"

"The final decision will be up to the Army Surgeon General, the chief of staff, and the Secretary of the Army. I can make recommendations based on your recovery and control of the cancer."

"I see." Briggs hesitated. "Damn, I would like a cigarette," he said. "When would you recommend the surgery be done?"

"Some time within the next week or two. I would advise against a longer delay. During the interim, X-rays, lab studies, and consultations need to be obtained. I would also like you seen by my consultant from Johns Hopkins, Dr. McClintock. He'll be here next Thursday evening."

General Briggs stood and extended his hand. "Colonel," he rasped, "thank you for your candor. My aide will call you this afternoon and firm up a schedule you would like me to follow."

JP squeezed the general's hand, then escorted him out.

Just before leaving the general turned and asked, "Who would do the surgery?"

"I would, with my chief resident, Major O'Connel. He's an old armor man from your alma mater, class of '59."

General Briggs nodded, smiled, and left.

Back in his office JP began writing in the general's medical record. Dave Strickland knocked, then walked in wearing green scrubs and carrying a cup of coffee.

JP looked up. "How's the kid with the dog bite?"

"Fine. He wants to go home. Because of the location and amount of tissue trauma the pediatricians started him on rabies antitoxin."

"That makes sense. What about the dog?"

"Impounded by the MPs and held for observation at the vets. There is one other development."

"Oh?"

'The general surgeons are going to explore Fabrezio's belly. They agreed with Roy French's concern about a sub-capsular spleenic bleed."

'That was a good pickup for Roy. I'm glad the air force trained their pilots to be thorough. If that capsule had ruptured it could have ruined our day, not to mention Fabrezio's," JP said. "Any word on the cadet from West Point?"

"Yes, sir. He'll leave Stuart Field about 1900 hours and arrive here a couple of hours later. Do you want me to alert the OR?"

"Nope. Been there, done that. In fact the assistant chief of anesthesia has volunteered to pass gas."

"Harry Resniek volunteered? The man has changed."

"You never can tell about people," JP said knowingly. "You should have seen Harry on his first day here."

Strickland settled back in his chair and sipped from his coffee mug. "I have a feeling you're going to tell me."

"You'll enjoy this. Pass it on only to very select individuals."

"Trust me, Colonel."

"Harry finished his fellowship at Hopkins one day and drove down here to report for duty the next. He had been excused from the three-week orientation course at Fort Sam because of the acute need here for an assistant chief of anesthesiology. Harry had no uniforms, no idea of military protocol, and no ID. What he did have was hair down to his shoulders, a beard, loud sports shirt, baggy pants, and sandals."

Strickland smiled as he conjured up a picture of a hippie Harry Resniek.

JP continued. "When Harry couldn't get into the regular parking lot because it was full he swung into the quadrangle."

"The sacred lot where only the anointed may park?"

"You got it. Only one space was vacant. Guess which one."

Strickland started to laugh. "Not the commanding general's."

"Precisely. Since the spot was vacant Harry reasoned it only logical he should park his car in it."

"This is getting interesting," Strickland said, leaning forward.

"Harry had never been to Walter Reed, but had been told the anesthesia department was on the fourth floor. He took the first elevator he came to, which happened to be the elevator used for patient transport. When the doors opened on the fourth floor he stepped out. Instead of turning right to go to the anesthesia department and OR he turned left into the corridor that led to Ward 8."

"The VIP ward."

"Right. Ike was a patient on the ward at the time. Three Secret Service agents were in the hall outside his room. On the TV monitor they saw a strange man with long hair, beard, sport shirt, slacks, and sandals approaching the door to Ward 8. As soon as Harry stepped through the door they had him spread eagle against the wall and handcuffed.

"Harry insisted he was the assistant chief of anesthesia and had papers to prove it in his car. The agents agreed to take him to his car. When they reached the quadrangle parking lot, Harry's car was gone. The MPs had it towed for being in the general's spot. By now Harry had become quite agitated. He was sure his car had been stolen. He was in handcuffs, being taken to jail. His first day in the army had turned into a nightmare."

"I can't wait to hear the rest of the story, boss," a grinning Strickland said.

"I can't wait to tell it," JP said, chuckling as he recalled the episode. "Steve Hall, the chief of anesthesia, happened to see Harry being stuffed into a car by two tough-looking guys. He rushed over and banged on the rear fender of the car just as it left the curb. The driver slammed on the brakes. The agents jumped out with pistols drawn. Steve said the first thing that came to mind. 'God damn it, where the hell are you taking my assistant chief?' Luckily Steve was in uniform.

"The agents looked at Steve, then at Harry and then back at Steve. 'Colonel, you've got to be kidding,' one of the agents said."

"Poor Harry," Strickland said, his voice dripping with false sympathy.

"Steve vouched for Harry, got him released, and drove him to the towing company lot to claim his car. Harry had to pay a twenty-five-dollar towing fee and ten-dollar parking fee to get his car."

"That's one hell of a story, boss."

"Don't ever tell Harry where you heard it."

Thelma's voice reverberated through the room. "The OR is ready for Dr. Strickland, and Colonel, Commander Glover from Bethesda is on line one."

JP waved to Strickland as he left, still chuckling. He reached for the phone. Bart Glover was the chief of head and neck surgery at the Bethesda Naval Medical Center and JP's navy counterpart. A medical corpsman in World War II, he had served with the 3rd Marine Division on Guam and Iwo Jima, where he received two Purple Hearts and a Silver Star. Although Glover had never forgiven JP for going into the Army Medical Corps instead of the navy, the two were good friends. They frequently consulted each other on complex surgical cases, VIPs, and administrative matters.

"What's up, Bart?" JP asked.

"Have you seen Jason Grove's column in this morning's paper?"

"I'm in the army, Commander. I don't have time to read the morning paper. What did Mr. Groves say?"

"Well, he rather vividly described the deplorable latrine facilities at Walter Reed, particularly Wards 20 and 21. He also reported that the lack of air conditioning during the hot summer months was responsible for unusually high infection rates, and repeated efforts to obtain funds for new plumbing and air conditioning had been stonewalled by Pentagon bean counters.'

"Mr. Groves seems to have gotten his facts right. I wonder where he got his information."

Bart Glover laughed. "I have to tell you, JP, you were the first person to come to mind when I asked myself the same question."

"You have a suspicious mind, Commander."

"That may be. Any time you would like to transfer to the navy let me know. The navy has lots of modern flush commodes."

"I'm sure they do, and they need every one of them considering what else the navy has in great abundance."

"Are you ever going to get over having been a marine?"

"Probably not. Thanks for the alert, Bart. I'd better call the CG before he calls me."

"Good luck. Let's get together this week for dinner at the club with our wives. I have a couple of cases I'd like to run by you."

"Friday or Saturday evening is best for us. I'll check with Kathy and call you tomorrow. There's a general with Stage Three cancer or the larynx I want to discuss with you."

Just as JP hung up Thelma informed him, "General Worden is on line three."

Damn. He didn't waste any time. JP snapped up the phone. "Good morning, General."

"JP, have you seen the Jason Groves column in this morning's paper?"

"No, sir, but a friend just briefed me."

"Well, I suggest you read it. It has stirred up a hornet's nest over on the hill. I've been notified that tomorrow at ten the chairmen of the House and Senate Armed Services Committees will be here to inspect the hospital. Wards 20 and 21 will be hit first, then the rest of the hospital. I want you and Joe Mangonis to escort them through your wards."

"It will be a pleasure, sir," JP said with alacrity.

"You sound inappropriately pleased. I won't ask if you know who informed Groves of our plumbing and air conditioning problems." The general chuckled. "I have my suspicions. Whoever he or she is did us a great favor. Maybe now I'll be able to shake supplemental money out of DOD."

"Sometimes it takes a nuclear device to get the enemy's attention, General."

"True, but we wouldn't want to overdo the use of nukes, now would we?"

"Oh no, sir. I would hope the informant or informants have the good judgment to be more circumspect in the future."

"Good." The general hung up.

Over the intercom JP told Thelma, "Get me Joe Mangonis in urology, please."

"Colonel, I just took a call from Major Dreicher at West Point. Cadet Carter has started to bleed through his packing. The departure time from Stuart Air Force Base has been moved up to 1300 hours."

JP made some quick mental calculations. The T–39 Saberliner should land at Andrews at about 1430 hours, then twenty minutes to helicopter Carter to Walter Reed and about an hour to prepare him for anesthesia and surgery. "Please alert the OR and neurosurgery for a 1600 start time."

"Yes, sir. Do you want me to notify Mrs. Franklin you won't be home until late?"

"I'd better talk to her, Thelma. It's been happening so often she is getting touchy."

"I don't blame her."

"Whose side are you on?"

"Hers of course. I'll get her for you.

In less than a minute Kathy Franklin was on the phone. "Honey, there's an emergency coming down from West Point," JP told her. "It's a cadet bleeding with juvenile angio. His surgery will go at least seven hours."

Kathy's soft southern voice asked, "Are you sure you didn't arrange this because tonight is PTA at Woodlin?"

"You know me better than that."

"Precisely. And, JP, I've had five phone calls about a Jason Grove's column in this morning's paper that mentions your ward."

"Wasn't it thoughtful of someone to go to the effort of writing Mr. Groves about the sad conditions on Wards 20 and 21? General Worden has just told me Groves's column shook up the Pentagon. Tomorrow a senator and a representative are coming to inspect the hospital."

"Do you have any idea who wrote the letter to Jason Groves?"

"Kathleen, this is not a secure phone."

Kathy Franklin laughed. "You will never change, but I love you anyway."

"Back at ya, kid. See you tonight."

Thelma walked in with some papers for JP to sign. "Well, how did she take it?" she asked.

"Better than expected. And would you believe I'll miss a PTA meeting tonight?"

★

Monday, April 14, 1969, 1630 hours
Walter Reed Army Hospital, Washington D.C.

Cadet Thomas Carter had been in the ICU about thirty minutes when JP walked in, looked around and spotted him. A thin young man, Carter was sitting up in bed, blood dripping in one arm and Ringer's lactate in the other. The end of a Foley urinary catheter protruded from each nostril and was taped to his nose. The balloon ends were in the upper throat, expanded with saline to bring pressure on the bleeding tumor. Dried blood caked his face and neck. Periodically he spit blood and clots into a kidney basin. A young pretty second lieutenant nurse hovered over Carter as though he were a movie idol. Craig Entarde was in a chair beside the bed writing in a chart.

JP, his face somber, studied the miserable cadet for a long moment, then shook his head sadly. "Mr. Carter, you are one sorry-looking human."

Carter stared back at JP, trying to decide if this idiot in a white coat was really a doctor. Craig Entarde stood and introduced JP.

Carter brightened. "Yes, sir. They told me about you at the Academy when they learned I was coming here." Carter's voice was hoarse and nasal.

"Really, and what exactly did they tell you?"

"That you fell off the rocks at Blackcap Mountain and broke your leg."

JP turned to Craig Entarde. "How about that. After spending most of my off time for three years teaching clumsy frightened cadets to climb rocks, my only legacy is a single minor misfortune. The younger generation has no sense of gratitude."

Entarde tried to get the conversation back on track. "Lieutenant Sanchez just ran a 'crit on Cadet Carter. It's thirty-four after six units of blood. The seventh unit is going in now."

JP nodded, then dragged a chair over to the side of the bed and sat down. "Mr. Carter," he began, "I'm going to review the operation we have planned and the possible complications. When I finish you will have an opportunity to ask questions, then you will be given a twenty-minute written examination which will count one-third of your final grade."

Carter shook his head. He croaked to Craig Entarde, "Is he always like this?"

"Sometimes worse, much worse," Entarde admitted.

JP became serious. "I understand your mother will arrive tomorrow evening."

"Yes, sir. She's presiding at a trial that has something to do with espionage. A lot of the testimony is in closed court. She recessed the trial for four days."

"We will leave orders for her to be admitted to the ward as soon as she arrives with no limit on visiting hours."

"Thanks, sir... Colonel, I need to ask, what are my chances of being commissioned after surgery?"

"Ah, the cart before the horse." He looked at Captain Entarde. "Isn't that the way with young people these days," he said, shaking his head. "Mr. Carter, questions will be allowed later. For now I will discuss the extracranial part of the surgery. The neurosurgeons will be by to discuss the intracranial part."

JP reached for Carter's chart, opened it to a blank page, and drew a front view of a face, then marked in the incisions. "They will be placed to minimize visible scars," he explained. "The bulk of the tumor is in places ordinarily inaccessible because of the facial skeleton. Some bones of the face will have to be cut and some removed to get adequate exposure of the tumor." He shaded in parts of the cheek, upper jaw and nose to illustrate. "It may even be necessary to cut the lower jaw. Should it come to that, the jaw will be wired back together at the end of the operation."

JP flipped to a blank page and drew a cross section of the middle third of the skull Pointing with his pen to a golf ball size cavity under the base of skull, he continued. "This is the sphenoid sinus, a bony cavity capable of great mischief just by virtue of its relationship to adjacent structures. It serves no useful purpose that I know of. The roof of the cavity supports the brain and pituitary gland. The optic nerves, the nerves of vision, cross just in front. Each side of the sphenoid sinus is in contact with a large venous structure, the cavernous sinus, through which pass the internal carotid artery, the vessel that supplies most of the blood to the brain. Nerves to the eye muscles, face, and jaw also run through the cavernous sinus. Any questions so far?"

Carter shook his head.

"I reviewed your X-rays and angiograms. The tumor has not only filled the sphenoid sinus, it has eroded the roof and both walls. That means tumor is in contact with the lining of the brain, the pituitary gland, and the cavernous sinus. Tumor has also invaded the right eye socket, maxillary sinus, and cheek. It has extended out under the base of skull to enter the middle cranial fossa and brain."

What little color Carter had in his face drained away.

JP continued, "Mr. Carter, I must be candid with you. There is substantial risk that one or more of the structures mentioned may be injured during the removal of the tumor."

"I'm not sure what that means, sir?"

"It means you could lose all vision in one or both eyes, suffer a stroke, leaving you paralyzed on one side, sustain permanent brain damage which could impact reasoning, memory, and cognitive functions. You could develop meningitis, pituitary dysfunction, uncontrolled hemorrhage, or even die. Other than those, there's very little risk."

"Jesus Christ, sir, you have a way of putting things."

"Now for the good news."

"I can't believe there is any."

"Of course there is," JP assured. "Colonel Barfield and I have operated on seven patients with your kind of tumor, that is, tumor extending from the throat into the brain and other places. There were no cases of significant post-op infection, stroke, brain damage, uncontrolled hemorrhage, blindness, or death. Two patients developed reduced vision in one eye. Two had transient unilateral weakness of arms and legs, one patient had a brisk post-op bleed which was controlled in the OR. Four patients with erosion of the sphenoid roof developed temporary diabetes insipidus. That is, markedly increased urine output up to eight liters a day. Each patient was treated with pituitary hormone injections for several weeks until urine function returned to normal. All seven went back to school or work within an eight-week period post-op, and are doing well." JP paused, closed the chart and leaned back. "Now, Mr. Carter, you may ask your questions."

Cadet Carter remained silent for several moments. "I want to know how this surgery will affect my commissioning in June, sir?"

"Carter, you do have a one-track mind. Let me put it this way. If none of the bad things mentioned happen, there is a good possibility you can be commissioned with restrictions. One patient, a lieutenant, is now two years post-op and remains on active duty with certain restrictions on his assignments. Something like that can be worked out for you."

"Restrictions? What kind of restrictions?"

"We'll just have to wait and see. For now let's concentrate on separating you from your tumor." JP stood up. "Oh, about the written exam. You can forget it for now."

Chapter Five

Monday, 14 April, 1969, 1920 hours
Operating Room No.6, Walter Reed Army Hospital, Washington D.C.

Cadet Thomas Carter lay supine on the operating table, his body covered by layers of green sterile sheets. His shaved head, fixed to a metal frame off the end of the table, had been prepped. The face, neck, and upper chest also had been prepped. Sterile towels covered the head and face but left exposed the neck and upper chest. An anesthesia tube, extending from the corner of his mouth, was connected under the drapes to rubber hoses from the anesthesia machine by his hip. Three bottles of Ringer's lactate dripped slowly, two into arm veins and one into the right heart via a vein behind the collarbone. A clear plastic tube connected a catheter in Carter's bladder to a glass liter bottle taped to the floor under the operating table. Dark yellow urine dripped into the bottle. An ECG monitor on a shelf displayed ongoing tracings of heart activity. On a stool next to the anesthesia machine sat Major Harry Resniek critically surveying the scene through thick glasses.

Lieutenant Colonel JP Franklin stood on a foot stool behind Major Dave Strickland quietly observing. Forty minutes earlier Strickland, Terry O'Connel and Craig Entarde had entered the neck through a wide horizontal incision. After isolating the external, internal, and common carotid arteries on both sides, umbilical tape was looped loosely around each. The tapes could be selectively tightened to occlude the artery to control hemorrhage in the upper neck, face, base of skull, and brain.

The OR door was shoved open and the bear-like figure of George Barfield entered, followed by his chief resident, a much shorter, lighter, and younger Ben Toricelli. Their scrubbed hands and forearms held upright, dripped water from the elbows. JP glanced in their direction, then announced, "Look sharp, people. The brain doctors have arrived."

When Barfield stopped near the operating table the scrub nurse threw a sterile towel over his wet hands. As he dried his hands he watched Terry O'Connel lay sterile towels over the exposed neck for a moment, then turned to Toricelli. "The throat cutters have completed their preliminary tasks, finally."

"Our surgery is organized, meticulous, and anatomical, like a Bach fugue," JP shot back.

George Barfield looked at his friend of many years. "First time I've ever heard it described that way. You ready for us to start on the head?"

"Be our guests. Would you mind if Terry scrubs in with you?"

"Only if he swears an oath never to reveal the secrets of what we brain surgeons really do."

"You mean how crude and clumsy your surgery is?"

"Exactly," Barfield said, now grinning behind his mask.

"It's a deal." Moving to the door, JP turned. "I will leave Mr. Carter's fate in your hands while I tend to my heavy administrative responsibilities. Call me when you have the tumor exposed. Before I go, a word of caution. I won't describe Major O'Connel as aggressive, but if you find he has taken over the case don't say I didn't warn you."

★

Back in his office JP began sifting through papers from his in-basket. A red bordered cover sheet caught his attention. *Damn, a congressional inquiry.* The red border gave the recipient of such an inquiry seventy-two hours to forward a response concerning a congressman's or senator's constituent in the army. A blue border indicated a White House inquiry. It required a response in twenty-four hours. Occasionally a phone call came directly from the White House. When JP took over as chief nearly six years ago his predecessor had failed to warn him about such calls. Thus when a voice with a Texas drawl asked for information on a supreme court justice who was JP's patient, he refused. The Texas voice persisted. "Colonel Franklin, this is your President speaking." JP had responded, "You've got to be kidding," and hung up.

Minutes later the phone rang. It was the hospital deputy commander. "JP, you're lucky the President has a sense of humor." The one-sided conversation went downhill from there, ending with, "He's going to call back. You'd better tell him what he wants to know."

That evening at the dinner table JP had related a description of the call to his family. Jim, the oldest had asked, "Is that what you really told the President of the United States?"

"I thought he was a reporter trying to con me into giving out privileged information."

"When do you leave for Asmara, Dad?"

"Asmara. What do you know about Asmara?" JP had quizzed.

"I know its the capitol of Eritrea, which became a province of Ethiopia in 1962. The US Army has a hospital there.

"If I go to Asmara you guys go with me," JP had responded.

The entire family had groaned in unison.

JP smiled recalling the incident. Reaching to a pile of medical records on a table by his desk he pulled out the record of a twenty-two-year-old soldier, the subject of the congressional inquiry. The soldier, a private stationed at Fort Jackson, South Carolina, had received orders to Vietnam. Several weeks later he was referred to Walter Reed for evaluation of recurrent ulcer-like lesions in the roof of his mouth.

Concerned that the soldier might be exhibiting early manifestations of leukemia or immuno-deficient disease, JP had told Roy French to do a "million dollar" work-up. After three weeks of blood tests, biopsies, and X-rays the diagnosis remained elusive. Biopsies demonstrated only acute and chronic inflammation. Then a sergeant – a patient on the ward recovering from a neck wound – reported seeing the soldier repeatedly put the lit end of a cigarette in his mouth. Suspecting malingering, JP ordered the soldier's jaws wired together. The procedure was not only diagnostic but therapeutic. When the wires were removed ten days later the ulcers had miraculously healed. The soldier's malingering had cost the army and US taxpayers thousands of dollars in hospitalization costs, lost duty time, expensive lab tests and X-rays. Yet he wrote his congressman that incompetent army doctors had failed to diagnose his disease.

★

Two hours later JP gazed proudly at the empty in-box and the full out-box. Just as he reached for his coffee mug, Thelma walked in with a thick stack of papers and stuffed them into the empty in-box. 'This morning's distribution," she said. "A White House inquiry and two congressionals are in there." She removed the papers from the out-box.

JP groaned. "I feel like a hamster on a treadmill, Thelma. Vietnam would be a vacation compared to this," he said, indicating the in-box jammed with papers. He paused a moment, then told his secretary, "Type up another request for a change of assignment. Use the last request as a guide; just change the dates."

"Colonel, that would be a waste of my time. How many requests have you already submitted for a Vietnam tour?"

"Three, but the idea of George Barfield going and me staying conflicts with my Marine Corps-instilled sense of values."

Thelma shook her head sadly. "Brainwashed, that's what the marines did to you." As she walked out she flung back, "You don't know when you're well off."

For several minutes JP stared moodily at the papers stuffed into the in-box. When his pager went off he jumped, startled. A female voice came from the pager's speaker. "Colonel Franklin, this is Captain Eastman in the OR. Colonel Barfield has the tumor exposed and is ready for pictures."

Opening the lower drawer of his desk, he grabbed the clinic Nikon SLR with attached flash and headed to the OR.

★

Monday, 14 April, 1969, 2130 hours
Operating Room No.6, Walter Reed Army Hospital, Washington D.C.

JP entered the operating room with the Nikon draped off his neck. George Barfield and the two residents, Toricelli and O'Connel, were huddled around the head. He moved to stand behind Barfield. "What do you have, George?"

Barfield shifted to one side. "Take a look at this."

JP stepped on a footstool and peered down at the exposed brain. Toricelli gently retracted the right brain using two wide flat malleable retractors over cottonoids. Barfield pointed with blunt scissors to a fiery red thumb-like tumor extending up from the floor of the skull. "This is the largest intracranial extension I've seen," he said with a tinge of awe. "It's the first to penetrate the dura and push into the temporal lobe. Take some pictures while I figure out the best way to separate it from the brain."

JP stared at the tumor. "Thank God no one tried to take it out from below; it would have killed him."

"Let's hope we don't do that from up here," Barfield said ruefully.

Lifting the camera, JP peered through the viewfinder. "Move your big head out of the way, George." Focusing the camera, he began a series of flash exposures. When he finished he asked, "Well?"

"I think the tumor can be separated from the brain without taking brain tissue," Barfield said. "A small segment of the dura around the tumor will need to be resected, but that can be repaired with a piece of temporalis fascia." He held out his hand for a scalpel.

JP looked to the anesthesiologist. "Better start some blood, Harry."

★

Three units of blood later, the intracranial part of the tumor was handed off to the scrub nurse and bleeding controlled. "That's it," Barfield said, tossing a large hemostat into a kidney basin.

"You do good work, George," JP said, admiring the uninjured brain now clear of tumor.

Barfield pointing to a nickel-sized hole in the floor of the skull. "What do you want done with this?"

"Put a layer of Gel Film over it like the other cases," JP said. "We'll know when to stop as we come up from below. By the time the Gel Film dissolves, the tissues at the base of skull will have sealed off the defect. That's what we presumed on the others. So far it's worked."

Barfield nodded. "There is one problem."

"I hate that word."

"We couldn't get a clip on the right internal carotid artery proximal to where the ophthalmic comes off. If you still plan on embolizing the internal carotid with muscle I'll have to put the clip distal. If any muscle is carried into the ophthalmic it may result in a blind eye."

JP searched his limited experience for an answer. In previous cases bits of muscle inserted into the internal carotid artery were carried up to block feeder arteries to the tumor. The eye continued to receive blood retrograde from the opposite side with little change in vision. Now he faced the question of whether that had been necessary. He weighed the risks of severe bleeding inside the head and stroke against a blind eye and stroke. There was no precedent to guide him.

"I don't know the answer, George," JP reluctantly admitted. "I do know this cadet will never be commissioned with a blind eye."

JP watched Toricelli tidy up the brain prior to closing while he tried to make a decision. "I have an idea," he finally said.

"Let's hear it. I try to keep an open mind... so to speak."

"What do you think of holding off clipping the internal carotid and embolization for now. Instead, just lay the bone flap over the brain without wiring it back to the skull. If we get into uncontrolled hemorrhage removing the bulk of the tumor from below you can rush in, clip the internal carotid in the head, save the patient and be hailed a hero."

"I like the idea, especially the hero part," Barfield said, chuckling.

★

Thirty-five minutes later, JP, masked, gowned, and gloved, moved to the operating table. Carter's head and neck were now hidden under sterile towels but his entire face was exposed from forehead to lower jaw. The eyelids had been sewn closed to prevent drying of the eyes or injury by instruments. Terry O'Connel and Craig Entarde, with Dave Strickland assisting, began an incision under the right lower eyelid, carried it to the bridge of the nose, then down in the angle between the nose and face to the middle of the upper lip, which was split. Next, the skin and muscles of the right face were raised in a flap extending from the nose back to the ear, leaving exposed the facial bones on the right. The flap was then covered with a wet sponge and folded back.

The nasal bone was chiseled free on the right side and across the bridge, then fractured and turned to the opposite side as if turning a page in a book. Portions of the facial bone were progressively removed, leaving enough to maintain the facial framework. A red, multilobulated rubbery tumor was exposed filling the back of the upper throat. As bone removal continued, extensions of tumor were traced into the right orbit, cheek, and undersurface of the skull.

Using his fingers, JP tried to define the dimensions of the tumor. "This one's large, much larger than I thought.'

Harry Resniek popped up to look. From past experience he knew JP was master of the understatement.

"Let's get some pictures before the blood flows," JP said, turning to Craig Entarde. 'You're junior man, so you're elected."

After the photographs were taken JP told Dave Strickland, "You won't be able to remove the tumor in one piece. Just follow standard infantry tactics for dealing with road blocks."

"That translates to?"

Terry O'Connel injected, "Attack from the flanks, isolate and eliminate."

"Spoken like a true Academy man," JP said. "What he means, Dave, is to do a segmental removal until you get to the last pocket of resistance, which will probably be tumor in the sphenoid sinus. While you do that, Terry and I will try to keep the area clear of blood with suction and control bleeding by occluding vessels in the neck." He looked over to the anesthesiologist. "Harry, we're about to lose a lot of blood in a short time."

Resniek nodded and reached for two units of blood.

Dave Strickland picked up the cutting cautery and began slicing through the accessible tumor. Tissue sizzled and popped. Wisps of smoke drifted up. The pungent smell of burned tissue wafted through the room. Blood spewed from the cut surface of the remaining tumor and spilled over onto the drapes.

Harry Resniek rose from his stool and stared at the field. "Get six more units up here stat," he told the circulator. She moved to the wall phone and began dialing.

JP grabbed a handful of 4 x 4 sponges and jammed them on the spurting fountains of blood. Pressing down hard with both hands, he told Entarde, "Tighten the tapes."

"Which ones, Colonel? There are six."

"External carotids for now, Terry, get in here with those suckers. Don't be shy." He looked at Dave Strickland. "Keep going. You're doing fine."

As soon as the tapes around the external carotid arteries were cinched down, much of the bleeding subsided. "Well," JP said, sighing, "we know where the tumor is getting most of its blood supply."

An hour and twenty minutes and five units of blood later, Dave Strickland had removed all tumor except that which filled the sphenoid sinus, the golf ball-sized bony cavity supporting part of the brain and in contact with large venous cavities on its sides. He looked up. "Chief, how do I get this thing out?"

"Very carefully, David. Keep in mind that the optic nerves cross above the roof, the pituitary gland sits further back, the internal carotids ascend on either side in a delicate sac of venous blood, and behind the sinus is the brain stem. Other than those you have little to worry about."

"Thanks, sir. You're very encouraging."

"Use blunt dissection as much as possible to separate tumor from the bony walls and roof of the sphenoid. You may encounter areas where bone is missing and tumor is adherent to the dura or blood vessels. For those you will have to use sharp dissection."

"What about cautery?" Entarde asked.

"Not a good idea. It could fry the pituitary, optic nerves, or brain stem. Dangers exist even when using scissors or scalpel, but cuts can be more precise. Okay, Major Strickland, march on."

"This is tougher than flying the back-course ILS approach during my check-ride for an instrument rating," Strickland said. Beads of sweat began to accumulate on his forehead. The circulator moved behind him and wiped his forehead with an ABD pad.

JP was a strong adherent of the concept that a physician must do more than heal, he must teach. He must impart his skills to succeeding generations of physicians. However, in the passing of those skills the patient's well-being must not be jeopardized. It was a measure of a physician's worth as a teacher to recognize when that point had been reached and take over from the student.

To an observer JP seemed relaxed, almost cavalier. It was a ploy to take as much pressure off Dave Strickland as possible. Actually he watched Strickland's every move like a hawk, recording in his mind's eye his progress. If Cadet Thomas Carter ended up paralyzed, blind or dead, the ultimate responsibility would be his to carry for the rest of his life.

Dave Strickland insinuated an index finger between the firm rubbery tumor and the adjacent bony wall. The space he created was exploited by inserting closed scissors, then opening the blades. For several minutes all went well. It appeared that the tumor was about to be delivered when Strickland stopped and looked at JP. "Boss, we've got a problem."

"We? What do you mean, we?"

"I'm not kidding, Colonel," Strickland said, his voice rising in a pitch. "There's a nickel-sized defect in the roof of sphenoid where the tumor is attached to the dura. I could see the optic nerves above the dura."

"Try a little discrete brute force."

Strickland worked in silence, then shook his head. "It just won't free up." Before he finished the sentence a tremendous gush of blood suddenly flooded out, soaking drapes and spilling on the floor. JP threw in more sponges, shoving them down with two suckers. Entarde added two more suckers.

"Cinch down the tape around the right internal carotid," JP told O'Connel.

"Done, sir."

When the bleeding was only partially diminished JP knew things had gone critical.

"Shall I cinch the left internal?" O'Connel asked.

"No. I don't want to stroke him. Besides, the angio showed little or no blood to the tumor from the left. Harry, stay up with blood loss. Don't let his blood pressure drop."

The risk of stroke had rocketed. Removal of the remaining tumor would have to be done by sharp dissection almost blindly under a sea of blood and done fast. A wrong cut or tear, and blindness, stroke, endocrine dysfunction, meningitis, and death could follow.

As much as JP wanted Dave Strickland to finish the case he sensed that Strickland had reached his limit of skill. JP had no choice. "I'll take over now," he said quietly but firmly; Strickland stepped back. "Send for Dr. Barfield," he told the scrub nurse. In seconds the fingers of JP's left hand located the area superiorly where bone was missing and the tumor was adherent to the brain covering. He held out his right hand. "Metz." The scrub nurse plopped the long blunt-tipped scissors into his hand.

The scissors' blades disappeared into the rising pool of blood. JP felt the blades pass over the tips of his fingers to the area where the tumor was stuck to the dura. By feel and perhaps a sixth sense he dissected bluntly with the dull outer edges of the scissors, then snipped millimeter by millimeter with the inner sharp cutting edges.

Harry Resniek, busy hanging one unit of blood after another, glanced at the EKG monitor. "Better move it, Colonel, we're getting behind the power curve."

At that moment George Barfield, gowned and gloved, came up beside JP "Shall I go back in the head?"

"Give me a minute more, George," JP said as he continued to work. "It's almost…" Suddenly the remaining tumor, about the size of a lemon, popped up out of the blood. "Packing," JP almost shouted, "lots of it. God, there's a big hole where the sphenoid should be." The nurse passed him the end of a roll of one-inch gauze. In seconds he shoved its thirty-six-inch length into the sphenoid and reached for another roll. In less than a minute it was packed into the recesses left after the tumor had been removed. The bleeding began to diminish. JP held pressure on the packing with two large suckers.

"Easy on the pressure," George Barfield admonished, "the brain stem and pituitary are at risk."

"Right, "JP said, relaxing slightly. "Craig, open the tape on the right carotid. Let's see what happens." He held his breath.

To everyone's delight and relief, the massive bleeding did not resume. "Gentlemen," JP said with more than a little pride, "we have a winner."

Harry Resniek stood and gazed into the field. "There's no limit to the surgeon's ego. How about holding off any more manipulations until I get him stabilized?"

"You've got it, Harry. What's the blood loss?"

"Nine units, not including three the neurosurgeons lost doing their thing. Did you get all the tumor out?"

"I think so. We'll remove the packing and take a good look before repacking and backing out." He turned to George Barfield. "While we're waiting and watching would be a good time for you to check the head. If everything looks okay you can close."

"Colonel, what about a tracheotomy?" Terry O'Connel asked.

"Let's hold off. Harry can leave the endo tube in for tonight. Keep a trach set at the bedside in case Mr. Carter decides to extubate himself and becomes obstructed. I'll spend the night in my office to be available. I'd like you and Craig to work out a bedside shift for the rest of the night."

Dave Strickland leaned back. "If you don't mind, Colonel, I'd like to stick around too."

"In that case you can put Cadet Carter back together," JP said, stepping away from the table. Pulling off his gown and then his gloves, he grabbed Carter's chart from the anesthesia machine, pushed a sitting stool to the wall and sat down. Leaning back against the wall, he groaned. "George, I'm getting too old for this."

"I'll tell you one thing, old buddy," the neurosurgeon said.

JP looked up. "What's that?"

"If one of my kids has one of these tumors I want you to do the surgery."

A smile creased JP's mouth behind his mask. He had just received the ultimate compliment.

Chapter Six

Friday, 19 April, 1969, 1150 hours
Walter Reed Army Hospital, Washington D.C.

Thelma Hoffberg's Brooklyn voice beamed from the intercom. "Colonel Franklin, Captain Blanchard is on line one."

Fred Blanchard, a navy captain, was chief of head and neck pathology at the AFIP and a world expert in that field. Blanchard seldom called except to relay bad news. JP reached for the phone. "Good morning, Fred."

Blanchard wasted no time. "I just finished looking at Jaime Peterson's slides."

Jaime Peterson, the four-year-old son of an army major, had undergone exploratory surgery of the ear the day before. A friable tissue mass was found to have eroded much of the mastoid bone and base of skull. The mass was biopsied and sent to the AFIP along with two lumps removed from the neck. JP guessed the mass was malignant, most likely the same type of tumor that was killing Ricardo Diego.

Blanchard continued. "Your impression was correct. Biopsies of the skull base and mastoid showed osteomyelitis and rhabdo. Both neck nodes were positive for tumor."

"When I wrote the provisional diagnosis on the path slip I prayed I would be wrong. I guess the Almighty wasn't listening," JP said.

"It seems he seldom does listen in these cases. We'll just have to use the wits he gave us to come up with a cure. I'm curious. How did you arrive at that diagnosis?"

"Jaime developed a protruding left ear, left facial paralysis, a turned in left eye, and two palpable nodes in his neck, all within a three-week period. His X-rays showed extensive bone erosion of the mastoid and base of skull. That picture fits the character of a very aggressive malignancy. Embryonal rhabdo is about the most aggressive I know."

"That's pretty good reasoning for an ex-jarhead. I'm impressed."

"You navy people are always impressed by the brilliance of those who serve or have served as marines."

"You're right, but it's mostly because it's such an unexpected phenomenon." Blanchard paused. "I don't envy you breaking the news to the parents."

"I tried to get them to consider the possibility of an ominous outcome, but they're heavy into denial. They refused to consider anything but a happy outcome. I'm going to send them to Al McClintock at Hopkins and Helen Canelli at Children's for some outside opinions."

"What are your treatment plans?"

"I've called around the country. Current philosophy is still ultra radical surgery and radiation followed by several courses of chemotherapy. That's how we managed eight previous cases. We may have prolonged their lives a year or two, but all are dead now except one, and he's dying."

"I'm available to review Jaime's slides and discuss the pathology."

"He'll be presented at the head and neck tumor conference next Thursday evening. Will you have time for pizza at Luigi's afterward."

"You buying?"

"Affirmative."

"I'll have the time."

After hanging up, JP stared broodily out his window. In the years since graduation from medical school there had been many occasions when he had questioned the wisdom of the Almighty. This morning was one of them. A little boy with a fatal disease… it just wasn't fair.

Dave Strickland walked in carrying two mugs of coffee. Setting one on the desk near JP's right hand, he eased into a chair, sipped from the other cup and studied his boss. "You don't look happy, Colonel."

"Blanchard just called with Jaime's path report."

"Rhabdo?"

JP nodded.

"That's rough." No doubt Strickland was thinking in terms of his own two young daughters. After taking another sip of coffee he set his mug down. "I should pass this on," he said. "Last night one of the nurses on the peds ward reported overhearing Jaime's father tell his wife he would take Jaime to Mexico for Laitrile therapy if the tumor turned out to be malignant."

"Thanks for passing that on. I'm meeting with the parents this evening. I'll discuss Laitrile with them. As far as I know it has never been effective treating malignancies and may have caused deaths." He picked up the mug of coffee and sipped thoughtfully. "Tell me, Major, are there any happy developments on our service?"

"Actually, Colonel, there are. Pfc Fabrezius is back on our ward minus his spleen. I took a look at it before the general surgeons removed it. Its capsule was distended with blood and ready to rupture."

"Roy French made a great call. He probably saved Fabrezius's life. Any more good news?"

"Pfc Bailey is off the psych ward and back on the ophthalmology service. And Cadet Carter was unpacked this morning in the OR with only a slight bleed. His urine output is dropping on Pitressin."

JP chuckled. "We must have really beat up his pituitary. He was putting out six liters of urine a day."

"I'm going to keep him on the ICU for tonight. By the way, have you met his mother? She was anxious to meet you."

"Every time I went to see Carter she was gone. Is she really a federal judge?"

"Yes, sir. US District Judge for Southern California. She's with Carter now. She will leave this afternoon to go back to San Diego." Strickland leaned forward in his chair. "Don't tell my wife I said this, Colonel, but Carter's mother is probably the best-looking judge in the entire federal judicial system."

JP chuckled. "She must be to get that kind of response from a conservative Baptist Republican family man like you. I'd better get over there and meet her. I've never met a lady federal judge, even an ugly one."

★

To reach the surgical intensive care unit JP cut through the operating suite, then turned right. Several yards from the automatic doors he punched a saucer-like switch on the wall. Cool air from the ICU rolled over him as the double doors slid apart. Walking briskly to the nursing station, he passed several vacant beds, then a bed with a patient on a respirator, his head swathed in bulky dressings. Stopping at the nursing station he picked up Cadet Carter's chart from the chart rack, lifted the metal cover and studied the nurse's notes, EKG tracings, lab reports, and input/output record. Everything seemed within acceptable limits except excessive urine output, but it was sliding towards normal.

Carrying the chart, JP approached Carter's bed. A slender woman, her dark brown hair liberally sprinkled with gray, sat on the edge of the bed, her back to him. Her shapely legs were hard to ignore. He heard Carter say, "Mother, here comes Colonel Franklin."

The woman stood up, turned and stared. Her eyes went wide with surprise; her loud gasp shattered the quiet demeanor of the ICU.

JP, stunned at recognizing the woman, let the chart slip from his fingers. It hit the floor with a loud metallic clatter. When he kneeled to pick up the chart the woman's voice stopped him. "Leave it, Marine," she said as she came to him. Their embrace was primal, leaving both weak.

Holding her tightly, JP whispered, "Oh my God, Ann."

Suddenly both were frightened by the resurrection of powerful feelings long held dormant. Reluctantly JP released her but held her hands several moments longer.

Cadet Carter croaked from his bed, "Mother, what's going on?" When she didn't answer he raised his voice. "Somebody please tell me what's going on."

Federal Judge Ann Carter turned to her son. "Tom, Colonel Franklin and I were good friends once, very good friends. He wasn't a doctor when we met. He was a seventeen-year-old marine on his way to the war in the Pacific."

JP blushed.

Judge Carter continued, "We haven't seen each other in twenty-four years."

"And you recognized him after all those years?"

"He's changed very little. Besides, it's not difficult to recognize someone you once loved."

"Loved? What do you mean, loved?"

It was Judge Carter's turn to blush. "I'll explain later," she told her son, then turned to JP. "I must be in San Diego tomorrow to continue a trial. My plane leaves Dulles at three thirty. Can we go somewhere and talk for a few minutes?"

"My office. I'll have my secretary call you a cab. I'd take you to Dulles but I have a case starting at two."

"I understand." Judge Carter patted her son's shoulder. "I'll be back to tell you goodbye."

JP took Ann's arm and guided her towards the door, then down the hall. Turning left, they entered the lengthy corridor of the OR suite. Still somewhat shocked over the coincidence of their meeting after twenty-four years, both remained quiet. Ann took note of the gurneys and equipment parked outside operating rooms. Personnel in green scrub suits moved busily in and out of the rooms and along the corridor. Surgeons and nurses stared at Ann. Some looked questioningly at JP, others with envy. He blushed in response to their stares.

Feeling out of place, Ann asked, "JP, should I be here?"

"No problem," he assured her. "I walked the president's wife through here to Ward 8 last week." He indicated double doors at the far end of the corridor. "Through those doors and to the right is the VIP ward where we put presidents, cabinet members, senators, foreign pooh bahs, and Supreme Court justices. When you're confirmed to the Supreme Court you'll be eligible for Ward 8. I expect to see you nominated and confirmed in a few years."

Ann smiled. "JP, you still say the sweetest things. I remember what you said when we were lying on the beach in our swimsuits at the Hardaways' before you went to the Pacific."

"I don't."

"Let me refresh your memory, Doctor. You were rubbing suntan lotion on my back and telling me that when I started law school I would have the cutest derriere in the entire school."

JP grinned. "And you told me I was too young to talk like that." He stopped and studied Ann's back. "Put on a little weight since then, I see."

"Watch your mouth, Colonel. That's bordering contempt."

"Just kidding. That's the best-looking rear on any federal judge."

"And I thought surgeons were caustic and cynical."

"You've got us mixed up with lawyers."

He guided Ann into a short corridor to double doors, opened one of the doors for her, entered the head and neck clinic and stopped at Thelma's office. "This is Federal District Judge Ann Carter, Thelma. She is Cadet Carter's mother and an old friend from World War II days."

Thelma eyed Ann suspiciously for a moment, then smiled and greeted her warmly.

In JP's office Ann sat down and crossed her legs. Her skirt stayed discretely below her knees. From behind his desk JP quietly studied her. Except for graying hair and a few pounds added in the right places, she had changed little. He couldn't suppress a smile.

Ann looked at him. "What?"

"My assistant was right. You are a beautiful woman."

"Your assistant has excellent judgment."

For the next few minutes neither spoke, each painfully aware they would have only a short time together and wanting to absorb as much of the other's presence as possible. Thelma came in with two mugs of steaming coffee. She set one down by Ann as she studied her surreptitiously. The other she placed near JP. Ann smiled thanks and reached for the mug. JP raised his mug and gently touched it to Ann's, not taking his eyes from her face.

Ann broke the silence. "Twenty-four years ago I kissed a marine corporal goodbye at the Law Building in Denver. Who could have predicted we wouldn't meet again until today. Who could have predicted the marine corporal would become a surgeon, that he would operate on my only son and save his life?"

"Don't get dramatic, Judge."

Ann sipped her coffee, then continued. "When Dr. Dreicher at West Point told me a Dr. James Franklin would be in charge of my son's surgery I asked a friend in the FBI to check on him. They had quite a file. I learned that Dr. Franklin had a Top Secret clearance, his father-in-law was a retired general who had commanded the Defense Intelligence Agency, his brother-in-law was a lieutenant colonel in Vietnam on his second tour, and his wife was an artist with paintings in half a dozen galleries in D.C., Georgetown and Arlington. More importantly, I learned he had an international reputation as a head and neck surgeon and pioneered the surgery for Tom's kind of tumor. Obviously my FBI friend didn't check back far enough, an oversight which I will call to his attention when I return to San Diego. It never crossed my mind that my son's surgeon would be the marine I once loved."

JP spoke quietly. "There wasn't any doubt in my mind you would end up as a federal judge. Your dad and Henry would be very proud."

Ann's father, a federal judge, died in an accident before World War II. Ann worshipped him. Her brother Henry, a B–29 bombardier, was killed during the war when a Japanese kamikaze crashed into his plane on a raid over Tokyo. JP had met him once during the war. Henry, on a flight to Bougainville in the Northern Solomons, diverted his B–25 bomber to Stirling Island to meet him.

"How is Marie?" JP asked.

"Mama passed away last year. She didn't marry the gentleman from UCLA you met in San Francisco when you were on your way to Korea. After she received her PhD she joined the faculty at the university and was eventually promoted to full professor. Her students were her family and they loved her. She taught piano, harmony, counterpoint and performance until she was seventy-eight, then had a stroke. She lived less than a year after the stroke."

"She was a remarkable woman," JP said, recalling the vivacious, talented woman.

"Mama looked on you as a son, JP. She sensed that you would excel at whatever you chose. I doubt whether even she could have predicted your excellence would touch her grandson." Ann laughed softly. "I was convinced you would stay in the army as a combat officer and make it a career, or pick up on the organ and eventually enter the clergy." Her laugh was subdued. "That shows what a great judge of character I am, especially of someone I loved."

"No one is perfect," JP quipped. Hungry for news of other mutual friends, he asked, "What can you tell me about the Hardaways?"

Melissa Hardaway and her husband John were good friends of Ann and her mother. They "adopted" JP when he was a marine Pfc stationed in San Diego. Melissa, a church director of music and an organist, gave JP permission to practice on the organ at her church. It was during one of the practice sessions he had met Ann. Melissa's husband, John, a navy lieutenant commander and the executive officer of a destroyer at the time, had encouraged JP to become an officer. During the Korean War, John, by then a commander and skipper of a destroyer, supported JP's unit at Pohang with naval gunnery.

"John made vice-admiral in September," Ann said proudly. "He's been alerted to go to Vietnam next year."

"Outstanding. There's hope for us mustangs. What about Melissa?"

"She is professor and chairman… whoops, chairperson, of the organ department at San Diego. We meet for lunch every two weeks. I can hardly wait to tell her who Tom's surgeon was."

Ann leaned across the desk and fixed on JP's face. "There's something I have wanted to ask you ever since I received the telegram notifying me you wouldn't come to my graduation from law school." Anger crept into her voice. "You promised you would come. You promised you would be there. Why didn't you come? Was it because you met someone else? The letter you sent three months after I graduated explained nothing."

JP's face flushed with embarrassment and guilt. "There was no one else, Ann. I was in college thousands of miles from you, taking subjects so boring I spent most of my time with other vets in a tavern drinking beer and telling war stories. I had no goals, no real interests. I was drifting. The day before I was to leave for your graduation I got my grades for the spring quarter. I had flunked two courses and received a C in a third. I was about to be thrown out of college for academic deficiencies. You were about to graduate from law school, number one in your class. I was too ashamed to go to your graduation. I had nothing to offer you."

"But you promised."

JP stared at the floor, then out the window. He couldn't look at Ann. "That was the only time in my life I have gone back on my word," he began. "I got drunk the night before I was to take the bus for Frisco. By the time I quit throwing up I had missed the bus. I didn't have the guts to call or write. I spent the summer in the New Hampshire mountains trying to put my life into perspective. By the time I did, I had lost you."

Ann's voice wavered. "I loved you, JP. Do you think it mattered to me you were flunking idiotic college courses. I would have known why and would have understood. I could have given you support and love. I would have married you. But you wouldn't let anyone near you. You had to play the macho marine warrior who goes up into the mountains to find peace. Damn it, JP, that was a scenario for a movie, not real life."

Ann moved from her chair to the window. Turning she leaned back against the window seat. JP tried to ignore her physical beauty.

She continued, "The last I heard of you was in a newspaper article. You were a lieutenant given credit for breaking up a big North Korean attack. You had shot up a water can in the dark mistaking it for a North Korean. That initiated a battle that left over 200 North Koreans dead. God knows how many wounded."

Ann moved back to the chair, sat down and studied JP's face. "Now you're a doctor, a surgeon. Tell me, Doctor, what made you change from taking lives to saving them?"

JP recoiled at the bluntness of her question. "Your mother told me you had a waspish tongue."

"It's my legal training."

"You ought to leave it in the courtroom," JP snapped.

Ann persisted. "Did that decision have anything to do with the war?"

JP nodded. "Both wars. In World War II I did things I never dreamed I would ever do. I lost friends who were like brothers. You know about some of them. Brogan, the Chief, Icardi, and your brother. Henry was the first man I ever hugged out of love, and I hardly knew him. After losing all my friends I swore I would never let myself get close to anyone again. Then I lost you." He paused.

"After the Chief was wounded on Iwo he was evacuated to the hospital in San Diego. I went to see him when I returned stateside. An admiral, the hospital commander, told me the Chief had died of meningitis. I cried, Ann, I cried in front of an admiral. Jesus Christ, marines are trained not to cry." Tears trickled down JP's face as he relived the experience. In a moment he went on. "The admiral told me something that would impact my life, although I didn't realize it at the time."

"What was that?" Ann asked softly.

"He told me that when we lose someone close, someone we love, we have to live our own lives more fully to make up for the loss. I learned later that the admiral's only son was killed on Pelelieu. It took six years and the Korean War for me to understood what he had tried to tell me."

Ann looked at him expectantly.

"My platoon rescued wounded British soldiers and took them to an army MASH. A nurse I knew," he blushed again, "introduced me to some surgeons. They gave my platoon credit for saving the lives of the Brits. They gave me credit for keeping a wounded US helicopter pilot from bleeding to death."

JP spoke deliberately, almost in a whisper. "Ann, ever since I was seventeen all I had ever done was take lives. Even to rescue those wounded Brits I fired my platoon against two regiments of Chinese Communists. When I was about to run out of ammunition I called in an air strike. Between the air force and my platoon, hundreds of enemy were killed and many more wounded. You know what? I felt no sorrow, no guilt. I felt nothing at all. I was as depersonalized a killer as one could be. But the saving of just one life awakened a sense of immense accomplishment. It far outweighed anything I had ever done. It was an introduction to a dimension I never knew existed."

He took a sip of coffee, then continued, "Watching those MASH doctors operate, seeing their compassion, skill, and dedication, brought me to the realization that it was infinitely more noble to save lives than to take them. I knew then I had to become a doctor."

Ann reached across the desk and put her hands on JP's. "You are one complex person, Colonel Franklin."

JP grinned and pulled his hands from under Ann's, then grasped her hands. "And you, Judge Carter, are a fine judge of character. By the way, last week the Chief Justice of the Supreme Court sat in the very chair you now occupy."

"I hope that's a good omen," Ann said, laughing.

JP became serious. "Do you think it was a good idea to tell Tom we were once in love?"

"It was the truth. We did nothing of which to be ashamed. Our love was pure, innocent, and naive." She smiled wanly. "Your love allowed me to enter marriage with my virginity."

"You came pretty close to losing it," JP said, laughing.

"How well I remember," Ann said softly, a smile on her lips.

"I hope you didn't tell anyone I slept with you and didn't do anything."

"Not to worry; the reputation of the marines has been protected," Ann assured him. "Now, JP, I want you to tell me about your wife."

JP related how he met Kathy in El Paso, Texas. "She was the sister of my best friend, a fellow lieutenant. Her gentle southern ways just overwhelmed me. I fell deeply in love with her. Later she told me her dad was a lieutenant general, the deputy Third Army Commander. Nine months after we met we were married. On the day of our wedding North Korea invaded South Korea. Four days later President Harry Truman committed US ground forces to the defense of South Korea. Three weeks after that I was on a Flying Tigers Constellation headed for South Korea."

JP described his difficulties getting into medical school. "I set a Guinness Book of Records for medical school rejections. It was Kathy's love and support that kept me from giving up."

"You must love her very much," Ann said.

"I do, Ann. She's a very gifted person in her own right. She gave up what could have been a very successful career in art to become a medical officer's wife and raise three boys, a girl… and," he grinned, "a doctor."

"Have you told her about me?"

"Yes. It was after she found a drawer full of your letters and some photographs in my room at my parents' house."

Ann giggled. "That's what happened to me. Walter found your letters and photographs in a drawer in my bedroom. I won't ask you what you did with my letters if you don't ask me what I did with yours."

"Deal," JP said.

Ann remained quiet for several moments, seemingly debating something in her mind. Finally, she asked, "Is there any possibility of your going to Vietnam?"

JP was surprised Ann would ask such a question. There wasn't any reason he shouldn't tell her. "I've been trying to go to Vietnam for the past two years. The Surgeon General just turned me down for a division surgeon's slot in the 4th Division. He told me I was essential here. George Barfield, the neurosurgeon who did the intracranial part of Tom's operation, will leave next week to fill that slot."

"The army is showing much better judgment than you," Ann said.

"Maybe, maybe not."

"What's that supposed to mean?"

"Ann, what I tell you next is in confidence. Only Kathy knows."

"Of course."

"Counting my time in the Marine Corps and as a line officer, I'll have twenty years of active duty in three months. I can retire. One of my consultants, Al McClintock, the chairman of head and neck surgery at Hopkins, is going into private practice next year. He wants me to replace him at Hopkins or join him in his practice as a partner."

"JP, that's wonderful." Ann seemed genuinely pleased.

"That depends on your point of view. It does put me in a strong bargaining position to pressure the Surgeon General to change his mind."

Ann looked confused.

"It's simple. Either I go to Vietnam or I leave the army, take my retirement and my experience to Hopkins, or go into private practice with Al McClintock and make big bucks. I'm just waiting for the most propitious time to drop my nuclear bomb."

Ann was shocked. "But why, JP? Why risk your life, your career, all the experience and skills you have as a surgeon? I don't understand. For God's sake, JP, you have already been through two wars; you have done your share of killing."

"I'm not sure I'll be able to explain any better now than I did when I told you I was going back to the Pacific for the invasion of Japan." He chuckled. "You offered to quit law school and marry me to keep me from going."

"Don't change the subject. You're as much of a nut case now as you were then. What did the marines do to you?"

"They taught me honor, courage, and commitment. It's all there in the marine motto, Semper Fidelis... always faithful. But you wouldn't understand. What would you know about war anyway?"

Ann's eyes blazed. "I lost my only brother in the war. That was a loss from which I have yet to recover. I worried night and day through eighteen months of that war over the marine I loved, petrified he would come back to me a cripple or not come back at all. Instead, he came back a changed person with a wall around him I could never get through. Ten years after my first husband died during heart surgery I remarried. My second husband was killed in Vietnam two years ago. If this stupid war in Vietnam lasts another year my only son will be in it." Tears streamed down her face. "Don't you dare tell me I don't know about war."

JP recoiled as if slapped. "I didn't know, Ann. Please forgive me."

Ann fumbled in her purse and came out empty-handed. JP rose, retrieved a box of tissue from his examining room and placed the box on his desk near Ann. She took several tissues and dried her tears. "Dennis was a marine lieutenant colonel, a JAG officer. We had been married five years before he went to Vietnam. He was killed when the Vietcong mortared a firebase where he was conducting an investigation of friendly fire. I kept my first husband's name for professional reasons." Ann took some more tissue and blew her nose. She looked up, embarrassed. "I'm sorry I lost it. Federal judges aren't supposed to do that, you know." She sniffed and smiled. "Now, Doctor, explain your decision to go to Vietnam."

JP's words were measured. "Almost seven years of my life have been spent managing terrible wounds of the head and neck in mostly young men. In those seven years I've become probably the most experienced surgeon in the US, perhaps the world, managing such injuries. The cost of that expertise is beyond imagination. I could never permit that experience to become a justification for my not going to

66

Vietnam. To do so would surpass the cowardice of those who fled to Canada or to university classrooms to avoid military service."

Ann leaned over the edge of the desk towards JP. "Listen to me, you dumb marine. The war in South-east Asia is different, very different from World War II and Korea."

JP stared at the woman he once loved. His eyes flashed anger. "You don't know what you're talking about."

"Damn it, JP, just listen to me. I'm a federal judge. I know a lot more than you about many things, including government policies in South-east Asia." Ann's voice dropped to almost a whisper. "I must have your word, your solemn word that you will never repeat what I tell you."

"You have it, of course."

"The trial over which I have presided for the past nine weeks involves national security. During the trial I became privy to highly classified documents pertaining to the war in Vietnam."

"Ann, you shouldn't..."

"JP, be quiet and listen," Ann said in a judge-like tone that indicated she did not tolerate interruptions. "Those documents revealed that individuals at the highest levels of our government knew early that the war in Vietnam could not be won without a total national commitment, to include invading North Vietnam, mining and blockading its coast and harbors. That knowledge didn't deter them from continuing to waste the country's most precious resource, its young men. Yet their own offspring avoided military service through every subterfuge imaginable." She laughed bitterly. "Some even entered the clergy."

JP stared at Ann, not wanting to believe what she was telling him, yet knowing she would never lie.

Ann continued, "The attack on the Turner-Joy and Maddox in the Gulf of Tonkin never took place. It was a contrived incident to justify escalating the war and obtaining congressional support. Since then Congress and the Joint Chiefs have been repeatedly deceived, denied critical intelligence, and even lied to. There is information that certain high government officials or their families may be profiteering from the war. That is currently under investigation."

JP chose his words carefully. "Ann, whether or not our government has lied to or deceived us has no bearing on my decision to go to Vietnam. Americans are being wounded there. I have unique skills and experience that may make significant contributions to the acute care and rehabilitation of the wounded, not only in Vietnam but in any future military operations. I must go.

Ann's sigh was one of resignation. "You are the most idealistic and naive person I have ever known. I suppose those were some of the qualities that made me fall in love with you."

"We were teenagers then. We didn't know what love was."

"Maybe you didn't, Doctor, but I did." Ann stood up and went to the window again. Gazing through it, she said dreamily, "I can see the Washington monument and the Capitol dome." Turning, she leaned back against the window sill, half sitting on it.

JP, seeing her figure silhouetted against the background light from the window, could not ignore the powerful physical desire he felt for her, even after almost thirty years. He closed his eyes as though seeking strength from the darkness, frightened by the realization that he still felt love for this woman.

"Are you all right?" Ann asked.

His answer was a hoarse "Yes".

Ann returned to her chair and sat down. Her eyes reddened. "My work as a federal judge and my son are all I have. When Dr. Dreicher called from West Point to tell me Tom had a tumor that could be fatal or leave him crippled, I was terrified. That his life was saved by someone I... I once loved was a gift from God, a gift only God can understand." She reached across the desk for JP's hands. Holding them tightly, she said, "I will never be able to thank you enough or repay you."

A noisy electric clock on the bookcase ground seconds of quiet into minutes. JP broke the silence, his voice almost breaking. "Ann, your love sustained me through a terrible war and the loss of friends who were as brothers. That love meant more to me than you will ever know. It is I who will never be able to repay you."

Tears slipped down Ann's cheeks again. She stood up. "I must go."

"Thelma will call you a cab," JP said, rising. "I'll walk you back to the ICU."

Without hesitation they reached for each other. The embrace lasted only seconds. It would have to do for a lifetime.

★

Friday, April 19, 1969, 2020 hours
Walter Reed Hospital, Washington D.C.

Lieutenant Colonel JP Franklin hung up his white coat, eased into his blouse, then sat at his desk. Picking up the phone he dialed 9 and then his quarters. When Kathy answered he said, "Hi. What was for supper?"

"Chicken, but it's all gone."

"Even the tail?"

"Even the tail."

JP groaned. "Who took it this time?"

"Nancy."

"That little pig."

"How would you like a small steak preceded by a dry martini?"

"You know how to get to a guy. I'll be leaving on the eight thirty shuttle bus. By the way, Kath, do you remember Tom Carter, the cadet with the angiofibroma I told you about?"

"Of course. How is he doing?"

"Just fine. You'll never guess who his mother is."

Chapter Seven

Thursday, May 12, 1969, 1120 hours
Walter Reed Army Hospital, Washington D.C.

Lieutenant Colonel JP Franklin sat at his desk, thoughtfully gazing through the window at the Washington's skyline, then shifted his attention to the empty chair in front of his desk. It had been almost a month since Ann Carter had sat opposite him and warned that the Johnson administration had considered the war in Vietnam lost as early as 1966. Initially he was skeptical, but the knowledge that she had placed herself at great professional risk gave what she said the aura of credibility.

Over the past month he had questioned some of the officers and senior NCOs evacuated from South-east Asia to the head and neck surgery service. Many were bitter at the way the war was being fought. Although none would admit that the US was losing the war, none went so far as to claim that the US was winning the war. The United States was the most powerful nation on earth. Yet in eight years it had failed to defeat a peasant army that ran around in the jungle wearing black pajamas. It seemed he was living the Korean War over again. Political considerations had denied a US victory in that war and seemed working to deny a US victory in yet another war.

Cadet Tom Carter had been discharged a week ago, his head sprouting hair like a marine recruit after a month at Parris Island. His face and neck incisions were healing so well they would be almost invisible in six months. Carter, determined to graduate in June with his class and be commissioned, refused convalescent leave and returned to West Point to study for final exams. JP cleared him medically for a commission but prohibited any assignment to ground combat arms for two years.

General Briggs underwent removal of his larynx and a radical neck dissection two weeks ago. The good news from the pathologist was that all margins of the surgical specimen were clear of cancer. Although cancer was found in six of the forty-two lymph nodes in the neck, it had not escaped the capsule (covering) of any nodes. The thyroid nodule was benign.

JP took one last look out the window. The solid appearance of the Capitol's dome was reassuring. The United States was indeed the greatest nation on earth, and he was committed to keeping it that way. Ann Carter was unquestionably sincere, but she was also mistaken. She had to be. One way or another he would get to Vietnam to see for himself.

Thelma Hoffberg walked in with the morning's distribution. "I'll be gone during lunch hour to get my hair fixed," she told him.

JP gave her a sly smile. "You have a heavy date coming up, Thelma?"

"Not in the least," she said frowning. "One man in my life was enough."

Sifting through the papers, JP came across a letter with a return address of

"Department of the Navy, San Diego Naval Hospital". Taking an old scalpel from a drawer he sliced open the envelope, unfolded the letter and began reading.

Dear Colonel Franklin

This is a follow-up on your former patient, Jaime Peterson…

Now that was curious. Why would Jaime be in San Diego? A month ago, using threat and bribe, he had persuaded Jaime's parents to agree not to take him to Mexico for Laitrile therapy. The threat was that JP would obtain a court order giving him custody of Jaime for the duration of his cancer treatment. The bribe was to arrange Jaime's transfer to the Children's Hospital where he would be treated in a promising experimental program using only chemotherapy.

He read on.

Jaime was admitted to our service ten days ago with acute Laitrile toxicity, meningitis, pneumonia, dehydration, electrolyte imbalance, and renal failure. He died twelve hours after admission. Autopsy confirmed the admission diagnoses. Additional findings included embryonal rhabdomyosarcoma of the left temporal bone with invasion of the brain, base of skull, and metastases to the lungs, liver, and eight of thirty-two cervical lymph nodes.

The admission history elicited from the parents was somewhat fragmented and circumspect. Apparently they brought Jaime home from the Children's Hospital for a weekend furlough. Instead of returning to Children's they took him to a Laitrile clinic in Tijuana, Mexico. After a week of therapy Jaime's condition deteriorated and he became unresponsive. The parents then brought him here.

Attached hereto is the autopsy report and pertinent photographs. A copy of this letter, autopsy report, and set of slides have been forwarded to Captain Frederick T. Blanchard, USN, at the AFIP. If additional information is required, please contact me at the above number. If any slides were taken of Jaime during surgery I would greatly appreciate duplicates.

Charles W. Ling, Captain, USN
Chairman, Department of Pediatrics

JP reread the letter several times, then wrote a note to have duplicates made of Jaime's intraoperative slides and forwarded. He leaned back in his chair and stared out the window again. Poor Jaime. What a lousy trick for fate to play on him. The shrill *beep, beep, beep* of his pager snapped him out of his soul-searching melancholy. "Colonel, this is Terry. Call me at 7824."

The extension was the officer's ward. When JP dialed the number O'Connel answered with the first ring.

"What's up, chief resident?"

"Colonel, we just got an air evac from Vietnam, a Captain Alex Leichuk who says he knows you from the Academy."

JP easily recalled the thin, gangly West Point cadet with glasses. "Alex was one of the regulars in the cadet rock-climbing club. He could bring his ankle up to his ear, an advantage for a rock climber. We climbed together in the Shawangunks on Saturdays when we should have gone to football games at Michie Stadium. I used to take him flying and got him started taking lessons at the flying club."

"I was going to call his folks to tell them he was here," Major O'Connel said, "but the only next-of-kin listed in his records was an aunt. She is to be notified only in case of his death."

"That's probably right. Alex is an only child. His parents were killed in a car accident when he was quite young. He was raised by maternal grandparents, both of whom died while he was at the Academy. Kathy and I sort of adopted him. Last I heard he went to England as a Rhodes scholar after graduation. What's his problem?"

"He has one of the worst neck wounds I have ever seen. Eight weeks ago an RPG frag took away most of the cervical trachea and part of the cervical esophagus. The remaining trachea retracted into his chest. He was drowning in blood until a medic pulled the trachea out of the chest and fixed it to the skin of the lower neck with a safety pin. The medic managed to do it while a half dozen VC were trying to kill him and finish off Leichuk."

"Good God."

"Leichuk was dusted off to the 71st Evac. The trachea was sewn to the skin and the larynx exteriorized to funnel secretions away from the airway. The esophagus was repaired with an end-to-end anastamosis. Not only is he now able to swallow, but he has taught himself esophageal speech."

There was silence as JP digested the information. "I'll be right down."

When he entered Ward 10, the officers' ward, Terry O'Connel met him just inside the door and walked him towards Leichuk's room. "Captain Leichuk would never have lived to reach the hospital if it hadn't been for the medic," O'Connel said. "I hope he got a medal. What was Leichuk like as a cadet?"

"Impressive, Terry, impressive. He graduated number four, with a 3.96 GPA while keeping a hellacious schedule of non-academic activities."

JP touched O'Connel's arm. "By the way, what was your GPA at the Academy?"

"Three six, and I had to hustle to get that."

"Not bad. How did you end up in armor instead of the engineers? That's where all the brains go."

"I liked to ride in tanks and shoot big guns."

"I know the feeling," JP said, ruefully.

At Captain Leichuk's room Terry knocked on the door, then pushed it open. Alex was sitting up in bed, reading a newspaper. He looked up as JP and Terry O'Connel entered. "Colonel Franklin," he burped with his esophageal voice, and grinned widely.

JP walked briskly to the bed and grabbed Leichuk in a hug. "You dumb smack, didn't you learn at Benning to keep your head down?"

"Yes, sir," Leichuk belched out in a voice sounding much like a frog croaking. "I did great at Benning but not so good in Nam."

"I thought you would be back at West Point as a professor by now. How did you end up in Vietnam?"

"I finished two years at Oxford, was designated an 'Outstanding Scholar' and decided I had enough academia. Most of my classmates had been to Vietnam or were in Vietnam. I decided it was payback time so I requested to be assigned there."

JP focused on Leichuk's neck. A quarter-sized hole in the lower neck was the upper end of the trachea. It was the hole through which Leichuk breathed. Between the hole and the lower end of the voice box was almost a three-inch gap where the trachea had been torn away. Through the open lower end of the exteriorized larynx the undersurface of the vocal cords were visible. It was a condition he had seen only twice before. JP shined the beam from his penlight into the larynx. Neither vocal cord showed any motion, an indication that both motor nerves to the vocal cords were damaged. It was an ominous finding that would impact reconstruction.

"The surgeons in Vietnam couldn't agree on how to fix my windpipe," Leichuk croaked. "Some wanted to remove my voice box and close up. They said the gap was too large to be reconstructed. Others argued to let things heal as they were, then send me to Walter Reed. Obviously they won." He searched JP's face. "What do you think?"

JP hesitated. He tried to organize an answer that would not sound like no answer. "It's a little premature to come to any conclusions and make recommendations, Alex. We will need X-ray studies, an exam of your airway and esophagus in the operating room, and consultation with the thoracic surgeons. I'd also like you evaluated by our consultants in Baltimore and New York."

"I'm anxious to get this thing fixed and get back to duty, sir, and I'm willing to take risks."

"We'll try to keep the risks to a minimum." He turned to Terry O'Connel. "Let's brainstorm a game plan for Alex after rounds tomorrow evening." He turned to Leichuk. "Since you will be the subject of our discussion, feel free to attend and add your two cents." JP wanted Alex to be cognizant of the immense problems facing reconstruction of his airway. "Between now and then, go to the medical library, it's on the third floor north, and read up on tracheal reconstruction so you can engage in a meaningful discussion when we meet.

"Aye, aye, sir," Leichuk burped.

★

Thursday, May 12, 1969, 1655 hours
Walter Reed Army Hospital, Washington D.C.

JP initialed the last document from the in-box and tossed it into the out-box. With the in-box empty and no problems on the wards that couldn't wait until tomorrow, he was free to leave. Shedding his white coat, he slipped into his blouse and buttoned it. Then, carrying his briefcase and hat, he headed for the elevators. Just as he passed the residents' ward office Roy French stepped out.

"Taking the afternoon off, Colonel?" he asked, glancing at his watch.

"Rank still has a few privileges. Besides, I'm caught up on my work. Residents, by definition, are never caught up."

"I thought that applied only to second lieutenants."

"If anything comes up be sure to call Dave Strickland. He's on staff call."

French threw his chief a sloppy salute. "Enjoy your afternoon off, sir."

"Major French," JP began with strained patience, "should you have the opportunity to go aboard a US naval vessel, and I dare say some day you will, keep in mind that naval custom considers a salute inappropriate when one is uncovered." Without waiting for a response, he moved on to the elevator. When he reached the hospital's front entrance the 1650 shuttle bus to Forest Glen was still at the curb.

Climbing on board he saw all seats were occupied by patients dressed in blue pajamas and maroon robes. Setting his briefcase on the floor next to the driver, he turned to face the front of the bus, grabbing a metal rail to steady himself. The driver, a young woman in fatigues with a Pfc stripe on her jacket, reached for the door handle. Swinging the door closed she shifted gears and headed for the Sixteenth Avenue Gate. JP leaned down to see better out the windshield. After passing out the gate, instead of turning north on Sixteenth Avenue the bus crossed it and entered Rock Creek Park.

"New route?" JP asked the driver.

"Yes, sir. It's a little further in mileage but keeps us out of the evening rush traffic on Sixteenth. After 1900 we go back to the old route."

As the spring greens and browns in Rock Creek Park flashed by, JP told the driver, "This is my favorite route when I'm lucky enough to have our only car."

A patient in the first seat leaned forward and touched JP's sleeve. "Sir, please take my seat," he said, rising.

JP briefly regarded the soldier. Eighteen or nineteen, his face was pale and drawn from loss of weight. Seeing no crutches or visible dressings, JP concluded that the patient was convalescing from a belly or chest wound. Improvising a white lie, he told the patient, "It's against hospital regulations for a doctor to sit on the shuttle bus unless there are vacant seats."

The young soldier looked confused, then shrugged.

"You can hang on to my briefcase and hat."

"Sure, Colonel," the soldier said, reaching for the two and setting them on his lap.

During the trip to Forest Glen JP coped with a sense of guilt at having left the hospital so early. He tried to assuage the guilt by reasoning this would be the first time in over a month that he would be home before 2000 hours. Many nights it was later, much later. In the mornings it was routine for him to leave on the 0545 shuttle bus to Walter Reed. If he were lucky enough to have the van for the day he could leave twenty minutes later. Regardless, the kids would be asleep when he left in the morning, and often asleep when he returned at night. Some nights he didn't come home at all. Perhaps he should seriously consider Al McClintock's offer to go into private practice with him or take the head and neck chair at Hopkins. The schedule couldn't be any worse, and the pay certainly would be better.

Thirty-five minutes later the bus slowed to 15 mph to cross a bridge over double railroad tracks. In so doing the bus passed from civilian Silver Spring, Maryland, to military Forest Glen, a 2,000-acre army post sometimes referred to as Walter Reed

Annex or Disneyland East. Before World War II Forest Glen had been the site of the National Park Seminary, an exclusive finishing school for college-age women. Shortly after the US became involved in World War II the army purchased the entire complex, converting it to a center for convalescing patients from Walter Reed Army Hospital. Now almost thirty years later, Forest Glen continued to house soldiers recovering from the physical and psychological wounds of war.

To a stranger driving through Forest Glen for the first time it appeared a collection of strange foreign-appearing buildings set in a forest of tall pines, oaks, maples, and an abundance of shrubbery. The dominant building, a massive wood and stucco structure, resembled a nineteenth-century elite European hotel. Its extensive complex of rooms now housed convalescing patients; its immense ballroom hosted dances and USO shows. Scattered through the remainder of the post were offices, laboratories, a small post exchange, craft shop, barber shop, chapel, theater, driving range, military police station, fire station, and half a dozen quarters for senior medical officers and their families.

Most of the quarters were built in the early 1900s as sorority houses to represent foreign countries. There was a Spanish hacienda, English hunting lodge, Dutch windmill, Swiss chalet, German castle, and Japanese pagoda. The pagoda was rumored to have been brought to Forest Glen from the 1898 World's Fair. JP's quarters was the Swiss chalet.

Living in Forest Glen was akin to living apart from reality in Sleepy Hollow, indeed a sort of Disneyland East. It was a great place for children. Hundreds of acres of woods provided abundant opportunities for young imaginations to run wild, from playing Davy Crocket at the Alamo to commando capture of Field Marshal Erwin Rommel in North Africa. In the late spring of every year the military families and their civilian neighbors emerged like groundhogs for a barbecue, soft ball games, horse shoes, and socializing. For the doctors who lived in Forest Glen as well as the patients, crossing over the railroad bridge was the great escape from the ugly realities of war.

When the bus stopped by the post theater JP was first off. He stayed by the door to assist patients with crutches who had difficulty negotiating the steps. After the last passenger exited he heard his name called. Turning he saw a bird colonel coming towards him. "Good evening, Colonel Tompkins," he said, saluting.

"Step over here in the shade, Colonel Franklin. There's something I want to tell you."

JP knew little about Colonel Tompkins other than he was an infantry full colonel who appeared to be in his mid-fifties and worked at Forest Glen in some administrative capacity as his pre-retirement assignment.

"Yes, sir," JP said, curious.

"I have some good news for you, but first I want your word not to discuss what I tell you with anyone until it becomes official."

JP readily agreed.

"I'm a member of the promotion board that meets here at Forest Glen," Tompkins said. "The board just concluded the selection of Medical Corps lieutenant colonels for promotion to colonel."

JP wondered why Tompkins was telling him this. He had been a lieutenant colonel for only three years. It would be another three or four years before he would be eligible for promotion.

"You were selected for colonel from way below the zone," Tompkins said.

JP was stunned, then skeptical.

Tompkins explained. "Your selection was based on your prior combat experience in two wars, especially service as a commissioned officer during the Korean War, your awards, decorations, and professional achievements."

"I had no idea I was under consideration."

"The board found provisions in the regulations that allowed it to legally stretch the criteria to permit your promotion and that of three other medical officers. They, like you, had command experience in war as combat officers, have superb records as medical officers, and are eligible to retire or soon will be. The board considered it imperative to make every effort to keep you all on active duty, not only in recognition of your contributions to the country in wartime, but because of your leadership potential for the future of the Army Medical Corps."

JP was immensely pleased but still shaken. "I don't know what to say, Colonel Tompkins," he stammered.

The infantry officer smiled. "Just keep your mouth shut, Doctor. Don't even tell your wife."

"Yes, sir."

He shook hands with Tompkins, then walked him to his car. When JP reached the door to his quarters he heard whining and scratching on the other side. As soon as he opened the door ninety-five pounds of a female German shepherd named Greta leaped at him. He managed to catch her front paws before they reached his uniform, then eased her to the floor, alternately hugging and patting her while she whined and dribbled urine. Kathy, surprised by his early arrival, emerged from the kitchen wiping her hands on her apron. Dismissing Greta with a final pat on the head, JP went to Kathy, held her tightly and kissed her. "What's for dinner?" he whispered.

"That was never funny, JP," Kathy said. Nineteen years ago, after they had just been pronounced man and wife and were rushing from the chapel at Fort McPherson, JP suddenly pulled her to a stop, looked into her eyes and asked the same question. Over the years Kathy learned to counter his weird humor. Tonight she answered without a smile, "Dead chicken; that's what we're having for dinner, dead chicken."

"My favorite," JP said, removing his blouse, pulling off his tie, and rolling up his sleeves. Going to the kitchen he took a bottle of beer from the refrigerator, then returned to the living room. "Kids around?" he shouted to Kathy, now in the kitchen.

"Jim's at the track with the van. Paul is at a scout meeting, Frank is at cub scouts, and Nancy is across the street playing with Penny. There's a letter for you from George Barfield on the hi-fi cabinet."

"Thanks."

"How long has George been in Vietnam?"

"About two weeks."

JP picked up the letter and sank into a antique rocking chair by a large picture window that overlooked much of verdant Forest Glen. Greta plopped down by the rocker and let out a deep doggie sigh. Opening Barfield's letter, JP read:

> *This assignment is nothing like I anticipated. As division surgeon I spend most of my time flying in helicopters. That leaves little time for surgery. So far I've done only two cranies and one spinal fusion. I have managed to avoid most of the administrative requirements of this job by ignoring them. One of these days the chief of staff will catch on to my gold bricking.*

No sooner had JP taken a swallow of cold beer than the kitchen phone rang.

"I'll get it," Kathy called out. A moment later she called out. "It's Major Fenster. She said it was urgent."

Carrying the opened bottle of beer, JP hurried to the kitchen. If Mary Fenster was concerned enough to call him at home and classify it urgent, a catastrophe of major proportions must be taking place on Ward 21. He picked up the phone. "What's up Mary?"

Fenster's throaty feminine voice admonished him. "Colonel, did you forget Senator Vaughn had a five thirty appointment?"

JP immediately pictured the TV ad of the small town southern sheriff who had pulled over a speeding New Yorker and told him, "Boy, you in a heap of trouble." Senator Vaughn was chairman of the powerful Senate Armed Services committee. JP had met him when he came to inspect the latrine facilities after the Jason Groves article appeared in the newspaper.

"I really goofed, Mary," he admitted. "Thelma was gone to the hairdresser's when the senator's secretary called to set up an appointment. Without Thelma to remind me I just forgot. Is Major Strickland or any resident around?"

"No, sir. They're in the OR working on a medevac from Vietnam. They won't finish until after midnight."

An awkward silent interval followed. "Well," JP finally said, "I guess you're talking to the new CO of the hospital in Asmara."

"Where in the world is that?"

"You don't want to know."

"Don't pack just yet, Colonel," Fenster said, laughing. "The senator's relaxing in the resident's ward office with a cup of my coffee and an old *Life* magazine. He wants me to tell him about Vietnam."

"Mary, if it were within my power you would be an instant lieutenant colonel."

"I'm already on the list. That's good enough. I'll expect you and Kathy at my promotion party."

"Tell the senator I'm on my way."

Hanging up, he turned to Kathy who was peeling potatoes at the sink. "When is Jim due back from the track?" he asked.

"Around seven. Why?"

"I've got to get back to the hospital. Thelma was off this afternoon when Senator Vaughn's secretary called to make an appointment for him. I made it for five thirty and then forgot about it."

"I saw the senator on the TV news last night," Kathy said. "He seemed like a very nice man."

"In a few minutes your husband will find out just how nice. Right now I desperately need a car. Damn, I wish we could afford two cars."

Kathy went to the kitchen window and peeked out. "Carrie Marley's Carmen Ghia is parked in its space. Don't get your hopes up. She won't even let her husband drive it. You get back in uniform. I'll see what I can do."

Thirty-four minutes later JP braked the Carmen Ghia into his parking spot in the quadrangle, amazed he had avoided a speeding ticket. Climbing the stairs two and three at a time, he reviewed what little he knew about Senator Vaughn. During World War II the senator had been a regimental commander in Europe. After the war he entered state politics but remained in the army reserves as a bird colonel and soon was promoted to brigadier general. After a senate seat in his state became vacant in 1947 through death, he was appointed to fill the remaining term, then won the next election by a landslide. By 1967 his seniority landed him the chairmanship of the Armed Forces Committee.

When JP walked into the ward office Senator Vaughn was tilted back in a swivel chair, his feet on the resident's desk, sipping coffee and reading a two-month old copy of *Life* magazine. Tall, somewhat overweight, and in his late sixties he had a relaxed friendly face and snow-white hair cut short, military style. The senator set his cup on the desk, swung his feet to the floor, stood up and extended his hand. "Enjoy your afternoon off, Colonel?" he asked mischievously.

JP flushed, then grasped the senator's hand. "Sorry you had to wait, Senator. I wish I could come up with a better excuse than just having forgotten your appointment."

"Since it's the truth, Colonel, it will do nicely. In this city the truth is somewhat unique and is very refreshing. While I was waiting for you, Major Fenster told me some war stories and took me on a tour of your ward. The new latrine is quite an improvement over the last one."

"Thanks for all your help in getting it for us, sir, and the air conditioning."

"Next time something like that comes up you call me direct. There's no need for anyone to write to a newspaper columnist."

"Yes, sir."

"And that Major Fenster, she really runs a tight ship up here. The patients love her."

"We couldn't function without Major Fenster. Fortunately for the army she's on the list for promotion and will stay on active duty."

"The army is showing excellent judgment, one of the few times. Please notify my office when the promotion ceremony will take place. I'll try to be present."

What a nice guy, JP thought. *No wonder he keeps getting re-elected. Hell, maybe I'll move to his state just so I can vote for him.* "Let's go to my office, Senator," JP suggested. He led into the vacant, dark clinic waiting room, turned on some lights, then entered his office. After they were seated Senator Vaughn withdrew a thin packet of papers from his briefcase and placed them on JP's desk.

"Eight years ago," the senator began, "I had a parotidectomy for a benign mixed tumor." He touched the right side of his face in front of the ear where the skin was depressed. A thin surgical scar, barely visible, extended from above the hairline down in front of the ear to below the angle of the jaw. "This morning while shaving I thought I felt a small lump, right here." He placed his finger on the scar. "I'm not sure if what I felt can be dignified by calling it a lump. Just the same I thought I'd better have it checked out."

As the senator talked JP's training and experience as a doctor quickly overcame any awe he might have had for this politically powerful man. "Any pain, tingling, or numbness in your face?" he asked.

"No, sir. Since the operation I sweat a lot on that side when I eat. That's been the only problem."

Shedding his blouse, JP draped it over a chair, then slipped on a white coat and led the senator to the examining room. After a careful examination of the head and neck he concentrated on the surgical scar, admiring its near invisibility. "You had a skillful surgeon."

"He was my brother-in-law. The poor man had a stroke last year and is in a nursing home."

After gently running his fingers over the scar from several directions, JP confirmed the senator's impression. "The lump is definitely there. It's about the size of a pea, hard and fixed."

The senator said nothing.

JP took his silence as a request to continue. "It could be a local recurrence of the mixed tumor. Two percent recur after parotidectomy. The lump could be a benign cyst secondary to a retained suture, although it's a little late for that. Sometimes trauma will initiate a local inflammatory response in the scar tissue. Have you had any facial injury within the past two or three years?"

The senator, making notes on a yellow legal pad, stopped and looked up. "I was in a car accident two years ago and hit the right side of my face against the window."

"There is another possibility. The lump could be malignant."

Senator Vaughn blanched. "Could you take a small piece of the lump under local anesthesia to see what it is?"

"That wouldn't be a good idea. If the lump were malignant, or even if it were a recurrence of your previous benign mixed tumor, cutting into it would spill tumor cells and jeopardize later total removal. A new diagnostic technique involves using a needle and syringe to aspirate such lumps, but its reliability is yet to be established."

Vaughn wrote on his yellow pad.

JP went on. "There is another disadvantage to a biopsy. Even when pathologists have the entire specimen to examine they sometimes disagree on the diagnosis. A sliver of the tumor to examine could increase the margin for error in diagnosis."

JP reached to his bookcase and removed an anatomy book. Opening it to a diagram of the face he pointed to the facial nerve, a five-branched structure from a single trunk that emerged from under the base of skull in front of the ear. "This nerve moves the muscles on one side of the face including the eyelid. It normally is sandwiched between the superficial and deep lobes of the parotid gland, the salivary gland in front of the ear. If the nerve is injured the muscles of the face will be paralyzed on that side."

Senator Vaughn studied the diagram as JP went on. "The risk of injury to the nerve during initial surgery of the parotid is minimal. With subsequent operations the risk to the nerve becomes substantial because the nerve is just under the skin and its anatomy may be distorted by previous scar formation." He paused to let his words sink in.

The senator leaned back. He smiled wanly. "It wouldn't do for me to show up on the evening news with my face paralyzed on one side. According to my wife I have a fierce enough scowl as it is."

JP tried to reassure the senator. "The history and physical exam are against malignancy. The mass is not painful, is not rapidly growing or associated with satellite lumps, facial weakness, or regional metastases, that is, lumps in the neck. Everything points to a benign process."

The senator leaned towards JP. "What do you recommend?"

JP paused. A wrong decision could compromise the senator's well-being, his appearance, his career, and possibly even his life. His incapacitation or loss to his committee could put legislative support of national defense in jeopardy. JP chose his words carefully. "The lump and scar should be widely excised under general anesthesia. If the lump is benign nothing further need be done. If it is malignant, additional surgery may be necessary."

"What kind of additional surgery?"

This was not a time for diplomacy. "Some parotid malignancies can be cured by extensive local surgery. The more aggressive cancers require removal of part of the jaw, the facial nerve, cheek, the big muscle and vein in the neck along with adjacent lymph nodes. It might even be necessary to remove part of the temporal bone, that is, part of the skull and adjacent brain. Post-operative radiation and chemotherapy may be indicated."

The senator stared at the floor a moment, then looked at JP. "I'm going to need time to think this over, Doctor. I have important meetings coming up in the next three weeks."

"There's no urgency to operate right away. I would, however, advise against a delay of more than three or four weeks. And, Senator, you should know that the management of recurrent masses after parotidectomy is controversial among head and neck surgeons. I suggest you consider obtaining a second opinion before consenting to what may be an extensive and disfiguring operation that could impact your career."

"I appreciate your candor, Colonel. As a matter of fact I have an appointment with a Dr. McClintock at Johns Hopkins tomorrow afternoon. I'll discuss your recommendations with him and get back to you." He stood up and extended his hand. "Thank you, Colonel Franklin."

After escorting the senator to his limousine JP stopped at the Ward 20/21 nurses' station before going to his office. Major Fenster sat at a counter charting medications. She looked up when he walked in. "How did you make out with the senator?" she asked.

"Fine. Thanks for stepping into the breech and saving my army career." JP went to a small coffee pot on a hotplate and poured himself a half cup of coffee. When he took a sip he nearly gagged. "Good God, Mary, you didn't give this stuff to the senator?"

Major Fenster grinned. "It is a little ripe, isn't it, but the senator seemed to like it."

JP dumped powdered cream and sugar into the cup and stirred the gray mixture with a tongue-blade. "Do you know anything about the case in the OR?"

"Very little. The patient is a medevac direct from Vietnam. He arrived late this afternoon. Major O'Connel got a call from the ER during rounds. Right after that the residents and Major Strickland went to the OR."

JP went to the sink, poured out the contents of his cup, then rinsed out the cup at the sink. "So much for your coffee. I'm going to the OR to see what my people are up to. If you need me I'll be on my pager. And Mary…"

"Sir?"

"Thanks again for bailing me out."

"Any time, Colonel, any time."

★

Thursday, May 12, 1969, 1940 hours
Operating Suite, Walter Reed Army Hospital, Washington D.C.

The long green corridor of the operating room section was clear except for gurneys parked against the wall outside two of the operating rooms. Lieutenant Colonel JP Franklin, in a green scrub suit, cap, mask, and non-conductive sneakers, glanced through a window in the door of the first room. Joe Downs, chief of general surgery, was surrounded by three of his surgery residents. Downs's right arm was buried up to his elbow in an immensely obese belly. His eyes behind glasses had a faraway look.

Grinning behind his mask, JP pushed open the door wide enough to stick his head into the room. "Lose something, Joe?"

Downs looked up. "Yeah, the appendix. The damn thing is supposed to be in here somewhere."

Downs was a superb general surgeon who had operated on a host of the country's greats and not so greats. If the patient had an appendix in that mountain of fat tissue Joe Downs would locate and remove it.

"What are you doing here tonight?" Downs asked.

"That's what I'm about to find out."

JP moved to the next operating room and pushed through the door. Three surgeons were bent low over the neck of a patient. The tallest, Dave Strickland, straightened up. "Chief, you must be psychic. I was about to call you."

Terry O'Connel, his back to JP, asked, "How was your afternoon off, Colonel?"

"You wouldn't believe me if I told you." He moved closer to the table. "What do you have?"

Strickland looked across the table. "One big mess." He turned to the junior resident. "You're up, Rolf."

Rolf Hanley moved slightly away from the operating table. "Wilson Brady is a nineteen-year-old infantryman who was part of a patrol that was ambushed near Plei Mei four days ago. He was about to throw a hand grenade when it detonated prematurely."

JP was incredulous. "What do you mean the grenade detonated prematurely? Grenades have three to five second fuses."

"I know, sir, but witnesses saw this one explode just after the spoon flew off."

JP stared at the resident.

Hanley continued. "He sustained multiple wounds of the head, face, neck, and eyes. The left eye is so badly damaged that the ophthalmologists are going to remove it. The right eye is also injured but they think it can be saved. There are multiple fractures of the right mastoid, rupture of both eardrums, severed right facial nerve, and multiple fractures of the mid face, upper and lower jaws. There are two penetrating wounds of the neck which fractured the larynx and probably perforated the upper gut. Tuning forks indicated no hearing in the right ear, and the left ear is now draining pus."

A horrible thought crossed JP's mind. *The teenager on the table had no hearing in his right ear. If infection destroyed the hearing in his left ear he would become totally deaf. If repair of the fractured larynx failed, the teenager would be unable to speak. And if the ophthalmologists were unable to save the vision in the right eye he would be totally blind. The result would be a war's basic teenaged vegetable, one who was unable to see, hear, or speak.*

JP moved behind his assistant. "What's the game plan, Dave?"

Strickland tossed his scalpel into a kidney basin. It landed with a clunk. "We just finished a trach. Next we'll make a big apron flap based superiorly and repair the upper gut and larynx. The eyeball doctors will then come in and do their thing. When they finish we'll debride the right mastoid and ear fractures. Hopefully, we'll be able to find the severed ends of the facial nerve and splice in a graft. After that we'll explore the ears."

"What about the jaw and facial fractures?"

"If the ophthalmologists are able to save the right eye we'll do a limited reduction of the fractures to avoid trauma to an already compromised eye. The oral surgeons are willing to wait a few days to reduce the jaw fractures and put him in occlusion. The belly surgeons will finish up with a feeding gastrostomy."

JP sighed. He had hoped to spend the night at home with Kathy and the kids. Reluctantly, he told Strickland, "Dave, this looks like an all-nighter. How about me calling in Roy French and his team? We'll take care of the ears and facial nerve. You can have him back after that."

Strickland looked up. "That's the best offer I've had today."

JP picked up a thin manila folder from the top of the anesthesiologist's machine. "I'm taking his transfer records to my office. I want to see how well the premature grenade detonation is substantiated. The incident should be reported. Maybe the lot number can be traced to the manufacturer. There may be other grenades that are defective. If this was sabotage by cutting the fuse short, I'd like to find the guy responsible and make sure he's hung… after a fair trial, of course.

The bitterness in JP's voice made Terry O'Connel and Dave Strickland wince and look up. Later they would agree they had never seen such cold hardness in any man's eyes.

Back in his office hunger pains reminded JP he had missed dinner. He should call Kathy to tell her he would not be coming home tonight. He dialed his home phone number.

A young voice answered. "Colonel Franklin's quarters. Frank speaking."

"Hi, Frank. It's Dad. Is Mother around?"

"She at the arts and crafts building. She's teaching her painting class."

"I forgot. When she gets back will you tell her I have an all-night case and won't be home until tomorrow evening."

After a long interval of silence, Frank said, "Dad?"

"Yes, Frank."

"How come you're never home?"

"A lot of people get hurt in Vietnam and are brought to Walter Reed for us to fix. The patient we're going to operate on tonight is one of them."

"Oh, okay. Maybe I'll see you tomorrow."

"I sure hope so."

"Bye, Dad."

JP slowly lowered the phone to its cradle.

Chapter Eight

Friday, June 6, 1969, 1440 hours
Walter Reed Army Hospital, Washington D.C.

Lieutenant Colonel JP Franklin sat in his office, his feet propped up on the desk, eating a ham sandwich procured from a vending machine in the basement for seventy-five cents. Today was the first day in several weeks the operating schedule was not inundated with casualties from Vietnam. It was an opportune time to catch up on cases postponed to make time on the schedule for casualties. Thus far today six children of varying ages had lost their tonsils and adenoids to a resident's knife. About half had, in addition, tiny plastic tubes inserted through the eardrums to relieve recurrent ear infections. These cases were followed by Senator Vaughn, who lost the lump in his parotid region to JP's scalpel. The lump went to the hospital pathologist who froze a piece of the lump for a rapid examination. The remainder of the lump was placed in formalin to be processed for a more reliable examination days later. Senator Vaughn was on the recovery ward waking up from his anesthesia. And Roy French was finishing up removal of a thyroglossal duct cyst from the neck of a seven-year-old girl. The cyst, a remnant of the embryological descent of the thyroid gland from the base of tongue, had presented as a mid-line lump in the neck. Although benign, the cyst could become life-threatening if it became infected.

Washing down the last of the sandwich with lukewarm tea, JP headed back to the operating suite. Pushing through the door, he went to the table to stand behind Roy French. "How's it going?"

"I'll be finished as soon as I sew in the rubber drains."

JP noted the precisely placed sutures crossing the neck to close the incision. "You do good work, Roy."

"Thank you, sir."

"Keep it up and you could end up with my job… you're fired."

The senior resident turned around, grinned behind his mask, and went back to work.

"Make sure she stays in recovery overnight and a trach set is kept by the bed. If she were to bleed she could lose her airway in a hurry," JP said. "I'm going to recovery to see if Senator Vaughn is awake."

Harry Resniek popped up from behind the anesthesia screen. "Awake? Of course, he's awake. He's probably sitting up demanding breakfast."

"One thing about you, Harry; humility is not one of your long suits."

The anesthesiologist stared at JP through his coke-bottle glasses. "Well, sir, I can't say that you have ever impressed me as being long in humility."

Roy French looked up. "The senator's case sure went fast, Colonel."

"It did, didn't it," JP said. "Sometimes I surprise even myself."

"See what I mean about humility?" Resniek said from behind his screen.

"Thanks for your help on this case, Colonel," French added.

"All I did was stand opposite you and entertain you and Craig with my keen sense of humor."

French sighed. "Sir, now that I'm about to graduate I have to tell you that I've heard most of your jokes at least three times each year, and I've been here four years. That's a total of twelve times. I know the joke before you get past the opening sentence."

"Watch yourself, Major," JP warned. "The key words you spoke were 'About to graduate'. You have not graduated. And if by some stroke of luck you do graduate, your assignment isn't firm."

"I'm going to Vietnam. What could be worse?"

"There's always the hospital in Asmara," JP said, grinning.

Harry Resniek studied Roy French over the top of his glasses. "I didn't realize you would graduate next month. Watching you operate I was sure you had at least another year to go."

Roy French stopped operating and looked at the anesthesiologist. "At least in Vietnam I won't have to put with your incessant demeaning remarks."

Resniek became thoughtful behind his mask and glasses. "I consider almost all surgery residents as narcissistic nerds. You, French, may be an exception."

"Harry, what makes you so damn caustic?"

Resniek sighed. "I'll try to explain in terms simple enough for even a surgical resident to understand."

"Here we go again."

"Anesthesiologists function intellectually on a much higher plane then ordinary mortals. By virtue of their specialty they are forced to tolerate for hours surgeons and surgical residents whose egos far exceed their intellects and abilities. My cynicism is the natural response of a superior human forced to work under those conditions."

★

Lieutenant Colonel JP Franklin entered the recovery ward and headed for Senator Vaughn's bed. The senator was, as Harry Resniek predicted, sitting up in bed trying to talk the young lieutenant nurse into bringing him breakfast. A rubber catheter from under the skin of his right face was connected to tubing from the wall suction. When the senator saw JP he brightened.

"Doctor, I'm starved. When can I get something to eat? The lieutenant said it would be up to you."

JP glanced at the wall clock. "In three hours, Senator. Until then there's some risk of vomiting from the effects of the anesthetic and drugs."

Senator Vaughn groaned his disappointment.

"Time for some post-op checks," JP told him.

"Be my guest."

JP focused on Vaughn's face. "Close your eyes tight, Senator." Both lids came down with equal strength. No white sclerae showed. "Now show me your teeth." The senator's smile was somewhat grim but symmetrical. JP was pleased. All parts of the facial nerve were working. The hospital in Asmara was again remote.

"Can you tell me anything about my diagnosis?" Vaughn asked.

"Yes, sir. The frozen sections suggested a benign end-stage inflammatory process known as nodular fasciitis. There was no evidence of malignancy. It will take twenty-four to forty-eight hours for the permanent sections to be processed and read by the chief of pathology here at Walter Reed. Captain Blanchard at the AFIP will review the slides and diagnosis."

"That sounds good to me. When can I go home?"

"Tomorrow morning after I remove the catheter drain. I'll send you back to your room now. You can have a soft diet in a couple of hours and a regular diet thereafter."

"I'll lose weight if I stay around here."

JP smiled. The senator could afford to lose weight. "Just tell the nurse on Ward 8 what you would like to eat. She'll have it cooked up in the kitchen there. I'll come by to see you later this afternoon."

Vaughn held out his hand. JP grasped it firmly. "Thank you, Colonel."

"I should warn you, Senator. Secretary Waldenstern is on Ward 8. Stay away from him; he's infectious at the present time."

"I never let that rascal get close to me under any circumstance," Senator Vaughn said, chuckling.

While JP was writing orders on Vaughn's chart his beeper went off. "Colonel, this is Thelma. Could you come to my office?"

Thelma seldom made that kind of request. He wondered what was up. Taking a short cut through the operating room, he entered the head and neck inpatient clinic and then Thelma's office. "You rang?"

Thelma handed him a sheaf of papers. "Congratulations, full colonel designate."

JP took the papers, read a portion of the first page, and sat down. "It looks official, Thelma."

"Yes it does, and very well deserved."

"I'll be promoted on my wedding anniversary, June 26".

"What a nice anniversary present for the army to give you," Thelma said, looking at her calendar. "That's a little over two weeks from now. I think you should call Mrs. Franklin."

"I think you're right," JP said, heading for his office.

Moments later JP broke the news to Kathy. She let out a squeal of delight. "How wonderful. I can't wait to tell the kids, Dad, Mom, and the neighborhood. You will outrank my brother. You know, JP, I've never gone to bed with a full colonel."

"Steady woman," JP said, keeping a disciplined tone to his voice. "Try to control yourself. It will be three weeks before eagle pinning time." He paused briefly. "I believe that name on the colonel's list should do until the official ceremony."

"Hurry home, Colonel."

Thelma's voice suddenly blasted from the intercom. "Colonel, Alex Leichuk would like to see you if you have a few minutes."

JP reached for the "talk" lever on the intercom. "Always time for Captain Leichuk."

A moment later the tall captain, dressed in blue hospital garb and maroon robe, walked into his office. JP leaned back in his swivel chair. "What's up, Alex? Need more convalescent leave?"

"No, sir," Leichuk croaked.

JP motioned to a chair.

Leichuk settled into the chair and leaned forward. "Sir," he burped, "I'd like to discuss surgery to repair my windpipe."

"Do you want straight talk or a honeyed version?"

"Why do I think I'm not going to like what you're going to say?"

JP stood and walked to a small blackboard on the wall. "Time for a lesson in anatomy." Picking up a piece of chalk he drew a diagram of a neck and chest, then superimposed the larynx and trachea with the latter branching out into the lungs. Next he took an eraser and wiped away the trachea from the bottom of the larynx to where the neck joined the chest. "That's what the VC did to you, plus or minus a few millimeters. Bridging a defect that large will require extensive neck and chest surgery. Simply put, your neck and chest anatomy will have to be rearranged."

"First time I've heard it described that way," Leichuk burped.

JP sat down behind his desk. "Given the state of today's surgical techniques, an operation of that magnitude carries substantial risk of failure, complications, and even fatal outcome."

Leichuk took a pen and small notebook from his robe pocket. Opening the notebook he asked, "Do you mind if I take notes?"

"Not at all, since you will be given a written exam at the end of this briefing that will count one-third of your final grade."

"Sir," Alex burped, "you have used that line so often the ward nurse predicted you would use it on me."

"I'll have to come up with a new act." JP smiled, then continued, "The operation being considered would begin with the chest surgeons mobilizing the right lung to permit the trachea remaining in the chest to be pulled up into the neck. Unfortunately it can't be pulled up far enough to reach the larynx."

"How close will it come?"

"Within two or two and a half centimeters; about an inch."

"So close and yet so far, like the bridge at Nijmegen," Leichuk said ruefully. "Can the trachea be stretched?"

"Yes and no. An additional centimeter, maybe more, might be gained by incising the tissue between tracheal rings. The down side of that is it would compromise the trachea blood supply and add tension to the suture line which would put the repair in jeopardy."

"I climbed enough rocks with you, Colonel, to know you have a way out."

JP smiled. "You're right. The larynx will be severed from its muscle and tendon attachments leaving only its blood and nerve supply. It can then be dropped down two to three centimeters; that would be more than enough to allow it to be sewn to the

86

trachea without tension. Using mountaineering comparisons, at this stage of your surgery the Hinterstoisser traverse has been crossed and the ice fields overcome, but an almost impossible overhang remains."

Alex put down his pen. "Sir, I've never climbed the north face of the Eiger."

"Neither have I. What I'm getting at is that even though the obvious obstacles are overcome, there are subtle ones that remain."

"Sir, you're talking like some of my Oxford professors."

"I'll take that as a compliment," JP said, smiling. "I'll get specific. It's presumed both nerves to the vocal cords were destroyed by the RPG frag that took out your trachea. Both vocal cords are now paralyzed near midline and no recovery of vocal cord movement can be anticipated. The narrow gap between the cords is not wide enough to pass sufficient air into the lungs to sustain life."

"Colonel, are you telling me that after you put my windpipe back together I still won't be able to breathe without a tracheotomy?"

"Precisely."

"Will I ever be able to talk with a trach even though my vocal cords are paralyzed?"

"Probably. You will need to inhale through the trach, plug the lumen with your finger, then exhale past the paralyzed vocal cords. If they're close enough together a reasonable voice should result."

"If a trach helps me breathe and talk, why do I get a sense you're not happy with that result?"

"No matter where the tracheotomy is placed after the tracheal repair, it will violate the operative site. There is a high probability that infection will follow and place the repair in jeopardy."

"You don't paint an optimistic picture, Colonel."

"It's important you be made aware of the odds you face."

"If the operation is a success and infection is controlled, what then?"

"After six months to a year, depending on how you heal, the vocal cords can be moved surgically apart. The challenge then will be to create an airway sufficient to permit you to breathe adequately, but an airway not so large that food, liquids, and secretions spill into the lungs. The closer the vocal cords are to each other the better the voice, but the worse to pass air into the lungs. The further apart the vocal cords are, the poorer the voice and the greater the risk of aspiration, although the better the ability to breathe. Everything will be a trade-off, Alex, and the least important consideration in this equation is the voice." JP rose to his feet. "Would you like some coffee?"

"Yes, sir, black please," Leichuk burped.

JP went into the conference room and filled two mugs with coffee from a percolator. Returning to his office he placed a mug in front of Alex.

"Thanks, sir," Leichuk burped.

JP continued. "Look, Alex, there's no urgency for this surgery. In three or four years newer techniques, the use of prostheses, or even cadaver grafts may make the surgery safer and more certain of success. You have a brilliant mind. This may be the Almighty's way of telling you to develop that mind for some other purpose," JP stopped before adding, "other than killing people." He wondered if his own military career through two wars was behind that thought.

"In the meantime you could go back to school, get your Masters, PhD, or even law degree. You could end up a lawyer who sues doctors." JP smiled at the thought. "You're certainly bright enough to get into medical school despite your physical handicaps. I know people who could help you. Some day you could develop techniques to reconstruct tracheal injuries like yours."

It seemed Alex had not heard a word. "Colonel, I saw the specialists in New York, Boston, and Baltimore you recommended. They all said substantially what you did."

"At least we surgeons are consistent."

"I'm an infantry officer, sir. That's all I ever wanted to be. If the surgery will give me a fighting chance to stay on active duty and continue my military career, I'm willing to take risks and then some. I want to have the surgery as soon as possible."

JP sighed. "Okay," he said, reaching for the intercom. "Thelma, would you bring the OR scheduling book, please."

After he finished scheduling Alex's surgery for three weeks hence JP handed the book to Alex. "Please give this back to Mrs. Hoffberg."

Alex Leichuk stood up. "Thank you, sir."

When Alex was gone JP stared out the window, wondering if he had done the right thing. Mrs. Hoffberg's Brooklyn voice shattered his introspection. "Colonel Perigone's secretary is on line one." Perigone was assistant chief of pediatrics.

JP picked up the phone; a feminine voice answered. "Just a minute for Colonel Perigone."

A moment later a gruff male voice came on line. "JP, I was afraid you might be at the mess hall. I know what a chow hound you are."

"I'm not thirty pounds overweight and had my trouser waist let out every six months for the past two years. How can I help besides sending you a twelve hundred calorie diet?"

Perigone laughed briefly, then became serious. "I just finished examining the three-year-old daughter of the German air attaché, Colonel Dietler. He told me she complained of a sore throat since waking up this morning. An hour ago she started drooling. My exam was negative except for a temp of one hundred, red throat, drooling, and minimal inspiratory wheezes over her neck." Perigone paused as though embarrassed to ask, but asked anyway. "Would you mind taking a look at her?"

Something in Colonel Perigone's voice conveyed a subtle unspoken message. It reflected immense concern for the child's welfare despite inability to define reasons for the concern. "Send her right over, Joe. I'll take a look and give you a call."

"Thanks. They're on the way." The voice on the phone reflected undisguised relief.

Five minutes later the quiet of the head and neck inpatient clinic was shattered by the loud, wheezing sounds of a child's desperate efforts to suck air through a nearly blocked airway. JP immediately recognized the terminal events of a disease process that killed over a dozen children every year in the United States. Many not killed were left with severe brain damage. For this child only minutes, maybe less, separated her from a neurological catastrophe and death. JP catapulted out of his chair and ran to the waiting room.

An officer in the blue uniform of a Luftwaffe colonel stood at the receptionist's counter holding a small blonde girl in his arms. The girl's ashen complexion, purple lips, and eyes wide with terror left no doubt as to the diagnosis. Her cry, while weak, sounded normal. That observation eliminated croup as the primary pathology. As JP approached, the girl's eyes rolled up and her eyelids sagged.

"I don't understand," the girl's father almost sobbed, his voice tinged with a German accent. "She was breathing all right when we left Colonel Perigone's office."

"There's no time to explain," JP said, extending his arms. "Unless we put a tube in her windpipe she's going to die."

"Mein Gott."

Without another word the colonel passed his daughter to JP. Holding the limp girl in his arms, he turned and ran towards the double doors that led to the operating suite. Passing Thelma in the hall, he shouted, "Page Terry O'Connel. Tell him to get to the OR stat."

Pushing through swinging doors into the OR suite, he ran down the main corridor searching for someone to assist him with the girl. As chance would have, the corridor was empty of people. Time was running out. Desperate, he shouted, "Help, damn it, somebody help."

Chapter Nine

Far down the corridor a door to an operating room swung open. Harry Resniek exited pushing an anesthesia machine. Alerted by the urgency in JP's voice and then seeing him rushing down the corridor with a small limp girl in his arms, he shouted, "In here, Colonel." Then, pulling the anesthesia machine, he backed into the operating room, holding the door open.

JP brushed past him into the room and lay the girl on the operating table. Grabbing bandage scissors from the anesthesia machine he cut the girl's dress and undershirt in the midline from her neck to below her navel, exposing her chest and abdomen. By this time her face was blue and her lips purple. Her chest and abdomen showed no respiratory efforts, and her heartbeat was almost too fast to count.

"She's quit breathing, Harry," JP panted. "Her rate's nearly 200."

The anesthesiologist clamped a rubber mask over the girl's mouth and nose, then repeatedly inflated the anesthesia bag with oxygen and squeezed it to force oxygen into her lungs. "I'm not doing any good, Colonel. She has an airway blockage."

"Try intubating her."

"What do we have here, a foreign body?"

"No. Acute epiglottitis."

Moving to the wall cabinet, JP flung open the glass doors and scanned the shelves of sterile instrument packs wrapped in green sheets. Grabbing a pack he carried it to a Mayo stand and pulled open its wrapping, exposing a tray full of instruments. After he slipped on a pair of sterile gloves he dug into the tray, selecting a scalpel and a fine-tipped hemostat. Reaching for the girl's chubby neck with his left hand his fingers probed for the cricothyroid space, the 2 mm x 6 mm space between the Adam's apple and windpipe. In this small area only skin, fat, and connective tissue covered the airway. As his right hand poised the scalpel blade above the skin he looked up expectantly at Harry Resniek.

Less than a minute had elapsed since they had entered the operating room. During that time Harry Resniek had pried open the girl's jaw and slipped an L-shaped tubular instrument through her mouth into her throat. A small bulb at the far end of the blade furnished light. Elevating the tongue with the blade, Resniek glimpsed the epiglottis. He should have seen a thin, flesh-colored flap the size of an adult fingernail over the opening in the voice box through which air must pass to reach the lungs. Instead he saw a flaming-red structure the size of a swollen adult thumb blocking the airway. "You called it right," Resniek said, withdrawing the laryngoscope. "I'll never get a tube past that thing."

JP immediately plunged the scalpel blade through skin and subcutaneous tissue. A characteristic "give" told him the tip of the blade had entered the airway. After sawing the tissues horizontally for several millimeters he forced the sharp-pointed hemostat through the incision. Opening the clamp, he widened the incision and held it open, ignoring the mild bleeding. Resniek shoved a child's size plastic anesthesia tube through the hole. "I'm in."

JP withdrew the hemostat, then stabilized the tube with the fingers of his left hand. Resniek connected the free end of the tube to the hose from his machine and began squeezing the anesthesia bag to inflate the girl's lungs with oxygen. Still holding the tube with his left hand, JP felt the neck with his free right hand for the carotid pulse. "Her rate's down to thirty, Harry. She's going to arrest."

"No way," Resniek snapped. With his free hand he picked up a syringe with an attached needle from his anesthesia machine and passed it to JP, "Atropine; give her a half cc IV. Leave the needle in and start Ringer's." He reached for the anesthesia tube. "I've got it."

JP tied a rubber tubing around the girl's upper arm as a tourniquet and began searching the back of her hand for a vein.

"Move it, Colonel," Resniek prodded. "We're running out of time."

JP found a vein and slipped in the needle on the first attempt. Releasing the tourniquet, he injected the atropine, then twisted the syringe free of the needle hub and attached the tubing from a bottle of Ringer's lactate hanging on a pole. He looked up. "What's she doing now?"

Resniek stopped squeezing the anesthesia bag to feel the girl's neck for the carotid pulse. "Rate's up to sixty."

JP sighed. "That was close."

"She'll never come closer."

The OR door slammed open and Roy French rushed in, breathing heavily. Stopping just inside the door, he scanned the room. "Looks... like... the crisis... is over," he gasped.

JP took note of his panting chief resident, now back in uniform and white coat. "You're out of shape, French."

"Yes, sir, I know. You've had me so busy I haven't had time to work out. I get home so late at night, that's if I get home, all I can do is collapse in bed and fall asleep. My wife thinks I'm having an affair."

"You are," JP said, "with a very demanding mistress. What happened to Terry?"

"He's down in the ER with an emergency; another kid with a dog bite of the neck. This one is worse than the last. He's not expected to live."

"Go change into greens and wash up. I'll prep the neck for a tracheotomy."

Before the door closed behind Major French two nurses dressed in green scrubs entered, followed by a man wearing a green OR gown over his uniform. One of the nurses asked, "What can we do, Colonel?"

"One of you scrub in, the other circulate. Right now I need a prep set and instruments for a trach."

"You're going to do another operation?" a male voice asked.

Turning, JP stared at the man who had come in behind the nurses, noting his awkwardly tied mask and untied cap.

"Who the hell are you?"

"Father Ryan, the Catholic chaplain. Heidi's father asked she be given the last rites."

"Oops. Sorry, Father," JP apologized. "I am glad to know her name." JP glanced at the inert girl, then back at the priest. "The last rites might be a little premature. She could use some heavy prayers to wake up without neurological deficit."

The priest seemed shocked at the mention of brain damage.

"From lack of oxygen," JP explained. "We'll have to wait until she wakes up, if she wakes up, to determine how much damage."

"Oh my," the priest said. Moving next to the girl, he placed his hand on the her forehead. Harry Resniek watched, an expression of pained tolerance on his face.

"What's her heart rate now?" JP asked Resniek.

"Holding steady at sixty. I gave her a bolus of steroids. It may keep down brain swelling. How about sticking on EKG leads? I want to monitor her heart."

"I can do that, Major," the circulator said as she set a prep set on a Mayo stand and moved the stand close to the OR table. JP picked up several cotton sponges, dipped them in a bowl of germicidal soap, and began scrubbing Heidi's neck. He included Harry Resniek's gloved hand and the anesthesia tube. Minutes later, Roy French came into the room dressed in a green scrub suit, his wet forearms flexed. The circulator threw a sterile towel over his hands.

JP told French, "Go ahead and drape. I need to change and wash up." He turned to the chaplain. "Come with me, Father. While we change I'll explain about the second operation."

In the doctor's dressing room Father Ryan began searching through stacks of clean scrub shirts and trousers on a gurney. "One might assume from these that all surgeons are extra large."

"Only their egos, Father," JP said, grinning. Opening his locker, he pulled trousers and a shirt from a stack of scrub suits on a shelf and held them out. "These are mediums. You look like a medium to me."

"No one has ever described me in quite those terms," Father Ryan said.

"You can store your uniform in my locker, Father. I'll give you the lock combination." Stripping off his old scrubs, he tossed them into a cloth basket in a corner, then pulled on a clean set. Slipping his feet into bloodstained green sneakers, he leaned over to tie them.

"You were going to tell me about the second operation?" Father Ryan asked.

"Right. First I'd better explain about acute epiglottitis. It's an infection that targets the little flap over the entrance of the airway causing it to swell. Children are the usual victims but occasionally adults are seen with the condition. It begins with fever, sore throat, and difficulty swallowing. The voice is normal but weak and there is inspiratory stridor. Within two or three hours, sometimes less, the epiglottis becomes so swollen it blocks the airway. Severe brain damage and even death will result unless the obstruction is relieved. I don't know of any infection that can kill a normal healthy child so quickly.

"Every year at least a dozen deaths from acute epiglottitis are reported in the US. The number surviving with severe brain damage is not known, but I suspect it is substantial. Last year there were two deaths in the D.C.–Baltimore area and five who survived but sustained severe brain damage. One of the initial survivors was left cortically blind, that is unable to learn Braille. He eventually died. The mother, a prominent actress, apparently was unable to handle her grief and committed suicide."

JP straightened up, closed and locked his locker, then helped the priest tie his mask and cap. "Let's go out to the sink."

The chaplain held the door open. JP passed into the corridor and stopped at a sink outside the operating room. Turning on the water with his knee, he adjusted the temperature to just below what would produce a first degree burn. While he scrubbed his hands and arms with a brush soaked with germicidal solution he continued. "Heidi's situation was desperate by the time she reached the OR. She had lost consciousness and stopped breathing. When Major Resniek was unable to pass a tube into the airway I had to move fast. The quickest and safest route to the airway in the neck is through the cricothyroid space, the space between the larynx and the hard cartilage ring at the top of the trachea. Take your fingers and feel it just below your Adam's apple."

The chaplain probed his neck.

"My stab incision cut through a delicate membrane in that space. The longer a tube stays through that membrane the greater the probability that irritation and infection will produce scar tissue. That scar tissue will grow until it obstructs the airway. To reduce the risk of this complication a tracheotomy is made lower down in the neck as quickly as possible. The incidence of troublesome scar formation is minimal in that area."

JP rinsed his hands and then his arms. "How long have you been a priest, Father?" he asked.

"Almost twenty years. I entered seminary after the war."

Turning off the water JP held his flexed arms over the sink. As excess water dripped from his elbows he studied the priest. Even though there had been two wars after World War II, there was only one real war as far as World War II vets were concerned. "Were you in the war, Father?"

The priest chuckled. 'You might say that. I was a platoon sergeant with the 82nd Airborne until a German soldier ended my promising military career… and I ended his. We both survived and write each other regularly. He became a Lutheran minister after the war."

JP stared at the priest as though seeing him for the first time. "Father Ryan, I have truly misjudged you," he said. "This may sound a little weird, but you remind me of a buddy I had in the Marine Corps during the war who lost a leg. The last I heard he was in a seminary in Pennsylvania studying to become a priest."

"Do you remember his name?"

"Of course. Mick… Michael Icardi."

Father Ryan regarded JP with a mixture of surprise and curiosity. "The Almighty works in strange ways, Colonel. The Holy Fathers at the seminary I attended after the war had the wisdom to keep veterans together. It was done in the hopes that the veterans would ventilate their war experiences to each other and thereby reduce post-war psychiatric problems. Father Mick was my roommate in seminary."

JP couldn't believe his good fortune.

The priest continued. "Father Mick told me how a JP Franklin and a Navajo Indian named Jake Conrad kept him from drowning and bleeding to death after he was wounded. I take it, Doctor, you are that JP Franklin?"

"Yes, sir." JP felt a powerful yearning to see Mick Icardi. "Would you know where Father Mick is now?"

"As a matter of fact I do. I received a letter from him three days ago. I'll drop the envelope by your office tomorrow. It has his return address."

JP moved to the OR door, chuckling. "Knowing what Mick was like in the Marine Corps it's hard to picture him a parish priest baptizing snotty-nosed babies in a small town."

Father Ryan laughed. "I doubt he's baptizing many babies; he's a navy chaplain assigned to the marines on Okinawa. In his letter he mentioned having volunteered for a third tour in Vietnam. He hopes to be the division chaplain for the 1ˢᵗ Marine Division."

JP was incredulous. "Mick is on active duty as a navy chaplain, with an artificial leg?"

"No one is quite sure how that came about. Father Mick has tremendous persuasive powers."

JP grinned. "I'll say. He got me in more trouble than I care to remember."

"He's been on active duty as a chaplain for over fourteen years. He was promoted to commander three years ago."

"That rascal. So we're both 0-5s. At least I'll soon outrank him," JP said, thinking of his impending promotion to full colonel.

As they entered the operating room, JP's pager beeped. "Justice Brownlee is here to see you, Colonel," Thelma's voice announced.

Father Ryan raised his eyebrows. "Supreme Court Justice?"

JP nodded.

The circulator came over to JP and silenced the beeper's static, then went to the wall phone, checked the list of numbers on the wall and dialed Thelma's number. She held the phone to JP's ear and mouth. "I'm knee deep in an emergency," he told her. "I won't be able to see the justice for at least forty minutes. Is Major Strickland around?"

"Yes, sir."

"Tell him it's about time he started pulling his weight. Ask him to see the justice. If that's not acceptable to the justice I'll see him as soon as I can break loose."

Returning to the operating table, he said, "Okay, people, let's go to work."

★

Roy French, working in his usual methodical and meticulous manner, completed the tracheotomy in ten minutes and secured the curved plastic tube with umbilical tape, tying the knot to the side of the neck. JP stepped back, pulled his gown off over his gloves, rolled the gown up and tossed it into a cloth hamper. "Basket," he said proudly, ignoring the circulator's glare. Stripping off his gloves, he dropped them into a metal kick bucket, then picked up the stethoscope hanging on the side of the anesthesia machine. For several moments he listened intently to each side of Heidi's chest. "Good air sounds on both sides," he announced, "but we still need blood gases and X-rays."

"I've already sent for the tech, Colonel," the circulator said.

JP thanked her, then turned to Major French. "Nice job, Roy. Hardly a drop of blood."

"Don't start crowing about surgical skills just yet," Harry Resniek said dourly. "You don't know if she's going to wake up a vegetable, or if she's going to wake up at all."

Resniek's gloomy remarks wiped away any euphoria the OR team felt at finishing with a live patient. The OR door bumped open. A wheeled portable X-ray machine was pushed into the room by a female soldier-technician.

"We need an AP and lateral of her chest," Roy French told her.

The tech slipped a film cassette under the girl's back, positioned the X-ray tube over the chest, then donned a lead apron and handed one to Harry Resniek. Moments later she announced she was ready. Everyone except the tech and the anesthesiologist moved into the hall, precautions taken to avoid radiation exposure. After the X-rays were taken the tech pushed her machine into a corner, retrieved the exposed film cassettes and disappeared out the door.

The tension of waiting for Heidi to wake up was telling. Roy French, at the foot of the operating table, gave up trying to write an op note with a GI pen. Abruptly he threw the pen into a metal kick bucket with such force that it clanged louder than a fire gong. The scrub nurse jumped, startled. Harry Resniek quietly handed Roy one of his many pens.

JP's anxiety broke through his facade of calmness. He walked over to a tray of clean instruments and removed two Kelly clamps. Ignoring the chastising look from the scrub nurse, he alternately opened and closed the clamps, creating ratcheting noises that surpassed in annoyance the sounds of fingernails dragged across a blackboard. Father Ryan stood against a wall, his eyes closed. JP hoped he was praying.

The X-ray tech reappeared carrying two films, slipped them up into a viewbox and flipped the light switch. JP and Roy French stood behind her studying the films.

"Looking for anything in particular?" Father Ryan asked.

"Yes, sir, pneumothorax," Roy French said. "In a child the tips of the lungs balloon up into the lower neck with inspiration. During tracheotomy, especially emergency tracheotomy, there's substantial risk of nicking the pleura, that is, the covering of the lung. That will cause the lung to collapse like a punctured balloon. If recognized early the lung can be quickly expanded by inserting a chest tube. A delay in expanding a collapsed lung can compromise oxygenation, lead to pneumonia or even lung abscess. Collapse of both lungs is incompatible with life."

The X-ray tech asked, "Need any more films?"

"These are fine. Both lungs are up," Roy French said. "You do good work."

The tech beamed. "Thanks, sir."

After the tech left, pushing her machine ahead of her like a baby carriage, the room became quiet. Periodically, Harry Resniek listened over both sides of Heidi's chest with his stethoscope. Then without warning he disconnected the anesthesia hoses from the tracheotomy tube. "She's breathing on her own," he announced. "Let's get her on a gurney."

The circulator left the room, then reappeared pushing a gurney. With Harry Resniek supporting Heidi's head, JP and Terry O'Connel lifted the girl gently from the OR table to the gurney. Suddenly Heidi stiffened. Her mouth opened wide to cry out, but no sounds came forth because of the tracheotomy. Her eyes opened wide in terror. She began to struggle. Harry Resniek looked up and smiled. "She's okay." Tension rushed from the room.

JP slapped Father Ryan on the back. "You must carry a lot of weight with the Big Six upstairs. It's enough to make a guy consider becoming a Catholic."

The priest grinned behind his mask. "Confirmation classes start next Thursday at the post chapel."

"You wouldn't want a sinful Protestant in your church."

"Quite the contrary. Protestants make the best Catholics."

JP waved a salute at the chaplain. As he moved to the door he turned to Roy French. "Go with her to recovery. I'll call the pediatricians, fill them in on what's taken place and ask them to follow Heidi with us. Then I'll talk to her father."

★

Thirty minutes later JP collapsed into his swivel chair, leaned back and propped his feet on his desk. Holding a mug of coffee he gazed out his window at the dome of the Capitol and marveled at fate. First it brought Ann Carter back into his life through her son, Tom. Then it brought back Mick Icardi through Heidi Dietler. What would fate bring next?

Sipping thoughtfully, his mind drifted back twenty-five years to Mono, a tiny island in the Northern Solomons. JP had been part of a marine patrol made up of himself, Mick Icardi, the Chief, and led by Platoon Sergeant Harold McDougall. The patrol, guided by an exceptionally intelligent jungle-wise native, John Boreas, slipped into Mono from a PT boat. Their mission: to rescue two Army Air Corps pilots who had crash-landed in the waters off Mono three months earlier.

The pilots were found and led to a rendezvous with a PT boat. As the pilots were being loaded into a rubber raft from the PT boat, Japanese along the shore opened fire. Sergeant McDougall and John Boreas were wounded. JP, Icardi, and the Chief fought off the Japanese allowing the others to escape in the raft to the waiting PT boat. The three young marines retreated into the jungle, evading the Japanese patrols hunting them through the night. The next morning the three marines stole a canoe from a fishing village and attempted to reach a friendly island. Chased by a Japanese barge firing a mortar, Icardi was severely wounded in the leg and all three were dumped into the water when the canoe overturned. JP managed to get a tourniquet on Icardi's leg while the Chief fought off a shark by throwing hand grenades at it. Just as the three marines were about to be killed by rifle fire from the barge, a Marine F4U Corsair attacked and sunk the barge. Minutes later JP and his comrades were taken aboard a PT boat. Icardi was evacuated to the naval hospital on Guadalcanal where his leg was amputated.

The pace of the war was such that JP never heard what happened to John Boreas and Sergeant McDougall. Icardi wrote once when he was in seminary, then nothing. That Mick Icardi was a navy chaplain on active duty scheduled to go to Vietnam was hard to believe. That one of his closest marine comrades would serve three times in a war zone while he, JP, sat out the war pontificating in an ivory tower was unacceptable. Somehow he would find a way to go to Vietnam.

Dave Strickland walked in before the echo of his knock faded, a single sheet of paper in his hand. "Heard you had a cliffhanger," he said, easing into a chair.

"It's the closest I hope to come to losing a patient without losing the patient," JP said. "What is the justice's problem?"

"He complained of hoarseness, productive cough, and fever. His chest film showed a right middle lobe pneumonia. I admitted him to Ward 8 on our service."

"Wise move. He's pretty fragile because of his age."

"The internists will manage his pneumonia; we'll take care of his hoarseness," Dave Strickland said and then he began laughing.

"What's so funny?"

"When I told the justice he would be on strict voice rest he said, 'Young man, are you ordering me to keep my mouth shut?'"

"What did you tell him?"

"I told him that was precisely what I had in mind. He laughed, then asked for a pen and a pad."

"I'll go by and say hello to the justice. I know him from previous admissions, but you plan on staying on as his doctor. What about the kid with the dog bite?"

"He's in bad shape. The dog got the common carotid and jug, as well as the trachea. He was stroked and nearly bled out by the time the paramedics got to him. I just had a call from Terry O'Connel; the kid is posturing and has dilated fixed pupils. The pediatric neurologists are evaluating him now. The parents have been told their son is not going to make it."

JP winced. Again fate had shafted a child. "What kind of dog was involved?"

"I don't know, but the D.C. police have arrested the owner. Apparently the dog has bitten a number of children in the neighborhood. The dog owner had ignored court orders to restrain the dog or get rid of it." Dave Strickland leaned over and placed a sheet of paper on JP's desk.

"What's this?"

"Tonight's roster of patients for the head and neck cancer conference."

JP groaned. "Damn. I forgot. I hoped to have dinner with my family."

"I'll moderate for you at the conference."

JP scanned the list. "I'd better be there tonight. We've got some tough cases to discuss, but you can still moderate."

"Thanks a lot, boss."

★

After Strickland left JP picked up the phone and dialed his quarters. When Kathy answered he said, "Oh that southern accent really gets to me."

"This had better be my husband."

"I hate to tell you this, Kathy…"

"Then I don't want to hear it."

"I forgot that the head and neck cancer conference is tonight. I won't be home until after ten."

"JP, this will be the third night this week that you miss dinner. The kids are beginning to wonder if they have a father, and I'm beginning to wonder if I have a husband. When you finally get home you're so tired you collapse in bed and fall asleep." Kathy Franklin giggled. "JP, are you having an affair?"

Chapter Ten

Wednesday, June 25, 1969, 1015 hours
Walter Reed Army Hospital, Washington D.C.

The intellectual quiet prevailing in the hospital library was intermittently disturbed by the brief bursts of hushed voices or the occasional shrill beep of a pager. In a reading room close to the reference stacks, Lieutenant Colonel JP Franklin sat at a long oak table. Volume I of *Surgery in World War II* was open to the chapter on the repair of facial nerve injuries. The chapter was short, with no meaningful data or useful details on technique. Twenty-six cases were reported, summarizing the combined experience at a facial nerve center in Europe and one in the US. Considering the large number of casualties in World War II, that seemed a small and unenlightening series. Those data were compared to the experience at Walter Reed since 1964 when JP, then a major, joined the staff. Thirty-four facial nerves had been repaired in the past six years, two more cases awaiting surgery, and the war in Vietnam was far from over. Soon he would write up the Walter Reed series and submit the article to a surgical journal. He wondered if the North Vietnamese had a similar series. If they did, perhaps the data from the two countries could be pooled. Dream on.

Closing the book he settled back a moment to contemplate the events coming up the next day. At 1400 hours he would be promoted to full colonel, thanks to the efforts of anonymous conscientious line colonels and a general who comprised the promotion board. Kathy planned to get all four kids out of school and bring them to the hospital for the ceremony. Tomorrow night he and Kathy would quietly celebrate his promotion and their nineteenth wedding anniversary by having dinner at the Walter Reed officers' club. Next Saturday afternoon Sleepy Hollow (Forest Glen) would come alive for a few hours as the Franklins hosted a promotion barbecue for military and civilian neighbors. Frank and Nancy had delivered the invitations last week.

JP's beeper went off, startling him and several others. Thelma's voice cut through the library's quiet. "General Worden and General Bartlett are in your office waiting to see you."

Silencing the beeper's static, JP got to his feet, picked up his notes and returned the book to the stacks. As he headed for the stairs to his office he wondered why the hospital commander and the Assistant Surgeon General of the army would show up unannounced in his office. Then it hit him: that's what happens when there is tragic news to be delivered... *Oh God, Kathy, the kids.* He took the stairs three at a time.

His heart pounding and short of breath, JP rushed into his office. The two generals were studying framed photographs on the wall of the tanks and half-tracks JP commanded in the Korean War. They turned to face him; both appeared very somber.

General Worden said, "JP, there's been a terrible injustice concerning your promotion to colonel."

Relief flushed through JP. *Thank God it was not Kathy or the kids.* He stared at the hospital commander. "I don't follow you, General."

"General Bartlett will explain," Worden said.

The Assistant Surgeon General began. "You and three other Medical Corps lieutenant colonels were placed on the promotion list with the strong and unanimous recommendation of the promotion board. This was done despite the short time in grade you and the others had as lieutenant colonels. The legal basis which allowed them to override the existing time constraints was a Department of Army policy allowing consideration of prior military service, with extra weight given to time in combat as commissioned officers."

A growing anger began to seep through JP as he perceived where this conversation was leading.

General Bartlett continued. "In your case, JP, the recommendation was based on service as an enlisted marine in World War II, service as a commissioned officer during the Korean War, medals, awards, your considerable professional accomplishments as a Medical Corps officer, your appointment to the National Academy of Science, and the prestige you brought the Medical Corps from the civilian medical community. The board considered you and the others, whose backgrounds paralleled yours, as having exceptional potential that would impact the future of the Army Medical Corps. They realized all four of you were close to retirement and special inducement was indicated to encourage you to remain on active duty."

JP felt as though a sputtering grenade had just been dropped at his feet. He tensed for the detonation.

"Unfortunately a new Department of Army promotion policy went into effect ten days ago. Its requirements superseded those of the previous policy, the policy under which the board could recommend your promotion." Bartlett stared at the rug. Embarrassment flooded his face. "Somehow in the heat of the activities in South-east Asia and Europe, the revised promotion policy slipped by the Surgeon General and myself. No provisions were made for medical officers with backgrounds such as yours. Had we been aware of the ramifications of the new policy we would have amended it. The JAG reviewed both promotion policies yesterday and ruled the requirements of the new policy must prevail."

"And just what are those requirements, General?" JP asked softly. Bartlett looked so pained that JP almost felt sorry for him.

"The current requirements for promotion are sixteen years beyond graduation from medical school."

"And?"

"I'm afraid that's it."

JP was stunned. He began a slow burn. He stared at General Worden, then fixed on General Bartlett. "Sir, are you telling me that a medical officer's prior experience in wartime as an officer leading men in combat, his responsibilities in military operations and military intelligence, and especially his professional accomplishments count for

100

nothing in the promotion of lieutenant colonels to colonel?"

Neither general spoke.

"As I see it, the only requirement now for promotion to full colonel in the Medical Corps of the United States Army seems to be just having survived sixteen years out of medical school without screwing up. Ineffective and incompetent lieutenant colonels, repeatedly passed over for promotion and due to be separated or retired, will now be promoted and assume positions of great responsibility. They will be our next generation of leaders, the role models for young physicians and the pool for future Medical Corps generals," said JP, shaking his head in sorrow. "God help the Medical Corps."

General Worden's face was becoming red with anger. General Bartlett remained impassive. Both were silent.

"According to the new and enlightened promotion policy I won't be even eligible for promotion for another four years." JP took a deep breath, trying to get a handle on his growing anger, then continued. "I must tell you, General, that policy is a formula for driving out of the Medical Corps its most promising officers, officers whose only mistake was to serve their country in war while their contemporaries languished, warm and safe in medical school or some obscure clinic where they avoided responsibility for sixteen years. General Bartlett, the Soviets couldn't have come up with a better policy to sabotage the Medical Corps and the army. Tell me, General." JP said, his voice dripping with undisguised venom, "is there a mole in the Surgeon General's office, or is it just so inundated with passed-over horse holders and perfumed princes it can't function?"

General Worden's ruddy face turned almost purple. "God damn it, JP, watch your mouth."

Before JP could respond by telling the generals what they could do with their promotions General Bartlett, to his credit, interrupted. "It's all right, Robert. Colonel Franklin spoke the truth. We in the SGO dropped the ball and should be willing to take the heat." He walked over to a coat tree where JP's blouse hung on a hanger. Touching the silver lieutenant colonel's leaf on the shoulder, he turned to JP. "I promise you, the Surgeon General and I will do everything possible to get these leaves changed to eagles. You must realize that getting a revision through the Departments of Army and Defense takes time, a year at least, possibly longer."

JP, fighting to control his anger, bit his lip and remained silent.

"I know you will have twenty years of active duty in January and be eligible to retire. I have learned you are being aggressively proselytized by several medical schools to chair their departments of head and neck surgery. I know about the offers to go into lucrative private practice." General Bartlett chuckled. "At this point I must admit the Medical Corps is not in the best bargaining position."

JP couldn't resist a smile at General Bartlett's candor.

"Yet I hope this injustice doesn't sour you to the extent that you leave the army." General Bartlett reached out and placed both hands on JP's arms. "The army needs your experience, JP, your skills and your leadership."

Oh sure. Tell me about it. "General, I need time to sort this out, to contemplate how the army treats the people it considers of merit and potential, and especially to analyze the army's fixation on venerating mediocrity. Whether I leave the army or stay is a decision I must discuss with Mrs. Franklin." At that moment JP's predominant thought was, *Screw the army. I'm out of here.*

"Whatever you decide I would elicit your help in getting the promotion policy changed," General Bartlett said.

"You have that, General," JP said, responding almost by reflex, then wondering if he were about to fall into a trap.

"Good. Within the next day or two you will receive a request from the Surgeon General for your analysis of the impact of the new promotion policy on the future of the army Medical Corps. Don't pull any punches. Tell it like you see it. Will you do that for the Medical Corps and your country?"

JP fell into the trap. "Of course I will, General."

General Bartlett extended his hand. "This will work itself out, JP You will be a colonel, I promise."

Yeah, when all my hair turns white or falls out.

After shaking Bartlett's hand and then Worden's, JP watched the two generals leave. As soon as they were gone Thelma came into his office. "What was all that about?" she asked.

JP slumped into his swivel chair. "Thelma, you don't keep a bottle of Scotch in your desk, do you?"

By the time he finished explaining his aborted promotion Thelma was in tears. "It's not fair, Colonel, it's just not fair." She took a tissue from her pocket, wiped her eyes and then blew her nose. "What are you going to do?"

"I'm not sure. For now the hard part will be to break the news to Kathy and the kids. Damn it, Thelma, our entire neighborhood expects me to be promoted to colonel today. A big block party is planned for Saturday." He stared at his desk. "Maybe I'll get my kids to go door to door and explain to the neighbors how come their dad will remain a light colonel, maybe forever. How am I going to explain it to my kids? Hell, I can't even explain it to myself."

Tears again slid down Thelma's cheeks. "You're not going to leave the army, are you?"

"I'm giving that option serious consideration. Dr. McClintock wants me to take the chair at Hopkins when he leaves, or join him in private practice. You wouldn't believe what he predicted my income would be."

"I don't want to hear it," Thelma said, shaking her head and rushing from the room.

JP stared gloomily out the window and thought about Al McClintock's offers. Private practice would assure him an income at least eight times his current army income, and working with Al McClintock would be pure pleasure. For almost twenty years McClintock had been his mentor. It began in Korea during the Korean War. JP was a young first lieutenant in the 3rd Infantry Division commanding a platoon of four tanks armed with twin 40 mm cannons, and four half-tracks mounting four 50-caliber machine guns.

When Communist China's People's Liberation Army (PLA) opened its spring offensive in 1951, a British battalion attached to the 3rd Division was in danger of being overrun. Two US helicopters attempting to evacuate the wounded were shot down. The pilot of one was killed, the other severely injured. JP's platoon was tasked to give fire support to the battalion and evacuate the wounded. Not realizing they were up against a Chinese division the platoon expended most of its ammunition, inflicting hundreds of casualties. When it became apparent that JP's platoon would be overrun along with the British, he managed to contact an air force FAC who saved the day. JP's platoon escaped, carrying eighteen British casualties and the injured US helicopter pilot to a MASH where Al McClintock, then a Medical Corps major, was chief of surgery.

A young nurse, Kristy Goulden, was in charge of the MASH emergency room. She had taken care of JP months earlier when he was so gravely ill that he almost died. She introduced him to Major McClintock who gave him credit for saving the life of the helicopter pilot and many British lives. For some reason Major McClintock took an interest in the young lieutenant, invited him to watch surgery, and eventually encouraged him to go to medical school. Now McClintock, chair of the division of head and neck surgery at Hopkins, a brigadier general in the army reserve, and a consultant at Walter Reed, was about to leave Hopkins and go into private practice. He repeatedly urged JP to retire from the army, replace him at Hopkins or join him in private practice.

JP allowed the image of a five-bedroom home, a rag top MG, a pickup truck, and a white Lincoln in the home's three-car garage, and a Cessna 310 in the hangar at Hyde Field, briefly to dominate his imagination for several sweet minutes. Finally, he reached for the phone and dialed his quarters. Kathy's gentle southern voice came on line. "Hi, kid," JP began, "how would you like to be a civilian?"

"What?"

JP explained.

Kathy Franklin, the daughter of an army general and sister of a lieutenant colonel, JP's best friend, was outraged. She was also savvy enough to know that many military decisions could not lay claim to anything remotely related to common sense. Close to tears she finally said, "I can't think of a better way to wreck the Medical Corps."

"We need to talk, Kath. I have to be here tonight until late, but our anniversary night is still free. Let's go to the club at Bethesda and do our talking."

"I thought we were going to club at Walter Reed."

"I've had it with the army. I may transfer to the navy. They have flush commodes and air conditioning. Better yet, I'll transfer back to the Marine Corps. Maybe I'll get my corporal's stripes back."

"You show 'em, tiger. Shall I keep supper warm?"

"I don't think so. I'm staffing a late case."

"Can you tell me about it?"

"Sure. It's a GI shot through the neck two days ago. The wound was so bad that the docs in Vietnam put him on the next Medevac out to Andrews."

"I'll be thinking about you, JP, and especially about him."

"Would you explain to the kids why there won't be a promotion ceremony tomorrow and block party Saturday."

"I'll tell the kids about the promotion, but, JP, there's no reason to cancel the block party. There are tons of hamburgers and hot dogs in the freezer. Why don't we just change the theme from a promotion party to a non-promotion party?"

JP thought for a moment, then laughed. "That is a great idea, Kath. Now I know why I married you."

"I'm looking forward to tomorrow night with the navy," Kathy Franklin said.

★

Thursday, June 26, 1969, 1930 hours
Officers' Club, National Naval Medical Center, Bethesda, Maryland

The maitre d' led Kathy and JP past a half dozen occupied tables to a table set for two by a window overlooking dense green foliage, tall evergreen and oak trees. Kathy wore a black moiré faille dress bought eighteen years ago in El Paso when JP was an artillery first lieutenant. She looked stunning: her prematurely gray hair gave off a blond sheen in the artificial light of the dining room. The dress emphasized her slender figure, a wonder of nature considering four pregnancies. Officers cast admiring glances at her and women radiated envy, perhaps even jealousy. JP, following Kathy and the maitre d', wore his only suit, a dark single-breasted one Kathy gave him when he graduated from medical school twelve years ago. Since it still fit and looked new, he saw no reason to buy another.

"Is this table satisfactory, sir?" the maitre d' asked.

"Fine. Thank you."

The maitre d' held the chair for Kathy, then lit a small alcohol lamp on the table. As soon as he left, an attractive waitress in her mid-thirties came to the table. "Good evening, sir," she said. "Would you like to order something from the bar?"

JP looked to Kathy.

"White Zinfandel, please."

"Dry gin martini on the rocks with two olives," JP added. After the waitress left, JP studied his wife. "You are one good-looking woman. Mrs. Franklin. I'll bet half the women here would kill to have a figure like yours."

"JP, you're losing it even before your martini arrives, but thanks. That compliment means a lot to a forty-year-old woman who has birthed four children."

The waitress brought their drinks. "Would you like to see the menus?"

"In about half an hour," JP said. "We have some serious conversation to get behind us."

The waitress gave them puzzled glances. "I'll check back," she said.

JP lifted his martini glass towards Kathy. "Thanks for your love and support through the years, Mrs. Franklin." He took a big slug of martini.

Kathy smiled wanly as she sipped her white Zinfandel. "It looks like I'm going to drive home tonight."

104

JP took another gulp of martini, then reached into his pocket for the car keys and slid them across the table. Kathy discretely picked up the keys and dropped them into her purse.

"I called my dad this morning about the promotion fiasco," Kathy said.

"I guess that call was inevitable. What did the former head of the DIA have to say about his non-promotable son-in-law?"

"He wondered if the Soviets had sneaked a mole into the Surgeon General's office."

"Your dad and his non-promotable son-in-law think alike." JP lifted his martini. "To the general." He toasted so loudly that heads turned.

"JP, behave yourself," Kathy admonished. "Dad said to tell you to stay cool, not make hasty or stupid decisions, and let the dust settle before moving. These things have a way of working themselves out."

By now JP was feeling warm and fuzzy. "Your dad's okay for a general." He leaned towards Kathy. "How do you feel about my retiring and us becoming civilians?"

Kathy sipped her white Zinfandel thoughtfully. She set the wine glass down gently and looked at her husband. "I would be less than truthful if I said I didn't cherish the idea of a big house, a three-car garage with three cars, expensive clothing, and the kids college tuitions assured. But I must ask myself if that is what I really want for me, for you, and the kids. Remember, I come from a military family."

JP drained the remainder of his martini and motioned to their waitress for another.

Kathy continued, "Do you remember when you were a lieutenant in Korea and wrote what your platoon sergeant said when you told him you were leaving the army to go to medical school?"

JP grinned. "That Andreson was something else. Of course I remember. He said, 'Lieutenant, all you've ever known since you were seventeen is war. You can't stand civilian life. You can't even stand civilians.'" Tears came quickly. JP's lifted his empty martini glass in a silent toast. Andreson, who received a battlefield commission in Korea, had saved JP's life. He was killed several months after JP left the platoon. JP visited his grave in Arlington National Cemetery at least once a month to tidy up and place flowers. That Andreson's memory surfaced while JP contemplated leaving the army would impact any decision.

The waitress set a fresh martini on the table, picked up the empty glass, then looked at Kathy. "Ma'am?"

Kathy lifted her glass slightly. "I'm fine. I'm the designated driver."

"We're ready to look at menus," JP said.

Moments later the waitress returned with the menus, then left.

Kathy placed her hand on JP's. "You were supposedly a civilian in medical school, except you stayed in the active reserves, went to every weekly meeting and monthly weekend duty. Each summer except the last you went on extended active duty. Whoever heard of a medical student taking the Advanced Infantry Course at Fort Benning?" Kathy smiled at the ridiculous memory. "Face it, JP, you weren't a civilian even when you were a civilian. After you graduated from medical school you couldn't wait to get back on active duty."

She sipped the white Zinfandel. Setting her glass down, she continued. "The war, the army and medicine have given you something far more worthy than eagles on your shoulders and an extra couple of hundred dollars a month more in your pay. It's given you tremendous experience, judgment, and skills that probably exceed most head and neck specialists in the world except maybe your counterpart in North Vietnam. You are in a position to exercise those skills to rehabilitate young men who have given much for their country." Kathy Franklin fixed her blue eyes on her husband and leaned forward. "Are you going to turn your back on them because you're ticked off at the army for screwing up your promotion?"

JP clinked the ice in his glass, took a long swallow of martini, and gazed at his wife. "Kathleen Franklin," he said, his speech slurred, "your old man and mom raised one hell of a daughter."

Chapter Eleven

Sunday, October 12, 1969, 1205 hours

The past summer the weather in the Washington D.C. area had been no different from other summers. It had been very hot and very humid. Patients in Walter Reed Army Hospital had suffered little, thanks to the air conditioning installed the previous spring. A positive spin-off was failure of post-operative infection rates to rise as in previous summers. New dependable latrine facilities added immensely to patient comfort. Few patients enjoying these changes realized they were initiated by a single letter sent in early spring to newspaper columnist Jason Groves by person or persons unknown.

Autumn brought with it cooling temperatures, the annual spectrum of vivid fall colors, and the happy anticipation of Thanksgiving and Christmas. Twelve thousand miles away the war in Vietnam continued to dissipate the nation's most precious resource, its young men. National cemeteries around the country dug new graves daily, and military hospitals remained filled with casualties. For families with loved ones in uniform, the war could mean months of anxiety often culminating in sorrow. For the bulk of Americans, however, the war was remote and abstract, limited to selected grisly television clips in the evening news.

At St. Marks Episcopal Church in Silver Spring the war was kept so remote and so abstract that it seemed non-existent. The absence of prayers for those in harm's way, for their families, and for those killed or wounded left no doubt where the church and its clergy stood on the war. One of St. Marks's less devout members, Lieutenant Colonel JP Franklin, would have left the church long ago but for his responsibilities as a father and husband. St Marks had an excellent young people's program, and Kathy, born and bred in the south, took church very seriously.

Shortly after JP reported to Walter Reed in 1964 the family joined St. Marks and began to attend mass regularly. Several Sundays later during coffee hour JP, in a moment of naivety, invited the rector, Father Joshua Markam, a portly cleric in the image of Friar Tuck, to visit with wounded Episcopalians recovering on Ward 21.

"Absolutely not," Father Markam had responded indignantly. His response could not have been more charged if JP had offered to fix him up with a call girl. "I could not do that," the priest insisted. "It would conflict with my total opposition to the war and my condemnation of those who fight in the war or support it."

JP was stunned at first, then became so incensed that he got in the rector's face. "What about me, Father?" he demanded. "Do you condemn me also? After all I heal the wounded, some of whom return to the war. And I support my country in Vietnam."

"Oh no, no, JP, you are different. You are a doctor. You work to undo war's damage, and that is God's work."

"I'm very relieved to hear that, Father."

Disgusted by clerical dissimulation, JP turned and walked away. Since that day he remained aloof from Father Markam, tolerating the man only as a family obligation and in a spirit of Christian charity. Going to church had become a chore to be avoided when possible.

Sermons given by Father Markam or his clone, Father Strum, were incredibly boring, lacking substance and direction. Confabulation was the word that most often came to mind. As a matter of survival JP developed mechanisms which permitted him to cope during the sermons, yet preserve his special relationship with God. As soon as Father Markam or Father Strum began a sermon JP tuned it out, concentrating instead on studying the heads and necks of adjacent worshippers for physical evidence of pathology. When he ran out of subjects he reviewed in his mind each patient on the head and neck surgery service, past operations, impending ones, and the anatomy of the head and neck. Those techniques sufficed for sermons of average length and content.

The lengthy reading from the Book of Common Prayer that preceded the sacraments became another opportunity to resume the surreptitious search for head and neck pathology. The kneeling congregation presented a different perspective. Distended external jugular veins were more apparent. Today was no exception to this practice. Now, as Father Markam droned on, Kathy Franklin, kneeling by her husband, recognized the irreverent game he was playing and jabbed him in the ribs with her elbow. He grunted, turned and winked. JP's faith, as unorthodox as it might be, included a benevolent Almighty who responded to minor transgressions with charity and humor.

As the last hymn was sung, the adult choir shuffled down the aisle followed by the children's choir, with eleven-year-old Paul, the second son, bringing up the rear. When Paul saw his dad he grinned, revealing the stump of an upper incisor tooth broken several weeks earlier in a scooter accident. JP wondered what happened to the cap? Later he would learn that the cap came off while Paul chewed bubble gum during mass. Fortunately the cap remained in the gum. Unfortunately the gum was swallowed during the singing of the last hymn.

After the benediction JP turned to Kathy. "I'm going to stay for the Postlude," he told her.

Kathy studied the Order of Service, then looked up at her husband questioningly. "Litanies by Jehan Alain? I thought Bach and Franck were the only composers you recognized."

"Alain is special. He was one of France's most promising young organists and composers until killed in World War II."

Kathy regarded her husband with curiosity. In nineteen years of marriage he had never mentioned Jehan Alain. "I'll be downstairs gathering the kids and talking to Louise Barfield," she said softly. Stepping into the aisle, she genuflected, turned and joined the column of worshippers slowly moving out.

The organ sounded the simple theme of the Litanies, repeating it over and over as the music progressed in complexity and intensity until ending on full organ. Its last measures repeated the beginning theme, echoing it throughout the near empty nave. It was a magnificent reiteration of faith. JP was fifteen when he first heard the Litanies at an organ recital given by the great French organist, Joseph Bonnet, at the Church of the Advent in Boston. The world had been at war for two years. Poland, France, Belgium and Holland had been overrun by Hitler's armies. England and Russia were fighting for survival. The music had remained through the years in JP's memory, a painful reminder of the death of its talented young composer and the tragic waste that war visits on nations. JP went to his knees, this time in sincere prayer. He hoped God was listening.

Minutes later, in the Sunday School assembly room, JP spotted Kathy among dozens of socializing Episcopalians. She was in deep conversation with Louise Barfield, a slim, attractive woman in her late thirties. The Barfields had lived near the Franklins at Forest Glen for five years. The children in both families were roughly the same ages. When George Barfield, the assistant chief of neurosurgery, left for Vietnam and an assignment as the division surgeon in an infantry division, the Barfields moved from quarters in military Forest Glen to a house in civilian Silver Spring. Even though the two families were now separated by four miles instead of 400 feet, Kathy and Louise remained close and the children visited frequently.

As JP approached the two women, Louise Barfield looked up. "Just now finish atoning for your sins?" she asked.

"I was told my list was too long and to come back later. What has George been up to?"

"I was just telling Kathy about his last letter. He's flying a lot, even getting flight instruction in a small helicopter called a Loach. He wants to get a rotary wing pilot's license after he comes home."

"What a cushy job," JP said with some envy, "and to think he gets paid." Before Louise could answer, his pager beeped. More by reflex than conscious effort he jerked the pager from his belt and held it to his ear. The male voice from the pager was easily recognized. "Colonel, this is Craig. Call me at 7464."

Returning the pager to his belt JP told the women, "That's the surgical ICU extension and Craig didn't say please, an ominous sign. I'll be right back." He headed for the church office and a telephone. The office door was open and the lights were on. Crossing to a desk with a phone he dialed Walter Reed, then asked for extension 7464. After the third ring a disciplined female voice answered. "Four East ICU, Captain Appel."

"This is Colonel Franklin. Captain Entarde paged me for this extension."

"Just a minute, Colonel."

A moment later Craig Entarde spoke. "Chief, I hope I didn't interrupt a good sermon."

"Your timing was off. You paged forty minutes too late."

"Sorry about that. I need to discuss a patient from Vietnam who should go to surgery today."

"I'm listening."

"This is a forty-five-year-old air force lieutenant colonel named Sanderson. He was the CO of a FAC squadron in Vietnam until he was shot down a month ago. A special forces team in the area pulled him from his wrecked plane and got him to a PZ. A Dust-off evacuated him to the 47th Surg. On admission he had a four-inch bruise on his neck, was spitting up blood, had severe pain on swallowing, trouble breathing, and sub-cutaneous emphysema of the neck. After tracheotomy a fractured larynx was repaired and a NG tube put down for feeding. Six days later he was transferred to Japan."

"Sounds routine so far."

"Yes sir, but the story gets fuzzy. Two days after he arrived in Japan the NG tube was pulled and he was started on oral feedings. Within twenty-four hours he spiked a fever to 106, developed an inability to swallow, and was unable move his arms or legs. His white cell count was 36,000. Two spinal taps were negative. Despite the negative taps the neurologists considered meningitis the most likely diagnosis and started him on mega doses of antibiotics. Over the next seventy-two hours his temperature came down and his white cell count stabilized at 16,000. Cultures from blood and spinal fluid showed no growth."

"Anything on physical exam?"

"He looks as if he has just been liberated from Dachau. He's running a fast heart rate, about 120 with intermittent bursts of arrhythmia. His neck has early scars from his surgery and he still has a trach. He can't or won't move his head or extremities, but reflexes are normal. There's a soft bulging mass the size of a half grapefruit in the right neck. The skin over the mass is erythematous with three-plus pitting edema. The neurological findings were so bizarre that I asked Hank Brownlee, the neurology resident, to take a look at him. Hank spent over an hour with him, then had the chief of neurology come in and go over him."

"Colonel Pickens came in on a Sunday?"

Entarde chuckled. "Yes, sir. Wonders never cease. They decided they didn't know what Sanderson's problem was, but were convinced it wasn't meningitis or spinal cord injury."

"Did they make any recommendations?"

"Yes, sir. Colonel Pickens said to call you."

"Sanderson must be in bad shape if that's what Colonel Pickens advised. Why do you believe he needs an operation?"

Entarde took an audible breath, then plunged into muddy waters, "The neck swelling, pain, fever, and high white count, when considered with the history of trauma, add up to infection. The onset of sepsis so soon after the NG tube was withdrawn and oral feedings started may be coincidental, but it does suggest the feedings are related to the infection. The most probable relation between the two is a perforation of the pharynx."

"Keep going. You're doing fine so far."

"We know when Sanderson crashed his plane his neck hit the edge of the instrument panel with enough force to fracture the larynx. That force could have been sufficient to force fragments of the fractured larynx against the cervical spine,

110

perforating the pharynx sandwiched between."

"Anything else?"

"Yes, sir. It's apparent that the perforation wasn't recognized at the 47th Surg or it would have been repaired and tube feedings continued for three to four weeks. My assumption is that when oral feedings were started in Japan, food and liquids leaked through the perforation into his neck contaminating it."

"That's not bad for a Citadel graduate who majored in history. Now that you have somehow managed to stumble into the truth, Captain Entarde, what are your intentions?"

"Sanderson is on his way to radiology for X-rays of the neck and chest, contrast studies, and then to the operating room."

"What if the X-rays are inconclusive or negative?"

"He needs a neck exploration regardless of what the X-rays demonstrate."

"Then why get X-rays?"

"To quote my esteemed chief and mentor, 'Because I don't like surprises.'"

"By gosh, Captain, you may well graduate next June."

Entarde chuckled. "I've alerted anesthesia. They'll be ready to go whenever we give the word. Do you want an NG tube put down pre-op?"

"No. The tube might snake out into the neck through the perforation. I'd hate for a liter of blenderized diet to get dumped in his neck or chest. Ask the belly surgeons to do a gastrostomy after we finish up in his neck."

"Yes, sir. Anything else?"

"I'll meet you in X-ray in twenty minutes."

Hanging up, JP returned to the Sunday School assembly room. Kathy and Louise Barfield looked up expectantly as he approached. "I need to go to the hospital," he told them. "An air force light colonel from Vietnam with pus in the neck is in dire need of the blessed relief only the knife can bring."

Several women nearby stopped talking and turned to stare.

"JP, must you be so colorful?" Kathy admonished.

"Sorry. I forgot where I was." He turned to Louise Barfield. "Could you drop Kathy and the kids off at the Glen?"

"Be glad to. It's on our way."

"You might as well have lunch with us," Kathy invited.

JP squeezed Kathy's hand in lieu of a kiss, thanked Louise, then headed to the church parking lot.

★

Sunday, October 12, 1969, 1315 hours
Walter Reed Army Hospital, Washington D.C.

JP eased the Greebrier van into his space in the sacred quadrangle parking lot. After locking the van he headed for ground level double doors and entered a dimly lit basement passageway. Six and twelve-inch pipes wrapped with white insulation traveled overhead; lesser pipes ran along one side. The passageway communicated with others that extended underground to every part of the hospital, AFIP and WRAIR. A knowledge of the passageways was particularly useful during inclement weather. One could get to almost any part of the Walter Reed Medical Center complex without once going above ground. One could also get lost.

JP pushed through another set of double doors and emerged into a brightly lit hallway leading to the X-ray department reception room. The enlisted male tech on duty at the desk looked up from his newspaper. "The doctors are in the reading room, Colonel Franklin."

"Any good news in that thing?"

"Yes, sir. The light at the end of the tunnel is getting brighter."

"Let's hope it's not a train."

JP continued down a corridor to enter a large room, its walls lined with banks of X-ray viewboxes above waist-high counters. Dictating machines on the counters were separated by stacks of large gray envelopes stuffed with X-ray films. At the far side of the room Craig Entarde, one of the two chief residents since Terry O'Connel and Roy French graduated in June, and Gregg Brazelton, the junior resident, were seated in swivel armchairs intently studying plain films of the neck and chest. Both residents turned.

Entarde looked at his watch. "You beat your ETA, chief."

"A combination of skilled driving, little traffic, and no cops. What do the films show?"

Indicating a side-view film of the neck Entarde pointed with a GI pen to the space between spine and Adam's apple. "The retropharyngeal space is five or six times wider than normal. The widened space goes from the base of skull to the upper chest. I've never seen anything like this." He moved the pen to a front-view film and traced a 5 x 3 inch oval density. "That, sir, is the mother of all neck abscesses." Next Entarde went to the chest film. Indicating the midline structure containing the great vessels superiorly and the heart inferiorly he continued. "The mediastinum is markedly widened and there is air along the left border of the heart. The pericardium appears thickened."

The door to an adjacent room opened. A man of medium height in a green scrub suit entered with several films. Lieutenant Colonel Edward Nieland II, age forty-two, hair longer than regulation, and rimless glasses down on his nose, looked every bit the medical school professor he would become after retiring from the army in two months. Nieland, a1950 West Point graduate, the son and grandson of West Point graduates, had been sent to Korea with his entire class shortly after North Korea attacked South Korea in 1950. Almost one-third of his class was killed in less than four months after arriving in Korea. Most of those not killed, Nieland included, were wounded. After recovering from his wounds Nieland went to medical school, graduating at the top of his class. Like JP, he had been on the list for promotion to colonel when the new promotion policy mandated four more years before he could be considered for promotion. In disgust, Nielson requested retirement and accepted a professorship as head of the special studies department of a Texas medical school at ten times his army salary, not to mention his retirement pay.

Nieland slapped JP on the back. "I see they dragged the heavy artillery in for this case."

"Hello, Ed. Glad to see you're still around."

"Not for long. Have you decided to go to Hopkins?"

"No. I made the mistake of marrying an army brat," JP said. "What do the contrast studies show?"

Nieland slipped a side and front-view film of the neck onto dark viewboxes and flipped switches. Fluorescent bulbs flickered yellow then turned bright white. "These are the spot films," he said. "The pathology is so obvious that even a junior resident should be able to recognize it."

JP tapped Captain Brazelton on the shoulder. "Colonel Nieland has thrown down a gauntlet at your feet."

Greg Brazelton studied the films for several seconds, then indicated a narrow column of white radio-opaque contrast material streaming through a defect in the side wall of the pharynx and out into the neck. "This confirms the upper gut perforation, which appears to be at the level of the third and fourth cervical vertebrae." He outlined a rounded dense area distending the right neck. "And this most likely is an abscess."

"Not bad for a Georgia man," Ed Nieland said. Turning to JP he asked, "Do you want an angiogram?"

"It would be academic at this point, Ed. Besides, Sanderson sounds very fragile. I don't want to stress him any more than necessary. I would like to take a couple of minutes to go over him while he's here."

"He's still on the fluoro table."

Entering the semi-dark room, JP waited a moment for his eyes to adjust. In the red glow from several special bulbs in the ceiling he made out the form of a man lying supine under a sheet. He touched the man's shoulder. "Colonel Sanderson."

The man opened his eyes and tried to focus on JP without moving his head.

"I'm Colonel Franklin, chief of head and neck surgery," JP said. "I'm going to turn on the overhead lights to examine you. You may want to keep your eyes closed." JP reached for the light switch. The room was flooded with bright light.

JP quickly confirmed the physical findings in the neck described by Craig Entarde, then focused on the man's face. It appeared drawn and wrinkled from severe weight loss. It was the face of an old man, much older than forty-five. As JP studied the man's face an overwhelming sense of familiarity surged through him. It was a feeling of kinship, of brotherhood, an almost spiritual bonding. He continued to stare at the man's face, then shook his head in frustration because there was no recognition.

Turning off the lights JP told Sanderson, "Colonel, you have a life-threatening condition brought on by a hole in your gullet. For the last three weeks food and saliva have leaked into your neck setting up an infection which has progressed to an abscess that extends from below your skull down into your chest. It's imperative we operate right away to save your life."

Sanderson blinked acknowledgment.

"Captain Entarde will be right in to go over the planned surgery."

As JP was about to leave he suddenly grasped Sanderson's right hand and squeezed it affectionately. It was an impulse he couldn't understand. Pausing at the door he stopped and gazed thoughtfully at Sanderson, then turned and walked out.

★

Sunday, October 12, 1969, 1410 hours
Operating Suite, Walter Reed Army Hospital, Washington D.C.

Lieutenant Colonel JP Franklin, in a green scrub suit, cap and mask, slammed shut his locker, slipped on the combination lock and twisted its knob. Stepping into the corridor he headed for the sinks outside Operating Room No.6. Craig Entarde was already at one of the sinks scrubbing his hands and arms. Nodding a silent greeting, JP moved to an adjacent sink, turned on the water with his knee, adjusted its temperature. and reached to a wall-mounted dispenser for a scrub brush.

Entarde stopped scrubbing and looked at JP. "I asked the chest surgery resident to look at Sanderson's films and be available in case we need to crack the chest."

"Better pray it doesn't come to that. There is a heavy price to pay if the chest is opened when the neck is full of pus. Two patients in our series went on to massive sepsis and died after thoracotomy."

Methodically scrubbing his hands and arms, JP mentally reviewed Sanderson's case and six others. He told his chief resident, "This is our seventh case from Vietnam with deep neck infection secondary to unrecognized upper gut perforations. Three, like Sanderson, were from blunt trauma. The others were the result of penetrating wounds. I'll be the first to admit seven cases in five years isn't exactly an epidemic, but there may be similar cases at other military hospitals we don't know about. Considering the confusing clinical picture, extreme morbidity, and high mortality, it may be prudent to send out advisories to theater surgeons and to our sister services."

"I'd like to write up our seven cases, Colonel."

"You got it," JP said. "Who is our anesthiologist?"

"Major Resniek."

"That's a good omen."

Entarde rinsed the soap from his hands and arms. Turning off the water with his knee, he held his flexed arms over the sink for excess water to drain from his elbows, then started for the OR door. Before reaching the door he stopped, hesitated, and turned to face JP. "Sir, were you aware that the College of Surgeons has called for resident papers for the May meeting in San Francisco?"

"I'm the one who posted the notice on the residents' bulletin board."

"I could write up the Walter Reed experience with gut perforations from Vietnam and submit it."

"Captain Entarde, I am impressed by your dedication; I am also suspicious of your motives," JP said, fixing his gaze on the chief resident. "Isn't your fiancée a nurse at Letterman?"

"Now that you mention it, sir, I believe she is," Entarde said with a half grin.

"And if you presented a paper in San Francisco under army sponsorship you would be eligible for administrative leave, travel expenses and per diem."

"Yes, sir. Those thoughts did occur to me."

JP let Entarde endure several moments of anxiety. "Okay. Let me review your paper before you submit it. If it's accepted by the College I'll approve admin leave and TDY."

"Thanks, Colonel." A happy Entarde pushed through the door into Operating Room No.6.

A few minutes later, Lieutenant Colonel JP Franklin followed.

Chapter Twelve

Sunday, October 12, 1969, 1425 hours
Operating Room No.6, Walter Reed Army Hospital, Washington D.C.

Lieutenant Colonel Charles Sanderson, United States Air Force, lay supine on the operating table, head turned to the left. A plastic anesthesia tube, anchored to the neck skin by black silk sutures, had replaced the tracheotomy tube. Two black rubber hoses attached to the tube by a Y adapter connected Sanderson's airway to the anesthesia machine at the head of the table. Major Harry Resniek sat by his machine monitoring gauges, making notes on a printed form on a clipboard, and occasionally glancing at a cardiac monitor.

Captain Greg Brazelton, the third year resident, was hunched over Sanderson vigorously scrubbing the exposed neck, chest and abdomen with gauze sponges soaked in Betadine. JP, watching Brazelton with feigned disinterest, noted the abundant hair on Sanderson's chest and abdomen. "These air force people are animals," he told Brazelton. "Better shave his chest and abdomen down to his belly button in case we have to crack his chest." Brazelton reached to the prep set for a sterile razor. While he shaved the chest and abdomen, JP asked the circulator to focus the operating light on Sanderson's face. Again he felt an inexplicable closeness with the man. Before he could dwell further Brazelton draped a towel over Sanderson's face.

The scrub nurse, Carol Barnes, a diminutive pretty second lieutenant, detached herself from behind her Mayo stand next to the operating table. Carrying a hand towel, she draped it over JP's wet hands. Drying his fingers, he worked the towel to his hands and forearms. Lieutenant Barnes picked up a folded gown from her table, shook it out and held it so that JP could push his hands and arms into the sleeves. She then helped him with his gloves.

"Thanks, Carol," JP said, looking into the green eyes that had devastated more than one surgery resident. "What's the news from Vietnam?"

"Peter is flying cobras out of Pleiku. He's due for R&R next month. We're going to meet in Hawaii and get married." She paused. "I guess it will be a short honeymoon, Colonel," she said ruefully.

"War accelerates relationships, especially for those of us in the armed forces," JP said, recalling his own marriage of three weeks before leaving his bride for the war in Korea and a ten-month separation.

Harry Resniek looked up from his paperwork. "Well, well, the warrior-surgeon has arrived, finally," he announced in his heavy Brooklyn accent.

JP turned towards the voice. "How did we rate the assistant chief of anesthesiology on a Sunday afternoon?"

"When I heard you were staffing this case I decided it would be more exciting here than on the golf course. Besides, I was losing."

The circulator, an overweight civilian nurse named Helen Grogan, tied the straps on JP's gown. While waiting for Brazelton to finish prepping, JP wandered towards Harry Resniek. "How long before you leave the armed forces of your country?"

"Nine months, Colonel, nine long months."

"I'm going to miss you, Harry. You're the only genuine red-eyed liberal I've ever known. In two years at Walter Reed you have become a legend."

"Well," Resniek countered, "your Korean War buddy McClintock made you a legend at Hopkins. He's pushing hard for you to replace him as chairman."

JP felt the eyes of his two residents and Carol Barnes swing on him. He shrugged. "That intelligence has a reliability index of zero. Besides, I wouldn't know what to do with all that money." Anxious to change the subject, he asked Resniek, "What are you going to do when you leave the army?"

"Go back to Hopkins as assistant professor of anesthesiology."

"Oh no," JP said with simulated alarm. "You'll corrupt generations of medical students and residents with your liberal ideas."

Stepping back, JP watched Craig Entarde arrange four towels in a rectangle around Sanderson's bulging right neck, then he turned to the circulator. "Better slip in a Foley catheter before we finish draping, Helen. Major Resniek will want to keep track of urine output. We need two more suctions in the field for backup, and order up six more units of blood."

The circulator gave JP an incredulous look. "Aren't you overdoing it a bit, Colonel?" she asked caustically.

JP stared at her. "What do you mean?"

"You're not going to do anything more complicated than drain pus from an abscess. That's done all the time up here without catheters, extra suctions, and ten units of blood."

Craig Entarde looked at the circulator, first with surprise, then with pity as he might for someone unawares he or she was about to face a firing squad.

"Helen, it's not necessary for you to agree with what I ask," JP said, his voice a near growl. "It's just necessary for you to do it."

The circulator moved hastily to the telephone.

Turning back to Sanderson, JP caught a glimpse of a thin plastic catheter disappearing into the skin just above the collarbone. "Thanks for putting in a central line," he told Resniek. "You may talk like a liberal, act like a liberal, and associate with liberals, Harry, but in a crunch thank God you think like a conservative. There is hope for you."

Resniek snorted.

Minutes later Lieutenant Colonel Sanderson was draped with sheets; only the neck remained exposed. The surgeon, Craig Entarde, elected to stand on Sanderson's right, the scrub nurse, Carol Barnes, beside him with her Mayo stand covered with instruments. Greg Brazelton stood opposite Entarde, ready to assist with two suckers and the electrocautery by his hand. JP was next to Brazelton.

Entarde dipped the sharpened end of a wooden Q-tip into an opened vial of methylene blue, then made a series of dots on Sanderson's neck. Beginning under the right earlobe, the dots descended along the front border of the thickest muscle in the neck, the sternomastoid, to above the collarbone, then swung towards the midline. After connecting the dots he stepped back and looked at JP "How's that for an incision, Colonel?"

JP scowled. "Let's hope you're a better surgeon than artist."

"I am, sir, I am."

"In that case, start cutting."

Carol Barnes slapped a scalpel into Entarde's open palm. He swiftly cut along the blue markings, going through skin and underlying thin platysma muscle to a sheet of gray tough connective tissue, the deep fascia. Brazelton quickly smothered the brisk bleeding with 4 x 8 inch gauze sponges. As he sequentially removed the sponges he and Entarde applied mosquitoes to bleeding points. Entarde then raised the first hemostat. Brazelton touched it with the electrocautery blade. Almost immediately a sizzling pop was followed by the odor of burnt flesh and a wisp of white smoke.

"Coag is too hot, Helen," Entarde called out.

The circulator turned a knob on the cautery control box. "Down to three."

"That's better," Entarde said as he and Brazelton cleared the remaining hemostats. Using a fresh scalpel, he began to deftly raise a flap on each side of the incision.

"Stay above the deep fascia, Craig," JP counseled. "There's pus beneath it under great pressure."

Dissecting rapidly with the scalpel, Entarde exposed the bulging distended gray sheet of fibrous tissue. Watching his chief resident operate, JP felt a flush of pride not unlike the father who sees his Little League kid hit a home run with bases loaded. The thought of sports brought on feelings of guilt. This was the day Jim, his oldest son, would run in the most important high school cross-country track meet of the year. And he, Jim's father, would miss the meet as he had missed all previous meets except one. Even then he had arrived at the track only to learn Jim had already run.

Medicine was a mistress who jealously resented wives and children. She demanded total commitment.

Craig Entarde looked up. "Chief, how do you want me to go through the fascia?"

"Very carefully. An explosive decompression could cause a weakened artery or vein to rupture."

"How about aspirating first?"

"There you go, thinking like a real surgeon."

Carol Barnes passed Entarde a 50 cc syringe with a large bore needle. Indicating the needle, she said, "It's fourteen gauge, the largest we have."

Accepting the syringe Entarde warned, "Have a couple more handy."

The needle easily penetrated the bulging fascia. A creamy green material quickly filled the syringe with such force it pushed the plunger back. Disconnecting the syringe from the needle hub, Entarde left the needle sticking through the fascia. Pus streamed from the needle hub. A foul stench saturated the operating room. Quickly capping the syringe, he passed it to the circulator, then accepted another syringe and attached it to the needle hub. The fascia was beginning to wrinkle as it collapsed.

118

Within minutes four more full syringes were passed to Carol Barnes. "The ID Fellow will pick them up. His pager is 3-6-4," Craig Entarde told her."

Harry Resniek's masked face appeared above his anesthesia screen. Surveying the operative field through thick glasses, he sniffed several times. "The pus doctors have struck again," he intoned, sitting back down.

"You were warned there was PID," JP said.

"PID? What in hell is PID?"

"Pus in dere."

Resniek grimaced behind his mask. "That humor is worse than the pus. I'll be glad to leave here in nine months."

"You will miss us, Harry," JP said. "Now for the moment of truth. Go for it, Craig."

Entarde held out his hand. "Carol, a Debakey and Metz to me and a Debakey to Colonel Franklin."

Using the long delicate Debakey forceps, Entarde grasped the collapsed sheet of fascia, tenting it up. JP placed his forceps an inch opposite Entarde's, who then snipped a hole in the fascia between the two forceps with the long dull-tipped Metzenbaum scissors. Inserting one blade of the scissors through the hole and under the fascia, the other blade outside, he quickly cut the fascia up to the jaw and down to the clavicle. As the relaxed fascia fell open more pus streamed out.

"Don't be timid, Gregg," JP encouraged Brazelton. "Get in here with the suckers."

After most of the pus was cleared JP and Entarde applied toothed clamps along each edge of the cut fascia and pulled it apart. Next came ten minutes of vigorous saline irrigation. Fragments of necrotic tissue, decaying food, and more pus were flushed out.

"There's a pea and a bit of carrot," Brazelton said.

"Please," JP entreated, "I haven't had lunch."

Gradually a distorted cavity was defined, extending from the base of skull down to the chest inlet. Craig Entarde slipped his hand deep into the neck, his fingers probing for the dimensions of the cavity. He looked up, concern showing in his eyes. "Colonel, the abscess cavity goes under the SCM. I can feel carotid pulsations." A moment later he added, "The jug has a lot of adhesions around it... oops."

"What do you mean 'Oops'?"

"My finger just went through a hole the size of quarter in the back wall of the pharynx. It's almost against the vertebrae."

"That's about where the spot films showed it to be."

"Shall I try to close it?"

"No. Suturing that infected devitalized tissue at this late date would be a waste of time. The sutures would pull through as soon as tied down. The perforation will have to heal on its own while we try to maintain an environment favorable for healing. Dr. Brazelton, what does that mean in practical terms?"

"Controlling infection with daily antibiotic irrigations via indwelling catheters, long term use of drains, IV antibiotics, and nothing by mouth for four to six weeks, possible longer. He'll have to be fed through a gastrostomy until fluoroscopy demonstrates the perforation has closed."

JP beamed proudly at the third year resident. "Brazelton, you are a credit to the Medical College of Georgia, an institution well known for producing graduates who develop into outstanding surgeons."

Harry Resniek groaned. "Between the stench of the pus and the stench of your egocentric conversation I think I'm going to be sick."

JP grinned. He told Entarde, "Pull your ham hand out of there and let Greg feel the abscess cavity and gut perforation."

Brazelton, his gloved hand almost disappearing into the cavity, gently probed with his fingers. "I feel the adhesions, Colonel. What should be done with them?"

JP glanced at Entarde. "You're the surgeon, Craig. Tell him."

"Yes, sir. The adhesions form small pockets of trapped pus. They should be broken up and the pus cleaned out."

"It's apparent you have been reading more than history books, Captain Entarde. As soon as Greg removes his hand from the colonel's neck, take your stubby fingers, educated at great taxpayer expense, and gently break up the adhesions."

Craig Entarde's eyes took on a faraway took as he worked more or less blind, his hand deep in Sanderson's neck. Periodically bursts of green pus streamed into the field to be removed by Brazelton's suckers. Suddenly a look of alarm flashed across Entarde's face. "Chief..."

The operative field exploded with dark red blood. Within seconds blood spilled out of the abscess cavity, soaking the drapes and dripping onto the floor.

In a flash JP grabbed several lap packs from the instrument table and threw them into the open neck. The pads immediately floated up on the rapidly accumulating blood. "Pressure," JP ordered, "put pressure on those, Craig. Use both hands. Carol, more lap packs. Harry, are you on top of this?"

"Two units going in, two more on the way," the anesthesiologist said, standing and looking over his screen. What the hell happened?"

"The jug ruptured," Entarde said, his voice laced with guilt.

"Not your fault, Craig," JP assured him. "The jug was sitting there waiting for a good excuse to blow. Be glad it ruptured here with the neck open instead of on the ward." He placed both hands on the lap packs. "I've got these. As I roll them out you try to locate the tear in the jug and get a clamp above and below."

Working with a thumb forceps in one hand and long narrow pointed scissors in the other, Captain Entarde soon had the lower third of the internal jugular vein exposed. He stepped back, exhaling loudly. "It looks like an over-filled German sausage with a jagged hole in its side," he said as he exchanged the scissors for a vascular clamp.

"Don't be so descriptive," JP said. "I have a penchant for German sausage. While you're working down there watch out for the dome of the right lung. It may extend up into the neck when Harry bags him."

Sweat broke out on Entarde's forehead as he worked deep in a confined space to create a enough room around the outside of the jugular vein to apply the jaws of a clamp. He was working in a part of the neck packed with critical anatomy.

Helen Grogan reached in front of Entarde's head and wiped his brow with a gauze pad. Seconds later, a rasping sound announced that a clamp had closed below the rent in the vein.

"Got it," Entarde said, triumph filling his voice. A second clamp was closed above the rent. The ruptured segment of jugular vein was now trapped between the two clamps. The bomb was defused. Tension spilled from the operating room.

"Good going, Craig," JP said, lifting out the lap pads and admiring the dry field. "Get a couple of stick ties in the vein and we can go home."

Rolling the blood-soaked pads into a ball, JP tossed them into a metal bucket a dozen feet away. Surprised but pleased with his accuracy, he called out, "Basket." The circulator frowned as she picked the pads out of the bucket, weighing each, then laying them out on a plastic sheet on the floor to be counted.

When JP turned back to the table he saw dark blood oozing into the field. Then, as if a dam had given way, massive amounts of blood surged into the opened neck and spilled over. This time it was Entarde who grabbed lap pads and shoved them into the field. "The clamps tore off, Chief," he said. "The vein just fell apart. The lower stump is almost under the clavicle."

JP faced a critical decision. His fragmentary glimpse of the torn internal jugular vein had shown only enough length in the lower neck for one more attempt at clamping and ligation. If that failed the only option remaining would be to open the chest to gain control of the vein as it joined a larger vein draining into the heart. Opening the chest would expose the chest contents to bacterial contamination from the neck abscess. Based on prior experience the almost certain outcome would be death from overwhelming infection.

As much as JP wanted Craig Entarde to work his way out of this critical dilemma he had no choice but to take over. If Sanderson died it would not have been because the Viet Cong shot him down and tried to kill him. It would not have been because surgeons in Vietnam and Japan overlooked a perforated gullet. If Sanderson died the responsibility for his death would fall directly on Lieutenant Colonel JP Franklin and no one else.

"I'll take over now, Craig," JP told Entarde. It was a quietly spoken decision but one from which there was no appeal. The look of relief in Entarde's eyes made it apparent he felt no reluctance at turning loose.

At that moment Resniek's sharp Brooklyn accent fractured the hushed monotones. "Hold everything," he ordered. His eyes almost closed as he listened intently to the chest with his stethoscope. Abruptly, he jerked the stethoscope from his ears. "Mill wheel murmur!" he shouted, "he's got an air embolus. Everything is going off except oxygen." He began turning knobs on his anesthesia machine. "Watch it," he warned, "I'm elevating the head of the table."

Air embolus, the dreaded complication of head and neck surgery, had reared its ugly head. Air, sucked into venous blood through a torn vein, is carried to the right side of the heart. The air–blood mixture is beaten into a frothy mixture that markedly reduces oxygenation of blood and decreases cardiac output. The wicked combination leads to cardiac arrhythmia and cardiac arrest.

JP frantically tore the drapes and towels from Sanderson, throwing them on the floor. "Help me turn him on his left side," he shouted to Brazelton. This maneuver utilizes gravity to increase heart efficiency.

"He's showing PVCs, Colonel," Resniek warned.

JP glanced at the cardiac monitor. Clusters of the PVCs were becoming more and more frequent. "Harry, they're falling on the T-wave."

"I know it," Resniek said, squirting oxygen into his bag and squeezing the bag hard. "He's already had a bolus of Lidocaine. Let me see if I can aspirate air from the right heart through the central line." A moment later the monitor suddenly showed a low continuous wavy line. "Damn it, he's gone into fibrillation. Helen... the defibrillator."

The cardiac monitor's alarm went off with a shrill wheee... The bright yellow tracing on the green background of the monitor changed abruptly from a wavy line to a continuous horizontal line.

"That's it," Brazelton intoned solemnly, he's flat-lined. He's in cardiac arrest."

Death, always a silent spectator in any operating room, had moved to make its claim.

Chapter Thirteen

Sunday, October 12, 1969 1530 hours
Operating Room No.6, Walter Reed Army Hospital, Washington D.C.

Lieutenant Colonel Charles Sanderson lay naked on his left side, oblivious to the drama unfolding around him. Irreversible brain, heart, and kidney damage were only minutes away; death was not far behind. JP's calm voice belied the near-panic he was fighting as he fired off orders. "Greg, help me get him on his back. Craig, keep pressure on those laps. Helen, slip the CPR board under his back as we turn him. Carol, have a 30 cc syringe with an eighteen gauge spinal needle ready."

JP and the third year resident struggled to lift the limp Sanderson and turn him back to the supine position. "Come on, Brazelton," he prodded, "put your back into it" The anesthesia tube suddenly parted from its hose connection with a "whoosh". The sweet odor of the fluothane filled the room. In a blur of motion Harry Resniek reached over and reconnected the two.

"You move fast for someone who spends most of his time on his butt," JP told him. "Were you able to aspirate any air from the heart through the central line?"

"Not much. I'll try again in a minute. Go ahead and mash on his chest."

JP thumped Sanderson's chest with his fist. The cardiac tracing jumped, then resumed its flat line. Shoving a foot stool to the table, he climbed on it, placed the heels of his hands on Sanderson's chest and began chest compression.

"Easy," Resniek cautioned. "Don't break his ribs."

"That's the least of my worries. Somebody feel for a femoral pulse. Craig, keep pressure on that neck. We don't want any more air sucked into the jug."

"He's got a weak pulse down here, Colonel,' Brazelton reported, his fingers on Sanderson's groin.

JP nodded. "Harry, check his pupils."

The anesthesiologist lifted the lids and briefly studied the eyes. "Both are constricted."

"There's still hope."

After several minutes of closed chest massage, fatigue and aching arms forced JP to tell Brazelton, "I'm wiped out, Greg. Take over for a while." As soon as Brazelton resumed chest compression JP stepped away from the table. Massaging his aching arms, he turned to Harry Resniek. "What's he doing now?"

"Still flat-lined."

"What meds have you given?"

"Lidocaine, Bretylium, bicarb and calcium."

"Any last minute ideas before I stick a needle in his heart?" JP asked.

"Let's try a bolus of epinephrine. It may get his heart out of asystole and start it fibrillating. At least then we can try to shock the heart to a regular rhythm."

"You want me to give the epi intracardiac?"

"Hell, no. I'll give it IV. The CPR seems to be circulating blood. The last thing his heart needs now is a needle stuck in it by a head and neck surgeon.

JP watched the anesthesiologist snap off the top of a small glass vial with his thumb. Withdrawing the clear contents into a syringe, he injected it into the plastic IV tubing, then reached up to the valve on the tubing to increase flow from the hanging bottle of fluid.

"Ease off the chest a second, Greg," Resniek said, his eyes fixed on the cardiac monitor. The flat tracing abruptly began to undulate. An eternity of silence, actually seconds, was shattered by his elated voice. "He's fibrillating."

JP stared at the electrical picture of Sanderson's trembling ineffective heart. It was a picture of hope, the earliest phase of resurrection from the dead. If only the heart could be shocked into a productive rhythm.

The circulator pushed the defibrillator to the table and charged it. JP grabbed its two paddles and held them up for her to squirt conductive cream on the contact surfaces. Rubbing the two surfaces together, he placed one paddle high on the right chest next to the sternum and the other low on the left, over the apex of the heart. "Three hundred watts, Helen," he told the circulator, then warned, "Stand clear."

Craig Entarde pulled his hands away from the neck and stepped back. Harry Resniek disconnected the anesthesia tube and held up his hands. Brazelton stopped chest massage and straightened up.

After checking a second time to confirm no one was touching Sanderson, JP pressed the red "Discharge" button in the handle of the right paddle. Sanderson's body convulsed as the burst of electricity shot through him. Entarde quickly returned his hands to the neck; blood was already seeping through the gauze pads. All eyes were now fixed on the cardiac monitor. The undulating tracing of ventricular fibrillation continued.

"Damn it," JP muttered.

"Hit him again, Colonel," Harry Resniek advised.

A green light indicated the defibrillator was recharged. "Stand clear," JP called, then placed the paddles on Sanderson's chest.

"Wait, Colonel," Resniek called out. "Hold it."

JP lifted the paddles, looked at Resniek and then the monitor. Single normal tracings appeared periodically in the wavy tracing. The tracing rapidly evolved into a normal heart rhythm. "Thank you, Lord," JP sighed.

"I had something to do with it," Harry Resniek said.

"Thanks, Harry."

"Is that all?"

"How about dinner and drinks for you and Rhoda next weekend at the "O" club?"

"That's much better."

How absurd to reward someone with food and liquor for saving another man's life, thought JP. He remembered how, in Korea, he had rewarded a squad in his platoon each week with two bottles of Scotch whiskey for the highest number of kills. He still owed

124

dinner and drinks to the unknown air force forward air controller who saved his platoon and a British infantry battalion from being overrun by the Chinese. The Brits he rescued still owed him dinner and drinks for saving their lives. Life, at least in the military, seemed a bizarre series of dinner and liquor debts incurred for taking and saving lives.

Harry Resniek shattered his introspection. "Give me a couple of minutes to get him settled, Colonel." Placing he stethoscope back in his ears, he listened over the chest. "Murmur's gone; heart sounds are strong, a little fast. I've got a drip going to keep his pressure up."

Minutes later Resniek nodded to JP. "Okay, Colonel, have a go at him. Try not to let any more air into his heart. My own won't tolerate another flail like the last one."

JP moved to the right side of the table, the surgeon's side. Turning to the scrub nurse, he held out his hand. "Pickups and Metz please."

★

Sunday, October 12, 1969, 1605 hours
Head and Neck Inpatient Clinic, Walter Reed Army Hospital, Washington D.C.

As soon as JP entered his office he filled an electric tea pot with water and plugged it into an outlet. Collapsing in his swivel chair, he propped his feet up on his desk and closed his eyes. It seemed every muscle in his body ached. When he heard the water bubbling he unplugged the pot and poured the boiling water over a tea bag in a cup. Absent-mindedly, he bounced the tea bag up and down in the hot water, watching the orange color seep out of the bag and darken.

A nagging guilt plagued him for having taken the case away from Craig Entarde, more so because of the speed with which he had ligated the stump of the torn jugular vein in the lower neck. He shouldn't have made it look so easy. Aware of the devastating impact such an experience could have on a budding surgeon's self-confidence, he had forced himself to turn the case back to Entarde.

As he watched Entarde meticulously isolate and tie off the upper stump of the jugular vein close to the base of skull, JP grudgingly admitted to himself that Entarde's surgical skills were fast approaching his own. One day they might even surpass his. The thought, instead of making him feel threatened, elicited great pride. What more fitting tribute can there be to a teacher than having those he taught surpass him in excellence.

Sipping his tea, he grew introspective as he tried to define the powerful kinship he sensed each time he saw Sanderson. It continued to resist explanation. "I must be working too hard," he told himself.

The pager on his hip beeped, startling him. "Colonel, this is Craig. General surgery just finished the gastrostomy on Sanderson. He'll be going to recovery in about fifteen minutes. The cardiology fellow will see him there and follow up on the arrest. Chest X-ray shows no broken ribs or pneumothorax. Blood gases are in the green. Mrs.

Sanderson is in the surgery visitors' lounge if you want to stop by."

JP swung his feet back to the floor, took a final slurp of tea and headed for visitors' lounge.

★

Sunday, October 12, 1969, 1612 hours
Visitors' Lounge, Surgery Recovery Unit

When JP walked into the lounge Laura Sanderson was sitting on the edge of a sofa thumbing through a worn issue of the *Ladies Home Journal*. She immediately stood, searching his face for clues. He introduced himself.

"Captain Entarde told me you might stop by after surgery," she said.

Laura Sanderson reminded JP of Kathy. They were about the same age. Each retained a youthful slender figure. Both radiated an inner beauty and serenity. JP suggested they sit down. He briefly debated if he should tell her how close she had come to being a widow Considering her husband's tenuous hold on life, he decided it best to be candid. He related the events that had transpired in the operating room, including the air embolus and cardiac arrest, emphasizing a guarded prognosis. "It will be a few days before we'll know if he sustained damage to his brain, heart or kidneys."

Laura Sanderson was quiet as she tried to digest the mass of information dumped on her. Finally she asked, "Will Charlie be able to fly again?"

JP was initially surprised at the question. On the ordinary mortals' scale of priorities, survival was much higher than flying an airplane. As a pilot himself he understood what lay behind Laura Sanderson's concern for her husband's flight status. Flying was more than a profession for many military pilots, it was a way of life to which they had been born. Chained to the ground they were lost. He carefully weighed his words. "I don't want to crush hopes prematurely or raise false hopes, Mrs. Sanderson. You must understand air force regulations are very strict regarding injuries of the upper airway, upper gut and flight status."

Laura Sanderson interrupted. "Perhaps I should tell you about Charlie, Colonel. His dad was a fixed-base operator who taught him to fly when he was twelve. Charlie got his private license at sixteen. By the time he graduated from high school he had his instrument rating. The only reason he went to college was to get into air force ROTC. That was his ticket to pilot training and fighters. He's a superb pilot and leader. The young pilots in his squadron worshipped him. They would have followed him anywhere. I don't know of anyone who is more dedicated to his men, more committed to his country, or who demands of himself a higher code of ethics." Laura Sanderson paused. In almost a whisper she continued, "Colonel Franklin, the country is in great need of officers like my husband."

JP had never heard a woman describe her husband in such positive terms. He was so moved that he was unable to respond for a moment. Standing up, he told Laura Sanderson, "I will do my best to get Colonel Sanderson in good enough shape to meet air force minimum flight standards. When the time comes for him to apply for flight status, I'll do everything short of lie to get him back in the cockpit."

'Thank you, Doctor," Laura Sanderson said, getting to her feet and offering him her hand. Her grip was firm.

JP started to leave. At the door he hesitated, turned and faced Mrs. Sanderson. "I'd like to ask you something unrelated to your husband's condition."

"Of course.

"Has Colonel Sanderson ever mentioned knowing me?"

Mrs. Sanderson smiled for the first time since JP had met her. "No, sir. Charlie doesn't like doctors, especially military doctors. Other than flight physicals he's had very little to do with them."

"Your husband is a wise man," JP said. "I'll be leaving for home after I check on your husband. Both Dr. Entarde and Dr. Brazelton will be in the hospital throughout the night, and I'll be only a phone call and thirty minutes away if I'm needed."

"Thank you, Doctor, "Laura Sanderson said. "And please thank all the medical personnel who helped with Charlie. I am so grateful. God bless them and you."

As JP walked to the recovery unit Laura Sanderson's gratitude echoed in his mind. Medicine truly was the greatest profession to which man could aspire.

Chapter Fourteen

Sunday, October 12, 1969, 1740 hours
Forest Glen, Silver Spring, Maryland

A tired and hungry Lieutenant Colonel JP Franklin slowed the Greenbrier van to fifteen miles per hour just before reaching the bridge that crossed into Forest Glen from Silver Spring. Maintaining the snail's pace, he continued through the post to the chapel, where he turned right and coasted down a short hill into one of two parking spaces authorized for the occupants of the Swiss chalet. Leaving the van, he walked down a narrow sidewalk towards his quarters, passing the Chinese pagoda, currently occupied by Colonel Bradford Marley, the chief of psychiatry and his wife Carrie.

A fall chill was in the air, and a misty rain fell from an overcast sky. Nearing the Swiss chalet, JP spotted Greta sprawled by the door under the porch faking sleep but slyly watching him approach. He knew what would come next and braced himself. Suddenly ninety-five pounds of German shepherd jumped up barking like a puppy. Breaking into a run towards JP, she left a trail of puddles on the sidewalk. When she leaped at him he caught her front legs and eased her down to the sidewalk. "Greta, why is it you're the only female I affect like this?"

The door of the chalet was flung open. Six-year-old Nancy and eight-year-old Frank ran out. Kneeling down, JP alternately hugged each child and patted the now whining shepherd. The two children locked their arms around JP's neck. Standing, he lifted them off the ground and carried them into the house. Greta, in a jealous pique, jumped up and down beside them barking furiously.

Once inside JP shook off the kids and picked up the dog. Holding her upside down, he eased into an antique rocking chair and began rocking. To sooth the struggling barking dog he crooned the marine hymn. Nancy and Frank ran to their mother in the kitchen. "Crazy daddy is home," they shouted.

Kathy Franklin appeared, shaking her head disapprovingly. "JP, why can't you walk into the house like a normal person? And that's your only going-to-church suit." She began laughing.

"What's so funny?"

"What your reaction will be when Greta loses control of her urethral sphincter, which she does routinely when excited. Your singing isn't helping."

JP immediately placed the wildly barking shepherd on the floor. "It must be the marine hymn. After all, she is an army dog."

Greta streaked up the stairs to the second floor followed by Frank and Nancy. The house became quiet. JP stood up, brushing dog hairs from his lap. "Kathy, I hope you're not jealous of Greta. I mean you can sit on my lap any time."

"No way. I'm not taking second place to a shedding German shepherd with

128

urinary incontinence." She kissed her husband. "How did the case go?"

"A real flail. The patient would have died except for Harry Resniek."

"He always seems to come through on the tough cases," Kathy said.

"I'm going to hate to see him leave the army. He is such a great asset."

"Would you like something to eat?" Kathy asked.

"I'll settle for a beer and munchies for now," JP said. "I think I'll light a fire. This chilly weather is getting to me."

Kathy headed to the kitchen with JP following. In the kitchen he reached for the wall phone. "I'm going to ask Brad to make a house call," he said, dialing. JP and Brad Marley had become close friends when both were stationed at the Military Academy. He had hunted deer with Marley, taken him flying and even taught him the rudiments of rock climbing.

After a short conversation JP hung up. "Brad will be over in a couple of minutes," he told Kathy. Taking a bottle of beer from the refrigerator and a frosted glass from the freezer, he lifted the bottle cap and half filled the glass. Returning to the living room, he placed the bottle and glass on the floor by a rectangular pit which extended out from a massive flagstone fireplace. There was room for up to eight people to sit comfortably on the floor around the fire place with their feet in the pit. Above the fireplace mantle hung a huge copper serving tray given to Kathy's brother by the Shah of Iran when he had served as a military advisor to the Shah's army. Kathy acquired the tray from her brother because it conflicted with the Japanese, Korean, and Vietnamese furnishings in his quarters.

Kindling and logs were already set in the fireplace. JP reached to the mantle for a book of matches. Lighting a match, he held it to newspaper pages stuffed under the grate until the papers began to flame, then sat down facing the fledgling fire. Dreamily he watched tiny peaks of orange flame leap and grow into larger flames until a fierce fire burned. For a moment JP was back in Korea, commanding a platoon of self-propelled automatic weapons and observing the results of his Mayday to Sharkbait, an air force FAC. Sharkbait had brought in a tactical air attack on a division of Chinese Communist forces that was about to annihilate JP's platoon and a British infantry battalion. As the planes flew away they left behind tidal waves of flame that coalesced into a single firestorm. For the enemy hell had come to the battlefield that day. For JP, observing the carnage through binoculars, there was no compassion or guilt for the horror he had initiated. There was nothing at all except relief that he and his platoon had survived.

Kathy broke the spell. Carrying a plate with crackers, cheese, and raw vegetables she sat down on the rug beside her husband and handed him the plate.

"Thanks, Kath," JP said, taking a slice of carrot from the plate and setting the plate on the floor. "Where are Jim and Paul?"

"Paul is spending the night at the Barfields with Mike. Jim is at the church."

"How did he do in the track meet?"

"It was cancelled because of the weather. Barb Summerson picked him up and drove him to church."

"Does he have a way of getting home?"

"Barb will bring him."

JP grunted. "Anything going on between those two? It seems that he's over at the Summersons a lot."

"I think he's intrigued by Barb because she has her own car and lets him drive it." Kathy Franklin leaned against her husband, anxious for the reassurance of physical contact with him. For several minutes she quietly studied the leaping flames.

JP sensed an almost brooding pensiveness in his wife. "Is something bothering you, Kath?"

"I had a long talk with Louise Barfield after church. She misses George terribly. The kids have started showing the strain of being without a father. Mike has skipped school three times since George left for Vietnam. Louise has an appointment tomorrow with the assistant principal to discuss Mike's truancy."

JP said nothing. He watched the fire subside and begin to smoke. Standing, he moved to the fireplace. Adjusting the logs with a metal rod, he grunted with satisfaction as flames leaped up again. Aware that Kathy was watching him, he avoided her eyes.

Kathleen Franklin was not the average army wife of the average army doctor. Long before she became the wife of a doctor she had been the wife of a combat officer. She saw her husband go off to the war in Korea three weeks after their wedding, not knowing if she would ever see him again. For almost two years after he returned she was an integral part of the activities at combat arms posts. She had also grown up in a military family. Her brother was a lieutenant colonel on his second tour commanding an artillery battalion in Vietnam. Her father was a retired general whose last assignment was as the head of the Defense Intelligence Agency. Kathy Franklin knew much more about the inner workings of the army than the average army wife of the average army doctor, and she certainly knew her husband well enough to recognize evasion.

"JP, why was George Barfield selected to go to Vietnam as a division surgeon?" she asked pointedly. "He's a superb neurosurgeon, probably the best in the army, but he doesn't know a company from a battalion. He thinks a battery is something to stick in a flashlight."

JP flushed as he wrestled with guilt. He was reluctant to tell Kathy he had encouraged George Barfield to take the division surgeon's slot, a slot he himself had coveted but was refused. A feeble attempt to stumble through an answer that was no answer was cut short by a knock at the door. Grateful for the interruption, he leaped for the door. A tall, slightly overweight, florid balding man in his mid-forties stood in the doorway. Turning, JP called out, "It's the neighborhood psychiatrist." Under his breath he added, "Just in time."

"Carrie will be over in a couple of minutes," Brad Marley said, stepping in. "She's waiting on some stuff in the washing machine."

Colonel Bradford Marley, the chief of psychiatry at Walter Reed, went into that specialty by a somewhat circuitous route. Before beginning his psychiatry residency he had completed two years of surgery residency and then a year of OB/GYN residency. This background gave him a pragmatic insight into patients and a rapport with his

130

non-psychiatrist colleagues enjoyed by few psychiatrists.

Approaching the fireplace Marley's psychiatrist's antennae sensed tension between JP and Kathy. "You two in need couple's therapy?" he asked, part serious and part in jest.

JP held up a half-empty bottle of beer. "Kathy was trying to get me drunk so she could pump me for classified information."

"You're as bad as my dad," Kathy said, punching JP's arm. "When the army wants to suppress embarrassing information it classifies the information *secret*."

"How did you come by that information?" JP demanded. "That policy itself is *secret*." Turning to Marley he asked, "Beer or Scotch?"

"Scotch, on the rocks," Marley said, sitting down next to Kathy.

JP disappeared into the kitchen. Returning moments later with a tall glass filled with ice and amber liquid, he handed the glass to Marlowe. "Scotch with a twist of ice," he said, confirming its contents.

The three sat quietly before the crackling fire, enjoying its warmth and savoring the comradeship and intimacy that comes only to those who serve in the armed forces. Marley broke the spell. 'The FBI was asking around the neighborhood about you two last week."

"Really?" JP said, showing little interest.

Kathy looked up from the fire. 'They were asking about us? Like what?"

"Oh, questions such as were you or JP heavy drinkers? Did you have frequent arguments? Did you appear to be living beyond your means? Did you drive expensive cars? Things like that."

"What did you tell them?"

'The truth, of course," Marley said, now grinning.

"Such as?"

"Such as whenever I came over here JP would be drinking as he's doing now."

JP looked at Marley, then took a long swallow of beer.

"See what I mean? A binge drinker if I've ever seen one," Marley said with a straight face. "I told them about your frequent arguments, like the one I just aborted."

"I was afraid you might have exaggerated," JP said with feigned relief.

"What's going on, JP?" Kathy asked. 'Why is the FBI questioning neighbors about us?'

"They're on to me, Kath," JP said contritely. "It's time for me to come clean with you. I've been selling classified data to the highest bidder. I did it for you, honey, so you could live in the style to which you were accustomed."

Kathy laughed. "Tell me about it. Our only car is a six-year-old van that wheezes as if it has asthma. It's mistaken for a bread truck whenever we go to embassy parties. We're sent around to park in the rear so our van won't be seen among all the chauffeured limousines." She turned to Marley. "Come on, Brad, why is the FBI checking on us?"

"Relax, Kathy. All the chiefs of services at Reed must have Top Secret clearances because of the nature of their duties and the VIPs they treat. Every two years the clearances are reviewed and updated. This was just one of those reviews."

JP interrupted. "The FBI quizzed me about Brad three months ago. He can just sweat out what I told them."

"We better change subjects," Marley said. "What was the emergency that had you working on a Sunday?"

"You're not going to believe this flail."

"Try me."

"The patient was an air force light colonel named Sanderson who was shot down a month ago in the Central Highlands. He arrived yesterday, moribund from a deep neck abscess. We took him to the OR. After draining the abscess we were breaking up adhesions around the jug when it ruptured. There was blood all over the place. Before we could ligate the jug he got an air embolus, started throwing PVCs, went to V fib and arrested."

Marlow took a long sip of Scotch. "I'm afraid to ask what happened next."

"Thank God Harry Resniek was passing gas. He had put in a central line before surgery started. He aspirated the right heart and got out some air. When the patient arrested he gave him a bolus of epi IV. It started the heart fibrillating. I zapped the heart with the defibrillator and got a sinus rhythm."

"I'm glad I went into psychiatry," Marlowe said.

"For a while this afternoon I wished I had."

They became quiet again, watching the changing shapes of flames and shadows. JP, still wrestling with the strong feeling of kinship he felt with Sanderson, turned to Marley. "Brad, I'd like your opinion on something."

"As a friend or as a psychiatrist?"

"Well, both I guess."

"The two usually aren't compatible, but you are such a weird case, JP, I'm willing to make an exception."

"You're all heart, Marley," JP said, grinning. "This concerns Colonel Sanderson, the patient we operated on this afternoon. When I first saw him in the fluoro room I experienced a feeling of some sort of bond between us, a bond that was almost spiritual. For a moment I thought I recognized him, but I can't remember ever meeting anyone who looked remotely like him. Brad, it really shook me."

Marley swirled the ice in his glass and dreamily watched the fire. "You've been in two wars, JP. You must have come across hundreds of people in those wars. Sanderson was probably one of them."

JP shook his head. "That's too simple, Brad. You're a full colonel. You should be able to do better than that."

Marley's interest was becoming piqued. "What do you know about Sanderson?"

"Just what I learned from his records and his wife. He was a fighter pilot in World War II and Korea. In Vietnam he was CO of a FAC squadron. The day he was shot down he was holding over special forces being hammered by the VC. When the fighters he called for were delayed by weather he faked rocket runs to take the pressure off the friendlies. It worked the first time but not the second. He managed to crash-land near the snake eaters. They pulled him out of his wrecked plane, carried him to a PZ and called in a Dust-off."

"Anything else?"

"His wife told me he was a fine CO. The pilots in his squadron would have followed him anywhere. She described him as very dedicated officer who held himself to the highest standards."

The psychiatrist studied his friend, took another sip of Scotch and set the glass down. "Your patient sounds highly principled, much like someone I know. Perhaps you saw in Colonel Sanderson the qualities you admire, the standards you set for yourself and those under you. He may have symbolized your concept of the consummate military man, all dedication, commitment, and without compromise."

Marley picked up his glass and gazed at the remaining amber liquid. "I don't usually drink when I'm working," he said. Looking up, he continued. "Face it, JP, you're an idealist. It's not possible to have been in two wars and do what you did without being an idealist. It's the only way you can live with your memories. Colonel Sanderson is probably cut from the same pattern as you. You think you know him from somewhere because, in a sense, you do. He's the mirror image of yourself, except he wears a different uniform and flies airplanes instead of cutting people open."

JP glanced at Kathy. He blushed when their eyes met.

Marley continued. "In your zeal, maybe even desperation, to maintain your cherished idealistic concepts despite what you have learned about the real world, you created in your mind an individual who possesses the qualities you hold so dear. Those are the qualities with which you have endowed Colonel Sanderson. JP, I've known you almost ten years. In that time I've learned that you place dedication to medicine, devotion to your country, and loyalty to your comrades above all else except maybe your family, and sometimes I have wondered about that. I'd be willing to bet that Sanderson's efficiency reports are replete with those same adjectives."

A sadness crept into Marley's voice. "Unfortunately, you and Colonel Sanderson are living dinosaurs. In a few years you and others like you will become extinct, as will the values of integrity, patriotism, and loyalty, the qualities you military idealists hold so dear. The saddest part is that our country will suffer grievously because you and your kind will be gone.

Kathy squeezed her husband's hand, acknowledging how close Marley had come to the truth.

The loud ring of the kitchen telephone shattered the thoughtful tranquility encompassing the three. Kathy started to rise when JP stopped her. "Hang loose, Kath. One of the kids will answer it upstairs."

After two more rings the phone stopped ringing. A moment later Frank shouted from the stairs. "Dad, it's for you. Some colonel in Vietnam."

"Quit kidding, Frank. Who is it?"

"Honest, Dad. He said he was calling from a place called Lung Been."

JP stood. "I'll get it in the kitchen. Hang up when I tell you."

"Who would be calling from Vietnam?" Kathy asked.

JP tried to sound unconcerned. "Probably some Berry Plan surgeon who wants to send a patient direct to our service or discuss managing a wound." In the kitchen he picked up the wall phone. "Okay, Frank, hang up and thanks." When he heard the click of the hang-up he said, "Colonel Franklin."

A male voice answered. "This is Colonel Dick Green at Med Command in Long Binh. Can you hear me, Colonel Franklin?"

"Loud and clear, Colonel. What can I do for you?"

"I understand you and Mrs. Franklin are good friends of Mrs. Barfield."

JP's gut twisted. *Why did Colonel Green say "Mrs. Barfield" instead of "the Barfields?"* He tried to keep his voice calm. "Yes, sir. One of our kids is over at the Barfields' now."

"Colonel Franklin, there is no easy way to tell you this." There was a long pause. For a moment JP thought the connection had been broken. The voice from 12,000 miles away continued. "Colonel Barfield was on a flight to Firebase Eileen yesterday when his helicopter was shot down. The flight crew managed to get off a Mayday and their position before they went in. An ARVN ranger company found the wreckage before night. There were no survivors. The bodies were recovered."

JP stared dumbly at the wall phone. A gifted neurosurgeon was gone. Four children were left without a father, a wonderful woman was left a widow. And he, Lieutenant Colonel JP Franklin, Medical Corps, US Army, had been partially responsible.

The voice on the phone persisted. "Colonel Franklin, are you there?"

"Yes, sir," JP said, now fighting back tears. "Has his wife been notified?" He could not bring himself to say widow.

"Negative. That's my reason for calling. The CG at Reed, General Worden, is out of town. The deputy commander can't be reached. The admin officer suggested that because of your friendship with the Barfields you and Mrs. Franklin might be willing to call on Mrs. Barfield with the chaplain."

A numbness crept through JP. "Of course, Colonel Green. We'll go over there right away."

"Be sure to coordinate your visit with the chaplain," Colonel Green reminded.

JP stared at the phone. *Yeah, sure.*

After some additional meaningless words Colonel Green hung up.

JP leaned against the wall for several minutes. Wiping tears from his eyes with the back of his hand, he fumbled in his shirt pocket for his reading glasses, slipping them on to hide the redness of his eyes.

When Kathy saw her husband she was not deceived by the reading glasses. The anguish on his face gave him away. "What is it, JP? What was the phone call?"

JP sat down and began reciting in a monotone. "George Barfield was killed yesterday when his chopper was shot down. Kathy, you and I have been asked to go over to the Barfields with the chaplain and break the news to Louise."

Kathy gasped, then wept quietly.

JP reached for her and held her close, feeling the convulsions of her sobs. How precious life was, and how quickly it could be taken.

Kathy quickly regained her composure. She told JP, "I'll pack a few things and spend the night with Louise."

Brad Marley, his round face ordinarily pink, was ashen. "Carrie and I will stay here until JP gets back."

"Thanks Brad," JP said. "Tomorrow morning do you think Carrie could come over when I leave for Reed and get the kids ready for school?"

"Just give her a call before you go out the door." Leaning over, he hugged JP and Kathy, then quietly left.

Chapter Fifteen

The North Korean guard shoved Lieutenant Colonel JP Franklin into the semi-dark windowless cell. Blinking in the dim glow of a single naked bulb, Franklin glanced furtively around the cell. In the shadows of the far wall he perceived the form of a man lying on the floor. As he started towards the man a rifle butt smashed into his back, driving him to his knees. In great pain, gasping for breath and coughing blood, he began crawling towards the man in the shadows. A North Korean officer strode into the cell and looked down on Franklin with contempt. "You call yourself a doctor," he shouted, "you are no doctor; you are a fraud, a criminal, a murderer. You will pay dearly for your crimes." The officer turned and left. The guard followed, slamming shut the barred door. Their booted footsteps receded into silence. Franklin crawled to the man in the corner, felt his neck for a pulse and found none. The man was dead. He turned the man's head towards the light to better see his face. "Oh my God," he moaned. "George Barfield."

★

Monday, October 13, 1969, 0500 hours
The Swiss Chalet, Forest Glen, Silver Spring, Maryland

The persistent loud jangle of the alarm clock dragged Lieutenant Colonel JP Franklin awake. Turning off the alarm, he lay on his back staring into the dark, grateful for release from the gut-wrenching nightmare. He reached for Kathy but felt only emptiness. Her absence brought yesterday's painful events tumbling into consciousness. Although still numbed by George Barfield's death in Vietnam, he was anxious to check on Colonel Sanderson. In medicine, concern for the living must take precedence over grief for the dead.

Minutes later, shaved, showered, and in uniform, he made rounds on the kids. Five-year-old Nancy didn't stir when he stuck his head into her small bedroom on the third floor. Greta's black form was curled next to Nancy on the bed. The big shepherd, aware that beds were off-limits to dogs, feigned sleep, hoping her violation would be overlooked. "Don't make a habit of it," JP warned her. She responded by exhaling with an audible "woosh". Descending to the second floor, he checked on the three boys. All were asleep and quiet except Frank, who intermittently ground his teeth. Just before going out the door to the van, JP phoned Carrie Marley. "I'm leaving for the hospital now," he told her.

"I'll be over as soon as I get dressed."

Carrie would get the kids up, cook breakfast, make lunches, and see that they made the school bus. One thing about military families: they took care of each other. That was the military way, and it was one of the reasons JP loved being part of the armed forces of the United States. No other organization came close to that kind of camaraderie. Picking up his cap and briefcase, he stepped through the front door. Closing the door, he checked to be sure it was locked, then headed for his van.

★

Monday, October 13, 1969, 0605 hours
Walter Reed Army Hospital, Washington D.C.

A blast of cold air rushed over Lieutenant Colonel JP Franklin as the automatic doors to the surgical intensive care unit slid open. Entering, he passed several empty beds and then a bed with a patient whose head was swathed in a massive dressing. A series of tubes and hoses connected his tracheotomy to a mechanical respirator. Twelve times a minute the machine inflated the patient's lungs, then allowed them to deflate. Each cycle was accompanied by the loud "whishhhh-pooo" of the respirator's action. Before reaching the nurses' station JP passed two more occupied beds, one by a double above-the-knee amputee, the other by a single amputee, his leg taken off almost at the hip. Both were victims of booby traps.

Pausing at the nurses' station he nodded to the nurse. "Quiet night?"

"Not bad, Colonel. All the medevacs went to the wards before midnight except these four." She handed him Sanderson's chart.

Opening the chart, JP scanned the lab results, nurses' notes, doctors' progress notes, and consultant's notes. He grunted with dissatisfaction as he read the obscure note by the cardiology fellow. Closing the chart, he left it on the counter, picked up a cap and mask, and continued to a glass-enclosed room, one of three such rooms used to isolate septic post-op surgical patients. Through the glass he saw Craig Entarde moving about inside the room. Sanderson, the upper third of his bed raised to a 60-degree angle, appeared asleep.

Tying straps of his cap and mask, he slipped on a gown and gloves, then entered the room. "Good morning, Craig. Did you get much sleep?"

"A couple of hours, sir. I was called at about three when the colonel spiked a temp to 104°F. I drew blood for a culture and white count, ordered an aspirin suppository, cooling blanket and a chest X-ray. The X-ray showed only mild atelectasis of both lungs. I bronchoscoped him anyway through his trach."

"Get much out of his lungs?"

"Some pus and blood that must have leaked past the endo tube cuff during surgery."

"What about brain damage?"

"No neurological deficits other than those characteristic of military pilots."

JP grinned despite the early hour. "They're like surgeons; every one is a prima donna with an attitude problem. Were you able to make any sense out of the cardiology note?"

"No, sir. I called the cardiology fellow and asked about myocardial damage secondary to the arrest and massage. He wouldn't commit himself. He recommended serial EKGs and enzyme studies."

"Oh, to be a thinking doctor instead of a cutting doctor."

"And walk the wards with a stethoscope around my neck looking professorial," Entarde added. "Shall we change Colonel Sanderson's dressing?"

"Good idea. He smells pretty ripe."

Captain Entarde left the room, returning a moment later pushing a dressing cart. The noise of the activity in his room woke Sanderson. His eyes focused on JP's face.

"Good morning, Colonel," JP said cheerily. "We're going to change your dressing. Neighbors as far away as Georgia Avenue have complained about the smell." Taking a pair of bandage scissors from the dressing cart, JP began cutting through layers of bulky dressing over the neck. "Let me know when I start cutting skin. I'm not very good at this."

Sanderson, unable to talk because of the tracheotomy, raised his right arm. The middle finger of his hand pointed towards the ceiling.

"Some sort of fighter pilot signal?" JP asked innocently, tugging on the dressing. Dried blood and secretions adhered the dressing to skin with the firmness of glue. "Brace yourself, Colonel," JP warned. "You will experience brief excruciating pain followed by a dull ache." He then pulled hard on the dressing, ripping it and adhesive tape from the skin.

The pain brought tears rolling down Sanderson's cheeks. Silently, he mouthed, "Shit." When JP looked at him disapprovingly he added, "Sir."

"That will teach you to give the 'bird' to a dedicated military doctor," JP said with mock severity. Leaning over, he examined the operative site. Four rubber Penrose drains exited through the nine-inch skin incision at varying levels. Two irrigation catheters entered through separate stab incisions. The skin was swollen and red. Yellow-green fluid exuded from the drains. In the confines of the closed room the odor was almost overpowering despite the air conditioning; all thoughts of breakfast were suppressed.

JP nodded with satisfaction at what he saw. "After Captain Entarde cleans you up you will smell sweeter than you did on prom night," he told Sanderson. "In the meantime, Colonel, think kind thoughts. The last person you want to tick off is the guy who changes your dressing,"

★

Wednesday, October 22, 1969, 1355 hours
Silver Spring, Maryland

Viewed from Georgia Avenue, Rossini's Funeral Home appeared to be a Victorian-style home with a large front porch and green lawn. An electric sign standing on one corner of the lawn flashed the funeral home's name. Smaller signs and arrows directed cars to a driveway and parking area at the rear of the funeral home. Lieutenant Colonel JP Franklin, driving the family red and white Greenbrier van, followed the arrows. He took care to park some distance from the conventional cars. Stepping to the ground, he gave his uniform a final inspection. The brass Medical Corps and US insignia on his lapels sparkled from many encounters with a Blitz cloth. Four rows of World War II and Korean War ribbons adorned his left chest. A name tag, properly aligned, was fixed to the flap of the right breast pocket. Above it was the South Korean Presidential Unit Citation. Kneeling, he wiped a layer of dust from his polished shoes with a small soft cloth. Deciding he was presentable, he walked briskly to the funeral home's main entrance.

The reception area was tastefully furnished to give the ambience of an elegant, comfortable nineteenth-century parlor. Floor and table lamps provided a soft, tranquil glow. A thick rug muffled JP's steps as he walked to the receptionist's desk. Behind the desk a severe-looking woman in her late forties, hair fixed in a tight bun, watched him approach. When he reached the desk she asked, almost in a whisper, "May I help you?"

"I'm Colonel Franklin, the honor guard for Colonel Barfield," JP said softly, trying to emulate her subdued voice.

The receptionist consulted the page of an open book on her desk, then looked up. "Yes, Colonel Franklin, we have you scheduled from two to four this afternoon." She gestured to an oak door adjacent to her desk. "Colonel Barfield is in the chapel at the end of the hall."

"Are there any special instructions for honor guards?"

"Be sure visitors sign the log on the table at the rear of the chapel."

JP thanked her. Passing through the oak door, he entered a wide carpeted hallway. On the right a half dozen picture windows looked out over a garden struggling to stay green despite the late fall season. An eight-foot wooden fence partially blocked out the adjoining filling station and garage. On the left four rooms of varying sizes opened into the hall. Walking towards the chapel, JP glanced briefly into each room. The first three were furnished in the same nineteenth-century motif as the reception room. None contained a casket. The fourth room was different. Its walls abounded with prints of balloons, airplanes, and trains. A child's crib was next to the far wall. A red fire engine, dump truck, hobby horse, and tricycle were arranged discretely around the crib.

Curious, JP stepped into the room and moved towards the crib. He stopped when he saw a boy, no more than four years old, dressed in pajamas. His arm held a stuffed puppy close to his chest. The picture of another small boy and his puppy flashed from JP's memory, their bodies in a ditch near a village in North Korea. Innocent victims of war, they were mourned by no one except possibly himself. Shaking off the memory, he left the room and moved to the chapel.

Reluctantly, he walked down the chapel's aisle to the casket. The upper half of the casket's lid was propped open. George Barfield, visible from the waist up, lay on a bed of white, crinkly satin-like material. He was dressed in green "Class A" uniform, his tie knotted perfectly at the V of the collar. The brass insignia on the lapels of his blouse were not only highly polished but meticulously located in the prescribed positions. JP smiled, recalling that George was notorious for tarnished brass often mounted incorrectly. He reached into the casket and placed his hand over Barfield's as if to say, "Goodbye, old friend. I will miss you."

JP walked to the heavy oak table at the rear of the chapel. The visitors' log lay open, a pen in its seam. Several dozen signatures were on the first two pages. Picking up the pen, he signed his name. In the section for remarks he wrote "Brother officer". Laying down the pen, he turned, faced the chapel entrance, and assumed a relaxed parade rest position, his feet eighteen inches apart and his hands clasped behind his back. While he stood in that position he began to review the eulogy for George that Louise Barfield had asked him to give at the funeral the following day.

★

Thursday, October 23, 1969, 1040 hours
Saint Marks Episcopal Church, Silver Spring, Maryland

Lieutenant Colonel JP Franklin, looking sharp in his dress blue uniform, stepped from the funeral home's limousine, tucked his hat under his left arm, then helped a sedately dressed Kathy Franklin out. Together they climbed the steps to the church entrance where they were met by an usher. After glancing at JP's name tag the usher led to a pew behind the Barfields. JP noted that the church was filled with as many people as it had been on Easter Sunday. Today's mass, however, would not celebrate the risen Christ. It would honor a military officer fallen, not in battle, but on a mission of mercy. Kathy genuflected and entered the pew. JP nodded to the cross on the altar, then followed her. Both kneeled in prayer.

The organist began the memorial service with Jehan Alain's simple yet magnificent Litanies. JP had requested the music as an adjunct to the eulogy he would give. As the last notes of the Litanies echoed through the church, Father Markam ascended the pulpit. In sonorous tones he began reading the Order for the Burial of the Dead from the Book of Common Prayer. "I am the resurrection and the life, saith the Lord. He that believeth in me, though he were dead, yet shall he live…"

JP's mind easily drifted back to 1943, to another memorial service, his first, on tiny Stirling Island in the Northern Solomons. At that service seventeen-year-old Marine Pfc JP Franklin grieved for brother Marine Joe Brogan killed by a Japanese sniper. JP had tracked down and killed the sniper, a Japanese youth not much older than he. Now, twenty-six years later, JP was again grieving at a memorial service. His introspection was cut short. Father Markham was calling his name. Kathy squeezed his hand.

Stepping into the aisle, JP genuflected. Approaching the altar, he bowed to the cross and climbed steps to the pulpit. He gazed briefly at the flag-draped casket at the foot of the altar, then looked out at the hundreds who had come to pay their respects to George Barfield. They were relatives, friends, colleagues, former patients and even relatives of former patients.

Suppressing initial waves of stage panic, JP began. "This is not the first time that I have been part of a memorial service for a comrade killed in war. Two previous wars gave me ample opportunities to mourn the deaths of men who were brothers in arms, some of whom I loved as brothers. Now another war has taken the life of another comrade, a dedicated physician and a gifted neurosurgeon, a man I greatly respected and admired.

"George Barfield's life early was replete with commitments to God, to his fellow man, and to his country. As a teenager he served as an acolyte. As a Boy Scout he reached Eagle Scout, predominantly on merit badges awarded for community service. In college he became a Big Brother, working with disadvantaged boys from the inner city. While a medical student he worked as a volunteer with medical missionaries in Central America during summer vacations. As a neurosurgeon he earned an international reputation for his accomplishments in the management of brain tumors and head wounds. And as a teacher he inspired excellence and dedication in his residents by his own example. His commitment to the army and his country were such that he refused repeated offers to take chairs of neurosurgery at prestigious medical centers or enter lucrative private practice.

"You should know that George Barfield was not ordered to Vietnam. Let there be no doubt of that. When he learned that a division surgeon's slot had unexpectedly opened up in Vietnam he volunteered. In today's environment of draft resisting, draft dodging, and worse, you may ask what motivated a man of George's skill and potential to turn his back on prestigious, high-paying, and safe opportunities to place himself in harm's way?

"The best I can do is share what I recollect from conversations over beer at the officers' club and cigars at backyard barbecues. George was well aware that separation from his family would impose tremendous hardship on his wife and children. It was a hardship suffered by every family whose member goes into a war. George realized that most soldiers sent to Vietnam had little choice in the decision. They would be exposed to much greater risk of death or severe injury than he would. He reasoned those soldiers should rightly expect their country to provide the very best neurosurgical care should they be wounded. In the opinion of George's many surgical colleagues across the country," JP paused to smile briefly, "not to mention George's opinion of his own skills, he was the very best. That he would place his life in jeopardy to go to the aid of wounded fellow Americans in a hostile area defines the strength of his character. His unarmed helicopter, clearly marked with red crosses, was shot down by an enemy who has repeatedly shown disregard for international law and moral decency.

"George Barfield was a gifted individual, but he was not the first gifted individual to give his life for his country, nor, sad to say, will he be the last. At the beginning of this memorial mass the organist played a selection titled Litanies. The composer, Jehan Alain, was a gifted young French organist killed early in World War II. Now, twenty-eight years later, we can only speculate on how much the world lost with his death. The impact of the Alains and Barfields lost to war in the spring of their creativity will never be known. They are losses the world can ill-afford."

JP paused to take a deep breath. "How can we respond when someone we respect, admire, and love is taken from us by war?" he asked. "I have no words of wisdom of my own. I can only offer the words of an admiral, a doctor who commanded the Naval Hospital in San Diego during World War II. I had gone to the hospital to visit a marine buddy, paralyzed from the neck down when he was wounded on Iwo Jima.

The admiral informed me that my buddy had died. Even though marines were trained to be too tough to cry, I cried. It was then the admiral told me what I now pass on to you. 'When someone we love is taken from us in war, we must endeavor to live our lives in such a way as to make up for that loss.' I learned later that the admiral's only son, a marine lieutenant, had been killed on Pelelieu."

JP paused, gazed down at the flag-draped casket, then looked up. "Those of us who knew George can do him no greater honor than to take the admiral's words to heart."

★

Thursday, October 23, 1969, 1330 hours
Arlington National Cemetery, Virginia

The first lieutenant, commander of Second platoon, Delta Company, 3rd Infantry (the Old Guard), scanned his platoon. Dressed in army formal dress – blue uniforms, black shoes shined to a mirror polish – the platoon was ready to begin the procession to the grave site. George Barfield's flag-covered coffin lay on the caisson, a four-wheeled flat bed buckboard. Four black horses harnessed to the caisson stood patiently, their riders talking soothingly to calm them and patting their necks. A saddled riderless black stallion tethered to the rear of the caisson pranced, as though anxious for the procession to begin. Fixed to each stirrup of the stallion's empty saddle a highly polished black cavalry boot pointed rearward. Four casket carriers stood in a row at each side of the caisson. Behind the caisson the drummer, bugler and rifle team stood formed. A line of limousines and cars waited at a discrete distance behind the casket team. An overcast sky and fine drizzle added to the solemnity of the occasion.

JP was positioned next to the caisson's right front wheel and in front of the casket team. He heard the lieutenant call the funeral detail to attention, then give the order to move out. The four lead horses obediently clumped forward, hooves clattering on the slick pavement. JP marched alongside, doing his best to stay in cadence with the drum beat. The line of limousines and passenger cars followed slowly.

The funeral cortege descended a lengthy incline past rows of headstones, all similar and all arranged in precise military formation. As the horses pulled the caisson around a slanted curve, its metal-rimmed front wheels slid on the wet pavement towards JP. Only the strongest self-control enabled him to resist jumping out of the way.

"Way to go, Colonel," the soldier behind him whispered.

An open grave, the first on a mild rise of ground, came into view. The lieutenant brought the procession to a halt. JP let his eyes wander towards the grave. An awning supported by four poles and ropes hung over the grave, protecting it from the drizzle. A larger awning covered a half dozen rows of metal folding chairs. Behind JP, the casket team slid the casket off the caisson and carried it with military precision to the grave and gently placed it on the catafalque. The lieutenant indicated that JP should stand at the far end of the grave. Standing at parade rest just outside the awning, he watched the procession of limousines and cars come to a stop behind the caisson. Car doors opened and slammed. Mourners took seats. Many stood in the drizzle beyond the awning. Louise Barfield and her children sat in the front row. Kathy, with Brad and Carrie Marley, was in the fourth row.

A military chaplain and Father Markey shared the graveside burial rites. The ceremony lasted only minutes. Finally, the chaplain said, "Unto Almighty God we commend the soul of our brother departed, and we commend his body to the ground..." The noise of a low passing jet from Washington National Airport drowned out the rest. The lieutenant brought the rifle team to attention, faced them right, and gave the orders, "Ready, aim, fire." A volley of shots shattered the solemn silence. A second and third volley followed. The bugler snapped his instrument to his lips. After the mournful notes of taps faded, two men of the casket team lifted the flag from the casket. Holding it open, they folded it precisely into a compact triangle with the stars and blue background on top, then handed the flag to the lieutenant. He turned and presented the folded flag to Louise. It was over.

JP stayed by the grave until everyone had left. After a final look at the casket he walked to the road where Kathy waited. She gripped his arm. In silence they walked to the waiting limousine.

Chapter Sixteen

Thursday, December 18, 1969, 0800 hours
Walter Reed Army Hospital, Washington D.C.

"A letter from Second Lieutenant Tom Carter," Thelma Hoffberg said, placing an envelope on Lieutenant Colonel JP Franklin's desk.

JP picked up the letter and examined the return address: Class 26–B, Student Detachment, Fort Wolters, Texas. "What do you know, that rascal is in flight school despite the physical profile I gave him."

"How could he manage that?"

"How could who manage what?" Dave Strickland asked, walking into the office.

"Tom Carter," JP said, "he's in primary flight school at Wolters."

"I thought you restricted him from combat activities, Colonel."

"The restriction prohibited assignment to ground combat units for two years," JP said. "I don't believe the subject of flying came up."

"It seems you dropped the ball, Colonel."

"It appears that I did. Well, there's nothing I can do about it now," he said stoically, then broke into a grin.

"Colonel, you are a sly one," Dave Strickland said.

"Well, are you going to open the letter?" Thelma asked impatiently.

JP tore open the envelope, unfolded a single page letter and read aloud.

Dear Colonel Franklin,

You and Colonel Barfield did such a great job on me I was able to pass the flight physical with a waiver. A buddy in JAG advised me your profile restriction referred specifically to ground combat units. Since there was no mention of air combat units it could be assumed I was not disqualified for flight training.

JP looked up. "That Philadelphia lawyer. He's as bad as his mother."

"I wouldn't know," Thelma Hoffberg said, tongue-in-cheek.

JP threw her a chastising look, smiled as though recalling a pleasant memory, then continued reading.

If I don't kill myself and/or my instructor I will finish at Wolters number one in my class. In January I will go to Rucker for advanced training. I can't wait to get my hands on a Huey after five months of the damned H–23. I will get my wings in June and expect to be assigned to Vietnam.

I was sorry you and Mrs. Franklin weren't able to make my graduation from the

Academy. My mother wasn't able to make it either. For her that's par for the course. If you have occasion to visit Fort Rucker I'll be happy to take you for a ride. Say "hi" for me to Major Strickland and the residents. Give my love to Thelma. I know she is the one who actually runs that department.

"I didn't think he noticed," Thelma said.

JP ignored her comment and read on.

Thanks again for everything. Merry Christmas and best wishes to all.

Sincerely, Tom Carter

P.S. My mother was not happy with my decision to go for flight training. She thinks you were somehow involved in that decision.

JP put the letter down and looked around innocently. "I wonder what gave her that impression."

A phone rang in Thelma's office across the hall. Thelma picked up JP's silent phone and punched the flashing button. "Colonel Franklin's office, Mrs. Hoffberg." After listening a moment she said, "Yes, sir. He's right here." She held the phone out to JP. "Colonel Chun from Fort Benning."

Frederick Chun was a 1955 USMA graduate who spent three years as an infantry officer before going to medical school at Chicago. Graduating third in his class, he went on to an internship and head and neck surgery residency at Walter Reed. Finishing in 1967, he was assigned to Martin Army Hospital at Fort Benning, Georgia, the Infantry Center where he was currently chief of head and neck surgery.

JP waved Strickland to a seat, then spoke into the phone, "What's up Fred?"

"Chief, I hate to lay this on you so close to Christmas, but I have one hell of a problem here."

"Not Dr. Minter?"

"Yes, sir. I was ready to kill the son of a bitch. The hospital commander wanted to court-martial him."

JP switched the phone to the speaker on the intercom and mouthed to Dave Strickland, "It's about our buddy, Dr. Minter."

Colonel Chun continued, "He's been a problem since he arrived. He repeatedly showed up late for work, left early, and was difficult to contact when he was on call, much less come in to the hospital. Last week he requested fourteen days' leave over Christmas and New Year. I told him he could have a week and no more. Benning is running a heavy load of troops with AIT, OCS, and Airborne training. He responded by dragging his feet on seeing patients. Those he saw he chewed out for bothering him with trivial complaints. He went so far as to accuse some GIs of malingering. The asshole picked the wrong group. They were special forces just back from their third tour in Vietnam. He was lucky he didn't get thrown through a window.

"Two days ago one of his post-tonsillectomy patients, a sixteen-year-old girl, started hemorrhaging in the evening ten days after surgery. In addition to having been the surgeon Minter was on call. He refused to come in to the hospital claiming he couldn't leave his sick wife. The hospital called my quarters in a panic. Vivian and I were in Columbus visiting an Academy classmate. Luckily I had left a phone number with the babysitter. The Columbus police escorted me to Benning with red lights flashing and sirens screaming. The MPs met me at the gate and led to the hospital."

"Good God."

"Precisely, sir. I ended up ligating the external carotid artery and transfusing six units of blood. The girl arrested briefly during surgery but was quickly resuscitated."

"Did you find a bleeding cause?"

"Yes, sir. That idiot Minter had put a suture through one of carotid branches and failed to recognize it. After ten days the artery ruptured."

Dave Strickland listened intently and shook his head, incredulous.

"There's more, Colonel."

"I'm not sure I want to hear it."

"I threw Minter's ass off my service and banned him from the operating room. I told him I planned to write up court martial charges for negligence, endangerment, dereliction of duty, and conduct unbecoming an officer. Minter hired a lawyer and was going to sue the army and me for twenty million dollars."

"On what basis?"

"Demeaning his reputation, restricting his practice, and months of suffering under an incompetent superior."

"The last may be hard to defend."

"Come on, Chief. This isn't funny. He also claims I was responsible for his wife's miscarriage because of the stress I inflicted on her through him."

"What did the OB people say about that?"

"Nothing. She was never seen as a prenatal patient on the OB clinic. Minter said he had made the diagnosis of pregnancy and was managing her prenatal care. There was no confirmation of pregnancy."

"What about the products of conception after the miscarriage?"

"Minter claims he flushed them down the toilet. His wife refuses to come to the OB clinic for exams and blood tests. She got hysterical when the CID agents went to talk to her. There's another interesting fact."

"I can't wait to hear."

"Three weeks before her alleged miscarriage Mrs. Minter obtained a refill of a prescription for birth control pills. That was her third refill since she's been at Benning."

"I'll be happy to testify at Minter's court martial. I have some correspondence on him I've been saving."

"That may not be necessary. The JAG is going to offer him an immediate general discharge in lieu of a general court martial, on the basis of mental instability and incompatibility with military life. The general discharge and withdrawal of his hospital privileges should be a red light whenever he applies for state licensure and board certification."

"That sounds like a reasonable solution," JP said. "We're lucky to have gotten rid of him so easily, and he's lucky he isn't spending five years at Leavenworth. And now, Colonel Chun, let's get to the real reason for your call. You need a replacement for Minter."

"You always could read my mind, Chief."

"Stand by, I'll see what I can do." He lay the phone down, opened a lower drawer and extracted a thick manila folder. Thumbing through its contents, he removed several pages and studied them. Selecting one, he picked up the phone. "You still there, Fred?"

"Yes, sir."

"I've got just the man. You must live right."

"Colonel, I've learned through painful experiences to be wary of such expressions from you."

"You are so cynical for a young man. On second thoughts you can hardly be blamed after I sent you Dr. Minter. This time, though, you are really in luck. It so happens there's a Berry Planner finishing a five-year residency at Iowa this month. I'll bring him on active duty in January, waive the requirement for the three-week orientation course at Fort Sam, and send him to Benning. You can teach him how to wear a uniform and salute."

Colonel Chun remained suspicious. "Why is he finishing his residency in December instead of June like everyone else?"

"Last winter he skied into a tree at Keystone with enough force to lacerate his liver, rupture his spleen, and break his femur. He had to drop out of his program for six months while he mended after laparotomy, splenectomy and repair of the femoral fracture. He's fine now. Just don't take him skiing. His chairman considers him so outstanding he wants him to join his staff after he finishes his military obligation. I'll send you copies of his records so you can contact him."

"Thanks, Chief. You've made my Christmas. I knew there was a Santa Claus out there somewhere."

Hanging up, JP slipped all the papers except one into the manila folder and returned the folder to the desk drawer.

"That Minter, what a turkey," Dave Strickland said. "He's lucky he's not up on a negligent homicide or manslaughter charge."

"I need some coffee," JP said, standing up. "How about you?"

"No thanks, Colonel. I should get back to the OR. They should be about ready for Colonel Bendler."

JP watched him leave, wrote a note to call the SGO about Minter's replacement, then picked up his empty coffee mug and headed for the conference/coffee room. In the hall he almost collided with Colonel Sanderson dressed in civilian attire. "Charles, what are you doing here? You're on convalescent leave until the end of January."

"Doc, we need to talk."

"That serious? Okay. Have a seat in my office. Coffee?"

"Air force policy is to never turn down a free cup."

In the conference room JP filled two mugs with steaming coffee from an urn, then returned to his office and handed one mug to Sanderson. As Sanderson eased into a chair his eyes swept the framed diplomas, photographs, and certificates on the walls. "First time I've been in your office, Doc. Looks like you've been around."

"It's been an interesting life," JP said, mentally noting that Sanderson's voice had improved and now had a strange familiarity. Paradoxically, his face had filled out with weight gain and no longer seemed familiar. "What's on your fighter-pilot mind?"

"That's the problem, Doc, my fighter-pilot mind."

"You've lost me already."

"I need to go back to duty and flight status. Convalescent leave is driving me nuts."

'You and Laura just moved into a new house in Falls Church," JP said. "That should be keeping you busy."

"It did for the first two weeks. Now everything is squared away in the house; there's nothing to do."

JP looked at Sanderson suspiciously. "You're holding back something, Charles."

"And you're too damn smart. You should have been an intelligence officer."

"I was one of those before going to medical school. Now let's hear it."

"I have orders assigning me to the Pentagon, but my reporting date is contingent on my discharge from the hospital." Sanderson leaned forward. "I'm ready to go to work and get back on flight status. My wife tells me my voice is improving."

"It sounds that way to me too," JP admitted. "What will be your duties at the Pentagon?"

"Revision of the training syllabus for FACs, supervising its implementation, and training the first cadre of instructors using the new syllabus."

JP studied his patient. The man had combat skills, experience and judgment that could save American lives and help win the war in Vietnam. He was also a hard charger. Turning him loose prematurely could imperil his recovery. It was a dilemma JP faced with many of the wounded career officers and enlisted men. Over the years he had learned to compromise with these hard chargers and the needs of the service.

"Okay, Charles," JP began, "I'm willing to sign you out on limited duty after January 1, but you can forget flight status for now."

Sanderson leaned forward. "Come on, Doc. I'm well enough now to fly anything with wings."

"Where did you get that ego, Charles? You have two conditions, at least, that disqualify you from flight status according to air force regs."

"I'm listening."

"That's an encouraging sign. Your last barium swallow demonstrated residual stenosis… a narrowing of the lower pharynx and upper cervical esophagus. That's the first disqualifying condition. You're making good progress with dilatations, but you're not out of the woods. Just consider yourself fortunate that revision surgery wasn't necessary."

"And the second condition?"

"At your last exam three weeks ago your right vocal cord was fixed. It hasn't been possible to determine if the vocal cord is not moving because its nerve was injured, because it was fixed by scar secondary to trauma and infection, or both."

"But my voice has improved."

148

"So Laura has noticed. That could be a good or bad sign."

"What's that supposed to mean?"

"It could mean the vocal cord is beginning to recover movement. It could also mean that scar shrinkage is bringing the vocal cord closer to the opposite vocal cord. That could be bad because it would mean a reduction in the airway, which is disqualifying for flight. Simply put, Charles, you cannot fly in the United States Air Force with a compromised airway, a compromised voice box, and a compromised gullet."

"Could you to tell if the vocal cord is moving by looking today?"

"Probably," JP said, standing. "Let's give it a try."

He led into the adjacent examining room. Minutes later, the examination completed, they returned to the office. Sanderson sat down and took a sip of coffee.

"Well?"

"There's good news, bad news, good news and bad news."

"You're confusing me, Doc."

"That's a skill I learned as an intelligence officer," JP said. "The good news is that the right vocal cord is moving. The bad news is that it isn't moving much. The good news is that once the vocal cord begins to move after an injury, chances are good it will go on to complete or near complete recovery. The bad news is that it may take up to eight months to recover."

Thelma's voice came from the intercom. "Colonel, could you see the Secretary of the Army tomorrow afternoon?"

JP studied his schedule. "It's pretty full, Thelma. I'll come over there and see what can be worked out." Taking his schedule, he told Sanderson to hang loose. "Think kindly of the Army Medical Corps, Charles. After all, you could have ended up in an air force hospital."

Minutes later, after arranging to see the Secretary of the Army at 1730 hours the next day, JP returned to his office. Colonel Sanderson was standing with the coffee mug in his hand, studying JP's honorable discharge from the Marine Corps in November 1945. He went back to his seat. "I didn't know you were a marine in the war."

"Colonel Sanderson," JP said with strained patience, "let me enlighten you. There is no such thing as 'were a marine'. The reality is, once a marine, always a marine."

"That explains why you're such a hard ass."

JP grinned.

"What did you do in the marines?"

"That was two wars ago. You don't want to hear about that."

"On the contrary, Doc, I do. I may be on to something."

"Now what's that supposed to mean?"

"It's supposed to mean there's something familiar about you, a certain subtle arrogance that reminds me of someone. Seeing the Marine Corps discharge on your wall started to bring things into focus. Now I want to hear what you did in the Marine Corps."

JP was surprised at the tone of Sanderson's voice. It was as though Sanderson had given him an order. He checked his watch and shrugged. "I went to the Northern

Solomons in 1943 when I was seventeen as part of a ground defense detachment. The detachment provided local security and occasionally went out on patrols. Nothing much exciting."

Sanderson's eyes shined as he closed in. "Did one of those patrols take place on an island named Mono in the Treasuries?'

JP winced as if slapped. He stared at Sanderson. "What did you say?"

"I'm asking if you were you part of a patrol that rescued two Army Air Corps pilots from under the noses of the Japs on Mono in late 1943?"

JP continued to stare at Sanderson.

"*Keine antwort ist auch ein antwort*," Sanderson said. "You and your marine buddies saved my life and Dick Grundig's life."

JP sat, stunned into silence. Memories long suppressed by the horrors of war intruded into his consciousness. He and Sanderson stood up and looked at each other, disbelieving. Then Sanderson grabbed JP in a fierce bear hug. "You damned jarhead, I never had a chance to thank you and the others for saving my life back then. And now you saved my life again."

"Your air force buddies saved my butt more than once in Korea, so we're even."

At that moment Thelma Hoffberg walked in. The sight of her boss being hugged by a male patient took her by surprise. "Am I interrupting something?"

JP broke loose. "Thelma," he said, "you are not going to believe who this guy is."

"Try me, Colonel," she said, settling her rotund body into a chair.

JP looked at his watch again. "This has to be brief. I'm due in the OR in ten minutes."

"Doc, can we get together after you finish the operation?"

"Let's meet at the officers' club about six for dinner. I have to be back here at seven thirty for tumor board."

"Is someone going to tell me what this is all about?" Thelma complained.

"Sorry," JP said. "You start, Charlie. I'll fill in."

"Well, in July 1943 another pilot, Dick Grundig, and I were returning from an escort mission to Bougainville. We were flying P–38s. My plane had taken hits in the fuel line and was leaking fuel. Dick's had lost an engine; the other was running in the red and was about to quit. We decided to ditch close to an island named Mono seventy miles south of Bougainville. It was a small round island only six miles across. The natives were reportedly friendly. We had no idea there were three hundred Japanese marines on the island. They saw our planes go down, figured we swam to Mono, and sent out patrols to track us down. They would have found us if it hadn't been for a native, John Boreas.

"John had been educated by missionaries, spoke excellent English, and had no love for the Japanese military. He guided us to a cave up on a small mountain. One of his cousins brought food to us every week or ten days. Two months later New Zealanders and marines invaded Mono and nearby Stirling Island. They killed most of the Japanese but several dozen escaped into Mono's interior jungle. Because of the fluid situation Dick and I were unable to make contact with the Allied Forces. When they withdrew, the surviving Japanese started looking for us again. They caught John's cousin carrying a large amount of food and tortured him into admitting the food was for us. When he wouldn't reveal where we were hiding they cut off his head, then started looking for John. Warned by his relatives, John escaped in a canoe to Stirling Island, about four miles away. That's all I knew at the time. Doc, it's your turn."

"I didn't realize you would be so long-winded, Charles." He reached for the phone and dialed operating room six. "This is Colonel Franklin," he told the answering nurse. "I'll be a few minutes late. Major Strickland can start the case." He hung up.

"Come on, Doc," Colonel Sanderson urged. "I've waited all these years to hear your part of the story."

Thelma Hoffberg sat erect in her chair as though a queen. "Yes, Colonel. please get on with it."

"Right. When John Boreas reached Stirling he told his story about the two pilots to my CO, Captain Mueller, who decided his marines would rescue them. My two buddies from boot camp, Mick Icardi and Jake Conrad, a Navajo from Crown Point, New Mexico, volunteered with me to go on the patrol. Sergeant McDougall, our platoon sergeant, was in charge, and John Boreas was our guide. By that time John had been appointed an honorary corporal in the Marine Corps.

"Some time after midnight we left for Mono on a PT boat with John's canoe secured to the foredeck. Just before dawn the PT boat hoved to about a mile off Mono near Falami, a fishing village. We used John's canoe to reach shore. John led us to the mountain where he thought Charlie and his buddy would be hiding if they were still alive and hadn't been captured. At the base of the mountain we stumbled onto a patrol of eight Japanese who had just started to mortar the caves." JP hesitated. He didn't want Thelma to hear that the marines killed all the Japanese, that he killed one in a hand-to-hand fight. "After we dealt with the Japanese, Sergeant McDougall sent John Boreas and me up the mountain to get the pilots. Charlie, you tell it from there."

Colonel Sanderson sipped from his mug, swallowed and went into a paroxysm of coughing, turning almost blue. After he settled down JP told him, "See what I mean by not being ready for the cockpit?"

Sanderson glared at JP, then took up the narrative. "Dick Grundig and I were near our cave entrance. We heard a commotion down below, then a PA system blared in English spoken by someone who didn't speak English, calling on us to surrender. Dick and I went deep into the cave. A couple of mortar shells detonated outside the cave. There was a second or two of silence followed by many explosions, machine gun fire, and then quiet. About an hour later a young marine, your boss, Thelma, ordered Grundig and me out of the cave, threatening dire consequences if we failed to comply. He and John Boreas got us down a sheer cliff where we joined the rest of the patrol. They took us out to a beach to wait for a rubber raft from a PT boat.

"About midnight the raft showed. Just after Grundig and I climbed in the raft there were shots from the shore. Sergeant McDougall was hit. The marines threw him in the raft, then started firing their Tommy guns towards the shore. Another marine brought out John Boreas who had been wounded and dumped him in the raft. Your boss and the other marines refused to get in the raft. Instead they stayed to fight off the Japanese so that we could get away. That was the last I saw those three marines, none of whom could have been much over eighteen.

"The PT boat took us to Stirling Island. A marine gooney bird flew Dick Grundig, me, and the two wounded marines to the Navy Hospital on Guadalcanal. After ten days Grundig and I were flown to a hospital in Brisbane. We were in bad shape with malaria, dysentery, and starvation. While we were recovering Dick and I used to lie awake at night talking about the marines who rescued us, then stayed behind to fight off the Japanese. We figured their chances of survival were zilch. They had sacrificed their lives for us. Now I find one of them survived to save my life again." Sanderson sniffed. His eyes turned red. "It's your turn, Doc. What happened after we took off in the rubber raft?"

JP had not thought about that night for many years. Now the details came tumbling out with remarkable clarity. "The Chief, Icardi and I suppressed the shooting from shore with our return fire. After we reached the jungle we figured the Japanese would expect us to head south towards Stirling Island so we headed north. The Japanese were not fooled. The Chief sensed we were being tracked so he set up a daisy chain of grenades and the Japanese walked right into it. That bought us some time. At dawn we watched some natives beach a canoe, then 'borrowed' it and set out for Stirling, paddling like crazy. After about four hours we were dehydrated, sunburned, and about wiped out. A shell detonated behind us. A Japanese barge was closing in, firing a mortar from its deck. A second shell tore up Icardi's leg and capsized the canoe.

"In the water I managed to get a tourniquet on Icardi's leg while the Chief scared off a shark with grenades. By then bullets were hitting the water around us. As the barge closed in, the Chief and I decided to fake surrendering. When the barge got close enough we would throw grenades on board, but the Japs weren't buying it. They were really trying to kill us. Suddenly the barge blew up with a tremendous explosion. Even though we were two or three hundred yards away I felt the heat of the blast. Parts of the barge went hundreds of feet in the air. An F4U with MARINES emblazoned on the fuselage roared over us, then zoomed into a steep climb, rolling over and over. Minutes later a PT boat showed up and took us aboard."

"I want to hear what happened to the other two marines."

"Mick Icardi lost a leg. He wrote me months later he would enter a Jesuit seminary in Pennsylvania to become a priest. A couple of months ago I learned he was a chaplain with the marines on Okinawa. Next year he will go to Vietnam for a third tour, this time as the division chaplain for the 1st Marine Division. After he was evacuated to the Canal only the Chief and I remained from the boot camp foursome. We kept getting into trouble. I don't know whether it was from boredom or because of guilt that we survived when our closest friends didn't. We reached a point where we didn't give a shit... sorry, Thelma, I mean we just didn't care any more. Once we used an excessive amount of dynamite trying to dig a latrine in coral. We blew away a good part of Stirling Island. Another time we got drunk and collapsed a bunch of army tents. Captain Mueller threatened to throw the book at us. He told us we were more of a menace to the Marine Corps than the Japanese. To keep the army from filing charges against us he sent the Chief to the 3rd Division on Bougainville as a code

152

talker. I went to the 4th Division for the invasion of the Marianas.

"Months later I learned that the Chief had been wounded in the spine on Iwo Jima and was quadriplegic. He was evacuated to the naval hospital in San Diego where he died of meningitis. He wanted to be a doctor and minister to his people. I wanted to be a minister and organist. Now the Chief is dead, I'm the doctor and Mick is a priest."

Tears trickled down Thelma's cheeks. She stood up. Shaking her head, she fled from the office.

JP and Sanderson sat quietly, each deep in his own reminiscences. Finally, Sanderson asked, "Do you know what became of the others?"

"Sergeant McDougall and John Boreas recovered from their wounds. John was promoted to Honorary Sergeant in the Marine Corps. McDougall was given a direct commission as a second lieutenant. In Korea I heard through the grapevine that Captain Mueller was a lieutenant colonel commanding an infantry battalion in the 1st Marine Division, and Lieutenant McDougall was a captain and one of his company commanders. I have no idea what became of John Boreas. I can't picture a man of his intelligence spending his life on an island six miles in diameter."

"Christ, what a story. You ought to write a book, Doc," Sanderson said.

"Maybe after I retire."

JP's pager came alive with Dave Strickland's voice. "Colonel, we're ready for you in the OR with Colonel Bendler."

"Would that be Bruce Bendler?" Sanderson asked.

JP nodded. "You know him?"

"We went through flight school together. Last I heard he retired from the air force and went to work for Air America in Vietnam. What's his problem?"

"Three packs a day for twenty years; that's a sixty-pack-year history. He has cancer of the larynx – the voice box."

"Jesus Christ. What are you going to do?"

"Explore his larynx to determine if a partial or total laryngectomy will be required to cure him, then go with our decision."

"Did you know he shot down six MiGs in Korea and another during his tour in Vietnam before he went with Air America?"

JP shook his head. "He seemed like such a benign guy."

Sanderson laughed. "Doc, you are such a poor judge of character. Bendler is a tiger in the air. On the ground he has to fight off the women."

"It must be that air force charm. What does his wife say about that?"

"She divorced him years ago."

"Maybe the cancer will be a heads up for him, at least to give up smoking." JP stood up. "I've got to go, Charles."

"I can't wait to get to a phone to tell Laura who the surgeon was who saved my life."

JP indicated the phone on his desk. "Be my guest. Dial nine for an outside line. Don't exaggerate. On second thought, pour it on."

Chapter Seventeen

Wednesday, December 24, 1969, 2350 hours

On Christmas Eve most military personnel in the Washington D.C. area were at home with their families. Among the exceptions were the medical personnel at Walter Reed Army Hospital, whose personal lives were governed by a higher priority. That afternoon a medevac plane landed at Andrews Air Force Base from Vietnam carrying forty-two wounded and ill patients. They were loaded into a caravan of ambulance-buses and delivered to the Walter Reed emergency room. There a horde of interns, residents, and staff swarmed over them, reviewing records, conducting physical examinations, and writing orders for continued care. Six casualties were admitted to the head and neck surgery service. Of these, one required immediate surgery and was taken to the operating room. Other surgical services were as busy or busier operating. Thus on Christmas Eve, the lights burned in every operating room at Walter Reed Army Hospital. By 2330 hours Lieutenant Colonel JP Franklin, Captains Craig Entarde and Greg Brazelton finished five hours of surgery to repair a massive neck wound sustained by a nineteen-year-old corporal less than seventy-two hours before.

After wishing everyone in the OR a Merry Christmas, JP swung by the wards to check on the remaining newly arrived casualties admitted to his service, then headed for the Greenbrier van in the sacred quadrangle. Anxious to get home to help Kathy wrap Christmas presents, he pushed the van past the speed limit on dark, deserted Georgia Avenue. Only a scrooge would write a speeding ticket on Christmas Eve, he reasoned. The drive through northern Washington D.C. and southern Maryland was a collage of multicolored Christmas lights. Even Rossini's Funeral Home was brightly lit.

When he stepped into his quarters Kathy was sitting on the floor, an open manual of some sort in her lap. Greta, asleep by her side, opened her eyes long enough to confirm what her nose and ears told her, then went back to sleep. The eight-foot Christmas tree, bought from the Scout Troop at Forest Glen, was laden with ornaments and tinsel, its lights glowing white. Dozens of gaily wrapped presents were piled high around the tree.

JP went over, kissed his wife and patted Greta. "You wrapped all the presents. Bless you my, child."

"Your timing was impeccable, Colonel," Kathy said. "I just finished except for that." She waved the manual towards sheets of varying shaped gun-blue cardboards on the floor, the makings of a seven-foot submarine with a working telescope. "That thing requires an engineer with a PhD to assemble."

"Not when there's an M.D. around."

Kathy tossed him the manual. "Okay, hotshot, you're on."

JP quickly thumbed through the pages of instructions. "Piece of cake. Give me a couple of minutes to shed my uniform. I will then demonstrate how a talented surgeon with superior scientific intellect and manual dexterity will have this submarine ready for test dive in less than half an hour."

Three hours later the submarine was only partially assembled. The last hour included a continuous string of unflattering epithets hurled at the sub's designer and manufacturer. When the first streaks of dawn began chasing away the night the submarine was finally together, its working periscope actually working. JP lifted the conning tower and climbed in. "I must make a test dive before signing off on the sub," he told Kathy.

"You make your test dive, Commander, I'm going to bed." She headed for the stairs.

Minutes later JP followed. In bed he nudged his wife.

"What is it, Commander?"

"The sub leaked at two hundred fathoms. Frank will have to stay above that."

"Going that deep made you addle headed."

"No. I was that way before the dive."

They had hardly closed their eyes when Nancy and Frank banged on the door and crashed into the bedroom. "Jim and Paul are downstairs opening presents," they announced in unison.

That was how Christmas 1969 began. Christmas dinner included a sixteen-pound turkey awarded to Paul for the highest number of newspaper starts among paper boys with routes in the Silver Spring area. JP, as usual, fought Nancy and Frank over the turkey tail.

★

Thursday, January 8, 1970, 0630 hours
Walter Reed Army Hospital, Washington D.C.

Lieutenant Colonel JP Franklin stepped from the Walter Reed–Forest Glen shuttle bus and headed to his office by way of Ward 12, the officers' ward, to check on Alex Leichuk. Today was the first day of regularly scheduled surgery after the holiday schedule. It was also the day the head and neck service and the thoracic-cardiovascular service would jointly reconstruct Alex Leichuk's trachea. Because of the complexity of the surgery and the time involved, Alex was the only patient on the head and neck surgery schedule. He had been scheduled and cancelled three time in the past two months. Each time the cancellation was due to fever, neck infection, and pneumonia.

Reaching the Ward 12 nursing station he greeted the chief ward nurse, Captain Sherry Barnhardt, "Your husband make it home for Christmas?"

She shook her head. "No, sir. The intelligence people predicted increased MiG activity between Christmas and New Year. All leave for his squadron was cancelled."

"That's rough," JP sympathized.

"For me, but not for him."

"Explain that, Sherry," JP said as he pulled two charts out of the chart rack.

"Dan has credit for four MiGs and he's determined to get one more to make ace. Except for a few days leave now and then, he'll try to stay in Vietnam until he bags the fifth."

"He must be one hell of a pilot."

"He is, Colonel, but flying is not all he's good at... sir." Captain Barnhardt blushed.

"Speaking of aviators, how is our buddy, Colonel Bendler, God's gift to the world of aeronautics and the female gender?"

"He's convinced himself he's home free because you removed only half his larynx and the margins were free of cancer. One of the medics caught him sneaking a smoke in the latrine. After you told him he could talk, but only in very short sentences, he became so intrigued by his low gravely voice he talks incessantly. The young nurses think his voice is sexy."

"You'd better warn them. Beneath the shy boyish demeanor lurks a predator."

"I'll break his arm if he tries anything with my nurses," Captain Barnhardt said.

"Any problems during the night with Captain Leichuk?"

"No, sir. Temp, X-rays, and labs are normal. He just got his pre-meds. The OR should be coming for him any minute."

JP thanked her. Picking up a stethoscope from the desk, he went to the door of Alex's room, knocked, pushed open the door and walked in. Leichuk, lying on his side facing the wall, was asleep. Deciding not to awaken him, JP quietly left.

At Colonel Bendler's room the door was open. JP knocked and walked in. "Good morning, Bruce."

Bendler, sitting in bed reading a newspaper, looked up. "Good morning, Colonel." His voice was indeed low and gravely, but definitely not sexy.

"How goes it with half your larynx gone?"

"Not bad except for chocking when I try to swallow liquids."

"Any chills or fever?"

Bendler shook his head.

Opening Bendler's chart, JP checked the temp curve for the last forty-eight hours. It was within the normal range. He listened with the stethoscope over Bendler's chest. "Take deep breaths," he instructed. When he finished he told Bendler, 'Your lungs sound moist, raising the possibility of an early pneumonia."

"What does that mean?"

"It means you need a chest X-ray this morning and the pulmonary therapist will stop by and work on you for a few days."

"Not that chest pounding again."

"You got it, Colonel."

"I need a pass for Friday night. I have a date with a cute nurse."

"Talk to Captain Entarde."

"I did. He said I'm still at risk for complications and refused to give me the pass."

"Bruce, you're not even three weeks out from surgery and you're already easing back into the lifestyle that landed you here. You came within a millimeter of losing your entire larynx, and for the next five years you will be at risk of losing what remains and perhaps even your life."

"Colonel, I've lived on the edge most of my life."

"Well, it's time you pulled back. Your survival with cancer of the larynx has nothing to do with how well you fly a jet fighter or how many MiGs you downed. Your survival has everything to do with your lifestyle."

Bendler cocked his head towards JP. "I'm not sure I follow you, Doc."

JP pulled open the nightstand drawer. Reaching in, he removed an almost empty pack of cigarettes and a half full pint bottle of bourbon. He tossed the cigarettes on Bendler's lap, then went to the sink, poured out the bourbon and tossed the bottle into a waste basket. Bendler looked as if he were about to cry.

"You're playing Russian roulette, Bruce," JP said, trying to control his anger. "Three weeks ago in the OR the hammer fell on one of five empty chambers instead of the single loaded one. But the odds are changing. Stay in the game and you will end up playing with five loaded chambers and an empty one. If you survive that you can look forward to the day when all chambers are loaded."

"Where are we going with this, Doc?"

"For you it's either Doctor or Colonel, but definitely not Doc."

"Yes, sir," Bendler said with exaggerated deference.

"Bruce, there are a lot of miserable and painful ways to leave this world. I can assure you that cancer of the throat has got them all beaten. You can't breathe, you can't swallow, you can't shit because you can't strain, The cancer will erode the cervical spine and compress the spinal cord making you quadriplegic. The pain increases until it is intolerable. Mega doses of painkillers keep you knocked out most of the time until your lungs become infected and you die of pneumonia."

"Jesus, Colonel, you have a way of putting things."

"So it's been said. I'm trying to penetrate that thick fighter-pilot mentality of yours and warn you that your career in the US Air Force is in great jeopardy."

That caught Bendler's attention. "Hell, I have no career. I'm retired."

"My spies in the Pentagon tell me you are no more retired from the air force than I am from the army."

"Those bastards. What else did they tell you?"

"You are on the fast track for full colonel and possibly a star, despite, in my opinion, your lack of judgment and common sense."

"No kidding."

'You could blow it all very easily, Bruce. As it is the Air Force Surgeon General may decide to really retire you for medical reasons instead of that spurious retirement that allows you to work for Air America. Don't delude yourself, the recommendations of your doctors here at Reed will have considerable impact on the decision of the air force to keep you on active duty."

"That's a veiled threat if I've ever heard one."

"Take it any way you want. If you have any desire to stay on active duty I suggest you clean up your act. Give up the cigarettes, booze, and stop trying to live the mythical life of a hotshot fighter pilot. Find a lovely lady from Georgia, marry her and settle down to enjoy your retirement, assuming you live long enough to retire."

Colonel Bendler was quiet for a few seconds, then asked, "Will I be able to go on pass Friday?"

"Damn it, Bruce, you haven't heard a word I've said. Whether or not you go on pass will be up to Captain Entarde."

"But he's only a captain. I'm a lieutenant colonel. I don't take orders from a captain."

"The hell you don't. Captain Entarde is the medical officer in charge of this ward. You, Colonel Bendler, are his patient and subject to his orders. Leave this hospital without his permission and I'll nail your ass to the door."

"You threatening me, Doctor?"

JP glared at Bendler. "Test me and you'll learn how fast you will meet a medical evaluation board and find yourself a civilian."

"You son of a bitch. You really mean it."

"There is an easy way to find out if I'm bluffing."

Bendler muttered something under his breath.

"Speak up, Colonel. I can't hear you."

"I said it was just my luck to have an ex-jarhead for a doctor."

JP, suppressing a grin, turned and stormed out, slamming the door.

Sherry Barnhardt, pushing a medication cart down the hall, almost ran into him. "Problems, Colonel?" she asked.

"That idiot Bendler needs an ice cold enema."

Barnhardt laughed. "You write the order and I'll be happy to personally administer it."

"I'll bet you would," JP said, breaking into a smile. "Just send him down to X-ray for an AP and lateral chest. Have the pulmonary therapist pound on his chest with a sledge hammer b.i.d."

The pager on his belt beeped. Thelma's nasal voice pierced the quiet of the hallway. "Colonel, Dr. McClintock just walked in. He's in your office with a cup of coffee. He said to take your time."

★

Five minutes later JP walked into his office. Dr. Alfonse Joseph McClintock, M.D., F.A.C.S., Brigadier General, US Army Reserve, Professor and Chairman, Department of Head and Neck Surgery, Johns Hopkins School of Medicine, sat relaxed with a mug of coffee in his hand. JP greeted him cheerily. "Thanks for coming, Al. I know what a busy service you run at Hopkins."

"Alex is a fine young man. I'm pleased to help. How long before we start our part?"

"About an hour. Any problems parking?"

"None so far. I parked in your space in the quadrangle. What about you? Where did you park?"

"Kathy and Jim have the car today. I rode the shuttle bus from Forest Glen."

"You military people have so many bennies."

158

"Tell me about them." Easing into the swivel chair behind his desk, he leaned towards Dr. McClintock. "Didn't you tell me your fee for one operation on a private case was more than my monthly army pay?"

"That was to entice you to join me in private practice."

"I was tempted, especially after the promotion fiasco. Then my oldest kid insisted he wanted to go to Duke. His high school math teacher convinced him there were no other universities in the country if not the world. I told him there was no way I could afford the tuition at Duke without selling his brothers and sister."

McClintock chuckled. "Where did he finally decide to go?"

"Duke. He got an air force ROTC scholarship."

"I would have thought he'd go for army ROTC."

"He wants to be a pilot. He applied to all three services for a scholarship hoping to triple his chances. His army interview was by a captain who needed a haircut and asked questions requiring only one word answers, like yes or no. His navy interview was by three officers. When they learned he wanted to fly they asked, 'What do you want to do after you grow up?' The air force told him to be at Andrews at 0700 hours prepared to stay overnight. During the day he and other ROTC candidates went through physical exams and the usual administrative stuff. That night they were put up at the BOQ, squired by a bunch of young pilots who took them to the officers' club for supper. The next day they toured Andrews, went up in the control tower and down on the flightline. By the time I picked him up in the afternoon he had been so brainwashed by the air force that the other services ceased to exist."

McClintock laughed. "Well, the offer to join me in private practice will always be open. The chair at Hopkins is yours if you want it. I was pretty sure you would retire after your promotion was axed. Frankly I was appalled at the army's treatment of doctors who served their country as combat officers before going to medical school."

"You may have been appalled, I was pissed. But then I realized the incredible gift I had been given here at Reed, experience that came at tremendous cost to the country and its young men. As angry as I might be about my screwed up promotion I could not use it as justification to turn my back on wounded soldiers."

"I had you pegged in Korea," Dr. McClintock said. "You were a flaming idealist then and you haven't changed a bit."

"I was accused of the same offense by no less than a US District judge," JP said, remembering Ann Carter. "I have but one defense: the Marine Corps brainwashed me during my formative years."

"I'm convinced of that," McClintock said, chuckling. He studied JP quietly for over a minute. "Something has bothered me about you ever since Korea."

JP looked at him, curious.

"Would you mind if I asked a very personal question?"

"Ask away, my mentor and consultant."

"After you were wounded and brought to my MASH, your sergeant told the medics you deliberately placed yourself in full view of the Chinese when directing your platoon's fire. You ignored warnings to take cover even though bullets were hitting around you."

JP said nothing. It had been his hope to keep suppressed memories suppressed.

"Lucky for you the PLA were such poor marksmen that the best they could do was hit you in the leg. Several days after your surgery I asked you why you had placed yourself in such an exposed position. All I got was silence and a back to examine. It's been eighteen years since then, JP. Would you care to give me a more enlightening response?"

JP's gaze shifted to the black and white framed photographs of an M–19 and an M–16 on the wall. The M–19, a Chaffee tank fitted with twin 40 mm cannons, could pump out 240 rounds a minute, each round carrying a quarter pound of high explosive. The M–16, an armored half track mounting four 50 caliber machine guns on a turret, could fire 2,000 rounds a minute. In Korea JP's platoon had consisted of four of each. They were awesome weapons, loved by the infantry, feared and despised by the enemy.

JP shifted his gaze back to Dr. McClintock. "Al, do you have any idea of the devastation my platoon inflicted in Korea?"

"Indeed I do. Remember I was chief of surgery at a MASH. We treated Chinese and North Koreans as well as United Nations casualties. And I heard a lot of stories from patients about the Dusters and Quads."

JP spoke almost in a whisper. "I've shared this with only one other person – Kathy." He hesitated.

McClintock took a sip of coffee and waited patiently.

"One day we fired into a village where a company of North Koreans had decided to make a stand. Later we reconned the village to count the dead and look for the wounded. There were bodies and parts of bodies everywhere. One of my squad leaders asked me how to estimate the number of enemy KIA. I told him to count the arms and legs and divide by four. At the time I considered my response witty if not precise."

"Good God."

"That night I couldn't sleep. I thought it was just anxiety over the next day's mission. I gradually realized I felt no remorse over what I had done that morning. I felt no compassion for the enemy. In fact, I felt nothing at all. I was feeling guilty at feeling no guilt. The next couple of days were so intense with fire missions I reached a point where, for a brief moment, I just didn't care any more. I was sick of war, the impersonal killing, the waste of life on both sides. I had felt the same thing in World War II, but never to the point of recklessness. It was as if I dared the Chinese to kill me. I didn't think they would take me seriously.

"That brief lapse almost cost me my leg, not to mention my life. My platoon sergeant risked his life to drag me to cover. In the hospital I had plenty of time to think. By acting so irresponsibly I had put my platoon and our mission in jeopardy. My stupid behavior could have cost US lives and would have if it hadn't been for my platoon sergeant. Who knows what impact it could have had on the battle. When you asked why I put myself at such risk I was so overwhelmed with guilt I was too ashamed to answer."

Dr. McClintock remained silent for a while, studying his protégé. "What a blessing you turned to medicine."

"I have you and Kristy Goulden to thank."

"Odd that you mentioned Kristy," McClintock said. "I received a letter from her yesterday."

"How is she, Al?" JP asked almost too quickly.

Dr. McClintock's look left little doubt as to its meaning.

JP met McClintock's look straight on. He and Kristy, an army nurse, had been good friends in Korea and nothing more. Kristy saved his life when he nearly died of dysentery and medical incompetence. Later, she and Dr. McClintock oriented him towards medicine.

JP's eyes went to his uniform blouse hanging on a clothes tree in the corner, focusing on two shiny Medical Corps caduceus pinned to its lapels. First Lieutenant Kristy Goulden had given him the insignia in Korea. The accompanying note had read: "One day these will replace the crossed cannons you now wear."

Dr. McClintock continued, "Kristy is a light colonel now, chief nurse at the Seventy-First Surg at Pleiku. She's finishing her second tour and has extended a year."

"But why is she spending so much time in Vietnam? I thought she was married."

"She is, or was. Her husband was an air force fighter pilot shot down in '68. The word is that he's being held in a POW camp near the Laotian border. Kristy doesn't want to leave Vietnam as long as her husband is a POW and stands a chance of being rescued."

JP's thoughts went back nearly twenty years. "Kristy Goulden is about the most dedicated nurse I have ever met," he said with conviction. "She is the gold standard for a military nurse."

"I agree. She is a remarkable woman; she certainly deserves better."

JP noted Dr. McClintock's empty coffee mug. "Can I get you a refill?"

"No thanks, not with three to four hours of surgery coming up. Have you made a decision about doing a tracheotomy?"

"It wasn't much of a decision. The frag that wiped out Alex's cervical trachea wiped out both recurrent laryngeal nerves. Both vocal cords are paralyzed in the midline. There's hardly any space between them for air to pass. He couldn't breathe without a trach. I talked with Jeff Pease at UCLA and Irv Goldblatt at Sinai. Both agreed a trach is essential."

"I came to the same conclusion," McClintock said.

"I considered a cord displacement operation or even a cordectomy to improve the airway done with the tracheal reconstruction, but decided against either because of the repeated infections. We can always come back later."

"That's reasonable."

JP reached for the phone. After talking briefly with a nurse he hung up. "About forty minutes until the chest surgeons finish, time enough for you see a patient on the neurosurgical ward."

"Let's do it," Dr. McClintock said, standing up.

★

JP stopped Dr. McClintock outside the neurosurgical ward. "Let me review his history for you."

McClintock nodded.

"Gene Tofler is eighteen. He was a rifleman in Vietnam who became quadriplegic after his PC was blown up by a remote detonated mine. X-rays demonstrated multiple fractures of the third, fourth, and fifth cervical vertebrae. He was to undergo laminectomy and fusion in Japan when he began spiking a high fever. Initially it was thought due to malaria. Finally, the radiologist described changes consistent with deep neck infection and osteo of the cervical spine. That's when they decided to send him here.

"The day after he was admitted his temp went to 105. A white count was markedly elevated, about 38,000. A spinal tap was cloudy, with 500 white cells and a sugar of twenty. X-rays of the C-spine showed early demineralization of the fractured vertebrae."

"What organisms grew out of the spinal fluid?"

"Staph aureus, pseudomonas, and strep; all very bad actors. Anaerobic cultures are pending. We were asked to evaluate Gene for management of possible gut laceration and neck infection. We recommended exploration, insertion of catheters for intermittent irrigation with antibiotic fluids, and biopsy of the vertebrae for culture and microscopic exam."

"Sounds reasonable. Let's take a look at him."

JP placed his hand on McClintock's shoulder. "Al, this kid was the class valedictorian of his high school. He was a merit scholar and in Who's Who among high school seniors. He turned down a physics scholarship at MIT to enlist."

Dr. McClintock winced. "I wish you hadn't told me."

They entered the neurosurgical ward. A dozen metal beds lined each side of the ward. Young men lounged in blue and maroon pajamas, some with clean-shaven heads, others with turban-like dressings. A few wore football helmets. Three Stryker frames, body-length metal frames, were arranged at the center of the ward near the nursing station. Each held a paralyzed patient, his spinal cord shattered. It occurred to JP that but for the grace of God he could have been made quadriplegic by a bullet from a Japanese, North Korean, or Chinese rifle. But God had seen fit not to withdraw his grace from him. Why then did God withdraw his grace from Gene Tofler?

JP stopped at the first Stryker frame. Gene Tofler lay on his back strapped to the stretched canvas. Imbedded in his skull was a stainless steel apparatus resembling ice tongs. A rope ran from the tongs to the head of the bed, then over a pulley to hang attached to weights. A double hose connected a tracheotomy tube to a mechanical respirator. Unable to breathe without the respirator, move or even talk, Gene Tofler could only blink his eyes and mouth soundless words with his lips.

JP greeted the young man cheerfully. "Gene, I'd like you to meet Dr. McClintock, chief of head and neck surgery at Johns Hopkins and one of our consultants. He's here to take a look at you."

The eyes blinked several times ad the mouth soundlessly formed the word "Hi".

162

Al McClintock opened a packet of sterile gloves. Slipping his hands into the gloves, he warned the patient, "I'm going to push on your neck a bit."

The eighteen-year-old blinked his assent.

McClintock ran his fingers over Tofler's neck, probing, pushing, and exploring. "There's no erythema except along the surgical scars and the trach," he told JP. Pressing down hard on the skin with one finger for a moment, he quickly withdrew. A deep imprint of his finger remained. "About two plus pitting edema, suggestive but not diagnostic of abscess." Pulling off his gloves, he tossed them into a metal bucket and reached for the patient's chart. After studying the progress notes, X-ray reports, and lab slips, he snapped the chart closed and looked at JP. "I agree. Neck exploration and vertebral biopsy is indicated. I'd suggest a gastrostomy for feeding."

"Would you write that on the chart?"

McClintock reached into his shirt pocket, took out a pen and began writing.

JP's pager beeped. A feminine voice said, "This is Major Fenelli in the OR. The chest surgeons will be through in fifteen minutes."

"Were up," JP said.

McClintock finished his note, closed the chart and laid it on the bed stand. He gently touched Tofler's shoulder. "Good luck, Gene."

The eyes blinked and the lips formed the soundless words "Thanks, sir".

Chapter Eighteen

Thursday, January 8, 1970, 1130 hours
Operating Suite, Walter Reed Army Hospital, Washington D.C.

Lieutenant Colonel JP Franklin and Dr. Alfonse McClintock, dressed in green OR shirts, trousers, caps, and masks, stood at adjacent sinks outside OR No.6 scrubbing up. By the time they neared the end of the ten-minute ritual JP had become so quiet that Dr. McClintock asked, "Are you all right?"

"Yes, sir. I was thinking of what Gene Tofler and Alex Leichuk have ahead of them."

"At least Alex has a reasonably good chance for rehabilitation, but it's unlikely he'll make it back to duty. The future for Gene is grim. If he survives this and subsequent infections he has years in a VA hospital ahead. With the C-spine injured as high as it is and all his respiratory muscles paralyzed, it's doubtful he will ever be free of a respirator."

"My closest buddy in the Marine Corps was hit in the neck by a shell frag on Iwo Jima. He was made quadriplegic and died of meningitis a month after he was wounded. I visit his grave near Gallup every couple of years. He wanted to be a doctor. I often wonder if I'm as good a doctor as he would have been."

"You carry a heavy load from two wars, JP. I understand you go out to Arlington National Cemetery once a month to visit some graves."

"Yes, sir. One of them is my platoon sergeant from Korea, Andy Andreson. He saved my life. The other is George Barfield. He was the assistant chief of neuro here before going to Vietnam." JP lapsed into a moody silence, then suddenly said, "I hope this war is worth the price the country is paying."

"I have my doubts," Dr. McClintock said. "You have been in two wars. You were an intelligence officer before going to medical school. Those experiences should give you some insight. What is your understanding of our objective in South-east Asia?"

JP shrugged. "Keep the Communists from taking over South Vietnam."

"That's an end result, not a military objective. Let's try a different approach. If you were the chief of staff what would be your recommendation to the President for a victory in Vietnam?"

"Mine and blockade the east coast of North Vietnam. Bomb all meaningful targets, and cut the Ho Chi Minh trail. Then make an Inchon-like amphibious landing in North Vietnam. At the same time launch an attack from the south."

"Precisely, but that will never happen. The North Vietnamese, Chinese, and Soviets know it will never happen. And that, my young friend, is the crux of our Vietnam problem. North Vietnam can never be defeated in South Vietnam, no more than Nazi Germany could have been defeated in France."

"And that, my older friend," JP said, "is precisely one of the reasons I must to go to Vietnam. I must see for myself what we are doing there."

"Don't you have faith in our news media?"

"Give me a break, Al."

JP rinsed his hands and arms, then turned off the water with his knee. Holding his forearms up, he paused to let water drain from his elbows. "Time to go to work," he said, heading for the OR door. Turning to face out, he pushed the OR door open with his rear and held it open for Dr. McClintock, then followed him into the OR. The instrument nurse, Carol Barnes, moved quickly to drape sterile towels over their hands.

At the operating table Colonel William Henshaw, Chief of Thoracic Surgery, his hawk-like face hidden behind mask and glasses, glanced up from the partially closed twelve-inch incision on Leichuk's right chest. "Heads up, people," he said, "the relief team has arrived."

JP stood quietly, observing as the last few stitches were placed and tied down. "Bill, this is Dr. McClintock, my consultant from Hopkins."

"Glad to have you with us, sir," Colonel Henshaw said. He introduced the OR team. "My chief resident, Arlen Ritchie; I believe you know Craig Entarde. Lieutenant Barnes is scrub, Captain Tebaldi is circulating, and our anesthesiologist is the malignant and perpetually hostile Major Harry Resniek, who was so superbly trained at your institution."

Resniek looked up from behind his anesthesia screen. "Malignant? No. Hostile? No. Witty? Yes. Insightful? Yes. Hello, Al." His head bobbed down behind the screen.

Dr. McClintock acknowledged each person with a smile behind his mask and a nod. While he and JP gowned and gloved, Colonel Henshaw watched the two residents put in a chest tube, then he stepped away from the OR table and turned to JP. "Sorry our part went so slowly. There was more scar tissue in the thoracic inlet than we anticipated. We even ran into several unexpected pockets of pus. It made for very slow dissection."

Returning to the OR table, Colonel Henshaw held out his hand. "Babcock." Carol Barnes plopped an eight-inch-long smooth-jawed clamp into his palm. Opening the clamp, he gently grasped the upper edge of the trachea, now an inch and a half above the top of the breast bone. A plastic anesthesia tube exited from the trachea to disappear under the drapes. "This is all the trachea we could get out of the chest, and we fought scar tissue all the way to get it. I hope it will be enough."

JP studied Leichuk's neck. An inch gap remained between the top of the windpipe and the lower end of the Adam's apple. Ordinarily that much of a gap could be easily closed by severing the larynx from its muscle and tendinous attachments, then bringing it down in the neck trailing its arteries, veins and nerves. But Leichuk's neck had been subjected to massive trauma, surgery, and repeated infections. The remaining blood vessels and nerves were embedded in tough scar tissue. It was essential they be exposed and protected before the larynx could be mobilized.

"What do you think?" Colonel Henshaw asked.

"I don't know, Bill. The neck is socked in with scar."

"That's what we found in the thoracic inlet."

JP turned to Dr. McClintock. "Any words of wisdom, sir?"

"I agree on the importance of preserving the blood vessels to the larynx, especially the arteries. Losing one would put survival of the larynx in jeopardy. Losing both will probably result in necrosis of the larynx and an infected life-threatening mess making laryngectomy mandatory. We had a case like that at Hopkins last month." Dr. McClintock moved closer to the table. "Having heard my encouraging remarks, Dr. Franklin, how do you plan to go about isolating the superior laryngeal vessels and nerves in the mass of scar tissue without injuring them?"

JP smiled. McClintock was ever the professor and teacher, and JP would always be his pupil. "Well, sir, the situation is not unlike an infantry patrol that runs into a roadblock."

"Oh no. Here we go again," Craig Entarde groaned.

JP continued as though he hadn't heard. "A direct attack can be made on the roadblock. That is a hazardous and often costly reaction. Its equivalent in this case would be to attack the scar tissue directly with a knife, hoping to see the critical blood vessels before cutting them. I would prefer a more subtle flanking maneuver."

Dr. McClintock frowned. "JP, sometimes you make me wonder if allowing former combat officers into medical school is a good idea."

JP's grin behind his mask went unseen, but the grin was reflected in his eyes and was hard to miss. He went on. "The flanking maneuver, in this case, would be identification of the external carotid artery in an area of normal tissue. It should be easy to locate because of its large size and pulsations. It will be dissected up to its first branch, the superior thyroid artery. That will be traced to the superior laryngeal branch which will be followed into the larynx. Using this technique the critical vessels will always be in view as the dissection proceeds through scar tissue, going from the known to the unknown."

"That makes good sense," Dr. McClintock said, "but you certainly were circumspect."

Colonel Henshaw interrupted. "Before I leave, gentlemen, I want to make one plea. Please don't try to pull any more trachea out of the chest. What you see is what you get. Any traction on the trachea could tear loose the sutures holding it up in the neck. If that happens the trachea will fall back into the chest."

JP nodded understanding.

"I'd like to leave Arlen scrubbed in for any problems that might develop in the chest."

"Happy to have him," JP said.

Stepping away from the table, Colonel Henshaw pulled his gown off over his gloves, then stripped off his gloves. Accepting Leichuk's chart from Harry Resniek, he pushed a sitting stool against the wall, sat down and began writing on the chart. JP moved to the operating table to stand by Leichuk's neck on the right with Arlen Ritchie by his side. Dr. McClintock and Craig Entarde stood facing them on the left side of the neck.

The scrub nurse passed a scalpel to JP. "Starting to cut," he told the anesthesiologist, then he made a five-inch horizontal incision just above the prominence of the Adam's apple. Craig Entarde and Arlen Ritchie quickly applied sharp-pointed hemostats on bleeders, then touched the electrocautery blade to the hemostats. JP then made a similar incision three inches below the first. Using a new scalpel, he began undermining the skin. A minute later he tossed the scalpel into a kidney basin and held out his hand. "Fresh blade." After twenty minutes he was on his sixth scalpel blade, still mobilizing flaps. "The army must be buying all the civilian blade rejects," he said. "The sub-Q tissue cuts like leather." He slammed the scalpel into a steel kidney basin. It hit with a *clang*. He held out his hand. "Knife."

Finally, the skin flaps were mobilized. Attaching double skin hooks to the edges of the flaps, JP angled the handles to Arlen Ritchie and Craig Entarde. They retracted the flaps to expose the region of the external carotid artery. "Now the real operation begins," he said, holding out his hand. "Metz and thumb forceps."

"You picked the most difficult side to dissect," Dr. McClintock observed. "It has the most scar tissue."

"I thrive on challenges. Besides, I decided to give the easier side to you in deference to your status as revered professor." After a pause he added, "Age was also a consideration."

Carol Barnes slapped long dull-pointed scissors into JP's hand, then followed with long, delicate forceps. JP quickly located the external carotid artery. Not only could he feel it beating, he could see the transmitted pulsations. Exposing the surface of the artery, he rapidly dissected upward to the first and second branches, then followed the latter until it disappeared into dense scar tissue above the larynx. The speed of his dissection now diminished dramatically. By the time he exposed the superior laryngeal artery he was progressing at an agonizingly one to two millimeters with each snip of the scissors. A tear of the artery from overzealous traction or misdirected cut would immediately end the operation. Heat from the huge overhead operating light rivaled the sun. Sweat, accumulating on his forehead, threatened to drip into the open neck. Captain Tebaldi came to the rescue and wiped his brow.

"Thanks, Clarice," he said. "If I move any slower I'll be going backwards."

"I don't believe I have ever seen you operate so slowly," Dr. McClintock remarked drolly.

"My reputation as the fastest knife east of the Mississippi has been tarnished."

At last the right superior laryngeal artery lay pulsating, exposed from its take-off from the superior thyroid artery to its entrance into the larynx. Lying beside it was the corresponding vein and nerve. JP stepped back. "Just like in the anatomy books," he said, passing the scissors and pickups to Dr. McClintock. "Your turn, professor."

Watching Dr. McClintock operate on the left neck, JP marveled at the man's great skill and confidence. He wondered if he would ever be as good a surgeon. Sensing a presence behind him, he turned to see a tall young man in an oversized scrub suit, eyes above the mask wide with curiosity.

"We have a visitor," JP announced.

"I'm Second Lieutenant Mark Crespin, a fourth year medical student from Maryland. The chief of anesthesia said I could observe in here."

"He did, did he? Are you in the army scholarship program?"

"No, sir, air force."

"Bad answer, lieutenant." JP looked up. "Gentlemen, shall we allow this officer from an adversarial service to observe the army's superb surgical techniques?"

"You'd better," Dr. McClintock advised. "Your son will be an air force pilot one of these days. It is conceivable that Lieutenant Crespin could end up as his flight surgeon."

"Lieutenant Crespin," JP said, "Dr. McClintock has just made a compelling argument on your behalf. You may stay but only if you come closer for a better view."

Crespin pushed a footstool towards the operating table, then climbed on it to look over JP' shoulder.

"Nineteen years ago in Korea," JP continued, "a callow and medically ignorant artillery lieutenant was given the opportunity to observe one of our country's great surgeons operate on the neck of a wounded helicopter pilot. Today that lieutenant and that surgeon stand before you in this very room."

McClintock stopped operating and looked over his glasses. "JP, you're overdoing it."

"Yes, sir," JP said sheepishly. After introducing the operating team to Crespin he asked Craig Entarde to review Leichuk's history. When Entarde finished, JP turned to Crespin. "Well, lieutenant, now you know everything we know."

"I don't think so, sir. I'm still not sure what you're trying to do."

JP picked up the trachea in the lower neck with thumb forceps. "We hope to connect this windpipe…" he grasped the lower margin of the Adam's apple, "to the larynx here."

Crespin looked puzzled.

"You're not happy with that answer, Lieutenant?"

"No, sir. Captain Entarde said both vocal cords were paralyzed in the midline and the patient would need a tracheotomy. What's the point of this surgery to reconnect his airway if he is going to need a tracheotomy anyway? That's no improvement over what he had before you operated."

"A very penetrating question," Craig Entarde said. "The young man shows unusual intelligence for someone in the air force. To answer your question, Mark, as things stood before surgery the larynx was a useless appendage. However, once connected to the trachea several things become possible, all of them good. An almost immediate result will be the ability to inspire through the tracheotomy, plug the tracheotomy hole with a finger, and expire, forcing air up through the larynx. It is true that the vocal cords are paralyzed, but fortunately they are paralyzed in the midline, which is the optimum position for voice production. Unfortunately, it is also the worst position for breathing. If this operation succeeds, Captain Leichuk will have his voice back, something he doesn't have now. In the distant future, usually a year to eighteen months, the vocal cords can be surgically moved apart. While this reduces the quality of the voice by increasing air leak on phonation, it can enlarge the airway sufficiently to dispense with the tracheotomy. However, there can be an undesirable side effect. Care to guess what it might be?"

Crespin didn't hesitate. "Yes, sir. If the vocal cords are moved too far apart his voice may become so breathy it won't be understood. Also that wide an opening could increase the risk of food and liquid entering the airway making him susceptible to pneumonia."

JP was impressed. "This young man is definitely AOA material."

Craig Entarde agreed. "He's much smarter than he looks, and most deserving of reward, say pizza at Luigi's tonight after rounds."

While Craig Entarde had been talking Dr. McClintock completed the exteriorization of the vessels and nerves on the left. He passed the scissors and forceps back to JP. "Now for the moment of truth."

JP dropped the instruments in a kidney basin, then held out his hand. "Allis please." Carol Barnes passed him a toothed clamp which he secured to the lower edge of larynx. "Another." After placing the second clamp an inch from the first he swung the handles to Dr. McClintock, who grasped both and gently pulled downward. JP held out his hand again. "Knife." Carol Barnes slapped a scalpel into his hand with such force he winced. "Did I say something wrong, Carol?"

"I'm sorry, sir. Alex was my husband's roommate at West Point. I'm just up tight, that's all.'

JP searched her masked face. "It's okay if you drop out, Carol."

"No. I want to stay, sir."

JP nodded, then returned to the neck. Using the scalpel, he rapidly severed the strap muscles attached to the outside of the larynx.

"It's loose," Dr. McClintock said encouragingly.

Using skin hooks, JP brought the lower margin of the larynx down to within three millimeters of the trachea. Even with strong downward traction it would move no further.

"So close and yet so far," Dr. McClintock said.

"I'm tempted to pull up on the trachea to get another silly three millimeters," JP said.

"I hope you won't do that, Colonel," Arlen Ritchie immediately responded.

"Just kidding," JP said. He tested the mobility of the larynx by moving it sideways and up and down, then looked at Dr. McClintock. "It's held up by the inferior constrictor muscles. What do you think of sectioning the muscle?"

"It may alter his swallowing, but there seems no other option. Don't be overly aggressive. You could end up with the entire larynx in your hand as a free graft."

"We wouldn't want that," JP said, rotating the larynx away from himself and bringing the constrictor muscles on the right into view. He carefully sliced through its fibers until the smooth outer lining of the gullet became visible, then passed the knife to Dr. McClintock who repeated the dissection on the left. As the last muscle fibers were severed the larynx became mobile and was brought down easily to lie against the upper ring of the trachea.

"We have the field in sight," JP said. "Flaps twenty, gear down."

Thirty minutes later the larynx was securely joined to the trachea. JP critically inspected the anastamosis. "Perfect," he declared, "just perfect."

Dr. McClintock addressed the medical student. "Lieutenant Crespin."

"Yes, sir."

"It may be germane to your career as a medical officer in the United States Air Force to note that the ego of the military aviator is exceeded only by the ego of the military surgeon."

JP looked at Crespin. "Lieutenant, have you given much thought to the track you will pursue after internship?"

"Yes, sir. I want to enter a head and neck surgery residency."

"Good answer."

"Lieutenant Crespin demonstrates excellent judgment," Craig Entarde said. "Perhaps we should allow him to order pepperoni and sausage on his pizza."

JP examined the pulsating blood vessels to the larynx. Everything looks good. No thromboses. Even the veins are working, Let's move on to the tracheotomy. Craig, you and Arlen do the trach. Put it as high as possible without getting into the anastamosis. Keep up a running commentary so Lieutenant Crespin and the rest of us can figure what you're trying to do. Dr. McClintock and I will endeavor to assist."

★

Fifty minutes later JP and Dr. McClintock finished changing in the doctors' dressing room. "I feel pretty good about this case," JP told McClintock. "I think we did Alex some good."

"The next three weeks will be the most critical."

"We'll be watching him like hawks, Al. Thanks very much for all your help."

"You did the hardest part."

JP eased down on a wooden bench and stretched his legs while waiting for McClintock to finish tying his shoes. "I just had an interesting thought, Al."

"Care to share it?"

"Today five skillful surgeons worked almost eight hours to repair terrible damage inflicted on a gifted human being in less than a second by a uneducated peasant firing a simple rocket-propelled grenade."

"Best not to dwell on that," McClintock said quietly as he stood up. "It will have you going around in circles." He touched JP's arm. "Come, my friend. Walk me down to your parking space. If my car hasn't been towed away by the MPs I'll know you carry some weight around this place."

170

Chapter Nineteen

Friday, January 30, 1970, 1740 hours
Washington D.C.

The evening traffic southbound on Massachusetts Avenue was packed bumper to bumper and moving with irritating slowness. Trapped in the right lane, Lieutenant Colonel JP Franklin fumed at the snail's pace and his van's inclination to stall at slow speeds. He turned to his wife. "Doesn't anyone in this town work past five o'clock?"

"Maybe all these folks are going to the reception at the German Embassy."

"Let's hope not."

"I'm glad we're going," Kathy said. "I get to show off the dress I bought on sale last week at Woody's."

"Well, I'm not glad. I hate wearing dress blues. Embassy receptions are stuffy and boring."

"Then why are we going to this one?"

"Because Gunther Dietler arranged the invitation. He's such a nice guy I couldn't say no."

"The Dietlers are very grateful to you for saving Heidi's life."

"Any superbly skilled surgeon could have done as much."

Kathy studied her husband's face in the fading light. "JP, did anyone ever tell you that you are full of yourself?"

"You're the first," he said, grinning.

The traffic in the lane on JP's left began to speed up. In the driver's side mirror he spotted an approaching gap several cars long. "A window of opportunity approaches," he told Kathy. As the opening came abreast he jammed the accelerator down and jerked the van into the left lane, barely missing the rear of the car he was following. His speed was rapidly increasing when the tail lights ahead suddenly flashed red and the car abruptly stopped. JP slammed on the brakes. The van skidded to a stop inches from the rear bumper of the car ahead. The van's underpowered air-cooled engine stalled.

"Idiot," JP fumed.

"Him or you?" Kathy asked, laughing.

"Him, of course. Whose side are you on anyway?"

Ignoring the angry horns blowing behind him, JP cranked the engine, let it idle a few seconds, gunned it several times, then shifted into drive. The van lurched forward. "I hate driving in D.C.," he said. "In fact, I hate D.C. When I was a lieutenant with the Nineteenth Group at Meade my buddies and I calculated that the Soviets, if they decided to nuke D.C., would do it at rush hour on a Friday. Our CO convinced us the Soviets would never be so stupid as to nuke Washington and end the confusion."

The right lane was now moving faster than the left, so JP eased the van back into it. "I'll be glad for tomorrow."

"What happens tomorrow?"

"In the afternoon I'll be at 6,000 feet in clean fresh air somewhere over beautiful Virginia. I have a T–34 scheduled from two until dark."

"You be careful up there," Kathy warned, wishing he hadn't picked a day to fly when air traffic in the D.C. area was probably the most dense of the week. Minutes later she asked, "How was Alex Leichuk today?"

JP hesitated, reluctant to share his concern and dampening Kathy's one evening out in three weeks. Yet she deserved to know, inasmuch as she looked on Leichuk almost as another son, "Up until yesterday he was doing so well we discontinued his antibiotics. At about two this morning he spiked a fever to 104. Craig and Arlen went over him thoroughly. All they found were increased secretions with a musty odor around his tracheotomy. They made gram stains and cultures of the secretions, drew blood cultures, ordered a white count, neck and chest X-rays, and had the ID fellow check him. The X-rays were negative; the white count was elevated. He was started on mega doses of IV antibiotics and local irrigations. As a precaution he was moved to the ICU. Bill Henshaw and I went over him this morning and again before I left tonight without finding much significant. His white count and temp dropped to near normal. Arlen and Terry will spend the night in the hospital. They'll call if anything comes up."

JP flashed the van's indicator light for a right turn, then turned into a wide street lined by impressive mansions, some set on grounds large enough to be considered estates. Most were surrounded by eight-foot-high wrought iron fences. Shiny brass plates fixed to gates and sides of main entrances identified the buildings as embassies. Foreign flags hung limp from poles jutting out over entrances or extending from second and third floor windows.

"Embassy row," JP announced. Slowing the van, he scrutinized buildings on both sides of the street.

"Are you sure you know how to get to the German Embassy?"

"Trust me, woman; it's around here somewhere. At least it was in the winter and spring of 1950."

Kathy flashed a curious look at her husband. "That was before we were married," she said. "You were stationed at Meade and supposedly planning the D.C.–Baltimore air defense. Why would you know about the German Embassy back then?"

JP tried to be nonchalant. "It was just part of our planning. We were going to emplace forties and Quads on the roofs of government buildings. The beaten zone had to be predicted since they might impact sensitive properties such as foreign embassies. We worked mostly from maps and aerial photographs, but made ground recons to check out our plans."

"That sounds plausible," Kathy said, somewhat skeptically. "Actually it sounds too plausible."

JP looked sheepish. "Your problem is that you have too much of your dad in you." Kathy's father, a three-star general, recently retired as head of the Defense Intelligence

172

Agency.

"Well?"

"Well what, Kath?"

"I don't buy that tactical stuff. I want to know the real reason you're so familiar with the embassies."

"You would have made it big in the Gestapo," JP said. "Remember, this was before we were married."

'Unless my memory fails me, you and I were engaged during that period."

"Okay. What I told you about ammo fallout was the largest part of how I came to know the embassy locations. A small, miniscule, very insignificant part was an activity in which single second lieutenants engaged."

"And what, pray tell, was that activity?"

"It was all very innocent. Well, not quite innocent; maybe contrived would be more accurate."

"I'm listening."

"In the evenings we bachelor second lieutenants would put on dress uniforms, drive to D.C. and see how many embassy parties we could crash in one evening. For the price of the gasoline to make the round trip from Meade we could gorge ourselves on food and drink."

"You mean you just walked into the embassies without invitations?"

"Exactly," JP said smugly. "Bachelor second lieutenants and ensigns were in great demand."

Kathy eyed her husband. "In great demand by whom?"

"Ah, well… by single ladies, such as embassy personnel, daughters of embassy personnel, and even female foreign agents who thought they might pump us for meaningful intelligence while we tried to do the same to them."

"And how far did this quest for intelligence go?"

"Not very far. After all, what would a second lieutenant know that an enemy agent would want to know. The quest for intelligence never went as far as the bedroom, if that was your implication."

"That was precisely my implication."

"You need not worry. We were well instructed how to deal with those kinds of situations if they had threatened."

"Really. Tell me about it."

"We were told to act very drunk and sick. If that didn't work we were to stick out fingers down our throats to induce vomiting."

Kathy burst out laughing.

"Did I say something funny?"

"It's the image of you trying to throw up to keep from being seduced by a sultry female spy."

"It would have been all for my country."

"I think that would have been carrying patriotism a bit too far," Kathy said. "Tell me, James, did you ever pick up any meaningful intelligence at any of the embassies?"

"Not really. The people I talked to were pros at that kind of stuff. They never let anything slip except by intent."

As they drove down embassy row Kathy studied the opulent buildings and estates. "Some of these embassies belong to very poor Third World countries. How can their governments afford them?"

"My guess would be the generous largess heaped on those governments by our benevolent State Department in the guise of foreign aid pays for most of them. That and a little old-fashioned corruption."

JP slowed the van. "Keep an eye out. The embassy is somewhere around here on a hill with lots of trees and a long driveway."

"You're sure we're not going to crash the German Embassy tonight without an invitation?"

"Of course not, honey. We were sent an engraved invitation. I just happened to have misplaced it. But Gunther will be our escort. His wife can't come because Heidi is down with the flu."

A moment later Kathy pointed across the street. "Is that it?"

JP slammed on the brakes, again stalling the van's engine. "Good eye, woman." Cranking the engine he let it idle, then backed up. While waiting for traffic to pass they saw three chauffeur-driven black limousines approach from the opposite direction and turn into the driveway. The luxurious limousines were in marked contrast to the box-shaped white and red Greenbrier van. When no more traffic threatened JP turned the van left, crossed the street and passed through the embassy gates. As the van slowly climbed the driveway JP and Kathy studied the line of expensive cars parked against the curb, many still with chauffeurs.

"If we go up to the front entrance in this bread truck we'll be asked to park around back near the delivery entrance," a worried Kathy predicted.

"That's really astute, Kath. Find us a parking place before we get there."

Kathy nudged her husband. "There's a place between those two cars," she said, pointing.

JP eyed a gap between a white Lincoln Continental and a black Cadillac. "I think I can get this beast in there," he said confidently. Stopping the van parallel to the Lincoln Continental, he began backing into the space behind.

Kathy, admiring the Lincoln, sighed. "JP, can we have a real car some day?"

"Sure honey. After I go into private practice we'll have two cars, a white Lincoln Continental rag top for you, a red Thunderbird for me, and a red and white Cessna 310 for both of us."

"By that time we'll be too old to drive and you won't be able to pass the FAA flight physical."

The squeal of rubber scraping against the curb preceded an abrupt stop. JP shifted to forward. "That curved sidewalk and the dark is throwing off my judgment."

"Would you like me to park?"

"Have faith, woman." After three attempts JP finally jockeyed the van into the space, twice nudging the black Cadillac.

"That was masterful," Kathy said. "I wonder how much a new tire will cost?"

"Give me a break. The tire just took a little scuffing."

Setting the parking brake, JP reached out to the back seat, grabbed his dress blue uniform blouse and stepped to the ground. As he walked around the van's front to the passenger door he buttoned the blouse. Opening the door, he helped Kathy to the sidewalk. Her simple close-fitting black dress clung to her slender figure. He marveled at the physical attractiveness of his wife. Over the years his John Wayne imitation had improved, but the words remained the same as on their first date. "Miss Kathleen, you sure are a handsome woman."

Kathy responded as she always had, with an exaggerated southern accent. "Why, Culnel Franklin, you do cut a trim figure yourself." She gripped his arm. They walked up the driveway to the embassy entrance. "I see you're wearing your ribbons tonight," she said.

"You noticed." JP ordinarily disdained wearing ribbons or decorations on his uniform.

"Is there a reason?"

"I thought I'd dazzle the common folk tonight, most of whom think military doctors have done nothing more exciting than go to medical school."

"I thought medical school was pretty exciting."

JP smiled wanly. "It doesn't hold a candle to getting shot at, much less getting hit." Reaching under his blouse, he pulled a pager off his belt. "Would you carry this in your purse? Under my blouse it makes a bulge that gives the impression I'm carrying a weapon."

"Sure" Kathy said, opening her small purse. Slipping the pager on top of the purse's contents she snapped it closed.

Two men in dark suits greeted them at the embassy entrance. They spoke English without a trace of accent. JP identified himself and Kathy. "We're to meet Colonel Dietler. Has he arrived?"

"No, sir. Colonel Dietler phoned from Pope Air Force Base in North Carolina. He is temporarily delayed… some mechanical problems with his aircraft," one of the men explained. "He should be here within the hour. If we can be of any assistance, please call on us."

JP thanked the men. He and Kathy moved through an extensive foyer to a huge high-ceilinged room continuous with a second elongated room. Both rooms were flooded with people. The din of many conversations, in many accents and strange languages, filled the air. Foreign military officers in formal dress, even kilts, men in dark suits or tuxedos, and ladies in formal and semi-formal dresses, stood in clusters talking. Most men, officers included, held drinks in one hand, the other jammed into trouser pockets despite their formal military attire. Women sipped wine delicately from long-stemmed glasses.

JP whispered, "Okay, Kath, we've put in an appearance. Let's go home."

Kathy squeezed his arm. "Behave yourself, JP."

A waiter carrying an empty tray approached. "Sir, would you care to order drinks?"

"Cokes for both of us, please."

They watched the waiter disappear.

"Let's infiltrate the masses," JP suggested. "Maybe we'll see someone we know."

They moved through groups of isolated conversations, scrutinizing faces and uniforms without recognizing anyone. After several minutes JP focused on a short, heavy-set officer in a dark brown uniform, red flashes on his blouse lapels, his left chest smothered with ribbons. The officer's round face wore a scowl as he stood alone nursing a drink. JP, unable to identify the man's uniform, told Kathy, "Let's find out where he's from; it's probably a poor Third World country."

"I'll bet he's homesick and lonely," Kathy said. "Maybe we can make him feel welcome."

The officer, seeing JP and Kathy approach, smiled a greeting.

"Excuse me, sir, I'm Colonel Franklin; this is Mrs. Franklin. We were unable to identify your uniform or the country you represent."

The officer studied JP's face as if to memorize it. He spoke with a heavy Slavic accent. "I wear uniform of Soviet Army. I am Colonel Andrei Illyanovsky, Soviet Military Attaché." He extended his hand.

When JP grasped it he felt his own crushed. He grimaced and tried to squeeze back.

Kathy suppressed a giggle. Her warrior husband had failed to recognize the uniform of his most probable adversary. Illyanovsky took Kathy's hand. At that moment the waiter brought their cokes.

"You drink soda; you don't like Russian vodka?" Illyanovsky said scornfully.

"I don't believe we've ever had any Russian vodka, Colonel," JP admitted, slightly embarrassed.

"What? No Russian vodka?" The Soviet colonel was incredulous. "How can that be? You are senior officer of United States Army, yes?"

"Yes, sir. I am a medical officer."

"Ah, medical officer? You are doctor. In Soviet Union military doctors drink vodka, much vodka, maybe too much vodka." He shrugged. "Maybe you like Russian wine?"

JP admitted neither he nor Kathy had drank Russian wine.

Illyanovsky shook his head, unwilling to believe any respectable adult in the civilized world, especially a field grade military officer of the United States Army, could have gone through life without at least once drinking Russian vodka or Russian wine. He smiled benevolently. "You must come to Soviet Embassy. We will give you Russian vodka, wine, even Russian caviar."

"Why thank you, Colonel Illyanovsky," JP said. "That is very kind." As he spoke he reviewed in his mind the implications of a US military officer visiting the Soviet Embassy. It was not a career-enhancing activity.

"You will give card," Colonel Illyanovsky said. "I will send invitation."

"I don't have a card, Colonel," JP said.

"Then write name, address, and phone number on paper."

JP had no desire to offend the Soviet officer. He reached inside his blouse for a pen and a 3 x 5 card, then he remembered he never carried anything in his dress blouse that might create a bulge. He turned to Kathy. "Do you have a pen and piece of paper?"

176

"I think so," she said, opening her purse.

Colonel Illyanovsky, standing next to Kathy, glanced into her opened purse. At the sight of JP's pager his eyes widened. "Excuse me," he said abruptly, "I will bring paper and pen." Turning he melted into the crowd.

Surprised at the Soviet colonel's abrupt departure, Kathy asked, "What's the matter with him? JP, why are you laughing?"

"He thinks that we, I mean, he thinks that you are an American intelligence agent, a spy."

Kathy glanced at the pager in her open purse. "That's ridiculous. Surely a Soviet colonel can tell the difference between a pager and a tape recorder or transmitter."

"Apparently not," JP said, still chuckling.

Kathy closed her purse. "Do you think he'll be back? I'd really like to visit the Soviet Embassy."

"Look, Agent Ninety-Nine, the FBI photographs everyone who goes in and comes out of the Soviet Embassy. Considering what your dad did before he retired, the FBI would go berserk if they saw you go in there."

"It looks like I blew our chances anyway," Kathy said, obviously disappointed. "Did you see all the ribbons on Colonel Illyanovsky's chest? He has more than you."

"I'll bet he got some of them trying to dust my ass in Korea," JP said bitterly.

"The Russians were shooting at you in Korea?"

"Probably. Every now and then we heard Russian language spoken on our track radios. It sounded like an FO calling coordinates for North Korean artillery, then adjusting fire. Another lieutenant and I worked up a plan to capture a Russian FO. We were going to estimate his location by triangulating his transmissions and backtracking the trajectories of rounds he adjusted. Who knows, we might have snared Illyanovsky. But that's all past; we're buddies now with the Soviets."

"Don't bet on it," Kathy said.

Taking her arm, JP said, "Let's get in the chow line. I'm hungry."

Working their way through the masses, they reached a line of people moving slowly towards both sides of a long table loaded with food. They had just started a conversation with a French major and his wife when a white-haired lady in her sixties came up and introduced herself.

"Colonel Franklin, I'm Mary Ann Dixon, society editor for the *Washington Telegram*."

JP had never heard of the *Washington Telegram*, but Mary Ann Dixon seemed so genuine and motherly he didn't have the heart to tell her. Instead he said, "Yes, ma'am. How can I help you?"

"You and Mrs. Franklin are such a handsome couple. Would you mind if my photographer took some pictures of you both for our Sunday society page?"

JP looked at Kathy, who shrugged.

"Excuse us, please," JP told the French major. He and Kathy followed Mary Ann Dixon to a hallway near the front entrance. A man waited there with a small flash camera, but the camera didn't look like any professional photographer's camera JP had ever seen. By now he was wondering how Mary Ann Dixon knew his name. He began having second thoughts about being photographed when a flashbulb went off in his face. Psychedelic after-images filled his vision. As his vision began to clear a second flash blinded him again. He heard Mary Ann Dixon say, "Thank you so much, Colonel Franklin." By the time his vision recovered she and her photographer were gone.

A familiar voice with a German accent hailed them from the far side of the room. Lieutenant Colonel Gunther Dietler, wearing a dark blue Luftwaffe uniform, quickly crossed over. "My apologies for not being here to greet you, he said. "That woman, the one with the photographer who took your picture, do you know who she is?"

"Mary Ann Dixon, society editor for the *Washington Telegram*," JP said, not too convincingly.

Colonel Dietler almost doubled with laughter.

"Come on, Gunther, what's so amusing?"

"You Americans are so naive, so trusting. I do not know that lady's real name, but I doubt she works for a newspaper unless it is *Pravda* or *Izvetsia*. She is from the Soviet Embassy, she is probably KGB."

"Not that sweet gray-haired lady," Kathy said.

"I am afraid so. My dear friends, do not plan any trips to the Soviet Union unless you wish to spend time in a gulag."

Kathy laughed. "This is like being on the Maxwell Smart show."

"It isn't funny, Kathy," JP said, scowling. "I'll have to write this whole thing up for army intelligence as an encounter."

"At least now you know what a Soviet uniform looks like," Kathy said. Moving between JP and Colonel Dietler, she took their arms and guided them towards the food table. "Let's eat some good food while we can. I hear that food in the gulags is grim."

★

Saturday, January 31, 1970, 0220 hours
Quarters 12, Forest Glen, Silver Spring, Maryland

The phone on the nightstand rang for the third time before JP woke. Reaching for it in the dark, he knocked it off the night table. It hit the floor with a crash.

Kathy stirred. "What is it, honey?"

"Just the damn phone," he said, fumbling on the floor.

"Turn on the light."

"Don't need it." Lifting the phone on to the bed, he spoke into the mouthpiece. "Colonel Franklin."

"Colonel, this is Arlen Ritchie. Sorry to wake you."

A vice closed on JP's gut. It was axiomatic: phone calls from the hospital at this hour never brought good news.

Ritchie continued. "I have some tragic news, Colonel. Alex Leichuk just died from a massive bleed, probably a ruptured innominate artery. He was pronounced dead a few minutes ago."

JP groaned as though struck by a heavy fist. He hoped Ritchie hadn't heard. Trying hard to keep his voice calm, he asked, "What happened?"

"Alex suddenly started pouring blood from his trach tube and mouth about forty minutes ago. By the time we got to him he had no pulse. We couldn't resuscitate him."

"Have his next of kin been notified?"

"His parents are deceased. A distant aunt is the only person on the list. Craig is calling her now."

JP forced himself to ask, "Have you talked to path about an autopsy?"

"Yes, sir. They have a staff meeting from seven to eight. They'll do the autopsy after that."

Stunned by the news of Alex's death, JP could think of nothing further to say. He thanked Ritchie for notifying him and hung up. Sliding his feet to the floor, he padded to the bathroom, closed the door, sat on the edge of the bathtub and stared into the semi-dark. His skills as a surgeon, his years of experience, his dedication as a doctor, had counted for naught. He had failed Alex. He had been beaten by a teenage peasant with a rocket-propelled grenade.

The bathroom door opened. Kathy came in and sat next to JP. Reaching her arms around him, she drew him to her. "It's Alex, isn't it?"

Unable to contain his grief, JP buried his face in his wife's shoulder; his body shook with silent sobs.

Chapter Twenty

Saturday, January 31, 1970, 1040 hours
Walter Reed Army Hospital, Washington D.C.

Lieutenant Colonel JP Franklin felt no sense of enlightenment or relief as he exited the McNabb Auditorium, the official designation for the autopsy theater. His affection for Alex had almost kept him from attending the autopsy. A higher force, the physician's oath, and his obligation to Alex and future casualties, compelled him not only to attend the autopsy but to participate.

The cause of death was as Arlen Ritchie predicted. The innominate artery, a major vessel the diameter of an adult thumb located under the right collarbone near the midline, had ruptured. The artery's wall close to the neck had become devitalized and weakened by trauma and repeated infections. A post-operative infection further weakened the wall until it was unable to withstand the pounding arterial pressures. When the wall burst without warning Alex died from massive hemorrhage in one or two minutes. It remained for the surgeons and pathologists to gather and critically review the medical records, operations, post-operative course, and autopsy findings to define the mechanisms that led to Alex's death. Knowledge thus gained could be applied to preventing such tragedies in the future.

What remained for Alex was a memorial service, then transport to Arlington National Cemetery for burial near his father, a highly decorated World War II infantry officer. Alex's grave would be added to those of Andy Andreson and George Barfield – graves that JP would visit as long as he was in the Washington D.C. area. *How many more graves,* he wondered, *would be added to that list before he himself would be laid to rest at Arlington?*

For JP there was the heavy burden of sorrow to carry, for he had lost not only a patient but a friend. Returning to his office from the autopsy room, he slumped into the swivel chair behind his desk. For several minutes he stared morosely out the window, contemplating his future as a surgeon. Perhaps he should give up surgery and go into administration. A knock at his open door was followed almost immediately by the appearance of Lieutenant Colonel Charles Sanderson dressed in civilian clothing. JP looked up but said nothing. Sanderson settled into a chair.

"I just heard about Alex," he said softly.

"Bad news travels fast."

"Do you know what went wrong?"

"Yes. I operated on him."

'You hold yourself responsible?"

"I'd give my right arm to find someone else to hold responsible."

"How about the VC who fired the RPG?" Sanderson said, leaning forward. "Or better, the idiots who sent Alex to Vietnam in the first place?"

JP stared at Sanderson. "What are you trying to tell me, Charlie?"

Sanderson hesitated as if having second thoughts about what he intended to say. But the dam had broken; there was no stopping the flood of bitterness that poured forth. "The week before I was shot down I lost two pilots out my squadron. The week before that I lost one. Would you like to know what they were doing when they were shot down? Let me restate that. Would you like to know what stupid missions, I, their commander, assigned them on orders from my superiors?"

JP remained quiet.

"Their missions were to direct tactical air onto suspected trails, dirt roads, submerged bridges, truck parks, and the like. Many targets were under double and triple canopy jungle. The pilots had to go down on the deck just to find something to hit. Those worthless missions and others were selected by imitation ants in Washington whose knowledge of target selection came from watching World War II movies. They even mandated attack corridors despite intelligence describing heavy triple A defense."

Sanderson slumped back in his seat. Abject misery dominated his face. He looked as if he was about to burst into tears. "If I had possessed any integrity as a commander I would have refused those missions and dozens of others. I should have asked to be relieved. I didn't. Instead I started flying the more stupid missions myself to keep some of the younger and less experienced pilots from flying them."

JP stood, excused himself and went to the coffee urn in the conference room. Fortunately one of the residents had made coffee that morning. Filling two mugs he returned to his office and placed one in front of Sanderson.

"Thanks, Doc," Sanderson said, reaching for the mug.

After several sips he seemed to gain control of his emotions. "Look, Doc, you're not the only one in this war carrying a heavy load of guilt. I can bring up at least a dozen names of fine young men I wasted by sending them on meaningless missions. It's unfortunate that those who ordered those missions will never be held accountable. It's criminal that those who drummed up this stupid war will never be held responsible."

JP wanted to block his ears. He didn't want to hear that Alex's life had been wasted. He didn't want to know that Walter Reed was full of casualties that never should have been. He didn't want to hear the echo of US District judge Ann Carter's words.

Sanderson's voice would not go away "Doc, I would hate to see you become a casualty of remorse and guilt because you could not undo with a knife the damage done by another with a gun or a grenade."

JP's eyes reddened. For several seconds he could not bring himself to answer. "You know, Sanderson," he finally said, his voice cracking, "you're pretty smart for an air force pilot."

When Sanderson stood up to leave he noticed a folded FAA sectional map on JP's desk. A ball cap, aviator's sun glasses, and T–34 aircraft checklist lay on top of the map. He looked quizzically at JP, then sat back down. "You going flying today?" The tone of the question left little doubt that he really meant: *"You can't be serious about flying today."*

"You have a problem with that, Colonel?"

"How much sleep did you get last night?"

JP shrugged. "After the phone call this morning about Alex... none. But I'm in good enough shape to handle a T–34. I've got one scheduled this afternoon for a couple of hours. I'm not about to cancel it just because I'm a little down."

"Doc, maybe..."

"Maybe what?" JP snapped.

"Ah, maybe you'd like a passenger. You know, I haven't been in an airplane since the air evac brought me to Andrews."

Colonel Sanderson had made a correct call. Grief, guilt, fatigue and sleep deprivation was a combination that could be deadly to a pilot. The T–34 was a hot airplane and not very forgiving. It would get an inattentive pilot into trouble fast. But the need to break free of the ground, to feel the chains of responsibility fall away, to fly with the birds lured JP with a force more powerful than the sirens of Greek mythology. Fortunately, common sense began to assert itself. A highly experienced pilot on board wasn't a bad idea.

"Do you mind riding in the back seat?" JP asked.

"No problem. I've had two tours as an IP. I'm at home back there."

JP's eyes brightened. "Okay, Colonel. You have a flight. I'll pick you up in front of the hospital at 1300 hours."

Sanderson got to his feet and started to leave. JP called after him. "Charlie..."

Sanderson looked.

"Thanks."

★

Saturday, January 31, 1970, 1340 hours
Hyde Field, Clinton, Maryland

Lieutenant Colonel JP Franklin, Medical Corps, US Army, pulled the red and white Greenbrier van off the road onto a dirt parking lot and stopped behind the largest of three wooden hangars. Setting the parking brake, he turned off the ignition and turned to his passenger, Lieutenant Colonel Charles Sanderson, US Air Force. "Welcome to Hyde International Airport, home of the Andrews Air Force Base Flying Club."

Both men stepped down from the van. They were dressed alike: insulated short jackets, denim shirts, blue jeans, and sneakers. Ball caps and aviator's sunglasses completed the uniform of the day. After JP locked the van he told Sanderson, "We can take a short cut between these two hangars."

As they walked by the hangars Sanderson noted areas of peeling paint and bare wood. "I hope the airplane we're scheduled to fly is in better shape then these hangars."

"You'd better believe it," JP said. "The flying club's chief mechanic is a cranky retired air force master sergeant. He treats the club's planes as if they were his own. God help any pilot, regardless of rank, who abuses one of his airplanes."

Sanderson chuckled. "Doc, I know I owe you my life times two. I have a lot of confidence in you as a surgeon. You can operate on me any time, but flying is a different ball game. Before I risk my life with you tell me about your flying experience."

"You getting cold feet already?"

"Just being cautious. I've been in so many airplane crashes I'm developing an aversion to them. So tell me about your flight training."

"Well, let's see. I joined the Andrews Flying Club about twelve years ago when I interned at Reed. My first instructor was a tough lady of about thirty-five named Gwen. She had a figure that drove her students nuts."

"That include you, Doc?"

"I'll never tell," JP said. "Fortunately all dual flying up to my license was in a super cub. Gwen sat in the back seat from where she fussed at me most of the time. When she was pleased with my flying, which wasn't often, she would light up a cigarette and stay quiet. Cigarette smoke never smelled so good."

Sanderson laughed.

"The rest of my instructors were air force pilots, most of them a pathological lot who would rather fly than eat. The one who transitioned me to the T–34 was co-pilot on Air Force One. He would come off a long trip, then drive out here to instruct a couple of hours before going home. His wife was ready to kill him or divorce him. Many times he'd be in the back seat eating a Big Mac and fries while I did my best up front to get him airsick."

"Sounds like a half dozen guys I know," Sanderson said. "What was his name?"

"Phil Jensen. He was a major back then."

"Hell, I was his instructor in UPT. I taught him everything he knows about flying. He's a light colonel now, flying F–100s out of Danang and still married." Sanderson studied JP with increased interest. "So Phil Jensen was one of your instructors. He'd never turn you loose in the thirty-four if you weren't safe. How many hours do you have?"

"About 600 including eighty-five in the T–34. I have some bootleg time in multi-engines and a T–39, all arranged by grateful air force patients. As for tickets I have an instrument commercial. How about you? How many hours do you have?"

Sanderson grinned. "About 11,000, mostly in fighters, but I've flown practically everything in the air force inventory."

JP stood to one side and gaped at Sanderson. "That is awesome, Charlie. Have you ever flown a T–34?"

"No, but if it has wings, I can fly it."

JP shook his head in mock disgust. "Tell me, Colonel, are individuals selected to fly in the air force because they test high in egotism, or is egotism a quality nurtured during flight training?"

"I was about to ask the same question about surgeons."

"That's very unjust, Charles. Surgeons are a modest unpretentious group of dedicated professionals."

It was Sanderson's turn to shake his head.

They stopped at the edge of a macadam taxiway. JP pointed across to a grassy area where a single low-winged silver airplane was tied down amidst a covey of high-winged airplanes. "That's our bird," he said, "our only T–34. We used to have two until some clown, probably a fighter pilot, tried to take off with the tail still tied to a block of concrete. He got about six feet in the air dragging the concrete on the runway before he stalled and pancaked, almost totaling the airplane. I cried when I heard about it. There was not enough money in the club treasury to get the plane repaired, so it became a hangar queen, used for spare parts to keep the other one flying."

JP indicated a garage-sized wooden building with a gas pump in front. "I need to take care of some paperwork, check the weather and pick up the key, Charlie. You go ahead to the plane, turn loose the tie-downs and pull the chocks. Be sure to get the tail rope."

"Yes, sir," Sanderson said, throwing JP a sloppy salute.

★

For years the T–34 had been the primary trainer in the US Air Force and Navy. The acquisition of the T–37 jet trainer made the T–34 obsolete, at least in the air force. Its T–34s were donated to military flying clubs. Manufactured by Beechcraft, the T–34 was basically a Bonanza model with a conventional tail instead of the traditional V tail and tandem seating. Its gleaming aluminum covering and sliding canopy gave it the appearance of a small fighter plane. It was rugged enough to have been certified by the FAA for aerobatics.

JP loved the airplane and loved to fly it. This was apparent from the glow of excitement he exuded as he walked from the Flying Club office towards the plane. Waving a flat square piece of aluminum with a key hanging from it, he shouted to Sanderson, "We're legal and we have the airplane for the rest of the afternoon."

Climbing up on the wing root, he unlocked and removed a padlock on the canopy, then slid the front canopy open. Dropping his maps on the seat, he unlocked the control stick, then touched switches below the instrument panel. "Master and battery switches off," he called out. Leaning towards the back seat, he slid open the rear canopy, then jumped to the ground. "Let's do the walk around first. I'll go over the rear cockpit interior after you're on board." Sanderson appeared nonchalant, almost carefree.

As JP lifted the engine cowling, he sensed that Sanderson, watching like a mother hen, was already gauging his competence as a pilot. Assiduously following the checklist, JP checked the engine oil dipstick, spark plugs, wires and cylinders physically touching each part. On the walk-around he moved the elevators up and down, the rudder from side to side, and checked for birds' nests. At the wings he removed each gas tank cap and checked fuel quantity. "Both tanks are topped," he told Sanderson as he secured the second cap.

"It's reassuring to see that you are thorough," Sanderson said.

"That's a pathological trait among surgeons."

Completing the external inspection, JP turned to Sanderson, came to attention and saluted. "Sir, all parts are present and attached securely to the aircraft. You may now board."

Sanderson climbed up on the wing, swung a leg over the side and settled in the rear seat. JP, standing on the left wing root, leaned over and showed him how to adjust the seat, then helped him with his shoulder harness. "How does it feel to be strapped into a cockpit again?"

"Great. Just great," Sanderson said, a wide smile spreading across his face.

JP indicated a flat panel with switches and buttons on the right side of the cockpit. "Those are controls for the radios. I have the same controls up front plus the circuit breakers. I'll set the frequencies. The headset and mike boom are hanging on the hook by your right hand." He leaned over and touched a red handle at the edge of the cockpit. "This is the canopy emergency release handle. Since we're not wearing parachutes I doubt you will have occasion to activate it."

Straightening up, JP continued. "On the left are the throttle, mixture, and prop pitch levers. If you can't remember which is which, the knob on top of each lever has a large letter designating its function." He felt like a Little Leaguer giving advice to Ted Williams.

"At the top of the throttle is the button for intercom. On the side is the transmit button. Don't get the two mixed up. Trim wheels for rudder, elevators, and ailerons are by your left hand. That flat handle near the floor is the fuel tank selector switch."

Tapping the instrument panel, he said, "All the gauges are standard. Low on the right of the panel are two handles. The upper one is for hot air, the lower one is for cold air. All the way out is the closed position. All the way in is full blast. They can be set for any intermediate position to suit your comfort. Today is kind of chilly for me so I'll be using heat up front. If there are no questions I'll continue from the front seat."

Sanderson smiled tolerantly and nodded.

Climbing into the front cockpit, JP slid into the bucket seat. He glanced at a small round thermometer attached to the windscreen. It read 43° F. After buckling his seatbelt and shoulder harness, he told Sanderson, "I'll call out the pre-start checklist as I do each item. You can follow me along. You could do everything from the back seat except start the engine; that's front seat only. Ready?"

"Fire her up, Doc."

JP twisted in his seat to look at Sanderson. "I forgot to give you this." He passed back a folded paper barf bag. Facing forward he called out, "Here we go. Flaps neutral." He checked the lever and the flap indicator.

"Fuel selector, left tank. Fuel booster pump switch, left tank." His fingers briefly touched or manipulated each item. He continued rapidly down the checklist. "Trim tabs, aileron set for zero degrees; rudder: three degrees right; elevators: three degrees up.

"Mixture: idle cut off. Prop: full increase." He pushed the prop pitch lever forward. "Throttle: cracked." He inched the lever forward.

"Ignition: off. Carburetor heat: handle in and locked. Generator switch: on. Battery switch: on.

"Clear prop," he shouted, visually checking the propeller area to be sure no one was near, then he engaged the starter. After the propeller made two complete revolutions he flipped the ignition switch to "BOTH" and shoved the mixture lever to full rich. The 225 horsepower Continental caught after a single belch of blue smoke and settled down to a throaty purr. JP's eyes fixed on the oil pressure needle. When it reached the green marking on the dial he gave a sigh of relief. The instrument told him they would fly today.

Pressing hard on the toe brakes, he advanced the throttle. The RPM needle climbed to 1,000, paused, then went to 1,400. Easing back on the throttle, he switched on the radio, dialed in 123.6, the frequency for the Hyde Field tower, and slipped on his headset. After several seconds the sounds of static came through his earphones. The static always brought back memories of the radios in his M–39 command track in Korea. Pressing the transmit button, he reported, "Hyde Tower, T–bird Seven Nine Zero Four Delta, Aero Club parking, for taxi and take-off."

"Zero Four Delta cleared to runway two seven. Make your run-up short of two seven. Altimeter two niner niner seven. Winds one eight at nine gusting to fourteen. Report when ready for take-off. The only traffic for Hyde Field is a Cessna Three Ten on final. Rose Field reports heavy traffic.'

JP acknowledged. "Zero Four Delta."

Nine knots gusting to fourteen was a fair cross wind, but JP thought he could handle it. After checking the inverter switch and pilot heater he caged and uncaged the artificial horizon, then released the brakes. A short burst of power jumped the plane onto the taxiway. Turning the aircraft left, he headed for runway two seven.

Before reaching the runway JP braked the plane to a squeaking stop. As the Continental engine idled his physician's instincts began to conflict with the pilot in him. The passenger in the back seat was not only a patient, he was a military pilot who had not flown in over four months and was definitely hurting. JP pressed the intercom button on the top of the throttle. "Hey Colonel, think you can fly it?"

"I thought you'd never ask."

The voice in his headset was hauntingly familiar. It sent a chill through JP, but recognition eluded him. For now the airplane would take precedence over memories. "You do the run-up, Charlie; it will give you a feel for the airplane. I'll call the power and prop settings for the run-up, take-off and climb-out. Just don't press the transmit button instead of the intercom. If the club finds out I turned the airplane over to you my flying days will be over for a long time."

JP heard a "burp" in his headset as Sanderson acknowledged. He felt the stick shake and the rudder pedals move.

"Okay, Colonel, run it up to 1,800 RPM, then pull prop pitch until RPMs drop to 1,600."

Sanderson complied.

"Now go to 2,000. Check the right and left magnetos; maximum drop is seventy-five RPM."

The engine noise increased. The plane bucked and swayed. JP kept his feet jammed on the toe brakes. He noted the slight drop in RPM as each magneto was checked separately. "Pull carburetor heat; max drop is a half inch of manifold pressure." He watched the needle on the manifold pressure gauge start to recede, then go back up as the carburetor heat handle was pushed in.

"Looking good. Now go to full power, about twenty-four seventy-five."

The engine noise increased to an angry roar. The plane shook violently as if furious at being denied flight. Then the vibrations all but ceased and the noise settled down to a quiet purr as Sanderson throttled back to idle.

"I've got the airplane," JP said. He wanted to test the controls himself. After all, he was the command pilot. Finally, he pressed the transmit button. "Hyde Tower, Zero Four Delta, ready for take-off, two seven.

"Zero Four Delta, cleared for take-off. Expedite; a Cessna One Ninety Five just turned downwind for two seven."

"Zero Four Delta."

"Time to close the windows," JP said over the intercom. Reaching up, he slid his hatch forward, locked it, then looked over his shoulder to be sure Sanderson had done the same.

"Okay, Colonel," JP said. "The airplane is all yours. Let's go flying."

Chapter Twenty-One

Saturday, January 31, 1970, 1410 hours
Hyde Field, Clinton, Maryland

Lieutenant Colonel Charles Sanderson, US Air Force, eased the T–34 on to Runway Two Seven and turned upwind, the nose wheel splitting the white center line. Without braking he advanced the throttle to full power and moved the stick left to counter the crosswind. The sleek low-winged plane leaped forward, gathering speed as it rolled down the runway.

JP squeezed the intercom button. "Rotate at sixty five knots and let her fly herself off."

The macadam runway was full of bumps, and JP felt every one. As the plane went light on its gear the ride began to smooth out. Then the runway dropped away and the end numbers flashed by. "Gear up, fuel booster pump off," JP told Sanderson.

As if by magic the gear handle snapped up and three green lights on the instrument panel immediately glowed red. The muted whine of the gear coming up ended with subdued thumps as each wheel locked into its well. One by one the three red lights winked out. The fuel booster pump switch flipped to the "OFF" position.

"Climb out at 100 knots and 2,600 RPMs. At 400 feet make a steep left turn; that's to keep us out of the Rose Field traffic. Rose Field is at our two o'clock and three miles out. On weekends it's like a beehive over there." JP continually scanned for other airplanes. He took seriously the sign in the flying club office: YOU WILL NOT SURVIVE A MID-AIR COLLISION.

A glance at the rate of climb indicator showed the needle fixed at 500 feet per minute up. At 1,000 feet he gave Sanderson a southerly heading. Soon a wide river drifted into view. "Level off at 5,500. Stay at least two miles east of the Potomac and follow it south."

Slightly loosening his seat belt, JP began to relax. He reached forward and adjusted the hot air control knob. The heat felt good. It and the purring Continental engine had a tranquilizing effect. He leaned back and watched the verdant Virginia landscape pass lazily beneath the wings. Fluffy white cumulus clouds floated across an azure sky. Thoughts of Alex Leichuk and the sixty-three patients on the head and neck service had been left on the ground, to be retrieved after the plane was back on the ground and tied down.

The cold afternoon air was moderately turbulent. JP noted with envy that the needles on the flight instruments hardly moved despite intermittent heavy buffeting. He squeezed the intercom button. "A white farmhouse with two barns and a large pond will be coming up in a few minutes. Sing out when you see them."

In a few minutes Sanderson's voice came through the headset. "I have the target in sight."

188

The voice and phrase tugged at deeply embedded memories. Before JP could dig them out the voice asked, "What now, Doc?"

"Put the left wingtip on the farmhouse and turn to a heading of zero seven six. That heading for ten minutes at 140 knots should put us over a north–south railroad."

Precisely ten minutes later Sanderson reported, "We're over the railroad."

"That's the west limit of the club practice area. The north and south limits are those two highways off our wings. They're about fifteen miles apart. The east limit is the Atlantic shore. Stay below 10,000 feet. The air above that belongs to real airplanes. You can go as low as you want. The farmers don't seem to mind us dragging their pastures. Go ahead and do some climbing and clearing turns to gain altitude. I'll check the club frequency to see if anyone else is in the area."

Moments later JP reported, "The practice area is clear. Try some clean and dirty stalls to get the feel of the airplane."

After a half dozen beautifully executed power on and power off stalls with the gear and flaps up and down, Sanderson asked, "How about a couple of aileron and snap rolls?"

"We don't have chutes, Charlie. We could get into trouble with the FAA and the air force for doing aerobatics without them." The plane droned on as JP dwelled on Sanderson's request. "Oh what the hell, go ahead," he said. "The worst they can do to us is send us to Vietnam. If the wings come off the plane they won't find enough of us to bury."

The voice in JP's headset chuckled. "Now you're talking like a fighter pilot, Doc."

The plane rolled gently to the right, with a brief stop at exactly each ninety degrees until it was level again. JP admired the precisely executed four-point aileron roll, not realizing it was only a prelude to an eight-point roll. Incredibly the altimeter needle hardly moved during the maneuvers. Wondering if the needle might be stuck, he leaned forward and tapped the glass over the altimeter. The needle jumped slightly. It wasn't stuck. Sanderson was just a superb pilot.

The nose came up slightly. The plane suddenly snapped in a 360-degree roll to the right, came straight and level, then snapped to the left, again coming straight and level. Dirt and dust floated around in the cockpit. JP's headset flew off. He grabbed it and adjusted it back on his head, then squeezed the intercom button.

"Not bad for an invalid."

"I'm a born pilot," Sanderson said. "Watch this." He dropped the plane's nose into a steep dive. The airspeed needle swung past 180, hovering just outside the yellow caution arc on the dial. The nose came up. JP felt G-forces mashing him into his seat. The nose continued up until the plane clawed for the sky, its engine screaming. The airspeed rapidly bled off as the plane went vertical, then eased over on its back completing the first half of an inside loop. Almost reluctantly the plane gently rolled right side up, exactly at the same altitude as at the beginning of the dive. "The Red Baron would be proud of you, Colonel," JP said with undisguised admiration.

The plane suddenly snapped on its back. JP's seat belt and shoulder harness cut into him as he hung upside down, his feet dangling uselessly below the rudder pedals. Then the plane began rotating violently to the right. Glancing up where the sky should have been, he dimly noted the rotating green of Virginia. "Jesus," he moaned, "an inverted spin." Within seconds the spin degenerated into a vicious spiral, almost flinging the earphones off his head again. A wave of nausea flooded through him; he fought the urge to vomit. He had no desire to clean up that kind of mess. A momentary glimpse of the altimeter showed precious altitude rapidly spinning away. At that moment Sanderson's voice crackled in his headset, "You have the airplane, Doc."

JP had never been in an inverted spiral, much less recovered from one. It was all he could do just to keep from throwing up. Every time he looked up he saw the rotating ground rushing towards him. When he looked "down" past the wings he saw clouds and blue sky. The instruments were now a blur of light and dark as the plane rotated past the afternoon sun.

"Stay cool, Doc," the voice in his headset counseled. "You can get us out of this."

JP was stunned by the familiarity of the voice in his headset. He sensed recognition was not far off.

"Come on, Doc, do something," Sanderson's voice urged. "I've got a family." After a few more seconds and a 500-foot altitude loss the voice said, "Jam your feet on the rudder pedals and go full left rudder, then get the stick forward."

The crazy bastard was serious about making him recover. Still fighting nausea, JP worked his legs up against violent forces he never before experienced. His sneakers finally contacted the rudder pedals but kept falling away. He felt like a fly trying to climb up on a ceiling. Finally, he managed to shove the left pedal in as far as it would go and slammed the stick forward.

"Easy, Doc, easy. Okay, good," the voice said. "Now neutralize the controls."

JP relaxed the left rudder and hauled back the stick, estimating its neutral position. Amazingly the plane stopped rotating, but it was in a high speed inverted dive. Afraid to look at the altimeter, he prayed that Sanderson knew what he was doing, because he sure as hell didn't.

"Roll her level with ailerons and you've got it made," the voice assured him.

JP jammed the stick roughly to the right. The plane rolled rapidly level, but then continued the roll upside down again. "Damn it," he muttered.

"Try again. Doc," the voice encouraged. "Use finesse, like you did on me in the operating room."

Again JP slammed the stick to the right, then eased it quickly towards neutral as the plane turned right side up. He stopped the roll with opposite aileron just before the plane flipped upside down again. "Got you," he whispered with more than a twinge of pride. Easing back on the stick and throttle, he brought the plane straight and level before sneaking a look at the altimeter. "Oh, my God," he exclaimed, relief surging through him.

"Not bad for an army doc," the voice in his headset said, chuckling. "Ever think of transferring to the air force?"

"You're a maniac, Sanderson. I'm getting a psych consult on you as soon as I get you back to Reed."

"Aw, Doc, that was fun. Let's do it again," Sanderson said, chuckling.

"Not on your life. Let's get this thing on the ground. I don't feel so good."

"Roger. You're the boss, boss. Besides I've run out of targets; I mean maneuvers."

The identity of the voice in his headset suddenly exploded into JP's consciousness. Sanderson was the FAC pilot who, eighteen years before in Korea, had saved JP's platoon and a British battalion from annihilation by Communist Chinese troops. Since the incident JP had been searching for the man. He not only owed the FAC his life, he owed him drinks. Trembling with the knowledge, he twisted in his seat to look at the man to whom he would be everlastingly grateful. Sanderson sat serene behind his air force issue aviator's dark glasses.

A grim smile touched JP's lips as he pressed the intercom button. He had never forgotten the FAC's code name or his own. "Ah, Sharkbait, this is Damsel Two Six, Over." Only static came from his headset. "Sharkbait, this is Damsel Two Six. How do you read?" Still no response. JP turned. Sanderson's glasses hung from one ear. He appeared dazed, much like a boxer who had just taken a hard punch to the head.

"Wake up, Sharkbait," JP shouted into the mike. "I recognized your voice in my headset. I'm the lieutenant whose platoon you saved north of the Imjin in '51. I am Damsel Two Six."

"Jesus Christ," Sanderson said slowly. "Jesus Christ."

"Negative Jesus Christ. You will meet him later." JP shook the stick and see-sawed the rudder pedals. "I've got the airplane." Without waiting for a reply, he dropped the plane on its left wing tip into a steep turn. The stall-warning horn sounded briefly. Lowering the nose and bringing the wings level, he headed the plane back towards Hyde Field.

"Hey Doc, take it easy," Sanderson said meekly from the back seat. "We don't have chutes."

"Butt out, Sharkbait. You and I have a date at the 'O' club that's eighteen years overdue."

★

Saturday, January 31, 1970, 1830 hours
Quarters 12, Forest Glen, Silver Spring, Maryland

"I'll get it, Mom," eleven-year-old Paul shouted as he ran for the ringing telephone. After a moment he called out, "It's an Air Police lieutenant at Andrews. He wants to talk to you about Dad."

Kathy's heart almost stopped. She forced her legs to carry her to the phone. She knew JP had gone flying that afternoon. She had been aware of his lack of sleep and how upset he was over Alex Leichuk's death. She had urged him to cancel the plane, insisting he was in no shape to fly. Now the Air Police were calling. The call could mean only one thing: JP must have had an accident. Why else would the Air Police call?

Then she reasoned that if JP had been hurt or killed in a plane crash the Walter Reed hospital commander and chaplain would be at the door. Trembling, she picked up the phone. "This is Mrs. Franklin."

"This is Lieutenant Kroenig, Air Police at Andrews."

"Yes, Lieutenant."

"Is Lieutenant Colonel James Paul Franklin your husband?"

"Of course he is. What has happened? Why are you calling?" Kathy was close to panic.

"He and a Lieutenant Colonel Charles Sanderson are being detained by my men here at the Andrews officers' club, ma'am."

"Detained? What do you mean detained? What have they done?"

"They haven't done anything, ma'am, at least not yet. I'm sorry to tell you ma'am. but both are very drunk. They were about to physically engage… that is, fight half a dozen naval officers who objected to their loud behavior. That was when the bartender called the club manager who then called us."

Kathy's relief was boundless. But JP drunk? The most he ever drank during nineteen years of marriage was three beers in one week or an occasional martini. "Lieutenant Kroenig, are you sure you're talking about my husband?"

"Yes, ma'am. I checked his ID card, driver's license and pilot's license." Kroenig's voice conveyed amusement tinged with understanding. "Ma'am, could you get someone to drive you over here to pick up your car and Colonel Franklin? He's in no condition to drive."

"Yes, of course, Lieutenant. It should take me about an hour to get there."

"That will be fine. We'll be in the main bar."

It was closer to an hour and a half later when Kathy stepped from Carrie Marley's Carmen Ghia at the Andrews AirForce Base officers' club.

"Would you like me to wait?" Carrie asked.

"No. I see our van in the parking lot. Thanks for bringing me over on such short notice."

"Call me when you get back. I'm dying to hear what got into JP."

"So am I, and it better be good," an angry Kathy said. Slamming the car door shut, she headed for the officers' club entrance. As she reached the door another attractive woman about her own age began climbing the stairs. Her face reflected a mixture of concern and anger. Kathy held the door open for her. "Excuse me, but did you come here to collect a drunk husband?" she asked.

The woman's face brightened. 'You must be Kathy Franklin. I'm Laura Sanderson. The Air Police lieutenant told me your husband was being detained with my husband."

"I can't imaging what got into JP. In nineteen years of marriage I have never seen him drunk."

"Ever since Charlie found out the surgeon who saved his life at Walter Reed was the marine who rescued him from the Japanese during the war, he's talked about nothing else. But I have no explanation for this behavior. Charlie's not much for alcohol."

"Well, whatever the explanation it'd better be good," Kathy said, shaking her fist, "or else I'm going to feed him a knuckle sandwich. Come on, Laura, let's find out what those two clowns have been up to."

192

JP and Charlie Sanderson sat slouched at a table in front of the bar. Behind them, at a discrete distance, stood a young Air Police lieutenant and three burly enlisted men wearing AP brassards. JP glanced back over his shoulder at them, then confided to Sanderson, "You know, Charlie, Shore Police, Air Police, Military Police, they're all the same the world over." When he saw his wife and Laura Sanderson enter the bar he staggered to his feet. "Hey Kathy, over here," he shouted.

As the two women approached JP said loudly, "Kathy, you gotta meet this guy. He's Sharkbait, the FAC who saved my ass in Korea. I've been looking for him ever since that day. If it hadn't been for him and his air force buddies you would have been a widow after only nine months of marriage. When I finally tracked down the son of a bitch he was on my own service at Walter Wonderful."

"JP, that language is atrocious. Stop it."

Sanderson stood, put his arm around JP and addressed his wife. "Honey, this was one mean bastard in Korea. Only a real tiger would piss off two regiments of Commies. At least he had sense enough to call on the air force when he found himself in deep shi... do do. But can you beat this, Laura? He saved my butt when he pulled me off Mono in the Treasuries. Then I saved his in Korea. A couple months ago he saved mine again." A drunken cackle escaped Sanderson as he regarded JP. "My turn is coming up, Jarhead."

JP smiled stupidly. "No way, you dumb fighter puke. And remember, if I hadn't given you all that flight instruction this afternoon we never would have caught up with each other."

"Doc, you may be one hell of a surgeon, but as a pilot..."

"I'm a hell of a lot better pilot than you will ever be a surgeon."

"I'll drink to that," Sanderson said, reaching for his glass.

"Oh no, you won't," Laura Sanderson said, snatching away the glass. "Kathy, let's get our drunk warriors home before they get into real trouble."

Kathy turned to Kroenig. "Lieutenant, could your men help these two heroes out to our cars in the parking lot?"

"Yes, ma'am." He motioned to the three Air Police.

After JP was safely belted in the van Kathy walked to the Sanderson's car. She passed her card through the car window to Laura. "We're married to complicated men. Let's get together over lunch and talk about them and us."

Laura Sanderson took the card and looked at it briefly. "I'll be in touch."

Chapter Twenty-Two

Friday, March 20, 1970, 0955 hours
Washington D.C.

The first day of spring was warm and sunny. Yet the persistent black cloud of the Vietnam War hung over the nation's capital as if a corrosive poison gas, eroding the nation's unity and strength. Anti-war demonstrations were increasing in frequency and fervor. Draft-dodging American males were fleeing in greater numbers into Canada to sit out the war while their contemporaries bled and died in South-east Asia. President Nixon's program of Vietnamization was being hailed as the formula for "Peace with honor". Given the reputation of the Army of South Vietnam, the outcome of Vietnamization was predictable.

All these nation-shaking developments seemed to have had little impact on the young soldier driving the army shuttle bus from Walter Reed Army Hospital to the Forrestal Building in downtown Washington. He bounced and swayed happily to the rock rhythm from a boom box on the floor by his foot. He also managed to pass through every traffic light on 15th Street just as the light turned yellow. Lieutenant Colonel JP Franklin, the only passenger on the bus, marveled at the driver's skill and timing.

At Constitution Avenue the bus made a left turn, traveled less than a mile before turning right on 14th Street. Passing the Museum of American History, the driver eased the bus into the left lane before entering a short underpass. Exiting, he made a left turn, crossed the opposite lanes to a covered driveway and stopped at the glassed entrance of a modern white six-story structure.

"Pentagon North, Colonel, the Forrestal Building," the driver called out.

JP picked up his cap and attaché case from the seat beside him, stood and walked to the door. "I can't say much for your music," he told the driver, "but your timing at those intersections was impeccable."

"I wondered if you'd noticed, sir," the driver said, grinning.

The Forrestal Building, named after the first Secretary of Defense, James Forrestal, was newly built to house selected Department of Defense activities. The Army Surgeon General's offices had just completed moving into it from the Pentagon. JP, like the rest of the service chiefs at Walter Reed who served as consultants to the Surgeon General, hated going to the Pentagon. The bus trip from Walter Reed and back consumed over two hours, often longer depending on traffic. The isolation, immense size, and complexity of the Pentagon was intimidating. Just getting to a destination in the building was a time-consuming navigational chore, assuming one knew where one was going.

The Forrestal Building was only thirty minutes from Walter Reed. It was within easy walking distance of L'Enfant Plaza, fine restaurants, and museums such as the Aeronautical and Space Museum, Smithsonian Institute, and National Gallery of Art.

194

The Army Surgeon General's offices occupied the entire third floor of the Forrestal building. On that floor over a hundred military and civilian personnel, supervised by lieutenant colonels and colonels, MSC manipulated the enormous medical assets of the United States Army throughout the world. Clinical and related medical activities were managed in concert with senior Medical Corps officers, traditionally the chiefs of services at Walter Reed. The physician consultants provided professional input pertaining to all aspects of their specialties.

Today was JP's first visit to the Forrestal Building. He would meet with his Medical Service Corps counterpart, Lieutenant Colonel Joseph Macklin, MSC, to firm up assignments of some sixty head and neck surgeons scheduled to enter active duty in July for two years. They would replace sixty head and neck surgeons due for discharge after completing two years of active duty. They would join a like number already on active duty with one or more years to serve. The staggered rotation assured approximately 120 head and neck surgeons on active duty at all times.

Carrying his attaché case, Colonel Franklin entered the new but austere glassed lobby and stopped at a gate manned by an armed uniformed civilian guard. After handing the guard his ID card and signing a log, he was given a visitor's pass to hang on his blouse pocket flap. As he passed through the gate the guard told him, "Be sure to pick up your ID card on the way out, Colonel."

Walking through the lobby to the elevators, JP fished in his blouse inner pocket for a 3 x 5 card with directions to Colonel Macklin's office. The pocket was empty; the card had been left on his desk at Walter Reed. Luckily he remembered the number of Macklin's office: 3017. Standing between two banks of three elevators, he guessed which of the doors would open first and stood before it. It was his lucky day. The doors in front of him slid noiselessly open. He waited for two civilians in shirts and ties to step out, then walked in. At least he knew which of six buttons to press. The doors closed as silently as they had opened. There was no sensation of upward motion or stopping. The doors opened and he stepped out into a bewildering puzzle of corridors, offices, open and closed doors.

"Lost, Colonel?" a low husky feminine voice asked.

JP turned. An attractive woman in her early forties carrying a sheaf of papers came towards him. He couldn't help but notice how well her conservative business jacket and knee-length skirt fit her trim, athletic figure. Dark brown hair cut short left an impression that she was younger than she really was. Oversized glasses gave her a wise academic look. The lucky bureaucrat who employed her as his secretary was to be greatly envied.

"If I don't find room 3017 this morning the Army Medical Corps will go into an administrative crisis," JP told her.

"I wouldn't want that to happen," the woman said, laughing. "It so happens 3017 is just across the hall from where I work. Stay with me; I'll take you there."

"Lead on," JP said, falling into step beside her. As they walked he tried to memorize the turns they made so he could find his way back. The woman stopped in front of open double doors. "Room 3017."

"Thanks. You have made a major contribution to the defeat of world communism."

"I rather doubt that," she said, laughing again. For a moment she studied the four rows of ribbons on JP's blouse, the Medical Corps caduceus, and finally his name tag. "Colonel Franklin, you appear too young to have been a doctor in World War II."

"I had a different profession then. I was a marine rifleman."

"You still seem too young to have been in World War II."

"I enlisted when I was seventeen."

"And after the war you went to medical school?"

"Not exactly. I was a line officer during the Korean War. Medical school came after that."

"Now that is an interesting background for a doctor," the woman said. "I'm Margaret Ryan. I work in 3016 across the hall. Let me know if I can be of any further help."

JP thanked her. He watched her open a large frosted glass door and pass into the room beyond. Through the briefly open doorway he glimpsed an impressively furnished office. A brass plate on the wall beside the door read: ASSISTANT SECRETARY OF THE ARMY FOR MEDICAL AFFAIRS. *Lucky guy*, he thought.

Sighing, he turned and walked through the open doors of 3017 into a large windowless expanse of floor space divided into multiple offices by glass partitions. The clatter of typewriters blended with muted conversations intermittently penetrated by ringing telephones. He quickly spotted Lieutenant Colonel Joseph Macklin in his glass-enclosed space. Rapping on the glass, he walked through the open door. Macklin was almost hidden by stacks of brown folders on his desk. Additional stacks were on one of the two chairs in the office and on the floor.

"Why don't you have the air force drop this stuff on Hanoi?" JP asked. "It could end the war."

"That would be cruel, inhuman, and a violation of the Geneva Convention," Macklin said, grinning. "It's not as bad as it looks. I know exactly where everything is." He moved two of the stacks on his desk to a central position, then placed the remaining stacks on the floor. "Any trouble finding my office?"

"I had my own personal guide," JP said, "the good-looking secretary who works across the hall for the Assistant Secretary of the Army."

Macklin stared at JP "Was she about forty, five six, great figure, dark hair cut short?"

"You noticed her too?"

Macklin shook his head. "JP, you idiot, that was Dr. Margaret Ryan. The doctor is for her PhD in economics from Chicago. She doesn't work for the Assistant Secretary of the Army for Medical Corps Affairs. She *is* the Assistant Secretary of the Army for Medical Corps Affairs. She is your boss several levels removed."

'You're kidding," JP said, glancing in the general direction of room 3016. He looked back at Macklin. "You're not kidding. Well, all things considered, that's the best looking boss I've ever had… except for Kathy."

"I hope you didn't say anything stupid."

"I didn't have a chance."

196

JP helped himself to a styrofoam cup from a stack next to an electric coffee maker. Half-filling the cup with thick black liquid, he dumped in sugar and cream. Easing into a metal chair beside Macklin's desk, he stirred the coffee with a tongue blade and watched Macklin sort out and arrange records.

JP had worked with Joe Macklin for over a year and had developed great respect for him. The forty-five-year-old lieutenant colonel looked forty. Like JP he had been an enlisted marine in the Pacific during World War II. Well built and well preserved, Macklin was a pathological weight lifter and martial arts master. Receding jet black hair, cut short, and a facial scar left over from hand to hand fighting on Guadalcanal, gave him a ferocious but handsome look that intrigued women. He moved with such grace that many who knew him did not suspect that the former infantry battalion commander was walking with an artificial leg, the sequelae of a NVA mortar fragment wound.

"How's the new prosthesis?" JP asked.

"It hurts only when I'm jogging," Macklin said with a sly grin.

"When do you retire?"

"In October. I'll go on leave in September to start law school at Georgetown."

JP groaned. "Just what the country needs, another damn lawyer to sue doctors. Speaking of lawyers, any final word on Dr. Minter's legal problems?"

"Minter is history. He accepted a less-than-honorable discharge rather than face a court martial."

"In nearly six years I can't recall another Berry Plan doctor like that turkey."

"There have been a few in the other specialties. Thank God most Berry Planners are conscientious doctors. The orthopod who amputated my leg in Vietnam," he tapped his artificial leg, "was a prince. He's in civilian practice now but liked the army so much he went into the active reserves. He gets to D.C. once or twice a year for medical meetings and calls me. We meet for lunch and tell war stories." Macklin pulled a stack of brown folders towards himself. "Okay, Doctor, let's go to work."

JP popped open the clasps on his attaché case, lifted out a manila folder and extracted four sheets. Sixty-three names in alphabetical order were on the first three sheets with written remarks by their names. They were the head and neck surgeons who would enter active duty in July. The fourth sheet listed fourteen names; twelve were head and neck surgeons in Vietnam and two in Korea. Half would be up for discharge and half for reassignment. This morning he and Joe Macklin would review the records of each individual on the lists before making a firm assignment. The official data in the records would be supplemented by information that JP had accumulated from phone calls, letters, and meetings with either the doctors, their department chairmen, or both. Any confirmed extenuating circumstances would be considered when making an assignment.

JP closed his attaché case, set it on the floor and looked up. "Charge on, Colonel."

"Let's start with doctors coming on active duty who have special problems," Macklin suggested.

JP flipped to the last page of the four in his hand. "The first is Carl Holzer, who finishes at UT Dallas. He has a seven-year-old son with severe cerebral palsy and three normal children. The CP child requires almost full-time attention. It's doubtful Holzer's wife could manage by herself if he were sent overseas. I talked to the boy's pediatric neurologist. He confirmed that the boy requires ongoing specialized care. Holzer's program chairman told me he is brilliant and a hard charger. Holzer himself requested assignment to a hospital with a pediatric neurologist and physical therapists, preferably in this country."

"You have an assignment in mind?"

"You know I do. Letterman Army Hospital, San Francisco, will have a vacancy for a head and neck surgeon in July. It has a regular army pediatric neurologist with an interest in CP who is also an associate professor at the university."

Macklin scribbled a note on a piece of paper and attached it to the outside of Holzer's record. "Done," he said. "Who's next?"

"Just one more tough one. Mark Cranell at Michigan. His wife just finished a course of chemotherapy for acute lymphocytic leukemia. I talked with her doctor two days ago. Her clinical response was less than optimum. She is due for a repeat bone marrow next week. I suggested to Cranell he apply for a hardship deferment, but he preferred to come on active duty to take advantage of the medical benefits."

"I can't blame him. Do they have any kids?"

JP glanced at his sheet. "Two boys, six and four."

Macklin sighed. "That's a heavy load for any man to carry. Assign him where you think he'll get the best support for his family."

JP swept Colonel Macklin with a flash of affection. "Sometimes you make me suspect there's a real heart instead of a mechanical pump beating within your chest."

Macklin grinned. "You have a fatal tendency to overestimate people, JP. Where shall we assign him?"

"I talked with Charlie Breslin at Madigan Army Hospital, Seattle. He'd be happy to have Cranell as his assistant. He and his wife will organize the hospital officer's wives to give the Cranells all the support they need."

"You would think they were marines," Macklin said, making notes. "Next."

JP passed Colonel Macklin a single page. "This is the wish list of head and neck surgeons in Vietnam with a year to serve after returning stateside. They were promised any assignment they wanted after completing tours in Vietnam."

Macklin put on a show of displeasure. "Damn it, JP, you shouldn't make those kinds of commitments without checking with me."

"Macklin, you are so full of BS it's coming out your ears. Just don't leave me out on a limb. If any wish can't be met by the MSC godfathers let me know. I'll work something out to keep the doctor happy."

Macklin looked at the list. "I'll see what I can do," he said, setting it aside. "Let's move on to the newcomers."

One hour and ten minutes later all assignments had been firmed up except for the selection of a senior head and neck surgeon to go to Vietnam as consultant.

'You have someone in mind?" Macklin asked.

JP opened his attaché case and extracted a single sheet which he pushed towards Macklin. "This year we are very fortunate; we have a volunteer."

Macklin picked up the sheet, scanned it and tossed it down. "General Deering will disapprove this just like he did the others. Last time he told me he didn't want to see any more requests from you. Give it up, JP."

"I can't do that, Joe. For almost six years I sent head and neck surgeons to Vietnam. It's immoral for me to stay sheltered at Walter Wonderful when I've been so diligent in sending others into harm's way. Besides, my years at Reed have given me expertise managing wounds of the head and neck. It's payback time."

"Explain that?"

"It's time for me to take those skills to the battlefield or whatever you warriors consider Vietnam." He sipped his coffee and grimaced. "When did you make this stuff?"

"Don't knock my coffee. It's free."

"That's the best I can say about it," JP said. "Look, Joe, last year I learned of an unexpected opening for a division surgeon in Vietnam and applied for it. As you know General Deering turned me down. What you don't know is that I encouraged George Barfield to go for it. I persuaded him that a tour in Vietnam would enhance his military career and give him insight into part of the army he didn't know. Instead of enhancing George's military career Vietnam killed him. I ought to have enough guts to do what I encouraged George to do."

"JP, you've already been in two wars. You've paid your dues. It's not necessary for you to go to the war in Vietnam. Take the word of someone who had two tours there. Between our politicians and the South Vietnamese our country is being bled out in a war they started but don't intend to win."

"I've heard that story before," JP said bitterly, recalling the conversations with Judge Carter and Colonel Sanderson. "It doesn't apply to me. He leaned back in his chair, took another sip of coffee and set the cup down on Macklin's desk. "It's apparent I'm not getting anywhere with a frontal attack. It's time I went over to a flanking maneuver."

Macklin stared at JP. "Now what the hell is that supposed to mean?"

"Unless I go to Vietnam I will retire in four months with twenty-one years of active duty. In retirement I will receive over half my base pay for the rest of my life while I accept one of a number of lucrative offers, any of which offers rewards that make my army salary look like a pittance."

"Jesus Christ, you drop something like that on General Deering and he'll hand you your head." Macklin looked pained. He was well aware of JP's value to the army, not only as a surgeon and teacher but as an officer with potential for star rank. "Don't set off any nukes just yet. I have an idea."

JP smiled. "I knew an enterprising paper pusher such as yourself wouldn't let an old marine buddy down."

"Would you be willing to go through Airborne School?"

"What? Why would I want to do that? I'm not nuts."

"The 101st Airborne Division will need a replacement division surgeon in August. If you are jump qualified and none of the other potential replacements are, the division commander will exert a lot of pressure to get you, particularly if he is aware of your background as a marine and line officer in two wars.

JP regarded Macklin skeptically. "And how would the division commander be made aware of my background?"

"By one of his former battalion commanders who happens to be an MSC officer in the Surgeon General's office."

JP stared at the floor for a good ten seconds. Suddenly he looked up. "Macklin, you are going to make one hell of a lawyer. Okay. I'll go Airborne. Get me a slot."

Macklin shook his head. "It must be true."

"What must be true?"

"All former marines are basket cases."

"You should know." He looked at his watch. "How about this former marine taking you to lunch?"

"I wish I could," Macklin said. He indicated the stacks of brown folders in his office. 'Your urologist buddy Mangonis will be here this afternoon to firm up his assignment list. And I've got to get you a space in the Airborne School at Benning."

"Is that going to be a problem?"

"It could be. The age limit is thirty-six."

"How old were you when you went through?"

Macklin looked sheepish. "Forty."

Chapter Twenty-Three

Friday, March 20, 1970, 1236 hours
The Forrestal Building, Washington D.C.

Lieutenant Colonel JP Franklin returned to the lobby, turned in his pass to the guard and picked up his ID card. As he signed out he glimpsed at his watch; he had just missed the shuttle bus back to Walter Reed. The next bus was at 1400 hours; he had almost an hour and a half to wait unless he took a cab. But a cab would cost at least seven dollars plus tip; better the money be spent on lunch at one of the nearby restaurants.

Leaving the Forrestal Building, he walked south on 10th Street towards L'Enfant Plaza and the Loring Hotel. Climbing the stairs to the hotel, he entered its sumptuous lobby, paused and scanned for a restaurant. Spotting it at the far end of the lobby, he moved to the entrance and fell in behind a party of four men in dark suits. A severe-looking maitre d' took four menus from his stand and led the four men to a nearby table. After they were seated and the menus distributed he returned. "Table for one, Colonel?"

"Please, non-smoking."

"This way, sir."

The restaurant's interior resonated a quiet, dignified elegance. Intricate glass chandeliers suspended from a high ceiling gave off shimmering warm glows. Oil paintings, most in the style of western European sixteenth and seventeenth-century artists, hung from walnut-paneled walls. Several paintings resembled the cover painting on a box of Dutch Masters cigars. Unoccupied tables were set with a dazzling array of forks, knives, spoons and china on immaculate white tablecloths. Vivaldi's *Four Seasons* blended with subdued conversations and occasional laughter. The maitre d' stopped at a table set for two and reached for a chair. As JP was about to sit down a feminine voice behind him asked, "Colonel Franklin, would you join me, please?"

Turning, he recognized Margaret Ryan seated alone and moved to her table. "That's the best offer I've had today," he said. After he was seated the maitre d' handed him a folded menu, then faded.

Moments later a waiter appeared. After filling JP's water glass he asked, "Would you like something from the bar, sir?"

"I would, but I'd better settle for iced tea."

Dr. Ryan moved an empty wine glass closer to the waiter. "Another sherry, please."

JP waited for the waiter to leave, then told Dr. Ryan, "I have a confession to make."

Dr. Ryan waited, the suggestion of a smile on her lips.

"When you were kind enough to guide me to room 3017 I had you identified as the secretary for some lucky high level civilian bureaucrat. It never occurred to me that you were the high level civilian bureaucrat."

Dr. Ryan laughed. "Apparently someone has talked," she said. "But that's not an uncommon mistake you male chauvinists make."

"I'm glad you laughed when you said that," JP said. Opening the menu, he studied the contents briefly, then closed and set it down.

"That didn't take long," Dr. Ryan said.

"It seldom does when you know what you want."

She stared at JP through large round glasses. "How perceptive."

The waiter brought Dr. Ryan's sherry and JP's iced tea. "Are you ready to order, sir?"

"Cheeseburger with Provolone cheese, medium well, and fries," he said, handing the menu to the waiter.

When the waiter was gone Dr. Ryan said, "You military people order food as if you were sending classified messages."

JP grinned. "We hate to waste words."

Dr. Ryan leaned slightly towards JP. "Since this conversation began with a confession, I have one to make."

"This table carries the same confidentiality as the confessional," JP assured her.

"I have not sinned, Colonel. I have just made some blunders, one of which I am about to admit, but I will hold you to your vow of confidentiality. Deal?"

"Deal," JP promised.

"When I saw your name tag this morning I remembered having seen the same name on correspondence last year, but I couldn't recall the specifics. I asked my secretary, who by the way is a male, to pull your file."

"Find anything interesting?"

"Quite a bit. You have a fascinating background for a medical officer. After going through your file I remembered why I recognized your name."

"You saw it on a post office wall with my black and white photograph?"

"No, but then I haven't been in a post office lately," she said, laughing. "Actually it was because of comments you submitted to the Surgeon General on the current policy regulating Medical Corps promotions from lieutenant colonel to colonel. A copy of your comments was forwarded to me."

JP recalled the blunt, critical remarks he had written. "This may be a prudent time for me to keep my mouth shut."

"Only about what I tell you next. You will probably hate me after you hear it."

JP studied her comely face, partially obscured by the large-lensed glasses she wore. "That would be hard to do, but not impossible."

"Hear me out, Colonel. I was responsible for the development of the flawed promotion policy and its final review before it was sent to the Secretary of the Army."

JP was taken aback by Dr. Ryan's candor. His bitterness over the promotion policy broke through the wall of good judgment. "I may not be overwhelmed by your competence, but I still like you."

Dr. Ryan gave JP a stony look. For a moment he thought she would reach across the table to hit him. "I'll give you that one, Colonel," she said coldly. "Don't push your luck."

The tension was broken by the appearance of the waiter with the salad that Dr.

Ryan had ordered and her second sherry. "Sir, your cheeseburger will be along in a few minutes," he assured JP.

After the waiter left Dr. Ryan lifted her wine glass towards JP. "Truce?" she asked in a conciliatory tone.

JP lifted his tea glass. "Truce." He sipped the tea, then set the glass back on the table. "Better start on your salad before it gets warm."

"You have a weird sense of humor, Colonel Franklin, and an inclination towards insolence, but I still like you." She began to eat her salad, then stopped and looked up. "Would you like some of my salad while waiting for your meal?"

"You're not setting me up to get my French fries, are you?"

"How did you know?"

"My wife does it all the time."

"She and I have something in common," Dr. Ryan said.

Their eyes met; JP looked away, embarrassed. He picked up his fork, reached across the table and speared part of an artichoke and a black olive.

"You took one of my olives," Dr. Ryan said, feigning outrage. "That is going to cost you."

The waiter brought JP's cheeseburger and fries. "The plate is hot, sir," he warned.

While JP cut the cheeseburger in half Dr. Ryan reached over and took a handful of fries and put them on her bread plate. After munching thoughtfully on several she began, "Until reading your comments on the promotion policy I had no idea medical officers like you existed, much less were so severely wronged by a policy for which I was ultimately responsible."

By now JP was feeling somewhat more charitable. "I wouldn't have expected you to know, but someone on your staff should have straightened you out..." He blushed. "I mean, enlightened you."

"I'm still learning my job, Colonel. Admittedly, I have made mistakes. I presume you have made mistakes in your profession?"

JP wasn't sure she expected an answer. Playing safe, he nodded. Dr. Ryan went on. "I try not to make the same mistake twice and to rectify the mistakes I have made. I regret that one of my screw-ups so adversely impacted you and other very deserving Medical Corps officers. That damned promotion policy is one of my most grievous mistakes. Believe me when I say that the Surgeon General and I are working to correct it."

"I have to tell you, Dr. Ryan..."

"Please call me Margaret, at least in social situations."

"Margaret, in less than thirty days a dozen requests for retirement and resignation will hit the SGO from medical officers whose backgrounds parallel mine. Some are Military and Naval Academy graduates with experience in combat who subsequently went to medical school. Others have backgrounds closer to mine. They started as enlisted men and worked their way to officer status, commanded troops in combat, then went on to become doctors. Most can step into high income positions in private practice. Medical schools proselytize them with religious zeal for department chairmen."

JP paused for a sip of tea, then continued, "These men are a unique breed of officers. They love their country and the armed forces in which they serve. For most, myself included, military life is the only kind of professional life they have known since their teens. But believe me, Margaret, they are not the kind of officers to sit around languishing as lieutenant colonels for years while lesser men go on to colonel and, God forbid, higher. What you just told me gives hope for them. Perhaps they will reconsider leaving active duty. Unfortunately for me it may be too late."

"What do you mean?"

"I sent word to the Surgeon General through Colonel Macklin that I would retire this September unless given a tour in Vietnam."

Dr. Ryan's eyes widened. "My God, you ex-marines are anything but subtle." She shook her head. "Colonel, I wish I could help you with that assignment but I cannot. That is in a professional area which is the purview of the Surgeon General." She smiled. "I'll have to admit, you are in a very good bargaining position." She then reached to JP's plate and took another bunch of French fries.

JP stared at the pitiful remnants of fries on his plate. "Those are very fattening."

She quickly returned most of the fries.

"Would you mind if I asked you something personal, Margaret?"

"I have an idea what it will be... how did a female university professor of economics end up as an Assistant Secretary of the Army?"

JP blushed. "I hope your ability to read minds is limited to administrative matters. If not, I'm in big trouble."

Margaret Ryan seemed to glow. "Thank you, Colonel. I needed that. Work on your cheeseburger. I'll tell you how it all came to be."

JP picked up a half cheeseburger.

"Six years ago I was a professor of economics at Chicago married to a professor of psychology. In the mid-1960s he grew a beard, long hair, and began protesting against the Vietnam War. That led to his organizing and leading anti-war demonstrations. About the same time I was diagnosed with non-Hodgkin's lymphoma and treated with radiation and chemotherapy. My husband's anti-war activities, his beard, long hair, and the side effects of my therapy so devastated our marriage that it couldn't survive. I have often wondered if we ever really had a marriage." She shrugged. "Our divorce became final last year."

JP set the remains of his cheeseburger down and focused on Margaret Ryan. It was then he saw the suggestion of a small bulge in her left neck.

She continued, "During my convalescence from chemotherapy I became interested in politics and the Vietnam War. It didn't take long to perceive that evil men from the top down had led our country into a war through deception and intrigue, a war they had no intention of winning. In 1967 I went to work for the Republican National Committee and Richard Nixon's election. I believed then and still do now that he would end the war in Vietnam; at least get our troops out with a semblance of honor. I raised quite a bit of money on his behalf and campaigned for him. After he was elected President he called to thank me for my efforts and asked if I would consider serving in his administration. One thing led to another, and here I am." She lifted her wine glass and took a healthy slug.

The half empty wine glass was not lost on JP "I'd like to give you some medical advice, Margaret," he said. "Since it's free you may not think it worth much, but it does have substance."

"Oh?" Hazel eyes behind large round lenses studied him.

"There's a substantial body of evidence to indicate that malignancies may be exacerbated by alcohol."

Margaret Ryan's eyes reddened behind her huge glasses. "Listen to me, Colonel, when a woman is in her forties, may have one to three years to live, has no marriage or prospects of marriage, and can never have children, a couple of drinks have no more impact on the scheme of things than a gnat biting an elephant."

"You're being a little pessimistic. That's not the usual outcome for non-Hodgkin's lymphoma."

"Perhaps for the average case, but for some reason I haven't responded to treatment like the books indicate I should. But then, I have always been somewhat unorthodox in my responses," she said bitterly. She touched the lump in her left neck. "No doubt you noticed this."

"I did after you mentioned you were diagnosed with lymphoma."

"I'm going to Hopkins next week to have it biopsied."

"Look, Margaret, don't jump to conclusions. The lump may not be malignant. It could be some sort of lymphoid response to your previous chemotherapy or radiation. Even if it were malignant more effective drugs and treatments are being developed."

Dr. Ryan smiled. "The surgeon at Hopkins who will do the biopsy said the same thing."

"Would you object to telling me his name?"

"McClintock. A wonderful man. Do you know him?"

"He's one of my consultants at Walter Reed," said JP, smiling. "We go back a long way."

"Unfortunately he will be leaving soon to go into private practice in another state. He told me he hoped to be succeeded by an army head and neck... oh, my... you?"

JP nodded.

Margaret Ryan smiled. "Now that raises an interesting conflict of interest for me."

"I can save you some anxiety. I happen to be married to an army brat who will not hear of my leaving active duty as long as the Vietnam War continues. Also bureaucratic scheming by comrades in high places has begun which may result in an assignment to Vietnam. Dr. McClintock will have to find another successor."

"As Assistant Secretary of the Army I'm pleased. As a patient of Dr. McClintock I'm disappointed."

JP sneaked a look at his watch. "I have to leave, Margaret; the next bus back to Reed is in twenty minutes." Visually he swept the dining room for the waiter.

"No, Colonel. You were my guest. I'll take care of the check. Next time, if there is a next time, will be your turn."

JP hesitated, then agreed. As he shifted his chair back and started to rise he heard a familiar male voice.

"Colonel Franklin, I wish I had known you were here." Lieutenant Colonel Joseph

Mangonis moved to stand beside him, his eyes fixed on Margaret Ryan.

JP did his best to be discrete. "Dr. Ryan, this is Colonel Mangonis, chief of urology at Walter Reed."

Dr. Ryan gave Colonel Mangonis a tolerant smile. "With both of you here I'm beginning to wonder who is back at Reed minding the store."

"It has an inherent momentum that allows it to maintain its course without us," Mangonis said.

JP, anxious to get Mangonis away before he discovered who she was, interrupted. "Thanks for lunch, Margaret." He took Mangonis by the arm and guided him towards the lobby.

"Hey, I was hoping you would ask me to join you," Mangonis groused.

"I have to catch the shuttle bus back to Reed," JP snapped defensively.

"Does Kathy know you were having lunch and drinks in a classy hotel with a very attractive woman who paid for your meal?"

"You have a grubby mind, Mangonis, but then, that goes with your specialty."

"Watch it, Colonel. I know who wrote the letter to Jason Groves about the latrines on our wards."

"So do I, Colonel," JP said, punching Mangonis on the arm. "So do I."

★

Friday, March 20, 1970, 1450 hours
Walter Reed Army Hospital, Washington D.C.

The shuttle bus returning to Walter Reed from the Forrestal Building was driven by a soldier who lacked the skill and rhythm of the morning driver. He managed to arrive at every traffic light just after it turned red. By the time the bus stopped at the front entrance of Walter Reed Army Hospital the usual thirty-minute trip had degenerated to fifty minutes.

When JP walked into his office Thelma Hoffberg followed right behind him. She placed a half dozen message slips and a typed letter on his desk. Indicating the letter she said, "This has to go out in today's distribution to make the seventy-two-hour deadline on congressional inquiries."

JP reviewed the letter in less than ten seconds, signed it and handed it back. "How's that for compliance?"

Thelma ignored the remark. "Colonel Macklin called just before you walked in. He said to tell you to start getting in shape. You are to report to Fort Benning on Friday, May 8 for orientation. Airborne training will begin the following Monday."

JP reached for his calendar, turned the pages to May and made some notes.

Thelma regarded JP with the concern of a mother for a son who has made a most stupid decision. "Colonel, what have you done?"

"I'm going to join a very select and prestigious group of warriors, the paratroops."

"You're no warrior. You're a doctor," she said. "Besides, Airborne training is for young men. You're not a young man. You will only get yourself hurt or killed.

206

Remember, you have a family to consider."

"Thelma, Thelma, I'm overwhelmed by your confidence in my survival capabilities."

"I have always suspected the Marine Corps left you addle-headed. This just proves it." She left, shaking her head sadly.

JP chuckled and waited for her to reach her office, then over the intercom told her, "Please page Major Strickland and ask him to come by my office." He then reached to his in-box for the top paper.

Ten minutes later there was a knock at the open door and Dave Strickland walked in, a mug of coffee in his hand. "You want to see me, Colonel?"

"Yes, David. Have a seat."

"That sounds ominous."

JP smiled slyly. "I want to pass on several items from my trip to the SGO."

Strickland settled back in his chair and sipped from his mug.

"Item one. I checked on your promotion to lieutenant colonel."

"It's been so long ago since I made the list I forgot I was on it."

"Well, you can tell Gloria she can plan to pin on your silver leaves in three weeks."

A wide smile swept across Strickland's face. "I have you to thank for my early selection."

"I was thinking more of the future of the Medical Corps when I wrote your ERs. You are an exceedingly competent surgeon, teacher, and administrator, with immense leadership capabilities. You have the same pathologic compulsiveness for excellence as I have. The residents, patients, and staff like you. As a matter of fact, I like you. Maybe it's because you remind me of myself."

The look Dave Strickland bestowed on his boss was heavy with skepticism. "Colonel, why do I get the uneasy feeling you are going to tell me something I may not want to hear?"

"You are also very perceptive, David, that's another of your virtues. On May 8 I will go on three weeks' TDY to Fort Benning to attend Airborne School."

"Why would you want to do that, sir? In fact why would anyone want to do that?"

"I can speak only for me. This August there will be an opening for a division surgeon in the 101st Airborne. If I make it through jump school I'll have a good shot at that position."

Strickland sat mute for a moment as he pondered the significance of what he just heard. "I knew you were working to get to Vietnam, but I didn't think you were so desperate you would be willing to jump out of perfectly good airplanes."

JP smiled. "If I go to the 101st in August there is the question of a replacement for me here."

"I can work with just about anyone you pick," Strickland assured him.

"And I thought you were perceptive. How I misjudged you."

The direction of the conversation suddenly became apparent to Major David Strickland. He stared at JP.

JP continued. "I plan to recommend to the hospital commander and the Surgeon General that you replace me."

Strickland sat silent, stunned.

"You have been assistant chief almost four years. On at least a dozen occasions you functioned well as acting chief in my absence. You had a tremendous background in head and neck surgery before you came here, to which has been added the Walter Reed experience. That makes you one of the top head and neck surgeons in the military if not the country. Sometimes I worry that your skills as a surgeon are beginning to exceed mine."

Dave Strickland's somber face broke into a grin.

"The only impediment to your appointment as chief would have been your rank, but that will be corrected in three weeks. So, Lieutenant Colonel Promotable Strickland, unless you vehemently object, unless I flunk out of jump school, unless my assignment to the 101st falls through, it is my intent that you succeed me as chief of the head and neck surgery service and consultant to the Surgeon General."

"Colonel, I wouldn't want you to wash out of Airborne training, but frankly I hope you will be turned down for the division surgeon's slot. You're too valuable here."

"When my grandchildren ask what I did in the army I don't want to have to tell them, 'They gave a war and I didn't go.'"

"On that premise I should be the one to go to Vietnam. I'll even volunteer."

"No, you won't. You're too valuable here," JP said, chuckling.

"I'll accept the position as chief as an interim appointment on the condition that you come back here after you finish your tour in Vietnam."

"I couldn't do that, Dave. That wouldn't be fair to you. Besides, I've had my fill of the nation's capital." Opening the lower drawer of his desk, he removed a folder and passed it to Strickland. "This has all the regular army head and neck surgeons on active duty. Look it over. Let me know who interests you as an assistant. I'll send for his 201 file. Together we should be able to come up with someone who will be acceptable to you and the generals."

Strickland took the file and nodded. He thumbed through the pages, then set the file down. "While you were downtown did you pick up anything on your promotion?"

"As a matter of fact I did," JP said, recalling the lunch with Margaret Ryan. "It was an assurance at the highest levels that a revision of the promotion policy is in the works, but will take six months to a year before becoming effective."

"What happens if you are promoted while in Vietnam?"

"I will be eligible to command an evacuation hospital. Ever since I was a lieutenant in Korea I wanted to become an army doctor and command a hospital in a combat zone."

Dave Strickland sighed. "You know, sir, life around here would be much simpler if you dropped the idea of going to Vietnam."

"Maybe for you, Dave, but not for me."

Chapter Twenty-Four

Monday, May 11, 1970, 1045 hours
The United States Army Infantry School, Fort Benning, Georgia

The three steel towers rose 250 feet above the ground to dominate the main post's skyline. The towers, built for the 1939–1940 New York World's Fair, had furnished safe tethered parachute rides for civilians during the fair. At the onset of World War II the towers were purchased by the army, brought to Fort Benning and modified so the parachutes were no longer tethered. Once released the parachutes and the men harnessed to them floated free from 250 feet. Since that time the towers had introduced generations of aspiring paratroopers to the joys and terrors of parachuting.

In an open field a half mile from the towers, groups of soldiers dressed in fatigue trousers, combat boots and white T-shirts, sweated in the burning Georgia sun as they queued up before a half dozen crossbars. The soldiers, most in their late teens or early twenties, were volunteers who hoped to survive the grueling three-week Airborne course to earn the coveted silver badge of the United States Army paratrooper. Already that morning they had passed half a dozen physical tests designed to eliminate those unlikely to complete the three-week course.

Only one physical test remained, the dreaded horizontal bar chinning test. It was dreaded because of its well-deserved reputation for washing out more applicants than any other test, including the push-ups and the three-mile run. The test required the aspiring paratrooper to hang at full arm extension from a horizontal bar eight feet above the ground. Then, using arms only, lift himself until his chin reached over the horizontal bar, return to full arm extension and repeat the cycle five more times.

Standing quietly in one of the groups, Lieutenant Colonel JP Franklin, M.D., Medical Corps, US Army, pondered his chances of getting his chin over the bar once, much less six times. He lamented that for almost seven years he had led a sedentary life at Walter Reed. Only after learning he would go to Fort Benning for Airborne training did he begin a half-hearted regime of jogging and push-ups. It was half-hearted because he assumed that the United States Army was so eager to have an internationally recognized surgeon among its paratroop alumni it would do all it could to insure the surgeon would graduate.

It was at the orientation for incoming Airborne trainees the preceding Friday that this assumption was fatally shattered. During welcoming remarks the commander of the Airborne School, a lean and mean full colonel, informed trainees that on the following Monday they would be required to pass a qualifying PT test before beginning Airborne training. "Failure to pass any part of any test," he told them, "will result in immediate dismissal from the school, regardless of rank or position." He looked squarely at JP when he spoke those last words.

Concerned he might actually flunk the PT test and be sent home in disgrace, JP spent most of Saturday and Sunday running, doing sit-ups, push-ups, and chinning on the cross bar. By Monday morning he was a stiff mass of aching muscles and joints. That he survived the physical challenges of the tests thus far, and now stood in line behind a muscular second lieutenant and a thin teenage private at one of the crossbars, was mute testimony to the inherent reserves of a determined middle-aged man in the face of great adversity.

The PT tests were supervised by Black Hats – enlisted instructors who wore black baseball caps. Each Black Hat was a veteran of multiple day and night parachute jumps. Many had served at least one tour in Vietnam. Like their colonel they were lean and mean, very mean. During the training day the Black Hats exercised almost unlimited authority over both officer and enlisted trainees, an authority rivaling marine drill sergeants in boot camp. Regardless of rank a trainee always stood at attention when addressed by a Black Hat.

It was the private's turn at the crossbar. JP and the lieutenant watched, envious to the point of jealousy as the private double-timed to the crossbar. Rather than climb up on stirrups to begin his pull-ups he jumped for the bar from the ground. In seconds he had done seven pull-ups and was moving up for the eighth when the Black Hat made a note on his clipboard. "That's enough, leg," he told the teenager. "Quit showing off and fall in on the bleachers."

The private happily jogged away.

The lieutenant, a former rugby player at the Military Academy, also double-timed to the crossbar. Climbing up on the stirrups, he managed the first four pull-ups smoothly. On the fifth he began to falter, but with great effort raised himself high enough to get his chin over the bar. The sixth pull-up was accomplished amidst grunts, groans, and body twists. Later JP described them to the lieutenant as "characteristic of a grand mal seizure." Spent, the lieutenant dropped to the ground.

The Black Hat nodded towards the bleachers and the lieutenant jogged off, The Black Hat then looked at JP. "You're up, Colonel," he snapped.

JP walked slowly towards the crossbar, nurturing the illusion he was conserving strength. The Black Hat raised his voice. "We're waiting on you, Colonel." His voice carried an edge, as if to say, You'll never make it, old man. Drop out now and save yourself the humiliation of washing out.

The implication was not lost on JP. Determined to go home with jump wings or in a box, he stifled a rude remark that would have gotten him thrown out of the school. Moving to the two vertical bars, he climbed on the stirrups, grasped the crossbar, and eased out into space. The first three pull-ups went with a speed and rhythm that not only surprised him but confounded the Black Hat. By the time the fourth pull-up was completed his arms and back felt as though spikes had been hammered into them. Gasping, he began the fifth pull-up, praying for strength and thankful he was not overweight. Somehow he lifted himself high enough to slide his chin over the crossbar. Quickly he lowered himself to hang exhausted from the crossbar, much like a bat suspended from a cave ceiling.

The Black Hat moved closer, ready to pronounce him failed or dead, he seemed

210

not to care which. Before the fatal words could be spoken, JP somehow found strength to begin moving up again. Emulating the grunts, groans and twists of the lieutenant, and calling on the Lord for just one more burst of energy, he twisted, strained, and convulsed his body upward with enough momentum to reach the crossbar with his chin. Dropping to arm's length he hung for a moment, then collapsed in a heap on the ground.

"Fall in with the others in the bleachers," the Black Hat told him with no show of emotion.

As JP double-timed to the bleachers he threw a hateful look over his shoulder at the Black Hat. Damned if the son of a bitch wasn't smiling.

★

Each trainee was issued a pack, poncho, pistol belt, canteen, canteen cover, and steel helmet with a number. The helmet number was a reminder to the Airborne trainee he had lost his identity and rank if he had any. Lieutenant Colonel JP Franklin became number 286. During the first week of training 286 learned the hard way he was no longer a lieutenant colonel. A Black Hat caught him walking instead of double-timing to the next mock-up.

"286, drop and show me twenty," the Black Hat ordered.

Now twenty push-ups was ten more than the number usually imposed for minor infractions; 286 respectfully brought this to the attention of the Black Hat.

"286," the Black Hat patiently explained, "you are the most senior officer in the course. You receive more pay and enjoy more privileges than anyone else. Therefore, 286, more is expected of you. That is why you will do twenty push-ups instead of ten."

When JP hesitated the Black Hat got in his face. "You don't like sergeants do you, 286? And you especially don't like being told what to do by sergeants, right, 286?"

"The thought did occur to me, Sergeant," JP said, now standing at rigid attention.

The Black Hat persisted. "You're kind of insolent for a field grade officer, especially one who probably won't make it to graduation. You have an attitude problem, 286. That can get you killed."

JP bit his lip and remained silent.

"If you get yourself killed jumping out of an airplane it will reflect badly on my record as an instructor. Therefore it is my responsibility to develop in you the right attitude. Don't you agree, 286?"

JP, still in a brace, mumbled, "Yes, Sergeant."

"What? I can't hear you, 286."

"*Yes, Sergeant,*" JP shouted.

"That's better 286, you can forget the twenty push-ups."

"Thank you, Sergeant."

"Instead just drop and start doing push-ups until I get tired watching you."

JP glared at the Black Hat, then reached for the ground. After sixty push-ups he rapidly weakened' and collapsed with his face in the dirt.

"My, my," the Black Hat said, his voice dripping with sympathy, "a little out of shape, aren't you. Maybe you should quit and go home before you have a heart attack and die. That, too, would reflect badly on my record."

JP groaned.

"Get back to your squad, 286."

Still gasping, his arms screaming with pain, JP double-timed to where his squad waited. As he slowed to a stop a young private first class grinned. "You sure told him off, sir."

JP grinned back. "I did, didn't I?"

Each day of the first week began with thirty minutes of vigorous PT followed by a three-mile run in combat boots. The hot Georgia sun and ninety percent humidity left everyone drenched with sweat at the end of the run. Then came repeated jumps from mock wooden aircraft to the ground three feet below. The jumper landed on his feet, then collapsed into a coordinated leg/hip/butt roll know as a PLF. JP did more push-ups the first week than he had done in his whole life, Marine Boot Camp excepted. His evenings became a routine of soaking his aching body under a hot shower for twenty minutes, taking three aspirin and collapsing on his bunk.

During the second week the morning runs increased from three to three and a half miles. Dozens of terrifying jumps were made from thirty-four-foot towers. In these jumps the petrified trainee, wearing a parachute harness, stood in a mock aircraft doorway thirty-four feet above the ground. A Black Hat clipped a static line from the harness to a hundred foot cable that angled down from the tower to end at a soft berm. At the command of "Go" the trainee jumped or fell six feet to the end of his static line. Then bouncing up and down like a yoyo, he slid along the cable at a fast rate until stopped by the soft berm and two classmates.

Numerous PLFs were practiced from swing landing trainers. These were diabolical contraptions of harnesses and straps suspended from the ceiling of a shed. The trainee, secured to the harness, stepped off a ten-foot-high platform and swung in an arc away from the platform. He continued to swing back and forth like a pendulum over a bed of sawdust until the Black Hat, at some unexpected time, pulled a rope. This released the trainee, who dropped four to eight feet to make his parachute landing fall.

At the end of the second week 286 had his first experience with the 250-foot tower. As the ranking officer in the student class he was given the privilege of being the first to be raised and dropped from the tower. After securing himself into the parachute harness 286 glanced up at his parachute. It was open and attached to a round metal frame as wide as parachute's circumference. A cable ran from the center of the frame to an arm at the top of the tower. The cable would lift the metal frame, parachute and jumper 250 feet into the air. At a given signal the parachute would be released from the frame. Jumper and parachute would then float free to the ground.

A Black Hat came by to check 286's harness and safety strap, the latter a two-inch wide, sixteen-foot long strap looped around the metal frame that held the parachute. Both free ends of the safety strap were clipped to the parachute harness.

"When you reach the top," the Black Hat counseled, "unclip one end of the safety strap and pull it free of the frame. Then and only then unclip the other end and drop it. Do you understand, 286?"

"Yes, Sergeant."

Preoccupied with the safety strap, 286 neglected to tighten the harness straps around his thighs. This fundamental error was made manifest as soon as the Black Hat gave the order, "Lift number one."

Number 286 was suddenly jerked upward. Excruciating pain knifed through his body as the loose thigh strap caught his family jewels. The weight of his 152-pound body was now crushing his testicles. His agonizing scream was probably heard all the way to the Fryer Field drop zone in Alabama. Struggling frantically to take the weight of his body of his testicles, he failed to realize his ascent had reached the top of the tower and stopped. The view of Fort Benning at that height would have been spectacular under different circumstances.

From 250 feet below an amplified voice repeatedly commanded, "Drop your safety strap, 286."

Tears from the intense pain streamed down 286's face as he frantically unclipped one end of the safety strap and let it swing free. Then, forgetting the Black Hat's instructions, he unclipped the other end and let it go. Realizing his mistake, he could only watch, helpless, as both ends of the strap now hung over the metal frame some eight feet away. To release the parachute now would risk entanglement with the strap and possible fatal outcome.

The voice from below was contemptuous. "Tower, lower one."

286 slowly descended to a chorus of boos and hisses from classmates waiting their turns. When his feet finally touched the ground and his body weight was taken off his testicles, he almost fainted from relief.

The Black Hat marched over and stood over him, hands on hips and feet apart. "What the hell happened to you, 286? How come someone of your rank and experience cant follow simple instructions?"

"No excuse, Sergeant," 286 said, immensely relieved his voice was not high pitched. He was not about to tell the Black Hat what had happened.

As 286 tightened his thigh straps the Black Hat shook his head in disgust. "Report to me after your drop. You need to be impressed with the need to follow instructions." Then, using his electric megaphone, he bellowed, "Lift number one."

★

Monday, May 25, 1970, 1030 hours
Lawson Army Airfield, Fort Benning, Georgia

The first day of "Jump Week" began the third and final week of Airborne training for Lieutenant Colonel JP Franklin and over 600 classmates. By the end of the week they will have made five parachute jumps including two night jumps. They would then be authorized to wear the coveted silver "Parachute Badge" of the United States Army paratrooper.

Glitches had been operative during the morning. Excessive winds over the drop zone in Alabama delayed the mass jump by two hours. While waiting for the winds to slow, the jumpers spent almost two hours in a huge shed enduring great discomfort from tight parachute harnesses, heavy T–10 back chutes, lighter reserve chest chutes, and the oppressive oven-like heat of the shed.

Finally, word came that winds over the drop zone were within safe limits for the jump. As the would-be paratroopers, impeded by their constricting harnesses, waddled out of the shed, JP glanced at the portrait of a lieutenant colonel on the wall who was killed on his fifth jump. The colonel left a wife and four children. The similarity of the colonel and his family to his own was not lost on JP.

Once outside, the jumpers assembled on the concrete ramp into chalks. The first chalk, led by JP, waddled like a line of ducks to the port side of a parked C–141 Starlifter jet. A Black Hat stopped them short of the aft door. "Relax," he told them. That was the joke of the day.

The young private behind JP groused, "These straps are killing me."

JP turned. "There's a certain logic to keeping us chuted up for long periods," he told the private.

"Sir?"

"After an hour or two you become so miserable you'll do anything to get relief, including jumping out of an airplane."

The private grinned. "You're pretty smart for a colonel... sir."

"Watch it, son, or you may be jumping without a parachute."

The Black Hat suddenly shouted, "Airborne."

Ninety-eight voices thundered, "All the way."

"Follow me," the Black Hat ordered. He turned and climbed metal steps into the aircraft.

JP boarded next, not because he was the most senior officer, but because he was a doctor. He alone would jump on the first pass. After landing he would function as the doctor on the drop zone while the other students jumped. This arrangement came about after the commander of Martin Army Hospital, a good friend, prevailed on him to serve as the drop zone doctor. This would relieve the hospital, already short of doctors, of the requirement to furnish a doctor for the drop zone.

"Who will take care of me if I crash and burn?" JP had asked.

The friend merely shrugged and smiled.

Awkwardly JP climbed the steps into the cabin. The dimly lit interior seemed larger than a freight car. Canvas seats stretched between metal poles lined both bulkheads. A third and fourth row of seats were back to back down the center of the fuselage. The jump master, wearing a flight helmet with headset and boom microphone, directed JP to sit just forward of the door. After strapping himself in, JP studied his fellow jumpers as they shuffled on board and waddled to their seats. They were a subdued lot compared to the rowdy bunch that had screamed on cue the previous week, "Killers from the sky."

An electric motor whined. The door slowly came down from the ceiling like the lid of a roll-top desk. Four jet engines spooled up one by one and the giant plane began to vibrate and rock. The jump master leaned towards JP. "286, since you are the only one jumping on the first pass you are designated the wind tester."

"Wind tester? No one said anything to me about testing the wind."

"No sweat, 286. The ground people will monitor your descent. Based on your drift they'll adjust the plane's course on the next pass so the rest of the jumpers will land as close as possible to the center of the drop zone." He smiled wickedly. "Of course, if there's too much drift the drop will be cancelled."

"I'm sorry I asked," JP said.

The whine of jet engines increased briefly. The plane lurched forward. Minutes later the engine noise increased to a steady roar. JP felt himself pushed against his seat belt as the plane accelerated. The floor tilted up and the plane lifted from the runway. JP's mouth was so dry he had difficulty swallowing. A distended bladder transitioned from discomfort to pain. By the time the plane leveled off at 1,400 feet, abdominal cramps and nausea had been added to his misery. He closed his eyes and leaned against the canvas seatback.

Someone touched his arm. "Sir, are you okay?" a voice asked. The young private in the next seat, the one who thought JP was "smart" for a colonel, was staring into his face.

"I'm fine," JP lied. "I was just wondering what I was doing up here about to jump from an airplane."

"Yes, sir. I was wondering the same thing."

JP forced a smile, then shouted above the engine noise, "Airborne."

"All the way, sir."

The lieutenant colonel and the private shook hands.

★

The steady noise of the jet engines was tranquilizing. The five minute plus flight to the drop zone in Alabama seemed to take much longer. JP drifted into a semi-conscious state, but came wide awake when the engine noise markedly increased and the pungent odor of burning kerosene reached him. The cabin door next to him was open. Fourteen hundred feet below the green and brown Alabama landscape drifted by. The jump master stood in the doorway, leaned out slightly and looked ahead. Moving back into the cabin, he spoke briefly into his mike, then touched JP's shoulder. "One minute, 286."

JP's heart rate tripled. He wondered if the jump master's true meaning was that he had but one minute to live. It seemed only seconds later the jump master shouted, "286, stand up."

Mechanically JP rose, trying to balance himself on the pitching floor.

"286, hook up."

Fumbling with the metal clamp attached to his static line, JP reached up and clipped it to the steel cable that ran along the length of the cabin's ceiling. Grasping the static line just below the clamp, he stood, zombie-like, wondering if there was a face-saving way he could avoid jumping. The ninety-seven pairs of young eyes on him convinced him there was not. The only route back to Fort Benning for Lieutenant Colonel JP Franklin was out of the door.

The jump master inspected JP's harness, chutes, and static line, then slapped his back. "Check." Moving aft to the door, the jump master clipped his harness to an anchor and coolly observed the terrain below. A bell sounded. The red light above the door went out and a yellow light flashed. JP dreaded the next command.

"286, stand in the door."

JP shuffled the short distance to the door, dragging his static cord along the cable with his right hand. Turning smartly, he placed the toe of his left boot at the door's edge, his right boot slightly behind, his open hands outside the door flush against the fuselage. Refusing to look down, he gazed out past the wingtips, then let his eyes wander to the two huge jet engines swaying gently from pods under the wing. Ribbons of black smoke streamed from the engines. The stench of kerosene fumes was nauseating. Suddenly he felt a slap on his butt and heard the shout, "Go."

Like a Pavlov dog programmed by weeks of conditioning, JP leaped into the air. His hands moved to a death grip on the reserve chute buckled to his chest as he counted, "1,000, 2,000." First he saw a blur of green, then blue. He heard a loud *whack* and was jerked upright by a fully inflated parachute. An inexplicable euphoria passed through him as he realized he would not die on this jump. Descending softly in a noiseless environment, he looked up to see the shrinking C–141 against the blue sky, black smoke streaming from its four engines.

An amplified voice from below broke his trance. "286, slip to the left. Slip to the left."

Although JP couldn't see anyone he knew that Black Hats on the ground were monitoring the descent of their doctor. Glancing to his right, he saw he was drifting towards a large stand of pine trees.

"286, slip to the left," the voice again commanded.

Reaching up with his left hand, JP grabbed a handful of risers and pulled down hard. Immediately the parachute slid rapidly to the left. Surprised and frightened by the speed of slip, he released the risers. As the ground came up towards him he saw he was still being blown towards the trees. This time he eased down gently on the risers. The parachute slipped deftly to the left. By now the ground was coming up fast.

Just as his feet hit the ground he pulled down on both main straps, collapsing his chute and making a near-perfect parachute landing fall.

Getting to his feet, he gathered up his parachute and started towards a group of soldiers standing next to parked trucks and a UH1H Huey helicopter, a red cross conspicuous on its side. Waving with his right hand, he shouted, "The doctor is in."

Chapter Twenty-Five

Saturday, May 30, 1970, 0700 hours
Walter Reed Army Hospital, Washington D.C.

Lieutenant Colonel JP Franklin, Medical Corps, US Army, entered his office for the first time since leaving for Fort Benning and the Airborne Course more than three weeks ago. Although not officially due back for duty until Monday, he decided to come to the hospital on Saturday, make patient rounds at 0800 hours and catch up on three week's accumulated correspondence. To his surprise and pleasure his desk was clear of the usual pile of phone messages to be answered. Except for a few papers the in-box was empty. Newly promoted Lieutenant Colonel David Strickland had been a good choice to succeed him in August.

Removing his uniform blouse he hung it from a clothes tree, pausing to admire the silver Airborne badge under the ribbons on the left breast. The badge was well worth the three weeks of physical and mental abuse that consistently pushed him beyond what he was sure had been his limits. It was even worth the thousands of punitive push-ups imposed on him by the Black Hats. Now he was no longer a "Leg". He was "Airborne," a member of a unique and elite brotherhood.

The ringing telephone snapped him out of his reverie. He picked up the phone. "Head and neck surgery, Colonel Franklin."

"Joe Macklin, JP. Your wife told me I'd find you there. Congratulations on the jump wings. How was the course?"

"Rough."

Macklin laughed. "That's the way it's supposed to be."

"Joe, why do I suspect your call at 0700 hours on a Saturday morning is not a social call."

"You're right. Late yesterday afternoon the division surgeon for the 36th Division, Colonel Diblasio, was seriously injured in a chopper crash."

"Elwood Diblasio?"

"You know him?"

"We were lab partners in gross anatomy as residents at Reed. What happened?"

"His chopper was hit by ground fire on a routine flight. It went down hard in a field. He has a broken neck, JP. He's quadriplegic."

An interval of awkward silence passed as both men dwelled on the significance of a surgeon unable to move his arms and legs for the remainder of his life. Macklin ended the silence. "The Thirty-Sixth CG is desperate for a replacement..."

"I get the drift, Joe."

"Somehow the CG learned you were bucking to go to Vietnam."

"Some more of your back-channel manipulations?"

"Always looking out for a marine buddy," Macklin said. "After reviewing your background the CG put tremendous pressure on Med Command and USARV to get you a.s.a.p."

"I'm flattered. When would I have to be there?"

"In ten days; two weeks at the most."

"That's really cutting a short fuse. I'll have to talk it over with Kathy before I give you an answer."

"I must have it by Monday morning," Macklin said.

"You'll have it."

After JP hung up he leaned back in his swivel chair and gazed out the window at the Capitol's dome for several minutes. Perhaps in Vietnam he would learn answers that were not forthcoming from under that dome. He stood up, retrieved his blouse and slipped it on. After buttoning the blouse he looked down at paratrooper's badge on his left breast, then grabbed his hat and left for home.

★

Thursday, June 4, 1970, 1120 hours
Walter Reed Army Hospital, Washington D.C.

Thelma Hoffberg walked into Lieutenant Colonel JP Franklin's office without knocking and thrust a sheaf of stapled papers at her boss. "I believe you are expecting these," she said, her voice quavering.

JP scanned the top sheet, tossed the papers on his desk and looked up. "Why, Thelma, after seven years I thought you'd be happy to get rid of me."

Thelma broke into tears. "Oh for God's sake, Colonel, just shut up." Turning, she ran from the room.

JP stared after her for several moments, then picked up the papers.

DEPARTMENT OF THE ARMY

SPECIAL ORDERS   June 1, 1970
ORDERS 66
EXTRACT

5.TC 202. Following reassignment directed. Individual will proceed on PERMANENT CHANGE OF STATION as indicated.

FRANKLIN, JAMES PAUL 003–00–9234 LTC WRGH WRAMC WASH DC 20012

FOR THE INDIVIDUAL

Assigned to: USARV TRANS DET APO SF 96484 FOR FURTHER ASG IDC–4

Reporting date June 12 1970

PORT CALL DATE JUNE 10 1970

218

SUPPLEMENTAL INSTRUCTIONS ATTACHED (APPENDIX B, AR 310–30) 26, 36.

JP shuffled through the papers, briefly studying each page. The realization hit him: for the third time in his life he would be leaving those he loved to go to war. This time he would not be doing as a marine Pfc or army lieutenant to take lives. This time be would be going as a doctor to save lives. He reached for the phone and dialed his quarters.

★

Tuesday, June 9, 1970, 1930 hours
Officers' Club, Fort Meyer, Virginia

The rain had almost subsided when JP stopped the Greenbrier van at the entrance to the officers' club. He handed Kathy an umbrella. "Go ahead inside," he told her. "I'll find a parking place."

"You take the umbrella," Kathy said. "You'll need it more than I."

"I'm in uniform. Umbrellas are a no-no."

Kathy sighed acquiescence. "I'll wait for you in the lobby."

The main parking lot was filled with cars as was the adjoining auxiliary lot. Parked cars lined the few legally available curb spaces. JP wondered if he would run out of gas before finding a place to park. By luck he made a wrong turn into the parking lot of the post theater. Evidently the movie was not worth battling the elements; there were plenty of vacant spaces.

He put on his cap, reached to the back seat for his raincoat and stepped out into light misty rain. Quickly slipping on the raincoat, he set off on a quarter-mile hike in the general direction of the officers' club. In the mist and on unfamiliar territory he made several sightseeing excursions of Fort Meyer before stumbling on to the officers' club. Once inside he checked his raincoat and hat. Kathy, seated on a plush antique wing-backed chair, stood as he approached. Seeing her slight figure in the simple elegant black dress made him ache with the misery of knowing this would be their last night together.

"Where did you park?" she asked.

"At the post theater. Every other space was taken. What's going on here?"

"The Airborne Society is having its annual dinner. They've taken over the entire club except the main dining room. I just saw General Delmar."

"Who's he?"

"He was my dad's roommate at the Military Academy and is my godfather. Would you like to meet him?"

"Not particularly, at least, not tonight. I would like to be exclusively with my wife."

Kathy smiled a winsome smile. "Whatever you say, Colonel."

When they walked into the dining room they saw that every table but one was occupied. "I'm glad I called for a reservation," JP said.

The maitre d' led them to the only vacant table. It was set for two. After they were seated he removed the RESERVED sign. Whether it was coincidence or fate, it was the same table they shared nineteen years ago to celebrate their first wedding anniversary. JP had just returned from the Korean War.

"This place hasn't changed in nearly twenty years," JP remarked.

"That's what I like about it," Kathy said. "It has an aura of permanence, stability, and history. I can feel the presence of George Marshall and Ike."

The waiter appeared. JP ordered white Zinfandel for Kathy and a dry vodka martini on the rocks for himself. "Plenty of ice and olives, please."

"Do you remember it was at this table you told me you wanted to be a doctor?"

JP nodded.

"You have come a long way since then."

"Do you remember it was at this table you told me you were pregnant with our first child?"

This time Kathy nodded.

"With four kids you too have come a long way."

Kathy became pensive. "Who could have predicted you would go off to a third war twenty years after going off to your second war."

"And only three weeks after we were married," JP added.

"I was so sure that after the Korean War this country would have learned its lesson… apparently not."

"This country has learned too well how to get into wars and how to fight them," JP said sadly. "What it has forgotten is how to win them."

The waiter brought their drinks. Kathy lifted her glass. "To the war's end," she said, her eyes reddening.

JP touched her glass with his, took a long sip of martini, then set the glass down. "It's been over a month since I've been to church or taken communion. I'm beginning to feel like a sinner."

"The Lord realizes you have been busy clearing quarters and moving off post," Kathy said.

"Tell Father Markham how much I appreciated his help finding us a house to rent on such short notice. Maybe I'll write him a thank you note."

"It was a lucky coincidence that one of his parishioners was going to the west coast for a year and was looking to rent his house," Kathy said. "The beauty of the house is that each kid has a room. Greta is happy with the fenced backyard, and we are still in the same school district."

JP took another sip of martini. He set the glass down and reached for Kathy's hand. "You know that I pushed hard to go to Vietnam."

"You told me many times you wanted to go. At first I wasn't sure you meant it. After George Barfield was killed I sensed you were serious. After Alex Leichuk died I was sure of it."

"Now that it's about to happen I'm having second thoughts. I didn't realize how agonizing it would be to leave you and the kids."

"What about Greta?"

"And Greta."

220

"We'll do fine," Kathy assured him. "We have plenty of friends to give us support. And Dad comes up to the Defense Intelligence Agency at least once a month. He and Mother will continue to stay with us on those trips."

"I'm supposed to get a few days' leave after six months. We could meet in Hawaii or Thailand or I could come home."

"What would you prefer?"

"Come home; I could be with you and the kids… and Greta."

"I thought that's what you would say." Kathy squeezed her husband's hand. "I'd like to ask you a question, JP."

"Ask away."

"If you're promoted to colonel in Vietnam what will happen to your assignment as division surgeon?"

"I'll have too much rank to continue as division surgeon. I would have to move on, hopefully to command a hospital. Why?"

"General Delmar told me you would be given constructive credit for Command and General Staff College for your time as division surgeon. That's equivalent to graduating from the college. It would put you in line for the War College and possibly a star, especially now that you're Airborne."

JP swirled the ice and martini around in his glass, then sipped. "I don't believe you have asked the real question, Kathy."

"You're right. I want to know. JP, I need to know… are you going to Vietnam to get your ticket punched to enhance your military career, to make general?" Kathy's blue eyes searched her husband's face.

JP smiled at the thought. "There are a lot of reasons I want to go to Vietnam, Kath, but getting my ticket punched is not one of them."

"Are you sure?"

"I'm sure. I worked hard to become a doctor and then a surgeon. I'm tops in my field. I love working with patients and I love operating, as bizarre as that may sound. Conversely I am miserable in a non-clinical setting. I hate, no, despise administration. As a general I would have to give up medicine and instead, push papers for the rest of my professional life in the army. After a few years I would have to retire, my surgical skills and judgment obsolete and irretrievable after a long hiatus. There would be nothing left for me but to play golf and visit kids. I hate golf and the kids would soon tire of having their old man under foot. No, I am not going to Vietnam to get my ticket punched. I'm going for other reasons, some I have yet to define, much less understand."

Kathy reached over and grasped her husband's hand. "Thank you, Colonel Franklin."

"Ya know, Miss Kathleen, you're a real Georgia Peach," JP drawled in his best John Wayne imitation.

"And you, Cunnel Franklin, are high on martini. Let's order dinner."

★

Wednesday, June 10, 1970, 1120 hours
Dulles International Airport, Maryland

The shuttle was filled with passengers bound for the American Airlines flight 1192 to San Francisco. Its electric motors whined as the ugly bus-shaped vehicle eased away from the gate on its fat tires and headed for a waiting Boeing 707. A subdued Lieutenant Colonel JP Franklin turned to the window behind him for a final look at his gamily. Hopefully, he would see them again in six months, although conceivably it could be a year. It could even be never.

He spotted the kids and Kathy up on the observation deck. They were searching the windows of the shuttle as it drifted by. Suddenly, Jim and Paul waved, then Kathy, Frank, and Nancy. They were his family and he was leaving them. The shuttle made a turn and his family was gone. Depressed and already homesick, JP slumped in his seat as the shuttle took him further from his family. Closing his eyes, he rested his chin in his hand. Feeling his smooth chin, he recalled shaving that morning. Nancy had walked into the bathroom and tugged on his shirt. JP shut off the electric razor and looked down at his six-year-old daughter.

"Dad?" she had said.

"Yes, Nan."

"Dad?"

"What is it, Nan?"

"Are you going to get killed in Vietnam like Colonel Barfield?"

Chapter Twenty-Six

Friday, June 12, 1970, 1430 hours
TWA Flight 1174, 33,000 Feet and Sixty Miles North-east of Saigon,
Republic of Vietnam

The Boeing 707 dipped slightly and began a slow descent. Mid-cabin in a window seat a sleeping Lieutenant Colonel JP Franklin, Medical Corps, US Army, began to stir restlessly. The vivid dream of his last night with Kathy had been shattered by the voice of his seatmate, a special forces sergeant named Karl Dahlgren. He tried to ignore the voice and return to the dream, but the voice persisted. "Sir, we're making our descent to Bien Hoa."

Forcing open heavy eyelids, JP focused red eyes on Dahlgren.

"Good dream, Colonel? You were smiling."

"If it had been a movie it would have been X-rated," JP said. The vestiges of sleep rapidly drained, replaced by a total body throbbing ache. For almost twenty-eight hours he had sat, belted in his seat, except for trips to the plane's latrine and short walks during fuel stops in Hawaii, Wake Island, and Okinawa. His forty-three-year-old body was protesting the cramped inactivity. Leaning forward, he wiped moisture from the window hoping to see the ground. Instead he watched sunshine and blue sky disappear as the plane descended into a dark gray overcast. Lightning danced around the plane, rain slashed against it and turbulence shook it.

JP tightened his seat belt, settled back and regarded his seatmate of the past twenty-eight hours. His young clean-cut face and short military haircut gave him a preppie appearance. In civilian clothing he could have passed easily as typical Joe College, but the resemblance ended there.

Sergeant Dahlgren had already served two tours in Vietnam. The decorations on his khaki shirt included a Silver Star, Bronze Star with two Vs, two Purple Hearts, and a paratrooper's badge. A mild chuckle escaped JP.

"Something funny, sir?"

"Just thinking. It's taken me twenty-seven years to make it to three wars. It's taken you a little over three years to do the equivalent."

For a moment Dahlgren looked considerably older than his twenty-two years. "I hate to tell you this, Colonel," he said, "but the way this war is being fought I'll probably be coming back for a tour when I'm your age."

The plane abruptly banked, then dropped its nose in a steep descending spiral. Startled, JP grabbed for the arm rests.

Dahlgren smiled at his seatmate's white-knuckle response. "This is the routine approach into Saigon airspace, Colonel. It cuts down on hits by ground fire," he explained. "We should be landing at Bien Hoa in about five."

"I thought we were scheduled to go into Tan Son Nhut."

"There was a change. While you were asleep the pilot announced there had been some VC activity at Tan Son Nhut. He didn't say what, but the field was closed. All commercial aircraft inbound have been diverted to Bien Hoa."

As the overcast thinned, JP caught glimpses of greens and browns below through the window. The plane broke out of the overcast into a depressing gray world of rain. The terrain, a flat checkerboard of fields and rice paddies, was dotted by clusters of round, water-filled holes. Many of the clusters bordered populated areas. JP asked Dahlgren about the holes.

Dahlgren released his seat belt and leaned past JP to look out the window. "Those are B–52 bomb craters filled with rainwater."

"I didn't realize they bombed so close to populated areas."

"They do when people on the ground are desperate," Dahlgren said. "The B–52s saved my A Team and Mike Force up in the Central Highlands on my last tour, but the bombing was the most terrifying experience of my life."

"How do you mean?"

"An NVA regiment was assembling for an attack on our compound. Our strength was only a couple hundred Montagnards, their dependants, and twelve special forces including myself. There was no way we could have survived an attack by a force that size. I requested B–52s to bomb as close to our compound as possible without killing us. The raid was approved and we were given a time for the bomb drop. Within a minute of the designated time we received word on the radio of bombs away. We heard no planes. Suddenly the ground in the compound shook so violently that people were thrown off their feet. Bunkers and buildings collapsed. The noise was so painful and deafening that I screamed to relieve the pressure on my ears. The heat and dust seemed to suck all the oxygen out of the air. I was sure I was going to suffocate. Sappers in the wire were so stunned that they became disoriented. A few took off. We killed the rest except for a couple we took prisoner."

"What happened to the NVA regiment?" JP asked.

"We're not sure. All we found during a sweep for BDA were scraps of burnt clothing and bits of flesh. The intelligence people took the regiment off the NVA order of battle."

JP slowly shook his head. "Civilization had come a long way since warriors hacked at each other with swords... or has it?"

Electric motors whined. JP turned his attention back to the window. A flap under the wing had gone part way down. A minute later it went further until almost vertical. The plane seemed to wallow as it lost airspeed. The landscape rapidly transitioned from rice paddies to huts, then houses. Stores, street markets, and buildings swept by. Cobwebs of roads were packed with a variety of civilian vehicles.

The landing gear thumped down. The plane flashed over the runway numbers. Tires squealed and engines roared into reverse thrust. Rapidly decelerating, the 707 turned onto a taxiway and headed for the military terminal. Through his window JP studied rows of concrete revetments, each occupied by a small jet fighter. He looked at Dahlgren for clarification.

224

"Those are VNAF A–5s," Dahlgren said. "They're T–37 trainers reconfigured to carry ordnance."

"The VNAF pilots any good?"

"They are better than good. They are outstanding. Most will fly right down fifty-one caliber tracers to bail you out."

JP was surprised at Dahlgren's enthusiastic endorsement of the South Vietnamese Air Force. "What about the ground troops?"

Dahlgren's enthusiasm quickly faded. "Sir, if the ARVNs would fight like the VC or NVA, you and I wouldn't be needed here." Bitterness had crept into his voice.

"You're trying to tell me something, Sergeant."

"Only that not all ARVN units are committed to winning. They're not even committed to fighting. They're poorly led by incompetent and often corrupt officers, many of whom have no military backgrounds. Some officers may be collaborating with the VC and NVA. The units they command are so unreliable that they're more of a threat to us than the VC."

Dahlgren hesitated, reluctant to go on.

"Talk to me, Karl," JP said. "I've spent the last twelve years in an operating room. I need to know what I'm getting into out here."

"I can't tell you anything about the big picture, Colonel. I can give you examples from down at my level."

"Anything will help," JP assured.

"One of my buddies was assigned as an advisor to an ARVN infantry company in the Delta. When the company returned from an operation they brought back only one casualty, my buddy. He had been shot in the back. There are many similar stories. In one operation at the Michelin Plantation almost every US advisor was brought back dead."

A sense of gloom swept through JP. The light at the end of the tunnel was getting weak.

Dahlberg continued. "The last three months of my second tour I was assigned to MACV SOG. My team slipped into Laos to monitor the Ho Chi Minh trail, rescue POWs, grab prisoners for interrogation, and do BDAs. Many of those missions were compromised. The NVA were set up on the landing zone waiting for us, or they came after us with dogs and special tracking teams. We lost a lot of good men. When we complained we were told MACV wouldn't investigate for fear of making the Vietnamese lose face. MACV wouldn't even cut the Vietnamese out of the operations loop."

The tunnel was getting darker. "What about POWs? Were you able to rescue any?"

"Colonel, this is classified."

"You have my word."

"We rescued some ARVNS but no US. When we hit the camps we found most had been just abandoned. It was obvious the camps were warned. The POWs too debilitated to travel were bayoneted, shot, or had their throats cut. One had his belly slit open, a flame-thrower shoved in and fired."

JP didn't want to hear any more. His naivety was being brutally stripped away.

The plane squealed to a stop, swaying gently on its shocks. One by one its engines whined down into silence. A flight attendant opened the door at the front of the plane and swung it back against the fuselage. The rain had stopped: waves of hot, humid air flooded the cabin. On the tarmac two Vietnamese men in white coveralls rolled metal stairs up to the doorway. A US Army captain in starched fatigues scrambled up the stairs. Entering the cabin, a clipboard in his hand, he surveyed the rows of seated troops. "Gentlemen," he said, grinning, "welcome to the Republic of Vietnam."

★

The military terminal at Bien Hoa Airfield was a huge barn of a building with walls of metal siding, a corrugated metal roof supported by steel ribs, and a concrete floor. The interior was lit by rows of naked fluorescent lights hanging from the ceiling. On one side a long counter stretched the length of the terminal. Airmen in starched fatigues worked behind the counter, assigning military personnel and civilians on flights to destinations in South-east Asia.

Soldiers and marines lounged in cheap, metal-framed chairs padded with green plastic seats and backs. Some slept while others read paperbacks or talked to buddies. Suitcases, duffel bags, and packs were parked near their feet. Scattered through the terminal, groups of Vietnamese civilians, mostly women and children, stoically waited for space A flights. The combined odors of sweating bodies and frying burgers from an adjoining fast food service permeated the hot, humid atmosphere. A half dozen floor fans working full bore had little impact on the heat or odor.

JP and Sergeant Dahlgren joined passengers from the plane gathered by a sign that read: INCOMING OFFICERS AND NCOS. Nearby was a pile of duffel bags and suitcases. A corporal in starched khakis stood beside the luggage pile dispassionately watching. "Gentlemen," he finally began, "may I have your attention. I am Corporal Hobart. I will be your escort to the Ninetieth Replacement Depot. Please secure your luggage, be sure it's yours, and then assemble on me."

Minutes later the group had reformed. "Anyone missing luggage?" Hobart asked.

No one answered.

"Please follow me."

He led through the terminal and out of the main entrance to the first of three large olive drab buses parked against the curb. A GI armed with an M–16 stood by the open door of each bus. JP climbed on board with his luggage and nodded a greeting to the GI driver.

"Sir, leave your luggage at the front," the driver said.

JP saw that the first two seats on the right side of the bus had been removed to provide floor space for luggage. Dropping his duffel bag and garment bag, he moved to the seat behind the driver. Sergeant Dahlgren eased into the seat beside him, his khaki shirt already soaked with sweat. Glancing out of the glassless window, JP found himself looking through a heavy metal grill. He turned to Dahlgren. "Are the bars to keep passengers from escaping?"

Dahlgren laughed. "No, sir. They're to keep out grenades thrown by Vietnamese

226

whose hearts and minds we have yet to win."

As soon as the bus was loaded, the armed GI stepped aboard and nodded to the driver. The door hissed closed. The driver shifted gears and the bus moved out from the curb.

"How far to Long Binh?" JP asked Dahlgren.

"About twenty miles. It will take close to an hour because of the traffic."

JP turned his attention to the window. Traffic to and from the airport appeared light, consisting mostly of military vehicles. He was not prepared for the onslaught of civilian vehicles that threatened the bus as it timidly worked its way onto a six-lane highway. Cars, buses, trucks, motorcycles, and mopeds drove wildly through the streets as though there were no tomorrow. For some of the Vietnamese that might have been true. He turned to Dahlgren. "I'll never complain about Boston drivers again."

"Wait until you try to cross a Saigon main street on foot. It's dicier than a VC ambush."

"Do you know where you will be assigned?" JP asked.

"No, sir. I'll find out tomorrow."

Leaving the highway, the bus worked its way through lesser streets lined with small shops on both sides. Wide open store fronts displayed stalls and counters overflowing with produce, fish, chickens, and dry goods. Shocking was the plethora of mess kits, combat boots, fatigues, pistol belts, canteens, and C-rations. He looked to Dahlgren for an explanation.

"All that stuff was stolen from us or sold into the black market by the ARVNs, Colonel. There's a thriving black market operating in the open in all South Vietnam."

"What about the police?"

"They're a joke. The police, politicians, and ARVNs, especially the officers, are in on the black market profits." Dahlgren shook his head in disgust. "Our South Vietnamese allies make money off prostitution and dealing drugs to the GIs. Our own people are too timid to do anything about it except snag a pusher every now and then. After all, we are guests of the South Vietnamese government and we wouldn't want to piss off our hosts. They might ask us to leave."

Dahlgren studied the floor a long minute, then looked at JP. "Colonel, I never thought I would ever say this, but sometimes I have wondered if we were supporting the wrong side."

What little light remaining in the tunnel just disappeared.

The bus slowed to stop at a traffic light. A pedicab pulled up beside it. Through the grilled window JP studied the pedicab's passenger, a Vietnamese woman about his own age dressed in white. A coolie hat, secured by a strap under her chin, shaded a face that radiated a dignified regal beauty. Suddenly their eyes met. They stared at each other as if endeavoring to discern the thoughts of the other. The traffic lights changed and the bus moved forward. The pedicab turned into a side street. JP, struck by the woman's beauty, continued to gaze after the pedicab until it passed from sight.

Dahlgren had seen the woman and JP's reaction. "She symbolizes her country," he remarked cynically.

"How do you mean?"

"Very beautiful and very dangerous. She probably works for the VC."

A little over an hour after leaving Bien Hoa Airport the bus drove through the gate of the huge US base at Long Binh. JP marveled at the sheer size of the "military city" built by the United States Army and civilian contractors. The bus then turned again and passed under a sign: 90ᵀᴴ REPLACEMENT BATTALION. In less than a minute it squealed to a stop in front of a long, low wooden building with louvered sides. The driver turned to JP. "Sir, field grade officers report here." The door hissed open.

Sergeant Dahlgren stood up to allow JP into the aisle. The two shook hands firmly. "Thanks for the education, Sergeant," JP said.

"Take care of yourself, Colonel."

"You too, Sergeant."

JP pulled his duffel bag and garment bag out of the pile at the front of the bus. Carrying the garment bag and dragging the duffel bag, he stepped from the bus to a wooden sidewalk. The door hissed closed and the bus drove off, leaving behind the familiar stench of diesel fumes. Crossing the sidewalk to the building, he opened the door and entered a long windowless room. Fluorescent lights bathed the room in a cold white light. Two noisy floor fans disturbed the hot moist air. Metal filing cabinets and desks lined both sides of the room. Clerk typists were busy at typewriters. A prominent sign in front of a desk read: INCOMING OFFICERS REPORT HERE.

JP headed to the desk. Dropping his luggage on the floor, he stood before an obese staff sergeant, his face buried in an issue of the *Stars and Stripes*. A partially smoked cigar rested on an ashtray constructed from a C-ration can. After standing at the desk for over a minute, JP cleared his throat. The sergeant continued to read. Finally, the sergeant dropped the paper on his desk, took a drag on the cigar, exhaled and looked up. "Reporting in?"

JP noted that the sergeant failed to stand or include "sir" or "Colonel" in his greeting. "You are very perceptive, Sergeant," he said coldly.

"Be with you in a minute."

The sergeant sorted papers on his desk, then took time to relight his cigar. Finally, he held out his hand. "I suppose you have orders?"

Reluctant to begin his Vietnam tour on a sour note, JP stifled the impulse to cut the sergeant off at the knees. Instead he opened his duffel bag, withdrew a packet of papers and passed it to the sergeant.

Laboriously the sergeant got to his feet. Without speaking he walked towards an office at the end of the building. While waiting, JP reached into the open duffel bag and lifted out a framed photograph of Kathy and the kids. He was still looking at the photograph when the sergeant returned.

"Jesus," the sergeant said, "you haven't been gone from the States two days and you're already homesick."

Ignoring the sergeant, JP placed the photograph carefully back in the duffel bag.

The sergeant didn't realize when he was well off.

"All you medics are soft. You know nothing about war. While you're over here all you do is bitch about how tough you have it with all them nurses."

228

Several of the younger enlisted men twittered.

JP flushed. When he spoke it was loud enough to be heard throughout the office. "Sergeant…" he leaned closer to read the name tag above the right breast pocket of the fatigue jacket. "Sergeant Dunby, I presume one of the prerequisites for your staff sergeant's stripes was the ability to identify officers."

Suddenly the clatter of typewriters ceased and an ominous quiet flooded the room. Staff Sergeant Dunby saw a merciless hardness come across what he had considered to be the benign face of another naive doctor out of his element. The look and voice sent a chill through Dunby. Slowly he got to his feet.

JP continued. "And I presume that as a staff sergeant you were at one time aware of the military courtesies required by regulations to be extended officers, including Medical Corps officers."

By now the sergeant was standing at a attention. "Yes, sir," he whispered, reluctant for the other EM to hear.

"What? I can't hear you, Sergeant."

"Yes, sir," the sergeant said, somewhat louder.

"I still can't hear you. What did you say?"

"*Yes, sir,*" he shouted.

JP let thirty seconds of silence go by. "Sergeant, your demeanor suggests it may be necessary for me to discuss with your commander what I perceive as a compelling need for you to undergo a refresher course in the customs of the service. Perhaps an appropriate reduction in rank would motivate you to pay closer attention in the class on military courtesy."

The sergeant swallowed hard. "I wish you wouldn't do that, Colonel," he said in a contrite voice.

JP acted as if he hadn't heard. "You have one of the cushiest jobs in Vietnam, Sergeant. It would be a shame for you to leave it to hump in the bush as a platoon or squad leader of real soldiers. I wonder how long you would last before the VC, or more likely one of your own men took you out." The last brought a grim smile to JP's lips. To Sergeant Dunby it brought a look of terror.

"What's going on out here?" demanded an authoritative voice behind JP.

JP turned to face a six-foot-three major in his early forties. He was almost as overweight as his sergeant.

The major saw the silver leaf on JP's collar and quickly introduced himself. "Sir, Major Parmentier, acting commander of the field grade personnel section."

"I'm Colonel Franklin, just reporting in. I was just recognizing Sergeant Dunby on his military bearing and adherence to military courtesy. It not only reflected well on him but on his acting commander." JP emphasized "acting".

Sergeant Dunby's face was swept with relief.

Major Parmentier turned beet red. "Thank you, sir."

"It wasn't meant as a compliment, Major."

"Yes, sir, I understand," Major Parmentier said, glaring at Dunby, whose face resumed its concern.

After an embarrassing silence Major Parmentier cleared his throat. "Colonel, your assignment will be firmed up at USARV Med Command on the hill. Colonel Miller, chief of Medical Corps personnel, is expecting you. Transportation is waiting for you in front of this building."

"Thank you, Major."

"And, Dunby, I want you in my office after you escort the colonel to his transportation."

"Yes, sir," Dunby said. He handed JP back his orders and reached for his luggage.

JP stopped him. "That won't be necessary, Sergeant." Picking up his garment bag and duffel bag, JP headed to the door. Dunby rushed ahead to open it. Outside a jeep waited with a soldier standing beside the passenger seat.

JP faced Dunby. "You'd better pray we never meet again, Sergeant," he said icily.

Dunby went pale. He came to attention and saluted.

Ignoring the salute, JP turned his back on the sergeant and walked to the waiting jeep.

Chapter Twenty-Seven

Friday, June 12, 1970, 1610 hours
Long Binh, Republic of Vietnam

Carrying his luggage, Lieutenant Colonel JP Franklin approached the parked jeep. The soldier standing by it came to attention and saluted.

"Pfc Solano, sir. Are you the colonel going to Med Command?"

JP, his hands full, nodded.

Pfc Solano took the garment bag from JP and placed it in the back seat of the jeep. The duffel bag followed. JP climbed into the passenger's seat. Solano walked around the front, took his seat and cranked the engine. Shifting gears he made a U-turn and headed towards an area of elevated terrain half a mile away. On the way they passed rows of one- and two-storied wooden office buildings, barracks, motor pools, BOQs, and an officers' club. The road then began a gradual ascent through a section of neatly arranged trailer homes.

"Who lives in those?" JP asked Solano.

"Full colonels and brigadier generals. The two-, three- and four-star generals and admirals live in bungalows around the senior officers' mess up on the far side of the hill. They have it real tough."

"That gives you something to work towards, Solano."

"I don't think so, sir. Three months and I'm out of Nam and this man's army," Solano said, grinning happily.

"What then?"

"Probably college."

"Good answer," JP said.

The road ended in a wide flat partial circle at the top of the rise. Half a dozen elongated two-story office buildings were arranged in a rectangle. Solano stopped at the entrance of last building. A large sign above the glassed entrance read: MEDICAL COMMAND, US ARMY VIETNAM/FORTY-FOURTH MEDICAL BRIGADE. A maroon flag with a single star hung limp from a pole over the entrance.

"This looks like the right place," JP told Solano as he swung his feet to the ground. "I can get my gear." Reaching in the back, he lifted out the duffel bag and garment bag.

Although the driver of a vehicle is not required to salute when behind the wheel, Solano saluted.

JP snapped a salute in return. "Thanks for the lift, and don't forget college."

"Yes, sir, I mean, no, sir."

JP climbed wide concrete steps, pushed his way through the glass doors into the lobby and paused to study the directory. Waves of frigid air rolled over him cooling him so rapidly he began to shiver. He quickly found the office number for the Chief,

Medical Corps personnel. A minute later he was seated in a well-furnished reception room sipping coffee from a styrofoam cup and eating a doughnut.

A gruff voice brought him to his feet. "JP Franklin, how the hell are you?"

JP stood to face a tall, overweight, full colonel charging at him like an express train. "Ed Miller, I had no idea you had risen to such lofty heights of command."

"A few chosen ones must carry the heavy burden of administrative responsibilities in this conflict," Miller said with false modesty, extending his hand.

Grasping the hand, JP sensed a sweaty weak grip.

Colonel Miller led into a large glassed-in office furnished with plush leather chairs, a Japanese reel-to-reel tape deck, walnut speakers, refrigerator, hot plate, television, and an immense desk with a glass top. JP eased into a captain's chair beside the desk and watched his friend of many years move ponderously to a swivel chair behind the desk. Gesturing towards all the luxury items in the room, he quipped, "Way to fight a war, Ed."

Miller grinned. "This job has its perks."

JP tried to ignore the observation that Miller's face had filled out considerably since he last saw him. A waddle of redundant skin and fat dangled under his chin. His belly hung out over his belt like a partially deflated inner tube. The epithet "Saigon Warrior" came to mind. Sergeant Dahlgren had introduced him to a more appropriate phrase identified by the four letters: R.E.M.F.

Colonel Miller picked up a pipe lying on his desk and filled the bowl with tobacco from a large can. Fumbling in a drawer, he withdrew an odd-shaped lighter which he held over the bowl. Blue flame shot from the lighter; clouds of gray acrid smoke spewed from the pipe, Miller's mouth and nose.

"Good God, Ed," JP gasped, "you must have a death wish."

"Vietnam is a hard place to give up old vices. In fact, Vietnam is a place that engenders new vices. I'll quit smoking when I go home."

"I'm not a psychiatrist or a chaplain, so I won't touch that. However, as a head and neck surgeon I'm putting in a claim to do your tongue–jaw–neck dissection when you show up with cancer."

Furrows of concern passed over Miller's face. He placed his pipe carefully down on the desk and looked at JP. "Since you brought up the subject, would you mind taking a look at some white spots on my tongue?"

JP set his cup on Miller's desk and stood up. "Let's go next to the window." He turned Miller's head so the sunlight fell on his protruding tongue. "This is a hell of a way to do an exam. Okay, now touch the roof of your mouth with the tip of your tongue."

The undersurface of the tongue was an angry beefy-red color spotted with dirty white patches 2 to 3 mm in diameter. "Any pain, burning, or trouble swallowing?" JP asked.

"A little burning, mostly at the end of the day."

"How many bowlfuls do you light up a day?"

"About ten or twelve."

"And you suck on an unlit pipe between?"

232

"That's about it."

"What about alcohol?"

"One or two martinis before dinner."

JP looked skeptical.

"Well, sometimes two to three and a glass of wine, but not every day."

After feeling both sides of Miller's neck for lumps, JP returned to his seat and picked up his coffee cup.

"What do you think?" Miller asked. He resembled a prisoner just found guilty and who waits for the judge to pronounce sentence.

"I don't think the white patches are cancer… at least not yet. Most likely the patches are leukoplakia, which may or may not be a precursor to cancer. The mucosa of the undersurface of the tongue and floor of mouth looks definitely premalignant."

"I guess that's both good and bad news."

"I should warn you, Ed, my hallway consultation isn't worth much. You need a real exam by a head and neck surgeon. There's one at the 24th, 93rd and 98th Evacs here at Long Binh, so you won't have to go far. Whoever you see will want to excise those lesions for histologic exam. In the meantime, give up all tobacco and booze. Sometimes the leukoplakia subsides and the mucosa returns to normal by eliminating the irritating factors."

"Damn it, JP, you haven't been in Vietnam three hours and you're already screwing up my life."

"I'd screw it up even more if I had to whack out your tongue, part of your jaw, floor and mouth, and do a neck dissection. You would never be able to swallow again. Think of all that good food you'd have to blenderize and gravity swallow like a pelican."

The room became quiet interrupted only by the ring of a distant telephone. Colonel Miller ceremoniously lifted the can of tobacco from his desk, held it over a wastebasket and let it drop. Three expensive pipes followed. He looked as if he were about to cry.

"You're already a better man for having done that," JP said. "Just make sure you don't fish them out after I leave."

"We'd better get to your assignment before you end up admitting me to the hospital." Reaching to his hold box, he withdrew some papers and passed them to JP. "I know you had your heart set on going to the 101st, but the exigencies of the service had to take higher priority."

"I've always hated that phrase."

"What phrase?"

"Exigencies of the service. It's always used to justify shafting someone, in this case, me."

Miller smiled. "Med Command appreciates your coming over here two months earlier than you planned. I hope Kathy understands."

"She'll understand better if Med Command sends me home two months earlier."

Miller indicated the papers in JP's hand. "Those assign you as the division surgeon to the 36th Infantry Division. With 24,000 men it's one of the largest divisions in

Vietnam."

He stood up and went to a large wall map of South-east Asia and placed a stubby finger on the coast of South Vietnam. "I'll trace out the approximate AO of the 36th. The northern limit is here at Nghia Lam. Come down the coast 100 miles to Quang Dien, the southern limit. All the terrain from the coast between Nghia Lam and Quang Dien to the Laotian border belongs to the 36th."

"I thought it belonged to the Vietnamese," JP said. He stood up and went to the map, studied it for a moment, then returned to his seat. "Those boundaries encompass 10,000 square miles, Ed."

"You won't have to walk it, JP. You'll have your own chopper."

JP's face brightened. "Those are the right buzz words to make me happy I came."

"Just be careful where you take the chopper. Remember what happened to George Barfield and Elwood Diblasio."

"Any word on how Diblasio is doing in Japan?"

Colonel Miller shook his head sadly. "He died yesterday of respiratory complications."

JP spoke his thoughts. "He didn't have much future as a high quad."

"Remember, JP, those damn choppers are dangerous. It's not generally known, but two other medical officers have been shot down and captured, one in your AO."

An almost pathological fear of capture, a long-suppressed holdover from the Pacific War, surfaced in JP's mind. Despite the air conditioned coolness of the room he began to sweat.

Colonel Miller stared at him. "You okay?"

JP nodded. "I'm not used to this climate."

"It takes several days to get acclimatized."

"Where's the 36th Division headquarters?"

"At Phong Sahn, here on the coast halfway between Nghia Lam and Quang Dien. It's a huge base, almost as large as Long Binh. The medical battalion headquarters and division surgeon's office are located there."

"You know, Ed, the only division surgeon I have ever seen was in the 3rd Division in Korea when I was out-processing to go home. He signed a certificate attesting I had been properly deloused and was free of lice."

Miller laughed. "Your responsibilities will be a bit more involved. You will be responsible for everything medical that impacts the health and welfare of the 24,000 men in the division; from preventative medicine to evacuation of casualties."

"I hope I'll have some help."

Miller consulted a paper on his desk. "As of yesterday the 36th Division had assigned forty-six doctors, four dentists, two veterinarians, and fifty-seven Medical Service Corps officers. The MSCs include a sanitary engineer, psychiatric social worker, your battalion headquarters staff, plus medical administrators for the units to assist battalion surgeons."

"What about enlisted personnel?"

"Including the medical battalion and the medics in the field… close to 1,000."

"That sounds like an empire," JP said.

234

"You will wear three hats in the 36th Division. In a sense you will serve three masters."

"Don't you remember what the Bible says about serving two masters? The Lord probably considers three masters ridiculous."

Miller droned on. "Be that as it may, your first hat will be as division surgeon. You will be on the division headquarters staff with access to the three generals, chief of staff, headquarters staff members, and anyone else you want access to. You advise the division commander on all medical and related matters including medical support for military operations."

"That sounds simple enough. What's my second hat?"

"Commander of the medical battalion. The battalion has four clearing companies and a headquarters company. It comes under DISCOM. As the battalion commander you answer to the DISCOM commander, a full colonel. He makes out your ER."

"Who endorses it?"

"The ADC for supply, a brigadier general."

"And my third hat?"

"As of now you are the US Army's head and neck surgery consultant for South-east Asia. You should be available to give surgical or administrative counsel to any military doctor in South-east Asia. Whether you do it in person or by telephone is a matter for your judgment and the wishes of the 36th commanding general."

"From what you have told me so far, Ed, it looks as if I'll have a lot of spare time."

Miller lowered his voice. "JP, the division surgeon, especially of a division as large as the 36th, is a plum assignment. My spies in the puzzle palace have leaked to me that the Medical Corps promotion policy is about to be revised and you will be on the bird colonel's list. The eagles should come through in four to six months." He leaned back in his chair. "After you're promoted we'll see about getting you an evac hospital to command. When you rotate back to the States you will qualify for the War College. That should bring a star within reach." Miller settled back in his seat. "No wonder you were hot to come out here."

JP momentarily bristled at Ed Miller's implication that he was in Vietnam to get his ticket punched. Miller was just trying to guide a friend. "How do I get up to the 36th?"

"We'll arrange space for you to fly up to Phong Sahn on a C–130 the day after tomorrow."

"Why not tomorrow?"

"The 130s fly into Phong Sahn every other day. The flights are planned to land at night because of increased rocket attacks on the airfield during the day. While you're waiting you can draw fatigues, jungle boots, get some shots, and visit the largest post exchange in country. You can stay with me in my trailer. It's air conditioned, has a guest room, bathtub, shower, and full kitchen. It also has a freezer full of T-bone steaks. I make a great martini."

The prospect of spending two days in Long Binh did not sit well with JP. Somehow basking in an air-conditioned trailer, drinking martinis, and eating T-bone steaks seemed incompatible with war. "Ed, I really need to get up to the 36th as soon as possible. The chief of staff wrote asking me to expedite my arrival."

"I wish I could help, JP. Even generals have trouble getting private flights."

"Would you object to me making my own arrangements? I can get fatigues, shots, and whatever else I need after I get to Phong Sahn."

"Good luck, buddy. What do you have in mind?"

"I have friends in high places." He took out his wallet and withdrew a card. "Mind if I use your phone?"

Miller pushed the phone to him. 'Dial nine for off base. Is it long distance?"

"Bien Hoa."

"Just dial the number for the base and the extension. Do you have it?"

JP nodded. Holding up the card, he dialed the number written on it. When a voice answered he said, "This is Lieutenant Colonel JP Franklin. I'd like to speak to your chief operations officer, Mr. Bendler."

Chapter Twenty-Eight

Saturday, June 13, 1970, 0700 hours
Bien Hoa Airfield, Republic of Vietnam

The US Army sedan with Lieutenant Colonel JP Franklin riding up front slowly approached the sandbagged bunker guarding the auxiliary entrance to the airfield and stopped at the metal barrier. The snout of an M–60 machine gun protruding from the bunker's gunport swung ominously towards the sedan. A white helmeted ARVN MP, an M–16 slung over his shoulder, stepped from the bunker, scrutinized the sedan, then walked to the driver's open window. After scanning the sedan's interior he took the papers the driver gave him and returned to the bunker.

While waiting, JP noted the barbed wire fence and rolls of concertina wire bordering the airfield. Manned towers and bunkers every 200 to 300 meters guarded the perimeter as far as the eye could see. "I see they take security seriously around here," JP commented to the driver.

"Yes, sir. It got real tight after sappers blew up a bunch of airplanes last month."

The MP reappeared, returned the papers to the driver, then went to the barrier. Lifting it, he motioned for them to enter. As they drove through the gate he came to attention and saluted. JP snapped off a return salute.

Approaching the perimeter road, the driver slowed. "Which way now, Colonel?'

"Just a second."

After consulting a small spiral notebook he took from his shirt pocket JP pointed to a half dozen parked UH1H Hueys on the left. "Head for those choppers. A quarter mile beyond should be a concrete building with small planes parked in front. One of the planes will be a tail dragger with an oversized rudder, strange-looking wings, and a long nose. That's my ride."

Minutes later the driver brought the sedan to a stop several feet from the left wing tip of an ungainly high-winged single-engine aircraft. It rested at a steep angle on its two thick main gear and large tail wheel. The fuselage began with an oversized three-bladed propeller on an extended nacelle. It ended in a disproportionately tall vertical fin and rudder. The entire leading edge of the wing appeared to have fallen four or five inches away from the rest of the wing. Two men stood in the shade under the left wing. One, in his mid-twenties, was dressed in a loose-fitting flight suit and baseball cap. The other, considerably older, wore slacks and a sport shirt. Neither man wore insignia or rank.

JP opened the sedan's door and stepped out. The older of the two men, Bruce Bendler, a former patient, greeted him with a hug and warm handshake. "Colonel Franklin, it's been a long time since Walter Wonderful." The man's voice was low and raspy.

"Six months, Bruce," JP said. "You given up smoking yet?"

"Only five cigarettes since you cut my throat."

"That's a good start." Reaching to Bendler's neck, he felt the two six-inch almost invisible horizontal scars. "Beautiful," he said, "just beautiful. Vivid testimony to the superb skill of your surgeon."

"When it comes to egos, you surgeons make us pilots seem humble." Bendler gestured towards the younger man beside him. "This is your pilot, Joe Frieze."

"Glad to meet you, Colonel," the pilot said, gripping JP's hand. "Bruce has told me how you cut out a cancer from his voice box but left him still able to speak. The only problem now is he never says what I want to hear."

JP chuckled. "Women considered his voice sexy. At Reed he spent much of his convalescent leave trying to impress nurses and other young ladies with what a big wheel he was in South-east Asia. I came out here to check on his stories."

"Aw, Colonel, I want you to know I've settled down since my operation," Bendler said.

The sedan driver approached carrying JP's garment bag and duffel bag. Joe Frieze took them and headed to the open door in the plane's fuselage.

"Thanks for the ride," JP told the driver.

"Good luck, sir," the driver said, saluting.

Returning the salute, JP and Bendler followed the pilot. "Okay, Bruce, tell me what you meant by 'settling down'."

"That throat cancer was the first time in my life I faced the possibility of death when I had no control over the situation. It was a heads-up experience. I took your advice about Georgia women."

"I forgot what I told you."

"You told me to marry a Georgia girl. I married one from Atlanta; she works at the embassy."

"When did that happen?"

"Last month."

"I must say you air force types take a long time to mature. Congratulations."

"Look, Doc, I wasn't kidding when I wrote you about staying with us. Our villa is air conditioned. It has a couple of guest rooms; you can take your pick. Ernestine can whip up wonderful southern fried chicken and gravy on short notice. She can even arrange a date for you from the embassy."

JP shook his head, not without regret. "That wouldn't sit well with Kathy: she has definite old-fashioned ideas. Besides, I really need to get up to the 36th. All their operations are on hold until I get there."

Bendler looked at Joe Frieze. "What did I tell you about surgeons' egos?"

"Boss, how about arranging a date from the embassy for me next time I'm in Saigon?"

"You do well enough on your own, Frieze."

The pilot lifted JP's luggage through the open door, then climbed aboard and moved them aft to a storage area, fastening a webbed net over them. Bendler slammed the door shut. He and JP walked around the nose of the plane to the open door on the right side.

JP gestured at the plane's unusual configuration. "What kind of airplane is this, Bruce?"

Bendler patted the metal fuselage. "This, Dr. Franklin, is a Helio Courier, one of the best STOLS ever built. It will do things that will put a helicopter to shame. I believe it was designed in the early 1950s by some professors at MIT."

JP looked up at the wing. "How come the leading edge looks as if it's going to fall off?"

Bendler laughed. "I thought you knew something about airplanes. Doc. That strip of leading edge is called a 'slat'. It's spring-loaded to stay 4–5 inches in front of the true leading edge until wind pressure of about fifty knots forces it back against the true leading edge. When the slat is deployed forward, like it is now, the stalling speed of the plane is markedly reduced and lift increased. This bird can take off in less than 300 feet and land in a little over 200, depending on the windspeed, direction, and obstacles."

"Impressive," JP said. He shook hands with Bendler. "Thanks for getting me on this flight."

"No problem. Joe was going in your direction anyway."

JP climbed through the door and into the co-pilot's seat. Bendler followed, and stood behind him. "Watch yourself up in the 36th AO, Doc, it's full of bad guys. They would love to get their hands on a senior army surgeon, especially one known internationally. They have already shot down two doctors in your AO, killing one and capturing the other."

"I know about them."

"What you don't know is that the latest intelligence suggests that the North Vietnamese are selling US prisoners to the Russians. Chinese, and North Koreans. I'd hate it if that were to happen to you."

"So would I," JP said with a shudder. "Don't worry, Bruce. I'll be the paragon of caution up there."

"That's the kind of talk that worries me, especially coming from an ex-jarhead."

Jumping to the ground, Bendler turned and stuck his head back in the plane. "You know how to get in touch with me. The next time you're in Saigon, Ernestine and I will expect you for dinner. No more BS about your vital role in this bizarre activity euphemistically referred to as a war."

"Semper Fi, Bruce."

The door slammed closed.

JP waved through the side window, then buckled his seat belt and shoulder harness. He paused a moment to savor the wonderful smells of petroleum products, electrical wiring and worn leather that permeate the interior of a small airplane, then fumbled along the right side of his seat for the seat release lever. Finding it, he slid his seat forward, then reached for the headset and boom mike hanging over him. By the time it was adjusted comfortably on his head Frieze had started the engine. As the RPMs built up the headset came to life. Frieze's voice came through the intercom, "Colonel, we've been cleared to take off from the taxiway. There's a twelve-knot wind gusting to sixteen coming right down it." The engine noise increased and the plane began to move forward. "After we go to full power we'll be airborne before the wheels make one complete revolution," he added with a mischievous grin.

JP looked past the nose and whirling prop; blue sky filled the windscreen. "How can you see to drive this thing?" he asked.

"With the tail wheel dragging, you have to S-turn a lot and look out of the side windows. Once the tail comes up visibility ahead is as good as from any plane with tricycle gear."

JP watched Frieze go rapidly through a checklist while taxiing, his feet dancing on the rudder pedals to counter the gusting wind trying to push the big vertical fin around. Frieze increased power; the onset of loud metallic banging just outside his window was startling.

Frieze laughed at his response. "Those are the wing slats bouncing in and out."

"I thought we were losing parts off the wing."

"This is a rugged airplane, Colonel," Frieze assured. "It's easy to fly but tricky to land. Most accidents occur on landing; the most frequent injury is the pilot's pride. Like any other airplane it can't fly through mountains." Frieze spoke to the tower, then turned to JP. "Okay, Colonel, hang on." He shoved the throttle all the way forward. The engine noise increased to a powerful roar.

The plane seemed to leap into the air with hardly a ground roll. One second JP was looking down the taxiway, the next he was looking at blue sky. Frieze brought the nose way up to an obscenely steep angle. A glance out the side window showed the ground rapidly spiraling away. A sweep of the instruments made him shudder. The airspeed needle indicated fifty knots. Surely a plane this heavy and at this angle of climb would stall. The intermittent banging of the slats did little to comfort him. He turned to Frieze. "Does that damn noise ever quit?"

"What noise, Colonel?" Frieze asked, grinning.

At 2,500 feet they leveled off. By this time the noise of banging slats had subsided. JP loosened his seat belt. "That was spectacular. I felt like an astronaut blasting off."

"The big 350 Lycoming out front can really drag this beast around," Frieze said with the pride of a father boasting over one of his kids. He played with the throttle and prop pitch until the airspeed needle settled at 125 knots and the altimeter needle fixed at 2,500 feet. After trimming the airplane Frieze looked over at JP. "Bruce said you were a pilot; want to fly her?"

The question was akin to asking an alcoholic if he would like a free drink. In a flash JP's hands were on the wheel and his feet on the rudder pedals. "I've got it."

"You have the airplane," Frieze said. "Maintain a heading of zero six zero until we reach the coast, then turn north just out over the water. There are fewer bad guys out there who might shoot at us. If we have to make a forced landing the beach is a pretty good auxiliary strip."

Forty minutes later the white sandy shore along the coast passed under the plane, giving way to the blue South China Sea. "Well, Colonel, as the fighter pukes say, 'we're feet wet'." He looked down at the sandy beach just under the left wing. "Would you believe feet moist? You can turn to a heading of three five eight now and drop down to 2,000. If you keep the left wing tip over the shore line that will put us about the proper distance over water and headed more or less in the right direction."

"I'm impressed with your precise navigation, Joe."

The young pilot grinned. He slid his seat back and loosened his belt and harness. "We'll make a fuel stop at Cam Ranh Bay and get something to eat. They serve pretty good cheeseburgers and fries at a place near the terminal. We'll refuel again at Chulai, then go on to Phong Sahn."

"Where do you go after you drop me off?'

"Up to Quang Tri for tonight, then west tomorrow to who knows."

"Do you get down to Saigon often?"

"No, sir. That was my first in five months. I ferried the plane down to Bien Hoa for an engine change and new radios. It gave me a chance for some R & R in Saigon."

The morning air was beginning to warm up. JP adjusted the air vent to blow on him. By now he had developed a "feel" for the Helio Courier. Slower in speed and response than the T–34 he was accustomed to flying, the Courier was easier to fly. As it droned north over the South China Sea he felt a sense of detachment. The day was sunny, the winds calm, the air smooth, and the blue sky cloudless. He found it difficult to believe that 2,000 feet beneath the left wing young men just out of adolescence were killing each other. Soon he would become a part of that activity, but for now, flying this strange airplane at the terrifying airspeed of 125 knots, Lieutenant Colonel JP Franklin, M.D., Medical Corps, US Army, was at peace with the world.

★

Saturday, June 13, 1620 hours
120 Miles South of Chulai

Except for the landing and take-off at Cam Ranh Bay, Joe Frieze seemed content to let JP fly the Hello Courier. The plane's left wingtip continued to trace the edge of South Vietnam's shoreline, passing over fishing village after fishing village. Several miles out from shore, clusters of tiny round boats bobbed in the water among larger vessels. Curiosity finally got to JP. He dipped the right wing for a better look.

"LRDBs," Frieze informed him, "little round dink boats. The Vietnamese fish and dive from them, at least that's what they're supposed to be doing."

Minutes later Frieze announced, "The southern end of the American Division AO is just off the left wing." He pointed over the Courier's long nose. 'That prominent hill on the coast is Montezuma; a sophisticated outpost is on the summit. It gathers data on enemy activity from sensors scattered from the coast all the way to Laos and beyond."

"That's a great navigational aid," JP said.

"Yes, sir, it's hard to miss but not impossible. Just west of Montezuma is a north–south runway and some buildings. That's Fire Support Base Bronco, headquarters of the 11th Brigade. About five klicks west is Duc Pho, a village of about 3,000. It's a source of major problems for the Americal."

"What do you mean, problems?"

"Things like VD, TB, marijuana, amphetamines, heroin, and VC sympathizers. Even though the village is off-limits, occasionally a GI will sneak into the village and never return. It's not known if he was killed and buried, or captured and moved into Laos."

"Are you trying to shake me up, Joe?"

"No, sir. Just making sure you're well informed. About thirty klicks west of Duc Pho is the province's capital, Quang Ngai." Frieze reached behind his seat to a pocket and lifted out heavy binoculars. After peering through them a moment he passed them to JP "There's an unfinished cathedral at Quang Ngai. You can make it out with these."

Keeping his right hand on the wheel, JP took a quick look through the binoculars, spotted what he thought was the skeleton of a large building, then returned the binoculars.

Frieze continued. "An ARVN military hospital and the province hospital is located in Quang Ngai. So is an orthopedic hospital staffed by a Quaker doctor and his wife. The hospital makes and fits artificial limbs, mostly for kids. It also trains adult amputees to make and fit artificial limbs."

Impressed by Joe Frieze's intimate knowledge of the area, he asked, "How is it you know so much about this area?"

"I spent my first tour in '68 as a FAC flying Mixmasters out of Bronco. In my spare time I worked as a volunteer at the Quaker hospital helping kids learn to walk with artificial limbs."

JP studied the young pilot, concluding that his laid-back demeanor was a cover for a highly motivated and dedicated individual. "How did you get selected for a second tour so soon after finishing your first?"

Frieze grinned sheepishly. "I volunteered. Flying assignments in the States were boring after the flying I had done over here. The air force offered me two years at MIT to get a Master's in physics, then a three-year tour at the Academy teaching. The last thing I wanted was to be back in a classroom as a student or teacher. An opening with Air America came along. I was told it would be exciting and would look good on my record. It's definitely been exciting; I'm not sure it will ever appear on my record."

JP chuckled. "I've heard that story before."

Twenty minutes later Frieze touched JP's shoulder. "There's a river coming up at eleven o'clock," he said, pointing.

JP shifted his gaze from the instrument panel to the wind screen and nodded.

"That's the Song Tra Khuc. Just north is a cluster of hamlets called Son My Village. One, I can't tell which one from here, is Mylai." Frieze studied the area through the binoculars, then handed them to JP.

To steady the binoculars JP took both hands off the wheel and leaned to the left for a better view. The Courier's nose and left wing suddenly dipped. The engine noise increased and the altimeter started to unwind. "Damn it," JP muttered. Dropping the binoculars in his lap, he grabbed for the controls. Leveling off after loosing four hundred feet, his face glowing with embarrassment, he braced himself for caustic remarks from Joe Frieze.

The young pilot only laughed. "This airplane is like a spirited horse, Colonel, docile and benign until you give her a little extra rein. Then she'll turn around and bite you."

JP scanned the instruments, rolled in a little up trim, added power and regained the

242

lost altitude.

"Want to go back for a closer look at Mylai?" Frieze asked.

"I don't think so, Joe. Just reading about it was bad enough."

JP was aware of the alleged slaughter of old men, women, and children by troops of the Americal Division. He was highly skeptical that American soldiers would commit such atrocities and considered the report some sort of Communist propaganda trick.

Frieze must have discerned his thoughts. "At first I was sure the story had been cooked up by the press and the NVA to take the heat off the Communists for murdering 4,000 civilians in Hue during TET. Then I talked to a friend who worked in the CP on LZ Dottie. That's about twelve klicks west of Mylai and is the parent headquarters of the platoon involved in the massacre. According to him our troops went over the edge."

Again JP was hearing things he didn't want to hear.

"From what my friend told me I can understand why the massacre happened. I just can't excuse it. If I did, I'd be just as evil as the Communists."

"I don't follow you, Joe."

"For weeks patrols in the area of Mylai had taken heavy casualties, not from contact with enemy troops but from mines and booby traps, many set by old mama sans and children from Mylai. The GIs saw their buddies blown into raw meat. Those not killed had hideous injuries. One platoon got trapped in a minefield and had three KIAs and twelve WIAs in one day. Some of those GIs had legs blown off almost at the hips and their crotches shredded. That kind of stuff went on day after day without seeing a single Viet Cong, much less killing one."

JP stared at the young pilot. "I thought we were winning the war."

A hardness came over Frieze's face. "That's a myth, sir. We win all the battles, sure, but so many restrictions have been placed on ground and air activities that the war has become unwinnable. Even worse, idiotic target selection and rules of engagements have caused a lot of unnecessary casualties. Five of my close friends from the Academy have been killed or are missing." He paused and looked at JP. "You're not going to believe what I tell you next."

"Try me."

"When pilots flying up north reported missile sites and triple A being installed along the approaches to targets, they were forbidden to attack the sites. Only after the sites became operational and actually fired at our planes could they attack. Even worse, the pilots were prohibited from altering approaches to targets."

JP saw bitterness written all over Frieze's face. *My God*, he thought, *what are we doing to our young men?*

Frieze continued, as though once started he was unable to stop. "On any given day Haiphong Harbor is clogged with ships, including ships of our so-called allies and friends, delivering military hardware and supplies to the North Vietnamese. A classmate wrote me that a full colonel, a wing commander who led a flight up north to Haiphong, was court-martialed for violating the rules of engagement."

"What?"

"He fired at a triple A ship in Haiphong Harbor after it had fired on and hit two planes in his flight. Some of the colonel's shells hit a Soviet ship anchored beside the triple A ship." Frieze stared thoughtfully out the windscreen, then turned to JP. "Colonel, our bosses in Washington have decided it's better to allow Americans to be killed than to offend our enemies." He slumped in his seat. "I'd better shut up before I talk myself into big trouble."

"Haven't you heard of the doctor–patient relationship? What you have told me is privileged information, Joe," JP assured. Ahead, he made out a narrow stretch of land extending several miles from the mainland into the South China Sea. "That looks like Cape Cod."

"The similarity ends there," Frieze said. "That's the Batangan Peninsula. Ho Chi Minh was supposed to have been born there. It's full of VC sympathizers and VC. The Americal Division has been trying to pacify it for years. Engineers from Dottie built a road from QL 1 just north of Quang Ngai into the peninsula. They put in reinforced bridges and improved drainage to protect against floods. MEDCAPS have gone in there to inoculate kids and deliver babies. But GIs still get sniped at or blown up by mines and booby traps."

When the Chulai airfield came into sight Joe Frieze put his hands on the controls. "I've got the airplane, Colonel. We'll land here for fuel, then head up to Phong Sahn."

★

Forty minutes later they were airborne again headed north. Frieze let JP do the take-off, but it was a conventional take-off, not the spectacular blast-off as from Bien Hoa. Frieze pointed out landmarks as they flew: Monkey Mountain just south of Danang, the hospital ship Sanctuary out in Danang Harbor, the Haivan Pass north of Danang. "This is the AO of the 1st Marine Division, Colonel," he added.

"I may have an old marine buddy from World War II there as the division chaplain."

'That's really going way back… sir. I didn't think you were *that* old."

"Watch it, Frieze. I don't need you to fly this thing."

The pilot grinned and eased his seat back along the rails.

By now JP was beginning to feel the fatigue from hours of flying. He yawned repeatedly and his butt kept getting numb. Every now and then he squirmed in his seat seeking relief. Despite the discomfort he was reluctant to turn the plane back to Frieze. He had no idea when he would have another opportunity to fly while in Vietnam.

Finally, Frieze pointed to a flat brown area along the coast. "That's Phong Sahn coming up, Colonel."

In a few minutes JP could make out a long wide north–south runway in an immense area dense with buildings and roads.

Frieze reached to the radio knobs and tuned in the frequency for Phong Sahn approach. After establishing contact he transmitted, "Batman Four is five miles south over the coast at 2,000 for landing."

"Roger, Batman Four. What type of aircraft are you?"

"Batman Four is a Helio Courier."

There was a lengthy pause, then Phong Sahn approach came back. "Say again type aircraft."

Frieze smiled tolerantly. "Helio Courier is a high-winged single-engine STOL. I have one VIP O-five pax to drop off at the terminal."

"Understand, Batman. Will your pax require transportation?"

"That's affirmative. Notify the division surgeon's office the pax is their Six."

"Roger, Batman Four. You are cleared to enter left downwind for runway one seven. Winds one niner at ten gusting to fourteen. Altimeter two niner niner eight. Report turning base. No immediate traffic, but be advised, seven rockets hit the base thirty minutes ago.

"Batman Four." Frieze rolled in the barometric pressure in the altimeter's Kollsman window, then told JP, "Better start letting down, Colonel. Drop back to 1,800 RPM and enter downwind at 600 feet and eighty knots. I'll take the airplane after you turn final."

JP played with the throttle, prop pitch, and trim until the Courier was in a steady gentle descent. At slower speeds the Courier's controls became heavy. Glancing intermittently at the altimeter, airspeed, and runway, he leveled off at 650 feet, then lost fifty feet in his turn downwind. The left wingtip now traced the edge of the runway. The altimeter needle was fixed at 600 and the airspeed needle hovered at eighty. Proud of his precision flying, he told Frieze, "I'm beginning to like this weird airplane."

Joe Frieze grinned. "You're not doing badly for a doctor... sir.

"One of these days I'll show you how to take out an appendix."

"I might take you up on that, Colonel."

Frieze pointed out his window west to mountains six or seven miles away. "Colonel, can you see that gap between those two peaks?"

JP, his hands full trying to maintain 600 feet altitude and eighty knots airspeeed in the mid-afternoon turbulence, took a quick look and nodded.

"The VC fire 120-millimeter rockets through it. They aim for the airstrip, POL dumps, and division staff hooches. Most of the rockets land in the water and kill fish, but one of these days the VC are bound to get lucky."

JP flew a longer downwind than he intended. Frieze diplomatically asked, "Colonel, you going up to the DMZ?"

JP reddened, dropped a wing in a steep turn and added power.

"Bat Four, base," Frieze reported.

"Bat Four, continue approach."

JP made another ninety-degree left turn and lined the nose up with the runway. The Courier was still at 600 feet.

"Stay at this altitude, Colonel." Frieze then reported to the tower. "Bat Four, final."

"Bat Four, cleared to land."

"Okay, Colonel. I've got the airplane. I'll drop you off at the passenger terminal." Frieze partially lowered flaps and added power. The airspeed dropped off to seventy, then sixty. A barn-like building came into view. "There's the terminal," he said.

JP looked at the altimeter. It still read 600 feet. They were too high. No way could they land anywhere near the terminal from this height.

"Bat Four, are you making a go around?" the tower inquired.

"Bat Four, negative."

"Roger."

Frieze brought the flaps all the way down. The nose dropped into an almost a vertical dive.

JP slid forward. If he hadn't been restrained by his seat belt he would have ended up under the instrument panel. Holding on to his seat, he watched the ground rushing up and wondered if his Vietnam tour was about to end in a column of black smoke on the Phong Sahn runway. Just before the plane ploughed into concrete Frieze, brought the nose up into a high three-point attitude. The slats suddenly began a ferocious banging against the wings.

"That noise bother you, Colonel?" Frieze asked.

"What noise?"

"Hey, sir, you're halfway to becoming a Helio pilot," Frieze said, easing the near-stalled Courier onto the ground in a perfect three-point attitude. It seemed they had rolled only a hundred feet before stopping adjacent to a gate at the terminal. A half dozen GIs sat on benches outside the terminal. They had watched the unusual landing of the strange-looking aircraft. A large sign on the terminal roof read: WELCOME TO PHONG SAHN.

Frieze's hands moved deftly around the cockpit shoving knobs, pushing levers, and flipping switches. The big three-bladed prop spun down to a stop. The cabin was suddenly filled with a soothing quiet except for the descending pitch of the gyros spooling down. Unlocking his seat belt and shoulder harness, JP hung his headset on a hook, slipped his seat to the rear, and went loose. He was very tired, but it was a euphoric kind of fatigue as comes with the successful completion of a long and complex operation. Finally, he worked his way out of the seat and climbed down to the ground.

Joe Frieze handed him his garment bag and duffel bag, then jumped down.

JP stuck out his hand. "Thanks for the ride, Joe, especially the dual."

Frieze grasped JP's hand. "You did good, sir. I'm an FAA CFI. If you want to log the Helio time go ahead and sign my name." He took out a 3 x 5 card and pen from his pocket, printed a number and handed the card to JP. "That's my FAA license number. You can log four hours and fifty-seven minutes dual.'

JP slipped the card into his shirt pocket. "Thanks again, Joe. If you're back in this area look me up. I'll introduce you to some pretty nurses."

"Roger that, sir," Frieze said. Throwing JP a quick salute, he climbed into the plane and closed the door.

As JP picked up his garment bag and duffel bag an officer in fatigues, a major's leaf on one collar and caduceus on the other, emerged from the terminal, walked towards him and saluted. "Sir, are you Colonel Franklin?"

JP returned the salute. "I am."

"I'm Matt Peterson, the division psychiatrist. Welcome to Phong Sahn, sir."

"Thanks for meeting me," JP said, extending his hand.

Peterson's grip was firm. He reached for JP's duffel bag and suitcase. "My jeep... I mean your jeep, is parked outside the terminal."

"I'll be with you in a minute, Major," JP said. Turning, he watched the Helio Courier move towards the taxiway. Its speed rapidly increased. The tail came up, then its nose, and it transitioned to a crazy steep spiral upward. A wave of melancholy swept JP. Joe Frieze reminded him too much of Alex Leichuk, and Alex had bled to death early one morning at Walter Reed.

Chapter Twenty-Nine

Saturday, June 13, 1970, 1610 hours
Phong Sahn Air Terminal, Republic of Vietnam

Lieutenant Colonel JP Franklin, Medical Corps, USA, followed Major Matt Peterson, Medical Corps, USA, to the terminal. As soon as he stepped inside the permeating stench of feces and urine struck like a fist. "Gas attack," he gasped.

Matt Peterson laughed. "No sir, just stopped-up latrines."

"I hope you're going to tell me it's a one-time problem?"

"Afraid not, Colonel. It's been a recurrent problem during the four months I've been here."

"I didn't want to hear that. Who is responsible for waste management in Phong Sahn?"

"The engineers, but they're handicapped. The civilian outfit that installed the latrines used pipes too small to carry the load."

"Didn't the army insist on some sort of warranty, like six years or 60,000 flushes, whichever came first?"

Peterson smiled despite the stench. "No such luck, Colonel."

"We had a similar problem on my ward at Walter Reed. It dragged on for months until Jason Groves solved it for us."

"The syndicated columnist?"

JP nodded. "Someone sent him a letter deploring the inadequate plumbing on the ward. After the letter was published the stuff that ordinarily flowed through the pipes hit the fan. New latrines and plumbing were installed in less than three weeks."

"I don't think he can help us out here," Peterson said.

"You're probably right. Where do the troops go to relieve themselves when the latrines are stopped up?"

"Outside in a field."

"Not a good solution. Does the division surgeon have the authority to close down the terminal for health reasons?"

"I think so, Colonel, but that would be akin to dropping a nuclear bomb."

"Just having such a weapon in one's inventory can be very persuasive," JP said, smiling. "Besides, that seems to have been done de facto. I don't see anyone in here."

Emerging from the terminal's front entrance, JP took in a deep breath. "Ah, fresh air."

A jeep was parked facing the terminal. Leaning against the front fender was a soldier, his face so youthful that JP wondered if he had started shaving, He came to attention and saluted when he saw the two officers approaching. Both officers returned the salute.

"This is Pfc Jackson," Major Peterson said. "He's been the division surgeon's driver for the past two months."

"I'm very sorry about Colonel Diblasio," JP told him.

"He was a real nice guy, sir," Jackson said, taking the duffel bag and garment bag from Peterson. "It was a tough way for a doctor to go."

No more tragic than anyone else killed in this war, thought JP. His eyes swept the jeep, noting its well-kept appearance. Two radios in the back took up a third of the space. A ten-foot whip antenna, curved forward in an arc from its mount above the rear bumper, was secured by a cable to the front bumper. A microphone and speaker hung on the dash. The jeep's interior was neat and clean.

Jackson waited for Major Peterson to climb into the back seat, then handed him the duffel bag.

"I can hold the garment bag on my lap," JP told Major Peterson.

"Thanks, Colonel. That will give me room to breathe."

JP started to climb into the front passenger seat when the sound of a fast approaching jeep stopped him. The jeep turned into the terminal parking lot and skidded to a stop nearby amidst a cloud of dust. JP immediately recognized the driver, a close friend of many years, Colonel Louis Marchenko, a general surgeon turned psychiatrist after a heart attack. Currently he commanded the 350-bed 96th evacuation hospital on Phong Sahn.

Colonel Marchenko hopped out of his jeep and started towards JP, who tossed him a salute. The two friends shook hands, then hugged each other. "It's about time you got your butt out of that ivory tower and out here," Marchenko said.

"I really appreciate your coming down to meet me, Lou. How did you know when I would arrive?"

"Matt was kind enough to call me after he received word that your plane was inbound."

They briefly exchanged news about families. "I'd better not keep you any longer," Marchenko said. "Matt has a busy schedule set up for you the next few days. When you have a chance come over to the hospital and let me show you around. Kevin Brodie, the head and neck surgeon, is anxious to meet you. He finished a residency at Philadelphia last June."

"It's nice to know there is someone here who speaks my language."

Marchenko walked JP back to his jeep. "It's tragic about Elwood. It hit everyone at the hospital hard."

"Do you know what happened?"

"According to John Witherington, the chief of staff, it was the golden BB in its purest sense.

"I'm not sure I know what that means, Lou."

"One round from somewhere hit a vital part of the chopper's hydraulic system as it descended into an LZ to pick up wounded. No one saw any tracers. The helicopter stalled and dropped like a stone from a hundred feet. Fortunately there was no fire."

"What about the crew?"

"The medic and crew chief were thrown out when the chopper crashed. One had a skull fracture and subdural. The other sustained broken ribs and a pneumothorax. The AC was killed. The pilot survived with broken legs, pelvis, and back. JP, if you are going to fly Dust-off missions, keep in mind they are the most vulnerable of all the choppers in Vietnam."

"How do you mean?"

"The crews will go to extremes to reach and evacuate casualties, including going into hot LZs without gunship support."

"Don't they carry on-board machine guns?"

"Now you are being naive. That would be a violation of the Geneva Convention. The VC know the Dust-offs are unarmed and shoot at them with impunity."

"I'll try to keep that in mind, Lou."

As JP climbed into the jeep's front passenger seat Colonel Marchenko waved to Matt Peterson, then asked Jackson, "Those last wounds giving you any trouble?"

"No, sir."

"If they do we will want to see you in surgery clinic."

"Yes, sir."

"Take good care of Colonel Franklin, Jackson."

"Yes, sir, I will."

Marchenko picked up the garment bag and handed it to JP. "If I can be of any help, call me." He slapped the hood and waved them on.

Jackson started the engine and backed out of the parking space. Shifting gears, he drove onto the terminal road, raising dust as he drove.

JP turned to Peterson. "What's the schedule?"

"Today will be easy; get you squared away at your hooch, then go to division headquarters for a meeting with General Webster, the CG, and his chief of staff, Colonel Witherington. After that you'll be free until the 1800 happy hour at the generals' mess."

"Happy hour?" JP was incredulous. "I thought there was a war on."

Peterson shrugged. "Actually it's more of a social hour. General Webster desires his senior officers present at the mess during that hour unless they have cogent reasons for being absent. His reasoning does make good sense. Happy hour facilitates informal communicating among senior officers. It also makes the CG and the two ADCs available to the headquarters staff without their going through the delay of appointments."

"That does make sense, still… I presume chow will follow happy hour."

"Yes, sir. At the conclusion of the evening meal today I will present you to the mess."

"What does that mean?"

"I will review your background, then give you an opportunity to say whatever you wish."

"Would you like me to write out a brief biographical sketch?"

"That won't be necessary, Colonel. General Webster furnished me copies of your 201 file when you were being considered for the division surgeon's slot."

"Was that for background information or to evaluate my psychiatric suitability for the job?"

250

Peterson smiled. "Both, sir."

"Evidently I passed. What about tomorrow's schedule?"

"You're to meet with the division surgeon's staff in the morning, and the medical battalion staff in the afternoon. The following two days you will spend being oriented by the division headquarters staff and visiting major units on Phong Sahn including the 178th Brigade. Then come visits to the 9th Brigade headquarters at Quang Dien, about forty miles south, and the 174th at Ghia Lam thirty miles north. You can visit your clearing companies at the same time. After that you should be ready to go out to the firebases to meet the battalion commanders and battalion surgeons. In your spare time there's the paper work to be taken care of."

"Do we have a shredder? Just kidding."

Jackson brought the jeep to a stop at the junction with a wide two-lane road heavy with traffic. While waiting for a dozen trucks and jeeps to pass, JP asked, "Can you get AFRS on the jeep radios?"

Jackson smiled for the first time since meeting JP. "No, sir. The big radio transmits and receives on the medical battalion, division and emergency frequencies. The other radio receives only. It is set to the Dust-off frequency." He shifted gears and accelerated into a left turn.

JP turned back to Major Peterson. "What can you tell me about the CG?"

"General Webster was a nineteen-year-old sergeant in the Tenth Mountain Division during World War II. He earned a battlefield commission and Silver Star when he disabled a Tiger tank, killed the crew, and carried two of his wounded men to safety. Then he went back and did the same to a second tank. He was wounded taking on a third Tiger. In Korea he commanded an infantry company, received another Silver Star, and as a very junior major, was given command of a battalion. This is his second Vietnam tour. In '67 he commanded a brigade in the delta, was moved up to division as chief of staff, then promoted to brigadier general and made assistant division commander. He got his second star last November and took over the division in April. Education wise he has a PhD in political science from Rutgers."

"I am impressed," JP said.

Jackson gunned the jeep and turned left to follow a trailer tank truck. Major Peterson kept up a running commentary as they drove along the road.

"One end of this road eventually goes off base to connect with QL–1, a highway that runs north to Hanoi and south to Saigon. The other end of the road goes to the navy dock. The base is about ten miles long and half as wide. Located on it are the division headquarters, the airfield 178th Brigade headquarters, DISCOM, supporting units like division artillery, engineers, signal, quartermaster, scout dog platoon, battalion rear headquarters, and, of course, the two hospitals."

"What's the other hospital beside the 96th?"

"The 19th Surg with eighty beds. It's limited to general, chest, and orthopedic surgery whereas the 96th handles everything medical and surgical. Both hospitals treat Vietnamese civilians, ARVNs, VC and NVA."

Major Peterson leaned forward. "Colonel Witherington has been going berserk trying to figure how you managed to come up here in a spook plane."

JP grinned.

"And I'm sure Jackson would also like to know. Care to confide in your friendly division psychiatrist?"

"Like all things spook, keep this to yourselves. The flight was arranged by a grateful former patient who now runs Air America operations."

"Psychiatrists never seem to have those kinds of patients," Peterson said with some regret.

The road made a wide turn to the left, skirting a white sandy beach bordering the South China Sea. Dozens of figures in bathing trunks sunned in the sand. Others played volleyball, basketball and softball. A few walked along the shore.

"Where do they get the energy?" JP asked. "I feel wiped out."

"Supposedly after you've been here a while your metabolism adjusts to the climate and your pre-Vietnam energy level returns. I've been here four months and have yet to reach that level of recovery."

JP chuckled.

"That beach is for grunts on R&R from the bush. I send selected cases of combat fatigue from my mental health ward out there. Two or three days in the sun and sand can be very therapeutic."

"Sir," Jackson said, "I could use a couple days on the beach."

"Colonel, you should know something about your driver."

"He doesn't have a driver's license?"

Jackson smiled.

"He was a combat medic in the 9th Brigade until he was wounded giving first aid to casualties while under fire. That got him his second Purple Heart. He should have been evacuated back to the States, but talked personnel into keeping him here. After three weeks in the hospital he was assigned to the med battalion for convalescence. Colonel Diblasio made him his jeep driver. He figured that would keep him out of trouble."

"And has it, Jackson?"

"So far, sir."

After they had traveled a mile, Peterson pointed to a dense growth of jungle vegetation between the road and the sea. "In there is the 36th's version of the Ho Chi Minh trail. All newcomers must negotiate the trail at least once." Peterson smiled wickedly. "I believe that includes the division surgeon."

"You're kidding. What does it involve?"

"Surviving a 200-meter jungle and swamp trail infested with mines, booby traps, and camouflaged pits with simulated punji sticks. There's also a series of tunnels to negotiate."

JP turned to Jackson, "Have you gone through the course?"

"Yes, sir, twice."

"How was it?"

Jackson shrugged. "I got killed three times on each trip."

"What about you, Matt?"

"I went through it once, was killed eight times and fell into three punji pits."

'You're a natural jungle fighter, Matt. It's a good thing for the VC you're not humping in the bush with a weapon."

"I'll be watching for your score, Colonel."

The semi-tanker they were following indicated a right turn, then pulled off the road to park next to a water tower. Just beyond the tower were two circular vats about fifteen feet in diameter lined with a black material.

"That's the main water point for Phong Sahn," Peterson said. "The water is pumped out of a well and into the vats. After treatment with chlorine the water is pumped up into the water tank for distribution to units.

Jackson slowed the jeep to a crawl so JP could watch. The truck driver climbed to the top of the huge tank behind his cab, opened a hatch and reached for a hose hanging above him from the water tower. The scene was reminiscent of a western movie in which a steam locomotive filled up on water from a tank next to the railroad tracks.

"Who runs the water point?" JP asked.

"A civilian outfit from the States. They hire South Koreans to do the work."

"Does the division surgeon have responsibility for the water point?"

"In a way. Lieutenant Daniels, the division sanitary engineer, inspects the water periodically for chlorine concentration, impurities, and bacteria. The lab at the 96th processes cultures. Speaking of the 96th, that's it over there." He indicated many low buildings joined together by walkways 200 meters from the road. "The 19th Surg is on the west side of the airfield. It's commanded by a lieutenant colonel named Irvine."

"He's an old buddy. I'll have to give him a call."

"You regular army doctors seem to be part of one big family. Everyone knows everyone else."

"That's about it. You'd better sign up."

A three-quarter-ton truck without a canopy came towards them. As it passed, JP read the message painted in the space between the windshield and hood: ONLY WE CAN PREVENT FORESTS.

"Now what's that supposed to mean?"

"The truck belongs to the chemical detachment. They're in charge of defoliation and crop control. They spray defoliants such as Agent Orange from Hueys or C–123s. The VC don't take kindly to such tactics. If you're invited to go on a spray mission think twice before accepting."

"I'll think more than twice," JP assured him. He indicated a warehouse-like building adjacent to a parking lot filled with jeeps, trucks, and two parked Huey helicopters. "What goes on there?"

"That's the main post exchange. You can buy anything there from cameras to charcoal broilers. What they don't have in stock they will order from Japan or the States." Peterson pointed to a field on the left several hundred meters from the road. "Phong Sahn International Helicopter Airfield, commonly referred to as the Admin Pad. It's used for non-tactical helicopter traffic. Combat assaults usually form down on the airfield because so many choppers are involved. Your chopper will use one of the

VIP pads near your hooch."

The helicopter field resembled a miniature airport, with a glassed-in tower, antennae and spinning anemometer. Hundred-meter runways marked with numerals of compass headings crossed the field.

Jackson slowed the jeep. Easing to the right, he turned to a secondary road and started up a mild incline.

"If we had continued on that other road another half mile we would have come to a fork," Peterson said. "The right fork goes to your medical battalion, DISCOM, the signal battalion, scout dog detachment, engineers, and rear headquarters for the battalions of the 178th Brigade. The left goes to division artillery headquarters, the helicopter detachments including Slicks, Dust-offs, gunships, and Scouts. The road ends at a dock used by the South Vietnamese and US navy."

They began passing long wooden buildings on both sides of the road. Multiple sandbags dotted their corrugated metal roofs.

"Why the sandbags?" JP asked.

"To keep the roofs from being blown away by strong winds. During the monsoon season winds can reach sixty knots."

After passing a dozen such buildings Jackson slowed almost to a stop opposite a similar building. In front was a large poster of a frowning Uncle Sam pointing a finger at passers-by. The caption said, "I want you… to take your malaria pill."

"If you haven't already guessed, Colonel, that's the division surgeon's office. Next door is the division dispensary. A general medical officer runs it."

The jeep accelerated. As it continued up the road Peterson called out the buildings on the left and right. "AG, finance, personnel, Order of Battle, G–1, G–2, G–3, G–4, G–5, provost marshal, and chaplain."

A pack of at least a dozen dogs suddenly cut in front of the jeep. Jackson braked sharply to avoid running into them. The dogs, ignoring the jeep, continued on to disappear behind a large H-shaped buildings.

"What's the story on the dogs?" JP, asked. "They can't be all be pets."

"They come on base from outlying villages attracted by spilled garbage at the mess halls. They gather in packs and reproduce like rabbits. There must be hundreds of strays on base that go from mess hall to mess hall. That pack was headed for the consolidated mess."

"Have the vets done anything to reduce the dog population?"

"No, sir. Colonel Diblasio was pressuring them to send some heads to Danang for rabies examinations but they never did."

"I'll have to impress them to move on that or their own heads might be in jeopardy."

Peterson smiled. "We're coming up to the TOC on the left."

A cluster of dug-in and sandbagged buildings and bunkers came into view. Multiple antennae projected skyward from the buildings. An eight-foot double fence of barbed wire surrounding the buildings was patrolled by armed soldiers with German shepherd dogs. Large spotlights were installed at intervals along the fence.

Peterson explained. "The largest building is an amphitheater. The 0700 and 1700 hours briefings take place there as well as select briefings attended on a need-to-know

254

basis. You are expected to attend at least one daily briefing and preferably both. On any major operation you will be invited to the need-to-know briefings since you will be coordinating medical support for the operation."

JP nodded.

"The headquarters building is that white cottage beyond the field on your right. The CG, two ADCs, chief of staff, and their assistants have offices there. Those other buildings belong to the JAG."

Continuing up the road they reached a crest where the road dipped towards the South China Sea 200 meters away. Guard towers every 100 meters stood as silent sentinels along the shore, and 100 meters to the right was a long building with a thatched roof and thatched sides. It reminded him of a warehouse built by island natives in the South Pacific during World War II.

"What's that?"

"The main officers' club. They open at noon, have a short-order menu with sandwiches, burgers, fries, and soft drinks. The bar opens at 1600 hours. I hope you like rock music and loud singing."

"Why?"

"Once or twice a week the USO puts on a show at the club. Your hooch is the closest to the club."

JP frowned.

"Let's go on to the colonel's hooch," Peterson told Jackson.

They made a left turn, drove about fifty meters and parked next to a building about sixty feet long and half as wide. Raised off the ground, made of wood and painted blue, it and others like it were located at the edge of the bluff overlooking the South China Sea. On the opposite side of the road a dozen trailer homes were neatly arranged in a small community set off by white-painted wooden fences.

"Yours is the first hooch on the right, Colonel."

JP was admiring the trailers on the left. "Frankly, Major, I'd rather live over there."

"Most of us would, Colonel. That's where the Donut Dollies live."

"There are women there?"

"Yes, sir. Red Cross girls. They're involved in welfare and recreation."

"Can you translate that for me?"

"They run recreation centers here on the base, at Quang Dien and Nghia Lam. They visit firebases regularly to put on programs, play Scrabble, Monopoly, cards, organize song fests, or just talk with GIs."

"I didn't realize women went out to the firebases. Have any been hurt?"

"None so far, although their choppers have taken some hits. That's routine around here. Two of the girls were on a firebase last month when it was mortared. They were scared out of their wits but not hurt. The next day they went out again."

"I'm impressed."

"So were the GIs."

"Let's take a look at my condo," JP said, climbing out of his jeep. He waited for Peterson, then followed him along a wooden sidewalk to the first hooch, climbed three stairs to the door and entered a large room. The far wall was plywood with a door. The east wall consisted of windows looking over the South China Sea.

"The sunrises at Phong Sahn are spectacular," Peterson said.

Jackson stepped through the doorway carrying JP's duffel bag and garment bag. "Where would you like these, Colonel?"

"Right where you are is fine. Thanks."

After Jackson left, JP surveyed the remainder of the room. A counter divided the room into a sleeping and work section. On one side was a metal bunk, already made with a pillow, sheets and blanket. Another blanket lay neatly folded at the foot. A similarly made-up bunk was in a corner against the wall on the far side of the room. A desk, two wooden chairs, two lamps, and two metal wall lockers completed the furnishings.

"All the comforts of home," JP mused out loud. Indicating the door at the room's end, he asked, "Where does that go?"

"Father Deveraux's room. You share the hooch with the division chaplain."

"Oh, oh."

Peterson laughed. "Are you Catholic?'

"No, Episcopalian."

"Not to worry. Father is fairly tolerant of Protestants."

"That's reassuring."

"You'll meet him later. He went down to Phuc Hoa this afternoon to conduct a memorial service for a battalion chaplain and two others killed yesterday."

A sliver of anxiety shot through JP. "What the hell is going on here, Matt? In one month you lost a doctor and a chaplain."

"Just bad luck, Colonel. I have no other explanation."

"I know what happened to the doctor. I don't think I want to know what happened to the chaplain… what happened?"

"An infantry company returning from a three-week operation in the bush bivouacked their last night on an abandoned LZ. That's considered a no-no since the VC almost invariably booby trap an LZ after it's been abandoned. The battalion chaplain went out to spend the night. He was with the company commander and first sergeant the next morning when one of them detonated a mine. All three were killed."

JP stared out the window across an inlet of water. Half a mile away a helicopter settled down next to a group of buildings while another circled, waiting to land. Peterson, looking over JP's shoulder, explained, "That's the 96th Evac. The choppers are probably bringing in casualties."

Lieutenant Colonel JP Franklin, Medical Corps, USA, watched until the second chopper landed, then he turned away. For him the Vietnam War was just beginning to come into focus.

Chapter Thirty

The communal latrine was unoccupied when Lieutenant Colonel JP Franklin entered, naked except for a raincoat over his shoulders and wooden clogs on his feet. After shaving he hung the raincoat on a peg and entered the shower. He tried each of the six shower heads, selecting the one with the strongest spray. Adjusting the mix of cold and hot water until close to inflicting first degree burns, he moved into the spray, savoring not only the luxury of a hot shower but the privacy of showering alone, a luxury he would find rare in the foreseeable future. Twenty minutes later, dressed in clean fatigues, paratroop badge fixed to his left breast pocket, he stepped from his hooch to the board sidewalk and headed to the general's mess.

In a brief meeting late that afternoon with Major General Jeffrey Webster, the division commander, and his chief of staff, Colonel John Witherington, he was formally welcomed into the division and handed orders appointing him division surgeon and medical battalion commander. General Webster briefly mentioned three items requiring his immediate attention. The first was morale and discipline in the medical battalion headquarters, the second was a similar problem in Delta Company, a clearing company of the medical battalion at Nghia Lam. The third was a combat assault to take place in seven days on an abandoned special forces base at Qui Tavong near the Laotian border. The division staff would brief him in detail later about the operation.

Now as he walked to what remained of happy hour he marveled at the tranquility and beauty of the South China Sea only 200 meters away. The Vietnam War seemed as distant and abstract here in Vietnam as it did back in Washington D.C. The wooden sidewalk led past the division staff hooches, communal latrines, and bomb shelter. Not knowing when he might have to use the shelter he decided to take a closer look at it. About thirty feet long and six feet wide, the shelter was basically a trench dug into the ground, its sides built up by layers of sandbags extending on to a corrugated steel roof. Wooden steps descended four feet below ground level into a darkened interior, the floor was obscured by a layer of water. It took little imagination to envision every known species of viper lurking in that swamp at the bottom of the stairs.

Returning to the board sidewalk, he continued towards the mess, passing three bungalows, each beautifully landscaped with tropical plants bursting with color. The bungalows were quarters for the division's two assistant commanders and commander. JP would learn later each bungalow had two bedrooms, kitchen/dining room, sitting room/study, and a latrine with flush toilet and shower. They were in marked contrast to what he remembered of 3rd Division headquarters during the Korean War. Then, the commanding general's quarters was an eighteen-foot travel trailer pulled by a three-quarter-ton truck. The general's "mess" was a single table set apart from the other tables in the officers' mess tent. His latrine was a hole in the ground. Within reach were a covered can with toilet paper and a can of lime. This primitive facility was surrounded by a tarp for privacy.

The 36th Division general's mess, built in the form of a T, sat on the highest part of a bluff 300 meters from the South China Sea. The crossbar of the T contained the lounge and bar. The dining room and kitchen made up the stem. Entrance was through double doors into a foyer with shelves, coat rack, and hangers on one side and windows on the other. Today the coat rack was empty, but both shelves were partially covered with fatigue caps. There was a smattering of caps with black subdued colonel's eagles, but most caps showed lieutenant colonel's leaves. JP tossed his cap with the others, then pushed through swinging doors into the lounge.

The transition from oppressively hot and humid air to comfortably cool and arid air was abrupt but welcome, thanks to central air conditioning. The lounge was spacious, about half the length and width of a basketball court. One entire wall consisted of immense picture windows that looked out over a stone patio to a grand view of the Phong Sahn beaches and the ocean. A bar with eight stools was on the opposite side of the lounge. Adjacent to the bar a set of double doors presumably led to the dining room. The lounge was tastefully furnished with leather sofas, chairs, lamps, and tables. Taped background music blended with quiet conversations. In all, the lounge gave an aura of sophisticated elegance. If one had to fight a war, there was no question, this was the ideal way to do it.

JP spotted General Webster in serious conversation with Colonel Witherington and a bald-headed colonel whose left neck displayed a prominent surgical scar. Eighteen or twenty other officers stood in groups sipping drinks or beer. Some had gathered around a chest-high table intently watching dice rolled repeatedly from a cup. Scanning the room for a familiar face and finding none, JP focused on the bald colonel with the neck scar.

Moving closer for a better look, he saw that the scar extended down from behind his ear to disappear under the collar of his fatigue jacket. The colonel suddenly looked up and found JP's eyes on him. Embarrassed, JP turned away. Moments later Matt Peterson entered the lounge, saw JP and walked over. "Good evening, Colonel. Are you ready for your coming out tonight?"

"You'll be doing the all work," JP said. "How much of my 201 file did you review for your introduction?"

"All of it, Colonel," Peterson said.

"Do yourself and me a favor, Matt, leave out everything except my medical background, and cut that short."

Peterson grinned. "I hate to disobey my new commander on his first day, sir, but the chief of staff gave me a direct order to be complete. I am obliged to comply."

"What if I buy you a drink and authorize ten days' leave in Bangkok?"

Peterson considered the offer, then shook his head. "Sir, I cannot be bribed. Tell you what, I'll buy you a drink."

258

"I can see you and I are going to have problems," JP said. "Sprite will be fine."

A few minutes later Peterson returned from the bar with two tall glasses filled with ice and clear bubbling liquid. "Your Sprite, Colonel," he said, handing a glass to JP.

"Thanks," JP said, taking a long sip. "Who is the mean-looking bald colonel behind me talking to General Webster? The one with a long scar down his neck?"

Peterson looked past JP's shoulder. "That's Colonel Bruteau, the division aviation officer. He controls the rotary and fixed wing assets of the division."

"Do you know how he got the scar?"

"I heard it was from surgery during the Korean War."

The name Bruteau failed to stir any memories nor did the man's face. The scar did not appear his handiwork. JP sipped his drink. "Does division aviation officer mean that Colonel Bruteau is in charge of the Dust-off detachment?"

"No, sir. The Dust-offs come under an air ambulance battalion which has headquarters in Danang. The division surgeon can exert considerable influence on Dust-off operations, but that's based more on mutual respect and cooperation rather than official dogma. By the way, the doctor shot down and presumed captured in our AO three months ago was flying in a Dust-off."

"I wish you hadn't told me that."

"You'll meet the Dust-off CO, Major Jelnik tomorrow. He's on your schedule for 1000 hours."

"That's at the division surgeon's office?"

"Yes, sir. You'll be there all morning. In the afternoon you go to the med battalion headquarters."

JP was about to ask about morale and discipline problems in the med battalion when a GI in a white mess jacket and fatigue trousers pushed open the double doors next to the bar. Cradling a three-note chime in his arm, he struck the chimes several times, then turned and disappeared through the double doors.

"That's the equivalent of chow call," Peterson said.

General Webster led into the dining room followed by colonels, lieutenant colonels and a major. JP and Matt Peterson entered last. "The medics bring up the rear," JP remarked.

"That suits me, Colonel. I'm a little out of my class here anyway."

The dining room was arranged with two long tables on each side, each seating six. Large windows made up much of the walls on both sides. The head table was round with places for eight. Generals, full colonels, and visiting VIPs, sat at the head table. The staff rotated at the table by roster.

JP followed Matt Peterson to one of the long tables to stand behind a vacant chair. Scanning the dining room, he noted that every chair in the dining room had an officer standing behind it. Conversations subsided towards silence in preparation for the blessing.

JP took note of the spotless white linen tablecloths, linen napkins, sterling silver, decorative china, glass stemware and opened bottles of white and red wine. Salads were already on the table. JP's subtle frown went unnoticed except by a short middle-aged officer standing opposite him who smiled knowingly. The cross on his collar identified him as the division chaplain. A white-jacketed GI closed the double doors. The taped music stopped. Colonel Witherington nodded towards JP's table. "Father Deveraux."

The division chaplain's blessing was short, concise, and ended with his calling on God to protect the soldier in the field. Chairs scraped; officers took seats. Almost immediately white-jacketed GIs appeared with bowls of mashed potatoes, string beans, and platters of T-bone steaks. The taped music resumed.

Matt Peterson touched JP's arm. "Colonel, it's about time you met your hooch-mate, Father Deveraux."

The priest's grip was firm as they shook hands across the table. "Glad you're on board, Doctor Franklin. Your end of the hooch has been too quiet."

"Most people call me JP, Father Deveraux."

"Peter or Father Pete will do for me."

While the platters of food were passed around JP studied the priest. He appeared to be about fifty, in good physical shape, with a ruddy freckled face and crew cut hair predominantly gray. Watery blue eyes twinkled behind thick horn-rimmed army issue glasses.

Matt Peterson continued, "Father Deveraux played professional hockey before becoming a priest. Before that he was a platoon commander in the Americal Division on Guadalcanal until a Jap mortar shell nearly wiped him out." Next he introduced the remaining officers at the table and described their jobs. Al McGuire, division chemical officer; Tony Martinelli, G–2; Walt Collier, G–3.

When the platter of broiled steaks reached JP, he selected a steak he hoped was medium rare, then passed the platter to Peterson. Cutting into the steak he saw no pink. Damn! It was well done. He reached for the bottle of Merlot and half-filled his wine glass. *War*, he decided, *is hell*.

Conversations quickly turned to the day's activities. New to this environment and these people, JP remained discretely quiet, preferring to listen and develop a sense of his comrades. At one point he glanced at the head table and caught Colonel Bruteau looking at him. Later he saw Bruteau say something to General Webster, then nod towards him. The attention from the head table was becoming unnerving.

Al McGuire, the division chemical officer, described a near-disastrous spray mission flown that afternoon. "We went out to Tien Yap in a Huey fitted with fourteen-foot spray booms to defoliate a field of manioc. I spotted it a month ago near where a LRRP team reported an NVA way station on a route east from Laos."

"Why didn't you spray the field then?" someone asked.

"I wanted to wait until the manioc was about ready to harvest," Colonel McGuire said with a wicked grin. "Nothing happened on the first pass. On the second it was apparent the NVA were pissed off. They shot away four feet of the spray boom on the right. That pissed me off, especially since there are no more booms in our inventory. On the next pass I gave the door gunners permission lay down suppressive fire with their M–60s. That failed to intimidate the NVA. They shot off the other spray boom only two feet from its attachment to the fuselage. That was enough to convince me it was time to go home."

JP and the others laughed.

"I got in the last word," McGuire said. "Before leaving I called in the snakes and watched them work over the area. My problem now is that we are out of the defoliation business until new booms are delivered in about two weeks... unless, of course, our new division surgeon loans me two of his."

"I didn't know spray booms were in my inventory," JP said. "What are they used for?"

"Your preventative medicine section uses them for mosquito control.'

JP hesitated. He wasn't about to start giving away the store without first knowing what was in the store. Yet he felt an obligation to support division activities. "I'll have my preventative medicine officer call your office tomorrow and see what can be worked out."

"I'm going to like working with you, Doc," the chemical officer said, grinning.

Later in the meal JP told Father Deveraux, "An old marine buddy named Icardi is supposed to be assigned to the First Marine Division as the division chaplain some time this month. Do you know if he's arrived yet?"

"I don't think so. Chaplain Gillesby is not due to leave for another two weeks. I'll call down there tomorrow and ask if your friend is on board."

After waiters had cleared the tables they served coffee and dessert. As those were being consumed Colonel Witherington rose at the head table and glanced in JP's direction. The din of conversations abruptly subsided. "Gentlemen," Witherington began, "this evening we welcome our new division surgeon and medical battalion commander, Lieutenant Colonel James Paul Franklin, Medical Corps, who arrived early this afternoon aboard a spook aircraft. Perhaps one day he will tell us how he managed to arrange such a flight."

Witherington paused for the expected discrete chuckles, then continued, "Major Peterson, the division psychiatrist, will provide us with Colonel Franklin's background. When he finishes, Colonel Bruteau will add his remarks, and then General Webster will conclude."

As Peterson got to his feet JP wondered why Colonel Bruteau would want to make remarks about him. He had never seen the man before... or had he? Peterson removed several 3 x 5 cards from his fatigue breast pocket, looked at them briefly, then cleared his throat.

"Ten days in Bangkok..." JP whispered. "On second thought, two weeks."

Peterson smiled tolerantly. "General Webster, gentlemen, when I was notified that Colonel Franklin would leave his position as chief of head and neck surgery at Walter Reed to join the division, I decided to learn what I could about him from sources other than official records. My primary source of information was the current assistant chief of anesthesia at Walter Reed, a medical school classmate of mine. In this mission he was aided and abetted by Mrs. Franklin."

JP groaned and slumped in his seat. Damn that Harry Resniek. Twelve thousand miles was still too close to him. Payback time would come some day; a Franklin never forgets or forgives.

"Major Resniek wrote that Colonel Franklin was a superb surgeon, recognized all over the world for his expertise in the management of malignancies and trauma of the head and neck. That much is common knowledge in the academic medical community. What is not known, except by Mrs. Franklin and Colonel Franklin's closest friends, is that at the time he volunteered for Vietnam he was being recruited for the chair of head and neck surgery at Johns Hopkins. Why he turned his back on such a prestigious appointment to come to Vietnam is understandable if one examines his life."

Peterson paused for a sip of water, then continued, "Colonel Franklin began his military career in June, 1943, at the age of seventeen as a private in the United States Marine Corps. He served initially in the Northern Solomon Islands. Among his citations was one describing participation in a patrol which rescued two Army Air Corps pilots out from under the noses of the Japanese on the island of Mono in the Treasuries. Later he was part of a squad that destroyed bunkers, pill boxes, and neutralized caves in the Marianas. After eighteen months in the Pacific he rotated back to the States.

"When the war ended he was discharged a corporal. Enrolling as a freshman at Carlisle University in Atlanta, Georgia, he endured three years of academia before dropping out in 1948 to accept a direct commission as an army second lieutenant. After completing the branch basic course at Fort Bliss he was assigned to self-propelled automatic weapons. In Vietnam we know those weapons as Dusters and Quads.

"On June 26, 1950, Second Lieutenant Franklin married his best friend's sister, Kathleen Thompson, whose father, a lieutenant general, later headed the Defense Intelligence Agency at Fort Meade. The wedding day was also the day North Korea invaded South Korea. Four days later President Truman committed US ground troops. Three weeks after that Lieutenant Franklin was on his way to Korea. Eventually he commanded a platoon of Dusters and Quads in the 3rd Infantry Division – the 3rd Herd as some of us know the division. One incident, described in his records, gives a picture of the man who is now our division surgeon."

The dining room became deathly quiet. Even the GI waiters stopped clearing dishes and pouring coffee to listen.

"In April 1951 the Chinese began their spring offensive. Nearly two divisions of Communist Chinese Forces hit the British Commonwealth Brigade, an allied unit attached to the 3rd Division north of Uijongbu. Despite intense and repeated attacks by two regiments of Chinese, the British held. One battalion, almost surrounded, had a number of severely wounded who required urgent medical care. Two helicopters attempting to evacuate the wounded were shot down. One pilot was killed; the other pilot, severely wounded. Lieutenant Franklin was tasked with evacuating the British wounded and US pilot to a hospital.

"When Lieutenant Franklin's platoon reached the British battalion it came under heavy small-arms fire from at least one regiment of Chinese Communists. Lieutenant Franklin fired his platoon at the Chinese, killing and wounding several hundred. By then his platoon was almost out of ammunition and about to be overrun. Rather than pull out leaving the wounded, he made radio contact with an air force FAC, then

262

marked the target area with his remaining 40 mm cannon shells. The resulting holocaust visited on the Communists forces by the air force allowed the British to withdraw. Lieutenant Franklin then loaded the wounded on his armored tracks and delivered them to a MASH.

"Returning to the States Lieutenant Franklin was assigned as the S–2 of a Triple A Group charged with the air defense of New York City. A 'group' would be comparable to a brigade or regiment today. Of interest is the TO&E of a Triple A Group called for the S–2 to hold the rank of major. In 1952 Lieutenant Franklin went on inactive status to attend medical school. He was promoted to captain, artillery, in the reserves. Graduating fourth in his class he returned to active duty, Medical Corps, to complete an internship and a four-year residency program in head and neck surgery at Walter Reed. Assigned to the US Military Academy he was one of the founders of the cadet rock climbing club and served as a climbing instructor. In 1964 he was assigned to Walter Reed Army Hospital. Promoted to lieutenant colonel, he was appointed chief of head and neck surgery and consultant to the Surgeon General. In 1967 he was admitted to the National Academy of Science.

"This spring Colonel Franklin requested assignment to the 101st Airborne Division as division surgeon. To enhance his chances for selection he went through the Airborne course at Fort Benning, an ordeal many of you have yet to endure. It was our good fortune and the misfortune of the 101st that he was willing to leave his family and Walter Reed two months early to fill the vacancy left by the tragic loss of Colonel Diblasio."

Peterson put the 3 x 5 cards card back in his pocket. "So there you have him, gentlemen, your new division surgeon and medical battalion commander, Lieutenant Colonel JP Franklin."

A burst of applause followed. JP turned beet red. When the applause subsided Peterson addressed the head table. "Colonel Bruteau."

The tall bald colonel rose to his feet and cleared his throat. "I would like to return to the spring 1951 Chinese Communist offensive, and the two helicopters shot down attempting to evacuate the wounded British. You heard Major Peterson say one pilot was killed and the other severely wounded."

Bruteau stopped to massage the scar in his neck. "Gentlemen, I was that other pilot. I was not only bleeding to death from a neck wound but drowning in my own blood.

"After the Dusters and Quads were loaded with the wounded there was no room left for me. A young lieutenant had me put into his M–39 command track. Somehow he kept me from bleeding to death and asphyxiating while his platoon drove south looking for a hospital. I remembered nothing of this until I woke up in a MASH after two hours of surgery. The chief of surgery, a Major McClintock, told me a triple A lieutenant named Franklin saved my life. The next morning I saw Lieutenant Franklin for a few minutes when he stopped by to see how I was doing. That was nearly twenty years ago."

He rubbed his bald head. "I had a lot more hair then and my face after surgery was swollen like a beach ball. It is understandable that Colonel Franklin didn't recognize me today, but I recognized him. A man does not forget the face of the person who saved his life. I often wondered what became of the young lieutenant who saved my life." He looked at JP. "Now I know. His assignment to this division is a good omen. It is also payback time. My first order tomorrow will be that all aviation assets of the division are to be at his disposal." Bruteau sat down.

General Webster stood, a slight smile on what was characteristically a somber face. "In my search for a lieutenant colonel, Medical Corps, I reviewed the records of a number of eligible individuals, going back in some cases to the Korean War. The record that impressed me most was one which contained an ER written in Korea in 1951 on a first lieutenant commanding a platoon of Dusters and Quads. The rater had this to say about him: 'Lieutenant Franklin plans his combat operations efficiently and insures those plans are carried out. He is a strict disciplinarian who demands the best from his subordinates. This officer can operate with no or very little supervision.' The endorser also wrote: 'A calm quiet individual who displays initiative and common sense. He commands the respect of his subordinates by his technical abilities and leadership.' Gentlemen, you can readily understand now why this officer was my first choice as division surgeon. Since he is endowed with common sense, initiative and is a strict disciplinarian, I consider it appropriate to give him a free reign to do his job as division surgeon."

A slight smile creased JP's lips. His mind was already running in high gear. Free reign to him meant just that.

★

JP was quiet as he and Major Peterson walked from the general's mess. Finally, JP broke the silence.

"You overdid it with that introduction, Matt."

"It was worth giving up ten days in Bangkok."

Again they walked in silence. This time it was Major Peterson who broke it. "Colonel, I hate to dump this on you your first day, but you face a crisis in the medical battalion and one of the clearing companies."

"It's time to dump. What's up?"

"The med battalion has the highest rate of Article 15s, court martials, and AWOLs in the division."

"What's going on, Matt? You were the acting battalion commander as well as the acting division surgeon."

"No, sir. I'm a very junior major and relatively inexperienced. I was appointed only as acting division surgeon. Major Barbour, the medical battalion executive officer, was made acting commander after Colonel Diblasio's shoot down. Even before that it was my sense that Colonel Diblasio left running the medical battalion to Major Barbour while he spent most of his time in the division surgeon's office."

"I thought he did a lot of flying."

"He was terrified of helicopters, Colonel. I counseled him extensively on his fear of flying. The flight on which he was shot down was one of only five or six he went on since he was here. In a way I feel responsible for his death."

"From the little I know about a division surgeon's responsibilities out here, Matt, it is imperative he spend much of his time flying. Getting shot down is part of the risk that goes with the job." He stopped and stared at a partial moon, its yellow beams reflected off the water. "Beautiful, isn't it?"

"Yes, sir. Wait until you see the sunrise tomorrow."

"From what you told me, Matt, Major Barbour has been the de facto medical battalion commander ever since Colonel Diblasio was the division surgeon."

"That's about it. Colonel Diblasio rubber-stamped everything Major Barbour put in front of him."

JP lapsed into thoughtful silence as they walked. He looked up. "When did you say I was scheduled to visit the medical battalion headquarters?"

"Tomorrow afternoon at 1300 hours."

"Let's make a change without announcing it."

"Sir?"

"In the morning I will visit the medical battalion unannounced. Tell Jackson to pick me up at my hooch at 0700 hours, but don't tell him where I plan to go."

"What about the morning briefing?"

"You go. You can brief me at lunch tomorrow. And Matt…"

"Yes, sir."

"Not a word of my change of plans to anyone."

Chapter Thirty-One

Sunday, June 14, 1970, 0640 hours
Headquarters Staff Bivouac Area, 36th Infantry Division, Phong Sahn,
Republic of Vietnam

Lieutenant Colonel JP Franklin paced back and forth on the pavement outside his hooch, periodically glancing at his watch. Pfc Jackson was already ten minutes late with the jeep: it was not the best way to start off with a new commanding officer. While waiting JP reminisced over the breakfast he just consumed at the generals mess: orange juice, coffee, creamed beef on toast, three fried eggs, toast, and a doughnut. During breakfast he had gazed out the large picture windows at the first of many beautiful Vietnamese sunrises he would see. It was, to say the least, a curious introduction to modern warfare.

Concerned that Jackson might have had an accident, JP started back to his hooch to phone the medical battalion when a jeep careened around the corner and skidded to a stop. A very worried Pfc Jackson saluted. "Colonel, I'm sorry I'm late, sir."

"You got lost?"

"No, sir. I went to check out the jeep before breakfast and saw it had a flat tire."

A glance at the jeep's rear showed the spare tire missing. "Did you get the spare on in time to make it to breakfast?"

"No, sir. By the time I got it mounted I was running late. I thought I'd better get up here."

"Well, this is your lucky day, Jackson. You'll have a second chance at breakfast."

"Sir?"

"Head back to the med battalion," JP said, climbing into the jeep.

"But, sir, that's on your schedule for this afternoon."

"Not any more. I just exercised a commander's prerogative."

Jackson gave him a confused look.

"I changed my mind, Jackson."

Jackson shifted gears, made a U-turn and descended down the road they came up the day before, passing the plethora of buildings Peterson had identified. This time no dogs crossed going to the consolidated mess hall.

"I appreciated the salute," JP told Jackson. "but it's not required when you are behind the wheel of a military vehicle."

"Yes, sir, I know, but Major Barbour told me he'd give me an Article 15 if I didn't salute him. He said he didn't care if I was driving or not."

"He's the battalion exec?'

"Yes, sir."

JP did not wish to undermine his executive officer's authority. "For the time being, Jackson, continue to follow that policy."

When they reached the main road Jackson turned right. After a mile he turned right again to a dirt road. The terrain on both sides of the road gradually rose to wide pasture-like hills. Clusters of buildings and hooches dotted the terrain. JP asked about them.

"Those are the rear headquarters of battalions in the 178th Brigade, sir. There's also a rec center run by the doughnut dollies and a chapel."

Another mile brought them to a branch in the road. Jackson veered to the right. "Where does the other branch go?" JP asked.

"Division Support Command, the officer and NCO clubs, and the scout dog compound, sir."

A sign welcomed them to the 36th Medical Battalion. The battalion headquarters, like many units on Phong Sahn, was located close to the seashore. Approaching the headquarters building, they passed a fenced area on the left. Half a dozen 2.5-ton trucks were parked in the open. Another truck and a jeep were on jacks in an open shed.

"That must be the motor pool?" JP said.

"Yes, sir. To your right is headquarters and Alpha Company."

JP studied the double row of wooden structures, ten in all, each at least eighty feet long and thirty feet wide. "What are they?"

"Company headquarters, dispensary, emergency room, lab, minor surgery, X-ray and four wards; medical, surgical, psychiatry and civilian."

"We treat civilians here?"

"Yes, sir, even kids. We also have half a dozen Vietnamese women in training to be nurses. Last month we tried to take up a collection to send one of them to Saigon for more training."

"What do you mean, tried?"

"Major Barbour stopped us."

JP grunted. "What else is over there?"

"Clinics, sir; dental, optometry, and mental health. The smaller buildings beyond those are officers' quarters. The EM hooches, service club, and day rooms are on the other side of battalion headquarters."

"This place looks like a mini MASH," JP said.

"Yes, sir, except that there are no nurses, and casualties don't come here."

JP indicated a building set back several hundred meters from the cluster of officers' hooches. "What's that?"

Jackson took a quick look. "The exec's hooch. Captain Nichols the S2, S3, lived there with the last exec. He moved out when Major Barbour was made exec."

JP sensed there was more to that event than what Jackson was telling, but decided not to push the issue.

They were now in a wide flat area between the mess hall and battalion headquarters, a building twice as large as the ward buildings. At its rear was a concrete extension protected by layers of sandbags. Half a dozen antennae projected skyward from its roof.

"That's the commo shack," Jackson offered. He made a wide left turn towards battalion headquarters and parked in a space designated for the commanding officer. A sign hung from a post next to stairs leading to the entrance. It read: 36TH MEDICAL BATTALION. Underneath hung a second sign: LTC JP FRANKLIN, MC COMMANDING. Under that was a third sign: COMMAND SERGEANT MAJOR AB CHESSLER.

JP climbed from the jeep and turned to Jackson. "I should be here until eleven thirty. If I need you earlier how do I get in touch with you?"

"Just call the commo shack, Colonel. I always let them know where I can be reached." He saluted.

JP hesitated, then returned the salute. "Enjoy breakfast," he told Jackson. Climbing a half dozen stairs to a screen door he opened the door and entered an office area. A corridor on the far side led to the remainder of the building. A young clerk typist at a desk near the door looked up, jumped to his feet and shouted, 'Tenshun." An older man at a desk in the far corner set down a coffee mug, stood and came to attention. At least six foot three, muscular and in his early fifties, his short gray hair and craggy face gave him a youthful energetic look. He came over to JP and saluted. "Sir, Command Sergeant Major Chessler, 36th Medical Battalion."

JP returned the salute. "At ease, Sergeant Major. I'm Colonel Franklin, the new CO." He extended his hand.

"Welcome aboard, Colonel," Chessler said, gripping JP's hand. He introduced the clerk typist, Pfc Samuels.

JP looked around the headquarters. Seeing only enlisted personnel and little activity he asked Chessler, "Where are the officers?"

"All except Major Barbour are attending a breakfast conference at DISCOM, sir."

"And Major Barbour?"

"He called in sick this morning. He said he would try to be here this afternoon to brief you."

"Did he go on sick call?"

"No, sir." The command sergeant major appeared decidedly uncomfortable.

"Let's go to my office, wherever that is, Sergeant Major," JP said. "Bring your mug."

"Would the colonel like some coffee?"

"Maybe later."

Chessler walked to a closed door and opened it. Entering a darkened room, he flipped a switch turning on overhead fluorescent lights. A second switch started an exhaust fan built into the wall. JP surveyed his office. Windowless, it was at least four times larger than his office at Walter Reed and appeared even larger because of its spartan furnishings. The desk was a standard government issue metal desk painted green. Behind it was a swivel chair and behind that a wall with the battalion colors on a pole crossed with the US flag. A narrow rectangular conference table with six folding metal chairs occupied the forward part of the room. Another metal chair was by the desk. A huge map of the 36th area of operations was pinned to the wall and covered with acetate. He noticed it included a portion of eastern Laos. There were no markings on the acetate.

JP eased into the swivel chair and motioned Sergeant Major Chessler to the chair beside the desk. After Chessler was seated he asked, "Is Major Barbour out much due to illness?"

Chessler looked pained. He seemed reluctant to answer. "Sir, he calls in sick almost every morning but recovers by afternoon. When he's here he stays in his office most of the time."

Now that was a worrisome syndrome, thought JP. He leaned towards Chessler. "I have been told this battalion is setting some sort of record for Article 15s, court martials and AWOLs." He fixed Chessler with a quizzical look. "What's going on, Sergeant Major?"

Chessler sipped his coffee thoughtfully, then set his cup down. "Sir, I'm not sure I should be the one to answer that. It might be better if you asked the officers."

"I intend to ask the officers, Sergeant Major, but they're not here now and you are, so I'm asking you. You're the top NCO in the battalion. I'm sure you didn't get those stripes by evading answers to questions from your commander."

"No, sir, nor did I get them by putting down officers."

JP sensed a conflict of loyalties in Chessler's answers. He pushed a little. "From what I have heard of this battalion there is a breakdown in NCO and officer leadership."

Chessler winced. "Begging the colonel's pardon, sir, there is no breakdown of NCO leadership nor the leadership of most of the officers."

"Does that mean most but not all the officers?"

A wall seemed to have gone up between JP and his command sergeant major. After a strained silence Chessler said, "Colonel, I've been in the army twenty-four years and have always backed my officers. I also know that officers protect each other." He looked anxiously towards the doorway as if he feared he might be overheard.

JP perceived Chessler's reluctance to speak feely. He stood up. "Let's take a walk, Sergeant Major. Where is a nice, quiet, secluded area?"

"Down on the shore, Colonel. It's isolated except for the guard towers, and they're manned only from dusk to dawn."

"The shore it is," JP said, grabbing his fatigue cap off the desk.

On the way out Chessler told the clerk, Samuels, "The colonel and I are going down to the beach to inspect guard towers and bunkers."

Samuels looked skeptical. "Right, Sergeant Major."

Five minutes later JP and his sergeant major walked along the sandy shores of Phong Sahn. A hundred feet away the South China Sea, blue and calm, stretched east to the horizon. Half a mile out several small fishing boats, their masts silhouetted against the sky, bobbed gently. The scene was too placid, too beautiful for a country at war.

Chessler took out a pack of cigarettes. "Would the colonel object if I smoked?"

"Do you want me to answer that in my capacity as a doctor or as a battalion commander?"

A subdued chuckle escaped Chessler.

"Light up, Sergeant Major."

After Chessler had lit his cigarette they walked in silence. Suddenly Chessler blurted, "Sir, the problem in the battalion is Major Barbour."

JP said nothing, hoping his silence would encourage Chessler to continue.

"Colonel Diblasio, the last CO, spent most of his time up at the division headquarters writing reports. He came down to the battalion for a couple of hours once or twice a week, but left running the battalion to Major Barbour. Things were bad then, but after Colonel Diblasio was shot down and Major Barbour made acting CO, things got worse, much worse."

JP was hesitant to focus on Barbour as the source of the battalion's disciplinary and morale problems. Things may have deteriorated under Colonel Diblasio and Barbour could have been trying, albeit heavy handedly, to whip the battalion into shape.

Chessler continued. "Major Barbour gave Article 15s for the slightest infractions. He threatened practically everyone, even the officers, with court martial. There are half a dozen court martials pending now for insubordination and failure to obey orders."

"What's their status?"

"A buddy of mine in JAG has held them up on technicalities."

Chessler field stripped what remained of his cigarette and dropped the pieces into the breeze. Immediately he lit another. After a few drags he went on. "The young troopers and NCOs despise Major Barbour. He makes unreasonable demands and intrudes into their free time with chickenshit work details. When he talks to them he makes them stand at attention, then cuts them to pieces with demeaning remarks. He will haul a soldier into his office for the slightest infraction and give him a choice between an Article 15 and a court martial."

"How have the officers responded?"

"They met with Major Barbour and tried to get him to ease up. He kept them standing in a brace while he screamed at them for almost an hour, accusing them of mutiny and scheming to undermine his chances for promotion. Two weeks ago he submitted adverse ERs on each officer. If those go through, Colonel, none of the officers will ever be promoted; their army careers will be over." Chessler took a drag on his cigarette and exhaled. "Hell, sir, he even threatened to take my stripes."

JP desperately searched for an explanation other than the obvious. "You said Major Barbour calls in sick a lot?"

"Yes, sir, and he is sick, but it's the kind of sickness that comes out of a bottle. He got away with it when Colonel Diblasio was CO because the colonel was hardly ever here. When he did come he always telephoned battalion headquarters first and asked Major Barbour to have any completed paperwork ready for his signature. Most of the time I don't think Colonel Diblasio had any idea what he was signing. If it hadn't been for Captain Nichols this battalion would have fallen apart months ago."

"Captain Nichols?"

"He's both the operations and the intelligence officer. He's also taken care of much of the administration Major Barbour should have been doing. The troopers respect him. He's the one who screwed up the court martial charge sheets so the JAG would hold them up for corrections."

A Huey helicopter approached just off the shore. The throbbing beat of its rotors drowned out conversation. Both men stopped to watch it pass. Two GIs sat in the open door with their feet hanging out. One waved. JP waved back. When its noise faded JP told Chessler. "I'm grateful for your candor, Sergeant Major. Anytime you believe the guard towers and bunkers need inspecting, just say the word."

270

"Yes, sir," Chessler said, smiling.

JP looked at his watch. "We better head back."

As they neared battalion headquarters JP stopped and pointed to the hooch on the hill a quarter mile away. "Is that Major Barbour's quarters?"

"Yes, sir."

"I think I'll make a house call."

"Would you like Jackson to run you up there in the jeep?"

"No, thanks. I'll walk. I need the exercise. Just make sure Major Barbour doesn't know I'm coming."

★

It took JP almost ten minutes to climb the narrow dirt road ascending to the executive officer's hooch. A jeep was parked by the door. A quick glance showed papers scattered on the floor along with two crushed beer cans and a chain and padlock with key in the padlock. Walking to the door, JP knocked timidly as if a frightened private sent to fetch the executive officer. After waiting a discrete interval he knocked again, this time louder.

"Goddamn it," a hoarse voice responded. "I left orders not to be disturbed."

JP pushed open the door. The heavy odor of alcohol mixed with stale cigarette smoke rolled over him. A quick look around the darkened room revealed clothing scattered on the floor and piled on the spare bunk. Major Barbour was stretched out on his bunk, dressed only in boxer shorts and a T-shirt. On the floor by the head of the bunk a half-full bottle of vodka sat next to an empty glass. A burning cigarette rested on the bent edge of an empty C-ration can. Draped over the edge of a makeshift wooden chair was a .45 pistol in a holster attached to a web belt.

When Barbour saw the lieutenant colonel's leaf and Medical Corps caduceus on JP's collar he sat up, swung his feet to the floor and tried to stand. Staggering, he fell back heavily on his bunk. "Sorry, Colonel," he said, his speech slurred, "I thought you were coming this afternoon. I'm not feeling well. I've had terrible belly cramps and dizziness."

JP fought to control his anger. Without a word he walked to the chair and jerked the pistol from its holster. Removing the magazine, he pulled the slide back and let it snap forward several times to ensure no bullet was in the chamber, then let the hammer down. He slipped the pistol back in the holster and looped the web belt over his shoulder. The magazine went into his pocket.

"Wait a minute," Barbour protested. "What the hell do you think you're doing?"

"I'll tell you what I'm doing, Major," JP said, his voice icy, "I'm relieving you as executive officer as of right now and placing you under arrest pending court martial."

"Court martial? What the hell for?"

"Drunkenness on duty, dereliction of duty, and conduct unbecoming an officer. Those will do for starters. I'm sure I'll be able to come up with a few more charges later. From now on you are confined to quarters."

Barbour looked as though he had been slugged with a two-by-four. He glowered at

JP. "You fucking Medical Corps officers can't make it as doctors in the real world so you join the army," he shouted. "You don't know shit about the military. You show up here a day ago and now you want to court martial me?"

"You have the big picture, Major," JP said calmly and started to the door.

"I've got nineteen years in. You can't do this to me," Barbour screamed.

"I'm not doing it to you, Major. You have already done it to yourself. In my opinion you should have been thrown out of the army years ago." JP didn't trust himself to speak further.

Barbour lunged for the .45 hanging off JP's shoulder. "That's mine, goddamn it," he shouted as he tried to jerk the belt of JP's shoulder.

JP reacted instantly with a swift chop to Barbour's neck. The marine training from years ago was not forgotten, it had just lain dormant.

Barbour gasped, turned purple, bent over and vomited.

"Try that again and I'll really get mad," JP said. "Assaulting a superior officer will be added to the charges against you."

"You son of a bitch," Barbour spit out.

JP ignored the man. He picked up the half-full bottle of vodka and started to leave. At the door he turned. "Remember, Major, you are under arrest and confined to quarters. Break those restrictions and I'll have your ass thrown in the brig." In his anger JP had reverted to marine vernacular. "In case you don't know what a brig is, visualize a Conex with bars and you have the picture."

JP walked out and slammed the door behind him. Climbing into the major's jeep, he placed the holster, web belt, pistol and booze on the floor in front of the passenger seat. As he cranked the jeep engine, Barbour appeared in the doorway, red eyed, barefooted, and still in his underwear.

"That's my jeep," he shouted. "I signed for it. You take it and I'll get you for theft of a government vehicle."

JP stared at the pitiful officer a moment and wondered about a system that had allowed him to survive so long. Gunning the engine, he shifted into first and let the clutch snap out, leaving Barbour in a cloud of red dust. Minutes later he skidded into the executive officer's parking spot. Fastening the security chain around the steering wheel, he padlocked it. Taking the key, pistol and vodka, he climbed the steps to battalion headquarters two at a time and hit the screen door with the force of a runaway train. It flew open with a loud crash, startling the sergeant major who catapulted out of his seat, spilling his coffee.

"Jesus Christ, Colonel, I thought we had incoming."

"You did... your CO." He slammed the vodka bottle, Barbour's .45 pistol and jeep padlock key on Chessler's desk. "Major Barbour has been relieved as executive officer. He is confined to quarters. He no longer has any authority in this battalion nor is he authorized any equipment. Equipment already issued to him will be picked up. His jeep is parked outside. You have the key. If he needs to go anywhere have someone drive him but only after I give my permission. Any questions?"

"Yes, sir. What about his meals?"

"Have them taken up to his hooch. Has Captain Nichols returned from the

DISCOM conference?"

"Yes, sir."

"Ask him to report to me."

Chessler's eye's brightened. "Yes, sir."

As JP entered his office he growled over his shoulder, "Get me Colonel Watanabe on the phone."

"Colonel Watanabe?"

"The AG."

"Yes, sir."

Moments later Chessler knocked. "Sir, Captain Nichols is here."

"Send him in."

Nichols looked to be in his late twenties, slender, medium height, with an open, honest face and an affect that not only reflected self-confidence but inspired confidence. If snap judgments were valid, JP was about to make a wise choice for executive officer.

Nichols marched up to JP's desk, saluted and reported.

Returning the salute, JP offered his hand. Nichols's grip was firm and assured. "Have a seat, Captain."

Sergeant Major Chessler called through the door. "Sir, Colonel Watanabe on line one."

JP picked up the phone. Captain Nichols started to leave but JP waved him back to his seat.

"Colonel Franklin here," JP said. "We met briefly last night at the general's mess."

"Of course, Colonel Franklin. How can I help you?"

"I've just relieved my executive officer, Major Barbour. I'm charging him with a litany of offences including drunkenness, dereliction of duty, conduct unbecoming an officer, and assaulting a superior. After I cool down I'd like to give him a choice between resignation and a court martial. Can I do that?"

There was a chuckle. "Good God, Doc, it didn't take you long to start cleaning house."

"What about it?" JP was in no mood for idle banter.

"You can't do it by yourself. Between the JAG and me we can probably make either one happen."

"Good."

"Give me a few minutes to check his records and talk to the JAG." After a pause he asked, "You have anyone in mind for a replacement?"

"My S–2/S–3, a captain named Nichols."

"Douglas Nichols?"

JP looked at Captain Nichols. "Is your first name Douglas?"

Nichols nodded.

JP spoke into the phone. "Yes, do you know him?"

"I certainly do. He's a legend in the 174th Brigade. He was an infantry company commander with a prior tour in '68. He was wounded twice, awarded a Silver Star and two Bronze Stars with Vs. He has an MBA from Harvard. I tried to get him to transfer to the AG Corps after the last time he was wounded, but he insisted on MSC. He is on the list for promotion to major. I'm not sure what that status will be in view of the adverse ERs submitted by Major Barbour." Watanabe chuckled. "According to Major Barbour, you have the cream of misfit officers in your battalion headquarters."

"There's only one misfit down here, and that's Major Barbour. What can be done about those efficiency reports?"

"I'm glad you asked, Colonel. Would you believe my nit-picking sergeant found all sorts of flaws on the ERs that Barbour sent?"

"God bless your nit-picking sergeant," JP said.

"And just now I decided that because of those flaws all the ERs will need to be done over. It is unfortunate that Major Barbour won't be around to make the corrections and resubmit the ERs."

"That is indeed unfortunate," JP agreed. "Colonel Watanabe, it just struck me that you are a brilliant and gifted officer. How come you're not a general?"

"Give me a couple more months," Watanabe said, chuckling. "Is there anything else I can do for you while you have me in a good humor?"

"What about a replacement for Captain Nichols as S–2/S–3?"

"I'll see what I can do."

JP placed the phone on the cradle, turned to Captain Nichols and studied him a moment. "You heard?"

"Yes, sir."

"Feel up to the task?"

"All the way, sir. I 'ye been pretty much running the battalion unofficially for the last couple of months."

"Now you will get to run it officially as executive officer. That's the good news. There's also good and bad news about the efficiency reports Major Barbour submitted."

"Sir?"

The good news is that the AG considered them so poorly prepared they will need to be done over and resubmitted. The bad news is that you, as executive officer, will have to do the rating and I, as commander, will have to do the endorsing."

"That's bad news, sir?"

"Captain Nichols, you have no idea how I hate paperwork."

"What about my ER, Colonel?"

"I will personally rate you. The DISCOM commander, whoever that is, will be the endorser. I'll make sure he is fully appraised of your sterling qualities."

"I can handle that, Colonel," Captain Nichols said, grinning.

JP stood. "Let's go over to the mess hall, get some coffee and talk."

On the way out JP stopped at the command sergeant major's desk. "Cut orders appointing Captain Nichols executive officer as of right now. Send copies to wherever copies go. If you need us we will be in the mess hall checking out the coffee."

"Yes, sir." A broad grin swept Chessler's face.

A soon as JP stepped into the mess hall a voice shouted, "Tenshun."

"Carry on," he shouted back.

274

Captain Nichols led to a counter where a stainless steel pitcher sat on a hotplate. Reaching for a nearby mug, he filled it with coffee and handed it to JP, then filled a mug for himself and followed his commander to a table. A heavy-set man with sergeant's stripes on the sleeve of his white jacket walked rapidly to their table. "Sir, Staff Sergeant Robillard, mess sergeant for Headquarters and Alpha."

"Good morning, Sergeant," JP said. "I'm the new battalion commander, Colonel Franklin. And this," he indicated Captain Nichols, "is the new battalion executive officer."

Robillard stared from JP to Nichols and back, then flashed a wide smile. "Yes, sir. Would the colonel like some sweet rolls with his coffee?"

"No, thanks, Sergeant, but I do have a request."

The sergeant looked at JP expectantly.

"Please have the mess personnel stop calling 'Attention' when I walk in. It could discourage me from drinking your coffee."

After Sergeant Robillard left, JP and Nichols sat down facing each other. "I'll be candid, Captain Nichols," JP said, "I know next to nothing about a medical battalion. It's going to be up to you to educate me."

Nichols put down his mug. "I'll be happy to, Colonel. Where would you like to begin?"

"With the basics."

"Well, sir, the headquarters is organized as in most battalions. Major Barbour was the exec. Bill Wortham is the admin officer. I was intelligence and operations, I also functioned as communications officer. Don Fleury is supply. His responsibilities include maintaining the medical supply depot and issuing medical supplies and equipment to the clearing companies and battalion aid stations."

"Tell me about the clearing companies."

"There are four. Two are located here on Phong Sahn. Alpha is with the medical battalion headquarters here. Charlie is with the 178th Brigade. Neither treat casualties because the 96th Evac and 19th Surg are so accessible. However, both Alpha and Charlie accept patients from the hospitals; most patients are recovering from less serious wounds. They need a few weeks' convalescence before returning to duty. Alpha and Charlie also treat a variety of medical problems including selected cases of malaria, dysentery, VD, drug overdose, and combat fatigue."

"What about the other clearing companies?"

"Bravo is at Skunk Patch near Quang Dien, about forty miles south. The commander is Steve Wood. He's also the brigade surgeon for the 9th Brigade, which has its headquarters at Skunk Patch. Delta Company is at Dog Patch, thirty miles north and close to Nghia Lam. It's commanded by Jerry Millbarth who is the brigade surgeon for the 174th Brigade. Both clearing companies provide acute care for casualties who are so critical they might not survive the additional twenty-five to thirty minute flight to the 96th Evac or 19th Surg. Those clearing companies do cut downs, control bleeding, transfuse O-negative blood, treat shock, apply splints, do trachs, put in chest tubes and catheters, plus do a bunch of other stuff I don't understand. When the casualty is stabilized he's flown by a backhaul Dust-off to one of the two hospitals in Phong Sahn."

"What kind of surgical backgrounds do Wood and Millbarth have?"

"Captain Wood was drafted after finishing two years of general surgery at Mass General. He intends to go into urology and eventually do kidney transplants. He's an outstanding officer, medically and as a commander. The other two doctors with him have had lesser surgical training, but, thanks to Wood's teaching abilities, they have been brought up almost to his level."

"And Captain Millbarth?"

"Millbarth left a general surgery residency in the middle of his third year. He has a reputation for delegating much of the trauma work to the other two doctors in the company. Fortunately they are much more conscientious and skillful than their commander. Discipline and morale in Delta is very poor."

A telephone rang somewhere in the kitchen area. Moments later one of the cooks came to the table. "Colonel Franklin, there's a phone call for you."

JP started to rise. Excusing himself, he followed the cook through the kitchen to a small office. A telephone receiver lay on its side on a wooden field desk. He picked it up. "Colonel Franklin."

"Fred Watanabe."

"Yes, Fred."

"Here's what I learned so far about Major Barbour. Last February he was relieved as a battalion S–4 after only two months. He was almost court-martialed over some missing property. In April he was relieved as battalion S–3 after only a week, then spent two weeks in the detox program at the 98th Evac in Long Binh. Before he was assigned up here to the med battalion he was hospitalized on the closed ward at the 98th for acute depression and attempted suicide. A week ago he was notified he had been passed over for promotion a third time. He's on his way out of the army."

JP almost dropped the phone. "Fred, Barbour's a potential suicide right now. I'll get back to you." He slammed the phone on its cradle and ran out to Nichols. "Let's move out. I'll explain as we go."

276

Chapter Thirty-Two

Sunday, June 14, 1970, 0850 hours
36th Medical Battalion Headquarters Area

The executive officer's jeep, with Captain Nichols driving, skidded to a stop by Major Barbour's hooch. JP jumped out, rushed to the door and pounded on it. When there was no answer he tried to open the door. It was secured closed. He beat the door with his fist. "Major Barbour, it's Colonel Franklin. Open up."

The silence from within was ominous.

"We'll have to break in, Colonel," Captain Nichols said.

"I'm too old for this. Okay. On the count of three; you count."

When Captain Nichols uttered, "Three," both men slammed into the door. It exploded inward, crashing to the floor. They rushed through the doorway; Barbour's bunk was empty.

"He's on the floor between the wall and the bunk," Nichols said. Reaching for the bunk, he dragged it away from the wall. Barbour was lying prone, his head turned to the side and his eyes closed.

Kneeling beside the inert officer, JP rolled him on his back. "Hold his jaw up, Doug," he told Captain Nichols, "that will help his breathing. If he vomits turn his head to the side. I'm going to check him over."

JP's fingers probed the neck; the carotid pulse was weak, irregular, and almost too rapid to count. Lifting Barbour's T-shirt, JP watched the chest movements; respiratory efforts were shallow. Raising Barbour's hand, he studied the fingernail beds. Even in the poor light inside the hooch the purple hue of cyanosis was unmistakable. A quick check of the eyes revealed pinpoint pupils.

"You think he's had too much booze?" Captain Nichols asked.

"More than that, he's overdosed on a narcotic." JP moved to the head. "I'll take over the airway. We need help fast. Look for a phone."

"It's on the other side of the bunk on the floor," Captain Nichols said. Walking around the bunk, he picked up the phone and dialed. A moment later he said, "Bill, Doug Nichols. I'm at Major Barbour's hooch with Colonel Franklin, the new CO. Just a second for Colonel Franklin." He handed the phone to JP. "It's Bill Sandow, the Headquarters and 'A' Clearing Company commander."

JP held the phone with one hand while holding Barbour's jaw back with the other. He spoke rapidly. "We have a real flail here. Major Barbour has ODd on a narcotic and alcohol."

"That's a deadly combination, Colonel."

"Right now he's unresponsive, cyanotic, with a fast thready pulse and pinpoint pupils."

"I'll be right up with our emergency kit. It has equipment to intubate, lavage, and meds."

"Narcan?"

"Yes, sir. What about a Dust-off?"

"Good idea. I wish I'd thought of it."

After hanging up JP continued to monitor Barbour's airway. He told Doug Nichols, "Check around for a bottle of pills."

Captain Nichols began to systematically search around the bunk. "What is Narcan, Colonel?" he asked.

"It's a drug that reverses the respiratory depression of narcotics. It can be a miracle drug in some cases. Let's hope this is one of them."

After several minutes Nichols reported, "No luck on med bottles, Colonel. There is an empty vodka bottle."

JP grunted.

Nichols lifted the door off the floor, carried it outside and leaned it against the wall. A moment later he called through the open doorway, "A jeep just left Alpha company headed this way."

The sound of a fast-approaching jeep grew louder until it squealed to a stop outside the door. A tall officer in his early thirties walked into the hooch carrying an aluminum suitcase. He was followed by a medic carrying a cardboard box. The officer set the suitcase down by JP. "I'm Bill Sandow, Colonel. What can I do?"

"Give him two milligrams of Narcan IV stat; follow with a liter of Ringer's lactate TKO. While you're doing that I'll intubate him."

Sandow nodded. He opened the aluminum suitcase and removed a laryngoscope; its six-inch tongue blade collapsed against the battery handle. Rotating the blade away from the handle, he checked to be sure the bulb at its end was lit, then passed the L-shaped instrument to JP.

JP forced open Barbour's mouth and advanced the blade into the throat, elevating the tongue and epiglottis. "I hope he doesn't vomit." Gripping the laryngoscope handle with his left hand, he held out his right. The medic placed a cuffed endotracheal tube in the outstretched hand. JP threaded the tip of the tube through the vocal cords into the trachea, then withdrew the laryngoscope. "I'm in."

The medic attached a 10 cc syringe to the syringe lock on the anesthesia tube and looked at JP.

"Six ccs should do it."

The medic pressed the syringe plunger in until six ccs of air had been delivered to inflate the rubber cuff at the end of the tube. The inflated cuff functioned as a seal, making ventilation more efficient and protected the lungs from aspiration should Barbour vomit. While JP held the anesthesia tube steady the medic connected an AMBU bag to it. JP immediately began squeezing the bag, inflating Barbour's lungs with ambient air. Next the medic connected a tube from a small bottle of oxygen to the AMBU bag.

"IV is in, Colonel," Captain Sandow reported, "and he's had two milligrams of Narcan."

278

"If he doesn't respond in a couple of minutes give him another dose. How are you at putting down nasogastric tubes?"

"My specialty, Colonel."

"Put one down Barbour and lavage his stomach." He looked over to Captain Nichols. "How far away is the Dust-off detachment?"

"Only a couple of minutes' flying time, Colonel. The Dust-off should be here any second. I'll go guide it in."

The medic held out a smoke grenade. "I hope you don't mind purple, Captain."

Nichols grinned, took the grenade and went outside.

JP was impressed with the quick, efficient response from Alpha clearing company. "You people are on the ball," he told Captain Sandow. "I was worried after meeting Major Barbour."

"I can't blame you, Colonel," Sandow said as he adjusted the IV drip. "I learned to ignore him. It used to drive him nuts."

The hooch shook violently as a Huey helicopter passed not more than twenty feet over the roof, its noise intense. The noise diminished as the helicopter went outbound, then increased as it returned. It settled fifty feet from Barbour's hooch, its noise subsiding. Captain Nichols appeared at the door, followed by a medic carrying a folded stretcher. The medic pulled open the stretcher and set it on the floor beside Barbour. JP disconnected the AMBU bag from the anesthesia tube.

Barbour was quickly lifted to the stretcher and carried to the helicopter. JP climbed in, reconnected the AMBU bag and oxygen, then resumed squeezing the bag. As soon as Captain Sandow and the medics were on board the rotor blades spun up for take-off. Captain Nichols, standing on the ground, shouted through the door, "I'll send transportation to the 96th to pick you all up."

JP nodded.

The Huey helicopter lifted to a hover, then slowly flat-turned left, dipped its nose, and gathered forward speed. Passing over the shore, it flew over water at fifty feet. In less than two minutes the Huey eased on to the helipad of the 96th Evacuation Hospital. As soon as it went heavy on its skids medics rushed towards it pushing a gurney. Barbour's stretcher was transferred to the gurney. With JP still hanging on to the anesthesia tube and AMBU bag, and Sandow holding up the IV bottle they rushed Barbour into the emergency room.

Barbour's stretcher was placed on two metal sawhorses. Someone in a green scrub suit grabbed the AMBU bag out of JP's hands with the curt comment, "I've got the airway." A medic began cutting off Barbour's underwear. A nurse drew blood for blood gases and toxicology. Another nurse prepped Barbour's penis for an indwelling catheter, and still another attached EKG leads. Captain Sandow seemed to know everyone. He was immediately accepted as part of the ER team while JP remained a stranger on the fringes, passively watching.

Colonel Louis Marchenko walked into the emergency room and watched the activity for a few moments. When he saw JP he came over. "One of yours?" he asked.

"My med battalion exec. I relieved him a couple hours ago."

"Looks like he took it pretty hard."

"He has a history of alcoholism, depression, at least one suicide attempt and hospitalization on a closed ward."

"He should go to the closed ward at the 98th Evac down at Long Binh."

"Whatever you say, Lou."

Suddenly Barbour began thrashing about. He ripped off the EKG leads and tried to pull out the anesthesia tube. Medics grabbed his arms and held them against the stretcher sides until nurses tied them down with layers of four-inch gauze bandage.

Marchenko chuckled. "Looks like he's waking up."

"Narcan is a great medicine."

Marchenko studied JP's face. "You look like you've had a rough day and it's only nine twenty."

"I feel terrible about my exec, Lou. This was all my fault."

"What do you mean?"

"Barbour was falling down drunk when I first saw him. I relieved him and put him under arrest pending court martial. I wasn't aware he had been passed over for promotion a third time and was going to be forced out of the army. I didn't know about his psychiatric history. If I had I would have been more compassionate."

"Part of an alcoholic's successful manipulation is to dump guilt on everyone but himself, JP. You did him a favor by bringing things to a head, albeit rather abruptly. Remember too, in that battalion you are a military commander, not a psychiatrist or a doctor. Your first and only responsibility is to your command and its mission. Barbour clearly was a threat to both."

JP looked at his friend. "You know, Marchenko, you're quite bright for a general surgeon turned psychiatrist."

"You're not so dumb for an ex-jarhead. How about some mess hall coffee?"

"That's the best offer I've had today. Just a minute." JP went over to Captain Sandow. "I'll be in the mess hall with Colonel Marchenko. Join us when you're free."

"Sir. I'm going to stay here a while with Major Barbour. I'll send for my jeep when I'm ready to leave."

JP nodded. "Bill, your quick response back at battalion probably saved Major Barbour's life. We may never know if he will ever be grateful, but I certainly am."

Sandow blushed.

As Marchenko led from the ER towards the mess hall he told JP, "Bill Sandow is a powerhouse. He volunteers to work in the ER whenever he can break loose from the med battalion. We call him when we're short of doctors or have mass casualties."

"Those words are music to my ears after what I experienced this morning."

"Tell me about it, Doctor."

★

Sunday, June 14, 1970, 1220 hours
36th Infantry Division HQ Area, Phong Sahn, RVN

Private First Class Jackson brought the jeep to a stop in front of the division surgeon's office, the building with the poster of Uncle Sam pointing his finger and saying, "I want you to take your malaria pill."

Lieutenant Colonel JP Franklin climbed out of the jeep, studied the poster a moment, than turned to Jackson. "Uncle Sam makes me feel uneasy. I have yet to take my first malaria pill."

"It wouldn't look good if the division surgeon came down with malaria, Colonel."

"You have a point there."

"Do you want me to wait, sir?"

"No, I ate early lunch at the 96th. You can go back to the battalion. I'll be here for the rest of the afternoon, then walk to the briefing and my hooch. I'll send word when I'll need you tomorrow."

"Yes, sir." Jackson saluted.

"New policy, Jackson. That's not necessary for a driver behind the wheel. I don't want you wrecking my jeep."

Jackson grinned.

JP walked the length of the division surgeon's office to the far end, climbed three steps, opened the door and entered. A voice shouted, "Tenshun." There followed a scrambling of chairs, then silence except for the noise of a floor fan.

"As you were," JP called out. Visually he swept the office. The room was long, with two desks at one end and four desks on each side along the length, which ended in a partition with a doorway but no door. Filing cabinets and status boards lined both walls. Most of the enlisted men looked as if they just graduated from high school. Returning to their desks, they surreptitiously eyed JP.

A wiry officer in his early thirties came up to JP, stopped, came to attention and saluted. Rimless glasses on his intelligent face gave him the appearance of a college professor. "Sir, Captain Charles Dryer, administration officer, headquarters, division surgeon."

JP returned the salute, introduced himself and held out his hand. Dryer grasped it firmly. "Welcome aboard, Colonel. May I introduce the staff."

JP nodded. "Lead on, Captain."

He followed Dryer to the two desks at the end. A very tall thin captain and a husky first lieutenant of average height came forward.

Dryer began with the tall officer. "This is Captain Tom Moffet, the preventative medicine officer, and First Lieutenant Chris Daniels, the sanitary engineer."

JP shook hands with each, then listened to a brief summary of their duties. "I'd like to meet with you both later," he told them.

Dryer next introduced their enlisted assistants, then led down the row of desks, introducing the NCOIC, Master Sergeant Mickey Jordan, and five clerk typists. Finally, Dryer led through the doorway that lacked a door. "This is your office, Colonel."

The office was half the size of his office in the medical battalion. There was a desk, four metal folding chairs, a stacked metal bookcase and a filing cabinet. Large nails driven high in one wall served as coat hangers. A poncho hung from one of the nails. Tacked to the wall next to the desk was a map of Military Region I. On the wall across from the desk hung a stained khaki canvas pouch; dozens of its pockets were filled with surgical instruments. Curious, JP removed and examined several instruments.

Captain Dryer explained. "That's an NVA surgical kit, Colonel. It was found in an underground hospital west of Can Tuy."

"The instruments seem to be of pretty good quality," JP said, going behind his desk and sitting down. The desk top was clear except for a flip-type calendar, a full in-box, and an empty out-box." He told Captain Dryer, "No matter where the army sends me I can never escape the full in-box and empty out-box."

Dryer smiled sympathetically. "I'm afraid there's more paper for you on my desk."

JP groaned. "What happens to all this paper?"

"It goes to division to be filed," Dryer said with a straight face. "Would you like some coffee?"

"I'd better not. I just downed two cups at the 96th Evac. Have a seat and educate me on the function of the division surgeon's office."

Dryer eased into the metal chair beside the desk. He began, "We are the administrative headquarters for some 824 enlisted men, forty-seven medical officers, sixty-three medical administrative officers, four dental officers, and two veterinarians."

"I'm almost sorry I asked."

An hour later JP ran out of questions. Dryer stood. "Excuse me a minute, Colonel." He went to his desk and returned with a single paper. "This is your revised schedule for this afternoon and tomorrow."

JP glanced over the paper. "You gave me two hours off tomorrow afternoon."

"I thought you would need time to get into the paperwork."

"You're all heart, Captain. Who is the Major Jelnik you have scheduled for 1400 hours today?"

"He's the Dust-off commander. He asked to see you as early as possible."

JP nodded. He looked at his watch. "Would you send in Captain Moffet and Lieutenant Daniels."

"Yes, sir."

"If they're drinking coffee tell them to bring their mugs."

A curt knock startled JP. He looked up. Captain Moffet and Lieutenant Daniels stood in the doorway.

"Come in and have seats, gentlemen."

After the two were seated JP spent the first few minutes learning their academic backgrounds. Captain Moffet graduated from Johns Hopkins with a PhD in Public Health, then went to medical school and residency. He was not married, but admitted that he and a nurse at the 96th Evac were engaged. Lieutenant Daniels had a Master's degree in sanitary engineering from the University of Kansas. He was married and had a one-year-old daughter.

Over the next hour Captain Moffet briefed JP on health matters in the division. He covered malaria, trench foot, dysentery, food poisoning, hepatitis, skin diseases, snake bites, venereal diseases, and drug and alcohol abuse. Lieutenant Daniels reviewed sanitation, water purification, food preparation, trash and garbage disposal and insect control.

"That reminds me," JP said, "do we have spray booms that fit a Huey?"

"Yes, sir," answered Daniels. "We have five."

"How essential are they to your section?"

"Not very. I usually get a C–123 to spray for mosquitoes. They can cover a much larger area."

"Colonel McGuire, the chemical officer, is in great need of spray booms. The NVA shot up his last two on a defoliating mission a couple days ago. Give his office a call and see what can be worked out."

Lieutenant Daniels made some notes in a small flip-top notebook.

JP continued. "I'd like to get your thoughts on a couple of problems I more or less stumbled on to yesterday." He described the clogged commodes at the air terminal and the pack of dogs that almost collided with his jeep.

"Let's take up the clogged plumbing first. What are the potential health hazards?"

Captain Moffet spoke. "They're considerable, Colonel. Major concerns would be epidemics of dysentery and hepatitis. The risks increase when troops use the terrain around the terminal for latrines, especially during the monsoon season."

"Did Colonel Diblasio make any effort to get a handle on the problem?"

"Not really. As a result pressure was never put on the right people."

"Who might the right people be?"

"The installation commander, Colonel Holstrom, and the division engineer, Colonel Madison."

"Okay. I'll have a father–son talk with both these gentlemen. I understand I have the authority to close down the air terminal for health reasons if necessary."

"That's correct," Moffet said.

"It's nice to have a backup nuclear device," JP said, grinning. He opened the top middle drawer, found a yellow writing pad and pen, and wrote some notes. Looking up, he asked Lieutenant Daniels, "What about putting in alternate latrine facilities outside the terminal?"

"The soil isn't suitable for pit latrines, but a four holer using cut 55-gallon drums and some piss… excuse me, sir, urine tubes, could serve as backup."

"What I would like from you both are impact statements after you inspect the terminal," JP said. "Also a record of any previous efforts to deal with the situation."

Both officers wrote in their flip-top notebooks.

"I guess I'll have to get one of those," JP said, referring to the small green notebooks. "The second problem is the packs of dogs that run loose on the base. Have there been any dog bites?"

"None so far," Captain Moffet said, "but it's only a matter of time."

"Is there a policy if that happens?"

"Yes, sir. A course of anti-rabies vaccine is mandated unless the dog is captured and held for observation. If the bite is on the scalp, face or neck, the vaccine is begun immediately. My preference would be to send the dog's head to the path lab in Danang for exam rather than confine the dog and wait to see if it exhibits signs of rabies."

"Have any heads been sent as part of a survey?"

"No, sir. The vets are waiting until someone is bitten."

"Not exactly an enlightened policy. Let's encourage them to send some dog heads to Danang so the brains can be examined for rabies. We also need a program to reduce the dog population. And, Lieutenant…"

"Yes, sir?"

"Start pulling surprise inspections on garbage discipline at the mess halls. Report any mess hall you consider you consider a dog attraction. That includes the general's mess and officers' clubs. If anyone gives you a hard time let me know."

"Yes, sir."

JP thanked the two officers for the thoroughness of their briefings. "As you can see," he said, pointing to the doorway, "my door is always open." The remark was good for a laugh, since there was no door.

★

Sunday, June 14, 1970, 1400 hours
36th Infantry Division HQ Area, Phong Sahn, RVN

Captain Dryer stuck his head in the door. "Sir, Major Jelnik is here."

JP motioned Dryer into his office. "What can you tell me about Jelnik in thirty seconds?" he whispered.

"This is his third tour. He flew Loaches his first tour, Cobra gunships the second, and has commanded the Dust-off detachment in our division since April. He has a pocket full of Air Medals, three Purple Hearts, two DFCs, and a Silver Star."

My God, thought JP, *where do we get such men?*

"Send him in."

A short, wiry officer in starched tailored fatigues marched in, saluted and reported. His black hair was cut short. A thin moustache gave him a dapper carefree look. He looked to be in his mid-thirties. Cradled in his left arm was a brand new flight helmet, its headset cord neatly wound. JP returned the salute, shook hands, and invited the major to have a seat. Sergeant Jordan stuck his head in the door.

"Would the colonel or the major like some coffee?"

JP looked at Major Jelnik.

"A half cup, black, please," Jelnik said. Sitting down in a metal chair in front of the desk, he placed the flight helmet in his lap.

"That sounds good for me, Sergeant," JP said. He turned to Jelnik. "I've already flown today on one of your helicopters."

"Yes, sir," Jelnik said, smiling. "I heard it was a short flight. "How is Major Barbour?"

"His immediate problem has been resolved. He'll be going to the 98th Evac at Long Binh in a couple days for detox and therapy."

A clerk brought in two mugs of coffee. JP thanked him, then turned to Jelnik. "Tell me about the air ambulance detachment. Assume I know nothing and you will have overestimated my knowledge of Dust-off operations."

Major Jelnik reviewed every aspect of his detachment, its organization, maintenance schedule, pilot proficiency and upgrades, missions and aircraft losses. He gave statistics on aircrews killed, wounded, injured in crashes, missing and presumed captured or dead.

When he finished JP asked, "Any outstanding problems?"

"Yes, sir, two."

JP reached for the yellow legal pad and pen. He looked at Jelnik. "Fire away."

"The first concerns over-classification of medical evacuation requests." Jelnik went on to explain. "There are three classifications which determine the effort flight crews exert to evacuate a casualty. A classification of 'Urgent' carries the implication that the casualty will die or lose a limb if not promptly evacuated to a hospital. A ballpark figure is thirty minutes. When such a call received, day or night, regardless of weather in most cases, the aircrews will make a maximum effort to evacuate the casualty, sometimes going into a hot pickup zone without gunship protection. Those and bad weather are the situations in which we have lost most of our helicopters and crews."

Major Jelnik paused to sip his coffee, then continued.

"The lowest classification is 'Routine'. It describes a patient who would not incur significant medical complications by delaying evacuation up to twenty-four hours. Examples would be a sprained ankle, suspected malaria, dysentery, and fevers of undetermined origin. 'Priority', the intermediate classification, indicates a safety window of about twelve hours during which the patient can be evacuated before he gets into trouble.

"The classifications are judgment calls usually made by the enlisted medic in the field. Sometimes the medic, on his own initiative or on orders from a superior, will call in as 'Urgent' a condition of lesser seriousness. Over the last thirty days there have been seven incidents in which soldiers were evacuated as urgent when they were actually routine. Two involved hoist extractions at night, which are very hazardous as well as hard on the helicopter. Another helicopter took eleven hits and the on-board medic was seriously wounded while evacuating a GI with fever."

"I get the picture," JP said. "If you will give me a list of incidents, dates, times, and units involved I'll start with the brigade and battalion surgeons. If that doesn't get results I'll come down on the battalion commanders. If that doesn't work I'll really get mad. The sooner I'm notified of any new violations the more effective can my response be."

"Thanks, sir." Jelnik laid a paper on JP's desk. "These are the violations for the past month."

JP glanced at it, then looked up. "You came so well prepared on the first problem that I'm afraid to ask about the second."

"It concerns awards, sir. Many of my crews are very deserving of decorations including Silver Stars, DFCs, and lesser awards. Because of our organization the recommendations must go to Danang to battalion headquarters, then to corps headquarters and finally down to Saigon. By the time the award is authorized months have gone by, the subjects have been transferred, rotated, evacuated, or killed. Many of the recommendations have been downgraded. What is desperately needed is a mechanism for granting impact awards and eliminating the inordinate delay that currently plagues the process."

After some thought and doodling on the yellow pad JP said, "I'm almost sorry I asked, Major. I must admit I don't have the foggiest idea how to fix that problem. However, there must be someone around this sprawling modern army division headquarters who does know how. Give me a week to chase him down and see what can be done. Anything else?"

"One other, Colonel," Jelnik said. Taking the new flight helmet from his lap, he laid it on JP's desk. He turned the helmet so JP could see that his name was stenciled on it. "I understand you like to fly."

JP picked up the helmet and admired it lovingly. "Major, if you are trying to bribe me you have succeeded beyond your wildest expectations."

Jelnik smiled. "Sir, I would like to invite you to fly with the Dust-offs at your convenience."

"How would I go about doing do that?"

"Just come down to our flight operations, wait for a routine mission and go. Or we could call you when we have a routine mission going out. We'll try to screen out the hot LZs."

"That is very considerate, Major." He reached for the schedule Captain Dryer had given him. "I have a couple of spare hours tomorrow afternoon to catch up on all that paper," he said, indicating the overstuffed in-box. "Like the bumper sticker says: 'I'd rather be flying.'"

Chapter Thirty-Three

Monday, June 15, 1970, 1335 hours
Division Surgeon's Office, 36th Infantry Division, Phong Sahn, RVN

Lieutenant Colonel JP Franklin tilted back in his swivel chair, propped his jungle boots up on a corner of his desk, and regarded with satisfaction the empty in-box. Yesterday it had been crammed with papers. In a flurry of compulsive administrative activity lasting past midnight he had cleared it out. This morning he had the satisfaction of dumping the papers on Captain Dryer's desk, then went to briefings by the G–2, G–3, G–4, and G–5. The immense amount of information thrown at him by so many people on so many subjects in such a short time gave credence to the expression "drinking from a fire hose".

Tomorrow's schedule varied little in pace. It included briefings by the installation commander, JAG, AG, air force FAC commander, and the air force ALCE commander, whatever that was. In the afternoon he would fly forty miles south to Skunk Patch near Quang Dien, visit the B Company of his medical battalion, then fly out to one or two firebases. He looked forward eagerly to getting out of Phong Sahn.

Captain Dryer appeared at the door with at least a dozen papers in his hand and advanced towards JP's empty in-basket. "I hate to do this to you, Colonel."

"Then don't. You know, Charles, the army has more people writing papers and reports than it has fighting the war. No wonder we haven't won."

"I can't wait to read your response to this," Captain Dryer said, glancing at the top sheet in his hand.

"My response to what?"

"Bravo Company, 1st/35th on Beth Ann, had a VD rate of 128 per cent last month."

JP's feet hit the floor. "What? Let me see that." His eyes swept over the statistics. He passed the paper back to Dryer. "Put it on the bottom of the pile. I'll get to it some time."

"It's due at division tomorrow, Colonel."

"How is it we have so little time to process the report?"

"It arrived from the brigade surgeon seven days late."

"Is that Captain Millbarth, the D company CO?"

"Yes, sir. He has a hard time getting reports in on time."

"That's not his only problem. I understand morale and discipline are major problems in D."

"Yes, sir. That's the feedback we get here."

"I'd better get up there tomorrow and have a father–son talk with Captain Millbarth."

"That will be hard to do, Colonel. He's still on R&R in Bangkok. He's due back on the 17th."

"Okay. Set me up to pay him a visit the day after he gets back."

JP looked at the paper with the individual unit VD rates again and shook his head. "I don't believe this. Ask Captain Moffet to come in here, please."

Dryer dropped the rest of the papers in JP's in-box and left. Shortly after Tom Moffet knocked and walked in.

JP handed him the VD report. "Have you seen this?"

Captain Moffet scrutinized the figures and shook his head. "No, sir." He chuckled. "That certainly is a remarkable achievement for Bravo Company.

"What's the going rate for VD in an infantry company?"

"Between two and six percent, and that includes the people returning from R&R in Bangkok. I suspect there is a misplaced decimal point and the correct statistic is 12.8. I'll check the report with the brigade surgeon."

"If that report goes up to division the company commander will get his head handed him for sure." JP called out, "Captain Dryer."

"Yes, sir."

"What happens when reports are late at division?"

"Someone from G–1 calls and makes dark threats."

"Does that someone wear a rank higher than the silver leaf of a lieutenant colonel?"

"No, sir. Usually it's a major or a sergeant."

"Okay. Let's sit on this report until we can check out Bravo Company and their record-setting VD rate. The last thing I want to do my first week as division surgeon is wreck careers. I'm already off to a bad start."

"Yes, sir."

"Charles, it's not necessary to agree with everything I say."

A chuckle came from the other side of the doorway.

"If there's any flak from division about an overdue report, tell them the new division surgeon is pathologically compulsive about verifying all data, which up to a point is true. If that doesn't satisfy them have them call me. By the way, where is Beth Ann?"

"On a mountain top about sixty miles west of Nghia Lam."

"How in hell can so many people get VD out there and get it more than once in one month?" He handed the report Tom Moffet. "This is a problem that merits the attention of someone with an extensive academic background, someone with MD/PhD degrees."

"Nothing at Hopkins prepared me to cope with this kind of VD rate," Moffet said. "It sounds like an epidemic. I'll head out to Beth Ann tomorrow."

"How are you going to get out there?"

"Probably on the ash and trash flight in the morning, then hitch a ride back with whatever is going my way."

"I'm supposed to have a chopper available on a daily basis, thanks to my old buddy Colonel Bruteau. You can have it tomorrow morning. Schedule it through the medical battalion operations sergeant. I'll need it in the afternoon to go down to Quang Dien."

A telephone rang in the outer office. After a moment a clerk appeared in the doorway. "Sir, it's Major Jelnik on line one for you."

JP picked up his phone and punched the first button. "Colonel Franklin."

"Mike Jelnik, Colonel. Yesterday you mentioned you would like to fly a mission with the Dust-offs once or twice a week."

JP, watching Captain Dreyer stuff more papers into his in-box, asked, "You have something in mind that is compatible with my timid and non-violent nature?"

Jelnik laughed. "I think so, Colonel. We have a request from Firebase Nancy for a routine mission to pick up a GI with an FUO. The area around Nancy has been quiet for weeks. It should be a pleasant safe flight."

"Where do you want me to meet the Dust-off?"

"It can pick you up at the VIP pad near your hooch. Since it's a routine mission there is no rush. Whatever time is convenient for you."

JP looked at his watch. "How about in thirty minutes?"

"Fine. Don't forget your flight helmet."

JP picked up his fatigue cap and started out. Pausing at Captain Dryer's desk, he said, "I'll be flying with the Dust-offs this afternoon out to Nancy. Would you pass that on to the chief of staff's office?"

Captain Dreyer looked at JP with a mixture of concern and disbelief.

"Something wrong, Charles?"

"Ah, no, sir. It's just that we're not accustomed to the division surgeon flying Dust-off missions. That's what Colonel Diblasio was…"

"Relax, Charles. It's a boring routine mission to pick up a GI with a probable cold."

"Yes, sir," Dreyer said skeptically, then reached for his phone.

Twenty-five minutes later JP was in his hooch strapping a web belt with a brand new Colt 45 automatic pistol in a holster. The supply sergeant who issued the pistol told him it had not been fired since it left the factory. JP wasn't sure it would shoot, but the weight of the weapon on his hip was comforting… just like the old days. But he was a doctor now, and doctors did not shoot people. Then why was he carrying a weapon?

Slipping into a flak jacket, he grabbed his new flight helmet from the shelf in his locker, closed and padlocked the door, then headed for the VIP pads fifty meters away. The short cut to the pads was cross-country directly down from his hooch. An alternative route was the paved road which was almost six times the distance of the short cut. The generals used the road to drive down to their helicopters. It was also used to pick up arriving VIPs. Once at the pad he leaned against windsock pole and gazed out at the South China Sea only thirty meters away. Unmanned guard towers dotted the shore.

A Huey helicopter, red cross on its nose and sides, passed noisily over the staff hooches, flew out over the sea, then circled towards the VIP pads, flaring to a gentle touchdown. A young crewman with a red cross on his flight helmet climbed out and saluted as JP approached. Returning the salute, JP removed his fatigue cap and stuffed it in a pocket. Slipping the helmet on his head, he held the headset cord in one hand and climbed awkwardly on board. Settling into the canvas seat by the open door, he searched for a jack to plug in his four-foot long headset cord.

"I'll get it for you," the medic shouted. He took the cord and inserted it into a jack behind the seat, then helped him fasten his seat belt.

A voice came through the headset. "Welcome aboard, Colonel. Chief Warrant Officer Dawkins. I'm the AC. Lieutenant Strunk is the pilot, the medic is Spec Four Adams. Is this your first chopper flight?"

JP pulled the boom mike down, then fumbled for the mike button on his cord. "Except for a ninety-second flight yesterday," he said without elaborating.

'This should be an easy thirty-minute trip out to Nancy. Flight conditions are CAVU."

JP looked out the open door at the blue sky and billowy cumulus clouds. He pressed the mike button. "Great day for flying, Mr. Dawkins."

The Huey came up to a hover, turned towards the water, dipped its nose and picked up speed. Climbing to 2,000 feet it headed south-west. Below the flat brown-green mosaic of rice paddies along the east coast gave way to gentle green hills that climbed gradually to tree-covered mountains. Vietnam was a beautiful country, too beautiful a country to be at war.

The AC's voice broke through his reverie. "Colonel, the bald peak about eight klicks out at one o'clock is Nancy. We'll be there in four."

An excited young American voice broke the spell. "Mayday, Mayday, Mayday. Any aircraft this push. This is Paper Boy One, over." The call was repeated and ended with a desperate plea, "Please come in."

The AC transmitted, "Paper Boy One, this is Dust-off One Seven. Go."

"This is Paper Boy One. We have mass caz; three KIA, four WIA, all urgent. An APC hit a mine. We are at…" The voice gave the coordinates.

JP watched the pilot and AC consult their map. The pilot banked the Huey sharply into a sixty-degree left turn. "Paper Boy One, Dust-off One Seven is eight minutes your posit. What's the local situation?"

"The APC is burning and ammo is cooking off. Charlie is in tall grass and bushes three to four hundred meters east. There was heavy incoming small arms after the APC was hit. That has eased off but may start up when you come in range. You need gunship cover. Over."

"Roger, Paper Boy One. Has your higher been notified?'

"Negative. We can't raise it."

"Understand. Wait one, Paper Boy."

The AC switched channels and notified the TOC at Nancy of Paper Boy One's situation and asked for gunship support. After a pause the AC was told the gunships were on the way. It would take a minimum of twenty minutes for them to reach the coordinates given.

The AC looked over his shoulder at JP "Colonel, we have a problem."

"I never liked that word, Mr. Dawkins."

"Actually, sir, we have two problems."

"That doubles my dislike. Okay, let's hear them."

"I was told not to expose you to unnecessary danger. A hot LZ is definitely dangerous."

"The key word there is 'unnecessary', Mr. Dawkins. According to my briefing yesterday by your commander, an 'urgent' request indicates life-threatening

290

conditions. Proper interpretation suggests this situation entails a 'necessary' danger and therefore justifies exposure?"

Dawkins chuckled. "If you say so, sir."

"And problem number two?"

"The regs direct us not to go into a hot LZ without gunship protection. The gunnies are twenty minutes out."

"What do you suggest?"

"Drop you off at Nancy. By the time I return the gunnies should be on board."

JP had been given the perfect excuse to get himself out of harm's way. Regulations required gunship protection when going into an area where there was shooting. The gunships were twenty minutes away. That was plenty of time for him to be dropped off on a safe firebase and the Dust-off to reach Paper Boy One with the gunships. But a twenty-minute delay of medical care could be critical to the survival of a severely injured soldier, and there were four severely injured soldiers waiting for evacuation. Besides, he was a doctor; he should be where he was needed.

He pressed the mike button. "Bad answer, Mr. Dawkins. Think of something else."

"We could circle and wait for the gunnies, sir."

"Try again."

"Go into the LZ with you on board and without gunship support."

"You got it. Since you will be violating regulations would you like a direct order from me?"

"No, sir, that won't be necessary, but thanks for the offer, and Colonel, sir, I do admire your style."

The pilot touched the AC's shoulder and nodded towards the left side of the windscreen. A thin column of black smoke rose several hundred feet in the air. As they neared JP made out a wide dirt road running through a field of tall grass. The jungle came within twenty meters of the road on the west side and 200 meters on the east side.

The AC spoke into his boom mike. "Paper Boy One. I see black smoke."

"Roger, Three Seven. That's the APC burning. Ammo is still cooking off so stay clear. We are in the tree line forty meters north of the APC. Where are the gunnies?"

"They're going to be a bit late. We'll do this without them."

"Your call, One Seven, and thanks. Make your approach from the west and land close to my smoke. We will try to make the gomers keep their heads down with small arms and an M–60. Over."

"Roger, Paper Boy. Pop smoke now."

From a quarter mile away yellow smoke gushed from beside the tree line. "I have yellow smoke," the AC transmitted.

"Yellow is affirmed."

The AC turned to the pilot. "Okay, Randy, take her down. Remember, 2,000 feet per minute is too damn slow."

Hearing that, JP reached to tighten his belt just as the helicopter banked sharply and dropped from under him into a steep descending spiral. He gripped the tubular seat frame with both hands and watched the green-brown mosaic beneath rapidly evolve into a carpet of tree tops, then individual trees. Strong G-forces mashed him into his seat as the pilot leveled off, skimming over tree tops at a 115 knots. As soon as they passed beyond the tree line they flashed over the burning APC. The pilot banked steeply, the rotor tips cutting a swath in the grass. Leveling off, he hauled the nose up. Decelerating rapidly, the Huey dropped through grass and hit the ground with a bone-jarring thump.

The aircraft commander looked at the pilot. "Jesus Christ, Randy, what the hell kind of landing was that?"

"A safe one," the pilot said, his face pale.

JP didn't have the vaguest idea what to do. When he saw the medic jump to the ground he followed. His head was suddenly snapped back and the helmet jerked off his head by the four foot headset cord, which was still plugged into the jack. A grinning medic indicated that the goof had been witnessed by at least one. The medic's helmet cord was at least eight feet long.

Twenty meters away the jungle's edge was a wall of trees and shrubs. Streams of red tracers floated intermittently towards the opposing tree line 300 meters away and disappeared into the jungle. An occasional green tracer floated back. The helicopter's engine and rotor noise masked out any sound of gunfire.

Two GIs materialized from the tree line with the limp body of a GI between them, his arms over their shoulders, his feet dragging along the ground. The medic climbed back on board the Huey while JP remained on the ground. The GIs moved rapidly to the helicopter's door, stopping long enough to pass the casualty's head and shoulders to the medic. They then took off back to the jungle. As the medic pulled the man on board JP lifted his legs, noting the man's blood-soaked fatigue jacket and trousers. In the space of a minute GIs dragged two more casualties and dumped them on the helicopter's floor. The head and face of one was a mass of blood: the legs of the other were severely mangled.

JP started to climb on board when he spotted a GI jogging towards the helicopter with the inert form of a soldier over his shoulder in a fireman's carry. Since there was no more room on the helicopter's floor JP motioned the soldier to put his unconscious buddy in the side seat, the one ordinarily occupied by a door gunner. Air ambulances were not permitted to be armed.

A dime-sized hole appeared as if by magic in the helicopter's skin inches from JP's hand. Two similar size holes appeared just above his head. Glancing back over his shoulder, he saw puffs of dirt advancing towards the helicopter. *Bastards*, he thought. *So much for the Geneva Convention.* He half threw himself into the helicopter. The medic pulled him in the rest of the way just as the helicopter lifted to a hover.

Turning left, the Dust-off dipped its nose and skimmed over the grass building up speed. JP stood and moved to examine the casualties. Just then the helicopter banked sharply, throwing him off balance. He managed to steady himself by pressing his hand up against the helicopter's pleated ceiling. As the helicopter banked in the opposite direction his peripheral vision picked up the blurred image of the unconscious GI in the side seat rising out of his seat. A closer look showed the man's seat belt was undone; its two segments hung loose flopping in the rotor wash. JP castigated himself

292

for failing to check the man's seat belt. The sight of bullets creeping towards him had been so unnerving that he couldn't wait to get into the helicopter and out of danger. Now the unconscious soldier was about to fall to his death.

JP worked his way between the wounded on the floor to the rear edge of the open door. To reach the GI in the side seat he leaned out facing the rear and grasped the top edge of the door with his left hand for security. Abruptly the helicopter banked violently away from him. The casualty was again lifted out of his seat, this time much further. Unless stopped he would drop twenty feet into a mass of jungle tree tops tearing by at over one hundred knots.

Forcing his eyes from the blur of tree tops, JP made a desperate lunge for the unconscious soldier and managed to grab a handful of bloody fatigue jacket. The man's weight and another violent steep bank ripped his left hand from its tenuous grasp on the door edge. Still gripping the soldier's jacket, he felt himself being pulled out the door. The tops of trees sped by only a few feet below the helicopter's skids. JP was certain he was going to die. It would be an ignominious death, and after only three days in Vietnam. Kathy and the kids would be notified he had fallen out of a helicopter on his first Dust-off mission. What a humiliating way to go.

JP's momentum out the door was abruptly stopped. A sharp pain hit his abdomen as his webbed pistol belt tightened and its buckle dug in. The medic had perceived his predicament and grabbed his webbed pistol belt from behind at the last moment. For several seconds JP hung out the door trying to cope with the realization he would not die. Praying that the buckle on his web belt would hold, he pulled the flaccid casualty back into the side seat. The helicopter was now flying straight and level, reducing the risk of falling out. He brought both ends of the seat belt together over the GI's lap, threaded the locking lever through the hasp and flipped it over, locking the belt. Working himself back into the cabin, he briefly hugged the teenage medic who had just saved two lives, then turned his attention to the three casualties on the floor.

The medic had already cut the jacket and undershirt off the first casualty. A ragged two-inch hole in the left chest oozed frothy blood when the man exhaled. A quick check showed no other injury. JP shouted in the medic's ear, "Tape a Vaseline gauze pack over the hole and start Ringer's. Run it full bore."

The medic nodded.

JP kneeled to examine the next casualty. His legs were so severely injured that a few snips of scissors would complete the amputations. He checked the tourniquets on each thigh near the groin; both appeared to control bleeding. Then he loosened one of the tourniquets for a moment. No blood spurted from any vessels including a torn femoral artery. After tightening the tourniquet he felt the man's neck; the carotid pulse was absent. Lifting one eyelid and then the other, he saw that each pupil remained dilated despite bright sunlight.

Looking up at the medic, JP shook his head, then turned to the third casualty. The soldier's head and face were covered with gelatin-like congealed blood. Taking gauze pads from the medical kit, he wiped the blood from the head and face. Part of the scalp was missing. The edges of the remaining torn scalp spurted blood. Multiple fractures crossed the exposed skull but none were depressed. There was no visible leakage of clear fluid suggestive of cerebrospinal fluid.

The medic held his medical kit with its opening towards him. JP grabbed abdominal packs, placing them over the exposed skull and torn scalp then wrapped an elastic bandage over the pads, keeping most of the pressure on the bleeding scalp and the least over the skull fractures. The soldier suddenly vomited. Quickly turning the head to one side allowed most of the vomitus to spill out the corner of the mouth. Then the soldier began jerking chest movements characteristic of an obstructed airway.

The medic passed JP a rubber suction bulb. Aspirating residual vomitus and secretions from the mouth, he squirted the material out the door. Some of it was blown back in by the rotor wash. The airway remained obstructed and the man's complexion was turning purple. JP reached over and grabbed the medical kit from the medic. Digging into the interior, he found a scalpel with blade attached inside a sealed test tube, scissors, and a plastic anesthesia tube. Using the scissors, he cut off part of the tube but left a six-inch length with the tapered end preserved. Taking the scalpel, he cut into the space between the voice box and windpipe, the cricothyroid space. When he sensed that the blade had entered the airway he jammed the tapered end of the tube through the opening and stabilized it with his left hand. Vomitus and blood immediately oozed from the end of the tube.

The medic, anticipating the need, passed JP the rubber suction bulb. Covered with blood and vomitus, the bulb slipped from his hand, rolled to the floor's edge and fell out. JP looked to the medic for a replacement. The medic shook his head.

JP stared at the tube in the soldier's windpipe. Green gastric juices mixed with blood filled the lumen. The soldier's efforts to breathe were diminishing as he tired. Unless his airway was cleared, he would soon asphyxiate and die. Only one option remained and just the thought started JP retching. It took all his willpower to lean over and suck secretions from the tube. Spitting out the secretions, he repeated the cycle a second and third time. As he contemplated a fourth cycle he was so overcome by nausea that he barely made it to the door before vomiting. Luckily the helicopter was in a bank and most of the vomitus was sucked away by the rotor wash.

The helicopter began a rapid descent. In less than a minute it settled on the 96th Evac helipad. Medics and stretchers were everywhere. JP's role quickly changed from active to passive. He watched each casualty lifted to a stretcher. "Keep a hand on that tube," he cautioned the medics who carried the casualty with the cricothyrotomy.

After all casualties had been removed JP jumped to the ground, moved away from the helicopter and bent over, heaving over and over again until nothing came up.

The Dust-off medic came over to him. Concerned, he asked, "Sir, are you going to be okay?"

JP nodded affirmative, although at the moment he had his doubts. "You saved my life and that of the GI," he gasped. "I'll thank you officially if I ever live through this." When he saw his flight helmet in the medic's hand he told him, "Hang on to my flight helmet. Right now I never want to fly again, ever."

He bent over and heaved.

Chapter Thirty-Four

Monday, June 15, 1970, 1550 hours
Emergency Room, 96th Evacuation Hospital, Phong Sahn, RVN

By the time Lieutenant Colonel JP Franklin stopped vomiting and entered the emergency room, green sheets covered three of the four soldiers brought in minutes before. Dark red blood from under one of the sheets dripped to the floor creating a widening puddle. A medic walked by and dropped several olive drab towels on the puddle. The fourth soldier, the one with the fractured skull and emergency airway, lay naked on a stretcher. The segment of plastic tube that JP had placed in his trachea was replaced by a small diameter endotracheal tube connected to an anesthesia machine. A nurse anesthetist intermittently flushed oxygen into the soldier's lungs. A unit of blood, a blood pressure cuff inflated around the collapsible plastic bag, drained into the groin. A similar unit drained into an arm. Ringer's lactate ran wide open into the other arm. A doctor in a green scrub suit leaned over the soldier, compressing his chest with a regular rhythm, pausing intermittently for the anesthetist to ventilate the lungs. A chaplain stood close by administering the last rites.

JP stood alone in the background, his face, fatigues, and flak jacket mosaics of dried blood. No longer was he an active participant in the heroic efforts to preserve life; he was a passive observer of the failure of those efforts. The doctor compressing the chest abruptly stopped and glanced up at the cardiac monitor. The tracing was flat. Shaking his head sadly, the doctor stepped away from the casualty. The anesthetist pulled out the breathing tube. Nurses and medics disconnected the blood and fluid lines. The Vietnam War had claimed another young life, and another potential Jehan Alain or Walter Reed was denied to the world. JP turned away, his eyes filled with tears.

A nurse grasped his arm. "Come with me, soldier. I'll get you cleaned up and have a doctor take a look at you." As she tried to ease him towards an empty stretcher she reached for his .45 pistol. "Better let me take this."

JP reacted in a flash. Twisting, he grabbed her wrist in a vice-like grip. "I'm okay," he growled, "and nobody takes my weapon."

The nurse recoiled at the viciousness of his response. "My wrist, soldier, you're hurting it."

Releasing her wrist, JP stammered, "I'm sorry..." His eyes went from the name tag over her right breast to the subdued lieutenant colonel's leaf on her fatigue jacket collar. "Goulden," he mouthed, "Colonel Goulden." He shifted his gaze to her face. Recognition came slowly, for twenty years had passed since he last saw Kristy Goulden in Korea. Her face had lost some of its youthful perkiness, but retained a physical beauty now enhanced by maturity, confidence, and compassion. "Kristy?" he whispered.

At the sound of her name the nurse searched JP's blood-splattered face without recognition. His name and collar insignia were obscured by dried blood. Massaging her wrist, she said, "You don't know your own strength, soldier, and you still need to be checked by a doctor." Gingerly she grasped his arm and again tried to ease him towards a stretcher. When he resisted her voice hardened. "Listen, soldier, I'm a light colonel and don't you forget it. Give me any more trouble and I'll call the MPs."

JP was near the edge. "Goddamnit, Kristy, I'm a light colonel too. I'm also a doctor... or thought I was," he said bitterly, staring at the four sheet-covered bodies.

Kristy Goulden intently studied JP's face, trying to penetrate the caked blood and grime. "You're the division surgeon who brought in the four casualties?"

"They're all dead, Kristy. I didn't save a one, not a one." His voice trembled and he began to shiver in the cold air-conditioned emergency room.

Lieutenant Colonel Goulden walked to a cabinet and pulled out a folded white blanket. Shaking it open, she placed it over JP's shoulders. "How about some hot coffee, Colonel?" She still did not recognize him.

JP nodded. Wrapping the blanket around himself, he continued to stare at the four covered stretchers.

Kristy returned with a brown mug. "It's hot," she warned as she handed it to JP.

Lifting the mug, he slurped the black liquid. "God, that's good," he said, closing his eyes as if to erase the sights of the tragic afternoon. When he opened them he saw recognition in Kristy's eyes.

"JP," she gasped. "JP Franklin." In a burst of spontaneous affection she reached out and drew him to her, hugging him, blanket and. all. When she realized ER personnel were staring she quickly released him and blushed. "I can't believe you are here in Phong Sahn."

"I got here four days ago."

"Al McClintock wrote you were coming to Vietnam in August to be the 101st division surgeon. What are you doing in the 36th?"

"Exigencies of the service. Colonel Diblasio got himself shot down."

"That was so tragic. I took care of him while he was here."

"Al told me you were at the 71st in Pleiku. What are you doing here?"

"I heard through the grapevine there is an NVA POW camp in the 36th AO where US POWs are being held. Supposedly it's not far from the special forces compound at Qui Tavong which was overrun by the NVA in '68. Bill was shot down defending the camp. I transferred here to be as close to him as possible and keep up with any rescue attempts."

"Is something being planned?"

Kristy shrugged. "I don't know. Every time I try to find out I run into a wall of silence. In the meantime the frenzied pace of this place keeps me so busy I have little time to brood."

JP sipped his coffee. "You changed so little I was able to recognize you right away."

"If you get yourself cleaned up I might recognize you for sure," Kristy said. "Al McClintock has kept me up on your accomplishments since you graduated from medical school. He was very disappointed when you decided not to follow him at

296

Hopkins."

"I owe Al a lot, Kristy, but I owe my country more. I couldn't leave the army while this war is going on."

"You have come a long way from that young platoon commander who took on two regiments of Chinese to rescue a bunch of British wounded. That was the talk of the hospital for six months after you left. From what I've seen today you haven't changed at all. You're still stumbling into firefights and you're still rescuing the wounded."

JP glanced again at the four sheet-covered stretchers. "My track record was better as a line officer," he said bitterly.

"You can't hold yourself responsible, JP," Kristy said softly. "Those men were dead when they were picked up."

Sensing another chill coming on, JP pulled the blanket tighter around himself and sipped more coffee. "Did you know the 36th Division aviation officer was the chopper pilot I rescued on that operation in Korea?"

"You mean Colonel Bruteau?"

JP nodded.

"I know him from his visits to his pilots and aircrews in the hospital. That explains the scar on his neck."

"We'll have to get together for a threesome 3rd Herd reunion," JP said.

A tall young man, his green scrub suit fresh-stained with blood, an OR mask hanging below his chin, entered the ER, looked around and approached them. "Excuse me, sir, are you Colonel Franklin?"

JP stared at the man. His horn-rimmed glasses gave him a wise, all-knowing look.

Kristy quickly introduced him. "This is Kevin Brodie, the head and neck surgeon."

JP shifted the coffee mug from his right hand to his left and shook hands.

"Sir, I tried to contact you at your office and was told you had gone on a Dust-off mission," Brodie said. "When I heard that a doctor had done a cricothyrotomy on a Dust-off bringing in casualties I took a wild guess that it was you."

JP smiled. "Now that you've found me, what can I do for you?"

"I'd like to run a case by you."

Despite the psychological trauma of the disastrous afternoon, JP's interest was piqued. Medicine was a great healer, not only of the patient but of the physician. He sipped some coffee and looked questioningly at Brodie.

"The patient is about twenty; it's hard to be more specific because of his wound. It appears he was hit mid-neck by a high velocity bullet traveling upward. The bullet shattered the larynx, tore up the hypopharynx, went through the floor of mouth, tongue, palate, and exited the root of the nose just below the frontal sinus. It split his mid-face into almost equal halves, each half with an eye and part of a nose. We have packs jammed everywhere but haven't been able to control the bleeding, much less start reconstruction."

"Sounds challenging," JP said, then took another sip of coffee.

'That's an understatement, Colonel." Brodie paused and looked hopefully at JP "We wondered if you would give us a hand."

JP, his fatigue and grief swept away by the anticipation of demanding surgery, quickly responded. "Sure. I'll need to call my office and let them know where I am. If you'll give me the patient's name and unit, I'll see that his CO is notified of his condition."

Major Brodie seemed surprised and almost confused by the request. "Sir, we don't know his name or his unit. He's a Viet Cong found about eight klicks from Firebase Nancy."

JP's eyes flashed anger. "That's where we picked up those GIs after their PC was blown up. That son of a bitch in the OR or his buddies detonated the mine that killed seven GIs. They tried to kill me and the Dust-off crew." Recalling the experience drove JP over the edge. His voice became low and dripped with venom. "As far as I'm concerned, the little fucker can bleed to death."

Kevin Brodie, shocked by the vehemence of JP's response, turned pale.

Kristy Goulden was aghast. "You can't mean that, JP."

"The hell I can't." He turned and started to leave.

"Damn it, JP," Kristy said, grabbing his arm, "you're not a line officer any more. Stop thinking like one. You're a doctor now. You don't kill people and you don't let them die when you could save them."

JP glared at her, too angry to speak. He tried to shake off her hand but her grip was too strong.

Kristy continued. "You took an oath to save lives. You have no right to turn your back on that oath just because someone wears the wrong uniform."

In his intense anger JP almost blurted out details of a classified G–2 briefing that morning. He was told dozens of US POWs had died from the deliberate withholding of medical care, torture, and even executions by the Viet Cong and North Vietnamese. Instead he bit his lip and stared morosely at the mug in his hands, its trembling the only overt manifestation of the conflict within him. Finally, he lifted the mug and drained the remaining coffee. Setting the mug on a nearby Mayo stand, he pulled off his blanket, dropped it on an empty gurney and turned to Kevin Brodie. "Kristy is right, Major. Let's go before I change my mind."

★

Lieutenant Colonel JP Franklin, MD, Medical Corps, USA, followed Major Kevin Brodie, MD, Medical Corps, USA Reserve, into the doctors' dressing room. Metal lockers lined its walls. Green scrub shirts, trousers, caps and masks were piled on a shelf between two doors at the far end of the room. Long narrow benches at the center of the room reminded JP of a locker room in a gym. In one corner a large cardboard box was partially filled with bloodstained green sneakers. A clothes hamper for soiled scrubs and a trash container were the other items in the room.

Kevin Brodie indicated the two doors. "The one on the right has a commode; the other, a sink and shower."

"I'll just clean up for now so we can get started," JP said. "You don't happen to have mouthwash in your locker, do you?" He had to get the residual taste of vomitus out of his mouth.

298

"As a matter of fact I do," Brodie said.

He removed a padlock from a locker and opened the door. Reaching up to the shelf, he took out a bottle half full of blue liquid and passed it to JP.

"I'll probably use all of this."

"No problem, Colonel."

Minutes later a somewhat cleaner Lieutenant Colonel JP Franklin emerged carrying his bloodstained fatigue jacket and T-shirt. Rolling them into a ball, he tossed them into the trash barrel. "They'll never be clean," he told Brodie, "I don't care how many times they're washed."

"What happened to your pistol and flak jacket?"

"Kristy put them up for me in the emergency room."

Settling on a bench, he undid the laces of his jungle boots, dropped them on the floor and shoved them under the bench. Kevin Brodie went to the box of used sneakers. "Do you have a preferred size?"

"Nine and a half or ten."

While Brodie rummaged around in the box JP stripped off his fatigue trousers. It joined the T-shirt and jacket in the trash basket.

Brodie brought a set of green scrubs and a pair of OR shoes. "The scrubs are all large, Colonel. The nurses have the smalls and mediums." He held out a pair of bloodstained green OR sneakers. "These belonged to Ted Shackelford, our urologist, who went home last month."

JP accepted the sneakers and scrubs without comment. As he pulled on green scrub trousers Brodie noticed dried blood on his abdomen and thighs. "Colonel, you weren't hit, were you?"

"No, but it wasn't because the bastards didn't try."

Brodie sat down on a wooden bench and leaned back against the wall. He remained quiet while JP dressed. Finally, he said, "I'm sorry, Colonel, I mean about what you went through out there."

JP didn't answer. He slipped a foot into a sneaker and reached for the laces.

The young surgeon continued. "I don't know how to say this."

JP looked up, leaving the sneaker untied.

"Doctors here lead sheltered lives. Most of us are afraid to set foot off the hospital compound except to go to the main PX. We sleep on clean sheets, take hot showers, eat good food, and chase nurses. The only people we talk to are other doctors and all we talk about is doctoring." He paused, shifting his legs. "We have little idea what you experience when you go out to the bush. We know nothing of what the young GIs go through out there. What's more, we don't want to know. It's tough enough spending twenty hours a day putting these kids back together. It's even tougher when you start wondering what it's all for."

"I hope the price we're paying is worth whatever we're supposed to get out of it," JP said, thinking of the three dead left in the bush and the four sheet-covered bodies in the ER.

Brodie remained silent, watching as JP first tied the shoelaces in a flash of fingers, then standing up, checked out the sneakers. "How do they fit?" he asked.

"Not bad for hand-me-downs. If you don't make it as a surgeon you should do well as a shoe salesman."

"Yes, sir. I'll keep that in mind. Colonel, may I ask a personal question?"

"If I'm not obliged to answer it."

"In the ER it was apparent that you knew Colonel Goulden from long ago. I have never heard her speak to anyone like she spoke to you."

Better to start out with the truth then allow tongues to wag, thought JP. "You're right, Kevin, I do know Colonel Goulden from a very long time ago. Early in the Korean War I was hospitalized at a MASH with severe dysentery. I was near death from medical mismanagement when Kristy took over my nursing care. Later, when I was convalescing, the medics and patients told me Kristy's care saved my life. I never had a woman save my life, only guys. Kristy and I became good friends; nothing more. Months after I was discharged from the hospital my platoon brought some British wounded to the MASH where she was the ER supervisor. She and the chief of surgery, a man named Al McClintock, oriented me towards medicine. McClintock later became the chair of head and neck surgery at Hopkins and my mentor. He has remained close to Kristy through letters. I learned from him she was at Pleiku. I had no idea she was here."

"That's a remarkable story," Brodie said, handing JP a cap and mask. "Did you know her husband?"

"No. I never met him. I understand he was a superb pilot. He shot down two MiGs in Korea."

"She's gone through hell since he was shot down at Qui Tavong two years ago. I know she grieves for him although she manages to hide it well."

"Kristy is like a beautiful swan, Kevin," JP said, tying the straps of his cap and mask. "She will love only one man, and the commitment is for a lifetime."

"We sure love her around here."

"That's understandable. Okay, Dr. Brodie, I'm ready."

Kevin Brodie led down a corridor, tying his own mask and cap as he went. They passed through double swinging doors into a wide corridor. Six operating rooms, three on each side, opened into the corridor. Brodie stopped momentarily at the last door on the right, then pushed through into the operating room. JP followed.

The scene was familiar. Blood-soaked green sheets covered a supine form on an operating table. White glare from portable operating lights drenched one end of the table. Two masked figures in green hunched over the table, their mumbled conversation just audible over the noise of suction machines. IV poles stood as silent sentries at the sides of the table. Bottles of clear fluid and plastic blood bags hung from the pole's T-bars.

A nurse in an ill-fitting scrub suit and baggy OR gown counted 4" x 8" gauze sponges onto her Mayo stand. A mildly paunchy male, his face obscured by a mask and glasses, sat on a metal stool next to the patient's left hip. Intermittently he squeezed the football-shaped black rubber bag attached to an anesthesia machine. Black hoses ran from the machine to a plastic tube that disappeared into the patient's lower neck. Two male medics acted as circulators. One kneeled on the floor in a

300

corner counting dozens of blood-soaked sponges arranged in neat rows on a sheet. The other intently watched the surgeons at the operating table.

"I got him," Kevin Brodie announced proudly as if he had just bagged a trophy buck. "This is Colonel Franklin, from Walter Reed. He's the new division surgeon for the 36th Division."

Both surgeons looked up and nodded. Neither spoke, but their eyes reflected relief.

The anesthesiologist regarded JP from over the rims of his glasses. "I'm glad someone is finally here who knows what to do with this guy."

Kevin Brodie introduced each person, beginning with the surgeons.

"Elliot Franceschi," he said, indicating the surgeon on the patient's right. "Elliot trained at UCLA. Opposite him is Paul Reischwig from Utah. And the sarcastic gas-passer is Scott Marcella. We're not sure he ever went to medical school, much less finished an anesthesia residency. The scrub is Jill Webster. One of the circulators is Warrant Officer Bill Denslow. Bill was a gunship pilot until his cobra got nailed with an RPG. He's supposed to be on convalescent leave down at Cam Ranh Bay. He insisted on staying here and working in the OR because he wants to go to medical school. The other circulator is Spec Four Winkler."

JP gave Denslow a friendly nod and made a mental note to talk with him later. Pushing a foot stool nearer the table with his foot, he climbed on it and peered over Elliot Franceschi's shoulder. "What do we have?"

Franceschi lifted layers of blood-soaked gauze lap pads off the neck exposing a dime-sized hole surrounded by blackened skin in the mid-neck over the Adam's apple. Bright red blood gushed from the hole. "This looks like the entrance wound, Colonel," he said. "The powder burns suggest he was shot at close range. The larynx and hypopharynx are a mess." Placing dry pads over the neck, he nodded to Reischwig to apply pressure to the pads with his hands.

Moving to the patient's mouth, tightly packed with gauze, Franceschi continued. "The bullet came up through the tongue and palate. Packing the oral cavity and pharynx was the only way we could slow down the bleeding."

JP reached up to the rim of an OR light and focused its beam on the patient's mouth. Blood oozed out through the packs. "How do you feel about pulling the packs for a quick look?"

"I'd just as soon leave them in for now, Colonel."

"That's okay with me. Let's see the face."

Gingerly Franceschi lifted the bloody dressing covering the face. A jagged gash split the upper face and nose almost in the midline. Tissue and bone had exploded outward as the bullet exited. Holding half the face in each palm, Franceschi moved his hands apart, exposing a defect that extended rearward to the base of skull and throat. Blood quickly welled up in the defect and spilled onto the drapes. Franceschi and Reischwig hurriedly grabbed gauze pads and stuffed them into the defect.

"That's awesome," JP said.

"Yes, sir," Franceschi said. "We surmised either someone shot him at close range, or he was squatting with an AK between his knees when it discharged."

"I wish I had my camera," JP said ruefully.

"We've taken plenty of slides and will take more, Colonel. We'll be happy to give you a set," Franceschi said.

JP stepped from the stool and walked to a metal table. Two X-ray viewboxes and a small stack of films were on the table. Flipping the viewbox switches, he picked up the films and waited for the fluorescent lights to flicker into full glow. Holding each film briefly in the white light, he studied the images and offered his interpretations. Finished, he tossed the films on the table, flipped off the lights, and moved to the operating table. Stepping back on the footstool, he said, "Here's how I'd suggest you deal with this."

The surgeons looked up expectantly.

"Go after the bleeding first. If bleeding can't be controlled everything else will be a waste of time."

They waited for him to go on.

"Start with tapes around both carotids, common, external and internal. Most of the bleeding seems to be from the external carotid. If it's impractical to ligate the individual branches ligate the trunk. Try to spare one lingual artery; if both are ligated the tongue will slough. Once bleeding is controlled you can start putting him back together, beginning at the base of skull and working out. Use part of the tongue to reconstruct the floor of mouth and pharynx. Leave the larynx to the last. It may be the biggest challenge. Then do a feeding gastrostomy."

"You are going to scrub in, aren't you, Colonel?" Franceschi asked, a worried tremor in his voice.

"A herd of horses couldn't keep me out," JP assured. "Has the neurosurgeon cleared the dura in the frontal region?"

"Yes, sir. He's across the hall if we need him."

"Good. While Kevin and I wash up, go ahead and develop a generous U-shaped flap based superiorly. That should give plenty of exposure of both carotid sheaths, the airway, upper gut, and base of tongue."

"You make it all sound so simple," Kevin Brodie said.

"That's the consultant mystique," JP said, smiling behind his mask. "But like the fencing master I'm careful not to give away all my secrets. It would be catastrophic for my image if you all ended up knowing as much as I do." He looked up at the wall clock, then turned to Brodie. "This is going to be at least a seven-hour case, and that's an optimistic estimate." Pulling out his wallet, he extracted a card with some typed numbers on it. "Is there a phone around here?"

"Yes, sir, at the OR nurse supervisor's station," Kevin Brodie said.

"I need to notify the chief of staff that I'm going to miss happy hour and dinner at the general's mess; tonight of all nights."

"Is that going to be a problem?" Brodie asked.

"You bet it is. Would you believe lobster and Chardonnay is on the menu tonight, and a John Wayne movie is scheduled after?"

Kevin Brodie stared at him, disbelieving.

"I know, Kevin; it's a hell of a way to fight a war."

302

Chapter Thirty-Five

Lieutenant Colonel JP Franklin stepped back from the operating table, his gown and scrub suit saturated with blood. His feet, swollen after more than seven hours of standing, were ready to explode out of the hand-me-down sneakers. His back and legs felt as if he had been humping through the jungle with a ninety-pound pack. During the last three hours he had managed to first ignore, then suppress the warnings of a progressively distending bladder and the pangs of a food-starved stomach. Behind his mask he smiled. He was becoming the quintessential surgeon, one possessed of a large bladder and a small stomach.

From past experience he knew that massive overwhelming fatigue would soon descend on him like a truckload of bricks. But for now he was on a high, flushed with adrenalin and endorphins, by-products of a great case that had gone well. The Viet Cong's injured arteries were ligated, the face reconstructed, the pharynx and oral cavity repaired, and the shattered larynx rebuilt. Eventually the VC would be able to breathe, swallow and speak.

Scott Marcella, watching from his anesthesiologist's perch like a wise old owl, nodded approvingly as Kevin Brodie tied down the final sutures. "Just like downtown," he remarked, obviously impressed.

Brodie looked up at the anesthesiologist. "The ultimate triumph… approval from a cynic who seldom approves of anything."

JP untied his gown strap, pulled the gown off over his gloves and dumped it into a cloth basket. Ripping off his gloves, he tossed them into a metal kick bucket. Marcella handed him the patient's chart.

Easing down on a sitting stool, JP leaned back against the wall, closed his eyes and uttered a groan of ecstasy. After several minutes he opened the chart, found a blank sheet and began writing a consultant's note. When finished he returned the chart to Marcella, then told Kevin Brodie, "My hooch and other phone numbers are on the chart. The people at the other numbers should be able to get in touch with me if you need me. I'll try to stop by in a couple days to see how he's doing."

"Thanks for your help, Colonel," Brodie said. "I'll have the OR supervisor order you a pair of sneakers. It will be about two weeks before they get here. Tens okay?"

"Fine." JP looked down at his hand-me-down sneakers. "These have a salty look. I think I'll hang on to them for now."

In the doctors' dressing room JP used the latrine, washed, then changed into a clean scrub suit. Having discarded his bloody fatigues, he would have to wear the scrub suit back to his hooch. After lacing up his jungle boots he went by the emergency room to pick up his pistol, web belt, holster, and flak jacket. He hoped to see Kristy Goulden but she was off duty.

Looping the belt over his right shoulder, the pistol hanging low in its holster, he picked up his flak jacket and headed to the hospital entrance. Having missed the evening meal, he now battled hunger pains. A hot meal would have to wait until 0600 hours, when the general's mess opened for breakfast. Until then he would settle for a hot shower and several hours of sleep. Suddenly he stopped short; he had forgotten to send word to Jackson to come and pick him up. Now he would have to find a phone, wake Jackson, wait for him to dress, sign out the jeep and drive six miles to the hospital, a waste of precious minutes that could have been spent sleeping. Muttering a few choice phrases, he pushed through a set of doors to find a phone.

He had entered a semi-dark ward. A dozen occupied beds projected out from the walls on each side. At the nurse's station midway, a doctor in a white coat studied a chart under the yellow light of a goose-neck lamp. Opposite the doctor a nurse wrote in a loose-leaf notebook. As JP neared the nurse's station he recognized Colonel Marchenko, the hospital commander. Surprised to find him still working at such a late hour, he said. "Lou, you're killing my desire to command a hospital."

Marchenko looked up, then glanced at his watch. "You look like hell; just finishing up that VC?"

JP nodded.

"There goes your reputation as a fast knife."

"I charge by the hour. Wait until you get my bill. On second thought, let me use the phone to call my driver and I'll forget my bill."

"I'll do better than that," Marchenko said. "I'll drive you back to your hooch. It's the least I can do after the work you put in for us." He indicated the nurse. "This is Sandy Arness."

Arness, a husky but pretty captain, studied JP a moment. "You look like you could use some coffee, Colonel."

"A half cup, black, will keep me awake until I hit the sack."

Captain Arness left to get the coffee.

"It's so tragic none of the casualties you evacuated survived," Marchenko said. "I heard the Dust-off had eleven bullet holes in it."

"The bastards were probably aiming for the red cross on the chopper."

"JP, you had no business going into a hot LZ."

"I didn't have a choice, Lou."

"Of course you had a choice. You could have stayed out of the helicopter in the first place. Christ, you were lucky you weren't killed your first week in Vietnam."

Captain Arness returned with a mug half filled with coffee, a napkin with a dozen soda crackers, and a small opened can of Vienna sausage. "I thought you might be hungry, Colonel. This is all we have on the ward," she said apologetically.

"That looks like a feast, Sandy, thanks."

"There are a couple of cooks on duty now setting up breakfast," Marchenko said. "I can get them to fry you up some bacon and eggs."

"No, thanks, Lou. I'd better get to my hooch and a little sleep. Hell week continues tomorrow… I mean today."

JP made sandwiches of the Vienna sausage and crackers, washing them down with coffee. "That's the best meal I've had today, Sandy," he told the nurse. "I'm all set, Lou."

"My jeep is parked out by the hospital's front entrance."

Marchenko led from the ward, down a covered wooden walkway, past more wards, past the front office, and out of the entrance. The night was cool. A myriad of stars and a quarter moon shined overhead. Miles away in the west an occasional silent red or green tracer floated across the dark sky. Suddenly a burst of intense bright light lit a segment of the sky and drifted towards the ground.

Marchenko stopped at a parked jeep, turned and stared west into the night. "Looks like the Cong have hit a firebase. My people will be going to work in a few minutes."

JP tossed his gear in the back seat of the jeep, then climbed into the passenger seat. Through half-closed eyes he watched Marchenko unlock a padlock releasing the chain that fixed the steering wheel to a clamp welded to the chassis.

"Can't trust anybody these days," Marchenko remarked dryly, pulling the chain loose and throwing it in back. After pumping the gas pedal he turned the starter switch. The engine ground over and over but failed to start. He pumped the accelerator again and hit the starter. Again the engine growled without starting. The odor of raw gasoline was strong.

'You flooded the carburetor, Lou. Are you checked out in this thing?"

"It needs a tune-up. I'll wait a couple of minutes before trying again. If it doesn't start I'll get a six-by. That's the prerogative of a commander."

As they sat waiting JP began to drift into sleep. Marchenko's voice brought him awake. "JP, rumor reached me that you and Kristy Goulden greeted each other like long-lost friends."

JP wasn't sure Marchenko was asking a question or making a statement. "Lou, I hope you're not implying what it sounds like you're implying."

"Just looking for an explanation. The fact that I heard about it so early should give you an idea how these things get started. They can take on a life of their own very rapidly."

JP decided to be candid with Kristy's commander as he had been with Kevin Brodie. "Kristy saved my life in Korea, Lou. She played a major role in my decision to go to medical school. Nothing physical ever transpired between us other than one sisterly kiss on the cheek before I went out on a mission. We were both married then and we are now. We love our spouses and we take our marriage vows seriously. For me Kristy was the kid sister I always wanted but never had."

"Did you know that her husband may be held in a POW camp out by Qui Tavong?"

JP nodded. "She told me."

Marchenko reached to the ignition switch and cranked the jeep's engine. This time it started immediately. Fifteen minutes later, after weaving the jeep through the dark streets of the 36th Division headquarters, he parked next to JP's hooch and killed the engine.

"Aren't you concerned you might not be able to start it again?" JP tweaked.

"I'll take the chance just to give you some friendly counseling."

"About Kristy?"

"Precisely. It's only natural you should feel gratitude and indebtedness to someone who saved your life, more so for turning you to medicine. Just don't let your sense of gratitude and indebtedness plus Kristy's vulnerability lead you both into something that you and she will regret, not to mention your families."

JP was getting fed up with the innuendos. "For God's sake, Lou, back off. I love Kathy. I would never do anything to put our marriage in jeopardy. I have great affection, maybe even love for Kristy, but it's the kind of love a brother would have for a sister and nothing more. I would never do anything to hurt her."

"I'm glad you feel that way."

JP climbed out of the jeep and reached for his web belt, pistol, holster and flak jacket. "Not that I would ever consider doing otherwise, Lou, but between a hooch-mate who is a Catholic priest trained as a Jesuit, and a strict Southern Baptist buddy who is commander of the local hospital, I'm inalterably condemned to a life of celibacy until I go home."

Marchenko leaned over the passenger seat towards JP. "You really put your ass on the line today going into that hot LZ. I don't want to walk into my ER some day and see you laid out on one of those stretchers."

JP tossed his friend a sloppy salute. "A man's gotta do what a man's gotta do. Semper Fi, Lou."

"Dumb jarhead," Marchenko said, shaking his head. Cranking the engine, he shifted gears, made a fast U-turn and disappeared into the darkness.

Minutes later, JP, nude except for a towel around his waist and wooden clogs on his feet, clomped along the board walkway that led to the communal latrine shared by staff officers. Blinking as he entered the brightly lit shower, he glanced at a sign that admonished bathers: CONSERVE HOT WATER.

"Not this time," he muttered.

Adjusting the water temperature until it was as hot as he could tolerate he stepped under the strong spray. Dispassionately he gazed at the blood on his thighs and belly from the wounded GIs and the VC. It seemed incongruous that the blood of his comrades could not be distinguished from the blood of his enemy.

★

Tuesday, June 16, 1970, 0730 hours
Briefing Theater, 36th Division Headquarters, Phong Sahn, RVN

The briefing theater resembled a tiered classroom. The briefing officer spoke from a platform down in front. Sliding panels over the platform displayed a variety of maps and charts. The first row of seats consisted of comfortable leather swivel chairs for generals and full colonels. The remaining four rows of folding metal chairs were for officers of lesser rank. JP preferred to sit in the last row. He had learned he could nap back there with impunity during presentation of such exciting data as the number of eight-inch howitzer shells fired in the previous twenty-four hours.

The briefing had been under way for about thirty minutes. The weatherman made his predictions, the G–2 made his predictions of Viet Cong and main force intentions. Now the assistant G–3, a major, was about to complete his presentation. "The summary of casualties for the previous twenty-four hours is as follows. There were three US KIA and four WIA eight klicks west of Firebase Nancy when their APC was blown up by a probable man-detonated 155 mm shell." A pointer tapped the location on the map.

"Heavy enemy small-arms fire was received immediately after the mine exploded as the dead and wounded were carried to cover. It subsided only to recur when the Dust-off went in to pick up the four wounded. Although the Dust-off took several hits there were no further casualties. Two Cobra gunships worked the area expending their ordnance. The four casualties died en route to the 96th Evac or in the emergency room. A sweep of the area before dark found blood trails but no wounded or dead. There were two other KIAs and five WIAs, the result of booby traps in dikes between rice paddies eleven klicks south-west of LZ Harriet." Again the pointer tapped the map.

"There were no confirmed enemy KIAs and only one enemy WIA, a VC picked up west of Nancy and taken to the 96th. His condition, according to Colonel Franklin, is critical. It will be several weeks before he will be available for interrogation. In the same area three suspected VC, one a female, were detained and turned over to the ARVNs for interrogation. In other action… at 0340 hours this morning a mechanical device was detonated two klicks east of LZ Linda. A patrol swept the area at first light. They followed a blood trail to a dead mother tiger and two cubs."

JP's head fell forward. He was asleep.

Chapter Thirty-Six

Wednesday, June 17, 1970, 1310 hours
VIP Pad, 36th Division HQ, Phong Sahn, RVN

Lieutenant Colonel JP Franklin stood beside the windsock, scanning the cloudless Vietnamese sky for the UH1H Huey helicopter assigned him for the remainder of the day. It would take him to Skunk Patch near Quang Dien, headquarters of the 9th Brigade and the Bravo Company of his medical battalion. There he planned to meet with the company medical officers, tour the company area, then visit Fire Support Base Maria eighteen miles south-west of Quang Dien.

Cradled in his left arm was his flight helmet, its four-foot long headset cable rolled up loosely. A pistol in its holster hung from the webbed belt around his waist. Since his flight in the Dust-off yesterday four items were added to the belt: sheathed knife, canvas pouch with three magazines loaded with caliber 45 ball ammunition, lensatic compass, and full canteen.

From over the South China Sea a Huey helicopter noisily announced its approach. Its landing light, brilliant even in daytime, made it easy to spot. Nearing the helipad it made a 360-degree turn, then descended rapidly, flared and settled softly on the helipad. As JP started towards the helicopter he saw it was different from the Dust-off of yesterday. It had no red crosses on its nose or sides; what it did have was a door gunner in each side seat behind an M–60 7.62 mm machine gun.

The port side gunner stepped to the ground and saluted. Returning the salute, JP climbed on board and settled into the seat by the door. After belting in he put on his helmet and plugged in its headset cord.

On the flight deck the man in the right seat turned. "Good morning, sir. I'm Warrant Officer Dan Ranson, the AC. I'm going to be your regular pilot." Ranson didn't look a day over twenty. The bushy handlebar mustache he had grown in an effort to appear older only enhanced his youthfulness. After introducing the peter pilot and door gunners Ranson asked, "Will there be any change in your itinerary?"

"Yes. Cancel everything except Skunk Patch and Firebase Maria." Recalling the chief of staff's admonition to be present for cocktail hour at the general's mess, he added, "I need to be back in Phong Sahn by 1700 hours." He didn't want to miss the T-bone steaks and Cabernet Sauvignon scheduled for the evening meal.

The engine whine increased. The rotor blades whipped around. In his headset JP heard the pilot say, "Coming up." The helicopter lifted until its skids were about three feet off the helipad. "Hover test complete," the pilot reported. Slowly the Huey flat-turned until it faced the South China Sea. Dipping its nose, it began to move forward. Rapidly gaining speed, it dropped to just above the water, churning the calm surface with rotor wash, then climbed in a right turn towards the south-west. Intersecting a paved two-lane north–south highway it banked left and followed the road south. JP heard the AC call the artillery frequency inquiring about artillery firing with trajectories that might put them in danger of colliding with a shell along their route. Getting shot down by friendly fire was a hazard JP had not considered. It was a lousy way to go.

Artillery control responded on Ranson's first call. "Quang Dien is cold. Hortense is currently firing 105s west and south-west. Maximum height is 3,000 feet. If you stay over QL One and below 1,000 feet you should be safe."

"Roger, over QL One, below 1,000," Ranson repeated.

JP sat by the open door, fascinated by unfolding scenery of rice paddies and seashore. As he contemplated the beauty of Vietnam he became aware of his enviable assignment. He had assigned to him a helicopter, two pilots, two door gunners, and license to go anywhere in the 36th AO he wished. It was an exciting yet awesome opportunity. He had to remind himself that Vietnam, despite its beauty, was a dangerous environment, exceedingly hostile to helicopters and those who flew in them. He pressed the mike button. "Mr. Ranson, how long have you been in Vietnam?"

"One month into my second tour, Colonel."

"What did you fly your first tour?"

"The Loach… the Hughes light observation helicopter."

"That puts you way ahead of me in experience. I'll defer to your judgment the decision to abort any approach to a unit you consider hazardous."

"Thanks, Colonel." Ranson sounded relieved. "We should be at Quang Dien in about twenty. Right now we're over QL One, the north–south highway from Saigon to the DMZ. We'll go down on the deck in a minute. You'll see a lot more detail down there… but not for long," Ranson said, chuckling. "Are you expected at the medical company?"

"They were notified yesterday. They might appreciate a heads up that I'm on the way."

The Huey dropped to about twenty feet. Looking down, JP saw the Huey's shadow on the highway zipping down the highway chasing them. Traffic was light. An occasional truck, motor scooter, or bicycle shared the road with cattle and oxen. Acres of rice paddies stretched out on both sides of the road, their square dimensions marked by earthen dikes. A cluster of huts and one-story buildings flashed by. An area the size of a football field came up rapidly. It was filled with people, cattle, carts and trucks. Few adults bothered to glance at the low flying helicopter roaring past. However, children in a nearby schoolyard waved vigorously. JP and the door gunners waved back just as vigorously.

The Skunk Patch tower cleared the Huey for a straight-in approach. The Huey's nose came up. It climbing rapidly to several hundred feet to bleed off airspeed. When it leveled off it was lined up for a straight approach to the north–south runway.

"Cleared to air-taxi to Bravo Med," the tower instructed. "No traffic in the immediate area."

Descending to three or four feet over the runway the pilot slowed to about twenty knots and "taxied' down the runway on a cushion of air. For JP, taxiing an aircraft without wheels seemed unnatural. Parked on ramps to the left and right of the runway were Hueys, Loaches, Chinooks, Cobras, and even C–123 twin-engine transport planes. On the east side of the runway huge open-ended tent-hangars housed more aircraft.

The Huey made a 45-degree flat turn to the left and followed a taxiway to a group of a dozen wooden buildings not unlike the headquarters buildings at Phong Sahn: long, wooden, louvered and painted blue. Each building was surrounded by a wall of fifty-five gallon drums, presumably filled with earth. A white flag emblazoned with a red cross flapped from a pole in front of one of the buildings. The Huey hovered over a square of PSP and settled on a large red cross painted at the center. The jet turbine whined down and the rotor blade slowed.

JP pressed the intercom button. "I'll be here about an hour, Mr. Ranson. Keep Bravo Company headquarters informed where you are. I'll send word when I'm ready to move on to Maria."

"Roger, sir. We'll go on to the fuel farm, top off the tanks, then return to park to the side of the pad. One of us will be with the aircraft at all times."

Removing his helmet, JP set it on an adjacent canvas seat and unbuckled his seat belt. Slapping on his fatigue cap, he jumped to the ground just as a senior NCO appeared and saluted.

"Sir, First Sergeant Dockering. Welcome to Bravo Med."

Returning the salute, JP took note of the sergeant's weathered intelligent face, close-cropped hair, and walrus mustache. A cloth combat medic's badge and paratrooper's wings were sewn to the left breast of his fatigue jacket. JP guessed the sergeant's age to be in the late thirties.

The helicopter lifted off in a flurry of conversation-killing noise. After it faded Dockering continued, "Sir, Captain Wood sends his apologies for not meeting you. We just got in two wounded a few minutes ago. All the doctors are tied up in the emergency room. Captain Wood asked that I bring you there."

JP nodded. At the door of the emergency room he thanked Dockering. "I can take it from here, Sergeant," he said, finishing with "Airborne".

Dockering stared at JP a moment, then at the subdued jump wings sewn on his fatigue jacket. "All the way, sir."

Pushing through double doors, JP entered a long windowless room brightly lit by banks of fluorescent lights. Six stretchers set on sawhorses were arranged parallel to the wall on each side of the room. A wire cable ran the length of the room above the stretchers. Unopened bottles of IV fluids and packaged plastic IV tubing hung from the cables ready for immediate use. Shelves built into the wall were crammed with glass bottles of clear fluid, boxes of plastic tubing, sterile instrument packs, dressings, medications, and syringes. Malleable wire ladder splints of varying lengths and sizes hung from nails driven into the walls. Portable suction machines and green oxygen tanks were distributed among the stretchers. Shelves and cabinets in the center of the room contained stacks of green sheets and blankets. Except for the raspy noise of electric motors on the suction machines, the room was quiet.

310

At the far end of the room personnel in green were bent over inert figures on two of the stretchers. As he neared JP saw that the chest of one was bare and being prepped with disinfectant by a medic. Beside him a doctor filled a syringe with local anesthetic. The doctor looked up, glancing at the lieutenant colonel's leaf and caduceus on JP's collar.

"Colonel Franklin," he said, "I heard you were going to visit us today. I'm Ken Gruber. My helper here is Spec 5 Strahan."

Gruber pointed to a tiny wound between the fourth and fifth rib on the right. "This young man caught a grenade frag. His chest X-ray demonstrated a pneumothorax but very little blood. His cardiogram was normal. He's in some pain and short of breath. I'm going to put in a chest tube to get some expansion of the lung while waiting for the backhaul Dust-off."

JP nodded. He was about to offer help when a flurry of frenzied activity at a nearby stretcher grabbed his attention. Three people in green huddled around the neck of a struggling casualty. One worked desperately to clear blood from the oral cavity with a large sucker while attempting to clamp a bleeding artery deep in the throat with a long hemostat. The other two had their hands full trying to control vigorous bleeding from a three-inch horizontal incision in the lower neck.

The man with the sucker said, "I can't get it from up here, Steve. I'm going to pack."

"Don't pack until I get the trach in."

"Make it quick. He's bleeding faster than I can suck it out."

"Christ, Dick, I've got big problems down here. I sliced through an immense goiter trying to get to the trachea. It's bleeding like crazy." He turned to a medic standing behind him. "Hang another unit of O-negative, Randy."

The medic went several feet to a refrigerator, opened the door, hesitated, then lifted out a bag of blood. Returning, he hung the bag on an IV pole and connected it to the catheter in the casualty's arm. "Sir, there are only two units left."

"What's the word on resupply from the 96th?"

"They have twelve units ready to go. They'll send them as soon as a chopper is available."

"When will that be?"

"They're not sure. All choppers including Dust-offs are committed for the afternoon."

"We may have to give the last units to this patient. Pray that no more casualties come in needing blood."

JP cleared his throat. "Could you use another pair of hands?"

The doctor looked up. "Colonel Franklin. Sorry I couldn't meet your chopper. I'm Steve Wood, the CO, and sir, that's the best offer I've had today."

JP undid his pistol belt and placed it on a nearby stretcher. After removing his fatigue jacket, he accepted a cap, mask, and sterile gloves from the medic. As he slipped on the gloves he asked, "What do we have?"

"A nineteen-year-old who caught a grenade frag in the right lower jaw. It fractured the jaw and tore up the base of the tongue. From the way he's bleeding the frag probably severed the lingual artery. I'm trying to get in a trach. This damn goiter has complicated things."

The casualty began twisting and bucking as he struggled for air. JP told the doctor at the patient's head, "Forget clamping the artery. Concentrate on keeping the airway as clear of blood as possible while we get a trach in."

Taking the sucker from the medic helping Captain Wood, JP cleaned away enough blood to glimpse the cut bleeding surfaces of a markedly enlarged thyroid gland over the trachea. He looked up at Captain Wood. "That's a big one all right." Returning the sucker to the medic, he manipulated his fingers until half the goiter was between the thumb and forefinger of each hand and squeezed. The bleeding instantly slowed to a tolerable ooze. "Clean out the clots," he told the medic.

"That's remarkable," Steve Wood said.

"God's gift to the surgeon."

"Sir?"

"Fingers, Dr. Wood, fingers. Hurry up and get that trach in. My fingers are killing me."

Taking advantage of an almost dry field, Steve Wood quickly dissected down and exposed two to three cartilaginous rings of the windpipe. He looked at JP. "Do you believe in a flap or window to enter the trachea?"

"Surgeon's preference. Right now I have no idea where you are on the trachea. I doubt you do. Go up on the trachea, feel the cricoid, then count down three rings. That way you won't inadvertently put the trach too low, something that could lead to great unhappiness."

After confirming the location of the intended opening into the trachea, Captain Wood cut a square flap out of the front wall, then quickly rammed in a cuffed tracheotomy tube through the opening. Immediately the casualty coughed violently. Blood and sputum shot out the lumen of the tracheotomy tube with the force a bullet. The medic handed Wood a 10 cc syringe full of air. Connecting the syringe to a valve hanging off the trach tube he inflated the rubber cuff at the end of the tube creating a watertight seal. The airway was now secure.

JP glanced at the doctor at the patient's head. "Okay. Pack the mouth and pharynx. Don't spare the packing and pack it in as tight as you can." He watched Steve Wood slide a suction catheter through the tracheotomy tube and advance the tip into the lungs to clean secretions and blood out of the airway. The GI began to breathe more easily and his struggles subsided.

"Get a generous biopsy of the goiter, Steve," JP directed, "then put in some figure-of-eight sutures along the cut edge of the goiter. Take care not to nail my talented and highly skilled fingers."

Steve Wood looked up at JP and grinned. He sliced off a piece of the goiter, then told the medic assisting, "Two O silk suture on a large curved needle."

Finally, the last suture was placed and tied down. JP took his hands from the field. Massaging his fingers, he studied the dry field. "You do good work," he told Captain Wood. "Take a listen to his chest. We want to be sure we didn't give him a collapsed lung." He turned to the doctor who packed the oral cavity. "What's he doing up there?"

"Oozing through the packing but nothing spectacular. I think he'll do okay until he gets to the 96th."

Captain Wood turned to a medic behind him. "Check on a backhaul Dust-off, Randy. These two are ready to go."

A moment later the medic returned. "Sir, the standby chopper went out to make a pickup. Dust-off control estimates twenty-five minutes."

"Did you tell him we had two urgent cases?"

"Yes, sir. He said twenty-five minutes was the best he could do. All the choppers are committed. A platoon ambushed a company-sized NVA unit. There's one hell of a firefight going on west of Cindy."

Captain Wood looked at JP. "Sir, would you consider...?"

"Of course," JP said without hesitating. "Send one of your doctors along to make sure things stay under control. I'll stay here and let you show me around."

Ten minutes later both casualties had been loaded on JP's helicopter. JP climbed on board and went up to the flight deck. He put his hand on Dan Ranson's shoulder. "Let me know when you're back. I still want to go out to Maria this afternoon."

Ranson nodded. "We should be back in about an hour."

As JP moved back through the cabin he checked on the two casualties, shook hands with Dick Frances, the doctor accompanying them, and jumped to the ground. Steve Wood met him. "What would you like to see first, Colonel?" he shouted above the Huey's noise.

"The mess hall and some coffee."

Captain Wood nodded.

Both men watched the Huey lift off and head north. As its noise subsided conversation without shouting became possible. "Our real mess hall burned down last month," Steve Wood said as he led between two buildings. "The engineers are building a replacement. It will be completed in two more weeks. We're messing temporarily in a squad tent."

"How is that working out?"

"Functionally okay, but by mid-morning the heat inside the tent is brutal, even with the sides rolled up."

They entered the framed mess tent through a screen door. The interior was, as predicted, brutally hot. A half dozen picnic tables and benches were arranged down the center. A voice suddenly shouted, "Tenshun." Steve Wood immediate responded, "Carry on," then led to the serving counter. A swarthy rotund man in whites came up to them. "Sir, Staff Sergeant Forrester, Bravo Med mess sergeant."

Steve Wood introduced JP. "We could use some of your famous coffee, Sarge."

"Yes, sir, coming right up."

JP and Steve Wood moved to a wooden picnic table and sat facing each other. JP was visually checking the austere surroundings when Sergeant Forrester returned and placed a paper napkin with two doughnuts and two mugs of steaming coffee on the table.

"Thanks, Sergeant," JP said, reaching for one of the mugs and a doughnut. "Tell me about your mess hall fire."

"Well, sir, it was like this. We was frying up a batch of doughnuts for breakfast. The fat caught fire and spilled over. Then the fat accumulated on the wooden rafters over the stove caught fire. That's when we called the fire department."

Steve Wood interjected, "Colonel, the fire department on Skunk Patch consists of South Koreans supervised somewhat remotely by US civilians."

Forrester continued. "The dispatcher sent a fire engine to the wrong location. It took a while for the MPs to track it down and lead it here. When the engine's pump was activated a couple of spurts of water came out of the hose and then nothing. The pump had frozen for lack of oil."

JP chuckled. "At least you'll get a new mess hall out of it."

"Yes, sir," Forrester said. "Will the colonel be staying for the evening meal?"

"No. I'll be going out to Maria as soon as my chopper gets back from Phong Sahn."

After the mess sergeant left Steve Wood said, "Now I know the probable origin of the expression 'The fat's in the fire'."

JP grimaced. "That's pretty raunchy, Captain Wood." He took several sips of coffee, then leaned towards the young doctor. "How do you like commanding a medical clearing company in a combat zone?"

"Being responsible for 110 men, four officers, and the medical support of a brigade of 8,000 men in combat has been a very maturing experience, Colonel. It's the last thing I expected when I was drafted out of my general surgery residency. At the time I was looking forward to a urology residency and an academic career as a professor."

"You seem to have adjusted well to military life. Your clearing company is functioning first rate," JP said. "How do you get along with the brigade commander?"

"Fine. Colonel Prather has been very supportive. He makes sure I'm included in all the important briefings and planning. He comes down here every now and then to visit patients and just shoot the breeze."

"I met him briefly at the general's mess the other night," JP said. "He invited me to visit his brigade first."

"Will you see him today?"

JP glanced at his watch and shook his head. "I'll save that for another time since I've already spoken with him. I want to get out to the 1st/5th this afternoon."

"Did you know their battalion surgeon left for R&R in Bangkok yesterday?"

"I'm sorry to hear that. I had hoped to spend some time with him. I'll still go out to Maria; the battalion commander is expecting me."

"Sir, could I ask a favor?"

JP nodded.

"I planned to send one of my doctors out to Maria today to take sick call. From the way things are looking I'm going to need every doctor here. It would be a great help if you could take care of that sick call while you're out at Maria."

"Sure, no problem."

JP drained his mug and stood up. "How about the grand tour of Bravo Company?"

"Yes, sir. Coming right up."

★

Wednesday, June 17, 1970, 1415 hours
BLO, Skunk Patch, Quang Dien

Lieutenant Colonel JP Franklin followed Captain Steve Wood into the first of the company wards. Ten bunks were arranged perpendicular to the wall on each side; six were occupied. A small desk near the entrance served as the nursing station for a medic. "This is our surgery ward," Steve Wood explained. "We handle almost all minor wounds. The patients are kept here post-op until ready to return to their units. Cases from our brigade done at the hospitals at Phong Sahn and not evacuated out of country or Cam Ranh Bay are sent here to convalesce, leaving more beds available at the hospitals for the more seriously injured."

"That makes sense," JP said.

Wood led out of the ward and into the adjacent building. Its interior was similar to the ward just left. "This is the medical ward. What we treat here are the milder cases of malaria, dysentery, and patients convalescing from more serious illnesses after discharge from the hospitals at Phong Sahn."

"Do the hospitals furnish any kind of consultative backup?"

"It's almost exclusively by telephone. If things are slack here I let one of the docs go up to Phong Sahn to make rounds with the surgeons and internists. Occasionally they scrub in on a case or work a couple hours in the ER."

"I'll see what I can do about getting a surgeon and internist down here a couple of times a month to make rounds with you." He grinned. "Feel free to put them to work like you did me."

"That would be a big morale boost, Colonel. We're pretty isolated here."

JP was very impressed by Steve Wood. The young doctor had no military experience prior to being drafted. Yet here he was, running a medical clearing company as though he were a career Medical Corps officer. The ward door opened. First Sergeant Dockering stepped through and scanned the ward. When he spotted JP and Steve Wood he came over.

"What's up, Sarge?" Captain Wood asked.

"Message for Colonel Franklin from Chief Warrant Officer Ranson. He said he would be delayed about thirty minutes because of mechanical problems with the chopper. He's going to pick up a different chopper."

JP nodded. "Thanks, First Sergeant."

After Dockering left Steve Wood said, "This place would collapse without Sergeant Dockering. He and Lieutenant Smithy, the admin officer, make commanding a medical clearing company a piece of cake."

JP slapped Steve Wood on the shoulder. "Captain, you have just articulated the essence of a successful commander, and that after only four months in the United States Army."

Captain Wood smiled widely.

"What's the ward next door?"

"A combined medical and surgical ward for civilians. It has a small unit at one end for kids. The adults help look after them. We also have a couple of nurse trainees from

Quang Dien who work here during the day."

"Do they receive any pay?"

"The other docs and I chip in to fund their salaries."

Twenty minutes later the two were in Steve Wood's office drinking coffee when a strange-sounding helicopter buzzed in, landed close by, and shut down. "That's no Huey," JP said."

"It sounds more like a Loach."

"Probably Ranson with a substitute chopper," JP said, rising.

As they headed towards the door Chief Warrant Officer Ranson stepped in. "Sir," he said, "I'm ready to go out to Maria whenever you are."

"You flew the Loach in?"

"Yes, sir. It was the only bird available on short notice. It's all I flew my last tour. I'm still current in it as an IP."

JP turned to Steve Wood and extended his hand. "Thanks for your hospitality, Steve."

Wood grasped JP's hand. "Thanks for the help in the ER, the use of your chopper, and taking sick call at Maria."

After a parting salute JP and Dan Ranson walked towards the Loach. To JP, the Loach lacked the graceful aeronautical lines of the Huey. It closely resembled an ugly tear-shaped bug with a tail. As they neared he saw the Loach had only four seats; two in front and two in the back. It was beginning to look attractive. "Do I get to ride up front?"

"Yes, sir. Your helmet is on the left front seat. Colonel Bruteau passed the word you were interested in some rotary wing instruction."

JP nodded. The Loach was turning into a beautiful flying machine.

"Well, today is as good a time as any to start," Ranson said.

"Right on, Mr. Ranson."

Climbing into the Loach, JP put on his helmet, plugged in the headset cord, and secured the seat belt and shoulder harness. When the radio static came through the headset he pressed the mike button.

"Let's go flying, Mr. Ranson."

316

Chapter Thirty-Seven

Wednesday, June 17, 1970, 1555 hours
En Route, Fire Support Base Maria, 9th Brigade AO, RVN

As the Loach climbed towards 2,000 feet Chief Warrant Officer Ranson began with an identification of each control and an explanation of its function to Lieutenant Colonel JP Franklin. "The long-angled lever by your left hand is the collective. Raising it adds pitch to the rotor blade increasing lift. The handle rotates to function as the throttle."

JP nodded. He couldn't wait to get his hands on the controls.

"The stick between your legs is the cyclic. It tips the rotor blades whichever way the stick is moved. That changes the helicopter's attitude, much like the stick in a fixed-wing aircraft. The pedals rotate the tail propeller which gives directional control. Okay, Colonel, for the next few minutes you work the pedals. I'll take care of everything else. When you can hold directional control you can add the cyclic and finally the collective."

Sounds simple enough, JP thought. With his fixed-wing experience flying a helicopter would be a piece of cake.

"Okay, sir, you have the pedals. Maintain a heading of two four zero."

JP rested the heels of his boots on the floor and the soles on the pedals. Almost immediately the left pedal pushed towards him. The Loach dropped into a descending turn to the right. He shoved in the left pedal to stop the turn. Too much. The Loach began a left turn. Right pedal. Left pedal. Right pedal. JP fought the wildly oscillating Loach as he chased the spinning gyro compass.

Ranson chuckled. "The tail rotor on a Loach has tremendous torque, Colonel. You have to keep a heavy left foot to keep this bird straight. The heading you want to maintain is still two four zero."

Gradually JP gained enough directional control to keep the compass within five degrees plus or minus of 240 degrees. Over the next fifteen minutes he took over the cyclic, then the collective and throttle. Now he had total control of the aircraft, or was it the other way around. In seconds he was chasing the VSI, altimeter, and compass. The Loach bobbed up and down, weaving this way and that like an out-of-control yo-yo. His sorry performance was humiliating.

"Okay, Colonel, I've got it," Ranson said, taking the controls. "Different from flying a fixed wing, sir?"

"Just a little," JP said, struggling to salvage some of his pride.

"A cardinal principle of helicopter pilotage is to always fly as if the engine were going to quit. Sooner or later you won't be disappointed."

"What happens then?"

"A maneuver known as auto-rotation."

The engine noise suddenly subsided. The airspeed dropped off. Ranson continued. "The reaction should be to bottom the collective to take all the pitch out of the rotor blades and increase air resistance against the flattened blades. This will keep the chopper from dropping like a rock. At the same time haul back on the cyclic stick to keep the nose up, otherwise the chopper will try to dive into the ground."

To JP it seemed the Loach was already dropping like a rock. A glance at the VSI showed its needle moving past 2,000 feet per minute down. The hundred-foot altimeter needle spun away precious height. A look out of the bubble showed the ground rushing up at a horrifying rate, yet Ranson seemed as calm as if lecturing in a classroom. "Timing is critical in this maneuver," he explained. "If you add collective too early, the helicopter will stop its descent briefly, then fall through to crash and burn. Add collective too late and you get the same result. The only other factor to remember as you near the ground is that helicopters, like fixed-wing aircraft, land into the wind." The Loach rotated ninety degrees. "I'm going for that open patch of field just ahead."

At about fifty feet Ranson added a bit of collective, slightly slowing the descent. Then a few feet above the ground he added full collective. The Loach shuddered and thumped down on the ground. After a moment of silence he said, "That wasn't one of my better auto-rotations, but you get the idea. Now I will introduce you to hovering."

Soon a tense JP struggled with cyclic, collective, throttle, and pedals to keep the helicopter over one spot. He bounced the Loach from the ground to as high as twenty feet, then back down. The Loach slid backward, rotated, then climbed forward. Twice Ranson took over the controls to keep the Loach out of the trees. Sweat poured from under JP's helmet. Just as he felt he had finally gotten control of the wildly gyrating helicopter, Ranson came on the controls.

"I've got it, Colonel. I'm starting to get airsick," he said laughing. "You did good for only forty minutes dual. It took me almost five hours before I learned to stay ahead of the airplane."

"I hope there weren't any VC observing today."

Ranson chuckled. "We should plan on at least one hour to two hours a week of intense dual. After you get eight or ten hours' Loach time I'll transition you to the Huey. With your fixed-wing time you should be able to get proficient enough to get a chopper to the coast and crash-land near friendlies."

"That's a pleasant thought," JP said. He looked at the clock on the instrument panel. "It's almost 1630, Dan. We'd better head to Maria."

"On the way."

★

Wednesday, June 17, 1970, 1645 hours
Approaching Fire Support Base Maria

The 1st/5th Infantry Battalion Headquarters and its supporting units were entrenched on the flattened bald of a 900-foot high peak eighteen miles west and south of Quang Dien. The summit, once covered by a heavy growth of trees and jungle vegetation, had been vaporized nine months ago by a 10,000-pound bomb dropped out the rear of a US Air Force C–130 Hercules transport. After the fires burned themselves out and molten rock cooled, Rome ploughs were airlifted to the peak by Chinook helicopters. They completed preparations for construction of the firebase. Agent Orange, sprayed from air force C–123 transports, defoliated the dense verdant trees and shrubs that once climbed to the peak from the triple canopy jungle in the valley below. The result laid bare the approaches to the base, discouraging the Viet Cong from outright frontal assaults. It failed to stop an occasional rain of mortar shells falling on the base.

Comparatively speaking, Fire Support Base Maria was a safe oasis in a hostile and violent land. Spread over half a dozen acres it was a complex of unpainted wooden structures, partially dug in, partially sandbagged, and partially protected by ammo boxes filled with red dirt. Twenty-foot tall guard towers at strategic locations around the perimeter were manned twenty-four hours. GIs scanned the valley below with powerful binoculars during daylight. After dark they used starlight scopes, miracle instruments that collected ambient light from stars and moon to change night into an eerie green day. Tunnels of concertina wire and razor wire extended down several hundred feet from the perimeter to challenge ubiquitous VC sappers. Patterns of claymore mines faced away from the perimeter, set to blast challengers into shredded flesh at the squeeze of hand-held clackers.

Key structures, such as the Tactical Operations Center (TOC) and battalion aid station, were buried under sandbags. Multiple large and small bunkers, numerous fighting holes, two- and four-hole latrines, and even showers improvised from 55-gallon drums dotted the summit. A narrow road soaked with permapreme circled inside the perimeter. Three helipads near the TOC represented the only means of reaching or leaving the firebase other than walking. At one end of the base a battery of 105 howitzers protected by a ring of sandbags stood ready to support the battalion's companies in the field. At the opposite end of the base an unpainted wooden building built in the form of a T, the battalion mess, provided diners with imposing views of western Vietnam and less imposing meals.

Dan Ranson eased the Loach down onto a flat area several rotor-widths from the helipad and shut down the engine. The declining whine of the turbine was accompanied by that of the gyros spinning down. JP removed his helmet and tucked it under the seat, then unbuckled his seat belt and shoulder harness.

A tall, lanky soldier appeared at JP's door and saluted. "Sir, Sergeant First Class Zydma, battalion aid station NCO."

Returning the salute, JP climbed down from the helicopter.

"Captain Wood sent word you would be taking sick call, Colonel."

"Any time you're ready, Sergeant."

"I have twenty two men waiting at the aid station."

"Lead on, Sergeant."

"Colonel," Dan Ranson called out, "would you mind if I tagged along?"

"Sergeant Zydma may put you to work."

"That's okay by me, sir," Ranson said, joining up.

★

Wednesday, June 17, 1970, 1650 hours
Fire Support Base Maria

The battalion aid station resembled a small two-room fort. Its walls were a double layer of wooden ammunition boxes filled with dirt, its roof a triple layer of sandbags. The interior had sufficient room for about six ambulatory people and two stretchers on sawhorses. After seeing the primitive interior of the aid station it was easy to understand the rationale of over-flying the battalion aid station to take casualties to the clearing company for acute care or directly to the hospitals in Phong Sahn.

Sick call went fast. JP's experience taking cadet sick call during his three-year tour at the Military Academy stood him in good stead. He recalled mornings when the line of waiting cadets extended from the emergency room, down a corridor the length of the hospital, out the door, on to the sidewalk and beyond. He became a "quick-draw" diagnostician as a requirement for survival. Thus twenty-two patients now were a piece of cake. Dan Ranson was put to work arranging clinical records and taking temperatures. By the time sick call ended JP had given out generous amounts of analgesics, decongestants, laxatives, anti-diarrheal medications, and skin ointment. Three men were given light duty slips and two more placed on quarters. The rest were sent back to their units.

Lieutenant Colonel Mark Steglich, 1st/5th battalion commander, entered the aid station just as sick call ended and introduced himself. Steglich, West Point, Class of '54, had captained the rugby team at the Academy. After graduation he went on to Oxford as a Rhodes scholar. This was his second Vietnam tour. During his first in 1963–64 he commanded an infantry company for six months, then went to battalion headquarters as S–3. After promotion to major he served as the battalion executive officer until rotated back to the States to Command and General Staff College. Early in 1970 he returned to Vietnam as a lieutenant colonel to command the 1st/5th.

Colonel Steglich insisted on giving JP a walking tour of the firebase. Ranson was invited to join them. They ended up in the Tactical Operations Center where they were briefed by the S–3 on current battalion objectives. "We interdict the flow of supplies to the east coast from the Ho Chi Minh trail in Laos, protect local villages and hamlets, identify targets for the fast movers, and do bomb damage assessments." When the briefing ended Steglich stood up.

"Not a very aggressive way to fight a war, much less win it," he admitted almost apologetically. He glanced at his watch. "Can you stay for the evening meal, Doctor?"

"I thought you'd never ask," JP said. "I've smelled frying chicken for the last half hour. I will need to notify the chief of staff's office at division."

"We can do that for you through the TOC. You going to miss lobster tonight?" Colonel Steglich asked.

"That was last week. It's T-bone steak tonight. The truth is, I'd much rather eat fried chicken."

"Right on. This way, Doctor. You too, Mr. Ranson."

Minutes later JP, carrying a plastic tray, followed Colonel Steglich through the single chow line, accepting servings of mashed potatoes and canned peas. When he came to the vat of fried chicken his mouth watered.

"White meat or dark, sir?" the GI server asked.

"Dark, please."

A drumstick and thigh were dropped on his tray.

"Gravy?"

"Over everything."

"Everything?"

"Everything."

Spoonfuls of light brown gravy were ladled over the chicken, potatoes, and peas. Next, canned peaches were dumped into a compartment of the tray followed by two slices of white bread.

Colonel Steglich led to a table by a screened window in a section marked off for officers. Overturned clean cups and silverware, wrapped in paper napkins, indicated each setting. JP set his tray on the table and paused a moment to absorb the awesome view of the surrounding country, then eased down on the bench opposite Steglich.

"Thanks for pinch-hitting for our battalion surgeon," Steglich said.

"No problem. I was coming out here anyway."

JP cut off a piece of fried chicken, chewed and swallowed. "Your mess sergeant puts out great fried chicken."

"He's number one. I had to fight off brigade to get him. You have no idea the impact of tasty food on morale."

JP grinned. "Oh yes, I do," he said, spearing another piece of chicken with his fork.

"How many battalions have you visited?" Steglich asked.

"This is my first. Since I hit Phong Sahn a week ago I've been overwhelmed with briefings, orientations, introductions, and tours of all the units on the base. I would have come out here sooner had I known how good your cook was."

Dan Ranson eased down on the bench next to him. JP scrutinized the immense servings of potatoes, peas and bread that almost hid two pieces of fried chicken. "You on a diet?"

"No, sir. With only two pieces of chicken I have to make up calories with other foods."

JP smiled.

"Anything you picked up talking to medical personnel or during sick call I should know?" Colonel Steglich asked.

"Two GIs with troubling findings."

"How do you mean?"

"Both complained of chronic dry cough, which they amply demonstrated while talking to me. Their chest exams were negative, but their throats had a diffuse beefy redness suggesting chronic irritation. Since both denied a history of smoking cigarettes the possibility of smoking something else raised its ugly head."

Steglich stared at JP a moment. "You're suggesting marijuana?"

"What's your sense on its use in the battalion?"

Steglich played with his food for several moments. "It's not a problem in the bush. The troopers monitor each other. They won't tolerate anyone who isn't at his peak of alertness. Back here and at battalion rear it's a different story. Marijuana is definitely a problem although I don't yet have a handle on how much of a problem."

"How have you handled it so far?"

"Not too well, I'm afraid. I've been fairly lenient with anyone caught with one or two joints, relying on counseling by the battalion surgeon and threats by their company commanders. As a last resort company punishment is imposed, mostly fines, loss of privileges, and rarely a one-grade reduction in rank. Anyone dealing marijuana gets the book thrown at him. There were two courts martial convictions. Both men were sentenced to six months at LBJ and given bad conduct discharges." He reached for the pitcher of lemonade and filled JP's and Ranson's cups, then his own. "I'm the first to admit our policies dealing with marijuana don't reflect inspired leadership, but it's all we have. We're like the blind trying to navigate in a strange environment."

A loud *boom* from nearby so startled JP that he almost dropped his cup. A second, third and fourth *boom* followed, and then quiet.

Steglich laughed. "One of our 4.2s registering."

"Mortar shells are supposed to cough when leaving the tube," JP said, trying to hide his embarrassment.

"Not those mothers. They're high trajectory cousins to 105 howitzers."

"Any indication of substance use in the battalion other than marijuana?" JP asked.

"No heroin or opium, but there is a growing use of amphetamines. Most is sold at Nghia Havoc in bottles under the trade name Obesitol." He chuckled. "The label on the bottle has a picture of a fat Vietnamese woman. We suspect the stuff is made up and bottled in the village, probably somebody's backyard. The crime lab found large amounts of amphetamines in some samples, very little in others, all sorts of bacteria and a spirochete that causes leptospirosis."

Dan Ranson looked at JP.

"It's a spirochete carried by animals, primarily rats and dogs and is shed in their urine. The disease affects the liver causing jaundice. It's fatal in ten percent of the people who develop jaundice." He turned back to Steglich. "Yesterday I learned that an even more ominous problem has surfaced at Phong Sahn. This information is classified for now."

Steglich nodded.

JP turned to Ranson. "That goes for you too, Dan."

Ranson swallowed. "Yes, sir."

"The G-2 informed me that packs of cigarettes have been thrown over the fence onto the base in areas where they would be easily found by GIs. Some of the cigarettes were sent to the CID crime lab at Long Binh. Analysis showed marijuana heavily laced with heroin."

"Jesus!"

"There's more. In Saigon it's now possible for a GI to buy a capsule of pure heroin for as little as three dollars. The same heroin in the States would have a street value of about two hundred dollars. There have been several deaths from drug overdoses because of the purity of the heroin. It's only a matter of time before that high-grade low-cost heroin becomes available in our AO if not already here."

"Those bastards," Steglich fumed. "They destroy our young people and finance their war at the same time."

"That's the classified part, Mark. We're not sure that the VC or NVA are responsible."

"Why doesn't that surprise me?" Steglich said bitterly.

A tall, thin major in his early thirties set his tray down next to Colonel Steglich and slipped onto the bench. A handlebar mustache hid most of his upper lip. Short black hair, just beginning to turn gray at the temples, contrasted with his light tan complexion. Steglich introduced him as John Olivarez, his executive officer. After shaking hands JP introduced Ranson.

Major Olivarez turned his attention to Colonel Steglich. "Boss, we may have a problem out at Alpha Company."

"What's up, John?"

"Earl Mossberg fell and hurt his ankle two days ago."

"How serious is it?"

"He insists it's not a bad injury. He said he's done well on improvised crutches."

Steglich became thoughtful. "I don't know about Earl. He just made captain and this is his first company command. I'm not sure how much credence to give his self-estimate. What's the tactical situation out there?"

'They're going into night lager and will put out a half dozen ambushes on suspected trails."

Steglich looked at his watch. "It's going be tough getting a Dust-off out there this late on a routine medevac. He may not even need to be evacuated. I wish our doc were here."

JP cleared his throat. "Colonel, if I can have another piece of fried chicken I'll go out to Alpha Company, wherever that is, and check out Captain Mossberg's ankle. If he needs evacuation I'll take him with me back to Phong Sahn."

"You're on, Doc," Steglich said. "John, get the kindly old division surgeon another chicken thigh. Get one for Mr. Ranson too."

"My pleasure," Major Olivarez said, rising.

In a minute he was back with two chicken thighs on a plate. He handed the plate to JP who took a thigh, then passed the plate to Ranson. "Now you see the bennies of flying the division surgeon."

"I'm not so sure, sir," Ranson said, placing the remaining thigh on his tray. "I'll wait until I see where Alpha is located."

"I'll notify Mossberg you're coming," Major Rodriguez said. "When you're ready to leave, stop by the TOC for Alpha's location, call sign, and frequencies."

"I really appreciate this, Doc," Colonel Steglich said. "Let me know what you decide."

"You'll be the first to know after Mossberg," JP said, slicing off a large chunk of chicken thigh.

★

Wednesday, June 17, 1970, 1905 hours
Vicinity Alpha Company, 1st/5th Battalion, 9th Brigade AO

At 2,000 feet the evening air was cool and smooth. The Loach buzzed along serenely. Somewhere up ahead three GIs waited in the jungle next to a clearing to signal the helicopter with a strobe light. In the left front seat Lieutenant Colonel JP Franklin scanned the green carpet below. A glance at Dan Ranson showed he was doing the same. "Why don't they pop a smoke grenade?" JP asked. "It would be easy to see from up here?"

"The strobe is less likely to give away their position. It can be seen only from above. We should be getting close." He reached to the radio console, pushed a button, and transmitted. "Burnside, this is Redbird Three."

The response came almost immediately. "Redbird, this is Burnside. We hear you. You're about a klick north-east and getting closer. Stay on your present heading. Strobe is on."

"Roger, Burnside." A moment later Ranson said, "Okay, there it is."

"I don't see anything," JP said, searching.

"It's behind us now, but I have a fix on it." Ranson examined a map on his lap, then looked up. "Hell, sir, they picked an LZ on a hill. The last thing I want to do is dig a rotor into the side of a hill."

"That could ruin our day. Maybe they have a flat spot picked out we can't see from here," JP rationalized. "How come you're not turning back?"

"I'm going to make a couple of false landings before letting you off. Then I'll make a couple more after. The idea is to confuse the wily Cong. They won't know which landing is the genuine one; they don't have enough people or time to check out all of them."

"You're a sly one, Ranson."

"Hang on, sir."

Ranson banked the bach sharply to the left, then dropped it like a rock. JP felt himself lifted up against his seat belt. The altimeter spun down and the jungle rushed up. Ranson leveled off above the tree tops, yanked up the nose and suddenly they were on the ground.

"I almost lost it when you dropped this thing," JP said.

"Lost what, sir?"

"All that good fried chicken."

Ranson grinned. After a short interval on the ground to simulate discharging or picking up passengers, Ranson bounced the Loach up into the air, flew a half circle and settled to the ground again. He waited thirty seconds, then lifted off and headed for the bona fide LZ. This time JP spotted the strobe light.

"You're learning, sir," Ranson said, dropping the Loach.

As they neared the ground JP saw the only area clear of trees was the side of a steep hill.

"Colonel, I can't land there," Ranson said. "The best I can do is put a skid on that flat rock sticking out just ahead. You'll have to climb out on the skid and jump. I'll put your side close to the hill so you won't have far to fall... I mean jump."

"And I was just beginning to like you, Ranson," JP said, undoing his seat belt and shoulder harness. "I hope you're not planning on picking me up here. I would like to go back to Phong Sahn today, but not hanging on a skid."

"No, sir. I'll VR for another PZ while I'm flying around waiting on you."

"How much time do I have on the ground?"

Ranson studied the fuel gauge and clock. "About an hour. Please don't stretch it, sir. I might have to leave you."

JP nodded. Removing his helmet, he slid it under his seat. By this time Ranson had brought the Loach to about ten feet over the rock and began to ease down towards it. JP moved to a sitting position on the floor with his feet hanging out the door, then gingerly felt for the skid with one boot. After both boots were on the skid he grabbed the door sides with death grips and lifted himself to a standing position. Now all his weight was on the skid. He looked down. The rock was smaller than he had first thought. He would have to jump to the hill side, about three feet below the rock. "I'm really too old for this," he muttered, then jumped.

Landing hard on the sloping ground his downhill leg collapsed. He fell, rolling almost twenty feet before he could "self-arrest". As he lay panting, waiting for the world to stop spinning, a soldier with an M–16 materialized at his side and knelt down.

"Sir, sir, are you hurt?"

JP pushed himself to a sitting position and stared at the GI. The youthful face was all concern. "The only thing hurt is my pride, soldier."

Another soldier with an M–16 approached. JP made out subdued Airborne wings on his left breast. A third GI remained close to the jungle edge, an M–79 grenade launcher cradled in his arms.

"That was one hell of a PLF, sir," the GI with the Airborne wings said as he helped JP to his feet.

"You should have seen me come off the swing-landing trainer at Benning," JP said, brushing himself off. He removed his .45 pistol from its holster, cleaned debris off the butt and then returned it.

The GI introduced himself as Pfc Winters and the GI with him as Pfc Washington. "The surly man with the grenade launcher over there by the jungle is Pfc Caldoni."

"Which one of you picked this LZ?"

"I did, sir," Winters admitted sheepishly.

"I won't forget," JP said scowling.

"We'd better get moving, Colonel," Winters said. "It's about a five-minute fast hike to the CP. Caldoni will take the lead. I'll go next, then you. Washington will bring up the rear."

As they filed into the jungle JP began scanning the trees ahead for snipers. Old habits were hard to break. As an eighteen-year-old marine he had trekked through the jungles of the Northern Solomon Islands searching for snipers. Now, twenty-seven years later he was still trekking through jungle searching for snipers. It seemed he hadn't made much progress in twenty-seven years, but then, neither had the world.

★

Six minutes later, moving rapidly along an almost non-existent trail, Caldoni led into a tiny area of low growth hidden from the fading sunlight by triple canopy jungle. A half dozen GIs stood about eying JP with curiosity. Sitting on the trunk of a fallen tree was a captain in his mid-twenties, his right leg extended, boot off, and stockinged foot resting on the ground. Lying nearby on ponchos stretched out on the ground were two GIs. A short, muscular soldier with a red cross arm band, black hair cut almost to the scalp, had just completed starting an IV on one of the GIs and was adjusting its drip.

JP stopped the captain's salute and extended his hand. "Hi, I'm Colonel Franklin, the division surgeon, making a house call… so to speak."

"Earl Mossberg." The captain gripped JP's hand. "Battalion sent word you were coming." He indicated a wiry, athletic young man standing about three feet away, a CAR 15 slung muzzle down over his shoulder. "This is my platoon sergeant, Sergeant Ellison."

Sergeant Ellison saluted. "You're the first division surgeon I've seen in the bush in two tours, Colonel, sir."

JP returned the salute. "Any excuse to get away from a desk. And I'd just as soon not be saluted out here." JP recalled how Japanese snipers observed who was saluted, assumed they were officers and shot them. Indicating the two men on the ground, he said, "They look like they need a doctor."

"Yes, sir," Mossberg said, "much more than I. They both should be evacuated. You'd better look at them first." He called to the medic. "Gene, get over here and meet your consultant."

The medic straightened up, walked over and reported. "Specialist Four Gene Sato, sir. Second platoon medic."

"Tell me about your patients."

"Yes, sir."

They moved to the two supine men. Sato kneeled by one. "This is Pfc Granowski. Early this morning he experienced severe chills followed by high fever and headache. He became disoriented and had a brief episode of hallucinating. I think he has cerebral malaria and needs urgent evacuation."

Sato couldn't have been much older than nineteen. JP was impressed by his professional manner. After briefly examining Granowski, he looked up at Sato. "I agree. I'll take him back with me."

They moved to the GI on an adjacent poncho. Sato reached down and pulled the

326

man's right trouser leg up to the knee. A puncture wound of the calf was apparent. The leg was mildly swollen, with red streaks going towards the groin. "This is Pfc Rifkin. He fell into a punji pit about two hours ago." Sato reached down and picked up a four-foot length of bamboo and handed it to JP. "This went in about four inches."

JP studied the tapered end of the stick, noting the barb and dried blood. "Do they really put feces on these things?" he asked.

"Not that I could identify," Sato said.

JP returned the punji stick to Rifkin. "He can go with Granowski on my Loach. What about your CO?"

"I think his ankle is broken."

"I'll check him out. You round up some people to carry him and these two to the PZ. They're in no shape to walk. Do you have any antibiotics?"

"Yes, sir. Penicillin and tetracycline."

"Not much good for Rifkin's problem. Better let the orthopods at the 96th start him on their antibiotic preference."

JP returned to Captain Mossberg. "Your turn."

"What about Rifkin and Granowski?"

"Cerebral malaria and early infection from a punji stick wound. Both need to be evacuated." JP kneeled by Mossberg's foot and peeled off his sock. The ankle and foot were grotesquely swollen; the overlying skin was a mottled reddish purple. It was hot to the touch and lacked a palpable pulse. When he gently flexed the foot Mossberg winced and let slip a groan. Looking up, JP asked, "How and when?"

"When we crossed a stream two days ago I jumped for a rock, missed and fell. It seemed just a mild sprain at the time. I wasn't going to call it in but Sato convinced me it might be serious. I'm hoping it can be taped so I can walk with crutches."

JP shook his head. "Bad news, Captain. The ankle is broken. There's a hematoma, that is, a collection of blood over the fracture, and probably early infection. You need to be evacuated."

"Damn it, sir, I just got the company a month ago."

JP shrugged. "War is hell." Standing up, he asked, "You have someone in mind to take over the company?"

"We're short of officers. Besides being company commander I took over this platoon after its lieutenant was wounded. His replacement is due in next week, Sergeant Ellison can take over the platoon. He's been running it anyway." He grinned at Ellison who smiled back. Mossberg continued, "The weapons platoon commander, Bill Hanneford, is due for promotion to first lieutenant. He can act as company commander until my exec gets here from Skunk Patch."

"Sounds good to me," JP said. "I need to talk to my chopper pilot."

Mossberg motioned for his RTO to comply. After a minute or so the RTO handed JP a small speaker-mike. "Redbird, you enjoying yourself up there?"

"That's a Rog."

"You're needed down here right away. There are three who require urgent transport to the 96th. I hope you have a PZ picked out close to this CP."

"Roger. It's a sand bank by a stream 300 meters east of your position." A pause filled with static followed. "You realize I can carry only three pax?"

"You'll just have to come back for me, Redbird."

"Ah, sir. It will be dark in less than an hour, and there's a front out of Laos headed this way. It's due your posit about that time. Heavy rains and high winds are forecasted."

"You are full of good cheer, Redbird." JP could see no way out for him tonight. He wondered how he got himself into this situation in the first place. "Okay, Redbird. I'll stick it out here tonight. I wouldn't want to risk an expensive helicopter."

"What about me, sir?"

"Oh, yes. You too, Redbird. Now get that piece of junk on the stream bed."

"On the way, sir."

Chapter Thirty-Eight

Wednesday, June 17, 1970, 1950 hours
Alpha Company CP, 1st/5th Battalion, 9th Brigade AO

Spec Four Sato had rounded up four volunteers to carry Granowski using the ponchos as stretchers. Two husky six footers volunteered to carry Rifkin and Captain Mossberg piggyback. As the little caravan was forming up Mossberg told JP, "Colonel, I'm sorry you'll have to spend the night out here because of me."

"Don't sweat it, Captain. I was chasing bad guys in the jungle when you were in diapers," JP said with a cavalier air.

"Did you bring any gear with you?" Mossberg asked.

JP shook his head. "I didn't plan on spending the night."

"I'll leave my rucksack for you. It has raingear, a canteen of water, C-rations, and some other items you may find handy."

"Thanks. I was wondering how I'd make it through the night, especially if it rained. You better get word to Colonel Steglich you are being medevacked to Phong Sahn."

"I've already done that," Sergeant Ellison said. "I also told them you would spend the night with us and to pass that on to the 36th chief of staff."

"That should get their attention up at division. They'll probably go ballistic."

"Time to mount up, Captain," Sergeant Ellison said.

"Who's in charge?"

"Corporal Perez. The route is south-east about 300 meters to the small stream and waterfalls we crossed yesterday. The Loach will be on the stream bank somewhere in the vicinity."

"That sounds precise enough for government work," Mossberg said. He held out his hand. "Take care of the second platoon, Sergeant."

Ellison grasped the hand. "Will do, sir. It's been a pleasure."

"Back at you. Hope to see butter bars on you one of these days."

"Don't hold your breath, sir," Ellison said smiling. He called softly to a wiry short corporal in his late teens. "Okay, Perez, move them out."

The GIs standing by Granowski kneeled down and grabbed a handful of poncho. Lifting awkwardly at first, they moved behind the point man and Perez. Captain Mossberg and Rifkin climbed on the backs of their respective beasts of burden. JP fell in alongside Mossberg. "I'll walk to the PZ with you. I want to be around if Granowski has a seizure."

For twenty minutes the group maintained a steady pace, stopping twice for the GIs carrying Granowski to change sides, and those carrying Rifkin and Captain Mossberg to rest. The faint sounds of gurgling water reached them only to be masked by the increasing noise of a rapidly approaching Loach. As it passed overhead it was seen briefly through the thick canopy of vegetation seventy feet above the stream. JP wondered how Ranson would ever find a route to descend through that canopy. As if in answer the Loach's engine sounds diminished to a fast idle; it was down some fifty meters away, its idling jet engine an acoustic homing beacon.

Perez altered the route slightly. Minutes later the group broke out of the jungle and moved on to a narrow sandy bank. A dozen meters downstream the Loach rested on the bank, its rotor blades turning lazily. Above, a confluence of branches, leaves, and vines formed a vegetative roof except in one area, where nature had created an opening slightly larger than the diameter of the Loach's rotor arc. That Dan Ranson managed to guide his Loach down through that opening seemed a miracle. How he would fly the Loach back up through it with a full load was too frightening to contemplate.

When the group reached the Loach Granowski was strapped into the left rear seat and Captain Mossberg in the seat beside him. Over the engine noise JP shouted to Mossberg, "Keep a close watch on Granowski. If he has a seizure or becomes delirious he might undo his seat belt and fall out."

Mossberg nodded.

JP slapped him on the shoulder. "Good luck." He moved up to the pilot. "I don't know how you got this thing down through that stuff," he said, pointing up.

Ranson grinned. "Neither do I, sir."

"Do you have any idea how you're going to get out of here?"

"The reverse of how I got in."

"Humility is not one of your virtues, Mr. Ranson."

The young pilot became serious. "Sir, I really hate to leave you out here tonight."

"Don't risk coming back tonight. That's an order."

JP walked around the nose of the helicopter to Rifkin and made sure he was belted securely. When he started to leave Rifkin motioned vigorously. He looked as though he were about to cry. JP stuck his head through the open door. "What's the problem?" he shouted.

"My punji stick, sir. I forgot it," Rifkin said, pointing to where the GIs were standing.

JP trotted to the area and began searching. In a moment he found the four-foot length of bamboo. Picking it up, he jogged back just as Ranson lifted the Loach to a hover. JP thrust the punji stick through the door. Rifkin grabbed it, mouthed, "Thanks," and waved. Dan Ranson gave them both a tolerant glance, shook his head, and increased power.

JP moved to the jungle's edge to stand with the GIs and watch. The Loach backed up slowly about 100 meters and hovered over the stream as if an Olympic diver contemplating the most important maneuver of his life. For Warrant Officer Dan Ranson and his three passengers that was not far from the truth. The Loach's engine screamed in full power, its rotor blades became a mad blur in the fading light of dusk. Then the Loach moved forward, gathering speed at a phenomenal rate. Suddenly it blasted up through the opening, its blades shattering branches with ear-splitting cracks resembling rifle shots. A shower of branches and leaves floated to the ground.

"I never saw anything like that," one of the GIs said in wonderment.

"You and me both," JP agreed.

As Perez formed the men up for the trek back to the Alpha CP, the winds picked up. Light from the setting sun became obliterated by a pervading overcast. The rolling sounds of thunder some distance away resembled impacting artillery. In an effort to beat the rain Corporal Perez decided to jog the group back to the CP. By the time they had gone 100 meters JP was sweating like a pig, his chest heaving with air hunger. Twice he almost called out to Perez to slow down, but pride took control each time and he swore he would drop first. It was almost dark when they approached the CP perimeter and Perez slowed the group to a walk. JP moved up abreast of him.

"Corporal, are you trying to kill me?"

A sly grin spread over Perez.

"No, sir," he said, his Puerto Rican accent unmistakable. "Just trying to get you in shape for a night in the jungle."

★

Lieutenant Colonel JP Franklin, M.D., Medical Corps, USA, renowned head and neck surgeon, former chief of head and neck surgery, Walter Reed, Hospital, associate professor at two medical schools, member, National Academy of Science, sat shivering on a rotten wet log, huddled under Captain Mossberg's poncho, his head and face almost hidden by the poncho's hood. Winds gusting to forty knots blasted sheets of rain through the jungle. Each time lightning flashed he cringed in anticipation of the giant thunder claps that would follow. Rainwater leaked past the tightened poncho collar soaking his jacket and T-shirt. Water squished in his boots when he curled his toes. His trouser legs were soaked to the knees. Once, during nearly three hours of steady rain, he dropped off to sleep only to be abruptly awakened when he fell off the log into a puddle. Now a distended bladder added to his misery. Sooner than later he would be forced to get up and relieve himself. Hunger was eating away at his gut. Misery was reaching a new height, but at least the mosquitoes were gone.

What right did he have to complain? Most of the men of the second platoon were out in the jungle somewhere; teenagers for the most part, lying in ambush along suspected trails. How much greater must be their misery than his. They were giving this war the best of their youth, and it was apparent the best would not be good enough. They were fighting a war doomed to be lost because it was not being fought to win. Ann Carter had been right. For the first time in his life JP began to doubt his country's motives. Things would never be the same.

Eventually JP's mind slipped into a semi-dreamlike state. He was awake, but he was also asleep. He began to visualize Kathy and the kids, the wards at Walter Reed filled with wounded. God, he was homesick.

Almost as suddenly as the rain had started it stopped. The overcast dissipated and a half moon beamed its yellow light at the jungle. Within minutes the mosquitoes were out in hordes. Having been denied their blood meals for over three hours, they struck with vengeance. JP grabbed Mossberg's rucksack, fished frantically through it and withdrew a small plastic bottle and flashlight. Shielding the flashlight lens, he turned it on, confirmed that the bottle was insect repellent, and applied the oily substance liberally to his face, neck, hands, and legs. The mosquitoes were not at all impressed.

Reaching again into Mossberg's rucksack, he removed a box of C-rations. Tearing open the box he withdrew a can and read the label: CHOPPED HAM AND EGGS. Using the little P-38 can opener on his dog tag chain, he cut around the top and removed it. Setting the can aside, he cut the top off the second can and emptied out powdered chocolate, powdered coffee, crackers, heat tabs, toilet paper, and matches. He was examining the items when Sergeant Ellison appeared.

"Need help, Colonel?"

"A quick refresher course, Sarge; it's been a while."

Ellison took the empty second can and demonstrated how to cut slits in its side. Placing a heat tab on the ground, he lit it, then set the slotted can over it. "Okay, sir, there's your stove." He watched critically as JP grasped the can of ham and eggs by the sides and set it on the stove. "Ah, sir, next time you open a can of C-rats don't remove the cover. Just bend it back and use it for a handle."

"Right. To be truthful, Sergeant Ellison, I'm hoping there won't be a next time."

Ellison chuckled.

Using a plastic spoon, JP stirred the cold greasy chopped ham and eggs. He looked up at Ellison. "Anything exciting going on?"

"Yes, sir. A CIDG force from Ang Le ambushed a squad of VC about five klicks east of here. They killed four, picked up three AKs and an RPG. The rain washed out blood trails. They sent word that the surviving VC may be headed this way."

"I'm sorry I asked," JP said. "You'll have to enlighten me. I've been in Vietnam only a few days. What's a CIDG?"

"Civilian Irregular Defense Force. They are minority groups like the Montagnards and Hmong, trained and commanded by special forces A teams. The A team usually consists of two officers and twelve NCOs, all cross-trained. The team at An Ke lost its officers three days ago; one was KIA, the other was WIA and evacuated. It's now commanded by an old special forces buddy, Karl Dahlgren. He just arrived in country last week."

"Now there's a coincidence," JP said, "we had seats together on the plane from Travis. How is it you're not with special forces this tour?"

"Colonel Steglich convinced me I should go to OCS after this tour. He said I needed some regular troop duty to enhance my military future. That had a certain logic, so here I am, now a platoon commander without ever having gone to OCS."

JP pulled the wet poncho off over his head and draped it over a nearby branch to drain and dry. He shivered when a gust of wind hit his wet fatigues.

"I see you're Airborne, sir."

JP glanced down at the subdued jump wings on his fatigue jacket. "I went through Benning before coming out here. I've made only five jumps," he reluctantly admitted.

"That's how we all started, Colonel."

"How many jumps do you have?"

"A little over 700. I was an instructor in the skydiving club at Bragg. Out here I jump with the ARVN rangers every month to keep up my jump pay. Besides, I like to jump. If you're interested I have some buddies who are advisors with the ARVNs.

They can arrange for you to join them when they jump."

JP hesitated. He wasn't sure how General Webster would react to the idea of his division surgeon jumping out of airplanes with a bunch of ARVN rangers. Perhaps it would be prudent not to mention it until after he had jumped. "Have one of your buddies give me a call. Maybe we can work something out."

"Airborne, sir."

"All the way.

Reaching down to his "stove", JP tried to stabilize the can of C-rations by grasping its sides while he stirred the contents. Immediately he pulled back his hand. "Damn it," he muttered, waving burnt fingers in the damp air.

"Hot, sir?" Ellison asked, tongue-in-cheek.

"You might say that."

Taking out several folded tissues from his pocket, JP wrapped them around the can and gingerly tasted a spoonful of ham and eggs. "Not bad," he said, digging out a second spoonful. He devoured half the can before asking Ellison, "What's your impression of this war after two tours?"

"It sucks… sir."

JP was surprised at the bitterness in Ellison's voice.

Ellison continued without prompting. "We kill dinks by the thousands in South Vietnam, a few more in Laos and Cambodia. More dinks come down the Ho Chi Minh trail from the north to replace those we killed. In the meantime we lose good men to enemy contact, mines, booby traps, and, hell, even to punji sticks."

Again JP was still hearing things he did not want to hear. There seemed to be no end to it, and the worrisome aspect was that it was all consistent.

"Shit, sir, we wait until supplies sent by our British, French and other allies are offloaded at Haiphong, carried south down the Ho Chi Minh trail and then along trails east to the coast. And like tonight, we sit on those trails east hoping to bag a few dinks. It's a lousy way to fight a war and no way to win a war. I'm disgusted that our senior officers support such a worthless self-defeating policy."

JP said nothing. What was there to say?

★

It wasn't long before the rains returned, this time with even more viciousness than before. Cocooned in Captain Mossberg's poncho, JP prayed for a quick dawn. Gradually, he drifted into a troubled sleep. It seemed he had just fallen asleep when someone was shaking him. A voice kept repeating, "Sir, Colonel Franklin, sir."

Disoriented, JP stared wildly at the darkness around him.

"It's Specialist Sato, sir, the medic."

JP straightened to a sitting position. "Sato, you just broke up a great dream."

"Sorry, sir. Sergeant Ellison asked if you would come over to his position."

JP struggled to his feet. Water, accumulated in his lap, spilled onto his trouser legs and boots. Stifling choice profanity, he pulled the poncho hood further down over his head. "All set."

Sato led about ten meters to a spot where Ellison huddled with his RTO under a shelter rigged from a poncho. JP hunkered down at the entrance, doing his best to ignore the rain and his discomfort. "What's up, Sarge?"

Ellison waved a mike-speaker from a PRC 25 pack radio. "Sir, I'm in contact with Karl Dahlgren, the A team leader at Ang Le. He's asking for help with a medical problem in his compound. He called here to talk to Sato because his own medic is home on emergency leave. I told him you were here."

JP stuck his head under the poncho roof. At least it was protected from the rain. "What's the problem?"

"The six-year-old daughter of one of the Nung strikers has been throwing up since last night."

"That include fluids?'

"Yes, sir, everything. Karl asked if you could come over and take a look at her."

Tonight? In this weather? He must be kidding. I'm a forty-three-year-old man who hadn't moved around in a jungle at night in the rain since World War II. Surely I'll get lost, captured, wounded, or killed.

But medicine was a calling that transcended personal considerations. It allowed no margin for fears of personal safety, ethnicity, politics, nor anything else. A doctor was a doctor; he had taken an oath and was bound by that oath. Everything else was secondary. It was as binding as the oath taken by the clergy.

JP sighed. "How far to this camp, Ellison?"

"Five klicks, a little over two miles."

"Have you and Dahlgren figured out a way to get me over there in one piece?"

Ellison's smile was barely perceptible in the shadowy reflected beam from his flashlight. "Yes, sir. Washington will lead. He's the best we have for navigating the jungle at night. Sato will back him up. He's familiar with the camp and its approaches. He's been going over there to take sick call and do Medcaps whenever their medic has been gone. Caldoni, Winters, and Perez will bring up the rear. You'll have five of my best men protecting your aaa... I mean protecting you, sir."

JP was embarrassed. Taking five men from the platoon CP defense would seriously weaken it. "I was only kidding, Sergeant. I've been in the jungle before." He failed to mention it was twenty-seven years ago and he was in his teens. "Just give me one man who knows where he's going. I'll get by."

Ellison was firm. "No, sir. If something happens to you the paperwork for me will be endless."

JP grinned. "Ellison, you're going to make one hell of a second lieutenant. By the way, what's a Nung?"

"They're a tough, smart people of Chinese and Vietnamese extraction. They're tenacious in a fight and fiercely loyal to the special forces. The special forces guys love them and the feeling is mutual."

"You'd better notify battalion where I'm headed and ask they pass it up the line to the division chief of staff."

Ellison leaned towards JP and whispered, "Colonel, you going to get into trouble over this?"

334

"Probably. I'm not even supposed to be out here at all. Division is probably steaming over my just spending the night in the bush." He chuckled. "Wait until they learn their division surgeon is cruising around in VC-infested jungle at night." He shrugged. "What can they do to me, send me to Vietnam?"

"Sir, I admire your attitude."

"Airborne."

"All the way, Colonel."

JP turned to the waiting medic. "Let's go, Sato. If you and Washington get me captured or killed my wife will never forgive you. Neither will I."

★

For over two hours JP followed Sato and Washington at a pace so fast it could best be described as jogging. Twice they crossed streams swollen by the heavy rains, afterwards checking themselves and each other for leeches before continuing. JP stumbled intermittently in the near black jungle. He was disgusted with himself for not putting on a better show of jungle proficiency for the teenage soldiers escorting him. Once, half asleep and exhausted, he walked into a tree. Thinking it was Sato, he apologized, then kept on walking.

With the approaching dawn the rain eased, then ceased. Slivers of light began to infiltrate through the dense jungle canopy above. It was then that JP realized with a start that the size of his small group had doubled. Five armed Nungs had joined up with them. When? He had no idea. A Nung, walking beside him and noting his surprise, grinned sheepishly.

The Nungs led from the jungle, crossed an open field, then climbed a prominent hill to a fortified camp of several acres built in the form of a star. Rolls of concertina wire delineated the camp's perimeter. Approaching an opening through the wire JP spotted half a dozen claymore mines, all seemingly pointed at him. He hoped the rumor was false that claymore mines could be detonated by static electricity, as in a thunderstorm.

The odor of wood smoke from multiple cook fires permeated the early morning damp cool air. JP's stomach began to rumble, reminding him of his own hunger. A soldier wearing staff sergeant's stripes came towards him. JP recognized him immediately. They shook hands.

"Well, Karl, Vietnam isn't so big after all."

"It sure looks that way, Colonel. I never thought I'd see you again, much less out here and so soon."

"Us old marines get around. Congratulations on the fourth stripe."

"Thanks, sir."

"Shall we have a look at the young lady?"

"Yes, sir, this way."

Dahlgren led past sandbagged bunkers, one and two man fighting positions, and dug-in M–60 machine guns.

"The VC ever attack this camp, Karl?"

"Not since last week. We hit them with snakes and Spectre. The Cong really got bloodied, but that's no assurance they won't attack today. We're a thorn in their side."

"You're full of good cheer, Dahlgren. It makes visitors feel very comfortable."

JP followed Dahlgren down a row of huts. Constructed of mud and grass, with thatched roofs, each had one or two square openings in the front wall that served as windows and a larger opening that was the door. Dahlgren entered a hut without knocking. The single room interior was semi-dark. Minimal light from an overcast dawn came through the open door and windows. Smoke from a wood fire in a pit dug in the ground hung heavy in the room. It was difficult to keep from coughing.

A diminutive middle-aged dark oriental woman, a gaily colored skirt around her waist, met them. She smiled shyly and led to a bamboo-framed bed built close to the ground. A small girl lay on the slats, her eyes closed. Suddenly she sat up, leaned forward and began retching. The woman grabbed a bowl from the ground by the bed and held it under the girl's mouth. Saliva and gastric juices dribbled down from her mouth. The woman wiped the girl's mouth with a soiled cloth, then gently eased her back down on the bed.

JP knelt beside the bed. Talking soothingly even though he knew the child couldn't understand, he felt her forehead. The skin was dry and hot. He gently pressed on her eyelids. The globes felt shrunken and soft. He turned to Sato who was watching intently. "She's dehydrated from vomiting and fever. You wouldn't have a flashlight by any chance?"

Without a word Sato took an otoscope and tongue blade from his pack.

"Just like Walter Wonderful," JP said, hiding his surprise. After checking the otoscope's light he examined the child's ears, nose, throat. Passing the otoscope back to Sato, he shook his head. "Nothing significant except mild redness of the throat and lymphoid hyperplasia."

Gently he felt the girl's neck. Only scattered small non-tender lymph nodes in the posterior triangles were palpable. Reaching behind the girl's head he flexed the head as he watched her thin legs. He told Sato, "If she had meningeal irritation, she not only would have had a stiff neck, she would have involuntarily flexed her hips and knees. That's Brudzinski's sign. Is there a stethoscope in that rucksack of yours?"

Sato immediately pulled out a stethoscope. Its rubber tubing was brittle and cracked and the metal parts rusty. JP listened over both lungs, then over the heart. He shook his head. "Nothing but a fast heart, about 120. Now for the belly."

As soon as JP laid his hand on the girl's abdomen she cried out and tried to move away. He told Sergeant Dahlgren to ask the mother about the girl's bowel movements. After what seemed a lengthy conversation he reported, "She thinks it's been a couple of days."

JP stood up. "Well, my best guess is that she has an acute belly, probably appendicitis. She needs to have some lab studies and get into the hands of a real doctor." He turned to Sergeant Dahlgren. "Call for a Dust-off and classify it urgent. If you're given a hard time you can say that is the classification given by Cut Throat Six. If that doesn't shake them up let me talk to them. I will definitely shake them up."

"Yes, sir."

336

While Dahlgren was gone JP asked Sato, "Any medical supplies here, like IV fluids and antibiotics?"

"Yes, sir. Ringer's lactate in liter bottles and IM penicillin."

"She needs fluid replacement. Get a liter of Ringer's lactate, pour out all but 250 ccs and start an IV."

Sato looked uncertain. JP explained, "She's a small kid, about twenty kilos. Inadvertent fluid overload is a risk in kids. It can put them in congestive failure or produce cerebral edema, either of which could be fatal. Pouring out all but 250 ccs lessens that risk."

"What about antibiotics, Colonel? I read in a medical journal that using antibiotics is an alternate way to treat acute appendicitis."

This kid is sharp, JP thought. "Good idea. Give her a couple of million units of penicillin IM. Have the mother sponge her off with some cloths soaked in cool water. That'll help bring down her temp." He headed for the door. Over his shoulder he said, "I'm going to check out this place and see if I can scrounge a cup of coffee. If you have any trouble starting the IV give me a call."

As JP stepped out of the hut Sergeant Dahlgren returned. "Dust-off will be here in thirty-five."

"Great. Is there a cup of coffee around here?"

"Yes, sir. I can fix you a cup. Ah, Colonel, while you're waiting do you suppose you could take a look at a three of my Nungs. One has been coughing up blood, one has a huge lump in his groin, and the third has a large ulcer on the tongue and a big knot in his neck."

"You're determined to get your money's worth out of me today, Sergeant Dahlgren."

"Yes, sir. It's not every day the bacci 6 visits this place. In fact, I can't think of it ever happening on any of my tours."

"Well, believe me, I don't plan on setting a precedent."

Chapter Thirty-Nine

Thursday, June 18, 1970, 0740 hours
Special Forces Camp, Ang Le, 9th Brigade AO, RVN

Lieutenant Colonel JP Franklin stood beside the helipad at the special forces camp searching east into an overcast sky. The field jacket he had found in Captain Mossberg's rucksack, although several sizes too large, provided some warmth in the damp, chilly morning air. Hearing someone behind him, he turned to see Sergeant Dahlgren approaching with a canteen cup of hot coffee.

"I knew you would get into hot water coming out here, sir," Dahlgren said, "but I didn't think you would get busted down to captain."

JP looked down at his shoulder. "I'd better take off the railroad tracks before I go back."

Dahlgren extended the canteen cup to JP, handle first. "It's very hot, sir."

"It's about time you showed up with my coffee." JP slurped from the edge of the cup and let out a sigh of pleasure. "Your buddy Ellison is scheduled for OCS after he finishes his tour."

"I know, sir. He'll make a good officer."

"That's not where I was trying to lead with that remark, Karl."

"Sir, I'm happy to stay as a sergeant, maybe make master sergeant by the time I retire. Besides, I don't have any college. I was lucky to finish high school. Ellison has three years of college."

"You would be a shoo-in for an ROTC scholarship, Karl. It pays tuition, books, plus subsistence."

"I don't think so, Colonel. The idea of being in the same classroom with long-haired, pot-smoking, anti-war hippies leaves me leaves me cold. I'd probably get thrown out of school for decking one."

"Dahlgren, you are a bigot. You must learn to be more tolerant."

"Right, sir."

"If you change your mind about the ROTC scholarship let me know. I'd be happy to write some lies about you in the form of a letter of recommendation."

Sergeant Dahlgren looked at JP for a moment. "Thanks, Colonel. I'll keep that in mind. What do you think about my three Nungs?"

"Well, the one coughing blood has tuberculosis or lung cancer. He should go to the province hospital for chest X-rays. If it's TB it should be treated. If it's cancer school is out. The one with a lump in his groin has an inguinal hernia. It's easily reducible now, but there's always a risk the bowel can become strangulated and necrose, that is, die. It should be repaired while he is asymptomatic. If the surgeons at the province hospital won't do it get word to me. I'll see about having the surgery done at the 96th and arrange for a chopper to pick him up. The Nung with the big ulcer on his tongue has an advanced cancer that extends to the floor of mouth, jaw, and neck. He needs a big operation, one that removes most of his tongue, floor of mouth, part of the jaw, plus a neck dissection."

"He would never go for that, Colonel."

"That doesn't leave much. The only working X-ray therapy machine in South Vietnam is in Saigon. Even if we could get him down there the results would be minimally palliative."

"I'll talk to him about the surgery, sir, but I doubt it will do much good. The Nungs are a stoic people and family oriented. If they're dying they want to be with their families. Ah, sir, there is another problem."

"Damn, how I hate that word," JP said, then sipped from his canteen cup.

"The little girl with appendicitis… her parents refuse to let her be medevac'd unless they can go with her."

"That's okay with me."

"They want to know where they'll stay while she's in the hospital and about their meals."

"There are people at the 96th who take care of such mundane details, Karl. Tell the girl's parents not to worry."

The drone of a distant helicopter drifted into hearing. Again JP scanned the overcast. Moments later he spotted the Huey flying close to the ground. A Nung standing near the helipad threw out a sputtering smoke grenade. It rolled close to the helipad and began to spew out clouds of yellow smoke.

"What do you know," JP quipped, "my color."

"You can't prove it by me, sir," Dahlgren said.

JP turned to the young sergeant. "Thanks, Karl. I needed that."

★

Thursday, June 18, 1970, 0840 hours
Emergency Room, 96th Evacuation Hospital, Phong Sahn

Lieutenant Colonel JP Franklin, carrying the little Nung girl in his arms, walked into the emergency room trailed by the girl's mother and father. The Dust-off medic walked alongside while holding up the bottle of Ringer's lactate. A pretty major with Nurse Corps insignia rushed up to them. "Put her over there," she ordered, indicating a stretcher lying across two sawhorses. She took the IV bottle from the medic and hung it on a pole by the stretcher.

JP scanned the emergency room; it was devoid of doctors. "Where are the belly surgeons?" he demanded. "I radioed ahead that we were bringing in a kid with a probable hot appendix who needed an immediate laparotomy."

"They're tied up in the OR. It will be at least an hour before one of them can drop out."

"By that time this kid's appendix will have ruptured," JP fumed. "I'm going to the

OR to talk to them. Meanwhile get stat chest and belly X-rays, CBC, electrolytes, and a urinalysis. Catherize her for the urine specimen." He indicated the IV bottle. "That's her second 250 of Ringer's since seven this morning. Add some aqueous penicillin and run it TKO until someone sees her who knows what he's doing. Get a Nung interpreter over here and have anesthesia pre-op her."

The major had never seen JP before. His rank and Medical Corps insignia were covered by Captain Mossberg's field jacket from which the captain's bars had been removed. The odor of wood smoke and jungle dampness emanating from his cruddy fatigues was hard to ignore. His grimy unshaven face and unkempt hair gave him a fierce, wild look. Anger flared in the major's eyes.

"Just who do you think you are, bringing a Vietnamese kid in here and giving me orders."

Before JP could snap back a caustic response Lieutenant Colonel Kristy Goulden, Nurse Corps, US Army, walked into the ER and quickly appraised the developing confrontation. "He's okay, Mary Beth," she told the major. "This is Colonel Franklin, the new 36th Division surgeon. He's also our head and neck consultant."

"Oh," the major said, taken aback. Her face reddened.

Kristy continued. "Sometimes he comes on like a tornado. He can be surly, demanding, obnoxious and downright insolent... and those are his good qualities."

By now the major was grinning. "You seem to know him well, Kristy."

"Not really. We knew each other during the Korean War. I made the mistake once of saving his life." She turned to JP. "Are you sure this kid has acute appendicitis?"

"I'm not sure of anything except that she has some sort of inflammatory process going on in her belly, most likely a hot appendix. She needs a laparotomy."

"Okay. This is Mary Beth Densmore and don't expect her to apologize. You have no rank or insignia visible and you look like hell. She will get you a cup of coffee while I go to the OR and try to shake loose a belly surgeon."

"Thanks, Kristy," JP said.

Moments later the major returned with a mug of steaming coffee. "I forgot to ask if you wanted cream and sugar."

"Black is fine," JP said, accepting the cup. "Mary Beth, you should be aware that Kristy has a pathological tendency to exaggerate."

"Really, Colonel? Strange, I never noticed that before, and we're room-mates." Major Densmore indicated a desk. "Would you write orders for what you want done pre-op? Blank order and progress note sheets are in the drawers."

JP sat down at a desk, took another sip of coffee and set the coffee mug down. In the top drawer he found half a dozen GI pens. The appropriate forms were in a side drawer. *Hell*, he thought, *I don't know the kid's name*. He wrote: "Female Nung, age six," then the pre-op orders and finally a short admission note. By the time he had finished Kristy returned.

"What's the word?" JP said, getting to his feet.

"At least an hour. They just finished a splenectomy and have a lacerated liver and bowel resection to go..."

"Damn it Kristy, this kid can't wait that long."

340

"JP, would you let me finish."

"So finish."

"Tom Denhart, who is scrubbed in with Colonel Leicester, the chief of surgery, finished a fellowship in pediatric surgery before he came to Vietnam."

"Now that assignment makes a lot of sense."

"Just be quiet and listen. Tom will drop out and do the kid if you will take his place and assist Colonel Leicester."

JP groaned. After the night in the jungle what he needed desperately was a shave, hot shower, clean fatigues and hot food. The last thing he needed was two to three hours of surgery. Besides, he had to catch up on almost two days worth of paperwork at the division surgeon's office and the medical battalion. He shrugged. *The hell with it all.*

"Okay, I'll do it."

"Finish your coffee first. You look beat. Anesthesia will be down in a few minutes to pre-op the kid. I'll see about getting a Nung interpreter, finding the parents a place to stay, and get them a pass to the mess hall."

"Kristy, you are a real Florence Nightingale."

"Yeah, right," she said, looking at him quizzically. "What were you doing out at a special forces camp?"

JP smiled. "It was the culmination of a series of unanticipated events, all of which conspired against me."

"The last time I heard something like that you had taken on two regiments of Communist Chinese and almost gotten yourself and your platoon wiped out."

"I'm a slow learner," he said, then briefly reviewed the events of the past eighteen hours.

As Kristy listened her face clouded. "I don't believe this."

"You don't believe what?"

"I don't believe anyone with your rank and background would be so stupid as to traipse through the jungle at night with a bunch of teenage killers."

"They were not killers," he snapped.

"What do you think they do out there? You could have been killed, wounded or worse, you could have been captured."

"Back off, damn it. I'm in no mood for this, I'm probably going to catch hell from the general as it is. I don't need you to prepare me for the ordeal."

"Listen, you dumb jarhead. My husband is out there somewhere. More than likely he's chained to a tree like some wild animal. He was doing his job when he was shot down. What you did last night was not your job. JP, you haven't been out here a week and you have already put your life on the line twice that I know of. What is it with you?"

JP set his mug on the nurse's desk and looked into Kristy's green eyes. In his best John Wayne drawl he said, "It's that marine thing, ma'am. A man's gotta do what a man's gotta do." He turned, walked out of the ER, down the hall and entered the OR suite.

Minutes later, scrubbed and in greens, his mask tied over his cap, he pushed through the door into the operating room. "Hi," he said, "I'm Colonel Franklin, ready to assist." His voice startled everyone in the room. They stopped what they were doing and turned to stare at him. One of the surgeons stepped away from the table, pulling off his gown and gloves. "I'm Tom Denhart," he said. "What's the story on the girl?"

While JP briefed him the scrub nurse shook out a gown and held it for him to slip into. The circulator tied the straps behind him. He shoved his hands into gloves held by the scrub nurse, then bellied up to the operating table. The surgeon opposite him stared over the rims of thick glasses for a moment. "Welcome aboard. I'm Tony Leicester, chief of surgery. Grab a Dever and sucker. We'll go to work."

★

Thursday, June 18, 1970, 1310 hours
96th Evacuation Hospital, Phong Sahn

JP finished putting in the last suture closing the belly; Colonel Leicester cut off the excess length with suture scissors. Over the past two hours they had shared the surgery, with Leicester doing the complex parts and talking JP through the easy parts. "Never know when we might have to call on you to do some belly surgery," he explained. For his part JP, tired or not, was never happier than when he was cutting and sewing.

During the operation he and Colonel Leicester reviewed each other's backgrounds, education, families, friends, and acquaintances, ending on a first name basis. As Leicester cut the last suture he critically regarded the colostomy and closed belly.

"Not bad for a head and neck man."

"It certainly destroys the mystique you belly surgeons created about your specialty," JP said as he pulled off his gown and stripped off his gloves. "I'm out of here," he said, moving to the door.

"Thanks for your help," Colonel Leicester said. "Come back any time. We can always use an extra pair of hands."

Before leaving the operating suite JP checked each of the other five operating rooms. Three were unoccupied. There was no sign of the Nung girl in the other two. Stopping at the OR supervisor's desk he asked the plump nurse on duty, "Have they done the little girl yet?"

The nurse stood up. "Yes, sir. It was a hot appendix ready to rupture. She was taken to recovery fifteen minutes ago." Noting JP's haggard look, she asked, "Can I get you a cup of coffee and a couple of aspirin?"

"I think I'd prefer some chow. When does the mess hall close?"

The nurse glanced at her watch. "It stops serving at 1330 hours. Are you Colonel Franklin?"

"Right."

"There's a message from the 36th chief of staff." She shuffled among the papers on her desk. "Here it is. General Webster wants you to report to him in his office as soon as you finish surgery."

JP groaned. "I'll take that coffee and aspirin."

342

Thursday, June 18, 1970, 1415 hours
36th Infantry Division Headquarters, Phong Sahn

Lieutenant Colonel JP Franklin, M.D., Medical Corps, US Army, marched smartly into General Webster's office, saluted, and stood at attention.

"At ease, Doctor. We need to talk," the general said. "You know Colonel Witherington, my chief of staff."

"Yes, sir."

"Doctor, you are the first division surgeon I know of who spent the night with an infantry platoon in the boonies and then humped five kilometers at night to an A team camp."

"Yes, sir."

"Was it worth the risk?

"I'm not sure I follow the general's question?"

"Let me put it this way. Do you have any idea the windfall your capture or death would have been for Communist propaganda, especially coming after the death of our last division surgeon… and he hardly set foot off the base."

"General, under the circumstances I didn't have much choice."

"There are some who would differ with you, Doctor, myself included."

"Yes, sir."

"I admit I gave you carte blanche to go wherever you considered necessary in our AO. That appears to have been a lapse of judgment on my part."

JP remained quiet. Yes sir or no sir would have been a lose–lose response.

"I had no idea you would put yourself repeatedly in harm's way, and so soon."

"Sir. I was well protected last night and this morning."

General Webster smiled. "You may have a point there."

"How do you mean, sir?"

"Those young men, the teenagers who took you to the special forces camp… they have collectively two Sliver Stars, nine Bronze Stars with Vs, and six Purple Hearts. Corporal Perez; the young man who led the group, has one of the Silver Stars. He is only nineteen years old, but in his short life he's killed twelve Viet Cong, captured three, and directed an air strike on an NVA battalion headquarters that killed thirty-eight. He is about to receive his second Silver Star and be promoted to sergeant." The general smiled. "In many ways he reminds me of myself."

JP was shocked. Perez and the other GIs seemed like wholesome innocent boys not yet men. Then he remembered; once he too had been like them.

The general continued, "Since I took command of this division one medical officer was shot down and captured. Another was shot down and died later of his injuries. They were on routine missions, unlike the two soirees in which you engaged."

"Sir, may I speak freely?"

"Please do. That's the only way I can keep a handle on what goes on in my division."

"This division has 24,000 men scattered over 10,000 square miles. There is no way I

343

can function effectively as division surgeon if I'm motivated by the desire to avoid risk. I'm well aware of what awaits me should I get captured. Your G–2 made that abundantly clear when he briefed me. On the other hand I can't allow fear to take precedence over what I consider my responsibilities as division surgeon."

General Webster remained silent for several moments while he studied a paper on his desk, then he looked up. "I respect your sense of duty, Doctor. For that and other reasons not yet apparent to you I won't impose any restrictions on your activities. I do ask that you use caution in your travels, stay away from hot LZs, and keep the chief of staff informed of your itinerary when you leave Phong Sahn."

"Yes, sir."

"That will be all, Doctor," General Webster said softly. "I expect to see you at cocktail hour, and you will be sitting at the head table for the evening meal."

"General, while you are in a relatively good humor I wonder if I might make a request?"

"I think I'd better not agree to anything where you are concerned until I hear the entire proposal."

"The Dust-off detachment has experienced inordinate delays in processing awards through their multiple layers of headquarters. Considering the tremendous courage and airmanship those crews demonstrate daily they deserve better."

"What would you recommend?"

"That the processing of awards, particularly impact awards, be done through division rather than through the Dust-off chain of command."

"That sounds reasonable. What do you think, John?"

"No reason why it can't be done, General."

"Is there anything else while you have me in a good humor, Doctor?"

"Yes, sir. If and when the delayed decorations finally come through, could you be imposed upon to award them?"

"I would be proud to."

"Thank you, sir." JP came to attention, saluted, did an about-face, and marched out smartly.

After the door was closed General Webster turned to his chief of staff. "John, why do I get the feeling I've been had?"

"Well, general, that's what you get when you get an ex-marine for a division surgeon."

Chapter Forty

Friday, June 19, 1970, 0740 hours
36th Infantry Division Briefing Amphitheater, Phong Sahn, Republic of Vietnam

The daily 0700 hours briefing seemed to drag on and on. Throughout the nearly filled small amphitheater heads intermittently drooped, then snapped upright. The generals and full colonels in their leather swivel chairs down on the front row were showing signs of restlessness. In the last row, where it was possible to sleep without fear of discovery, Lieutenant Colonel JP Franklin, Medical Corps, USA, fought valiantly to stay awake. It was during the weather officer's discourse on isobars, temperatures, and winds aloft that he lost the battle. He awakened as the G–1 was finishing up his discussion of troop strength, troop losses, anticipated losses, anticipated gains, and a myriad of other less than exciting data.

JP's interest was kindled by the G–2 who reported that two new NVA battalions had infiltrated into the 9th Brigade AO from the Ho Chi Minh trail. His interpretations and predictions of another Tet offensive seemed a bit esoteric, but then, that was the traditional name of the intelligence game.

Next came the G–3, a tall, academic-appearing lieutenant colonel named Bruce Collier, an old friend and former neighbor of JP's when both were captains stationed at the US Military Academy. Collier pulled a huge map of Military Region I to the center of the platform, grabbed an eight-foot long wooden pointer and began. "This briefing covers the time period 0600 hours 18 June to 0559 hours 19 June. In the 174th Brigade area the 4th/59th on Firebase Daisy Mae, sixteen kilometers north-west of Nghia Lam," the pointer tapped the base location on the map, "was hit with a fifty-minute mortar attack beginning at 0140 hours this morning. During the attack sappers assaulted the perimeter with grenades, satchel charges and RPGs. Headquarters and Charlie Companies responded with claymore mines, automatic weapons, mortar, and M–79 grenades. Flare and gunships were called in. They were supplemented by Sandys using napalm and CBUs. The enemy withdrew at 0300 hours. Two US soldiers were killed and seven seriously wounded. Four of the wounded were evacuated by Dust-offs to the 96th Evac and three to the 19th Surg. Seven others were slightly wounded; they were treated on Daisy Mae by the battalion surgeon and returned to duty. A sweep of the area is currently under way. So far only body parts, bits of clothing, and blood-soaked ground have been identified."

The pointer moved south as Collier continued. His voice had a mid-western drawl. JP thought he sounded like Jimmy Stewart, the movie actor. "In the 178th Brigade AO at 1500 hours, F Troop, 8th Cav, working the hills twenty-five kilometers west of Phong Sahn, discovered a hooch with five rooms. The rooms contained bloody mats, medical dressings and other supplies including 800 pounds of rice." He tapped the map with the pointer. "The hooch appeared to have been used as an NVA medical aid station and hospital. The rice was confiscated; the hooch and other supplies were destroyed. The Cav is currently sweeping the area with help from the scouts."

The pointer tapped another area. "Delta Company, 3rd/41st, while maneuvering in the mountains twenty-eight kilometers north-west of Phong Sahn, discovered five fresh graves with male bodies. They were apparently killed by artillery fired in the area the previous day."

The pointer moved south to the 9th Brigade AO. "Bravo and Charlie Companies, 2nd/37th, began an early morning search and clear operations in the jungle of the Bai Chanh Valley thirty-eight kilometers west of Quang Dien. Bravo was to clear the high ground; Charlie the low ground. As Bravo moved across a grassy field the point platoon received intense rifle and machine gun fire. Artillery and helicopter gunships were called in. At times the enemy was so close individual combat took place. The enemy finally withdrew at about 1100 hours leaving fifty-three dead. The dead were identified as members of the 27th NVA Sapper Battalion. US loses were three killed and eleven wounded. All wounded were evacuated to the 96th Evac."

JP wondered if fifty-three enemy KIA versus three US KIA was a fair exchange. The parents and wives of the three KIA wouldn't think so.

The remainder of the briefing passed as JP drifted in and out of sleep. The G–4 utilized charts to show gasoline, diesel, and jet fuel consumed over the twenty-four hours and the amount remaining. Just as exciting was the number of 105 mm, 155 mm, and eight-inch shells fired in the past twenty-four hours. JP perked up when he heard that a single Duster had fired 230 rounds of 40 mm ammunition. He recalled from his own experience as a Duster platoon commander in Korea the basic load of a Duster was 240 rounds HE and sixty rounds AP.

The G–5 reported that a civilian Vietnamese truck had skidded on a turn and collided with a parked US Army two-and-a-half-ton truck in the village outside the Phong Sahn base. The army truck was soon surrounded by angry Vietnamese civilians threatening the GI driver. An ARVN soldier pulled the pin of a hand grenade and wedged the grenade beneath the rear wheel of the truck. If the driver had driven off the grenade would have exploded under the fuel tank. Only after the Vietnamese truck driver had been paid off in piasters by a US Army civic affairs officer was the army truck allowed to go. *So much for our allies*, thought JP. *It made one wonder if the United States was supporting the wrong side.*

Mercifully, the briefing finally ended. JP headed down the street to the division surgeon's office, about 300 feet from the briefing amphitheater. Entering, he was greeted by a chorus of chattering typewriters, then silence, a chorus of "Good morning, sir" followed by the resumption of typewriter chatter. The greeting was in contrast to the military protocol imposed by his predecessor, who had insisted on a wall-shattering "Tenshun", with everyone jumping to his feet and hitting a brace each time he walked in.

Tom Moffet, the preventative medicine officer, came out from behind his desk and

346

followed JP. "Colonel, if you have a couple minutes I can give you some feedback on the dog problem. Chris has the latest on the latrines at the air terminal."

"I can't wait to hear. Bring your coffee, in fact, bring me a cup." He paused at Captain Dryer's desk. "Did you manage to fill my in-box yesterday while I was gone?"

"Afraid so, sir.

"What's on my schedule today?"

"Major Jelnik asked to see you at 0900 hours. Colonel Witherington would like you to stop by his office at 0930 hours, and Colonel Collier has you scheduled for a briefing at 1000 hours. After that you're to fly to Dogpatch for lunch with Captain Millbarth and the Delta Med officers, then go on to Firebase Cynthia." He handed JP a sheet of paper. "That's your copy."

Walking into his office, JP eased into the chair behind his desk. The first thing he did was flip over two pages of the desk calendar to June 19, which put him two days closer to going home. He cringed when he glanced at the full in-box, then waited for Tom Moffet and Chris Daniels to pull up chairs.

Moffet set a mug of coffee on JP's desk.

"Thanks," JP said, and slurped the hot liquid. "What's new with the hounds of Phong Sahn?"

"Disturbing news, Colonel. During the week my sergeant and I made a rough count of the loose dog population on Phong Sahn base. We quit counting at 200. Last week the people in the vet's office put down five dogs captured at random. The heads were sent to the I Corps path lab in Danang for exam of the brains. Yesterday the lab called with the results."

"One of the heads was positive?"

"No, sir. All five heads were positive for rabies."

"Good God!" JP exclaimed, reaching for a yellow legal pad and GI pen. "Did the vet make any recommendations?"

"Just the obvious. All stray dogs must be captured and put down."

"Brilliant."

"There is a problem with capturing the dogs."

"There's that word again."

Moffet continued. "The dogs are wild for the most part and street smart. It will be near impossible to get close enough to capture several hundred dogs using a net or a noose on the end of a pole. Some dogs are vicious and may even attack."

"How about putting out poison?"

"That might get a few. The vet said the remaining dogs would wise up and ignore food with poison. Besides poison is risky in a populated area."

"I guess we'll just have to blast the suckers with a 12 gauge."

"You mean just shoot them?" Chris Daniels said, horrified.

"Unless you have a better suggestion, Chris. I'll talk to the provost marshal. Maybe he can put out a couple of MP hunter-killer teams."

"Sir, I don't think that would be a good idea," Tom Moffet said.

"Why not? It will cut down on the dog population."

"It could cut down on the MP population. Killing dogs with shotguns would be gruesome. The GIs wouldn't stand for it. They'd go after the MPs."

JP sighed. "Okay, you come up with a better idea."

"It's in your in-box."

JP glanced at the stuffed box. "Maybe you'd better tell me."

"It's a proposed regulation requiring that all dogs, in fact all pets in the division, be registered with the vet, immunized for rabies, and carry tags with the date of immunization, the owner's name and unit. All dogs must be under the owner's control at all times. Dogs running loose will be impounded."

"That sounds good in theory. Since most dogs will be non-immunized and running loose, how do you propose to capture them?"

"I talked to Captain Searly, the med battalion S–4. He talked to a buddy in the G–4 section who phoned the manufacturer of tranquilizer guns in the States. Somehow he arranged for two guns and a generous supply of darts to be sent air mail. They should arrive within the next two or three days. The vets will do the rest, including publicity in the division newspaper. I will write up some material for the division newspaper, describe the health threat that stray dogs represent and the need for control."

JP put down his pen and took a sip of coffee. "You're making my job too easy, Tom. Is there anti-rabies vaccine available in case someone is bitten?"

"Yes, sir. It's at both hospitals. Apparently the vaccine is not infallible even when given early."

"Is there some basis for that?"

"The latest USARV monthly medical bulletin described a marine in the 1st Marine Division who died three months after he was bitten by a dog with rabies. He had received the full course of anti-rabies shots."

"That's an attention getter. Be sure to put that in the newspaper article. Anything else?"

"Yes, sir. Chris and I need to visit tactical units in the field to make random urine collections to test for malaria prophylaxis. Chris wants to inspect water purification techniques, food preparation, and sanitation on the firebases."

"Okay. My chopper is yours when I'm not using it. You know how to schedule it. Just stay out of hot LZs, don't get captured, and above all, don't bend my chopper." He turned to Chris Daniels. "You have a report on the air terminal plumbing crisis?"

"Yes, sir," Daniels said grinning. "Engineers cleared the stoppage the day you told me about it. There have been two more incidents, both cleared within six hours of when reported. The installation commander has authorized construction of a two-holer and four urine tubes as backup, so to speak."

"I guess that's progress," JP said, laughing.

"Anything else?"

"No, sir," both officers said in unison.

Captain Dryer stuck his head in the door. "Sir, Major Jelnik is here."

"Send him in."

Major Jelnik waited for Moffet and Daniels to leave, then entered. He carried a large manila envelope thick with papers.

"Have a seat, Mike. Coffee?"

"No, thanks."

"How are things in the Dust-offs?"

"Fine, sir. We've gone two weeks without loosing a bird," the Dust-off detachment commander said. "Have you recovered from your exciting medevac last week?" he asked, grinning.

JP leaned forward. "I'll be candid; that was the worst experience I have ever had in three wars. Four dead out of four wounded is not an enviable record for a doctor. And making the pickup under fire is very unnerving when you can't shoot back. That's the first time in my life I've had that experience. Your people do it every day and many times under much worse conditions. It's a shame that recognition has dragged because of the bureaucracy."

"I'm glad you feel that way, sir," Jelnik said, placing the manila envelope on JP's desk.

"What is that?"

"Duplicates of the requests for awards and citations pending on my air and ground crews plus witness substantiations. There are forty-seven, some go back as far as three months. Several people are in for two and three awards."

JP pulled the envelope towards him. "I started the ball rolling with General Webster the day before yesterday. As soon as these awards are approved he will present them at a formal ceremony."

"That will mean a great deal to my men, Colonel."

"Anything else I can do for the Dust-offs, Mike?"

"No, sir. You have done more than I hoped for."

JP stood and picked up his fatigue cap and the large envelope. "I'm on my way to see the chief of staff now. It should be a propitious time to drop this in his lap... so to speak."

★

Several minutes later JP entered Colonel Witherington's office.

"Have a seat, Doctor," the chief of staff said. "This won't take long." He slid a single paper along the desk.

JP picked up the paper and studied it.

"That is this month's schedule for the Ho Chi Minh trail and the firing ranges at Phong Sahn. General Webster has given you ten days to become qualified with the M–14 and M–16 rifles, the M–79 grenade launcher, the 45-caliber pistol, and the two types of hand grenades. During the same ten days you will negotiate the Ho Chi Minh trail as many times as necessary to achieve a passing grade. Failure to qualify with any of those weapons or pass the Ho Chi Minh trail with a minimum score in that time period will result in your being confined to the Phong Sahn base until you do qualify. Is that clear?"

"Yes, sir," JP said, suppressing what would have been a huge grin. Now he knew how Brer Rabbit felt after Brer Bear threw him into the briar patch. Next to surgery he loved to shoot guns, all guns, big and small.

The G–3's office was about two blocks from the chief of staff's office. Identical on the outside to a dozen adjacent blue-painted wooden-louvered buildings, including the division surgeon's office, it was identified by the small sign that hung from a post at the front entrance. Much of its floor space was occupied by desks and file cabinets. Clerk typists banged away at typewriters; NCOs and company grade officers moved busily around the room. The noise of clattering typewriters and ringing telephones blended with low-pitched conversations. This was the administrative section of G–3.

When Lieutenant Colonel JP Franklin walked in, the stench of cigarette and cigar smoke hung heavy despite the efforts of two large floor fans. "This place stinks," he announced as he eased into a folding metal chair by Colonel Collier's desk.

The gray-haired officer at the desk looked up. Leaning back, he reached for the stub of an unlit cigar resting on an ash tray fashioned from a brass 105 mm shell. "Were you referring to Vietnam in general or my office in particular?"

"Both. If you're going to light that thing the least you can do is offer an intact one to your guest."

"I thought you were down on cigars."

"I weaken on rare occasions. This doesn't happen to be one of them, but I enjoy the luxury of refusing."

"Okay, Doctor, would you like a cigar?"

"As a matter of fact, I would."

Accepting the proffered cigar JP stuck it in his pocket, ignoring Collier's glare. "Never know when that rare occasion will arise."

"You jarheads never forget how to scrounge."

"That's how marines managed to survive through the years, what with the army, navy, and now the air force taking the best of everything."

Lieutenant Colonel Bruce Collier, Infantry, West Point, '56, and Lieutenant Colonel JP Franklin, Medical Corps, became friends when both were stationed at the Military Academy and lived in adjacent quarters of a duplex. Collier, then a math professor, had been, in addition to his regular duties, the officer in charge of the cadet parachute club. JP, in addition to his medical duties, had been the officer in charge of the cadet rock climbing club which he helped start with his daughter's godfather. Over backyard barbecues and cold beer JP would try to convince Collier that jumping out of perfectly good airplanes was an exceedingly dangerous activity and could be hazardous to one's health. Collier, in turn, worked to convince JP that climbing rocks was an insane activity that could end up in a world of hurt. It was poetic justice when each broke a leg. Collier made a bad landing on a windy day; JP fell while climbing alone without protection.

On Saturday afternoons when the cadets were to play football at Michie stadium, the entire neighborhood, men, women, and children, would board buses to be transported to the stadium, that is everyone except JP and Collier. Both officers, recovering from their broken legs, sat on their small communal front porch, casted legs propped on the metal rail, smoking cigars while enduring the caustic taunts of fellow officers.

350

"I'd better get down to business before you clean me out of cigars and steal all my personnel," Colonel Collier said. "What do you know about Qui Tavong?"

"Never heard of it until the day I arrived. General Webster mentioned it briefly. Come to think of it I never heard of Phong Sahn until a month ago."

"JP, you must have been living on an isolated island."

"I suppose some people would consider Washington D.C. in that light."

Colonel Collier stood up. "Let's go back to the conference room. It's quieter there and I can use the wall map to orient you. Coffee?"

JP shook his head. "My kidneys are in afterburner from all the coffee I've had this morning. I'll be flying up to Dog Patch this morning and then out to Cynthia in the afternoon. Hueys don't come equipped with relief tubes."

Colonel Collier chuckled. "Just don't try pissing out the door while in flight. On second thoughts, everyone ought to try that just once.

JP followed the G–3 towards the rear of the building. Once inside the conference room Collier closed and locked the door, then moved past a table and chairs to an acetate-covered map of Military Region I. He turned to JP. "Can you read a map?"

JP bristled, rising to the bait. "I'm a former marine, Bruce."

"I know; that's why I asked." Collier became serious. "From here on everything is classified *secret* and above."

JP nodded.

Collier turned back to the map and tapped with his finger. "You are here," he said, chuckling.

JP leaned forward. "No kidding. I wondered where I was."

The finger moved almost a hundred miles north-west to indicate an airstrip and village four miles east of the border with Laos. "This is Qui Tavong. In the early 1930s the French built a fort there and later a crude airstrip."

JP moved to the map and studied the area Collier indicated. The contour lines indicated that Qui Tavong was a flat plateau surrounded by triple canopy forests and mountain ranges extending into Laos, some with peaks up to 3,000 meters.

"In the early 1960s the special forces established a line of camps along the Laotian border to monitor traffic on the Ho Chi Minh trail. The base camp was at Qui Tavong. The NVA, as might have been predicted, resented the threat to their supply line into South Vietnam. By '68 they had eliminated all the special forces camps in the area except the one at Qui Tavong. This was garrisoned by about 500 Montagnard CIDGs and a company of ARVN Rangers, all supervised by a special forces A Team. A village adjacent to the fort, which is the real Qui Tavong, was home to about 300 civilians, mostly CIDG dependants."

Collier's finger indicated a red line in Laos running east–west to the border. "This is Route 884. In early '68 the NVA began widening it. At the same time they extended it to meet Route 16 in Vietnam. Route 16 continues east to Quang Dien which is 8 klicks south of us. These roads and trails have became one of the principle NVA supply routes to the east in Military Region I."

JP took a final look at the map and sat down. "You're going to tell me that Qui Tavong became a threat to the NVA that could not be tolerated."

"That's pretty good for an ex-marine," Collier said. "In August '68, the 5th NVA Division of about 6,000 men wiped out Qui Tavong's outposts one night and attacked the fort at dawn. When it became apparent that the fort could not hold, an emergency airlift was instituted. Air force C–130s, supported by tactical aircraft and gunships, evacuated over 900 people from Qui Tavong before it was overwhelmed. Tragically, the last C–130 with about a hundred CIDG, their dependants, and a dozen Green Berets on board, was hit by ground fire as it was taking off. It crashed just off the strip. The wreck with what remains of the bodies is still there. Seven special forces troopers who stayed behind as a rear guard have not been heard from since that day.

"The air force lost two fighters which were shot down. Both exploded on impact with no survivors. An air force FAC was also shot down. The pilot crash-landed his 0-2A. He established radio contact with an overhead fighter. However, an hour later he failed to respond to repeated calls by SAR aircraft. It was presumed he was captured. He's been carried as a probable POW ever since."

"Would that be Colonel Goulden?"

Collier turned pale. He looked as though he had been slugged. "Jesus Christ, JP, that information is highly sensitive. Very few people are authorized access to it and you're not one of them. How in the hell did you know about Goulden?"

"His wife is chief ER nurse at the 96th. I knew her during the Korean War. She gave me some details of his shoot down."

Collier remained quiet for several seconds as though debating something within himself. "I suppose as division surgeon you are authorized to know what's going on. General Webster told me to use my judgment in briefing you."

"So far you have demonstrated excellent judgment, Bruce. Don't blow it now."

"If you reveal any of this to anyone, JP, especially Colonel Goulden's wife, you will put a lot of American lives at great risk including the lives of POWs who might be in our AO."

"I understand, Bruce, and you have my word."

"For the past two months SOG teams have been watching the portion of the Ho Chi Minh trail across the border from Qui Tavong and along Route 884. They reported a substantial increase in traffic, not only of supplies but of men entering South Vietnam from Laos. G-2 suspects the NVA are making a major effort to lay up supplies and build up units before the monsoons hit in October. There is strong indication they are preparing for an offensive as soon as the monsoons end.

"An NVA prisoner, a captain snatched by a SOG team, has told interrogators of a POW camp in Laos just over the border from Qui Tavong. It is a camp where POWs are collected before moving as a group up the Ho Chi Minh trail to Hanoi. The captain also revealed there is a POW camp somewhere on this side of the border with captured US airmen. He didn't know where the camp was but heard rumors that the POWs were about to be moved to the camp in Laos. The most disconcerting information he revealed was that prisoners physically unable to travel will be executed."

"Do you think that's true, Bruce?"

"I know it's true. We have photographs to prove that it happened at other POW camps.

352

"That's what the Japs did to POWs in World War II," JP said. "In Korea the Chinese were more humane. They left the very sick or seriously wounded POWs by the side of the road to be found by UN forces."

"Don't expect that in this AO."

JP remained silent.

Colonel Collier continued. "General Webster decided several months ago to make a combined US–ARVN assault on Qui Tavong. He wanted to wait until the NVA had built up maximum supplies at their way stations and when the roads were functioning with the greatest traffic. Twice we had D-day scheduled and twice it was cancelled. D-day is now in three days. Two battalions of the of the 174th Brigade, plus division air assets, engineers, EOD, artillery, rangers, and medics will take part in the operation along with one regiment of ARVNs. Air force and marine tactical aircraft, C–123s, and C–130s will participate."

"What about evacuation of casualties? Qui Tavong is almost a hundred miles from Delta Med or the hospitals here at Phong Sahn."

"The medical portion of the operation was worked out by Colonel Diblasio, Captain Millbarth, the brigade surgeon, and the brigade S–3. You don't have anything to do in the way of planning except to monitor the operation and get some idea how the division operates on a combat assault."

"I'm scheduled to go Delta Med this morning. I'll review Millbarth's plans and see what I can do to help."

"Any questions?"

"Only one. Are there plans to go after the POWs in the camps in Vietnam or Laos?"

Collier's face flushed. "That's not a subject for discussion."

JP smiled. "You just answered my question. Bruce, I want to be part of any POW rescue effort that might rescue Colonel Goulden's husband. I'll go as a medic. I owe it to his wife; she saved my life in Korea."

"You're out of your mind, JP. You will just screw things up. Bright Light missions are extremely hazardous. The SOG people are well trained to do what they do. They're in superb physical condition and they work together as a team. You're an out-of-shape middle-aged doctor and an outsider. You would be a burden to the team and would certainly compromise the mission. Besides, you took an oath as a doctor to preserve life. Could you violate that oath and kill to protect members of your team?"

JP's shoulders slumped. "You're right, Bruce."

"You can best support any Bright Light mission by keeping your mouth shut and stay as far away from the SOG team as possible. Remember, JP, not a word of this to Goulden's wife. The missions will be canceled if there is the faintest whiff that security has been compromised."

Chapter Forty-One

Dog Patch was located in the northern third of the 36th Division AO and four miles east of the coastal town of Nghia Lam. From a Huey helicopter half a mile out and 600 feet up, it was apparent why Dog Patch had received at least part of its name. It appeared an immense flat treeless area of orange-brown dirt, its surface marked by unpainted wooden buildings, some partially dug in, their exposed portions protected by walls of stacked ammo boxes filled with earth and layers of sandbags. In the monsoon season Dog Patch became a boot-sucking, tire-sucking quagmire of mud with many of its wooden sidewalks under water.

The 174th Brigade headquarters and its supporting units, including Delta Company of the 36th Medical Battalion, were located at Dog Patch. Like Bravo Company at Quang Dien seventy miles south, Delta was one of the few medical clearing companies in Vietnam providing emergency care for the severely wounded. Captain Jerry Millbarth, Medical Corps, US Army Reserve, commanded Delta Company and served as the brigade surgeon, advising the brigade commander on medical matters.

As the Huey passed over the end of the single runway, Chief Warrant Officer Dan Ranson in the right seat spoke to his peter pilot. "We're cleared to the Delta Med helipad. Fly down the strip to mid-point, then turn east on the next taxiway. Look for a big rectangle of sandbags with a red cross. That will be the roof of the Delta Med emergency room. The helipads are about a hundred feet north."

The Huey swept down the strip at fifty feet and banked right. "I have the pads," the peter pilot reported. "There are three; does it matter which one I land on?"

"Your choice, but don't shut down. We need to top off the tanks at the fuel farm. There's a front due out from the west this afternoon. We may have to fly over or around it. Running out of fuel is not an option."

"I hear you, boss," the young warrant officer responded.

The Huey began a steep descending turn to the left. Leveling off, it nosed up and settled on to the helipad. JP, recalling his own inept efforts at landing a Loach a few days earlier, was impressed. "Beautiful," he said over the intercom. "I couldn't do better."

"Considering your last flight, Colonel, that demonstration of superb pilotage gives you something to work towards," Dan Ranson said.

"I have always maintained that a student's progress, whether a surgeon or a pilot, reflects the capabilities of the teacher. Don't you agree, Mr. Ranson?" JP was scheduled for another hour's dual with Ranson the next day.

"I agree up to a point, Colonel. Beyond that, self-preservation overwhelms the teacher."

"You win that round, Ranson," JP said, laughing, "but remember, your day is coming."

"Boss, I think you're in trouble," the peter pilot said.

JP undid his seat belt. Before taking off his helmet he told the flight crew, "We'll be here for lunch. Plan to leave for Cynthia at about 1330 hours."

Storing his helmet under the seat, he climbed to the ground. After a wave to the door gunner he walked towards a figure in fatigues standing off to one side. As he neared he saw the man wore captains bars and a caduceus on his jacket collar. His fatigues, at least one size too large, appeared to have been slept in.

The captain was in his early thirties, of average height, overweight and in need of a haircut and shave. His down-turned lips and sad eyes gave him the appearance of a circus clown. Other than those pithy observations, the captain appeared to be a fine specimen of a military officer.

Instead of saluting his commander the captain stuck out his hand. "Welcome to Dog Patch and Delta Med," the captain said without much enthusiasm. "I'm Jerry Millbarth, Delta Med commander."

Reluctant to embarrass the man at their first meeting, JP ignored the lack of military courtesy and grasped the hand. The captain's grip was weak and sweaty.

"Are you up here for a particular reason?"

Again the man failed to accord his commander the courtesy of a "sir' or "colonel". And again JP suppressed a rebuke. Instead he said, "I wanted to meet you; also discuss the Qui Tavong operation." He glanced at his watch. "Shall we eat lunch first?"

"This way," Millbarth said, leading off.

"How was Bangkok?" JP asked as they walked towards the mess hall.

"Miserable. It rained every day except the day I left to come back to Vietnam."

"At least you had a few days with your wife."

"She didn't come. I was by myself." Millbarth offered no explanation. "The mess sergeant has some T-bone steaks for our lunch," he said.

JP wondered if Millbarth meant steaks were obtained just for himself and his guest, for all the company officers, or for everyone including enlisted personnel. A weak alarm began to sound. It became louder when they passed several enlisted men who walked by without saluting. Millbarth seemed not to notice.

JP let it go for now. While he was not pathological over strict adherence to military protocol, he believed that moderate military courtesy was essential to discipline and morale. He preferred a loose informal kind of leadership that made for a warm working environment but left no doubt who was in charge. However, Captain Millbarth was stretching this philosophy.

The mess hall, an unpainted wooden structure, its upper third open but screened for ventilation and light, resembled half a dozen others he had seen in Phong Sahn and on fire support bases. The officers' section was a single table set off from the enlisted dining area at the far end of the mess hall.

"Mess kits are already on the table," Captain Millbarth said. "We needn't go through the chow line. The mess sergeant will bring our steaks, potatoes, and vegetables."

As JP followed Millbarth through the enlisted section towards the officers' table he glanced at the mess kits of the enlisted men. He saw no T-bone steaks nor well-picked T-bones. What he did see were Vienna sausages, watery asparagus, and mashed potatoes soaked with water from the asparagus. It didn't seem right that in a combat zone, even one as benign as Dog Patch, officers would dine on steaks while enlisted personnel ate Vienna sausage. He felt the same sort of uneasiness when dining in the general's mess. At least there the food was purchased separately using the considerable monthly mess dues assessed to each member.

This was not the general's mess. This was the company mess of the medical battalion he commanded. As commander JP could set direction. Thus when he reached the officers' table he grabbed a mess kit and canteen cup. "I don't want to put your mess sergeant to any inconvenience," he told Millbarth, "I'll just go through the chow line." Before Millbarth could object JP moved quickly to the end of the chow line to stand behind a private first class. A very upset Millbarth had no choice but to follow.

The Pfc turned. When he saw the light colonel's leaf on JP's collar his eyes widened. "Sir, you're not really going to eat this stuff, are you?"

"That bad?"

"The mess sergeant is hard core VC, sir."

JP chuckled. He noticed that Millbarth was not smiling.

"I thought officers had their own separate menu," the Pfc said.

"Not any more," JP said, looking straight at Captain Millbarth.

As he followed the Pfc along the serving line he glanced into the kitchen. The cooks and mess personnel wore filthy aprons over fatigues. Most were without hair cover. Scraps of food littered the floor. JP winced when he saw a cook step on some food and keep walking.

After half-filling his canteen cup with warm lemonade he waited for Millbarth, then walked to the officers' table and took a seat. Millbarth sat opposite. They were soon joined by three other officers whose trays contained Vienna sausage, watery asparagus, and mashed potatoes soaked with water from asparagus. The word was out.

Millbarth introduced the three officers. The executive officer, Dominic Cruessi, was a thirty-year-old UCLA med school graduate drafted at the beginning of his third year of general surgery at LA County Hospital. He was of medium height, with a studious face behind army horn-rimmed glasses and a confident, compassionate demeanor. Married and with two children, Cruessi would return to complete his surgical residency when he left the army.

Captain Delbert Caldwell, DDS, Dental Corps, was twenty-nine. He had come on active duty right after completing dental school. He owed the army considerable payback time for his four-year ROTC undergraduate scholarship and his four-year army-sponsored scholarship in dental school. He was also married and had two small children.

First Lieutenant Will Tatum, MSC, was the Delta Med administration officer. A business major in college he was commissioned through ROTC. He managed the bulk of Delta Company's administrative requirements. Tatum was single but was dating a nurse at the 96th Evac.

A third Medical Corps officer, Ben Jamison, had rotated back to the States eight days ago leaving Delta Med one medical officer short. When the table talk turned to a replacement JP reached into his fatigue jacket pocket, removed a folded paper and passed it to Millbarth. "That's a short bio of Brent Mann, due here in a few days as Jamison's replacement."

Millbarth scanned the sheet and scowled.

"As you can see," JP said, "Mann will be a problem initially."

"He's had very little surgical training," Millbarth complained. "He finished a straight pediatric internship and was drafted before completing his second year of peds residency."

"That's right. He will need some fast surgical training and close supervision, but he could be a big help with pediatric problems."

Millbarth was not happy. "Couldn't we get someone with a stronger surgical background?"

JP shook his head. "Afraid not. The pool has dried up. The 96th Evac has agreed to take Mann for three weeks OJT. They promise to work him day and night in their emergency room and scrub him in on surgery."

"But that would mean we would be short a doctor three weeks after he gets here."

"His time at the 96th will be well worth the hardship it might impose here. If you get behind the power curve call me and I'll see what I can do. But you should get Mann down to the 96th before he starts treating casualties."

Millbarth nodded reluctantly.

During the remainder of lunch JP tried to keep the conversation light and lace it with subtle humor. He got few laughs. The officers seemed restrained and uncomfortable. He sensed Delta Med was not a happy place. Its commander's sloppy appearance, lack of military discipline and courtesy, and his attempt to ingratiate himself by serving steaks instead of the regular menu, was forcing JP to consider relieving him. But he was reluctant to do it so soon after relieving his battalion executive officer.

As soon as Cruessi, Caldwell and Tatum finished eating they excused themselves, leaving only JP and Millbarth at the table. JP set down his fork and wiped his lips with a paper napkin. "This place seems as good as any to talk, Captain."

"What did you have in mind?"

JP fought a growing aggravation with Captain Millbarth. Simple courtesy required he be addressed as "sir" or "colonel". Millbarth had consistently ignored such courtesies. Suppressing his displeasure, JP said, "I'd like to hear what you have planned for the medical support of the Qui Tavong operation."

"Nothing to worry about," Millbarth assured. "Every contingency is planned for to the last roll of adhesive tape and unit of blood."

For some reason JP was not reassured. "Who will be the medical officer in charge at Qui Tavong?"

"Gary Neville, the battalion surgeon from the 3rd/5th."

"What's his background?" JP asked, hoping Neville was not another budding pediatrician.

"He was training as an ER doc when he was drafted. He's been with the 3rd/5th as battalion surgeon for four months. This will be his third big operation with them."

"He sounds qualified," JP said, making a mental note to check Neville's 201 file and talk to his battalion commander. "What happens if Captain Neville is taken sick, wounded, or just overwhelmed?"

"I guess I'd have to find a replacement from one of the other battalions."

"You better alert someone now so he can familiarize himself with the operation and be prepared for a possible sudden departure. His battalion commander also needs to be notified."

Again Millbarth reluctantly nodded assent.

"What about supporting medics?"

"Gary's NCOIC is an old hand. He knows how to fast-construct a protected battalion aid station in a high-threat area. The other EMs were field medics for six months before moving to the aid station."

"Qui Tavong is fifty minutes' flying time from Phong Sahn. What are the plans for picking up casualties from the field and providing acute care before flying them back to Phong Sahn?"

"The aid station will have equipment and supplies to function as an acute care facility. The Dust-off detachment will furnish four helicopters, two for pickup of casualties in the field and delivery to the aid station, and two for backhaul to Phong Sahn after casualties have been stabilized."

JP asked about resupply.

"That will be done through Lieutenant Tatum and the medical battalion supply depot. Low-titer O-negative blood will come direct from the two hospitals in Phong Sahn on backhaul Dust-offs returning to Qui Savong."

JP had to admit, Millbarth seemed to have the medical support well planned. Then why did he feel so uneasy. "I want to be notified immediately if problems develop with any aspect of the operation," he told Millbarth. "And I'd like you to go out to Qui Tavong the first day to be sure everything is going well with the construction of an aid station."

Millbarth turned pale. "I don't have a helicopter," he croaked. "I have no way of getting out there."

"I expect there will be a lot of traffic going to Qui Tavong from here," JP said. "As brigade surgeon you should have no trouble hitching a ride. I'm sure the brigade commander would be delighted to have you go along in his C&C chopper."

Millbarth's voice wavered. "Gary Neville is perfectly competent to manage things by himself. There is no need for me to go out to Qui Tavong and interfere in his operation."

"Your purpose in going, Captain Millbarth, is to do what you can to support Neville, not interfere with him."

"I don't see it that way. I should be here in the brigade TX and monitor what goes on at Qui Tavong. And I'll be needed in the emergency room to take care of casualties
358

from there."

JP took a deep breath. "The casualties from Qui Tavong will be flown directly to the hospitals in Phong Sahn. The aid station at Qui Tavong will function as a mini clearing company. There won't be any need for casualties to come here."

Millbarth dug in his heels. "I disagree. Perhaps we should discuss this with the brigade commander."

JP's voice carried an edge. "You are free to discuss it all you wish with the brigade commander. Keep in mind I am your commanding officer and I have just given you a direct order to get your sorry ass out to Qui Tavong on the first day, You will message my office a full report of your visit when you return."

Millbarth recoiled as if slapped.

"Is there any part of that order you do not understand?"

"No."

That did it. JP stood and fixed his eyes on Millbarth's face. "Captain, I am very close to hitting you with an Article 15."

"You can't do that."

"The hell I can't. Just try me. Get on your feet and stand at attention when addressed by a superior."

Millbarth slowly rose, his face beet red.

"I remind you of the simple requirements of military courtesy. You will salute a superior and address him by his rank or by the term 'sir'. Is that clear?"

"Yes," Millbarth hissed.

"What? I missed the colonel and the sir part."

"Yes, sir… Colonel."

JP gave Millbarth a withering look of disgust. "Get yourself presentable and your company in shape, Captain, or you will be facing big trouble." As he started to leave he said, "Don't bother walking me out. I can find my way." Returning Millbarth's sloppy salute he walked briskly from the mess hall, slamming the door behind him. His mind was made up. As soon as the Qui Tavong operation was up and running, Millbarth would be history.

★

Friday, June 19, 1970, 1329 hours
Charlie Med Helipad

Climbing on board the waiting Huey, JP noted half a dozen bulging orange bags marked US MAIL on the floor. Stacked next to them were four large unmarked cardboard boxes. Taking a seat by the door, he eased on his flight helmet and plugged in the headset cord.

"Enjoy your lunch, Colonel?" Dan Ranson asked.

"I'd rather not discuss it." JP said morosely. "What are we delivering besides mail?"

"Surrender leaflets, sir. The brigade psy war officer asked if we would drop them off on our way to Cynthia."

"By 'drop them off' do you mean scatter them on top of the wily Cong and NVA?"

"That's affirmative, sir, that is if you're willing."

JP shrugged. "Why not? It will be my most direct participation to win this bizarre activity called a war. What's the weather?"

"Mild drizzle and light fog starting halfway out to Cynthia. We'll probably low level when we reach the mountains. Do you get airsick easily?"

"Only when I'm scared."

★

Friday, July 19, 1970, 1410 hours
Sixteen Miles South-east of Fire Support Base Cynthia

Belted in the seat next to the open port side door, JP watched the green rolling landscape 2,000 feet below change from flat to verdant treeless hills abundant with vegetation. Above the Huey scattered fluffy white clouds transitioned to dirty gray overcast, blotting out the sun. Ranson's voice came through the headset. "We're coming up on the drop area, Colonel, but there's a problem."

"Damn it, Mr. Ranson, you know I hate that word."

JP heard a chuckle. "Sir, there's a twenty-five to thirty knot head wind up here out of the west. Our ground speed is down to eighty. If the leaflets are dropped from this altitude most will end up in the South China Sea."

"Can I just kick the boxes out and let the VC and NVA make their own distribution?"

"I don't think that will work, sir. How do you feel about going down on the deck?"

"Last time I did that I almost fell out."

"Not to worry. There's a monkey harness under your seat. Strap it on and clip the anchor strap to one of the O rings on the floor. With the harness on, even if you fell out you wouldn't fall far… unless, of course, the anchor strap broke."

"You are a comfort, Ranson. What about the door gunners helping?"

"Since we're going down on the deck we'd be a lot safer if they stayed on the guns."

"Right. Good thinking."

Minutes later, JP tightened the harness straps around his waist, found an O ring on the cabin floor and clipped in the anchor strap. He was able to move to the door but no further. Kneeling by the boxes, he tore open the top of each, then restacked them. Finished, he took out several leaflets from the top box, examined one, then stuffed them into his pocket to send to the kids as souvenirs. Returning to his seat, he belted in and reported he was set.

"We're going down now, sir. When we level off you can start dumping leaflets. We'll fly a left race track pattern for a complete 360, then decide if we need to repeat it."

JP burped his mike button twice.

The peter pilot dropped the nose and headed for the ground. Leveling off at twenty feet, he banked the Huey in a tight left turn. JP struggled to his feet and unsteadily moved to the starboard door and leaned out against his anchor strap. For a moment he stared at the door gunner, who grinned and gave him a thumbs up. Grabbing a fistful of leaflets, he slam-dunked them into the rotor wash, then reached for the next batch. By the time the Huey reversed course he had emptied the top box and threw it out. As he developed confidence in the security of the monkey harness he moved more rapidly, emptying the second box while still on the downwind leg. He was warming to the task. Throwing out the empty box, he reached into the next. With each handful he shouted into the wind, "Take that, you dirty commie pinkos." This was total war.

The Huey lifted up into a climbing turn. "How's it going back there, Colonel?" Ranson asked.

"One and a half boxes to go."

"You up to another run?"

"Why not. Semper Fi."

The Huey made a sharp left bank, dropped down like a hawk and leveled off.

Again JP threw out fistful after fistful of leaflets. Abruptly, the helicopter banked sharply to the right and began to jink violently, throwing him hard against the limit of the anchor strap. "What the hell?" he muttered as he tried to recover. Then he saw the strings of green tracers lazily passing by the door, The port door gunner suddenly began firing. Empty brass bounced around the cabin. One went scorching down JP's back. "Son of a bitch," he yowled as he tried to shake the hot shell out despite the monkey harness.

The Huey lurched up. "We're out of here, Colonel."

JP pulled the remaining boxes of leaflets to the door and kicked them out.

"Bombs away," he shouted.

Chapter Forty-Two

Friday, June 19, 1970, 1535 hours
En Route to Fire Support Base Cynthia

Cynthia was the most western of the 174th Brigade's firebases. Only fourteen kilometers east of the Laotian border it was built on the flattened summit of a small mountain. Its base, partially circled by a river on three sides and an almost vertical rock wall on the fourth, was in a region of almost impenetrable jungle, mountains and valleys. Like many other firebases in the region it could be reached only by helicopter; the flight to Cynthia from Dog Patch averaged fifty minutes for a Huey. Well positioned on its summit was a battalion of infantry, the 2nd/43rd, a company of ARVN Rangers, and a battery of 105 mm howitzers. The only other artillery support was from a battery of 8 inch howitzers firing at extreme range. AC–130 gunships and tactical air support were thirty-five minutes away.

As Lieutenant Colonel JP Franklin's Huey flew west towards Cynthia, overcast gradually blotted out the afternoon sun. Low-hanging clouds obscured many of the taller mountain peaks. Wisps of smoke-like clouds streamed past the helicopter's open door. At 2,000 feet, the damp air was chilly. A few drops of rain splattered against the Huey's windscreen, then rapidly progressed to sheets of water. The peter pilot uttered an oath and activated the wipers. In the blink of an eye the sky and ground became obscured, then white. Suddenly they were flying in a ping-pong ball. JP, shivering in a seat by the door, buttoned the top button of his fatigue jacket and wondered if he were about to end his career on the side of a mountain.

CWO–2 Dan Ranson told his peter pilot, "Do a 180 and ease down to the deck. There are no mountains back where we came from, only rice paddies."

The Huey started a slow descending right turn. After losing 500 feet the rain diminished, then stopped. Gray clouds, beaten by the rotor blades, broke into smoky fragments and scattered. Ranson's head seemed on a swivel as it turned back and forth like a radar parabola scanning for a target.

"Make a ninety-degree descending left turn and look for a river."

By now the Huey was down to 300 feet. "That it, boss?" the peter pilot asked, tilting the helicopter.

"Good eye. Go for it."

The Huey dropped to tree top level, banked left and approached the river at a 45-degree angle. "When you intersect the river go down to twenty feet and follow its course in a general westerly direction," Ranson said.

The peter pilot looked at Ranson, shrugged, and dropped the Huey towards the river. The airspeed was approaching 120 knots when he threw the Huey into a sharp right bank and gingerly eased downward. Tree tops and vines whizzed by the open door in a continuous blur, then tree trunks and shrubs, and finally the Huey was skimming so close to the water that its rotor wash left a trail of misty spray.

"I've got it," Ranson said, taking the controls.

JP sensed the change on the controls. The Huey went even lower. An engine failure or pilot error in this environment at this speed would have General Worden and the Walter Reed chaplain calling on Kathy within twenty-four hours. JP had to admit, flying at 105 knots over the water's surface, trees and vegetation tearing by twenty to thirty feet from the tips of the rotor blades, was a mix of terror and exhilaration. He was willing to bet Ranson was having the time of his young life.

Suddenly the port door gunner cut loose with his M-60.

"See something, Winters?" Ranson voice came through the intercom.

"Three dinks with weapons on the bank; three more naked in the water."

"You get any?"

"I don't think so, sir. We were there and gone too quick, but we sure scared the hell out of them."

The co-pilot reached for a map. "I'll call in the coordinates to Cynthia."

The Huey continued to follow the river's course, banking violently at its curves and turns. "Colonel, the rivers make great navigational aids out here," Ranson said. "You want to be certain to follow the correct branch or you could find yourself the guest of the Cong or Pathet Laos."

JP burped his mike button twice.

The Huey's nose came up. Its airspeed bled off as it climbed a mountain, its skids not more than ten feet above the tree tops. Nearing the summit the airspeed dropped further. Dense trees and jungle foliage gave way to stands of leafless trees and dead shrubs, testimony to the effectiveness of Operation Ranch Hand. Easing over rolls of concertina wire strung between barbed wire fences, the Huey reached the summit, then gained another ten feet. It slowly flat-turned and headed for purple smoke spewing up a hundred meters away.

Looking down through the door, JP saw a myriad of sandbagged bunkers, fighting positions, and complexes of unpainted wooden buildings. As the Huey passed over an outhouse its door opened and a GI emerged, tightening his belt. He glanced up, waved, and went his way. The Huey finally settled on a PSP pad, scattering purple smoke. The engine whined down and the rotors slowed.

"How long do you expect to be here, Colonel?" Ranson asked.

"About an hour, more or less, probably more than less.'

Ranson reached for an UZI hanging on his armored seat back. "I'm going to check this thing out."

"Don't shoot yourself or your peter pilot," JP warned. "I'm not ready to fly this thing back to Phong Sahn on my own." Jumping to the ground, he walked away from the Huey and almost collided with a young captain holding a salute.

"Sir, Captain Brian Knowles, Battalion Surgeon, 2nd/43rd."

Returning the salute, JP extended his hand. Knowles's handshake was strong and confident. "How are things going out here?" JP asked.

"Lonely and boring, Colonel. You're the first staff surgeon to visit in the five months I've been out here."

"What about the brigade surgeon?"

"I met him at Dog Patch the day I reported to brigade. I haven't seen him since."

JP nodded sympathetically.

"Sir, before we go to the aid station, Colonel Armistead, the CO, asked that I bring you by the TOC. He'd like to meet you.

"Lead on."

The battalion tactical operations center was a partially dug in and sandbagged structure with three small rooms that served as offices/sleeping areas and one large room. The latter was crammed with radios, maps, tables, computers, phones, and desks. A half dozen enlisted men and two officers, a major and a captain glanced at JP when he walked in, then continued working. A short, muscular man in his mid-forties greeted JP, introducing himself as Lieutenant Colonel John Armistead, the battalion commander. "We appreciate your coming out here, Doctor," he said. "I'm sure Doc Knowles is happy having someone to talk to about medicine."

Colonel Armistead indicated several folding metal chairs in front of an upright map covered with acetate. "Take seats. I'll give you an overview of what the battalion has been and is doing."

After JP and Captain Knowles were seated Colonel Armistead went to the map. Using a pointer, he identified Cynthia, the Laotian border, and three trails marked in red winding through what appeared to be some of the worst mountain terrain JP could recall having seen on a map. "The NVA are saturating these trails with caravans of supplies heading east from the Ho Chi Minh trail. Our task has been to interdict the trails with ambushes and identify targets for artillery and fighter bombers. We have been reasonably successful in doing just that. However, there has been a predictable response on the part of the NVA. They now consider us a major threat to their supply effort.

"Two main force regiments have been identified moving into this area." The pointer tapped. "We anticipate they'll be giving our units in the bush a hard time. It's only a matter of time before they attempt an assault on Cynthia, We have LRRP teams, our own units, and the ARVN Rangers searching for the NVA regimental headquarters and the main bodies of troops. When we locate them we'll call for the B–52s."

Armistead went on to cite statistics. "Over the previous thirty days the battalion captured four tons of rice, ninety SKS or AK–47 rifles, thousands of rounds of rifle ammunition, one 51-caliber machine gun and six RPGs. It destroyed ten bunkers, six tunnels, and an underground hospital. Enemy losses were 109 confirmed KIA. There were probably more. The enemy are quick to carry off their dead and wounded. After the B–52s there's not much left to count."

"What about our own losses during those thirty days?" JP asked.

"We lost twelve killed, thirty-one wounded, and two missing. Fourteen of the wounded were returned to duty. The others were eventually evacuated out of country."

If this were a war of attrition we would be winning, thought JP.

364

After Armistead concluded his briefing he thanked JP for visiting the firebase. "Come back when you can spend the night. I have a guest bunk in my office and an almost inexhaustible supply of beer and cigars."

"Those inducements are hard to resist. I'll get word to you in a couple of weeks and bring my sleeping bag." The two colonels shook hands.

As JP walked with Captain Knowles towards the battalion aid station he asked, "How do you get along with your CO?"

"Too well. He doesn't want to me leave when my six months are up."

"How do you feel about that?" JP asked.

"I never thought I would say this, Colonel, but I am in some conflict."

"How do you mean?"

"In my five months out here I've become very close to many of the officers and EMs. I feel especially close to Colonel Armistead. He's a good man and a superb commander. He realizes the US is not going to win this war in the traditional sense and he's not willing to waste US lives for a spectacular victory or a high enemy body count. He does aggressively search out the enemy and attacks only when he has the advantage. I will definitely feel guilt when I leave, but for a doctor this place is the pits professionally. I'm desperate for medical challenge."

The battalion aid station was built two-thirds below ground level and one-third above. The exposed portion was protected by ammo boxes filled with dirt and stacked to a corrugated steel roof. The roof itself was covered by a double layer of sandbags protected from the elements by a black tarp. A half dozen collapsed stretchers leaned against the roof. Two GIs sat on the roof smoking.

Captain Knowles led down six steps to an entrance covered by mosquito netting. Pushing through the netting he shouted, "Tenshun."

Entering behind him JP called out, "As you were." Surveying the garage-sized room, he focused on four medics sitting around an examining table, each holding a hand of cards. Varied colored bottle caps were in neat piles in front of each medic. A medic with staff sergeant's stripes on his sleeve stood up, came over to JP and saluted.

"Sir, Spec Six Westover, NCOIC, Battalion Aid Station 2nd/43rd."

Captain Knowles introduced the other three medics.

"Go ahead and play out the hand, Sergeant," JP said. "I wouldn't want to be responsible for someone losing a big pot."

One of the medics laughed. "There's one big pot around here that does need losing," he said. "That's the one hanging over the sarge's belt."

Westover glanced down at his beltline and grinned. Turning to JP, he asked, "Would the colonel and captain like some coffee?"

"I thought you'd never ask."

"Please."

Westover turned to one of the medics. "Eisen, get the colonel and Doc some of our premium brewed coffee."

A moment later a canteen cup partially filled with thick black liquid was thrust at JP. He slurped the hot liquid, then took a seat at the table. Captain Knowles eased into another seat and indicated to Westover to join them. The younger medics disappeared to perform real and imagined duties.

JP began, "As you know, I've been in the division only a few days. Part of that time I've been visiting firebases to get a sense of the medical support in the division, meet medical personnel, principal officers, and identify problems affecting the health of the units." He stopped and sipped coffee from the canteen.

"Well, Colonel, there is a serious problem developing in this battalion," Brian Knowles said, "and it impacts discipline and combat efficiency."

"You must be referring to marijuana and drugs."

"Yes, sir. I have no idea how to deal with it."

"Don't be too hard on yourself. I have no idea how to deal with it either. In fact, at the present time the army has no idea how to deal with the drug problem. It was a struggle for the army just to admit it had a drug problem. At least now that the problem has been recognized, the search for a solution can get under way."

"Is Med Command going to come out with a drug policy?"

"Afraid not. They have left development of a drug program up to each division. I have no experience in this area. Fortunately, Matt Peterson, the division psychiatrist, has had some; three months of his residency was spent in a state prison system working with convicted drug users. I put Matt in charge of developing a drug program for the division. Between the two of us we have a program nearing completion. It will be at least another week or two before it's ready to submit to the general for approval."

"Can you give me some idea of what to expect?" Brian Knowles asked.

"Sure. The program will begin with a two-day symposium at the 96th Evac for all division medical officers. Speakers will include psychiatrists, psychologists, social workers, criminal investigators, JAG, and even the chaplain. In addition to lectures covering legal aspects, pharmacology, toxicology, and the neurological effects of drugs, there will be workshops and open forums on management. Matt has talked his former chairman at Pennsylvania into moderating the symposium. Fortunately, the chairman is a reserve colonel and can be brought on temporary active duty."

"What about the war during the two days of the symposium?"

"I'll request the general put the division in a defensive mode so most of the doctors can attend. Considering the crisis nature of the problem I'm sure he will agree."

JP drained the coffee from the canteen cup and set it down. "There's more. Beginning next week the provost marshal, JAG, chaplain, and I will give a program at the reception center to every group of incoming troops. Our presentation will cover the medical, legal, moral, and administrative ramifications of drug use. We'll also fly out to firebases and recreation centers to give the same presentation and hold rap sessions."

"What about the GIs already on drugs, especially heroin?" Sergeant Westover asked.

"That's one of our thorniest problems because of the legal ramifications. Major Peterson advocates some sort of amnesty program to include inpatient medical treatment and counseling at the Alpha medical clearing company for drug users who voluntarily turn themselves in. After completing the program they will be returned to their units. They will not be subject to any punishment nor will there be any adverse

366

remarks on their military records. Those who choose not to enter the amnesty program and are subsequently identified as drug users, and those who are recidivists, will face jail time and BCDs."

A rustling of the mosquito netting turned all eyes towards the doorway. The tall major from the TOC entered and came over to JP. "Sir, Bravo Company's second platoon point man was accidentally shot. There are no choppers on the base to go to the bush to pick him up except yours. Would you consider sending it?"

"Of course," JP said, rising.

"I'll go with it," Brian Knowles said, reaching for a medical rucksack.

"That won't be necessary, Doc. The man is dead."

Brian Knowles sagged. "Who was it?"

"Michael Harrison; he was leading a patrol. He must have become disoriented and walked right into a first platoon ambush."

A long gloomy silence followed. Sergeant Westover finally broke it. "Do you know who shot him, sir?"

'Yes; Billy Neal."

"Oh Christ," groaned Westover. "He's Michael's best friend; he's engaged to marry Michael's sister."

JP moved to the door. "I'll get my chopper crew started."

When JP reached the Huey he saw only a door gunner stretched out across the four canvas seats at the rear bulkhead reading a paperback. "Go round up your crew on the double," JP told him. "I'll explain when everyone is here."

In less than a minute Dan Ranson and his peter pilot hurried towards the Huey with the two door gunners following. "What's up, sir?" Ranson asked.

JP reviewed what he had been told. "The GI needs to be evacuated."

Ranson turned to his peter pilot. "I'll get the coordinates, frequency, and call sign from the TOC. You crank up this beast and be ready to go.

By the time Ranson returned, layers of smoke-like clouds had descended on to the firebase and winds had picked up. It was treacherous flying weather, especially in the mountains. JP took Ranson aside. "The soldier is dead, Dan. Don't push it."

Ranson nodded, tossed him a salute and climbed into his seat. JP stepped back. The engine noise increased. The Huey lifted to a hover, air-taxied to the plateau's edge, hesitated, then plunged out of sight into the valley, taking its noise with it.

For fifteen minutes JP, Brian Knowles, Sergeant Westover, and several enlisted men waited quietly in the mist, each wrapped up in his own thoughts. One of the medics had an unzipped body bag draped over his arm. Sergeant Westover lit a cigarette.

"Does this happen often?" JP asked Westover.

"Only once in the seven months I've been here, Colonel. A short arty round killed two men and wounded three. Shit, sir, there's no worse way to die in war than killed by your buddies."

But accidents happen in war, thought JP. He had seen them in the Pacific and again in Korea. Even he had been accused in Korea of firing his platoon of self-propelled automatic weapons into friendly troops, a charge quickly proven without basis. The troops – green combat engineers – were unaccustomed to flat trajectory automatic weapons firing eight to ten feet over their heads and impacting only a hundred meters in front.

The sound of an approaching Huey stopped conversation. All eyes turned towards the sound. The Huey lifted up from the valley, rose above the plateau, made a half circle and descended towards the landing pad. Westover field stripped what remained of his cigarette.

As the helicopter settled onto the pad JP made out a soldier sitting on the floor, rocking back and forth with the inert form of another soldier in his lap. An M–16 lay on the floor by his right hand. As the turbine's noise subsided the soldier's plaintive sobs were clearly heard. They tore at JP's heart.

The medic with the body bag went to the helicopter's door and started to climb on board. In a flash the soldier had the M–16 pointed at the medic's chest. "Get away from Michael with that fucking body bag."

The medic's eyes widened. "Take it easy, Billy," he said, backing off. Ranson and his peter pilot turned in their seats and stared, but otherwise remained still. The two door gunners calmly uncoupled their M–60s and carried them away.

Captain Knowles moved to the door. "Better let me take a look at Michael, Billy."

"It won't do no good, Doc. He's dead. My best friend is dead and I killed him," he wailed, rocking back and forth, his dead friend's head in his lap. "Oh, Doc," he sobbed, "how can I face his mom and dad; his sister… we were going to get married…"

"They'll understand, Billy, I know they will. It was an accident," Captain Knowles said, moving to climb on board.

Billy Neal swung the M–16 towards the young doctor. "Back off, Doc. Michael's not going anywhere in a body bag."

JP moved next to Brian. He spoke quietly. "Billy, I'm Doctor Franklin, the division surgeon."

Billy Neal stared at him with bloodshot eyes. "So?"

The M–16 muzzle swung to JP.

"This is my chopper, Billy. I'll take Michael back with me to the 96th Evac. They'll take good care of him there, and no body bag until after he reaches Graves Registration. You can come with us if you want."

"I can come with you?"

"You have my word."

"And no body bag?"

"Not until after Michael leaves the hospital."

The M–16 muzzle wavered. Billy turned the rifle around with the butt extended. JP, certain that Billy was going pass the rifle to him, reached for it. Suddenly Billy put the muzzle in his mouth.

"No! Billy, no!" a horrified JP screamed, leaping for the weapon.

The world exploded in a blast of noise and red. Blood, brain, and bone splattered over JP's face and fatigues. For a moment he thought he would pass out. Wiping his face and eyes with his sleeve, he saw blood spurting from a gaping defect in the side of Billy's skull.

368

"Jesus Christ!" Brian Knowles said, climbing on board. "Jesus Christ."

"He's got a chance," JP said, jamming his fingers into the defect. He felt for the spurting vessels with his fingers. Blood continued to pour out the wound, then slowed to an ooze. "Mash his chest, Brian. He's arrested."

"I'm on him," the young battalion surgeon said, thumping the chest and beginning closed chest heart massage.

JP's fingers slipped into a large defect deep at the base of Billy's skull. "Forget it," he said, withdrawing his fingers. "Billy blew away his brain stem."

The medic with the body bag started to climb on board again. JP waved him away.

"I promised Billy that Michael would not go to the 96th in a body bag."

"What about Billy?"

"I guess that includes him. Get them on stretchers and cover them with sheets. I'll take them back with me to the 96th."

"Not Graves Registration?" Sergeant Westover asked.

"I gave my word. They go first to the 96th." JP looked down at his bloody hands and blood-soaked fatigues. "I need to clean up."

"There's soap and cold water in the aid station," Brian Knowles said, his face white as a sheet. "I'll go with you. I need to do the paperwork on Michael and Billy."

"What can I do, Colonel?" Dan Ranson asked.

"Be ready to leave for the 96th as soon as I get back."

Inside the aid station JP removed his fatigue jacket. Using a scrub brush, soap and water, he tried to clean off the blood and brain fragments from the jacket and the insignia on its collar points. He succeeded only in making a bigger mess. 'The hell with it," he finally said. Rolling up the jacket, he tossed it into a nearby trash bin. "I'd never wear it again anyway." Glancing at his blood-soaked T-shirt he pulled it off and threw it in with the jacket, then began scrubbing his face and hands.

"You'll freeze dressed like that in this weather, sir" Sergeant Westover said. "I'll scrounge up a field jacket from supply; about a size thirty-eight?"

JP nodded.

"I don't think we have any lieutenant colonel's insignia. I can ask Colonel Armistead for some of his."

"That's not necessary. He has enough on his mind."

A medic handed JP a clean towel. As he was drying his hands and face Brian Knowles looked up from his paperwork, pen poised. "Colonel, I'm not sure how to record the circumstances of Billy Neal's death."

"I thought it was obvious?"

"That's what I'm getting at, sir. An official conclusion of suicide as the cause of death will have to be line of duty: no. That may cause problems with insurance and other death benefits. Even if it doesn't, it would be emotionally devastating to both families to learn that Billy committed suicide grieving over having killed his best friend."

JP pondered the ramifications of what Captain Knowles had told him. "I understand," he finally said. "As far as I am concerned Billy's death was an accident. He was handing me his rifle when it accidentally discharged. I'll put a note in the record to that effect."

"Thanks, Colonel. It's a small thing, but I think it will mean a lot to both families."

★

Friday, June 19, 1970, 1815 hours

Fifty-five minutes after leaving Firebase Cynthia the Huey touched down on 96th Evac Hospital's helipad. Medics waiting with gurneys pushed them to the Huey's door. The stretchers with Michael Harrison and Billy Neal were slid on the gurneys and rolled into the emergency room. JP followed.

A doctor dressed in fatigues, a major's leaf on his collar and a stethoscope draped around his neck, walked to the gurneys. Lifting the sheet over Michael Harrison, he stared a moment. Replacing the sheet, he went to Billy Neal's gurney, raised the sheet and briefly examined the facial and head wound. Dropping the sheet, he turned around scowling. "What idiot had these dead grunts brought in here?" he demanded.

The four young medics standing by the gurneys turned towards JP. A lieutenant nurse working at a desk stood up and started towards them.

JP was shocked at the major's callous denigrating tone. Walking up to the major, he said, "These men were brave US soldiers killed in the line of duty. You will show them the greatest respect when you speak of them."

The major backed away, his eyes searching JP's borrowed jacket for name and rank. Seeing none, he felt on safe ground to explode. "Goddamn it, you don't bring dead grunts into my emergency room. They're supposed to go directly to Graves Registration. Now I'll have to do all the paperwork."

"I feel for you, Major," JP said contemptuously, handing him manila envelopes with Billy's and Michael's records.

The doctor opened the envelopes, slipped out the records and scanned them. He looked up. "What's this bullshit about Neal's accidental death? The wound is clearly self-inflicted. I'm calling it suicide."

"Look, Major, you weren't there. I was. I had a fatigue jacket sprayed with Billy's blood and brains to prove it. I say it was an accident."

"I don't know who you are," the major snapped, "and frankly I don't give a shit. Neal's death was suicide and that's how it's going down on his records." He shouted to the medics. "Shove these two into body bags and get them over to Graves Registration."

"No," JP said.

"No? What the hell do you mean, no?"

"Before Billy's accident I promised him that Michael would not be put in a body bag until Graves Registration. It may seem a small thing to you, Major, but a promise is a promise. I'm extending it to Billy. I'll escort them over to Graves. I'm asking you again to record Billy's cause of death as an accident. It would mean a great deal to the families of both men."

The major was outraged. "You have a hell of a lot of nerve. You bring two bodies into my ER without body bags. Look at the mess they made; there's blood all over my gurneys. Then you tell me I can't stick them in body bags. Now you want me to change my diagnosis as to Neal's cause of death. You are a menace; I want you out of my emergency room."

The nurse and medics watched in disbelief as the major, who was the same height as JP but thirty pounds heavier, grabbed JP's arm and tried to propel him towards the door. In a blur of movement, JP twisted out of the grasp, locked the major's arm behind his back and slammed his face down on an empty gurney. Blood spurted from the major's nose.

"You miserable scumbag," JP growled. "A hundred of you aren't worth one Billy Neal or Michael Harrison."

"Call the MPs," the man screeched.

"What is going on here?" an authoritative feminine voice demanded. When JP turned to face the speaker she exclaimed, "Oh no, not again."

JP released the major's arm. He had the look of a cat caught with its paw in the goldfish bowl.

Lieutenant Colonel Kristy Goulden, Nurse Corps, US Army, sighed. "JP, how is it every time you come into my ER you create chaos?"

"It's just the marine way, I guess."

"My nose," the major moaned, "it's broken."

JP felt the nose. "No such luck."

The major backed away. "I'm going to press charges against you."

"Charges? What charges, Charles?" Kristy asked.

"I'll tell you. First he brought two dead grunts in here instead of taking them to Graves. He insisted one was an accidental death when it was an obvious suicide. He refused to allow the bodies to be put into body bags and then he assaulted me."

Kristy turned to JP. "Well?"

JP shrugged. "Those are the facts." Then he explained the circumstances of Michael's and Billy's deaths, his promise to Billy, and the desire to keep Billy's death from being officially declared a suicide. "The major disagreed over the circumstances of Billy's death. He then became violent and tried to physically throw me out of the ER. I was forced to defend myself."

Kristy went over to the medics and nurse and talked quietly with them. When she returned she told JP, "Come with me."

He followed her to where the major now sat at a desk pinching his nose.

When the major saw JP approaching he shouted, "Keep that son of a bitch away from me before I hurt him."

Kristy burst out laughing. "Charles, you're lucky this ex-jarhead didn't get mad. Now just shut up and listen. There are five witnesses who will testify as to your disrespect for the dead soldiers, your use of foul and profane language, and that you assaulted Colonel Franklin forcing him to defend himself."

"Colonel? He has no insignia on his collar."

"That's because my fatigue jacket was splattered with Billy Neal's brains and blood," JP interjected. "I had to dispose of the jacket."

Kristy flared at JP. "Be quiet and let me handle this." She turned back to the major.

"Colonel Franklin has written a note that Billy Neal's death was an accident. Do you dispute it?"

"Of course. That's bullshit and he knows it."

"Watch your dirty mouth, Charles, or I'll write you up myself for conduct unbecoming an officer."

"I'm calling it as I see it – a suicide."

"Charles, do you remember a young nurse you sent home last month with the diagnosis of hepatitis. The feedback I got from the States was that she was three months' pregnant. How could you have missed such an obvious diagnosis? I wonder who the father was, or is? And do you recall grabbing me one night in the ER and trying to kiss me when you thought there was no one around... and you a married man. Well, there were two witnesses. They wanted to report the incident to the CO. I told them to forget it. Perhaps I should reconsider and report the incident."

The major's shoulders stumped. He reached for the records. "Since Colonel Franklin was a witness to Neal's death I'll have to accept his version."

"Wise decision, Charles." Kristy said. She turned to JP. 'You look awful. I'll get you some coffee."

"Not now, Kristy. I want to take Billy and Michael over to Graves."

"All right. I'll arrange for an ambulance and go with you."

JP reached over and squeezed Kristy's arm. "Thanks for the help."

"Any time."

"You know, Goulden, you can be a real hard ass when you want."

"Nothing like an ex-marine I know."

Several minutes later an ambulance backed up to the ER doors. JP insisted on helping to carry the stretcher with Michael into the ambulance, then the stretcher with Billy. When he started to climb in the rear of the ambulance Kristy stopped him.

"Don't you want to ride up front?"

JP shook his head.

"In that case I'll ride back there too."

The drive to Graves Registration and the morgue took less than three minutes. Stepping down from the ambulance, JP gazed at the severe barn-like building. "I don't think I want to go in there," he told the medics.

"We can take them from here, sir," one of the medics said.

"I'll go with them," Kristy said. "I know the captain who is the mortician."

In moments Kristy was back. "Now you can ride up front. The medics will ride in back." She climbed into the cab beside the driver. JP climbed in beside her and slammed the door shut.

"Tell the driver how to get to your hooch," Kristy said. "We'll take you home."

"Go out to the perimeter road and head east to the admin pad. I'll guide you from there." He slumped against the door, exhausted. He felt Kristy move against him. Her body was hard and muscular, yet he felt nothing. Inside he was as if dead. He closed his eyes.

Minutes later the ambulance stopped at JP's hooch. When he stepped to the ground Kristy followed and stopped him. "You mustn't hold yourself responsible for

372

Billy's death," she told him.

"If not me, who? The VC? The NVA? Ho Chi Minh? The army? Who, Kristy, who?" He was near tears.

"I'll tell you who, JP, your country; it is responsible."

She put her arms around him and hugged him tightly as a sister would a brother she loved. Releasing him, she climbed back into the ambulance and was gone.

Chapter Forty-Three

Saturday, June 27, 1970, 0540 hours
MARS Network Station, 36th Infantry Division Headquarters, Phong Sahn, RVN

The small waiting room of the MARS station was austerely furnished with six metal folding chairs and a low table covered with a plethora of old magazines, many with missing covers. Two improvised windowless phone booths occupied one side of the room. A small sign with black numbers on a red background identified each booth as No.1 and No.2. Presiding over the waiting room was a young corporal who sat on a tall stool behind a waist-high counter. In a separate room behind the corporal radio operators manned short wave radios.

MARS was the communication offspring of military short wave radio operators in Vietnam and amateur radio operators (HAMs) in the United States. The soldier in Vietnam, through the military operator, established short wave communications with the HAM operator in the States, who then completed the link to the soldier's home as a collect call using commercial phone lines. The long distance charge was for only the distance between the HAM operator's location and the soldier's home. The HAM operators participating in the program were volunteers who never charged a penny for their time or the use of their very expensive equipment.

The MARS network allowed military personnel to talk to their families at a fraction of the cost of a long-distance commercial call from Vietnam. Even if one could have afforded the commercial rates from Vietnam to the US, those phone lines were restricted to official business and therefore not available. The disadvantages of MARS were many. Calls were limited to three minutes once every two weeks. Each party was required to say "Over" when ready for the other party to respond. Transmission and reception were at the mercy of unpredictable atmospheric conditions. Most aggravating of all was the caller's awareness that two or more strangers were monitoring his personal and often intimate conversation.

Lieutenant Colonel JP Franklin, M.D., USA, had accepted these disadvantages and now sat in the MARS station waiting room thumbing through old issues of the *American Rifleman*. He had been sitting there since 0500 hours when the MARS station opened, hoping to make a three-minute call to Kathy. Since leaving Forest Glen and Walter Reed, he and Kathy had written each other every day. Her letters arrived irregularly, often in clusters of three and four. In each letter she wrote she had received no mail from him. She was close to asking friends in the Pentagon to investigate.

JP continued to reassure her in the letters she didn't receive. He considered calling on the MARS network sooner, but contemplation of the procedures involved were intimidating and he readily found ways to avoid using it, preferring instead to put his thoughts on paper in the relaxed environment of his hooch or office. But Kathy's concern over the lack of mail from him was reaching crisis proportions. A MARS call would not only reassure Kathy, but might shed some light on where his letters had gone. That, plus growing homesickness and a longing for Kathy, overcame his reluctance to use the MARS. This morning the alarm went off at 0430 hours. After a shave and a shower, JP got dressed and set off for the small wooden frame building with the thirty-foot tail strange antenna.

The door of booth No.2 abruptly opened and a Pfc exited. He thanked the corporal at the counter and left. The corporal consulted the sign-in clipboard on the counter, then looked up.

"Colonel Franklin, you're next sir; booth two."

Dropping the *American Rifleman* on the table, JP stepped into the closet-like booth. Dim light from a low wattage bulb hanging from the ceiling illuminated the dirty white porous acoustic tile lining the walls and ceiling. A standard black telephone sat on a chest-high shelf. Closing the door gave an illusion of privacy. He picked up the phone.

"Kathy?"

"Stand by, Colonel," the military operator said, "I'm having trouble making contact with the HAM in Dallas."

While waiting JP's phone somehow was patched to the phone in the adjacent booth. He heard a young male voice talking.

"I know it's rough on you, honey, but it's rough on me too. Over."

"When we got married I didn't know it would be like this. I can hardly stand living with your folks. Your mother is driving me up the wall. She thinks I'm an airhead and don't know nothing about being a mother. I have migraine headaches and I'm tired all the time. The kids keep getting sick or into trouble. Terry got sent home from school yesterday for throwing a book at the teacher. Ricky got into a fight in the schoolyard. I have to see the principal tomorrow about both of them. I think he's going to expel Terry. Over."

"Have you seen a doctor about the headaches? Over."

"Last week. He told me it was just nerves." The woman began sobbing. *"You got to come home."*

A male voice interrupted. "Thirty seconds."

The GI caller said, "Honey, honey."

The military operator's voice interrupted again. "She can't hear you. She didn't say over."

The conversation was suddenly cut out of JP's phone. Another military operator's voice said, "Colonel, your party is on the line. Say over when you want the other party to respond."

JP listened for Kathy's voice.

"Go ahead, sir."

"Kathy?"

"Kathy?"

"You must to say 'Over', sir," the military operator reminded.

"Over."

Kathy's soft southern accent came across 10,000 miles. "JP, it's so good to hear your voice."

"Kathy, how is everything going?"

"She can't hear you, sir. She needs to say 'Over' so the HAM operator in Dallas can switch his set from transmit to receive."

"JP, can you hear me? Over."

"I hear you fine, but I'm having trouble with this 'Over' business."

Static.

"Say over, sir."

"Over."

"Were all fine. Jim went to air force ROTC summer camp. He got an hour's dual in a T–37 jet. Paul is at Boy Scout camp and has earned two merit badges already. Frank goes to Cub Scout Camp Wewantcha at Andrews this weekend. That will leave just Nancy and me. We miss our men folk, JP. Over."

"Have you received any mail from me? I've been writing every day. Over."

"None until yesterday. I was getting concerned so I checked with. the post office. They were holding eighteen of your letters because the written address couldn't be read. JP, the post office man asked that you to print our home address from now on so they can read it. Over."

A voice broke in. "Thirty seconds, sir."

"Kathy, my three minutes are almost up. I love you. I miss you and the kids so much. Over."

Kathy's voice came over garbled. "JP, I…"

Static."

"What?" What?"

The military operator broke in. "Sir, she said she loved you."

"Uh, thanks."

"You had about ten seconds left, Colonel, but we lost contact with the HAM. Sorry."

JP hung up, opened the door and headed out to the general's mess for breakfast. The MARS experience had been anything but satisfying. In fact it had been depressing. He couldn't shake the distressing conversation he overheard between the young GI and his wife. The war was taking its toll on military families. He was thankful for Kathy's strength and love.

At the general's mess he ordered his favorite breakfast, creamed beef on toast and two eggs over-medium. As he sipped coffee and read the daily news summary sheet Bruce Collier, the G–3, slipped into the seat facing him.

"Good morning, Doctor."

JP looked up. "Good morning, Bruce."

"I understand you busted the Ho Chi Minh trail the day before yesterday."

"Bad news travels fast."

"You were killed nine times and fell into four punji pits. That's almost a record."

"That was my first trip through the trail. I did better yesterday and passed."

"Just barely."

"Give me a break, Bruce. It's been nearly thirty years since I've done that sort of thing. Did you see my scores with the .45 pistol, M–14 and M–16?"

Collier shrugged. "They were acceptable."

"Acceptable, hell. I shot expert with all of them. I almost max'd with the M–14 using open sights and a scope, with and without a noise-suppressor. I'm definitely sniper material... was sniper material."

★

Saturday, June 27, 0740 hours
Briefing Theater, 36th Infantry Division Headquarters, Phong Sahn, RVN

The morning briefing was unusually boring. All three generals and chief of staff were in a question-asking mode. This led to prolonged complex answers which led to more questions. JP stirred in his seat, aware that the briefing would go on for at least another forty-five minutes. Eager to get to his office and tackle accumulated paperwork, he searched for an escape route. His motives stemmed less from a conscientious desire to deal with administrative responsibilities than from the desire that nothing should interfere with his seventh and eighth hour of dual instruction scheduled in the afternoon with CWO–2 Dan Ranson. Flying, whether fixed or rotary wing, was the ultimate psychotherapeutic activity.

Easing out of his chair, he quietly climbed the aisle stairs to the rear door while enduring the envious, even jealous glances of his contemporaries. Luck was with him; he made it out unnoticed by the powers seated in the swivel leather chairs. As he walked the block to the division surgeon's office he reviewed his previous hour of dual with Ranson two days ago. During the last fifteen minutes of flight he sensed a budding mastery of taking off and hovering. Now he was anxious to prove that it had not been a delusion.

Much of the pleasure of flying the Loach had been eroded by the constant dread that at any moment Ranson would chop power and announce, often with glee, "Engine failure." Then came the sickening drop accompanied by the knowledge that an error in split-second timing would result in death or serious injury. Out of the dozen auto-rotations that JP attempted all would have theoretically ended in fatal crashes had they been done close to the ground. Despite this, JP couldn't wait to get his hands on the Loach's controls.

When he entered into the division surgeon's office the sounds of a half dozen typewriters stopped momentarily. A chorus of "Good morning, Colonel" greeted him, then the typing resumed. Pausing at the coffee pot to fill his mug, he took a sip, then told Tom Moffet and Chris Daniels, "We need a short meeting. Bring your coffee."

He walked into his office, glanced at his desk, then went to the door. "Captain Dryer, you filled my in-box again after I worked so hard yesterday to empty it."

Dryer looked up from his desk. "Yes, sir. I knew you would be disappointed otherwise. There is one worthy item in all that mess."

"And that would be…"

"Orders promoting Captain Nichols to major."

"Captain Dryer, this may be the start of a great day."

When Dryer looked confused JP explained. "I talked to my wife this morning, the first time since leaving to come to Vietnam. Now with Nichols's promotion and flying this afternoon, Vietnam is taking on the aura of the ideal assignment." He failed to mention that tonight's dinner at the general's mess would include lobster followed by a John Wayne western.

Captain Dryer regarded his boss with skepticism. "I don't think I would go that far, sir," he said laconically. "Will you need your jeep this morning?"

JP nodded. "I'll go down to the medical battalion when I finish here. I've got to pin major's leaves on Doug Nichols."

"He certainly deserves it," Dryer said with some envy.

'Your day is coming, Charles," JP assured him.

"By the way, Colonel, do you know anyone in the 1st Marine Division?"

"Why do you ask?"

"There's a letter for you from the 1st Marine Division chaplain."

JP beamed. "I told you it was a great day, Charles. The letter must be from an old marine buddy from World War II. He lost a leg in the war, the good war, that is, for you of the younger generation. He became a priest, then talked his way into active duty as a navy chaplain."

JP rushed back into his office. Sifting through the papers in the in-box he found Mick Icardi's letter.

18 June 1970

Dear JP,

After all these years I am finally going to catch up to you. I tried to call you at Walter Reed last month when I went home on leave from Okinawa. I ended up having a lengthy conversation with Mrs. Hoffberg. She explained you had departed for Vietnam two months early and went to the 36th Infantry Division instead of the 101st. She also told me what a big deal head and neck surgeon you have become.

I joined the 1st Marine Division two days ago as the division chaplain. You will never guess who is here so I will tell you. Captain Mueller, our old CO who once threatened to throw you in the brig, is now a major general and the division commander. Our dear former platoon sergeant, Hal McDougall, is a lieutenant colonel and commands the second battalion. His exec is former Corporal Jim Pinezy, now a major.

When I reported to the division here I told General Mueller you were with the 36th as its division surgeon. He tasked me with getting you here for a reunion of our old defense detachment. I have been authorized to invite you, bribe you, coerce you, or send a Force Recon Team to kidnap you. Take your pick.

I realize you are knee deep in the responsibilities of a new assignment Therefore I will try to convince General Mueller to be reasonable and wait for a slack period when your general can spare you for a couple of days to come down here on TDY.

God works in strange ways. Obviously he meant for us to get together or he wouldn't have started this war. Give my best to Chaplain Deveraux. Keep an eye on him; he is definitely bishop material.

Love in Christ,
Your old marine buddy
Semper fi

Michael J. Icardi, Commander
Chaplain Corps
United States Navy

JP read the letter a second time, and then a third time. He looked up at a knock. "Come on in."

Tom Moffet and Chris Daniels trooped in and sat down. JP indicated Father Icardi's letter and explained his relationship with the priest. "Don't be surprised if one of these days I slip down to Danang," he told them.

"What I want to discuss now is my visit last week to Delta Med at Dog Patch. I was very concerned with what I saw. Sanitary conditions in the mess hall were unsatisfactory; that included cooks and mess personnel. The food was ill-prepared and one level above nauseating. Who knows what pathogens were floating around in it. Discipline and military courtesy was non-existent. The CO, Captain Millbarth, was given a week to get his company in shape. The week was up a couple of days ago.

"I'd like you both to go up there and give that outfit a white-glove going over. Arrange to take one of the senior NCOs or a warrant from food service with you to check food preparation. The mess sergeant is in dire need of a heads up or a reduction in rank. The GIs may end up fragging him if the chow gets any worse. That thought crossed my mind after eating his cold Vienna sausage, asparagus, and mashed potatoes soaked in asparagus water."

"It must have been pretty bad," Tom Moffet said, grinning. Taking his spiral notebook from his fatigue jacket pocket, he began writing.

"While you're up there check on the drinking water, sanitation, waste disposal, and dog population."

"Should we let them know we're coming?" Chris Daniels asked.

"Let it be a surprise," JP said, smiling grimly. "Try to arrive at Delta Med at meal time so you can share their chow. Don't let the CO, Millbarth, talk you into letting the mess sergeant bring your food to the table. Insist on going through the chow line."

"Day after tomorrow okay, Colonel?" Moffet asked. "My jeep won't be out of maintenance until then."

"I'd prefer you not drive up there, Tom. If you were to stop to change a tire or worse, break down, you could be in big trouble. You could find yourself surrounded by a bunch of non-smiling armed peasants in black pajamas. Go ahead and schedule the chopper."

"We used it last week to go out to troops in the bush to collect urine samples."

"Any test results back?"

"Yes, sir. Every unit we tested passed except Bravo and Delta, 2nd/9th. They were eighteen and twenty-six percent negative for Dapsone and Chloroquine/Promiquine."

JP considered the data. The random tests indicated that approximately one-fifth of both companies had not taken anti-malarial pills. The conclusion was inescapable: one-fifth of each company was at risk for incapacitation by malaria. The percentage could be higher since the test subjects were selected at random. Others not tested could be equally negative. Such personnel losses could cripple a unit's combat effectiveness and result in unnecessary casualties, perhaps even defeat in battle.

Tom Moffet continued. "I told both company commanders that those data reflected on their leadership and could put their military careers in jeopardy. Both promised to put pressure on platoon officers, sergeants, and medics. I'm going out there to recheck in a few days."

JP made some notes on a yellow pad, then looked up. "I will hold your report until I've had a chance to counsel the battalion commander. We'll go with the retest results this time, and there had better be no negative urines. Anything else?"

"Yes, sir. The tranquilizer guns arrived with 500 darts," Daniels said."

"How are they working out?"

"Somewhat bizarre. There is such a variation in dog weight that the vet hasn't figured out the proper dosage to tranquilize the dogs and not kill them with overdosage. Some of the dogs might be GI pets, so he's erring on the underdosage side. As a consequence half the dogs shot have run off with the darts still sticking in them."

"Maybe war should be fought with tranquilizer darts rather than bullets. Humans should be treated at least as humanely as wild dogs with rabies." JP laughed at his own joke, then addressed the young sanitary engineer. "How are things at the air terminal?"

Daniels grinned. "I've been out there three times in the last week, Colonel. Every commode tested flushed successfully. Would you like an official report?"

"That won't be necessary."

Captain Dryer came to the door. "Colonel, your jeep is here."

"Thanks, Charles. Anything else to discuss before I leave?" JP asked.

"No, sir," they answered, rising.

JP opened the top desk drawer and took out a box set of subdued gold major's leaves. "I bought these at the PX a week ago for Captain Nichols's promotion." Slipping the leaves into his pocket he dialed the medical battalion headquarters.

"Command Sergeant Major Chessler, sir."

"This is Colonel Franklin. Good morning."

"Good morning to you, sir."

"Is Captain Nichols in the building?"

"Yes, sir. Does the colonel wish to speak to him?"

"Definitely not. I'll be at the battalion in about ten minutes bringing a set of major's leaves and orders promoting him to major. Would you ensure that no one, especially Captain Nichols, leaves battalion headquarters until after he is promoted."

"I understands sir, and I will be discrete. He won't suspect a thing."

After hanging up, JP picked up Doug Nichols's promotion orders and headed for the door. "I'll be at battalion headquarters for the rest of the morning," he told Captain Dryer. "If you need me this afternoon you can reach me through the aviation detachment."

JP's jeep driver sat next to a clerk typist; both were reading paperbacks. "Let's go, Jackson," JP said as he breezed by. Reaching the jeep before his driver, he climbed in, turned on the radio and tuned in the Dust-off frequency. Except for static, all was quiet. Maybe the war had taken a holiday.

Jackson climbed in and started the engine. "Battalion, sir?"

JP nodded.

Jackson shifted gears and let out the clutch. The jeep gathered speed.

They drove in silence for less than a minute before Jackson turned to his commander. "Sir, did you have a chance to look over my request for transfer back to the infantry?"

"Not really, Jackson. I stuffed it my desk drawer hoping you would forget about it."

"Sir, I'm a combat medic," Jackson persisted. "I belong with the troops. The 2nd/45th is my unit and it's going to Qui Tavong. I should be with them."

"You've already been wounded twice, Jackson. Why push your luck?"

"A lot of my buddies have been wounded more times than that, sir, and they are still humping, Nothing personal, sir, but I hate being a jeep driver."

"It's a good thing I'm not sensitive."

Jackson was bright, conscientious, dependable, and sometimes laughed at his jokes, thought JP. He had become almost like a younger brother or a son. He was not the type to hide and quiver with fright in a firefight. When his comrades called, "Medic," Jackson would respond no matter what, unless… JP forced the thought from his mind. He had no right to deny wounded GIs the care of a skilled medic. Damn it all, no one told him being a division surgeon entailed this kind of decision.'

"Sir?" Jackson persisted.

JP caved in. "Okay. I'll approve your request."

Jackson decided to push his luck. "Sir, could you do it this morning?"

"I guess so."

"And could I use the jeep to run the request through DISCOM and division headquarters so I can make the Qui Tavong operation?"

"Be back by noon."

★

Saturday, June 27, 1970, 0915 hours
Headquarters, 36th Medical Battalion, Phong Sahn, RVN

When JP walked into battalion headquarters Sergeant Major Chessler stood up.

"Tenshun."

"As you were," JP called. "Sergeant Major."

"Sir?"

"I'm going to approve Pfc Jackson's request for transfer to the 2nd/45th effective immediately. I can drive the jeep myself until you find a replacement driver."

"Yes, sir. He's been bugging me about the transfer ever since he submitted it last week. He must have gotten to you."

JP nodded. "He did. Give me a minute to approve his request, then round up everyone in headquarters and Alpha and herd them into my office."

At his desk JP opened the top drawer and removed Jackson's transfer request while Jackson hovered expectantly outside his office door. "Get on in here," he told the jeep driver.

Jackson entered the office and stood uneasily at JP's desk.

"You sure this is what you want?" JP asked.

"Yes, sir."

JP scrawled his name on the request. Standing, he handed the paper to the young medic. "Take care of yourself, and that's an order."

"Yes, sir. Thank you, sir."

He came to attention, saluted, did an about face and walked out.

JP stared after him. He shook off an overwhelming feeling of sadness. A jeep started up outside battalion headquarters and drove away, then a knock at the door aborted growing self-recrimination.

Seven officers including Captain Nichols and twelve enlisted men filed into the office and came to attention. Only Captain Nichols did not know the reason for the meeting.

"Please stand at ease," JP said, then fixed his eyes on his executive officer. "Captain Nichols," he said in a loud voice.

"Yes, sir," Nichols answered, snapping to attention.

"How is it you are out of uniform?"

Nichols paled and tried to examine himself. "Sir?"

JP waved some papers. "It says here you are a major, yet what I see on your collar is a set of captain's bars."

Nichols's grin would have faced down a grizzly bear. "I didn't expect this for another two months if at all, Colonel, considering Major Barbour's ER on me."

"Fortunately, Major Barbour's efficiency report on you was lost. A pity," JP said, smiling. "Front and center, Captain Nichols." JP moved around to the front of his desk and stood beside Nichols. He passed some papers to Chessler. "Command Sergeant Major, please read the promotion orders."

"Yes, sir, my honor." Chessler assumed a rigid stance. "Attention to orders.

Everyone in the room came to attention and faced the sergeant major.

"Headquarters, US Army Vietnam, Special Orders 3033, June 20, 1970, paragraph four. By direction of the President..." After a litany of paragraphs, sub-paragraphs, numbers, and letters Chessler came to the important part. "Announcement is made of the promotion of the following named officer, Douglas A. Nichols, Captain, Medical Service Corps, to Major, Medical Service Corps, with date of rank 14 June 1970."

JP turned to Doug Nichols, removed the captain's bars from his right collar and placed it on his desk. Taking the major's leaf from his pocket, he pinned it on Nichol's collar. "That looks good on you, Major. Congratulations." He extended his hand.

"Thank you, sir," Nichols said, then whispered, "for saving my career. He gripped JP's hand.

★

The rest of the morning went fast. The disciplinary residua from Major Barbour's reign of terror had been reduced to two miscreants. Both elected non-judicial punishment under Article 15, the Uniform Code of Military Justice, rather than face court martial. It was a decision that, once made, could not be appealed regardless of the punishment meted out by a commanding officer.

The first case was a corporal who threatened a Pfc with a knife. Although the corporal had no prior offenses, JP reduced him one grade and fined him two-thirds of his pay for three months. The corporal's face reflected shock at the severity of his punishment.

"You have a wife and two children?" JP asked.

"Yes, sir."

'Your punishment will undoubtedly impact their welfare. The loss of two-thirds their income for three months will hurt them much more than you."

"Yes, sir. They're having a tough time as it is. Our parents are helping. I guess they will have to help more."

JP continued. "You can now see that your behavior impacts people important to you even though they may be 10,000 miles away?"

"Yes, sir."

"What if the other man decided to defend himself using a knife or a gun? You could be facing murder charges instead of an Article 15, or you could be dead and he could be facing a murder charge."

"Sir, I was lucky this time. There will never be another, I swear."

"Let's hope so," JP said.

He let the corporal sweat through a minute of silence while he wrote on an official form. Setting the pen down, he looked at the man. "I am going to suspend your sentence."

"You mean I get to keep my stripes... sir?"

"And your pay. However, you mess up during the next three months and the entire sentence will go into effect."

"Yes, sir. Thank you, sir." A beaming corporal saluted, did an about face and marched out.

The second case, a private who had gotten drunk and started a fight, marched in and saluted. JP let him sweat for several minutes, then looked up. "This will be your third Article 15. It will put you in line for a general discharge instead of an honorable discharge. Is that what you want? How are you going to explain it to your kids and grandkids?"

The private paled, as though the ramifications of what he had done finally got through to him.

"When do you DEROS?" JP asked.

"In fifteen days, sir. When I get back to the States I process for discharge."

"Can you stay out of trouble until you leave the battalion?"

"Yes, sir."

"Lucky for you no one was hurt in the fight you started," JP said. "I'm going to drop all the charges against you. Doing so will get you an honorable discharge. Mess up again while you are in this battalion and I'll throw the book at you."

After the private left newly promoted Major Nichols walked in. "I've never seen two GIs walk out of Article 15 hearings with such big smiles," he said, chuckling. "If you have time, Colonel, I have a few things to discuss."

"Now that you're a major I must be more sensitive to what you have to say."

Nichols settled into a metal folding chair and placed a clipboard on JP's desk. Most of what he reviewed from the clip board was of an administrative nature. Nichols had dealt with them so effectively that JP approved his decisions without making any changes.

"The last item, Colonel, is our new S–3 sergeant, Wade Harrel."

'Tell me about him."

Nichols grinned slyly. "He was my platoon sergeant during my first tour in '68 when I was down in the Delta. On this tour he came to the 36th as a platoon sergeant down in the 9th Brigade. After five months he was moved to battalion headquarters as operations sergeant. He was flying a recon in a Loach when he was shot down. The Loach pilot was severely injured and Harrel sustained a broken arm. Because of nightfall, deteriorating weather and NVA closing in they couldn't be rescued. Sergeant Harrel, carrying the injured pilot, somehow slipped past the NVA and humped 16 klicks through the worst kind of jungle. Three days later he stumbled into an ARVN ranger patrol. They called in a Dust-off. Harrel and the pilot were evacuated to the 96th. When I learned he was over there I paid him a visit."

"Why do I suspect a conspiracy?"

"To be honest, sir, I suggested to Sergeant Harrel that he might be interested in filling our vacant operations sergeant's slot. In fact I told him if he didn't apply for it I would break his other arm."

"He sounds like, one hell of an NCO. I'm looking forward to having him in the battalion. When will he report in?"

"He's over at division processing in this morning. He should be here late this afternoon."

"I'll try to get back to meet him after flying with Dan Ranson." He looked at his watch. "How about lunch, Major?"

"Sounds good; fried chicken today."

"My appetite just tripled."

A phone in the outer office rang. A moment later Pfc Samuels knocked. "Colonel, there's a Major Brodie at the 96th Evac for you."

"Excuse me, Doug," JP said. Going behind his desk, he picked up the phone and sat down. "What's up, Kevin?"

384

"Colonel, I need you over here, like right now. I have a challenging case."

JP hesitated. A fried chicken lunch and two hours of dual in the Loach now hung in the balance.

Brodie continued. "A GI took a mortar frag through the upper neck. It chipped the lower margin of both mandibles fracturing them, shattered both submaxillary glands, lingual glands, tongue and floor of mouth. The hypoglossal and lingual nerves were severed on both sides. The tongue is paralyzed. The hyoid bone is pulverized and the epiglottis is hanging by a shred. He can't swallow, talk, or breathe."

"Good God, Kevin, how did he live long enough to reach the hospital?"

"That's a fascinating story. I'll tell it to you when you get here."

"I'm on the way."

Flying and fried chicken were just shifted to the back burner.

★

Saturday, July 27, 1970, 1220 hours
96th Evacuation Hospital, Phong Sahn, RVN

"I've never had any experience repairing bilateral hypoglossal nerve injuries," Kevin Brodie confessed to JP as they scrubbed at the sink outside the operating room.

"You won't be able to say that after today," JP said. "I had seven at Walter Reed. Tell you what, Kevin, let me do the easy side first. Then, having seen how a skilled and talented surgeon manages such wounds, you can do the other side."

Major Brodie chuckled. "And I thought I was a prima donna."

"Now, what's the story on this casualty? Why isn't he dead?"

"You're not going to believe this, Colonel."

"Try me."

"As soon as the GI was hit he went down with acute airway obstruction and profuse bleeding. The combat medic, desperate to get in an airway, attempted an emergency tracheotomy. It was a gutsy decision on his part; he had never done a trach on a human, only on goats. With all the bleeding, the struggling patient, the disturbed anatomy, and an ongoing firefight, the medic became disoriented and realized he could not complete the trach. He screamed for help on the radio."

Brodie rinsed his hands and arms, soaped and began scrubbing again.

"Don't stop now," JP pleaded.

"The battalion surgeon, Jack Wendell, happened to be in the TOC when the medic's call came in. The CO gave him permission to use his Loach. Wendell grabbed his medical rucksack and headed for the coordinates. The LZ was still hot when they arrived but they went in anyway without gunship backup. The Loach took multiple hits; one hit knocked out the radios. The GI was moribund when Jack reached him. With the medic assisting, Jack managed to get a hole in the trachea and kept it open with a spread Kelly clamp. The GI was carried in a sitting position to the Loach and strapped in a rear seat with Jack still keeping the trach hole open using the Kelly. During take-off the Loach took additional hits. The pilot was hit mid-thigh and shoulder."

By now JP was so mesmerized by Brodie's account that he stopped scrubbing to listen.

"They made it here, but since their radios were out they were unable to alert the ER, so no one met them. The pilot, despite his leg and shoulder wounds, helped Jack carry the GI into the ER. Kristy Goulden had heard the Loach land and went to the ER to check on it. She got out a trach tray and helped Jack complete the tracheotomy. By that time the place was flooded with people."

"What a story. How is the Loach pilot?"

"He should be back flying in six to eight weeks."

"I'll want to talk to the chopper pilot before I leave today and get the details."

"Why is that, sir?"

"I'm going to recommend Jack Wendell for the Silver Star and the Loach pilot for the Distinguished Flying Cross. Not only that, but I will ask General Webster to present the awards," JP said, rinsing his hands and arms. "Okay, Doctor Brodie, let's go to work."

Chapter Forty-Four

Sunday, June 28, 1970
96th Evacuation Hospital, Phong Sahn, RVN

The operating rooms had been busy since the previous afternoon, when a platoon of the 178th Brigade stumbled into an NVA company thirty-two kilometers west of Phong Sahn. The encounter was brief but very violent, leaving dead and wounded on both sides. By nightfall the NVA faded away, pursued by Cobra and AC–130 gunships. A steady stream of helicopters delivered US wounded to the 96th Evac and 19th Surg. Lieutenant Colonel JP Franklin, who had gone to the 96th Evac in the afternoon to do one case with Kevin Brodie, operated through the night and early morning. It was his first experience with mass casualties; one in which he learned to hate the sound of an incoming helicopter.

At dawn that morning, elements of two battalions of the 174th Brigade and a regiment of the 1st ARVN Division began a combat assault on the airstrip at Qui Tavong, the abandoned special forces base on the Laotian border. Swarms of Cobra gunships prepped the area around the airstrip with mini-guns and rockets, then began search and destroy missions. Troop-carrying Hueys touched down briefly to disgorge heavily armed infantry. While the infantry secured the airstrip and then extended the defensive perimeters, C–47 helicopters began landing personnel, bulldozers, graders, supplies, 105 mm howitzers and mortars. Engineers began clearing mines and filling bomb craters in the strip. A tactical operations center was set up and communications established with Dog Patch and Phong Sahn. The lack of immediate NVA response was a measure of their complete surprise.

Lieutenant Colonel JP Franklin had planned to fly out to Qui Tavong early as an observer, but the casualties kept coming. Each time he was about to break loose from the 96th to go out to Qui Tavong, another casualty was brought in for him to manage. There were so many with facial and neck wounds that he and Kevin Brodie operated in separate rooms. By 0400 hours the helicopters had stopped coming, and by 0830 hours JP was able to drop out. He headed for the doctors' dressing room.

JP learned early to keep a set of clean fatigues, underwear, socks, shaving gear and toilet articles in his locker at the 96th. They were a blessing this morning. Dressed in clean fatigues after a shave and a shower, he felt reasonably human. Famished, he headed for the hospital mess hall. Minutes later, his tray loaded with dehydrated eggs, bacon, toast, cereal, milk, and a mug of coffee, he found a vacant table in the officers' section. He was in no mood for idle conversation. Easing down, he began to eat mechanically, washing the food down with coffee, oblivious to the half dozen conversations going on around him and fighting off sleep.

"How about some company?" Kristy Goulden said, setting her tray opposite his and sitting down facing him.

JP looked up, waved his fork at her, and resumed eating.

"I hear the 96th got their money's worth out of you," Kristy said.

"Yeah, and then they made me pay for my breakfast."

Kristy examined the tray loaded with food. "You seem to have gotten your money's worth."

"I'm not sure when I'll get to eat next."

"What's that supposed to mean?"

"My chopper's going to pick me up here…" he looked at his watch, "in thirty minutes. After I stop at my hooch to pick up a weapon and flight helmet I'm heading out to Qui Tavong."

"That's where my husband was shot down," Kristy said. "What's going on out there?"

"The 36th is in the process of assaulting the airstrip as we speak."

"That will mean more casualties."

"I'm afraid so."

"JP, are there plans to search for POWs in the area?" Kristy's eyes were pleading.

"I can't discuss anything like that. Please don't ask any more questions."

"Why not? Why can't I ask if anyone is going to try to rescue my husband from a POW camp? How long does he have to be out there chained like an animal before someone tries to free him?"

JP looked around. People at the adjacent table had heard. "Kristy, for God's sake, be quiet."

"Damn it, JP, I won't be quiet. I love my husband. Even though he's less than a hundred miles from here I haven't been able to get a bit of information about him from the people he was trying to protect when he was shot down. Nobody cares what happens to him. You're my friend and even you don't care."

"Kristy, if you don't shut your mouth you will get a bunch of good people killed." JP was seething and his voice cut like a whip.

"What do you mean?"

"This hospital is full of Vietnamese workers from Nghia Lam; some are VC sympathizers, some may even be VC. It's hard to tell; they all look alike. They keep their ears open for the kind of stuff you have just been shouting."

Kristy's shoulders slumped. "Can't you tell me anything, anything at all?"

JP shook his head.

"Can't or you won't?"

JP shrugged but didn't answer. Kristy's agony was tearing him up inside.

"You're just like the others fighting this stupid macho war."

She burst into tears, abruptly pushed away from the table, grabbed her tray and left.

★

Sunday, June 28, 1970, 1040 hours
Ninety-six Kilometers East of Qui Tavong at 2,000 Feet

As soon as JP had belted himself into the helicopter at Phong Sahn he began to drift to sleep. Dan Ranson's voice came through his headset.

"Tough night, sir?"

"That's putting it mildly, Mr. Ranson."

"I heard there were some real bad cases."

"The worst was a multiple injury case, a nineteen-year-old hit by an RPG. He was a joint effort; just about every specialty was involved in his surgery. The neurosurgeon removed a frag from the brain with me helping. Then he helped me repair a transected trachea, esophagus and smashed larynx. At the same time the general surgeons resected eight feet of small bowel, removed the spleen, part of the liver, and one kidney. While this was going on the orthopods amputated both legs and an arm."

"Good God, sir… is he going to make it?"

"It's doubtful, Dan. When I left the hospital he was on his thirty-fifth unit of blood. He was bleeding from all his wounds, his BP was in and out of shock, his one kidney had quit putting out urine, and he was showing multiple cardiac arrhythmias. Other than that, the poor bastard is in good shape," JP said bitterly.

Ranson remained quiet for several minutes. The helicopter droned on. Ranson came back on the intercom. "Did you to get anything to eat, Colonel? We have C-rats on board."

"I managed to get breakfast at the 96th."

He didn't mention he lost his appetite after the flare-up with Kristy and dumped most of his breakfast in the garbage can. "I'm going to sack out, Dan. Wake me when we're close to Qui Tavong." He took off his helmet and set it on the seat beside him. Leaning back against the bulkhead, he closed his eyes. The recurring image of Kristy's tears nagged at him, bringing tears to his own eyes and deep feelings of guilt. He could have hinted to Kristy in so many words of the impending search for POW camps in the Qui Tavong area. He could have given her a glimmer of hope. After all, he owed her his life.

But Bruce Collier had told him that too many POW rescue missions had been compromised because of security leaks. Not only had the missions failed, but highly trained, dedicated personnel were lost. As much as he might have wanted he could not divulge anything that could remotely jeopardize a POW rescue effort. His feelings for Kristy were secondary. He would bear his guilt as just another burden of the war. Hopefully, one day soon Kristy would understand.

★

JP felt his arm shaken. Opening his eyes, he saw the door gunner pointing to the helmet on the seat. Slipping the helmet over his head, he heard Dan Ranson's voice.

"Colonel, we're five minutes out from Qui Tavong."

JP burped the transmit button twice, then gazed out the door at the many 5,000-

and 6,000-foot mountain peaks set in a green-purple range of lesser mountains that stretched west to the horizon. He squeezed the mike button. "Mr. Ranson, have you or your peter pilot ever been out here?"

"Negative, sir."

"How will you know if we have crossed into Laos?"

"According to a Goshawk I talked to in the club, the ground fire in Laos is much more intense."

"I'm sorry I asked."

JP glanced at his watch; it was almost noon. Perhaps it was a good thing that his visit to Qui Tavong had been delayed by three hours. Captain Neville, the battalion surgeon in charge of the aid station, was capable and experienced, as was his NCO. They needed time to organize and begin construction of the aid station. The last thing they needed was a light colonel who knew little about building aid stations looking over their shoulders.

The engine sounds diminished as the pilot reduced power and lowered the nose into a sharp descent. Ranson reported his position to the airstrip control at Qui Tavong and requested landing instructions. "We would like to set down at the battalion aid station."

"I have no idea where that is," the tower operator reported. "Set down wherever you want. Field elevation is 1,270 feet. Winds out of eight at twelve. Altimeter is 29.9. Two Chinook cargo helicopters just departed to the south-east. You will have to make your approach from the south-east as well. Exercise caution. Flights from the other quadrants reported taking heavy ground fire eight klicks out."

Seconds later the Huey skimmed over lush, green tree tops. Amidst the mountains and rolling hills an oasis of an extensive flat area with a runway came into view. The Huey slowed and continued to descend, passing over bulldozers, trucks, and graders moving about on the runway. Near the north-east end of the runway lay the burnt hulk of a C–130 Hercules cargo plane, a grave for the hundred souls killed when it was shot down two years ago. Graves registration personnel were already at the site, processing remains.

"I don't see an aid station, Colonel," Ranson reported.

"How about a white flag with a red cross?" JP suggested.

"No, sir. I do see a couple of parked Dust-offs."

"Go for them."

As the Huey neared the Dust-offs JP saw three men in fatigues standing with their backs to the clouds of red dust raised by the settling helicopter. The engine whined down and the rotor blades slowed. JP removed his helmet and moved up to the flight deck. "When is the latest we should head back to Phong Sahn?" he asked Dan Ranson.

"About 1900 hours, sir. It's not healthy to fly around Vietnam at night, especially this part."

"Understand," JP said. Grabbing his rucksack, he climbed to the ground and slapped his fatigue cap on his head. Adjusting the .45 pistol and canteen to comfortable positions on his hips, he headed for the three men who now stood watching him approach.

He scowled as he passed an open tarp on the ground piled high with medical supplies. Much of the supplies were covered by a thin layer of red dust. Four stretchers lay on the ground, their canvas portions also loaded with medical supplies. Two metal sawhorses were set up in the open, each with a stretcher. There was no evidence of an aid station under construction. For some reason six hours had been lost.

One of the three figures detached himself from the other two and walked towards JP. "Sir, can I help you?" he asked without saluting.

JP studied the man's young innocent face, the improperly positioned captain's bars and caduceus on his collar, and the brand new fatigues. "Who are you?"

"Captain Mann, the battalion surgeon."

"The pediatrician who just came in country?"

Mann blushed. "Yes, sir. I reported in to Charlie Med last night."

"Where is Captain Neville and his NCO?"

"Captain Neville left for the States yesterday on emergency leave. His wife, who was eight months pregnant, was in an auto accident. She had an emergency hysterectomy for a ruptured uterus and developed a severe post-partum sepsis."

"Were they able to save the baby?"

"Yes, sir. The baby is doing fine."

"What about Neville's NCO? Where is he?"

"He's in the 96th Evac with acute hepatitis."

"Talk about bad timing," JP said, removing his fatigue cap. Wiping his brow, he replaced the cap. "I'm Colonel Franklin, the division surgeon.

"Yes, sir, I figured that."

"Let's take a walk, Captain. We need to talk."

After they had gone a short distance Mann blurted, "Sir, I sure am glad to see you."

"That demonstrates excellent judgment, Captain. Do you have a first name?"

"Yes, sir. It's Brent."

"Okay, Brent, let's get back to my original question. What are you doing out here?"

"Well, sir, when I reported to D Company yesterday it was just after Captain Millbarth had been informed that Captain Nevile would be going on emergency leave and his sergeant was in the hospital with hepatitis. Captain Millbarth told me he didn't have any choice but to send me out here as Neville's replacement."

"Was there any discussion about your lack of surgical experience and the loss of a critical NCO?"

"Yes, sir. I told Captain Millbarth that my surgical inexperience made me dangerous treating casualties. He said not to worry, that I was intelligent and would learn fast. He gave me a manual on emergency surgical procedures."

"I see," JP said. His day was not going well at all. "Do you know if Captain Millbarth intends to send a replacement for the NCO in the hospital?'

"No sir, he doesn't. He said I would have to get along with the two medics he was sending with me."

JP glanced at the two teenagers standing near the medical supplies. They looked overwhelmed.

"Has Captain Millbarth been out here today?"

"In a way, sir."

"What does that mean?"

"He came out with me on the chopper, then went right back."

"Did he get out of the chopper?"

"Only to run to another chopper that was leaving to go back to Dog Patch."

Outwardly calm, JP silently endured his growing anger at fate and especially at Captain Millbarth. "If the NVA hit this place in the next twenty-four hours we will be in deep trouble," he told the young doctor. "I hope you won't take what I say next personally, but sending you out here was a major lapse of judgment."

"Colonel, I couldn't agree with you more. Where do we go from here?"

"As a commander I need to make some decisions, then communicate my decisions to those I trust to implement them. You can put that in your book of pearls in case some day you become a commander."

"Yes, sir," Captain Mann answered, not sure whether JP was kidding or was serious.

"Do you happen to know where communications is?"

"Yes, sir. It's next to the TOC." He pointed to a cluster of antennae by a tent several hundred feet away.

"While I flood the atmosphere with radio transmissions, see if you can locate a flat area suitable for an aid station. Nearby mounds or berms that offer protection from incoming fire would be a plus."

"Is there anything else I could do, Colonel?"

"Yes. Pray that the NVA were caught with their pants down today."

★

Walking towards the commo tent, JP saw half a dozen GIs stripped to the waist, filling and stacking sandbags around the outside of the tent. Inside, a sergeant supervised three radio operators sitting at banks of radios on wooden tables. The hum of a diesel-powered generator came from some distance away.

"Can I help you, Colonel?" the sergeant asked.

"I hope so, Sergeant. I'm Colonel Franklin, the division surgeon. I need to talk to my med battalion at Phong Sahn."

"Sir, I can authorize only urgent communications."

"What I have to communicate is urgent. It will become very urgent if we start taking casualties."

The sergeant thought for a moment, then tapped one of the radio operators on the shoulder. "Give the colonel what he wants."

"Thanks, Sarge." JP handed a card with his medical battalion frequency and call sign to the radio operator. "I need to talk to Mac Five. I'm Mac Six."

The RTO looked at JP, curious. "That's a strange call sign, sir. I've never heard it before."

JP grinned. "I made it up last week. It's short for Mac the Knife."

"Oh." The operator turned to his radio. Several minutes later he stood and handed JP his headset with its boom mike. "Press the button on the cord to transmit, sir."

JP sat down and adjusted the headset over his ears. "This sure beats MARS," he said, then squeezed the transmit button. "This is Mac Six. Over."

"Mac Five. Go."

JP described the predicament at Qui Tavong to Major Nichols, then asked, "Has Sergeant Harrel reported for duty? Over."

"Affirmative. He standing right next to me. Over."

"Good. Get together with him and load two Conexes with medical supplies. Be sure to include a fridge, generator for the fridge, lights, wiring, low-titer O-negative blood, 1000 sandbags, six man-sized shovels, four Coleman lanterns, germicidal solution, an autoclave, and anything else you and Sergeant Harrel consider important for an aid station. Call the aviation detachment and request two Chinooks to fly the Conexes out here at first light tomorrow. If you have trouble getting the Chinooks insist on talking to Colonel Bruteau or his exec. Since I haven't bent one of their choppers yet you can use my name liberally. Over."

"Copy; two Conexes and supplies at first light. Anything else? Over."

"I'm just getting started, Mac Five. Sergeant Harrel is to accompany the supplies out here and supervise construction of the aid station. He should plan on being here until a suitable replacement can be found. Next item: round up two medics and send them out with Sergeant Harrel. One of them should be experienced. Over."

"Roger, Sergeant Harrel and two more medics. Over."

"Call Captain Millbarth at Delta Med. Tell him you are passing on a direct order from me. My chopper will stop by in the morning to pick up Captain Cruessi and bring him here. He should plan on being here for three weeks. Captain Mann, who is out here now, will go to the 96th Evac tomorrow for three weeks' OJT, then return to replace Cruessi. Better let Colonel Marchenko know that Mann is coming. You can expect Millbarth to gripe about being shorthanded. Tell him he can rotate the reserve battalion surgeon through Delta Med. If Delta gets overloaded Millbarth is authorized to shift casualties to Alpha and Charlie in Phong Sahn or the 96th Evac and 19th Surg. Over."

"Wilco, sir. Anything else? Over."

"I will spend tonight out here and possibly tomorrow night. Call the chief of staff's office and let him know what's going on." He paused to review in his mind if he had missed anything and decided he had not. "That's it from here. Anything for me? Over."

"Four letters from your wife. I'll send them with Sergeant Harrel. Over."

"Bless you. Mac Six out."

JP pulled off the headset and placed it on the table with the radio. Standing, he asked the operator, "How is it that transmission and reception are so clear and without static despite all the mountains around us?"

"There's an air force plane cruising above us. We transmit to it and it relays the transmissions."

JP thanked the operator and the sergeant, then walked to his helicopter. Dan Ranson and the crew chief door gunner were on the cabin roof examining the rotor shaft. "Missing something?" he called out.

"No, sir. Just checking the Jesus nut."

"Dan, I'm staying here tonight. You can go back whenever you're ready. In the morning pick up Captain Cruessi at Delta Med and bring him out here."

"Problems, sir?"

"You might say, or better, I'm trying to prevent problems."

"Need any C-rats, Colonel?"

"I brought some in my rucksack."

"Yes, sir."

"Since you are going back empty, check with the tower before you leave for anyone needing a lift to Phong Sahn."

"Wilco, Colonel, I hate to keep leaving you in these situations."

"I'm getting used to it, Dan. Have a safe flight back."

★

"What do you think of my battalion aid station site, Colonel?" Brent Mann asked when JP returned.

JP surveyed the tennis court-sized area. A berm twelve feet long and three feet tall partially protected the side of the aid station that would face the perimeter. The remainder of the terrain was mildly raised in the other three quadrants to provide lesser protection. "I'm impressed. We'll try to build you a little Walter Reed."

"I thought I would be building it, sir."

JP shook his head. "I have other plans for you, Brent. Tomorrow you will go to the 96th Evac for three weeks' OJT in the emergency room. After that you will return out here to remain until the end of the Qui Tavong operation, which should be some time in September."

"I was hoping to spend time in a hospital, but that's not exactly what I had in mind."

"I don't think you will see much in the way of pediatrics except for the occasional wounded child. You can expect to be working day and night with no time off. If there is nothing going on in the ER you will scrub in on surgery. If there's any spare time you will spend it making rounds on the surgical wards."

"And I thought I was through with my internship."

"Think of it this way. You have a three-week rotation on the best trauma service in the world. For now, let's get on the physical side of military medicine."

"Where do we start?"

"We start by digging, Captain Mann. We need a hole large enough to partially bury a three-car garage."

Mann reached for an entrenching tool.

JP stared at the young doctor a moment, then shook his head. "Hold off using that thing. I'm going to see if I can capture one of the bulldozers down on the strip."

★

Lieutenant Colonel JP Franklin walked to the edge of the runway and observed the trucks, scrapers, and bulldozers improving the strip. Much as a tiger would stalk an impala, he remained immobile, seeking out the closest dozer. One just finished shoving dirt into a bomb crater and started moving towards him. He waited until it was almost past, then ran out in front of its blade, waving vigorously. His timing was impeccable. The dozer clanked to a stop, its throbbing, diesel polluting the clean Vietnamese air. The driver, who was probably in his late teens, sat high on his throne regarding JP with curiosity.

JP climbed up on the dozer's tread. When the driver glimpsed the lieutenant colonel's leaf on JP's collar he killed the dozer's engine and saluted. "Good afternoon, sir. Pfc Wurton."

"Private First Class Wurton," JP began in his best fatherly tone, "I'm Colonel Franklin, the division surgeon."

"Yes, sir. How can I be of service to the colonel?"

"Now that is a fine attitude, Wurton. You are definitely OCS material."

"Sir, why do I get the idea you want to borrow my dozer?"

"Only if you come with it. The truth is, Pfc Wurton, I am in desperate need of about an hour of dozer time to excavate ground for a medical aid station. I want to get the station built before we start taking casualties."

Wurton looked at his wristwatch. "I finished my runway job thirty minutes ahead of schedule and I have a half hour for lunch coming up. Yes, sir, I can do it. Just show me where."

JP climbed into the seat next to Wurton and pointed.

Wurton cranked the big diesel and the dozer charged ahead. The smell of diesel fumes, the lurching of the dozer, and the clanking of its treads brought to JP memories of a day twenty-seven years ago. He was a teenage marine riding shotgun on a bulldozer working on an airstrip on a Pacific island. Three of his close friends were riding other dozers on the strip. He saw one of his friends shot by a Japanese sniper. Driven by hate and revenge, he tracked down the sniper and killed him.

Wurton slowed the dozer to a stop by the medical supplies. "Where do you want me to start, sir?"

"What? Oh, sorry, Wurton, I was just thinking how little progress the world has made in twenty-seven years," JP said, returning to reality. "I'll get off here and walk the outline. Start any time."

★

In less than fifty minutes Wurton had excavated a wide deep pit large enough to accommodate a three-car garage and then some. Over the noise of the idling diesel he shouted, "Anything else I can do for you, Colonel?"

Climbing up on the tread, JP took a pen and small notebook from his pocket. "I need your full name, serial number and unit. I'm going to send a letter of thanks through channels to your CO."

"Aw, sir, you don't have to do that." Wurton's face, already red from the sun, became even redder.

"Yes, I do. It would have taken to the war's end for me and my crew to dig something as large as that with entrenching tools." After getting Wurton's information, JP jumped to the ground. "Thanks again," he shouted. Wurton saluted. The huge diesel engine roared, and the dozer lurched forward.

Removing his pistol belt with its holstered pistol and canteen, JP placed it carefully on the tarp with the medical supplies. Then he peeled off his fatigue jacket and undershirt. Folding each neatly, he set them on the tarp beside the pistol belt. Naked to the waist, he picked up an entrenching tool and waved it at Captain Mann. "Grab one of these and follow me. Your men too. We need to fine-tune this hole in the ground."

Two hours later, JP, his hair matted, sweat pouring off his face and bare chest, stopped shoveling and went over to his canteen. Pulling it out of the canteen cover, he unscrewed the cap and took several swallows of warm water. He glanced at the Brett Mann, bare to the waist, digging like a beaver. It was probably the hardest work the young doctor had done in years.

A major with engineer insignia on his collar appeared from over a berm and walked over to Brett Mann. "Who the hell is in charge of this detail," he demanded, "and you stand at attention when addressed by an officer."

Mann turned pale despite the sun and heat. He nodded meekly towards JP.

The major strode over and stood in front of JP. "Are you in charge of this detail?"

JP looked the major in the eyes, smiled, then took another swig from his canteen before answering. "I guess you could say that."

"You guess? Hell, man, don't you know? Never mind. Did you commandeer one of my dozers to excavate that ditch?" he asked, pointing to the large pit in the ground.

"I wouldn't go so far as to say 'commandeer'," JP said. "Is there a problem?"

"You're goddamn right there is a problem, soldier. I'm responsible for dozens of engineering projects here. Dozer time is valuable. I'm the one who allocates their use."

"Major, I apologize and take full responsibility. I should have gotten your permission, but we were running out of time, the dozer was in the area, and the operator was kind enough to help us out. If there is blame it should fall on me."

JP took another swallow from his canteen.

"Damn it, stand at attention when I'm talking to you, soldier. This entire work detail has shown little discipline and you have bordered insubordination."

"Really?"

"Soldier, I want your name, unit, and the name of your commanding officer."

JP slowly screwed the cap back on his canteen. "My name, Major, is JP Franklin. My unit is the 36th Medical Battalion, and…" He turned his back on the major, set the canteen down by his pistol belt and picked up his fatigue jacket. Slipping it on, he faced the major again. "The commanding officer of the 36th Medical Battalion is," he looked down at his name tag, "what do you know, Lieutenant Colonel JP Franklin."

The major took one look at the lieutenant colonel's leaf pinned to JP's right collar and the airborne wings on his left breast, swallowed hard, and turned red.

"Now, what was it you were saying, Major?" JP asked in a benign tone.

A subdued major came to attention and saluted. "Sir, Major Jake Hawkins, Corps of Engineers, Exec, 36th Engineer Battalion. Sir, I have really jammed my foot in my mouth."

"Relax, Major," JP said, grinning and offering his hand. "Lieutenant colonels don't ordinarily dig ditches. You had no way of knowing my rank with my jacket folded on the tarp. I may have even baited you a bit. But I think you should apologize to the battalion surgeon, Captain Mann. He's the one whose heels you locked. You are in risky business out here, Major, and the battalion surgeon is the last person you want pissed off at you." He waved for Brent Mann to come over and introduced him to Major Hawkins. They shook hands.

Major Hawkins eyed the hole in the ground left by the bulldozer and two hours of shoveling. He shook his head. "May I ask, sir, what exactly you are trying to do here?"

"Getting a site ready to construct a battalion aid station," JP explained. "We have Chinooks due tomorrow morning with Conexes full of medical supplies."

The major glanced at his watch. "Tell you what, Colonel, let me get some men, equipment, and an officer over here to give you a hand."

Chapter Forty-Five

The main force NVA in the Qui Tavong area had been stunned by the sudden reoccupation of the airstrip by US and ARVN Forces four days ago. Before they could react, helicopter scouts, Cobra and AC–130 gunships were beating up what NVA units they found. Mohawk aircraft fitted with classified computerized equipment to sniff out Communist urine, detect body and campfire heat, prowled the air around Qui Tavong while US and ARVN troops aggressively patrolled the jungle. Air force, navy, and marine fighter bombers, guided by the ubiquitous FACs flying OV–10s, discouraged the enemy from massing its troops. Fighting was limited to small units clashing violently.

The first casualties had arrived at dusk on the first day when the aid station was still a hole in the ground. A GI on a patrol had triggered a mine, killing himself and severely wounding three comrades. JP, Brent Mann and the medics worked furiously out in the open by flashlight to save the wounded. When the three left aboard the backhaul Dust-off for the fifty-five-minute flight to Phong Sahn they were still alive. Bleeding had been controlled and Ringer's lactate flowed into their veins. Their chances of surviving the flight to Phong Sahn would have been infinitely better had they been given O-negative blood, but there was none to give.

Between casualties, JP, Brent Mann, the medics, and even the elite helicopter crews filled and stacked sandbags. Major Jake Hawkins and his crew of engineers worked through the night to complete construction of the aid station. JP repeatedly berated himself for being lulled into a sense of security by Captain Millbarth's reassuring words. He swore he would never take anything for granted again in a combat area. Had he learned anything at all as a lieutenant in Korea?

The next morning Dan Ranson's helicopter settled down beside the nearly finished aid station. JP welcomed Captain Dominic Cruessi, the incoming battalion surgeon, then shook hands with a departing Captain Brent Mann. JP had been impressed with Mann's intuitive responses dealing with the casualties. He had shown excellent judgment, manual dexterity, and was a rapid learner. He had shouted to Mann over the helicopter's noise, "As a pediatrician you make one hell of a surgeon."

The young doctor had grinned, saluted, and climbed aboard the helicopter. It powered up, lifted to a hover and was soon out of sight. Fifteen minutes later a Chinook helicopter landed with Sergeant Harrel, two medics, and a Conex filled with medical supplies. Sergeant Harrel turned out to be a powerhouse of organized energy. By the time JP left for Phong Sahn on the afternoon of the second day, the aid station was complete and functioning as a mini clearing company with Captain Dominic Cruessi in charge.

Now, four days after D-day, JP was at his desk in the division surgeon's office scanning the casualty report which summarized the first three days of the Qui Tavong operation. The US had lost seven killed and nineteen wounded, primarily from mines and booby traps. The NVA had suffered 106 confirmed killed and three captured. Statistically, the US was winning the war of attrition. That should be of some comfort to the next of kin of the young GIs killed.

Initialing the report, he tossed it into his out-box, and pondered the three nagging problems that hung on him like persistent toothaches. The most serious was Captain Millbarth, the Delta Med commander. The man was a coward, not fit to command. Yet if he were relieved there would be no immediate replacement. JP had no choice but to hang on to Millbarth until Brent Mann finished his three weeks' OJT at the 96th Evac and returned to Qui Tavong to relieve Dom Cruessi. Cruessi would then return to Delta Company to assume command. At that time Millbarth would become history. It was a game of musical chairs, a game JP despised.

The second problem was the Delta Med's first sergeant. Sergeant Major Chessler considered him an ineffective NCO, a poor leader for whom the enlisted men held no respect. He spent most of his time in the orderly room or his bunkered hooch, living in terror of being fragged. Little wonder the enlisted men in Delta Med did not salute officers and even addressed them by their first names.

The third problem was the Delta Med mess sergeant. A lazy individual and a poor cook by any standards, he was despised by the enlisted men. He allowed his subordinates to run the mess while he stayed in his cubby hole office, wrote letters and read paperbacks. Considering the quality of the chow it was a miracle he had not been fragged already. He had to go.

Getting to his feet, JP picked up his coffee mug and walked into the outer office to the desk of Master Sergeant Mickey Jordan. An NCO of the old school, Jordan had worldwide connections with just about every senior NCO in all four services and possibly even in some foreign services. If ever a position were to be created as an enlisted equivalent to the chairman of the joint chiefs, Master Sergeant Mickey Jordan would be JP's choice to fill it.

Jordan started to rise but JP waved him down, set his mug on his desk and pulled up a metal chair. "Sergeant Jordan, we need to talk."

"Yes, sir. This must be about Delta Med."

"How did you know?"

"I've been hearing bad things about Delta Med for the past two months, mostly about the lax discipline and lousy food. I tried to get Colonel Diblasio interested, but he kept telling me not to worry, that things would work themselves out." Jordan grinned. "After I heard how you managed your exec at the med battalion the first time you met him, I figured it wouldn't take long for you to get on Delta Med's case."

"It's taken me longer than it should have, Sarge. Now I'm stuck for three more weeks with a company commander I want relieved. And there are two senior NCOs up there who should be relieved."

"Yes, sir, I know about them." Master Sergeant Jordan reached into the top middle drawer of his desk, removed two manila folders, and passed them to JP. "Colonel, those are the records of two NCOs in the division who were just promoted. They now have too much rank to stay in their current assignments and they need new homes."

JP picked up the folders but didn't open them. "You know these men?"

"I know them well. Sergeant Hansel was an outstanding platoon sergeant in the 101st his last tour in '67. He was wounded twice, both times when he carried casualties out the line of fire. He won the Silver Star, made sergeant first class in '68, and was an instructor at Ranger School for two years. He would be a no-nonsense role model for the young troopers and would do a good job for you at Delta Med as first sergeant."

"Sounds like our man," JP said. "What about the replacement for the mess sergeant?" JP glanced at the name on the second chart. "Sergeant Grendell."

"Grendell is a master chef, sir, not a mess sergeant. He graduated at the top of his class at Cooks and Bakers school. I met him when he was the acting mess sergeant at my last outfit. The chow was so good that guys were fighting to get transferred into my outfit. A half dozen officers' messes are after Sergeant Grendell, but frankly, sir, he doesn't care much for officers… no offense intended, Colonel."

JP smiled. "None taken, Sergeant. When can those two be on board at Delta Med?"

"Hansel by tomorrow afternoon; Grendell in three days."

JP stood up. "Make it happen, Sergeant."

"Aye, aye, sir."

JP studied Jordan suspiciously. "Were you ever in the navy, Master Sergeant Jordan?"

Jordan made a face. "No way, sir. I served a hitch in the Marine Corps during the war. When my four years were up I decided the Marine Corps way of life was hazardous to my health, so I enlisted in the army. By the time I went through jump school, rangers, special forces, Korea, and two Vietnam tours I realized I had made a big mistake. It was too late to go back to the Corps."

"You old jarhead," JP said, sticking out his hand. "Platoon 445, Parris Island, June '43"

"Semper Fi, sir, Platoon 326, P1, August '42."

★

The voice on the phone sounded annoyed. "This is Captain Millbarth. What is it you want?"

Just the tone of Millbarth's voice pissed off JP. "It's not what I want, Captain, it's what I, as your commander, am about to order you to do."

"And what might that be?"

JP was having trouble controlling his anger. "I am ordering you to relieve your first sergeant and your mess sergeant."

"What? You want me to do what? I won't do that. Those are good men and I will defend them."

"That is very commendable, Captain. I just wish your judgment could have matched your loyalty to your men.

400

"You will reconsider?"

"I will not. In case it has slipped your mind, Captain, permit me to remind you. I am your commanding officer. Not only can I order you to relieve your first sergeant and mess sergeant, I have done it."

"I protest."

"Protest all you want, Millbarth. Orders have already been cut at battalion. The first sergeant's replacement will arrive tomorrow afternoon and the mess sergeant's replacement will arrive in three days. Their records will be sent to you by the afternoon courier."

"I vehemently disagree with those decisions."

"You are free to disagree with my decisions, Captain Millbarth, just make damn sure you comply with them. You can tell your first sergeant and mess sergeant they are lucky they are not meeting an evaluation board. And I remind you again, Captain Millbarth, you will address me as colonel or sir."

After an inordinate delay Millbarth answered, "Yes, sir, but I'm putting you on notice. I will discuss this action with the brigade commander and the IG."

"Your brigade commander was informed of my intended action and concurred. As for the IG, you are always free to seek his counsel. I will expect you to call this headquarters by 1700 hours today to report you have complied with my orders. If you fail to do so you should consider yourself under arrest pending charges of willful disobedience."

JP slammed the phone into its cradle. *That miserable yellow son of a bitch. How did he ever get into medical school? How did he ever survive to graduate?*

A sharp knock at his door made him jump.

"Sorry, sir," Sergeant Jordan said, "I didn't mean to startle you."

"It's okay, Sarge, just coffee nerves. What's up?"

"A GI named Benson requests permission to speak to the colonel. He says it's urgent."

GIs did not ordinarily request to talk to the division surgeon. In fact, this was the first time JP could recall a GI ever having done so. "Send him in," he said, curious.

A moment later a soldier in his late teens marched in, came to attention in front of JP's desk and saluted. "Sir, Pfc Benson, Bravo Company, 1st/43rd, requests permission to speak to the division surgeon.

JP returned the salute. "Stand at ease, Benson."

The soldier clasped his hands behind his back and moved his feet apart.

"You told the sergeant you wanted to discuss something urgent with me?"

"Yes, sir." Benson began swaying. "Sir, may I have permission to sit. I feel dizzy."

JP nodded and indicated the chair by his desk.

As Benson moved to the chair and eased down, his movements appeared labored, like that of a tired old man.

"Sir, four days ago my company was airlifted to battalion rear here in Phong Sahn after three weeks in the bush. The company is scheduled to go out again tomorrow for another three weeks. Sir, I don't think I can hump three more weeks in the bush. I didn't think I'd make it through the last three."

"What's the problem?"

"I feel weak, dizzy and nauseated most of the time. It's all I can do to get out of my sack in the morning."

"Have you been to see your battalion surgeon?"

"Twice sir, Captain Westin. He couldn't find anything wrong. He told me I would have to go back out with my company."

"What's your assignment in Bravo Company?"

"I'm an acting squad leader, second platoon, sir. I'm supposed to make corporal next month."

This made no sense. Malingerers were seldom appointed squad leaders or promoted to corporal. "How long have you been a squad leader?" JP asked.

"About two months."

"How many times were you on sick call during that time?"

"Sir, I have never been on sick call since I been in the army until I saw Captain Westin two days ago.

Pfc Benson did not present the history and appearance of a malingerer, and that triggered an alarm in JP's medical mind. "I need to examine you, Benson," he said, getting to his feet. "Let's go next door to the dispensary."

Walking ahead, JP observed Benson moving slowly and with effort. "Are you short of breath?" he asked.

Benson nodded. "Yes, sir. I don't understand. I ran track in high school; now I don't think I could run across the street."

JP held the dispensary screen door open and watched Benson laboriously climb the four steps to the door and enter the reception area. In the morning's sunlight his skin appeared chalk white.

A medic sitting at a small desk jumped up when he saw JP. "Morning, Colonel. Having your own sick call today?"

"It looks that way, Ownings. This soldier needs to be logged in and a record made, then take him back and get him stripped for a PE."

After writing Benson's full name, rank, serial number, and unit on a log sheet, Spec 4 Ownings transferred the information to a clinical record sheet. He led Benson down a hallway; both disappeared into a room. After they left, JP summarized Benson's complaint on the record sheet.

Minutes later, Ownings called out, "All set, Colonel."

JP entered the small examining room. Benson, stripped to his shorts, lay supine on an examining table with a thermometer sticking out of his mouth. Ownings unwrapped a blood pressure cuff from Benson's upper arm and rolled up the cuff. "BP is ninety over fifty, sir; pulse is 120." Withdrawing the thermometer, Ownings studied it, then looked up. "Temp is 102."

JP slipped on disposable gloves, reached for an otoscope and examined both Benson's ears. The drums were intact but pale. Pulling down each lower eyelid, he saw that the conjunctiva was a weak pink color instead of the normal red. The mucous membranes of the oral cavity had a similar washed-out color. The neck was negative except for multiple non-tender movable lumps the size of grapes. Similar lumps were

402

found in the axillae and groin.

JP reached for a stethoscope hanging off an IV pole. Auscultation of the chest revealed good breathing sounds over both lungs, but the respiratory rate was almost three times normal. The heart rate was abnormally rapid and accompanied by ejection murmurs. Returning the stethoscope to the IV pole, JP warned Benson, "I'm going to push on your belly."

As soon as JP pressed down on the abdomen Benson jumped. "Ouch… sir."

Proceeding more gently, JP discerned a liver enlarged six fingerbreadths below the lower rib margin and an exquisitely tender spleen the size of a grapefruit. Pulling off his gloves, he asked, "When did you last see Captain Westin?"

"This morning. He's supposed to go back to Wanda this afternoon."

"That your firebase?"

"Yes, sir."

JP turned to wash his hands at a sink. Benson had the clinical findings of a life-threatening disease, probably leukemia or lymphoma. Having come to that conclusion, JP now faced a dilemma. He could admit Benson directly to the 96th Evac, bypassing Captain Westin, the battalion surgeon. If he did that, word would spread through Benson's battalion that Captain Westin had failed to diagnose a serious illness. Westin's effectiveness as a doctor in the battalion would be destroyed. However, if Captain Westin were to admit Benson to the hospital his reputation would be protected. Before making a decision JP wanted to know if Benson was an isolated case of missed diagnosis for some reason on Captain Westin's part, or was Benson characteristic of a pattern that could impact the combat efficiency of Westin's battalion.

"You can get dressed now," JP told Benson. "Did you eat breakfast this morning?"

"No, sir. I was too nauseated."

"How do you feel about lunch? It's about that time."

"I am getting a little hungry."

"The consolidated mess is up the street. Go up there, get some coffee or tea and anything you feel you can hold down. After you finish come back here."

"What do you think, sir?"

"I'm not sure. I need to consult with Captain Westin."

Picking up Benson's medical record sheet, JP returned to his office, stopping first at Captain Dryer's desk. "Charles, I'd like to see the 201 file on Captain Westin, the battalion surgeon for the 1st/43rd. I'd also like to talk to Westin's battalion commander or exec, I don't know their names."

In less than a minute the admin officer had removed Westin's folder from a filing cabinet and placed it on JP's desk. Opening the folder, JP began reading.

Westin was thirty-one, married, and had two small children. A graduate of the University of Nebraska School of Medicine he had been elected AOA in his junior year. Westin was drafted out of his first year of internal medicine residency. After taking the three-week orientation course at Fort Sam Houston, San Antonio, Texas, he was sent to Vietnam as a general medical officer. The black and white full-length photograph stapled to the folder showed Westin to be a handsome young man with wavy hair at the edge of regulation length. A thin mustache graced his upper lip adding a tinge of maturity to his youthful appearance.

A voice called out, "Sir, Colonel Densmore, 1st/43rd, is on line two."

JP picked up the phone and identified himself, then briefly reviewed Benson's case.

"I'm wondering why Pfc Benson came to see you," Colonel Densmore remarked. "We have a first rate surgeon in our battalion."

"That's what I wanted to discuss with you, Colonel Densmore. Benson was seen twice by your surgeon, Captain Westin. Both times Captain Westin recommended duty. This raises some concern in my mind as to Captain Westin's judgment."

"Captain Westin has been an outstanding battalion surgeon. The men respect him and his judgment; so do I."

"Are you aware of any problems that might effect his performance? Any scuttlebutt from the NCOs or EM that might indicate a trend?"

"No sir, absolutely none. Todd is a very conscientious gung-ho kind of doctor. What you just told me is a departure from his usual performance."

"Has anything occurred recently that might have impacted his performance... some personal or financial problem?"

"None. He's very devoted to his wife and little girls." Colonel Densmore paused. "He did become very depressed after a tragic incident several weeks ago, but snapped back to his normal upbeat self after a few days."

"Can you tell me about the incident?"

"Do you remember Chaplain Sandborne?"

"Sure. He was killed a couple of weeks ago along with a company commander and first sergeant. A booby trap was detonated when the company night-lagered at an abandoned firebase."

"Good memory, Colonel. Well, Chaplain Sandborne was Todd Westin's hooch-mate. He and Todd were very close."

"I see."

"Tell me, Colonel Franklin, what are your plans for Benson?"

"Based on what you've told me I'll return him to Dr. Westin. If he's half the doctor you consider him to be he'll have Benson in the hospital by mid-afternoon. If he doesn't, I'll have to take over."

"I realize you could do that now, and I appreciate your letting Todd handle the admission. He's a good man. He'll come through."

After hanging up JP went to the doorway and asked a clerk to get Captain Westin on the phone. "He may be at the 1st/43rd battalion rear aid station."

Several minutes later Westin called. JP asked him if he remembered seeing Pfc Benson.

"Yes, sir, I saw him this morning on sick call. He complained of loss of energy. I thought he was goofing off so I marked him duty."

"Benson was here a few minutes ago. I'm going to return him to you to be re-evaluated. Call me back to discuss your findings and any action you take."

There was a long silence, then a subdued, "Yes, sir, send him right over."

As soon as JP hung up a clerk knocked. "Sir, Pfc Benson is here."

JP walked the length of the office to Benson, who was sitting on the edge of a desk.

"How was lunch?"

"Better than C-rats, sir."

"I just talked with Captain Westin. He'd like you to return so he can check you over. My jeep driver will run you to the 1st/43rd."

"Thanks, sir." Benson's gratitude was in his voice.

★

Thursday, July 2, 1970, 1150 hours
Division Surgeon's Office

A phone in the outer office rang five times before it stopped. Most of the office personnel were at lunch. "Colonel," a voice finally called, "Captain Westin on line one."

"Thanks."

JP picked up the phone. "Colonel Franklin."

"Colonel, I want to give you a follow-up on Pfc Benson, but I'd like to do it in person. Do you have time to see me this morning?"

JP looked at his watch. "Sure. Come on over."

"I'm on the way."

Ten minutes later Captain Todd Westin walked in. He looked exactly as he did in his photograph except that his hair was a bit longer. JP met him at the doorway, shook hands, and escorted him into his office. "Coffee?"

"No, thanks, sir."

"Have a seat," JP said, indicating the chair by his desk.

Westin eased into the chair, then shifted uncomfortably. "Sir, after I re-examined Pfc Benson I took him over to the 96th Evac and discussed his history and findings with Colonel Anderson, the chief of medicine. On my physical I had found general lymphadenopathy, an enlarged liver and spleen. Blood studies showed severe anemia and a white count of 60,000, mostly immature lymphocytes. He was close to impending heart failure. Colonel Anderson had me do the admission PE and write admission orders. The admitting diagnosis is acute leukemia. After Benson is stabilized he's going to be evacuated directly to Walter Reed."

JP sipped his coffee, looked at Westin, but said nothing.

Westin finally broke the silence. "I really dropped the ball on Benson." When JP didn't answer he continued, "I was in a hurry to finish sick call and get to a meeting. I made a snap judgment that Benson was trying to stay out of the bush. It was a terrible blunder. I hate to think what could have happened had he gone into the bush in his condition." Westin placed an elbow on JP's desk and leaned forward. "I want to thank you for giving me a chance to redeem myself."

"I understand you and Chaplain Sandborne were very close," JP said.

Westin seemed surprised that JP knew about the chaplain. "Yes, sir. Bill and I shared the same hooch for five months. Both of us went on R&R in Hawaii together with our wives."

"His death must have hit you pretty hard."

"It was devastating, sir. Bill was the kindest, most dedicated man I've ever known. What kind of God would allow a man like that to be killed? It makes no sense."

"I doubt that God selects who lives and who dies in war. It's man and luck that do the selecting."

Westin slumped back in his seat. His eyes reddened. After a moment he looked at his watch, then stood up. "I'd better be going, Colonel. A chopper is going to pick me up at the admin pad in an hour to go back to Wanda. I need to get back to battalion rear and pick up some medical supplies."

JP cast a jaundiced look the pile of papers in his in-box, then made an easy decision. "What say I go with you. I need to visit your firebase and meet Colonel Densmore. Today seems as good a day as any."

"Sir, that would be fine."

"Give me a couple of minutes to get my gear and rucksack from my hooch." As the two moved through the outer office towards the door JP stopped at Captain Dryer's desk. "On a diet?" he asked the admin officer.

"No, sir. I'm going to lunch as soon as I finish this report."

"So you can put it in my in-box?"

"How did you guess, Colonel?"

"I wouldn't rush if I were you, Charles. I'm going out to Wanda with Captain Westin in his chopper."

"How do you plan on getting back, sir?"

"Hitch a ride on the late afternoon ash and trash chopper. If that doesn't work out I'll spend the night." He turned to Westin. "Do you have a spare bunk in your hooch?"

"Yes, sir."

"See, Charles? I'm all set."

"Colonel, I can't help but wonder if your going out to Wanda is a ploy to avoid tackling the papers in your in-box?"

JP grinned. "You can wonder all you like, Charles. Just don't come to any conclusions. Would you notify the chief of staff's office where I'm going? Tell them I'll probably miss cocktail hour and possibly dinner."

Dryer nodded and reached for the phone.

JP turned to Westin. "All set, Todd. Let's go."

As they neared the door a phone rang. JP ignored it and would have kept going had a clerk not called out, "Colonel, phone call; Major Brodie at the 96th."

"Hang loose, Todd. This should take only a minute."

JP went to the clerk's desk and picked up the phone. "What's up, Kevin?"

"Sir, I need you over here right now."

"Kevin. that's what you say every time you call."

"Colonel, this is serious. An eleven-year-old boy was setting out some sort of booby trap when it detonated. Most of his face was blown away. Both eardrums and both eyes were ruptured. The ophthalmologist said the eyes will have to be removed. There are two small wounds in his mid neck. X-rays show metal frags up against the cervical vertebrae. His right arm is gone from the elbow down."

"Good God!"

"I did a trach so he could be put to sleep. The orthopods are debriding his arm to mid humerus. I let them go first because they promised to be finished in an hour. Our part will take at least four hours."

"I'll be there in fifteen minutes."

After hanging up, JP returned to Captain Westin. "Todd, I'll have to postpone my visit." He briefly summarized the case at the 96th.

"Thanks again for the second chance," Captain Westin said, extending his hand.

JP shook it warmly. "You should thank Colonel Densmore. He expressed such a high regard for you I had no choice."

Captain Westin came to attention and saluted. It was a sharp, snappy salute, not bad for a two-year man. JP returned the salute with one just as sharp and snappy. "Have a pleasant flight, Todd. I sure wish I were going with you."

★

Thursday, July 2, 1970, 1330 hours
OR No.2, 96th Evacuation Hospital, Phong Sahn, RVN

The casualty was small, even for an eleven-year-old Vietnamese male. The bulky dressing on the right upper arm stump resembled a large white boxing glove. His facial features appeared to have been wiped away by a giant sander. The skin, a diffuse purplish red, was peppered with hundreds of tiny bleeding pits. Patches of skin were peeled away exposing facial bones. The eyes, flattened and torn, were retracted into their sockets. Fragments of nasal bone and cartilage remained tenuously attached by pedicles of tissue. Portions of the lips were missing. What remained of the lips was charred and contracted into a snarl exposing shattered decayed teeth. The external ears were shredded and both eardrums ruptured. The ossicles had been torn from their attachments and lay loose in the middle ear spaces. A markedly swollen neck showed two small holes in the skin oozing blood and saliva. Low in the neck an anesthesia tube exited from the trachea.

JP was shocked at the extent of the injuries. He was looking at a deaf, blind, one-armed child with devastating facial injuries. A thought intruded: *allowing the child to die would be a humane alternative.* But JP was a doctor, dedicated to preserving life. He was committed to using every bit of his judgment and skill to save the boy's life and set the stage for his rehabilitation. There could be no other alternative.

The OR door swung open and Kevin Brodie walked in, his arms dripping from the scrub. "What do you think, boss?"

"I think I'd better grab a quick lunch in your chow hall. We're going to be here a long time."

★

Thursday, July 2, 1970, 1830 hours
OR No.2, 96th Evacuation Hospital, Phong Sahn, RVN

Lieutenant Colonel JP Franklin pulled his gown off over his arms, then ripped off his gloves. "I'll write an op note while you finish up," he told Major Brodie. Accepting the chart from the anesthesiologist, he moved stiffly. Easing down on a sitting stool, he leaned back against the wall and groaned. "You know," he said to no one in particular, "the simple act of sitting down takes on great meaning after five hours of surgery." Opening the chart, he flipped pages to a blank progress sheet and began printing.

The operation could hardly be classified as a success. The face was scrubbed clean, minimally debrided and partially reconstructed. The nose was repaired with function as the objective rather than appearance. Mucosa was used to reconstruct the inner lining of the upper and lower lips. Both external ears were debrided and prepared for eventual reconstruction. Repair of the eardrums and middle ears was deferred until infection had been eliminated and an operating microscope was brought from the 95th Evac in Danang. There were only two such microscopes in Vietnam; the other scope was in Saigon. The neck was explored. Luckily the larynx was minimally fractured and easily repaired. The hole in the upper gut was debrided and closed primarily with interrupted sutures. Both frags were removed and the neck drained. In two or three days the eye doctors would remove what remained of the eyes.

The door swung open. The OR supervisor stuck her head into the operating room, looked around and focused on JP. "Colonel Franklin, Colonel Goulden just called. She asked that you stop by the emergency room after you finish here."

JP suppressed a groan; not another case. He looked up from the chart. "Thanks, Marj." Getting to his feet, he handed the chart back to the anesthesiologist. "Call me if things go sour. I'm going to the ER."

"Let's hope there's not another case waiting down there," Kevin Brodie said.

"I doubt there is," the anesthesiologist interjected. "I haven't heard a chopper come in for at least an hour."

When JP walked into the ER he saw no activity. The litters and gurneys were empty. A nurse and a medic sat at desks doing paperwork. JP walked over to the nurse. "Lieutenant, I'm Colonel Franklin. Colonel Goulden asked me to stop by here after I finished in the OR."

The lieutenant looked up. "Just a minute, Colonel." She reached for the phone.

As soon as Kristy walked into the ER, JP became alarmed; her eyes were red and puffy.

"Kristy, what's wrong? What's happened?"

Kristy's gaze shifted from JP to folding screens at the far end of the ER, then back. "JP, did you know Captain Westin?" she asked, her voice wavering.

"He's one of my battalion surgeons. I talked with him in my office this morning. If it hadn't been for the wounded kid in the OR I would have flown out to Wanda with him this afternoon. What do you mean, did I know Captain Westin?" Realization hit with the force of a dropped safe. He glanced at the screens, then at Kristy. "Oh God, no."

"JP, I'm so sorry."

"What happened?"

"I was told his chopper was on final to Wanda when an RPG hit the tail boom. The chopper dropped from about eighty feet, hit the ground, exploded and burned. They never had a chance."

"How many?"

"Seven. The AC, pilot, and door gunners were taken to the morgue. They wore nomex flight suits, so they could be identified. The other three wore fatigues and were so badly burned that identification was difficult. No dog tags were found on the bodies; they may have melted in the explosion and fire. I asked graves registration to leave the three unidentified here to give you a chance to ID Captain Westin. JP, I know I'm asking a lot…"

"It's okay, Kristy," JP said. He walked slowly to the screens. Behind them three stretchers were neatly arranged on the floor, each with a green sheet over a human form. The sweet smell of burned flesh mingled with the odor of jet fuel. Kneeling by the first stretcher, JP lifted the sheet and studied the charred remains of a human being. Replacing the sheet, he went to the second stretcher and then the third. The thought occurred, *If it had not been for Kevin Brodie's call, there would have been a fourth stretcher.*

Covering the last body, he stood, faced Kristy and shook his head. "I can't tell, damn it, I can't tell which one is Todd." He turned away before she could see his tears, paused, then walked out.

Chapter Forty-Six

Monday, July 6, 1970, 0930 hours
1st/43rd Battalion Chapel, Battalion Rear, Phong Sahn, RVN

The chapel was almost empty now. When the memorial service ended a few minutes ago it was filled with the comrades of the dead who had come to honor them. On the altar a tall brass cross overlooked four flight helmets and three steel helmets; one of the steel helmets had a red cross painted on each side. The helmets represented the seven Americans killed when their helicopter was brought down by a rocket-propelled grenade.

A chaplain's assistant moved to the altar carrying a large cardboard box. Lifting each of the helmets, he loaded them into the box, closed the lids, then carried the box to a room behind the altar to be stored, presumably until the next memorial service. A Signal Corps corporal disconnected wires that ran from a microphone at the pulpit to a reel-to-reel tape deck on a metal folding chair in the front row. Rewinding the tape, he removed the reel and slipped it into a brown envelope on which was printed the names of the honored dead and the date. Duplicate tapes of the memorial service would be made and mailed to each next of kin. After the Signal Corps corporal left only one person remained in the chapel.

Lieutenant Colonel JP Franklin, Medical Corps, US Army, sat gazing at the cross on the altar as he wrestled with grief, guilt, and cowardice. Four days ago, after viewing the charred remains of Todd Westin, he was overcome by a crushing sense of guilt. Westin had been killed in a fiery helicopter crash. He, Lieutenant Colonel JP Franklin, would have died with him but for the last minute call from Kevin Brodie. In a bizarre convoluted way an eleven-year-old child, injured as he set up a device to kill Americans, had saved his life. Why should he have lived when Todd Westin and six others died? Was that really God's intent? If so, God worked in strange and convoluted ways.

That afternoon another memorial service would be held for the same dead men at Firebase Wanda, forty miles south-west of Phong Sahn. Lieutenant Colonel JP Franklin was to have attended but had backed out, giving the feeble excuse of pressing administration responsibilities. That was a lie. He cancelled a flight lesson scheduled the next day with Dan Ranson for the same reason; that too was a lie. He delayed flying out to Qui Tavong, again for the same reason; and that was also a lie. Lieutenant Colonel JP Franklin had not only become a liar, he had become a coward.

Grief and guilt had been displaced by an even more powerful force: an irrational overwhelming terror of flying. Fueled by the knowledge that George Barfield, Elwood Diblasio and Todd Westin died in helicopter crashes, not to mention hundreds of non-physicians, Lieutenant Colonel JP Franklin was convinced that all helicopters

410

were death traps. He was certain that if he flew again he would die; he would never see Kathy or his children again. They would never see him again. His charred remains would be too great a challenge for any mortician, and too gruesome to be viewed in an open casket. No, he would never fly again. He was innovative and would find plenty of justification to stay on the ground.

"Colonel, are you okay?" a voice inquired. Major Michael Jelnik, the Dust-off detachment commander, eased into the seat next to him.

JP looked up. "I'm fine, Mike," he lied. "What are you doing here?"

"Jeff Holcomb, the AC on the chopper shot down, was my friend. We were in flight school together. He was the best man at my wedding."

"I'm sorry, Mike."

"Thanks, sir. Did you know Doc Westin?"

"I met him the day he was killed." JP said, then abruptly changed the subject. "Did you want to see me about something, Mike?"

"It can wait, Colonel. Would you mind if I sat with you?"

JP nodded.

Neither man spoke for a while, then JP broke the silence. "Mike, I was supposed to fly out to Wanda with Todd Westin the afternoon he was shot down. The only reason I didn't go was to help out with a case at the 96th Evac." JP hesitated. It was not his nature to ask for help. He had learned to handle his fears ever since he was a teenage marine in World War II. But this fear was different. It was as overwhelming as it was irrational. He turned to Major Jelnik. "I'd like to ask you something, Mike."

"Sure, Colonel."

"Have you ever been afraid to fly? More than afraid, terrified, breaking into a sweat just at the thought?"

Major Jelnik stared at the wooden chapel floor. He spoke slowly, almost in a monotone. "Yes, sir. Flying Cobras on my last tour I saw three of my closest friends shot down and killed. Dozens of other friends were lost; some missing, some killed, and some horribly disfigured by burns. There were times I was so fearful of flying I stayed awake nights dreading the dawn and another mission. There were days when I used any excuse to avoid flying, even faking illness. I was so ashamed of myself I was ready to turn in my wings."

JP studied the Dust-off commander, searching for the clues that had sustained him. "You still fly regularly, Mike. You're a superb pilot and a legend to your young pilots. They talk about you going into hot LZs without gunship support to evacuate casualties. How could you do that, given your fear of flying?"

"Colonel, this is in strictest confidence."

"Of course."

"It's not the fear of flying that I had to overcome. I love to fly. It was the fear of death or crippling injury. According to the shrinks those are normal responses, considering the kind of work I do. My responsibilities as a commander and a leader do not allow me the luxury of showing fear. To do so would be very destructive to my young pilots. It would certainly threaten our mission."

"How did you overcome those fears?" JP asked, desperate for the magic words.

"To be candid, sir, I haven't overcome my fears. I learned to control them, ignore them, and suppress them. Every pilot I know who has flown combat missions has faced the same kinds of fears. Some drown them in booze. Some give up flying. Most decide fear cannot rule their lives. One way or another they come to grips with it and go on. The most powerful incentive is the realization that the lives of comrades depend on you. It is unthinkable that you would let them down because of fear."

JP remained quiet while he considered Jelnik's words. Finally, he said, "You know, next to surgeons you aviators are pretty smart people."

Major Jelnik got to his feet. "Colonel, if you're treating someone who has a fear of flying I would be happy to talk to him."

"You just did, Mike."

★

Monday, July 6, 1970, 1505 hours
Three Miles East of Qui Tavong at 2,000 Feet

The airstrip controller's voice instructed, "Cleared for a straight in approach from the east, winds calm, altimeter 29.06. Traffic departing to the north. Report a quarter mile out."

Dan Ranson acknowledged. "Take her down," he told the peter pilot.

Lieutenant Colonel JP Franklin, M.C., USA. went light in his seat as the Huey started a gentle descent. He was calm and relaxed, even berating himself at having been such a wimp about flying. Suddenly the Huey jerked violently to the side.

"Son of a bitch," the peter pilot gasped. "Did you see that? Did you see that?"

"Go for the deck, go down," Ranson shouted on the intercom.

The Huey dropped like a stone, leveling off just above the tree tops, then making a wide 360-degree circle.

"What happened?" JP asked.

"We almost collided with a 155 mm shell. It went by in front of the windscreen like a big, pointed black bird."

"You're kidding."

"No, sir. The asshole in the tower cleared us through an artillery firing zone." Ranson got on the radio to the tower. "You dumb shit," he told the tower operator, "do you have any idea what you just did?"

A long interval of static followed, then, "Sorry about that, sir."

"You're going to be a lot sorrier after I talk to your CO. If you clear another bird through that fire zone I'll come back and blow away your sorry ass with my guns."

JP chuckled despite the brush with death. As much as he had flown with Ranson, both as passenger and student, he had never seen him lose his cool, much less use profanity. Certainly as a student he had given Ranson plenty of reason to cuss.

"Sorry about the language, Colonel," Ranson apologized. "I don't mind being shot down by the enemy. That's part of the stupid game we play over here. But I get bent out of shape at the idea of being shot down by my own side. As soon as we land I'm going to have a father–son talk with that idiot's commander."

Considering that Chief Warrant Officer Ranson wasn't much over twenty-two years old, and that he would be talking with a captain or major close to thirty years old, JP wondered who would be father and who would be son in that conversation.

Minutes later, the Huey settled to the ground fifty feet from the battalion aid station and shut down. Two Hueys with red crosses were parked nearby. Ranson unlocked his belt and shoulder harness. Taking off his helmet, he turned to JP. "When would you like to head back, sir?"

"As late as possible without flying at night."

"Make it 1915 hours. There's a weather front due out of Laos at about 2100 hours. I'd like to beat it back to Phong Sahn."

JP nodded, then turned to take a salute from Captain Dominic Cruessi, the acting battalion surgeon. "Hello, Dom, I brought you fourteen units of O-negative blood," he said, returning the salute.

"We were down to our last two units, Colonel. These will fill our fridge."

Dragging a large insulated cooler by the handle to the edge of the door, JP jumped to the ground. "Grab the other handle," he told Cruessi. After asking the door gunner to bring his rucksack he and Cruessi, carrying the cooler between them, headed towards the battalion aid station.

"This thing weighs a ton," Cruessi complained.

"Except for the blood it's full of ice," JP grunted, "and a couple of six packs of beer."

"Bless you, my Colonel."

"How are things going?"

"So far, all casualties have been from action out in the bush. Besides US, we've treated about a dozen ARVN and three NVA. There were only seven US deaths in all and they were from basically fatal wounds. I'm dreading what we'll have to handle when the NVA attack this base."

"What do the deep thinkers think?"

Cruessi looked at JP and grinned. "They are thinking logically, as do all deep thinkers."

"I'll bet they predicted the NVA would attack Qui Tavong when they have amassed sufficient strength. However, given our massive air support, it is unlikely they can afford the horrendous casualties required to overrun the base. As an alternative they will try to make it sufficiently painful for us so that we will think twice about staying out here."

"That's brilliant, Colonel. I never realized you were a deep thinker."

"I was an intelligence officer before going to medical school, and that was quoted from page 23, paragraph 4, subparagraph alpha, of the *Complete Intelligence Officer's Briefing Manual* by Sun Tzu, modified to fit the existing situation."

Approaching the battalion aid station and the two parked Dust-off helicopters, JP asked, "Are those the front haul, backhaul, or one of each?"

"Both front haul. One of the backhaul choppers medevac'd a wounded NVA to Phong Sahn early this morning. It took some hits just east of the strip but made it to the 19th Surg. It won't be ready to fly until tomorrow morning. The other left for Phong Sahn fifteen minutes ago with three urgent cases. Right now we are short backhaul choppers until one returns from Phong Sahn."

"My chopper is available for backhaul to Phong Sahn."

"That would be a big help, Colonel. There was one other casualty today but we decided not to evacuate him. His name was Grumpy."

"Grumpy?"

"Yes, sir: Grumpy is a German shepherd scout dog who got a grenade frag in the thigh muscle of his left leg. When I started to debride and clean the wound Grumpy lived up to his name. If it hadn't been for his handler you would be looking for a new battalion surgeon."

JP laughed.

"You should see the ingenious dressing I improvised to keep Grumpy from licking his wound."

"Sounds like a case report for the College of Surgeons."

"Sir, Grumpy's handler put him in for a Purple Heart. What do you think the chances are of it going through?"

"They should be very good. Those dogs have saved a lot of American lives. Let me know if the paperwork meets any obstacle. When it's awarded I'd like to attend the ceremony."

"I'll pass that on to Lieutenant Bow Wow."

"Lieutenant Bow Wow?"

"Bill Langford. He's the CO of the scout dog detachment."

The battalion aid station, begun as a four-foot-deep pit encompassing the area of a three-car garage, had been made fort-like by layers of sandbags and stacks of ammo boxes filled with dirt around an inner support of heavy wooden beams. It was so sturdy, thanks to Major Hawkins, that it probably could withstand hits by all but heavy mortar shells, satchel charges, or armor-piercing shells. A dozen collapsed stretchers leaned against one side. An L-shaped wall of sandbags protected each of the two entrances. A sign read: LITTLE WALTER REED WEST. APPOINTMENTS NOT REQUIRED.

The interior was well lit by half a dozen naked bulbs hanging from a wire along the ceiling. Twice that many gooseneck floor lamps stood ready to supplement the ceiling lights. Three pairs of metal sawhorses were set up at the far end of the interior to accept stretchers. Another six or eight sawhorses were collapsed and stacked against a wall. Shelves improvised from wooden crates were crammed with bottles of IV fluids, packs of sterile instruments, and dressings. A small autoclave was set on several stacked ammo boxes, and a waist-high refrigerator sat on the floor humming noisily.

Three medics and a staff sergeant quickly mobilized up from a card game, an activity that seemed epidemic at battalion aid stations in South Vietnam. Two medics relieved JP and Cruessi of the cooler and moved to the refrigerator.

"This is my NCOIC, Sergeant Lofgren," Cruessi said, introducing a muscular young man in his twenties and then the three medics. "Sergeant Lofgren replaced Sergeant Harrel."

JP nodded to the medics. He asked Sergeant Lofgren, "Any problems keeping the blood cold?"

"No, sir. The engineers ran us a line from their main generator. If the generator goes down we have the small put-put you sent out. It's okay for the fridge and lights, but can't handle the autoclave."

"How about blood resupply?"

"No problem so far. Each backhaul Dust-off comes back with six or more units."

"There are two six packs in the cooler with the blood I brought. Is there going to be enough room in the fridge for those?"

Lofgren shook his head sadly. "I don't think so, Colonel."

"Then I guess the beer should be consumed before it gets warm."

"Yes, sir. Thank you, sir."

"I have some letters for my former jeep driver who is a medic in the first platoon, Delta Company. Would you happen to know where that is?"

"Yes sir. Delta is part of the perimeter defense. The first platoon is about a hundred meters south of here. Would you like me to deliver the letters?"

"I'll do it. I want to be sure he's behaving himself. I'll be back in about fifteen minutes."

"That will be about chow time, Colonel," Captain Cruessi said. "I'll meet you here."

★

Private First Class Jackson was well know by the men in the first platoon. JP was quickly directed to a pup tent next to a bunker. Kneeling down, he peered into the tent. Jackson, fully clothed, was asleep. He debated whether to leave the letters and not wake him, but the winds were picking up. The letters might end up in Laos. He shook Jackson's foot.

Jackson stirred and struggled to a sitting position.

"Sleeping on the job again I see."

"Oh, hello, sir," Jackson said, blinking.

"How is it going?"

"Pretty good, sir. I was out on an ambush last night with the second squad."

"I brought you mail from the battalion," JP said, taking a packet of letters from his pocket. "Some of them smell of perfume." He studied the back of an envelope. "What does S.W.A.K. mean?"

Jackson blushed. "It's a kind of a code, sir, between me and my girl."

JP smiled and handed the letters to Jackson. "Okay, you can go back to sleep."

★

Dom Cruessi held up a mess kit. "Colonel, you ready for supper?"

"I've been ready for the last two hours."

"This is our guest kit," Cruessi said, handing JP the mess kit with its knife, fork, and spoon hanging off the handle. After picking up another mess kit, he led out of the aid station. "The field kitchen and mess are on the other side of that hill," he said, pointing.

The field kitchen and serving line consisted of a tent fly covering three gasoline stoves, two metal work benches, an assortment of pots, pans, and a water buffalo. A three-quarter-ton truck backed up to one end of the tent fly served as a storage area. The serving counter, made of planks laid over empty wooden ammo boxes, was loaded with pans of food. Servers behind the counter ladled food from the pans into mess kits.

It was a picture JP had witnessed so many times in two previous wars. "Some things never change," he remarked as he and Dom Cruessi passed down the serving line, their mess kits extended.

"How do you mean, Colonel?"

"This mess is no different than the ones in World War II and Korea. One would think even if nations had not learned how to keep from waging wars, at least they could come up with an improved field kitchen for the troops who have to fight them." He looked down at the two Vienna sausages, mashed potatoes, and carrots swimming in carrot juice. "The food hasn't changed either."

"It beats the boned chicken and beef with noodles in C-rats."

"You have a point, Dom, but not much of a point."

After filling canteen cups with coffee they looked for a place to set their mess kits. A jeep drove up and parked a few feet away. The driver climbed out with his mess kit clinking and headed to the chow line.

Cruessi led to the jeep and set his mess kit and canteen on the hood. "A table with a view of colorful Vietnam and Laos, monsieur," he said with a flourish of his hand to the west.

"A bottle of your best Merlot, waiter."

"Monsieur will have to settle for mess hall coffee. The war, you know," he said, shrugging apologetically.

JP used the jeep's narrow front fender for his table. Turning, he scanned the mountain ranges extending west. "It's hard to believe the Ho Chi Minh trail is only a few miles west."

"Four miles west, to be exact, Colonel."

Both men heard the distant rumble of thunder. Gray-black clouds began to accumulate in the west. "That front was not due for another two hours," Cruessi said. "Maybe it will put the war on the back burner."

"Don't bet on it," JP said. "I'd better head back to Phong Sahn after we finish chow."

The two men ate in silence for a minute or two. JP broke the silence. "Dom, we have a little privacy here. I need to discuss a delicate subject."

"Oh, oh. That has an ominous ring, Colonel."

"When Brent Mann returns here and you go back to Charlie Med, I'm going to relieve Jerry Millbarth."

Dom Cruessi took a sip of coffee. "It's been a long time coming. Colonel Diblasio almost relieved Jerry a half dozen times but kept putting it off. I suspect he reasoned if he put it off long enough he would go home and his successor would take care of the problem."

"What I don't understand is why Jerry has been so ineffective," JP said. "I checked his records. He made AOA his junior year and graduated seventh in his medical school class. He was allowed to complete the second year of a five-year general surgery residency before he was drafted. His department chairman described him as brilliant and a hard worker. He should have been an outstanding clearing company commander. Instead he's been a disaster."

"Colonel, Jerry is very angry over having been pulled out of his residency to spend two years in the army. He'll be two years behind many of his former contemporaries when he returns. All the good fellowships and research grants will be taken by the time he leaves the service. And he's especially bitter over having been sent to Vietnam."

"He did have the option to sign up for the Berry plan. That would have assured him of completing his residency before being called to active duty."

"I know. Jerry gambled and lost. He's a very poor loser. I played the same game and lost too, but I feel lucky because what I'm doing is related to surgery, and, like it or not, I have become part of my country's history."

"I like your attitude, Dom."

"Jerry has another problem that has put him into intermittent depression; it certainly reinforced his anger and bitterness."

JP sipped his coffee and waited for Dom to continue.

"Jerry's wife is working on her PhD in sociology at Berkeley. Four months ago she wrote to him saying that she had moved in with another graduate student, a man twice her age who is active in the anti-war movement. She wants a divorce as soon as he returns."

"That's rough," JP said, his level of sympathy rising. "Does he have any kids?"

"No, sir. He wanted kids but his wife refused to stop birth control pills."

"Jerry may be better off than he realizes. I appreciate your sharing that information. It puts an entirely different perspective on Jerry Millbarth."

"How do you mean, sir?"

"My original plan was to take Jerry over North Vietnam in a C–130 and throw him out."

"Wouldn't that have been a bit extreme?"

'You're right," JP said, smiling. "Now I'll try to get him an assignment where he can get psychiatric counseling and possibly work under the supervision of surgeon with academic qualifications. It would be almost like another year of surgical residency, maybe better."

"Hey, sir, I'd like an assignment like that."

"No way, Dom. I have other plans for you."

"Oh, oh."

"The day you return to Delta Med you will be appointed commanding officer."

Captain Cruessi stopped chewing and stared at JP. "Do I have a choice?"

"Nope."

"In that case I accept, on the condition I can fire the current first sergeant and mess sergeant."

JP smiled knowingly, then went into his best French–Spanish accent mode. "Ah, mon capitaine, you underestimate the efficiency of your commandente."

The whine of a Huey electric starter was followed by the increasing noise of the turbine engine firing up and the *whup–whup–whup* of rotor blades biting the air. A moment later, a Huey with red crosses on its nose and sides rose from the far side of the berm, turned south and flew out of sight, its engine noise fading. Dom Cruessi picked up his mess kit. "They're going after someone, Colonel. I'd better get back to the aid station."

★

Twenty minutes later, a faint throbbing noise gradually increased until the aid station shook as a Huey passed low over its roof to land a 100 feet away. Before its sounds subsided, medics carried a stretcher through the entrance. A young soldier, his face ashen, stared up at the ceiling as the stretcher was lowered over a pair of sawhorses. A triple pad taped over the left abdomen and chest was soaked with blood. A second stretcher, carried by the Dust-off crew, appeared in the entrance. As it passed by, JP saw that the bulky dressing covering the left thigh was so drenched with bright red blood it was draining onto the stretcher to form a puddle. A belt around the upper thigh used as a tourniquet had come loose. After the Dust-off crew placed the stretcher on a pair of sawhorses, JP reached down and cinched the belt tight. The bleeding slowed dramatically.

Although it was JP's nature to take charge and give orders – after all, he was a lieutenant colonel and the battalion commander – in this situation he bit his lip and told Captain Cruessi, "It's your show, Dom."

"Take the leg, Colonel. I'll take the belly."

JP slipped on sterile gloves. Using bandage scissors, he began cutting off the thigh dressing, pleased that Dom Cruessi didn't hesitate to take charge. Delta Med would be getting a good commander.

By the time JP cut away the leg dressing, a medic had an IV in each arm with Ringer's lactate running. "Start two units of blood," JP ordered. "He isn't moving much. Has he had any meds?"

The medic looked at the medical tag. "Yes, sir. Two syrettes of morphine."

"That stuff probably pooled when he went into shock. Watch his breathing when his pressure comes up." Morphine was a respiratory depressant.

A medic manipulated a gooseneck lamp, sending its yellow beam over a badly shattered upper left leg.

"I need suction and wide malleable retractors," JP said. An electric motor hummed and a suction tube was pressed into his hand.

Using retractors and suction, JP step laddered his way into the depths of the wound, then leaned the retractors to the medic opposite him. "Hang on to these." Fingers probed now for the femoral artery. He looked up. "I can't find it. It must be transected and retracted. Someone ease off on the tourniquet a bit."

A stream of blood shot from the wound, missing JP's face by inches.

"I said ease it off, not take it off."

A feminine voice said, "Sorry about that." The blood flow diminished.

JP looked up into the attractive intelligent face of a woman in her late thirties or early forties. Her oversized fatigues failed to hide her lithe figure. Her hair, prematurely gray, was tied in a ponytail, giving her a perky youthful look. "Good God! A woman!" exclaimed JP.

"You are very good at gender ID, Colonel," the woman said.

"And to think, I'm not a gynecologist. Who are you?"

"Linda Gardner, journalist with the *Baltimore Eagle*."

"Never heard of either."

'You keep this up and you will hear and read of both."

JP stared at the woman. "Okay, Miss Gardner, when I tell you, loosen the tourniquet slowly, and I mean slowly."

Taking the two retractors from the medic, he worked them deeper into a conglomerate of torn oozing muscle and bone fragments, sucking away clots as he went. "Okay, the retractors are yours," he told the medic. His fingers again explored deep into the wound. "Ouch, darn," he muttered, jerking his hand away and looking at a finger.

"What sir?"

"I just got nailed by a spicule of bone. I hope this guy doesn't have hepatitis."

Intent on locating the proximal end of the torn artery, he leaned over until his forehead brushed against the hot metal shade of the gooseneck lamp. "Damn it," he said, jerking back.

"You're just a hazard to yourself," Linda Gardner said.

JP glared at her, shook his head and smiled in spite of himself. "Okay, Gardner, sorry, Miss Gardner, loosen the tourniquet."

Blood began to bubble from high in the wound. Using the sucker, JP followed the blood to its spurting source, the transected proximal end of the femoral artery. Straddling the finger-thick artery with the jaws of a hemostat he closed the clamp. "Got you, you son of a bitch," he said, immensely relieved. "Is someone checking respiration?"

"Yes, sir," a voice said. "It's shallow and twelve."

"Better start oxygen."

Looking up, he saw Linda Gardner's eyes on him and flushed. "Sorry about the language."

"I've heard worse."

Within minutes, both ends of the femoral artery and its accompanying vein were ligated. "Cut the sutures long, very long," JP told the medic. When the medic looked at him questioningly he explained, "The surgeons at the 96th will have an easier time finding the vessel ends than I did just by chasing the sutures." Ripping off his gloves, he told the medic, "Go ahead and dress the wound. I'll help you with the splint." He turned to the woman reporter, "You did well for a wo... I mean, lay person."

"My dad was a GP in Alabama. I used to help him in the operating room with mill accidents and shotgun wounds when I was in high school."

A distant rumbling stopped conversation a moment.

"If that ain't thunder we're in a world of hurt," a medic opined.

The rumbling grew louder, intermittently shattered by deafening claps of thunder. A heavy rain now pounded the aid station's roof.

JP went to where Dom Cruessi was working. "How's it going?"

"Not good. This kid is bleeding into his belly and has a collapsed lung. I have a chest tube in with a condom on the end. I'm not sure how much good it's doing. I almost lost him from cardiac tamponade; I had to tap his pericardial sac. He'll die unless we get him to the 96th a.s.a.p. How about your case?"

"Bad femoral fracture with transection of the femoral artery and vein. If we can get him to the 96th soon the leg might be saved. There's a Mass General-trained vascular surgeon there."

Another rolling thunderous noise shook the aid station. A moment later Dan Ranson walked through the entrance. "Colonel, we've got a problem."

"How many times do I have to tell you, Ranson, I hate that word."

"The front just rolled in two hours early. Ceiling is down to 200 feet and visibility is less than an eighth of a mile. It's pouring rain, winds are gusting to forty-five knots and forecasted to increase. We're stuck here for the night."

"Colonel," Captain Cruessi called out, "there's another problem. All the backhaul choppers are gone."

"What about using a front haul chopper to take these casualties to Phong Sahn?"

"That would leave us with only one Dust-off. If that went down there would be no chopper for extraction, and those two have the hoists with jungle penetrators."

JP went over to his young helicopter pilot. "Dan, we have a problem."

"Sir, you know how I hate that word."

"One of these kids will die and the other will lose a leg and probably die unless they both get to the 96th soon."

"Colonel, if I try to fly in this weather all of us will probably die."

"I'll go with you, Dan. We can all go out in a blaze of glory."

"Colonel, are all ex-marines as gung-ho as you?"

"More so. I was below normal."

"Let me ask you, Colonel, would you go with me because these kids really need you, or would it be to buck me up?"

JP didn't answer.

"I thought so." Ranson went over to the casualties and looked at them briefly, then returned. "Okay, sir, I'll make the flight, but only on my terms."

"That's a pretty gutsy statement for a CWO-2 to make to a lieutenant colonel. Okay, what are the terms?"

"You, my crew chief, and door gunner all stay here. Unless my peter pilot volunteers, he'll stay too."

JP nodded assent.

"Can one medic handle both casualties?"

"I think so," JP said. "He just needs to keep the IVs going with blood."

420

"Okay. Load the casualties on board. I'll take one medic, but he'll have to volunteer."

Almost immediately three young voices said in near unison, "I'll go."

JP could have hugged each medic.

"Go draw cards," Ranson told them.

"You're not leaving me here," the peter pilot said. "This place is dangerous."

Ranson slapped him on the back. "Go get our bird ready."

Linda Gardner stepped forward. "I must get back to Phong Sahn to file my story line."

Ranson, his young face heavy with concern, gave Linda Gardner a look that would have curdled milk. "Sorry ma'am, but no. This flight stands a good chance of ending up a pile of black smoke on the side of some mountain."

"I'm a certified correspondent," Gardner said, waving her USARV press card. "You can't keep me off your helicopter."

"It wouldn't matter if you were the Secretary of Defense, ma'am. You are not flying with me tonight."

JP spoke up. "Miss Gardner, Mr. Ranson, as young and boyish as he appears and acts, is still the aircraft commander. The Huey may be a small aircraft as aircrafts go, but it's all his. Like the captain of a ship or an airliner, aboard his craft his word is law." Now that wasn't quite true, but it did sound impressive and it fit the situation. "There will be plenty of flights to Phong Sahn in the morning. You can catch one of those."

Gardner began to protest, but the look JP gave her cut her off at the knees. She shrugged, accepted the inevitable, took out a spiral notebook from her pocket and began writing.

"See what you've done, Mr. Ranson," JP admonished. "She's putting you and me down on her hate list."

Minutes later medics carried stretchers with the two wounded soldiers covered by ponchos, out into the night and rain to the helicopter and slid them onto the floor. JP and Dom Cruessi, their ponchos dripping, climbed on board. Using flashlights, they checked the casualties and their IVs, then gave the medic last minute instructions. Strong winds violently rocked the helicopter.

The two door gunners removed their M-60s and ammunition, closed one door and slid the other partially closed. Rain pelted the Huey. The peter pilot was already in his seat and going through pre-flight procedures. Dan Ranson climbed into the right seat, pulled off his poncho, rolled it up and tossed it to the rear.

JP saw the reflection of the red instrument lights on their young faces and began having second thoughts. If they were killed he would have five deaths on his conscience instead of two. Moving up behind Ranson and the peter pilot, he touched Ranson's shoulder. "How are you fixed for fuel, Dan?"

"Topped off the tanks right after we arrived, Colonel."

"Look, Dan," JP said, "if it doesn't look right, don't push it. Losing two is better than five."

"Getting cold feet, sir?"

"You're damn right. All you have to do is fly this bird. I have to stay on the ground and sweat you people out."

"No need to sweat, sir. My peter pilot is ready for his AC upgrade, so you have two of the best up front. We'll corkscrew up through this stuff until we're 1,000 feet above the tallest peak around here, then take an easterly heading until picked up by Phong Sahn radar. It can vector us to the airfield and the runway with a GCA."

"Don't make it sound so simple, Ranson. I might try it. I'll be at the tower or commo shack until we get word you landed in Phong Sahn. As soon as you head east send your compass heading and airspeed every five minutes until Phong Sahn radar has you."

Ranson gave JP a puzzled look, then nodded assent. The implication was obvious. If the Huey went down its approximate position could be estimated from the radio log.

"Good luck," JP said, touching both Ranson and the peter pilot. He thanked the young medic for volunteering, climbed to the ground and slid the door shut. He moved out beyond the rotor arc to stand with Dom Cruessi, Linda Gardner, the medics, and the two door gunners, all huddled under ponchos, hoods pulled down low."

The Huey's starter whined, the jet engine fired, and the rotor began to turn. The red rotating light and navigation lights came on briefly, then went out. The Huey went to full power, rising several feet, slinging rain at hurricane speeds. It rotated ninety degrees, began lifting almost straight up, then began a tight climbing spiral. Within seconds it was lost in the overcast and darkness. Its engine noise lasted for a minute longer, then faded. Only the sounds of heavy rain remained.

Dom Cruessi turned to Linda Gardner. "It would be best if you spent the night in the aid station. There's plenty of room and it's about as dry and protected as any place here. We'll fix you up with a couple of blankets and a stretcher."

"That's the best offer I've had today," she said.

"You'll need a bunk too, Colonel."

"Just a place for my head."

"Little Walter Reed West has the finest of guest facilities in western South Vietnam."

Chapter Forty-Seven

Monday, July 6, 1970, 2345 hours
Battalion Aid Station, Qui Tavong, Republic of Vietnam

A jubilant Lieutenant Colonel JP Franklin returning from the airfield tower pushed past the hanging tarp and entered the battalion aid station. Pausing to let rainwater drain off his poncho, he pulled the poncho off over his head. A single bulb hanging from the ceiling cast a yellow glow outlining the interior. The remaining bulbs had been twisted in their sockets until dark. On the dirt floor eight stretchers lay side by side. Blankets outlined figures trying to sleep on five of the stretchers. Dom Cruessi sat on the sixth, his back against the wall, reading a medical journal. The seventh stretcher was empty. Two folded army blankets lay at the foot. A few inches, away Linda Gardner sat cross-legged on the eighth stretcher, a blanket over her shoulders, horn-rimmed glasses down on her nose. As JP approached, she stopped writing in her notebook and looked up over the top of her glasses.

Captain Cruessi closed his medical journal. "What's the word, Colonel?"

"The word, Dominic, is good. They made it."

"Thank God," Gardner whispered.

JP continued. "They broke out at 11,000 and headed east. Phong Sahn radar picked them up thirty miles out and gave them a GCA approach to the airfield. The weather made it too hairy for a landing at the 96th Evac. An ambulance picked up the casualties at the airfield. Both are still in surgery; so is Mr. Ranson."

"Why Ranson? Was he hurt?" Cruessi asked.

"No, he was just curious to see what surgeons do. A nurse I know arranged for him to observe surgery. Who knows, the experience may be pivotal in Mr. Ranson's life."

"How do you mean, Colonel?" Linda Gardner asked.

"I know of another line officer who fell in love with surgery watching his first operation during the Korean War. In fact, that very same nurse was the catalyst."

"Maybe I should interview her," Gardner said. "I smell a story. What's her name?"

JP wished he had kept his mouth shut. "Miss Gardner, the nurse is a very private person. She wouldn't be interested in an interview."

"Shouldn't that be her decision and mine?"

"Right now, Miss Gardner," he snapped back, "it is my decision."

The last thing Kristy needed was a reporter probing into her personal life. With an ongoing Bright Light mission that might rescue her husband, the publicity could be disastrous.

Linda Gardner flushed, then changed the subject. "What's the weather for tomorrow? I really need to get out of here."

"Tomorrow will be another beautiful sunny day in Vietnam," JP said. "Tonight I'm ready for sleep." It was then he realized that the only empty stretcher was the one next to Linda Gardner. He gave Dom Cruessi a withering look.

Cruessi shrugged. "She wants to ask you some questions."

"That should be an interesting interview technique," JP said, sitting down on the end of the stretcher. Unlacing and removing his boots, he moved up to the head of the stretcher, dragging both folded blankets. Using one for a pillow, he unfolded the other for cover and stretched out. "It's been a long day," he said turning towards Gardner. She sat cross-legged on the stretcher next to him. He watched her write in her notebook for several minutes. "If you were a hundred pounds heavier you could pass for a modern-day Buddha," he told her.

Gardner gave him a look over her glasses that would have turned most mortals to stone. "You are just overflowing with goodwill, Colonel. I'll start off with some easy questions you should be able to answer."

"Okay."

"What is your full name?"

JP suppressed a smile. He dropped his voice almost to a whisper. "Look, Miss Gardner, Captain Cruessi, the medics, Warrant Officer Ranson and his crew carried the ball here. I'm like you, more spectator than participant. I would prefer you leave me out of anything you publish."

"That, Colonel, will be my decision."

JP sighed. "Touché."

Gardner allowed herself a half smile. After JP finished giving her the information about his background, she put down her notebook and pen. Removing her glasses, she slid to the end of her stretcher. "Don't go to sleep just yet, Colonel. I'll be right back." Feeding her stockinged feet into jungle boots, she announced loudly, "I need an escort to the latrine."

Four supposedly sleeping teenage medics immediately popped up on their stretchers and reached for M–16s and flashlights.

"Hold it, you guys," Sergeant LeGrande said, laughing. "Two should be more than enough to keep Miss Gardner from harm. Smithson and Lin, go with her."

After the three struggled into ponchos and were about to leave, one of the medics, so embarrassed that his face glowed, handed Gardner a roll of toilet paper. All three clumped out into the night, medics with M–16s under their ponchos, Gardner with the roll of toilet paper under her poncho.

After they disappeared into the night JP sat up. "How long has she been here?" he asked Dom Cruessi.

"She came in early this morning from Phong Sam with the backhaul Dust-off. She's been interviewing Dust-off crews, me and the medics. She asked to go out on a Dust-off mission that required a hoist extraction. I refused. To make sure she didn't make an end run I told the Dust-off pilots to ignore her charm and good looks."

"That's hard to do," JP said. "I guess we should try to keep her happy."

Cruessi laughed. "You didn't get off to a very good start, Colonel."

JP flopped back down and pulled the blanket up to his chin. "Yeah. God, I'm tired." He was drifting into sleep when Linda Gardner clumped back with her escorts. Her grunts and other noises as she pulled off her poncho and boots, then squirmed herself back on the stretcher from the front end, brought JP fully awake. Turning towards her, he mumbled, "Stealth is not your long suit, Miss Gardner."

"You'd be surprised, Colonel," she said. "I'm glad you're still awake."

"How could I be anything but with you around."

"Since we're spending the night together, please call me Linda."

"Okay, Linda, and you can call me Colonel."

Gardner adjusted her glasses down on her nose, then picked up her notebook and pen. "Shall we continue?"

"Will this be an on-the-record interview, or will it go down as pillow talk?"

Chuckles came from under Captain Cruessi's blanket.

JP turned to look at him. "What's so funny, Dom?"

"I was thinking of headlines that could show up on the front page of the *Baltimore Eagle*."

"Such as?"

"Division surgeon sleeps with beautiful woman reporter. Reveals all."

The four medics on stretchers at the far end snickered under their blankets.

"I like the headline, Captain Cruessi," Linda Gardner said, "especially the part about the beautiful woman reporter. I just might use it."

"My wife will not react kindly to such a headline," JP warned. "She has very old-fashioned values."

"I'll be discrete," Gardner promised.

"Okay, take your first shot."

"Now that's an interesting way for a doctor to put it. First I'll ask the question reporters traditionally ask. How do you think the war is going?"

JP hesitated. If he were a having a candid conversation with Father Deveraux he would articulate his growing concern that the US was fighting a no-win war which it would eventually lose. But Linda Gardner was no priest. She was a smart, savvy, attractive woman sitting on a stretcher close to him radiating feminineness. She was so close, in fact, that he could easily reach out and touch her.

"Colonel, did you hear my question?"

"Sorry. Just getting a little sleepy. What was the question?"

Gardner repeated it.

"I'm the wrong person to ask such a question. I've been in Vietnam less than a month. That's hardly enough time to find the PX, mess hall, and latrine, much less pontificate on the progress of the war. Besides, I'm a doctor. My perspective of the war is skewed."

Again Linda Gardner studied him over her horned-rimmed glasses, her pen poised over her notebook. "Colonel Franklin, I've been a reporter long enough to recognize evasion. If I don't get serious answers from you I might have to make up my own."

"I just gave you an answer. It must have sailed over your head."

"Okay, we'll let that one lie for a while. Next question. Why are you here?"

"That's an easy one. I'm an army officer. Army officers go where the army tells them to go. I was told to go to Vietnam, and that's why I'm here."

"Where did you learn to be so elusive?"

JP grinned. "In spy school."

"You're playing games with me, Colonel, and I don't like it." Gardner was becoming angry.

JP felt as if compelled to explain an answer to a child, knowing the child could not understand the answer. "Linda, you're a civilian. Civilians are different from us… military people. We live differently, we think differently, we associate with other military people for the most part, and we are motivated by values you civilians cannot comprehend."

"Are you telling me I would not understand the answer to a simple question like why you came to Vietnam?"

"You have that right."

"Try me anyway, Colonel."

"What motivated me and many career officers and men are values such as honor, courage, commitment, loyalty to comrades, love of country, and the conviction that what the US was doing in Vietnam was right."

"Now that you have been in Vietnam for a month do you still feel that way about our being here?"

JP hesitated. He leaned over to Gardner and whispered hoarsely, "No."

Gardner closed her notebook, put it and her pen on the ground between her stretcher and JP's. She then took off her glasses and set them down on her notebook. She was well aware that JP was watching her. "Let's finish this in the morning, Colonel," she said softly. "You look as if you could use some sleep."

JP pulled the blanket up to his chin. "Goodnight, Linda."

"Goodnight, Colonel."

★

Tuesday, July 7, 1970, 0045 hours
Battalion Aid Station, Qui Tavong, Republic of Vietnam

Loud booms and shock waves shook the battalion aid station and its occupants as would a giant earthquake. Dirt and dust sprinkled down from the ceiling. The single burning bulb swayed madly, flickered, went out, then came back on. Three more shells burst close by within seconds. A brief silence was followed by shouts in English and Vietnamese, then came multiple lesser explosions. Sporadic M–16, AK–47 and M–60 machine-gun fire was accompanied by intermittent explosions. Shouts and screams permeated the dark night.

The medics and Dom Cruessi were already up stacking their stretchers. Dark bulbs were twisted into brightness. JP and Linda Gardner were the last to lace up their boots and stack their stretchers. Sergeant LeGrande went to the entrance and pushed his head out past the tarp. At that moment a brilliant orange flash lit up the area and a tremendous *boom* rattled the aid station.

Linda Gardner jumped. "My God, what was that?"

"The NVA torched a Chinook down on the strip," LeGrande said laconically.

"What's our security?" Dom Cruessi asked.

"Two grunts with M–16s and one with an M–79, sir. The colonel's two door gunners and their M–60s are out on the perimeter."

A voice from outside called, "Wounded coming in." In a moment the tarp over the entrance was pushed aside and a GI carrying the front of a stretcher appeared.

Captain Cruessi looked questioningly at JP.

"You're still boss man here, Dom."

Together they examined the first casualty as his stretcher was placed over the waiting sawhorses. The GI, shot through the head, was unconscious. A large segment of posterior skull was missing. Brain, blood, and cerebrospinal fluid oozed through the defect. Just as Cruessi reported the pupils dilated and fixed, the casualty arrested. Cruessi sighed sadly and turned to a medic. "Wrap a bandage around his head and take him outside."

As the medic began to dress the head wound JP said, "Hold up a second." He studied the dead soldier's bloody, distorted face, then reached for the man's dog tags. "Oh God, no," he groaned.

"What is it?" Linda Gardner asked.

"It's a kid named Jackson. He was my jeep driver."

"I'm so sorry."

Before JP could dwell long on his guilt and grief the medic touched his shoulder. "Sir, there are more casualties coming. This man needs to be taken outside to make room."

JP nodded, tears slipping down his face. "I'll help carry him." He failed to see Linda Gardner watching him.

★

Tuesday, July 7, 1970, 1030 hours
Qui Tavong, South Vietnam

There had been no sleep after the first mortar round detonated. Everyone, including Linda Gardner, worked feverishly to deal with the inflow of wounded. JP and Dom Cruessi were awed by her compassion, coolness under fire, and her stamina. Linda Gardner was quite a woman.

Just before dawn the NVA broke off their attack. By the time the sun rose in the morning, only a chilly dampness, multiple puddles, and soft wet ground remained as reminders of the previous night's storm. In the battalion aid station piles of bloody fatigues and bloody dressings were grim reminders of the battle.

By dawn, nine severely wounded GIs had been treated. Considered "urgent", they were evacuated to Phong Sahn aboard a Chinook. Seventeen lesser wounded GIs, classified "priority", were evacuated at dawn. Three GIs, Pfc Jackson included, were in body bags down on the airstrip awaiting routine transportation to Graves Registration.

Two GIs only slightly wounded were sent back to their units. After the last of the wounded had left and the aid station cleaned, GIs began lining up by the entrance for sick call. JP and Captain Cruessi divided up the patients. By noon all had been seen.

Dom Cruessi handed JP a canteen cup with warm coffee. "Thanks for all your help, Colonel."

"I should thank you for the chance to be a doctor."

"Any time, Colonel."

"Have you seen Linda Gardner?" JP asked.

"She's down on the strip trying to hitch a ride back to Phong Sahn," he said, chuckling. "Once those pilots get a look at her she won't have a bit of trouble." Cruessi reached for his canteen cup and sipped. "Colonel, she was a lot of help with the casualties."

"She told me her dad was a GP in Alabama. She used to help him with trauma cases. He must have been a good teacher."

"Just seeing a woman out here had a calming effect on the wounded."

"Not only the wounded," JP quipped, smiling. "I think I'll go down to the strip and thank her."

"I have a feeling she would appreciate that."

When JP reached the airstrip he spotted Linda Gardner sitting on an ammo box, her pack beside her. She appeared very tired and forlorn. He stifled the urge to hug and hold her. Instead he sat down beside her. "You were going to leave without saying goodbye?"

"You seemed so busy and preoccupied."

"And you didn't finish my interview."

"I blame the Communists for that."

"I want to thank you for pitching in during the attack. Doctor Cruessi and I appreciated the extra set of hands. Your dad trained you well. Just your presence did much to calm the wounded."

"They did a lot for me." Tears slid down her face. "I had forgotten what it was like to be useful." She sniffed and wiped her eyes. "Sorry about the tears, and I'm sorry about your jeep driver."

JP shrugged. "One of the burdens I will carry from this... this war." He almost said "stupid war".

Gardner reached over and briefly squeezed his hand. She had understood.

"Where do you go from here?" JP asked.

"To Hue, Dong Ha, and then home."

"Watch out for those marines up on the DMZ."

Linda Gardner smiled. "They're harmless. I slept with an ex-marine once. He didn't do a damn thing."

★

Returning to the battalion aid station, JP saw Captain Cruessi writing a letter. "To your wife?" he asked.

"Yes, sir. I write to her every day."

"Would you mind if I slipped a note in with your letter? You must promise not to read it."

Cruessi gave him a curious look. "Not at all, sir, and I promise not to read it."

JP printed a short note. It said:

Your husband is one of the most dedicated, compassionate, and competent physicians I have encountered. He is also one of the nicest people.

After signing the note with his title, he folded it and passed it to Cruessi.

"Do you have any idea when your chopper is due back, Colonel?"

"Not really. Whenever it shows, I guess."

"Colonel Simmons, CO of the 2nd/46th, has invited us to lunch."

"You realize, Captain Cruessi, that it is a singular honor for medics to be invited to lunch with an infantry battalion commander. However, it is an even greater honor for the battalion commander when the medics accept. The truth is, Colonel Simmons lived three row houses up from my quarters at West Point. I took out tonsils on two of his kids and a thyroglossal cyst on a third. What's he offering?"

"Fried chicken, mashed potatoes, gravy, string beans, and Dutch Master cigars. He said he'd send transportation whenever you're ready."

"I accept, and I'm ready now."

A few minutes later, a GI timidly entered the battalion aid station and went to Sergeant LeGrande. "I'm Colonel Simmons's driver, here to pick up two doctors."

Le Grande shouted to Dom Cruessi. "Captain, Colonel, your ride is here."

"You know where we'll be," Cruessi told LeGrande. Slapping on his fatigue cap, he led out of the aid station with JP following. At the jeep JP waited for Cruessi to climb into the back seat, then settled into the front passenger seat.

The 2nd/46th battalion headquarters mess was in a tent partially protected by a hip-high wall of sandbags. The officers' mess was typical of many battalion messes in the field: a single wooden folding table and two benches set off from nearby similar tables, the enlisted mess. Officers and enlisted personnel went through the same chow line.

"Dark or light, sir?" the server asked JP.

"Dark, please."

A drumstick and thigh were dropped on his tray.

"Gravy?"

"Over everything."

A burly mess sergeant standing behind the server moved forward. "Colonel, there are seconds on chicken today."

"You have any chicken tails back there?" JP asked.

The mess sergeant laughed from the belly up. "Hell, no sir, We throw those things away. Even the Montagnards won't eat them."

After they were seated at the table Colonel Simmons looked at JP. "Chicken tails?" he inquired.

"What's wrong with chicken tails, Fred? They and turkey tails are my weaknesses.

If the NVA ever wanted me to switch sides they would need only to offer an endless supply of turkey and chicken tails."

"We all have our weaknesses," Simmons said. "Mine are thighs."

"Mine are breasts," Dom Cruessi added, then burst out laughing. "Freud would have a ball with this conversation."

Two captains came through the chow line and joined them. Colonel Simmons introduced the captains as his S–2 and S–3.

"Any handle on this morning's attack?" JP asked the S–2.

"Yes, sir. We came out way ahead on body count, and that didn't include what may have been dragged away including wounded who die later. There were numerous blood trails. Patrols are out with dogs tracking them. On the minus side we had three KIA and twenty-five WIA, lost a Chinook and a Huey. A Chinook was damaged but is salvageable. Alpha Company on a patrol this morning located an NVA supply cache. They captured an assortment of automatic weapons, RPGs, satchel charges, ammo, and about ten tons of rice."

"What will you do with all that rice?" Cruessi asked.

"What we can transport out we give to the ARVNS to distribute to Montagnards and others in our AO. The rest we try to make unpalatable by mixing it with dirt, burying it, urinating on it, or just dumping it out on the ground and hoping for rain."

A major came straight to their table. Simmons introduced him as his exec, Glenn Burson. "What's up, Glenn?" he asked.

"Charlie Company just reported that their second platoon found a complex of bamboo and thatched buildings sixteen klicks west of here. The buildings were so heavily camouflaged that the platoon almost walked by without seeing them. Some of the rooms contained bandages, instruments, and medical supplies. There was even a kitchen with partially cooked rice."

"Has that intel been forwarded to brigade?" Colonel Simmons asked.

"Yes, sir. But that's not all the platoon stumbled into. Two rooms had leg irons fixed to the floor and walls, some with dried blood. The platoon commander, Lieutenant Hollingsworth, believes that POWs were held there until very recently. He wants to go after them."

Simmons didn't hesitate. "Tell Hollingsworth to back off. If the NVA guards believe the prisoners are about to be rescued they will kill them. Besides, the POWs will be in Laos by now. The only chance of rescuing them is to intercept and kill the guards before they can kill their prisoners."

Simmons turned to JP. "We're forbidden to cross the border into Laos, even to rescue our own people," he said bitterly.

"Our esteemed State Department?"

"Precisely, except out here we refer to them as State Depart... ah, forget it. Luckily the restriction doesn't apply to Montagnards and Hmongs." He looked up. "Anything else, Glenn?"

"Yes, sir. Scratched into the floor of one of the rooms which had leg irons were four last names. The names were forwarded to brigade."

JP's interest was more than tweaked. "Major Burson, those four names scratched on the floor, would one of them be Goulden?"

Burson, stunned by JP's question, stammered, "Yes, sir, but how did you know?"

"You've got to watch this doc, Glenn," Simmons said. "He's a lot smarter than he acts." Simmons turned to JP. "Tell us how you knew about Goulden? It could be useful information."

"He was the FAC who went down during the battle here in '68. He was on the ground and communicating until night. The next morning when a rescue attempt was made he never answered calls. He's been MIA since. The chief ER nurse at the 96th Evac is Goulden's wife and is a friend. I learned about him through her. In addition, I was briefed about two weeks ago by Colonel Collier, the G–3," JP said with a shrug to indicate he could tell no more.

★

Tuesday, July 7, 1970, 1450 hours
Battalion Aid Station, Qui Tavong, Republic of Vietnam

JP, Captain Cruessi and Sergeant LeGrande scanned the sky to the east while leaning against the sandbagged wall of the battalion aid station.

"When is your chopper due, Colonel?" LeGrande asked.

"Whenever it gets here, Sarge," JP said. "I enjoy a low priority in its use unless I declare an emergency." He grinned. "If it looks as if I'm to spend another night out here I will declare an emergency."

"Well, sir, you can't fault our hospitality," Captain Cruessi said.

"What do you mean?"

"We did set you up to sleep with a good-looking lady reporter."

"You set me up all right, Captain, and I won't forget it."

The sound of an approaching helicopter drew their eyes to the east. A speck in the sky materialized into a Huey. Suddenly it plummeted earthward, leveled off at fifty feet and thundered overhead at high speed. Pitching up several hundred feet in a graceful climbing turn, it dived for the aid station, flaring at the last moment and touching down near the three men.

"I don't think that's my bird," JP said. "Dan Ranson doesn't hotdog like that. It's not his style."

"What about his peter pilot?"

"He's more conservative than Ranson. Besides, that bird has two door gunners. Ranson left his door gunners here."

"Someone in the cockpit just waved," Sergeant LeGrande said.

JP picked up his rucksack. "Ranson may have had problems with his bird. This is probably a substitute. Sergeant, will you alert Mr. Ranson's door gunners. Tell them to bring their M–60s."

By the time JP and Captain Cruessi reached the Huey its engine had shut down. Except for the spooling down of the gyros, quiet prevailed. JP stuck his head through the door. The AC removed his helmet and looked over his shoulder. "Good afternoon, Colonel. Ready to go back to a life of luxury."

"Mr. Ranson. Was that you hotdogging over the runway?"

"No, sir. I'm much too mature to engage in such puerile antics."

"Your peter pilot?"

"Yes, sir. My new peter pilot. This is his first flight with me; he is a bit unrestrained."

The co-pilot removed his helmet, turned around and grinned insolently. "Hello, Colonel."

"Tom Carter! What are you doing here? Your profile restricted you from combat."

"I'm not flying combat, sir, just VIPs under the tutelage of one of the greatest pilots in Vietnam."

"Is that what Ranson told you he was?" JP shook his head in disgust and threw his rucksack on board. "I'll talk to you later." Turning, he shook hands with Captain Cruessi. "Take care of yourself, Dom, and thanks for the hospitality."

"Come back often, Colonel," Cruessi said.

"Don't count on it."

JP climbed into the Huey and took a seat against the rear bulkhead. When he tried to shove his rucksack under the seat he found most of the space filled with coils of rope. Easing on his helmet, he plugged in the headset cord and waited for the radios to come on. While waiting, he reached down and pulled out neatly coiled Plymouth Goldline climbing rope. Piled on top were sling ropes and a dozen carabiners. As soon as the Huey was airborne and climbing he pressed the mike button. "All right, Ranson, what have you and Carter been up to?"

"You mean the rope, sir?"

"The unused 7/16th Plymouth Goldline climbing rope to be precise."

"Ah, yes, sir. We brought a team out from Phong Sahn. That equipment belongs to them."

"So why wasn't it used?"

"Lieutenant Carter's superior airmanship under my guidance allowed us to set down in a cleared patch of jungle no larger than the diameter of the rotor blades, thus avoiding the need for the team to rappel in, not to mention the danger."

"You know, Ranson, modesty among pilots seems about as prevalent as virtue among prostitutes. Where did you drop off this team?"

"I'm sorry, sir, I'm not at liberty to tell you."

"You just did, plus answering the one I was about to ask. Excuse me while I go into my prayer mode."

As the Huey passed through 500 feet it started a gentle turn to the south-east. JP gazed down at the variegated blanket of the third layer of jungle canopy.

"Colonel," Tom Carter's voice came through the intercom, "my mother asked me to keep an eye on you out here. I heard you slept with a very pretty lady reporter last night. What should I write my mother…Sir?"

"Just fly the damn airplane, Carter."

"Helicopter, sir. Helicopter."

A voice burst into their headsets clear and excited.

"Mayday, Mayday, Mayday. Any aircraft this push. This is R.T. Texas. Over."

Over the intercom JP heard Ranson's voice. "Damn, that's the team we inserted." He transmitted. "This is Kelly Six. What's up, Texas? Over."

"Good to hear your voice, Kelly. We have one US POW who is an urgent medevac. Three other POWs and their guards are three klicks west.'"

"How about picking up you and the POW, then dropping you off to intercept the other POWs and their guards?"

"Bad idea, Kelly. There's no PZ within reach and the gomers are after us with trackers and dogs. The NVA guards had started to cut this POW's throat when we ambushed them. He's bleeding like stink and is having a lot of trouble breathing."

"I'll try to get you a Dust-off with a jungle penetrator. What's your posit?"

The Huey began to circle, drifting west towards the Laotian border. Team Texas sent their position in code. Ranson transmitted it to Qui Tavong with an urgent request for a Dust-off. Back came the report that all Dust-offs were on missions. It would be at least thirty minutes before one became available. Ranson transmitted this information to R.T. Texas.

"Kelly, this guy won't last that long. He was in bad shape before the dinks cut his throat."

In frustration, Ranson slammed his fist against the rubberized edge of the instrument panel.

JP pressed the mike button. "I have an idea, Dan."

"Sir?"

"Get me over the SOG team. I'll rappel down with my rucksack, patch up the POW as best I can, then hitch him and me to the rappel rope. You lift us up, take us to a safe place, lower us to the ground, land, bring us on board and head for Qui Tavong."

"Sir, I can't let you do that. That team is in Laos; the dinks are already after them with trackers and dogs. If you get captured or killed in Laos I'll spend the next thirty years in solitary at Leavenworth."

"Come on, Ranson, where's your team spirit?"

"Aw hell, sir, I never should have hooked up with an ex-marine. Okay, Colonel, if you're willing so am I, but I'll have to check with the rest of the team first."

Tom Carter responded by turning the Huey west and beginning a gradual descent. The two gunners responded by charging their M–60s and firing test bursts. The two passenger door gunners gave thumbs up. JP had never felt so proud to be a member of the armed forces of the United States as he did at that moment. He wished Linda Gardner could have been on board; then she would have understood.

Chapter Forty-Eight

Tuesday, July 7, 1970, 1520 hours
Five Kilometers East of the Vietnam–Laotian Border at 2,000 Feet

Chief Warrant Officer–2 Ranson transmitted, "Texas, this is Kelly Six, Over."

"Go, Kelly."

"We have a possible solution. We have Mac Six on board."

"Say again, Kelly."

"The division surgeon, he's a neck specialist."

"How is he going to get down here?"

"If you can find an opening through the canopy wide enough he'll rappel down using the gear you left behind."

"The guy must be nuts."

"He's an ex-marine."

"That explains it. Has he ever rappelled before?"

"Sir, have you?"

"I used to teach rock-climbing at West Point."

"I heard that, Kelly. How are you going to get him and the POW out?"

"Variation of a McGuire rig."

"Understand. Mac Six should come down sterile."

"Whoa," JP broke in, "that's asking too much."

A chuckle came through the headset. "Kelly, stand by."

A minute or two elapsed, then R.T. Texas was back. "Kelly, there is an opening in the canopy one hundred meters east of our posit. Two men are now heading there on the double. They will talk you to them, then shoot a flare."

"Do they have strobe?"

"Negative. It was damaged in the ambush."

"Estimate your coordinates in three. Snakes and a slick with STABO should be with you in thirty."

"Call them off, Kelly. We'll be long gone. We will need fast movers with delayed bombs to penetrate this canopy to get the gomers' attention."

While Ranson relayed that information to Qui Tavong JP uncoiled ten feet of Plymouth Goldline rope. Holding up the free end, he looked inquiringly at the crew chief/gunner, who pointed to hinged metal rings set flush with the floor. Lifting a ring, JP fed the rope end through it, tied it in a single bowline and jerked hard to test its security. He tied the other end of the rope to his rucksack. He did the same with a second rope but tied its end to a different ring. Through his headset he heard Texas report, "Kelly, I hear a chopper a half klick north-east of our posit. Over."

"Roger, Texas. I'm going to reduce power a couple of times."

434

The engine sounds became muted, recovered, became muted, then recovered again.

"Kelly, we ident. You are approaching our posit."

JP tied a sling rope around his thighs and waist so as to form a seat harness. Capturing the sling rope with a carabiner at his buckle, he tested the carabiner's gate for function.

"Kelly, you're much louder. First flare on the way."

Half a kilometer away a tiny burst of bright light suddenly appeared 400 feet over the jungle, then began a slow erratic descent.

"There it is," Tom Carter said, slightly banking the Huey.

"Texas, can you risk one more flare?"

"No sweat. The gomers know where we are."

Fifty meters away the second flare shot up out of the jungle canopy.

"Okay, Texas, we have the PZ," Ranson radioed.

The Huey slowed to a hover, then inched forward until it was over the entrance to a vertical tunnel six to eight feet wide, a tunnel extending down almost a hundred feet through leaves, branches, vines, and hiding God only knows what kinds of man-eating varmints.

The crew chief placed a folded canvas tarp over the floor's edge at the door to keep the ropes from scuffing, then began to lower JP's rucksack but quickly pulled it back up, shaking his head. "Sir, the rucksack is too light," he told Ransom. "It's getting whipped around so bad I'm afraid it will snag."

Ranson squirmed out of his heavy chicken jacket and passed it back. "Try this for ballast."

The crew chief, after tying the chicken jacket to the rope ends, fed out the twin ropes. JP followed the rucksack and heavy jacket down through the hole in the forest growth until they disappeared. When the ropes went slack almost a hundred feet had been played out. A chilling thought crossed his mind. *If I go down that rope I may never come back up.*

Over the intercom Ranson told JP, "Colonel, give your wallet, insignia, ID, dog tags, wedding ring, and any papers or letters to the crew chief."

JP removed the chain from around his neck with his dog tags and wedding ring, then took from his pockets his wallet and two letters from Kathy. He gave them a mournful glance then passed them to the crew chief who stuffed them into his pocket. "If you lose that wedding ring you may as well leave me in Laos," JP told him. "There's no point in my going home. My wife will never believe I lost it in Laos."

"Not to worry, Colonel. I'll guard it with my life."

The crew chief took out his penknife; using the small blade, he cut from JP's fatigue jacket the lieutenant colonel's insignia, caduceus, name tag, and the US Army label. "Okay, sir, now you are sterile."

Dan Ranson slipped his Uzi off the back of his seat and offered it to JP – the ultimate sacrifice. JP shook his head and patted the .45 pistol on his hip. Reaching down, he grabbed the leather thongs hanging from the holster's tip and tied them around his mid-thigh as did the gunfighters of the old west.

"Colonel, you don't have to do this," Ranson said.

"Getting cold feet, Ranson?"

"Yes, sir."

"Just keep me out of the trees... and don't forget to come back for me." JP hesitated, reluctant to say what he felt he must say next. "Dan, if the ropes get snagged and you feel the helicopter is in jeopardy, have the crew chief cut the ropes. That's an order. I'll be pissed off if it's carried out, but I'll understand."

Ranson nodded but he wasn't smiling.

JP removed his helmet and tossed it on the seat. He jammed his fatigue cap on his head and moved to the door. Standing with his back to the door, he reached for the ropes and looped them twice through the carabiner, then checked the gate to be sure it was closed securely. If it opened during descent he would have to make a spectacular PLF.

Slipping on leather gloves, he gingerly backed to the doorway and leaned out over the jungle, using tension on the rope to steady himself. Bending a knee, he lowered the free leg until his boot contacted the skid, then brought the other boot down. A quick glance back over his shoulder showed the canopy of trees only a few feet beneath the skids. Fear took hold and he began to shake uncontrollably. The shaking quickly passed: he hoped no one had seen it. A moment later his cap blew off. He watched it sail onto a tree top.

The Huey moved almost imperceptibly as the crew chief guided the pilot until the ropes were almost in the center of the opening, then he gave JP a thumbs up.

JP responded with a sick smile and shoved off from the skid, dropping ten feet before braking. The ropes held: he was in control; he would live. He dropped another ten feet. Branches tore at his face and fatigues. He began to twist in a sea of green and purple, becoming dizzy. The palms of his hands were beginning to burn despite the leather gloves. Suddenly he collided with the ground. A soldier in camouflaged fatigues grabbed and steadied him while he unclipped from the ropes. Another soldier untied the rucksack from the ropes but left the chicken jacket attached. He spoke briefly into a hand-held radio. A moment later, the chicken jacket rose swiftly and disappeared in green foliage. Seconds later, the Huey's sound was gone.

A strange quiet permeated the jungle broken seconds later by a crashing sound as twelve men in camouflaged fatigues broke out of the jungle. Two US and two Montagnards carried a limp, six-foot scarecrow of a man on a poncho, his torn, filthy black pajamas hanging in shreds. As they set the scarecrow gently on the ground, blood dripped from a bulky neck dressing. The man was conscious, his eyes wide open with panic. Gurgling sounds accompanied each breath.

JP kneeled by the scarecrow's neck. Reaching behind him, he dragged his rucksack alongside. Looking up, he asked, "Any medics here?"

"Yes, sir." A tall GI in his mid-twenties moved forward and kneeled down on the opposite side of the neck. "Sergeant Rudolph, sir."

JP tossed him bandage scissors and a pair of rubber gloves from his rucksack. "Cut the dressings but don't remove them. Keep pressure on the midline and on your side of the neck." Opening up a pack of large thick gauze pads and a pack of sterile surgical

436

instruments, JP laid them on the opened instrument wrapping on the ground beside him. "Anyone have a flashlight?" he asked.

"Yes, sir," another GI said, shining the beam of a flashlight on the neck. A Montagnard moved up with a second flashlight.

"Follow where I'm working with your light," JP instructed. Slipping on a pair of rubber gloves, he grabbed a thick gauze pad and a hemostat. Carefully lifting the lower edge of the neck dressing, he blotted fresh blood and wiped away clots revealing a gaping eight-inch horizontal cut across the lower neck. Blood and air bubbled up from the wound. The POW moved continuously as he struggled for air and coughed out blood.

"What do you think, sir?" Sergeant Rudolph asked.

"The cut went through the thyroid gland and severed the trachea. I've got to get in an airway before he drowns in blood or asphyxiates. Keep pressure on the dressing."

JP reached into his rucksack, fumbled around and finally came out with a 10 cc syringe attached to a tracheotomy tube with an inflatable rubber cuff at its tip. He set it down on the instrument wrapping. Using a combination of pressure, manipulation, and blotting with gauze pads, he exposed the lower end of the severed trachea. Grabbing the tracheotomy tube, he shoved it into the trachea. The POW coughed violently, spewing blood over JP's face.

"Thanks a lot," JP said, jerking away and wiping his face with his sleeve. He quickly inflated the cuff, sealing off the trachea from blood that could have drained into the lungs. The POW's agitated movements stopped. Now he lay quietly, breathing easily.

Several Montagnards stood very close, intently watching. He caught a glimpse of other Montagnards setting out mechanical devices and tried to ignore why they might be doing it. Sergeant Rudolph, obviously impressed, said, "That's probably the fastest tracheotomy in medical history."

"The NVA who cut his throat did all the work," said JP, stitching the tracheotomy tube to the skin. "That reduces the risk of the tube becoming dislodged," he told Rudolph. "Now we tackle the cut thyroid gland."

JP turned to his rucksack and removed several packs of "0" black silk already fixed to large, curved, round needles. "You are about to witness crude surgery at its best," he told Sergeant Rudolph. Grasping the needle with a needle holder, he took big bites through both halves of the thyroid. Using a running locking stitch, he brought the bleeding cut surfaces tightly together and tied down the suture. The bleeding diminished to an ooze.

"We're making progress, Sergeant," JP told Rudolph. "Let's check the rest of the neck."

As JP rolled the bloody dressing up towards the midline he exposed a severed left external jugular vein. Ordinarily the diameter of a pencil this vein was twice as large. Clamping both ends of the vein, he ligated each segment.

"I'll bet the anterior jugs are cut too," he mused.

Rolling the dressings further towards the midline his prediction was rewarded by a rush of dark blood. He quickly clamped and ligated the vein ends. "Sometimes I hate it when I'm right."

A mild ooze continued from deep in the wound. He decided to ignore it for now. The skin was rapidly closed with interrupted sutures placed far apart followed by a pressure dressing, taking care to leave the tracheotomy exposed.

"I know it looks like dog surgery, but we're pressed for time," he told Rudolph. "I'll do better at the 96th." Leaning back, he observed the closed neck and trach tube. "It's really not bad for government work." Standing up, he pulled off his gloves. "Who is in charge here?"

A husky six footer, his head shaved bald and covered by a bandana, stepped forward. He couldn't have been much older than twenty. "Sergeant Blaisdale, sir. I'm the One Zero."

"One Zero?"

"I'm the NCO in charge."

JP studied the young sergeant's face a moment, disbelieving. "I've done all I can do here for this man. You can call back my bird."

Blaisdale lifted the radio to his lips.

JP scanned the US SOG team and the Montagnards. Turning to Sergeant Rudolph, he asked, "Who stopped the NVA from killing this man?"

Rudolph pointed to a grinning, wiry Montagnard. "Sergeant Y'Sam. He shot from the hip and nailed the gomer in the forehead. Damndest shot I ever saw."

JP turned, saluted the still grinning Montagnard, then bowed low in a gesture of recognition and thanks. Kneeling again, he tried to clean the POW's face of blood and grime with a gauze pad. Someone passed him an uncapped canteen. He poured water on a pad, soaking it, then gently wiped. The POW's face was gaunt, dirty and bearded; his eyes sunken, his shoulder-length hair filthy, matted and infested with lice. His body was almost skeletal, indicating great loss of muscle mass. The body and extremity skin was covered by multiple weeping sores. The penetrating stench of body odor, feces, urine, and fresh blood was nauseating. JP wondered if this could be Kristy's husband. Whoever he was, he was somebody's husband, or son, or brother.

JP leaned close to the POW's ear. "Hang in there, partner," he told him. "We'll have you out of here before you know it. You think you had it rough? Wait until you get my bill for making a house call in Vietnam."

Sergeant Blaisdale interrupted. "Sir, I hate to tell you, but you ain't in Vietnam.

JP smiled knowingly, then began throwing instruments into his rucksack.

The distant barking of dogs froze everyone for a moment. "They're on to us," Blaisdale said calmly.

The sound of an approaching helicopter drew attention upward. The noise of beating rotor blades was soon overhead. The chicken jacket appeared, descending slowly on the double rope. Sling ropes and carabiners hung off the jacket.

"I'd better do this," JP said. Standing he reached for one of the ropes and twisted a length of it into a figure-of-eight knot. He did the same with the second rope, then slipped a carabiner into the loop of each rope. While he tied his own sling rope harness, the two sergeants did the same for the POW. Sergeant Blaisdale held out the chicken jacket to JP who shook his head and pointed to the POW.

After the jacket was secured on the POW's chest Blaisdale and Rudolph lifted him to a standing position and held him while a third GI clipped the sling rope harness to the carabiner in the rope loop. JP checked to be sure the connections were secure, then clipped himself to the second loop. Grasping the POW from behind, he nodded to Sergeant Blaisdale, who then spoke into his radio.

While they waited, JP told Sergeant Blaisdale, "Help should be here in five to ten minutes."

"We can't wait, sir. The gomers will be on us by then. They'll shoot down any chopper hovering like yours. Don't sweat us, sir. We'll E and E across the border. We have plenty of toe-poppers to slow down the gomers and some teargas powder for the dogs."

"Keep my rucksack if you want," JP said.

"I'd rather booby trap it for the gomers, sir," Blaisdale said, smiling.

The lift, when it came, was much milder than anticipated. Networks of branches scratched and clawed at them both as they were dragged upwards. JP did his best to protect the POW's face and keep the tracheotomy tube opening clear. A wave of overwhelming guilt swept through him as he lost sight of Rudolph, Blaisdale, and the SOG team. He should have stayed.

Suddenly they were above the canopy of tree tops and moving slowly towards the east although lagging behind the Huey. The breeze felt good on his cuts and scratches. Gazing up the 130 feet of Plymouth Goldline tethering him and the POW to the Huey, the ropes appeared thin and fragile. Recalling the data on 7/16 Plymouth Goldline from his rock-climbing days at West Point was reassuring: it had a breaking strength of 5,025 pounds and would stretch to almost half its length before breaking.

Ahead JP saw a small clearing; it was apparent that the Huey was heading to it. He made some hasty calculations. Landing in that clearing, then carrying the POW to the helicopter and taking off would use up six or seven minutes, possibly more. Another five minutes would be required to reach Qui Tavong. The POW had lost much blood and was extremely tenuous. Those seven minutes could be crucial to his survival. And what if the NVA were waiting to ambush them at the clearing. They routinely tried to cover possible PZs. It would be tragic for the POW to be killed so close to freedom, not to mention himself.

Holding the POW as best he could with one arm, he waved with the other arm until he caught the door gunner's attention, then pointed towards Qui Tavong. The gunner waved; the Huey altered course, gained altitude and continued east. By the time it reached Qui Tavong the sling rope was cutting into JP's crotch, bringing back painful memories of the debacle on the 250-foot tower at Fort Benning.

Once over the battalion aid station the Huey descended slowly, lowering them both to waiting medics and Captain Cruessi. Ranson's flying was so skillful that the POW settled on a stretcher with only slight guidance by the medics. JP uncoupled himself from the ropes and removed his sling rope. The medics unhitched the POW, picked up his stretcher and rushed to the aid station with JP and Captain Cruessi jogging to keep up.

"I didn't think I'd see you back so soon, Colonel," Cruessi said.

"Neither did I. Another five minutes in that damn sling and I would have ended up with a high-pitched voice and really sterile."

★

Tuesday, July 7, 1970, 1950 hours
Qui Tavong, Republic of Vietnam

Dusk approached as medics carried the POW on a stretcher back to the Huey, now waiting in flight idle. In the aid station his dressing had been removed, the neck checked, and a new dressing applied. A catheter was placed into his bladder, his lungs were sucked clean through the trach tube, and he had been given two units of low-titer O-negative blood. Another two units dripped in now. He would be given another two units on the way to Phong Sahn. JP was treading a thin line, giving him enough blood to keep him alive but not so much blood as to overload his fragile cardiovascular system and put him in heart failure.

Inside the Huey the medics hung the blood bags from hooks in the ceiling. JP climbed on board with a flashlight. Shining the beam on the bulky neck dressing, he saw it was still white, a positive sign. After waving to Cruessi he moved up to Dan Ranson and Tom Carter. "If this thing has an afterburner now is the time to use it," he shouted above the engine noise. "This guy is in such bad shape he may not make it."

The Huey leaped into the air.

★

Tuesday, July 7, 1970, 2100 hours
Thirty Miles West of Phong Sahn at 2,000 Feet

Dan Ranson's voice came over the intercom. "Colonel, Phong Sahn approach has Colonel Marchenko at the 96th patched in and standing by."

JP pressed the mike button. "Lou, ready to copy? Over."

"Pen and pad all set. Over."

"I'm bringing a severely malnourished, sick, repatriated US POW with his throat cut by the NVA. He was anemic to start with and has lost a lot of blood but is not actively bleeding now. He's on his fifth and sixth unit. These are his injuries: severed trachea, possible severed esophagus, severed thyroid gland, severed both external and anterior jugular veins, possibly the left internal. His medical condition is extremely tenuous. He will require medical evaluation and fine-tuning before he can be put to sleep."

"We are ready for him. Captain Cruessi alerted us forty minutes ago. Phil Anderson is waiting in the ER. There is a problem…"

"There goes that damned word again."

Marchenko continued. "Kevin Brodie has his hands full with a GI shot through the face and neck. He estimates another three hours. Are you in good enough shape to do the case?"

440

JP had planned on doing the surgery anyway. "Affirmative. I'll need an assistant."

"That too may be a problem. We are stretched thin."

Dan Ranson's voice interrupted. "Sir, could I help?"

"Okay, Lou, I have an assistant. Will you notify the 36th chief of staff on what's coming down?"

"Already have. He will be over to talk to you."

JP stifled the word a groan. "See you in thirty. Out."

Tom Carter's concerned voice was now in the headset. "Dan, you're really pushing this beast. The gauges have been in the red for the last ten minutes."

"If it makes you nervous don't look at them," Ranson said, his voice strained.

A minute later Carter's voice came through again. "Aw hell, Dan, the chip detector light just came on."

"Override the son of a bitch."

★

Tuesday, July 7, 1970, 2130 hours
Approaching the 96th Evacuation Hospital Helipad, Phong Sahn

The bright yellow lights around the 96th Evac's pad made it easy to spot at night from several miles away. Dan Ranson didn't slow the Huey until the last few seconds, then he eased it onto the pad with hardly a bump. Medics, waiting outside the ER door, double-timed to the Huey, pushing a gurney. Before the helicopter whined down to idle they had removed the stretcher with the POW, placed it on the gurney, and were racing back to the ER. JP removed his flight helmet, leaned back and listened to the music of the gyros spooling down. The odor of superheated metal was now almost overwhelming. Moving up to the flight deck, he patted Tom Carter and Dan Ranson. "Is this thing going to blow up, Dan?" he asked.

"No, sir, but it's going to cost the taxpayer a bundle to fix."

"Thanks for what you did today, especially for not leaving me stuck on a Laotian tree branch."

"It got a little dicey while we were hovering over the PZ the second time," Tom Carter said.

"What do you mean?"

"The engine gauges went into the red and stayed there until we reached Qui Tavong. They did it again coming back and stayed in the red."

"That explains the smell. I thought it was me."

"Colonel, we're going to leave the bird here," Ranson said. "I don't think it's safe to fly. Tom will go to the detachment, close out the paperwork and arrange for a Chinook to lift it to maintenance in the morning. That leaves me free to help you in the operating room."

"I'll be in the ER for the next few minutes. Meet me there when you finish what you have to do here."

"I'm finished now."

"All right then, let's go."

★

Tuesday, July 7, 1970, 2235 hours
Emergency Room, 96th Evacuation Hospital, Phong Sahn

Lieutenant Colonel Philip Anderson, III, M.D., M.C., USA, chief of internal medicine, sat at a desk writing in a chart. He looked up as JP and Dan Ranson approached. "Don't push me, JP," he said defensively. "It will take at least an hour, probably longer to run tests, stabilize him, and review X-rays before he can be put to sleep."

"You call the shots, Phil. Many brave people put their lives on the line to get him here, and he's been through hell. We can't risk losing him."

Colonel Anderson nodded. He studied the scratches and dried blood on JP's face. "You don't appear in much better shape. When did you last eat?"

"Around noon."

His thoughts drifted to R.T. Texas. He wondered when they last ate.

"You have a long case ahead of you. Get something to eat and some fluids. I'll honcho the POW and send someone to find you when he's ready to go."

"Thanks, Phil. I should warn you. A delegation of brass from the 36th may show up to interrogate the POW. They can be very persistent, even intimidating. Our concern is the patient's welfare. Use your judgment as to how far to let them go with the interrogation. If you need backup, call me. I'll be in the chow hall." He turned to CWO–2 Ranson. "Let's wash up, Dan, and get something to eat."

After several minutes of washing his hands and face, JP looked in the mirror and winced at the number of scratches and welts.

"Those branches really did a number on your face, Colonel," Dan Ranson observed.

"It's all your fault."

"At least I didn't leave you out there," Ranson said grinning.

"I wish we could have brought the SOG team out."

"Those teams are tough, Colonel, probably the toughest in any army. You should feel sorry for the NVA."

When they entered the mess hall only five or six people, nurses and medics, were at the bench tables. The serving line was empty of food except for a pan of bacon and one of hash brown potatoes. A cook in whites appeared.

"Eggs, gentlemen?"

"Any limit?" Dan Ranson asked.

The cook studied Dan's haggard face and sweat-stained flight suit, then JP's scratched face and bloody fatigues, noting the lack of rank, insignia or name. "For you two there's no limit."

"Go for it, Mr. Ranson," JP said, smiling.

"I'd like six eggs scrambled and four slices of toast."

The cook looked at JP. "Sir?"

"Three scrambled and two toast should do it."

Soon both carried mugs of hot coffee and trays laden with food to a table. Sitting down, JP sipped the coffee and groaned with pleasure.

Ranson was digging into his half dozen scrambled eggs when Kristy Goulden came in, looked around, spotted them and came over to their table. Her eyes were red; she had been crying. JP knew immediately that the POW rescued was not her husband. When she sat down beside him he started to introduce Dan Ranson, then remembered they had met when she arranged for him to observe surgery on the casualties from Qui Tavong.

"Can I get you something from the chow line?" he asked.

"Just coffee, black."

"I'll get it," Dan Ranson said, popping up and heading for the coffee urn.

"Kristy, I am so sorry the POW wasn't Bill," JP said. "I wished it could have been him. God, how I wanted it to be him."

Kristy wiped her eyes with a napkin, then blew her nose. "Don't say that, JP. He's somebody's loved one. I'm happy for her, or them."

Ranson returned with a mug of coffee and set it in front of Kristy, then resumed his seat and attacked his eggs.

Kristy focused on JP's face. "You look like you were in a fight with a tiger and came out second best." Her eyes fixed on his bloodstained fatigue jacket, then went to the lightened areas where the cloth insignia had been removed, then back to his scratch-laden tired face. It was then she realized what he had done. "Oh JP, thank you, thank you so much for trying."

"We wouldn't have made it if it hadn't been for Mr. Ranson and his peter pilot."

Ranson stopped eating and blushed.

Kristy looked up beyond JP. "Your welcoming committee has just arrived."

JP looked back over his shoulder. A grim Colonel John Witherington bore down on them with the division G–2, Lieutenant Colonel Tony Martinelli. JP introduced Dan Ranson and Kristy, explaining, "Her husband was shot down in the Qui Tavong area in '68."

"I know all about Colonel Goulden," Witherington told Kristy. "As soon as we sort all this out I'll have Colonel Franklin brief you. And you, Mr. Ranson, your escapades are well known in division headquarters. I believe Colonel Bruteau has scheduled a meeting with you tomorrow."

Dan Ranson groaned.

"Colonel Goulden, would you and Mr. Ranson please excuse us?" Colonel Witherington said.

Kristy stared at the 36th Division chief of staff a moment, then without a word picked up her mug and moved to a far table. Dan Ranson followed, carrying his tray.

After they were out of hearing Witherington took off. "Doctor, what in hell did you think you were doing, going into Laos and playing soldier? You were not authorized to cross the border. By doing so you disobeyed standing orders; you violated agreements between our State Department and the government of Laos. You put a valuable helicopter, its crew, and yourself at great risk. Do you have any idea the repercussions that would have followed had you been captured and put on display, dead or alive? What the hell is with you marines?"

Witherington's remarks set JP seething. In his fatigued state, facing another six hours of surgery, he had had it with this goddamned war and its stupid rules. "Colonel, some very brave men risked their lives to rescue that POW. They are still out there and in great peril. I wasn't playing soldier out there. I wasn't playing at all. I was a doctor trying to save the life of a dying comrade, one of our own. His throat was cut, he was bleeding and choking to death. He would have died had I not gone in to help him. And, Colonel Witherington, sir, marines, even ex-marines, do not turn their backs on comrades in need. So write me up for a court martial. I really don't give a shit any more... sir."

Witherington suddenly broke into a smile. "Relax, Doc, take it easy. I was only kidding. I would have done the same thing had I been in your place. My little act just now was to mollify the State Department assholes if division gets any flak about what you did. I will be able to assure higher authorities you have been appropriately counseled and there will not be a repetition... will there?"

JP sipped his coffee, set the mug down, and stared at Witherington without answering.

Colonel Witherington continued. "Tony Martinelli is in pre-op now interrogating the POW. Will that put the POW at any risk or delay his surgery?"

"I don't think so, Colonel. He won't be able to speak; he'll have to write out the answers to your questions."

"Recovering a POW is a major coup, Doctor. Unfortunately you cannot be recognized for your participation. As far as the division is concerned, you were never in Laos and you never rescued anyone. I must order you not to discuss any aspect of the rescue with other than authorized individuals."

"Colonel, I don't really care for myself, but my chopper crew and the SOG team deserve to be recognized and decorated for what they did. I and the POW probably would be stuck on a tree limb in Laos if it hadn't been for the airmanship of Warrant Officer Ranson and his crew. I'm writing them up for medals."

"Don't waste your time, Doctor. The constraints on you apply to them. They were never in Laos and therefore could not have done what you would claim they did."

"What about the SOG team that rescued the POW?"

"Doctor, you are not listening to me. The rescue didn't happen. The SOG team was never there. They are never there, wherever there happens to be."

JP shook his head sadly. "I have to tell you, Colonel, this is the most screwed up war I have ever been in."

"I have to agree with you, Doctor, but those are the rules sent down from higher and we have to play by them. For now I want you to go over what transpired from the time you heard the Mayday to the time you arrived here. I've got to brief the generals when I leave here."

JP sipped coffee and set the mug down. "Colonel Witherington, I'm not sure you are cleared for that kind of intelligence." The hard look from the chief of staff convinced him he shouldn't push the issue. He shrugged. "I'll take a chance," he said

444

with a crooked grin. He went on to describe in meticulous detail every facet of the rescue including the emergency surgery in the jungle. When he finished he asked, "Any word on the SOG team?"

Witherington shook his head. "Yes, and it's all bad, Doctor. Twenty minutes after you departed, the team made contact with a large NVA force. We had tac air over them but the triple canopy jungle made rockets, napalm, and gun runs useless. Their last radio message reported one US and four Montagnards KIA. All the rest of the team were wounded, some two and three times. Their last radio transmission requested bombs with delayed fuses on their positions."

"No," JP gasped.

"It wasn't for nothing, Doctor, believe me. What I tell you next is highly classified, disseminated only to those with a need to know. You do not have a need to know, but I'm going to tell you anyway. It's the least I can do in recognition for what you did."

JP sipped his coffee and waited.

"R.T. Texas reported the coordinates of an NVA division headquarters just over the border in Laos. The location is apparently a staging area loaded with trucks, artillery, armor, and ammo dumps, all in preparation of assaulting Qui Tavong in the next week or two. As we speak the B–52s are on the way."

"Are any other teams trying to intercept the POWs?"

"There were three, but they were pulled out because of the 52s."

Lieutenant Colonel Martinelli appeared holding a mug of coffee. He sat down next to JP.

"Was he able to tell you anything, Tony?" Witherington asked.

"Quite a bit, sir." Taking a flip-top green notebook out of his fatigue jacket pocket, Martinelli opened it. "Our man is Air Force Captain Charles Barrington. He was a bird dog pilot shot down in '68. The others imprisoned with him were all air force pilots, Laroux, Watanabe, and Goulden. Goulden was considered the camp troublemaker. He took no shit from the guards. They beat him regularly on general principle and kept him locked up most of the time. He made three unsuccessful attempts to escape but was recaptured within days. When the NVA got word that US troops were in the area they bugged out, taking patients and POWs with them. All POWs have malaria, dysentery, skin diseases, bleeding gums, loose teeth, lice, and chronic cough, probably tuberculosis. Barrington was in such bad shape that he couldn't keep up with the others. At first the NVA were going to shoot him. They decided against it because the shots would have been heard. They drew lots to see who would cut his throat. The guy with the knife had just started when the SOG ambush opened up."

"Does he have any idea where the others were taken?"

"He overheard the guards talk about a holding area for prisoners near the Ho Chi Minh trail. Prisoners collected there were to walk north or ride empty supply trucks returning to North Vietnam. There were rumors of US POWs to be traded to the Russians or Chinese for war supplies."

"What can I tell Colonel Goulden's wife?" JP asked pointedly.

There was an awkward silence.

"For God's sake, Colonel," JP pleaded, "she's one of us. She's hurting for even the slimmest shred of hope her husband is alive. This is her second eighteen-month tour just to be close to him. We can't leave her twisting in the wind."

Colonel Witherington sighed. "All right, but before you tell her anything, explain the classified nature of these operations. Any compromise will increase the danger to her husband and other POWs, not to mention rescue teams."

JP nodded.

"You can tell her what we know, including his physical condition. You can even tell her that three SOG teams will be inserted within the next forty-eight hours to search for the camp in Laos. But for God's sake, Doctor, don't tell her about the B–52s."

"Thanks, Colonel," JP said.

★

Wednesday, July 8, 1970, 0520 hours
96th Evacuation Hospital, Phong Sahn, RVN

JP washed and dried his face and hands in the doctors' lounge. Still in scrubs, his blood-specked mask hanging off his neck, he slipped on a white coat found hanging in an open locker. Surgery on the rescued POW, Captain Barrington, ended half an hour ago. He was now on the recovery ward attached to a mechanical respirator.

The operation had gone slowly but well. The cut thyroid gland was debrided and repaired. The severed external and anterior jugular veins were ligated again above and below. A horizontal cut in the sausage-size internal jugular vein on the left was sewn closed. The trachea had not been completely severed; its membranous posterior wall was intact. That made reconstruction so easy the tracheotomy tube was left out. As JP put in the last skin stitches he sent word for Kristy to meet him in the mess hall.

Now as he walked to the mess hall JP smiled at Dan Ranson's performance as a surgical "assistant". At first hesitant, awkward and insecure, Ranson quickly became an adept assistant who hung on JP's every word, did exactly as he was told, was amazingly dexterous, and instinctively knew what to do next. After the surgery ended Ranson confessed that surgery was almost as much fun as low-leveling in a Huey.

When JP entered the nearly deserted mess hall, Kristy was sitting at a table, holding a mug of coffee with both hands. He stopped by the coffee urn picked up a mug, filled it with coffee, and went over to her table. "Good morning, Colonel," he said cheerfully as he sat down on the bench beside her.

Kristy studied his face. "You look worse than you did yesterday."

JP grinned. "After nearly two days in the field and six hours of surgery, I probably don't smell so good either."

"What did you want to tell me?" Kristy asked.

"Colonel Witherington cleared me to bring you up to date on what we know about your husband. What I tell you is highly classified. I need your word you will treat it as such."

Kristy looked at him with a mixture of fear and hope, then nodded.

"The news is good and bad. The POW we rescued is an air force captain named Barrington. He had been imprisoned with your husband and two others since '68 at a camp just this side of the border."

Kristy drew in a deep breath; her eyes sparkled with hope.

"When the camp was about to be overrun by US troops yesterday the NVA bugged out, taking the POWs with them. Barrington was so weak he fell behind. The other three went on ahead with the guards. Barrington thinks they might be headed to a POW camp thirty-two kilometers from the border in Laos, and eventually to Hanoi via the Ho Chi Minh trail."

Tears formed in Kristy's eyes and ran down her face. She made no effort to wipe them away.

"Barrington related that your husband made three attempts to escape, but was recaptured each time."

"What did they do to him for trying to escape?"

JP swallowed. "You don't want to know." He omitted the information that B–52s were on the way to saturate-bomb the area where her husband might be.

"What about the team that rescued Captain Barrington?" Kristy asked. "Were they able to furnish any more information on Bill?"

JP stared at the table.

"What is it, JP? Talk to me."

"They didn't make it."

"Not any of them?"

When JP didn't answer Kristy groaned. "Oh my God."

She buried her face in her arms and sobbed.

JP put his arm around her and held her convulsing body against his.

Chapter Forty-Nine

July 8, 1970 to September 7, 1970
36th Infantry Division Activities, Phong Sahn, Military Region I,
Republic of Vietnam

By the beginning of September Lieutenant Colonel JP Franklin, M.D., Medical Corps, US Army, had turned eighty-seven pages of the flip-over calendar in his division surgeon's office. As chief medical officer for 24,000 soldiers distributed over 10,000 square miles he had flown 110 hours visiting firebases, special forces camps, troops in the bush, and ARVN counterparts. At least once a week he accompanied a battalion surgeon to a village or hamlet to provide medical care as part of the Medical Civic Action Program. Twelve more hours were flown with the Dust-off helicopters evacuating casualties. Another nine hours were logged as dual in the Loach. He now was sufficiently proficient to take off, hover over an area somewhat smaller in size than a football field, and thump down hard in what Dan Ranson sometimes described as "an arrival", and at other times "a controlled crash". Simulated engine failures continued to terrify him. Occasionally, Ranson accused him of trying to kill them both. Soon he hoped to transition to the Huey.

Three to five times a week he operated at the 96th Evac, sometimes with Kevin Brodie, at other times without him. During the ten days while Brodie was on leave, he operated almost every day. The plethora of head and neck trauma, not only among US forces but ARVNs, NVA, VC, civilian adults and children, advanced his judgment, skills, and confidence as a surgeon far beyond what he imagined possible. In moments of reflection he questioned his value as the division surgeon. Medical support throughout the division seemed not at all affected regardless of where he was and how he spent his time. It was a humbling revelation.

When Brent Mann returned to Qui Tavong after three weeks' OJT at the 96th Evac, Captain Cruessi went back to Delta Med to replace Captain Millbarth as commander. Millbarth seemed relieved when JP told him he was being reassigned, as if a heavy load had been lifted from his back. He was transferred to the convalescent hospital in Cam Ranh Bay to work under the close supervision of a senior surgeon and receive psychiatric counseling. Dom Cruessi, assisted by a very capable first sergeant and a superb mess sergeant, pulled Delta Med out of the morass of low morale and poor discipline.

Since the deaths of Todd Westin and Jackson the division had lost seven enlisted medics killed in action. Nine medics sustained wounds so serious that they were evacuated to hospitals in the United States. Most medics became casualties when they braved enemy fire to give aid to wounded comrades. A Dust-off crew of three was killed when it was shot down approaching a hot LZ to pick up some wounded.
448

Another four were killed when their Huey collided with a Cobra gunship. The Cobra's rotor blade came through the windscreen decapitating the AC and co-pilot. JP was obliged to attend every memorial service for the medics killed and write letters of condolences to the next of kin.

In late July the decorations for the Dust-off crews finally came through, all thirty-seven of them. JP was invited to join the commanding general's party during the presentation ceremonies. Since then, decorations for the Dust-off detachment were processed within three weeks or less, with impact awards pinned on the recipient within a day or two.

The drug amnesty program was now fully operational. The mental health ward of Alpha Clearing Company had its thirty-six beds constantly filled with drug users anxious to free themselves of drug dependency without incurring criminal records, bad conduct discharges, and jail time. It was too early to determine the success of the program. However, a disturbing trend was beginning to appear. While the use of marijuana, amphetamines, and LSD declined, the use of heroin increased. Heroin addiction was much more difficult to treat and the recidivism rate was high. Heroin impacted small unit cohesiveness, combat efficiency, and discipline. Much of it was sold at bargain prices by the enemy. Lectures, rap sessions, vivid descriptions of the damaging effects of drugs on body and mind, threats of court martials and prison contributed somewhat to the reduction of drug use but failed to eliminate it. It was estimated that between 0.2 and 0.5 percent of the division were heroin addicts.

Division contact with the NVA and VC during this three-month period was limited to short, violent platoon- and company-sized firefights. Helicopter gunships, artillery, and tactical air gave US ground forces a tremendous advantage over what was frequently a numerically superior enemy. Consistently defeated in the field, the enemy melted into the jungle after each battle, dragging its wounded and, when possible, its dead. It left behind mines and booby traps to take their toll, not only of US forces but civilians.

During the past three months the enemy had suffered over 1,700 killed and an unknown number wounded. Given the enemy's primitive medical capabilities it was presumed that many of the wounded died. Its most serious defeat was in the Phuoc Uyen Valley, where the 7th NVA Regiment suffered 590 killed. Captured were 122 tons of rice, 502 assault rifles, 32 crew-served weapons, and tons of ammunition. Wherever the enemy stood and fought it was defeated. After so many US wins it was time to declare victory and go home.

With the approach of the monsoon season the Qui Tavong operation began to wind down. The NVA, despite suffering heavy losses from the B–52 raid in July, managed to recover sufficiently to make two major attacks on the airfield. Defeated each time, they suffered heavy casualties. Search and destroy missions during July and August by US and ARVN troops crippled the NVA's effort to build up of its forces and supplies in the east.

★

Monday, September 7, 1970, 1830 hours
Headquarters Staff Bivouac Area, 36th Infantry Division, Phong Sahn, RVN

Lieutenant Colonel JP Franklin, returning from the communal shower with only an army raincoat over him, clumped along the wooden boardwalk in his clogs to his hooch. Minutes later, dressed in fatigues – washed, starched, and ironed by hooch maids – he slipped his feet into jungle boots polished to a spit shine by the same hooch maids. He was now dressed for happy hour and dinner at the general's mess.

A knock at the door that separated his hooch from that of the division chaplain was followed by the appearance of Father Peter Deveraux. In one hand he carried a half-full bottle of Scotch, in the other two glasses with ice.

JP looked up from tying his boot. "Father Pete, is it communion time for shanty Protestants?"

"Not really. If you desire the blessings of the sacraments you will have to enlist. Confirmation classes begin week after next." The priest poured a generous jigger of Scotch into each tumbler and passed one to JP.

"To peace," he said, holding up his glass.

JP lifted his glass. "To peace, brotherly love and all."

"You mock it, Doctor, but I'll still drink to peace."

The cold liquid burned JP's throat. "You serve up good Scotch, Father Pete. If this is what you serve at communion, sign me up."

"A blasphemous Catholic is bad enough in the eyes of God. A blasphemous Protestant has no hope at all."

The coarse ringing of the telephone aborted JP's response. As he reached for it he told Father Deveraux, "Never good news this time of day."

The voice in the receiver was quickly identified as the commander of the 96th Evac. "What's up, Lou?"

"It's what is taking place as we speak that's up."

"And what might that be, Colonel?"

"The monthly officer's barbecue. You missed the last three, you cannot be allowed to miss this one."

"How about my hooch-mate, Father Deveraux?"

"The good Father is always welcome."

Peter Deveraux shook his head, pointed towards the general's mess, and left.

"Lou, apparently your hospital is beyond redemption as far as the division chaplain is concerned. He's going elsewhere. I'll be there in thirty minutes."

Breaking the connection he waited for the dial tone, then dialed the chief of staff's office. The assistant chief of staff, Major Jerry Van de Mere, answered.

"This is Colonel Franklin, Jerry. Would you pass on to Colonel Witherington my regrets for tonight. I'll be at the 96th Evac attending a mandatory professional function."

"Doctor, you have set a record for missing happy hour and dinner at the mess."

"I cannot be expected to give up a T-bone steak and serious conversation about

450

medicine for spaghetti, meatballs, and talk about football."

"Are you sure it's not the pretty nurses?"

"You have an evil mind, Van de Mere."

Van de Mere was laughing when JP hung up. Next he dialed his battalion headquarters and asked that his jeep be sent immediately.

★

Monday, September 7, 1970, 1910 hours
96th Evacuation Hospital, Phong Sahn, RVN

Jackson's replacement as JP's jeep driver was Neil Groves, a nineteen-year-old South Carolinian who had raced motorcycles competitively while in high school. He was so good at it that he dropped out of high school to race full time. He was doing quite well financially until his draft board caught up with him. After basic training at Fort Jackson, SC, and AIT at Fort Benning, Georgia, he joined the 36th Division in March. Wounded three times before his nineteenth birthday he was taken out of the infantry and assigned to the medical battalion as JP's jeep driver. Extremely bright and a fast learner, he worshipped helicopter pilots and was determined to become one.

JP had introduced Groves to Chief Warrant Officer Ranson, who quickly gave Groves the facts of life. Without an education he didn't stand a prayer of going to flight school. JP and Dan Ranson encouraged Groves to enroll in USAFI correspondence courses to obtain his high school equivalent. JP began preliminary paperwork for Groves to be considered for an army ROTC scholarship when he was ready to enroll in college.

As they neared the 96th Evac officers' club the booming pulsating noise of rock music rolled over them like an avalanche. By the time Groves parked the jeep at the end of a line of assorted military vehicles, the noise was so intense one had to shout to be heard.

The hospital officers' club and its patio, like many officer and enlisted clubs in Phong Sahn, was built on a bluff overlooking the South China Sea. Two years ago, after engineers and medical personnel had completed the patio, chains of Christmas tree lights and Japanese lanterns were strung as decorations for the first barbecue. The decorations were still there, having survived the monsoons and even a typhoon. Remarkably, most of the original lights still worked. Over the intervening two years scores of grateful patients and other interested officers contributed wood, cement, and skills to make the club a favorite hangout for not only medical officers, but officers from combat arms, Dust-off, slick, and gunship units. All were willing volunteer laborers in an environment of attractive, mostly unmarried, young females.

Barbecue grills, constructed by welding split 55-gallon drums side to side, emitted massive clouds of gray smoke as T-bone steaks, hot dogs, and hamburgers flamed. Picnic tables and benches, constructed from lumber requisitioned at "midnight" by a gifted marine lieutenant, filled much of the patio. An orthopedic surgeon, utilizing skills acquired in a five-year training program, built a portable bar that was considered a wonder of mechanical engineering.

After Groves pulled out the parking brake, JP sat, shuddering at the sheer volume of taped music blasting from three speakers. The impact on his ears rivaled the noise of his platoon in Korea firing sixteen 50-caliber machine guns and eight 40 mm cannons at the same time. He and Groves watched a dozen or so couples on a cleared section of the patio, their bodies undulating to the music's beat, each seemingly lost in his or her own world of performance, oblivious to their partners. The men, in their mid to late twenties and early thirties, wore absurd sports shirts, equally absurd slacks or shorts, and sandals. The women, several years younger, were dressed in short shorts or miniskirts. A few personnel were dressed like JP, in fatigues and combat boots. The scene made JP wonder if the war was an illusion. Finally, he turned to Groves. "This isn't for me. Let's get out of here."

Groves's eyes were fixed on a particularly attractive young nurse in a miniskirt. "Sir, could I take your place? You can have the jeep."

"You're too young and immature for this place, Groves. Let's go."

As they started to back away an authoritative male voice stopped them. "Step away from the jeep, Colonel."

Lou Marchenko grabbed JP's arm and guided him out of the jeep.

Kristy Goulden stood next to Marchenko. "I told you if he showed up at all he would take one look and leave."

JP nodded towards the deafening music. "Can you blame me?"

Marchenko smiled. "I wouldn't be here if I weren't the commander. You need to be here because as soon as you are promoted you will command a hospital. Therefore it is incumbent on me to make you cognizant of a hospital commander's responsibilities." He looked at Kristy Goulden. "If I'm obliged to attend, so is my chief ER nurse."

JP shrugged. "Never let it be said I turned down a free steak meal."

"What about Taejon, Korea, October 1950?" Kristy asked.

"God, woman, you never forget."

"Or forgive."

JP turned to Groves. "I'll call you when I'm ready to leave. It should be around 2130 hours."

"Sir, are you sure you don't need me around for protection?"

"If things get out of hand I'll send word," JP said, smiling.

"Yes, sir."

Groves saluted, shifted gears, and drove off, a wide grin covering his face.

Marchenko, still holding JP's arm, eased him along the periphery of the dancing couples. "You'll be sitting at the commander's table," he said. "Follow Kristy. I'll bring you a beer and steak. How do you want it?"

"The beer cold and the steak medium well."

"Kristy?"

"Sounds like a good call, Colonel. Make mine a petite steak and substitute Fresca for beer." She turned to JP "This way, Doctor." She worked her way past clusters of young men and young women eating, sipping beer, and talking. JP failed to recognize
452

many of the nurses. The reason was the traditional one given by male chauvinist surgeons: he had never seen the nurses with their clothing on – only wearing scrub suits, gowns, masks, and caps. Trailing Kristy by two or three steps, he couldn't help but notice how well her fatigues fit the contours of her slight figure.

"How come you're not in a miniskirt?" he asked.

"I go on duty in a couple of hours," she said over her shoulder. "Besides I don't own a miniskirt." She stopped at a table near the far edge of the patio. "This is the commander's table. It's like the others except it's furthest from the speakers. You can almost carry on a normal conversation here." She turned to the two people already at the table. "You know Kevin Brodie."

JP blinked at the garish sport shirt topped off with a Vietnamese coolie hat. Four empty cans of beer were arranged neatly in front of him and he was working on the fifth. An unlit cigar dangled from a corner of his mouth. Brodie waved, a silly stupid grin on his face.

"I thought I knew him, but now I'm not sure."

Brodie whipped out a Dutch Masters cigar from his pocket. "Colonel, have a cigar from the proud papa of a seven-pound boy."

"Hey, congratulations, dad," JP said, extending his hand.

Brodie tried to stand but collapsed down on his seat. "Just a little unsteady… sir.

JP looked at the cigar longingly.

"Don't even think of it while I'm here," Kristy warned. She indicated the other officer. "This is the new chief of orthopedics, Carl Broadmeyer. He signed in two weeks ago."

Broadmeyer started to rise but JP quickly stopped him by reaching across the table and shaking hands. Broadmeyer's ham-like hand had a grip that would have made a blacksmith wince. He had the physical build to go with blacksmithing. JP slid on to the bench opposite Broadmeyer and Brodie. Kristy sat next to him.

"I'm glad to finally meet you, Colonel," Broadmeyer said. "I heard a lot of good things about you down at Med Command. Colonel Marchenko tells me you operate here so often he considers you part of the staff."

"The commanding general better not get wind of that. I'll end up taking sick call on some remote firebase for the rest of my tour. Where were you assigned before Vietnam?"

"Tripler, Hawaii, as assistant chief of orthopedics."

"Hot stuff coming," Lou Marchenko announced. "Here you go, Colonel Goulden," he said, laying a paper plate in front of her, "a petite steak, medium well, and a baked potato." He pulled a can of Fresca out of his pocket, "…and your cocktail." He set another plate in front of JP. A still smoking T-bone steak covered most of the plate leaving little room for the potato. "T-bone, medium well, and a cold beer," he said, extracting a can of beer from another pocket.

"I'm impressed by your hospitality, Colonel, and especially by your waitering," JP said.

"I became skilled in the latter waiting on tables in my undergraduate fraternity. It was that or starve."

"It must be reassuring to know that if you don't make it in medicine you have another profession on which to fall back."

JP popped open his can and took a long swallow of cold beer. Coming up for air, he set the can on the table and attacked his steak.

"I have a confession to make," Marchenko told JP as he eased down on the bench.

"It's not within my job description to grant absolution."

Marchenko continued. "I suggested to Carl he sit at our table tonight to discuss a problem with you."

"Are you telling me I was set up?"

"Think of it this way. You're getting a T-bone steak, all the beer you want, and pleasant company."

"I prefer to think of it as a set-up."

"Okay, have it your way, but listen to what Carl has to say. It could impact your division." He nodded to Broadmeyer. "You're up, Carl."

Broadmeyer put down his knife and fork. "Colonel, it's my understanding that medics who go out into the field are issued a number of single-dose morphine syrettes for use in easing pain of the severely wounded."

"That's correct. The syrettes are issued by the battalion surgeon, his administrative officer, or the NCOIC of the battalion aid station. The medic is accountable for each syrette," JP said, wondering where Broadmeyer was going with this conversation.

A corporal in fatigues touched Kristy on the shoulder. "Ma'am, there's a phone call for you from Quang Dien."

Kristy stood and excused herself. "JP, watch my steak."

JP nodded, then turned back to Broadmeyer. "You were saying, Carl?"

"In the two weeks I've been here at the 96th my service has treated eight extremity abscesses on wounded, and the patients were not all orthopedic cases. All the abscesses were at sites of morphine injections given by medics in the field."

"What?" JP put down his knife and fork. Broadmeyer's shot across the bow had gotten his attention.

"Yes, sir. I went back one year through the hospital records here and at the 19th Surg. Only three abscesses at morphine injection sites were recorded until two months ago. Since then there have been eighteen."

Marchenko added, "That doesn't include wounded who received morphine injections but didn't live long enough to develop abscesses."

Broadmeyer continued. "There was a common complaint among the wounded who did develop abscesses. The morphine given in the field failed to alleviate pain, even after a second and third injection."

"Do you think the source of abscesses is a contaminated batch of morphine syrettes from the manufacturer?" JP asked.

"That was my first thought, sir. As I looked further I discovered that all the abscesses developed in casualties from the 9th Brigade, specifically from one battalion, the 3rd/48th at Firebase Maxine."

"Defective syrettes from the manufacturer could still be the cause," JP insisted.

"Possible, sir, but unlikely."

"You're leading up to something I don't think I want to hear, Carl," JP said.

454

"The syrettes distributed to the 3rd/48th have the same lot number as syrettes distributed to the other two battalions in the 9th. Only casualties from the 3rd/48th developed injection site abscesses. If that lot had defective syrettes at the time of distribution the abscesses would have shown up in casualties from the other battalions instead of just one battalion."

JP was stunned. The implications were devastating. With all abscesses developing in one battalion he had to assume the syrettes had been altered at the 3rd/48th Battalion aid station before distribution to the medics. Only three people at the aid station would have had the opportunity: the battalion surgeon, his admin officer, and the NCOIC.

Kristy returned from her phone call, slid back into her place next to JP, and noted the somber faces. "You must be discussing injection site abscesses."

Marchenko nodded. "We dumped the problem into the division surgeon's lap," he said. "Was the phone call important?"

"Yes, sir. Bravo Med sent word they have three casualties to evacuate as soon as they're stabilized. One is a bilateral traumatic above-the-knee amputee from a mine, one is an AK penetrating neck wound, and one is a grenade frag penetrating belly wound."

JP indicated Kevin Brodie. "He's in no shape to operate on anyone's neck. Have the OR call me when the casualty has been fine-tuned by anesthesia. I'll come over and do the case."

"Appreciate that," Lou Marchenko said.

JP took a final bite of his steak, swallowed it down with beer, and stood. "I need to get moving on this. Carl, I want to thank you for picking up and following through on the abscesses. I'll keep you informed how things work out. I imagine your testimony eventually will be required."

"I'll be available, sir."

JP turned to Marchenko. "Dr. Broadmeyer is an impressive young man, Lou. You'd better get rid of him before he takes your job."

"He can have it any time," Marchenko said, laughing. "Leave your plate. We'll take care of it."

"How about your jeep driver running me back to my hooch? It will save me half an hour."

"Sure. He's down in my office. Tell him I said to take you home."

Kristy stood up and stepped away from the bench. "I'll walk you out to your ride."

As they walked towards the administrative part of the hospital Kristy gestured back towards the patio. "I'm getting too old for that kind of partying."

"You've changed since Taejon. I'll bet you voted Republican last election."

"I didn't vote at all. Both candidates were losers."

When they had gone some distance from the patio Kristy suddenly asked, "What can you tell me about the Bright Light teams in Laos looking for Bill's POW camp?"

JP turned to her in dismay. "For God's sake, Kristy, that's highly classified. Whoever passed that information to you took a terrible risk of compromising the missions."

"I would never do anything to jeopardize a mission, JP. You know that."

"Damn it, Kristy, just asking puts the mission in jeopardy." JP's anger quickly melted. Kristy seemed so miserable and vulnerable. "I'm sorry," he said. "Bright Light missions are closely guarded. Even I am kept out of the loop unless medical input is needed. If you had asked me about the missions two days ago I would have had to report it as a breach of security. The missions would have been scrubbed. Now that the teams are on site nothing can be done except hope and pray. I shouldn't be telling you even this. How did you find out about the missions anyway?"

"Don't push me, JP. I gave my word."

"That won't wash, Kristy, not when lives are at risk.

Kristy sighed. "Okay, one of the team members told me."

"Now why would he do that? Those guys are the most close-mouthed in Vietnam."

He abruptly stopped. The look of suspicion he flung at her left little doubt of its meaning.

Kristy winced as if slapped. She grabbed JP's arm, turning him towards her, eyes blazing with anger. "Don't you ever look at me like that again if you value our friendship."

Stunned by the vehemence of her response, JP stammered, "I deserved that and I apologize; I know you better. I'm still broken up over losing the SOG team that rescued the air force captain. We've lost two more teams since then. Security leaks are suspected."

Kristy's voice wavered. "What little was told me, and it was precious little, was by a team member I had taken care of in the ER when he was a casualty. He thinks I saved his life, like an idiot lieutenant I took care of in Korea."

"That idiot lieutenant still remembers and will always be grateful," JP said. "Look, Kristy, teams are going into Laos all the time to track down reports of POWs. Some POW reports are bona fide, others are enemy efforts to entrap the teams, and still others are fake stories made up by people seeking rewards. Every person beyond those actually involved in the mission adds risk to the team members and the mission's success."

"Okay, Colonel. I can live with that. Will you promise to tell me if things look hopeful for my husband's rescue."

JP nodded.

"So, Colonel, what you're going to do about the defective morphine syrettes?"

JP smiled. "Can you be trusted to keep your mouth shut?"

"Don't be an ass, JP."

"I have a gut feeling I'm over my head, Kristy. I'm going to need help."

"Well, that's a unique admission for you."

"Now who's being an ass?"

"Sorry. Who are you going to ask for help?"

"I'll start by dropping this on the sheriff tonight."

"Who?"

"The provost marshal. He'll get the CID and the JAG involved."

"What about the person responsible?"

"Identifying him has top priority."

"And when he is identified?"

"I'll nail him to the brig door."

★

Monday, September 7, 1970, 2115 hours
36th Division Staff Bivouac Area, Phong Sahn, RVN

JP knocked on the door of Lieutenant Colonel Douglas Hanneford's hooch several times before giving up. Hanneford was either dead or not in his hooch. A dark figure on the board sidewalk along the hooch called out, "If you're looking for the sheriff he's still at the general's mess watching the movie."

Turning, JP made out the rotund form of Lieutenant Colonel Charles Baker, the division finance officer, alias Money Bags Six. "Must be a good movie. The sheriff seldom sticks around after dinner for the movie."

"It's Double O Seven with James Bond.'

"I'm surprised you're not watching it. You're a big James Bond fan."

"Writing to my wife takes precedence."

As JP returned to the board sidewalk he asked Baker, "What happened to my jump pay this month?"

"What jump pay? It's been over three months since you last made any authorized jumps. You're not current; hence no jump pay."

"I made three jumps with the ARVNs at Quang Dien last month."

"They were not authorized. The general hit the roof when he learned you jumped with the ARVNs. I'm surprised you haven't heard from him."

"I haven't been around much."

"Considering the general's reaction I decided it wouldn't be a good idea to try to talk him into backdating an authorization, at least for now. You're welcome to try."

"No, I don't think so."

"Let's give things a couple of weeks to settle down, then I'll see what I can do," Baker said, then moved on.

When JP entered the lounge at the general's mess the movie had just ended. The lights were on and the projectionist was rewinding the 16 mm film. Most officers were leaving amidst a steady stream of remarks about the prowess of 007 in the field and the bedroom. JP spotted the hulk of Lieutenant Colonel Douglas Hanneford sprawled in a leather chair reading a magazine. Going over, he tapped the provost marshal on his shoulder. "Doug, we need to talk."

The provost marshal rose to his full six foot four inches. "Let's get a Pepsi and go out on the patio."

A few minutes later, they were seated in comfortable cushioned patio chairs viewing the beauty of undulating moonlight on the South China Sea. JP related what he knew about the epidemic of abscesses. "Suspicion focuses on the battalion aid station," he concluded.

"It certainly looks that way," Hanneford said thoughtfully. "Who in the aid station issues syrettes to company medics?"

"The battalion surgeon, his administration officer, and the sergeant in charge of the aid station."

"How can I help?"

"The morphine supply in the aid station needs to be confiscated and tested. The personnel should be interrogated, their personal effects searched, and whatever else you crime stoppers do in solving crimes."

"Okay. That can be arranged. If you give me the names of those three key personnel I'll run background checks on them. What are you going to do about the syrettes already with medics in the field?"

"Tomorrow I'll have the 9th Brigade surgeon and his people go out to the field, pick up the syrettes and issue fresh syrettes with a different lot number."

"What about resupply?"

"The battalion commander will be given a supply of syrettes to keep in his safe to be issued to medics only with authorization of one of his officers. Right now I don't trust anyone in that aid station."

"Sounds good so far," Hanneford said. "Do you want the syrettes collected from the field also analyzed?"

"Definitely."

"No problem. Be certain the syrettes are collected under the supervision of an officer and placed in a plastic bag. The officer should sign his name with the date, location, and the medic's name on a card or paper, place it in the bag and then seal it. Bring the bags to me; I'll take care of the rest."

"How long before we get the results from the lab?"

"Five days to ten days; sooner if the request is classified urgent."

"The results may help identify the responsible person before he does more harm."

"Okay. Urgent it is. I'll assign two MPs and two CID agents to the case. The agent in charge will be Chief Warrant Jesse Rodriguez. What time tomorrow do you want them and where?"

"How about 0800 hours at the admin pad. I'll arrange for a chopper. First stop will be Quang Dien and the 9th Brigade, then on to Maxine."

"Anything else?"

"Nothing I can think of. I'm new at this game."

The provost marshal stood up. "You know, Doc, the thought of some wounded kid getting a shot of contaminated ineffective morphine drives me up the wall. I want the bastard responsible."

"So do I, Doug. So do I."

Chapter Fifty

Wednesday, September 9, 1970, 0840 hours
9th Brigade Headquarters, FSB Skunk Patch, Quang Dien, RVN

The UH1H Huey helicopter with Second Lieutenant Thomas Carter, USMA '69, at the controls, flared over the mid-portion of Skunk Patch's 6,000 foot runway. Leveling off at four feet, it hovered a moment, then air-taxied to the helipad outside Bravo Company's emergency room and gently touched down. It was a vivid demonstration of skillful airmanship. Lieutenant Colonel JP Franklin, belted in by the door, felt compelled to compliment the pilot.

"Carter, you're a show-off."

"Thank you, sir."

Dan Ranson cut in. "Plenty of room for improvement."

The engine whine and rotor swish subsided. Undoing his seat belt, JP removed his flight helmet, set it on the floor under his seat and turned to Chief Warrant Officer Jesse Rodriguez seated beside him. "I'll go to Bravo Med first, then brigade to brief Colonel Prather." He glanced at his watch. "Meet back here at ten."

Rodriguez nodded. "Sergeant Casper and I will be at the MP station if you need us."

JP moved up to the flight crew. "Dan, will you be ready to depart at 1000 hours for Maxine?"

"Yes, sir. We're going to go top off the tanks, then return and shut down over there," he said, pointing to a cleared area fifty meters away.

JP slapped on his fatigue cap and jumped to the ground, The door gunner, already on the ground, saluted. Returning the salute, JP headed for the Bravo Company orderly room. He paused briefly to watch a flight of twelve Hueys in staggered formation pass overhead heading west.

As soon as he stepped through the doorway into the orderly room a young clerk jumped to his feet and shouted, "Tenshun." The muscular middle-aged first sergeant at an adjacent desk started to rise.

"As you were. Carry on," JP called out.

The sergeant continued to rise, walked over and saluted. Before he could report JP returned the salute. "How are you, Sergeant Dockering?"

"Fine, sir. If Captain Wood had known you were coming he would have been here to welcome you."

"I didn't send word on purpose. Step outside and I'll explain."

JP led the way some distance from the orderly room. "What I tell you next is to be discussed only with Captain Wood."

"Yes, sir."

JP described the epidemic of abscesses at morphine injection sites in casualties from the 3rd/48th and the impending investigation. "Your doctors will be out in the boonies most of the day collecting morphine syrettes carried by the medics and replacing them with syrettes from a different lot. By the way, Sergeant, where are your doctors?"

Dockering looked uncomfortable. "Sir, they... ah, they may still be in their sacks. They were up all night with a Vietnamese woman in prolonged labor. She delivered twins an hour ago."

"That's a first for the medical battalion," JP said. "There must be some sort of award for such a medical milestone. If there isn't one I'll make one up. How are the babies and the mother?"

"Fine, sir. Just fine, sir." The sergeant beamed with pride, as though he himself had delivered the twins. It was apparent he was proud of his doctors and shared in their triumphs. He reached for the phone on his desk. "I'll inform Captain Wood you're here. It won't take him but a minute to get dressed and come to the orderly room."

"That won't be necessary, Sergeant. I'll just go on to his hooch. What I have to tell him and the other doctors won't take long. You might alert Captain Wood I'm on the way, but tell him I said to stay in the sack," JP said, starting to leave, then stopped. "Where is the officer's hooch?"

"Behind the emergency room, sir."

"Right. Thanks."

JP found the hooch without any trouble, knocked twice then walked in. The single room was long, furnished with six metal bunks, six metal wall lockers, an assortment of tables, chairs and bookcases, mostly improvised from wooden ammunition boxes. Medical books and journals lay scattered on the tables. Three of the six bunks were occupied by blinking, sleep-starved doctors dragging themselves into consciousness from deep sleep.

"I always suspected you guys spent most of your time in the sack," JP said in a loud voice.

"Good morning, sir," said a groggy Captain Steve Wood, the company commander. He swung his bare feet to the floor and reached for fatigue trousers.

"Stay put, Steve," JP ordered. "That goes for the rest of you. Is there any coffee around this place?"

"Yes, sir, behind you on the table against the wall."

JP walked to an improvised table and studied a percolator, a can labeled "Coffee", and some mugs. "How do you work this thing?"

Dick Frances sat up. "Just plug it in, sir. It's already loaded with water and coffee."

JP reached down, found the hanging cord and inserted it into an outlet behind the table. Almost instantly the percolator began bubbling. A delicious odor of brewing coffee wafted through the hooch. JP pulled a chair close to the doctors' bunks and sat down. "I heard you people had a tough delivery last night."

"That's the understatement of the year, Colonel," Steve Wood said. "The woman showed up last night with a history of having gone into labor eight hours before. She had no prenatal care. Thank God this wasn't her first pregnancy." Wood chuckled. "We didn't know there was a second baby until it... she presented. None of us had

460

ever delivered twins or even seen twins delivered."

"That must have been a bit of a shock."

"We were on the phone with Colonel Powell from the time the woman showed up until the second baby was delivered. He led us through the deliveries by the numbers. I don't think he got much sleep."

Powell, the commander of the 3rd Field Hospital in Saigon, was formerly chief of OB/GYN at Walter Reed. He was one of the top obstetrical specialists in the country. As the Walter Reed tradition required, Powell took care of the staff doctors' wives. He was often the topic of conversation at officer's wives' club luncheons. Invariably one of the wives would mimic his high-pitched warning before inserting a cold vaginal speculum during gyn examination. "This may feel a bit chilly, heh, heh, heh."

The percolator stopped gurgling. "Does that mean coffee is ready?" JP asked.

"Yes, sir."

JP went back to the table and filled four mugs with coffee. Picking up two, he carried one to Steve Wood and the other to Dick Frances. Returning to the table, he picked up the remaining two, handed one to Al Gruber and kept the last for himself.

"Army life is changing for the better," Gruber said.

"How do you mean?"

"First time I've been served breakfast in bed by a colonel."

"Don't let it go to your head," JP snapped. Sitting down, he slurped the hot coffee. "Not bad for government issue."

"It's not GI, sir," Dick Frances said. "My wife sent me a can of Columbian Special."

Steve Wood set his mug on the floor and looked at JP questioningly. "Colonel, why do I get the feeling you came down here for more than just to make us coffee."

"Very perceptive, Captain," JP said, becoming serious. "There's a situation at the 3rd Battalion that probably involves one or more of the medical personnel in the aid station. It's going to require all our efforts today to get the situation under control." He went on to describe the high number of injection site abscesses. "They were all traced back to the 3rd Battalion. It was apparent from the records that the syrettes had been tampered with between the time they were issued at brigade medical supply and the time they were injected into casualties by medics."

Steve Wood was horrified. "Good God, sir, the medics out in the bush still may be carrying some of those tampered syrettes."

"That's the reason they must be picked up a.s.a.p. and fresh syrettes issued."

"And that's why you are here."

"Steve, you're getting smarter by the minute. Here's what I would like you and your doctors to do." JP then outlined the plan for confiscating the syrettes and issuing new one. "When I leave here I'll go to brigade to brief Colonel Prather on the situation and hit him up to put a helicopter at your disposal. The chopper pilot can get the coordinates and call signs of each unit from the 3rd Battalion TOC."

JP paused to sip his coffee, then looked at each officer. His voice took on a hardness. "Do not go into any hot LZs. That's an order. I've been attending too many memorial services lately."

"Colonel, you don't suspect Jay Dinkons, do you?" Dick Frances asked.

"Everyone assigned to the aid station, including the battalion surgeon, is a suspect. The CID is working on that aspect. We, you and I, have two urgent objectives. One is to reduce the risks of contaminated syrettes being used on casualties. The other is to be sure the syrettes picked up are properly labeled so they can be used as evidence."

"Shall we tell our people why we're picking up the syrettes?"

"No. Make up some sort of cover story. We don't want to tip off a suspect and give him opportunity to dispose of critical evidence."

Frances sighed. "I've seen some bad things since I've been out here, Colonel, but this is the worst. I can't believe an American would put another American at such risk."

"There's no accounting for human nature when drugs are involved," JP said. Getting to his feet, he took his mug over to the table, set it down and turned. "Steve, I need to borrow your jeep for about half an hour to go to brigade."

"Sure, Colonel. I'll call the first sergeant." Captain Wood reached for the phone on the floor by his bed.

★

Wednesday, September 9, 1970, 1020 hours
Fire Support Base Maxine

Fire Support Base Maxine, home of the 3rd/48th Infantry Battalion, was located on the top of a mountain sixty-four kilometers south-west of Quang Dien and Skunk Patch. The summit, shorn of all vegetation, was easy to spot from the air. It was the only bald summit in an extensive range of tree-covered mountains. Chief Warrant Officer Dan Ranson made his approach by maintaining 2,000 feet until just over Maxine. Below on the firebase red smoke was clearly visible streaming south-west from its source. Ranson dropped the Huey into a steep spiraling descent. In less than a minute the Huey flared over Maxine and settled on to the helipad, raising immense clouds of red dust.

Lieutenant Colonel JP Franklin, M.C., USA, made out the lanky form of the Lieutenant Colonel John Nielson, Infantry, USA, leaning into the rotor wash and hanging on to his hat. Nielson, another of JP's West Point neighbors, was a mustang, having worked his way up to officer status from private. After earning a PhD from Princeton in history Nielson turned down faculty positions at three universities to go to West Point as a professor of history. Completing four years of teaching at the Academy, he insisted on going to Vietnam. Now on his third tour, highly decorated, and on the list for full colonel, JP considered him well on his way to a first star.

Chief Warrant Officer Jesse Rodriguez touched JP's shoulder. "Colonel, we'll need to be left alone at least for the next hour with the aid station personnel. I have warrants from the JAG authorizing search of the battalion aid station and the personal effects of the three individuals you named as having access to the syrettes. When we're through I'll find you and report."

JP nodded. As soon as he climbed down from the helicopter Nielson approached, saluted, and extended his hand. Snapping a return salute, JP grabbed the extended hand of his friend. "How are you, John?"

"I was fine until Colonel Prather's call this morning. What the hell's going on, JP?"

"Let's go somewhere we can talk."

"The mess hall's as good as any. This way."

JP barely managed to stay up with Nielson's rapid pace without breaking into a run. Breathless, he asked, "You always move this fast?"

"Only when I'm anxious to learn why my brigade commander calls me out of the blue and tells me to expect the division surgeon and CID agents within the hour, give them a free hand and keep my mouth shut."

"Relax, John. This problem is mine although it affects your battalion."

The mess hall was a long, low, wooden building with screened windows all around, its sides partially sandbagged. As soon as the colonels entered, a high-pitched voice shouted, "Tenshun."

Nielson immediately called, "As you were." Passing a half dozen vacant tables, Nielson stopped at one in a far corner. "This should do for privacy," he said. In less than a minute a mess man wearing a green T-shirt and fatigue trousers brought a stainless steel pitcher of steaming coffee and two mugs. Nielson filled the two mugs with coffee, shoved one towards JP and took several sips from the other. Setting the mug on the table, he said, "Okay, tell me, what's going on in my battalion."

JP related what was known about the injection site abscesses. He discussed the reasoning that implicated the 3rd Battalion aid station and plans for dealing with the problem. "The CID are in the aid station right now confiscating all syrettes for analysis and evidence. They'll also interrogate the medical personnel. The JAG authorized search of their hooches and personal items."

When JP finished, Nielson seemed in deep thought. Suddenly he stood. "I'll be back in a couple of minutes." He turned and walked from the mess hall.

While waiting, JP sipped coffee, taking in the panoramic view of adjacent mountains and the lush green valley stretching west. Minutes later, Nielson returned as abruptly as he had left.

"You must have made a decision," JP said.

"The only one I could have made under the circumstances."

"You cancelled today's operations."

Nielson nodded. "We had two company assaults planned for late this morning. I scrubbed both. There is no way I will allow my men in harm's way when casualties may be injected with pain meds that are not only ineffective but may cause harm. Brigade will probably raise hell after they laid on so many choppers."

"You needn't worry, John. After I briefed Colonel Prather I suggested he put out an order canceling today's missions for the 3rd. He refused; he said the 3rd was your battalion and how you fought it was up to you."

Nielson smiled. "Now you know why I love working for that man."

"While we're waiting on Mr. Rodriguez, John, what are your impressions of the senior personnel assigned to the aid station?"

Nielson poured himself more coffee, sipped it, then set the mug down. "Sergeant Braunwin, the NCOIC, is on his third tour. He was a medic with the special forces his last two tours. He would still be with them except he was badly wounded. Your buddies at Walter Reed wanted to give him a medical discharge. He talked his way into remaining on active duty, then volunteered for a third tour. He is one of the few people I know with two Silver Stars. I'd trust him with my life."

JP sighed. "That pretty well eliminates him. What about the admin officer?"

"Lieutenant Ambrose, from the day he joined the battalion, has been like a kid on his first camping trip. He's been out here more than he's been at battalion rear, which is where he's supposed to be. When he's not in the aid station he's in the TOC or the fire control center. He's already learned to compute fire missions on the FADAC. He really should be wearing crossed cannons instead of a caduceus. If I hadn't forbidden it he would have gone out on patrols. He's engaged to marry a nurse at the 19th Surg." Nielson shook his head. "JP, you're going to have to look elsewhere for a villain."

JP had to admit, neither Sergeant Braunwin or Lieutenant Ambrose seemed likely suspects. Reluctantly he said, "That leaves the battalion surgeon, Jay Dinkons."

"As you know, Jay joined the battalion two months ago, about the same time as Braunwin and Ambrose. He has turned down repeated invitations to fly with me, spend time in the TOC, or even try get to know my staff. He takes his chow to his hooch and eats alone. When he's on the firebase, which is not often, he's in his hooch reading or writing letters. He hasn't been able to establish rapport with the troops or, for that matter, with Mark Evans, the battalion chaplain, who is his hooch-mate. The men avoid Jay when they're sick; they much prefer going to Sergeant Braunwin."

JP recalled Dinkons's strange effect when he first reported in to the division. He had spent an entire morning taking Dinkons on a tour of the medical battalion, Alpha and Charlie Clearing Companies, the two army hospitals, and the Phong Sahn base. In the afternoon he flew with him out to Maxine, stopping at several firebases along the way for Dinkons to meet his contemporary battalion surgeons. Dinkons acted disinterested, asked no questions, and seemed to have his attention focused elsewhere. JP assumed the man was homesick and undergoing a kind of culture shock. Since that day JP had visited Maxine three times. Each time Dinkons was at battalion rear. It was apparent Sergeant Braunwin was carrying the medical ball on Firebase Maxine. As a result he began pressuring Med Command for a replacement.

"I'll admit Jay is kind of strange, John," JP said, "but he's a doctor. A doctor would never do anything to harm those under his care. We will have to look elsewhere."

The screened door to the mess hall opened. Chief Warrant Officer Jesse Rodriguez walked in and looked around.

"Over here, Jesse," JP called out.

When Rodriguez reached the table JP introduced him to Colonel Nielson.

Nielson touched the stainless steel pitcher. "Coffee is still hot, Jesse. Grab a mug from the rack."

"Thanks, Colonel."

When Rodriguez returned with a mug he set it on the table and slid on to the bench while Colonel Nielson poured coffee. Rodriguez took several timid sips, then set the mug down.

"Anything you can tell us?" Colonel Nielson asked.

Rodriguez took out a small green flip-top notebook from his fatigue jacket pocket and thumbed through its pages. "Sir, all morphine syrettes have been confiscated from the aid station and properly labeled. Blood and urine samples were taken from everyone assigned to the battalion aid station. Captain Dinkons was the only one of the three who was reluctant to cooperate until we showed him the court order. We interrogated all personnel assigned to the aid station and searched their personal belongings."

Rodriguez closed the notebook and slipped it into his fatigue jacket pocket. "There is only one suspect at this time, sir, and I'm sorry to say it is Captain Dinkons. As of now there isn't enough evidence to make an arrest, but I expect it will not be long in coming."

JP felt as though he had been kicked in the stomach. One of his own doctors was under suspicion of committing a heinous crime. "Jesse, could you elaborate on what you have discovered so far?"

"Yes, sir. One week after Captain Dinkons took over as battalion surgeon he had the combination lock changed on the safe in the aid station. He is the only one with the combination. All narcotics, including morphine syrettes, are stored in the safe. According to Lieutenant Ambrose and Sergeant Braunwin, Captain Dinkons was the only person to issue morphine syrettes to medics in the past two months, or any other controlled substance."

Rodriguez paused for a swallow of coffee, then continued, "A search of Captain Dinkons's personal effects turned up four small syringes and half a dozen 27-gauge needles in a locked foot locker."

JP explained to Nielson. "27-gauge needles are very fine needles that make tiny puncture holes." He turned to the CID agent. "Did Captain Dinkons give any explanation for the syringes and needles in his locker? They could have been there for bona fide medical reasons."

"Yes, sir. He said he was allergic to insect bites and occasionally had to give himself epinephrine by injection. The needles and syringe were confiscated and will be sent to the crime lab for analysis of residue and fingerprints. Captain Dinkons's medical records will be checked for a history of allergy to insect bites."

JP desperately wanted to believe Dinkons innocent, but the evidence, circumstantial though it might be, was damning. He could not risk leaving Dinkons as battalion surgeon. He looked at Colonel Nielson. "John, I don't have any choice. I'm going to relieve Captain Dinkons."

"I concur with that, Colonel," Chief Warrant Officer Rodriguez said. "I recommend he be taken to Phong Lahm and be restricted until the lab and background checks are in."

JP shrugged agreement. "I'll keep him around battalion headquarters. I'd appreciate it if you would put the lab studies on a fast track."

Rodriguez nodded.

"JP, what about medical coverage for my battalion?" Nielson asked.

"I'll have the brigade surgeon or one of his staff come out here on a daily basis for sick call. Anyone with a condition that Sergeant Braunwin considers serious can be evacuated to Bravo Med at Skunk Patch. Once we know the results of the lab tests I'll know what to do about a replacement."

"One more thing, sir," Jesse Rodriguez said. "I will initiate a much more thorough background check on Captain Dinkons than is ordinarily done. Who knows what that will turn up."

"Thanks for all your work, Jesse," JP said, standing up. He took a final sip of coffeee. "I guess I'd better go tell Captain Dinkons the bad news."

★

Sunday, September 13, 1970, 1020 hours
Headquarters, 36th Medical Battalion, Phong Sahn, RVN

Four days had passed since the episode on Firebase Maxine. Lieutenant Colonel JP Franklin had been caught up in the challenges of a division surgeon and medical battalion commander. The division had been active, aggressively attacking concentrations of NVA and their supply lines in South Vietnam in anticipation of the coming monsoon season. The incidence of malaria and dysentery increased. Two medics had been killed and five others wounded. JP had been called to the 96th Evac three times to operate on complex injuries. The last case lasted nine hours. Thus he had little time to dwell on Captain Dinkons, and even less time to write Kathy. Some of his daily letters were only one or two short paragraphs. Now he sat at his desk in the medical battalion office doing what he hated doing most, reviewing and signing papers.

Sergeant Major Chessler wrapped on the doorway with his hammer like fist. The building shook. "Sir, Agents Rodriguez and Ambrose to see you."

JP went quickly to the door and extended his hand. "How are you, Jesse?"

"Fine, sir." Rodriguez said, grasping his hand. "You remember Agent Ambrose?"

"Sure."

JP shook hands with Ambrose. He gestured towards chairs in front of his desk.

Rodriguez eased into one of the chairs, placed an attaché case on his lap and opened it. Removing a sheaf of papers held together by a large metal clip, he looked up. "Colonel Franklin, you are Captain Dinkons's commanding officer?"

"That is correct."

"These are for you, sir."

Rodriguez laid the papers on JP's desk.

JP thumbed through the dozen or so sheets, then looked up. "How about summarizing what's in here. I'll read them later."

"Yes, sir. Those papers include reports from the crime lab at Long Binh. One hundred and sixty three morphine syrettes were collected from medics in the field. Sixteen contained ordinary contaminated water and minimal traces of morphine. A spectrum of organic, inorganic, and bacterial contaminants was identified in the water."

"Good God!" JP exclaimed, shocked at the revelation.

Rodriguez continued, "Six of thirty-seven syrettes taken from the safe in the battalion aid station were found to have water and similar contaminants. Two syringes and four needles taken from Captain Dinkons's foot locker had traces of morphine. Another syringe had the residue of ordinary unsterile water similar to the water found in the tampered syrettes. Captain Dinkons's fingerprints were found on all three syringes and syrettes."

JP sat quietly as the significance of what he had just been told registered.

"There's more," Rodriguez said. "The blood and urine samples from Captain Dinkons were positive for breakdown products of morphine. All the others tested were negative."

JP leaned forward, still refusing to believe one of his doctors could have done such a thing. "Jesse, if as you are suggesting, a fine needle and small syringe were used to aspirate morphine from the syrettes and replace it with ordinary water, a hole would have remained in the syrette through which water would have leaked, especially when the tube was squeezed. The medics would have reported it."

"You underestimate the cleverness of the addict, Colonel. The label on the syrette was partially lifted and the needle inserted in the area ordinarily covered by the label. After the morphine was aspirated and replaced with water, the hole was covered with a drop of collodion. The collodion not only filled the hole left by the needle but acted as glue for the label."

JP thumbed absent-mindedly through the papers Rodriguez had given him. The print seemed blurred. This was an aspect of war he had not contemplated. He wanted no part of it, yet it had become part of him.

"There's more," Rodriguez said.

"I'm not sure I want to hear it, Jesse."

Rodriguez continued, "The background investigation of Captain Dinkons revealed that he abruptly left a surgery residency towards the end of his first year. He was able to start an emergency medicine residency, but dropped out after six months. He was in a family practice residency when he was drafted."

"What's the interpretation of that?" JP asked.

"Sir, there's no need for interpretation. The medical administrators of all three hospitals gave sworn statements that Dinkons was suspected of stealing drugs. There was insufficient evidence to prosecute so he was allowed to resign."

JP shook his head sadly. "I'm going to recommend trial by general court martial. How soon can an Article 32 investigation take place?"

"If you can get the paperwork to the JAG today he'll have an officer appointed to do the investigation by tomorrow. Because of the seriousness of the impending charges against Captain Dinkons and the risk of bodily harm once the GIs learn what he has done, the JAG suggested confinement pending the Article 32 investigation and subsequent trial."

JP nodded assent.

Rodriguez closed and locked his attaché case. Standing up, he said, "With your permission, sir, Agent Ambrose and I will place Captain Dinkons under arrest, handcuff him, and read him his rights."

Chapter Fifty-One

Tuesday, September 22, 1970, 1300 hours
36th Medical Battalion, Phong Sahn, RVN

Lieutenant Colonel JP Franklin, M.D., Medical Corps, US Army, read with some dismay the general court martial proceedings in the case of the United States Army versus Captain Jay W. Dinkons, Medical Corps, US Army Reserve. Dinkons, through his military counsel, had requested and was granted trial by a military judge in lieu of a board of officers. He then pled guilty to the most serious charge with the stipulation he would not serve jail time. The military judge sentenced him to two years confinement and a dishonorable discharge, then suspended the confinement. By now Dinkons was on a jet flying home and sipping martinis, but he was taking with him a felony conviction and a dishonorable discharge. He would never be able to hold a narcotics license or vote in a national election. Although states varied in requirements for medical licensure, it was unlikely that an accredited hospital would appoint him to its staff.

Corporal Samuelson knocked on his door. "Sir, Mr. Ranson is on line one."

"Thanks, Sammy." JP picked up the phone. "What's up, Dan?"

"Colonel, my chopper needs a flight this afternoon to check out new air-nav equipment and it's about time you transitioned to the Huey. Are you interested?"

"When and where?"

"The detachment helipad at 1400 hours. I want to go through the start-up procedures with you on the UH1H. Who knows when you might have to do it and under what circumstances. After today's flight I'll give you the Tech Manual on the Huey to study."

"Does that mean I'll get an exam one of these days?"

"You better believe it, Colonel. It will come like an engine failure, when you least expect it."

"You know, Ranson, I've always thought you were a hard ass."

★

Tuesday, September 22, 1970, 1410 hours
86th Aviation Detachment, Phong Sahn, RVN

"Well, sir," Warrant Officer Ranson told Lieutenant Colonel Franklin as they completed the walk-around external inspection of the Huey, "if this were flight school I would grade you marginally satisfactory. You really should use the checklist instead of relying on memory."

JP blushed. He knew that Second Lieutenant Thomas Carter, standing nearby, had heard. "Carter, you write anything about this to your mother and I'll find some way to ground you."

"Sir, the thought never crossed my mind," Tom Carter said, grinning.

"Okay. We're set to go," Ranson announced. "Lieutenant, you are junior man besides being extra baggage this flight. Grab a fire extinguisher and stand by. Colonel, you take the left seat."

JP opened the left door, put his foot on the step and climbed up and into the seat, working his leg around the cyclic. Carter, standing on the skid, handed him his flight helmet, then helped him with his shoulder straps.

After locking his seat belt and shoulder straps, JP slipped on his helmet, adjusted the earphones and plugged in the headset cord. Reaching for the flip-type checklist he turned to the page on pre-start.

Ranson walked around the front of the Huey, climbed into the right seat and belted in. He quickly checked the position of the circuit breakers, dialed in the radio frequencies, then reached up to the overhead console. "I'm activating the igniter circuit breaker, Colonel, then I'll turn on the master switch."

A moment later the gyros began to spool up and radio static came into JP's earphones. Ranson's voice on the intercom followed. "There's a trigger on the cyclic. Squeeze it to the first click for intercom, to the second click for transmit. All set?"

JP nodded.

Ranson waved to Tom Carter who was standing beside the fuselage with a fire extinguisher. On the intercom he told JP, "Follow me lightly on the controls, Colonel. I've got my left hand on the collective and am rolling the handle, which is the throttle, to the indent starting position."

JP felt the handle rotate.

"On the collective handle is a trigger switch. I'll squeeze it to initiate the electric starter."

The starter motor whined. Above the helicopter the rotor blades began to turn. Then came a loud hissing sound.

"The second noise indicates fire has caught in the turbine. It's imperative now to watch the exhaust-gas temperature gauge, EGT for short." Ranson tapped the instrument. "The needle will go into the red initially but should return to the green after a few seconds. If it stays in the red there is high probability of a hot start."

JP squeezed the cyclic's trigger to the first click. "What then?"

"Shut down, bail out, and let the fireman do his thing."

The EGT needle shifted to over the green marker. Above, the rotor blades spun faster. "Okay, sir, call out the gauges to be monitored in the six pack."

JP touched each instrument as he named it: "Transmission pressure, engine oil pressure, engine oil temp, fuel pressure, amp meter, and exhaust gas temp."

"Now check the warning lights for high and low RPMs, the master caution and chip detector lights."

"Negative lights," JP reported.

"I'll do the take-off," Ranson said. "Follow me on the controls. Once we're clear of

Phong Sahn airspace you can take over and head to the practice area. We'll do a little air work this afternoon, then practice take-off and hovering. Carter, you all set back there?"

"Roger, except I forgot my motion sickness pills."

Ranson grinned. He squeezed the cyclic trigger to the second position. "Duke control, this is Duke Four, ready to go."

"Ah Duke Four, stand by."

The Huey vibrated with a synchronized rhythm; the turbine sounds transitioned from noise to sweet music.

"Duke Four, Duke control. Do you have Mac Six on board?"

"Roger, sitting right next to me."

"Your flight has been scratched. You are to shut down and report to flight operations immediately. Mac Six has an urgent telephone call from the chief of staff. He can take it in here."

The engine sounds died and the rapidly turning rotor blade began to slow. JP, cursing the gods of war, pulled off his helmet. Unbuckling the seat belt and shoulder harness, he opened the left door and climbed down to the ground. "I wonder what this is about," he groused to Dan Ranson as they walked to the operations shack.

"Beats me, sir."

Entering the shack, Ranson and Carter disappeared into a small room. JP continued on to a counter where a corporal handed him a phone.

"Colonel Franklin, sir," he said.

"John Witherington, Doctor."

"Yes, sir."

"We've just received an unusual request from General Mueller, the commanding general of the 1st Marine Division. One of his battalion commanders sustained a serious wound of the neck and had been taken to the hospital ship, *Sanctuary*. Apparently the neck wound is so devastating that there is talk of removing the larynx. The navy head and neck surgeon assigned to the *Sanctuary* is on leave. General Mueller requested you be sent to the *Sanctuary* as a surgical consultant."

"General Mueller was my CO during World War II, Colonel, and the current 1st Division chaplain was a close buddy. I've been looking for an excuse to visit them."

"Fate works in strange ways, Doctor. Do you have anything pressing that would preclude your going?"

"No, sir."

"Good. The general has authorized you TDY with the navy to serve as a surgical consultant for twenty-four hours, longer if necessary. Just keep us informed. You can keep the chopper with you or send it back."

"I'll probably send it back unless the weather turns bad."

"Don't let those jarheads brainwash you, Doctor."

"It's too late, sir."

After hanging up, JP called his medical battalion and the division surgeon's office to let them know he would be gone for one, possibly two days. Then he walked out to the helicopter. Dan Ranson and Tom Carter followed a few minutes later. The door

470

gunners were already belted in, their M–60s installed.

"You want to fly it up there, Colonel?" Ranson asked.

"I'd better not, Dan. We're pressed for time. Besides, flying a helicopter is hard work. I have long hours in the operating room ahead of me. By the way, have you or Carter ever landed a helicopter on a ship?"

"No, sir."

"I'm sorry I asked."

★

Tuesday, September 22, 1970, 1545 hours
Approaching Danang from the north over the coast of South Vietnam

Second Lieutenant Thomas Carter maintained the Huey at 2,000 feet over South Vietnam's white sandy coastline. Through the open door Lieutenant Colonel JP Franklin saw Danang appear in the distance. South Vietnam's third largest city and one of its major seaports, Danang reminded him of Seattle. Carter altered course slightly to the east and began a gradual let-down over the water. Tiny fishing boats littered the sandy shore for miles. Clusters of larger boats undulated at anchor in the water just off shore. Small one- and two-roomed huts lined the shore; the afternoon sunlight glinting off their shiny corrugated metal roofs. West towards the main part of the city the dwellings became progressively larger, evolving into closely packed rows of three- and four-storied buildings. Carter banked east; miles ahead the South China Sea met the sky.

"I just had a pleasant thought," JP announced over the intercom.

"What's that, sir?"

"If we stay on this heading for five days we'll be home."

"That thought occurs to me regularly, Colonel."

A white passenger ship with a huge red cross on its side materialized in the distance. JP keyed his mike. "Is that the *Sanctuary* coming up at ten o'clock?"

"Negative, sir," Ranson said. "That's the *Heligoland*, a West German hospital ship. It takes care of civilian casualties. The *Sanctuary* is further east. We should be close enough now to give them a call and get a radar vector."

Sanctuary approach answered on the first call. Ranson punched in four numbers on the Huey's transponder and pressed the "Squawk" button.

Sanctuary approach confirmed radar contact and gave a course heading to the ship. "Surface winds are out of the north at twelve gusting to eighteen with a pitching deck. Set down on the number one pad on the fan tail."

In a few minutes Dan Ranson pointed through the windscreen. "There she is at one o'clock."

"It looks awfully small, Dan," said Tom Carter.

"It will get bigger as we get closer," Ranson assured him.

Carter brought the Huey down to 300 feet above the water.

JP, looking forward through the open door, saw the *Sanctuary*'s stern lifting and falling, Straight down, multiple breaking waves reflected a choppy sea. He tightened his seat belt and gripped the tubular frame of the canvas seat. This was not a good place for an auto-rotation.

Despite the winds and turbulence, Carter maintained a stable approach, bringing the nose up and slowing the Huey to ten knots as they neared the *Sanctuary*'s stern. A windsock on a deck above the helipad whipped about like an angry cobra. Four firemen in silver textured fireproof suits, fire extinguishers at the ready, stood in nearby protected areas. As soon as the Huey crossed over the edge of the stern, "ground effect" gave it slight lift. Carter brought the Huey to a brief hover, then eased forward slowly. The *Sanctuary*'s stern rose and fell with a pulsating regularity. Just as the stern reached its zenith Carter reduced collective and wedded the Huey to the ship with a thud. Immediately crewmen ran to the Huey and secured it to the deck with cables. Ranson shut down the engine.

"Great landing, Tom," JP said.

"I don't know; he had me worried," Ranson interjected. "Do you want us to stay, Colonel?"

"No. You better head back to Phong Sahn while the weather holds. I have no idea how long I'll be here. I'll hitch a ride back tomorrow."

"We'll take off as soon as we top off the tanks, use the latrine and try to scrounge some coffee."

"Mr. Ranson, on board a US naval vessels the latrine is called a head," JP explained.

"Yes, sir, a head it is."

With his fatigue cap firmly on his head, JP climbed down and walked briskly towards two figures standing by a hatch. One was a middle-aged officer in a short-sleeved white uniform, the four stripes of a captain on his shoulder boards. The other was a younger man who wore a doctor's white coat over green operating scrubs, a stethoscope stuck in one pocket.

JP saluted the navy captain. "Sir, would it be superfluous for me to ask permission to come aboard?"

Returning the salute, the captain grinned. "Under the circumstances, Colonel, I have no choice but to say 'Permission granted', and welcome aboard. I'm Captain Pederson, the skipper." He indicated the man in green scrubs and white coat. "This is Commander Farnsworth, chief of surgery. The hospital commander, Captain Herman, is in Saigon at a hospital commander's conference."

JP shook hands with both men.

The captain continued, "Commander Farnsworth will be your host. Anything I can do for you while you're on board please call on me. You will be welcome on the bridge at any time."

JP thanked the captain. "My chopper crew could use some coffee."

"No problem. The deck control chief will see to it and anything else they need. Thanks for coming, Colonel."

He turned and disappeared through a hatch.

Farnsworth said, "Colonel, we have a few minutes while the orthopods finish debriding and packing the patient's thigh wound. How about some coffee and doughnuts before we go to the OR? I can brief you on the case."

"That's the best offer I've had today."

Farnsworth led through metal double doors held open by two seamen. JP smiled his thanks. As he and Farnsworth walked down a wide passageway Farnsworth asked, "Have you ever been on a hospital ship?"

"This is my first. I may take your captain up on his offer to visit the bridge. Ever since I saw Ronald Reagan as a ship commander in a World War II movie I wanted to stand on a ship's bridge and report, 'I have the conn', then pull that lever thing back and forth and order 'full speed ahead'."

Farnsworth smiled. "That might be arranged." He paused at an open doorway. "This is the officers' ward room. There's a medical library with an enlisted librarian down the hall. It has a good selection of medical texts, bound and current journals."

The room they entered was the size of a classroom. Furnished with leather armchairs, tables, a television, and reel-to-reel tape deck, the room had a warm, comfortable ambience. Farnsworth led towards a table covered with a white linen tablecloth. An electric coffee urn occupied one end of the table. Next to the urn a silver tray contained cups, saucers, and spoons. A smaller tray held packets of sugar and powdered cream. On a nearby table another tray was loaded with doughnuts and cookies. An aroma of fresh bakery mixed with that of coffee reminded JP he was hungry.

Farnsworth reached for a cup and saucer. "Help yourself to doughnuts, Colonel. I'll bring your coffee. How do like it?"

"Black, please," JP said, placing three plain doughnuts on a plate and moving to a nearby table. Sitting down, he waited for Farnsworth to bring the coffee. After Farnsworth was seated JP thanked him, took a sip of coffee and followed it with a bite of doughnut.

"The ward room stays open twenty-four hours a day," Farnsworth said. "Mess personnel keep the coffee and doughnuts fresh. If you want something more substantial there is chow available most of the day for crews going on and coming off watch."

"I've always admired the navy's lifestyle," JP said.

"If one has to be in Vietnam as a doctor," Farnsworth said with a slight smile, "a hospital ship is as good a place as any."

"Do you ever get off the ship?"

"Occasionally I fly over to the 95th Evac in Danang and give the army a hand when things here are quiet. I go to the province hospital twice a month to help out on difficult belly cases. I've been teaching the Vietnamese surgeons how to close colostomies."

"Tell me about our patient," JP said.

"He's a forty-eight-year old marine lieutenant colonel who was commanding the 6th Battalion. About four hours ago he was hit by mortar frags when he was visiting one of his companies in the bush. He sustained wounds of the thigh and neck. The thigh wound had considerable soft tissue damage but no bone fractures. The femoral vessels and nerve were intact although the femoral nerve appeared contused."

Farnsworth took a sip of coffee, then set his cup on a saucer.

"The neck has a single entrance wound just to the left of the laryngeal cartilage. There is no exit wound. As soon as the colonel was hit he developed acute upper airway obstruction and lost his voice. Fortunately, his battalion surgeon happened to be close by and somehow cut down on the trachea, got in an airway, and managed to control the bleeding. The colonel's C&C chopper brought him here. On physical exam the neck was markedly swollen. There was a dime-sized entrance wound in the left mid-neck. On palpation, the laryngeal cartilage felt like cracked egg shells. There's crepitation from the mandible to mid-thorax."

JP remained quiet as he assimilated the information and formed an image of the injury.

"Any X-rays?"

"Yes, sir."

"Jeff, you and I are the same rank. There's no need to sir me. I go by JP."

"The navy is strict on protocol. I thought I'd better give you the benefit of doubt. After all, sir, you are the consultant."

"True, but I operate best in an informal environment."

"Whatever you say, JP. The X-rays are in the OR. I can summarize them for you."

"Please do."

"The soft tissue lateral of the neck showed massive infiltration of air through neck tissues. The air obscured most of the anatomy. The chest films showed widening of the mediastinum and air under the pericardium."

"What about the mortar frag?"

"It's embedded in the anterior wall of C–4."

"Any evidence of spinal cord damage?"

"None. He was able to move upper and lower limbs. Bill Porter, our neurosurgeon, cleared him for a neck exploration. Both he and the orthopods would like to see that frag out, but only if it can be removed easily. If we run into any problems they will be available to consult or scrub in."

JP finished his second doughnut. "The navy makes excellent doughnuts," he said, reaching for his third.

"We really appreciate your coming up here, JP. Before Barry Templeton, our head and neck man, left on leave, he said to call you if we had any big problems in the neck. He was sure you would find a way to help us out."

"That name sounds familiar," JP said. "Is Templeton an ex-navy corpsman, sort of thin, red-faced, with freckles and receding red hair? He was with the marines at the Chosin Reservoir in 1950."

"Good memory. Barry remembered you from your lectures at the AFIP Basic Science Head and Neck Course. He especially remembered the party at your quarters for air force, navy, and army head and neck residents taking the course. He said your wife was a phenomenal cook."

"What I wouldn't give for some of her cooking now," JP said wistfully.

"There is another aspect of this case of which you should be aware."

JP remained silent.

474

"The 1st Mar Div commanding general has called me twice this afternoon to check on the casualty. Apparently he and the casualty served together during World War II and the Korean War. The general will probably come out this evening or tomorrow morning to visit casualties and present awards. I'm sure he'll want to talk to you."

"Thanks for the warning," JP said. "Actually I'm looking forward to seeing him. He was my CO during part of World War II."

"You were in the marines?"

JP nodded. "Almost three years."

"I'll be damned. So was I. Semper Fi, Colonel."

"Small world, commander. Semper Fi."

The two doctors, both former marines, shook hands again.

Chapter Fifty-Two

Tuesday, September 22, 1970, 1545 hours
USS *Sanctuary*, off the Coast of Danang, RVN

Commander Jeffrey Farnsworth and Lieutenant Colonel JP Franklin, masked, gowned, and gloved, pushed through the doors into one of the *Sanctuary*'s operating rooms. Colonel Franklin scanned the air-conditioned room, noting its gleaming modern equipment. "Just like downtown," he told Farnsworth. Both men moved towards the operating table where two surgeons stuffed gauze into a gaping thigh wound. The older of the two surgeons looked up. "We'll be through as soon as we wrap the leg, Jeff."

"How did it go?"

"Piece of cake. There was a lot of soft tissue destruction mixed with scar tissue from World War II wounds. That leg seems to attract metal." The surgeon lifted the packing briefly to expose a gaping defect in the mid-thigh. "We did a generous debridement."

Farnsworth and JP peered over the surgeon's shoulder. "Definitely generous," Farnsworth said. "What's the prognosis for rehab?"

"Pretty good if no post-op infection or major vessel thrombosis develops. The defect will be closed in Japan or the Philippines in ten days or two weeks. Over the next year much of the deformity will fill in. The leg will never be a thing of beauty, but then it wasn't before it got hit. After physical therapy he should be able to get around reasonably well with a cane and a distinguished limp."

"You do nice work for an orthopod," Farnsworth said.

"Coming from a belly surgeon that has to be a compliment. I understand the neck wound is so bad it may be necessary to take out the larynx."

"That decision will be up to Colonel Franklin," Farnsworth said, indicating JP. "He's the army's head and neck top gun from Walter Reed, now the 36th's division surgeon." Farnsworth turned to JP. "Colonel, the older of the two gentlemen at the table is Commander Sam Reiner, chief of orthopedics. His assistant is Lieutenant Dave Warner. Dave has been anxious to meet you."

"Any particular reason?"

"Yes, sir," Warner said. "I heard a lot about your work at Walter Reed from Jerry Templeton. He talked almost as much about Mrs. Franklin's wonderful cooking at the Basic Science Course Party."

"I'll pass on to her that she won the hearts of the navy through its stomach. It sounds like Jerry is orienting you towards head and neck surgery."

"More than that, Colonel. I've been accepted for the program at Bethesda to start next July."

"In that case, would you like to scrub in on the neck?"

"Sir, I thought you would never ask."

Farnsworth nodded towards a lit bank of viewboxes covered with X-rays. "Those are his films?"

JP moved from viewbox to viewbox, studying each film. When he finished he turned to Farnsworth. "I don't see anything more than what you described." He pointed to a jagged 1 cm metal lucency at the anterior surface of a cervical vertebra. "The frag must have lost most of its momentum by the time it hit the spine. There's no fracture, just a few bone chips. If it had gone another centimeter he would have been quadriplegic. You're positive there was no extremity weakness before he was put to sleep?"

"Yes, sir. The spine was cleared as stable by the chief of neurosurgery and the chief of orthopedics, who now stands before you."

"That's right, Colonel," Commander Reiner said. "The C-spine is solid."

"He's lucky," JP said, backing away from the viewboxes.

"Very lucky," echoed Reiner.

JP continued, "There is an additional injury that should be considered; it's one that can be disastrous if not recognized and treated."

"What's that, sir?"

"The pharyngeal perforation."

Jeff Farnsworth went to the viewboxes and examined the films. When he turned away he had a perplexed look. "JP, do you really see a pharyngeal perforation on these films?"

JP smiled. "You're right. I don't see a perforation. What I do see is widening of the retrovisceral space." His finger outlined the area between the vertebrae and the upper gut. "Even more compelling is consideration of the anatomical relation of the larynx, pharynx, and C-spine. There is no way for the frag to have entered the neck where it did, and end up embedded in the vertebra without having passed through the anterior and posterior walls of the pharynx."

"Did you seen anything on the X-rays that would incline you to take out the larynx.?" Farnsworth asked.

JP shook his head. "No, but that's not a decision I would base on X-ray findings anyway. My experience at Reed and thus far in Vietnam has tilted me towards conservatism. Even with massive laryngeal injuries such as from blunt trauma, shotgun blasts, dog bites, and high velocity bullets, if the patient survives long enough to reach the operating room it is possible to salvage something that resembles a larynx. Multiple operations may be necessary to rehabilitate the patient, but at least he has something on which to build. If life-threatening infection or aspiration pneumonia develop later a laryngectomy can be done."

"I guess that covers the subject," Commander Farnsworth said.

At the operating table Dave Warner applied the last strip of tape to the bulky thigh dressing. Commander Reiner checked the dressing, pulled off his gown and gloves and turned to JP. "He's all yours, Colonel. Good luck."

Dave Warner finished prepping the patient from jaw to nipples, then slipped on sterile gown and gloves while JP and Jeff Farnsworth covered the patient with layers of green sheets, leaving only the neck and upper chest exposed. JP picked up a sharpened wooden applicator, dipped the pointed end into an opened vial of methyl blue that the scrub nurse held for him. Using the applicator as a pen, he drew a U-shaped incision beginning under one ear and extending to the other, with its horizontal segment low in the neck to include the tracheotomy. "This is my favorite incision for extensive neck injuries," JP explained. "It gives great exposure and can be modified, depending on the injury. For lesser injuries one or two horizontal incisions are preferred or a single vertical incision along the anterior border of the sternomastoid muscle."

Completing the outline of the incision, JP dropped the applicator on the Mayo stand. The scrub nurse immediately handed him a scalpel. He now faced his most frequent dilemma in the operating room, the conflict between the surgeon who loved to operate and the teacher who loved to teach. He held the scalpel handle towards Jeff Farnsworth. "Go ahead and start off. I'll take over when we get to the larynx."

Although JP hated to admit it, Farnsworth's elevation of the skin flap and exposure of the injured larynx were as good, if not better, than he could have done. Farnsworth continued on, meticulously defining the mass of cartilage fragments and torn soft tissue where once there had been a well-formed rigid Adam's apple. For JP, who liked to consider himself the "fastest knife east of the Mississippi", it was a humbling revelation. "Jeff, if you were in the army instead of the navy I'd feel threatened."

Farnsworth smiled. "Thanks, Colonel. Now what?"

Retracting the injured larynx and trachea to one side with his fingers, JP asked for an army–navy retractor.

"You mean navy–army, Colonel," the scrub nurse corrected, passing him a ten-inch long flat metal bar, its ends bent at right angles,

"Right. Navy–army; I forgot I'm in hostile country."

He slipped the retractor over his fingers and pulled the conglomerate of injured larynx, trachea, pharynx and esophagus towards him. Dave Warner worked the suction to keep the area clear of blood.

"Now, Jeff," JP continued, "work down towards the cervical spine on your side using blunt dissection, stay on the outside of the constrictor muscle and be careful not to poke through the muscle into the pharynx; there are enough holes in it already."

After several minutes inserting closed scissors, then opening the blades to spread apart tissue, Farnsworth looked up.

"I'm there."

"Insinuate a finger between the spine and back wall of the pharynx and create a working space 3–4 cm long. You will probably feel the perforation in the back wall of the pharynx before you see it. Same goes for the frag."

The OR was silent except for the hiss of air conditioning and the suction. Farnsworth suddenly looked up. "I feel the frag, JP. Oops, it just came loose." Using a pair of thumb forceps, he reached into the depths of the wound with its spoon-shaped

478

jaws. Moments later the forceps emerged with a dime-sized jagged metal fragment in its jaws. Farnsworth dropped the frag into a metal emesis basin. It landed with a metallic clunk.

"Shucks, you're supposed to let your consultant do that," JP said, feigning disappointment. He inserted the army–navy's longer limb deeper into the space created by Farnsworth's finger dissection. Lifting up, he leaned over the over to examine the defect, then explored with his fingers. When he had finished he told Dave Warner to do the same and describe his findings.

The young surgeon's eyes took on the characteristic faraway look of surgeons when forced to rely on tactile sensations to provide critical information. "Well, sir, the periostium over C–4 is shredded. There's a small shallow indentation of the anterior wall. I can feel sharp edges and tiny particles of bone or metal, but the vertebra feels solid."

"Very good. Keep going."

"My finger just fell through a hole in the back wall of the pharynx."

"You have the makings of a real head and neck surgeon, or at least your fingers do. If the upper gut perforation had been undiagnosed, secretions, food, and liquids would have leaked out into the neck setting up potentially fatal infection." He turned to Jeff Farnsworth. "Go ahead with aggressive irrigation, then debride the edges of the perforation until they bleed, and close it with interrupted sutures."

Thirty minutes later the perforation in the back wall of the pharynx was closed. JP then instructed Farnsworth to cut the end of one of the narrow neck muscles and swing the muscle between the spine and repaired perforation. "The muscle will function as a batten, bring in a blood supply to enhance healing and reduce the risk of infection."

Next, the perforation in the front wall of the pharynx was located and repaired in a like manner. After examining both repairs, JP indicated satisfaction. "Now for the main event. I think I'd better tackle the larynx, Jeff."

"I think I agree, Colonel."

JP called for a headlight and loupe. The corpsman–circulator brought an apparatus that resembled a coal miner's light. Slipping the headband over JP's head, the circulator tightened it. "That's not too tight, is it, sir?"

JP winced. "Better loosen it a little before I have to go to a smaller hat size."

"Sorry about that," the circulator said, readjusting the headband. "How is it now?"

"Much better, thanks."

Next the circulator eased thick black eyeglass frames over JP's ears. A pair of tubular lenses with 3X magnification were fixed to the eye part of the frame.

"You look as if you're wearing night vision goggles," the scrub nurse said, passing JP a sterile towel.

Grasping the towel to avoid contaminating his gloves, he adjusted the light to form a spot about twenty inches away, then focused each lens on the light spot. Returning to the operating table, he held out his hand. "Debakey forceps and Lincoln scissors." Using the delicate forceps and the pointed tips of the narrow-bladed scissors, he began dissecting into the jumble of torn tissue and fragmented Adam's apple cartilage.

Dave Warner, cleaning away blood with a sucker, remarked, "It looks like a boiled egg after someone slammed it with a fist. I just don't see how anything that mutilated can be reconstructed."

"Think positively, Dave, like the farmer's kid who was sent to clean out the barn. Knee deep in horse manure, he started shoveling like crazy. 'With all this manure,' he told himself, 'there must be a pony in here somewhere.'"

Over the next two hours JP meticulously defined from the amorphous conglomerate of tissue, muscle, a dozen irregular fragments of cartilage, the largest the size of a dime. Suddenly, he looked up. "Jackpot." He uttered. In his forceps he held a 1 cm long strip of muscle. "Would you believe this is the left vocal cord? It's still attached to the arytenoid," he said, indicating a 4–5 mm bone-like triangular structure. "Now all we have to do is find the opposite vocal cord and arytenoid, rebuild the Adam's apple and reattach the vocal cords. Then we can go home."

Four hours from the time the skin incision was made the larynx had been reconstructed and closed over a finger cot stuffed with sponge rubber. The finger cot functioned as an internal splint to maintain cartilage and tissue in their anatomical positions until healed. It would be removed in three to six weeks.

"We're ready for the irrigation catheters," JP told the scrub nurse. "A couple of No.6 Red Robinsons will do. After we finish in the neck we'll need to put in a feeding gastrostomy."

"Why not just put down an NG tube, Colonel?" Dave Warner asked.

"It will be four to six weeks, perhaps longer, before oral feedings can be started. An NG tube for that length of time would compromise the pharyngeal repairs by mechanical irritation and serve as a source of infection. The gastrostomy bypasses the upper gut, keeping it at rest thereby giving it the best chance to heal."

"Belly surgery is my specialty," Jeff Farnsworth said. "Dave and I can do the gastrostomy after we finish in the neck."

The pulsating noise of an approaching helicopter grew louder, then quickly subsided as it settled on the *Sanctuary*. Minutes later, the helicopter's noise increased, then faded.

"More work for somebody," the scrub nurse opined.

Thirty minutes later Farnsworth and Warner were placing the skin sutures when a tall figure in green scrubs entered the operating room. Approaching the operating table while holding a mask over his nose and mouth, he stopped by JP.

"Colonel Franklin, I'm Tony Durgan, chief of anesthesia."

"Why do I have the feeling you didn't come in here just to meet me?"

"You're very perceptive, sir. We just got in a young marine shot through the face and neck. Could you give us a hand?"

JP looked at Commander Farnsworth. "Can you finish up?"

"Sure, Colonel. Go ahead and drop out, and thanks."

Stepping back, JP undid the belt of his gown, pulled off the gown, tossing it into a cloth basket. "I'll look in on this patient and put a note on his chart after I finish the next case." Stripping off his gloves, he turned to the chief of anesthesiology. "Let's go have a look at this wounded tiger."

480

★

Wednesday, September 23, 1970, 0640 hours
USS *Sanctuary*

A tired and hungry Lieutenant Colonel JP Franklin, white coat over green scrubs, entered the officers' mess. Many tables were occupied by male officers in khaki uniforms sporting a variety of collar insignia other than Medical Corps. Nurses young and old, pretty and otherwise, dressed in white, were scattered among the tables. It was reassuring to see women in skirts instead of trousers. JP looked for an empty table. Having operated almost continuously through the night, he was in no mood for idle conversation with strangers. All he wanted was a place to sit quietly, have coffee and something to eat.

A young white-jacketed steward met him at the door. The steward led to a table in front of two large portholes overlooking the water. In the distance the lights of Danang continued to flicker. A small discreet sign on the table read: COMMANDERS AND ABOVE. JP eased into a cushioned arm chair facing the port holes, his back to the diners. The steward laid a check-off menu and pencil before him, then turned his cup over in its saucer. A moment later he filled it with steaming black coffee. "I'll be back in a minute for your order, sir," he promised.

"I'll be here," JP assured him, reaching for the coffee. After several sips he studied the menu, then checked off, "Eggs, over-medium, creamed beef on toast, hash brown potatoes, sausage." He omitted the orange juice. Over the past fourteen hours he had sucked through a straw enough orange juice to float an aircraft carrier. It had been his only sustenance as he went from one case to the next for a total of four cases, the last ending twenty minutes ago.

Sitting in the chair, nearly blind with fatigue and lack of sleep, he mentally reviewed the four operations, remembering he didn't write an op note on the first patient, the marine lieutenant colonel. In fact, he did not know the colonel's name. Those were minor omissions, he rationalized, attributable to the exigencies of war and easily corrected after a substantial breakfast.

As the coffee's warmth and caffeine took hold, he allowed his mind to drift. Twenty-six years ago, when he was an eighteen-year-old marine hunting Japanese in the Pacific jungles, who could have predicted that one day he would eat breakfast in the senior officers' mess aboard a naval hospital ship after operating on four wounded marines.

The sound of another landing helicopter elicited a silent groan as he contemplated the arrival of more casualties and more surgery. He wondered if he would ever get off the *Sanctuary*. After a minute or two the helicopter's engine noise subsided, leaving him curious as to why it had shut down instead of taking off. Reaching for one of the single sheet daily news summaries scattered on the table, he read of US military triumphs throughout South Vietnam and the success of President Nixon's Vietnamization program. If the US were winning the war with such overwhelming certainty how come the enemy didn't know it?

JP was so engrossed reading that he failed to perceive that a two-star marine general had entered the mess accompanied by a navy commander, a marine captain, and the ship's skipper, Captain Pederson.

Conversations in the mess subsided noticeably as curious diners watched the four officers walk briskly to JP's table and stand behind his chair. JP, oblivious to their presence, continued to read the news summary and slurp coffee.

The general's voice was gruff and unusually loud. "He always had an insolence about him that bordered insubordination when in the presence of superiors."

Startled, JP sensed a haunting familiarity to the voice and struggled to identify it.

"On your feet, Marine," the general commanded.

Pushing back his chair JP slowly got to his feet, his face burning. Who the hell was this turkey to harangue him? Turning, he found himself face to face with a stocky white-haired two-star marine general wearing jungle fatigues. Next to the general stood a similarly dressed navy commander, a subdued chaplain's cross on his collar and a funny smile on his face. Behind thick-lensed glasses his eyes twinkled. The two officers elicited a vague familiarity, but JP's sleep-starved mind refused to drag up the proper memories.

The general grabbed JP in a bear hug. "You dumb jarhead, what the hell are you doing in an army uniform?"

JP's eyes dropped to the name printed on the general's fatigue jacket. Recognition came like a bolt of lightning. Stunned, he gasped. "Captain Mueller... sir?" Glancing beyond the general to the chaplain, he now recognized the basic good looks, ruddy complexion, and still black curly hair. "Mick Icardi. Oh for Christ's sake." He broke loose from the general and threw his arms around the chaplain.

"I'll say a prayer to absolve you of blasphemy, you irreverent Protestant," Father Icardi said, pounding JP on the back.

The general cleared his throat. "Let's take seats, gentlemen." As they sat down General Mueller asked the waiting steward, "Has Colonel Franklin ordered a good breakfast?"

"I believe so, sir."

"Bring us all what he ordered."

JP kept his eyes shifting from General Mueller to Father Icardi, trying to bridge twenty-seven years. "General," he began, "the last time I saw you was in '44. You handed the Chief and me our transfer orders. I remember your parting words."

"And they were..."

"You two get the hell out of my sight before I throw you both in the brig."

General Mueller turned to his aide, Marine Captain Goldenson, and the ship's skipper, navy Captain Pederson. "Colonel Franklin was Private First Class Franklin at the time. He and his Navajo buddy Jake Conrad were the most destructive pair of marines I had ever come across. They blew away nearly half my island. Later they almost started a war with the army when they sabotaged a bunch of the army's squad tents. I had to get them off the island before court martial charges could be brought against them. Together those two were more of a menace to the Marine Corps than the Japanese."

482

When the general turned back to JP his voice saddened. "Father Icardi told me about the Chief's death. I know you and he were very close."

"Yes, sir. We were like brothers. He wanted to be a doctor."

Mueller studied JP for a long minute. "It's an interesting coincidence that his best friend became a doctor." Abruptly the general changed the subject. "How is Hal McDougall?"

JP was confused. *Why would General Mueller ask about his World War II platoon sergeant?* "Sir, the last time I saw the sarge was in '43 off the coast of Mono. After he was hit by a sniper's bullet, Mick... Father Icardi and I got him in a rubber raft to be taken out to a waiting PT boat."

JP's mind, kicked by a surge of adrenalin and caffeine, was now racing at top speed, recalled the orthopedic surgeon's comment in the OR that the patient had been wounded twice in the leg in World War II. McDougall had been wounded twice in the leg. Realization finally flowed over him. "Jesus Christ," he whispered, "I operated on my old platoon sergeant."

"Watch that language," Father Icardi warned. "I have some influence with the Big Six upstairs, but two blasphemies in less than an hour may stretch it."

JP stared at the priest. As a marine, Pfc Mick Icardi could out-profane most DIs.

"Doctor," the general said with mock dismay, "you didn't know the name of the man on whom you operated?"

JP's face reddened. "That's about it, General. I was told he was a lieutenant colonel and a battalion commander. I let it go at that. While we were closing Sergeant... Colonel McDougall, I had to drop out to operate on another wounded marine. Before I finished the second case I was asked to operate on a third case and then a fourth, which I finished just before coming down here. Come to think of it, I don't know any of their names. I do know their injuries and the details of my surgery."

He stopped talking when three stewards brought plates loaded with eggs, creamed beef on toast, and hash brown potatoes. After setting the plates down in front of the officers they brought pots of steaming coffee.

"Well, I imagine that's what really matters," General Mueller said. "Go ahead and start eating, Doctor. You look like you could use a square meal. You can tell me about Mac between mouthfuls."

"Yes, sir."

Lifting his over-medium eggs with his knife and fork he placed them on the creamed beef. After several generous mouthfuls washed down with coffee, he reviewed in detail McDougall's injuries and the prognosis for rehabilitation. "If all goes well, and that's a big if, he may be fit for limited duty in about a year."

General Mueller looked as though he had been kicked in the gut. "Thank you for your candor, Doctor. Even as a Pfc you were one for speaking your mind." Becoming serious, he said, "We're indebted to you for coming up here to operate on some of our marines. Your commanding general was most generous in letting you go."

"He gives me pretty much a free reign, sir."

"General Webster briefed me on your liberal interpretation of that term."

Mick Icardi set his cup in its saucer and chuckled.

"Something funny, Father?" General Mueller asked.

"More amusing than funny, General."

"Explain please."

"Here we are, three senior officers in three different military services: army, navy, and Marine Corps. All of us began our military careers as enlisted marines after surviving boot camp."

"There are four of us," the general interposed. "Captain Goldenson, my aide, will be a field grade officer soon. He began his career as an EM before going to college and through the platoon commander's program at Quantico."

Captain Pederson, the ship's skipper, broke in. "Five, General. I was a marine sergeant in the war before going to Annapolis."

General Mueller then added a sixth. "Your old corporal, Jim Pinezy, was Mac's exec. I moved him in as battalion commander as soon as I heard Mac was wounded. He's a major now but I expect silver leaves won't be long in coming."

Father Icardi wondered out loud. "Where would the officer corps of the armed forces be today without enlisted marines to draw on?"

"Minus some of its finest officers," General Mueller said. "Colonel Franklin, do you think Mac has recovered enough from anesthesia for us to see him for a few minutes?"

"Yes, sir. He is one tough bird."

General Mueller laughed. "Now that's a prophetic observation. Today, in addition to a Purple Heart, Silver Star, and Air Medal, I have a set of eagles to pin on him. His promotion orders to full colonel came through yesterday." He looked at JP and Father Icardi. "How would you two like to pin eagles on your former platoon sergeant?"

JP beamed. "General, nothing would give me greater pleasure."

"It's worth a tour in Vietnam just to do that," Father Icardi added.

"By the way, Colonel Franklin, if you're thinking of returning to the 36th today, forget it. You are officially on TDY to the 1st Marine Division until 1200 hours tomorrow, at which time one of our helicopters will fly you back to Phong Sahn. Tonight you will be guest of honor at my mess. Father Icardi has graciously offered you the spare bunk in his hooch. I suspect you and he have much to talk over."

"Aye, aye, general," JP said.

Chapter Fifty-Three

Wednesday, September 23, 1970, 0750 hours
USS *Sanctuary*

The *Sanctuary*'s skipper, Captain Pederson, led General Mueller from the officers' mess along a passageway. Walking briskly behind them, Lieutenant Colonel JP Franklin playfully punched Commander (Father) Michael Icardi's arm.

"You, of all people, a priest. I can't believe it."

Father Michael Icardi punched back. "You, of all people, a hotshot surgeon. I can't believe it."

"Surgeon, yes, but hotshot, no. I'd rather you think of me as brilliant or gifted."

Father Icardi rolled his eyes. "Have mercy on this immodest Protestant, Lord, and thanks for bringing us together."

"This stupid war had something to do with it," JP said bitterly.

The priest was startled by the vehemence in his friend's voice. "Our leaders will have to answer to God one day for what they have done to our country and its finest young men."

Captain Pederson stopped at elevator doors and pressed the "UP" button. The doors immediately opened. "These elevators are well trained," he quipped as they filed in. The doors closed; the elevator went up one floor. When the doors opened the strong smell of disinfectant reached them. Captain Pederson stepped into another wide passageway with the others following.

Arriving at the entrance of the recovery ward, the group burst through its double doors. A lieutenant commander nurse catapulted from her seat at the nurses' station and hurried to meet them. In her late thirties, with short blonde hair and a full-bodied figure, JP thought she was still very attractive. Maybe he had been away from Kathy too long.

General Mueller smiled at the nurse as she came to greet him. "Good morning, Betty. How is Colonel McDougall?"

"Doing nicely, General. He's been awake off and on."

"What do you have in the way of data?" JP asked.

Never having seen JP before, the nurse hesitated. Glancing at his white coat, the mantle of a physician, she concluded he must be the consultant surgeon described in the op note. "Vital signs are stable, Colonel Franklin," she reported. "His temp was 38, urine output 60 ccs an hour. BP was 110/50, heart rate was 120 with intermittent PVC when he arrived from the OR. His rate is down now to 80 with no more PVCs. Hematocrit at 0700 hours was 34 after 8 units of blood and 3 liters of Ringers. The white count was 14,000; blood gases, lytes were normal, and the portable chest film showed an opaque chest."

"Was he sitting up when the films were taken?"

"His back was elevated thirty degrees, as it is now."

Concerned that blood and secretions may have leaked into the lung, JP asked for a stethoscope. The nurse removed the one from around her neck. passed it to JP, then led to McDougall's bed.

Lieutenant Colonel Harold McDougall lay supine, eyes closed, his back and head elevated into a semi-sitting position. A bulky dressing filled the space between his chin and collarbones except above the breastbone where a tracheotomy tube exited. JP, using the stethoscope, listened intently over each side of the chest as the others watched. He suppressed a frown when he heard unmistakable sounds of air passing through fluid on inspiration and expiration.

"I'd better clean him out," he concluded.

Reaching to a nearby suction machine, he flipped its toggle switch. The machine's electric motor sounded like a small outboard motor running at full speed. Slipping on sterile gloves, he withdrew a sterile plastic catheter from its package and fitted it to the end of the tubing from the suction machine. Threading the free end of the catheter through the tracheotomy tube into the trachea, he advanced it as far as it would go. Slowly withdrawing the catheter, he intermittently thumbed the control hole, creating intermittent suction. A stream of dark red-stained thick fluid passed through the tubing to the collection bottle. As the catheter was being withdrawn McDougall suddenly awoke. Coughing violently, he struggled to push JP's hand away.

"Good morning, Sarge," JP said cheerfully. He reinserted the catheter. McDougall coughed even more violently, gasping for breath. "That's for putting me on mess duty on the ship going overseas," JP said, withdrawing the catheter.

Fright and anger emanated from McDougall's eyes as they swept over the faces surrounding him. Spotting General Mueller and Father Icardi at the foot of his bed, he relaxed and fixed on JP's face.

"I've got to do this a couple more times, Sarge," JP said, threading the catheter through the trach tube. "Your lungs are full of crud. You smoked too much." McDougall settled back, resigned to a fate over which he had no control. After two more suctions JP again listened over the chest with the stethoscope. His serious expression gave way to a smile. "Much better," he told the nurse, returning her stethoscope. "Thanks."

General Mueller moved in and grasped McDougall's right hand in a gesture of affection and greeting. "How are you doing, Mac?"

Unable to make any sound, McDougall mouthed, "Fine, sir." His eyes shifted from the general back to JP.

"Mac, I'd like to introduce you to your surgeon," General Mueller said, indicating JP. "He's the 36th Division Surgeon who flew up here to operate on you." The general paused. "On second thought, an introduction may be superfluous. Take a good look at your surgeon."

McDougall stared without recognition.

"Mac, this is Lieutenant Colonel James Paul Franklin, one of the country's top head and neck surgeons. During World War II Colonel Franklin was Private First

Class Franklin, US Marine Corps, and a member of your ground defense platoon. It was he and Father Icardi who threw you into the rubber raft off the coast of Mono after you were hit in the leg. They stayed behind with the Chief to fight off the Japs so you and the two Army Air Corps pilots you rescued could get out to the waiting PT boat."

McDougall's eyes' reddened as memories were dragged from the depths of his anesthesia-clouded brain. Recognition flashed across his face.

JP leaned over the bed and hugged his old platoon sergeant. "I'm getting fed up with bailing you out every time you are wounded," he whispered.

McDougall took a tissue from a box in his bed, wiped his eyes, then gestured for writing material. The nurse placed a yellow legal pad and pencil next to his right hand. Fumbling with the pencil, he finally secured it and scrawled a sentence on the pad. JP studied the distorted writing for a moment, then broke into a wide grin. McDougall had written: "I never really thought you were a shithead." JP passed the pad to General Mueller who chuckled and passed the pad to the others.

Father Icardi glanced at the pad and placed it back on McDougall's bed. "I didn't see anything on the pad about 'gifted' or 'brilliant'."

By this time Captain Goldenson had rounded up nurses, corpsmen, and doctors. They gathered around McDougall's bed. A Silver Star recipient deserved an audience.

General Mueller continued, "Mac, we have some medals for you. My aide, Captain Goldenson, will hit the highlights of the citations."

The captain cleared his throat. "Attention to orders."

Everyone, including General Mueller, stiffened. Special orders and citations were then read awarding Lieutenant Colonel Harold McDougall, United States Marine Corps, his third Silver Star, fourth Purple Heart, and fourth Air Medal. General Mueller took the medals from a small velvet-lined tray held by his aide. After pinning the medals to McDougall's gown over the left upper chest, he squeezed McDougall's hand.

McDougall's lids began to droop as the awards ceremony ended. They fluttered open when General Mueller leaned over the bed and whispered, "Got something else for you, Mac. Your promotion came through yesterday." Straightening up, the general continued. "I will now read, with great pleasure, orders promoting Lieutenant Colonel Harold McDougall to Colonel. When I finish, two former privates first class of Colonel McDougall's World War II defense platoon will pin on his eagles."

Captain Goldenson stepped forward and handed a shiny silver eagle to JP and one to Father Icardi.

"You ready for this, Mac?" General Mueller asked.

McDougall smiled for the first time since his surgery, nodding affirmative.

The general put on his reading glasses. "Attention to orders. Headquarters, United States Marine Corps…"

When the general had finished JP and Father Icardi stepped forward. Each moved to a side of McDougall's bed, pinched up a segment of gown over his shoulder and pinned on an eagle. Both stepped back smartly, slapped on their fatigue caps and saluted smartly.

"Colonel," Father Icardi said, "it seems you owe each of us a dollar."

General Mueller grasped full Colonel McDougall's hand. "Congratulations, Mac. I wore those eagles for seven years. May they bring you the good luck they brought me."

McDougall's eyes reddened again. He mouthed a soundless, "Thanks, General."

"We're having your promotion party tonight at my mess along with Colonel Franklin as our guest of honor," General Mueller said. "I realize you can't be there, but not to worry. All drinks and hors d'oeuvres will be billed to your account." Mueller squeezed the new colonel's hand again. "I'll be back in a couple of days to check up on you."

Outside the recovery ward General Mueller stopped JP. "Doctor, I have a few more marines to visit, then I'll leave for my headquarters. I will expect you to leave with me. Father Icardi is hereby detailed to make sure you are on my chopper when it takes off."

JP slapped on his fatigue cap and tossed his old CO a French flat-handed salute.

"But of course, mon general."

★

Wednesday, September 23, 1970, 1025 hours
USS *Sanctuary* Helipad

JP and Father Icardi stood by the skids of General Mueller's silent helicopter waiting for the general and his aide. "I'll be glad to get off this tub," JP said.

"Why is that? You're being treated like a VIP."

"I've never felt secure on anything that could sink."

JP stuck his head through the helicopter's door and examined its interior, noting the plush vinyl-covered seats and banks of radios. "This is like General Webster's chopper."

"All generals travel first class," Father Icardi said.

"They must get their choppers from the same dealer."

While they waited JP asked Father Icardi, "How did you get yourself assigned as the 1st Marine Division chaplain?"

"You want the truth?"

"I expect nothing less from a priest."

"When General Mueller took over the division he traced me to Okinawa and sent word suggesting I put in for a transfer. That was just a formality. From what I heard later he was ready to have me kidnapped had I refused. When I learned that the old sarge and Jim Pinezy were in the division a herd of horses couldn't have kept me away. If it had been possible, General Mueller would have had you transferred into the division."

The sounds of an approaching helicopter drew their attention skyward. A Huey with a red cross on its side rapidly descended towards the *Sanctuary*. It crossed the stern and settled on the deck.

"I'd better take a look," Father Icardi said, starting towards the helicopter.

"I'll go with you."

A double door in the superstructure opened and four corpsmen spilled out followed by two more pushing gurneys. They arrived at the helicopter's door at the same time as Father Icardi and JP. Two stretchers, each with a severely wounded marine, were lifted from the helicopter's floor and placed on the gurneys. IV bottles juggled by corpsmen waved erratically over the stretchers as the gurneys raced towards the doors.

JP, almost jogging, scanned the marine on the first gurney. Both legs were gone from above the knees, the stumps smothered in massive blood-soaked dressings. Over the abdomen several layers of thick pads dripped bright red blood. The young marine's complexion had a gray mottled hue. "He may not make it, Mick," JP told the priest.

"I'll go with him for the last rites," the priest said.

JP dropped back to the second gurney. The marine's left hemi-face and upper neck were covered by a bulky dressing oozing blood. Lifting the dressing slightly, JP exposed a mix of bone fragments, skin and torn muscle. One eye was hanging out of its socket. Blood oozed from a torn, distorted oral cavity. Exposed fractured bones and loose teeth were mixed with facial muscles and skin. Low in the mid-neck the end of a plastic tracheotomy tube protruded from a crude incision. The upper neck was a cluster of muscle and cartilage. *Good God*, thought JP, *what a mess. And some peasant did it in less than a second with an AK–47.*

Jeff Farnsworth appeared from a hatchway and briefly examined each casualty. He shouted to JP, "Can you give us hand with the face and neck?"

JP nodded, then yelled to Father Icardi. "Mick, I'm going with this kid."

As they approached the open doors leading to the ship's interior General Mueller stepped out. Quickly taking in the scene, he told JP and Icardi, 'You two belong here. I'll send a chopper for you when you're ready to leave."

JP, his mind already in the operating room, seemed not to have heard.

★

Wednesday, September 23, 1970, 2320 hours
1st Marine Division Headquarters Staff Bivouac Area, Danang, Republic of South Vietnam

Lieutenant Colonel JP Franklin, a towel wrapped around him, entered Father Icardi's hooch after a hot shower in the communal latrine. Slipping on a set of green scrubs "borrowed" from the *Sanctuary*, he crawled between the clean cool sheets of the guest bunk and lay on his back, hands clasped behind his head. Father Icardi was still in the latrine shaving after his shower. A small lamp on an upturned ammo box by his bunk gave the room a subdued yellow glow.

While waiting for his friend he reviewed his last case, the marine with part of his face and neck shot away. The eye was so badly damaged that it had to be removed by the eye surgeon. The bony roof of the eye socket, a shelf which supports the brain, was found fractured with a large fragment of bone driven up through the dura into the brain. JP assisted the neurosurgeon to debride the brain and repair the dura. He helped the eye surgeon remove the damaged eye. then helped the oral surgeon repair the fractured jaw and wire the remaining teeth into occlusion. Next the oral surgeon assisted him in repairing a severed facial nerve, facial lacerations, explore the neck, and reconstruct a disrupted pharynx and fractured larynx. Under Jeff Farnsworth's tutelage, JP constructed a gastrostomy. Seven hours after the marine had landed on the *Sanctuary* he was taken to the recovery ward, having received the ultimate in the care of wounded, a team effort with each specialist contributing his expertise. If the country was sending its best young men to get blown apart in war, it was also sending its best surgeons to put them back together. But the best were not good enough for the marine with the traumatic amputation of his legs and the abdominal wound. He died on the operating table.

JP turned his head slightly and stared at Icardi's empty bunk, then at the artificial leg propped against the wall. He found it difficult to reconcile the wild teenage marine Pfc of World War II with the dedicated Catholic priest, now the 1st Marine Division chaplain.

Clumping sounds on the wooden walk outside the hooch ended when the hooch door was shoved open by the end of a crutch. Commander Michael Icardi, Chaplain's Corps, United States Navy, hobbled in on his crutches. Sitting down on his bunk he extended his single leg. "It's been a long day," he groaned, glancing at JP. "What are you doing awake? Twenty-two hours of surgery with no sleep should have put you under long ago."

"Too much going on. Besides, I'm curious."

"About what?"

"Why a marine with one leg would become a Catholic priest and how he managed to pass the physical for a commission and active duty as a chaplain?"

Father Icardi didn't answer for several moments. He slipped under a sheet and adjusted his pillow. "I'll tell you," he said finally," but you'd better not fall asleep."

"Not a chance. I've waited twenty-seven years to hear this."

"Before I was put under anesthesia on Guadalcanal the doctor told me he would try to save my leg. When I woke up after surgery my leg was gone. I was devastated. God had abandoned me. I had prayed regularly that I survive the war in one piece; obviously God was not listening. Several days after my surgery the Catholic chaplain came by to see me. He asked if I would like to take communion at my bedside. I told him no thanks. Since God had turned his back on me, I wanted nothing to do with God. The chaplain told me to quit feeling sorry for myself and to think of brother marines who had given so much more than I, including their lives. Because I survived when so many did not, I was obliged to do something with my life that would justify my survival. Later, on the hospital ship going to San Diego, I had plenty of time to think. I decided I could best honor the sacrifices of my brother marines by serving the Lord."

JP propped himself up on an elbow. "That's an inspiring story, Mick. I'm impressed by your commitment to the Lord, and I'm especially grateful to the chaplain on Guadalcanal who set you straight."

490

Both men were quiet as each retreated into his own thoughts. JP finally broke the silence. "Amputees are disqualified for commissions and active duty. How did you manage both?"

Father Icardi grinned. "Prayer, my son, prayer, and maybe a little politics."

"Now we're getting to the truth."

"First I had to convince my bishop that I was worthless as a parish priest. That wasn't very difficult since he had already formed that opinion of me. Then I persuaded Bu Med that a one-legged chaplain with combat experience as an enlisted marine would have an immense advantage over a two-legged chaplain, not a former marine, who lacked combat experience. And a chaplain who knows his way around in the jungle would quickly establish rapport with the troops, especially when he goes out to the bush to give communion."

"That would be true of a chaplain with two legs. How did you convince Bu Med that a chaplain with one leg could really hump it in the jungle?"

"I had one of my parishioners take home movies of me playing basketball with some teenagers from my church. I sent the film to Bu Med." He paused and grinned. "What Bu Med didn't know was that it took three weeks for the ulcers on my stump to heal after making that movie."

JP shook his head in wonderment. "The Navy Surgeon General still had to approve your request. Wasn't he a bit skeptical? I certainly would have been."

"It didn't hurt my request for waiver that my bishop and the Navy Surgeon General were roommates at Boston College and played on the BC football team."

"Father Mick, you haven't changed a bit since you were a marine. You're still a master manipulator. I'm surprised you're not Pope."

"Give me time. I'm working on it," Father Icardi said, smiling.

JP became serious. "I learned this is your second tour. On your last one you went through the siege of Hue during Tet. You got a Navy Cross for dragging the crew out of a burning helicopter seconds before it exploded, a Silver Star for carrying two marines out from enemy fire after they were wounded. I also heard that you go humping with the grunts in the boonies."

"You've been checking up on me, Doctor. Who can object to taking the word of God where it's most needed, especially when God and the commanding general consider it a good idea."

"Don't push your luck, Mick."

"Any time the Lord wants me I'm ready."

"Damn it, you don't have to put him on notice you're available."

Father Icardi smiled. "Who are you to preach to me on taking risks? Your division chaplain told me about your adventures."

"Any time the Lord wants me, I'm ready."

"Touché. And now, Dr. Franklin, tell me how you went from a shy, bumbling marine private first class who twice flunked the grenade course at Pendleton to, as you humbly put it, a gifted, brilliant surgeon."

"I need to be careful what I say around you."

"You didn't marry the girl you met in San Diego?"

"No, it didn't work out, Mick. We broke up after my third year of college. Neither of us had been in love before. I think we unknowingly used each other to learn how to give and accept love."

"You used to boast about how smart she was. What happened to her?"

"She's a federal district judge who has been nominated by the President to the Court of Appeals."

"You're right. She was and is smart. Probably smarter than you. Strange you should know so much about her."

"You have been hearing too many confessions from sinful Catholics, Father Mick. Her son was a cadet at West Point a couple of years ago when he turned up with a bad tumor of the upper throat. I operated on him. Now he's the peter pilot on my chopper."

"You have a chopper?"

"Sure, don't you?"

"The army gets the best of everything," Father Icardi said with some envy. "Tell me, what led to your decision to become a doctor?"

"That's a long boring story."

"We have the rest of the night."

"You're a hard man, Mick. Sorry, I can't get used to calling you Father Icardi."

"Father Mick will do. That's what the grunts call me."

"Okay, Father Mick. After the war ended I started college as a history major. I wanted to learn why a country sends its best young men to kill the best young men of another country. During the first three-quarters I made the dean's list although I didn't learn much about war. Then I began hanging out at a local tavern, drinking beer with a bunch of student-vets and telling war stories. I cut classes at college for the classes at the tavern. My grades tumbled. I had no idea what I wanted to do with my life. One day I told my history prof to shove his course. I was going to quit school and go back to the Marine Corps. Then in a campus paper I read that the army needed second lieutenants. I was offered a direct commission without going to OCS. I grabbed it like a drowning man would grab a life preserver."

JP shifted on his bunk hoping to find a less uncomfortable spot for his hip. "How come the Marine Corps stuffs its mattresses with rocks?"

"It keeps the young marines lean and nasty. Carry on with your story, my son."

"After graduating from branch basic school I was assigned to Fort Bliss, near El Paso. While at Bliss I fell in love with my best friend's sister. She was a twenty-year-old soft-talking Georgia girl who just graduated from the University with a BA in art education. Nine months later we were married. It was the day the North Koreans invaded South Korea. As soon as I reported off my honeymoon I was handed orders to Korea. I've hated Communists ever since."

"That must have been rough for a newly wed," Father Icardi sympathized.

"I cried all the way to Korea. Over there I commanded a platoon of self-propelled automatic weapons. One day another officer and I came across a wounded Korean boy and took him to a civilian hospital in Taejon. The boy died in the hallway before he could receive care. In a way I felt responsible for the kid's death because I wasn't able

492

to do anything to save him. Months later, after the Chinese began their spring offensive, a British battalion was about to be overrun. My platoon was sent to evacuate their wounded. We used up most of our ammo firing at the Chinese, called in an air strike, then took the wounded to a MASH. A nurse I knew introduced me to a couple of the surgeons. They gave me credit for saving the lives of the Brits and invited me to observe surgery. Seeing those doctors work to save lives touched something in me, Father Mick. Except for you I never had saved anyone's life. All I had done was take lives. It was the spiritual awakening that turned me to medicine, much as the spiritual awakening that turned you to the church. I had to become a doctor."

"That's an amazing story," Father Icardi said, "You ought to write a book."

"Maybe some day I will."

Chapter Fifty-Four

Tuesday, September 29, 1970, 1835 hours
36th Infantry Division Headquarters Staff Bivouac Area, Phong Sahn, Republic of Vietnam

A freshly shaved and showered Lieutenant Colonel JP Franklin, wearing clean, starched fatigues and polished boots, finished reading a "Thank You" note from Colonel Harold McDougall, USMC, now at Bethesda Naval Hospital in Maryland. He had written:

> For an army surgeon your recommendation carried a lot of weight with the navy. They flew me directly to Bethesda from Danang. When I arrived at Bethesda Captain Glover came by to see me. He told me I had the best for a surgeon. Still, it's hard to believe that anyone so discoordinated to have flunked the grenade course twice at Pendleton could rise to such lofty heights. One never knows about young marines; they're all sleepers. Captain Glover plans to remove the stent in two weeks. I'm anxious to try out my voice; also I can hardly wait to eat a Big Mac instead of blenderizing it and squirting it into my gastrostomy. Enclosed is the dollar I owe you.
>
> Best wishes and thanks, Semper Fis/Mac

JP put the dollar in his wallet for a good luck charm and headed for the general's mess. The lounge was crowded. Why wouldn't it be? The menu tonight included lobster, rice pilaf, and white wine. Looking around, JP saw Father Peter Deveraux sitting at the bar nursing a drink. He walked over, greeted the priest, then ordered a gin martini on the rocks. While waiting he noted the contents of the glass in the chaplain's hand. "Father Pete, that doesn't look like Fresca to me," he commented.

"It's Scotch and water. I convinced the Almighty that I deserved something stronger than a soft drink tonight."

"A special occasion, or is the war just grinding you down?"

The priest looked at him a moment, then swung around on his stool. "Let's go sit at a table."

JP picked up his drink and followed the chaplain to a small round table next to a picture window. Sitting down, he sipped his drink and looked expectantly at the priest.

Father Deveraux leaned towards JP. "I just received word that something terrible happened to Marty Brandon, the chaplain for the 2nd/28th."

"Was he hurt?"

"No, at least not physically. He was visiting units in the field this afternoon using the battalion commander's Loach. At Delta Company he was asked to take a GI to the mental health ward at the medical battalion because the man was acting so bizarre. On the way to Phong Sahn the GI suddenly unbuckled his seat belt, shouted 'Geronimo', and jumped out of the Loach at 2,000 feet."

"Good God. Was the body recovered?"

"No, at least not yet. The Loach pilot followed the GI down; he called for the Blues and guided them to the spot where he saw the GI go in."

"How is Chaplain Brandon dealing with the experience?" JP asked.

"Not very well. He thinks he should have stopped the GI. If any of the Blues are killed or injured looking for the body he will blame himself."

"That kind of guilt trip isn't justified, Peter. The Loach is a small helicopter with two seats in the back, each by an open door. If a passenger decides to unbuckle his belt and jump, there's not much the other passenger can do to stop him. If there were a struggle both could fall out or cause the helicopter to crash."

"I wasn't able to convince Chaplain Brandon of that," the priest said. "I was wondering if you would you have time tomorrow to talk with him."

"Sure. Have him stop by my office or I can go out to Mindy to see him. Let me know which he would prefer." JP stirred his martini with a swizzle stick. When he looked up he saw the tall form of Colonel John Witherington approaching their table. "Brace yourself, Peter, here comes trouble."

Both officers started to rise but the chief of staff stopped them with a wave, then dragged a chair to the table and sat down.

"Good evening, gentlemen."

"Good evening, sir," JP and Father Deveraux chorused.

"Any news on the man who jumped from the Loach?" the priest asked.

"I got word a few minutes ago. The body was recovered. It's being taken to the 96th Evac for autopsy and toxicology studies. His pack, which remained on the Loach, was searched by the CID. Three small pills were found wrapped in toilet tissue and identified as LSD."

"What a tragedy for the family," Father Deveraux said.

"That it is, Father. Under the circumstances it may be appropriate for you rather than Chaplain Brandon to write the letter of condolence to the family."

"I agree, sir," Peter Deveraux said.

The chief of staff turned to JP. "Doctor, any suggestions how to prevent this from happening again?"

"I just learned of it a few minutes ago, Colonel, but a few things already have come to mind."

"Let's hear them."

"The event should be widely publicized in the division newspaper and the *Stars and Stripes* as a consequence of LSD. It will be included in the drug orientation lectures given to all incoming personnel. I will notify Med Command to put out a bulletin that anyone suspected of LSD intoxication in the field be evacuated by Huey or Chinook with two escorts and restraints. I'll check with the division psychiatrist for additional measures."

Witherington grunted approval.

When he didn't leave but instead sat quietly sipping his drink, JP became suspicious. "Colonel, I've been around you long enough to sense you're about to drop something unpleasant on one of us."

"Your instincts serve you well, Doctor," Witherington said, smiling almost evilly.

JP took a slug of martini and waited for the shoe to drop.

"A female reporter named Wendy Brewer representing the *Chicago Gazette* is due to arrive at 0830 hours tomorrow by U–21. She wants to spend several days in our AO."

"What's so bad about that, sir?"

"At least three reasons. She opposes the Vietnam War."

JP chuckled. "So do most of us out here."

"She hates army officers."

"She must know some of the same officers I do," JP said, smiling. "And the third reason?"

"She asked specifically for a conference with the division surgeon."

JP groaned.

"General Webster was impressed with how well you managed the lady reporter from the *Baltimore Eagle* at Qui Tavong… what was her name?"

"Linda Gardner."

"Right. Linda Gardner. She wrote some very positive articles about the division. Considering your success with Ms. Gardner, General Webster decided you would be the most appropriate officer to act as Ms. Brewer's escort."

"Sir, the word 'escort' used in reference to the opposite sex carries a certain inference."

Witherington laughed. "I'll defer its interpretation to your judgment, Doctor. Meet her plane down at the airfield, make her feel welcome, and take her to her quarters. She'll be staying with the Donut Dollies, trailer No.6. Get her squared away in her quarters, give her a guided tour of the area, dazzle her with your footwork, then bring her to the general's mess for lunch. The general and I will take over until the evening. You pick her up at her quarters and escort her to the mess for happy hour and dinner. You and she will be seated at the general's table."

"Sir, respectfully, I had a tough time explaining Linda Gardner's articles to my wife. And frankly, sir, I don't have the time to babysit a female reporter, especially one who hates military officers."

"War is hell, Doctor," Witherington said, standing up. "The general does appreciate your willingness to take on this extra responsibility."

He left, laughing.

★

Wednesday, September 30, 1970, 0130 hours
36th Division Headquarters Bivouac Area, Phong Sahn, Republic of Vietnam

The phone rang and rang in Lieutenant Colonel JP Franklin's hooch, then lapsed into silence. Moments later it rang again. This time its noise was supplemented by Father

Deveraux banging on the connecting door. "JP, for the love of God, answer the phone."

Dragged into consciousness, JP groped for the phone in the dark, shoving it off the table to crash to the floor. Fumbling for the lamp, he knocked it off the table. Its bulb shattered with a *pop*.

"Damn it all," he muttered. He hoped the division chaplain hadn't heard. Locating his flashlight, he turned it on, found the phone cord and reeled in the phone as if pulling in a fish. He put the phone to his ear, listened to the disconnected buzz, then set the phone on its cradle. It immediately rang. He jerked up the phone. "Colonel Franklin."

"Colonel, Kevin Brodie at the 96th."

"Brodie, it's almost 2 A.M."

"I hated to wake you, sir."

"Sure you did."

"Colonel, I have a major flail here. I need your help. An eight-year-old Vietnamese girl was severely bitten in the neck by a dog last night at Quang Dien. Her larynx was crushed and almost torn loose with the pharynx. The left internal jug and carotid were ripped in two. GIs rushed her to B Med. A cuffed endo tube was shoved into the trachea, the jug and carotid ligated. She was transfused with low-titer O-negative blood and sent her up here."

By now JP was wide awake, his mind churning. "Any neurological deficits?"

"No, sir. Reflexes are intact. She arrested twice, once at Quang Dien and once here in the ER. Anesthesia needs about forty minutes to get her stabilized before she can be put to sleep."

"What about the dog?"

"Its head is on the way to Danang to be checked for rabies."

"Okay. I'll get my jeep and come over."

"Colonel Marchenko's jeep is already on the way to pick you up."

"Brodie, you're getting too efficient. Have some strong coffee ready."

"I've done better than that. Stop by the mess hall when you get here. The night-shift cooks will fix you some bacon and eggs."

"Bless you, my son."

★

Wednesday, September 30, 1970, 0705 hours
96th Evacuation Hospital, Phong Sahn, Republic of Vietnam

Lieutenant Colonel JP Franklin, M.D., Medical Corps, USA, walked out of the front entrance of the hospital to his waiting jeep.

"Good morning, sir," a cheerful Pfc Jack Groves greeted.

JP grunted something inaudible as he climbed into the front seat.

"Tough night, sir?"

"That would be an understatement, Groves. I need to go to my hooch, shower, change uniforms, then go to the air terminal to pick up a female reporter who hates officers."

"Yes, sir," Groves said, smiling as he shifted gears. "Sir, I heard about the Vietnamese kid with the dog bite of the throat. How's she doing?"

"Pretty good, all things considered. We put most of her voice box, windpipe, and gullet back together. If she doesn't stroke, and an almost inevitable infection is controlled, she has a good chance for near normal breathing, swallowing, and voice in nine months to a year, possibly sooner."

"When will you know about the stroke?"

No answer.

"Sir?"

Still no answer.

Groves glanced to his right just as a sleeping Lieutenant Colonel Franklin was moving to fall out of the jeep. Quickly reaching over, he grabbed a handful of fatigue jacket. He drove the remaining five miles to JP's hooch steering with his left hand and gripping his sleeping passenger with his right. As the jeep slowed to a stop the squealing brakes awakened JP.

"Sir, we're at your hooch."

Slowly JP reached for the ground with his feet, then turned to face his driver. "I'll be about twenty minutes."

★

Wednesday, September 30, 1970, 0813 hours
Phong Sahn Airfield, Republic of Vietnam

Private First Class Groves parked the jeep behind the barn-like passenger terminal at the airfield. JP glanced at his watch. Fifteen minutes until Wendy Brewer's U–21, a six-passenger Beechcraft King Air turbo-prop, was due to land.

"I'm going to the ALCE to check on her flight, then meet the plane," JP told Groves. "Do you have something to read?"

Groves reached to the jeep's glove compartment and removed a paperback, flashing the title *Lord Jim*.

JP recalled the powerful impact that Joseph Conrad's novel had had on him when he read it in high school. "You reading that for pleasure?"

Groves grinned. "Not exactly, sir. It's part of the assignment for my USAFI English course."

"How do you like the story so far?"

"It's kind of hard to follow, but I'm hanging in there."

"Don't weaken," JP, said, stepping to the ground.

Entering the terminal, he was hit by the stench of feces. Stepping into the latrine, he saw a row of full commodes with feces and toilet paper floating. Leaving the latrine, he walked over to the vacant passenger counter.

"Anyone here?" he shouted.

An air force sergeant emerged from a doorway behind the counter. "Yes, sir. Can I help you?...Oh, oh, Colonel Franklin."

"Sergeant Cassidy, you know the division can't function with its air terminal commodes stopped up."

"Yes, sir, the engineers have been called. They'll be here later this morning..."

"Very good, Sergeant. The shit must be kept flowing if we hope to defeat the wily Cong."

Leaving a grinning Sergeant Cassidy, JP exited the terminal on its airfield side and stepped out on a large expanse of concrete where passenger aircraft usually parked. He walked several hundred feet to a small two-story wooden building identified by a sign: AIR LIFT CONTROL ELEMENT. Climbing external stairs, he entered a small room sparsely furnished by a desk, two tables, chairs, telephones and radios. Maps of the local area, Vietnam, and South-east Asia hung on one wall. On another wall was an acetate-covered board marked with columns titled: TYPE A/C, ARRIVAL, DEPARTURE, FLY OVER, ORIGIN, DESTINATION. A counter separated the work area from the entry area. While JP tried to decipher the entries on the schedule board an air force sergeant came over to the counter.

"Can I help you, Colonel?"

"I want to check on an army U–21 inbound from Bien Hoa with an 0830 ETA."

"Yes, sir. It will arrive about ten minutes late. It ran into severe turbulence south of Quang Dien."

"Thanks, Sergeant. Your boss around?"

"No, sir. Colonel Withers is in Danang at a meeting. Would you like a cup of coffee while you're waiting?"

"Black, please."

The sergeant went to a glass coffee pot on a hotplate, poured coffee into a styrofoam cup, and set it on the counter.

JP took a short test sip, then a longer one. "The air force makes good coffee. I think I'll relax on the bench outside the terminal, soak up sun, and enjoy the scenery. Thanks again, Sergeant."

Descending the stairs to the concrete apron, JP walked back to the terminal, and eased down on the nearest of two long wooden benches lining the wall on both sides of the terminal entrance. Gazing thoughtfully west across the apron, taxiway and main airstrip, he sipped his coffee. Two air force F–100s idled at the end of the runway, side by side. The deafening noise of their engines spooling up rolled over the ground. They began moving forward, rapidly gaining speed. Almost simultaneously two ear-splitting explosions came from the two jets as they cut in their afterburners. Thirty seconds later they were out of sight except for two sun-bright glows in the blue sky that rapidly diminished. Quiet reigned again.

Five miles from the western side of the field, mountains and Viet Cong-controlled territory began, yet it all seemed so calm and peaceful. Vietnam was such a beautiful country. No wonder it had been coveted by so many foreigners who now lay buried in the pages of Vietnam's history. He wondered if such a fate awaited the United States. Or would the United States and North Vietnam' become bosom buddies, as happened with other former US adversaries.

The twin engine turbo-prop plane painted in US Army olive and white colors, passed over the end of the runway so quietly that JP would have missed it had he not been looking in that direction, He watched it touch down, slow almost to a stop, then turn on a taxiway and head towards the terminal. *What a beauty*, he thought. What he wouldn't give to fly it. He envied the flight crew. They not only got to fly the plane but they were paid to do it.

The plane came to a stop fifty feet from where he was sitting. The engine noise abruptly ceased. The propellers quietly spun down to lazily rotate, then stopped. JP stood up, tossed his styrofoam cup into a trash bin and walked out to the plane. The door in the fuselage opened out, then swung down to form stairs. A young warrant officer in a nomex flight suit, aviators wings on his left chest, scrambled down. Seeing JP, he saluted and identified himself as Warrant Officer Benedict, the co-pilot.

JP returned the salute. "Welcome to Phong Sahn, Mr. Benedict."

"Yes, sir. I was beginning to wonder if we would make it after we flew into a cell south of Quang Dien. Our radar was out so we didn't spot the storm. Even I started to get airsick. Excuse me, sir."

He turned to face the door.

A slender woman, about thirty-five, wearing tight-fitting fatigues and no hat, appeared in the doorway, hesitated, then unsteadily began to slowly descend the stairs. The warrant officer reached for her elbow. JP studied the woman's face. A high forehead was partially covered by a bang; brown hair was tied in back into a ponytail. She could have been described as pretty except for the scowl that dominated a very pale, ashen face. As soon as she stepped on to the concrete she leaned over and vomited. "Oh God," she moaned, accepting several tissues from the warrant officer.

JP waited until she recovered a bit, then introduced himself. "I'm the 36th Division Surgeon."

The reporter stared at him a moment, then bent over and vomited again.

"I wish you wouldn't do that, Ms. Brewer," JP said. "It's giving me an inferiority complex." Brewer did not laugh. "Sorry about the rough flight," he added solicitously.

"That army chow I had for breakfast and those two assholes flying me through a storm with broken equipment are perfect examples why this war is so screwed up."

The pilot appeared in the doorway with a small suitcase and a bulging GI rucksack. He passed both to the co-pilot. "I'll carry these to your vehicle, Colonel," the co-pilot said.

"My jeep's on the far side of the terminal."

When Brewer started for the terminal entrance she stumbled. JP reached out to steady her but she pushed his hand away. "I don't need help from an army quack who couldn't make it in private practice."

JP stifled a crude retort. He tried to stay unobtrusively close enough to catch her if she fell. The last thing he wanted on his hands was a bitchy female reporter with a broken hip. Inside the terminal they were immediately assaulted by the pungent fecal odor of obstructed commodes.

Brewer took one sniff and vomited on the floor. "Goddamned army," she moaned, "can't even keep the shit flowing. How in hell do they expect to win the war?"
500

JP bit his lip. It seemed a reasonable question.

When they exited the terminal Groves hopped out of the jeep and jogged to them. "I can take those, sir," he told the co-pilot, reaching for the luggage. As the co-pilot turned to go back to the terminal JP thanked him.

"Good luck, sir," the co-pilot whispered.

Brewer glared at his departing back. "What the hell did he mean by that?"

JP ignored the question. He told her to sit in the back of the jeep. "You'll be more comfortable there. If you feel you are going to vomit, just lean over the side." Assisting her over the front passenger seat he noted there was no wedding band on her left hand. He smiled grimly. A husband would have had two choices: either run away or kill her. Right now he himself would be inclined to take the latter route.

Groves wedged the suitcase in the back next to the radio and handed the pack to JP, who held it on his lap. "Where we going, sir?"

"Donut Dolly area. It's across the street from my hooch."

The road from the airport to the main road was dirt sprayed with permapreme, the petroleum compound that soaked into the ground, making it temporarily hard and water resistant. After months of heavy traffic a series of humps, bumps, and ruts developed. Groves did his best to avoid them but succeeded only partially. Brewer began retching, then complained bitterly. "He doesn't drive any better than those two cretins fly who flew me up here."

Donut Dollies was the informal and affectionate term given by GIs to the young, attractive and extrovert Red Cross workers who volunteered to go to Vietnam. Most were college graduates and in their early or mid-twenties. At Phong Sahn the Donut Dollies were housed two to four in comfortable trailers located across the road from the division staff hooches. Some trailers had white picket fences around them; a few had flower gardens.

The Donut Dollies ran recreation centers in rear areas for the troops. Others flew out to firebases where they visited with troops, played group games such as Scrabble, and distributed ditty bags with toilet articles. They brought with them paperbacks, records, tapes, magazines, coffee and doughnuts. They were the only women, other than reporters and VIPs, authorized to fly in helicopters to firebases and LZs.

When they reached the staff bivouac area Groves slowed, then pulled the jeep off the road and parked next to a wooden board sidewalk that led between trailers. JP glanced over his shoulder at Brewer, now asleep with her head back and her mouth open. He stifled a grin at the speculation of some poor guy waking up in the morning with a hangover next to her.

"Keep an eye on her," he told Groves. "I'll take her bags to her trailer, then come back for her." He leaned close to Groves and whispered, "If she wakes up don't panic."

In the four months that JP had been in the 36th Division he had never ventured into the Donut Dolly area, even though it was only across the road from his hooch. That was more than he could say for some of the other division staff. He scanned the first trailer for the location of its number, then quickly found trailer No.6. Its door was open except for the screen door. He knocked at the side of the door.

A pretty young woman in shorts and a halter appeared, pushed open the screen door and regarded JP, who stood quietly, holding the pack and suitcase. "I was told to expect an overnight guest," she said, smiling, "I didn't know it would be you, Colonel Franklin. Please come on in."

"Hello, Jenny," JP said, looking at his watch. "Don't you people ever work?"

"Give me a break, Colonel, This is my first day off in three weeks. Who is my house guest?"

"A lady reporter named Wendy Brewer. She has an attitude problem. She hates everyone in general and the armed forces in particular. She's also suffering from airsickness. All things considered she may not be in the best humor. Where do you want her stuff?"

"Down the hall, first room on the right. That's Carol Wendling's room. She won't be back until some time next week."

"Pray that your guest is long gone by then."

Carrying the luggage, he went through a kitchenette to a small living room/dining room, then into a hall. As he passed the bathroom door he cast an envious glance at the commode, shower and sink. Entering the bedroom, he dumped the suitcase and pack on the floor next to an army metal bunk. A small dresser with mirror completed the furnishings. An assortment of female cosmetics, lotions, comb, hairbrush neatly arranged on the dresser brought forth longing for Kathy. He had been away too long, and still had seven more months to go. He returned to the kitchenette. "I'll be right back with Brewer."

"Take your time, Colonel."

"She'll probably sleep for a couple of hours, shower, and change clothes. She wants to interview me, so give my office a call when she's ready. I'll send my jeep for her."

As JP moved to the door Jenny placed her hand on his arm and stopped him. "Colonel Franklin."

"Yes Jenny?"

"Why are you doing this to me?"

JP shook his head sadly. "War is hell."

Chapter Fifty-Five

Wednesday, September 30, 1970, 1215 hours
Division Surgeon's Office, 36th Division, Phong Sahn, Republic of
Vietnam

"Colonel," Captain Dryer called from his desk," phone call for you on line one."

"Thanks Charles," JP said, picking up the phone. "Colonel Franklin."

"This is Jenny, Colonel. Your friend just told me she's not interested in lunch at the general's mess. She doesn't have very high regard for army food or army officers."

"If you ignore her endearing personality how is she doing?"

"She slept until a few minutes ago. She went to the bathroom and threw up on the floor. I had to clean up the mess. You owe me, Colonel."

"The entire division owes you, Jenny. You are making a great contribution to the defeat of the wily Cong."

"Tell me about it."

"I'll be in my office for the rest of the afternoon. When Brewer wants to come down give me a call."

Hanging up, JP resumed work on the papers from his in-box. He looked up when Master Sergeant Jordan knocked on his door.

"Sir, there's a Green Beret sergeant out here named Dahlgren to see you if you have the time."

JP stood up. "Always time for Sergeant Dahlgren."

Dahlgren walked into the office carrying a crossbow and half a dozen arrows in one hand. In the other he carried a thin knife in a leather sheath with two short straps.

"Good afternoon, sir," he said.

"Karl, what brings you out of the bush and into civilization?"

"I come bearing gifts from the Hmongs and the special forces."

"Those are for me?" JP asked, eying the crossbow and knife with more than a little greed.

"Yes, sir. The father of the little girl you diagnosed with acute appendicitis made the crossbow and arrows for you."

Dahlgren placed them on JP's desk.

JP picked up the crossbow. He hefted it and sighted along its shaft. "I've always wanted one of these."

Dahlgren laid the sheathed knife on the desk. "And this, sir, is from the special forces. We figured any doctor gutsy enough to hump through the jungle at night to see a sick Hmong kid deserves recognition by the Green Berets."

JP reached for the knife. Withdrawing it from its leather sheath, he examined its fine steel and razor edge.

"It's a backup knife, Colonel, to be carried strapped above the ankle under the pants." He placed his foot on a chair and pulled up his right trouser displaying a similar sheathed knife strapped to the leg above the boot.

"Karl," JP stammered. "I am deeply touched. These gifts will always mean a great deal to me."

"I'm glad you like them, Colonel. Be careful with the crossbow. It looks primitive, but it will put the arrow through an Atlanta phone book at twenty yards. The knife is sharp enough to use for shaving."

"I'll keep that in mind if my razor breaks down."

"Well sir, I've got to catch a flight back to my Hmongs. You come out and see us."

"No way. You'll put me to work."

"You got it, sir."

"Take care, Karl. And thank the little girl's father."

After Dahlgren left JP picked up the crossbow and examined it. The stock was crudely engraved and painted in yellow, red, and blue. He struggled for five minutes to work the bow string back to its detent. After placing an arrow on the stock's groove he alerted everyone in the main office to stand clear. "I'm going to check out this weapon."

"Just a second, Colonel," Tom Moffet said. He quickly drew a bullseye target on a sheet of typing paper and tacked it to the wooden wall behind his desk, then moved out of the way.

"All clear on the firing line," someone shouted.

From thirty feet away JP sighted along the top of the stock, computed Kentucky windage and elevation, then squeezed the crude trigger. There was slight whoosh followed by a thud. The arrow missed the paper target but embedded itself in the wall inches away.

"That's impressive," JP said. Walking to the arrow, he grasped it and pulled. Nothing happened. He pulled harder. The arrow still would not budge.

Setting the crossbow down on a desk, he gripped the arrow with both hands and pulled back steadily. The arrow slipped from his hands.

"Try using this, Colonel," one of the clerk typists said, handing him a pair of pliers.

As hard as he tried with the pliers, the arrow would not give. Finally, he broke off the shaft flush with the wall. When he compared the length of the shaft remaining with that of an intact arrow it was at least an inch shorter.

"Well, are you juveniles through playing," a female voice asked sarcastically.

JP turned to see Wendy Brewer standing just inside the doorway.

"Ms. Brewer, welcome to the division surgeon's office." He held out the crossbow. "Want to try it. I'll load it for you."

"I have no time for games."

"I see you're in your usual bubbly good humor," JP said, examining his broken arrow. "What can I do for you?"

"You can answer some questions if you don't mind."

"Frankly Ms. Brewer, I do mind… did mind. But higher authority insists I cooperate with you, so have at it. It might be easier on both of us if we go back to my office."

"Lead the way."

In his office JP stood, waiting for Brewer to sit. "Did you hitch-hike down here?"

"I walked. Is that so unusual?"

"No, I walk it almost every day."

"Well, bully for you."

Captain Dryer stepped into the office. The look he gave JP was one of abject pity. "Ma'am," he said to Brewer, "would you like coffee?"

"Black. Make sure it's hot. I despise lukewarm coffee and the people who serve it."

"Yes ma'am. Sir?"

"Same for me, please, but I'll still like you if it's lukewarm."

Brewer flashed JP a look that would have turned lesser men to stone, then settled into a metal chair at the side of the desk, ignoring two more comfortable wooden armchairs in front of the desk. Evidently she had showered, washed her hair, put on clean fatigues and even a hint of makeup. Cleaned up, she wasn't a bad-looking woman, although still very pale.

"How do you feel?" he asked.

"Let's can the bullshit," she said, taking a spiral notebook and pen from her bag. Opening the notebook, she picked up the pen and fixed him with her eyes. "Your full name, rank, and hometown."

The Gestapo had nothing on this, woman.

Captain Dryer entered, carrying two steaming mugs of black coffee. He set them down on the desk. "The coffee is boiling hot," he warned.

Brewer ignored him and the coffee.

"Thanks," JP said. Reaching for a mug, he took a timid but audible test slurp.

"Do you have to do that?" Brewer snapped.

JP glared at her, then slurped coffee so loudly that it could have been heard in Hanoi. The slug of steaming coffee burned his mouth and throat. "Damn it," he gasped hoarsely.

A hint of a smile crossed Brewer's face. "Let's get back to the questions."

JP nodded.

"Where did you go to medical school?"

"Medical College of Georgia, Class of '57."

"Did you have any training beyond medical school?"

"A rotating internship, a year of general surgery and three years of head and neck surgery residency at Walter Reed Army Hospital plus postgraduate courses at Columbia P&S, Mount Sinai, and UCLA."

"What were your assignments after you completed your training?"

"The Military Academy at West Point for three years, then back to Walter Reed as assistant chief for two years and chief for five."

Brewer stopped writing, reviewed her notes, then fixed on JP. "Let me get this straight. You graduated from medical school in 1957?"

JP nodded.

"And ten years later, that's five years after completing your residency, you were made chief of a surgical service in the most prestigious military hospital in the world?"

"No one else wanted the job."

"I should have realized army hospitals were staffed by incompetents."

"Now why would you say that?"

"I have my reasons," Brewer said bitterly.

JP thought he saw tears forming in her eyes. They disappeared so fast he couldn't be sure he saw them. Tears were something he had been sure Wendy Brewer was incapable of producing. The sight of them made him curious about this woman.

Her voice still maintained the same bitchy accusatory tone as before. "Did you take the oath of Hippocrates, Colonel Franklin?"

Strange question; where is she going? wondered JP. "I did, along with seventy-six classmates at graduation from medical school." He reached for his coffee mug and took a timid sip.

"Well, Colonel," Brewer said as if a prosecutor about to nail a defendant, "having taken the Hippocratic oath, how is it you now violate that oath by serving in a military force that has inflicted and is inflicting great suffering on a peace-loving people?"

JP almost spilled his coffee. He set his mug down and stared at Wendy Brewer. "What did you say?"

"You heard me, Doctor." The "doctor" was spoken in a voice dripping with contempt. "I'm referring to the search and mostly destroy missions, the B–52 and fighter-bomber raids, missions that have caused enormous destruction, tens of thousands killed and many more injured. You poison the Vietnamese people with defoliants and burn them horribly with napalm. I have been documenting these atrocities for the past month, so don't bother denying them."

"Have you also documented the 4,000 bodies of men, women, and children murdered by the Communists and buried in mass graves outside Hue during Tet? Have you photographed the bodies of murdered village chiefs, or their raped and disemboweled wives and children? Have you talked with surviving villagers who were forced to watch these atrocities as warnings the same would happen to them should they refuse to support the Communists? Have you seen the bodies of beheaded American soldiers, their bodies grotesquely mutilated? Or American soldiers who had their bellies sliced open, flame-throwers shoved in and ignited? Lady, for someone who has supposedly made a study of atrocities in Vietnam you are incredibly naive. In fact, I would go so far as to say you don't know what the hell you're talking about."

"That's all propaganda put out by MACV to cover their own atrocities and you know it, just as you are aware of the inequities of a conscription that drafts the sons of the poor, disadvantaged, and uneducated to be used as cannon fodder while the sons of the wealthy and privileged hide out in college classrooms and the National Guard."

JP remained silent. There was some truth in what Wendy Brewer had just said, but like much else the press reported, it was only a selected segment of truth used to support a preconceived agenda. He leaned towards the reporter. "The sons of two of my medical colleagues at Walter Reed are currently serving in Vietnam as grunts. They volunteered. The sons of two generals I know were killed in Vietnam. I would hardly classify those young men as poor, disadvantaged, and uneducated."

"That doesn't prove a thing."

"It does to me."

"Colonel," a clerk typist called out, "phone call on line two."

"Excuse me," JP said, lifting the phone. "Colonel Franklin."

"Kevin Brodie, sir. I need help."

"What do you have this time?"

"A six-year-girl whose trachea and cervical esophagus was transected by a mortar frag."

"Good God, how did that happen?"

"This was election day in her village. The VC mortared the village to discourage people from voting."

"I'll be right over."

"Take your time, Colonel. She won't be ready to go to the OR for another hour."

After hanging up JP turned to Wendy Brewer. "That was the head and neck surgeon at the 96th Evac. He asked me to help him with a case." JP described the Viet Cong shelling of the little girl's village and her injuries. "Why don't you come with me?" he suggested. "You can take all the photographs you want to document a VC atrocity."

"No, thanks. The story of the shelling is just a ploy to shift blame to the Viet Cong for something the U.S. Army did."

"The mortar frag is still in her, Ms. Brewer. You can watch me remove it. Hell, you can even have it. Take it to an ordnance expert for ID. I'm willing to bet you will learn it was manufactured in a Communist country."

"All that would demonstrate is how clever you people are in covering over your own atrocities," Brewer countered.

JP slumped back and sighed. "You do have a problem with the truth."

Master Sergeant Mickey Jordan knocked, stuck his head through the doorway. "Phone call for you, Colonel. You'll have to take it out here."

That was curious. JP had two phones on his desk, each with four buttons for four different lines. Any incoming call to the division surgeon's office could be answered on one of the two phones. He threw a glance at his phones. One of the buttons was flashing; he hoped Brewer hadn't noticed. Excusing himself, he followed Jordan to his desk and picked up the phone lying on its side. "Colonel Franklin."

"Just a minute for the G–2, sir."

Lieutenant Colonel Tony Martinelli, the head of division intelligence, came on line. "Doctor, how are you making out with the inquiring reporter?"

"It started out as a disaster. It's now approaching catastrophe."

Colonel Martinelli chuckled. "I asked your sergeant to get you away from her."

"Good thing; we were about to duke it out. What's up?"

"I just received word from USARV that Brewer's press credentials have been withdrawn. Her miserable ass is being thrown out of the country. The State Department, South Vietnamese government, and Association of News Journalists all have concurred."

"What did she do, murder someone?"

"Worse. A week ago Brewer was detained by the ARVNs in a province hospital in

Hue. She was caught photographing without permission an eighty-year-old Vietnamese woman who had second and third degree burns over most of her body. In Brewers rucksack the ARVNs found the draft of an article condemning US and ARVN employment of napalm in Vietnam."

"Those kinds of accidents happen although the FACs and other pilots put themselves at great risk to prevent them. That doesn't seem like justification for kicking her out of the country."

"Doctor, I can't believe you're defending her."

"I can't believe I'm defending her."

"You will probably change your mind after hearing this. The woman that Brewer photographed was not burned by napalm. She was burned when her kerosene stove exploded after she substituted gasoline for kerosene. ARVN intelligence developed the exposed film in Brewer's camera and her rucksack. They traced the photographs to people burned or injured in car crashes, fires, and other similar incidents. Not a single photograph was of a bona fide napalm burn."

"She's somewhat of a zealot, Tony, but I didn't think she would go that far."

"There are plenty of reporters out here with integrity who try to report the war objectively even if not to our liking. If Brewer's photo subjects had been of true napalm burns, she would not have been stopped. But she's over here to prove something, truth be damned."

"What do you want me to do with her?"

"Don't answer any more questions. Send her over here. I'll drop the grenade on her. She'll be on tomorrow's C–130 flight to Bien Hoa and out of the country by the next day."

"Colonel Martinelli, you have made my day."

He hung up, a broad smile on his face.

"Good news, sir?" Sergeant Jordan asked.

"The best, Sergeant. Only the war's end would be better."

★

Wednesday, September 30, 1970, 1915 hours
General's Mess, 36th Infantry Division Headquarters, Phong Sahn, Republic of Vietnam

Every seat in the dining room was taken by division staff and authorized guests, which included several senior nurses from the two military hospitals in Phong Sahn and a traveling Miss America from several years ago. The occasion was the very popular monthly seafood fest, a meal of lobster, shrimp, scallops, with all the trimmings including white wine. At one of the tables Lieutenant Colonel JP Franklin, M.D., Medical Corps, US Army, was finishing his salad and hungrily contemplating the main course.

The division communications officer, Joe Hardy, sitting opposite JP, put down his fork, took a sip of Chablis, and smiled at JP. "I heard you babysat a lady reporter today."

"There are some activities in war one is compelled do even though doing so is against one's better judgment. Escorting Wendy Brewer was one of them. Fortunately, she declined the invitation to break bread with the division staff and will be leaving tomorrow for Bien Hoa."

Lieutenant Colonel Bill Meyerhoff, USAF, commander of the FAC squadron, Zoomie Six, interjected, "I heard she was a first-rate bitch."

JP smiled. "That was one of her more redeeming qualities. Had she remained I would have urged her to fly with the commander of the FAC squadron to obtain an aviator's perspective of war."

"I've had my fill of airsick back seaters," Meyerhoff said disgustedly, looking at JP.

"If I had known that FAC pilots flew inverted most of the time I wouldn't have eaten such a big breakfast."

"Doc, you threw up all over my airplane. I had to fly with the canopy open for a week to get rid of the stench."

"You lie, Meyerhoff. I used a barf bag very skillfully."

A white-coated GI replaced JP's salad plate with a larger plate on which reposed broiled lobster meat, shrimp, and scallops on a bed of rice. Another white-coated GI tapped JP on the shoulder. "Phone call, Colonel Franklin. You can take it out in the bar."

JP stood and for a moment gazed longingly at his plate, then growled at his table mates. "Touch my plate and you die." As he left the dining room several diners waved sympathetically. Phone calls at this time and at this place were always bad news. Entering the bar, he slid onto a stool and picked up the phone. "Colonel Franklin."

A feminine voice answered. "Colonel, this is Jenny Russel."

"Yes, Jenny?"

"There's something really wrong with Wendy Brewer. This evening I talked her into taking some chicken soup. About ten minutes later she vomited that up. Sir, she's still vomiting."

"I heard you were a lousy cook, but not that bad. Anything else?"

"Yes, sir. She's had some bleeding from the vagina."

"Enough to soak a towel?"

"No, sir. It stained her panties and the sheet."

A sense of guilt passed through JP. Had he been too quick to attribute Brewer's vomiting to airsickness? Its persistence and now vaginal bleeding were ominous.

"Jenny."

"Yes, sir."

"Keep Brewer in bed. Don't let her get up for anything, even to go to the bathroom. I'm on my way." Without waiting for an answer he hung up and took off. Grabbing his cap as he passed through the foyer, he jogged the quarter mile to Jenny Russel's trailer. She was waiting at the door and let him in.

"How is she?" he asked as he entered.

"She quit throwing up but has started to complain of belly cramps." Jenny led him to Wendy Brewer's room.

The small bedroom was lit by a lamp on a bedstand. An oscillating fan on the floor swept the room with a warm breeze. Wendy Brewer lay supine on top of a sweat-soaked sheet, dressed only in a T-shirt and panties. Her eyes were closed. She was breathing rapidly and sweating profusely. A pan was on the floor by the bed.

JP turned to Jenny Russel. "I need more light."

Jenny flipped a wall switch by the door. The room was flooded with bright light from a ceiling fixture.

Brewer's eyes opened and stared at JP. "You bastard," she said with her usual malice, "you knew I was going to get thrown out of the country. You didn't have the decency to tell me before I talked to that son of a bitch Martinelli."

"Save your venom, Wendy. Where do you hurt?"

"My gut," she moaned, rubbing her fingers over her umbilicus. "God, it hurts. Are you going to give me something for pain?"

"Maybe later. Is the pain steady or does it come and go?"

"Damn it, I don't know. It just started."

JP took her wrist. Her pulse was rapid, about 140.

"I'm going to feel your belly," JP told her. Placing his right hand on her abdomen, he gently applied pressure.

"Ouch," Brewer cried out. "Go easy. You're hurting me."

Her abdomen was tight as a drum and exquisitely tender. JP noted the right lower quadrant scar. "Have you had an appendectomy?"

"In high school."

'That's unusual. Most people have them out in hospitals."

Brewer almost smiled in spite of herself.

JP sat on the side of the bed. "When did you have your last period?"

"What kind of question is that? It's none of your business."

"Wendy, this is my business. Answer the question."

Brewer glared at him. "Three months ago," she wailed, then burst into tears.

JP stood up and turned to Jenny. "I need to use your phone."

"It's in the kitchen."

Wendy Brewer lifted her head. "What is it? What are you going to do?"

JP looked down at her. "I think you're several months pregnant and threatening abortion. I can't tell if it's a tubal pregnancy or a normal one. You need to be hospitalized and looked after by a doctor who knows what he's doing."

"What if I refuse?"

"You will lose the baby."

"I never wanted it in the first place. This is such a lousy world for a kid to grow into. I'd be doing the little bastard a favor. Bastard," she said bitterly, "bastard. That's just what it is, a bastard." She began to sob.

Jenny Russel sat down on the bed, took Brewer's hand, held it tightly and looked up at JP. "Are you going to call for an ambulance, Colonel?"

"Yes, but to take her only to the VIP pad; it's about a quarter of a mile from here. A Dust-off will fly her to the hospital."

"I'm not flying in any army helicopter," Brewer insisted.

"Wendy, our concern now is to save the baby. That should be your concern too. If

510

you went all the way to the hospital by ambulance at night on Phong Sahn's roads you would abort for sure."

"How did I get myself in such a mess?" she wailed.

JP leaned over and squeezed her free hand. "It's not such a mess. You have a precious little life inside you fighting to live, and you're among friends now." He straightened up. "Don't go away. I'll be right back."

Chapter Fifty-Six

Wednesday, September 30, 1970, 2240 hours
Ward No.3, 96th Evacuation Hospital, Phong Sahn, Republic of Vietnam

There was no obstetrical ward at the 96th Evacuation Hospital. However, the US Army Nurse Corps, on short notice, improvised one at the far end of Ward No.3 – a ward partially filled with recovering wounded within days of returning to duty. Wendy Brewer was afforded a modicum of privacy by three folding screens arranged around her bed. Inasmuch as she was on strict bedrest the problem of latrine use had yet to be addressed. For the time being a bedpan would suffice.

The absence of an obstetrical ward was not unexpected, since the history of war had failed to demonstrate the need for an obstetrician at a hospital in a combat zone. Fortunately for Wendy Brewer, Lieutenant Colonel Fred Henschel, the chief of anesthesia, had been a family practitioner for eight years before going through a three-year anesthesia residency. As a family practitioner he had logged over a thousand deliveries. He felt quite comfortable taking over the care of Wendy Brewer when she arrived unexpectedly on the helipad. Within minutes he had her sedated and Ringer's lactate with antibiotics running into a vein.

JP, who had accompanied Brewer on the helicopter to the hospital, had stayed with her until she fell asleep, then left for a cup of mess hall coffee. Before returning to his hooch he decided to look in on her one more time. Entering a darkened Ward No.3 he walked past beds with sleeping GIs to the far end of the ward. Brewer, in blue pajama tops, lay quietly on her back in bed, her eyes closed, a sheet pulled up to just above her hips. A lieutenant nurse brought a clean bedpan and set it on the floor just under the bed. Fred Henschel sat on the edge of the bed writing on a chart.

"How is she doing, Fred?" JP asked.

"Good. All parameters indicate a uterine pregnancy. The contractions have stopped and there's been no more bleeding. I talked to Harvey Powell at the 3rd Field a few minutes ago. He agreed that conservative management is the way to go. There is no reason at this time to interrupt the pregnancy."

"I'm not up on my OB, Fred. How common are cramps and bleeding in the first trimester?"

"Well, they're not uncommon. During the first twenty weeks about thirty percent of women will experience cramps and mild bleeding. Of those, only ten to fifteen percent will go on to abort. All things considered, Ms. Brewer stands a good chance of carrying the baby to term." Colonel Henschel stood up, snapped the chart closed and hung it on the foot of the bed. "Getting her over here by chopper was a prudent move," he said. "If she had come by ambulance she probably would have lost the baby."

"The Dust-offs came through again."

"I'll be back in a few minutes," Henschel said. "Mind keeping an eye on her?"

"Not at all."

JP pulled up a chair to the side of the bed and sat down. For several minutes he watched Brewer's regular breathing. A nurse took her blood pressure and pulse, wrote the figures on the chart, then showed JP the chart. All the numbers were normal. He nodded thanks.

After a while JP began to yawn. It had been a long day. He stood and stretched.

Brewer opened her eyes and looked at him. "Please don't leave," she said pleadingly.

"Hi! How do you feel?"

"Better. How's my baby?"

"Doing okay."

Brewer shifted slightly. "Colonel, I want to thank you for what you did for me."

"I would have done as much for any bitchy pregnant reporter."

Despite her discomfort, Brewer smiled. "I deserved that. I feel I owe you an explanation."

JP remained silent.

"The baby's father was a major named Dave Partridge in the 101st Airborne. We were going to be married in Vietnam, then decided to wait until his tour was up so we could have a church wedding in the States. I have never been married; I wanted to do it up big the first time. Two months ago Dave was severely wounded. He died during surgery at Phu Bai."

"I'm so sorry, Wendy," JP said. "That explains a lot."

"There's more. When I learned of his death I became very bitter over the war. I blamed army doctors and not the VC or NVA for Dave's death. I vowed to do everything possible to end the war, even lie. That was wrong. I deserved to lose my press accreditation." She turned away. "I'll probably lose my job."

JP reached over and squeezed her hand. "Don't run up the white flag just yet, Brewer. You're going to have a kid who will need a mama with an income."

"When I'm sent home in disgrace my reputation and credibility will be destroyed. There will be no place in journalism for me."

"How about if you are sent home just pregnant?"

"I don't follow you, Colonel."

"You forget what schemers we military people are. The division PIO, Denny Kirsten, is a master manipulator. He has all sorts of connections at MACV and the press. Considering your stress coping with the death of your fiancé in combat and the problems of a tenuous pregnancy, a convincing argument could be made that you were acting under great duress which clouded your judgment. I believe Major Kirsten could be persuaded to exercise his considerable influence and arrange for your accreditation to be reinstated, provided, of course, that you go home and take care of yourself."

"Why would you do that for me after all that the grief I caused you? And Denny Kirsten hates my guts."

"Wendy, for all practical purposes you are an army widow. You are carrying an army brat, an Airborne one at that. It's axiomatic; we in the army take care of our own."

★

Wednesday, September 30, 1970, 2350 hours
Headquarters Staff Bivouac Area, 36th Infantry Division, Phong Sahn, RVN

Lieutenant Colonel JP Franklin turned off the lamp by his bunk, then propped himself to a semi-sitting posture and gazed out the windows. A partial moon cast a pale yellow glow over the smooth South China Sea. The water's tranquility gave no hint of the deadly games being played inland less than thirteen minutes flying time from his hooch. Out there young Americans were trying to survive the night in a hostile jungle plagued by heat, rain, insects, reptiles, tigers, and a committed enemy. Sleep was a luxury they could ill afford if they wanted to live.

The door at the opposite end of the building banged open. Footsteps followed. A light was turned on, its glow shining under the door between JP's room and the adjoining one. The division chaplain, Father Peter Deveraux, had returned from his Wednesday evening poker game.

"Been sinning again tonight, Father?" JP called out.

"Ah, Doctor, you're still awake. The good Lord saw fit I lose twenty-two dollars and thirty cents, most of it to Protestants."

"If you had been a Baptist you would have been at a Wednesday night prayer meeting. You would have ended the day wealthier by twenty-two dollars and thirty cents."

"It was the Baptist chaplain who took most of my money."

"That is the Lord's way of urging you to repent your sinful ways."

"Enough of this. I'm going to turn in, Don't forget your prayers."

"I'll ask that you be dealt better cards next Wednesday."

★

Thursday, October 1, 1970, 0210 hours
Division Surgeon's Hooch, 36th Infantry Division Area, Phong Sahn, Republic of Vietnam

The pounding on the door of his hooch wrenched JP from a deep sleep. "Colonel Franklin, Colonel Franklin," a husky voice shouted.

"Just a minute," JP called out. Groggy with sleep, he fumbled for the lamp switch, then blinked when the room was bathed with light. Pulling on fatigue trousers, he slipped his feet into wooden clogs, clumped to the door and unhooked the latch. When he pushed open the door yellow light from behind him streamed on to a hatless muscular young man of medium height wearing black pajamas. A 357 Magnum was snugged in a shoulder holster. His face, caked with dust, sagged from fatigue. JP stared as if to penetrate the dust, for the man had a vague familiarity.

"Sir, I'm Captain Durden, CO of the A team at Phu Than," the man reported. "I need to talk to you about a serious problem."

Shaking the cobwebs out of his head, JP invited the captain in. "Have a seat," he said, indicating the guest bunk.

Durden settled on the bunk and leaned back against the wall, closing his eyes for a moment. JP pulled a chair close to Durden and waited.

"Sir, I apologize for waking you at this hour. I would have been here earlier but my chopper made a forced landing west of Can Tuy. I had to hitch a ride here. I came straight to you rather than work my way up through channels in order to save time."

JP, now fully awake, continued to study the young captain's face. Recognition came swiftly. "I know you from West Point, Durden," he said. "You joined the Rock Climbing Club in your plebe year. You made up for your lack of climbing skill and judgment with brute strength."

"Good memory, sir," Durden said, managing a small grin. "Some people say that's what I've been doing since I graduated."

"The last time we climbed together was at the Gunks," JP said, remembering fondly the weekend trips when he would take cadets to the Shawangunks, a popular rock climbing area near New Paltz, forty miles north of the Military Academy.

"That's right, sir. You talked me into climbing the 'Dentist', which was one grade higher than I ever want to climb again."

The door between JP's room and the chaplain's opened. Father Deveraux stepped in, wearing a dark blue bathrobe and slippers. "Doctor, I find it incredible you are up at two in the morning reminiscing about your rock climbing days. Don't you doctors ever sleep?"

"Not when one of my former climbing protégés comes banging on my door." JP introduced Durden. "He's come with a problem so compelling it was worth risking the wrath of a lieutenant colonel at two in the morning." He turned to Durden. "This'd better be good. Sam."

Durden leaned forward. Speaking in a low voice, he began. "First I should give you a little background. About two months ago the Montagnards at Bai Chan became fed up with the Viet Cong taking much of their rice harvest as tribute, conscripting their young men, and murdering their elders to intimidate the others into cooperating. The Montagnards requested they be moved to a secure area. The South Vietnamese government moved them to Phu Than, close to the Ruff Puff compound where my team is located. We were tasked with the security for the Montagnards. Until the Montagnards harvested their own rice crops and manioc they were to be furnished rice captured by US units and turned over to the ARVNs for distribution. USAID contributed fish powder and canned milk to the ARVNs to be passed on as a supplement to the children's diet."

"Why weren't the rice and supplements given directly to the Montagnards?" Father Deveraux asked.

Durden smiled bitterly. "Our civilian bosses in Saigon wanted to create the image of a benevolent and caring South Vietnamese government. So far, only inadequate amounts of rice have been delivered and no canned milk or fish powder."

"You're painting a village with malnutrition," JP said, "especially the children."

"It's much more serious than that, Colonel. Three days ago some of the Montagnard kids came down with diarrhea, vomiting, coughing and high fever. By the second day some of the kids had convulsions and passed blood with their stools. Eight kids died that day and eleven more died the next day, that was yesterday. Before I left the village I counted a dozen very sick kids and another thirty beginning to have diarrhea and vomiting."

"What about the adults?"

"A few have diarrhea, but nothing as severe as the kids and no deaths." Durden stopped, as though he had run out of words. He looked at JP. "Sir, I tried to get help from the ARVNs. There's a battalion of infantry with its headquarters five klicks north of us. The CO told me they couldn't spare doctors or helicopters. Is there anything you can do?"

"Lets hope so," JP said, glancing at his watch. "There's no point in going out there in the dark. Besides I need a couple of hours to get things organized."

"What is that fine mind of yours thinking?" Father Deveraux asked.

"Captain Durden described what sounds like an epidemic of bacterial dysentery… shigellosis. Cholera and typhoid fever are other possibilities but much lower on the suspect list. My fine mind is considering a medical team, led by a real doctor, to go out to Phu Than with medical supplies and backup to stay long enough to control the epidemic."

Durden looked perplexed. "Sir, aren't you a real doctor?"

"Sam, there are some who, having seen me operate, would consider that a legitimate question," JP said smiling. "The blunt truth is, correcting dehydration and electrolyte imbalance in young children with fever, diarrhea, and vomiting is very tricky. It would be best done by a doctor with experience in pediatric medicine and infectious diseases who will function as a team leader out there. I can coordinate the operation, furnish medical personnel, supplies, transportation, and whatever else might be needed. As a doctor I'll work out there under the supervision of the team leader."

Now the chaplain looked perplexed.

"Something wrong with my plan, Father?"

"This is a war zone, JP. Where are you going to find army pediatricians out here?"

"You underestimate your division surgeon and hooch-mate," JP admonished. "My operating at the 96th Evac and 19th Surg, giving lectures, and attending their… er… professional functions has given me excellent rapport with the hospital commanders and their staffs. For example, I know that Lieutenant Colonel Phil Anderson, the chief of medicine at the 96th, was chief of pediatrics at Madigan before he took an internal medicine residency and then an infectious disease fellowship. He would be the ideal person to lead this team." JP paused, mentally reviewing what he knew about Anderson. "I'm afraid there may be a problem with Colonel Anderson."

"What do you mean?"

"Neither I nor his hospital commander can legally order him to Phu Than, much

516

less order him to remain out there for several days. Frankly, a situation like this has never come up." JP sighed. "Let's hope he'll volunteer."

"You think he might be reluctant?" the chaplain asked.

"Reluctant is putting it mildly, Father. Colonel Anderson has a pathological fear of leaving the security of the hospital compound. He hasn't set foot off it since arriving in Phong Sahn five months ago. He also has a phobia of flying in helicopters, having treated people who were badly injured and burned in crashes. Other than those shortcomings he is the perfect candidate."

"Is he Catholic?" Father Deveraux inquired.

The implication of the priest's question sank in. JP grinned. "I certainly hope so, Father."

"Any other doctors with pediatric backgrounds who could, as you put it, volunteer?" the chaplain asked.

"The chief of anesthesia at the 19th Surg, Trevor Holcomb, was a pediatrician before opting for the quiet of the operating room. I doubt he can be spared to spend a couple of days in the boonies. I hope to convince him to supervise the care of any kids so sick they require hospitalization. There is one other doctor in the division with training in pediatrics. Brent Mann, at Delta Med, was drafted out of his second year of pediatric residency. I don't think I'll have much trouble getting him to volunteer. From what I hear his CO can't keep him out of helicopters. He's been agitating for an assignment as a surgeon to an infantry battalion."

"Sounds like my kind of guy," Durden said quietly from the guest bunk.

JP turned to the young special forces captain. "Sam, I don't want to sound like a worrier, but I'm responsible for the safety of the people I send. What's the security and risk factor at the Montagnard village?"

"My A Team has one other officer and nine NCOs. Our Mike force consists of 180 Ruff Puffs dug in on a hill two klicks from the village. An ARVN battalion headquarters is eight klicks away, and we are within range of a 105 battery on Duckville. The Ruff Puffs make daily sweeps around the Montagnard village. One platoon is deployed at night in an ambush configuration."

"Have the patrols picked up any sign of VC activity?"

"I was afraid you'd ask that, Colonel. Last month the Ruff Puffs killed eleven Viet Cong, captured two and confiscated their weapons. That was twice what it was the month before. So far, there's been no shelling or probing of the village, but the VC are in the area and their activities appear to be increasing. That is not a good sign, sir."

"How am I going to get Colonel Anderson to volunteer after I tell him what you just told me." JP broke into a grin. "I'm not sure I want to go."

"Let's hope Colonel Anderson doesn't ask about security."

"You're a sly one, Durden. Be careful you don't end up working for the CIA. I will have to brief Colonel Anderson about the risks and take the chance he'll still volunteer."

"Yes, sir. What can I do?" Durden asked.

JP looked at the grimy captain fighting to stay awake. Without a word he walked to his locker. Opening the door, he pulled out a clean towel, a set of green scrubs, and a red bulging ditty bag with toilet articles. Tossing them on the guest bunk, he said, "You, Captain, can go shave, shower and try to get some sleep. I'll schedule a chopper for 0630 hours." He glanced at his watch. "It's 0245 hours now. You should be able to get a couple of hours' sleep. I'll wake you in time for breakfast." He reached for the phone. "In the meantime I have work to do."

JP took his phone over to his bunk and sat down. Placing the phone beside him, he dialed the medical battalion. When the duty NCO answered he ordered up his jeep. Next he dialed the hooch of the 36th's chief of staff. The phone rang six or seven times before a muffled voice answered, "Witherington."

"This is Colonel Franklin."

"Don't you doctors ever sleep?"

JP quickly described the situation in the village and his intentions.

Witherington remained silent several seconds. "That's pretty risky, Doctor," he finally said. "VC activity in that area has increased in the past month. I'm sure they will want to use the dead Montagnard kids as examples of the South Vietnamese government's negligence and perhaps even culpability. They will not take kindly to your meddling in what could be a great propaganda coup for them. Once they learn that high-ranking medical officers are in the village it will become a target hard to resist."

"I realize that, Colonel, but nineteen kids have died. More will die unless the epidemic is controlled. Aside from the humanitarian aspects, this would be an opportunity to demonstrate to the Montagnards and South Vietnamese that the US Army is committed to their welfare."

Witherington paused. "You have stated your case well, Doctor. Okay, you're authorized to take whatever personnel and supplies out there you consider necessary. The doctor from the 96th must be a volunteer and have his commander's blessing."

"Yes, sir. Ah, sir… about our security. Considering your assessment of the VC reaction would it not be prudent to beef up the defenses?"

"Doctor, sometimes I get the idea you are bucking for my job."

"No chance, sir. I don't like the idea of division surgeons calling me at two in the morning."

"We'll put a scout with a high ship over the area during the day and a night hawk after dark. They'll be in communication with our ground forces in the area. In addition, we'll beef up village defenses with a company of rangers and alert the ARVN battalion. You know, it just wouldn't do for our division surgeon to get captured."

"That's very thoughtful of you, sir."

"I was thinking of the paperwork," Witherington said, chuckling. "You should plan to brief the general at 0700 hours."

JP hesitated. He didn't want to push his luck too far with the chief of staff. But to hang around just to brief the general at seven would delay getting to the village until almost 0900 hours.

"Colonel, I'd like to beg off the briefing. I hope to be out at Phu Than by 0700 hours."

"Very well, Doctor. I'll brief the general in the morning. Plan your schedule to be back

518

in time to brief at 1700 hours. I will want your assessment of the situation at Phu Than and its impact on the division's medical capabilities. Do you want to use my chopper?"

"No, sir. I had one scheduled for 0830 hours. I'll just reschedule it."

"Be sure to fill in the G–5 before you leave. By the way, how is that obnoxious reporter Wendy Brewer?"

"Mother and child are doing well as of two hours ago."

"Keep me informed."

"Aye, aye, sir."

"Colonel Franklin."

"Sir?"

"You're in the army now. Knock off that marine/navy stuff."

Next, JP phoned his medical battalion exec, Major Nichols. "Doug, I need to borrow Sergeant Harrel again for several days." He went on to describe the situation at the Montagnard village. "Sergeant Harrel will be in charge of the logistics out there. He should plan on staying for several days." Hanging up, JP looked up the number of Tom Moffet's hooch and dialed it. The preventative medicine officer answered on the first ring.

"You must have been waiting by the phone for it to ring," JP said. Briefly he again described the epidemic and his plans. "I need you and Chris Daniels out there to work on water and waste sanitation. Bring your toothbrushes in case you decide to stay."

The next call, to Delta Med at Nghia Lam, had to go through a sleepy Vietnamese female operator who spoke poor English and might have been a VC sympathizer. When Dom Cruessi picked up the phone JP gave no details. "Have Brent Mann standing by the helipad to be picked up at 0650 hours. Tell him to pack for three to four days."

Finally JP dialed Colonel Marchenko's trailer. A sleepy voice answered.

"It's a pleasure for me to wake up someone at the 96th for a change," JP said. "For too long it's been the other way around."

"I have a bad feeling about this call."

"I want to borrow your chief of medicine for a couple of days."

All sleep was swept from the Marchenko's voice. "You want to do what?"

JP explained.

"You'll never get him to volunteer, JP. Just the sight of a helicopter makes him airsick, and physical courage is not Phil's long suit."

"I have a secret weapon."

"Good luck."

By the time JP dressed and shaved, Pfc Groves was knocking on his door. "Be out in a minute," he called out. After buckling on his web belt with its holstered pistol, he strapped the knife that Sergeant Dahlgren had given him to his right leg, then knocked on the chaplain's door. "Father Pete, ready?"

"On the way."

Setting his alarm clock for 0530 hours, he placed it on an ammo box next to the now sleeping Durden, then headed out to his jeep.

"What's up, Colonel?" Groves asked.

"I'll tell you on the way to the 96th."

Father Deveraux materialized out of the dark. "A cheery good morning to you, Pfc Groves."

"Good morning, Father."

JP tilted the front passenger seat forward to allow the chaplain to crawl into the back seat, then replaced the seat and slid into it. "Drive on," he said. On the way to the 96th he described the epidemic to Groves.

"Gee, sir, I sure would like to go with you."

"We'll have a full load going out. If we bring some kids back we may be over the chopper's lift load. Maybe you can be worked in on one of the subsequent flights."

The darkness hid Groves's disappointment.

★

Thursday, October 1, 1970, 0405 hours
96th Evacuation Hospital, Phong Sahn, RVN

Colonel Louis Marchenko was in his office when JP and Peter Deveraux walked in. Seeing the priest, he said, "Good morning, Father. What brings you out at this hour with a brain-damaged ex-marine?"

"I'm the moral muscle if Colonel Anderson drags his feet volunteering."

"Ah, the secret weapon. Do you want me to go with you, JP?"

"It may be best if the guy who makes out Phil's ER isn't around when we put the question to him. Your presence would be too intimidating."

"You have a point there. You know the way to the BOQ?"

JP nodded.

"Anderson's room is No.21. It's a corner room on the second landing. I'll phone him he's about to have visitors but I won't reveal the purpose of your visit. Let me know if the hospital can help in other ways."

"Thanks Lou."

Leaving Marchenko's office, JP and Father Deveraux walked along a lengthy covered wooden walk, past half a dozen wards, through the emergency room and out to the helipad. Turning right, they passed Marchenko's thirty-five-foot trailer and came to a wooden two-floored building resembling a cheap motel. The door of each room opened on to a deck that ran the length of the building. A single naked bulb burned under a metal shade at each corner and mid-deck casting ominous shadows. Four hundred feet away were four similar buildings, the nurses' quarters. Unseen in the dark was a volleyball court and a tennis court separating the nurses' quarters from the BOQ. *Hardly insurmountable obstacles*, thought JP.

Reaching the second landing, JP stopped at Room No.21. A diffuse glow behind drawn curtains indicated that its occupant was awake. The door was immediately opened to JP's knock. Phil Anderson, dressed in fatigue trousers and a T-shirt, stood barefoot in the doorway. A tall man in his early forties, his intellectual face not quite awake, repeatedly blinked behind rimless glasses. Beyond him the small room was furnished with a single metal bunk bed, small desk, two chairs, and a crude homemade bookcase crammed with medical books. A reel-to-reel tape deck sat on top of the bookcase along with reels of tape. The desk was covered with medical journals and papers.

"JP, Father Deveraux, come in," Anderson said. "Lou Marchenko said you would explain the purpose of your visit at this crazy hour."

"Phil," JP began, "what I'm about to ask may sound even crazier."

Anderson motioned to two chairs, then sat on his bunk.

JP continued. "There is a large number of children in a village at Phu Than who are severely ill with diarrhea, vomiting, dehydration, electrolyte imbalance, and malnutrition. They are at great risk of dying, Phil; nineteen children have already died."

"Good God, JP, say no more. Of course I'll be happy to take care of the kids. Just get them here as quickly as possible."

"Phil, I don't think you understand. There is an epidemic in that village. It's likely there are more than thirty children who require intensive treatment. There's no way they can be medevac'd here. What I'm asking is that you go out to Phu Than and lead the medical team to treat those kids."

Anderson turned pale. "You want me to do what? No way, JP. You're nuts. Phu Than is a dangerous place. All Vietnam is a dangerous place. Flying in a helicopter is a dangerous activity. Look at what happened to Diblasio, Barfield, and Westin. There's no way I'll get in a helicopter, much less go out to some village in the middle of Viet Cong territory. And damn it, Father, quit looking at me that way."

"Phil, the Almighty blessed you with a brilliant mind. Your country gave you superb training and immense professional opportunities. As a result you have a tremendous capacity to heal. Most men would sell their souls to be able to do what you can do. The sick children in that Montagnard village may die for lack of skilled medical care. The Almighty gave you the ability to deliver such care. Are you going to sit there on your bunk in your bare feet and tell the Almighty you prefer the security of your miserable little room to saving the lives of children?"

Colonel Anderson stared from the priest to JP then back to the priest. His shoulders slumped. "What kind of help would I have out there?" he asked softly.

"Brent Mann from Delta med will be your assistant," JP said quickly. "He's had almost two years of pediatric residency. You'll have at least two enlisted medics full time. Tom Moffet, the preventive medicine officer, and Chris Daniels, the sanitary engineer will be out there. Tom has an M.D./PhD from Hopkins and boards in Public Health. Chris has a Master's in Sanitary Engineering. My med battalion operations sergeant will be in charge of logistics and we'll have our own chopper. I'll function primarily as your gofer, getting whatever you need from division medical supply and the hospitals. I'll also be out there part time, but you will be in charge."

Anderson stood up and reached to a shelf for his shaving kit. Turning, he looked at Chaplain Lieutenant Colonel Peter Deveraux. "Damn it, Father, how did I ever get talked into this?"

"It's God's will, Phillip."

Chapter Fifty-Seven

Thursday, October 1, 1997, 0630 hours
Phong Sahn, Republic of Vietnam

Chief Warrant Officer–2 Dan Ranson and Second Lieutenant Tom Carter landed their UH1H Huey helicopter at the admin pad and shut down. Ranson climbed out, took one look at the mountain of supplies and the eight passengers waiting to be transported to Phu Than and shook his head. "No way," he muttered. Walking rapidly over to Lieutenant Colonel JP Franklin, he saluted. "Sir, we need to talk." It didn't take him long to convince Colonel Franklin that a second helicopter would be required.

Ranson cut through the administrative obstacles and arranged for a second Huey. By the time it arrived his helicopter was loaded. It departed for Phu Than with JP, Phil Anderson, Sam Durden, and Sergeant Harrel on board. The second helicopter, with the remainder of the supplies, Tom Moffet, Chris Daniels, and two medics, took off five minutes later for Nghia Lam to pick up Brett Mann, then continue on to Phu Than. The mission of mercy was under way.

★

At 2,000 feet the early morning air was cool and invigorating. JP, seated behind the co-pilot and facing the open door, watched villages and hamlets pass beneath the Huey's skids. From this altitude they appeared as small islands of habitation in a vast ocean of rice paddies. Ahead, a river gently snaked east–west for several miles, then curved sharply to the south.

At the river's bend a neat pattern of hooches couched in fields of green fanned out in a semi-circular pattern from the east bank. Sunlight flashed off dozens of shiny metal roofs, off the mirror-like river, and off the rice paddies. Vietnam appeared too peaceful and too beautiful to be at war.

Captain Sam Durden, seated on a rear bulkhead seat, leaned towards JP and touched his arm. He pointed to a cluster of brown-colored hooches on an elevated area of cleared flat ground west of the river. "That's the Montagnard village," he shouted.

"What about the village on this side of the river?"

"Vietnamese."

"Any diarrhea there?"

Durden shook his head. He then pointed to a high cone-shaped hill with a flat summit several kilometers from the Montagnard and Vietnamese villages. "My Mike Force compound is up there. We'll land there, pick up a couple of interpreters, then

522

head to the Montagnard village."

JP nodded.

Captain Durden unbuckled his seat belt and moved forward to stand behind Tom Carter and Dan Ranson. Indicating the hill he had just shown JP, he handed Ranson a slip of paper, returned to his seat and buckled in. "I gave them the team's radio frequency and call sign," he explained.

Tom Carter dropped the Huey's nose, then banked into a steep descending spiral. JP turned to look over Carter's shoulder at the instrument panel. The VSI needle swung towards 2,000 feet per minute down; the airspeed needle rotated into the yellow arc and the altimeter needles unwound. A look out of the door showed the ground rushing up to meet them. Carter leveled off just over the tree tops, unloading Gs on the Huey's rotor blades and passengers. After passing beyond the trees, the Huey dropped to just above the river's surface, churning water as it skimmed at 120 knots.

JP threw a glance at Phil Anderson. The 96th's chief of medicine had his eyes shut tight and his jaw clenched. Both hands were fixed with white-knuckle grips on his seat's metal frame. At least he hadn't thrown up.

Approaching the hill's base, the Huey nosed up and climbed several hundred feet, bleeding off much of its forward speed. Clearing the hilltop it flared, hovered a moment, then settled on a square of PSP, throwing up clouds of red dust. As the dust settled JP saw that the high side of the summit was terraced into three levels. A dozen living spaces had been dug into each level and fortified by stacks of green plastic sandbags, leaving only narrow entrances.

"You live up here, Sam?" JP asked.

"Yes, sir. It ain't much, but it's home." Unbuckling his seat belt, he moved to the door. "I'll be right back," he shouted over his shoulder. Jumping to the ground, he jogged to one of the entrances and disappeared into the interior's darkness.

JP undid his belt and moved to the seat beside a very pale Lieutenant Colonel Anderson. "How are you doing, Phil?"

"I'll never forgive you and Father Deveraux for coercing me into this," Anderson said.

"Hey, you volunteered, remember?" JP said, grinning.

"With a gun at my head. Why did we land up here?"

"To pick up a couple of interpreters. We'll be leaving soon," JP said, patting Anderson's shoulder. "Hang tough, Phil," he said, then returned to his seat.

Several minutes later Captain Durden, followed by two young Ruff Puffs carrying M–16s, climbed into the helicopter. The Ruff Puffs looked not much older than fifteen. They couldn't have weighed more than one hundred pounds. After they were belted in the Huey lifted up and eased to the edge of the hill. Passing over the concertina wire it dropped into the valley. Phil Anderson again gripped his seat frame and shut his eyes. In less than a minute the Huey settled on the sandy east bank of the river several hundred meters from the Montagnard village. A narrow trail led from the river bank through four-foot tall grass towards the village.

Unbuckling, Captain Durden moved to the door. "We go as grunts from here, gentlemen."

A group of Montagnard men emerged from the trail and moved to the Huey's door. They were small-boned, wiry, and dressed in a variety of clothing from loincloths and long black shirts to fatigues. Durden, JP and Sergeant Harrel loaded each man with boxes of medical supplies until only gas lanterns, cans of water, cans of gasoline, and two trunks remained.

"You may as well get some heavy labor out of me," JP told Durden as both jumped to the ground.

"If you say so, sir."

Turning towards the door, they grabbed the handles of the first trunk and dragged it out of the door. JP grunted as his right arm took up the trunk's weight. Carrying the trunk between them, they started up the trail. A look over his shoulder showed Phil Anderson and Sergeant Harrel about twenty paces behind, carrying the second trunk. More Montagnards passed them going down the trail for the remainder of the supplies.

The trail began as a mild incline; it steadily increased in grade until it became a punishing climb. The effort of carrying the heavy trunk and climbing the steep trail soon had JP sweating and gasping for breath.

"Out of shape, Colonel?" the special forces captain tweaked.

"Watch it, Durden. Don't make me regret getting you off the rocks when you got stuck climbing the 'Dentist'."

The special forces captain flashed a grin.

Halfway up the trail the caravan was greeted by a dozen giggling barefooted children dressed in black, thigh-length shirts or short pants. The small children wore nothing at all. All quickly distributed themselves among the beasts of burden and ostensibly helped carry the supplies. JP noted protruding bellies and stick-like limbs on many of the children. There was little doubt that these children were victims of chronic malnutrition. As they neared the Montagnard village the second Huey – the one that went to Nghia Lam – circled overhead, then landed next to Dan Ranson's helicopter on the river bank.

Just before reaching the village the trail widened, leveling off as it passed through a gap in concertina wire that circled the village. A dozen meters beyond the wire began rows of primitive huts constructed of brown mud and straw. Three larger framed buildings stood out among the other buildings, their thatched sides contrasting with the much smaller mud and straw structures. Corrugated metal sheets formed the roofs of all buildings. The skeletal structure of two more large buildings was taking form adjacent to a cleared central area which could be considered the village "square". A maze of narrow trenches connected sandbagged shelters, bunkers, and fighting holes.

Forty to fifty men, women, and children stood in loose groups in the village square, quietly watching the approaching caravan. Durden and JP carried their trunk to the edge of the area and set it down. Massaging his aching right arm, JP watched Phil Anderson and Sergeant Harrel exit the trail carrying the second trunk. Anderson's fatigues were soaked with sweat and his face twisted with pain. He looked as if he were about to become a casualty. If that happened there was no backup plan. JP suppressed the urge to even speculate on one.

Montagnards emerged from the trail, carrying supplies from the second helicopter. Bringing up the rear were Tom Moffet, Chris Daniels, Brett Mann and two enlisted medics.

Two of the older Montagnard males, the village elders, detached themselves from the crowd, came forward and greeted Captain Durden effusively. Durden returned the greetings, then introduced JP as the chief *bacci* who had come with his assistants to examine the sick children and make them well. Durden then looked to JP. "How would you like to proceed from here, Colonel?"

JP was aware he had the rank and authority to take charge of the group. However, he also realized that it would be Phil Anderson's experience, expertise, and efforts that would determine the outcome of the epidemic. Considering Anderson's reluctance, even resistance to "volunteer", it was with considerable anxiety that JP decided Anderson should direct the medical effort in the village. He told Captain Durden, "Colonel Anderson will be in charge out here. Better check with him."

A dubious Sam Durden turned to Anderson. "Sir?"

Colonel Anderson's response was as surprising as it was reassuring. He moved to the center of the group of Americans and began speaking with the confidence and poise of a medical school professor organizing ward rounds. "Here's how we'll work this," he began. "First we identify all the sick children in the village and place them in one of three categories. The 'critical' cases are children in immediate danger of dying. They will require medevac a.s.a.p. to the 19th Surg. The next group are the 'serious' cases – children too sick to be treated at home but not so sick they require evacuation. They will be managed in an improvised pediatric ward. The remaining children will be considered 'routine' and taken care of in their homes… er… hooches."

"How do you want to triage the kids, Phil?" JP asked.

"We'll split the M.D.s into two groups. Tom Moffet and I will start with the hooches at the north end of the village. Colonel Franklin and Brent Mann start at the south end. One interpreter is to go with each team. Every hooch should be checked for sick children. Classify each child into one of the three groups I described, then go on to the next hooch. Hopefully, by the time we run into each other we will have checked all the hooches. At that time we'll review everything and decide who goes where." He looked at JP. "Colonel, will we have a helicopter available for evacuating the critical kids or do we need to arrange for Dust-offs?"

JP could not believe that Phil Anderson was the same individual who, only a few hours ago, almost had a heart attack when it was proposed he spend several days and nights in a Montagnard village. So awed was he by Anderson's transition from lamb to tiger that he failed to respond.

"JP?" Anderson persisted.

"Sorry, Phil. You asked about a chopper." He pointed to the forms of two Hueys parked on the Ruff Puff compound two kilometers away. "One of those is ours for as long as we need it. Just tell me when."

Anderson nodded, then continued. "Lieutenant Daniels, I want you to survey the village for risk areas that might be contributing to this epidemic, such as contaminated water supply, latrine facilities, garbage disposal, rodent control, and anything else in the sanitary line. Sergeant Harrel…"

"Yes, sir."

"We need a hut large enough to be used as a ward for twenty kids. When you find it have the medical supplies brought in to it. Set up the gas lanterns, water cans, soap, and towels. Anything the villagers can contribute by way of pallets for the kids will be appreciated." Anderson paused and looked around. "Did I overlook anything?"

There was no response. "Okay, let's get started."

JP started off towards the south limit of the village with Brent Mann and the Ruff Puff interpreter.

Captain Durden caught up to them. "Colonel, do you mind if I go along?"

"We'll put you to work, Sam."

"That will be fine with me, sir."

As the four approached the first hut JP scanned its exterior. Constructed of red-brown clay and straw, its front wall had two wood-framed but glassless windows and a wooden door. Several bundles of firewood leaned against the wall near a window. Only two or three feet separated the hut from the side of the adjacent one. An open door exposed a dark, smoky interior not unlike the huts at Karl Dahlgren's special forces camp. The embers of a cook fire glowed at the bottom of a pit dug in the mid-floor.

A short, thin, dark woman with black hair, piercing dark eyes and wearing a soiled waist-high sarong, greeted them at the door. She led into a single room dominated by a "queen-sized" bed of bamboo strips. It lacked mattress, sheets, or pillow. A naked infant, not more than four years old, lay on his side on the bed, his spindly legs drawn in the fetal position with his thighs cradling a distended abdomen.

"He looks pregnant," Durden remarked.

"Get his name and as much of a history as possible," JP told him. Durden took out a pen and green flip-top notebook from a pocket. He began conversing with the mother through the Ruff Puff interpreter. JP kneeled down and felt the child. His skin was wrinkled, hot and dry. Flexing the head forward on the chest produced no resistance or pain, reducing the possibility of meningitis. Palpation of the eyeballs through closed lids revealed them to be shrunken. Placing his ear flat on the infant's chest, he listened intently. Breathing was rapid but shallow. The sounds of air bubbling through fluid were clearly audible despite the chatter between Durden, the Ruff Puff, and the mother. The heart rate was almost too fast to count. Examination of the abdomen indicated the liver was enlarged to three centimeters below the margin of the lowest rib and fluid distended the belly. The reflexes were depressed. When he pinched the skin to elicit pain the infant responded with a weak cry that rapidly subsided. JP stood up and nodded to Brent Mann. "Your turn. When you finish we'll compare notes."

When Mann had finished JP asked Durden for the child's history.

"He's four years old. Three days ago he developed fever, vomiting, and bloody and watery diarrhea. He had about fourteen stools yesterday and eleven so far today. He's vomited everything the mother tried to feed him, passed very little urine, and doesn't cry any more."

"You aced that test, Durden," JP said. "You're a cinch to make it in medical school."

"I'll give that some thought, Colonel."

JP turned to Brent Mann. "Doctor?"

"My impressions," Mann said as he stood up, "are severe malnutrition, hepatomegaly, ascites, protein and vitamin deficiencies, bacterial dysentery, severe dehydration, electrolyte imbalance, bilateral pneumonia, and possibly early congestive heart failure. Colonel, this is one sick kid."

"I agree. He could die any time. Put him on the list for immediate evacuation to the 9th Surg".

The infant began a weak cry. As he rolled from one side to the other shiny mucosal tissue resembling a deflated red balloon protruded from the between the gluteal folds.

"Damn," Brent Mann said, "I missed a rectal prolapse."

"So did I," JP said.

"A what?" Durden asked.

Brent Mann turned to the young special forces captain. "In prolapse, the rectum is turned inside out because the anal sphincter muscles have been weakened from severe diarrhea."

"Oh."

Sam Durden was obviously impressed by Brent Mann's academic manner and his expertise. Medicine was a dimension in which Durden, as intelligent as he was, entered as a total stranger. A tiny ember of interest had just flamed in Sam Durden.

"Let's go on to the next hooch," JP said. As they walked the short distance he noted the perplexed look on Brent Mann's face. "Something bothering you?"

"Yes, sir. Considering the diarrhea, vomiting and fever these kids have had for the past three days I can understand how they became dehydrated and out of electrolyte balance. What I don't understand is the malnutrition. That has contributed as much as anything to their susceptibility to intestinal infections, and it may have been indirectly responsible for the large number of deaths."

JP turned to Captain Durden. "Didn't you tell me rice, fish powder, canned milk and vitamins was furnished to the South Vietnamese to give these kids?"

"Yes, sir, but very little of it has been delivered."

"That's pretty obvious when you look at these kids. We need to check up on our so-called allies."

"Sir, you don't think...?

"That's precisely what I think, Captain," JP said, taking out his own flip-top notebook and GI pen.

★

Fifty-five minutes later JP, Brent Mann and Sam Durden met with Phil Anderson and Tom Moffet in the village square. Mann presented his and JP's findings. "We examined nineteen children. Three are critical and should be evacuated a.s.a.p. Seven are close to critical; they can be treated here with IV fluids, electrolytes and antibiotics.

Nine kids can be managed in their hooches."

Tom Moffet then spoke. "Colonel Anderson and I identified four children who require immediate evacuation, eight who require fluids, electrolytes, and antibiotics, and eleven who can be managed in their hooches."

Colonel Anderson made some notes in his own green flip-top notebook, then looked up at Sergeant Harrell. "How's our pediatric ward coming?"

"Sir, the storage shed behind you is about the best I could find. As soon as it's emptied the Montagnards will fix up twenty pallets for beds. I estimate it should be ready in about an hour."

"Good. It will have fifteen admissions as soon as it's ready. I'll give you a hand getting it set up as soon as we get the critical kids on their way."

JP touched Durden's arm. "Time to radio for the choppers, Sam."

In less than five minutes the noise of approaching helicopters interrupted the conversation. The two Hueys sailed over the village and settled down by the river.

"Let's get those seven kids down to the choppers," Colonel Anderson ordered.

"Sir, before we move those seven kids to the choppers some decisions must be made," Captain Durden told Colonel Anderson.

"What do you mean?"

"These people are very close to their children. Each child going to the 19th Surg will have two parents who will insist on accompanying their child. Fourteen parents and seven severely sick kids is going to be a logistic problem on the choppers and at the 19th Surg."

"You know these people, Captain. What would you suggest?"

"Have the parents pick two sets of parents to go with the kids. They will look after all the kids as their own. That's the way these people are."

"We could take lessons on child rearing from the Montagnards," Colonel Anderson said. "Okay, Captain, follow through on that." He turned to JP. "What's the 19th Surg doing to get ready for these children?"

"Trevor Holcomb is setting up a peds ICU. Four Vietnamese student nurses will be assigned to it; they will be under the supervision of two US army nurses with backgrounds in pediatric nursing."

Colonel Anderson tore a sheet from his notebook and handed it to JP. "That's a list of what I'll need in addition to what was already brought out."

JP read the items aloud, "Ringer's Lactate, five percent glucose, IV and liquid oral ampicillin, trimethoprim sulfamethoxazole, vitamins, sugar, salt, tea, Coca Cola, canned milk, protein source, rice, and disposable diapers... disposable diapers?" JP looked up. "Come on, Phil, where am I supposed to get disposable diapers in Vietnam?"

Anderson smiled. "I can dream, can't I? We'll manage without them. I could use four more medics and a couple of nurses."

"Medics won't be a problem; they'll fight to come out here. There's no way I can approve the request for nurses. They would be an added incentive for the VC to hit the village. I hate to think of the repercussions if a nurse were captured."

"Okay. I have no desire to motivate the VC into attacking us. When are you

528

coming back?"

"Right after I brief the general at 1700 hours."

"I'll have drawn bloods on all the kids for lab tests by then."

"The chopper that brings me will head back to Phong Sahn as soon as it's unloaded. The bloods can be sent back with it. The results should be ready by morning."

"Sir, I have some needs," Chris Daniels said.

"You aren't going back to Phong Sahn?"

"I'd like to stay out here."

JP studied the young sanitary engineer, then shrugged and pulled out his notebook and pen. "Okay," he said, "go on."

"I could use a dozen Lister bags and five gallons of powdered chlorine." When JP looked up Daniels explained, "This village gets its drinking and cooking water from the river. They also wash clothes and bathe in the river."

"I get the picture."

"I'll also need ten gallons of lime. Sanitation here is primitive. I'm going to show them how to dig pit latrines, garbage pits, and how to use the lime to cover excrement. I could use all the insecticide bombs the division can spare. This place is overrun by bugs. If you bring any cats they'll have field day out here."

"Right," JP said, looking up from his notebook. "Cats, is that spelled with a K or a C?" Smiling, he tore out the page and stuffed it in his wallet along with Anderson's list. "I'll bring out what I can. The rest will be brought out tomorrow. If you think of anything else, Captain Durden can radio it in to the med battalion." He turned to the division preventative medicine officer. "What are your plans, Tom?"

"I'd like to stay and help out with the kids. I can make hooch calls."

JP smiled and nodded permission. "Good thing you two brought toothbrushes." He looked around. "I'm surprised no one mentioned food. I'll bring out C-rations and lots of water. Hopefully, tomorrow I'll be able to get you a hot meal. Does everyone have a weapon?"

Only Phil Anderson had come without a .45 or M–16. JP unbuckled his webbed belt with its holstered .45 and handed it to Anderson. "You'll have to widen the belt a half dozen notches," he said chuckling, "and don't shoot yourself in the foot."

Then he addressed the group. "Some time this afternoon a company of rangers will arrive to reinforce the village defenses. In addition, during the day a scout helicopter and gunship will be prowling the area. At night a gunship equipped with infrared scopes and miniguns will be looking for trouble." He stepped back. "I guess that's it. I'll be back in about six hours with chow and supplies."

Within minutes Captain Durden was herding the parents and their critically ill children down the trail towards the choppers. As soon as the crew chief gunner saw JP coming down the trail he alerted the pilots. Electric starters whined followed by the ascending pitch of turbines firing up. Rotor blades turned with increasing speed and noise. When JP climbed into Dan Ranson's Huey one set of parents was already seated, each with a critically ill child. Tom Carter, standing behind his seat, held the remaining child while waiting for JP to belt himself in. JP held out his arms for the child.

As the child settled whimpering into JP's lap, Carter stepped back and surveyed the cabin. "If only my mother could see this."

"What do you think she would say?"

"It's a hell of a way to fight a war."

"In my mind, Tom, it's the best way."

Chapter Fifty-Eight

Thursday, October 1, 1970, 1350 hours
Headquarters, 36th Infantry Division, Phong Sahn, Republic of Vietnam

Colonel John Witherington, the chief of staff, looked up from his desk at JP's knock and beckoned him in. "What's the situation at Phu Than, Doctor?"

"Grim, Colonel. Grim," JP said, moving to a chair by the desk and sitting down. "Nineteen children dead in two days. Seven children so critical that they may die. They're now hospitalized at the 19th Surg. Fifteen children are near critical; they will be treated at the village in an improvised pediatric ward. Another twenty, although very sick, can be managed in their hooches."

"The general desires that the division support the Montagnards every way possible. They have been among the most dependable and loyal of our allies. If you have any trouble getting what you need let me know."

JP remembered the last item on his list. "Sir, would you happen to know where I can get hold of disposable diapers?"

Witherington laughed. "As a matter of fact I do. For some obscure reason a diaper company in the States donated 10,000 disposable diapers to the division. That was a fortuitous gift considering the developments at Phu Than. The G–5 has the diapers stored somewhere. Tell him to give you what you need. Anything else?"

"Yes, sir. I have come up against something that has left me unsure how to proceed."

Witherington stared at JP a moment. "Doctor, I believe this is the first time I've heard you make that kind of admission."

"I'm mellowing, Colonel."

"So what is this problem?"

"There is severe malnourishment in that Montagnard village, particularly among the children. I believe the malnutrition contributed significantly to increased susceptibility for infection and reduced capacity to deal with it."

"Is it a matter of getting more food to the Montagnards?"

"In a manner of speaking, yes and no."

"You have lost me, Doctor."

"It's my understanding that fish powder, canned milk and captured rice was given to the South Vietnamese government in the Phu Than area to be distributed to the Montagnards."

"I believe that is correct. It's a policy articulated out of MACV and the State Department."

"Well, little if any of those items were delivered to the Montagnards at Phu Than."

Witherington leaned towards JP. "Doctor, do you realize the serious implications of what you just said?"

"Yes, sir, but the deaths of nineteen Montagnard children also have serious implications."

Several more seconds of silence followed. Finally, Colonel Witherington said, "I'll put the G–2, provost marshal, and CID on it. There are also some Vietnamese assets I cannot reveal other than to tell you that they are highly principled and very skilled in black market investigations. They consider integrity a matter of Vietnamese honor. Now, what else?"

"When the operation at Phu Than ends I will submit the names of all US personnel involved for awards."

"I'll go along with whatever you recommend as long as it's not the Medal of Honor. Is that it?"

"One more request, Colonel."

"And what might that be?" Witherington said, sighing.

"I would like to skip the briefing this evening."

"I think you have given me enough information to carry the ball for you."

"Thanks, sir, and thanks for the extra protection out at Phu Than, especially the Rangers."

"There are additional assets if you need them, including the Blues, Spectre and fast movers. Get us a worthy enough target and we'll bring in the B–52s."

"I hope none of those will be needed."

"Let me diverge a bit, Doctor, since you mentioned the Rangers."

"Yes, sir."

"What's your impression of the A Team commander out at Phu Than, Captain Durden?"

"He's an exceedingly competent and conscientious officer. I am trusting him with the lives of the people I've taken out there, not to mention my own life."

Witherington smiled. "Durden is one of the officers under consideration to command the Ranger company when its present commander rotates. If you feel strongly about him put it in the form of a written recommendation. In fact, consider yourself just appointed to the nominating committee."

★

Thursday, October 1, 1970, 1430 hours
Mess Hall, 19th Surgical Hospital, Phong Sahn

Lieutenant Colonel JP Franklin filled his mug with coffee, then followed the hospital commander, Lieutenant Colonel Kenneth Irvine, M.C., USA, to a table. Taking a seat opposite Irvine he asked, "Any word on the kids I brought in?"

"I talked with Trevor just before you walked in. All the kids are severely dehydrated, hypokalemic and hyponatremic. Two kids have pulmonary TB, one is close to liver failure and congestive failure. Trevor tapped his belly and removed a liter of fluid. That helped the kid's breathing somewhat. We were able to reduce the prolapsed rectum on the same kid. I'm not sure how stable it will be while his diarrhea continues. If it – the prolapse – recurs it can be surgically repaired later.

"Ken, I really appreciate the support you are giving these kids. I would be in a real bind without it."

"Look, JP, I'm a doctor. I took the same oath as you."

"I didn't realize what I was swearing to when I said 'I do' at med school graduation. Certainly I never expected to be chasing around Indochina trying to locate sacks of fish powder and cartons of canned milk."

"Funny you should mention that."

"Mention what?"

"Fish powder and canned milk. One of our Vietnamese nurse trainees is from Phu Than village. Last weekend she went home to visit her folks. She saw they had a bag of fish powder and some cans of condensed milk. Since these were rare items in Vietnamese households she asked her parents about them. She was told the fish powder and canned milk were brought to Phu Than by some ARVN soldiers and sold to the local stores as surplus supplies."

"Like hell they were surplus," JP said.

Colonel Irvine continued. "This morning, after she was assigned to the Montagnard kids you brought in, she saw how malnourished they were. She mentioned to her supervisor that it was a pity the surplus fish powder and canned milk sold in her village couldn't have gone out to the Montagnard village. Her supervisor passed that information on to me."

JP pushed back from the table and stood up. "Ken, you have no idea how important that information is. I need to pass it on to the chief of staff."

As he started to leave Colonel Irvine called after him. "Hey, marine, be careful out there. Even with a score card it's difficult to distinguish enemy from friends."

When JP called Colonel Witherington's office a first lieutenant answered. "The colonel hasn't returned from a meeting with the air force," the lieutenant reported. "If it's urgent I can try to get a message to him."

"It's urgent," JP said, repeating the substance of what Ken Irvine had told him.

"Where can Colonel Witherington reach you if he has any questions?"

"That may be hard to do. I'm going to take a load of medical supplies out to Phu Than, then make a social call on the local ARVN battalion commander."

★

Thursday, October 1, 1970, 1450 hours
LZ at the Montagnard Village, Phu Than, Republic of Vietnam

As the Montagnards carried away the last of the supplies from the helicopter JP was about to climb back on board when Captain Sam Durden came jogging out of the trail.

"Hey, Colonel, you're not bugging out, are you?"

"Not really. I picked up some information on the missing fish powder and canned milk." JP related what Colonel Irvine had told him. "I'm going make a social call on the local ARVN battalion commander to see if he can enlighten me on how food supplements donated by the US for the Montagnard kids ended up selling in Phu Than village."

"Ah, sir, that may not be a good idea."

"What do you mean? I thought it was a great idea."

"That battalion commander could be big trouble. He has the reputation of being mean as a snake."

"Really? A snake is precisely the species I'm looking for, Sam. All I plan is to ask for his cooperation in tracking down the soldiers who sold the canned milk and fish powder in Phu Than."

"Sir, nothing goes on in that battalion without Colonel Minh's knowledge and approval. I would recommend waiting until we get some muscle before going over there."

"That could take days. These kids don't have much time. They need that milk and fish powder." JP turned, climbed into the Huey and slapped Dan Ranson on the back. "Let's go."

Captain Durden came to the door. "Hold up a minute, Colonel. Let me get some men and go with you."

"Durden, you may not be the greatest rock climber to come out of the Academy, but your judgment out here has been pretty good. Okay, I'll wait on you and your men."

Minutes later, Captain Sam Durden, armed with a .45 pistol and a Car–15, climbed on board followed by three of his special forces men. One carried an M–16, one an M–79 grenade launcher and .45 pistol, and one a mean-looking repeating 12-gauge shotgun. Add the two door gunners with their M–60 machine guns and the Huey would carry formidable firepower. JP himself was unarmed; his .45 pistol was still with Colonel Anderson.

After taking off JP shouted to Captain Durden, "Have you ever been to the ARVN battalion headquarters?"

"Yes, sir. I was a guest at their mess a couple of times."

"We are going to drop in on them without calling ahead. After all, we ugly Americans must live up to our ugly reputations."

"Colonel, the ARVNs are very touchy on the subject of protocol."

"Is that so? Well, I'm very touchy about essential food stolen from children and sold on the black market."

Captain Durden shrugged. "You're the boss, sir."

"For an infantry officer it doesn't take you long to get the big picture."

Ten minutes later the Huey settled on a square of PSP in front of the ARVN battalion headquarters. A dozen unarmed ARVN soldiers in the area stopped to watch. Nearby the South Vietnamese yellow and red flag snapped from a flagpole in front of a Quonset hut. Adjacent to it, at ten-foot intervals, were five more similar Quonset huts.

Durden pointed to the first hut. "That's the battalion headquarters."

"What are the others?"

"One is a mess hall; I'm not sure about the rest, probably supply and storage."

Before the rotor blades stopped turning a Vietnamese major appeared at the door.

534

He waited for JP to climb down, then saluted and reported in excellent English.

"Sir, Major Huong, 2nd Battalion executive officer."

JP returned the salute, then introduced himself. "I believe you know Captain Durden."

"Yes, sir. How are you, Sam?"

"Fine, and you, sir?"

"Same."

"Colonel," Major Huong began, "I apologize for the lack of a courtesy party to greet you. We had no advance notice of your arrival."

JP overlooked the subtle rebuke. "I came to see Colonel Minh."

"I am very sorry, sir. The colonel left an hour ago to visit one of his companies. He should return shortly. May I be of assistance?"

JP sized up Huong. Wearing unstarched fatigues, in his mid-thirties, there was something about the man that suggested he would rather be commanding an infantry company in the bush than a desk in battalion headquarters. Huong had an aura of integrity and commitment. JP decided to play straight.

"Major, I'm trying to locate missing supplies of fish powder and condensed milk given the South Vietnamese government by my government for distribution to the Montagnard village just west of here. The supplies were never delivered. As a result the children in that village developed severe malnutrition and dysentery. Nineteen children have died. Seven more children, in danger of dying, were taken to the 19th Surgical Hospital in Phu Than for treatment. Several dozen children are currently being treated in the village."

"What does that have to do with the 2nd Battalion, Colonel?"

"I have reliable information that fish powder and milk have been sold to stores in Phu Than village by ARVN soldiers."

Major Huong paled, then reddened, as though slapped hard across the face. When he spoke it was in a low voice and the words were deliberate. "Colonel, does your presence here imply you suspect someone in this battalion may be involved in the sale of those items?"

"This is the closest ARVN unit to Phu Than village. It seemed logical to at least consider the possibility that personnel in the battalion may have knowledge of or actually be involved in a black market operation."

"Colonel Franklin, that reasoning may be logical, but it has no resemblance to reality. Colonel Minh would never allow such an activity to take place in his command. He is an honorable man." Huong's voice lacked conviction and it piqued JP's interest.

"Major Huong, would you mind if we looked around while waiting for Colonel Minh?" he asked innocently, glancing at the five Quonset huts adjacent to the battalion headquarters.

Suddenly, Major Huong realized that Captain Durden's men had already drifted to the Quonset huts and were now peering through windows.

"Colonel Franklin," Huong said testily, "you have no right or authority to enter this compound and engage in a witch-hunt. I must insist that you order your men to stop what they are doing and leave immediately, You are not welcome here."

JP turned to Captain Durden. "Get your men back to the helicopter."

After Durden's men had assembled at the chopper he returned. "Colonel, may I talk to you in private?"

"If it concerns our purpose here Major Huong has every right to listen to what you have to say."

"Yes, sir. My men reported that only one of those Quonset huts has barred windows covered by blankets. Its door is much more solid than the others and is secured by heavy hinges and two padlocks."

JP looked at Major Huong.

Huong hesitated, as if trying to put together previous events that, at the time, seemed insignificant, but now... "No one enters that hut without Colonel Minh," he said. "He has the only keys. I have never been in it. It is my understanding the hut contains critical battalion supplies to be used only in an emergency."

JP sensed that Major Huong had come to a conclusion that was not pleasant for him to contemplate.

Huong continued. "As executive officer of this battalion my loyalty is to my colonel. I must insist, Colonel Franklin, that you wait in headquarters for Colonel Minh to return."

Before JP could respond a Loach shot over the headquarters building, wheeled to the left and dropped onto the landing pad. A short, Vietnamese officer in starched tailored fatigues, shiny paratrooper boots, a pearl-handled revolver stuffed in a shoulder holster, jumped to the ground and almost ran to where JP and Huong were standing. He wore the rank of a lieutenant colonel, infantry. JP noted that he wore no parachutist's badge, his paratroopers boots not withstanding.

"Major Huong," the officer shouted in English, "what the hell is going on here?"

Before Huong could answer JP introduced himself, reviewed the epidemic in the Montagnard village and its probable causes. "We are searching for the missing fish powder and canned milk, Colonel Minh. And we are attempting to identify the ARVN military personnel involved in the distribution of these items to stores in and around Phu Than."

Colonel Minh's voice was low and decidedly threatening. "So you come unannounced with your armed men to my battalion headquarters as though Kempetai on a raid. Well, Colonel Franklin, you have come to the wrong place. There is no fish powder or canned milk in this compound, nor has there ever been." He glared at JP. "I find your inferences insulting. I am an officer of the Army of the Republic of Vietnam." Dark eyes fixed on JP. "You dare question my word?"

"Colonel Minh, one of my men observed that the fifth Quonset hut," JP pointed, "seemed unusually secure for ordinary supplies. Perhaps those missing items are stored there without your knowledge."

Colonel Minh's eyes narrowed. "Impossible. I have the only keys." His anger prevented him from realizing the implications of what he had just said.

"In that case, sir, you cannot object to an inspection of the hut, the one with two padlocks to which you have the only keys."

Minh's face clouded. "You insult me, Colonel Franklin. My general will hear of

536

this. I will see you are severely reprimanded. Now, sir, you take your men and get the hell out of my battalion area immediately."

JP did not take kindly to that sort of talk from anyone, least of all an officer of equal rank. "Colonel Minh," he said quietly, "your manners are atrocious and your demeanor unbecoming an officer."

Sam Durden winced, then groaned.

"How dare you speak to me in such an insulting tone?" Minh shouted, his voice at a high pitch. He fumbled with the pistol in his shoulder holster.

Suddenly, JP found himself looking down the barrel of a cocked snub-nosed 38-caliber pistol The bullets visible in the cylinder seemed larger than 40 mm armor piercing shells. *Oh shit*, thought JP, *I've pushed him over the edge.*

Before he could blink the metallic sounds of M–16s being charged echoed as Captain Durden and his men loaded their weapons and spread in a half circle around Minh. A half dozen ARVN soldiers, attracted by Minh's shouting, ran for their own weapons. The door gunners in JP's helicopter charged their M–60s. It seemed that another historical gunfight was about to erupt at the OK Coral.

Major Huong paled, incredulous at the actions of his commander. "Colonel Minh," he croaked, "sir, please put away your weapon."

"Shut up, Huong."

Major Huong moved between JP and Minh, making himself a shield to protect JP.

"Goddamnit, Huong, get the hell out of the way. Do you want to get shot too?"

"Sir, I cannot let you do this."

A Huey helicopter roared overhead, circled sharply and landed a hundred feet away. Clearly visible on its side was the crest of the 7th ARVN Division. Two figures immediately emerged and strode briskly towards Minh, Huong, and JP. A stocky well-built Vietnamese in fatigues, the insignia of a major general on his collar and cap, led. Behind him was a US Army full colonel.

JP recognized Major General Pham van Giang, the 7th Division commander and Colonel Fred Bertolucci, the 174th Brigade commander. As they approached General Giang shouted, "Colonel Minh, put down your weapon."

Minh glared past Huong at JP. The pistol muzzle didn't move, neither did JP.

"Colonel Minh, you will hand your weapon to Major Huong immediately. That is an order," General Giang said.

Minh hesitated; he looked uncertain.

"Colonel Minh, do as I ordered or I will have you shot right now."

Slowly Minh lowered the pistol, then extended it to Major Huong, butt first. Huong quickly unloaded the pistol and stuck it in his belt.

JP looked around to be sure that Durden and his men had unloaded their weapons. Durden's nod and smile indicated they had.

General Giang now stood in front of Colonel Minh. "Explain your actions."

"Sir, this, this colonel invaded my headquarters with armed men. They arrived unannounced. Major Huong failed to resist their spying. I arrived just in time to put a stop to their activities."

The general's eyes reflected a mix of anger and humiliation. Indicating JP, he said,

"This man is a doctor. You were going to shoot a doctor? Did you not inquire as to why a doctor would come to your headquarters?"

"He told me it was to locate missing supplies."

"What were those supplies?"

"Some milk, rice, and fish powder."

"And…"

"I assured him those supplies were not in my headquarters."

"Records indicated those supplies were delivered to your battalion two months ago for distribution to the Montagnards."

"They were given to the Montagnards within three days after being received here."

"All of them?"

"All of them."

"There is one problem with that, Colonel Minh. None of the supplies, specifically the fish powder and canned milk, were received by the Montagnards. And I understand they have appeared for sale in Phu Than village. How do you explain that?"

"General, for many weeks I have suspected that the Montagnards were selling those items on the black market. What you just told me confirms it."

"Do you really think that the Montagnards would watch their children die from malnutrition in order to make a profit?'

"They are very unscrupulous, General."

General Giang looked thoughtful. "Yes, I suppose that is a possibility. But then, why were you so resistant to the arrival of these men at your headquarters?"

"They violated protocol, sir."

"And you have nothing to hide from their prying eyes?"

"No, sir, nothing at all."

"Then you cannot object to our inspection of your headquarters."

Minh remained silent.

General Giang, ignoring Minh, told Major Huong to lead to the Quonset huts. The doors to the first four huts were opened. The general peered into each, then moved on. At the fifth hut he stood at the heavy door and stared at the padlocks.

Major Huong apologized. "Sir, I do not have keys to these locks. Only Colonel Minh has the keys."

"General," Colonel Minh interrupted. "I assure you, on my word of honor as an officer, there is nothing of interest in there. Only military materials that are kept secure to prevent pilfering."

General Giang was adamant. "Unlock the door, Minh, or I will have the locks shot off."

Moving with great reluctance, Colonel Minh removed a small ring with two keys from his pocket, unlocked and removed both locks. The general kicked open the door, stepped inside, then beckoned the others to enter. The far end was piled high with bags labeled "Fish Powder". Cartons of canned milk were stacked against a wall. General Giang was livid. He called for Colonel Minh. There was no response. He repeated Colonel Minh's name. The response was the sound of a jeep cranking up, its engine gunned, then abruptly stopped. Moments later Colonel Minh appeared from a corner of a Quonset hut escorted by Captain Durden and his men.

The general minced no words. "Minh, you are a disgrace to your uniform and your country. You make me profoundly ashamed. You are relieved of your command and placed under arrest." He turned to Major Huong. "You, sir, are appointed acting battalion commander. You will see that Colonel Minh is properly restrained and placed aboard my helicopter under guard for transport to my headquarters for trial by court martial. You will also see that the material in this hut is inventoried, then delivered to the Montagnard village as soon as possible."

"Yes, sir."

He turned to JP. "Colonel Franklin, my apologies for your treatment here. I thank you for exposing this thief. The Montagnards will receive their supplies and then some."

"Thank you, General. If you will excuse me and my men, sir, we will return to the Montagnard village. Some very sick children are there who need continued care."

As JP, Durden and the three Green Berets walked towards JP's chopper Durden let out a sigh. "Colonel, I don't know if I want to hang around you any more. You live dangerously."

"Look who is talking." JP shrugged. "I guess I did push Minh a bit too far."

"That, sir, is an understatement."

A voice called from behind. "Hold up there, Colonel Franklin."

JP stopped and looked over his shoulder. Colonel Bertolucci was walking towards him. "Better go on to the chopper, Sam. I don't think you want to hear what he's going to say to me. I'm not sure I want to hear it."

JP turned and saluted the full colonel brigade commander.

"Jesus Christ, Doc, what were you trying to do, start World War III?"

JP grinned. "You got here just in time, Colonel, like the old Seventh Cavalry. How did you know I was out here?"

"I got a call from John Witherington. After he received your message and, knowing you, he figured you were about to declare war on our ARVN allies. He told me to pick up General Giang and get out here on the double. Thank God Giang is such a straight arrow."

"Thank God for Major Huong. Did you see him put himself between Minh's pistol and me?"

"If there were more like those two we wouldn't be needed in Vietnam at all," Colonel Bertolucci said. "Come on, Doc. I'll walk you to your chopper."

"You know, that was the first time I have ever looked into the business end of a loaded .38. I can tell you, it is an awesome sight."

Chapter Fifty-Nine

Friday, October 2, 1970, 1740 hours
VIP Pad, 36th Division Headquarters, Phong Sahn, Republic of Vietnam

Lieutenant Colonel JP Franklin, M.D., Medical Corps, US Army, carrying his rucksack and M–16, climbed aboard the idling UH1H Huey helicopter. Laying the M–16 across the two center rear seats, he belted into the seat by the door and put on his flight helmet.

"How did the briefing go, Colonel?" Chief Warrant Officer–2 Dan Ranson asked over the intercom.

"Short and sweet. The general let me brief first, then leave. He wanted me out at Phu Than before dark."

"Considering Lieutenant Carter's night-flying proficiency that was a prudent decision," Ranson said. "This is the first time I've seen you with an M–16; are you expecting trouble?"

"Not really. I loaned my .45 to Colonel Anderson the first day at the village. After three wars I feel naked traveling without a weapon," JP explained. He felt for the comforting bulk of the "backup" knife strapped to his right leg under his fatigue trouser. "Did the 19th Surg send over the lab reports on the kids?"

"Yes, sir," Ranson said, waving a large manila envelope.

JP glanced at the boxes of medical supplies stacked on the cargo deck. He smiled when he spotted a dozen cardboard boxes labeled DIAPERS, then leaned back against the bulkhead and closed his eyes. The events of the last twenty-four hours came tumbling out. The first night at the Montagnard village had been one of frenetic activity. Phil Anderson put him to work starting IVs. Threading a needle through wrinkled skin into a tiny collapsed vein in a dehydrated struggling infant was a formidable effort. All too often the effort failed and surgical exposure with direct cannulation of the vein became necessary. Light from gasoline lanterns supplemented by wavering flashlights held by tired medics helped little, and the light attracted a spectrum of insects which seemed to thrive on the spray from insecticide bombs. Phil Anderson and Brent Mann moved constantly, giving orders while they themselves worked. By the time dawn came JP felt as if he had been a medical student on his first day in the pediatric ICU. Now, recalling the experience, he felt a deep sense of accomplishment. In the bizarre environment of the Vietnam War, where killing the enemy and counting their bodies was the name of the game, saving young lives had introduced a modicum of sanity into the formula.

JP's only sleep in the last twenty-four hours had been on the flight back to the 36th Division Headquarters that morning. After a shower, shave, clean underwear and fatigues, he spent most of the day playing catch-up in the division surgeon's office and the medical battalion. He ate lunch at the medical battalion, then went to the 19th Surg to check on the Montagnard children. Sadly, one of the seven children had died during the night. It was the first child he had seen in the village, the one with pneumonia, congestive heart failure, enlarged liver, ascites, kidney failure, and cachexia. One other child was deteriorating. The remaining five were holding their own. As the Huey leveled off at 2,000 feet JP's last thought before falling asleep was of the child who had died. He was as much a casualty of war as if he had been shot.

★

Twenty-seven minutes after taking off, the Huey made a low pass over the Montagnard village, then landed on the river bank. JP unbuckled his seat belt and went up to the flight deck. "As soon as you are unloaded head back to Phong Sahn," he told Dan Ranson and Tom Carter. "Pick me up about noon tomorrow."

"Yes, sir."

JP grabbed his rucksack and M–16, jumped to the ground and started up the trail. Halfway to the village he passed Sergeant Harrel leading a column of Montagnards down the trail to unload medical supplies from the helicopter. Just as he reached the improvised children's ward Brent Mann stepped out, saw JP and started to salute.

JP stopped him. "Hey, knock off saluting out here."

"Welcome back, Colonel. The betting pool was four to one you wouldn't show up after the ordeal last night."

"Did you win or lose money? Think twice before answering, Captain."

Mann grinned. "I won a bundle. The least I can do is treat you to drinks and a steak dinner at the O club."

"I accept, and I appreciate your faith in me. I won't ask who the losers were but I have my suspicions," he said. "How did you and Colonel Anderson manage today with the four medics?"

"Good, sir. Ah, well, sir, the medics… I mean, some of our help… a lot of our help was not from medics."

JP stared at Mann. "You're trying to tell me something."

"A nurse from the 96th Evac came out here on the resupply chopper this morning."

"You mean a female type US Army nurse?"

"Yes, sir. She told Colonel Anderson she was on a three-day leave, had her CO's approval to come out here and was ready to help."

"The hell you say. The medical personnel I authorized to come out here did not include nurses." The noise of a Huey winding up and taking off stopped the conversation for a moment. After it passed overhead and quiet returned he proclaimed, "She will be on the next chopper out of here."

Brent Mann gave him a look that clearly meant "Don't bet on it".

Turning, JP pushed past mosquito netting and entered the semi-dark shed. The odors of cook fires were quickly replaced by stronger odors of feces and disinfectant. He set his rucksack on the ground near the entrance, leaned his M–16 over it, and surveyed the interior. Three gasoline lanterns hissed away on empty ammo boxes creating islands of bright white light diminishing peripherally into shadows. Children and infants lay on straw mats arranged neatly in rows. One or both parents squatted by each child, sponging with water and encouraging the child to drink from a paper cup. Medics moved quietly, taking temperatures, checking IVs, and giving meds.

In one corner Phil Anderson and a slender woman in fatigues, her back to JP, had just immobilized a small boy in a half sheet. The woman held a thin struggling leg while Anderson probed for a vein above the ankle with a needle on a syringe. A medic held an IV bottle and the tubing ready to be connected to the needle. After three failed attempts the boy began to cry. His mother, standing in the shadows, moved to comfort him.

Colonel Anderson looked up and saw JP approaching. "The cutting doctor has returned." He pointed to the child's leg. "This kid just pulled out his IV. I'm not having much luck getting another back in. How about doing a cut down?" The woman assisting turned around and smiled.

JP ignored Anderson and stared at the nurse. "Kristy, I should have known it would be you," he said angrily. "Damn it, I didn't authorize you or any other nurse to come out here. You are going back on the next bird."

Kristy's smile vanished. "Would you mind discussing my being here after you do the cut down," she said coldly. "This child is still severely dehydrated and needs fluids."

JP glowered at her. "Prep the ankle," he snapped.

"Yes, sir," Kristy said with exaggerated deference. She reached for a bottle of germicidal soap and sterile gauze sponges. "The gloves are stacked on an ammo box near the door." Squirting soap on the sponges, she began scrubbing the boy's ankle while the medic held the leg.

JP found the packaged gloves and began pawing through them. "These are all nines. What happened to the seven-and-a-halfs?"

"They were used up; only nines are left."

Grabbing a packet of size nine gloves, JP ripped it open with a vengeance. "I suppose I should be grateful they're not tens," he groused, moving back to the little boy and kneeling down.

Kristy, ignoring JP's petulance, passed him a syringe filled with Xylocaine. After infiltrating skin and subcutaneous tissue with the local anesthetic, he paused while it to took effect. Then, picking up a knife handle with an attached pointed blade, he made a one-centimeter horizontal incision in the skin just above the inner ankle. Using a fine-pointed hemostat, he quickly exposed a branch of the saphenous vein and passed two silk sutures under the vein, leaving a two-centimeter gap between sutures. Tying the lower suture in a blur of fingers, he left the upper one untied.

Kristy reached down and stabilized the vein using the sutures while JP cut a tiny slit in the vein. He then fed a small diameter sterile plastic catheter into it. Blood dripped from the hub on the distal end of the catheter before Kristy could connect it to the IV tubing. JP tied down the upper suture, cut the sutures just above the knots, and closed the skin with two more sutures. Looking up at the IV bottle, he was pleased to see fluid dripping steadily. "How about that for speed?" he asked no one in particular, his anger dissipated.

542

"I've seen surgical interns do faster cut downs," Kristy remarked caustically.

"You're a real joy personality," JP said, accepting a small curved needle and suture on a needle holder.

"Look who's talking."

After securing the tubing to the skin with the suture JP taped another six inches to the skin, then checked again to see if fluid was still dripping from the bottle. He called over to Phil Anderson. "How fast do you want this IV to run?"

"Kristy will take care of it," Anderson said.

JP shrugged. "Okay. What do you want me to do next?"

"Go outside and cool off," Colonel Anderson said as he walked over. "While you're out there I want you to think about this. In the few hours Kristy has been here she's given tremendous help. Besides assisting me, supervising the medics, giving meds, and controlling the IVs, she's been instructing the Montagnards how to clean up their kids, how to get the kids to take meds and fluids, and dozens of other chores I didn't have time to do and the medics weren't trained to do."

"Phil, do you have any idea of the danger she faces out here?"

"No, but it's no different than the danger we all face. She's a nurse, JP, an army nurse. She accepts risks in order to do what she's trained to do, just like you and I do. You can be a horse's ass and send her back to Phong Sahn. You certainly have that authority. But you'll be handicapping me and hurting these kids."

At that moment Kristy touched JP's arm. "Let's go outside," she said.

They moved to the door. JP held up the mosquito netting for Kristy, then followed her into the night. "First time anyone has called me a horse's ass," he grumbled.

"Now that is hard to believe. To what part of a horse's anatomy would you prefer to be compared?"

"Come on, Kristy, back off. You know I never would have given my permission if you had asked to come out here."

Kristy turned to face him. "If you're really concerned over the welfare of these kids you will let me stay."

"You're living in a dream world, Kristy. This is a dangerous place. There are bad people out here and they do bad things to other people. Even our so-called allies may actually be our enemies. Kristy, if anything were to happen to you out here it would be my fault. I could never forgive myself."

"Listen, you retarded jarhead, I didn't work to save your life in Korea so you could stop me from saving other lives. You heard Colonel Anderson; I'm needed here." She moved towards him until almost in his face. "Tell me, Colonel, do you really want to mix IVs, give shots, and chart meds on each patient? Do you really want to teach the women how to change diapers, or even what diapers are for."

JP was beginning to weaken. He had no desire to do any of those.

"Vietnam is my second war and this is my second tour. All I have done in both wars was take care of severely wounded young men. It's starting to get to me, JP. I desperately need to do something to balance my distorted perspective of nursing. I need to help care for these kids. I need it for me as well as for them."

JP remained quiet.

"I can't keep from thinking my husband is somewhere out there," she gestured towards the west. "Being here, working with these people, helps me feel close to him." She started to sob.

JP stifled the impulse to take her in his arms. Lou Marchenko's warning about vulnerability stopped him. He didn't even have a Kleenex to offer.

Kristy sniffed several times. "I'm sorry I got weepy," she said. "I'd better get back to the kids. I'll leave in the morning."

"No," JP said, "you made your point." He hesitated, as if reluctant to go on. "Please stay, Kristy, you're needed here. I'll clear it with division."

Kristy touched JP's face with her fingers. "Thank you, Colonel."

JP chuckled softly.

"Something funny?"

"I'll bet your husband never won an argument with you."

Kristy's winsome smile was lost in the night. "Whatever made you think that, Colonel?"

★

Sunday, October 4, 1970, 2310 hours
Montagnard Village, Phu Than

Three days had passed since Lieutenant Colonel JP Franklin had mobilized a medical team under Lieutenant Colonel Phil Anderson and transported the team to Phu Than along with hundreds of pounds of medical supplies. Since then no more children had died in the village although two died at the 19th Surgical Hospital. All the remaining children were off IVs, their diarrhea slowed or stopped. They were taking fluids and even rice by mouth. Tonight was the last night he and the other medical personnel would spend in the Montagnard village. In the morning all US medical personnel would return to Phong Sahn. It was planned for Phil Anderson or Brett Mann to visit the village once daily to check on the children.

The day after the confrontation with Colonel Minh at the ARVN battalion headquarters, sacks of fish powder, rice and crates of canned milk were delivered to the Montagnard village in a steady stream. Major Huong visited the village daily bringing boxes of fresh fruit. On his last visit he left an invitation for JP to attend his promotion to lieutenant colonel and assumption of command ceremony as 2nd Battalion commander. There was hope for South Vietnam with officers like Huong.

With nothing to do and feeling not at all sleepy, JP slipped out of the makeshift pediatric ward, leaving behind twenty-three sleeping children and a snoring Phil Anderson. Brent Mann and Kristy were making rounds before trying to get some sleep themselves. Easing down on some sandbags, he stared thoughtfully into the night. He turned to a shuffling behind him. Sam Durden materialized out of the dark.

"Good evening, Colonel."

"I was hoping to see you before leaving, Sam."

"I'm going to miss you all out here. It's been one hell of an adventure. West Point never prepared me for anything like this."

"You were the key person in saving these kids, Sam. If it hadn't been for you many more would have died."

"Aw, sir, all I did was sound the alarm. You medics did the rest."

JP studied the shadow of the young captain's face. "I never suspected modesty to be a quality among you macho infantry types."

"You underestimate us, Colonel," Durden said. "I should tell you the Montagnards are very grateful for what you and your team did."

"It was Colonel Anderson's team, Sam. He organized the response and supervised the medical management. I was just a high paid gofer."

"I never would have suspected modesty among surgeons… sir."

"Touché."

The sounds of a Huey helicopter broke the night's quiet. The sounds increased to a thunder as its rotors beat the air over the village, then diminished until no longer heard.

Durden looked at his watch. "Night hawk is a little late coming on station."

"He's been a great comfort the last two nights. He must have given the VC second thoughts about any action against the village."

"Yes, sir. It's been so quiet here I almost cancelled tonight's mission."

"What stopped you?"

"Nothing tangible, just a gut feeling. We've been patrolling aggressively for the past three days without coming across any VC. That's suspicious in itself."

"You know, Durden, you're pretty smart for an infantry officer. You would have made a good marine."

"Thanks, sir," Durden said, grinning. He reached into his fatigue jacket pocket, produced two Dutch Masters cigars and offered one to JP.

"It's been a while since I smoked one of those," JP said, reaching out.

"I hope you have a strong stomach, Colonel. They're kind of dry."

After lighting up the two officers sat quietly, enjoying the cool night, each other's company, and the knowledge they had achieved something positive in a country gone crazy with killing.

Durden broke the silence. "Colonel Goulden told me you were a line officer in the Korean War."

JP exhaled a cloud of smoke and thoughtfully studied the ash on the end of his cigar. "She ought to know."

"What do you mean, sir?"

"It's a convoluted story. In Korea I almost died in an army hospital from dysentery and medical mismanagement. When the hospital commander learned of my condition he took charge of my case and assigned a young second lieutenant nurse to salvage me." JP smiled grimly as he recalled the high fevers, bone shaking chills, severe cramps, and almost continuous diarrhea and vomiting.

"Weeks later, when I was recovering, a ward medic told me about a nurse who had taken care of me almost around the clock. He said her care saved my life."

"Colonel Goulden?"

"Good shot." Gripping the cigar with his teeth, he drew in a mouthful of smoke, then blew it out into the night. "Six months later, during the Chinese Spring Offensive, I was ordered to take my platoon of Dusters and Quads and rescue some British wounded. They were part of a battalion about to be overrun by the Chinese. When we reached the Brits we started taking fire. I decided to teach the Chinese a lesson and fired my platoon against what appeared a battalion of Chinese on the forward slope of a mountain."

JP paused to relight his cigar, then continued. "You know, Captain, in war things are never what they seem. On the backside of that mountain was the better part of a Chinese division massed for a final assault on the Brits. After my platoon opened fire the rest of the Chinese came pouring over the crest. It was obvious we would run out of ammo long before the Chinese ran out of Chinese. We were about to go down in history as another Little Big Horn. An air force FAC saved us and the Brits. He brought the fires of hell down on both sides of that mountain. We picked up the casualties and took them to a MASH. Guess who the nurse was in charge of the ER."

"Kristy Goulden."

JP nodded. "Kristy introduced me to a couple of surgeons doing an emergency tracheotomy. They let me watch and even explained what they were doing. The patient was one I had given first aid to in my M–39. The MASH surgeons gave me the credit for saving his life. From that time I was committed to becoming a doctor." JP lowered his voice to hoarse whisper. "I owe Kristy my life and, in a way, the caduceus I wear on my collar."

"What a story, Colonel. You should write it up in a book."

"Maybe some day I will."

"Do you know anything about Kristy's husband?" Durden asked.

"Yes and no. I never met him. He was from your alma mater, class of '48. Apparently he was one hell of a fighter pilot. In the Korean War he shot down two MiGs. He and Kristy met in Japan in December 1950 when both were on R&R. They were married three weeks later. He was on a second tour as a FAC in '68 when he was shot down at Qui Tavong."

"Do you think he's still alive?"

JP puffed thoughtfully on his cigar. "Sam, what I tell you next is classified."

"Yes, sir."

"He was definitely alive in July; beyond that I can't say. I learned he is hard core. He's given his captors a rough go, escaping three times only to be recaptured, beaten close to death, and thrown into a cage. He has malaria, parasites, possibly tuberculosis, vitamin deficiencies, and is on a near starvation diet. How long he can endure those conditions is anyone's guess."

"Those bastards. Does Kristy know?"

JP nodded. "I told her."

Neither officer spoke for several minutes, each lost in his own thoughts. Suddenly Captain Durden asked, "Is there an age limit on applying for medical school?"

JP puffed contemplatively on his cigar. "Sam, are you just being curious or do you have a specific reason for asking?"

546

"Both, sir. This is my second tour in Vietnam. I'm on the list for major. When 1 DEROS I'm set for Command and General Staff College. I'll probably fill a battalion exec slot. I'll never command a battalion in combat, at least not in this war, not the way we're fighting it."

JP smiled in the dark. "So are you seriously considering medical school?"

"Sir, you should have been an intelligence officer."

"Actually, I was an intelligence officer before going to medical school."

Kristy Goulden's voice interrupted. "Did someone mention having been an intelligent officer before going to medical school, or did he say he was an intelligence officer?"

"Pull up a sandbag and have a cigar, Colonel Goulden," JP invited. "Captain Durden is treating. He and I were discussing my past and his future."

"No thanks on the cigar, but I'd love to hear about your past and his future, especially your past."

The dark sky was fractured by a stream of red fire as if from a hose squirting flaming gasoline. The sound of a helicopter was obliterated by three or four seconds of what sounded like the moaning of a chainsaw. The stream of fire abruptly ceased, then resumed for two or three more seconds.

Durden shoved himself up from the sandbags, tossed down his cigar and ground it with his foot. "Night Hawk's found something. We need to go on full alert." He disappeared into the night.

A blinding flash inside the perimeter was followed by a *boom* that shook the ground and deafened ears. JP and Kristy, their night vision destroyed by the flash, could only stare without seeing.

"I've got to get back to the kids," Kristy said. As she started towards the shed a second flash/boom was followed by a third and fourth, then too many to count. JP grabbed Kristy and pulled her behind a pile of filled sandbags and covered her body with his. A flare popped into life hundreds of feet above the perimeter and began its erratic descent. Ruff Puffs ran in all directions, their shouts mingled with the wails of women and cries of infants. The night had become a collage of flashes, booms, single and multiple shots. Four more helicopters were over the village, their miniguns spraying the adjacent jungle. The night was suddenly lit by a tremendously bright flare. The drone of a C–130's turbo engines reached the village.

"Oh my God," Kristy cried out, "JP, the perimeter."

JP turned. The descending flare cast a green-white light on a glistening near-naked figure in a loincloth worming through the concertina wire less than a hundred feet away. His hand dropped to his hip for his pistol. "Oh shit."

"What?" Kristy whispered.

"My pistol… Anderson has it, and my M–16 is in the shed."

Silently they watched the sapper crawl free of the wire, stand and briefly survey the village, then begin moving towards the shed with the sick children. He would pass close to the sandbags where JP and Kristy had taken refuge. In his hand he carried a rectangular object half the size of an attaché case.

JP reached down, pulled up his pant leg and started to lift out the hidden knife when Kristy jabbed him in the back with a hard object. "Ouch, damn it, Kristy," he whispered.

"Will this help?" she asked, pushing the handle of an entrenching tool into his hands. "I found it next to the sandbags."

Gripping the handle with both hands as if it were a baseball bat, JP stood waiting, ready to swing. As the dark figure came abreast of the sandbags JP stepped out and swung the shovel with all his strength, striking the sapper's chest with such force that the wooden handle snapped. The sapper stumbled back, then fell on his face as if shot. His deadly satchel charge hit the ground and bounced out of reach. No sparks squirted from it. Thank God it hadn't been armed.

Jerking the knife from the scabbard on his leg, JP threw himself on the sapper's back but slid off before he could get a grip. "The son of a bitch is covered with grease," he grunted to Kristy. Just as the sapper reached for his satchel charge JP cupped the man's chin with his left hand. With great effort he forced back the sapper's head, exposing his neck. For a brief moment JP was no longer a doctor, trained to save lives. He was the marine, trained to take lives. The knife blade flashed in the eerie green light of the descending flare.

"No, JP!" Kristy screamed. "No."

The knife hesitated.

The sapper twisted violently, fueled by fear of impending death. JP forced his left forearm across the sapper's throat and locked his wrist with his right hand. Tightening the hold, he compressed both carotids, jugulars, and the windpipe. Despite this the sapper continued to struggle to reach his satchel charge. "Get rid of that thing," JP shouted to Kristy.

She kneeled down and picked up the satchel charge and threw it aside.

In his peripheral vision JP glimpsed another sapper a dozen feet away running towards the children's shed. A spray of sparks started from his satchel charge. Just as he was about to throw it he fell, cut nearly in two by an M–60 machine gun. His satchel charge hit the ground ten feet from the children's shed. It lay sputtering and shedding sparks.

Kristy ran to the satchel charge and scooped it up by the handle without stopping.

"Throw it," JP yelled as he struggled to subdue the greased sapper. "Get rid of it."

Kristy ran towards the perimeter with the sputtering satchel charge, then stopped and began turning around and around like a discus thrower.

"For God's sake, Kristy, throw it," JP screamed.

The charge sailed out over the concertina wire as six more sappers worked through it, then detonated. The blast and heat were intense. In the brilliant flash he saw Kristy's small form thrown in the air and slammed on to the ground. The sappers in the wire, dazed by the blast and concussion, tried to stand, became entangled in the wire, and turned to escape.

The sapper under JP launched a furious effort to get loose, then abruptly went limp. JP rolled him over on his back. The man was unconscious, except that he wasn't a man, he was a boy no more than sixteen. His chest sagged inward on the right as he made violent efforts to breathe. Palpating the chest, JP felt the unmistakable sharp ends of fractured ribs. He was no longer a threat.

JP left him and ran to the inert form of Kristy. Kneeling. he felt her neck and found a strong regular carotid pulse. His eyes and hands swept over her body, probing, squeezing, and feeling for evidence of injuries.

Kristy stirred, opened her eyes and fixed on JP. "Colonel Franklin, what do you think you're doing?" There was a faint smile on her lips.

JP flushed with embarrassment. "I thought you were hit. I was checking for wounds."

"Did you find any?"

"No."

"Maybe you should check again."

"Damn it, Kristy, you scared the hell out of me."

"I didn't know you cared." She sat up. "How did I do?"

JP grinned. "You have one hell of an arm. That charge so scared the daylights out of the sappers in the wire that they took off." He held out his hand. When she grasped it he helped her to her feet. "You okay?"

"Just shaken up. What happened to the sapper you hit with the shovel?"

"Oh, oh, I forgot about him." JP ran back to where he had left the unconscious sapper. Kristy followed. "He's got broken ribs and a pneumothorax," he told her. "He needs a chest tube." Kneeling down, he grasped the unconscious VC under his arms and dragged him towards the shed.

The sounds of firing and explosions subsided until only intermittent single shots broke the night's quiet. Half a dozen buildings burned fiercely illuminating figures running about the village. The smoke obscured vision, burned eyes, and made one gasp for breath. Sam Durden abruptly appeared. "Let me give you a hand, Colonel." He reached down and picked up the sapper's feet. As they carried the sapper towards the shed Durden said, "That was a great throw, Colonel. It broke up the attack on this side of the perimeter. Your timing and accuracy were impeccable. I'm going to write you up for a Bronze Star with a V."

"Sam, I had my hands full with the sapper we're carrying. Muscles here," he nodded to Kristy, "grabbed the satchel charge and threw it."

"Then I'll put her in for a Bronze Star."

"You can't do that."

"Then you do it, Colonel."

"I don't think you understand, Sam. Kristy is a nurse; nurses don't engage in combat. Hell, she's not even supposed to be out here."

"You're right, Colonel. I don't understand."

"Let me put it this way. Kristy's courageous action never happened. It couldn't have happened because she was never here."

"Sir, I have to tell you, this is the most screwed-up war I have ever been in."

Chapter Sixty

Monday, October 19, 1970, 0330 hours
Staff Bivouac Area, 36th Infantry Division, Headquarters, Phong Sahn, Republic of Vietnam

The monsoon season was well into its second week. The fury of rain and wind increased with each succeeding day. Occasional brief remissions brought sunlight, calm, and the false hope that the interlude of nature gone wild had ended. Then the rain and wind returned with vengeance.

In his hooch Lieutenant Colonel JP Franklin, cocooned beneath two blankets, poncho, and raincoat, drifted in and out of sleep, shivering in the penetrating bone-crunching damp cold. Torrents of rain, driven by gale winds, slashed at the walls and windows of his hooch with a fierce intensity. The sudden screech of tearing metal brought him wide awake and reaching for his pistol. When droplets of water began to splash on his face he was left with the inescapable conclusion that part of the roof had blown away.

A look at the luminescent dial of his travel clock showed two hours before the alarm went off at 0530 hours. The cold and noise made going back to sleep a lost cause. He decided to dress, then write Kathy a letter. Reaching to the lamp by his bunk, he pressed the small switch at its base. A subdued click failed to produce the expected light, confirming the second power outage in five hours. Next, he fumbled on the counter by his bunk for his flashlight. It slipped from his grasp, rolled off the counter and hit the floor with an ominous thump. He retrieved the flashlight from under his bunk, but it, like the lamp, refused to light. Groping his way to his locker, he found a spare flashlight. "This is going to be one of those days," he told himself, turning on the flashlight.

Moving his bunk from under the leaking ceiling, he set his steel helmet sans liner upside down under the dripping water. Stiff from the cold and dampness, he dressed slowly, wallowing in misery until a tidal wave of guilt washed away his self-indulgence. He was relatively safe and dry, except for the water dripping from the ceiling. He was sheltered from the fierce wind and rain beating at his hooch. A few minutes' flying time away thousands of young Americans in a hostile jungle were enduring the severe weather without shelter or security. Braving the elements, they searched out the enemy even as the enemy searched for them. It was a brutal way for adolescents to come of age, assuming they survived long enough to come of age.

The phone's loud ring startled him. He reached for it, well aware that no phone rings at 0330 hours with good news. He picked up the receiver. "Colonel Franklin."

The slow southern voice of the Dust-off commander came through the phone. "Colonel, this is Major Jelnik. I hated to wake you, sir." Jelnik sounded clearly troubled.

"That's okay, Mike. I've been awake waiting for your call since part of my roof blew away a few minutes ago.

Jelnik laughed in spite of the hour.

"What's up?"

"That's the problem, sir. Nothing is up or will be up in this weather."

"It's too early for riddles, Mike."

"About thirty minutes ago we received an urgent request from the 3rd/7th on Firebase Lucy for an immediate medevac. The request was relayed through Beth Ann because Lucy's radio couldn't reach us."

JP's mind tracked through his knowledge of firebase locations. He had gone out to Lucy only two weeks ago with a new battalion surgeon, Tim Mosher. His recollection of the last few miles of the flight were vivid. Lucy was in the midst of Vietnam's tallest mountains and surrounded by triple canopy forests. Flying in those mountains, even on a calm day, was hazardous. At night it was not only hazardous, it was deadly.

Major Jelnik continued. "Here's the situation, Colonel. Last night two GIs ingested an unknown quantity of C–4 and beer. A couple of hours later they began to vomit, urinate blood and act so crazy they had to be restrained. Then they began to have convulsions."

"What's the battalion surgeon doing for them?"

"That's part of the problem. He went to the battalion rear two days ago for some medical supplies. He's been stuck there since because of the weather. Sergeant Burdick, the senior medic at Lucy, is doing his best, but those GIs really need hospitalization."

"I know Burdick. He's a good man, but this is way over his head. In fact it's way over my head."

"Colonel, this is the worst weather I've encountered in Vietnam, and I'm on my second tour. The ceiling is practically on the ground. Visibility is zilch. Winds are gusting to sixty knots. God only knows what they are in the mountains around Lucy."

"I'm getting the picture, Mike," JP said, glancing into the blackness and chaos outside his windows. The two GIs at Lucy were at risk of dying unless medevac'd promptly to a hospital for definitive care. However, any attempt to fly out to Lucy in the current weather and darkness was certain to end up a smoking tragedy on some mountain side.

Jelnik's voice reflected his anguish. "Colonel, I won't authorize a medevac mission to Lucy unless given a direct order, and then I'll fly the mission myself without a peter pilot."

"No one is going to order you to fly against your professional judgment, Mike, so calm down."

"Thanks, sir." Major Jelnik sounded as if a crushing weight had been lifted from his shoulders. "Just before calling you I called the air force forecaster at Danang. He wasn't very encouraging although he did say a high pressure cell was moving this way out of Laos. He couldn't predict its route, speed, or duration, but there is the possibility of a short break in the weather some time within the next eight hours. Colonel, if there is any hope of making it out to Lucy and back we'll go."

"I know that, Mike."

"Sir, what are the chances of the two GIs pulling through if treatment is delayed?"

"Good question. Frankly, I don't know the first thing about C–4 toxicity. I need to talk to a real doctor. Then I'll work with Captain Mosher and Sergeant Burdick to manage the two GIs at Lucy until they are evacuated."

"I'll call you as soon as there's a break in the weather. Where will you be?"

"Probably the division TOC. The best radio communications are there. If I'm not in the TOC I'll leave word where I can be reached."

★

JP placed a call to the battalion rear of the 3rd/7th infantry battalion. As he waited for the duty officer to answer he thanked the Lord the phones were still working.

A voice answered. "Lieutenant Findlay."

JP identified himself and explained the situation on Lucy. "Would you pass this information to Captain Mosher and have him meet me at the division TOC. Between the two of us we will practice medicine by remote control."

"Colonel, do you want Captain Mosher to call you back?"

"Negative. I'll be on my way to the TOC. Just tell him what I told you."

The next call was to the medical battalion commo section and through them to Pfc Groves. The first response was a muffled "Hello?"

"Groves, Colonel Franklin. I need a ride from my hooch to the TOC. I'll explain on the way."

"Be there in fifteen minutes, Colonel," Groves said, now wide awake.

"Wear a wet suit and drive carefully. Some of the roads may be flooded. If you get into trouble use the radio to call for help."

"Yes, sir."

After hanging up JP retrieved his 36th Division wallet from the locker and removed a card with names and phone numbers. Holding the card up in the flashlight's beam, he dialed one of the numbers listed.

A sleepy voice answered. "Colonel Anderson."

"Good morning, Professor. This is Colonel Franklin."

"JP, for God's sake, it's not even 4 A.M."

"I realize you internists chose that specialty so you could sleep at night and think profound thoughts during the day. Here in Vietnam we surgeons cannot indulge that luxury. There's a war on and I need help."

"Cut the crap. I'm well versed in your wily ways, JP. I still have nightmares over that VC attack at the Phu Than Montagnard village."

"Just think how proudly you will wear the Bronze Star with V on your chest when you go home."

"JP, what the hell do you want?"

"I need to tap that computer brain of yours."

The sound of yawns came over the phone.

"I need to know how to manage C–4 and alcohol toxicity, and don't talk fast. I want to take notes." JP described the situation at Lucy.

"You're in luck. C–4 toxicity was discussed at the quarterly medical meeting at Long Binh last week. I have the data somewhere around here. Hang on."

While waiting JP adjusted the flashlight to shine its beam on a yellow paper pad in his lap. Holding a GI pen, he was ready when Anderson returned.

"Okay; as of last week six US soldiers and two marines in Vietnam had reactions from the ingestion of C–4 plastic and alcohol that were serious enough to require hospitalization. The youngest patient was twenty, the oldest, thirty-five. The average amount of C–4 ingested was 77 grams; the most was 180 grams. Alcohol consumption varied from two beers to six. There is no clinical or research data on the chemistry of alcohol combined with C–4. The informal consensus at the meeting was that alcohol not only potentiates the toxic effects of the C–4, but breaks it down into something like formalin."

"That sounds ominous. Were there any deaths?"

"No. All patients underwent prompt treatment. Four with severe renal and liver damage were evacuated to the States. Two of the four required renal dialysis at the 3rd Field in Saigon. There was no discussion at the meeting of the impact of delayed treatment on outcome. Presumably it would have serious long-term sequelae or even be fatal."

"You will have two cases to report at your next meeting," JP said. "What's the recommended management?"

"Primarily supportive. It should begin with immediate gastric lavage."

"Both GIs at Lucy have had severe vomiting for several hours."

"It's probably too late for lavage to be of any value. The airway needs to be protected against aspiration of gastric contents. There will be enough problems without adding chemical pneumonitis. Control of seizures is paramount. Sodium amobarbitol or Paraldehyde should stop the convulsions. Phenobarb IM can be given to prevent further convulsions. Anoxic brain damage is always possible with convulsions, so oxygen may be prudent, especially during seizures. You getting all this down?"

"Doing good, Professor. Keep going."

"Renal insufficiency or total renal failure secondary to kidney damage can result."

"Both GIs at Lucy are urinating blood."

"Not a good sign. They need indwelling catheters to measure hourly urine output and specific gravity. If they stop putting out urine a test dose of mannitol or furoscimide should be given to jump-start the kidneys. If that doesn't work the condition has progressed to total renal failure. The only hope for survival then would be renal dialysis."

"That's great. The only artificial kidney unit is at the 3rd Field in Saigon."

"You'll have a hell of a time convincing the air force to take two patients to Saigon in this weather."

"What about aqueous hemodialysis or peritoneal dialysis? Could you do that here?"

"Of course, but in the past both modalities failed to remove significant quantities of RDX, the probable toxic factor in C–4. To make matters worse, RDX is lipid soluble."

"It accumulates in the central nervous system and body fat?"

"You're pretty smart for an ex-jarhead."

"I'm a closet wannabe internist."

Anderson chuckled. "You surgeons are too self-oriented to hack it in the world of internal medicine. By the way, I discharged the last of the Montagnard kids yesterday. I need a chopper to get him back to his village."

"As soon as there's a break in the weather I'll have one on your pad. Where can I reach you if I need more of your expertise?"

"Let's see, it's after four now. There's no point in going back to sleep. I'll be in the mess hall drinking coffee and working on an article for the Archives."

"I admire all you brains in internal medicine."

"Someone must do the thinking for surgeons. After breakfast I'll be making rounds. Call the front office and ask them to send a runner."

"Thanks, Phil."

"Good luck. You have a real tiger by the tail."

★

Monday, October 19, 1970, 0425 hours
36th Infantry Division Tactical Operation Center, Phong Sahn, Republic of Vietnam

The MP stood under a wooden shelter at the TOC's entrance, his wet poncho shining in the reflected beam of a floodlight. Sighting JP, he saluted, then asked for his ID card. JP, his collar and shoulders already soaked during the short walk from his jeep, returned the salute, fished out his ID card and handed it to the MP. The MP shined the beam of his flashlight on the card, then on JP's face causing him to blink in the bright light. Returning the ID card, he apologized. "Sorry, sir. I recognized you, but I still had to check."

"That's the only way to go," JP assured him. "In a few minutes a Captain Mosher, the surgeon for the 3rd/7th will be here. He's not on the authorized list, but it's important he be admitted. I'll square it with the duty officer."

"No problem, sir. Don't forget to sign in."

JP thanked him, pushed open the door and entered the TOC. Pulling his poncho off over his head, he draped it on a vacant chair to drain, then signed the log book. The TOC, brightly lit by a backup generator, seemed unusually quiet except for the static from multiple speakers. Teletype machines and computers, like their enlisted operators, appeared to be resting. Other enlisted men moved around the room carrying papers or marking maps and status boards with red and blue grease pencils. Two officers, a captain and lieutenant colonel, studied a wall map covered with acetate and penciled markings. They turned to see who had entered.

The lieutenant colonel, David Berger, came over to JP. Of average height, with a rounded face, western mustache and receding hairline, he told JP, "I know what brings you here at 0430 hours."

"Mike Jelnik must have called."

"Right. He filled me in on the problem at Lucy. My commo people are trying to establish communications with Lucy by working a patch through Beth Ann. If that's successful you'll be able to talk to Lucy directly."

"You people are on the ball," JP said with a twinge of admiration.

"Always. How about some coffee?"

"Thought you'd never ask."

Berger returned with a mug of steaming coffee and handed it to JP.

Cupping the mug with his hands, JP absorbed its warmth, then slurped the hot black liquid. "No war could go long without coffee."

"Then let's eliminate the coffee bean and go home."

"Great idea, David. Run with it. What's happening in the division?"

"Nothing much except for the excitement at Lucy. The monsoons have kept down casualties. If we can't have peace, at least let's pray for an extended monsoon." Berger moved to a wall map of the 36th Division AO. "Two mechanical devices were detonated during the night. One in the 174th AO, here," he punched the map with a stubby finger, "and here. The OP on Daisy Mae detected metal moving in this area at about 0130 hours." His finger swung in an arc over an area near the coast.

Sensors, triggered by three pounds or more of metal, had been seeded along trails traveled by Viet Cong and NVA. The sensors transmitted not only the location but direction and rate of travel of the metal. It was assumed that anyone traveling at night with three or more pounds of metal was up to no good.

"So did you fire the mission?" JP asked.

"Surely you jest. By the time we got political and military clearance from the ARVNs the target disappeared. Sometimes I wonder about our South Vietnamese allies."

JP bent his head and slurped coffee, then looked up. "You're not the only one."

A radio operator on the far side of the room called out. "Colonel Berger, we're patched through to Lucy."

"Outstanding. Tell them to stand by," Berger shouted back. Turning to JP, he asked, "Want to talk to Lucy now?"

"Let's wait a couple more minutes for their battalion surgeon. I'd like him to carry the ball as much as possible. Any problem with him coming in here?"

"No. Just tell the MP at the entrance."

"I already did," JP said, easing down on a metal chair. "What's flying in the AO?

"Only bullshit. Everything else is grounded from the DMZ south to Phan Rang. The navy cancelled all carrier-based missions for the third day."

JP slouched in his seat and morosely contemplated his options. All portended ill for the two individuals convulsing out at Firebase Lucy. While waiting for Captain Mosher he printed on a yellow pad a management outline for C–4 and alcohol toxicity. As he was finishing there was a rustling at the entrance and Tim Mosher, battalion surgeon for the 3rd/7th, appeared, dripping water from his poncho. A short muscular man in his late twenties, he had a youthful face, thin mustache and close-cropped black hair.

"You look a little damp," JP said by way of a greeting.

"Good morning, Colonel," Mosher said, pulling off his poncho. "One would think the army could come up with a more efficient rain gear than this damn poncho. It funneled water down my neck and back. My legs are soaked up to my knees."

"The poncho hasn't changed since World War II. You'll have to admit, once the army comes up with a bad idea they stick with it." JP introduced Mosher to Colonel Berger, who handed him a cup of coffee.

"We're ready to talk to Sergeant Burdick at Lucy," JP said.

Colonel Berger nodded. "Be a minute or two."

JP reviewed with Captain Mosher the management outline for C–4/alcohol toxicity he had printed on the yellow pad. "The best we can hope for is to control seizures, provide oxygen, maintain renal function, and prevent aspiration."

The RTO called to Colonel Berger, "Sir, it will be a few more minutes. Sergeant Burdick has his hands full right now."

"That doesn't sound encouraging," Captain Mosher said.

"When Burdick comes on line, Tim, I'd like you to talk to him. Get an update on the situation and guide him through the management steps we just reviewed."

"Yes, sir. May I have your notes?"

JP handed him the pad. "I'll be next to you. If something comes up we can't handle, Colonel Anderson, the 96th chief of medicine, is a phone call away."

The RTO shouted across the room. "Sir, I have Sergeant Burdick."

Mosher went to the radio console. The RTO handed him a mike. "You know how to work this, sir?"

Mosher nodded and squeezed the mike button. "This is Skull Base Six. How do you read? Over."

"Broken, lots of static. Over."

"What's the situation out there, Tony? Over."

"Bad, sir, real bad. I stopped the seizures with Amytal, but they keep recurring every half hour. Over."

"Okay. You can follow the Amytal with IM phenobarb. There's some in the drug locker. What's their neurological status? Over."

"Mostly lethargic, but drifting in and out of unresponsive. Over."

"Do you think you could slip a Foley into each man? It's important to measure urine output and specific gravity. Over."

"I can try, sir. Over."

"Those two are at great risk for renal failure. If they quit putting out urine try twenty-five of Mannitol. Over."

There was a long pause. "Sir, one of the men is having a seizure. I need to go. Over."

"I'll be standing by the here. As soon as the weather breaks we'll be coming out there."

"Thanks, sir. Skull Base out."

Mosher handed the mike back to the RTO, picked up his mug of coffee, went to a chair and sat down. He looked at JP. "What now, Colonel?"

556

"We tough it."

★

JP was on his third cup of coffee. The last report from Sergeant Burdick was that one of the men had quit putting out urine and failed to respond to Mannitol.

Captain Mosher, sitting beside JP, suddenly burst out. "Damn it, sir. I feel so helpless here. I should be out there."

"I share that feeling, Tim. For the present there's not much we can do but sit here and sweat. Even if you were out at Lucy you couldn't do more than Sergeant Burdick is doing."

A corporal called out JP's name and held up a phone. JP took the phone and identified himself.

"Mike Jelnik, sir. How are things at Lucy?"

"Medically deteriorating. One man has quit putting out urine."

"I just finished talking to the chief air force meteorologist in Danang. He predicted a possible break in the weather any time after 0700 hours with a two to three-hour duration."

"What do you mean by break?"

"Half-mile to mile visibility, ceiling up to 1,000 feet, diminished rain and calm winds. It may be a little dicey to go out to Lucy but worth a try. I've scheduled the very best pilots to fly the mission."

"Do I know them?" JP asked, curious.

"Yes, sir. I'm going as AC. Dan Ranson volunteered to go as my peter pilot."

"Mike, has anyone told you modesty was not one of your virtues?"

"All the time, Colonel."

"I'll be going with you as the flight surgeon."

Captain Mosher, standing close enough to hear JP's part of the conversation, interrupted. "Sir, it's my battalion and those GIs are my men. It's my responsibility to go."

JP studied the young doctor a moment, nodded, and spoke into the phone. "Correction Mike, Captain Mosher, the 3rd/7th battalion surgeon, will be going with you as flight surgeon."

"Roger, sir. Have him at our operations as soon as possible. We'll take off as soon as the weather hints at breaking."

JP felt obliged to add a caveat, if for no other reason than to salve his own conscience. "Mike, the first priority is the safety of your crew. If things start to go sour, turn around and come home or set down in a safe spot. As much as I want to save those two GIs their rescue is not worth three more lives."

"Yes, sir. I understand."

JP hung up. He turned to the battalion surgeon. "Okay, Tim, let's see if I can get you a ride to Dust-off Ops."

Chapter Sixty-One

The MP's helmeted head, dripping rainwater, appeared in the doorway. "Captain Mosher, your transportation is here," he called out.

"Be right there," Mosher said. Picking up his web belt and holstered pistol from the chair, he fastened it around his waist. "I don't know why I carry this thing. I would never shoot anyone," he told JP.

"Remember the words of Sun Tzu."

"Sir?"

"Do not commit wholly to a strategy yet to be fought.'"

Mosher pulled his poncho over his head. "Did Sun Tzu really say that, Colonel?"

"I think so. It's the kind of thing he would say."

JP walked the young battalion surgeon to the TOC entrance, shook hands and pulled open the door. Captain Mosher stepped out into the heavy rain and disappeared into the darkness.

Closing the door, JP walked to a wall map and studied the terrain between Phong Sahn and Firebase Lucy. The contour lines for six miles around Lucy indicated an array of frightening tall peaks, treacherous valleys and box canyons. When he turned away he saw Colonel Berger watching him. "I'm sorry I looked at it," he said.

Berger tried to assure him. "They'll do fine. Mike Jelnik is one of the best pilots in the division. If you don't believe it just ask him."

"Mike is modest to a fault. Only if pushed will he admit he is the best pilot in the division." JP reached for his poncho. "In the six months I've been in the 36th I've seen many aircrews like Mike and Dan Ranson risk their lives to save comrades. It does much to restore my confidence in the future of our country."

"I get the same feeling. We have the best and the brightest over here. The draft dodgers and war protestors back in the States will spend the rest of their lives trying to live down their guilt and shame."

"I wish I could be sure of that," JP said. "It wouldn't surprised me if the draft dodgers of today didn't end up as the 'heroes' of tomorrow."

"No way. The country would never allow such a thing," Berger said. He watched JP pull on his poncho. "We monitor the Dust-off frequency here if you want to stay and listen."

"I need to go over to the ALCE and talk to Joe Withers about borrowing a C–130 from the air force." He reached for a phone. "First I'd better make sure he's there."

Monday, October 19, 1970, 0615 hours
Air Lift Control Element (ALCE), Phong Sahn Airfield, Republic of Vietnam

The four miles from the TOC to the airfield was ordinarily an eight-minute drive. Today it took almost thirty minutes. Visibility varied between ten and fifty feet, intermittently dropping to zero when wind slammed rain against the windshield with such intensity that the wipers became ineffective. Despite ponchos and the heavy canvas rooftop, JP and Groves were wet and shivering by the time they pulled up to the ALCE building and parked.

"Chain up the jeep and come inside," JP said. "It's dry in there and they're bound to have hot coffee… or cocoa," subtly referring to Groves's youth.

Climbing the outside stairs to the second floor, JP entered the small reception area and walked to the counter, leaving a trail of puddles and wet footprints. An overweight master sergeant greeted him. Lifting the end section of the counter, he said, "The boss is in his office, Colonel. Go right in."

As JP passed through the opening he inclined his head towards Groves who had just entered the reception area. "Would you have a cup of coffee for my driver?"

"Yes, sir. How about you?"

"No, thanks. I'll need both hands free to defend myself against your boss."

"Good luck, Colonel."

He knocked on the doorway of Joe Withers's office, then entered. Withers, talking on the phone, gestured towards a folding metal chair by the desk. Easing into the chair, JP studied the array of framed reproduced paintings on the walls. They were of P–38s shooting down Zeros, F–51s shooting down Yaks, and F–4s shooting down MiGs. The paintings represented planes flown by Withers in World War II, Korea, and Vietnam. In three wars he had shot down a total of four enemy planes, one short of making him an ace.

Lieutenant Colonel Joseph Withers, USAF, was in his late forties, slight of build, with wavy white hair and a trim white mustache. His pale blue eyes seemed to be always searching for that elusive fifth enemy plane which could make him an ace.

Withers finished his phone conversation, hung up and regarded JP with suspicion. "The only time you come up here is when you're after something the air force has and doesn't want to give up."

"Joe, you are so cynical for a middle-aged has-been fighter pilot. Are you here so early because you are dedicated or because you can't sleep?"

"Neither. I was on the night shift. I go off duty at seven. What is it you want from the air force this time?"

"I want to borrow a C–130 and a crew for a day."

Withers's eyes widened. "You want what? What the hell for?"

"Pick up two very sick GIs from the strip here and fly them to Tan Son Nhut."

"Is that all you want? I must admit, Doctor, your demands are becoming quite modest."

JP described the situation at Lucy and the urgent need to get the GIs to Saigon. "Without renal dialysis they will die, Joe. The only artificial kidney in Vietnam is at the 3rd Field."

"Where are the GIs now?"

"Still at Lucy. A Dust-off is going to try to get out there to pick them up and bring them here."

Withers was incredulous. "In this weather?" He leaned back in his chair, becoming thoughtful. "That pilot has balls." Picking up the phone on his desk, he said, "Give me a couple of minutes. I'll see what can be worked out."

JP stood up. "I knew the air force and its most brilliant fighter pilot would come through. I'll grab a cup of coffee."

Back in the larger office JP told the sergeant, "I've changed my mind about the coffee."

"Yes, sir." The sergeant headed for the coffee pot. Returning with a full mug, he warned, "Watch it Colonel, the coffee is boiling hot."

"Right, thanks."

While JP sipped the hot liquid he noticed the empty waiting room. "Any idea what happened to my driver?"

"He checked on his jeep a couple of minutes ago and found the canvas top partially ripped off. He borrowed some wire and tape. He's out there trying to fix it."

Scattered bits of a one-sided conversation escaped from Withers's office, ending with, "Okay. That's how I'll put it to him." A moment later he appeared at the door of his office and beckoned to JP. "Bring your coffee." He waited until JP was seated. "There's good news and bad news. Which do you want first?"

"The bad. It should be downhill from there."

"Don't bet on it. The weather from here to Danang is forecasted to worsen over the next twelve hours. That doesn't present much of a problem for a C–130 at Danang. As long as the pilot can see the runway lights and center line he can take off. But trying to put one of those monsters down on the runway here in this weather would flirt with disaster."

"So how could there be any good news?"

"The weather at Tan San Nhut is predicted to improve over the next twelve hours."

JP leaned towards Withers. "Are you telling me if we can get the two GIs to Danang the air force will fly them to Saigon?"

"That is precisely what I'm telling you. For an ex-marine you have surprisingly clear thinking."

"Colonel Withers, for your information there is no such thing as an ex-marine." JP settled back. "I'm impressed by the weight you carry in the air force for a lieutenant colonel. I'm also curious; how did you manage to get a Herky bird so quickly?"

"Easy. The 130 squadron CO is my brother-in-law."

"Now that's really being connected. What about the crew?"

"The best aircraft commander in the squadron has already spoken for the flight."

"I am overwhelmed. If you'll give me his name I'll ask General Webster to write his

CO a letter of commendation and recommend an award."

"That won't be necessary; my brother-in-law has enough decorations and commendations. More will only make him harder to tolerate."

★

Monday, October 19, 1970, 1120 hours
52nd Air Ambulance Detachment, 36th Infantry Division, Phong Sahn, Republic of Vietnam

Lieutenant Colonel JP Franklin walked into the Dust-off flight operations room, pulling the door closed and shutting out gale winds and punishing rain. The detachment executive officer, Captain Wilfred Bock, and his operations sergeant stood behind a seated radio operator gazing morosely at the hissing speakers on shelves above the radios. Bock's face carried an anxious expression not unlike a father waiting for his young daughter to come home on prom night. Hearing the door close he turned. "Good morning, sir."

"Any word, Will?" JP asked, pulling off his poncho.

"They made it to Lucy forty minutes ago. We haven't heard anything since."

Draping the poncho over a chair, JP watched it drip water on to the floor forming an expanding puddle.

"What did the air force say?" Bock asked.

"Yes and no. They have a plane available with a volunteer crew. Getting off the ground at Danang will be no problem and Tan San Nhut should be above minimums for the next twelve hours. Any attempt to land here at Phong Sahn in this weather is out." JP sat down and contemplated the floor. Suddenly, he looked up. "What do you think Mike's chances are of making it to Danang in this weather?"

Bock thoughtfully sipped coffee from a mug, then set the mug down next to a stack of *Flying* magazines on a table. Walking to a wall map, he studied the coast of South Vietnam from Phong Sahn to Danang. After a moment he turned to JP. "It's possible, Colonel. Phong Sahn radar could vector them to the coast, then turn them south just off shore. Once over water they could let down until they saw breakers, then angle to the shore. Most of it is white sand to Danang. Going that route rather than inland would reduce the risk of flying into Monkey Mountain or some other obstacle."

"If they are down on the deck how will they know when they reach Danang?"

"They should be able to identify the 95th Evac. It's a large hospital compound spread out from the shore and is hard to miss. Most of the buildings have red crosses on the roofs. Once they have the hospital in sight they will have several options. They could take a bearing from the hospital to the main airfield, gain altitude to get identified by Danang radar, then be vectored to the airfield for a GCA or ILS approach. If they had enough visibility to see rooftops they could low level to the airfield. Mike has flown to Danang a number of times, so he's familiar with the terrain. I don't think he's been up there in anything like this." He gestured towards a window being raked by rain.

"Would they have enough fuel to make Danang from Lucy without refueling?"

"Probably. I'm sure Mike topped off his tanks at Lucy if fuel was available. Even with full tanks, though, fuel will be a big question. A Huey bucking strong winds will consume fuel at a phenomenal rate. Another consideration is the possibility of getting lost or the need to fly much longer routes than anticipated."

JP sat down next to the table with the stack of *Flying* magazines. He pulled off the top magazine and studied the cover, a beautiful yellow Super Cub flying over verdant Virginia farm country. Giving in to nostalgia, he showed the photo to Captain Bock. "I took my FAA check ride in a beauty like this, except it was painted red. Thirty minutes into my flight test the FAA inspector asked if I would mind if he flew the cub a while. He didn't turn loose until after we landed almost an hour later."

"I've never flown a tail dragger," Bock said, gazing lovingly at the Super Cub as if it were a beautiful woman.

Bock and JP jumped when one of the speakers came to life. Mike Jelnik's voice blasted through the static. "Bandaid, Bandaid Six, Over."

The radio operator grabbed for his mike. "This is Bandaid. Go Bandaid Six."

"Is Bandaid Five available?"

Bock catapulted out of his seat and took the mike. "Right here, Mike. What's your situation?"

"At 7000 feet 2 miles west of Phong Sahn. I can't see a thing. We went on instruments as soon as we lifted off Lucy. The turbulence up here is something fierce. Dan Ranson and I have had to be on the controls together most of the time. The chopper is leaking like a sieve. Everyone is soaked. The two GIs are sedated and secured on stretchers lashed to the floor. Doc Mosher is anxious to get them on the Herky Bird to Saigon."

"Ah, Mike, there's a problem with the 130. It can take off from Danang; it just can't land here at Phong Sahn."

"You're trying to tell me something, Will."

"That's a Rog. If you can get the GIs to Danang, the air force will take them to Saigon."

An interval of static followed. "Stand by while I make some calculations and take a vote."

JP thumbed absent-mindedly through the *Flying* magazine, studying the photos and advertisements on each page.

"Bandaid, Bandaid Six."

"Go, Six."

"Okay. Everyone on board voted for Danang. So much for their good judgment. We topped off the tanks at Lucy so we're good on fuel. What have you worked out for a route?"

Bock outlined the flight plan he had reviewed with JP. "I'll call Danang to let them know your route and ETA. Do you have their frequencies and calls?"

"Roger."

"I have the division surgeon here. Does Doc Mosher have anything for him?"

"I don't think so. The doc is airsick as hell. Right now he has his head in a barf bag.

562

The turbulence is so bad even Ranson is beginning to look a little green. I'll get word to you when we land. Bandaid Six, out."

Continuous static followed. The ring of a telephone seemed almost anticlimactic. JP casually watched the operations sergeant pick up the phone and heard him say, "Yes, sir. He's right here. Just a minute." He extended the phone to JP.

JP took the phone.

"Captain Cruessi, sir."

"Dom, what's happening up there at Dog Patch?"

"Charlie Med is about to wash away in a sea of red mud, Colonel. Some of my men have started building an ark and collecting animals. But that's not what I called you about."

"I didn't think so," JP said, chuckling.

"I just finished talking with Gary Dreysdale, the 5th/46th battalion surgeon at Donna. From what he told me I had no choice but to declare Bravo Company ineffective."

"Good God. Why?"

"The company was out in the bush for almost eight days. They were ankle to hip deep in water. Most of the company is down with immersion foot."

"What do you mean by most of the company?"

"Over a hundred men and officers."

"Has Captain Dreysdale triaged the company to see what he's dealing with?"

"Yes, sir. It's not as bad as it sounds. Seventy-eight men have only edema and erythema of the skin over one or both feet. Gary confined those men to their hooches, advised them to wear sandals, and keep their feet as dry as possible. They even eat in their hooches… C-rations. Twenty-four men have mild to moderate breakdown of skin with varying degrees of secondary infection. Gary has them bunking in the mess hall. He and his medics are managing them with aggressive local therapy and systemic meds including antibiotics."

"How are they working meals with twenty-four men and forty-eight smelly feet in the mess hall?"

"The resupply choppers haven't been able to reach Donna for three days because of the weather. The battalion ran out of fresh food two days ago. The mess hall is closed as far as serving meals. Everyone is on C-rations, MREs, or LRP rations."

"Let's hope the VC and NVA are having similar problems. Any severe cases?"

"Yes, sir. There are seven with extensive skin breakdown, ulceration, and draining pus. Some have chills, fever, exposed muscle and bone. Gary has them in the chapel. He's doing what he can for them until a Dust-off can make it out to Donna to evacuate them. They need aggressive therapy including debridement. Gary thinks that at least half will require skin graft or flaps."

"How long did you say they were out in the bush?" JP asked.

"Eight days."

"That's clearly a breakdown in command, Dom. Three days is max out in the bush in this kind of weather unless circumstances are compelling. Did Gary advise the company and battalion commanders of the high probability of immersion foot if they pushed that time limit?"

"Yes, sir, repeatedly until the battalion commander, Colonel Rushmore told him to keep his mouth shut. The company commander tried to bring in his troops on the fourth day but was given a direct order by the battalion commander to continue the mission."

"Is there anything on paper?"

"No, sir, but there are plenty of witnesses."

Captain Cruessi then described in great detail a chronology of events ending with the relief of the company commander and court-martial charges against him. "Colonel, Gary Dreysdale was so pissed off at the battalion commander that he tried to get to Nghia Lam to alert me and brigade. Colonel Rushmore stopped him and restricted him to his hooch and the aid station. When Gary tried to radio me from the battalion TOC Colonel Rushmore charged him with breaking restriction and will court martial Gary unless he accepts an Article 15. Gary is going to file a complaint with the IG claiming Rushmore is making the company commander the fall guy for a disaster that was clearly of Rushmore's making."

"It sounds like the wrong officer was relieved. How is he taking it?"

"Very hard. Being relieved of command means the end of his military career. A court martial will makes things much worse. He's a West Point graduate; an army career was his goal since he was a kid."

"How far has this thing gone, Dom?"

"I'm not sure, Colonel. I tried to see the brigade commander this morning to present the company commander's side, but he had already left for Phong Sahn."

"Flying in this weather?"

"No, sir. He's traveling by jeep in a convoy."

"His reasons must have been compelling to go that route, considering the weather."

"Probably concerns Bravo Company."

"By the way, what's the company commander's name?"

"Zeller, William Zeller. He's..."

"Cupcake? You mean Cupcake was the company commander?"

"You know him, sir?"

"He was a regular in the cadet rock climbing club at the Academy. I taught him everything he knows about rock climbing. He is one straight arrow."

"His company has the lowest casualty rate of any company in the division and one of the best combat records. I looked it up."

JP was silent as the ramifications of what he had been told ran through his mind. A young officer with immense potential was about to have his career destroyed by a superior officer whose motives and competence were questionable.

"Dom, as soon as I finish here I'll head over to the chief of staff's office and drop this in his lap. The information you've given me is convincing. A good defense counsel should be able to run with it. Now, what else can I do for the 174th Brigade?"

"Stop the rain."

"I'll talk to Father Deveraux."

564

"I need a chopper to evacuate the worst cases from Lucy."

"I'm in the Dust-off detachment now. I'll pass the word to their operations officer. Anything else?"

"That's it, Colonel. I'll be going out to Donna with the first chopper."

"Keep me informed."

JP gently placed the phone on its cradle and turned to Captain Bock. "Donna needs priority evacuation evac of seven GIs with severe immersion foot." He described the current situation, then stood up. "I'm out of here for the chief of staff's office." He reached for his poncho.

Chapter Sixty-Two

Monday, October 19, 1970, 1305 hours
36th Infantry Division Headquarters, Phong Sahn, Republic of Vietnam

Lieutenant Colonel JP Franklin entered the outer office of the chief of staff. The assistant chief of staff, Major Jerry Van Demere, working at his desk, looked up. "Good afternoon, Colonel Franklin. What brings you to the head shed?"

"Good afternoon, Jerry. I need ten minutes of your boss's time."

"He just went to an emergency meeting with General Webster and Colonel Fisher, sir. I don't how long he'll be in there. I can call you at your office when he's free."

"I'd better wait. I have my own emergency to discuss," JP said, pulling off his poncho. Taking a seat on a leather sofa, he picked up a recent copy of the *American Rifleman* from a coffee table.

"Care for a Coke or Pepsi while you're waiting, sir?"

"No, thanks. When did Colonel Fisher get here?"

"About twenty minutes ago; he drove down from Nghia Lam. Nothing is flying in the division."

Almost nothing, thought JP, smiling knowingly. He wondered where Mike Jelnik and Dan Ranson were with the two GIs from Lucy. Then he speculated about what motivated the 174th Brigade commander to drive forty miles to Phong Sahn from Nghia Lam in such foul weather. Finally, he concluded that Colonel Fisher's meeting with General Webster and Colonel Witherington was related to the immersion foot fiasco at Bravo Company. His concern now was how best to approach the delicate subject of defending a junior officer against serious charges brought by his commander.

Colonel Witherington walked in, nodded to JP and went hurriedly to his assistant's desk. "Jerry, I need the service records of Lieutenant Colonel Henry Rushmore and Captain William Zeller right away." Turning to JP, he asked, "Doctor, are you waiting to see me?"

"Yes, sir," JP said, rising. "It concerns the two officers whose records you just requested and their involvement with the immersion foot epidemic at Bravo Company."

Witherington studied JP for several seconds, then made a decision. "You'd better come in and discuss it with General Webster and Colonel Fisher." As JP moved to the door Witherington stopped him. "Forget the formalities."

The commanding general's office was spacious. A huge glass-topped desk dominated one side of the room. A number of armchairs, several tables with lamps, and a leather sofa were placed strategically around the desk.

Colonel Witherington explained JP's presence to General Webster. "Colonel

Franklin may have information pertinent to our discussion of Colonel Rushmore and Captain Zeller."

"Always interested in a marine's perspective," the general said. "You know Colonel Fisher."

"Yes, sir."

"We were neighbors at West Point," Colonel Fisher added.

"Have a seat, Doctor," General Webster invited. "What's the word on the two GIs out at Lucy?"

"Major Jelnik and Warrant Officer Ranson made it out to Lucy an hour and a half ago with the battalion surgeon, Captain Mosher. They picked up the two GIs and now are somewhere between here and Danang."

The general glanced at Witherington and Fisher. "In this weather that must be some sort of flying miracle." He turned to JP. "Why are they going to Danang?"

JP explained about the C–130's ability to take off at Danang and the great risks of trying to land at Phong Sahn. "Sir, considering the hazards and skills involved I would like to recommend Distinguished Flying Crosses for the flight crew and the Air Medal for the doctor."

"That sounds reasonable. I'll be happy to approve them. I have a bit of good news for you, Doctor, but first tell us what you can about the disaster at Lucy?"

JP cleared his throat. "Let me say at the outset that I am acquainted with Captain Zeller. He was a member of the cadet rock climbing club at West Point during the time I was an instructor in the club. I consider him a friend although I haven't seen him since 1964."

"You're not going to allow that to color your judgment, are you?"

"No, sir. I would be here even if Captain Zeller were unknown to me. What took place in Bravo Company compromised the health and combat effectiveness of an entire company; it could have impacted the effectiveness of the division."

"We are well aware of that, Doctor," General Webster said. "From what Colonel Rushmore told Colonel Fisher, relieving Captain Zeller was justified. If the Article 32 investigation confirms what Colonel Rushmore claims took place, there are grounds for court martial on charges of willful disobedience and negligence."

"General, there was willful disobedience and negligence, but not on Captain Zeller's part."

"Now what is that supposed to mean, Doctor?"

"According to Captain Cruessi, the brigade surgeon, and Captain Dreysdale, the battalion surgeon, Captain Zeller was well aware of the USARV regulation that stipulated a three-day limit for troops in the bush during continuous heavy rains. The intent of the regulation was to reduce the incidence of immersion foot."

"I would think his awareness of that regulation compounds his culpability in this matter," General Webster said.

"It would, sir, except that certain events supported by enlisted men and officers of Bravo Company indicate otherwise."

General Webster gave JP a hard look. "Go on, Doctor."

"Captain Zeller terminated Bravo Company's mission on the fourth day and was returning to Lucy. When Colonel Rushmore learned of this he ordered Captain Zeller by radio to resume the mission. Captain Zeller protested, pointing out the increased risk of immersion foot. Colonel Rushmore then flew to Bravo Company's CP and gave Captain Zeller a direct order to proceed with the mission or be relieved and face court martial. He told Captain Zeller the NVA were out there somewhere and Bravo Company would stay in the bush until it produced NVA bodies and weapons."

"That is a very serious allegation, Doctor," General Webster said, his face grave. "Are there witnesses to this?"

"Yes, sir, Bravo's three platoon commanders, the company's first sergeant, a platoon sergeant, two squad leaders and Captain Zeller's RTO."

"Please continue, Doctor."

"When Captain Dreysdale, the battalion surgeon, learned that Bravo Company was being kept in the field beyond the three-day limit he reminded Colonel Rushmore of the USARV regulation and the increased risk of immersion foot. He was told the mission took precedence over any stupid regulation. When Dreysdale persisted Colonel Rushmore told him to keep his mouth shut, then restricted him to the battalion aid station. The following day Captain Dreysdale tried to alert by radio Captain Cruessi, the brigade surgeon, of the growing threat of immersion foot in Bravo Company. Colonel Rushmore caught Dreysdale in the TOC about to send a message. He is preparing court-martial charges against him for breaking restriction."

"That certainly is not the story Colonel Rushmore told Colonel Fisher," General Webster said.

"There's more, General."

"I'm not sure I want to hear it, Doctor, but go on."

"Captain Zeller tried to take his company over high ground to reduce exposure to wet environment. When he reported his position to the battalion TOC Colonel Rushmore promptly ordered a different route, one which led through rice paddies and a marsh. By the sixth day in the field Bravo Company's progress was markedly slowed by an increasing incidence of immersion foot. Colonel Rushmore berated Captain Zeller for his lack of progress and again threatened to court martial him if he didn't move on. By the end of the following day, the seventh day, Bravo Company was so inundated by immersion foot that it was immobile. Captain Zeller reported the situation and requested termination of the mission. Colonel Rushmore accused Captain Zeller of being soft on his men. Colonel Rushmore then flew out to Bravo Company during a break in the weather. When he saw how many men were crippled by immersion foot he went on a screaming tirade against Captain Zeller in front of his men, relieved him and placed him under arrest."

General Webster turned to Colonel Fisher. "Were you aware of this, Charles?"

"Partially, but with a much different perspective. Rushmore sent me word that the Bravo Company commander had gotten his company lost in the bad weather and would be delayed returning to Lucy by several days. I ordered him to find the company and return it to Lucy immediately. The next day I received information that Bravo Company was actually into its seventh day in the bush. When I questioned Rushmore he told me that Captain Zeller had disobeyed his order to return to Lucy."

568

"Why would he do that?" the general asked.

"Rushmore described Captain Zeller as a glory hound who drives his company hard and often ignores orders," Colonel Fisher said.

"How long has Rushmore been in command?" the general asked.

"About two months, sir. In his first month he relieved three of the four company commanders. With Captain Zeller's relief it's now four of four."

The general became thoughtful. "I remember interviewing Rushmore when he reported into the division. I told him my desire was to minimize US casualties, and killing ten or fifteen NVA or VC a week would have no impact on the war's outcome. There was no need to get our own people killed or hurt for reasons that would matter little in a few years. Although he readily agreed I don't think he heard a word I said."

There was a knock at the door. Witherington rose, went to the door and opened it. Captain Laird entered and handed him two thick folders. "Thanks, Jerry."

"Sir, there's a phone call for Colonel Franklin on line two from Dust-off operations. The caller said it was urgent."

General Webster picked up a phone on his desk and held it out. "I hope it's good news. We could use some right now."

JP accepted the phone. The message was short and sweet. An immense smile crossed his face as he hung up. "It's definitely good news, general. A C–130 with the two GIs and Captain Mosher aboard just took off from Danang for Tan Son Nhut."

"Any problems on the flight to Danang?"

"Some. The helicopter's chip detector light went on when they were just north of Danang, then the gearbox failed. Major Jelnik managed to set down near some marines. The marines loaded the two GIs and the battalion surgeon into a truck and drove them to the airfield."

"What about the helicopter's flight crew?"

"Major Jelnik, Warrant Officer Ranson, and the crew chief will stay with the Huey until a Chinook can bring it back. The word is that the marines have adopted them and refuse to let them leave."

The general smiled. "Marines – what would we ever do without them?" He looked at his chief of staff. "Let's get an ID of the marine unit involved and its commander. They deserve a letter of thanks."

"Yes, sir," Witherington said, making notes on a yellow pad. "What about the C–130 crew?"

"By all means. Anyone who flies in this weather deserves a medal… or a psychiatric evaluation." The general turned back to JP. "Do you have an estimate when Bravo Company might be operational?"

"It's capable of defending the firebase now while recovering, but it shouldn't be depended on as the battalion reserve except in an extreme situation. Two and possibly three weeks will be required before Bravo can be considered truly operational although it will be short at least seven people."

"Would a break in the weather help?" the general asked.

"Definitely. Sunshine does wonders to speed up recovery."

General Webster picked up a paper on his desk and glanced at it. "The latest met forecast predicts a window of good weather starting the day after tomorrow and lasting two to three weeks followed by several months of almost continuous rain." He turned to Colonel Fisher. "Well, Charles, it's your brigade, your battalion commander, and your company commander. As the concerned father asked the young man calling on his daughter, 'What are your intentions?'"

"Hold off on the Article 32 investigation. Instead send the IG out to Lucy to talk to the people in Bravo Company. If what the doctor has told us is substantiated, I will relieve Colonel Rushmore, quash the court-martial charges against Captain Zeller and reinstate him as Bravo Company commander."

"That may take several days, Charles," Colonel Witherington said. "The IG moves slowly and ponderously. There's no telling what Rushmore might do with his battalion during the interim."

"You're right, John," Colonel Fisher agreed. "I'll bring him to brigade where we can keep an eye on him. I'll put his battalion in a defensive mode. My three, Major Harkins, was an acting battalion commander for a month before he came up to brigade. He is a level-headed, cool individual who came up through the ranks. He's been a superb operations officer. I hate to lose him, but he's on the list for promotion so I would have lost him sooner or later."

General Webster picked up a thin stack of papers stapled together, looked at JP and smiled. "Speaking of promotions, Doctor, yours will be effective some time in late October or early November. This is the list that just came out from DA." He held out the papers.

JP catapulted to his feet, took the papers and studied them briefly. Finally, he would command a hospital.

"Congratulations, Doctor. The promotion is well deserved and, I understand, somewhat late in coming," General Webster said. "The promotion ceremony will take place here in my office."

"Way to go, JP," Colonel Fisher said, standing up and shaking his hand."

"I second that," Colonel Witherington said, "and from now on we are on a first name basis."

"Thank you, sir, I mean John," JP said, gripping the extended hand.

"After you are promoted, Doctor," General Webster continued, "you will have too much rank to remain here as division surgeon, much to my regret and, in many ways, relief. You can bet your replacement will not have had any association with the Marine Corps." The general showed a shadow of a smile. "Do you have any preferences for the remainder of your tour?"

JP felt like a traitor, about to abandon his brothers in arms. He hesitated, then finally gave way to his heart's desire. "Yes, sir. I want to command an evacuation hospital."

"We'll see what we can do. Is there any other information you wish to pass on?"

"No, sir."

The general stood and extended his hand. "Thank you for your input, Doctor."

As JP was leaving Colonel Witherington's outer office a phone rang. Captain Laird called out, "It's for you, Colonel; Major Brodie at the 96th Evac."

JP sighed. "Tell him I don't want to talk to him."

Laird relayed the message. "He says it's urgent."

"It's always urgent," JP said, taking the phone. "What now, Kevin?"

"Boss, I need you over here, like right away."

"That's what you always say."

"This time I really mean it."

"What do you have?"

"An-eight-year-old girl, the daughter of a village chief. The VC came into their village early this morning, killed her mother and father, then shot her in the face and neck and left her for dead. A LRRP team heard the shooting and investigated. When they found her they called a Dust-off."

"You have a way with words, Brodie. I'll be over in a few minutes on one condition."

"What's that, sir?"

"You let me do the case."

"Deal, sir."

★

Tuesday, October 20, 1970, 0115 hours
36ᵗʰ Division Staff Quarters, Phong Sahn, Republic of Vietnam

Lieutenant Colonel JP Franklin made a second and then a third search of the top shelf in his wall locker, confirming it was void of anything edible. He had missed lunch, he had missed supper, he had just finished eight hours of surgery, he was tired and he was pissed. Taking his ire out on the locker, he slammed the door shut with a massive swing. The resulting metallic crash rivaled the blast of an exploding 120 mm rocket. Within seconds Father Deveraux, dressed in a T-shirt, trousers and sandals appeared at the connecting door.

"Problems, my son?"

"It's been a rough day, Father. I was just feeling sorry for myself."

"And you took it out on an innocent locker?"

"Damn right. It was supposed to have some goodies in it. Instead the cupboard was bare and I'm hungry as hell."

"If some day you become familiar with hell, Doctor, a distinct possibility in your case, hunger will be the least of your concerns. When did you eat last?"

"This morning."

"Stand by, doctor, the Church will be your salvation."

The chaplain disappeared into his room. Moments later he reappeared carrying a two-foot length of plank on which was arranged an open jar of pickled pig's feet, a dozen salted crackers spread out on a facial tissue, and a can of cold beer from the chaplain's small fridge.

JP's eyes widened. He reached for the beer, popped open the can, took a long swallow and burped. "Father Pete, you just saved my life."

"Doctor, saving your life is of no great concern of mine. Saving your soul is."

Chapter Sixty-Three

Thursday, October 29, 1970, 2035 hours
Staff Bivouac Area, 36th Infantry Division, Phong Sahn, Republic of
Vietnam

Lieutenant Colonel JP Franklin entered the field grade officers' communal shower, turned on his favorite shower head, and manipulated the hot and cold handles until the water temperature was as hot as he could tolerate. Stepping under the strong spray, he closed his eyes for a moment as a relaxing warmth seeped through his exhausted body and the water washed away blood from half a dozen wounded GIs. It had been a day of mass casualties beginning at dusk yesterday when helicopters began delivering wounded to Phong Sahn. By mid-morning the next day twenty-seven severely wounded Americans had been medevac'd to the 96th Evacuation Hospital and fourteen to the 19th Surgical Hospital. Eleven dead were taken to Graves Registration. There had been so many head and neck cases among the wounded that he and Kevin Brodie divided the cases and operated in separate rooms assisted only by a nurse or medic.

The battle began unexpectedly yesterday afternoon. An infantry company of the 174th Brigade stumbled into elements of a NVA battalion just east of the Song Krong River eight kilometers from the Laotian border. The US battalion commander quickly committed the remainder of his battalion. By nightfall parts of a second US battalion had been airlifted to high ground west of the river. The NVA battalion found itself trapped between two US battalions, its back against the river.

The withering fire of two infantry battalions supplemented by helicopter gunships and air force fighter bombers took a fearsome toll of NVA until dark. An AC–130 Spectre with NOD, 20 kw searchlight, four 7.62 mm miniguns and four 20 mm Gatling cannons, added to the carnage through the night. The NVA fought furiously to break out. A second NVA battalion, moving to assist its comrades, ran into an ambush set by the US battalion on the west side of the river. It too was decimated by the helicopter gunships and Spectre. By mid-morning the battle had ended. The Song Krong ran red with Communist blood. The remnants of two NVA battalions slipped across the border into their Laotian sanctuary to refit. The US battalions returned to their firebases, and the jungle returned to its natural inhabitants. Although the battle ended in a clear US tactical victory, nothing had really changed.

JP turned off the water and dried himself. Returning to his hooch, he dressed in clean, starched and ironed fatigues, then headed to the general's mess. Although the evening meal had long ended he knew there would be something to eat waiting for him. While still operating at the 96th Evac he had sent word to the mess sergeant he would be late and requested a plate of leftovers be set aside. The mess sergeant was happy to comply; two months earlier JP had operated on the mess sergeant's wounded brother.

572

Entering the semi-dark lounge he saw that a short film on football classics was showing. Scattered through the lounge, a dozen shadowy figures slouched on chairs and sofas intently watching the action. Football was not high on JP's list of interests. Hardly glancing at the screen, he walked to the bar and slid onto a stool. The bartender, Corporal Luttrel, limped towards him from the far end.

"Is that leg giving you trouble?" JP asked over the sound of the movie monologue and noise of the projector.

"It did this morning, sir. It's better now."

"Any swelling, redness, fever, chills?"

"No, sir."

"Stop by the dispensary tomorrow and let the doctor take a look at it."

"Yes, sir. Can I get you something from the bar?"

"Sprite on the rocks. Anything stronger will put me under the bar."

Luttrel reached for a glass, filled it with ice, then set the glass and a cold can of Sprite on the counter. "I'll tell the mess sergeant you're here."

JP popped open the Sprite can and poured the liquid over the ice in his glass while watching Luttrel limp to the end of the bar and out a door.

Corporal Ben Luttrel, age nineteen, was recovering from his fourth wound, received when he ignored enemy fire to drag a wounded comrade to safety, killing two Viet Cong in the process. With three previous wounds in seven months, a Silver Star, and two Bronze Stars, Luttrel had been assigned to the general's mess as a safe billet to finish out his tour.

Taking a sip of Sprite, JP turned to watch the movie. The football classic had mercifully ended and the movie *MASH* was just beginning As he watched the credits and the supposed South Korean background he couldn't help but dwell on his own experiences as a lieutenant in that war, a war that ended in a stalemate because politicians would not commit to winning. Now the politicians were repeating history, and more of America's finest young men were dying. Twenty-five years from now would their sacrifices have any meaning?

Behind him he heard Luttrel slide a plate onto the bar. "All set, sir. Watch the plate; it's hot."

Turning to the bar, JP's eyes feasted on a small thick steak, scrambled eggs, and hash browned potatoes.

Luttrell set utensils wrapped in a linen napkin next to the plate. "Sergeant Hardesty said to tell you the mess is out of spaghetti and meatballs. He hoped steak and eggs would do. If the steak's not done as you want, let me know."

"It looks beautiful," JP said, cutting off a piece and chewing it thoughtfully. "Excellent, just excellent," he said, looking up.

"I heard you were operating all day at the 96th," Luttrell said.

"Everyone was operating, even doctors from the clearing companies. It was a mass caz, most from your old outfit."

"I hope they kicked a lot of ass… I mean, butt, sir."

"From what I heard they did just that."

After several bites of food washed down with Sprite, JP turned to watch the movie.

Before he could discern the theme of the story the film broke and lights came on. Groans followed. While the film was being repaired some officers returned to the bar for fresh drinks. The JAG, Lieutenant Colonel Jesse Wilmont, eased on to the stool next to JP and stared jealously at his plate. "How do you rate steak and eggs when all we got was spaghetti and meatballs?"

JP swallowed a mouthful of scrambled eggs and hash browns, then grinned at Wilmont. "The mess personnel are expressing their gratitude to the Medical Corps in general and to a dedicated military physician in particular." He took a swallow of Sprite.

"In my next life I'm going to medical school instead of law school."

"I don't know, Jesse. Admission requirements are pretty stiff for medical school."

Wilmont punched JP lightly on the arm, picked up his drink and returned to his seat.

The ceiling lights went off and the movie resumed. As JP was finishing his meal the phone on the bar rang. Luttrel answered. "Yes, sir, he's right here," he said, handing the phone to JP "It's Colonel Witherington."

JP took the phone. "Yes, sir," he said.

"Doctor, a medical disaster has hit Delta Company, 3rd/7th." He paused. "Just a minute, my hot line is ringing."

While waiting JP recalled he had visited the 3rd Battalion only a week ago. There was no hint of an impending medical problem, much less medical disaster. The battalion surgeon, Chris Snyder, was a Wisconsin graduate who survived a surgical internship at Cook County Hospital in Chicago before being drafted. Snyder was highly regarded by his battalion commander.

Witherington's bass voice came through the phone." Okay, Doctor, you still there?"

"Yes, sir."

"That call was the air force confirming that an AC–130 Spectre just took off from Danang for Delta Company area."

JP wondered why Witherington would want a four-engine turbo-prop gunship for a medical emergency.

"I'll make this brief, Doctor," Witherington continued. "You're going to have lots to do in a short time. Here's the situation. Delta Company was setting up for night lager five klicks south-west of Firebase Jeannie. A hot meal was flown out to them at about 1700 hours. Two hours after eating the meal the entire company was inundated with vomiting and diarrhea."

"What about the battalion surgeon?"' JP asked.

"The surgeon was with the company and ate the same meal. He is too sick himself to be of any help, but he sent word he's certain the problem is food poisoning."

By now JP's mind was spinning in high gear; fatigue from twenty-four hours in the operating room had been wiped away. "I'll get up a team and head out there."

"I've allotted you two slicks. Warrant Officer Ranson is the flight leader. The slicks should be at the admin pad in twenty minutes. Major Alsos, the assistant G–3, will brief you there. Any questions?"

574

"No, sir, at least not at the moment."

"Is General Webster still there?"

"Yes, sir. He's watching the movie."

"I need to brief him."

JP laid the phone down, walked to where General Webster sat and tapped him on the shoulder.

Back in his hooch JP sat on his bunk, reached for the phone and dialed his executive officer's hooch. As he waited he went to his locker, pulled out his pistol belt with the .45 pistol in ifs holster and tossed it on the bunk.

"Major Nichols."

"Doug, Colonel Franklin. I'm going to need you to marshal your fine administrative talents into superfast mode."

"No problem, sir. What's up?"

"Delta Company 3rd/7th is in the bush south-west of Jeannie with food poisoning. You have a pen and pad handy?"

"Just a second… all set, Colonel."

"These are medical supplies to be taken from the supply depot, delivered to the admin pad a.s.a.p. and loaded on two slicks." He recited a list of items he had compiled in his mind, "Normal saline, Ringer's lactate, five percent glucose, IV tubing, syringes, needles, minor surgery packs, flashlights, extra batteries and bulbs, Thorazine suppositories and injection, Demerol, Lomotil, sugar, sodium, potassium chloride, Kaopectate, and water."

"What about toilet paper and soap?"

"Now you're thinking like a lieutenant colonel. Throw in some IV Ampicillin."

"Anything else, sir?"

"I need two doctors, six medics, and the venerable Sergeant Harrel, your operations NCO. I'll take Mark Turley as one of the doctors. You should be able to get along without your HQ & A Company commander for a day or two. I'll take Tom Moffet, my preventative medicine officer. You and Sergeant Harrel select the medics. Try to get volunteers and have them at the admin pad in thirty minutes. Make sure they bring weapons and ammo."

"Anything else, Colonel?"

"I need my jeep. As of now you are the acting battalion commander. Don't try a coup while I'm gone."

Nichols laughed. "Not a chance, Colonel."

Next, JP alerted the two US Army hospitals in Phong Sahn to the possibility of receiving critically ill casualties with food poisoning.

The door between his room and the chaplain's opened and Father Deveraux stepped in. "I couldn't help overhearing. Could you use an extra hand?"

"Always room for a representative of the Lord, Father."

"Take me a minute to get my gear," the priest said moving to hi s door.

"Peter, do you have any kind of weapon for protection?"

"Of course."

"Good. Bring it."

"I will, you can bet on it."

JP secured his pistol belt around his waist. Removing the .45 pistol from its holster, he dropped the magazine from the receiver and squeezed down the bullets to be sure there were seven. Next, he pulled back the slide, checked the empty chamber, then pressed down the slide stop allowing the slide to slam forward. He squeezed the trigger, the hammer snapped forward. Then he fed the magazine back into the receiver and returned the pistol to its holster. He checked each of the three magazines in the canvas pouch on his belt; all were fully loaded.

Each time he went through this routine he wondered if he could use the pistol to kill a human being. The thought caused him to reach down and touch the bulk of the hideout knife strapped to his leg. If Kristy hadn't stopped him he would have killed with it the night the VC attacked the Montagnard village. Closing the locker door, he secured it with a combination lock. As he reached for his fatigue cap Father Deveraux reappeared.

"All set," the division chaplain announced.

JP noted the web belt around the chaplain's waist; two canteens hung from it but no pistol. "I thought you were going to bring a weapon for protection, Peter."

"I have," the man of God insisted.

"I don't see it."

Father Deveraux took a small Bible from his pocket and waved it. "This is the only weapon I need for protection."

★

Fifty minutes after JP had hung up the phone in the general's mess he stepped from his jeep in the lighted parking area of the admin pad. The pad itself was dark except for strings of parallel yellow and blue lights. The twelve-foot tower showed only a dim light in its observation windows. Out on the PSP apron a two-and-a half-ton truck pulled away from the silhouettes of two parked Huey helicopters. A group of darkened figures clustered between the helicopters, Turning, JP waited for Father Deveraux to struggle from the jeep's back seat to the front and stumble out, carrying his rucksack.

"Putting on a little weight, Father?"

"Not at all," the division chaplain said defensively. "Jeeps are being made smaller than in the past."

JP grabbed his web belt with pistol and fixed it around his waist, then reached for his rucksack. Pfc Groves, the driver, leaned towards JP. The look of envy on his young face was lost in the dark, but his words were not. "Sir, do you remember promising I could go with you on a mission?" The emphasis was on "promising".

JP studied the young former infantryman. "Seems to me I remember saying something like that."

"What about now, sir?"

"Do you have a weapon?"

Groves reached into the back seat and held up an M–16, a pouch of magazines, a web belt with two canteens, and a rucksack.

576

JP shrugged. "Okay. Secure the jeep and leave the key with the NCO in the tower. Call the first sergeant and have him send someone to pick up the jeep tonight."

"Yes, sir," Groves said happily, reaching for the lock and chain.

JP and Father Deveraux started off towards the darkened forms between the two Hueys. "You know, Father," JP said, "if the wind blows in the right direction the NVA will not only figure out Delta's location but its predicament."

"You have the weirdest sense of humor for a doctor," the chaplain said. laughing.

"I know, and that joke smells. Come on, Father, let's get things moving."

As they approached the darkened group of figures between the Hueys, one figure detached itself from the others and walked rapidly towards them. Stopping in front of Father Deveraux, he saluted. "Sir, Major Alsos, are you Colonel Franklin?"

JP spoke up. "I'm Colonel Franklin, Major. You just saluted the division chaplain, Father Deveraux. I will admit that in the dark he does appear to be mature and intelligent enough to be mistaken for the division surgeon."

"The egotism of surgeons knows no bounds, Major," Father Deveraux remarked caustically.

Major Alsos, confused by the banter between the two senior officers, thought it prudent not to respond.

"I understand you are to brief us," JP said.

"Yes, sir."

"Let's go over to the others so they can hear what they're getting into."

When they reached the group JP nodded a greeting to the two doctors, Sergeant Harrel and medics, then went over to Dan Ranson and Tom Carter. "You know where we're going?"

"I have the coordinates of the LZ. I'm not sure how much good they'll be in the dark. I also have the radio frequency and call."

"Let's hear what Major Alsos has to say."

Major Alsos moved closer to the group and coughed. "May I have your attention." After everyone had gathered around him he continued. "The situation at Delta Company is desperate. We believe that the NVA already suspect Delta's vulnerability and will almost certainly try to take advantage of it. With that in mind Charlie Company, 3rd/7th less one platoon, is being transported from reserve on Jeannie to the Delta bivouac area for perimeter defense. That is considered less than adequate if the NVA attack in force. Two special forces A Teams and their Mike Forces will aggressively patrol south and west of Delta. A Ranger company should be taking off any time now from the airstrip here. It will be inserted to patrol north and east. A reserve battalion at Quang Dien has been alerted for possible insertion if things get dicey.

"Air cover will be two Night Hawks; four Cobra gunships are on call at Jeannie. Four more Cobras are on standby at Phong Sahn. A Mohawk went on station half an hour ago. Just before I left the TOC it reported two groups, estimated twenty to thirty bodies, eight to ten klicks west of Delta Company. Zoomie Six has assured us he can have tactical air over the target in thirty minutes. A Spectre is on its way to Bravo from Danang."

"What about artillery?" Ranson asked.

"Right. A battery of 155s on Mabel and a battery of eight-inchers on Juliet can reach sixteen to twenty klicks west and south of Delta. You pilots be sure to coordinate with the TOC on Jeannie when approaching the area. We don't want anyone colliding with an eight-inch shell."

"That could ruin our day," Dan Ranson observed dourly.

"A Night Hawk will meet you over Jeannie and escort you to the LZ about three klicks south-west. Watch for stumps when you land." Alsos paused. "Any questions?"

Sergeant Harrel asked, "Any larger NVA units in the area other than that reported by the Mohawk?"

"Yes and no. An NVA regiment has been identified just over the border in Laos. One of its battalions has been operating defensively in the area around Jeannie to keep open the supply line east. If there is trouble it will be probably come from that battalion."

Dan Ranson asked, "Can you tell us anything about the LZ?"

"The LZ was cut in a bamboo field. It was the only area where an LZ could be cut, given the terrain and need for speed. Unfortunately its small size allows only one chopper to land at a time. A hundred meters west of the LZ towards Bravo the bamboo transitions to double and triple canopy jungle. Bravo Company is located in that jungle 600 meters from the LZ." He paused again. There were no more questions. "This concludes my briefing. Good luck."

"Thanks, Major," JP said. Then he addressed the group. "Chaplain Deveraux, Sergeant Harrel, Pfc Groves, and one medic ride with me in Mister. Ranson's helicopter. The rest ride in the other one. Let's mount up."

★

Two Huey UH1H helicopters, one slightly above, behind and to the left of the other, flew westward through the night towards Fire Support Base Jeannie. Two thousand feet below a black void stretched wherever one looked. An occasional tiny yellow dot twinkled in the void. Periodically the dark night was streaked by distant red and green tracers. None came close to the two helicopters. Intermittently small portions of the darkness some distance away were turned to day by descending flares. Clusters of brief flashes gave mute evidence of heavy guns firing or impacting shells detonating.

Lieutenant Colonel JP Franklin, Medical Corps, US Army, belted to the canvas bench seat next to the open door, gazed down at the monotonous panorama of black. He speculated what fate might await them should the helicopter make a forced landing. Shuddering at the thought, he shifted his gaze up towards the heavens. A partial moon glowed, bathing a layer of fluffy clouds in yellow.

Releasing the lock on his seat belt, he moved carefully past boxes of medical supplies stacked on the floor to stand between Ranson and Carter. Holding on to the armored seat backs, he surveyed the red-glowing instruments. The altimeter needle was fixed at 2,000 and the airspeed needle vibrated at 95 knots. Carter had the controls. Ranson turned and shouted "We'll be passing over Jeannie any time now, then we'll turn to a heading of two four zero for two minutes, twenty seconds and at 95 knots. That should put us close enough to see the LZ's strobe light."

"Any word on the LZ?"

"It's cold. I just finished talking to the snake leader. He's taking his Night Hawks to support an A Team that stumbled into an NVA patrol eight klicks from the LZ. We're on our own."

Tom Carter touched Ranson's arm and nodded towards the center of the windscreen at a cluster of tiny lights on ground. As the lights passed beneath he banked the helicopter to the left. Ranson reached to the instrument panel and punched the button on the stopwatch. JP watched the magnetic compass numbers peel from 264 to 240. The airspeed needle still indicated 95 knots and the altimeter remained at 2,000. As the sweep hand of the stopwatch completed its second minute a flashing narrow vertical cylinder of light came into view.

"I've got it," Carter said.

Returning to his seat, JP belted. in. "The LZ's is dead ahead," he told the chaplain.

"I wish you had used a less descriptive adjective," the chaplain said.

JP smiled. He cinched his seat belt tight and advised the others to do the same. He had experienced Carter's combat approach to landings many times. It was scary enough in daylight; at night it was terrifying.

The helicopter entered a steep left bank, then suddenly tried to drop from under him. Only the secured seat belt prevented him from becoming airborne. Moments later he was mashed into his seat as the helicopter leveled off. Through the door he saw the vague dark blurred forms of tree tops only a few feet below the skids. If Carter screwed up now they would end up in a gigantic ball of orange flame and black smoke. Death would be quick; it would also be dramatic.

The Huey flared like a goose braking to a landing. Slowing even more, it transitioned to an almost vertical descent. Leaning out the door and ahead, JP saw the white beams of half a dozen flashlights pointed at the ground outlining an LZ not much wider than the Huey's forty-four-foot rotor arc. Both door gunners leaned out, feeding information to the pilots of clearances for the main rotor and tail propeller blade. At the last moment the Huey's landing lights came on, destroying everyone's night vision. The helicopter settled gently to the ground.

Chapter Sixty-Four

Tuesday, October 29, 1970, 2330 hours
Delta Company Night Bivouac Area, Five Kilometers South-west of
Fire Base Jeannie, Republic of Vietnam

The landing light went out, plunging the brilliantly lit LZ into blackness. The engine and rotor noises rapidly subsided as power was reduced to idle. JP, his night vision temporarily destroyed by the glare of the landing light, fumbled for his seat belt lock. The loss of night vision, combined with the insult to his vestibular system by Tom Carter's dramatic approach, left him momentarily blind and dizzy. He took his time climbing out of the helicopter, feeling with his foot for the skid and then the ground. The cargo compartment light came on. Although not very bright, it illuminated the helicopter's interior enough to help re-establish orientation.

"This is your rucksack, Colonel," Groves said, passing it out.

JP took it, then moved quickly from under the rotor wash out to the periphery of the LZ and dropped it on the ground. Father Deveraux caught up to him. "For a couple of seconds I was sure I was going to meet my maker," he shouted over the engine noise, dropping his rucksack beside JP's.

"Carter's a nice quiet guy on the ground, but in the air he's a holy terror," JP shouted back.

"As long as the terror is holy we should be safe."

Just as Sergeant Harrel joined the two a voice behind them asked, "Sirs, is one of you the division surgeon?"

Turning JP made out the outline of a GI, an M–16 slung over his shoulder and a radio on his back. Even in the dark he saw that the GI was not much over twenty.

"I'm the division surgeon, Colonel Franklin."

"Corporal Truette, sir, with some men from second platoon, Charlie Company."

JP introduced Father Deveraux and Sergeant Harrel. "The sergeant will supervise unloading the helicopters."

"We need to move fast," Harrel said. "There's another chopper waiting to land as soon as this one clears the LZ. How many men are with you, Truette?"

"Eleven besides me, Sarge. Five are deployed around the LZ for security. The rest can help unload the chopper and carry supplies. How do you want to work it?"

"One medic and the colonel's driver will stay on the chopper and pass out the supplies to the rest of us. The supplies should be carried out to the perimeter and stacked near the trail that goes back to Delta Company. We'll do the same with the second chopper. After it leaves we'll organize a caravan."

Corporal Truette nodded, then called to his men. "Okay, you guys, form up at the chopper's door, grab a box and take it over there." He shined the beam of his flashlight at the thick trunk of a bamboo tree.

As Truette and his men lined up at the helicopter's door Sergeant Harrel. fell in behind the last man. JP pulled on the chaplain's fatigue jacket. "Come on, Padre, let's go to work." He moved behind Sergeant Harrel. When he reached the helicopter, Groves handed him a cardboard box containing eight one-liter bottles of IV fluid.

JP grunted at the weight as he lifted the box to his shoulder.

"Out of shape, sir?" Groves asked, tongue-in-cheek.

"Don't tempt me into leaving you out here, Groves," JP threatened.

By the time JP returned for his third load the cargo floor was empty. The helicopter's engine noise picked up as it went to take-off power. Dust and debris stung his face and hands. A moment later brilliant light flooded the LZ. The helicopter lifted off, the light went out and darkness prevailed.

Father Deveraux ruminated, "How can the pilots see anything after looking into that light?"

"They are wily fellows, those pilots," JP said.

"What do you mean?"

"One uses the light to land or take off, sacrificing his night vision. The other wears a set of special glasses that cuts out most light, preserving his night vision. When light is turned off, the pilot wearing the special glasses removes them and takes the controls. If there are no glasses one pilot just shuts his eyes, so I've been told by an IP who had too many beers."

The sounds of the departing Huey were quickly replaced by the louder *whup, whup, whup* of the approaching second Huey. This time JP and Father Deveraux turned to face the perimeter, closed their eyes and waited. Again came the bright glare and the hurricane wind whipping up dirt and debris. The helicopter settled, darkness returned and the noise subsided.

"Let's welcome the new arrivals," JP said.

They reached the helicopter just as Tom Moffet and Mark Turley climbed down. "Welcome to LZ Sal Monella," JP shouted. "Have the medics stay on board to pass out supplies. You two join the chaplain and me as beasts of burden. We officers must lead by example."

Behind him Sergeant Harrel grinned.

As soon as the helicopter was unloaded it went to full power. Everyone turned his back to the flying debris. Again brilliant light flooded the LZ; the helicopter lifted up a few feet, hesitated, then began climbing. The landing light went out returning the LZ to darkness. Corporal Truette touched JP's arm. "Colonel. we better get moving. The NVA will probably send a patrol to check on the activity here."

"Right," JP agreed. "Corporal, before we go I want to make one thing clear."

"Sir?"

"You are the jungle warfare pro here. Don't be intimidated by all the commissioned rank. Just tell me what my people and I should do to present the least threat to our common survival."

Truette couldn't suppress a chuckle. "Yes, sir."

"How far to Delta's position?"

"About 600 meters through some pretty dense jungle." Truette shined his light on the mound of stacked supplies at the perimeter. "Those boxes are pretty heavy, Colonel. I don't think anyone will be able to carry more than one at a time."

"You said you have eleven men with you?" Sergeant Harrel asked.

"That's right, Sarge, but five are for security; two leading, two bringing up the rear, and one with me on the flanks. That leaves six to carry supplies."

Sergeant Harrel added himself, JP's driver, Groves, and the four medics. "That's six more," he said.

JP spoke up. "I'm volunteering Doctors Turley, Moffet, and myself."

"There's no way the Church is going to be left out," Father Deveraux interjected.

"That's sixteen people to carry," Truette said. "I counted twenty-one cartons; we'll have to leave five behind."

"We should be able to get along without them," JP said. "We brought more supplies than I thought would be needed."

"In that case we'll booby trap what we leave behind."

A worried Father Deveraux asked, "Corporal, aren't you concerned an innocent civilian or child might find the supplies and set off the booby trap?"

"Father, there are no innocent civilians or children out here; only the gomers and us." He turned to JP and handed him a roll of tape and a knife. "Fluorescent tape, sir. Cut off a piece and stick it on your rucksack. It gives off enough light in the dark to be seen two to three feet away. It will make following the man in front easier. I don't want to lose anyone."

JP sliced off a three-inch length of tape, then handed the tape and knife to Father Deveraux. After sticking the tape on his rucksack, he hefted it onto his back and moved to the pile of supplies. Lifting a carton to his shoulder, he groused, "They haven't gotten any lighter."

The caravan formed into a ragged line. JP was number three man; the chaplain, number four. Each man carried a heavy carton of medical supplies on his shoulder or in his arms plus a weapon except Father Deveraux.

Truette came up to JP. "We're ready to move out, sir. The point man is Pfc Sabin. He has eyes like a cat. His backup is Pfc Leveque. The booby trap is set with six grenades wired as a daisy chain to detonate in series."

"That should get their attention."

The ragged line of twelve GIs, four medics, an operations sergeant, a jeep driver, three doctors, and a chaplain began shuffling along an almost invisible trail. Truette, walking beside JP, spoke into his radio mike. "Bushwack two is moving."

The column passed from the bamboo grove, where moonlight filtered to the ground, into the triple canopy forest, where no moonlight filtered to the ground. JP stumbled repeatedly, each time uttering a subdued "damn it". Once he tripped over a vine, nearly dropped his carton of fluids and almost collided with Leveque. His response escalated to "Goddamnit". This brought an immediate whispered reproach from Father Deveraux behind him. After twenty minutes Truette called a rest.

JP eased his heavy carton to the ground, then helped Father Deveraux with his load. He noticed that the priest was breathing rapidly and almost wheezing on

582

inspiration. "You okay, Father?"

"Just a little old for this kind of activity."

"That makes two of us. I'm beginning to think I haven't made much progress in the last twenty-seven years."

"What do you mean?"

"Back in World War II I carried boxes of ammo at night on jungle trails as a marine Pfc. Now here I am, about to make full colonel, still carrying boxes at night on jungle trails. The only difference is that back then fluorescent moss instead of fluorescent tape was used to keep track of the man in front."

"But you have made progress, Doctor, immense progress. Instead of carrying bullets to take lives you are carrying medicines to save lives. I wish the rest of the world could have made comparable progress."

"You know, Father Pete, you're pretty smart for a priest."

Truette gave the order to load up and move out. JP kneeled down and lifted the heavy carton of IV fluids to his right shoulder. Seconds later the column began moving. The steamy heat of the jungle night, the heavy weight on his shoulder, and the hordes of mosquitoes attacking despite or because of repellent, was draining his strength. At least it wasn't raining.

JP moved closer to Leveque. "How much further?"

"About 200 meters, sir."

"Right now that sounds like 200 miles."

"Would you like me to carry that box, sir?"

"I'd rather you continue carrying that M–79."

The column had traveled another fifty meters when the muffled *boom* of an explosion shattered the jungle's quiet. Rapid explosions quickly followed.

Truette came abreast of JP. "The dinks were closer than I thought, Colonel. It was probably a patrol checking the chopper activity at the LZ."

"When they get a look at what we left behind it won't take them long to figure out the rest," JP said.

"All six grenades went off, sir. I'm sure some of the patrol got wiped out. The rest will be hotdogging after us madder than hell. If they get in front of us we'll be in deep shit… sir. We'd better pick up the pace."

JP stifled a groan.

The new pace, while not double time, was considerably faster than the easy shuffle at which the column had been moving. JP's breathing now came in gasps. He shifted the load from his shoulder to up front, holding it with both hands against his chest. Then his arms began to give out so he moved the load back to his right shoulder, ignoring the pain from the chaffed area. At times asked himself, *What the hell am I doing here? I could have been safe and comfortable at Hopkins as chairman.* After a burst of perverse reasoning he concluded that Hopkins would have been boring. This was better.

"Hold up, Colonel," Leveque whispered. "Pass the word."

JP repeated the message to the chaplain behind him, then moved closer to Leveque. "What's up?"

"We're almost inside an ambush kill zone, sir. Sabin's gone ahead to give the password and clear us through. He'll make sure the guys know dinks may be following us."

Soon the column was moving again. The thought that half a dozen teenagers were waiting patiently somewhere in the dark ahead ready to kill wiped out fatigue. In his haste to get through the kill zone JP kept bumping into Leveque and apologizing. He lost track of time. Then the column came to another stop. A voice beside him said, "I'll take that."

JP handed his load to the outstretched arms of a GI, one of a group sent out to meet the column and escort it. As they neared the Delta Company area they were greeted by the permeating stench of feces. The NVA would have no trouble finding Delta Company. The odor brought back memories of Korea's rice paddies and honey buckets. One thing about wars in the Far East: the smell of feces has remained relatively constant.

The column passed through Delta Company's perimeter. The yellow-white beams of dozens of flashlights punctured the darkness. The ground was littered by a plethora of figures; some vomiting into cat holes, and some squatting as they attempted to direct streams of liquid feces into cat holes. Others lay on their sides in fetal positions, alternately groaning and retching.

JP fell back to Sergeant Harrel. "Have them stack the supplies in a central place, then come and find me. I'll be trying to get a handle on the situation here."

Two figures materialized from the darkness.

"Colonel Franklin?" a voice asked softly.

"Here," JP answered. The figures moved towards him.

"I'm Captain Timmons, Charlie Company commander. I have responsibility for Delta Company's defense. This is Spec Four Wendt, my top medic. I'd like to give you a quick brief, sir."

"Give me a minute to collect the people who came with me, Captain. I want them in on it."

JP quickly gathered the two doctors, division chaplain, Sergeant Harrel, four medics, and his jeep driver. "Looks like we didn't lose anyone on the way here. Okay, Captain, you're on."

"Yes, sir. About eighty people are down and totally ineffective. When they're not vomiting they're squatting. Some are doing both at the same time: others are passed out. My men have dug a bunch of cat holes. I can't vouch for the accuracy of the people trying to use them, so watch where you step. My men have also dug one-man fighting holes in case we're attacked. If you have to use one make a visual or sniff recon before jumping in."

"What's the water situation?" Tom Moffet asked. Water was not only critical for replacement of lost fluids and electrolytes, but for more basic functions such as hand washing.

"It's tight," Captain Timmins said. "We brought extra canteens and a dozen five-gallon cans. My men are limiting themselves to one canteen a day until things settle down."

"Any water points in the area? We brought plenty of purification pills," Moffet said.

"There's a small stream about half a klick from here. I'd rather not send anyone out

584

there until I get a handle on the local tactical situation. The NVA are quite good at setting up ambushes around water points."

"What's the status of the battalion surgeon and Bravo Company commander?" JP asked.

"Both are in bad shape. I saw them a couple of minutes ago. Chris Snyder was squatting over a cat hole and Fred Pinson, in between heaving his guts, kept insisting he had to get back to his troops."

"Would that be Frederick Alphonse Pinson the fourth?"

"Yes, sir. You know him?"

"As a cadet he was my oldest kid's assistant scoutmaster when we were stationed at West Point."

"It's a small world, Colonel."

The sounds of someone close by vomiting emphasized the urgency of Delta Company's predicament. "We'd better get to work," JP said.

"How can I help, Colonel?" Captain Timmons asked.

"Give me all your medics."

"There are only two: Specialist Wendt and Frazer."

JP faced the doctors and medics. "There are six medics here; two will go with each doctor. Start off treating the sickest people first." He turned to the two Charlie Company medics. "Wendt, you and Frazer work with me."

"Where do you want me?" Groves asked.

JP had forgotten his jeep driver. He thought a moment. "Circulate among the doctors and bring them whatever supplies they need." He turned to Sergeant Harrel. "Where are the medical supplies?"

"In a shallow hole over there," Harrel said, shining the beam of his flashlight at stacks of boxes twenty meters away. "There are also a couple of dozen bamboo staves to use as IV poles that Wentdt and Frazer prepared."

"That answers my next question before I had a chance to ask it," JP said. "Many thanks," he told the two medics. "Okay, let's start healing the sick." As the group dispersed he asked Captain Timmons, "Where are Snyder and Pinson?"

"Over on the other side of the supplies. Is there anything else I can do for you, Colonel?"

"Keep the NVA off our backs."

"You got it, sir. If you need me just yell." Timmons disappeared into the darkness.

Father Deveraux came up to JP. "How can I help?"

"Peter, most of these people are miserable. Could you cruise the area and reassure them that food poisoning is like a horrendous drunk: great unhappiness for a short period but recovery in less than twenty-four hours."

"You have a unique way of putting things, Doctor," the chaplain said.

A series of sharp explosions several hundred meters outside the perimeter ripped through the night. A flurry of M–16 fire followed, then subsided except for sporadic single bursts of fire. No one spoke for several seconds.

"The dinks must have walked right into the kill zone," Spec 4 Wendt said.

"It sounded like a wipeout," the medic named Frazer added. "I didn't hear any AK fire."

JP gazed thoughtfully in the direction of the firing, then turned to Wendt and Frazer. "Let's go to work."

★

Fred Pinson, the Delta Company commander, was huddled on his side, knees drawn up to his elbows, groaning. A few feet away lay the battalion surgeon, passed out. JP kneeled next to Pinson and felt his forehead. The skin was warm and dry. The carotid pulse in the neck was 100. He shook Pinson's arm. A groan escaped from Pinson as he tried to focus his eyes on the dark figure beside him.

"You West Point wimps just can't hack it," JP berated his son's former assistant scoutmaster.

"What the hell?"

JP shined a light on his own face.

Recognition came after a long moment of staring. "Major Franklin."

"It's colonel promotable now, Fred. How do you feel?"

"Terrible, sir. I can't stop vomiting or shitting."

"Other than that?

"Other than that I feel fine. Oh... oh Lord." Pinson began retching, sat up and leaned over a small hole in the ground and vomited. Wiping his mouth with his sleeve, he lay back down. "Colonel," he said just above a whisper, "you should take care of my men first."

"I see it in a different perspective, Fred. You're the most important officer in Delta Company. The sooner you are on your feet the safer this company will be. Besides, there are two doctors and four medics already treating your men." He turned to Spec 4 Wendt. "Give him fifty of Thorazine IM and start an IV with Ringer's lactate. Run it in full bore."

"Yes, sir."

"What's my diagnosis?" Pinson groaned.

"You don't want to know," JP said "Well, maybe you do. You and your company are down with food poisoning, probably staphylococcus, possibly salmonella. You are dehydrated from vomiting, diarrhea, fever, and inadequate fluid intake. You're going to be started on IVs to replenish fluids and electrolytes. You'll be given shots to control your vomiting. Someone will bring around a canteen with sugar and salt water. Take sips even though you're nauseated. As soon as you can hold down liquids you'll get oral meds for diarrhea."

Taking a roll of toilet paper from a box that Wendt had set nearby, JP placed it on Pinson's chest. "In the meantime, Captain, I'll leave you with your own personal roll of TP. Rank does have its privileges."

"You're all heart," Pinson groaned, adding, "Colonel... sir."

Chuckling silently, JP told Frazer, "Come on, we've spent enough time on this crock."

They moved several feet to the battalion surgeon's inert form on a spread out poncho. Kneeling, JP found physical findings similar to Captain Pinson: hot, dry skin and fast pulse. Grasping the surgeon's shoulder, he shook it. "Hey, Snyder, you going to sleep all day? There's work to do."

The young doctor stirred, then rolled on his side with his back to JP.

"How's he doing, sir?" Frazer asked.

"Not good. He's burning up; his pulse is 140. Take a feel." He moved back slightly.

Frazer placed his hand on the doctor's face, then pressed his fingers into the mid-neck just in front of the sternomastoid muscle. "Christ, sir," he said, straightening up.

"If I weren't here how would you treat him?"

"Like you did Captain Pinson, sir, with IVs, anti-emetics IM, and follow-on antidiarrhetics, possibly antibiotics."

"Why would you include antibiotics?"

"Because his high fever suggests not only dehydration but sepsis."

"Very good. I wouldn't fault you for using antibiotics, although my preference would be to hold off in acute staph food poisoning, which this appears to be. It's a self-limiting process and recovery is usually in six to twelve hours. Symptoms are due to endotoxins rather than the staph organism. Antibiotics have no effect on endotoxins." JP stood up. "Go ahead and follow through with your recommendations on Dr. Snyder, but omit antibiotics for now. Then catch up to me. I'll find you someone else to work on."

Ten minutes later JP was starting an IV on a third GI when he heard his name called. "Over here," he shouted back, blinking his flashlight off and on.

Captain Timmons appeared. "Sir, we have a problem."

"Some of our people hurt in that ambush?"

"No, sir. We were lucky. Seven enemy were KIA, two got away but left blood trails. We'll follow those at first light. We captured an NVA lieutenant. He's the problem, he's got severe M–16 wounds of both legs."

JP's eyes swept the darkened night lager position. Close to a hundred GIs were somewhere in that darkness, prostrated by food poisoning and vulnerable to an attack by the enemy. As division surgeon his first obligation was their welfare, but he was also a doctor, committed to easing suffering, no matter who was doing the suffering. There was little doubt someone shot through both legs by an M–16 on auto fire was suffering. JP sighed. He would try to meet both responsibilities. "We'll do the best we can until he can be evacuated," he told Timmons.

"Yes, sir. Where do you want him?"

"How about over by the medical supplies. What's his status?"

"He's unconscious."

"He won't need a guard. Just have someone get me when he's there. Any update on what's going on in the area?"

"It's pretty fragmentary, Colonel. There's enemy movement two to three klicks south-west heading in this direction. A Spectre has been vectored towards it." Timmons sighed. "It's going to be an interesting night."

"Your words are of little comfort, Captain."

Chapter Sixty-Five

Friday, October 30, 1970, 0130 hours
Delta Company Night Bivouac Area, Five Kilometers South-west of
Fire Base Jeannie, Republic of Vietnam

"Damn," Lieutenant Colonel JP Franklin said softly. His fourth attempt to start an IV in the arm of a prostrate GI resulted in an expanding mass under the skin. Pulling off the rubber tourniquet, he placed a dry sponge over the growing hematoma and pressed down hard. "Sorry, soldier, I'll have to try the other arm again."

"Sir, have you ever done this before?" the GI moaned.

Despite fatigue JP couldn't suppress a smile. "You wouldn't want to know, soldier." He looked up at Spec 4 Wendt holding a flashlight. "Care to give it a try?"

"Yes, sir. Could you hold this for me?" he asked, extending the flashlight.

Taking the flashlight, JP shined its beam on the soldier's other arm. Wendt wrapped the rubber tourniquet around the upper arm. "Make a fist," he told the soldier. With his index and middle finger he palpated a distended vein in the forearm, cleaned the area with an alcohol sponge, and slipped the needle with its catheter into the vein on the first try. Removing the needle but leaving the catheter, he connected the tubing from the IV bottle to the catheter.

"That was pretty slick," JP said, passing strips of tape to Wendt to secure the tubing to the soldier's forearm. "If word of this gets out my reputation will be ruined."

"Don't worry, Colonel. I'll never tell," Wendt promised.

The soldier stirred. "But I will… sir."

"Give him fifty of Thorazine IM," JP growled. "Be sure to use a large bore needle with a barb."

"I was just kidding, sir," the soldier said.

"So was I," JP said, moving towards another soldier.

Rays of incredibly bright light suddenly penetrated the overhead jungle canopy as if a giant flashlight had been turned on. The faint drone of turbo-prop engines grew louder, then subsided as the light moved away. Moments later, a weird moaning noise resembling a chorus of mooing cows drowned out the fading engine sounds.

"Spectre, sir," Wendt explained. "He uses the light to mark out a target box, then fires into it with miniguns and Gatling cannons. It is awesome."

The moaning noise abruptly stopped and quiet returned. Shuddering at man's inhumanity to man, JP shined his light on a nearby figure sitting on the ground, an M–16 cradled in his lap. "How are you doing, soldier?" he asked.

"Better than an hour ago, sir. I'm almost hungry."

"When did you last throw up?"

"About thirty minutes ago."

"And your last BM?"

"Five minutes ago."

The man's forehead felt cool and his pulse was normal. JP gave him a Lomotil tablet from a bottle he carried in his pocket. "Take it with some water. It should slow down your diarrhea. A medic will be by in a few minutes passing out sugar water. Drink as much as you can but only in small amounts."

"Yes, sir. Thanks."

JP and Wendt started towards the supine form of another GI when shuffling sounds at the perimeter caught their attention. They pointed their flashlights towards the sounds. The bright beams painted four GIs carrying an inert figure on a poncho improvised into a stretcher. "That must be the NVA lieutenant," JP told Wendt. Waving his flashlight, he shouted, "Over here," then pointed his light to the ground nearby. "Set him down there."

The GIs eased the stretcher with its inert bloody figure onto the ground. As the sides of the poncho flattened, blood spilled out. One of the GIs said bitterly, "I should have killed the son of a bitch when I had the chance."

JP shined his light on the GI. He couldn't have been more than eighteen. Kneeling beside the stretcher, JP shined his light on the NVA lieutenant's face. Why wasn't he surprised when he saw that the prisoner was almost as young as the soldier who shot him? Scanning the head, neck, chest, arms, and abdomen he saw no evidence of wounds. Then the flashlight's beam fell on the NVA's legs.

Wendt gasped. "Holy shit, sir. It looks like someone tried to amputate his legs with an M–16."

Both mid-thighs were shredded mixtures of clothing, muscle, and bone spicules. A tourniquet of 1/4-inch nylon rope was tied securely just below each groin. Slight amounts of blood oozed from the wounds.

JP felt the neck for a carotid pulse. It was rapid, weak and thready. "He's in shock," JP told Wendt.

"Yes, sir. He's lost a lot of blood."

"Let's start an IV with Ringer's in each arm. You take the left." Turning to the watching GIs, he pointed his light momentarily to the boxes of medical supplies. "One of you men get a box and put it under his legs."

The GI who had expressed regret over not killing the NVA prisoner moved to the supplies and returned carrying a large cardboard box. His buddy raised the prisoner's shattered legs so the box could be placed beneath, then gently lowered the legs on to the box.

In less than a minute JP and Wendt had an IV going in each arm. "Run it wide open," JP told the medic, then stood and adjusted the flow on the IV he started.

"Should the wounds be covered, sir?" Wendt asked.

"Right. We'll cut off what's left of his trousers, then wrap the wounds with ABD pads and tape."

When they had finished, JP stood and faced the four GIs who were still watching. "Which one of you put on the tourniquets?"

There was a short interval of silence. Finally, one of the soldiers spoke up. "I did, sir."

Much to JP's surprise it was the GI who had shot the NVA lieutenant. "I thought you wanted to kill him." It was more of a statement than a question.

The soldier looked at his boots and said nothing.

"Your tourniquets saved his life," JP said. "There's not much more we can do for him here. I'll try for an extraction with the jungle penetrator at first light."

"Do you want a guard on him, Colonel?" Wendt asked.

"No. He's in no shape to go anywhere. Let's get back to our people. Check him every five minutes and loosen the tourniquets for brief periods."

"Yes, sir."

Three minutes later JP was trying to start an IV on a soldier whose almost continuous retching made it impossible to find a vein. He shouted to Wendt working on another soldier, "I need fifty of Thorazine and a hand here as soon as you finish with that man."

"Be there in two, Colonel."

As JP turned back to the soldier his peripheral vision picked up the shadow of a man half a dozen yards away crawling crab-like.

A GI shouted, "The gomer, he's trying to get away."

Comprehension came in a flash. The wounded NVA prisoner was pulling himself over the ground using his arms and dragging his shattered legs. But he wasn't trying to escape, he was going for an M–16 lying next to a sleeping soldier.

Exploding into a run, JP jerked his .45 pistol from its holster, jacked a round into the chamber and aimed, all in a single swift motion. His finger took up the trigger slack. At this distance he couldn't miss. The NVA was dead meat.

The NVA must have heard the pounding boots rushing towards him and made a desperate lunge for the M–16. Grasping its stock with one hand, he rolled on his back, charged the weapon and brought the muzzle up to point at JP's chest. At that distance the NVA couldn't miss. Yet there was no blast, no searing pain.

An inexplicable force stayed JP's trigger squeeze for a micro second. By then he had reached the NVA. As his momentum carried him past he delivered a vicious kick to the M–16, tearing it from the man's grip and sending it clattering into the darkness. Three GIs grabbed the NVA and pinned him to the ground. Suddenly his body went slack. Blood loss had dragged him into unconsciousness.

A voice behind JP gasped. "Man, that mother is bleeding."

Quickly unloading his pistol, JP shoved it into its holster, then kneeled by the unconscious enemy soldier. "Somebody shine a light." The beams from two flashlights fell on the man's legs. Both tourniquets were gone. Blood spurted from the massive thigh wounds.

"Damn," JP muttered. Reaching over to each groin, he shoved a hand down hard compressing the underlying femoral artery and vein. "Get a couple of tourniquets," he shouted to Wendt.

In seconds Wendt returned with two short lengths of nylon webbing. Kneeling opposite JP, he looped the webbing around the upper thigh of the right leg. JP pulled his hand away as the webbing was tightened and secured. The left thigh was managed in like manner.

"Looks like that did it," Wendt said, noting the hemorrhage had slowed to a mild ooze from both thighs.

"Not bad for government work," JP added. "Let's see what he did to his arms."

A limited hematoma in each forearm indicated where the IVs had been pulled out. "Praise be for small blessings," JP said. "Let's get him back to his bunk."

Three soldiers and Wendt lifted the unconscious NVA's head and body while a fourth supported his legs. Awkwardly, they followed JP's flashlight beam back to the improvised stretcher. Two bottles of Ringer's lactate lay on their sides with most of their contents drained out on the ground.

"How's our supply of Ringer's?" he asked Wendt.

"I'll check, sir." In a moment he returned with two bottles. "Not counting these, Colonel, there are two dozen left."

JP made quick calculations. Most of the truly inundated soldiers were receiving intravenous fluids. Some were beginning to recover. "I think we can spare another two," he said. He and Wendt worked to restart IVs in different veins, now almost flat due to the shock-level blood pressure.

A GI asked, "Sir, would you like me to stay around to be sure he doesn't pull out his IVs?"

JP looked up. The soldier who volunteered to act as "nurse" was the same one who shot the NVA in the ambush, then applied tourniquets to both legs saving his life. "Good idea," he said. Shining his flashlight beam on the man's fatigue jacket, he read aloud his name, "Sanford."

Sanford moved closer to the supine, unconscious NVA lieutenant, kneeled down and shined his light in the man's face, studying it. He then stood up looked at JP. "Sir, do you mind if I ask you a question?"

"Go ahead. I reserve the right not to answer it."

"Yes, sir." Sanford hesitated.

"Did you forget your question?"

"No, sir. My buddies and I wondered why didn't you shoot the gomer when you had the chance. He sure as hell was trying to shoot you."

It was JP's turn to hesitate. He could not tell Sanford he had killed many times in other wars. He could not describe the revulsion he felt when he saw parts of bodies hanging from tree branches knowing he was responsible for such carnage. There was too much he could not tell Sanford. Instead his response was almost no response. "Doctors don't kill people except maybe by committing malpractice."

Sanford laughed nervously. It was apparent he was far from satisfied with JP's answer.

JP castigated himself for his cavalier response. He realized that Sanford was searching for answers to explain his own action. "It's more complicated than that," he added. "To be truthful, Sanford, I'm not sure why I didn't shoot, just like you can't explain why you didn't kill him when you had the opportunity, why you applied tourniquets to save his life."

"Maybe some day the answers will come, Colonel."

"In the meantime you better keep an eye on our mutual patient."

Captain Timmons appeared from the darkness. "Did I miss some excitement, Colonel?"

"I suppose what took place could be described as excitement."

"Sir?"

"Our North Vietnamese guest decided to reward our hospitality by attempting to kill as many of us as he could, starting with me." He described the incident.

"Jesus Christ, Colonel. Why didn't you shoot him?"

"That's the same question put to me by Sanford just as you came up. Frankly, I don't know how to answer it."

Timmons shrugged. "Well, sir, it seems fate is conspiring to keep him alive. Maybe some day he'll be one of Vietnam's great writers or its president."

"Maybe even a doctor," JP said with a smile. Moving several yards away from the GIs and the POW, he motioned for Timmons to follow. "Step into my office, Captain."

"Yes, sir."

"How does it look for getting a Dust-off in here for a hoist extraction?"

"In the dark?"

"That NVA is in such bad shape I don't think he'll last until daylight. Chances are good he'll lose both legs even if he survives."

"Well, sir, enemy activity in the area seems to have subsided. I just finished talking with battalion. The Rangers, Blues and Mike Forces are bedded down in ambushes. Spectre did a number on a probable reinforced platoon. It has enough fuel to stay on station until dawn. The Mohawk hasn't sniffed out any more Communist ammonia close to us. There are two Night Hawks up looking for trouble, and two snakes are parked at Jeannie. They can be on station in five minutes. So to finally answer your question, Colonel, a Dust-off using a jungle penetrator would be reasonably safe here, assuming there is a crew crazy enough to fly out here in the dark to evacuate a wounded enemy soldier."

Timmons removed a cigar from his jacket and peeled away the cellophane. Biting off the end, he spit it out, clenched the cigar between his teeth and lit it. He took out a second cigar and held it out. "Care for a Dutch Masters, Colonel?"

"I'll smoke it later," JP said, grabbing the cigar before Timmons could withdraw the offer. He slipped it into his fatigue jacket pocket, patted the pocket, thanked Timmons and continued. "What you're telling me is that the POW can be medevac'd with minimal risk to the Dust-off?"

"Yes, sir."

"Okay. Send in the request and classify it 'urgent'. Make sure the Dust-off crew are volunteers and understand they are to pick up an enemy soldier."

"Yes, sir." Captain Timmons started to move away, stopped and returned. "Colonel, I'd like to ask you a question."

"Fire away, Jeff."

"Why are we doing this?"

"I wish I knew."

592

Fifty minutes later the familiar sounds of a descending Huey helicopter broke the night's quiet. From the center of the Delta Company compound a vertical column of bright white light began to repeatedly flash upward. JP had just handed a soldier a Lomotil pill when Captain Timmons approached with his RTO.

"Colonel, the Dust-off's about to lower the jungle penetrator. It should come down close to the strobe."

JP nodded. "Wendt," he called out to the Charlie Company medic.

"Yes, sir."

"Round up some help and bring the POW."

"Yes, sir. What about his IVs?"

"Close off the valves, pull the tubing out of the bottles and tape the ends into sterile gloves, then tape the gloves to his arms. The medic in the Dust-off can restart the IVs."

Several minutes later Wendt and four soldiers appeared carrying the NVA POW in the improvised poncho stretcher and set him on the ground near the flashing strobe light. Captain Timmons came from the opposite direction, his RTO trailing. He spoke into the hand mike/speaker. The noise of the hovering Huey became intense. Its hurricane-like downdraft whipped branches violently.

A soldier shouted and pointed. "There it is."

A yellow pipe-like apparatus three feet long and about six inches in diameter descended slowly with its cable from the undersurface of the canopy of branches and leaves. Shining his flashlight upward, JP was pleased to see it had come through the least dense area. When the penetrator was within a foot of the ground Timmons spoke again into his mike. The descent of the penetrator stopped.

"Okay. Let's get him aboard," JP shouted above the helicopter's racket. Stabilizing the penetrator with one hand, he released an arm-like seat, then undid the security straps. The GIs carried the wounded NVA to the penetrator, lifted him to a sitting position and lowered him onto the seat bar while JP guided his legs so as to straddle the seat. Wendt then secured the NVA to the penetrator with the straps.

"Colonel," Timmons called out, "the pilot's reporting engine temp in the red. He said to move it."

JP checked each strap to be sure it was secure, then told Timmons, "All set. Take him away."

A moment later the POW began to slowly rise. He disappeared into the canopy, breaking off pieces of branches. A large chunk of branch hit JP on the head. He gingerly touched the expanding lump. "The son of a bitch is getting his last licks," he growled.

"What was that, Doctor?" a voice behind him asked.

JP turned. "Father Deveraux, why are you always around when I wish you weren't, and never around when I need you?"

The priest grinned. "Because when you don't want me around is when you need me most."

"Oh Lord, here comes a battlefield homily."

"Actually, you've given me an idea for a sermon. Come by Sunday morning and you'll get the full blast."

"Me go to a Catholic Mass? I'd be thrown out of the Episcopal Church."

"Have I ever told you that Episcopalians make the best Catholics?"

"Peter, why is it I never win an argument with you?"

"That's because the Lord is on my side. Who or what do you have on yours?"

"Logic, Father, logic."

"That's not as good."

"I give up. How are things going in the rest of this field hospital?"

"About twenty of the very sick have already started to recover. Your two medical colleagues and their assistants are about to finish up. They said to tell you one of them will make rounds through the rest of the night. They'll call you if they need you."

JP had planned to stay up and circulate among the ill soldiers, but Mark Turley and Tom Moffet were mature, competent, and conscientious physicians. They could be trusted to act responsibly. Suppressing his innate inclination to micromanage, he pulled out Timmons's Dutch Masters cigar and unwrapped it. Biting the tip and spitting it out, he flamed the other end and blew out great clouds of smoke. "After I've smoked this thing," he told Father Deveraux, "I'm going to get some sleep. It's sure nice not to be needed."

★

Dawn had come at 0530 hours but sunlight failed to penetrate the jungle canopy and early morning mist until an hour later. JP had been awake since 0430 hours. Unable to go back to sleep he wished, fervently for the sun to hurry up and rise. Several feet away the division chaplain snored placidly and nearby Specialist 4 Wendt snoozed silently. JP decided to let both sleep unless they were needed. After washing his face with a small amount of water from his canteen, he brushed his teeth, rinsed his mouth, combed matted thinning hair, slapped on his fatigue cap, and started to make rounds. He almost stumbled into Chris Snyder, the battalion surgeon. "What are you doing up? I was sure you would be dead by now."

Snyder laughed. "If I had gotten any worse I would be dead."

"How do you feel?"

"I'd like to crawl into a hole and sleep for a week."

"If you feel that way you better lay back down."

"No, sir. I need to start acting like a battalion surgeon instead of a wimp with a cheap hangover. I feel as if I let down Delta Company when they needed me most."

"You're too hard on yourself, Chris. Food poisoning has defeated armies, lost wars, and wiped out nations."

Snyder searched JP's face. "I never read that in any history book."

JP grinned. "Neither did I. I just made it up. Have you had a chance to see Captain Pinson this morning?"

"Yes, sir. He's still pretty sick. I started another IV on him. He was up most of the night with dry heaves. If he doesn't come around by noon I think I'll medevac him to the hospital."

Two cheerful voices greeted them. "Good morning, Colonel, good morning Chris." Tom Moffet and Mark Turley joined them, both holding full canteen cups of coffee.

JP stared at the two. "Well, well, the gruesome twosome. What a sorry pair of officers. Your uniforms look as if you slept in them and they're filthy. You both need shaves and have bags under your eyes."

"You don't look so good yourself, Colonel," Tom Moffet said, "and your disposition is foul."

"It might improve if my junior officers would share some of their C-ration coffee."

"Be happy to. How about you, Chris?"

"No way, thanks."

JP removed his canteen cup from its canvas holder on his web belt then slipped the canteen back into the holder. Locking the cup's handle, he held it out. Both Turley and Moffet poured part of their coffee into the cup. Taking a timid sip, JP almost burned his lip. "How did you get it so hot?"

"One of the GIs showed us how to use C–4 to heat the water," Mark Turley said.

JP took another careful sip. "This is excellent, just excellent. Thank you, gentlemen." He sipped again. "How are the troops this morning?"

"About half the company is on its feet, so to speak," Tom Moffet said. "Most of the others should be up and about by this afternoon. There are a couple of people I'm worried about; Mark has another. They will need to be medevac'd if they don't show improvement by noon."

"Does the division preventive medicine officer have any idea how this near disaster came about?" JP asked Tom Moffet.

"As a matter of fact I do."

"I can't wait to hear."

"This is from the Delta Company first sergeant.'

"He should be a reliable source."

"Yes, sir. The day before yesterday the company cooks set out marmite cans of hot food on the helipad pad in the morning to be picked up by the resupply chopper and taken out to Delta for its noon meal. The chopper never showed because of mechanical problems. The cans stayed on the pad in the hot sun until that evening. One of the cooks noticed them out there and had them put in the reefer."

"Oh, oh," JP said. "I think I know where this is going.'

"The next morning the cans were brought out to the pad again. They sat in the sun until 1600 hours, when the resupply chopper finally picked them up and took them out to Delta. I think you know the rest of the story."

"Not quite. What was the chow?"

"Ham, potato salad and peas."

"Potato salad; I should have known."

Father Deveraux joined the group. "What's so bad about potato salad? It's my favorite."

"It's also one of the best culture medias for the rapid growth of Staphylococcus aureus."

Chapter Sixty-Six

Saturday, November 7, 1970, 0600 hours
36th Infantry Division Staff Bivouac Area, Phong Sahn, Republic Of
Vietnam

The persistent ringing of phone dragged Lieutenant Colonel JP Franklin from a deep sleep. Only three hours ago he had collapsed on his bunk still fully clothed after finishing a marathon case at the 96th Evac. Shaking the remnants of sleep from his head, he reached for the phone. The caller was the 9th Brigade commander, Colonel Paul Prather, and his voice was loaded with anger.

"What's up, Paul?" JP asked. He and Prather had been friends since both were stationed at West Point in the early 1960s.

"A big time problem with the new doctor you assigned yesterday to the 4th/9th at Maggie. I'm ready to court martial the son of a bitch."

"You mean Captain Snell?"

"That's exactly who I mean."

"Good God. He hasn't been in your brigade twenty-four hours. What's he done?"

"It's what he hasn't done. He spent last night here at Quang Dien in your clearing company. This morning he was supposed to go out to Maggie. Hank Cosgrove, his battalion commander, made a special trip in from Maggie to welcome him and take him out there. Snell refused to get in the helicopter."

'What?" JP came wide awake. "Did he give any reason?"

"The candy ass claimed his extensive education and training made him too valuable to risk flying over enemy terrain and living in the jungle for six months."

"Didn't Hank describe the beauty of Vietnam that surrounds Maggie?"

"Come on, JP, this is serious. Snell is facing big trouble. Did he indicate to you yesterday that he would do this?"

"I spent most of morning briefing him. He wasn't happy about his assignment to Maggie, but gave no hint he would refuse to go. In fact he was looking forward to flying in a helicopter for the first time in his life and spending the night with the doctors in Bravo Med. Something must have spooked him."

There was a pause before Colonel Prather answered. "You may be right. One of our slicks was shot down yesterday evening. Three GIs were killed and one wounded. The AC and peter pilot we badly burned. All of them were taken to Bravo Med for emergency care. Snell may have helped take care of them."

"That would have shaken any new guy his first day."

"Look, JP, the last thing I want to do is court martial a scared doctor just in country, but if Snell isn't out at Maggie by noon today that is precisely what I will do."

596

JP did some fast thinking. Snell was in a pissing contest with his superiors, a contest he would surely lose. "Paul, can you hold off until I come down there for a father and son talk with Captain Snell."

"I was hoping you would do that. I won't take any action until I hear from you. By the way, I've been alerted to be at the general's office day after tomorrow for your promotion.'

"That is the big day from what I hear."

After Colonel Prather was off the line JP called the JAG, Lieutenant Colonel Jesse Wilmont, and described Captain Snell's actions.

The 36th Division chief lawyer's response was grim. "It's clearly a case of failure to obey a lawful order from a superior. By so doing he denied medical care for the wounded and sick in a combat zone as well as avoided hazardous duty. That puts a very serious spin on the charge. If this doctor wants to avoid committing professional suicide he'd better get his butt out to Maggie."

"If he were found guilty what sort of penalty might he expect?"

"Anything from a suspended sentence and a dishonorable discharge to life imprisonment at hard labor. Given the anticipated mood of a court martial board made up of line officers who daily risk their lives and the lives of their men, the doctor would almost certainly face prison time at hard labor. In a declared war he could face a firing squad."

"Thanks, Jesse. That information gives me some talking points."

Next, JP called the aviation detachment. The duty NCO answered.

"This is Colonel Franklin. I need my helicopter for the morning to go to Quang Dien and hopefully out to Maggie."

★

Saturday, November 7, 1970, 0810 hours
Bravo Medical Clearing Company, Skunk Patch, Quang Dien, Republic of Vietnam

Lieutenant Colonel JP Franklin found Captain Richard Snell, M.C., USA, in the mess hall eating breakfast by himself. He took a seat across the table from him.

Captain Snell looked up. "Colonel Franklin, I wondered about the chopper that just landed."

"Look, Dick, I hate to ruin your breakfast but we need to talk."

"There's nothing to talk about, Colonel," Snell said defiantly. "I saw what happened to those people from the helicopter that was shot down. I don't want to end up like one of them."

"I think you'd better hear me out."

Snell sipped coffee from a mug. "Okay."

JP let the lack of protocol slip by. This was not the time to get military with a scared doctor determined to commit professional suicide. "Dick," he began, "the military functions on the basis that orders will be obeyed, otherwise there would be chaos. That is why the military will take a very dim view of an officer who refuses to obey an order from his commander, particularly in a war zone."

"What could they do, shoot me?"

"If this bizarre activity were a declared war you would definitely run the risk of a firing squad."

Captain Snell paled.

"That is unlikely. What is possible, in fact probable, is that you will face a general court martial. If you are convicted for failing to obey a lawful order from a superior to avoid hazardous duty, you will spend some time in prison at hard labor and be given a dishonorable discharge. Not many doctors have been court-martialed for failure to obey: in fact, you may be the first. The board could decide to send a message with your sentence."

JP saw that Snell had stopped eating and was listening attentively. He continued. "A general court-martial conviction is equivalent to a federal felony conviction. You will never be able to vote, hold a federal or state government position, be issued a narcotics license, or own a weapon. States vary on granting a medical license to a convicted felon and hospitals have even stricter staff requirements. I doubt that a training program would accept a felon into residency. A dishonorable discharge will deny you all VA benefits, including loans, GI Bill, and job preference.

"Dick, we all face risk out here and we all, at one time or another, are forced to deal with what can best be described as a pathological, paralyzing anxiety about being killed or injured. It's a part of war that cannot be avoided. Each person must deal with that anxiety in his own way or it will destroy him."

The look on Captain Snell's face suggested that JP may have gotten his attention. "I'm going to get some breakfast and sit at another table," JP said standing up. "If you decide to go out to Maggie I'll take you out there in my chopper and help break the ice with your commander. If you refuse to go, I'll arrange for a defense counsel. From the way Colonel Prather and Colonel Wilmont talked this morning when I discussed your actions you can expect pre-trial confinement."

With that JP left a thoroughly shaken Captain Richard Snell and headed for the serving line. He was hungry. Loading a tray with French toast and bacon, he took his tray to a vacant table, sat down and began eating. Minutes later, Captain Snell came over with his tray.

"May I join you, Colonel?"

"Please do."

"Colonel, if your offer still stands I'm ready to go out Maggie. I'll need a few minutes to get my gear."

"My Huey is parked just off the clearing company helipad. Warrant Officer Ranson is the aircraft commander." He looked at his watch. "I'll meet you there at 0900 hours."

When JP had finished breakfast he went by 9th Brigade Headquarters. Luckily Colonel Prather was in his office.

"How do things stand?" Prather' asked.

"I had to hit Captain Snell over the head with a 2 x 4, but I think I got his attention.

I'll take him out to Maggie and square things with Hank Cosgrove."

"Thanks, JP. I appreciate the support. I'll send word out to Hank to expect you."

"Snell thinks we're going straight out to Maggie, Paul. But once we're airborne I'll take him on an orientation tour of the 9th Brigade AO. We'll be delayed getting out to Maggie until around 1300 hours."

"JP, you sneaky rascal."

★

At 0900 hours when JP walked to his helicopter Dan Ranson and Tom Carter were examining the tall propeller. "See anything exciting?" he asked.

"Just a nick at the tip of the blade," Ranson said. "I doubt if it has unbalanced the prop. I'll have it checked when we get back to Phong Sahn."

JP examined the small nick, then felt it with his fingers. "It doesn't feel like much."

Ranson nodded and started for the AC's door. "Do we go to Maggie from here, Colonel?"

"In a convoluted way. That shoot down yesterday spooked Captain Snell about flying in helicopters. I don't know if he'll show up to go to Maggie he's so scared. If he does show up I want to demonstrate that flying around Vietnam is reasonably safe. Until we're airborne act as if we are going to Maggie. Once we have Captain Snell where he can't back out we'll take him on a grand tour of the 9th Brigade AO and end up on Maggie."

"Sir, I never realized you were so devious."

"Marines always rise to the occasion. What's the weather out west?"

"Rain and fog but nothing unmanageable."

"Here comes our VIP now," Tom Carter said, looking towards the Bravo Med orderly room.

When Captain Snell reached the Huey he handed his duffel bag and suitcase to the port side door gunner, then climbed on board.

"Take the seat by the door," JP suggested. "You'll get a much better view from there than where I'm sitting."

After Captain Snell was belted in JP passed him his flight helmet. "You can listen to the flight crew with this on. If you want to talk with them press this button." He held up the transmit button on the cord.

While Snell fiddled with the helmet JP called out, "All set Dan."

The electric starter whined. In a minute they were airborne and climbing.

"How long is the flight to Maggie?" Snell asked JP.

"Ordinarily twenty minutes, but first we're going to go on a tour of the AO."

Captain Richard Snell blanched.

★

Saturday, November 7, 1970, 1530 hours
Eight Kilometers South of Phong Sahn at 2,000 Feet

"Colonel, do you want off at the VIP pad?" Dan Ranson asked JP over the intercom.

"Negative. Drop me off at the 96th Evac."

There was a chuckle in the headset. "I thought Captain Snell would bail out when you told him we were not going straight to Maggie."

JP grinned evilly, recalling Snell's reaction. "He's a better man for it, Dan."

Four hours after leaving B Med at Skunk Patch, a well-informed Captain Richard Snell, M.D., Medical Corps, US Army Reserve, entered the battalion TOC at Maggie for yet another briefing, this time by his battalion commander and two company commanders.

The itinerary had included every firebase in the 9th Brigade. Snell met his battalion surgeon contemporaries and went on tours of their firebases and aid stations. Each battalion commander or exec personally briefed Snell in the TOC. After a lunch of fried chicken on Jeannie they visited two OPs. Then, on impulse, JP took Snell to Karl Dahlgren's special forces camp. JP was greeted with such adulation by the Hmongs that Captain Snell was truly overwhelmed with envy. Sergeant Dahlgren gave Snell a briefing that rivaled that of the G–2 at division. Finally they had flown along the Laotian–Vietnam border and "drifted" over to Laos.

"I can never figure out where that damned border is," Dan Ranson had complained.

JP identified parts of the Ho Chi Minh trail for Snell, lectured him on the significance of the trail and his battalion's part in interdicting supplies and troops moving east from it. The high point of the flight came when Snell spotted a huge elephant moving leisurely across a clearing. He scrambled to his pack for his camera.

Dan Ranson turned to look at JP who nodded. The Huey dropped until it was close enough for Snell, an amateur photographer, to go almost berserk taking dozens of photographs before the elephant stampeded. Euphoric over what he had just photographed, Snell shouted to JP, "Wait until my wife sees these pictures." It seemed that Captain Richard Snell, M.C., US Army Reserve, had just discovered Vietnam.

Now as the Huey neared the 96th Evacuation Hospital JP speculated on what the day had cost the US taxpayer. All things considered, keeping Captain Snell out of Leavenworth Prison was not a bad investment.

★

Saturday, November 7, 1970, 1545 hours
96th Evacuation Hospital, Phong Sahn, Republic of Vietnam

Walking through the emergency room, Lieutenant Colonel JP Franklin, M.C., USA, was greeted warmly by nurses and medics. It was a good feeling to be accepted by the clannish hospital personnel. Soon he would leave their friendship to begin anew in another hospital, this time not as a consultant but as the hospital commander.

Passing out of the emergency room, he continued down the covered boardwalk to the POW ward, knocked on the door and waited. A tall burly MP opened the door. "Can I help you, Colonel?"

"I'm Colonel Franklin, the division surgeon, here to see a North Vietnamese lieutenant brought in a week ago with severe leg wounds. I don't know his name."

"Yes, sir. That would be Second Lieutenant Dai. He's the one in traction next to the nurses' station. You will have to leave your weapon with me, sir."

JP undid his web belt with its holstered pistol and handed it to the MP.

"Any hidden weapons, sir?"

JP nodded, pulled up his right trouser leg, undid the hideout knife that Sergeant Dahlgren had given him, and passed it to the MP.

The MP studied the knife, then JP, but said nothing. He appeared fascinated by the knife and impressed that a doctor would carry it.

Walking to the nurses' station JP recognized the duty nurse, Captain Trina Ferguson, a perky young woman whose blonde hair was cut so short it was boyish. However, the remainder of Captain Ferguson was definitely girlish. Engaged to an infantry company commander, she had extended her time in Vietnam by six months so that their tours would end simultaneously and they could be married in the States.

"Good afternoon. Trina," JP said. "How is Lieutenant Dai?"

Captain Ferguson looked up. "Hi, Colonel." She handed him Dai's chart. "Both legs are still warm with good pulses."

"Any neurological deficits?"

"No, sir. He can wiggle his toes and he can feel pin pricks."

"Incredible. I was sure he'd lose at least one leg. The vascular surgeon and orthopods have wrought a miracle."

"Two miracles: one for each leg," Ferguson said. "We're lucky to have Major Danforth here."

"Mass General trains its vascular surgeons well. Lieutenant Dai had the best."

"Unfortunately Lieutenant Dai doesn't see it that way."

JP looked at her questioningly.

"Colonel, he's very depressed about being wounded and captured."

"I'm not sure I wouldn't feel depressed if someone tried to amputate my legs with an M–16."

"It's more than that, Colonel. He's convinced our only purpose in keeping him alive is to pump him for information."

After thumbing through Dai's chart JP returned it to the nurse, then walked to the foot of Dai's bed. Dai, dressed in a pajama top and boxer shorts, lay supine with both legs hung up in traction. Bulky dressings covered his mid-thighs. His hair was cut short, almost to the scalp, which made his youthful handsome face appear even more youthful. His eyes were closed as if asleep.

JP pulled a chair to beside the bed, sat down, and studied the man he came within a hair of killing. When Dai failed to stir after several minutes Captain Ferguson came over and gently shook his shoulder.

"Lieutenant Dai, you have a visitor."

"He understands English?" JP asked.

"Yes, sir, and speaks it better than you and I... well, better than I anyway," she said, smiling.

Dai opened his eyes and fixed them on JP.

"Lieutenant Dai. this is Colonel Franklin, the division surgeon." Captain Ferguson said by way of introduction.

Dai continued to stare. "Are you here to get intelligence from me?"

JP chuckled. "You are only a second lieutenant, Dai. You couldn't possibly know anything that would interest me."

The hint of a smile touched the corners of Dai's mouth but quickly vanished. "Then what is it you wish of me?"

"A question has occurred to me."

"I expected it would."

"This has little to do with military matters."

"Then what?" Dai squinted at JP. Recognition suddenly lit his face. "You are the doctor who treated me in the jungle, the one who almost shot me."

"I'm impressed you were able to see and remember."

"That is not all I saw."

JP waited.

"I saw how quickly that pistol appeared in your hand, how quickly it was loaded and aimed, not at my chest but at my head. You say you are a doctor, but no doctor handles a weapon with such speed and control. An ordinary soldier would have aimed at my torso. You aimed at my head. You are no ordinary doctor. You, sir, have been trained to kill."

JP, surprised at Dai's perceptiveness, was momentarily speechless.

"So, tell me, Doctor, why did a trained killer hesitate to kill an enemy about to kill him?"

JP chose his words carefully. "Your perception about me is accurate, Lieutenant, but only up to a point."

"I don't understand."

"A long time ago I was a marine who fought the Japanese. The Marine Corps had trained me well to kill. I am a doctor now, committed to saving lives, not taking them. The other night in the jungle you saw my training as a marine surface when I perceived a threat to me and my comrades. When I began to squeeze the trigger my training as a doctor stopped me from firing."

"You would have let me kill you?" Dai said, incredulous.

"That is something you and I will never know, Lieutenant."

Dai was silent for almost a minute. "In many ways you remind me of my father. He talks in riddles as do you."

"Is he in the North Vietnamese Army?" JP asked.

"He is a general," Dai said, then realized he had revealed more than he should have.

"He must be very proud of the son who became an officer."

Dai smiled bitterly. "My father is a surgeon who specializes in head and neck surgery. In the war with the Japanese he was a soldier of the Viet Minh. He fought the Japanese. He and others rescued many American airmen and furnished important intelligence to the OSS. After the war your country rewarded their loyalty by supporting France in taking away our freedom and independence. Your country stood aside while the French threw my people into medieval dungeons. General Giap's wife died in one; his sister was beheaded by the French in such a prison."

JP was not familiar with Indochina's history, but something in the way Dai spoke rang of truth.

Dai continued. "My father wanted me to become a doctor, but I decided I must first help unite my country and drive out the foreigners." He smiled wanly. "My countrymen have been driving out foreigners for centuries. We have become quite good at it."

JP looked at his watch. "I must go, Lieutenant," he said, standing up. "Before I do I would like to ask the question I planned to ask before we were somehow sidetracked."

"I will answer only if it has no military significance. I owe you that much for not killing me."

"You had the opportunity to kill me, Lieutenant, and did not. The question is why?"

Lieutenant Dai stared at JP, then turned his head away. "After I was shot I was convinced I was dying," he said, his voice distant. "My legs were useless, the pain intolerable and I was bleeding. If I didn't die I was certain to be a cripple, reduced to begging on the streets to survive. I wanted to die, Colonel, if not of my wounds, then by my enemy. It would redeem my disgrace of capture. You were my enemy: yet if I had shot you then you could not have killed me." Dai turned to face JP. "It was my misfortune I chose an enemy to kill me who no longer believed in killing."

JP shook his head. "You Vietnamese are such strange people. Will I ever understand you?"

Lieutenant Dai looked up at JP and smiled. "That is precisely what I was thinking about you Americans."

★

The main officers' club on Phong Sahn was a long barn-like structure on a bluff looking out over the South China Sea. A thickly thatched roof and bamboo matted sides covered a solidly built structure that had withstood many typhoons. A spacious interior was kept comfortably cool by the thick roof and air conditioning. Most of the floor space was filled with plastic covered tables and chairs. An area clear of furniture served as a dance floor and doubled as a stage for traveling USO shows. Across one end of the room a counter functioned as a bar from 1600 hours until closing at 2300 hours. Soft drinks, cheeseburgers, fries, and steaks could be obtained after 1100 hours. An Akai reel-to-reel tape deck wired to half a dozen Sansui speakers blasted out music and songs in a variety of beats and accents. The relaxed informality and lovely Vietnamese waitresses made the club a favorite hangout for young warrant officers and company grade officers. Senior officers often stopped there after work for a cold beer.

Since the club was only 300 meters from his hooch, Lieutenant Colonel JP Franklin sometimes dropped by for a quiet, relaxed beer on the covered patio. He often brought his mail or writing material. Today there was no mail, so he brought a writing pad and pen, intending to write Kathy about the young NVA lieutenant. After picking up a can of cold beer at the bar he headed out to the patio and selected a table in a secluded area. Popping open the can, he took a long refreshing drink, then gazed east across tranquil blue waters to the horizon. His wife and kids were only 12,000 miles away. How he missed them. A familiar voice dragged him away from his introspection.

"Hi, Colonel, mind if we join you?" A smiling Dan Ranson, dressed in flowered short pants, a colorful short-sleeved shirt, and sandals stood with a can of beer in his hand. Beside him was a grinning Tom Carter, similarly dressed and equipped.

JP stared at the them. "You two are a disgrace in those outfits," he snapped.

"We'll take that as affirmative, sir," Ranson said as he and Carter pulled out chairs and sat down.

"I'm sorry I missed your promotion, Tom," JP said. "but it's never too late to offer congratulations."

"Thanks, sir. I heard you were humping in the jungle with grunts at the time."

"If we had gone much further the grunts would have had to carry me." He fished in his fatigue jacket pocket, removed two shiny silver first lieutenant's bars and placed them in front of Carter. "I wore those through most of my Korean tour. I asked Kathy to send them to me after I learned of your promotion. When you get back to the real world I hope you will wear them."

Carter picked up the two silver bars, examined them carefully, then slipped them into his pocket. "Thanks. Colonel. They will mean a lot to me."

"I hope to give you my captain's bars one of these days," JP said.

"Promotion was not the only big event for Tom last week, Colonel," Dan Ranson said.

"Oh?"

"He was upgraded to AC."

Carter grinned. "Mr. Ranson had to get rid of me before I killed him with my flying. Upgrading me to AC was the quickest way."

"Does your mother know about your upgrade and promotion?" JP asked.

"Yes, sir. I called her on MARS. She sounded proud and upbeat. She asked for a photograph of the ceremony."

JP smiled. "She must be mellowing in her old age." He changed the subject. "I understand you both have asked for transfer to the Dust-off detachment."

"Yes, sir," Tom Carter said. "With you leaving after you are promoted things won't be the same. Besides, flying Dust-off missions is as close as we can come to what you doctors do."

JP took a sip of beer, then set the can down. "There's always a next step."

"You mean medical school?"

Ranson joined in. "We talked about that a lot when we were flying together. We wondered if a couple of over-the-hill aviators could become doctors?"

604

"Anything is possible, and you are hardly over the hill. Age shouldn't be a problem. How old are you?"

"Twenty-two," Ranson answered.

"How were your undergraduate grades?"

"Not very good. I quit college after two years to sign up for pilot training. Actually I quit before I got thrown out for academic deficiencies."

"You would be surprised how many brilliant surgeons overcame similar backgrounds," JP said, recalling his own dismal three-year undergraduate academic record. "These days a low GPA, even for just a year or two, is a severe handicap to medical school admission, but handicaps are meant to be overcome, Dan. You will have two years in which to redeem yourself academically. If you maintain a near 4.0 average during those two years, particularly in courses known to be premed killers, like organic chemistry, comparative anatomy, and genetics, and if you do well on the MCATs and dazzle the admission committee with your footwork during interviews, you have an excellent chance of being accepted."

"That's encouraging, sir. My military commitment ends in nine months. It's a toss-up between medicine and law as to what I go for."

"Let me give you a some fatherly advice, Dan. Unless you want to be a doctor more than anything else in the world, forget medical school." JP turned to Tom Carter. "What about your grades at the Academy?"

"Three point eight nine."

"Smart ass," Ranson said.

"Listen up you two," JP said, "you both are shoo-ins for the army scholarship programs once you're accepted to medical school. The scholarship furnishes full tuition, books, and fees plus pay and subsistence of a second lieutenant."

"I didn't realize the army had that kind of program for doctors," Ranson said.

"There's also one for dental, law, vet, and theology schools," Carter added.

"When either of you start sending out applications, let me know. I'll be happy to write letters of recommendation and do anything else I can to help."

"Thanks, Colonel," both men said.

Ranson stood. "Sir, if you will excuse me I'm going to get a haircut while the barber is still here."

JP studied the pilot. "Good decision, Dan. You're about two weeks overdue. With that shirt and long hair you look more like a hippie than a chief warrant."

After Ranson left JP and Carter quietly sipped beer and watched small fishing boats bob up and down a quarter mile from shore.

Tom Carter turned to JP. "Do you know when you are going to be promoted?"

"The rumor is it will be the day after tomorrow in the general's office. The head shed is being pretty closed mouth about it."

"You don't want to stay on as division surgeon?"

"I'll have too much rank, Tom. Besides, I want to command a hospital. Rumor is that it will be the 98th Evac at Long Binh, but I haven't been able to confirm that. Even my spies at Med Command have gone underground."

"I wrote to my mother that you would be promoted. She said to congratulate you.

Melissa Hardaway also sent her congratulations. She said you have come a long way from the marine Pfc she knew during the war."

"How is your mother, Tom?" JP said softly.

"She's fine. Did you know the President nominated her to the Court of Appeals?"

"Yes, I did; I wasn't at all surprised. She is a remarkable woman and that appointment is well deserved. She'll sail through the confirmation hearings."

"Sir, I realize my mother is a brilliant judge. Her brilliance and dedication to law have been a wall between us ever since I was a kid. Now that I'm an adult I feel I hardly know her."

Carter continued. "From the way you two greeted each other on the ICU after my surgery it was obvious your relationship was more than casual."

JP, recalling the episode, smiled but remained quiet.

Carter went further. "Sir, can you tell me anything about my mother that would help me know her better?"

JP fiddled with his can of beer. It was almost empty. He held up the can; a Vietnamese waitress hurried over. "How about you?" he asked Carter.

"Yes, sir." He leaned towards JP expectantly.

"Two more beers, please," JP told the waitress. "No, make it three."

"You want glass?"

JP shook his head, then turned to Carter. "I met your mother in September 1943. I was almost eighteen, a marine Pfc on weekend liberty in San Diego. Your mother was eighteen, a pre-law student at the university who would start law school the following summer."

"At nineteen?" Carter asked, incredulous.

"No. She would still be eighteen."

"Good God, what a brain," Carter said, obviously impressed. "How did you two meet?"

"I was reconning churches in Dago for one that would let me use the organ to practice. The first church I checked out the organist was having a problem with a siphon."

"A what?"

"Carter, didn't they teach you anything at West Point?"

"Nothing about pipe organs.

JP sighed, then explained with great patience, "A siphon is a pipe that that continues to sound after the key is released. I managed to fix it. The organist was so impressed that she gave me carte blanche to use the organ."

"That was Melissa Hardaway."

JP looked at Carter suspiciously. "Tom, you know more than you're letting on."

Carter blushed. "Melissa and my mother are very close. She's been like an aunt to me. John Hardaway encouraged me to go to Annapolis. I decided I didn't want to end up on anything that could sink, so I picked the Military Academy."

"I heard he's a vice-admiral assigned to MACV."

"Yes, sir. He may get another star when he goes back to the States."

"There's hope for us mustangs," JP said. "When I was in Korea his destroyer

606

supported my unit with naval gunfire and flares. When he found out I was in one of the units he was supporting he visited me, bringing enough beer and steak for the entire battery."

"That sounds like the admiral," Carter said.

"To get back to how I met your mother... I was practicing the Bach Passagalia and Fugue in C-minor when she walked in, listened for a while, then invited me to a church supper for servicemen. Afterwards we played ping-pong until after eleven. Did you know your mother is a hell of a ping-pong player?"

"No, sir, we never played ping-pong; she never had time."

"Challenge her some time. She'll probably whip your aa... butt like she did mine. Because we finished playing so late I took her home on the bus. Lucky for me it was the last bus. Your grandmother insisted I spend the night. By the time I left on Sunday night your mother and I were deeply in love. I had never been in love before and neither had she. It hit us like tons of bricks."

The waitress brought three cold beers and set them down.

"I've got these," JP said, placing script on her tray. After she left he picked up his beer. "To the new first lieutenant, and his mother, the about-to-be-confirmed justice of the appellate court."

"I'll drink to the latter," Carter said, touching JP's can with his.

JP continued. "Your mother and I were together every time I could get liberty. We knew I'd be leaving soon to go overseas. I went AWOL twice to be with her; my buddies covered for me. I even bought a forged three-day pass to show MPs if I were stopped."

"You, sir? Forged pass? AWOL?" Carter sounded disbelieving.

"Good God, Carter. Haven't you ever been in love?"

Carter turned red. "Sir, if you and my mother were so much in love, why didn't you marry?"

"A lot of my buddies did get married before shipping out to the Pacific. Your mother and I came close, very close."

"What stopped you?"

"Not what but who. Melissa talked to me one day about the heavy casualties that marines were taking in the Pacific. She told me if I really loved your mother I would not risk saddling her with a crippled husband or leave her with memories of a dead husband and perhaps a baby who would never know its father. I hated Melissa for those words, but I knew she was right. I loved your mother too much not to heed them."

"How long were you overseas?"

"A year and a half. When I returned your mother was finishing her first year of law school with a 4.0 GPA and an invitation to join the law review."

"That's my mom," Carter said, not without an overtone of pride.

"I spent a week in Denver with her, attended classes, did research in the law library. It was so boring I almost went nuts. I learned in one week to hate law and lawyers."

"You and Shakespeare," Carter said, laughing.

"Your mother loves the law, Tom. It's her entire life, other than you."

"I know, sir, She pressured me to go to law school after I finished the Academy." Carter grinned. "I decided flying would be more fun." He became serious. "When you came back from the Pacific why didn't you marry her?"

"Because I was getting ready for the invasion of Japan. The same constraints prevailed then as when I went overseas the first time."

"Damn it, sir, I'm confused. You could have married her after the war."

"No. We both were nineteen when I came back, but I was not the same person she had known before I went overseas. I did things in the war I never dreamed I would ever do. I lost two of my best friends, another was crippled. I carried a heavy load of guilt for having survived the war intact when others had given so much. I had given nothing. I had no goals, no commitments. All I had were memories. I tried college, but after three years it had become an academic disaster while your mother made straight As in law school. I began to hang out in a local tavern, drinking beer with the other vets and telling war stories. By the time your mother graduated from law school number one in her class I was at the bottom of my class, about to be tossed out of college for academic deficiencies."

"Jesus Christ, sir, you? I can't believe it."

"Believe it. I missed your mother's graduation from law school after promising to be there. It was the only time in my life I failed to keep my word. I don't think she has ever forgiven me. Two months later I got my Dear John."

A long interval of silence ensued. Finally, Carter broke the quiet. "Thank you for sharing that with me, Colonel."

"If you breathe a word of this conversation to your mother I will rip the rotor off your chopper and wrap it around your neck."

"Sir, could I ask one more question."

JP sighed. "All right, Lieutenant, what is it?"

Carter remained quiet.

"Well, are you going to ask?"

"No, sir, I guess not."

At that moment Dan Ranson returned from the barber. JP and Tom Carter stared at his head.

"Something the matter?"

"Good God, Dan, who cut your hair?" Carter asked.

"The Vietnamese barber. The GI barber had left. Why?"

"I'm betting the barber was VC and used a machete."

Chapter Sixty-Seven

Monday, November 9, 1970, 1340 hours
36th Medical Battalion, 36th Infantry Division, Phong Sahn, Republic of Vietnam

A warm afternoon sun had chased away the overcast sky and heavy rain of the morning, bringing into focus the beauty of the Vietnamese seashore. The South China Sea, angry and violent just a few hours before, was now calm and serene. It was a day befitting promotion ceremonies, especially promotion from lieutenant colonel to colonel. According to tradition the rank of such magnitude as full colonel empowered its recipient to leap over tall buildings in a single bound and give advice to God.

Lieutenant Colonel James Paul Franklin, Medical Corps, US Army, walked along the sandy seashore several hundred meters from his medical battalion headquarters and contemplated his promotion. In a little over an hour the subdued black leaf of a lieutenant colonel on his collar point would be replaced by the subdued black eagle of a colonel. Although Lieutenant Colonel Franklin (Promotable) had no desire to leap over tall buildings in a single bound, nor did he aspire to give advice to God, he did want to command a large army hospital in a combat area. The eagle to be pinned on his collar at 1500 hours would be the ticket to that command. A few days after his promotion he would fly 600 miles south to take command of the 98th Evacuation Hospital on the huge military base of Long Binh, twenty miles from Saigon. Of the three hospitals on Long Binh, the 98th, with 425 beds, was the largest. According to rumors it was also the hospital with severest morale and discipline problems. Nevertheless, commanding the 98th Evac would be the culmination of a dream nurtured from the days when he was a platoon commander in Korea.

The warm moist breeze blowing off the South China Sea and the near-solitude of the shore did much to calm JP's growing excitement and anticipation. A hundred meters away a young soldier and his German shepherd dog frolicked along the shore as they gradually moved towards him. Suddenly the shepherd alerted and growled in his direction. A word from the soldier quieted the big dog, who then sat quietly watching JP with suspicion as he drew nearer.

The soldier saluted. "Pfc Moxley, sir, from the scout dog platoon. This is Pfc Bruno."

JP returned Moxley's salute, then glared down at the sitting dog. "Private First Class Bruno, don't you know you are required to salute an officer?"

Moxley sprang to his dog's defense. "Sir, Bruno is a sharp dog; he knows his regs. Show the colonel, Bruno. Salute."

Bruno emitted a doggie whine, then lifted his right front paw to his nose.

JP quickly snapped a return salute in return.

"He's going to apply for OCS when we get back to the States, sir," Moxley said.

"He'll probably make general before I do. Can I pat him?"

"No sweat, sir, as long you're not VC."

Kneeling down, JP patted the great dog's head. "Bruno," he whispered, "I get promoted to full colonel today."

The shepherd whined again, lifted his right paw and placed it in JP's right hand.

★

Monday, November 9, 1970, 1455 hours
Headquarters, 36th Infantry Division, Phong Sahn, Republic of Vietnam

Dressed in clean, starched fatigues and spiffed jungle boots, Lieutenant Colonel JP Franklin (P) entered the division headquarters building. The foyer and hallway was crowded with lieutenant colonels and colonels standing in a loose double line stretching to the closed door of the commanding general's office. JP joined the end of the line.

"It's about time you showed up," a voice said.

"Don't you people have jobs?" JP retorted.

"He hasn't been promoted yet, but he's already talking like a colonel," another voice added.

JP grinned. In the past six months these men had grown from total strangers to something akin to brothers. Working closely with them in a give and take atmosphere, he had developed great respect for their integrity, intelligence and commitment. Almost all had at least one tour as line officers in combat before joining the division; some had two. Now they were getting in their last digs, for after the eagle was pinned on his collar things would never be the same. Line officers took rank seriously, especially the rank of full colonel. They would no longer address him by his first name, or "Doc". He would soon be "Colonel" or "Sir".

The approach of a low-flying helicopter caused heads to turn towards the sound. The helicopter passed so low over the headquarters it shook the building.

"Hotdog pilots," a voice muttered.

The door to the general's office opened. Colonel John Witherington's 6'3" frame filled the doorway. "Gentlemen, please come in," he said, stepping aside.

The cluster of senior officers filed into General Webster's spacious office. The general, standing in front of his desk, motioned for JP to join him. His aide, Captain Selznick, stood beside the general. On the general's desk lay a packet of papers, a Bronze Star medal, an Air Medal, and a single black subdued eagle. The division's two brigadier generals, Barrett and Simpson, were several feet to the general's left. Both generals smiled and nodded at JP.

JP would miss flying with General Barrett, the ADC for maneuver. On those flights the general kept up a steady chatter on Indochinese history, terrain analysis, and local tactical activities. He gave learned lengthy discourses on conventional and unconventional jungle warfare, and thought nothing of crossing the border and low-leveling along the Ho Chi Minh trail. A paratrooper from World War II, General Barrett had jumped into St. Mere Eglise with the 82nd Airborne Division as a second lieutenant two months out of OCS. Later he fought in Greece and Korea.

John Witherington looked at his watch and cleared his throat. "Gentlemen, rest easy. We're waiting on some VIPs." He looked at JP, winked, then continued. "After the ceremony refreshments will be served in my office across the hall. Tonight happy hour will be on Colonel Franklin."

"Way to go," someone muttered.

A shuffling of feet in the hall drew everyone's attention to the door. Navy Commander (Father) Mick Icardi entered followed by Marine Major General Carl Mueller and finally a naval officer dressed in khakis, three stars on his collar. JP was surprised and pleased to see Mueller and Icardi, but was stunned by the appearance of the short stocky vice-admiral. The wrinkled weather-beaten face was perplexingly familiar.

General Webster spoke. "Gentlemen, the 36th Division is honored to have three special guests from our sister services. Vice-Admiral John Hardaway, Naval Liaison to MACV, Major General Carl Mueller, Commanding General, First Marine Division, and Commander Michael Icardi, division chaplain, First Marine Division."

JP's mind spun back in high gear back to World War II. The admiral, then a lieutenant commander, and his wife Melissa had befriended him when he was a seventeen-year-old marine stationed at Camp Pendleton. He and then Ann Gallagher had spent many happy weekends at the Hardaways' beachside home outside San Diego before he shipped out to the Pacific. Their paths crossed again early in the Korean War at Pohang Dong, a sea coast town. Hardaway, a commander, was the skipper of a destroyer that provided flare and naval gunfire support for JP's unit. JP studied the man's face. Except for wrinkles, white hair, and a pound or two weight gain, the years had been kind to John Hardaway. That he would travel hundreds of miles to attend the promotion of a friend he hadn't seen in twenty years spoke much for the man.

General Webster nodded to Captain Selznick, who stepped forward and stiffened.

"Attention to orders."

Every officer in the room, including the admiral and four generals, came to attention. Selznick, speaking in a clear, crisp voice, read orders awarding the Bronze Star to Lieutenant Colonel James Paul Franklin. The citation described his actions in controlling the epidemic of Shigelosis in the Montagnard village at Phu Than and the saving of many lives. "His loyalty, diligence, and devotion to duty were in keeping with the highest traditions of military service and reflect great credit upon himself and the United States Army."

General Webster removed the Bronze Star medal from its padded container on his desk, stepped in front of JP who stood rigid. After pinning the medal to JP's fatigue jacket over the left breast pocket the general stepped away, remaining at attention.

Captain Selznick continued. This time he read orders and citation awarding the Air Medal to JP "...for sustained hazardous aerial flights over hostile territory in support of ground forces in the Republic of Vietnam." General Webster pinned the Air Medal next to the Bronze Star, then faced the assembled officers.

"Stand at ease."

As the officers relaxed General Webster continued. "I will now depart from the traditional promotion ceremony by giving up my prerogative to pin the eagle of a full colonel on Colonel Franklin. Major General Carl Mueller, US Marine Corps, acting on the premise of once a marine, always a marine, graciously consented to fly here to do the honors. In World War II General Mueller, then a captain, was the commanding officer of then Private First Class JP Franklin, US Marine Corps. As told me by General Mueller, the last words he spoke to Pfc Franklin before transferring him was, 'Get the hell out of my sight before I change my mind and throw you in the brig.'"

JP flushed, recalling the captain's anger after he and his buddy admitted to collapsing half a dozen army squad tents while drunk. The memory brought back a smile and then a flush of sorrow. His buddy, the Chief, wounded in the spine on Iwo Jima, had died six weeks later.

Major General Carl Mueller, United States Marine Corps, marched briskly to face JP, his face frozen.

Again Captain Selznick intoned, "Attention to orders," and again the officers snapped rigid. Selznick rapidly read orders promoting Lieutenant Colonel James Paul Franklin, Medical Corps, US Army, to Colonel with date of rank October 19, 1970.

General Mueller removed the subdued black lieutenant colonel's leaf from JP's right collar and handed it to Captain Selznick. General Webster then passed a subdued black eagle to General Mueller, who pinned the eagle on Lieutenant Colonel JP Franklin's right collar, making him a colonel.

"General," JP said, "I can't think of anyone I would rather have pin that eagle on me except my wife Kathy."

"Congratulations, Colonel," General Mueller said, shaking JP's hand. "You have done the Marine Corps proud, albeit you did it in the army." He removed a folded paper from his pocket. "Colonel McDougall sent me this note and requested I give it to you." He handed JP a folded piece of paper. JP flipped it opened, glanced at the printed words and blushed. His World War II platoon sergeant had written: "The army must be really hard up for colonels." JP quickly stuffed the note into his pocket.

As General Mueller moved away Admiral Hardaway grabbed JP's hand, shaking it vigorously. "Good going, mustang. From what I've heard about you at MACV this promotion is well deserved."

JP eyes reddened. "Admiral, I can't tell you how much your being here means to me."

"You'll get your chance. I'm spending the night with you."

General Webster injected, "I offered the admiral my bungalow, but he insisted on sharing your hooch. He will be with me the rest of the afternoon for briefings. We'll see you tonight at the mess."

The remaining two generals came by next, followed by the rest of the officers. Lou Marchenko punched JP on the arm. "Come by before you leave for Saigon, Colonel. I'll orient you in on the challenges of commanding a hospital."

"Thanks, Lou." JP searched the room. "Isn't Kristy coming?"

612

Marchenko handed JP a small pink envelope. "She asked me to give this to you. She planned on coming but was asked to cover the POW ward for a nurse whose husband just came in from six weeks in the bush."

"That sounds just like Kristy. I'll try to stop by tomorrow and give her a chance to congratulate me."

"How about lunch? I'll make sure she's there."

"Done," JP said, slipping the envelope into his pocket. He looked up just as Commander (Chaplain) Father Michael Icardi grabbed his hand, then fingered the eagle on JP's collar. "I always figured you to be officer material," he said, hugging JP.

"From what my spies in the 1st Division tell me, you're up next."

"Only if the Lord wills it."

"Will you and the general be staying for dinner this evening?"

Icardi shook his head. "Sorry. The general and I head back to Danang as soon as we can break away."

JP looked the priest in the eyes. "Mick, did you have anything to do with getting General Mueller and Admiral Hardaway up here?"

"Like the utterances of the confessional, that information is classified."

"You miserable schemer. You'll never change," JP said, hugging the priest again.

General Webster interrupted. "Colonel Franklin, I'll be taking General Mueller to his helicopter in about ten minutes. Will you see that Father Icardi is there?"

"Yes, sir."

Admiral Hardaway came up to JP. "If you will show my aide where your hooch is he'll drop off my gear."

JP nodded. After the admiral and generals left he punched Father Icardi on the arm. "Come on, Mick. I'll give you a lift to the VIP pad. Old crippled marines shouldn't have to walk."

★

Monday, November 9, 1970, 1510 hours
VIP Pad, 36th Infantry Headquarters. Phong Sahn, Republic of Vietnam

As JP and Father Icardi approached General Mueller's silent helicopter the door gunner and a second lieutenant with naval aviator's wings stepped from the cabin, came to attention and saluted. They were unable to mask their surprise when JP returned the salutes and added, "Semper Fi."

Father Icardi explained. "Don't let the uniform and rank throw you. He used to be one of us. I'm not sure where he went wrong."

JP grinned. "The Marine Corps didn't have a medical corps. I wasn't about to join the navy."

The co-pilot and door gunner chorused, "Right on, sir."

The officer occupying the right seat in the cockpit turned and introduced himself as Captain Konrad, the aircraft commander. He indicated the young second lieutenant. "That's my peter pilot, Lieutenant Feingold. We're both Canoe U-graduates."

"I won't hold that against you," JP said, "particularly when you both showed such superb judgment by taking commissions in the Marine Corps."

Father Icardi chuckled. "I wonder if Admiral Hardaway would agree with you."

"Admiral Hardaway loves the navy," JP, said, "but he's the consummate admiral. He thinks in four dimensions, navy, Marine Corps, army and air force, not necessarily in that order. From what I remember of his philosophy, all four are part of the same family dedicated to getting the job done. His being here attests to that."

JP moved to the helicopter's doorway and scanned the spotless interior, leather plush seats, banks of radios, and electric binoculars. He nodded approvingly.

Father Icardi put his arm over JP's shoulders. "One more promotion and you'll get one of these."

"It will never happen, Mick."

Father Icardi saw the glint of bitterness in his friend's eyes and changed the subject. "It was nice having you only a few miles away after all these years."

"Senior chaplains must have meetings in Saigon, Mick, and my hospital is only twenty miles away. Let me know when you're in town; I'll send a Dust-off for you.

"Aye, aye, mon Colonel," Father Icardi said, saluting with a flat-handed French salute. As soon as JP returned the salute Father Icardi held out his hand. "You owe me a dollar, Colonel. That was your first salute after promotion."

JP started for his wallet, then hesitated. "No way. A German shepherd named Bruno saluted me when I told him I was practically a colonel. As far as I'm concerned, Bruno gave me my first salute."

"It won't wash, Colonel," the priest said, still holding out his hand.

JP took out a dollar in script from his wallet and slapped it into the outstretched hand.

Father Mick smiled and handed it back. "Put it in the offering… the Catholic Mass at the 98th Evac. The hospital commander is expected to attend all services."

The helicopter's starter whined. Over his shoulder JP saw an approaching sedan. He grabbed Icardi in a bear hug, then pushed him into the helicopters doorway. "Get out of my AO, padre."

★

Monday, November 9, 1970, 2130 hours
General's Mess, 36th Infantry Division Headquarters, Phong Sahn, Republic of Vietnam

Vice Admiral John Hardaway, USN. and newly promoted Colonel JP Franklin, M.C., USA, sat relaxed on the patio of the general's mess. Each held a brandy and a just lit Dutch Masters cigar. The admiral puffed vigorously on his cigar until its tip glowed red in the dark. He studied JP for a moment. "The last time we met was after your platoon started a firefight with a North Korean regiment at Pohang. At the time you were hell-bent to stay a line officer for the rest of your career. Now you're a rather famous surgeon. What happened?"

"People change, Admiral. After two wars I came to the conclusion saving lives was more noble than taking lives." He exhaled a cloud of cigar smoke.

"Melissa and I managed to keep up with your career through Marie Gallagher. After she died in '68 we were in the dark until Ann wrote that you were the surgeon who operated on Tom. That was a shocker."

"Nothing compared to my reaction when I saw Ann with Tom on the ICU at Walter Reed."

"You recognized her after almost twenty-five years?"

"Ann was part of my physiology for over five years. I could never forget her or what she meant to me."

"When Melissa learned from Ann that you were coming out here she told me to check up on you. I did precisely that. So, Colonel, you can run, but you can't hide." The admiral chuckled at his own humor.

JP smiled and sipped his brandy. "Ann told me that Melissa was on the faculty at San Diego."

"She has her PhD and is professor and chair of the organ department. She also spends two months a year giving recitals and teaching in the US, Canada, and Europe. Next summer she's scheduled for a series of recitals in Australia and New Zealand."

"You must be very proud of her."

"I am. You may have wondered why we never had children. You're a doctor, so I can pass this on to you. In 1939 Melissa sustained a ruptured uterus in a car accident. A hysterectomy was done to save her life. Her music, the organ, and teaching became her passion. She is phenomenal, both as a teacher and a performer."

"I hope I can hear her play one of these days."

"You can. She has a dozen recordings under the 'Classic' label. I'll have her send you some tapes. What about you? Melissa reminded me that as a teenage marine you were a very proficient organist who loved Bach."

"The last time I touched an organ was at the Fort McPherson chapel twenty years ago. I played the Bach Fantasia and Fugue in G minor for Kathy trying to impress her before I proposed."

"Obviously you succeeded," the admiral said, laughing. He then became serious. "JP, you have a fine future in the army. Your records indicate you will receive credit for C&GS for your work in the 36th. You are scheduled for the War College when you DEROS. I read strong recommendations in your file including one from General Webster that you be promoted to brigadier general as soon as eligible."

JP shook his head. "It's not going to happen, Admiral."

Admiral Hardaway puffed thoughtfully on his cigar, then set it on an ashtray on the table beside him. "Mind telling me why?"

JP took a long slug of brandy. His eyes watered. He momentarily lost his voice as the brandy burned his throat.

Admiral Hardaway laughed. "You marines have never learned to drink anything more sophisticated than beer."

When JP recovered he said, "Sir, I will be candid with you."

"Please do."

"After what I have learned in Vietnam I have decided to retire as soon as my payback time is up for accepting promotion." He swirled the remnants of brandy in his glass. "Except for college and medical school, admiral, military life is all I've know since I was seventeen. Even in medical school I was active in the reserves. I loved the military, its high ideals and its values. To me Indochina was a small colored spot on the world map, an area about which I knew little and cared less."

He sipped his brandy, then continued. "At Walter Reed my wards stayed filled with casualties from Vietnam; I was so busy trying to put young men back together that I paid little attention to the politics of the war, I took for granted that my country was an honorable country. I trusted it not to commit its young men to war unless the reasons were compelling. And once committed I was confident my country would be dedicated to winning."

Admiral Hardaway puffed on his cigar. "Maybe it's best this conversation end."

JP drained his brandy. The three stars on Vice-Admiral Hardaway's collar blurred. "You asked, sir," he said, his speech slightly slurred.

Admiral Hardaway remained silent.

"I wasn't in Vietnam long before I started picking up on things I didn't want to know: the absurd tactical restrictions, limitations, and bizarre objectives imposed on ground and air commanders, tactics so costly in men yet doomed to accomplish little. Admiral, I learned our young men are being nickel and dimed to death to support a corrupt ally, many of whom are in collusion with the enemy."

JP stopped, took a drag on his cigar and exhaled. "I have to tell you, sir, this war sucks."

Admiral Hardaway set his brandy on the table and gazed at streams of moonlight on the South China Sea. "It is so peaceful and tranquil out there," he said. Pointing to a cluster of lights a mile to the west, he asked, "What's over there?"

"The 96th Evacuation Hospital. If a chopper brings in a casualty you will see the helipad lights go on."

The admiral seemed to study the hospital's lights and at the same time debate something within himself. Finally, he looked over at JP. "What I tell you next is highly classified. Please treat it as such."

"Yes, sir."

"The US has already begun disengaging in South Vietnam. Equipment is being transferred from our stocks to the ARVN. Over the next two years the entire defense of South Vietnam will be turned over to ARVN. The US will be gone."

"But sir, the ARVN couldn't achieve a stand-off with the north when they were supported by half a million US troops with its tactical air. It is ludicrous to believe they will achieve greater success on their own. We have lost over 50,000 of our finest young men; there are hundreds of thousands more who have been crippled. What the hell was it for?"

Admiral Hardaway sighed. "JP, like you I began my military career at seventeen as an enlisted man. I cherished the same values that motivated you to choose the military for a life's work. I too have been plagued by the misgivings you described." The admiral's voice hardened. "And like you, Colonel, I raised my hand in an oath to obey

616

the orders of my military and civilian commanders. As long as you and I wear these uniforms, JP, we are bound by that oath. There can be no other way."

An immense blinding bright flash lit up the sky over the 96th Evac. A powerful *boom* swept through the quiet night. Moments later, yellow flames flickered upward. A distant siren began its undulating wail.

JP catapulted out of his chair. "Oh my God," he gasped.

"What was it?"

"A rocket; it hit the hospital."

Chapter Sixty-Eight

Monday, November 9, 1970, 2210 hours
96th Evacuation Hospital, Phong Sahn, Republic of Vietnam

Eleven minutes after the rocket detonated at the 96th Evac, newly promoted Colonel JP Franklin drove on to the hospital compound in a borrowed jeep. Wood smoke hung heavy in the air, burning his eyes and throat. He paused briefly at two parked fire trucks. Their headlights and powerful spotlights brightly illuminated the charred skeletal remains of a hospital ward. Shadowy figures, their shouts a mixture of Korean and English, scurried about dragging hoses. Shifting gears, JP drove on to the emergency room and parked near the entrance.

Pushing through the swinging doors, he entered the emergency room. Cold air rolled over him carrying the sweet smell of blood. He saw little activity except for two medics aggressively mopping the floor. Six stretchers, parallel to each other, lay across metal sawhorses. Six dead lay on the stretchers, their bodies outlined by the green sheets covering them. Beyond the stretchers a nurse and medic sat at a desk talking.

Moving rapidly past the stretchers, JP stopped at the nurse's desk.

The nurse, a first lieutenant, looked up. Her eyes, red and puffy, went from the colonel's insignia and caduceus on JP's collar to the name tag over his right breast pocket. "Can I help you, Colonel?"

"Any survivors?"

"Yes, sir, four. They're in surgery." Her voice wavered. "This makes no sense, Colonel. Why would they rocket a hospital? They killed some of their own people." She pulled tissues from a box on her desk, wiped her eyes, then blew her nose.

JP shook his head. "Nothing in this war makes much sense, Lieutenant. I'm going to the OR. Maybe they can use an extra hand."

Passing out of the emergency room, he headed down the covered boardwalk and turned into the passageway leading to the OR suite. The doors to the OR opened and Colonel Lou Marchenko emerged. When he saw JP he grasped his arm, "I'm glad I ran into you. Let's go to my office."

"Can't it wait, Lou? I could be of help in there," JP said, gesturing towards the OR.

"They're managing okay," Marchenko said firmly.

JP shrugged. Docilely, he walked with Marchenko down the lengthy boardwalk to the administrative part of the hospital. Marchenko was unusually quiet. As they entered the commander's office Marchenko flipped a switch on the wall by the door, turning on overhead fluorescent lights. "Have a seat," he said, nodding towards a worn leather sofa against one wall. JP sank into one of its frayed cushions. Marchenko pulled a GI metal armchair opposite him and sat down. A shudder passed through JP. In the bright fluorescent light Marchenko's face was a mask of sorrow.

Marchenko leaned forward. "There's no easy way to tell you this, JP."

"For Christ's sake, Lou, tell me what?"

"One of the KIAs was a nurse."

A hand grabbed at JP's gut and squeezed. "No," he moaned. "No, not Kristy."

"I am so sorry. God, I am so sorry."

JP buried his face in his hands. His body convulsed with the sheer intensity of his grief. After several minutes he gained some control. "What happened?"

"She was taking vital signs on that hardcore NVA lieutenant. She must have heard the rocket. According to the lieutenant, Kristy leaned over him as if to shield him just as the rocket came through the roof and exploded. A frag, one that would have almost certainly hit the lieutenant, hit Kristy instead."

JP felt he too had received a mortal wound, so great was his agony. "Oh God, Lou," he moaned, "she saved my life and I wasn't there to save hers. I was drinking brandy and smoking a cigar while she was dying. God, forgive me." Suddenly he turned on Marchenko, eyes blazing. "What kind of route step hospital are you running?" he shouted. "One of your own people is wounded and your collection of amateurs couldn't save her?"

Marchenko turned red. His voice became almost inaudible. "Listen to me, JP, Kristy died instantly. The frag severed her spine, aorta, vena cava, and tore up her lungs. She bled out in seconds. There was nothing anyone could have done."

JP stared at the floor, then up at Marchenko. 'That NVA son of a bitch; if I had killed him when I had the chance Kristy would be alive."

"I don't think Kristy would have seen it that way. You're a doctor, JP. You save lives; you don't take lives."

"I was better at taking lives. Maybe I should start taking a few NVA lives starting with that little NVA bastard."

"Go easy on the lieutenant, JP. He is so depressed about Kristy he tried to take a gun from an MP and shoot himself."

Minutes ticked by in quiet. Finally, JP stood up. "Where is she, Lou?"

"In the emergency room. I'll go with you."

As they walked JP realized that Marchenko himself must be suffering in his own personal hell. "I'm sorry I lost it back there, Lou. Kristy was very special."

Marchenko squeezed JP's arm. "It's okay, I understand."

They entered the emergency room and stopped at the nurse's desk. Colonel Marchenko told the duty nurse, "Colonel Franklin is going to stay with Colonel Goulden for a while."

The lieutenant nodded understandingly.

Marchenko led past the first five stretchers and stopped at the sixth. "I'll be in my office," he said softly. "Stop by on your way out."

As JP moved to the head of the stretcher he sensed he was being watched by the nurse. His hand trembled as he grasped the edge of the sheet. Lifting it and folding it down, he gazed at Kristy's face. In death, as in life, Kristy was a beautiful woman. Reaching down, he gently brushed hair from her forehead.

The doors at the far end of the ER slammed opened and two GIs walked in. JP heard one tell the nurse that they were from Graves Registration. The nurse handed him some manila envelopes. The GIs moved to the first stretcher, lifted it and carried it out. Minutes later, they returned for the second stretcher. After five stretchers had been carried out they came for the sixth.

As they neared JP glared at them. "Get the hell away from her," he growled.

The GIs, shocked at the vehemence of his words and awed by the eagle on his collar, backed away, confused.

The nurse threw a look in their direction, then quickly came over. "Come back in an hour," she told the GIs.

"Yes, ma'am," they said in unison and quietly left.

JP stood by Kristy's body as if an honor guard. In his grief he lost all concept of time. He was startled when the nurse touched his arm. "Colonel," she said softly, "the people from the Graves Registration are back. They will have to take Kristy."

JP slumped, acquiescing to the reality of Kristy's death. He leaned over and gently kissed her forehead. It was the first time he had ever kissed her. Then he pulled the sheet over her face, turned and walked out of the emergency room.

★

It was after midnight when JP stepped through the door of his hooch. Admiral John Hardaway, dressed only in a T-shirt and shorts, was on the guest bunk, his back propped against the wall. Papers were spread out on his lap and the bunk. A half-cocked .45 pistol lay on the bunk within easy reach of his right hand; a partially open attaché case sat on the floor beside him. He regarded JP over the tops of his black-framed glasses. "I heard it was bad."

JP sat down wearily on his bunk. "Yes, sir. Six killed; three POWs, two medics, and a nurse."

"Did you know the medics or the nurse?"

"I've known the nurse since we were both second lieutenants during the Korean War."

He described his hospitalization in Korea and how Kristy not only saved his life but oriented him towards medicine. He reviewed the circumstances of her husband's shoot down and the operation at Qui Tavong that almost rescued her husband.

"Anything new on him?" Admiral Hardaway asked.

"Just recently a Hatchet Force reported learning of a prison in Laos somewhere near the Vietnamese border. POWs are being collected there before being shipped north to Hanoi."

Admiral Hardaway looked at JP, incredulous. "You know a great deal of classified material for someone who has no need to know."

"I have grateful patients and loyal friends," JP said flatly without apology. "Speaking of friends, Admiral, I'd like to ask you something."

The admiral nodded.

"Is there a possibility Kristy could be awarded the Medal of Honor?"

That got the admiral's attention. "On what basis?"

"On the basis she sacrificed her life to save the life of a patient. Isn't that the same as the soldier who throws himself on a grenade to save his buddy?"

"I'm afraid that would be a stretch for at least three reasons, JP. First, she couldn't have known the life of her patient was at risk in time to act; second, no woman has ever received the Medal of Honor; and third, the life she saved was that of an enemy."

"You're right, sir. In war we're supposed to kill our enemies."

"In a perverse way that happens to be true."

"If Kristy had followed that edict she'd be alive and her enemy would be dead."

"That too may be true," Admiral Hardaway said. He paused, as though in deep thought, then said, "Have her commander submit papers for a Silver Star. I'll see what I can do when they gets to MACV."

"Thanks, sir."

"When do you leave to take command of the 96th Evac?"

"It was to be in about a week, but I'm going to delay."

"Considering how anxious you have been to command a hospital you must have a compelling reason for the delay."

"Yes, sir, but that information is classified."

The look Vice-Admiral Hardaway gave JP made it clear he was not accustomed to that kind of answer.

JP relented. "It's really classified information, Admiral. Please treat it as such."

"You can trust me, JP," the admiral said with the hint of a smile.

"The Hatchet Force I told you about, it has located a POW camp in Laos about fifty klicks north-west of Qui Tavong. Eight US and seven ARVN are in the camp; all are in very bad physical condition. A Bright Light team is going out day after tomorrow to attempt a rescue."

"What's that got to do with your delay going to the 98th?"

"I'm going as the medic. I don't know when I'll be back."

The admiral sat straight up. "The hell you say. How did you arrange that?"

"The One Zero leading the team is a grateful patient and a friend. I imposed on our friendship."

Hardaway shook his head. "There must be a better explanation."

"No, sir. If Kristy's husband is alive there's a good chance he may be in that camp. If he is rescued I want to be the one to break the news that Kristy was killed. It's the least I can do for Kristy."

"JP, do you have any idea what those SOG people do on those missions?"

"My friends have kept me well informed."

"And you consider yourself qualified to go as a member of a SOG team?"

JP said nothing.

"I understand your motives, JP, and I admire your courage. Right now I don't have much regard for your judgment."

"Sir?"

"You are not the highly trained marine warrior you were twenty-five years ago. You are a middle-aged has-been warrior, out of shape physically, rusty as hell with weapons, and lack the intensive constant training required of SOG team members.

Would you be able to kill an enemy about to kill one of your team members?"

JP stared morosely at the floor.

"Hell, you couldn't even shoot an enemy who was going to kill you. If you go on this mission you will put yourself and your team members in great peril, compromise the mission, and probably get yourself killed or worse, captured. I can't believe General Webster gave you permission to go."

JP shook his head. "He hasn't; I haven't asked him."

"You dumb jarhead; are you trying to get yourself court-martialed?"

"Admiral, after today I really don't give a shit."

"Since you told me your plans in confidence I won't violate that confidence by informing General Webster. However, unless you give me your word you will not participate in the Bright Light mission I will call MACV and have the mission cancelled."

JP reached down, untied his bootlaces, kicked off his boots and stretched out on his bunk. Raising himself up on an elbow, he looked at Admiral Hardaway. "You have my word, sir. Please don't scrub the mission." Flopping on his back, he stared at the ceiling. The tears came easily.

★

The memorial service for Kristy and the two medics killed in the rocket attack on the hospital was held in the division chapel three days later. On the altar two steel helmets, each with a red cross, rested in front of the brass cross. Between the helmets was Kristy's white nurse's cap. Off to one side, concealed under a white cloth, a tape recorder preserved for the next of kin the audible portions of the service. The chapel was almost filled with doctors, nurses, and enlisted staff from the 96th Evac and the 19th Surg. Former patients, both enlisted and officers, somehow made it in from the jungle for the service. That they would come was the ultimate tribute to Kristy.

After Kristy's death JP put out the word there would be no going away party. However, when the NCOs of the medical battalion headquarters organized a beer, steak, and cigar party for him he felt obliged to attend. Kristy would have wanted him to go.

The day after the memorial service JP's replacement arrived.

Lieutenant Colonel William Harlingen, forty-three, had been chief of surgery at the 85th Evacuation Hospital at Phubai. Vietnam was his second war. During the Korean War he had been a navy corpsman with the 1st Marine Division. Wounded at the Chosin Reservoir he spent over a year at Bethesda Naval Hospital recovering. The experience spurred him on to medical school and an army general surgery residency at Walter Reed.

JP kept Harlingen busy eighteen hours a day with orientations, meetings, and flights to units in the 36th Division AO. Even at night a steady conversation about the duties of the division surgeon continued until one or the other fell asleep. The intensity of his orientation helped keep his mind off Kristy and her husband. Finally, it was time for the change of command ceremony. The medical battalion, supporting units, division staff and friends were assembled in a large field next to the medical battalion headquarters. General Webster took the battalion colors from Colonel JP Franklin and passed them to Lieutenant Colonel William Harlingen. By that simple act Colonel JP Franklin went from a person with immense responsibility and authority to a person with no responsibility or authority. That night he slept more soundly than he had in months.

★

Saturday, November 14, 1970, 1300 hours
96th Evacuation Hospital, Phong Sahn, Republic of Vietnam

"When are you scheduled to leave for Saigon?" Colonel Lou Marchenko asked Colonel JP Franklin.

"A chopper is going to fly me to Danang in the morning. I'm booked on a C–130 flight from Danang to Tan Son Nhut leaving at noon."

"We're going to miss you around here," Marchenko said. "You could have had this hospital if you had been willing to wait six more weeks."

"This hospital has too many memories," JP said, thinking of Kristy. "What are your plans after you DEROS, Lou? You would be a natural to command a medical center like Walter Reed."

Marchenko shook his head. "I'm going to retire. GW has made me an offer to chair their department of psychiatry. I have accepted."

"I'm sorry to hear that, Lou. You're the kind of officer the Medical Corps needs desperately. I was sure you would stay on and make general. What happened?"

Marchenko swiveled his chair around to a partially filled Silex coffee pot on a hotplate. Lifting the pot, he swiveled back to offer JP a refill.

"No, thanks." He waited for Marchenko to fill his mug and return the pot. "You haven't answered my question?"

Marchenko sipped his coffee thoughtfully. He set the mug on his desk and leaned towards JP. "I'm a lot like you. I grew up believing in honor, integrity, and patriotism. I had a blind faith in my country. When we became involved in Vietnam I was convinced that our motives were honorable, that we were doing the right thing and were committed to winning. But patients from Vietnam on my psychiatric wards at Letterman were telling me different stories. I didn't believe them because I didn't want to believe them. When I got over here I learned what they told me was true."

JP interrupted. "Lou, I think I know what you're going to say next. Please don't say it."

Marchenko pushed his chair back and stood. "You're right. Thanks for stopping me."

"I'm going to miss you, Lou," JP said, standing. "The army is going to miss you." He held out his hand.

Marchenko grasped it firmly. "Thanks, Colonel, and thanks for all your help in the operating room with the tough cases and mass caz."

"I'm the one who should thank you. I'm a better surgeon because of the experience."

"With the tickets you will have punched over here you should be a shoo-in for a star."

"No way. I love surgery and teaching too much to give it up for a star."

"Is that the only reason?"

"No. Like you, I've found out things out here I wish I hadn't. It's like learning that the priest of your church is an adulterer. I'll retire after I pay back the two years for my eagles."

Marchenko nodded his head sadly. As he walked JP to the door he asked, "Will you have time today to see the NVA lieutenant?"

JP felt a surge of hate. "Why the hell would I want to do that?"

"For your own peace of mind as well as his."

"Now what's that supposed to mean?"

"Lieutenant Dai is on a massive guilt trip about Kristy being killed while shielding him. He's severely depressed about the possibility of being confined to a wheelchair for the rest of his life in a country that does not take kindly to the handicapped. He's convinced he's a traitor for allowing himself to be captured alive. He may try to escape just to give the MPs an excuse to shoot him."

"If he's so hot to get himself killed I'm not so sure we should try to stop him," JP said bitterly.

"I don't want to see you leave Phong Sahn carrying that kind of hate."

JP sighed, "Sometimes I despise psychiatrists as much as I do the NVA. Okay, Colonel, I'll see him. What ward is he on?"

"Five Bravo."

JP threw Marchenko a sloppy salute, then walked out of the office and into the corridor. Ward 5B was close to the administrative part of the hospital and easy to find. The entrance door was locked. He knocked; the door was opened by an MP.

"I'm here to see Lieutenant Dai."

The MP nodded. "Bed six, Colonel."

As he neared Dai's bed an ARVN MP standing nearby moved discretely away. Dai watched JP approach without expression. When JP stopped beside the bed Dai said blandly, "If you had killed me when you had the opportunity the nurse would still be alive."

"That thought has crossed my mind more than once, Lieutenant."

"Then why didn't you kill me?"

JP shrugged. "One must do what one believes to be right at the moment. I made a mistake."

"By sparing me you condemned me to the life of a cripple. I must bear guilt for the rest of my life that a woman, an enemy, died that I might live. Colonel, I do not wish to live the life of a cripple, nor live with the weight of the nurse's death on my conscience, nor bear the disgrace of my capture."

JP moved closer to Dai. "Lieutenant, I'm getting fed up with your self-pity. You are making me hate you more than I already do."

Dai's face reddened,

"The chances of your becoming a cripple are slim if you take care of yourself. All

624

parameters indicate you will walk again."

Dai glared at JP.

"If the nurse died protecting you, and it appears she did, you must accept her gift of life. You have spoken many times of honor. Well, if you have any honor, Lieutenant, you will not let her death be wasted. Honor mandates you to make your life worthy of her sacrifice. You owe her that much."

JP paused as though waiting for Dai to say something, but Dai remained quiet.

JP's voice softened. "This war must end one day. Your country will desperately need you and others like you to lift it from years of war."

Dai's face was impassive. JP wondered if he had heard a word he said. It didn't matter. "I will not see you again, Lieutenant. I leave tomorrow for Saigon to command a hospital."

Dai did not respond.

"Goodbye, Lieutenant."

As JP walked to the door Dai called after him. "Colonel Franklin... sir."

JP stopped and turned.

"Thank you, Colonel."

JP nodded, then walked out of the ward.

Chapter Sixty-Nine

Monday, November 16, 1970
Aboard a C–130 Hercules Transport Aircraft, en Route to Tan Son
Nhut Airport, Saigon

When flying as a passenger on military transports in Vietnam, one of the perks accompanying the rank of male colonel or female of any rank was an invitation from the aircraft commander to ride in the cockpit. The airline passenger seats against the rear bulkhead and an overhead bunk were far more preferable to the windowless, noisy, drafty cargo compartment with its canvas seats. Thus it was on the C–130 Hercules flying from Danang south 300 miles to Cam Rhan Bay, that Colonel JP Franklin had stood between the AC and co-pilot during most of the flight. Only on the take-off in Danang and final approach at Cam Rhan Bay did JP belt himself into one of the passenger seats. Conversation had been limited to airplanes, flying, and the performance of the C–130 transport compared to the F–4 fighter. The flight crew was impressed by a Medical Corps colonel who seemed to have such an intense interest in airplanes. When JP related that his son was in air force ROTC and hoped to fly C–130s one day, the AC, a major, turned to him. "Colonel, after we depart Cam Rhan and reach altitude, would you like to fly from the right seat?"

Thus it was that Colonel JP Franklin, Medical Corps, US Army, found himself in the co-pilot's seat with his hands on the wheel and feet on the rudder pedals. The co-pilot, a second lieutenant who had flown the leg from Danang to Cam Rhan Bay, retired to one of the passenger seats and promptly fell asleep.

"Maintain 27,000, a heading of one nine zero and 320 knots," the AC directed.

The C–130 Hercules was a pleasure to fly, readily responding to finger pressure on the yoke and toe pressure on the pedals. In minutes JP was flying the huge transport using only thumb movements of the trim-tab button on the yoke. The look he gave the aircraft commander was loaded with envy and even a trace of jealously. "I can't believe you actually get paid for doing this," he said.

For the next thirty or so minutes the painful memories from seven months of war were wiped from JP's consciousness. Even his grief over Kristy's death was suppressed by the euphoria of piloting the four-engine turbo-prop and sensing its responsiveness to his commands. Some 12,000 feet below the aircraft torrential rains and high winds battered the earth under a dirty layer of clouds, but up here at 27,000 feet there was only blue sky, sunshine, and the steady tranquilizing throbbing of four smoothly running turbo jet engines. It was a heady thirty minutes, enough to make an army doctor consider transferring to the air force.

The AC's voice intruded into JP's headset. "Colonel, we're entering Saigon airspace. Better let the lieutenant take his seat."

Reluctantly, perhaps even resentfully, JP relinquished his seat to the lieutenant. Again he stood between the AC and co-pilot and watched as the co-pilot flew a near perfect ILS approach to one of the runways at Tan Son Nhut. Just before touchdown JP buckled himself back into the passenger seat.

After rollout and taxi the co-pilot skillfully coordinated squealing brakes, throttles, and a small wheel by his right hand to inch the monstrous aircraft into a space between two parked C–130s. The throbbing noise of its four turbo engines abruptly ceased. Whirling propellers transitioned from blurred discs to individual blades, then slowed to a drifting rotation until finally stopped. JP undid his belt, stood up and reached for his fatigue cap. Moving up to the flight crew, he patted the co-pilot on the shoulder. "That was masterful."

The AC twisted in his seat. "For once he remembered everything I taught him." The co-pilot, busy flipping switches and turning knobs, grinned.

"I really appreciate the flight time," JP said.

"Any time, Colonel. You did good."

"If you ever come to Long Binh look me up at the 98th Evac."

"Will you introduce me to a pretty nurse?"

JP glanced at the wedding band on the AC's left ring finger. "I don't think your wife would approve, but I can promise you drinks and a steak dinner. That goes for your co-pilot, and since he is single there may be a pretty nurse who would love to meet a daring air force pilot."

The co-pilot turned around. "All right."

After shaking hands with the AC, co-pilot and flight engineer JP climbed down to the cargo compartment now empty of passengers. He walked its massive length and down the ramp to the tarmac. His duffel bag, suitcase, and Montagnard crossbow wrapped in canvas with its arrows were just beyond the ramp. The odor of burned kerosene hung heavy in the oppressively hot humid Saigon atmosphere. It was almost suffocating. The almost steady thunder of departing C–130s, fighter bombers in afterburners, C–141s, helicopters, and civilian aircraft, rolled over the airfield.

Hefting the duffel bag so that it hung off his left shoulder, he picked up the suitcase and crossbow, then headed to the terminal. Several hundred meters across the tarmac an olive army bus, red crosses on its sides, backed up to a C–141 Starlifter's rear ramp. JP stopped to watch. The back of the bus opened. Figures in blue pajamas, some on crutches, some assisted by orderlies in white, hobbled out of the bus, crossed to the C–141's ramp, and entered its dark green interior. Others from the bus were carried into the aircraft on stretchers.

Entering the terminal, JP found himself in a morass of US, ARVN, and other military personal mixed with civilians. As a colonel he was authorized to use the VIP lounge; another perk. After a short search he found the lounge. Before he could enter a soldier standing by the door made eye contact with him, then approached.

"Colonel Franklin?"

"Yes."

"Pfc Beringer, sir, from the 3rd Field. I have Colonel Powell's sedan outside. I'm to take you to the 3rd Field Helipad. A Dust-off will pick you up there and take you to your hospital."

Harvey Powell, former chief of OB/GYN at Walter Reed, was a good friend who now commanded the 3rd Field Hospital in Saigon. The Medical Corps was a small family.

JP slipped the duffel bag off his shoulder. It hit the floor with a thud. He told Beringer, "I'll carry the suitcase and crossbow if you'll carry the duffel bag."

Beringer picked up the duffel bag with one hand and led out the terminal's front entrance to an olive drab 1967 four-door Plymouth sedan parked at the curb. A plate on the front bumper prominently displayed a colonel's silver eagle. Beringer opened the trunk, tossed in the duffel bag, then reached for the suitcase. JP climbed into the front seat, holding the crossbow and arrows.

A South Vietnamese police officer wearing a white helmet, a "white mouse", walked over to the sedan and studied the serial number on the hood. JP nodded a friendly greeting. The white mouse responded with a stony glare. Beringer climbed in and cranked the engine.

"You didn't steal this did you, Beringer?" JP asked.

"No, sir. My taste runs to red ragtops."

Waving to the suspicious white mouse, Beringer boldly pulled out into the heavy traffic. Even with Beringer's courageous driving it took thirty minutes to reach the 3rd Field Hospital. The helipad, across the street from the hospital, was large enough to accommodate two Hueys or one Chinook. Several meters from the helipad a faded red windsock hung limp. Beringer drove on to the pad and parked a few feet from a waiting Huey, its red crosses prominent. When JP stepped from the sedan he was met by the Huey's AC.

"Sir, Chief Warrant Officer Slade," he said, saluting. "We're ready to take off whenever you are."

JP snapped a return salute. "Mr. Slade," he said in a near John Wayne drawl, "I've been ready for this flight a long time."

Slade, turned and led to the helicopter. JP climbed on board, took a seat near the door and fastened his belt. A medic crewman helped Beringer load JP's luggage on to the helicopter's floor, then checked to see that JP's seatbelt was fastened. "Is this your first flight in a chopper, Colonel?"

JP smiled. "No. I had a few flights up north."

★

The flight to Long Binh was at 500 feet and took less than twenty minutes. From this altitude Saigon appeared like any other far-eastern city; overpopulated, overbuilt, and dirty. Houses and apartment building of all sizes and shapes were jammed together amidst stores and shops. Narrow and wide streets appeared flooded with streams of traffic. The helicopter dropped its nose and began a gentle descent.

Sitting by the open door, Colonel JP Franklin, M.C., USA, strained for his first glimpse of the hospital he would command. It would be the culmination of a long-time dream. It would also be a challenge, for he had been told by General Draughn, the Med Command commander, "Morale in that hospital is so low it can't go any lower. The surgeons are close to revolt. Get down there and straighten up that place, JP."

A heliport larger than two football fields drifted into view. A dozen Huey helicopters with red crosses were parked in revetments made of 55-gallon drums and sandbags. Beyond those were as many Cobra gunships similarly protected. A road along one edge of the heliport separated it from a massive complex of buildings that covered at least two city blacks. The roofs of many of the buildings showed large red crosses painted on white square backgrounds. JP counted at least sixteen buildings formed of four Quonset huts jointed to from a perpendicular cross. A thick wall of concrete at least eight feet tall surrounded each building. Excitement and euphoria flooded through JP. He was looking at the hospital he would command; it was his hospital.

The Huey flared and settled. Two figures stood next to a parked jeep leaning against the rotor wash and holding their caps. The Huey's engine noise subsided. JP undid his belt. Carrying his crossbow and arrows, he went forward to the flight crew, shouted his thanks, then climbed down to the ground. The medic pulled his duffel bag and suitcase off the floor and started for the jeep. JP followed. As he neared the two figures he saw one was wiry, about his own height, in his mid-thirties with a handlebar mustache. The subdued gold leaf of a major was on one collar, a MSC caduceus on the other. The second figure was at least six inches taller, older, and heavier. He wore sergeant major's stripes on his sleeves. Both advanced towards JP, stopped and saluted.

"Welcome to the 98th Evacuation Hospital, Colonel Franklin," the major said. "I'm Major Jeff Dunbar, executive officer. This is Sergeant Major Gorbach, the hospital sergeant major."

Returning their salutes, JP shook hands with both. "Thanks for sending the chopper and meeting me."

"No problem, sir. How was your flight?"

"Beautiful, just beautiful," JP said, recalling the thirty-minute dual in the C–130.

"The sergeant major will take your luggage in the jeep, Colonel. We can walk to the hospital from here."

JP, with some reluctance, handed the crossbow and arrows to the sergeant major, then turned to Major Dunbar. "Lead on."

Jeff Dunbar led across the road to a wooden bride spanning a wide drainage ditch. JP frowned when he saw a gurney on its side in the ditch. He wondered how long it had been there. He said nothing to Major Dunbar but decided to keep track of how long it remained in the ditch.

The bridge connected to a covered boardwalk which led to double doors. Pushing through the doors, the two were greeted by cold air as they entered a long green-painted room brightly lit by overhead fluorescent lights. Half a dozen metal sawhorses, some with empty stretchers, lined one wall; gurneys lined the other.

"This is the emergency room, Colonel," Major Dunbar said.

JP scanned the room, noting anesthesia and suction machines, IV poles, cabinets, and shelves stuffed with sterile packs, packs bottles of IV fluids and meds. Several portable OR lights and X-ray machines were parked in one corner; others were scattered through the room. Exiting through another set of double doors, he and Major Dunbar entered a wide corridor; two passageways led from the corridor.

Indicating the one on the right, Dunbar explained, "This goes to the X-ray department; the other to the lab and blood bank." Continuing down the corridor, Dunbar indicated another set of double doors. "That goes to pre-op. It's mirror image of the ER. Casualties going to the OR are fine-tuned there and anesthetized. On the other side of pre-op is the OR suite with eight operating rooms, and beyond that is the post-op and surgical ICU."

JP was impressed by the efficiency of the hospital layout. "Whoever designed this hospital knew what he was doing."

Major Dunbar led past storage rooms, offices, and open spaces to enter another corridor from which three offices opened. A continuation of the corridor led to a very large open office with desks and file cabinets. GIs in T-shirts and Vietnamese women in tight-fitting dresses labored at typewriters. "This is the administrative part of the hospital, Colonel."

"Where's headquarters company?"

"About half a dozen buildings from here," Dunbar said. "Next I'll show you your office." Returning to the corridor, they entered the largest to the three offices. "This is yours, Colonel. Mine is next door. The chief nurse, Helen Schroyer, has the third".

The room was spacious, almost as large as General Webster's. A huge metal desk and executive leather swivel armchair was flanked by four waist-high bookcases crammed with medical texts and journals. A conference table, armchairs, and leather sofa occupied the front two-thirds of the room. Floor and table lamps supplemented the overhead fluorescent lights. A small radio rested on top of one of the bookcases. A television set in a metal swivel frame hung from the ceiling.

"This is impressive," JP said. "The only thing missing is a rug and wet bar."

Major Dunbar indicated the two phones on the desk. "The hospital has its own MARS station. You can be patched into it any time you want."

"What's the usual wait time between calls?"

"Two weeks, but Colonel Malthus made calls two and three times a week, mostly to his stockbroker."

"He was my predecessor?"

"Yes, sir."

JP went behind the desk and kneeled by one of the bookcases. Scanning the books he pulled out several new-appearing medical texts and checked publishing dates. He looked up a Dunbar. "These were published this year. Are there duplicates in the hospital library?"

"No, sir. We're authorized only one copy. Colonel Malthus insisted that all new texts and journals be brought to him for review. Somehow he never got around to reading them."

"Where's the library?"

"Next door in building twenty-nine alpha."

JP slid into the swivel chair behind his desk and sank into its soft plushy cushion, then stood up. "Jeff, I won't last thirty seconds in this thing after a noon meal on a hot

630

Vietnamese day, air conditioning not withstanding."

Major Dunbar smiled, pulled out a green flip notebook and made an entry.

"While you have that thing out, make a note to have these books and journals taken to the hospital library. From now on all new texts and journals go to the library. Is there a librarian?"

"Yes, sir. She's a Vietnamese woman with a PhD in library science from the Sorbonne. Her husband was an ARVN Ranger officer killed during Tet. She has a nine-year-old son. The librarian job is practically her only income. She gets next to nothing from the Vietnamese government."

JP wondered how a nation that failed to take care of its war widows and children could expect to win a war. "That's rough," he finally said.

Major Dunbar flipped his notebook closed and slipped it into his breast pocket. "Colonel, I need to find out you where you want to live."

"With my family in Silver Spring, of course. I didn't realize I had a choice."

"You do have a choice, sir," Dunbar said, smiling, "but it's somewhat limited. As a full colonel you can live in a trailer up the hill near the senior grade officers' club. It's about six miles from here. You would rub elbows with MACV and USARV big brass. Colonel Malthus lived up there."

"Tell me more."

Somewhat reluctantly Major Dunbar continued. "The trailer is furnished, has three bedrooms, bath with tub and shower, kitchen, dining room, closets and air conditioning. The grounds have been landscaped and are maintained by a gardener. You would be the trailer's only occupant."

"You're kidding."

"No, sir."

"What a great way to fight a war. What's my other option?"

"Half a hooch here on the hospital compound. I live in the other half. Each half has air conditioning, TV, small fridge, sink, two-burner hotplate, two metal bunks, GI desk and a small table."

"You forgot the latrine."

"It's a couple hundred feet away."

JP didn't take long to make his choice. The seed to command a hospital had been sown during World War II when, as a nineteen-year-old marine just back from the Pacific, he had gone to the San Diego Naval Hospital to visit a wounded comrade. The hospital commander, an admiral, had planted the seed. The seed blossomed during the Korean War. Now that he finally had a hospital to command in a war zone he wasn't about to do it by remote control from a fancy trailer.

"I'll take the other half of your hooch."

Relief flooded Jeff Dunbar's face. "Somehow I knew you would. I had the hooch maids clean and polish up the place."

From a clipboard Dunbar removed a sheet of paper and laid it on the desk. "This is a roster of senior personnel currently present for duty with whom you will want to meet. Their 201 files are on your desk." He pointed to a stack of records. "If you will indicate on the roster the times you wish to meet with them as a group or individually

I will make the arrangements."

"I'd rather meet with each chief of service on his own turf, make rounds, then spend some time with him," JP said, picking up the sheet and studying it. On it were the chiefs of medicine, surgery, psychiatry, radiology, pathology, chief nurse, chaplain, sergeant major, and head of the Red Cross. "I don't see the chief of anesthesia and chief of professional services on here."

"Major Resniek is both. He's in Hawaii on R&R."

"Harry Resniek? From Walter Reed?"

"Yes, sir. Do you know him?"

"He was the assistant chief of anesthesia at Reed." JP looked puzzled.

"Something wrong, Colonel?"

"I'm wondering what he's doing out here. Harry was the most anti-war, anti-Nixon liberal I ever met. His obligatory two years were up last summer. He was supposed to join the faculty at Hopkins. How long has he been out here?"

"About four months. He's carried a heavy load. He and Colonel Malthus clashed on his first day."

JP chuckled. "Knowing Harry I shouldn't wonder."

"Their shouting matches were legendary. Malthus finally shut Harry up by threatening to court martial him."

"Is Harry's 201 file in that stack?" JP asked, pointing to his desk.

Dunbar nodded.

JP thumbed through the files and pulled out Resniek's records. Scanning the pages, he suddenly looked up. "I'll be damned."

"Problems, Colonel?"

"Yes, me. I'm turning out to be a very poor judge of character. Resniek not only extended for one year beyond his obligatory two years, he did it contingent on his coming to Vietnam. That rascal volunteered, something he vowed he would never do. I'll never understand New Yorkers." JP dropped the file on top of the stack. "Jeff, when Harry went on R&R did he know I would be coming in as Colonel Malthus's replacement?"

"I don't think so. We didn't know who would replace Colonel Malthus until three days ago. Harry was in Hawaii by then."

"When is he due back?"

"In one week."

JP grinned evilly. "Let me get a good night's sleep and I'll devise an appropriate reception for our chief of anesthesia and chief of professional services. For the price of a martini I'll tell you a story about Harry that will initiate grand mal convulsions of laughter." He glanced at his watch: 1650. "Anything critical I need to know before you show me my quarters?"

"Yes, sir. There are some disciplinary cases in the works. The most serious is the impending general court martial of the chief of surgery, Major Palowski."

"General court martial? You're kidding. Good God! You're not kidding. What did he do, kill someone?"

"Not quite although he may have contemplated it. He was three days late getting back from R&R in Bangkok. Colonel Malthus read him the riot act and threw the book at him to set an example for the other doctors."

"Oh, for God's sake."

"There's more."

"I don't want to hear it... tell me anyway."

"Before going on leave Major Palowski was the moving force in building a new schoolhouse and clinic in An Ke, a small village eight miles from here."

"He should be commended for that, not court-martialed."

"Yes, sir. Most of us feel that way. Unfortunately Palowski used army lumber scrounged from the engineers and army trucks to transport it without authorization. Nurses, doctors, and EM went out to An Ke on what little spare time they had to help. Malthus got wind of it and wrote up additional charges including unauthorized use of government vehicles, stealing government property, conduct unbecoming an officer, and misuse of army personnel."

JP was too stunned to respond.

"The Article 32 investigating officer recommended non-judicial punished at the very most, but Colonel Malthus was determined to make an example of Major Palowski. He insisted on a general court martial."

Coming forward, JP placed both elbows on his desk. "What can you tell me about Major Palowski?"

"Major Resniek considers him an outstanding general surgeon and our best chest and vascular surgeon. He's always been eager to pass on his skills and judgment to the other doctors. When we've had mass casualties he's worked around the clock without complaint, setting an example for the other doctors. Before Colonel Malthus left for the States a group of doctors and nurses came to see him about dropping charges and putting Palowski in for a Legion of Merit. Colonel Malthus told them to get the hell out of his office."

JP slowly shook his head. "Your former commander sounds like a jewel. I certainly will try to live up to the standards he set."

Dunbar paled.

"Just kidding, Jeff. Has a trial date been set for Palowski?"

"No, sir. The charge sheet and Article 32 report are with General Draughn. He hasn't acted on them yet."

JP had met General Draughn when the general had visited the 36th Division in September. Draughn had planned to spend a day and ended up staying four days. JP arranged for him to fly in the front seat of a Cobra gunship. The downside was that Draughn had thrown up all over the cockpit. During a mass casualty influx at Quang Dien JP had the general, an internist, carrying stretchers, starting IVs, and assisting the Bravo Med surgeons. Since then General Draughn has blamed JP for aggravating his bad back.

"I know the general," JP said, smiling. "If you will remind me tomorrow I'll call his office and request the charge sheet and Article 32 investigation be returned for my review. After that I'll talk to the JAG to see what can be done to get Palowski off the hook and keep it legal. Anything else hanging fire?"

"Nothing that can't wait until tomorrow."

JP stood up. "How about showing me my hooch and then the mess hall. I need to get unpacked and some food in my gut."

★

"This is it," Major Jeff Dunbar said, stopping at a square wooden building set in a cluster of similar buildings. "It doesn't look like much, but it's home."

JP scrutinized the building from the outside. Not much larger than a two-car garage it had screened windows on two sides; an air conditioner protruded from one wall. The dirt around it had been recently raked. "I see we have a groundskeeper," he said. "Who else lives in this area besides you?"

"The registrar, chief of the lab, motor officer, adjutant, supply officer, headquarters company commander and his exec."

"Where are the doctors billeted?"

"In double-decker barracks at the north side of the compound, about 300 meters beyond the mess hall. The nurses' quarters are a hundred meters on the other side of the road. Colonel Malthus had the engineers build an eight-foot barbed wire fence around it and put an MP at the gate. No male visitors are permitted."

JP smiled. Men have climbed mountains, swam rapids, and fought dragons to reach their loves. Somehow a fence seemed a minor obstacle. He pushed open the door to this hooch, stepped in and glanced around. The single room was as Dunbar had described but larger than he had imagined. His luggage had been placed by one of the bunks. He reached up and switched on the TV. A black and white picture came into focus with a GI reading the news. "It works," he said, switching off the TV.

"My room is on the other side of that wall," Dunbar said, pointing. "If you need me just bang on the wall."

"I'll keep that in mind. Let's go eat."

On the way to the mess hall Dunbar showed him the latrine's location. "The hot water's cold much of the time and the cold water's warm. Wear a raincoat or poncho at night when you visit it. Squadrons of VC mosquitoes hang around the light over the door waiting to attack."

Changing course, they reached a covered boardwalk. Dunbar pointed to an area on the far side containing several dozen benches and a small shelter protecting a movie screen. "This is our outdoor movie, Colonel. If you will send word to the sergeant major that you plan to attend, the projectionist won't start the movie until you arrive."

JP gave Dunbar an incredulous look. "Was that Colonel Malthus's policy?"

"Yes, sir. Sometimes he wouldn't show up after he said he would. The troops would wait thirty and forty minutes, sometimes in the rain."

JP indicated a shelter over half a dozen wooden chairs. "What's that?" he asked. "It blocks the view of everyone behind it."

"That's for the commander and his guests."

JP shook his head in disgust. "Put out the word; the movie will start on schedule."

"Yes, sir," Dunbar said enthusiastically. His green flip-top notebook came out.

"And get rid of that hideous private box."

The two continued down the covered boardwalk another fifty meters to a street. Crossing the street, they reached a concrete walkway leading to an elongated T-shaped wooden structure. Dunbar opened the screened door and held it open.

"Welcome to the 96th Evac mess hall, Colonel."

JP stepped into a room wider and much longer than the Quonset hut wards he had seen earlier. It was furnished with an assortment of plastic-covered metal tables and chairs. The din of mess hall conversations noticeably diminished as JP followed Jeff Dunbar to the single chow line that served both officers and enlisted personnel.

"The word is out," whispered Dunbar, "that the new CO is eating in the mess."

"Is that so unusual?"

"It is here. Colonel Malthus took all his meals at the senior officers' mess on the hill or cooked his own in his trailer."

Picking up a tray, napkin and utensils, JP slid the tray on tubular rails to the serving line. When he saw the main course he stifled a groan; meatballs, spaghetti, and asparagus. As they came off the chow line two pretty Vietnamese women took their trays.

Major Dunbar explained. "The women will bring our trays to whatever table we select, then take requests for beverages."

JP followed Major Dunbar through a wide doorways into the officers' dining room. A dozen four-place tables were squeezed into two-thirds of the floor space. The remaining floor space was occupied by a large raised platform with two tables pushed together. As Dunbar led towards the platform he greeted doctors and nurses at tables along the way. JP sensed that he himself was being studied with more than casual interest.

Dunbar stepped up on the platform. "This is the commander's table."

JP hesitated. The thought of dining elevated on a platform like some oriental pooh-bah clashed with his sense of command, at least in a military hospital.

"Jeff, would you mind if we sat at one of the other tables?"

Dunbar immediately stepped off the platform as if his feet had been on a hot grill. He moved to the nearest table. "How's this, Colonel?"

"Fine," JP said, sitting down. "Anywhere but up there."

He thanked the Vietnamese girl for carrying his tray and ordered iced tea. Looking around the mess, he noted that the walls were bare and the windows obscured by soiled cloth curtains. Gingerly he tasted the spaghetti and found it lukewarm, watery and near tasteless.

"Who's the mess officer?" he asked, setting down his fork.

"There is none. Colonel Malthus decided that Sergeant Varney, the mess sergeant, could handle the mess without an officer looking over his shoulder."

"Really?" JP played with the tasteless mess on his tray. "Let's appoint a mess officer to oversee what is, in reality, a mess. Is there an MSC gourmet cook in headquarters?"

"Captain Hoagland, the adjutant. He barbecues behind his hooch almost every night. He hates the chow here."

"What's his background?"

"Nothing to do with cooking. He has a Master's in accounting."

"Perfect man for the job," JP said. "Tell him one of his first acts as mess officer is to go over Sergeant Varney's records including headcount, requisitions and deliveries, then match them up with the menus for the last couple of months. Also he's to eat at least one meal a day in the mess hall. If he has a problem with that tell him to discuss it with me. By the way, where is the chow prepared for the wards?"

"Here in the mess."

"I was afraid of that. Is there a dietician on the staff?"

"No, sir. The last one DEROSed two months ago. Colonel Malthus didn't requisition a replacement. He said Sergeant Varney could handle it."

JP sighed. "I think we have a problem here." Before he could elaborate the Vietnamese girl set a glass of iced tea near his tray. After taking a drink of tea he ate some of the food on his tray. The asparagus almost made him gag. A slug of tea chased away the taste. His eyes drifted to the platform. "You know, Jeff, that platform really bugs me."

"How so, Colonel?"

"It takes up so much floor space; the other tables are forced into a more crowded arrangement. I will never eat up there. How much of a problem would it be to get rid of the platform?"

"None at all, Colonel." Again the green notebook came out. "Do you want a table designated for the commander?"

"Not really. I want to feel free to join any table. It's good way for the staff to have access to the commander without going through the formality of making an appointment, which most are reluctant to do. And it's my way of learning what's really going on in the hospital. People are much more relaxed at a dining table with their commander than standing at attention in front of his desk." He reached for his glass of iced tea and drained it.

"If you would like more tea or anything else, set the salt shaker on top of the pepper shaker. One of the girls will come over."

JP followed Dunbar's instructions and soon had a full glass of iced tea.

"It seems awfully quiet around here for a war zone," he remarked.

"There have been no casualties in the past forty-eight hours."

"Has that happened before?"

"Just once, then all hell broke loose."

"I'm sorry I asked."

Chapter Seventy

Monday, November 16, 1970, 1930 hours
98th Evacuation Hospital, Long Binh, Republic of Vietnam

Returning to his hooch from the mess hall, Colonel JP Franklin turned on the air conditioner and began unpacking. Lifting starched but wrinkled fatigues and khakis out of his suitcase, he flattened them on his bunk, then searched for coat hangers in the lockers and dresser. Finding none, he banged on the wall between his room and Major Dunbar's.

Jeff's voice came through the wall. "Colonel?"

"Do you have any extra coat hangers?"

"Yes, sir." A few moments later Dunbar knocked on the door and handed JP a dozen wire coat hangers. "If you need more, just yell. I'm drowning in them."

After hanging the uniforms in the wall locker JP emptied the suitcase and duffel bag. Photographs of Kathy and the children went on his desk. He was now ready for a shower. After undressing he slipped on his raincoat and stepped into clogs. Picking up his ditty bag and towel, he headed for the latrine. As Jeff Dunbar had predicted, hordes of insects were on patrol around the single naked bulb over the latrine's entrance. Sensing JP approaching, they attacked. A desperate dash got him through the screen door. Left outside were all but a few determined mosquitoes which had given dining a higher priority than living.

The interior of the latrine was dimly lit by low wattage bulbs. The shower was blessed with plenty of hot water. It and soap washed away the grime of the 600-mile trip from Phong Sahn. Just as the relaxing effects of the hot water began to seep through his body. JP glimpsed a foot long dark shadow furtively dart across the floor. His reaction was swift and decisive. "I'm out of here."

Back in his hooch he slipped on shorts and a T-shirt, then crawled between clean sheets. An effort to write Kathy a letter drifted into illegible scribbles as drowsiness progressed inexorably to sleep.

Three hours later he was dragged awake by persistent scraping noises inside the hooch. Listening intently, he tried to identify the sounds. His hand searched for the reassuring feel of his pistol. Then came the realization that the pistol had been turned in to battalion supply back at Phong Sahn. He had yet to draw one from headquarters company supply. A flush of adrenalin brought him fully awake. Gathering courage, he switched on the bedside lamp. What he saw made him gasp.

Half a dozen monstrous cockroaches scurried from the light to the shadows. At least three inches in length they were the biggest roaches he had ever seen, San Antonio roaches included. Sliding his feet into clogs, he treaded gingerly to the small pantry. A search among cans and bottles left by previous occupants was rewarded by a can of aerosol insecticide. From its heavy weight he guessed it was almost full.

Declaring total war, he embarked on a search and destroy take-no-prisoner mission, but the enemy was nowhere to be seen. "Miserable VC bugs," he taunted, "come out and fight like men." When no roach appeared to take up the challenge he the sprayed insecticide into cracks, crevices, along baseboards, under furniture, around cabinets, and finally saturated the air in the room. The resultant fog and stench were untenable. Throwing on his raincoat, he grabbed an old issue of *JAMA* and retreated to the latrine.

Returning thirty minutes later, he opened all windows and turned on a floor fan that rumbled like an M–24 tank. Soon only a mild residual odor of insecticide remained. A search for blood trails was negative. The commie roaches had retreated from the field of battle. With a sense of fulfillment JP placed the can of insecticide on the chair by his bunk; it was where he usually placed his pistol when he had a pistol. Sliding between the sheets again, he switched off the light. Staring into the darkness, he fervently wished that he had chosen to live six miles away in a three bedroom trailer. Now it was too late. If word leaked out he had been chased out of his hooch by cockroaches the humiliation would be too much to bear.

An intermittent subdued sound, *plop… plop, plop… plop*, began to intrude on the otherwise quiet hooch. The sound was not unlike that of a soft boiled egg falling on the floor from a height of several feet. In a swift continuous motion. JP turned on the light and swept up the can of insecticide; his trigger finger took up the slack of the firing button. He was primed to kill. The light from the lamp was as if an illumination flare had burst over a battlefield. Dead roaches lay over the floor. Others on their backs groped the air with spiny legs in their final agonal tremors as their comrades labored up the walls much as mountaineers would have struggled up sheer rock faces. Most peeled off the wall to strike the floor with the now familiar *plop*. The few hardy climbers that reached the ceiling hung upside down until, weakened by the toxicity of modern chemical warfare, they submitted to gravity.

Enough of this, thought JP. Concluding there would be no further sleep in this hooch tonight, he hurriedly dressed in clean fatigues. After closing the windows he delivered a coup de grace to each of the dying roaches, emptied the remainder of the insecticide into the room, then left, closing the door tightly.

Initially he started for his office to tackle the papers he had seen spilling out of his in-box, then changed his mind and decided to visit some wards. After all, he was a doctor; his love was the care of patients, not the processing of papers. That was Major Dunbar's specialty.

The sprawling hospital compound was poorly lit by an occasional light on a pole. A tall water tower with a flashing red light on its summit helped maintain orientation. After passing several darkened buildings he reached one with a small light over the door illuminating a sign identifying the building as Ward 9-B. Entering, he found himself at the rear of a semi-dark green tunnel-like ward with metal bunks on both sides of a center aisle. Shadows of patients moved restlessly, their limbs or stumps wrapped in bulky dressings suspended by ropes, pulleys and weights. A strong medicinal odor permeated the air intermingled with the pungent smell of pus. At the distant end of the ward a well-lit nursing station was central to the ward and three similar ones.

The nurses' station was vacant when JP reached it. Subdued voices drew his attention to swaying flashlight beams at the far end of one of the other wards. The vague forms of a nurse and two medics moved around a patient's bed, adjusting his traction and talking soothingly. While waiting for them to return, JP pulled a chart from the chart rack, sat down and began reading.

The patient, a twenty-two-year-old corporal, had detonated a land mine near the Cambodian border. He suffered traumatic amputations of both legs. Following admission to the hospital, the stumps were surgically revised to above-the-knee amputations. Before JP could read further the chart was torn from his grasp.

"What do you think you're doing?" an angry female voice demanded.

JP looked up into the gray eyes of a slender nurse in her early thirties, captain's tracks pinned to her right collar. Her name tag read "Jordan". Two menacing orderlies, one well over six feet tall, stood protectively beside her. He slowly got to his feet. "I should have let you know I was on your ward, Captain," JP apologized. "You were busy with a patient so I decided to wait."

Captain Jordan regarded him suspiciously, her hand on the phone. "Who are you? What are you doing on my ward?"

"I'm Colonel Franklin, the new hospital commander. Why I'm cruising around the wards in the early morning is another story almost too embarrassing to discuss."

"How do I know you're not one of those lousy war correspondents after a story? They have pulled all sorts of stunts to get stories including masquerading as medical officers. You'd better have some ID beside that eagle on your collar or I'm calling the MPs."

JP took out his wallet, removed his army ID card and handed it to Captain Jordan.

She stared at the photo, then at JP. Her face turned crimson. "Oh my, Colonel Franklin, I am so sorry."

The two orderlies faded into the dark, leaving the captain to work her way out of her embarrassment. She identified herself as Sharon Jordan, night nursing supervisor for the four wards. "The last hospital commander never visited the wards," she explained.

"You did the right thing, captain," JP assured her. "I don't ordinarily cruise around at night visiting wards. Tonight there were special circumstances beyond my control… roaches in the wire so to speak." He went on to describe the roach assault and his counterattack.

When Captain Jordan stopped laughing she asked, "Will that make you change your mind about living on the hospital compound?"

"No, That would be retreating in the face of the enemy. Marines, even ex-marines, do not have the word 'retreat' in their vocabularies. It was expunged from their brains in boot camp. I'll stay and fight."

Sharon Jordan laughed again. "My husband is a company commander with the 7th Marines," she said. "He told me that, beside retreat, there was no word for promotion in the marine vocabulary."

JP laughed. "I thought that just applied to enlisted men."

A distant dull *whomp* and echo was quickly followed by five more *whomps*, their echoes reverberating into a coalescing rumble, then silence.

"Rockets," JP said, rising. He had heard enough go off at Phong Sahn.

A nearby siren began to wail. The sounds of multiple helicopters starting up and the pounding noise of rotors soon shattered the early morning quiet.

"That many choppers taking off can only mean one thing," Captain Jordan said. "Mass casualties."

"I'd better go to the ER," JP said. He had taken only a few steps when he turned back. "Ah, Captain Jordan, could you spare one of your orderlies to guide me to the ER?"

★

It took almost four minutes to reach the emergency room. Twice the orderly made wrong turns and became lost in the maze of boardwalk paths that wound through the darkened hospital complex. Each time the orderly, profoundly shaken up for getting his new commander lost, apologized profusely.

"Don't worry about it," JP assured him. "I stay lost most of the time and nobody seems to notice."

The orderly grinned.

JP recognized several buildings seen earlier during his orientation with Major Dunbar. "I can find my way from here," he told orderly.

"Yes, sir." The orderly saluted then fled before JP could return the salute.

Chuckling, JP walked along the outside of the emergency room and crossed the bridge over the drainage ditch, gratified that the gurney he had seen in the ditch earlier was no longer there. Crossing the street, he walked fifty feet to the helipad where he had landed only a few hours before. Yellow lights defined the periphery of the helipad. A spotlight shined on a limp windsock. Two medics waited by the helipad with a gurney loaded with folded stretchers. More medics pushing gurneys streamed from the emergency room. JP moved into the background.

A brilliant white light penetrated the darkness as a helicopter approached. In seconds it settled on the pad, its noise drowning shouts of the medics. Three inert figures on stretchers were carried from the helicopter and loaded on the gurneys. Empty stretchers were taken aboard the Dust-off which immediately took off. As JP followed the gurneys with wounded towards the emergency room he heard another helicopter approaching.

The quiet emptiness of the emergency room of yesterday was replaced by doctors, nurses, and medics who descended on the three casualties. Shoelaces were untied or cut, jungle boots and socks pulled off while fatigue jackets, trousers and underwear were cut away. At the same time blood was drawn for type, X-match and basic lab studies. IVs were started. Doctors examined for wounds while anesthesiologists and nurse anesthetists took charge of the airway and vital signs. Other nurses prepped the genitalia for insertion of urinary catheters. Three more casualties were wheeled in. Medics prepped chests, doctors put in chest tubes and did cut downs. One patient required a tracheotomy while another underwent open chest heart massage. Portable

X-ray machines rolled from one casualty to another.

The emergency room double doors slammed open once again. A medic appeared guiding a gurney behind him while a second medic pushed. JP glanced at the casualty as he passed. Partially burned fatigue jacket and trousers exposed blackened skin and charred muscle over the chest with exposed white of the ribs showing. Wisps of gray smoke continued to emit from the tissues accompanied by the pungent odor of burnt flesh. Another gurney rolled past. JP glimpsed a large mass in the casualty's right neck. He was followed by three more casualties and four walking wounded assisted by medics. By the time the casualties stopped coming, seventeen were in the emergency room.

JP felt a great sense of pride as he watched the tragedy of war unfold in the emergency room and the medical personnel respond. The acute care they were providing rivaled and probably surpassed the best manned emergency rooms in the world. Few, if any, trauma centers could manage such numbers of acute major trauma with such skill, and for good reason. Medical personnel in Vietnam did not go home to families at night. They did not work regular shifts; they did not have off Saturdays and Sundays. The primary thrust of their lives during their twelve months in Vietnam was to work, every day and all day if necessary. It was the ultimate practice of medicine. Eating and sleeping were secondary considerations often overridden.

A lanky major went from stretcher to stretcher, paused at each to read the field medic's tag; briefly examined the casualty, then spoke to the attending doctor or nurse. In his early thirties, his rimless glasses and Wyatt Earp moustache gave him a wise, professorial appearance. When he spotted JP, a stranger, he came over. "Any of these your men, Colonel?" he asked.

"I hope not, Major. I'm Colonel Franklin, the new hospital commander."

The major stuck out his hand. "Bill Palowski, chief of surgery. I was told you arrived this afternoon."

So this is the surgeon Colonel Malthus wanted to court martial. "Can you use another pair of hands?" JP asked.

Palowski stared, disbelieving, but quickly recovered. "Yes, sir. One of the casualties has a complex neck injury. Would you take care of him?"

"Sure, but I thought a head and neck surgeon was assigned here."

"He tore up his knee playing touch football last week and was evacuated to Japan. There's not telling when he'll be back, or even if he'll be back."

"In that case I'm your new head and neck surgeon until a replacement arrives."

"Yes, sir. Follow me."

Palowski led to a soldier lying on a stretcher, a green sheet up to his shoulders. A man in his mid-thirties, built like a wrestler and dressed in scrubs, sat at the casualty's head holding a black rubber anesthesia mask over the soldier's mouth and nose. Palowski introduced the man as Captain Joe Wendell.

"Joe is a nurse-anesthetist; he is so capable he can put me to sleep any time."

Captain Wendell grinned.

"Colonel Franklin is the new hospital commander, Joe. He will do the case."

JP nodded a greeting.

Palowski studied the medic's tag tied to the soldier's wrist, then turned to JP "This is Private Willy Benson who arrived in-country yesterday afternoon and was billeted at the 90th Replacement Battalion for processing and assignment. He was asleep in his bunk when the rockets hit his billeting area. A single frag entered the left side of the neck fracturing the larynx. There is no exit wound. He has partial airway obstruction, is aphonic, and has a large hematoma in the right neck."

JP moved in and began examining the soldier.

"Would you like an assistant to help in surgery, Colonel?" Palowski asked.

"Definitely," JP quickly responded. This would be a tough case. He would be operating in a strange OR with people he didn't know. It was not the best combination of circumstances. He would need all the help he could get.

"Excuse me a minute, sir," Palowski said.

JP's exam confirmed the fractured larynx and hematoma. The finding of pinpoint right pupil and dry right face was ominous. They indicated that the right cervical sympathetic nerve was severed. Given its close anatomical relation to the carotid artery and the expanding hematoma in the right neck, the conclusion was inescapable: the major artery carrying blood to the right side of the brain was injured, perhaps severed.

Palowski returned with a thin individual of medium height in trail. The man's face was so youthful that JP wondered if he had finished college much less medical school.

"Colonel, this is Jack Bednard. He completed a straight surgical internship at Saint Jo's in Iowa City before he was drafted. He was a battalion surgeon with the 4th Division for six months before being assigned here. When he finishes his military obligation he'll start a head and neck residency at Colorado."

JP shook hands with the young doctor, then thanked Palowski. "I can take it from here, Major."

"If you need anything give me a call."

JP nodded his thanks, then turned to the nurse-anesthetist. "What's his status, Captain?"

"He's had very little blood loss except for what is in the hematoma. His BP is normal but he's tachycardic, about 130. He was very agitated until I mixed a little anesthetic with the oxygen."

"Agitation is probably from anoxia secondary to partial airway obstruction from the fractured larynx. The hematoma is aggravating the obstruction by displacing the airway to the left."

"It's more than that, sir." Wendell handed JP a small paper pad with barely legible printing: "My brother Charley?"

JP returned the pad and looked at Wendell without understanding.

"He and his twin brother arrived in country together. His brother was wounded by the same rocket that got him."

"What's his brother's status?"

Wendell shook his head sadly.

"Does he know?"

Again Wendell shook his head.

What a waste, thought JP. "Is he ready to go to the OR?"

"Yes, sir, unless you want me to try to intubate him here."

"No. Let's get him in the OR and get set up first."

As they rolled the gurney out of the ER towards the operating suite JP turned to Captain Bednard. "Jack, don't let my eagles intimidate you. Ask about anything that concerns you. In return I'll ask you things I think you should know."

"Oh, oh. I feel like I just stepped into my residency."

"You may as well as get used to it, Captain Wendell."

As they passed a door Wendell said, "That's the doctor's dressing room, Colonel. You can change in there."

"I'm not going to take time for a full change. We need to get started on this man before that time bomb in his neck explodes."

Less than a minute later JP was back, still wearing fatigue trousers and boots, but having exchanged his fatigue jacket for an oversized green scrub shirt. A mask and cap completed the change.

Captain Wendell was apologetic. "Sir, Colonel Kelly won't allow that kind of partial dress in the OR."

"Who is Colonel Kelly?"

"She's the light colonel who runs the OR. Even Colonel Malthus was afraid of her, the few times he showed up in the OR."

"She'll just have to bend the rules. If our patient suddenly obstructs or that hematoma ruptures, I don't want to be caught in the dressing room with my pants down."

Wendell stopped the gurney outside an operating room. JP pushed the door and held it open with his back. The gurney was wheeled in and the soldier transferred to the operating table. Wendell introduced JP to the scrub nurse, First Lieutenant Sandy Thorpe, and the circulator, Spec 4 Gary Mesner. Thorpe, already gowned and gloved, was laying out instruments on a curved table. "I opened a pack for neck exploration, Colonel. Any special instruments you would like?"

"I'll need four working suckers, a vascular and a trach set."

Wendell pushed the anesthesia machine to the head of the table. "It will take me a couple of minutes to get up, Colonel. The lab data and X-rays should be here any time."

"I have a question, sir," Jack Bednard said. "Why didn't you want him intubated in the emergency room?"

"Any attempt to push an anesthesia tube into his trachea through the fractured larynx could precipitate total obstruction requiring a crash tracheotomy."

"Well then, why wasn't an elective tracheotomy done in the ER under local anesthesia?"

"That grapefruit in his neck is full of blood under systolic pressure. It's like an overinflated balloon, ready to rupture. The only thing keeping the blood in check is the layer of deep fascia now stretched thin by the expanding hematoma. A tracheotomy, whether a crash type or elective, must incise into the fascia containing the hematoma. When that incision is made, arterial blood will shoot out as if from a fire hose. It can be very dramatic or chaotic, depending on your point of view. There is a much better chance of controlling the bleeding and saving the patient's life if that catastrophic event takes place in an operating room. Good lighting, plenty of suction, proper instruments, and experienced assistants can mean the difference between life and death."

An X-ray technician materialized carrying four films which he slid into a bank of viewboxes on the wall.

"I ordered chest and neck films in the ER," Wendell explained.

JP and Bednard examined the films. Bednard pointed to a 9 mm shiny lucency at the fourth cervical vertebra. "There's the frag; it's small."

"Still potentially deadly," JP added. "It looks superficial to the spinal cord, which is a blessing."

"Will you try to remove it?"

"Only if I stumble into it. If extensive dissection were required to find it I'd just as soon leave it and drain the area. If the dura has been penetrated or there is spinal fluid leakage, I'll call for the neurosurgeon."

The OR door slammed open with a bang. A full-bodied female in green scrubs stomped into the room, her florid face partially hidden by a mask. She appeared in her late forties, with the build and look of a chief matron in a high security prison. She swept the room with a glare and finally fixed on JP. "You there, with the shirt and fatigue trousers, out."

"Colonel Kelly," Bednard whispered.

JP turned to face the irate OR supervisor, examining her as if she were a laboratory specimen. "Excuse me," he said politely.

"You heard me, get out of this operating room. Who the hell do you think you are, coming in here dressed in dirty fatigues and boots?"

"I'm a new surgeon who reported in yesterday. Right now I'm trying to save this man's life. He has a smashed larynx, can't breathe, and has a hematoma filled with arterial blood that can rupture at any moment. And right now you are interfering with his care."

The supervisor glared at JP "You damn surgeons are nothing but a bunch of overpaid prima donnas. You all think you can come in here and get away with violating all the rules. Well, not as long as I'm the OR supervisor." She grabbed JP's arm as if to shove him towards the door.

JP's voice lowered to a growl and cut like a knife. "Take your hand off my arm and get out of here. You are placing this soldier's life in jeopardy."

Colonel Kelly dropped her hand as if she had grabbed a hot stove. "You can't talk to me like that."

"I just did. If you want to make an issue of it report me to your commanding officer."

"That's exactly what I intend to do."

Colonel Kelly turned and stormed out.

Chapter Seventy-One

Tuesday, November 17, 1970, 0240 hours
Operating Suite, 98th Evacuation Hospital, Long Binh, Republic of
Vietnam

The operating room was quiet except for the *beep beep* of the cardiac monitor. Private Willy Benson lay on his back, his breathing labored as he worked to inspire air through his injured larynx. His neck had been scrubbed, then isolated with sterile towels and his body draped with sterile sheets. The skin incision, marked as a line with methylene blue, started under the right earlobe and descended over the front third of the hematoma, the grapefruit-sized collection of blood in the mid-neck. An inch above the collarbone the blue line swung left over the trachea to the left side of the neck. Colonel JP Franklin, a sterile gown over his T-shirt and fatigues trousers, stood on the patient's right, his gloved hands folded above his waist. Opposite him Captain Jack Bednard shifted nervously. All eyes were on the nurse-anesthetist, Captain Joe Wendell.

"A couple of minutes more, Colonel," Wendell said.

The waiting was necessary for the topical anesthetic, sprayed into Willy Benson's throat, to produce sufficient numbness to allow the interior of the larynx to be examined without his gagging, struggling, or vomiting. If the examination revealed an opening through the injured larynx sufficient to pass an anesthesia tube past the vocal cords into the windpipe, the tube would be passed and Benson put to sleep. There would be little danger of his drowning in his own blood while surgeons worked to expose and control bleeding from the injured carotid artery.

If the tube could not be passed Private Willy Benson would be in big trouble. A tracheotomy would be necessary before he could be put to sleep. At some point during the tracheotomy it would be necessary to cut into the thin sheet of connective tissue that restricted the blood from the injured carotid artery. The result would be massive catastrophic hemorrhage in an awake patient who would be drowning in his blood. The surgeons would face the dual critical needs of completing the tracheotomy before Benson asphyxiated and controlling the hemorrhage before he bled to death. It was a scenario JP dreaded, having been through it five times already. So far he had been lucky; there had been no deaths, but two patients suffered mild strokes. He hoped his luck wouldn't give out on this soldier.

The waiting was beginning to get to JP, patience never being one of his virtues. Subtly he prodded Captain Wendell to move on. "Whenever you're ready, Captain."

Wendell was not to be hurried, JP's eagles not withstanding, "Another minute or two, Colonel."

The seconds ticked by with agonizingly slowness. Finally, Wendell reached for a laryngoscope, an instrument with a battery-containing handle at right angle to a curved six-inch blade, a lit bulb at its end. Slipping the blade into Benson's mouth, he advanced it down the throat, lifting the base of tongue and epiglottis to expose the vocal cords. After a moment he moved his head out of the way.

"Take a look, Colonel."

JP leaned over; his glance was no more than three or four seconds, then he motioned to Jack Bednard. While Bednard looked, Benson became tense, then began to struggle. Wendell quickly removed the laryngoscope, sprayed more topical anesthetic into the throat, then replaced the mask over Benson's nose and mouth, blasting him with oxygen.

"Bag him gently," JP said. "The last thing we want is to force air into his neck." He looked over at Captain Bednard. "What did you see?"

Bednard hesitated. His view had lasted less than six seconds.

"We're waiting, Captain."

"I'm not sure, Colonel. I didn't get much of a look."

"You got more of a look than anyone else. Take a flying guess; you won't be graded."

"Well, sir, the anterior half of the false and true vocal cords are so disrupted that I couldn't identify anything. All I saw was torn tissue, fragments of cartilage, and blood. The posterior half looks intact. A small tube might pass."

"That's right on target," JP said. "You may do well at Colorado."

Captain Wendell asked, "Okay to give him succ before passing the tube, Colonel?"

Succynlcholine, a potent muscle relaxant, would paralyze all muscles, including the muscles of respiration. The patient would stop breathing. Unless a tube were quickly passed and oxygen administered, brain damage and death would become realities. Without the use of a muscle relaxant the patient would struggle and possibly inflict additional damage to the already injured larynx, precipitating complete airway obstruction. Urgent tracheotomy would be required under the worst of circumstances.

JP was faced with a decision. Captain Wendell was not a physician but a nurse with special training in anesthesia. To JP he was an unknown quantity. If he were allowed to attempt passage of the anesthesia tube he could create a life-threatening crisis. Major Palowski had described him as a highly competent and skilled nurse anesthetist. Such an opinion from his chief of surgery was a powerful endorsement. Considering all aspects, including his own ability to deal with a possible surgical disaster, he decided to risk the muscle relaxant and give Wendell the opportunity to pass the tube. "Go ahead and give him the succ," JP told Wendell. "You get two tries to intubate, then it's my turn." There was no compromise in his voice.

After saturating Benson with oxygen Wendell picked up a small syringe and injected its contents into the IV tubing. Almost instantly Benson became inert and stopped breathing. Wendell inserted the laryngoscope through Benson's mouth, exposed the vocal cords, then reached for an anesthesia tube. Advancing the tube, he stopped, backed off, advanced, stopped and then withdrew the tube. "It won't go," he said. "I need a smaller tube." He withdrew the laryngoscope and slapped then mask

646

over the patient's nose and mouth.

JP noted that Benson's color was still pink and his heart rate as shown on the cardiac monitor had not changed. Moving closer to the head of the table, he saw beads of sweat forming on Wendell's forehead.

Captain Wendell removed the mask, inserted the laryngoscope again, then slid the smaller anesthesia tube deftly through the injured larynx into the trachea on the first try. "I'm in," he announced.

"Outstanding," JP said, his voice laden with relief. A major hurdle had been passed. "How much blood is up here?"

"Two units."

"Better hang both running full open. Have another six units standing by. Keep ahead of blood loss; easier than trying to catch up." He turned to the scrub nurse." All four suckers working, Sandy?"

Lieutenant Thorpe nodded.

"Okay. Knife please,"

The handle of a scalpel was slapped into his palm.

Very slowly and carefully he cut through the skin, subcutaneous tissue and the thin platyma muscle just under the skin along the outlined incision. Beneath lay the stretched sheet of fascia bulging with blood under pressure, a booby trap set to explode. He told Jack Bednard, "That fascia is so thin; it's just looking for an excuse to blow up in our faces. One tiny nick would do it."

Using blunt scissors, he undermined the skin flap on each side of the incision, then emplaced two blunt-toothed self-retaining retractors, ratcheting the jaws apart. The outer visible half of the hematoma, a red balloon ready to burst, now lay exposed. The layer of connective tissue holding back the blood was stretched until it was almost transparent.

Throwing a glance at the scrub nurse, JP asked, "Vascular clamps and umbilical tape ready, Sandy?"

"Yes, sir. Do you think you'll need a shunt?"

"No, but have one ready in case I change my mind. Okay, Jack, get ready with two suckers; you too, Sandy. Things are going to happen in a hurry. Don't worry about handing me instruments. I'll get what I need off the Mayo stand or the table. When I make a hole in the fascia all hell will break loose."

JP checked the IV poles. One blood bag was collapsed. "Start another unit, Joe, and keep up his BP. That's his insurance against stroke." He reached to the Mayo stand and picked up long delicate Debakey forceps and blunt-tipped Metzenbaum scissors. Pinching the tensed bulging fascia with the forceps, he looked up. "Fire in the hole," he said and snipped.

A stream of blood an inch wide shot up from the hole to splash on the operating light, painting its lens red. Bednard instinctively jerked back. Ignoring the fountain of blood and working by feel, JP slipped a scissor blade through the hole he had made and in seconds had cut the fascia from below the ear down to the collarbone. Blood now bubbled fiercely out of the incision in massive pulsations, soaking drapes and pouring on to the floor. Tossing the pickups and scissors aside, JP shoved both hands into the expanding pool of blood. Working his fingers deep into the neck, he felt the pulsations of the cigar-sized carotid artery and the powerful stream of blood emitted through a tear in its side. Grasping the artery and its adjacent internal jugular vein below and above the tear with his fingers, he squeezed. The bleeding immediately slowed to a stop.

"The jug is severed and the carotid has a hole in its side," he announced. "I think I've got them. Get in here with those suckers and clear out the blood."

Four suckers, like four vacuum cleaners, slurped away the lake of blood until JP's fingers could be seen compressing the jugular vein and common carotid artery. A small amount of blood oozed from around his fingers. He looked up at Jack Bednard and smiled. "Dramatic, wasn't it?"

A very pale Captain Bednard nodded.

"Aren't you glad we didn't try this in the emergency room?"

Captain Bednard didn't answer. He was staring at Lieutenant Thorpe. Her eyes had rolled up and she was drifting. "Mesner," he shouted, "grab Sandy, quick."

The circulator was behind Lieutenant Thorpe in a flash. Supporting her from the armpits, he eased her onto a sitting stool. JP, still squeezing the carotid and internal jug, asked, "Want us to call a relief, Sandy?"

Sandy Thorpe slowly stood up and shook her head. "The only relief you would get is Colonel Kelly."

"God help us," JP moaned.

"I'm okay now," Lieutenant Thorpe insisted.

JP nodded. He turned to Wendell. "How's he doing?"

"Good. Pressure's 110 over 60; pulse is 120. He lost about four units in that episode."

JP grunted. "Okay, Jack, your turn to play surgeon. While Sandy keeps the field clear and I have my fingers in the dike, you work a vascular clamp over each end of the severed jug and clamp them off. Then get an umbilical tape around the carotid above and below the tear and cinch them down. Watch out for the vagus and cervical sympathetic nerves."

"Yes, sir." Bednard reached to the Mayo stand for the clamps.

Much to JP's surprise and relief, Captain Bednard clamped the jugular vein and controlled the carotid artery with tapes in less than three minutes.

"Good going," JP said, removing his hands and massaging his fingers. "Now we move fast. I'll suture the carotid tear first so he can start getting blood up to his right brain. Thank God he's right handed... or is he? I never checked."

"I did, Colonel," Captain Wendell said." He's right handed."

The young circulator asked, "What's so important about which hand he uses?"

Jack Bednard explained, "The motor cortex for a right-handed person is on the left side of the brain. Since the left carotid is intact he is still getting blood to that side, which considerably lessens the risk of stroke, assuming Captain Wendell manages to keep his BP up."

JP removed his hands from the neck and watched for bleeding. The field remained relatively dry. "Okay, gentlemen... and lady, let's go to work." He held out his hand.

"Suture."

★

Two hours and twenty minutes later, the rent in the right carotid artery had been repaired, the ends of the severed internal jugular vein ligated, and the larynx reconstructed around a stent. JP then assisted Captain Bednard with the tracheotomy.

A medic entered the OR. "Colonel Franklin?"

"Hyo," JP said as he tied down a suture placed by Bednard.

"There's a neck case being medevac'd from the Delta. It will be here in about forty minutes. Major Palowski asked if you would take care of it."

JP groaned. He glanced at the wall clock: 0520 hours.

"Yes, of course."

After the medic left, Joe Wendell asked, "Do you want him to have any heparin, Colonel?"

"What? No. Hold off. His blood has been thinned enough, considering all the blood and fluids he's received. By the way how much blood has he received?"

"The twelfth unit is going in now."

"Better ease up of the blood. He shouldn't lose much more unless my repair falls apart."

"Where did you learn to sew like that, Colonel?" Jack Bednard asked.

"A long time ago, in Marine Corps boot camp at Parris Island." JP chuckled as he recalled the twelve weeks of absolute hell back during World War II. "My DI kept finding buttons on my uniform I'd forgotten to button. He would finger the button and ask if I wanted it. If I said no he'd cut off the button and throw it away. If I said yes he'd cut off the button and hand it to me. Sometimes he'd cut off a button just to see how fast I could sew it back on."

"I didn't know you were a marine," Bednard said. "My dad is a marine."

"It's small world, Jack, especially among marines. When did your dad join up?"

"He enlisted out of high school during the war. He was in on the invasion of Saipan and Tinian. After the Japanese surrendered he was discharged, went to Harvard on the GI Bill and graduated Phi Beta Kappa. He went through OCS and became regular Marine Corps. He's been in ever since. He just finished his second tour over here as a battalion commander with the 1st Division. He's up for bird colonel."

"He's a true mustang," JP said. "Where is he stationed now?"

"He's home on thirty days' leave. His next assignment would have been the Pentagon, but he turned down the promotion and put in his papers to retire. He said he didn't want to continue as part of his country's disgrace. I'm not sure I understood what he meant."

JP understood. Having himself discerned the true face of the Vietnam War, the colossal dissimulation, corruption, and tragedy it encompassed. "I'm sorry, Jack," he mumbled. Moments later, dead on his feet, he began to sway.

Captain Bednard, at least fourteen years younger, seemed unphased. When it came time came to close the skin incision he asked, "What suture do you prefer, Colonel?"

JP didn't answer. Bednard's voice seemed so distant.

"Colonel," Bednard persisted, "Colonel Franklin, I'm losing you."

JP looked up. "Sorry, Jack. What did you say?"

"Sutures for the closure?"

"Your choice. Can you close with Sandy's help?"

"Yes, sir."

"I'm going to crash on the gurney outside the door. Before you close, flush everything with a ton of saline. Put in four Penrose drains and a Red Robinson catheter for irrigation. If one of those drains crosses my artery repair you will be dropped into Cambodia without a parachute."

"Yes, sir."

"Wake me when the next case gets here."

Sandy Thorpe moved next to the table opposite Bednard. She would retract and cut sutures. JP pulled off his gown and tossed it in a basket. Tearing off his gloves, he dropped them in a kick bucket. As he left the OR he said over his shoulder, "Call me if you need me. I'll be right outside."

After setting the brakes on the gurney JP climbed up and stretched out on its rubber mat, took a deep breath and fell asleep. He had no idea how long he had been asleep when he felt himself being shaken. Fighting his way to consciousness, he suddenly became alert and sat up, concerned that Willy Benson had gone sour.

A female voice lashed at him. "You can't sleep out here."

JP stared bleary eyed at the squat figure of Colonel Kelly, the OR supervisor. "I could if you would leave me alone."

"You again," she said. "You're nothing but trouble. Colonel Malthus never tolerated your kind of behavior in the operating room. I'm going to make sure the new commander doesn't."

"You do that." JP lay back down.

"If you're so damn lazy you have to sleep during duty hours you can use the floor in the dressing room."

Colonel Kelly's loud voice attracted interest from other operating rooms. Heads protruded from doors, then hastily withdrew under her threatening glare. An exhausted JP, in no mood to deal with her antics, rolled over and faced the wall, his back to her.

Incensed by JP's intransigence, Colonel Kelly shouted, "I've had it with your insolence. The new commander will hear of your insubordination. I'm going to request he prefer court martial charges against you."

"You do that too," JP said quietly to the wall. Then he was out like a light.

★

Tuesday, November 17, 1970, 1530 hours
Office of the Commander, 98th Evacuation Hospital, Long Binh,
Republic of Vietnam

Colonel James Paul Franklin, shaved, showered, and dressed in clean fatigues, entered his office. He took one look at the overstuffed in-box, turned around and walked out, colliding with an elderly Vietnamese woman pushing a broom. "I'm so sorry," he apologized.

The woman smiled and bowed. "Yes," she said, bowing again.

Not knowing what else to do, JP bowed in her direction. "So sorry," he repeated.

She smiled, bowed again, then resumed pushing her broom.

Jeff Dunbar, who had observed the collision, explained, "Mama San is our cleaning woman; she is very formal. Every morning when we first meet we bow to each other. I say, 'Good morning, Mama San, did you make many rockets last night?' She always responds by bowing and saying, 'Yes, Major, make many rockets.'"

JP shook his head. "I don't know about this place. First I'm run out of my hooch by a regiment of VC cockroaches. Then I operate through the night. When I come into my office I find my in-box filled with meaningless papers. Now you tell me the sweet old lady that cleans my office is a VC sympathizer who makes rockets at night. I've had it with this nut farm, Jeff. I'm going back to Phong Sahn."

Dunbar laughed. "Stay, Colonel. The place grows on you. I heard you had a tough night."

"It was much tougher on the kids we treated," JP admitted. "How come so many were wounded?"

"Five 122 mm rockets hit the replacement depot. Three landed in unoccupied area and did little damage. The other two hit tents full of GIs who had arrived in country eighteen hours before. They hadn't even started processing. Seven were killed outright, two died during evacuation. The rest ended up here. One of the dead and one of the wounded were twin brothers. The surviving brother is the first casualty you operated on."

JP shook his head. "What a waste." The words slipped out.

"Not from the VC's point of view," Dunbar said bitterly. "How is Willy Benson doing?"

"He's moving his arms and legs and knows he's in Vietnam. I almost cried when I told him his brother had been killed."

"This war really sucks, Colonel."

"I've heard that phrase before," JP said. "Is there any coffee around this place? I need an afternoon jolt."

Dunbar led across the corridor into a small supply room. A coffee urn percolated on a table. Some cups were on a shelf under the table top. He kneeled down, rummaged through the cups, and came up with a large heavy cup. Emblazoned in red on the side was the word COMMANDER. Holding it out he said, "This belonged to Colonel Malthus."

JP looked skeptical. "I don't think I want to use it."

"It's clean and safe, Colonel." Dunbar assured. "It was run through the autoclave in the OR three times after Colonel Malthus left."

"I'm surprised no one threw it away or smashed it with a hammer." Filling half the mug, JP waited for Dunbar to fill his. Together they headed back to JP's office. Easing down in his chair, JP propped his feet up on the desk and thoughtfully sipped coffee, then set the mug on his desk. "What can you tell me about Colonel Kelly?"

"Oh, oh. Don't tell me you two have clashed already?"

"It was a one-sided confrontation. She did the yelling and screaming; I did the listening. I was too preoccupied or too tired to do much else. Right now I'm neither."

"Well, Harry Resniek tried to get rid of Colonel Kelly from his first day here."

JP smiled. "Harry, for all his New York City liberal philosophy, does not tolerate fools or assholes, regardless of political persuasion."

"Just about every other day Harry would walk in here and demand that Colonel Kelly be relieved. One morning he and Colonel Malthus stood toe to toe and screamed at each other about Colonel Kelly. Colonel Malthus finally ordered Harry to shut up and leave or he would be court-martialed."

"Kelly and Malthus really love to bandy that threat around."

"Yes, sir. It's the ultimate big stick. Almost every week two or three surgeons complained to Colonel Malthus about Colonel Kelly. He'd listen, then throw them out of his office. The OR nurses complained to Colonel Schroyer, the nursing supervisor. When she tried to talk to Colonel Malthus he would nod, then do nothing. Hell, sir, he even threatened to court-martial me."

"Probably with some justification," JP said laughing. "Why do I get the feeling you're not one of Colonel Kelly's admirers."

"I didn't realize I was conveying that impression. I can tell you this, Colonel, she can be very intimidating. She even tried to get Major Palowski court-martialed for insubordination."

"That speaks well for Palowski." JP thoughtfully sipped coffee. "Let me ask you a hypothetical question, Jeff."

"Yes, sir."

"If Colonel Kelly were relieved, is there anyone on the staff who could replace her and be an improvement?"

"Yes, sir. Harry Resniek wanted to put Denise Endres, the assistant supervisor, in charge of the OR. He didn't get to first base with Colonel Malthus."

"What can you tell me about Endres?"

"She's a major on her second tour, up for promotion to light colonel. She's married to Mark Endres, the Dust-off commander. Major Resniek considered her so outstanding that he wrote her up for an award. Colonel Kelly trashed it. Speaking of trashing, Colonel Kelly's ER on Denise is so bad that if it goes forward it will kill her promotion. I've held it up pending your decision."

JP smiled. "I've had a little experience of dealing with that sort of thing. It's amazing the number of administrative errors one can find if one knows what to look for. Would you bring me the 201 files on Kelly and Endres? And I would like to meet with the chief nurse as soon as possible."

"That's Helen Schroyer. Yes, sir."

"What's she like?"

"Well, she's in her early fifties and will retire after this tour. She is sort of like everyone's mother or grandmother. It's easy to picture her bending over a hot stove on

Thanksgiving Day baking pumpkin pies, a bunch of grandchildren around her. She's had a tough time trying to protect the nurses, especially the OR nurses, against Colonel Kelly." Dunbar started to leave. "I'll get the files on Kelly and Endres."

"Get Schroyer's file too," JP said.

After Dunbar left JP stared thoughtfully at the wall. What a lousy problem to have dumped on him his first day as CO. Being a hospital commander was not turning out to be what he had expected.

In a few minutes Major Dunbar returned with three brown folders and laid them on his desk.

"Give me a few minutes to look these over, Jeff," JP said. "Then we need to talk."

After Dunbar left JP opened Kelly's folder and began reading. When he had finished he pulled out a top drawer, found the Long Binh telephone directory and turned to the section on Med Command. He located the number for the nursing consultant, then picked up the phone. Fortunately she was in. The conversation took much longer than he anticipated but it was worth the time.

Just as he hung up Lieutenant Colonel Mabel Kelly stormed into his office without knocking. "I'm Colonel Kelly," she announced. "I want to talk to you about disciplining one of the surgeons."

JP took a sip of coffee while keeping his eyes fixed on her face. He was surprised that Kelly had not recognized him, then remembered she had never seen him without a mask and cap. Finally he put the mug down. "I didn't see you scheduled for an appointment with me today," he said innocently. "What did you say your name was?"

"Kelly, Lieutenant Colonel Kelly. I am the operating room supervisor. I never needed an appointment with Colonel Malthus and I certainly don't intend to start now with you."

"Really. How interesting."

Kelly tried to gauge JP's blasé reaction. She continued. "I want to report one of the new surgeons for insubordination, disobedience, and violation of my OR regulations. I demand he be given non-judicial punishment with a fine and official reprimand."

"Anything else?"

"Yes. I want you to meet with the surgeons and reiterate my authority over them. They have become a very insolent group, thanks to that liberal Resniek from New York. And I want Resniek disciplined for undermining my authority."

"Finished?"

"For now, yes."

"Sit down, Colonel Kelly."

"What?"

JP voice had dropped to an icy coldness. "I said 'sit down', unless you prefer standing at attention with your heels locked together and toes at a forty-five-degree angle."

Kelly jerked as though slapped. "You can't talk to me that way."

"I can, and I did. Now make your choice."

Kelly slowly sank down into an armchair. Things were not going the way she expected with this new commander.

"Colonel Kelly, my sense after just twenty-four hours commanding this hospital is that you are a serious threat to its operation and morale." He stood up and went to the door. "Major Dunbar," he called out, "would you step in here, please."

Jeff Dunbar walked in, glanced at Colonel Kelly, then stood by JP's desk.

JP continued. "Colonel Kelly, as of this moment you are relieved as operating room supervisor. When you leave my office you will return to the OR and then to your quarters, collect your personal items and leave the hospital compound. You will not return under any circumstance except in a patient status. Should you return you will be placed under arrest. Is that clear?"

Colonel Mabel Kelly was on her feet. "Who the hell do you think you are? You can't relieve me."

"For openers I'm your commanding officer, but not for long. Not only am I authorized to relieve you, I just did."

"We'll see about that," Colonel Kelly said. She started to leave.

"Just a minute. I did not dismiss you."

Colonel Kelly stopped and turned to glare at JP.

"I had an interesting discussion about you with the nursing consultant at Med Command, Colonel Lopez."

That got Kelly's attention.

"Among the things I learned was that you set a record for IG complaints against your superiors at your last four assignments. You also set a record for destroying or attempting to destroy the careers of highly competent nurses by submitting adverse efficiency reports. There's more, a lot more" JP said, tapping Kelly's 201 File.

"What do you mean?"

JP leaned forward. "For instance, Colonel Malthus didn't just retire, did he? In fact, if he hadn't voluntarily retired he would have faced a general court martial for conduct unbecoming an officer. We both know the kind of conduct that was being considered as unbecoming, don't we, Colonel Kelly? And you, being party to that conduct, still on active duty in Vietnam, remain vulnerable. Is that not so, Colonel Kelly?"

Kelly sank into a chair. She resembled a deflated balloon.

"Now, let us take up the subject of the insubordinate surgeon; the surgeon happened to be your commanding officer."

That really rocked Colonel Kelly.

"Your behavior in the operating room this morning, your method of reporting to your commanding officer a few minutes ago, and your demeanor while in his presence as witnessed by Major Dunbar, would justify court martial charges of insubordination. Inasmuch as your divorce from Mr. Kelly is not yet final, those charges could be added to original charges of conduct unbecoming and adultery. Adultery is still a crime under the Uniformed Code of Military Justice, or didn't you know that?"

Colonel Kelly sat stiff, her face getting redder.

JP continued. "You are to report to Colonel Lopez at Med Command when you leave the hospital compound. She will have orders for your return to the States and subsequent retirement."

Mabel Kelly shot out of her chair. "We'll see about that, and all the other bullshit

654

you handed me. I have friends in high places. I'm going to get you, Franklin. When I finish with you you'll be lucky to command a dispensary in Asmara."

JP turned to Jeff Dunbar." Add threatening a superior officer to the charge sheet."

Kelly glared at JP, then started to leave.

JP's voice cut like a whip. "Colonel Kelly." She stopped as if she had run into a brick wall. "For the second time I must remind you that you are not dismissed."

Kelly stomped back and stood in front of JP's desk with her hands on her hips, her feet apart.

JP sighed. "The position you should be in is 'Attention'. Do you have any idea what that is?"

Mabel Kelly slowly brought her feet together and dropped her hands in a sloppy semblance of attention. JP doubted if she had ever stood at attention in her life. If looks could kill, the hospital would have needed a new commander and Kathy would have been a widow.

"Colonel Kelly," JP said quietly, "you are dismissed."

Kelly started out.

"Colonel Kelly," JP said with more patience than he thought he possessed, "you will return and render your commander the military courtesy which is his due."

Kelly returned, stood at attention in front of JP's desk, made what could be best described as a half-ass salute, did an about-face, and marched out.

JP told Dunbar, "Make a record as a witness of what transpired here, date, sign it and keep it in your safe. I'll do the same."

"Yes, sir. Seriously, Colonel, are you really going to court-martial her?"

"Good God, no. I just want to be rid of her." JP stood up. "Let's go to the chow hall. I'm starved."

"Would you care to stop by the officers' club for a drink?"

"Not a bad idea, especially after Colonel Kelly. Does the club serve martinis?"

"The best. Our bartender came from the fanciest French restaurant in Saigon."

"How did that happen? Did he lose his job?"

"In a way. The Viet Cong blew up his restaurant."

"That's the VC for you; no class."

Chapter Seventy-Two

Tuesday, November 17, 1970, 1620 hours
Headquarters, 98th Evacuation Hospital, Long Binh, Republic of
Vietnam

Major Jeff Dunbar entered Colonel JP Franklin's office. "Sir, I have Colonel Schroyer on the phone. She can come over now if you have time."

"Fine. Tell her to come ahead."

Major Dunbar returned to his office. In a moment he was back. "On the way."

"Spoken like a true cannon cocker. Now tell me about our chief nurse."

"The feedback I get from the doctors, nurses and EM is that she is outstanding. She not only has everyone's affection but their respect, mine included. For the last two months she has been in a losing battle with Colonel Malthus and Colonel Kelly. A strong rumor was beginning to circulate that Colonel Malthus planned to relieve her and make Colonel Kelly chief nurse. As soon as Harry Resniek heard the rumor he went to see General Draughn. The general told him he could have five minutes; their meeting lasted two hours. The next thing we knew Colonel Malthus was on his way back to the States, Harry was on his way to Hawaii on R&R, and you were assigned here."

JP shook his head. "What a nightmare."

"It's been a rough two months for Colonel Schroyer, and this is her third tour in Vietnam."

"Does she have a family?"

"Yes, sir. She has two sons. One is navy fighter pilot on Yankee Station. The other is an infantry lieutenant with the Americal Division. A daughter is a nurse at the 85th Evac at Phu Bai. Colonel Schroyer's husband is the 4th Division chaplain. He comes up here every two or three weeks for a day or two. If it's over a weekend he conducts the Protestant service."

"The hospital has a chapel?"

"Yes, sir, with a full-time chaplain, Ted Donaldson. He's a Baptist from Texas. We even have an electronic organ."

"What about an organist?"

"One of the nurses, Sharon Jordan, majored in organ performance before switching to nursing."

"We've met," JP said, smiling. "She nearly threw me off her ward when she caught me reading a patient's chart."

"She's capable of doing that," Dunbar said, laughing. He pulled out his flip-top notebook. "When do you want to start seeing the chiefs of service?"

"Tomorrow afternoon beginning with the chiefs of orthopedics and internal

656

medicine. In the morning I'll be at Med Command talking to the JAG and General Draughn about Pawloski's court martial. I'll also see Colonel Lopez about the adverse ERs that Kelly and Malthus turned in. If you would make up a list of the impacted individuals I'll pick it up in the morning before going to Med Command."

"No problem, sir."

"What sort of transportation is available for hospital headquarters?"

"We're down to one jeep. We had three; one was totaled in an accident; the other has been in maintainance a month waiting on parts. Because of a shortage of enlisted personnel there is no assigned driver. When Colonel Malthus was here he kept the jeep with him as his own private vehicle. The rest of us had to use 21/2 and 3/4-ton trucks if we needed to go anywhere. After he left I assigned our only jeep to the sergeant major. Officers and senior NCOs can check it out through the sergeant major's office."

JP did a quick comparison analysis. As a lieutenant colonel he had his own jeep and driver plus a Huey helicopter with flight crew and door gunners. Now as a full colonel he was relegated to driving himself in a jeep he shared with others and scheduled with the sergeant major. He wondered if he had taken a step forward or backward.

"That sounds like a reasonable arrangement," JP said. "Let's continue it. I will need the jeep for most of tomorrow morning."

A knock at the open door interrupted their conversation. They both stood as a matronly woman in her early fifties walked in. Somewhat stocky, her gray hair combed back neatly and fixed in a bun, she had a soft kindly face. Wire-rimmed glasses were perched on her nose. Lieutenant Colonel Helen Schroyer, Nursing Corps, US Army, certainly looked the part of everyone's mother or grandmother. Jeff Dunbar introduced her.

JP came around his desk and shook hands. "Please have a seat, Colonel. Coffee?"

"No, thank you."

"I appreciate your coming on such short notice," JP said. Returning to his seat, he began. "There has been an unexpected development impacting the operating room staffing that requires your immediate attention."

Colonel Schroyer leaned forward, anxiety written over her face.

JP went on to describe the events leading to Colonel Kelly's dismissal. "With her departure the hospital is faced with the need to appoint a replacement OR supervisor. Since you are the most knowledgeable concerning the nurses I would like your recommendation."

Helen Schroyer beamed. "Major Denise Endres would be my choice," she said without hesitating. "If Major Resniek were her he would strongly endorse her appointment. Denise is not only competent, she is well liked and respected by the surgeons, anesthesiologists, nurses and EMs."

JP looked at Major Dunbar. "Make it happen, Jeff."

Helen Schroyer shifted uneasily. "Colonel Franklin, Major Endres is due for promotion in three weeks. Her efficiency report rated by Colonel Kelly and endorsed by Colonel Malthus two weeks ago was so adverse that it will put her promotion in jeopardy."

"Major Dunbar has made me aware of that and adverse ERs on others. I have an appointment tomorrow morning at Med Command with Colonel Lopez to see what can be done about them. My impressions of the rater and endorser are that neither were administrative giants. Past experience suggests it is highly probable," he paused to stifle a smile, "that significant administrative and clerical errors were made which invalidate those ERs. In all probability they will need to be rewritten. Unfortunately the original rater and endorser are no longer available." He sighed. "I'm afraid redoing them will mean a lot of work for you and Major Resniek."

"It will be a pleasure for me, Colonel Franklin."

"I thought you would see it that way, Colonel Schroyer," JP said with a slight grin. "In the future, Major Endres will rate the OR nurses; the chief of anesthesia, Major Resniek, will endorse them. Major Endres will be rated by Major Resniek and you will be the endorser. Is that arrangement satisfactory?"

"Very much, Colonel."

JP continued. "I have been told that Colonel Malthus separated the OR personnel from nursing service."

"Yes, sir. He did that shortly after he arrived. Then he made Colonel Kelly the operating room supervisor with no one over her as a supervisor except himself."

"That is a somewhat unorthodox arrangement, would you agree?"

"It is highly irregular. In every other hospital the operating room personnel are under the nursing service."

"Well, I think we should conform to tradition. Do you have any objections to the OR personnel being placed back under the nursing service?"

"None at all. In fact, I was going to urge you to do just that."

JP turned to Major Dunbar. "Make that happen too, Jeff."

Jeff Dunbar asked, "Colonel, did you want to discuss awards at this time?"

"Right. Colonel Schroyer, resubmit write-ups on your personnel for awards you consider deserving. Any supportive document, such as statements from supervisory M.D.s, M.S.C.s, and even patients will be helpful. Anyone DEROSing should have the paperwork submitted a.s.a.p. so that the awards can be presented before he or she leaves."

JP leaned back in his chair and sipped coffee. "That does it for now, Colonel Schroyer, at least for me. Is there anything you wish to bring up?"

"Yes, sir, just one."

JP leaned forward. "Just one? I'm getting off easy."

"Colonel Malthus cancelled my daily meeting with the hospital commander. I would like it reinstated."

"Fine. What time would you like to meet?"

"0800 hours would be convenient for me."

"Consider it reinstated. If I'm tied up in the OR or somewhere else, Major Dunbar will sit in for me. You should understand you need no formal time to meet with me. I'm available any time." He stood up. "Colonel Schroyer, thanks again for coming at such short notice."

"It is I who should thank you, Colonel. A heavy load has been lifted from my shoulders."

658

After she left JP told Jeff Dunbar, "My instincts tell me we have one fine chief nurse."

"Your instincts serve you well, Colonel."

JP headed for the door. "I'm going to check on my post-op patients, then head for the mess hall."

"Are you still interested in a martini at the club first?"

"Definitely. Does the officers' club serve meals?"

"Only what can be cooked on a grill."

"Maybe I'll check out the cheeseburgers and fries. I'll meet you there in thirty minutes."

★

Tuesday, November 17, 1970, 1810 hours
Officers' Club, 98th Evacuation Hospital, Long Binh, Republic of Vietnam

The original hospital officers' club was built in 1967 as a small square wooden structure at the edge of the hospital compound adjacent to the Dust-off detachment. The Dust-off commander at the time, a very perceptive single young officer, was aware that the hospital's staff included almost a hundred females nurses and a dozen donut dollies, most of whom were unmarried and attractive. He came to the very logical conclusion there was no need for an officers' club in his own compound and devoted his resources to developing the hospital officers' club. Succeeding Dust-off commander followed his example.

Over the ensuing years the club evolved into a plush, elongated, air-conditioned structure with two tennis courts, volleyball courts, covered patio and garden. Little wonder that officers from all four services in the Long Binh/Bien Hoa area actively supported the club, not only with their cash but their labors. Even the older and more senior field grade officers found reasons to stop by for cocktails at the end of the day.

When Colonel JP Franklin entered the club he was greeted with a blast of cold air carrying the smell of beer and cigarette smoke. The throbbing bass beat of a rock band rolled out from giant speakers. About forty officers, evenly divided between males and females, sat at tables or at the bar. The females, dressed in fatigues, miniskirts, or shorts, were, for the most part, young and attractive.

JP spotted Jeff Dunbar at a table in a corner furthest from any speaker. Walking over, he tossed his cap on the table, sat down and surveyed the club. The main room was a combination dining room, dance floor, bandstand, and bar. Behind the bar swinging double doors with porthole windows led to a kitchen. At one end of the main room, open double doors let him see into a smaller room which had been the original club. It was now furnished with two ping-pong tables, a billiard table and several pinball machines. Beyond the end of the bar French doors led to a garden patio.

JP turned back to Jeff Dunbar. "This is a classy place; I can see why it's so popular."

"Sir, I don't think it's because of the facility."

The music changed to a slow dreamy beat. JP turned to watch a young warrant officer and nurse dancing cheek to cheek. More couples moved towards the dance floor. "I'm beginning to understand," he said.

"How is Private Benson doing?" Jeff Dunbar asked.

"Physiologically good. Psychologically bad. He's devastated over his brother's death. I wish I could have been more comfort. Doctor's don't deal very well with death; it is the ultimate defeat."

"The chaplain routinely visits all the patients in post-op and ICU at least once a day. I'll make sure he understands about Benson."

"It will take a very special kind of person to comfort Benson. I was obviously not the person."

"I think Ted Donaldson is. He's an infantry retread like me. He was a Green Beret lieutenant over here in '62. He was wounded and knocked unconscious by a ChiCom grenade. When he came to he was a prisoner. For two months he was moved west into Cambodia then north. One night he slipped out of his leg irons, killed his two guards, took their weapons and made his way back into South Vietnam. Just before making contact with US forces he ran into a VC patrol. He killed seven before he was wounded in the chest and belly. Left for dead by the VC, he was discovered by US troops who called in a Dust-off. After he recovered from his wounds he went to seminary, then came back on active duty as a chaplain. The wounded GIs here in the hospital can identify with him. He speaks their language."

"His story reminds me of a priest I know sort of like him."

A beautiful Vietnamese woman appeared at the table wearing an au dai. The tight-fitting dress with the slit side accentuated her delicate figure. Jeff Dunbar introduced her as Suzie, a waitress. In a heavy Vietnamese accent Suzie asked, "You want to order drinks?"

"Gin martini on the rocks with big olives," JP said.

"I'll have the same," Dunbar added.

Suzie repeated the orders and left.

"Who is in charge of the club?" JP asked.

"Technically you are, Colonel."

"You're kidding."

"No, sir. Since the club is on hospital grounds the hospital commander has overall authority over it. That never meant much to Colonel Malthus. He never set foot in the club or had anything to do with it. He was always at the senior officers' club on the hill with the brass."

"Who really runs this club, Jeff?"

"Well, the club officer is a Dust-off pilot, John Blalock. His dad owns a chain of restaurants and two nightclubs in Missouri. John is going to take over as CEO when he gets out of the army so he's eager for any food service experience. Sergeant Fertig, the Dust-off detachment supply sergeant, manages the club in his off hours. He get a salary from the club profits. The day-to-day operations are done by Mr. Lim. He was an ARVN infantry captain who lost a leg during Tet. He's salaried, as are the
660

Vietnamese cooks, waitresses, bartenders, and bus boys. Dues are twenty dollars a month. The whole operation is watched over by USARV. They inspect the books once a month and make spot inspections. Sometimes I think the inspections are just an excuse to come here for drinks."

Suzie brought their drinks on a tray. "Vodka martini with big olives for colonel," she said placing the glass in front of JP, "and vodka martini on rocks with big olives for major. Sixty cents, please."

"I'll get these, Jeff," JP said, reaching for his wallet. He placed a dollar in script on her tray.

"You want to order food?"

"I like the ambience here," JP told Dunbar. He turned to Suzie. "Double cheeseburger, well done, and French fries."

Suzie wrote on her pad. Jeff Dunbar ordered a ham and egg sandwich with fries.

After she left JP lifted his glass. "To comrades."

"To comrades," Jeff Dunbar repeated, raising his glass.

Taking a sip, JP commented, "A very good martini." Setting his glass down, he fixed his eyes on his executive officer. "I've learned a lot about the hospital personnel, but so far I know nothing about my XO."

"Well, sir, I graduated from the Citadel in '63 with a degree in business and a regular army commission. I went Airborne Ranger. A year later I was in Vietnam as an infantry platoon leader. Two years later I was back, this time as company exec. When my CO was wounded I was made company commander and promoted to captain. After four months I was pulled up to battalion as the three. On a VR one day my Loach was shot down and the pilot killed. My left shoulder was shattered by a bullet and my ankle broken. The crew chief/gunner got me out of the chopper. For eight days he dragged me through jungle evading VC patrols, some with dogs, hunting us. Somewhere we stumbled into a special forces camp. I owe that guy, Dick Tresgus, my life."

"What became of him?"

"He went back to flying. Two weeks after he started he was shot down and killed." Jeff Dunbar held up his glass in a silent toast. JP touched the glass with his.

Dunbar continued. "I spent six months at Tripler Hospital in Hawaii recovering. My discharge profile kept me from going back to the infantry so I wrangled a transfer to the MSC, and here I am, on my third tour, a hospital XO."

JP shook his head, awed. "Where do we get guys like you, the chaplain, and Tresgus?"

"From all over, Colonel. There are lots of us."

"Thank God for that. There's hope for the country. Are you married, Jeff?"

"Yes, sir. My wife is a nurse at Tripler."

"Any kids?"

"None yet. We plan on starting a family when I get back." Dunbar sipped his martini, then swirled the ice around in the glass before setting it down. "Colonel, there's something about Colonel Malthus and Colonel Kelly I didn't tell you that perhaps I should have. I held back because as far as I knew it was rumor. I didn't want to prejudice you."

"Go on."

"You may have surmised from Colonel Kelly's behavior that she was accustomed to having her way with full backup by Colonel Malthus."

"Now why would I have gotten that impression?" JP asked, smiling.

"Sir, the rumors were that Colonel Kelly and Colonel Malthus had a ah... special relationship."

"You mean they engaged in activities considered unbecoming officers, like violating one of the ten commandments?"

Jeff Dunbar flushed. "That's about it, sir."

JP smiled at his exec's discomfort, then took him off the hook. "When I talked with Colonel Lopez at Med Command she read me parts of a CID investigation on Malthus and Kelly. You're not telling me anything I didn't already know, so don't worry about it, Jeff." He took another sip. "This is really a good martini." Setting the glass down, he looked at his XO. "You seem to know a lot of rumors, Jeff. Any rumors on what assignments Colonel Malthus had before taking command of the hospital?"

"My spies in Med Command told me he was an obscure lieutenant colonel who hadn't practiced medicine in twelve years after screwing up several patients. He had been passed over for promotion to colonel three times and was probably the most senior lieutenant colonel in the Medical Corps. He was about to be forcibly retired when the DA published a revised promotion policy for Medical Corps officers last year. Malthus was picked up on the first go around, promoted to colonel and allowed to continue on active duty."

"How well I remember that policy," JP said bitterly. "I'd still be a lieutenant colonel if it hadn't been for some very dedicated people. Colonel Malthus is a prime example of the adverse impact when merit takes a back seat in the selection for promotion. And then, of course, there are the really outstanding people who quit in disgust."

"Yes, sir. There have been a bunch like Colonel Malthus in Vietnam and not only in the Medical Corps. God only knows how much damage they have done to the army." Jeff Dunbar took a slug of martini, then examined the glass. "Colonel," he said, "I'm sure glad you're here."

"That's just martini talk, Dunbar," JP said, grinning. "You haven't seen my dark side."

"Maybe not, but my spies in the 36th Division filled me in on you."

"Your spies?"

"Sam Durden, for example."

"Oh, oh. How did you come to know him?"

"Sam was a young second lieutenant platoon commander in my company before I went to battalion as the S–3. He wrote me a letter about you."

"That rascal. I knew I should have felt left him on the rocks at the Shawangunks. What's he up to?"

"He was just made CO of the Ranger company."

"Really? I wonder how that came about," JP said, tongue-in-cheek.

A tall, handsome officer in his mid-thirties, wearing a nomex flight suit, approached their table. JP noted the Master Aviator's wings and major's leaves. Jeff Dunbar stood up.

"Colonel, this is Mark Endres, CO of the Dust-off detachment. Mark, Colonel Franklin is the incoming hospital CO."

"I know all about Colonel Franklin," Major Endres said. "Mike Jelnik called me yesterday from Phong Sahn about him."

JP stood and shook hands. "You guys have a network of spies that surpasses the CIA."

Endres laughed. "Mike filled me in on your rotary wing experience, Colonel."

"Major Jelnik exaggerates a lot, but he's a great pilot," JP said. "Join us for a drink, Major?"

"Sir, I'm meeting my wife in a few minutes. Can I take a rain check on the drink?"

"Actually I was going to meet with your wife later this evening. That won't be necessary if you and she will join us now."

Endres shrugged and sat down.

Suzie appeared with two plates. "Cheeseburger fries for colonel; ham egg sandwich and fries for major." She looked at Mark Endres. "You order drink?"

"Scotch and soda on the rocks with a twist of lemon."

Suzie nodded and left.

A striking blonde in close-fitting fatigues entered the club, looked around and headed for their table. Mark Endres stood when he saw her coming. JP and Jeff Dunbar rose.

"Colonel," Mark Endres began, "I'd like you to meet my wife, Denise. She's the assistant OR supervisor."

Denise Endres extended her hand. Her grip was firm and confident.

After they sat down Suzie miraculously appeared. Denise ordered iced tea. "I go back on duty at midnight," she explained. "Colonel Kelly decided I could get by without sleep."

"That schedule may not be valid," JP said. "It would have to be approved by the new OR supervisor."

Denise Endres stared at JP without comprehension. "Sir?"

"I have some very distressing news, Denise. This afternoon Colonel Kelly was overcome by an insatiable desire to retire from active duty as soon as possible. Despite her invaluable contributions to the 98th Evacuation Hospital and the US war effort, I had no choice but to accede to her wishes."

Jeff Dunbar choked on his martini.

JP continued. "Inasmuch as you are the next senior nurse in the operating room and, as I understand, on the list for promotion, Colonel Schroyer strongly recommended you to succeed Colonel Kelly as OR supervisor. The orders are probably being cut as we speak." JP emphasized that the recommendation to appoint her OR supervisor was made by Colonel Schroyer and that he was just following her wishes.

Denise Endres stared at JP as if he had jut slapped her with a dead mackerel.

Suddenly, she smiled. "Mark," she told her husband, "I've changed my mind. Order me a gin martini on the rocks."

★

It was past 2200 hours by the time JP returned to his hooch. After writing a seven-page letter to Kathy he sealed the envelope, wrote FREE in the right-hand corner where the stamp would have gone, and turned out the light. Thirty seconds later he himself was out. When the phone began ringing he was so deep in sleep that he was oblivious to its noise. The thumping on the wall and Jeff Dunbar's voice brought him into the world of consciousness. "Colonel, answer your phone."

JP turned on the light, ignored half dozen roaches on the floor scurrying for cracks, and reached for the phone. "Hello," he muttered.

"Colonel Franklin, you awake?"

"Hmm. I doubt it."

"This is Bill Palowski, Colonel. There are nine wounded on the way in. Two are head and neck cases. Are you up to taking care of them?"

"Who did you say you were?"

"Come on, Colonel, wake up. We need help."

Chapter Seventy-Three

Friday, November 20, 1970, 1020 hours
Headquarters, 98th Evacuation Hospital, Long Binh, Republic of
Vietnam

Colonel JP Franklin was drawing a fresh cup off coffee from the coffee maker in the storage room when Major Jeffrey Dunbar stuck his head in the doorway. "Sir, Harry Resniek just called; he's at Tan Son Nhut. He has a ride to the 3rd Field helipad. Mark Endres will have a chopper standing by there to bring him here."

"Harry doesn't know I'm the new commander, does he?"

"No, sir."

"Good. Now here's how we'll work our nefarious scheme. You meet his chopper when it lands here and tell him the new commander wants to see him immediately. He will ask why. Tell him the commander has declared him AWOL for returning eleven hours late from R&R and is considering punishment under Article 15 as a warning to others."

"But Colonel, Harry isn't overdue. He has until midnight to sign in."

"Major Dunbar, must I remind you that I am a full colonel and the hospital commander. If I say Major Resniek is AWOL, he is AWOL."

"Sorry, sir. I lost my head," Dunbar said contritely.

"Okay. I will continue. The news that he is considered AWOL will almost certainly set Harry off like a rocket. As you walk him over here describe his new commander as extremely rigid and a martinet; a role model for aspiring SOBs who makes Colonel Malthus seem like a prince. Impress upon Harry he would do well to report to the new CO in the proper military manner." JP chuckled. "You know, Jeff, I doubt that Harry has the slightest idea how to report to anyone in a military manner. You will have to give him a crash course on military protocol on the way here."

"Won't he recognize you as soon as he walks into your office?"

"Jeffrey, Jeffrey, what little faith you have in your commander's ingenuity. When he walks in to report I will have my feet on the desk and an open *Stars and Stripes* in front of me. He won't be able to see my face and I'll disguise my voice. Then I'll let him stew for a minute or two. By then he should be close to meltdown."

"Sir, I hope don't mind my saying, you are a most devious person."

"Thank you, Major Dunbar. I consider that a compliment."

★

JP was so engrossed in the statistics of a report on casualty admissions that he paid scant attention to the thumping beat of a low-flying helicopter as it passed low over the hospital, rattling windows and roofs. Moments later Jeff Dunbar appeared at the doorway. "Colonel, I'm on my way to meet Major Resniek."

"I'll be waiting," said JP, grinning evilly.

After Dunbar left JP signed the report and tossed it into his out-basket. Picking up a copy of the *Stars and Stripes*, he leaned back in his swivel chair, swung his feet up on the desk, and opened wide the double-page newspaper, hiding his face. A few minutes later there came a timid knock at the door.

"Enter," JP growled.

A very subdued Major Dunbar whispered reverently, "Sir, Major Resniek is here as you ordered." The only thing Jeff Dunbar didn't do was genuflect.

JP, feet on desk, hand over mouth to muffle his voice, and *Stars and Stripes* in front of his face, snapped, "It's about time he showed up. Send him in."

There was a shuffling of marching feet, then a heavy Brooklyn accent announced, "Sir, Major Harry Resniek reporting to the commanding officer as ordered."

Ignoring him, JP ostensibly continued to read the paper.

After seconds of silence Resniek reported again but louder. "Sir, Major Harry Resniek reporting to the commanding officer as ordered."

JP rattled the newspaper. "I heard you the first time, Major."

More seconds ticked away. Resniek finally boiled over. "Goddamnit, Colonel, you could at least have the courtesy to put that newspaper down and return my salute."

JP dropped the paper, swung his feet to the floor and leaned forward. "Hello, Harry," he said, widely grinning.

Resniek's anger gave way to shock. He stared at JP, disbelieving. "Oh for Christ's sake." He then sank into a chair. "Aw, Colonel, you really got me that time."

Jeff Dunbar, laughing, offered Resniek a mug of coffee. Resniek reached for the mug.

"How was Hawaii?" JP asked.

"It could have been better, Colonel."

"What does that mean?"

"Well, by the time I reached Hawaii I had a rip roaring URI. And just before Rhoda's plane landed in Hawaii she started her period."

"Now you know what is meant by 'war is hell'," JP said, laughing. "Well, at least you got some sunshine and rest."

Resniek continued. "Last I heard you were trying to win the war single-handedly up in the 36th Division."

"Where did you get that distorted information?"

"Some of the surgeons from the 96th Evac and 19th Surg were down here last month to take the general surgery boards. After the exams they got high at the club and gave me an earful." Resniek placed his mug on JP's desk. "Colonel, while you're in a reasonably good humor and maybe even feeling a little guilt at the low-life reception you just laid on me, let me lay a few problems on you."

"Wouldn't you rather unpack, take a shower, and change uniforms?"

"This is too important for delay."

"Go ahead."

666

"Now that Colonel Malthus has gone, the most serious problem is Colonel Kelly, the OR supervisor. She is incompetent and a bitch, and those are her good points. The surgeons ignore her but she runs the OR nurses ragged. When Malthus was here she would run to that asshole; then he would get on my case. He told me her orders were his orders and I'd better obey them. He even went so far as to threaten me with a court martial if I didn't make sure Colonel Kelly's orders were implemented."

JP allowed himself a smile. "And to think you volunteered for Vietnam."

"Biggest mistake of my life."

"Well, there has been a development concerning Colonel Kelly which should meet with your approval."

"I can't wait to hear."

"The day after I arrived here Colonel Kelly decided to retire despite my pleas that she stay on. As we speak she should be somewhere back in the States processing for retirement."

Harry Resniek stared at JP with awe. "You didn't waste any time."

"I had some help," JP said modestly. "What's next on your wish list, my son?"

"The chief of surgery, Bill Palowski, is up on general court martial charges…"

"You're wasting my time, Resniek. Two days ago I talked with the JAG and General Draughn about Palowski's court martial. I have been given full authority to deal with the charges as I see fit. The general was more than happy to dump the whole mess on me."

"What do you plan?"

"Palowski will report to me this afternoon at 1600 hours. I haven't quite decided how things will go," JP said, stretching the truth.

"Can I give you some input about the man?" Resniek asked.

"You'd be wasting more of your time and mine. I already know your opinion of Major Palowski. It's substantiated by the surgeons and nurses with whom I talked. I've also seen Palowski in action. Now what else?"

"Who's in charge of the OR now that Colonel Kelly is gone?"

"Denise Endres. And that reminds me. Her last ER is to be returned along with many others because of significant clerical errors. They will have to be redone and resubmitted. You will be the endorser for the OR nurses except for Major Endres. In her case you will be the rater and Colonel Schroyer will be the endorser. By the way, the OR nurses are back under the chief nurse. Anything else?"

"Well, there is one more…"

JP interrupted. "If it's awards and commendations, just resubmit the paperwork. I've already told Med Command to expect a large number from us. They agreed to take a lenient attitude because no requests for awards had come from this hospital since Colonel Malthus took command."

Harry Resniek slurped some coffee and looked at his commander. "You know what, Colonel? I should go away more often."

"Now, Major Resniek, I have a question for you."

Resniek looked up expectantly.

"What are you doing still on active duty and in Vietnam? You were to have left the army last June and go to Hopkins, where your ultraliberal pontifications would contaminate young impressionable doctors for generations to come. In those heady discussions you and I had at Walter Reed I recall you were violently opposed to the US involvement in Vietnam. I was sure you would take part in an anti-war demonstration and get arrested. In checking your 201 File I learned you extended one year and volunteered for Vietnam. Explain yourself."

"I'm in Vietnam because of you, Colonel," Resniek said bluntly.

"You're talking in riddles, Harry."

"In those discussions we had you were so damn sincere and convincing that the US was morally obliged to defend South Vietnam. I became concerned that you might be right and I might be wrong. As you know, Colonel, I am seldom wrong."

"That's a crock."

"I decided to come over here to see for myself what my country had gotten itself into."

"You are something else, Resniek. What have you learned?"

"Are you sure you want to hear this?"

"I can handle it."

"It was just as I suspected; you were wrong and I was right. I learned this was not a morally justified war; I'm not sure it's legally justified. Our fearless leaders, most of whom have never heard a shot fired in anger, suckered us into this war, a war they have no intention of winning. They certainly have no intention of risking their own miserable draft-dodging offspring. Over here I have learned first hand the terrible cost in American blood of their duplicity, and much to my sorrow I have become a party to it."

"You know, Resniek, for a New York City liberal with a PhD from Columbia and an M.D. from Hopkins, you're not so dumb. Twenty years from now I may agree with you. For now don't let those thoughts intrude on your duties as a doctor and military officer."

★

Major William J. Palowski, Medical Corps, United States Army Reserve, Chief of Surgery, 98th Evacuation Hospital, knocked sharply at the door of the hospital commander.

"Enter," Colonel JP Franklin called out.

The chief of surgery marched smartly up to his commander's desk. "Sir, Major William J. Palowski reporting to the commanding officer as ordered, sir."

JP scrutinized Bill Palowski's cleanly shaven face, his recent PX haircut, and his clean, starched fatigues. Even though he couldn't see Palowski's boots he was willing to bet they were polished. It was obvious someone had coached him. "Stand at ease."

Major Palowski moved his feet apart and clasped his hands behind his back.

JP continued. "General court martial charges have been brought against you by Colonel John Malthus, the previous commander, for the following offenses: absent without leave, using a US government vehicle without authority, driving a US government vehicle without a license, misappropriation of US government property, insubordination to a superior officer, and misuse of military personnel. Do you understand the nature of these charges?"

"Yes, sir."

"I have thoroughly investigated the merits of the charges and discussed them with the USARV Judge Advocate General and Brigadier General Draughn, commander of Medical Command. As a result of these discussions I have been given full authority to adjudicate these charges as I see fit."

"Yes, sir."

"I am prepared to offer you non-judicial punishment under Article 15 of the Uniform Code Military Justice. Should you accept such proceedings there would be no appeal from my decision and any penalty I impose. Is that clear, Major Palowski?"

"Yes, sir."

"Should you decline to proceed under the provisions of Article 15 I would have no choice but to recommend a court martial. A conviction would carry the stigma of a misdemeanor or felony conviction with its untoward ramifications. Conviction under Article 15 carries no such stigma and, depending on the punishment imposed, may not even appear in your 201 file other than a note that the matter was adjudicated."

Major Palowski turned pale. He was clearly concerned. "Sir, I accept Article 15 proceedings."

JP pushed a sheet towards Major Palowski. "This document articulates your rights and the implications of Article 15 proceedings. Sign and date where you see an X."

Palowski leaned over the desk, scanned the sheet, picked up a pen from the desk and signed. He straightened back up.

"Major Palowski, after reviewing your performance as chief of surgery, the high esteem in which you are held by the professional and enlisted staff, the inestimable American and Vietnamese lives you have saved, and after consideration of the motives that guided your use of a government vehicle and supplies, I have decided all charges against you will be dropped except the charge of insubordination to your commanding officer. That is an offense which cannot be tolerated."

JP could hardly keep a straight face. "I am therefore issuing you an oral reprimand. Inasmuch at is it oral, the reprimand cannot appear in your 201 File nor will it go beyond this office."

Relief flooded through Major Matt Palowski.

"Wait outside while my decision is typed up for you to acknowledge by signing. Before you go let me give you a word of advice. The next time you want to go out to that village or any other village for humanitarian purposes, discuss it with me or Major Dunbar. There are ways of keeping such activities legal and even obtaining material and technical support. Besides, we will probably want to go with you."

"Yes, sir," a beaming Major Palowski replied.

"That is all. You are dismissed."

Palowski took one step backward, saluted, did an about-face and marched out.

★

JP was out by the coffee table again filling his cup when Jeff Dunbar joined him. "Colonel, you made one happy surgeon this afternoon. When the word gets out there will be a lot of celebrating at the club tonight."

"Those charges were absurd, Jeff. It would have been ludicrous to pursue them. Besides, Major Palowski, has done so much good here that he deserves a little slack. Speaking of the club, what say we knock off while things are slack and head over there for a martini?"

"Colonel, you're the kind of commander an XO would want to emulate."

As they started to leave they heard Colonel Schroyer call out. "Colonel Franklin, I need to talk to you."

JP waited for her to catch up. "Let's go back to my office, Helen. You too, Jeff."

Once in his office JP waited for the chief nurse to seat herself, then took his seat. Jeff Dunbar remained standing.

"A problem has come up that I have never encountered before," Colonel Schroyer began.

"Sounds challenging, Helen," JP said.

"One of my nurses, Lieutenant Downing, reported to me this afternoon that she has heard a male voice in the room next to hers for the past three nights."

"Is there a nurse assigned to that room?"

"Yes, sir, Lieutenant Belson. Lieutenant Downing didn't report it earlier because she didn't consider it any of her business. Last night was different. She heard loud voices in an argument and Lieutenant Belson sobbing almost hysterically. Lieutenant Downing became concerned and decided to report the incident."

"Did Lieutenant Downing see a male in the nurses' quarters?" JP asked.

"No, sir, but she has heard some of the doctors talk about an unknown officer who has shown up in the male BOQ latrine the last three mornings. No one knows who he is or where he works, and he's not very communicative."

"If Lieutenant Belson is married the male could be her husband?"

"Lieutenant Belson's records indicate that she is single. Besides, when a married nurse is visited by her husband we arrange a room for them other than in the BOQ or nurses' quarters."

JP looked at his executive officer. "What do you think, Jeff?"

"Sounds like someone is spending part of the night in the male BOQ, then slipping over to the nurses' quarters when the coast is clear, returning before dawn."

"What about the barbed wire enclosure and the MP at the gate?"

"Aw, come on, Colonel."

"He goes under the wire?"

"You got, it, sir."

"Army intelligence is looking for people like you," JP said. "How about coming up with a plan to nail this turkey."

Major Dunbar didn't hesitate. "I'll talk to some of the doctors in the BOQ. Whoever sees the phantom will call me immediately. I'll also coordinate with the MPs so we'll have some muscle on board when we confront the phantom."

"You must have been a whiz as an S–3. Okay. Let's do it."

670

Saturday, November 21, 1970, 0605 hours
98th Evacuation Hospital, Long Binh, Republic of Vietnam

JP was just about to leave his hooch for the mess hall and breakfast when the phone rang. He picked it up. "Colonel Franklin," he said into the phone.

"This is Jeff Dunbar, Colonel. Our phantom is shaving in the BOQ latrine. The MPs are on they way."

"I'll meet you outside the BOQ," JP said and hung up. It took three minutes at a fast walk to reach the BOQ.

Jeff Dunbar moved out of the shadows by the entrance. "Good morning, Colonel."

"Good morning, Jeff. It looks like your simple plan is about to bear fruit." He scanned the empty road leading to the BOQ. "I wish the MPs would hurry. I don't want this turkey to get away."

A moment later the lights of a jeep turned into the road. Soon the jeep pulled up to the BOQ and parked. A 6'3" MP captain stepped from the jeep's passenger seat. An equally tall but heavier MP sergeant got out from the driver's side and locked the steering wheel with a chain. They came over to JP and Major Dunbar.

"Sir, I'm Captain Ferranti, the exec of the MP detachment. This is Master Sergeant Almond. Our CO decided we should come since there is a high probability that the suspect is an officer."

"I appreciate your helping on short notice," JP said. "Your know Major Dunbar?"

"Yes, sir. Everyone knows Major Dunbar. He's the Long Binh tennis champion. He's beaten me every time we play, and I thought I was good."

JP looked at his exec. "I'm learning something new about you every day."

"How would like to work this, Colonel?" Captain Ferranti asked.

"You're the professional, Captain. You call it."

"Yes, sir." Ferranti turned to Jeff Dunbar. "Anything new?"

"Bill Schandler will identify the subject by nodding or pointing to him. You'll know Schandler from the orange and purple towel wrapped around his waist."

"That would be hard to miss," chuckled Ferranti. "Lead the way."

Major Dunbar led into the BOQ, then down a long hall to the communal latrine. Five males, in various stages of undress, stood at sinks shaving, brushing teeth, or combing hair. One male, an orange and purple towel around his waist, stepped away from the sink and whispered to Jeff Dunbar, "He's still in the shower."

Major Dunbar passed the information to the MPs, who then took positions by the shower entrance, their arms folded over their chests. In a few minutes a pudgy man of medium height in his late thirties or early forties emerged from the shower, a towel wrapped around his bulging middle. The MPs glanced at Bill Schandler who nodded affirmative.

Captain Ferranti stepped in front of the man. "Excuse me, sir," he said almost apologetically. "I'm Captain Ferranti of the MPs. I'd like to ask you a few questions."

The man stared at Ferranti and the MP sergeant. "Certainly, Captain."

"Sir, are you a member of the hospital staff?"

"No. One of the doctors here is a friend. He invited me to stay with him while I was at Long Binh on TDY. I leave today to go back to my unit at Danang."

"Your name and unit, sir?"

"Dalton, Colonel Mercer Dalton, US Marine Corps. I'm with the 1st Marine Division."

"And the friend's name with whom you are staying?"

"Smithy, Captain Charles Smithy, Medical Corps. Actually, Captain, Charles is more like a young brother than a friend."

Major Dunbar took Ferranti aside and whispered, "Captain Smithy DEROSed last week. His name card probably is still on the door."

Ferranti nodded and returned to Colonel Dalton. "Do you have your personal belongings in Captain Smithy's room, sir?"

"That's right. What the hell is this all about, Captain?" Colonel Dalton said, a little righteous indignation creeping into his voice.

Ferranti ignored the question. "Sir, when did you last see Captain Smithy?"

"Just a few minutes ago. He was asleep. He had been operating until early this morning."

"Colonel," Captain Ferranti said firmly, "let's go to Captain Smithy's room. You can show me your ID and TDY orders; this will all be straightened out."

"Look, Captain, there's no need for all of us to go barging up to Charles's room and waking him," Colonel Dalton said. "He needs his rest and I have to catch a plane at Bien Hoa at 1100 hours. I'm on a tight schedule."

"Not to worry, Colonel. If everything checks out we'll make sure you don't miss your flight."

"Tell you what, Captain," Colonel Dalton countered, "to keep from disturbing Charles, give me a few minutes to get dressed. I'll bring my ID and orders down to you."

"Sorry, Colonel, but we'll have to go with you." Captain Ferranti turned to JP. "We'll take it from here, sir."

"It's all yours, Captain."

"We'll stop by your office before we leave."

"Appreciate it, Captain, and thanks."

★

Back in his office JP, his feet on his desk, sipped coffee from what had been Colonel Malthus's mug. He debated whether to go to breakfast or wait for Ferranti, when Helen Schroyer knocked and walked in.

"Good morning, Helen. Please excuse my lack of manners," he said, not moving from his position. "Have a seat."

Colonel Schroyer eased into an armchair. "I heard you were operating last night."

"An ARVN shot through the face."

"Colonel, I'm not sure how to tell you this. It is somewhat awkward."

672

"Lieutenant Belson?"

"Yes, sir. I just talked with her. She told me her last period was two months ago. She thinks she's pregnant."

"I suspect she's right, and the father is a miserable marine full colonel from Danang named Dalton?"

"No, sir. The father is a marine major named Osterman stationed in Danang as a brigade supply officer."

A flush of anxiety passed through JP. His feet hit the floor just as Captain Ferranti's huge form filled the doorway. "We may have the wrong man," he told Ferranti. "The man we want is a marine major named Osterman, not a full colonel named Dalton."

Captain Ferranti gently but firmly guided Colonel Dalton into the room, except that now Colonel Dalton, dressed in a marine fatigue uniform, wore major's leaves on his collar points.

"Colonel Franklin," Captain Ferranti said, "meet Major Osterman alias Colonel Dalton." Ferranti handed JP an ID card.

After studying the picture and name on the ID card he returned it to Captain Ferranti without comment.

Ferranti continued. "We briefly interviewed Lieutenant Belson. She identified Major Osterman and gave a statement. She stated she and Osterman have had sexual relations over the past five months whenever he came to Long Binh on TDY or leave. He gave her a ring and promised to marry her. When he learned she was pregnant he tried to coerce her into getting an abortion by a Vietnamese doctor in Saigon. He even offered to pay for it. That precipitated the argument overheard by Lieutenant Downing."

JP looked at Osterman with contempt. "You are a real gentleman."

Captain Ferranti explained, "When Major Osterman came to Long Binh he scouted out the doctor's BOQ for a vacant room; there were always two or three. He would stay in a vacant room until late in the evening. When everything was quiet he slipped into the nurses' quarters and Lieutenant Belson's room."

"Where do we go from here, Captain?" JP asked.

"I talked with my superior who talked to the USARV JAG. The army has no jurisdiction over marines when marine authorities are available. The JAG said to leave it to your discretion."

"So much for lawyers," JP said, grimly.

A ray of hope came into Osterman's eyes only to be dashed when JP told Jeff Dunbar, "Chase down Major Osterman's CO and get him on the phone."

Jeff Dunbar told Major Osterman. "Come with me, Major." The two MPs followed Osterman and Dunbar out.

JP looked at Helen Schroyer. "You'd better take Belson off the nursing schedule for now. We should get her over to Harvey Powell at the 3rd Field for an exam and prenatal care. I'll call Colonel Powell as soon as I get rid of Major Osterman." He shook his head. "This is really a new one for me, Helen. What's been done in the past with pregnant nurses?"

"Those who are single are sent home and discharged. The army takes care of prenatal care, delivery, and postnatal care."

"Does this sort of thing happen often?"

"I don't think so. Lieutenant Belson is the first since I've been here."

Jeff Dunbar stuck his head in the door. "Sir, Colonel Pinezy, Osterman's CO, is on line one."

For the moment the name Pinezy elicited no recognition. JP picked up the phone and pressed the flickering button. "Colonel Franklin."

A voice asked, "Colonel Franklin, by any chance would you be the doctor who operated on Harold McDougall?"

Recognition flashed. "Jim Pinezy, you rascal. I've never forgiven you for putting me on the roster to guard the South Pacific beer supply."

There was a chuckle at the other end. "I've come a long way since then, Pfc Franklin, so have you."

"Hey, I made corporal on Iwo. General Mueller told me you replaced McDougall as battalion commander. I was sorry I didn't get to the change of command ceremony."

"They say war is hell."

"Are you still commanding a battalion?"

"No, General Mueller made me a brigade exec. For the next two weeks I'm acting brigade commander while the CO is on leave."

"How is it going?"

"It's a little more stressful than commanding a battalion."

"I'm afraid what I tell you tell next may stress you a bit more."

"Go ahead. I can handle anything the army can lay on me."

"One of your officers, Major Osterman, has been having an affair with one of our nurses, a young second lieutenant. Osterman had been staying in vacant rooms in the BOQ, then sneaking into the nurses' quarters. The nurse is now two months pregnant. He wanted her to get an abortion on the economy."

"That bastard."

"The MP report will probably included giving false information to a commissioned military police officer, and impersonating a superior officer, a full colonel."

"Hell, that's one rank above me, his commander."

JP laughed.

"What else has he done?"

"Well, he stayed in our BOQ without authorization, failed to pay the BOQ fee, entered a restricted area, the nurses' quarters, and got one of the nurses pregnant. Apparently he promised to marry her. Maybe we can have a shotgun wedding before he leaves."

"That better not happen, JP. He's already married and has three children. I'll add adultery and conduct unbecoming to the charges. He's a disgrace to the Marine Corps."

"What do you want me to do with him, Jim?"

"Tell him to get his sorry ass up here as soon as possible and report to me."

"Consider it done. Do you ever come to Saigon?"

"I DEROS in one month."

"Call me with your ETA. I'll have someone meet you and bring you here. Certainly you can delay going home one day to see an old World War II marine buddy."

"I'll do that. It's been a long time since you and the Chief got drunk and destroyed an army bivouac area."

"Twenty-seven years go fast, and that story grows with each telling."

"Right. Congratulations on making colonel."

"Thanks. Tell General Mueller and Father Icardi the welcome mat is always out at the 98th Evac. We have some private VIP rooms that double as guest rooms."

"I'll keep that in mind. Semper Fi, JP."

"Back at you, Jim."

After JP hung up he went into Jeff Dunbar's office where Captain Ferranti waited with Major Osterman. "You can turn him loose on his own recognizance. He has time to catch his flight back to Danang. On arrival he is to immediately report to Colonel Pinezy."

A subdued Major Osterman rose from his chair and walked out.

"Do you want me to write out a summary?" JP asked Captain Ferranti.

"I don't think that will be necessary, Colonel. I have enough information with Major Osterman's and Lieutenant Belson's statements. Copies will be forwarded to Osterman's commander."

Both turned to the door as heavy footsteps approached running Colonel Schroyer slowed to a stop at the doorway to Jeff Dunbar's office, panting.

"You're out of shape, Helen," JP quipped. "What's up?"

"Lieutenant Belson is in the ER. She OD'd and she's bleeding."

Chapter Seventy-Four

Saturday, November 21, 1970, 1110 hours
Emergency Room, 98th Evacuation Hospital, Long Binh, Republic of
Vietnam

Colonel JP Franklin hit the double doors of the emergency room at a run; the doors slammed open. At the far end of the room Lieutenant Belson's naked form lay on a stretcher. A green sheet, stained with blood, covered her legs and hips. Two plastic bags of blood hung from IV poles, their life-saving contents streaming into her veins. A plastic breathing tube, inserted through her mouth into her trachea, was connected to an anesthesia machine. Joe Wendell, stood at her head, rhythmically squeezing a black bag to ventilate Belson's lungs with oxygen.

Jack Bednard, leaning over her face, had just passed a nasogastric tube through the left nostril into the stomach. While he secured it to the nose with strips of adhesive tape thick yellow gastric juices dripped from the end of the tube. A medic passed him an empty 50 cc syringe. Connecting the syringe to the end of the NG tube, he sucked out as much of the stomach contents as he could, then began lavage with saline.

Rick Eberhardt, one of the emergency room doctors, folded the sheet away from Belson's hips and thighs exposing thick gauze pads soaked with blood. Removing the pads, he dropped them into a kick bucket, cleaned away blood and clots with a towel, then prepped the vaginal area with germicidal solution, a losing battle against the bleeding. While he tried to keep the area free of blood using suction and gauze pads, a nurse, First Lieutenant Betsy Robinette slipped a urinary catheter into Belson's bladder, then connected it to a bottle on the floor.

"What's her status, Rick?" JP asked.

"We're staying up with blood loss so far, Colonel. Her BP is 100/60; she's holding her own. She reacts only to painful stimuli; her pupils are constricted and her reflexes are depressed. From the way she's bleeding I suspect she has retained products of conception but I can't rule out the possibility of an attempted self-induced abortion."

"Any idea what she OD'd on?"

"There was an empty bottle of Seconal and a quarter empty bottle of gin by her bunk. Colonel, we have done about as much as we can here. She needs a D and C. If that doesn't control the bleeding she'll need a hysterectomy. That's not a decision I feel comfortable making on a twenty three-year-old. I'd like to send her over to Colonel Powell at the 3rd Field. In fact, I've already requested a Dust-off; I hope you don't object."

"Not at all. I'll call Colonel Powell to let him know what we're sending. When will she be ready to go?"

"She's ready now."

"Okay. You and Joe Wendell go with her on the Dust-off."

"Right, boss."

JP walked over to the ER supervisor's desk. Major Sally Westman, the supervisor, looked up as she hung up the phone. "The Dust-off will be on our pad in five minutes, Colonel."

"Good. I need to use the phone, Sally. Do you have a phone directory?"

"Yes, sir. If you need the 3rd Field's phone number it's on the card under the phone."

JP quickly found the number for the 3rd Field Hospital commander's extension and dialed it. A female Vietnamese voice with a French accent answered.

"This is Colonel Franklin, commander of the 98th Evac. I urgently need to talk to Colonel Powell."

"One moment please, Colonel Franklin."

While waiting, JP picked up a pencil from the supervisor's desk and began tapping it against the desk top.

Colonel Powell's voice came through. "JP, what's up?"

"We have an acute OB emergency here, Harvey, a two-month pregnant second lieutenant nurse, about twenty-three, who OD'd on Seconal and gin. She is bleeding so heavily that the ER doc is suspicious of an attempted self-induced abortion. We're not making any progress here; our experience with miscarriages and attempted abortions is zilch."

"Send her on. I'll alert the OR for a D and C and possible hysterectomy."

JP watched Belson's stretcher lifted and carried towards the ER door. "She's on her way to the chopper now. She should be there in fifteen minutes. Joe Wendell, one of our nurse-anesthetists and Rick Eberhardt, the chief ER doc, will accompany her."

"We'll take good care of her, JP. I'll call you as soon as things stabilize."

"Thanks, Harv."

After hanging up JP walked out to the helipad and watched the Dust-off with Belson take off and disappear. As he re-entered the emergency room a Huey helicopter came in low and fast. The thunder beat of its rotor wash shook buildings The sounds abated rapidly as it touched down. In the emergency room Harry Resniek and the assistant chief of surgery, Jerry Meacham, waited with Betsy Robinette and Sally Westman.

JP walked up to the nursing supervisor. "More casualties, Sally?"

"Just one; a lieutenant with a chest wound. He arrested in the Dust-off on the way here. "Major Westman's voice shook.

"What is it, Sally?"

"He was fragged by one of his men, Colonel."

The report hit JP as if a knife in his heart. The Vietnam War was slowly eroding his world based on discipline, honor, and loyalty. Fragging – the killing or attempted killing of officers and NCOs using fragmentation hand grenades – was an escalating practice in Vietnam. It was a practice that had devastating impact on discipline, morale, and combat efficiency. Young company officers were often intimidated into decisions that evaded contact with the enemy rather than risk being murdered by their own men high on drugs.

The double doors of the emergency room burst open: medics pushed through a gurney. A young lieutenant lay supine on a stretcher, his face a mask of purple pallor, his fatigue jacket soaked with blood. The stretcher was lifted to a pair of sawhorses and the ER team descended on him. "There's no pulse, BP, or respiration," Lieutenant Robinette reported. In less than a minute Harry Resniek intubated the lieutenant and began to ventilate him. IVs were started; blood under pressure poured into veins. A jagged tear no larger than a quarter in the left chest wall chest wall oozed bright red blood.

Jerry Meacham leaned over the lieutenant and briefly examined the wound, then began external cardiac massage. Blood poured from the chest wound. Meacham shook his head. "This won't hack it. He's got a chest full of blood. I'm going to crack his chest."

Betsy Robinette pushed a Mayo stand close to Meacham's right hand, set a wrapped sterile tray of chest instruments on the stand and ripped open the wrapping.

Harry Resniek looked to JP and shook his head.

JP shrugged as if to say the decision to open the lieutenant's chest was Captain Meacham's and not his. He moved towards the stretcher to assist Meacham when Captain Bednard walked into ER. Meacham called over to him, "Jack, put on gloves and give me a hand."

By the time Jack Bednard had pulled on a pair of gloves and bellied up to the stretcher Meacham had started. He swiftly cut through the skin and muscles between the fourth and fifth rib. Jack Bednard placed the rib spreader and stabilized the claws while Meacham ratcheted the spreader, opening a three- to four-inch gap in the chest wall and breaking two ribs in the process. Blood and blood clots now poured from the opened chest. "Suction," Meacham pleaded, "and somebody fix that light."

Lieutenant Robinette pushed two suckers into the chest; one stopped up almost immediately. She quickly brought in another. Meacham, ignoring the ineffective suckers, shoved both hands into the chest and began scooping out blood clots. "Now get those suckers in here," he said, "and somebody fix the damn light."

After a third sucker was introduced and the spotlight adjusted, Meacham slipped his left hand into the chest and grabbed a suction from Betsy Robinette with his right. Jack Bednard strained for a look.

"I'm elevating the left lung now, Jack, to get to the mediastinum," Meacham explained. He held out his right hand. "Long Metz... Forget it," he said, pulling his hand back. "The mediastinal pleura is in shreds. The aorta has a big hole in it and the vena cava is severed."

"Jerry, he's been over five minutes without a pulse or BP," Resniek said. "We have no idea how long he was that way before he got here."

Meacham began to massage the heart. More blood flowed from the chest. "Give me a Debakey vascular hemostat. I'm going to cross clamp the aorta."

"Jerry, his pupils are fixed and dilated," Resniek said, "and he's up to eight units of blood." He stood up, peered into the open chest and shook his head sadly. "You can't fix that."

"Goddamnit, Harry, I can try."

Captain Meacham worked the open jaws of the vascular clamp around the garden hose-sized artery leading from the heart. The ratchet sound of the clamp closing was heard above the noise of the suction machines. "Oh shit," he groaned, "it tore off. The aorta is too friable to hold a clamp. It will never hold sutures."

JP suppressed the urge to order Meacham to quit. This was Meacham's case; the decision when to give up was his.

Meacham's shoulders suddenly slumped. Finally, he had accepted defeat, not by a Viet Cong or an NVA, but by a murderous American soldier. He straightened up. "Go ahead and extubate him, Harry." He glanced up at the wall clock. "Time of death is precisely 1208 hours. Jack, close the chest."

Almost in tears Captain Jerry Meacham, M.D., Medical Corps, US Army Reserve, stepped away from the table and ripped off his gloves, trembling from the effort to keep his emotions under control. JP understood his grief. Doctors are very poor losers, and Jerry Meacham had definitely lost.

JP went over and put an arm over Meacham's shoulders. "Jerry, the lieutenant was dead as soon as he was hit," JP said, his thoughts momentarily drifting back to Kristy's Goulden's fatal wound.

"This was such a waste, Colonel," Meacham said, bitterly, "such a fucking waste."

"This whole stupid war is a waste, Jerry."

★

When JP returned to his office from a late lunch, Jeff Dunbar was seated at the conference table with a full colonel military police officer, a chief warrant officer, and Captain Carl Hoagland, the adjutant who was recently appointed mess officer "in addition to his other duties". No one was smiling.

"Oh, oh," JP said as he walked in.

Jeff Dunbar stood up and made the introductions. Colonel Martin was the Long Binh provost marshal and Chief Warrant Officer Trent was an agent from the CID. After they stood and shook hands, Dunbar continued, "They're here to give an update on the mess hall. Carl will give the background."

Hoagland started to rise but JP waved him down.

"Sir, the day after you appointed me mess officer I began an examination of the mess hall records. It quickly became apparent that a significant discrepancy existed between the number of rations requisitioned by the mess sergeant, the daily headcounts, the patient population, and total number of officers and enlisted men assigned to the hospital. Judging from the records and ration requests, our mess has been feeding half the population of Saigon."

"You mean one of the cooks has been cooking the books?" JP asked.

"That's about it, Colonel."

"Didn't anyone at the ration dump get suspicious?"

"They certainly should have, Colonel Franklin," the provost marshal interrupted, "and that's the basis of another investigation."

Captain Hoagland continued, "After discussing these findings with Major Dunbar we both went to the Long Binh provost marshal and JAG with our data. They brought in the CID. That's when Mr. Trent became involved. He will describe the results of his investigation."

Chief Warrant Officer–3 Trent cleared his throat. "Sir, we infiltrated a young CID agent into the mess hall as a cook's apprentice. He gave a cover story of having been just released from the Long Binh jail after serving a sentence for dealing marijuana. On his second day at work he began to show symptoms of drug withdrawal. The next day the mess sergeant, Sergeant Varney, took him aside and asked if he would be interested in making extra money with an added benefit thrown in. All he had to do was drive a truck to a certain address in Dong Lop."

"That's a village between here and Saigon, Colonel," Jeff Dunbar explained.

Mr. Trent continued. "Our agent agreed. He made the run yesterday. On the way to Dong Lop he stopped long enough for CID agents to examine the truck's cargo. Would you believe frozen meat, fresh produce and cartons of canned goods?"

"That explains all the spaghetti and meatballs we've been getting," JP lamented.

Trent smiled. "After the truck's cargo was marked and photographed, the truck continued to Dong Lop with our agents following. The truck was unloaded at a small warehouse. The driver was given two sealed envelopes, one for himself, the other for Sergeant Varney. The driver's envelope contained fifty dollars and three capsules of pure heroin. Sergeant Varney's envelope contained 600 dollars. The money and heroin were marked and photographed. Sergeant Varney's envelope was delivered to him at the mess hall. We managed to get photographs of his accepting the envelope and counting the money."

"Have you arrested Sergeant Varney?" JP asked.

"That's what we wanted to discuss with you," Colonel Martin said. "We traced ownership of the warehouse where the stolen goods were delivered to an ARVN colonel. The implication of an ARVN colonel and the distribution of heroin suggest more than simple stealing government property and black market racketeering. We have enough evidence now to hang Sergeant Varney, but we need more time to define what else and who else is involved. For those reasons we would prefer to hold off any arrests for the next week or two."

"Do you have any idea how long this has been going on?"

"The records at the ration dump and the mess hall suggest it began with Sergeant Varney's arrival. We are convinced it could not have continued to the extent it has without the support and collusion of higher-ups."

"Good God, Colonel, you don't think…"

"We consider all possibilities, Colonel Franklin. Right now it looks bad for Colonel Malthus. His decision to eliminate the position of mess officer and hospital nutritionist makes no sense from a hospital commander's perspective. It does make sense in that it left Sergeant Varney in sole charge of feeding over 600 people and facilitated his thievery. With that in mind we requested that the FBI investigate Colonel Malthus's bank accounts and other assets to determine if they were consistent with his military salary. Colonel Malthus's retirement has been delayed pending the outcome of this investigation."

JP, stunned that a senior medical officer might be implicated, remained quiet.

"I am at liberty to tell you there has been a major break in the case," Chief Warrant Officer Trent continued. "The name of the previous mess hall truck driver was obtained from the mess hall records. We learned he DEROSed to the States three weeks ago. He has been arrested and has agreed to cooperate with investigators and the JAG in return for a lenient sentence. He will be returned to Vietnam."

JP looked at Captain Hoagland. "Carl, you stirred up a hornet's nest. You need to go into law enforcement."

"I came to the same conclusion, Colonel, and applied to law school at Fordham."

"Oh no, not another lawyer."

Colonel Martin got to his feet. "Well, Colonel Franklin, that's where we stand now. I came with Mr. Trent to ask for your cooperation in this case."

"Of course."

"We need things to continue here as before without any hint of an investigation. We want to avoid alerting the subjects."

"You realize you're condemning hundreds of hospital personnel and patients to a lousy Thanksgiving."

"Yes, sir. I promise to make up for it as soon as this case is wrapped up. The Long Binh quartermaster owes me."

JP turned to Jeff Dunbar. "What do you think, XO?"

"It's all in a good cause, sir. I just hope we don't end up with spaghetti and meatballs on Thanksgiving."

Chapter Seventy-Five

November 29, 1970, 1250 hours
Mess Hall, 98th Evacuation Hospital, Long Binh, Republic of Vietnam

"Would you like another helping, Colonel?" asked the mess man behind the serving line.

Colonel JP Franklin scrutinized the semi-liquid material in the main compartment of his tray. "What is it, Garnett?"

"Beef Stroganoff, sir."

"You're putting me on."

"No, sir. That's what Sergeant Varney said it was."

"At least it isn't spaghetti and meatballs."

The mess man gave his commander a sick smile. "Sir, that's for tonight."

"Garnett, you have made my day," JP said, then continued along the serving line. Spinach, mashed potatoes and jello were added to his tray. The jello began to melt as soon as it landed on the hot tray. At the end of the serving line a Vietnamese woman took his tray, then followed him to a vacant table.

The Vietnamese woman set his tray down on the table. "You want drink?" she asked.

"Water, iced tea and black coffee, please."

"You want three drinks?" the woman asked, incredulous.

JP smiled and nodded. "Is that okay?"

The woman shrugged. "You colonel, you boss; it's okay." She went off.

The practice of having a Vietnamese woman carry trays for able-bodied fighting doctors, nurses, and admin officers of the United States Army did not sit well with JP. His initial reaction had been to discontinue the practice. "Why can't we carry our own trays?" he had asked Jeff Dunbar. His executive officer explained the facts of life to his commander. The women were daily hires. Every morning they lined up outside the gate hoping to be selected for a day's work. If they were stopped from carrying the trays in the mess hall they would be out of jobs. All were widows of ARVN soldiers and most had kids to feed. The hospital jobs, meager as they were, provided most of their incomes. JP was left with little moral choice but to allow the practice. Nevertheless, it bothered him.

He was bothered more by his recollections of double amputees and paraplegics in ARVN uniforms begging on the streets of Saigon. Even active duty ARVN troops were sometimes forced to beg or engage in some sort of illegal activity to sustain themselves and their families. In many units ARVN officers stole the pay and ration money intended for the troops. He recalled having read somewhere that the early manifestations of a decaying nation was its failure to honor its military men, its military widows and their families. Based on these criteria South Vietnam was a decaying nation.

682

What troubled JP even more was the disgraceful treatment by his own country of servicemen returning from Vietnam. Confrontations, insults, spitting on uniforms and other humiliating acts were common. Even the grieving widows of servicemen and the wives of POWs/MIAs were not immune to abuse by their countrymen. Many wives and widows received phone calls and anonymous letters exalting the deaths or capture of their loved ones in Vietnam as "acts of God, well deserved for having served in an immoral war". Other wives and widows were plagued with proposals to meet for sexual trysts, establish relationships or assistance with investing insurance money; sometimes all three.

He recalled one of his patients at Walter Reed, the attractive widow of a navy pilot killed when his plane, returning from a mission over North Vietnam at night and in severe weather, crashed into the rear of his carrier. She confided in JP that she was so plagued by a persistently obnoxious caller that she was considering suicide. Apparently the caller had gotten her name from newspaper obituary pages. It was a simple matter to get her phone number and address from the telephone directory. This was a far cry from World War II, when the community rallied around its war widows, protected and supported them.

The widow was so distraught that JP referred her to Brad Marley for psychiatric counseling. He also called a former marine buddy from World War II, now a detective in the Arlington Police Department, and described the widow's ordeal. The detective persuaded the widow to move in with her parents for a few weeks. He then installed a sexy policewoman in the widow's apartment. The policewoman, whose brother had been a marine killed in Vietnam, had volunteered for the assignment with alacrity. In a week she had the anonymous caller phoning three and four times a day. All the phone calls were legally recorded.

At the end of the first week the lowlife came to the widow's apartment unannounced and forced his way in, breaking the chain lock. The policewoman resisted his advances and backed away, pleading for him to leave. He pulled a knife and threatened to kill her unless she submitted. The policewoman, an accomplished kick boxer, delivered a powerful kick to the man's groin. As he doubled over she kneed him in the face, smashing his nose. At that moment two police officers exploded from a bedroom, wrestled the man to the floor and handcuffed him.

The man was charged with attempted murder, attempted rape, assault with a deadly weapon, forcible entry into a home, and harassment. The district attorney, with a son in Vietnam, rebuffed the man's efforts to plea bargain and the case went to trial. The man was convicted on each count by a jury. The judge, whose son, an air force pilot shot down over North Vietnam and MIA, imposed the maximum sentence for each conviction, with the sentences to run consecutively. The publicity given to that case dampened the enthusiasm of other lowlifes who had been harassing service wives and widows.

A young female voice asked, "May we join you, Colonel?"

Looking up, JP saw First Lieutenant Mandy Hershorn, a very good-looking psychiatric nurse. With her were Captains Charles Ventress and Bill Morely, both fully trained psychiatrists but not yet certified by the American Board of psychiatry.

"Please do," JP said.

After the three were settled and drink orders taken, Lieutenant Hershorn asked, "Any feedback on Cindy Belson?"

"Quite a bit. She had an emergency D&C which stopped the bleeding. She was going to be evacuated to Japan to recuperate but she insisted she stay in Vietnam to finish her tour. She'll be coming back here in a week. Colonel Schroyer will put her on limited duty until Belson feels strong enough to go full time."

"That's great," Mandy said. "She has a lot of friends here."

"What's new and exciting on the psychiatric wards?" JP asked the two psychiatrists.

"Strange cases, Colonel," Captain Ventress said, "so strange that you might have trouble believing them."

"Any time a psychiatrist is impressed by a patient's behavior it is notable."

"We had three admissions this morning. Two were self-inflicted wounds and one a case of sleepwalking."

JP timidly swallowed some beef Stroganoff and winced. "Speaking of self-inflicted wounds…" Laying down his fork, he picked up a slice of bread and began buttering it.

Ventress smiled and continued. "Both SIWs were of the foot, the left foot to be precise."

"You psychiatrists are really up on your anatomy."

"The story gets better, Colonel. The self-inflicted wounds occurred within thirty minutes of each other. Both patients were rear echelon troops and in the same unit. In fact they were close buddies living in the same hooch. They were never exposed to danger or hardship, so the motives for the SIWs are hazy."

"How serious are the wounds?"

"Both have shattered bones and torn ligaments. They will be on crutches and need physical therapy for months."

"Why are they on the psych ward?"

"The orthopods were reluctant to keep them on their wards for fear the patients with bona fide combat injuries would attack them. Then there's the question of what may have been an inappropriate relationship."

"I'm heartened you people still consider that kind of relationship inappropriate," JP said. "What's the story on the sleepwalker?"

"He's an officer on a brigade staff down in the Delta. Two nights in a row he tried to climb into a bunk with a sleeping officer. He was lucky he didn't get shot. Each time he claimed he was asleep and had no recollection beyond getting into his own bed."

"You believe that?"

The psychiatrist shrugged. "We're trained to objectively consider what our patients tell us. We don't make value judgments."

"Does that mean you have no opinion on the beef Stroganoff?"

"We do make exceptions for extreme circumstances."

Mandy Hershorn interrupted. "Colonel, you've made some great changes since you took over as CO."

"I have a feeling you haven't finished, Mandy."

"You're right, sir. When are you going to focus on the mess?"

"Some people consider the food here excellent."

Lieutenant Hershorn showed a sick smile. "Can you name anyone other than the mess sergeant?"

"Off hand… no."

"I ate dinner over at the 93rd Evac yesterday. Their chow was far superior to ours, and their Thanksgiving dinner was out of this world."

"You may find this hard to believe, but the chow here will improve substantially in a week or two."

"I've heard that line before, Colonel."

"But not from me. Trust me, Mandy."

"I've heard that line before too, Colonel."

JP studied the attractive young nurse. "I'll bet you have," he said, chuckling.

A Vietnamese woman came to the table and stopped by JP's chair. "You Colonel Franklin?"

JP nodded.

"You have phone call."

Rising, JP excused himself and went to one of several telephones scattered around the dining room. The caller was Lieutenant Colonel Wes Takita, the division surgeon for the 4th Division and a friend from internship days at Walter Reed.

"I always know where to find chow hounds," Colonel Takita said.

"I'll bet you have already eaten lunch at the 4th Division general's mess."

"How did you know? Look, JP, I have a case here that's way over my head."

"That's an unusual admission for you."

"One of the most significant lessons I learned since my internship was humility, or the art of knowing when to punt."

"I'm impressed. What do you have?"

"The patient is a twenty-four-year old corporal named Benjamin Fonsica. He was in good health until two days ago when he experienced belly cramps and loose stools. Yesterday he complained of dry mouth and double vision. Today he has difficulty swallowing and loss of pupillary reflexes. Whatever disease he has seems to be progressing rapidly. All lab tests including a spinal tap were normal or negative."

"You have some thoughts, I hope?"

"Guillian-Barre Syndrome and polio crossed my mind, but there is a hooker. A week ago he received ham canned by his grandmother in Nebraska. He ate some of the ham at that time. Three days later he ate some more. Two days after that the belly pain and diarrhea began. That history brought up the possibility of botulism."

"I've never seen a case."

"Neither have I, much less treated one. I hope someone on your staff has."

"I doubt it."

"At least you have a neurologist and an infectious disease type at your hospital plus a sophisticated lab. I'd like to send Fonsica to you."

"Fine. We accept all challenges. Do you have a time estimate?"

"He should be there in about ninety minutes."

After hanging up JP returned to his table, summarized the patient's history for the psychiatrists and was rewarded with blank stares. "Thanks a lot," he told them. He ate a few more bites of Stroganoff, then picked up his tray, handed it to one of the Vietnamese women hovering nearby and returned to his office.

★

By the time Corporal Benjamin Fonsica was admitted to the internal medicine ward his condition had deteriorated considerably from the one given on the phone by Colonel Takita. His speech was difficult to understand, saliva drooled from the corner of his mouth and his respiratory efforts were weak. Lab tests revealed anemia, a drop in platelets, and an inability to concentrate urine. Five specialists – internal medicine, infectious disease, neurology, neurosurgery, and JP – examined Corporal Fonsica, then gathered at the nursing station to discuss management.

The neurologist, Lieutenant Colonel Earl Wendling, summed up everyone's thoughts. "I don't know what Fonsica has, but he appears to be dying of it. His respiratory muscles have just about quit working and he can't handle his secretions. He needs an immediate tracheotomy and respiratory support on a ventilator. If his urine specific gravity continues to fall or he stops putting out urine he will require renal dialysis."

"What about the possibility of botulism, Larry?" the chief of internal medicine, Major Ted Lefkoff, asked.

"That's a strong possibility. So far it hasn't been ruled out nor has it been established. If the diagnosis were botulism there is no antitoxin in Vietnam, Japan, Korea or Okinawa. The only botulism antitoxin I know of is in San Francisco, and that's almost thirty hours away by jet."

"Is there someone in the States who is an expert on botulism?" JP asked.

"None in the continental US, but there is one at the University of Hawaii. I can't think of his name but I have it in my files."

"Hawaii gives me an idea that will cut flying time considerably for the patient and a plane carrying the antitoxin," JP said.

"I'm with you, Colonel," Wendling said. "We send Fonsica to Tripler in Hawaii and arrange for the antitoxin to leave Travis in California on a jet for Hickam."

"You read minds well, Larry, but saying it is one thing, getting two airplanes out of the air force is another. That's my problem. Yours is to go ahead with the tracheotomy and keep Fonsica alive. Ask Bill Palowski to do the trach and Harry Resniek to monitor the airway. This kid's hold in life is tenuous."

★

Back in the headquarters building JP walked into his exec's office. Jeff Dunbar, working at his desk, looked up. "Good afternoon, Colonel," he said.

"That's a subject open to debate on any given day in South Vietnam." JP sat down by Dunbar's desk. "Here's my problem, XO," he said, then related the medical history

686

of Corporal Ben Fonsica. "If the diagnosis is botulism and he does not received antitoxin he will die. The problem for us now is to get a C–141 from the air force, have it fitted with a respiratory unit, then get Fonsica on the way to Tripler a.s.a.p. We will also need a second plane from the air force to fly the antitoxin from Travis to Hickam."

Major Dunbar stared at his commander. "I must say you think big, sir."

"That is the essence of high command, XO. Maybe you should write that down."

"Sir, did you consider the expense of such an operation?"

"Only as an interesting statistic. I'm a doctor, Jeff, and there is nothing about expense in the Hippocratic oath."

"How can I help?"

"You can get me the name and phone number of the air force officer who owns all the C–141s in Vietnam."

Dunbar reached for his phone. "Give me a few minutes, Colonel. I've never done this before."

"Neither have I, Jeff."

★

The operating suite was quiet when JP entered. He found Harry Resniek in his little cubbyhole office reading the December issue of the *AMA Archives of Anesthesiology*. "Why read that, Harry?" he asked. "Don't you know everything there is to know about gas passing?"

"I do, but I like to read other people's ideas, then tear them apart."

"The people or their ideas?"

"Both," Resniek said, grinning.

"You are one intellectual son of a bitch, Harry."

"And you, sir, are a fine judge of character."

"How did the trach go on Fonsica?"

"Fine. We got him on a respirator just in time. You should have seen the crud we cleaned out of his lungs. He is going to need meticulous respiratory care if he's going to survive long enough to reach Hawaii."

"That brings me to my next question."

"Which would be?"

"Are you willing to accompany Fonsica to Hawaii if I sweeten the offer with a three-day layover before you returned?"

Resniek's eyes widened behind his coke-bottle glasses.

"Of course that would be contingent on your not having a URI and Rhoda not having a period."

"We can meet those requirements, Colonel... I hope."

"One of the phones in my office is a regular telephone to the States. You're welcome to use it to call your wife, but you will have to call collect."

"Do you know when the plane will take off?"

"Not yet. In fact I don't know yet if we have a plane."

"I knew this was too good to be true."

"Oh ye of little faith from Brooklyn. You must learn to trust your commander. I'll get two airplanes from the air force if I have to go to General Abrams himself to get them."

★

When JP returned to his office after eating early chow he found a paper on his desk with the name, Brigadier General Vernon Lanassa, USAF, and the telephone number of his office at Bien Hoa Airfield. Flopping into his chair, he dialed the number, went through several secretaries and aides until a gruff voice came on line.

"Lanassa."

"General, this is Colonel Franklin, commander of the 98th Evacuation Hospital at Long Binh."

"Yes, Colonel, I know about you."

"Oh, oh."

"Colonel Withers at Phong Sahn alerted me that you were coming to this area. He also warned me of your propensity for making absurd demands on the air force."

"I'm afraid Colonel Withers's assessment may be accurate, General."

"Let me be the judge of that, Colonel."

"General, I desperately need a C–141 fitted with a respiratory unit to carry a patient to Hickam as soon as possible. I also need a plane to carry a supply of botulism antitoxin from Travis to Hickam."

"Is that all? Hell, I had an idea that Withers was exaggerating."

JP explained Fonsica's medical predicament.

"I'll see what can be worked out and call you back in thirty minutes."

"Thanks, General. You are always welcome at the 98th Evac."

"I hear you have one hell of an officers' club."

"Yes, sir. It does enjoy that kind of reputation."

"I'll have to check it out. Tell me, Colonel Franklin, is it true you messed up the rear cockpit of an air force OV–10 while at Phong Sahn?"

"I'm afraid so, sir. I never expected most of the flight to be flown inverted. The barf bag furnished by the air force failed to function under those conditions. Frankly, sir, I believe the many hours Colonel Withers has flown in the inverted configuration has adversely impacted his cerebral function."

General Lanassa laughed. "I knew that years ago. Okay, Colonel, I'll call you back."

After hanging up JP went into Jeff Dunbar's office.

"How did you make out with the general, Colonel?" Dunbar asked.

"Well, he hung up laughing."

"I take that as a positive sign."

"He said he'd call back in thirty minutes. Do we have a Red Cross representative in the hospital?"

"Yes, sir, three."

"I'd like the Red Cross to notify Corporal Fonsica's next of kin in person, explain the gravity of his condition and urge them to get on the next plane to Honolulu."

"I checked Fonsica's personnel records, Colonel. The only next of kin is his wife who works as a waitress. I doubt she has the money to fly to Hawaii and back."

"Maybe the Red Cross or Army Emergency Relief can help out."

"Yes, sir. I'll get them started on it."

★

True to his word General Lanassa called back thirty minutes later. "Here's what has been worked out, Colonel Franklin. A medevac 141 had been scheduled to leave Bien Hoa tomorrow morning at 1100 hours. The departure time has been moved up to 2300 hours tonight. The plane is being fitted with a respiratory unit as we speak. Most of the patients on that flight are coming from your hospital. Can you have them out at the plane by 2100 hours?"

"Yes, sir."

"A plane has been laid on at Travis to leave with the antitoxin for Hickam Air Force Base in two hours. Now, is there anything else the air force can do for the army?"

"I can't think of anything off hand, General. If I do I'll call you."

"I was afraid you would say that."

★

Thursday, December 3, 1970, 0730 hours
98th Evacuation Hospital, Long Binh, RVN

When Colonel JP Franklin walked into his office after a breakfast of watery, reconstituted, dehydrated eggs the elderly Vietnamese cleaning woman stopped dusting his desk and looked up. He bowed deeply towards her. "Good morning, Mama san."

"Good morning, Colonel," she said, bowing deeper in return.

"Did you make many rockets last night for the VC?"

Her grin revealed brown-stained teeth. "Yes, yes, make many rockets for VC." With that she left the office as Jeff Dunbar walked in.

"Good morning, boss."

"Good morning, XO. You don't think she's serious about making rockets, do you?"

Dunbar laughed. "No, sir. Her son was a VNAF flight commander shot down trying to help a Mike Force in trouble. She likes working here just to be around military people."

"I didn't get any calls last night. That was a good omen."

"Yes, sir. There was call earlier this morning from Mr. Trent. He would like to come by this morning to talk to you. There are some development concerning Sergeant Varney and the mess hall he wants to discuss."

"While on that subject, I want Varney out of the mess hall one way or another before Christmas. What's being done about a replacement?"

"He's already on board."

"You mean there is another sergeant first class working in the mess hall?"

"Yes, sir, but without his stripes. He was a brigade mess sergeant who got drunk and beat up three MPs so badly that they required hospitalization. As a result he was court-martialed and busted to private."

"Jeff, I don't think we want that kind of person as our mess sergeant. He doesn't sound any better than the man he's replacing."

Major Dunbar laughed. "That's the cover story the CID arranged for him, Colonel. Working as a private will give him insight into the operation of the mess hall and the people who work there before he officially takes over."

"Where did you find this mess sergeant?"

"At Cam Rhan Bay in the convalescent center."

"Now how did you manage that?"

"I called the exec up there who is an old infantry buddy and asked him to survey patients about to return to duty for an outstanding mess sergeant. He called back and gave me the name of First Sergeant Melvin Quinn. Sergeant Quinn arrived here a week ago. He was briefed by the CID on the type of evidence they required."

"You are one tricky rascal, Dunbar. I'm not sure I can trust you."

There was a knock at the door. Both men looked up. Chief Warrant Officer Trent and two MPs filled the doorway.

JP indicated the chairs around the conference table. After they were seated he asked, "You have some follow-up on the mess in my mess hall?"

"I hadn't heard it put quite that way, Colonel," Trent said, smiling. "Our little sting operation turned out to be a big sting. It involved not only US personnel but ARVN officers, enlisted men, and civilians. An extensive black market and drug distribution ring has been broken up. We have five GIs in custody. Three already have asked to plea-bargain in exchange for lenient sentences."

"Outstanding."

"We have a warrant for the arrest of Sergeant Varney."

"Be my guest."

"The JAG has authorized pre-trial confinement at LBJ. A JAG representative will coordinate with you on the charges to be drawn up against Sergeant Varney."

"You and your men have done fine work, Mr. Trent. I'm very grateful. Once the chow improves around here everyone will be grateful."

"There is another development of which you should be aware, Colonel."

"What is that?"

"Do you recall the provost marshal mentioning that the FBI was looking into your predecessor's bank accounts and assets?"

"Vaguely."

"They have learned that Colonel Malthus, over a five-month period, had sent his bank in Philadelphia 47,000 dollars in excess of his military salary."

"That bastard," JP said, his voice laced with venom.

"My sentiments, sir. His retirement has been held up so he can be returned to Vietnam to stand trial." Trent and the MPs stood up. "With your permission, Colonel, we will place Sergeant Varney under arrest and read him his Miranda rights."

"You have my permission and my blessing. Come by the mess hall in a week and check out our chow."

"I just might do that, Colonel."

After Warrant Officer Trent and the MPs left, JP asked Jeff Dunbar, "How would you like to write up Captain Hoagland for some sort of commendation for my signature?"

"Be happy to, Colonel. He deserves it."

"Let's give the sheriff and his deputies enough time to clear the hospital compound, then go over, officially greet our new mess sergeant and try out his coffee."

"There's another bit of good new s concerning the mess hall."

"And what might that be, XO?"

"Colonel Martin, the provost marshal, arranged through the system for us to draw double rations of steak, hamburger, and chicken for two weeks."

"After what our people had to eat for the last six months they will think they died and went to heaven."

"I was surprised you didn't start taking your meals at the senior officers' mess on the hill."

"Don't think that didn't cross my mind, considering the dues I have to pay to belong to that outfit."

The sergeant major rapped on the door jamb, "Sir, you have a phone call from a colonel at Tripler."

"Thanks, Sergeant Major." JP picked up the phone. "Colonel Franklin," he said.

"Theo Paranakes, Colonel. I'm chief of medicine at Tripler."

"Yes, sir."

"I want to give you a follow-up on the patient, Benjamin Fonsica, with suspected botulism."

"I can't wait to hear."

"A very strange case, Colonel Franklin. By the time Fonsica reached the ward he was sitting up, asking for something to eat and demanding the tracheotomy be removed."

"You're kidding. I knew the air force could do remarkable things with their airplanes but this is beyond belief."

"Today he was decanulated. He's going about the ward as any active healthy twenty-four-year-old."

"What happened to my provisional diagnosis of botulism?"

Paranakes laughed. "Dr. Armitage, the world expert on botulism at the university, went over Fonsica as soon as he was admitted. His conclusion was that whatever disease Fonsica had it definitely was not botulism. Administration of antitoxin would have been inappropriate."

"I guess I pushed the panic button a little prematurely."

"These cases are such enigmas, Colonel. Under the circumstances I would have done the same thing. I suspect we will never know the true diagnosis. On the other hand the case demonstrates what happens when a cutting doctor tries to emulate a thinking doctor." Paranakes laughed at his own little joke. He added, "The Red Cross flew Fonsica's wife to

691

Hawaii. She is staying at the guest house on Tripler and Fonsica has an overnight pass tonight."

"Let's hope he doesn't work himself into an exacerbation. Colonel, I appreciate the follow-up."

"There are a few more tests cooking. I don't expect them to be any more enlightening than the test results already back."

After hanging up JP started for Jeff Dunbar's office when the sounds of two short bursts of M–16 fire several hundred meters away startled him. Half a dozen rapid single shots quickly followed, and then quiet.

Jeff Dunbar was in the hall. "That sounded close, boss, like the mess hall."

"Varney." JP started out the door.

"Hold up, Colonel. You don't have a weapon. Besides the last shots were from .45s. The MPs were carrying .45s. There were no answering shots from the M–16, so Sergeant Varney has been disarmed, wounded, killed or escaped. If he's escaped you're better off here." Dunbar stepped into his office, then quickly returned, strapping a .45 pistol and holster around his waist. "I never took the oath to preserve life," he said. Removing the pistol from its holster, he jacked a round into the chamber.

"Sometimes it pays to have an ex-infantry type as XO."

Moments later the phone rang. JP grabbed it viciously.

"Mr. Trent, sir. There's been a shooting."

"Damn it Trent, I can hear. What happened?"

"When we went to arrest Sergeant Varney he took off with an M–16. He shot Captain Hoagland and one of my men, then said he was coming after you. In the exchange of gunfire Varney was killed."

JP was momentarily overcome; one man dead, two wounded, all because of him. "What about Captain Hoagland and the MP?" he asked softly.

"They were taken to the emergency room, sir."

JP hung up. "Let's go. Hoagland and an MP were shot. They're in the ER now and Varney is dead. I wish to hell I had left things alone."

"You don't really mean that, Colonel," Jeff Dunbar said.

As they went out the door the phone rang in JP's office. "Hold up, Jeff. This could be about Hoagland." JP returned to his office and picked up the phone. "Colonel Franklin," he said.

"Bill Palowski, sir. I've just finished examining Carl Hoagland and Corporal Dunforth, the MP."

"What's the word, Bill?" JP's heart was pounding.

"The MP was hit in the abdomen and spine. He's paraplegic. He going to the OR for a laparotomy and probable tying off of the lumbar spinal cord."

JP groaned. A young man paralyzed from the waist down for life. "And Carl?"

"A shattered left humerus with probable nerve and vessel damage. The neurosurgeon will repair the nerve; I'll repair the artery."

"I'll be over as soon as I call Hoagland's wife."

After hanging up JP repeated to Jeff Dunbar what he had been told. "Three casualties, Jeff; two wounded and one dead, and not a single VC or NVA around to blame. What a tragic waste, Jeff. What are we doing to ourselves?"

Chapter Seventy-Six

The wounding of Carl Hoagland and the military policeman torpedoed hospital morale, sinking it to great depths. Morale sank even lower when the policeman died a week later of overwhelming sepsis. JP, weighed down by heavy guilt for having been indirectly responsible, considered asking to be relieved. Then a sudden influx of casualties brought the hospital to near inundation. The intensity of effort required to manage the plethora of wounded was therapeutic. While Carl Hoagland and the MP were not forgotten, the urgent need to care for the acutely wounded forced hospital personnel, including the commander, to compartmentalize grief and move on.

The provost marshal honored his pledge to arrange for extra rations to be issued to the hospital mess. Sergeant First Class Quinn turned out to be a jewel. In less than a week as mess sergeant the food improved to near-gourmet quality. By Christmas the reputation of the mess was such that GIs from adjacent units flocked to the hospital for Christmas meals. In the spirit of Father Christmas JP followed his XO's advice, turning a blind eye to the large number of unauthorized personnel eating in the hospital mess.

The days passed rapidly from 1970 to 1971. Hospital personnel came to accept their new commander as accessible, competent, hard working, with a weird sense of humor. Jeff Dunbar proved so capable an executive officer that JP turned most of the administrative aspects of the hospital over to him. Harry Resniek, as chief of anesthesia and chief of professional services, became the father/confessor to the professional staff, earning their respect by his intellect, competence, candor and common sense. In late January he was promoted to lieutenant colonel. His promotion party left the officers' club in shambles and most of the staff with hangovers.

By mid-February JP was so desperate to see Kathy and the kids that he considered going AWOL. Instead, he appointed Harry Resniek acting hospital commander, took ten days' leave, and flew to the US on a chartered jetliner packed with military personnel. The plane was forty minutes out from New York's La Guardia Airport when a flight attendant's distressed voice came from the PA system.

"If there is a doctor on board, please come to the front of the aircraft."

JP, in an aisle seat in the aft section, hesitated, curious to see how many doctors would respond. He was positive there were other doctors on board. Seeing no movement, he undid his belt, stood up and moved forward in the aisle, convinced he had discovered the ultimate test to identify "real" doctors. When a flight attendant on an aircraft urgently called for a doctor, whoever stood up was a real doctor.

Near the front row a pretty flight attendant was kneeling beside an inert soldier on the floor in the aisle. Although crowded for space, JP managed to kneel opposite her with the GI between. "I'm Colonel Franklin, a doctor," he said. "What can you tell me about him?" He looked at her name tag, "Nancy."

"Not much, Doctor. He was returning to his seat after using the latrine when he collapsed on the floor and had a convulsion."

There was no fecal odor and the GI's trousers at the crotch were dry, evidence that the GI did not lose bowel or bladder control and raising some doubt as to the nature of the seizure. JP felt the neck for a carotid pulse; it was fast and thready. Unbuttoning the GI's shirt he raised the T-shirt. The chest movements were slight, indicating shallow breathing.

JP looked up at the flight attendant. "I need a flashlight."

In a moment she handed him a heavy flashlight. Turning it on, he shined its bright beam into each eye. Both pupils were contracted to pinpoints. "Let's take a look at his forearms," JP said. Each rolled up a sleeve.

The flight attendant held up a forearm. "This is what you're looking for," she said.

The multiple puncture wounds on the forearm left little doubt. "How did you know?" JP asked.

"My husband is a Port Authority police officer at La Guardia and my dad is a doctor in the military."

JP nodded. "Is there portable oxygen on board?"

"Yes, sir."

She was gone less than a minute, returning with a green tank the size of a fire extinguisher. It was connected to a plastic hose with a rubber mask attached at the end.

Taking the tank, JP turned the circular knob to full open and placed the mask over GI's mouth and nose. He told the flight attendant, "My guess is that he's overdosed, probably heroin. His breathing is depressed. He could arrest at any time. He needs urgent hospitalization."

"You need to talk to the captain, sir," the flight attendant, Nancy, said. Standing, she motioned to another flight attendant. "Keep that mask over his face, Brenda. I'm going to take the doctor to the cockpit."

"Brenda, if he should vomit," JP told the second flight attendant, "turn his head to one side and clean out his mouth with your fingers. If he stops breathing give him mouth to mouth." Ignoring her frightened look, he followed Nancy to the cockpit door. She unlocked it with her key and disappeared inside. In a moment the door opened and she beckoned him to enter.

The captain, a balding man in his late fifties, removed his sunglasses and regarded JP for a moment, then extended his right hand. "Jim Farhensen, Doctor."

"JP Franklin." He winced at the grip.

"What's the situation back there?"

"What I've seen suggests a drug overdosage with respiratory depression; possibly a suicide attempt. He could stop breathing at any time. He needs medical treatment as soon as possible."

"We're only twenty minutes out of La Guardia. If you say so I can clear us through the traffic by declaring a medical emergency. That would be faster than trying to get cleared to an alternate field."

"Okay. Do it."

The captain nodded and slipped on his sun glasses.

JP left the cockpit and returned to the unconscious soldier. "I'll watch him from here on," he told Brenda, the second flight attendant.

A slight reduction in engine noise was followed by the sensation of lightness as the plane began a gradual descent. The flight attendant, Nancy, brought a small tote bag and a thick brown envelope. "These were in the overhead bin. Both have his name."

"Thanks." JP opened the folder and slipped out several dozen sheets of military jargon. The top sheet made reading the others unnecessary; it was a bad conduct discharge, more than likely for drug use and possibly drug dealing. Some of the soldier's pallor could have been due to time in prison. Little wonder he tried to end his life; his troubles were just beginning. After copying down the GI's name and service number, he returned the papers to the folder and stuffed them in the tote bag.

Seventeen minutes later the plane taxied to a gate at La Guardia Airport. As soon as the door opened two paramedics came on board, lifted the unconscious soldier and carried him down the aisle. JP went back to his seat, slipped on his blouse, picked up his briefcase and caught up with the paramedics as they carried the GI out the door and loaded him onto a gurney. He related his findings and impressions for the paramedics as he walked alongside the gurney to the waiting ambulance.

"Thanks a lot, Colonel," one of the paramedics said as they lifted the gurney and GI into the rear of the ambulance. "We'll take good care of him."

JP watched the ambulance move into departing airport traffic, its red lights flashing and siren whooping. Suddenly, remembering his connecting flight to Washington National Airport he jogged back into the terminal, up a flight of stairs and down a long corridor. The plethora of empty seats at the scheduled gate was an ominous sign.

The middle-aged female gate agent gathering up papers behind the counter looked up sympathetically. "I'm so sorry sir," she told him. "Your plane departed the gate five minutes ago." She eyed the ribbons on his blouse, the shining caduceus on his lapels and the silver eagles on his shoulder. "Let me see what I can do." She picked up the phone with one hand and extended her other. "May I have your ticket?"

Handing her his ticket, JP sat down in the nearest seat and fumed at fate. Kathy and the kids were expecting him home in two hours; he wasn't going to make it.

The woman talked for several minutes, made changes on his ticket, then looked over at JP and smiled. "Colonel Franklin," she called, holding out his ticket.

JP leaped to his feet.

"You're booked space available on the next flight to Washington National, Flight 712, departing at nine tonight. There are lots of empty seats. You shouldn't have any trouble boarding. Your luggage left on the flight you just missed. It will be waiting for you at National."

JP gave her his most appreciative smile. "Thank you, ma'am."

"I wish you wouldn't call me ma'am. It make me feel so ancient."

"Thanks, miss."

"That's better," she said. "I'm sorry I couldn't get you on an earlier flight. If you're hungry there's a nice restaurant just beyond the American Airline ticket check-in. I'll be eating there myself in half an hour."

696

JP mumbled something like, "Maybe I'll see you there," and fled.

With over three hours to kill he headed for the pay telephone, dialed the operator and placed a collect call to Kathy.

"JP, it's so good to hear your voice. Where are you?"

"I'm stuck here at La Guardia for the next three hours." He explained about the GI and missing his flight by five minutes.

"Do you want us to meet you at National?"

"No, I'm flying space available. That's always iffy. I'll call you from National, then take a cab home."

"We'll all be up waiting."

"I'm sorry about missing the plane, Kath. This is a hell of a way to start my R&R."

"Don't you worry about it, JP. I'll make it up to you after you get home."

"That kind of talk is enough to make me skip the plane and run to Sliver Spring."

Kathy laughed. "Save your strength, Colonel; you'll need it after you get here. I'll be waiting for you. In the meantime get something to eat."

JP found the restaurant as per the airline lady's instructions. He started to enter when an insulting grating voice stopped him.

"Hey, Colonel, back from killing babies?"

A gangling unshaven man in his mid-twenties, dressed in faded dirty jeans, greasy hair hanging below his shoulders, came up to JP and began fingering his campaign ribbons. "How many babies did you kill for each one of these?"

The man was at least a foot taller than JP, thirty pounds heavier and twenty years younger. JP considered breaking his wrist, but decided instead to try to avoid a confrontation. He brushed the man's filthy hand from his uniform and started to turn away when the man grabbed his arm and turned him.

"Hey, you fucking murderer, I'm talking to you."

JP slowly put down his bag. It had been thirty years since he had occasion to use hand-to-hand combat, and then he had killed a Japanese. Now he wondered if he were going to spend his R&R in jail or in a hospital. A burly 6'3" marine corporal stopped a dozen feet away. For several seconds he quietly watched the confrontation, then moved towards JP and the hippie.

"Excuse me, Colonel," he said in a soft gentle voice. In a move almost too fast to see he delivered a massive punch to the scumbag's mid-gut, doubling him over, gasping and retching. The marine followed up by smashing the heel of his dress shoe down on the man's instep. If the man could have caught his breath he would have screamed.

The marine was solicitous as he firmly grasped the man's arm and twisted it behind his back. "Sir, you seem to be ill; let me help you." He guided the groaning and limping hippie towards the nearest latrine. A passing Port Authority policeman stopped the two. Quickly sizing up the situation, he told the marine, "Thanks for your assistance, Corporal. I'll take care of him from here."

The marine returned to where JP stood, somewhat stunned by the burst of events. "I'm sorry as hell about that, Colonel," he said.

"Thanks for saving me from what could have been a night in jail or several weeks in the hospital." He extended his hand. "I'm Colonel Franklin."

"Corporal Josephson, sir." The marine's grasp was firm. "Glad I was around to be of help."

"Tell me, Corporal Josephson, are there circumstances that permit a marine corporal to drink beer and break bread with an army colonel?"

"No, sir. The regulations are very clear on that subject."

"Well, what about drinking beer and breaking bread with an army colonel who was once a marine corporal."

"Sir, the regulations are less clear on that subject."

"Semper Fi, Corporal. Follow me… and that's an order."

"Aye, aye, sir."

★

Ten days' leave translated into two days' traveling time to get to Silver Spring, Maryland, two days' traveling time back to Vietnam, and more or less six days at home. If only the time remaining in Vietnam would pass as fast. With Jim, the oldest, in his first year of an air force ROTC scholarship at Duke, only three kids, Paul, Frank, and Nancy were at home. Fortunately, all were of school age and were in school much of the day. That left Kathy and JP free to be on what could be considered an extended honeymoon.

One morning after the kids left for school, Kathy was in the kitchen washing the breakfast dishes while a restless JP sat on the rug in the living room half-heartedly watching a TV talk show. Greta, the German shepherd, lay against him, her head in his lap. Suddenly he shouted, "Kathy, come in here quick. You've got to see this."

Kathy appeared, wiping her hands on her apron. "I've got to see what?"

JP nodded towards the TV. "That."

A young man, dressed in well-tailored suit and tie, was being interviewed by the attractive morning show hostess. His clean-cut look, short haircut, and form-fitting suit made him seem the kind of young man every father hoped would date his eligible daughter. Introduced as a former air force first lieutenant who had flown fighter bombers in Vietnam, he was pimped by the hostess to describe his experiences.

The former fighter pilot spoke in a clear, educated, believable voice. His appearance and demeanor reeked integrity and credibility. "My targets," he began, "were schools, hospitals, and villages. Time and again I saw my napalm burst in schoolyards where children were playing. I watched as they ran in all directions engulfed in flames." The lieutenant became so overcome by remorse he was unable to continue for several minutes.

The hostess oozed sympathy. "It must have been horrible for you."

Finally, the handsome former lieutenant was able to pull himself together. "I'm okay now," he said bravely. "I can continue. I must continue so that the world will know the war crimes this country has been committing."

"What did the air force do when you told them that bombing schools and hospitals was criminal and immoral, that you couldn't go on doing it?" the hostess prompted.

"I was grounded and sent to Wilford Hall Hospital in San Antonio for psychiatric observation. After a month I was given a medical discharge and threatened with court martial if I spoke out about bombing civilians. But I must talk about it. I'm willing to risk a military court and jail, even the firing squad, to set my country on the path back to morality and righteousness."

"You are one of the most courageous and heroic persons I have ever met," the hostess gushed as she embraced the former lieutenant.

"He's also a lying son of a bitch," JP added.

"He seemed so authentic and sincere," Kathy said, ignoring her husband's profanity.

The next television segment included a peace activist just returned from Hanoi. He had brought with him dozens of watercolor paintings which he claimed were painted by schoolchildren in North Vietnam and presented to him when he visited their village. The camera focused on a crude simple painting the size of a business letter. "This is an eight-year-old girl's recollections of a US aircraft releasing its napalm pods over her village." He went on to the next picture. "This is the little girl's school. It shows that napalm has burst in the schoolyard and covered her schoolmates with flame. Some of the children are running".

For ten minutes the activist showed one horror painting after another, all allegedly showing atrocities committed by US war planes.

JP stood up, went over to the TV and turned it off. "My God," he told Kathy, "if that's what people in this country are fed day after day no wonder they despise the military."

"That is why I quit watching television."

"Why do the networks put that stuff on when the most superficial investigation would have exposed it as fraud? Whose side are they on anyway?"

"JP, there are people in this country who are determined to get the US out of Vietnam by any means. Many want to see a North Vietnam victory and the United States humiliated. They actively work towards it. They support North Vietnam financially and do everything they can to hamstring the United States. It doesn't matter that their perfidy prolongs the war and costs American lives. In time of war what they do would be considered treason. And speaking of perfidy, our so-called friend and allies across the water are setting a precedent for it."

"What do you mean?"

"They have no hesitation taking our foreign aid, stealing our military secrets, and trading with our enemies at the same time."

JP stared at his wife. "How do you know that?"

"Remember, my dad headed up the DIA before he retired."

"That old codger. I always thought he was smarter than he looked."

"That's a coincidence," Kathy said, laughing. "He said the same thing about you." Taking off her apron, she tossed it on a chair. "Come on, Colonel, let's go to Woody's and spend some of those big bucks you full colonels get. After that you can take me to lunch at the Vendome."

"Good God, woman, you think expensive."

★

The night before JP was due to leave for Vietnam was a Saturday night. He and Kathy left the kids with a babysitter, the sixteen-year-old daughter of the chief of pathology. Then they drove to the officers' club at Fort Meyers, just over the DC border in Virginia. The main parking lot was full so they cruised the adjacent auxiliary lot where Kathy quickly spotted a vacant space.

"Coming out here is becoming a family tradition when you go off to war or return from war," Kathy said.

"This is the last time," JP said firmly. He set the parking brake, placed the gear in park and turned off the engine. "I've had it with war, Kath."

"What does that mean?"

"There are no more good wars, only wars."

"That's what I've thought all along."

The officers' club was filled to capacity. Kathy had made a reservation even before JP arrived home, so she and JP were assured a table. As luck would have, the maitre d' took them to the same table where they had celebrated their first wedding anniversary after JP returned from the Korean War, a decorated first lieutenant. Now, twenty years later, they were sitting at the same table sipping the same drinks; he gin martini on the rocks, she a glass of white Zinfandel. JP chuckled.

"What is it?" Kathy asked.

"This place never seems to change; only the people who come here have changed."

"Have you changed, JP?"

JP took a long sip of martini. "Yes, I have, Kathy. I have lost my innocence. I no longer trust my country, have faith in its leaders, or believe what they tell me. Most of the senior officers I know feel the same way. It has seriously weakened our country." He paused to sip his martini." "We have sacrificed 50,000 of our best young men for nothing. We will have hundreds of thousands of crippled young men to care for to remind us of our folly."

"I dreaded the day when I would hear those words from you," Kathy said. "My dad predicted I would hear them, and one day soon." She reached over and grasped JP's hands. "Well, Colonel, where do we go from here?"

"I'll stay on active duty until the war ends and the troops come home, then I'll take the best offer."

"Are you sorry you didn't retire earlier and go to Hopkins?"

"No, not at all. The time I've spent in Vietnam has been a tremendous experience, not to mention coming of age. It's an experience few men have been privileged to have. I have been very lucky in that respect, Kath."

Kathy sipped her wine, then smiled at her husband. "Did you know you talked in your sleep last night?"

"Whatever I said were lies, all lies, and that's the truth."

"You're worried, aren't you?" Kathy said, laughing. "Well, you can rest easy. I couldn't understand much of what you said. Next time I'll pay closer attention and take notes."

700

"Was there anything you understood?"

"A few phrases. You kept repeating 'Cease fire, cease fire', then some profanity."

"I never realized it, but that's the best order I ever gave as a lieutenant. Let's order some chow. I'm getting dizzy."

That night in bed JP held Kathy in his arms, neither of them able to sleep. Then came the tears and they came easily for both of them. If Vietnam had taught them anything it had taught them how to cry. They wept for the dead, they wept for the crippled, and they wept for their country.

★

Friday, February 19, 1971, 1620 hours
Washington National Airport, Washington D.C.

JP, in uniform, shiny eagles on his shoulders, checked in at the ticket counter while Paul and Frank hauled his bags onto the scale next to the counter. Nancy clutched her father's hand. After receiving his boarding pass they all headed to the gate. The two boys ran ahead while JP and Kathy, Nancy between them holding both their hands, followed at a much slower pace. At the gate they sat quietly until passengers started to board.

"This is the part of R&R I don't like," Kathy said.

They waited until the final call. JP stood, shook hands with Frank and Paul, then kneeled and hugged Nancy. Finally, he held Kathy to him. "See you in a couple of months, kid." He hugged everyone again, kissed Kathy, and headed down the jetway. Once in his seat he bemoaned how fast his leave had gone.

That morning he had stumbled out of bed at 0500 hours and driven Paul around on his paper route. After breakfast the family had gone to 0800 hours mass at St. Marks. Father Markam was still the rector and his sermons were as boring as ever. Try as he did JP was unable to relate to anything Markam said. The priest lived in his own little world, a world where the sun shone and everyone was united in brotherly love. The good priest just didn't get it.

Chapter Seventy-Seven

Before boarding his charter flight at La Guardia Airport for the flight back to Vietnam, Colonel JP Franklin bought several newspapers to catch up on activities in Vietnam. During his six days at home he had paid very little attention to the war. In fact, he made every effort to avoid news of the war, routinely turning off TV and radio news broadcasts. What few he had watched early in his leave were patently biased in favor of North Vietnam and the Pathet Lao. Even though his son Paul had delivered forty-seven newspaper every morning to forty-seven middle-class homes in Silver Spring, JP had seldom glanced at the headlines of leftover papers, much less read any articles. The extra papers were utilized to line the bottom of paper grocery bags from the commissary, converting them to garbage bags. It was the best use he could devise for the newspapers and it manifested his contempt for their contents.

After the plane reached altitude the flight attendants came through the cabin taking orders for before-dinner drinks. JP ordered a gin martini on the rocks. With his tray table down he sipped his martini and read about Operation Lai Kahm, the incursion of the ARVN into Laos. The objective was to cut the Ho Chi Minh trail, destroy North Vietnam assets in Quen Loi, a Laotian town eighty-two kilometers west of the Laotian border, and forestall an invasion into Military Region I. The operation, a test of President Nixon's program of Vietnamization, was strictly an ARVN ground operation. The Cooper-Church amendment prohibited participation of US ground forces including advisors and artillery forward observers. However, air support by US Army air assets was permitted. What a stupid way to fight a war.

The operation required reactivating the old US Army base at Hung Nghia fifteen kilometers from the Laotian border, and the special forces camp at Phang Lei, only two kilometers from the border. US Army troops were tasked with opening and protecting highway No.18 from Thang Chi on the coast 130 kilometers west to the Laotian border, and providing security for Hung Nghia and Phang Lei. For JP, who was well aware of ARVN military capabilities, Operation Lai Kham was another defensive "offensive" operation characteristic of the flawed US/ARVN strategy. It would have little impact on the outcome of the war other than to hasten eventual Communist domination of South Vietnam. His response to all this was to down the first martini and order a second.

★

Wednesday, February 22, 1971, 0800 hours
98th Evacuation Hospital, Long Binh, Republic of Vietnam

Colonel JP Franklin, Medical Corps, US Army, bowed low to the elderly Vietnamese cleaning woman in his office." Good morning, Mama san. Did you make many rockets for the VC while I was on leave?"

The wizened old woman bowed lower, her broom extended behind her. "Yes, made many rockets for VC."

JP smiled, more in frustration than cynicism. Would he ever understand these people? Would they ever understand him? After she left Jeff Dunbar breezed in.

"Welcome back, boss. How were things back in the zone of interior?"

"Screwed up as usual. More important, what's happened here?"

"Plenty of activity for the hospital," Dunbar said, pulling out his green-covered notebook and taking a seat. "This is the breakdown of admissions while you were gone: thirty-seven surgical, seven burn, fifty-six medical, nineteen psychiatric, and two snakebites, neither of which was from a venomous snake. In addition there were twenty-two adult civilian surgical; three pediatric, and seven VC or NVA. Our current census is seventy-one surgical, ninety-one medical, thirty-one psychiatric, and nine burn."

"Sounds like you all earned your pay. Any problems?"

"No, sir. Harry Resniek, Bill Palowski, and Helen Schroyer have worked well together."

"What about the mess hall?"

"The only problem has been keeping unauthorized personnel from eating there."

"God bless Sergeant Quinn. Surely there must a commendation for him somewhere."

"I'll see what can be worked up."

"What's the word on how things are going down south?"

"The ARVNs are getting their butts whipped and we are losing a lot of helicopters and crews."

"Does that Fort Benning-damaged mind of yours have some kind of interpretation?"

"Some of my buddies are at Hung Nghia and Phang Lei. They've kept me well informed."

"What have they been telling you?"

"Well, General Thao who commands II Corps, is out of his league. He's never commanded anything as complex as Operation Lai Kham. General Quang, the CG of the 5th ARVN Division and the same rank as General Thao, is so pissed off over having been given a lesser command that he refuses to leave his villa in Hue. The entire ARVN operation is riddled with petty jealousies and lack of experience. One wonders what in hell they've been doing for the last ten years besides letting us fight their battles. The one good division is the 7th ARVN under General Than. He's a solid, dependable and capable commander, but he's the only one. I worked with him part of my first tour. Most of the other senior officers are prima donnas, maybe even corrupt prima donnas whose aspirations far exceed their abilities?"

"Do I detect a tenor of bitterness, Major?"

"Hell, sir, the ARVN have never fought well against the North Vietnamese main forces, and that's when they had US advisors, forward observers, ground and air FACs and tactical air. In Laos they are on their own and falling on their faces. Their ability to communicate with higher headquarters is limited. The VNAF has been no help. They are unable to coordinate their missions with the ground troops and their leadership is deficient."

"You have made me sorry I asked."

"Do you want to hear more, Colonel?"

"Not really, but go on."

"The NVA are now using T–54 medium tanks which outgun the ARVN M–41 light tanks. And I heard through the grapevine that the NVA had procured copies of the ARVN battle plan for Operation Lai Kham weeks before D-day. They were waiting."

"You paint a grim picture, Jeff. What's your prediction?"

"The ARVNs will get their asses whipped and run like hell back to South Vietnam. In a year or two the US will be out of Vietnam and Vietnam will once again be one nation. We will have lost over 50,000 men as the price for the privilege of being humiliated by a third-rate nation."

"They can use people like you on the joint chiefs," JP said, settling at his desk. "Speaking of policy making, I went by the MSC division at the Forestall Building to check up on you while I was on leave."

"Oh, oh."

"For reasons that defy explanation you are considered an officer of immense potential. I did my best to set the career people straight but got nowhere. Despite being a very junior major you are eligible for promotion to light colonel from the secondary zone. In the meantime you are scheduled for Command and General Staff College at Leavenworth when you leave here."

"This is just between you and me, Colonel."

JP nodded.

"After I finish my tour in Vietnam I'm resigning to work on a Master's/PhD program in hospital administration."

"I thought you were gung-ho army, Jeff."

"I was, Colonel, but that was before I saw what this war has done to the army and the country. I have seen too many men who excelled in dedication, courage, intellect, and integrity wasted by a nation that went on to denigrate their sacrifices."

JP remained quiet. He didn't want to respond, for Jeff Dunbar had just articulated his own thoughts. "Let's get some coffee, Jeff," he said, getting up.

At the coffee table JP filled Dunbar's cup and passed it to him. "Any important correspondence I need to get on?"

"No, sir. I was able take care of everything. A phone call from D.C. came for you about an hour before you signed in."

JP stopped filling his mug and looked at Dunbar.

"It was from a Federal Judge Carter; she said it was a personal matter and asked that you call her collect." He handed JP a paper from a memo pad.

JP stared at the numbers on the paper. "Judge Carter is an old friend," he said without explaining. "The last I heard she had been nominated to the Court of Appeals. Her son was one of my chopper pilots up in the 36th." He shrugged. "I guess I'd better call her."

704

Returning to his office, he sat down at his desk and reached for the phone. The delays and confusion trying to place a collect person-to-person call to the District of Columbia was beyond belief. Thirty minutes later he quit in disgust and asked the operator to bill him for the call. In less than a minute a male voice came on the line. "Watergate Apartments."

"Fourteen eleven, please."

The phone rang twice. A female voice, not Ann's, answered. "Fourteen eleven."

"This is Colonel Franklin in Vietnam calling for Judge Carter."

"Yes, Colonel. This is Ellen Blanton, Judge Carter's secretary. Just a minute please. Judge Carter is across the hall with a friend."

While JP waited his anxiety level reached new heights. Ann had never called him since 1945. And what was she doing in D.C.? Her district was Southern California.

Ann's voice came through loud and clear. "JP, thank you so much for returning my call."

"Ann, I realize this is not a social call…"

"It's about Tom. He was shot down in Laos two days ago."

JP didn't want to hear what would come next.

"Everyone but Tom on the helicopter was killed. Tom was shot through the shoulder; he broke a leg in the crash. After he was free of the wreckage he tried to stand up and was shot in the chest."

"Good God! How was anyone able to get in there to medevac him?"

"He was rescued by an army Ranger team led by his West Point roommate, Joe Felzer. Joe is now in trouble with the army and State Department for violating orders to stay out of Laos. There's talk of court-martialing him."

JP bit his lip to suppress verbalizing his opinion at the way the war was being fought. Instead he asked, "Do you know Tom's status now?"

"Yes and no. I've had two phone calls from a lieutenant colonel in the Pentagon. I was told Tom developed shock lung syndrome and kidney failure after his surgery at the hospital at Trang Ha. The day before yesterday he was flown to the 3rd Field Hospital in Saigon to be put on the artificial kidney." Ann's voice broke for a moment. "JP, my only son may be dying. I need to be with him in Saigon, not here in D.C. before the senate judiciary committee."

"Is that the hearing for your appointment to the Court of Appeals?"

"Yes, but that is no longer germane. My son is the most important thing in my life. I'm scheduled to fly to Vietnam in the morning; I'll be staying at the embassy."

For the second time since JP had known Ann she seemed close to breaking down. The first was when she had learned that her brother had been killed on a bombing mission over Japan and he had volunteered to return to the Pacific for the invasion of Japan. She was willing to drop out of law school and marry him to stop him. JP would have to do now as he did then, set her straight.

"Ann, your grief over Tom has clouded your judgment. There's a good chance Tom may not be here when you arrive." He didn't mention Tom could be in a body bag on his way to the States. "Your appointment to the Court of Appeals is something you have worked towards all your life. Before you make a decision that impacts that appointment give me time to go over to the 3rd Field and get a handle on Tom's condition if he's still there."

There was a long pause. JP could hear Ann breathing. "I'll be here at the Watergate until time to go to the airport in the morning."

As soon as the connection was broken JP dialed Dust-off operations and identified himself. "I need to go to the 3rd Field right away if you have a bird available," he told the operations officer.

"It's been a quiet day, Colonel. We have twelve birds sitting on the ground just waiting. Come over and take your pick. I'll have a crew for you."

"I'm on my way."

★

The 3rd Field Hospital had been established in two city blocks of permanent buildings in Saigon not far from Tan Son Nhut Airport. It had the aura of a stateside hospital. The doctors wore khaki uniforms instead of fatigues and the nurses wore white uniforms with skirts. Much of the hospital was air conditioned. Colonel Harvey Powell, the commander, was one of the country's top obstetrician/gynecologists and a close friend.

Thirty minutes after making the call to Dust-off operations JP knocked at the door of Colonel Powell's office and walked in. Colonel Powell stood up and held out his hand. "JP, what brings you to Saigon? I thought you despised the city."

"I do," JP said, gripping his friend's hand, "but I was asked to look in on a casualty injured in Laos who was evacuated here two days ago from the 18th Surg with shock lung syndrome and renal failure."

"That would be Lieutenant Carter."

"Right. How is he doing?"

"Fine. The shock lung diagnosis was an overzealous diagnosis, and his kidneys recovered on the plane coming down here from Trang Ha. Urine output and specific gravity have been normal since he arrived. The air force seems to work miracles with their airplanes."

"So I've noticed. What's Carter's status now?"

"He has a left shoulder wound which will require additional surgery; a compound fracture of the femur being treated with traction, and three broken ribs which are being ignored. If he continues to improve he'll be medevac'd to the States in about five days."

A tremendous weight was lifted from JP's shoulders. "Harv, in addition to being the son of a good friend Tom Carter was one of my chopper pilots when I was at the 36th. His flying skills bailed me out of bad trouble more than once."

"Did you know he had been recommended for the Distinguished Flying Cross?"

"Good God, no. What did he do?"

"Why don't I let him tell you. It's a fantastic story," Colonel Powell said, rising. "I'll take you to him."

Tom Carter's room was spacious and well lit by two windows. Carter lay on his back on one of the two beds in the room, his leg up in traction, his left arm in a cast. The other bed was unoccupied. A pulmonary therapist was encouraging Carter to cough when JP and Harvey Powell walked in.

"Lying down on the job again I see," JP quipped.

Tom Carter brightened. "Colonel Franklin. I hoped I would see you before leaving for the States."

"I'm about through for now, Lieutenant," the therapist said. "I want you to keep working on deep breaths and coughing."

"Yes, ma'am. I don't want that pneumonia bug."

Colonel Powell followed the therapist through the door. "Stop by on your way out, JP," he called back.

JP pulled a chair up to the bedside and sat down. "You've gotten yourself into a hell of a mess, Carter."

"Yes, sir. How did you know I was here?"

"Your mother called about an hour ago. She's convinced you're dying. She's about to dump her confirmation hearing before the judiciary committee and fly out here."

"My mother? Fly out here? You're kidding. She was never willing to compromise her goals before."

JP moved his chair closer. "You're wrong. Tom," he said a little bit too quickly.

"What do you mean?" Carter asked, leaning towards JP. He began to cough. "Oh God, that hurts."

JP ignored the question other than to say, "I'll explain some day when you're a little more mature."

"Colonel," Carter continued, "you've got to convince my mother to go on with the hearings. That appointment means so much to her."

"Your mother has a tendency to ignore advice given by those who know more than she does, but I'll do my best."

A pretty young nurse came into the room. "Temperature time, Lieutenant," she said and slipped a thermometer under Carter's tongue, then held his wrist to measure his pulse.

Removing the thermometer, she studied it a moment. "You have a slight fever and your pulse is fast."

"You do that to me every time, Shelly."

"Behave yourself, Lieutenant," the nurse said as she left.

Tom Carter turned to JP. "Do you have any idea where in the States I'll be sent?"

"Most patients pick hospitals closest to their homes. The services try to comply."

"I'd like to go to the San Diego area, but there's no army hospital there."

"That shouldn't be a problem. The services often take each other's casualties. I'll talk to Colonel Powell on my way out."

Carter's eyes suddenly reddened.

"Tom, are you hurting?"

"Yes, sir, hurting terribly, but it's not the physical pain. The people here keep me pretty much doped up for that."

JP waited.

"I lost my crew, Colonel, and Dan Ranson was killed with his crew."

If JP had been struck in the chest by a knife the pain could not have been more intense. Bit by bit the war was tearing him apart inside. "How did it happen?" he asked hoarsely.

"The ARVNs were getting slaughtered and screaming for medevacs. We had flown missions all day. The last one was at dusk; we decided to risk it. Dan's ship was lead; I was number two. As Dan made his approach to the LZ he transmitted that his ship had just taken an RPG hit on the tail rotor; he had lost all pedal control. As calm as ever, his last message reported going inverted. Then I saw a huge fireball and smoke. I decided to make a try for the LZ to pick up the ARVN wounded. As I came in I saw a machine gun in the trees firing at me. My ship took hits; my hydraulics went out and just about every annunciator light flashed red. I lost control and crashed in a left turn. The chopper exploded. My peter pilot and medic were killed. I was ejected and hit the ground hard. I tried to stand up but my right leg wouldn't work. I found a stick and, using it as a crutch, I tried to reach the tree line. Then a tremendous blow hit me in the chest and I passed out. I was told later a 51-caliber shell had hit my chicken jacket. A few broken ribs is a cheap price to pay for survival."

"It's a miracle you survived the crash. It was even more of a miracle you were medevac'd out of that LZ."

"If it had been up to my country I'd still be out there," Carter said bitterly.

"Your mother told me about Joe Felzer."

"Yes, sir. His Ranger team was at Phang Lai. He was monitoring radios in the TOC when he heard what happened to my ship. He commandeered two slicks, loaded his rangers on board, and talked some snakes into going with him as escorts. The gunships prepped the LZ with rockets and miniguns. The rangers laid down a base of fire while I was dragged to their chopper and loaded on board. The gunships made more runs and we took off. One ranger was hit in the leg, and another got a scalp wound. The chopper I was on took twenty-six hits, but we made it to Hung Nghia and B Med. The chopper had to be junked it was so badly damaged. From Hung Nghia I was evacuated to the 22nd Surg at Phang Lai."

"What a story! Thank God for your buddy Felzer."

"Colonel, he was placed under arrest when we returned pending court martial for taking US ground troops into Laos in violation of orders and the Cooper-Church Amendment. The charges were quashed the next day, not because they were absurd but because the adverse publicity was certain to tarnish the army's image, or what was left of the army's image."

JP stood up, went to then window and gazed at the heavy traffic in the street. "It's a screwed up war, Tom. It always has been a screwed up war and always will be a screwed up war. I'll never get over losing Dan Ranson, or so many others."

"Sir, you have no idea how much he respected you."

"I think I do, Tom, and that's what makes his death so much harder to accept."

"Did you know he was planning on going to medical school?"

"He would have made a great doctor," JP said, recalling how rapidly Dan Ranson adjusted to assisting at the surgery of the rescued POW. "I'd better call your mother

708

before she does something stupid."

"You're the only one who has ever talked about her like that. You make her sound… human."

"She is human, Lieutenant, very human. I can vouch for that," JP said, thinking back twenty-five years.

"Tell her I'm resigning from the army as soon as I can."

"You have any idea what you want to do after you leave the army?"

"Yes, sir. Dan Ranson and I talked a lot about going to medical school after we finished our tours. Now that he's gone I'll have to go for both of us."

JP reached over and hugged Tom Carter, then quickly left before Carter saw his tears.

★

JP walked into Harvey Powell's office.

"Carter is quite a young man," Powell said.

"He wants to go to medical school."

"He'll be an outstanding doctor." Colonel Powell stood up. "My office is yours, JP Just give my secretary the number you want called and she'll put it through."

"Thanks, Harv."

The secretary placed the call using official phone lines. If anything was official business this call was. The call went through in less than two minutes. Ann answered the phone, her voice laden with fear and anxiety. "Were you able to see Tom?"

"Of course. I just left his room. He's trussed up like a Thanksgiving turkey but he's out of danger."

"Thank God."

"Hey, army medicine should get some of the credit."

"Anything you say, Colonel."

"Tom's kidneys are working fine. His shock lung was due more to fractured ribs than actual lung contusion with A/V shunts."

"A/V what?"

"Forget it. He's stable and should be on his way home in four or five days. When I told him you would skip the senate hearing and dump your career to come out here he looked as if he would cry."

"Only one other time in my life was I willing to give up my career; then too it was for love."

"Yes, I know," JP said ruefully.

"You didn't tell Tom?"

"No, but I should have, Ann. I believe it would mean a great deal for him to know that his mother has a tender side. You should tell him."

"I'll think about it," Ann said. "Does he know to what military hospital he will be sent?"

"He asked for the Naval Hospital at San Diego. I don't think going there will be a problem."

"That's not very far from the Federal Courthouse. I'll be able to see him every day."

"He's fine young man, Ann, and a hell of a pilot."

"Did he indicate what he wanted to do after he recovered from his injuries?"

"As a matter of fact he did. He plans on resigning from the army and going to medical school. With his grades at the Academy he will have no trouble getting in."

There was a long silence. "Thank you, JP. It seems each day I owe you more and more."

"Ann, I had nothing to do with Tom's decision to study medicine."

"You would say differently if you read the letters he sent me. Much of what he wrote was about you."

It was JP's turn to remain silent. "I suppose it's too much to hope for that he didn't mention my helicopter flying."

Ann laughed. "Sorry, Colonel. Tom was quite descriptive."

JP groaned.

"By the way, JP, my neighbor across the hall sends her congratulations on your promotion and getting a hospital to command."

"Ann, I don't know anyone who lives at the Watergate."

"Of course you do. You and she had lunch together last April at the Loring Hotel."

More silence. "Oh, Margaret Ryan? I didn't know she lived at the Watergate. Honest. How is she doing?"

"Not very well. She's recovering from another course of chemotherapy. She had to resign as Assistant Army Secretary because of health. She has a full-time nurse with her. I check up on her several times a day when I'm here."

"She must have played some part in my promotion. Tell her thanks for me."

"We have had several very interesting conversations about you, Colonel," Ann said, laughing.

"I'll bet."

"We concluded that your wife Kathy must be a very remarkable woman."

"You got it right. Ann, I'd better end this call. God knows what it's costing the taxpayer. Unless there's significant change in Tom's condition I won't call again. Look for him at San Diego in about a week or ten days. Good luck with your hearings. They wouldn't dare not confirm you. And tell Margaret Ryan to hang in there. I owe her lunch."

Chapter Seventy-Eight

During the months of March and April the 98th Evacuation Hospital statistics demonstrated a continuing and encouraging decline in admissions. Enlisted and commissioned staff who DEROSed were not replaced. The other two hospitals at Long Binh, the 24th and 93rd Evacs, published similar statistics. It was apparent that the involvement of the United States in the Vietnam War was winding down. President Nixon was making good at least one part of his campaign pledge: to extricate US Forces from South-east Asia. It remained to be seen if other portions of his pledge, the "Vietnamization" of the war and "Peace with Honor", would come to fruition.

★

Tuesday, April 29, 1970, 1250 hours
98th Evacuation Hospital, Long Binh, Republic of Vietnam

Colonel JP Franklin returned to his office after a long relaxed lunch at the hospital mess. On his desk lay three letters from Kathy. Opening the envelope with the earliest postmark, he removed a folded newspaper page with an attached note.

Dearest,

I was reinforcing the bottom of a garbage bag with pages from one of our great newspapers when this article caught my interest. My first inclination was to follow through with the garbage. It would have been a fitting response to the contempt for truth shown by the editors when they buried the article on page ninety-six, opposite the obituary page. Then I remembered your childish outburst when you watched the subject of the article on TV, so I decided to send the article. Your instincts served you well. Come home. We need you.

Love,
Kathy

Unfolding the page, JP focused on an article circled in red ink. A single column wide and about four inches in length including the heading, it was so inconspicuous that it probably went unseen by anyone reading the newspaper. Kathy had found it only because the primary function of newspapers in the Franklin household was to reinforce brown paper grocery bags for use as garbage bags. The article summarized a press release by the Department of the Air Force. It referred to an interview on national television several months earlier of a former fighter pilot. During the interview the pilot described in vivid detail atrocities and war crimes he had committed in Vietnam on orders of his superiors.

JP recalled watching the interview with Kathy when he was home on leave. The pilot had come across as a clean-cut, conscientious and sincere young American. He had related how he dropped bombs and napalm on schools and hospitals, then machine-gunned men, women and children who tried to flee. Tormented by guilt and shame, the pilot had turned in his wings, resigned from the air force and gone public.

The articles, obviously condensed and edited from what must have been an extensive air force press release, revealed the fighter pilot to have been actually an airman second class – equivalent to army private first class. He had served on active duty for a total of eleven months, all at bases in the United States including two months in an air force disciplinary barracks. Ultimately given a bad conduct discharge he was currently under criminal investigation by the Justice Department for felony impersonation of a commissioned military officer.

JP slapped the article on his desk. "I knew it," he said aloud, "I knew that turkey was a fraud."

"You knew which turkey was a fraud, Colonel?" Major Dunbar asked as he walked in.

JP thrust the article at his exec.

Dunbar's face clouded as he scanned the article. "It would have been so easy for the show's producers to have verified the man's authenticity," he said, laying the article on JP's desk.

"You and I know why it wasn't done, Jeff, just as we know why the newspaper failed to address that question in the article, why it took over two months for the truth to be printed, and why the truth was buried in near-microscopic size next to the obituary page."

"It would have been more appropriate to have printed it on the obituary page," Dunbar said bitterly. "Truth is certainly dead among journalists."

JP opened a lower drawer in his desk and dropped in the article. Closing the drawer, he looked up. "Where are crusading editors like Steve Wilson of the *Illustrated Press* and his top reporter, Lorelei Kilborne?"

"Who?"

"Forget it. You're too young." After a moment JP relented and explained, "They were characters in a half-hour radio drama broadcast once a week in the late 1930s. My buddies and I listened to it religiously. Edward G. Robinson played the part of Steve Wilson. Claire Trevor played Lorelei Kilborne."

"Oh?"

"I admired their integrity and commitment. I suppose that program shaped some of my values. I almost went into journalism because of it."

"You're kidding, Colonel. What changed your mind?"

"My high school counselor advised me to forget college and go into a profession which would give me an opportunity to work with my hands. Eventually I gravitated to surgery," JP said, laughing, "Anything new since I left for lunch?"

"Yes, sir. General Draughn's aide called. The general requests your presence for cocktails at his quarters at 1700 hours today followed by dinner at the senior officers' mess."

712

"I should call the club and check out tonight's menu. If it's the meal from hell – spaghetti and meatballs – the conversation, for some unknown reason, is almost certain to focus on football. I may have to invent a surgical emergency."

Major Dunbar chuckled. "It's too late for that, Colonel. I told the general's aide that you would be delighted to accept the general's invitation. His sedan will pick you up in front of hospital headquarters at 1645 hours."

"Where did I go wrong with you, XO?"

★

JP was still at his desk reading and signing reports when the sergeant major informed him that the general's car had arrived. Wearing clean, starched fatigues and spiffed jungle boots, JP walked from his headquarters building out to a clean, shiny 1969 Plymouth four-door sedan. The corporal-driver saluted, then opened the rear door and stood at attention.

Returning the salute JP told him, "I'd rather ride in front. I get car-sick in back seats."

The corporal regarded JP skeptically, then grinned. Slamming the rear door shut, he opened the front door.

★

The senior officers' club and mess on Long Binh was a remarkable structure constructed of stone, wood, and glass. Its architecture and ambience rivaled that of exclusive country clubs in the United States. Built on one of the highest elevations of Long Binh, it had a commanding view of the base and the rural countryside. Tennis and volleyball courts abounded; only an eighteen-hole golf course was missing.

Half a dozen three-bedroom cottages were strategically located adjacent to the club. Built of stone and wood in the same motif as the senior officers' club, they were occupied by generals, admirals, and their aides. Bird colonels lived in three bedroom air-conditioned mobile homes set on lower levels. The grounds were beautifully landscaped and maintained. They gave JP cause to periodically regret not having chosen to live in one of the trailers and taking his meals at the club. Every month when he paid the club's hefty dues his regret turned to pain.

Brigadier General Beverly Draughn, the Medical Command commander, was an internist by training. Vietnam was his first war, so to speak. Twelve years earlier he had abandoned clinical medicine to climb the administrative ladder to the stars. It was rumored that he was a strong candidate for an eventual third star and appointment as Army Surgeon General.

★

Precisely on time JP rang the door bell of the general's cottage. An orderly, a young GI in a starched white jacket, starched fatigue trousers and highly polished boots, opened the door. Brigadier General Draughn stood behind him, a short, heavy man with a florid wrinkled face and a head of thinning white hair cut short.

"Glad you were able to make it, JP," General Draughn said, extending his hand. "I never know when you surgeons will have to run to the operating room."

JP grasped the general's hand in a firm grip. "Things have quieted down, sir. Let's hope they stay that way."

"Amen to that. What would you like to drink?"

JP turned to the orderly. "Gin martini on the rocks, please."

"I thought you preferred vodka," General Draughn said.

"I'm ticked off at the Soviets for a variety of reasons. This is my way of getting back at them."

"Best way to fight an enemy," General Draughn said, smiling.

"Sir?" the orderly asked the general.

"Scotch and soda with a twist of lemon today, Jerry."

General Draughn motioned JP to a leather sofa framed in oak; he moved to a straight-back leather chair next to a flagstone fireplace and leaned towards JP. "How is your hospital adjusting to the slowdown?"

"Very poorly, sir. The troops are restless; they're not accustomed to so much leisure time. Keeping the doctors busy has been a challenge; conferences, lectures, baseball and volleyball have their limitations. They want to be put to work or sent home."

General Draughn nodded understandingly. "The 98th was a basket case until you took it over. You have done a splendid job as commander."

JP wondered if the general's use of the past tense was prophetic.

"General Webster wrote to me that you were the best division surgeon he had ever seen," General Draughn began. "He strongly recommended you be considered for further command and increased responsibility. Admiral Hardaway, before he departed for San Diego and retirement, left no doubt in my mind that you should be promoted to general and eventually be considered for surgeon general. He also made that abundantly clear to COMUSMACV."

JP was truly embarrassed yet pleased. He admired and respected General Webster. He idealized Vice-Admiral John Hardaway who, as a lieutenant commander in 1943, became a role model when JP, then a seventeen-year-old marine stationed at Camp Pendleton, spent weekends with Ann Carter as guests at the Hardaways' beach house in San Diego. Recently, John Hardaway turned down a fourth star and a shot at CNO to retire. It was a decision that JP understood. Hardaway, like JP, was an officer who had come of age with World War II values of integrity, courage, and loyalty. He loved his country and cherished its ideals. He saw those values trashed by the war in Vietnam. With his retirement, the country, the armed forces and especially the navy, had suffered a grievous loss.

The white-jacketed orderly brought the drinks on a tray, momentarily interrupting conversation. JP lifted the martini from the tray and nodded thanks. The general took his Scotch and water, waited for the orderly to leave, then raised his glass.

"To comrades."

714

"To comrades," JP echoed, lifting his glass. The faces of Kristy Goulden, Todd Westin, Mike Jackson, George Barfield, Alex Leichuk, Andy Andreson, Joe Brogan, the Chief, and many others flashed through his mind in a nanosecond. He wondered which comrades General Draughn had in mind when he proposed the toast; perhaps one killed by a moped while crossing a Saigon street.

The general continued, "As you know, the US military involvement in South Vietnam is diminishing. Troops are being withdrawn from combat units and sent home. Transfer of military ordnance, munitions and materiel to the ARVNs is being done at an accelerated rate."

"Yes, sir." JP was willing to bet that much of the equipment and supplies would find its way to the Viet Cong and North Vietnamese. Hell, he wouldn't be surprised if some were sold back to the United States.

"With the diminishing US troop strength in Vietnam there has been a corresponding and blessed reduction in casualties," the general said. "We now have an opportunity to reduce the number of US Army hospitals in Vietnam."

"That is good news, general."

"Of the three hospital commanders on Long Binh you not only have the longest time in Vietnam, but served much of that time in an infantry division. The other hospital commanders have had no similar experience. With this in mind the decision was made to close the 98th Evac."

JP took a big gulp of martini, set his glass down on marble-topped table, focused on General Draughn and waited.

"Personnel at the 98th with less than nine months in country will be transferred to the 93rd and 24th Evacs. Personnel with more than nine months will be reassigned back to the States." General Draughn must have read JP's mind. "Closing your hospital leaves you in need of an assignment."

"Yes, sir. That thought occurred to me."

"I can offer you any assignment in South-east Asia. If you wait three more months and extend another nine, you can have my job; it's being downgraded to colonel."

"General, in all candor I can't think of any assignment in South-east Asia I would want, especially yours."

General Draughn smiled. "The Surgeon General predicted that would be your answer. You should know that both General Webster and Admiral Hardaway strongly recommended you be included in the next class at the War College. The Surgeon General concurred has reserved a space for you."

"Sir, I haven't been to the Command and General Staff College; I understand that is prerequisite for the War College."

"No problem; you have been given constructive credit for C and GSC based on your work as division surgeon and medical battalion commander. The leadership you demonstrated at the 36th Division and as hospital commander indicated a strong capacity for command. After you graduate from the War College you can look forward to a tour in the Pentagon with the high probability of a first star. After that, who knows?"

JP reached for his martini, drained it and returned the glass to the table. Another three years or more in the Washington D.C. area had little appeal; duty in the Pentagon as a colonel or even a brigadier general had even less. Before he could respond the general continued.

"A week after you reached Phong Sahn we began hearing of your adventures. At one time we considered pulling you out before you got yourself killed or captured. Your performance at the 36th, your military background as a marine in one war and a line officer in another, earned you the great respect of the line officers with whom you served. You demonstrated a capacity to establish rapport, not only with enlisted and commissioned personnel in the army of all ranks, but with personnel in the air force, navy, and of course, the Marine Corps. That kind of relationship is unachievable for those of us whose military experience has been limited to the Medical Corps. JP, you could do a lot for the Medical Corps in the post-war years."

"Sir, may I speak freely?"

"Of course." Noting that JP's glass was empty except for ice, General Draughn asked. "Another martini?"

"Sounds good, sir."

"Gerry," the general called out.

The orderly appeared from the kitchen. "Yes, sir?"

"Another martini for Colonel Franklin and Scotch and soda for me, please." General Draughn turned back to JP. "You were about to speak freely," he said, chuckling.

"Yes, sir. What I want to say is that I must decline the War College and the possibility of promotion to general."

General Draughn fixed JP with a glare. "Many line officers of high rank went to a lot of trouble to be sure that the powers-that-be were made aware of your potential," he said coldly. "Even senators, Supreme Court justices, a Secretary of Defense and of State are in your corner. What the hell is your problem?"

JP was momentarily taken aback by the general's response, but with his inhibitions dulled by the martini he charged on. "Sir, I'll try to explain."

"Yes, please do."

"I became a doctor at an age older than most and by a circuitous route through two wars. That route involved the taking of lives, many lives. In Korea I encouraged and rewarded my platoon by giving the squad with the most kills each week two bottles of Scotch, a day off and no officer or NCO harassment. I subscribed to a philosophy of war articulated by my platoon sergeant after I told him I had been credited with saving the life of the chopper pilot. He said, 'Lieutenant, saving lives is a good thing, but battles are not won by saving lives. Battles are won by killing the enemy. In the long run that is what really saves lives, the killing.'"

"Good God," General Draughn interrupted, turning pale. "Go on," he urged.

"I had an opportunity to watch surgeons at a MASH work to save the lives of some British wounded that my platoon had rescued. The surgeons gave me credit for saving the life of the helicopter pilot. In a bizarre way the killing in which I had engaged in World War II and Korea helped me to see that the saving of lives, even one life, was a great and noble achievement. I was convinced that I had to become a doctor; for me

716

there could be no alternative." He reached for his martini.

General Draughn sat silent, waiting for him to continue.

"Since that decision my life has been dedicated to medicine. It was a commitment that took precedence over all else, including in many ways my family. My years at Walter Reed and my time here in Vietnam have made me one of the most experienced head and neck surgeons in the world, particularly in the area of war trauma. Having come this far as a surgeon, I have no desire nor intention of turning my back on that expertise to wear a star and push papers for not only the remainder of my military career, but the remainder of my professional career. Surgeons grow stale very rapidly in the non-operating mode."

The white-jacketed orderly entered with the drinks. He set the martini on the marble table within reach of JP's hand and the Scotch and water on the flagstone hearth, close to the general. Picking up the empty glasses, he left. JP lifted his glass for a sip.

"Are there other reasons for your decision?" General Draughn asked, his voice softened. It was as if he sensed a nobility he could never achieve.

"Yes, sir. Our participation in this war will end soon. Except for a few outstanding officers the ARVN leadership is corrupt, inept, and driven by nepotism and turf preservation. Some are even traitors. My knowledgeable friends up north have told me that the ARVN will not have a prayer of prevailing against the NVA when US support is withdrawn. When that happens, General, it will be obvious to the world that we achieved nothing in Vietnam. The price for nothing was over 50,000 of our country's young men killed, thousands missing, and hundreds of thousands so badly injured that they will be handicapped for life. As nation we will have lost not only the war, but our self-respect." He picked up his glass and took a healthy swallow of martini, almost draining the glass.

"General," he continued, "it is inevitable that the defense budget will be severely cut and the armed forces drastically reduced. That reduction will impact the Medical Corps. There will be an epidemic of hospital closures. AMA accreditation for residencies will be irretrievably lost and a hemorrhage of outstanding doctors from the armed forces will surely follow. As a general officer there would be little I could do to reverse that process. Sir, I have no desire to be a participant in the dismantling of a military medical system that has been the finest in the history of the world. Nor can I, in all conscience, be part of a process that will markedly weaken the capacity of this country to defend itself."

General Draughn swirled the ice around in his glass, then took a swallow. Lifting the glass to JP, he said, "You, Colonel Franklin, are one idealistic son of a bitch."

"I accept the compliment, General," JP said smiling.

"Your assessment of the future for the armed forces is remarkably close to mine and that of the Surgeon General. That is precisely why strong-willed senior medical officers who engender respect among the military and civilian hierarchy will be desperately needed to deal with those changes."

JP studied his now empty martini glass. "Sir, I fear that any strong-willed Medical Corps general officer, regardless of the number of stars on his shoulders, will have no more impact on Congress, the defense budget, and the Medical Corps than a man trying to disperse fog with a shovel."

General Draughn shook his head sadly. "You do have a unique way of putting things, Colonel."

"Yes, sir. So I've been told."

"We had better get back to the problems at hand. When would you like to leave for the States?"

"As soon as possible, General. I'm just spinning my wheels here."

"Can your executive officer, Major Dunbar, handle the hospital's closure?"

"I'm sure of it, General. He's been the de facto commander ever since I thought I took command. He made commanding a hospital a piece of cake. He is a superb officer. I could not leave the hospital in better hands."

"So you indicated in ERs you submitted on him. Apparently the Medical Service Corps agrees. You can tell Major Dunbar that on May 11 he will be promoted to lieutenant colonel. And as for you, JP, you can call Kathy to inform her you will leave in two days on a medevac flight into Andrews. You will be carried on the manifest as the flight surgeon." He indicated JP's empty martini glass. "How about another before we go to the club?"

"I'd better not, General. I might get talked into something I would regret later."

★

Friday, April 30, 1971
Somewhere over the Pacific Ocean

The US Air Force four-engine C–141 medevac jet had reached a cruise altitude of 35,000 feet after taking off from Bien Hoa Air Base. The aft three-fourths of the plane's cargo space was configured with tiers of stretchers and a nurses' station. Every stretcher was occupied by a casualty. At the forward part of the aircraft passenger-type airline seats facing aft took up the remaining fourth of cargo space. The aircraft's first stop would be Tachikawa Air Base in Japan. Casualties would be offloaded and taken by ambulance-bus to the US Air Force hospital to spend the night. There they would be checked for untoward developments that might preclude continuing on to the United States. Dressings would be changed, casts inspected, and medications given. The next morning, after breakfast, they would be loaded back on the aircraft. After a refueling stop at Anchorage, Alaska, the plane would proceed to its final destination: Andrews Air Force Base in Washington D.C.

In the passenger section Colonel JP Franklin sat facing rearward. Carried on the manifest as the flight surgeon he was also the medical escort for a young first lieutenant diagnosed with acute lymphocytic leukemia. Flying backwards for the first time in his life, with no window to look out to maintain spatial orientation, he was soon fighting the sensation he was facing forward. The conflict between vestibular mechanism, lack of visual input, and the plane's motions had him with his face buried in a barf bag soon after take-off. Fortunately, the air force flight nurses were of hardier stock. They managed the patients nicely without his help.

The following day, the plane touched down at Andrews. Stretchers with casualties were offloaded from the aircraft, carried into four waiting ambulance-buses and secured in tiers. JP accompanied the lieutenant with leukemia as he was carried on board on of the buses. The convoy of buses, led by two MP cars, their red/blue lights flashing, proceeded off base on to the highway and headed for Walter Reed Army Hospital. For Colonel James Paul Franklin, M.D., Medical Corps, United States Army, his Vietnam odyssey had come to an end.

Glossary

105s	A cannon with a bore diameter of 105 mm
201 file	A military personnel record
4.2	A mortar with a bore diameter of 4.2"
AC	Aircraft commander
ADC	Assistant division commander
AFIP	Armed Forces Institute of Pathology. A facility located on the grounds of Walter Reed Medical Center. Its scientists are world-renowned for expertise in their fields of medical pathology.
air evac 141	A C–141 four-engine transport jet used by the air force to transport casualties
AIT	Advanced Individual Training. The special training after basic training
anastamosed	To join or sew together, as with the ends of a severed nerve
Andrews	Andrews Air Force Base
angiogram	A radio-opaque dye study of arteries
anterior	Front
AO	Area of operations
AOA	Alpha Omega Alpha, the honor medical society
AOD	Administrative officer of the day
AP	Armor piercing, a shell that can penetrate armor
APC	Armored personnel carrier
aphonic	Unable to make sounds using larynx
AFRS	Armed Forces Radio Service
arrhythmia	An abnormal heart rhythm
Article 15	Non-judicial punishment administered by a commander to deal with minor offenses

720

ascites	A collection of fluid in the abdominal cavity
atelectasis	A consolidation or collapse of the air spaces of the lung
atropine	A drug which blocks the inhibitory effect of the parasympathetic system on heart rate
AWOL	Absent without official leave, a punishable offense
b.i.d.	Twice a day
bacci	Doctor in Vietnamese
back course ILS	Instrument landing system flown 180 degrees from the regular direction. It is more difficult because the localizer needle is the reverse of its regular direction and control corrections are opposite to that ordinarily made.
BCD	Bad conduct discharge, a lesser type discharge than the more serious dishonorable discharge
BDA	Bomb damage assessment
beaten zone	The area in which bullets will eventually impact the ground
Berry Plan	A plan which assured a doctor in training that he would not be drafted until he completed his training, at which time he would be called to active duty. Doctors who chose not to participate in this plan risked being drafted out of their training programs at any time.
betadine	An idodine-like cleansing liquid utilized to "sterilize" the skin of the operative field
Bliss	Fort Bliss, an artillery/air defense post in El Paso, Texas
blues	The dress blue formal uniform
BOQ	Bachelor officers' quarters
Bravo two sixes	B–26 medium bomber
Bright Light	Missions to rescue prisoners of war in South-east Asia
bronchoscope	A rigid or flexible tube with a light at its end. It is used to enter the trachea and bronchus to examine and/or clean out the lungs.

BU Med	Bureau of Medicine (Navy) pronounced "Bew Med"
C&C	Command and Control. Refers to the helicopter utilized by a commander in controlling the battlefield
C&GS	Command and General Staff College, Fort Leavenworth, Kansas
C–123	A workhorse transport plane with two reciprocating engines
C–4	A plastic explosive that resembles putty or crazy dough
C–4	The fourth cervical vertebra
cachexia	A general wasting condition associated with starvation, cancer or other debilitating disease
CAVU	Terminology meaning ceiling and visibility unlimited or perfect flying weather
CBU	A bomb which releases anti-personnel bomblets over a large area
CCF	Communist Chinese Forces
chicken jacket	Heavily armored vest worn by flight crews
central line	A plastic catheter inserted into a major vein in the lower neck and fed into the right heart. It is utilized for measuring various pressures and delivering medications.
cervical esophagostomy	an opening into the esophagus of the neck which communicates with the skin of the neck. It is utilized as a route through which a patient can be fed.
CFI	certified flight instructor
CG	Commanding general
chalk	A line of parachute jumpers
chip detector light	A red light that glows on the instrument panel of a helicopter to indicate a piece of metal has entered the gearbox and the transmission is in imminent danger of failure. An immediate landing is recommended.

722

clavicle	Collarbone
CMH	Congressional Medal of Honor. Actually, the correct term is Medal of Honor
CNO	Chief of naval operations
CO	Commanding officer
Cong	Viet Cong; local Communist soldiers
Communist ammonia	Detection of ammonia in urine characteristic of Communist troops. This was done by aircraft fitted with sophisticated "sniffing" capabilities.
concertina wire	stiff rolls of razor sharp wire placed around positions to hamper access by enemy forces
constrictors	Muscles in the gullet that squeeze when it contracts, propelling food into the esophagus
cottonoid	A compressed strip of cotton prepared so as to hold its form. It comes a variety of sizes, from peanut size to 1" x 4". They are used to protect delicate structures during surgery.
cranies	Craniotomies: surgery which exposes the brain
C-rations	Individual preserved meals
crepitation	A crackling sensation on palpation which denotes infiltration of air in the underlying tissues
D&C	Dilatation of the cervix and curettage of the uterus or womb
DA	Department of the Army
decanulated	Removal of a tracheotomy tube from the trachea or windpipe
Dever	A wide curved retractor
DFC	Distinguished Flying Cross
DI	Drill instructor: a sergeant in charge of training recruits in Marine Boot Camp
DIA	Defense Intelligence Agency
DISCOM	Division Support Command. The superior headquarters of the Infantry Division Medical Battalion
DOD	Department of Defense

dura	Covering of the brain
Dust-off	Air ambulance, a UH1H Huey helicopter
E&E	Escape and Evasion
edema	Swelling due to extravasation of fluid into tissues
Eglin	Eglin Air Force Base, Florida
enucleated	Refers to surgical removal of the eye
ER	Emergency room
erythema	A coloring of the skin which varies in intensity from a mild pink blush to a fiery redness
FAC	Forward air controller. A pilot who discovers and marks targets for fighter bombers
fast movers	Jet fighter bombers
foley	An indwelling rubber catheter with a balloon at its end. Ordinarily it is inserted through the urethra into the bladder to constantly drain urine. The balloon, when inflated, prevents accidental extrusion of the catheter.
forties	Cannons with a bore diameter of 40 mm. Two are usually mounted on a converted tank. Direct fire weapons, they are exceedingly accurate.
frontal lobe	The front part of the brain
FUO	Fever of undetermined origin
G–1	Officer responsible for administration at division level and higher
G–2	Intelligence
G–3	Training and Operations
G–4	Supply
G–5	Civil Affairs
gastrostomy	A surgical connection between the stomach and the skin of the abdominal wall to permit insertion of a tube for feeding
GCA	Ground-controlled approach. A method of guiding an aircraft to a runway using radar on the ground which displays to the operator the altitude and

direction of the approaching aircraft in relation to the ideal approach to a runway. The operator than transmits to the pilot the position of his plane in relation to the ideal approach or corrections to reach that approach.

HE	High explosive
hematocrit	The relation of red cells to plasma after blood has been centrifuged and reported in millimeters. This provides insight as to the blood status of the patient. Normal is 40 mm to 50 mm with some variation, depending on age.
hemostat	Clamps of various sizes and shapes with pointed noses used to clamp bleeding blood vessels to control bleeding
hepatomegaly	Enlargement of the liver
Hmongs	A primitive mountain people found in Vietnam and Laos
hypoglossal	The twelfth cranial nerve which controls movement of one side of the tongue
hypokalemic	An abnormally low potassium level in the blood
hypocalcemic	An abnormally low calcium level in the blood
hyponatremic	An abnormally low sodium level in the blood
hypopharynx	That part of the pharynx or gullet that leads from the oropharynx to the esophagus in the neck
ICU	Intensive care unit
ID	Infectious disease
ILS	Instrument landing system – a system which displays on an instrument the relation of an aircraft to an imaginary ideal approach to the end of a runway
intracranial	Inside the cranial cavity
IP	Instructor pilot
JAG	Judge advocate general: military lawyers
Jesus nut	The nut which secures the rotor of a helicopter to the shaft. If the nut should come off in flight, the presumed consequence is that everyone on board

would meet Jesus.

jug	Internal jugular vein, the main vessel in the neck that drains blood from the head and neck
Kempetai	Japanese secret police during Word War II, with a reputation for ruthlessness that rivaled the Gestapo
KIA	Killed in action
lap packs	Large gauze packs used commonly in the abdomen during surgery or other areas when appropriate... exoskeleton of the voice box
laryngectomy	Surgical removal of the voice box
laryngoscope	An L-shaped instrument with batteries in the handle and a curved blade with a light at its end. It is used to expose the voice box, vocal cords and adjacent structures.
larynx	Voice box
LBJ	Long Binh Jail, a military prison located at the military base of Long Binh, about twenty miles from Saigon (Ho Chi Minh City)
LRRP	Long-range reconnaissance patrol. Small groups of specially trained soldiers who infiltrate into enemy territory
Leavenworth	Military prison located at Fort Leavenworth, Kansas
Letterman	Army hospital at Presidio in San Francisco
LZ	Landing zone
MACV	Military Assistance Command Vietnam. The senior US military headquarters in Vietnam
Marine F4U	Gull-winged propeller-driven fighter plane of World War II
Marine Gooney Bird	Affectionate nickname given to the military version of the Douglas DC 3 transport plane
MARS	Military affiliate radio stations: A system of radio/telephone communications between military short wave radio stations in Vietnam and amateur radio operators (HAMs) in the US. It enabled a caller in Vietnam to talk to his family in the US at a fraction of the cost of a regular telephone call. The

HAMs volunteered their services.

Mayo stand	A metal L-shaped stand of adjustable height used to hold instruments near the operative field
MCAT	Medical College Aptitude Test
MEDCAP	Medical Civic Action Program. A program in which US Medical Corps officers and medics or corpsmen would visit native villagers weekly or biweekly to manage medical conditions
mediastinum	The membranous envelope or partition containing the heart and great vessel. It separates the left lung from the right lung.
middle fossa	The middle portion of the base of skull which support part of the brain.
Mixmaster	Cessna O 2A Skymaster, a high-winged four-passenger aircraft with a propeller in the rear and one in front. It was called a "Mixmaster" because of its characteristic sound which resembled the electric kitchen utensil working at full speed.
Mohawk	Twin-engine high performance low-winged aircraft with side-by-side seating for pilot and observer. It was loaded with sophisticated equipment for detecting enemy presence.
mosquitoes	Fine tipped clamps for controlling small bleeding vessels of delicate dissection
MSC	Medical Service Corps: non-physician commissioned officers who work in the medical field
nasopharynx	The highest portion of the pharynx, the part behind the nose and below the base of skull
Navion	The civilian version of the military L 17. It is a low-wing four-passenger monoplane with retractable landing gear.
necrosis	Death of local tissues
NG (nasogastric) tube	A plastic tube approximately forty inches in length which is placed through the nose and passed into the stomach for lavage or feeding
night lager	A night defensive formation used by units in the field to protect against attack from any direction. It

is roughly circular in shape and resembles in theory the circling of prairie wagons done by settlers in the west when stopped for the night.

OCD	Officer candidate school
OJT	On the job training
O 1 Bird dog	A Cessna high-wing single-engine observation plane with a tail skid used by forward air controllers
OP	Outpost. An observation and listening post of variable distances from a unit's position
Operation Ranch Hand	The operation of defoliation using Agent Orange sprayed by C–123 aircraft
ophthalmic	Pertaining to the eye
ophthalmologist	A physician who specializes in management of conditions involving the eye and vision
OR	Operating room
orbit	Eye socket. Second meaning: the circling of an aircraft
orthopod	Physician slang for orthopedic surgeon
ossicles	The three tiny bones (malleus, incus, stapes) in the middle ear which mechanically transmit sound energy from the tympanic membrane (eardrum) to the inner ear
osteo	Osteomyelitis, infection involving bone
PE	Physical examination
pediapods	Physician slang for pediatrician
Penrose drain	Thin, collapsed rubber tubes of varying lengths and widths placed into wounds or operative sites to facilitate drainage of fluids or pus
pericardium	The thin connective tissue sac containing the heart
permapreme	A petroleum preparation used to create a temporary water-repellent hard surface on dirt roads
peter pilot	Co-pilot on a helicopter
pharynx	The portion of the gullet from the base of skull to the opening of the esophagus in the neck

728

PLF	Parachute landing fall. A method of landing in which the feet, lower leg, thigh and buttocks progressively contact the ground in a coordinate roll
pneumothorax	Collapse of a lung
prepped	Cleansing of the skin of the operative site with germicidal soap
provost marshal	The chief law enforcement officer
PSP	Perforated steel planking
Push	Vernacular for radio frequency
puzzle palace	Military vernacular for the Pentagon
PVC	Polyvinylchloride
PZ	Pickup zone
Quads	Vernacular for quadruple mounted fifty-caliber machine guns fixed to an electrically driven turret in the bed of an armored half-track
R&R	Rest and relaxation
radical neck dissection	An operation to remove the lymph nodes, muscles, nerves, and veins on one side of the neck in continuity with a primary malignancy of the head or neck
railroad tracks	Captain's bars, which consist of two parallel silver bars
Red Robinson	Rubber catheters of various diameters which are inserted deep into a partially closed operative site for irrigation with saline or antibiotic solution
resident	A physician in training for a particular medical or surgical specialty after graduating from medical school. The training period varies in length from two to five years, depending on the specialty.
Ringer's lactate	A salt solution that resembles blood plasma. It contains sodium lactate, sodium chloride, calcium chloride and potassium chloride in one liter of distilled water. It is used as an emergency solution to replenish lost blood but is not a substitute for whole blood or packed red cells.
ROTC	Reserve Officers Training Corps, a military curriculum at selected civilian colleges and

	universities which leads to a commission as a second lieutenant and active duty
RPG	Rocket-propelled grenade, a shoulder launched rocket used against vehicles, light armor, bunkers, and personnel
Ruff Puff	Regional forces/popular forces, a local militia trained by special forces
Sandy	A 1–E Skyraider, a single-engine low-wing propeller-driven attack aircraft capable of carrying a heavy bomb load, rockets, and extensive automatic weapons. It can remain a long time over targets and remain flying even after sustaining substantial damage.
SAR	Search and rescue
SCM	Abbreviation for sternocleidomastoid muscle, the thick oblique muscle on each side of the neck that extends from the mastoid bone to the breast and collarbone
Scrubs	Green shirt and trousers worn in operating rooms
Six-by	Vernacular for the 2.5-ton truck with a 6' x 6' bed
Slick	UH1H Huey helicopter
snake	Cobra gunship
snake eater	Vernacular for the special forces, who are trained to live off the land for long periods, sometimes sustaining themselves by capturing and eating snakes
SOG	Studies and Observation Group. Elite soldiers trained to infiltrate into enemy area, identify targets, snatch prisoners, plant sophisticated equipment, assess bomb/artillery damage, and rescue allied prisoners of war
space A flights	Space available flights
Specialist 6	Equivalent to sergeant first class
Spectre	A C–130 four-engine transport equipped with miniguns, Gatling guns, 105 mm cannon, and flares
STABO	A rope/harness method of extraction from areas where a helicopter cannot land

sternal notch	The indentation at the top of the breastbone
STOL	An aircraft capable of short take-offs and landings
Stridor	Loud, high-pitched respiration
Stuart Field	Stuart Air Force Base, located about twenty miles from the US Military Academy, West Point, NY
sub-Q tissue	Vernacular for subcutaneous tissue, the tissue under the skin
sub-dural	That which is immediately beneath the dura or covering of the brain
T-6	A T-6 (Texan) a single-engine propeller-driven low-wing aircraft with tandem seating, originally used as an advanced trainer but used during the Korean War by forward air controllers
T-39	North American executive twin jet which carries six to eight passengers
tachycardia	Abnormally fast heart rate
TDY	Temporary duty
temporal lobe	A portion of the brain roughly in the middle and adjacent to the temple
temporalis fascia	The tough connective tissue covering the muscle over the temple, the temporalis muscle
TKO	To keep open; it applies to the rate at which intravenous fluid is delivered so as to keep the vein from becoming obstructed by a clot
to bag	To capture
toe poppers	Small mines that can be dropped by those being pursued to discourage the pursuers. When a mine is stepped on the resultant explosion is sufficient to blow off toes, incapacitating the individual.
trachea	Windpipe
triple A	Anti-aircraft artillery
umbilicus	Belly button
UPT	Undergraduate pilot training
URI	Upper respiratory infection
USAFI	US Armed Forces Institute. The institute provides

high school and college level courses for members of the armed forces.

vasopressor	A drug that will raise blood pressure
VNAF	South Vietnamese Air Force
VR	Visual reconnaissance
VSI	Vertical speed indicator, an aircraft instrument which display vertical speed up or down
water buffalo	A 500-gallon water tank on a trailer chassis with spigots at one end
white cell count	The number of white blood cells per unit of volume. Normal is 5,000 to 10,000. Above 10,000 suggests infection, blood disease or blood cancer. Below 5,000 indicates disease of the immune system or bone marrow.
WIA	Wounded in action
Woodlin	A grammar school in Silver Spring, Maryland, about twenty miles from Washington D.C.
Woody's	Woodward & Lothrop, a popular department store in Silver Spring, MD
WRAIR	Walter Reed Institute of Research
Zoomie Six	Zoomie refers to aviators in the Forward Air Controller squadron. Six is the number that designates its commander.

Printed in the United States
36587LVS00004B/2

9 781932 077506